Case Problems in Finance

THE IRWIN SERIES IN FINANCE, INSURANCE, AND REAL ESTATE

Stephen A. Ross
Sterling Professor of Economics and Finance
Yale University
Consulting Editor

FINANCIAL MANAGEMENT

Block and Hirt
Foundations of Financial Management
Eighth Edition

Brooks
PC FinGame: *The Financial Management Decision Game*
Version 2.0—DOS and Windows

Bruner
Case Studies in Finance: *Managing for Corporate Value Creation*
Second Edition

Eun and Resnick
International Financial Management

Kester, Fruhan, Piper, and Ruback
Case Problems in Finance
Eleventh Edition

Helfert
Techniques of Financial Analysis: *A Modern Approach*
Ninth Edition

Higgins
Analysis for Financial Management
Fourth Edition

Levich
International Financial Markets: *Prices and Policies*

Nunnally and Plath
Cases in Finance
Second Edition

Ross, Westerfield, and Jaffe
Corporate Finance
Fourth Edition

Ross, Westerfield, and Jordan
Essentials of Corporate Finance

Ross, Westerfield, and Jordan
Fundamentals of Corporate Finance
Third Edition

Stonehill and Eiteman
Finance: *An International Perspective*

White
Financial Analysis with an Electronic Calculator
Second Edition

INVESTMENTS

Bodie, Kane, and Marcus
Essentials of Investments
Second Edition

Bodie, Kane, and Marcus
Investments
Third Edition

Cohen, Zinbarg, and Zeikel
Investment Analysis and Portfolio Management
Fifth Edition

Hirt and Block
Fundamentals of Investment Management
Fifth Edition

Lorie, Dodd, and Kimpton
The Stock Market: *Theories and Evidence*
Second Edition

Morningstar, Inc., and Remaley
U.S. Equities on Floppy
Annual Edition

Shimko
The Innovative Investor
Version 2.0—Lotus and Excel

FINANCIAL INSTITUTIONS AND MARKETS

Flannery and Flood
Flannery and Flood's BankMaster: *A Financial Services Simulation*

Rose
Commercial Bank Management: *Producing and Selling Financial Services*
Third Edition

Rose
Money and Capital Markets: *Financial Institutions and Instruments in a Global Marketplace*
Sixth Edition

Rose and Kolari
Financial Institutions: *Understanding and Managing Financial Services*
Fifth Edition

Santomero and Babbel
Financial Markets, Instruments, and Institutions

Saunders
Financial Institutions Management: *A Modern Perspective*
Second Edition

REAL ESTATE

Berston
California Real Estate Practice
Sixth Edition

Berston
California Real Estate Principles
Seventh Edition

Brueggeman and Fisher
Real Estate Finance and Investments
Tenth Edition

Lusht
Real Estate Valuation: *Principles and Applications*

Smith and Corgel
Real Estate Perspectives: *An Introduction to Real Estate*
Second Edition

FINANCIAL PLANNING AND INSURANCE

Allen, Melone, Rosenbloom, and VanDerhei
Pension Planning: *Pensions, Profit-Sharing, and Other Deferred Compensation Plans*
Eighth Edition

Crawford
Law and the Life Insurance Contract
Seventh Edition

Crawford
Life and Health Insurance Law
LOMA Edition

Hirsch
Casualty Claim Practice
Sixth Edition

Kapoor, Dlabay, and Hughes
Personal Finance
Fourth Edition

Kellison
Theory of Interest
Second Edition

Skipper
International Risk and Insurance

Case Problems in Finance

Eleventh Edition

Edited by

W. CARL KESTER
James R. Williston Professor of Business Administration

WILLIAM F. FRUHAN, JR.
George E. Bates Professorship

THOMAS R. PIPER
Lawrence E. Fouraker Professor of Business Administration

RICHARD S. RUBACK
Willard Prescott Smith Professor of Corporate Finance

All of the Graduate School of Business Administration
Harvard University

IRWIN

Chicago • Bogotá • Boston • Buenos Aires • Caracas
London • Madrid • Mexico City • Sydney • Toronto

Irwin/McGraw-Hill

A Division of The McGraw·Hill Companies

CASE PROBLEMS IN FINANCE

The authors of the previous edition of this book were William E. Fruhan, Jr., W. Carl Kester, Scott P. Mason, Thomas R. Piper, and Richard S. Ruback.

Case material of the Harvard Graduate School of Business Administration is made possible by the cooperation of business firms and other organizations which may wish to remain anonymous by having names, quantities, and other identifying details disguised while maintaining basic relationships. Cases are prepared as the basis for class discussion rather than to illustrate either effective or ineffective handling of an administrative situation.

This book is printed on acid-free paper.

2 3 4 5 6 7 8 9 0 DOW DOW 9 0 9 8 7

ISBN 0-256-14596-2

Editorial director: *Michael W. Junior*
Associate editor: *Maureen M. Harrington*
Marketing manager: *Katie Rose*
Project supervisor: *Karen M. Smith*
Production supervisor: *Karen Thigpen*
Senior designer: *Crispin Prebys*
Prepress buyer: *Heather D. Burbridge*
Compositor: *Shepard Poorman Communications Corp.*
Typeface: *10.3/12 Times Roman*
Printer: *R. R. Donnelley & Sons Company*

Library of Congress Cataloging-in-Publication Data

Case problems in finance / W. Carl Kester . . . [et al.]. — 11th ed.
    p. cm.
  Includes index.
    ISBN 0-256-14596-2
    1. Corporations—Finance—Case studies. 2. Business enterprises-
-Finance—Case studies. I. Kester, W. Carl.
  HG4026.C279 1997
  658.15—DC21   96–49239

http://www.mhhe.com

Introduction

Many readers might be meeting the case method of instruction for the first time. More often than not, the experience is a frustrating one, for cases typically end at the critical point, in the words of some, "just when they seem to be getting someplace." At that point, readers are left to make their own way. It may be helpful, therefore, to know from the outset what case problems are and what advantages we believe can be gained from their use.

The heart of the case method of instruction is the use of problems to train students to discover, and then to fix in mind, ways of thinking that are productive in the subject area. Appropriate use of theory and the acquisition of factual material and procedural skills are also important goals, but the main objective is an ability to handle different types of managerial problems intelligently.

The word *decisional* is sometimes used to contrast the case method with *expository* teaching. For example, most of the cases in this book are descriptions of actual business situations. The facts are those known to some executive or other decision maker; they present an immediate financial problem needing resolution. Some cases emphasize the preliminaries of decision making—the difficulty of isolating and defining the crucial problem or of determining whether enough information is at hand to make an intelligent decision. The majority of cases, however, are "issue" cases; they present reasonable alternative courses of action that might have been followed in the given situation. Sufficient information is given to place readers in the decision makers' positions. From this vantage point, students are challenged to analyze the problem and to decide on the course of action to be taken.

The cases themselves depict a wide range of financial problems and business situations. Reference to the Contents will show that problems have been drawn from most of the major areas covered in financial courses. Cases have been selected from a variety of industries and from different time periods. Cases are also included that illustrate different phases in the life cycle of business firms and problems of cyclical decline as well as of prosperity.

Organization of the Book

The sequence of this book's major sections reflects our decisional approach. We begin in Part I with **Estimating Funds Requirements,** a topic that is typically either omitted from a first expository course in finance or would occur at the end of such a course. We begin with this topic because obtaining sufficient funds to maintain ongoing operations is the first responsibility of a financial manager. Although this subject is not glamorous, it enables students to focus on concrete problems that require decisions.

This analysis naturally leads to a discussion in Part II of **Long-Term Financing and Liability Management.** The cases in this section begin with an exploration of **debt policy.** This is followed by an examination of **capital markets** and specific types of **financial securities.** Here we address the question, "In what markets and in which specific ways should companies raise new funds, or distribute cash back to providers of capital?" An important new module included in this edition of *Case Problems in Finance* is **Derivative Instruments and Risk Management.** It is incorporated in the Long-Term Financing and Liability Management section, because knowledge of derivative instruments and risk-management techniques enhances students' understanding of how companies might lower their cost of capital by issuing securities in whatever form and market that affords them a pricing advantage (e.g., yen-dollar dual currency and Eurobonds), then—using derivative instruments—transforming the liability into a liability consistent with their debt.

Part III, **Valuation and Investment,** exploits the capital markets and financing foundation developed in Part II, and the forecasting skills developed in Part I, to build a valuation paradigm based on discounted cash flow and cost-of-capital concepts. The valuation skills built in the **Investment Decisions** and **Cost-of-Capital** modules are then applied to a variety of major corporate finance problems found in the **Mergers, Acquisitions, Restructurings, and Corporate Governance** module. The book concludes with three new cases that provide a **Comprehensive Overview** of the course. Each of these cases involves a major investment decision and an associated financing decision.

The order of the individual cases also reflects our managerial focus, which contrasts with the capital market focus that underlies the organization of most expository textbooks and courses in finance. We believe that the ordering of materials from the managerial viewpoint is the most effective way to teach managerial corporate finance. One cost of this approach, however, is that it is often difficult to relate readings in popular textbooks to specific cases. We have therefore included several notes to provide students with essential background materials.

New Cases and Notes

In this edition, 34 of the 63 cases and notes are new. Of these 34 cases and notes, 30 are completely new to this edition and 4 are updates of notes and cases from the tenth edition. The new materials in this eleventh edition of *Case Problems in Finance* reflect the changing financial environment as well as advances in the theory and practice of financial management. In our judgment, the materials in the **Introductory** section and the sections on **Estimating Funds Requirements** and **Debt Policy** consist of well-tested cases providing a very teachable sequence that offers a good opportunity to stress fundamental techniques of analysis.

The **Capital Market Efficiency and Security Pricing** section retains a core of material from the tenth edition, but adds to this core some successful new material. The sequence of cases provided in this module affords an examination of weak- and semistrong-form market efficiency ("Jupiter Management Company"), and strong-form market efficiency ("Anheuser-Busch and Campbell Taggart"). These cases are followed by others that examine opportunities to create value through financial execution arising from various real-world deviations from market efficiency. A new case in the module, "Dividend Policy at FPL Group, Inc.," deals not only with the topic of cash distribution policy, but also with the broader issue of information asymmetries and the potential signaling effects of changes in financial policies and various other financial execution decisions.

The new **Derivative Instruments and Risk Management** module introduces students to three basic classes of derivative financial contracts: options ("The Keller Fund's Option Investment Strategies"), forwards and futures ("Tiffany & Company"), and swaps ("The B.F. Goodrich–Rabobank Interest Rate Swap"). Once considered financial esoterica, these derivative instruments are now common tools of financial management. Their use by managers is addressed in this module within the context of three major types of risk—foreign exchange risk, interest rate risk, and commodity price risk—that modern financial executives are often called upon to control. The use of corporate diversification as a risk management device is also examined in the "Phelps Dodge Corporation" case.

Several of the cases included in the **Financial Execution** module make use of this foundation in derivative instruments. Knowledge of options, for example, aids in the analysis of the convertible bond and warrant-bond financing alternatives confronted in the "MCI Communications Corporation (1983)" case. The "Intel Corporation (1992)" case primarily concerns a dividend and share-repurchase policy decision faced by Intel in 1992. However, a basic knowledge of puts and calls will aid students' understanding of some of the innovative financial execution alternatives facing Intel and discussed at the conclusion of that case. Likewise, analysis of the financing alternatives described in the "R.J. Reynolds International Financing" case depends on an understanding of how swaps and forwards can be used to hedge exchange-rate risk. Knowledge of options also comes into play in the **Investment Decisions** module, where a new case, "Arundel Partners: The Sequel Project" and a new note, "Capital Projects as Real Options: An Introduction," are used to introduce the application of option-pricing techniques to the valuation of **real options.**

This edition of *Case Problems in Finance* includes five new cases that deal with problems of **international finance** or **international capital markets,** or are international in the scope of their administrative setting. Among these are "Tiffany & Company," "The B.F. Goodrich–Rabobank Interest Rate Swap," and "R.J. Reynolds International Financing," the contents of which were briefly described above. In addition, the "Compañia de Teléfonos de Chile" case in the **Financial Execution** module introduces students to the use of American Depository Receipts (ADRs) by non-American companies to escape the constraints of illiquid and partially segmented capital markets at home. "MSDI—Alcala de Henares, Spain" in the Investment Decisions module provides students with an introduction to problems of **cross-border valuation.**

This new edition also includes four new cases that focus on financial problems and decisions commonly faced by **new ventures and private corporations.** 'Kochman, Reidt & Haigh, Inc." focuses on the problem of estimating and financing the external funding needs of a small, rapidly growing, working capital-intensive cabinetry maker. "U.S. Bank of Washington," while broadly about the subject of bank lending, also gives students an appreciation of the challenges faced by new ventures in trying to source capital in a form well suited to their needs and opportunities. "Netscape's Initial Public Offering" and "Eskimo Pie Corporation" are cases concerning the unique problems of valuing and selling stock in **initial public offerings** (IPOs).

Finally, three new cases have been added to the **Mergers, Acquisitions, Restructurings, and Corporate Governance** section. "Time, Inc.'s Entry into the Entertainment Industry (A)" examines the much-publicized 1989 bid for Time, Inc., by Paramount Communications in the wake of Time's announced merger with Warner Communications. This case raises issues about company valuation, acquisition strategies, bidding strategies, and corporate governance. The "Marriott Corporation: The Cost of Capital" case concerns Marriott's Project Chariot, which involved the restructuring of Marriott's businesses and, more importantly, its debt in such a way as to affect the value of many of its outstanding bonds. The "Duckworth Industries, Inc.—Incentive Compensation Programs" case examines the general topic of **value-based management** and, in particular, focuses on the use of **economic value added** (EVA) as a basis of establishing incentive compensation programs.

Inevitably some instructors will regret that some of their favorite cases have been omitted in this edition. The editors share this feeling. If an instructor is especially eager to continue to use certain cases that were dropped in this edition, they can be ordered separately from Harvard Business Publishing, 60 Harvard Way, Box 230–5C, Boston, MA 02163 (www.hbsp.harvard.edu).

Using This Book

All of these cases are designed to provide a basis for class discussion; as such they are not intended to illustrate correct or incorrect solutions to management problems. It need hardly be added that the discussion they provoke will move along more realistic lines if students also have a standard finance text or reference book available and use it freely for background information not provided by this casebook. In addition, students will need to acquire proficiency in a number of analytical techniques useful in handling the quantitative aspects of cases.

Case problems confront students with the necessity of making decisions, and this is perhaps their greatest value. Students cannot stop with an understanding of the facts and a listing of items that deserve consideration. Mastery of these matters is merely the jumping-off point for class discussion. To be effective, students must actually think the problem through to a decision, explain their analyses to classmates, and defend their ideas. The need to choose among balanced alternatives and to discuss the decision intelligently is a great force in learning. It helps to provide that elusive quality of judgment that is often missed when excessive reliance is placed on the application of theoretical models.

Since the cases present business situations that post debatable alternatives of action, they contain problems that can be narrowed but not settled by the usual techniques of financial analysis. Judgment must enter into the process of decision making, so unanimous agreement as to the best decision is neither expected nor desired. This ambiguity also contributes to the initial frustration of many students who have been working with scientific and technical problems in which a mechanistic approach can more frequently be counted on to yield a single "right" conclusion.

When analyzing case problems, readers should not overlook intangible human factors. The choice between financial alternatives in many, if not all, cases depends in part on the decision maker's disposition for risk taking and on other matters of judgment and taste.

Work with cases might require more student time than normal textbook reading assignments. However, the satisfaction of handling problems that introduce the complexities involved in actual business decisions is normally sufficient to compensate for the extra time required.

W. Carl Kester
William E. Fruhan, Jr.
Thomas R. Piper
Richard S. Ruback

Acknowledgments

To the business executives who contributed the material for the cases in this volume, we express our sincere gratitude. In the development of these cases, they gave liberally of their time, and in most instances they made available to us facts about their businesses that are normally held confidential.

We wish to acknowledge our debt to Pearson Hunt, Charles M. Williams, James T. S. Porterfield, Leonard C.R. Langer, Robert F. Vandell, Alan B. Coleman, Frank L. Tucker, James E. Walter, Erich A. Helfert, Victor L. Andrews, David W. Mullins, Jr., J. Keith Butters, and Scott P. Mason, whose names have appeared as editors in earlier editions of this book. Their influence will be obvious to anyone who has used prior editions of *Case Problems in Finance*.

Thirty-five members or former members of the faculty of the Harvard University Graduate School of Business Administration authored, coauthored, or supervised the writing of the cases used in this edition or earlier versions of these cases. In addition to the editors of previous editions of this volume, we wish to thank Carliss Y. Baldwin, Robert W. Bruner, William J. Bruns, Michael E. Edleson, Benjamin C. Esty, Kenneth A. Froot, Robert R. Glauber, John P. Goldsberry III, Bruce C. Greenwald, Samuel L. Hayes III, Timothy A. Luehrman, Ronald W. Moore, Lynn Sharp Paine, Kevin R. Rock, Erik R. Sirri, and Peter Tufano for the use of cases for which they are responsible as author, coauthor, or supervisor. We also extend our thanks to the research associates and students of the Harvard University Graduate School of Business Administration who assisted in the writing of the cases in this volume under the supervision of faculty members.

We are grateful to Harvard Business School's Division of Research, which provided financial support for the development of the cases in this book. The copyright on all cases appearing here is held by the President and Fellows of Harvard College.

Most of all, we would like to express our special appreciation to Jane Manilych for her expert editorial support, and to Brenda L. Fucillo and Rita D. Colella for their invaluable assistance in the preparation of this volume. Their care and expertise in editing the manuscript and putting it into proper form for publication has contributed importantly to its quality.

The editors assume full responsibility for the contents of this edition, but they are keenly aware of their obligation to their predecessors and colleagues.

W.C.K.
W.E.F., Jr.
T.R.P.
R.S.R.

Contents

Derivative Instruments and Risk Management

Financial Execution

PART III: VALUATION AND INVESTMENT

Investment Decisions

Cost of Capital

PART IV: REVIEW AND SYNTHESIS

Part I

Financing Current Operations

Assessing a Company's Future Financial Health

Assessing the long-term financial health of a company is an important task for outsiders considering the extension of credit and for insiders in their formulation of strategy. History abounds with examples of firms that embarked upon overly ambitious programs and that subsequently discovered that their portfolio of programs could not be financed on acceptable terms. The outcome frequently was the abandonment of programs in midstream at considerable financial and organizational cost to the company, its vendors, its employees, or its creditors.

The key issue in assessing the long-term financial health of a company is whether the corporate system of goals, product market strategies, investment requirements, and financing capabilities are in balance.

> At any given period every enterprise has a defined business mission which is realized in its established competitive positions in particular product markets. Corporate strategy centers on these competitive positions. This strategy may include a harvesting mode for a few mature and relatively unprofitable business units. But for most of the firm's product markets it is designed to maintain an existing market position or expand that position against primary competitors. Competitive strategy therefore dictates that the firm grow at least as rapidly as aggregate industry demand grows. The firm's targeted growth rate of sales must meet (or exceed) the expected growth rate of the industry.[1]

Thus, the starting point for assessing a firm's long-term health must be a thorough investigation of (1) management's goals for the company and for each of the product markets; (2) the strategy planned for each product market; (3) the likely response of competitors; and (4) the market, competitive, and operating characteristics of each product market. The analyst is well advised to devote substantial time to exploring these areas, as the entire financial system of the company is driven by the economic and competitive environment of its established product markets. The firm's strategy and sales growth in each of its product markets will heavily determine the investments

---

1. Gordon Donaldson, *Managing Corporate Wealth* (New York: Praeger, 1984), pp. 64–65.

in assets needed to support these strategies; and the effectiveness of the strategies, combined with the response of competitors, will strongly influence the firm's competitive and financial performance and its resultant access to funds to finance the investment in assets.

The following are some of the questions that seem important in assessing a company's future financial health. The sequencing of the questions corresponds to that suggested by Figure A.

1. What are management's goals for the company?
2. In which product markets does management plan to compete?
   a. What are management's goals in the various product markets?
   b. What is the strategy in each product market?

FIGURE A
Factors in Determining a Financing Plan

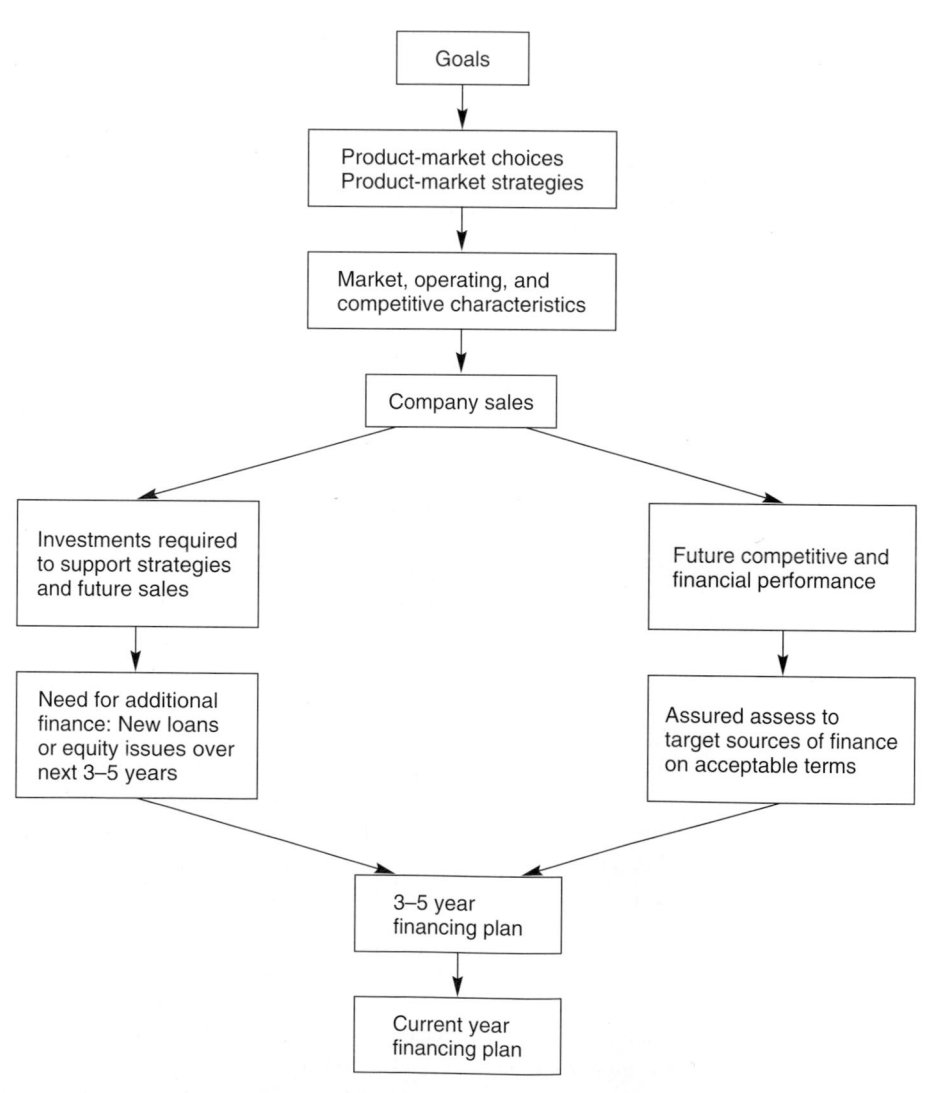

3. What are the market, competitive, and operating characteristics of each product market?
   a. What is the growth of primary demand in each product market? Are sales seasonal? cyclical?
   b. What are the strategies of the company's competitors?
   c. What are the company's operating policies?
   d. What are the main market, competitive, and operating risks?

4. What volume and nominal sales growth are likely for the company's units, individually and collectively?

5. What investments must be made in accounts receivables, inventory, and plant and equipment to support the various product market strategies? What will happen to the level of total assets over the next 3–5 years?

6. What is the outlook for profitability?
   a. What is the trend in reported profitability?
   b. What are the underlying financial accounting practices?
   c. Are there any hidden problems, such as suspiciously large levels or build-ups of accounts receivable or inventories relative to sales?
   d. Is the level of profitability sustainable, given the outlook for the market and for competitive and regulatory pressures? (Figure B summarizes market and industry factors that can adversely affect a firm's future performance.)

7. Will the company need to raise additional finance over the next year, or over the next 3–5 years, to carry out strategically important programs?
   a. Does the company have a seasonal financing need? If so, how large is it, and what will be the perceptions of suppliers of finance at the time of the need?
   b. Does the company have a long-term need for additional finance? If so, how large is it, and what will be the perceptions of suppliers of finance at the time of the need?
   c. Will the company have a need for additional finance if it encounters adversity?

8. How soundly is the company financed, given its level of profitability, its level of business risk, and its future need for additional finance? (Access to target sources of finance depends on future competitive and financial performance and on the soundness of the company's existing financial structure.)
   a. How current is the company in the payment of its suppliers?
   b. Is the company close to its borrowing limit according to restrictive covenants?
   c. Is the company within its capacity to service the debt? What is the maturity structure of existing debt?
   d. Are there any hidden problems such as unconsolidated subsidiaries with high debt levels or large contingent or unfunded liabilities?

9. Does the company have assured access on acceptable terms to external sources of funds in amounts needed to meet its seasonal, long-term, or adversity needs?
   a. Can the company raise equity funds?
      (1) Is there a market for the shares?
      (2) How many shares could be sold?
      (3) At what price could the shares be sold?
      (4) Would management be willing to issue new shares?

FIGURE B
Sources of Downward Pressure on Above-Market Returns

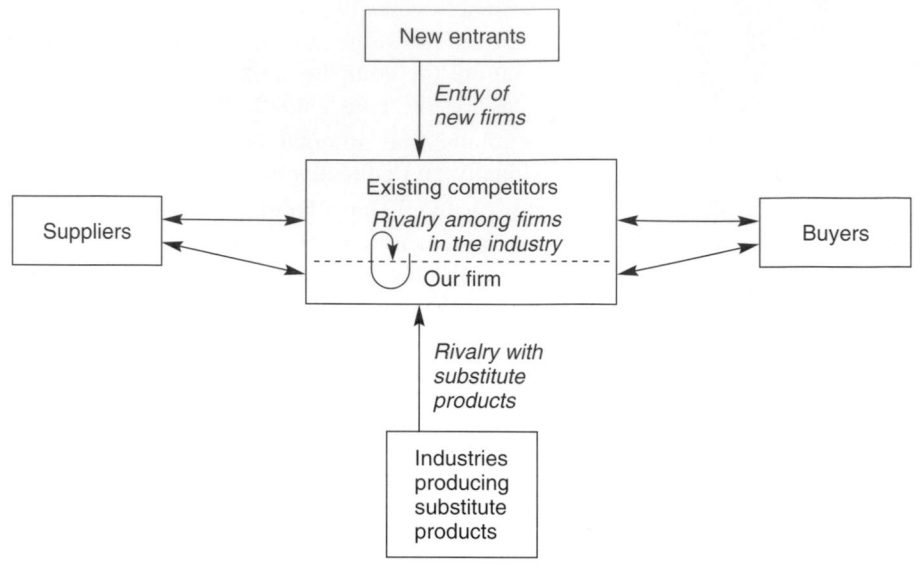

b. Can the company raise long-term debt?
   (1) Who are the target suppliers?
   (2) What are their criteria for lending?
   (3) How well does the company meet these criteria?
   (4) How much additional long-term debt can the company raise on accept-
       able terms?
   c. Can the company raise short-term debt?
   d. Does the company have assets that could be sold to raise funds? How
      quickly could they be sold?
10. Are the company's goals, product market choices and strategies, investment
    requirements, financing needs, and financing capabilities in balance? (Figure C
    diagrams the interrelation of these management and financial considerations.)
11. Will the company's goals, strategies, investment requirements, financing
    needs, and financing capabilities remain in balance if the firm is struck by
    adversity?
    a. What are the main regulatory, competitive, and operating risks? What com-
       bination of them might reasonably be expected to occur?
    b. How would management respond in strategic and operating terms?
    c. What would be the implications for future financing needs? For future
       financial performance?
    d. Will it be possible to raise the finance needed on acceptable terms, given
       the financial suppliers' perceptions of the firm's strategic, competitive, and
       financial performance?

Clearly, many of these questions cannot be answered by using only the information contained in a company's published financial statements. Many require an under-

FIGURE C
Testing for System Balance

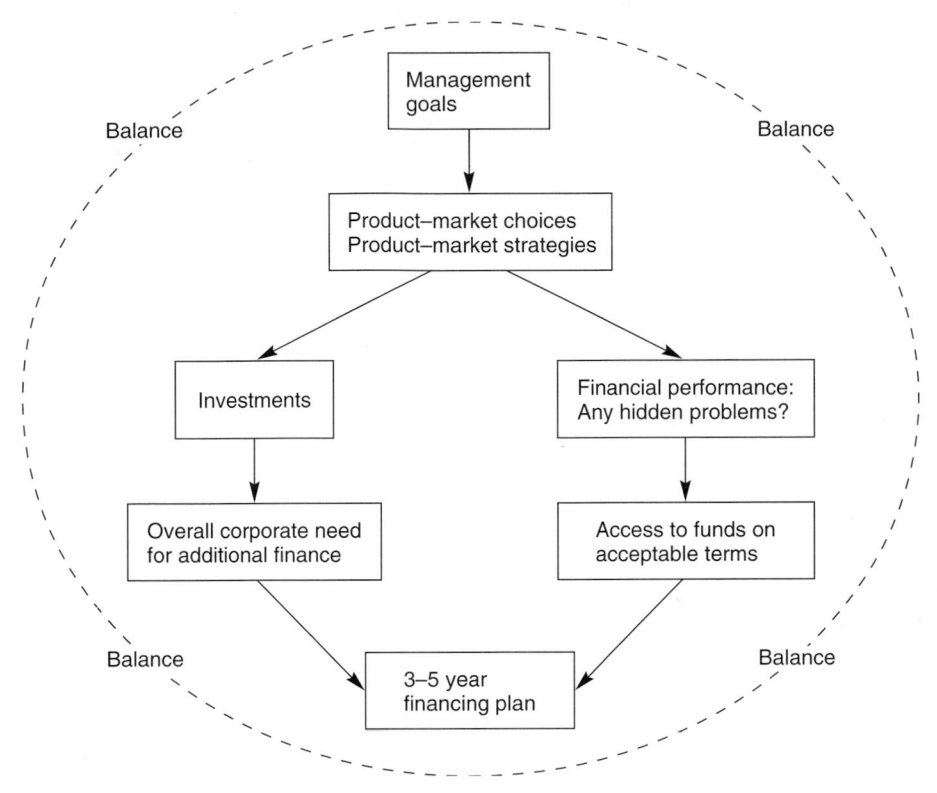

standing of (1) future industry structure and competitive behavior; (2) the competitive and operating characteristics of the business; (3) the long-term goals and plans of management; (4) the lending criteria of various segments of the capital markets; and (5) the soundness of management. Analysis of the published financial statements and their footnotes is only *one part* of a complete analysis of a company's future financial health.

It is also clear that the evaluation of a firm's financial health can vary substantially, depending on the perspective of the individual making the evaluation. A bank or supplier considering the extension of seasonal credit may consider a company a very safe bet, whereas a long-term lender dependent on the health and profitability of the company over a 15-year period may be very nervous.

The remainder of this note provides familiarity with the financial ratios that can be useful in answering some of the preceding questions. Exhibits 1 and 2 provide financial statements for 1992 and 1996 for a hypothetical company. The following section (Financial Ratios and Financial Analysis) presents four types of financial ratios and then asks a series of questions concerning the financial statements in Exhibits 1 and 2. Use the equations to answer the questions and fill in the blank spaces in the text. Your analysis of the statements should also answer two overall questions: Has the financial condition of the company changed during the 4-year period? What are the most significant changes, as indicated by the financial ratios?

Financial Ratios and Financial Analysis

The two basic sources of financial data for a business entity are the income statement and the balance sheet. The income statement summarizes revenues and expenses over a period of time, such as for the year ending December 31, 1996. The balance sheet is a list of what the business owns (its assets), what it owes (its liabilities), and what has been invested by the owners (owners' equity) at a specific point in time, such as *at* December 31, 1996.

From the figures found on the income statement and the balance sheet one can calculate the following types of financial ratios:

1. Profitability ratios
2. Activity ratios
3. Leverage ratios
4. Liquidity ratios

Profitability Ratios: How Profitable Is the Company?

Profitability is a necessity over the long run, for the level of profitability strongly influences (1) the company's access to debt finance, (2) the valuation of the company's common stock, (3) the company's willingness to issue common stock, and (4) the company's sustainable sales growth.

One measure of the profitability of a business is profit as a percentage of sales, as determined by the profitability ratio equation:

$$\frac{\text{Net profit after taxes}}{\text{Net sales}}$$

The information necessary to determine a company's profit as a percentage of sales can be found in the company's _____ .

1. Magnetronics's profit as a percentage of sales for 1996 was $_____ divided by $_____ , or _____%.
2. This represented an increase/decrease from _____% in 1992.
3. The deterioration in profitability resulted from an increase/decrease in cost of goods sold as a percentage of sales, and from an increase/decrease in operating expenses as a percentage of sales. The only favorable factor was the decrease in the _____ .

Management and investors are often more interested in the return earned on the funds invested than in the level of profits as a percentage of sales. Companies operating in businesses requiring very little investment in assets often have low profit margins but earn very attractive returns on invested funds. Conversely, there are numerous examples of companies in very capital-intensive businesses that earn miserably low returns on invested funds despite seemingly attractive profit margins.

Therefore, it is useful to examine the return earned on the funds provided by the shareholders and by the "investors" in the company's interest-bearing debt. To increase the comparability across companies, it is useful to use EBIAT (earnings before interest but after taxes) as the measure of return. The use of EBIAT as the measure of return also allows the analyst to compare the return on invested capital (calculated before the deduction of interest expense) with the company's estimated cost of capital to determine the long-term adequacy of the company's profitability.

4. Magnetronics had a total of $_____ of invested capital at year-end 1996 and earned before interest but after taxes (EBIAT) $_____ during 1996. Its return on invested capital is calculated as follows:

$$\frac{\text{Earnings before interest but after taxes (EBIAT)}}{\text{Owners' equity plus interest-bearing debt}}$$

In 1996 this figure was ____%, which represented an increase/decrease from the ____% earned in 1992.

From the viewpoint of the shareholders, an equally important figure is the company's return on equity. Return on equity is calculated by dividing profit after tax by the owners' equity:

$$\frac{\text{Profit after taxes}}{\text{Owners' equity}} = \text{Return on equity}$$

Return on equity indicates how profitably the company is utilizing shareholders' funds.

5. Magnetronics had $_____ of owners' equity and earned $_____ after taxes in 1996. Its return on equity was ____%, an improvement/deterioration from the ____% earned in 1992.

Management can "improve" (or "hurt") its return on equity in several ways. Each method of "improvement" differs substantially in nature. The analyst must get behind the return-on-equity figures and must understand the underlying causes of any changes. For example, did return on sales improve? Did the company's management of assets change? Did the company increase the use of borrowed funds relative to owners' equity? These three possible explanations are combined in the Du Pont system of ratio analysis:

$$\text{ROE} = \frac{\text{Net income}}{\text{Sales}} \times \frac{\text{Sales}}{\text{Assets}} \times \frac{\text{Assets}}{\text{Equity}}$$

Activity Ratios: Are There Any Hidden Problems?

The second basic type of financial ratio is the activity ratio. Activity ratios indicate how well a company employs its assets. Ineffective utilization of assets results in the need for more finance, unnecessary interest costs, and a correspondingly lower return on capital employed. Furthermore, low activity ratios or a deterioration in the activity ratios may indicate uncollectible accounts receivables or obsolete inventory or equipment.

Total asset turnover measures the company's effectiveness in utilizing its total assets and is calculated by dividing total assets into sales:

$$\frac{\text{Net sales}}{\text{Total assets}}$$

1. Total asset turnover for Magnetronics in 1996 can be calculated by dividing $_____ into $_____ . The turnover had improved/deteriorated from _____ times in 1992 to _____ times in 1996.

It is useful to examine the turnover ratios for each type of asset, as the use of total assets may hide important problems in one of the specific asset categories. One important category is accounts receivables. The average collection period measures the number of days that the company must wait on average between the time of sale and the time when it is paid. The average collection period is calculated in two steps. First, divide annual credit sales by 365 days to determine average sales per day:

$$\frac{\text{Net sales}}{365 \text{ days}}$$

Then, divide the accounts receivable by average sales per day to determine the number of days of sales that are still unpaid:

$$\frac{\text{Accounts receivable}}{\text{Average sales per day}}$$

2. Magnetronics had \$_____ invested in accounts receivables at year-end 1996. Its average sales per day were \$_____ during 1996, and its average collection period was _____ days. This represented an improvement/deterioration from the average collection period of _____ days in 1992.

A third activity ratio is the inventory turnover ratio, which indicates the effectiveness with which the company is employing inventory. Since inventory is recorded on the balance sheet at cost (not at its sales value), it is advisable to use cost of goods sold as the measure of activity. The inventory turnover figure is calculated by dividing cost of goods sold by inventory:

$$\frac{\text{Cost of goods sold}}{\text{Inventory}}$$

3. Magnetronics apparently needed \$_____ of inventory at year-end 1996 to support its operations during 1996. Its activity during 1996, as measured by the cost of goods sold, was \$_____ . It therefore had an inventory turnover of _____ times. This represented an improvement/deterioration from _____ times in 1992.

A fourth activity ratio is the fixed asset turnover ratio, which measures the effectiveness of the company in utilizing its plant and equipment:

$$\frac{\text{Net sales}}{\text{Net fixed assets}}$$

4. Magnetronics had net fixed assets of \$_____ and sales of \$_____ in 1996. Its fixed asset turnover ratio in 1996 was _____ times, an improvement/deterioration from _____ times in 1992.

5. So far, we have discussed three measures of profitability. They are
   (a) _____
   _____ (b) _____
   _____ and (c) _____
   _____ .

   We have also discussed four activity ratios, which measure the effectiveness of the company in utilizing its assets. They are (d) _____
   (e) _____
   (f) _____
   and (g) _____ .

6. The deterioration in Magnetronics's operating profits as a percentage of total assets between 1992 and 1996 resulted primarily from _____
   _____
   _____
   _____
   _____ .

Leverage Ratios: How Soundly Is the Company Financed?

The third basic type of financial ratio is the leverage ratio. The various leverage ratios measure the relation between funds supplied by creditors and funds supplied by the owners. The use of borrowed funds by profitable companies will improve the return on equity. However, it increases the riskiness of the business and, if used in excessive amounts, can result in financial embarrassment.

One leverage ratio, the debt ratio, measures the total funds provided by creditors as a percentage of total assets:

$$\frac{\text{Total liabilities}}{\text{Total assets}}$$

Total liabilities include both current and long-term liabilities.

1. The total liabilities of Magnetronics as of December 31, 1996, was $_____, or _____% of total assets. This represented an increase/decrease from _____% as of December 31, 1992.

Lenders—especially long-term lenders—want reasonable assurance that the firm will be able to repay the loan in the future. They are concerned with the relationship between total debt and the economic value of the firm. This ratio is called the total debt ratio at market.

$$\frac{\text{Total liabilities}}{\text{Total liabilities + Market value of the equity}}$$

The market value of the equity is calculated by multiplying the number of shares of common stock outstanding times the market price per share.

2. The market value of Magnetronics's equity is $14,275,000 at December 31, 1996. Its total debt ratio using market values was _____.

A second ratio that relates the level of debt to economic value and performance is the times interest earned ratio. This ratio relates earnings before interest and taxes—a measure of profitability and of long-term viability—to the interest expense—a measure of the level of debt.

$$\frac{\text{Earnings before interest and taxes}}{\text{Interest expense}}$$

3. Magnetronics's earnings before interest and taxes were $_____ in 1996, and its interest charges were $_____ . Its times interest earned was _____ times. This represented an improvement/deterioration from the 1992 level of _____ times.

A fourth and final leverage ratio is the number of days of payables ratio. This ratio measures the average number of days that the company is taking to pay its suppliers of raw materials. It is calculated by dividing annual purchases by 365 days to determine average purchases per day:

$$\frac{\text{Annual purchases}}{365 \text{ days}}$$

Accounts payable are then divided by average purchases per day to determine the number of days of purchases that are still unpaid.

$$\frac{\text{Accounts payable}}{\text{Average purchases per day}}$$

It is often difficult to determine the purchases of a firm. Instead, the income statement shows cost of goods sold, a figure that includes not only raw materials but also labor and overhead. Thus, it often is only possible to gain a rough idea as to whether a firm is becoming more or less dependent on its suppliers for finance. This can be done by relating accounts payable to cost of goods sold

$$\frac{\text{Accounts payable}}{\text{Cost of goods sold}}$$

and following this ratio over time.

4. Magnetronics owed its suppliers \$_____ at year-end 1996. This represented _____% of cost of goods sold and was an increase/decrease from _____% at year-end 1992. The company appears to be more/less prompt in paying its suppliers in 1996 than it was in 1992.

5. The deterioration in Magnetronics's profitability, as measured by its return on equity, from 15.2% in 1992 to 10.7% in 1996, resulted from the combined impact of _____

_____

_____ and _____

_____ .

6. The financial riskiness of Magnetronics increased/decreased between 1992 and 1996.

Liquidity Ratios: How Liquid Is the Company?

The fourth basic type of financial ratio is the liquidity ratio. These ratios measure a company's ability to meet financial obligations as they become current. The current ratio, defined as current assets divided by current liabilities,

$$\frac{\text{Current assets}}{\text{Current liabilities}}$$

assumes that current assets are much more readily and certainly convertible into cash than other assets. It relates these fairly liquid assets to the claims that are due within 1 year—the current liabilities.

1. Magnetronics held \$_____ of current assets at year-end 1996 and owed \$_____ to creditors due to be paid within 1 year. Its current ratio was _____, an improvement/deterioration from the ratio of _____ at year-end 1992.

The quick ratio, or acid test, is similar to the current ratio, but it excludes inventory from the current assets:

$$\frac{\text{Current assets} - \text{Inventory}}{\text{Current liabilities}}$$

Inventory is excluded because it is often difficult to convert into cash (at least at book value) if the company is struck by adversity.

2. The quick ratio for Magnetronics at year-end 1996 was _____, an improvement/deterioration from the ratio of _____ at year-end 1992.

A Warning

The calculated ratios are no more valid than the financial statements from which they are derived. The quality of the financial statements should be assessed, and appropriate adjustments made, before any ratios are calculated. Particular attention should be placed on assessing the reasonableness of the accounting choices and assumptions embedded in the financial statements.

The Case of the Unidentified Industries

The preceding exercise suggests a series of questions that may be helpful in assessing a company's future financial health. It also describes several ratios that are useful in answering some of the questions, especially if the historical trend in these ratios is examined.

However, it is also important to compare the actual absolute value with some standard to determine whether the company is performing well. Unfortunately, there is no single current ratio, inventory turnover, or debt ratio that is appropriate to all industries, and even within a specific industry, ratios may vary significantly among companies. The operating and competitive characteristics of the company's industry greatly influence its investment in the various types of assets, the riskiness of these investments, and the financial structure of its balance sheet.

Try to match the following five types of companies with their corresponding balance sheets and financial ratios, shown in Exhibit 3.

1. Electric utility
2. Japanese trading company
3. Aerospace manufacturer
4. Automobile manufacturer
5. Supermarket chain

In doing this exercise, consider the operating and competitive characteristics of the industry and their implications for (1) the collection period, (2) inventory turnover, (3) the amount of plant and equipment, and (4) the appropriate financial structure. Then identify which one of the five sets of balance sheets and financial ratios best matches your expectations.

EXHIBIT 1

Magnetronics, Inc., Consolidated Income Statements for Years Ending December 31, 1992 and 1996 (thousands of dollars)

	1992	1996
Net sales	$32,513	$48,769
Cost of goods sold	19,183	29,700
Gross profit	13,330	19,069
Operating expenses	10,758	16,541
Interest expense	361	517
Income before taxes	2,211	2,011
Federal income taxes	1,040	704
Net income	$ 1,171	$ 1,307

EXHIBIT 2

Magnetronics, Inc., Consolidated Balance Sheets at December 31, 1992 and 1996 (thousands of dollars)

	1992	1996
Cash	$ 1,617	$ 2,020
Accounts receivable	5,227	7,380
Inventories	4,032	8,220
Current assets	10,876	17,620
Net fixed assets	4,073	5,160
Total assets	$14,949	$22,780
Notes payable, banks	$ 864	$ 1,213
Accounts payable	1,615	2,820
Accrued expenses and taxes	2,028	3,498
Current liabilities	4,507	7,531
Long-term debt	2,750	3,056
Stockholders' equity	7,692	12,193
Total liabilities and stockholders' equity	$14,949	$22,780

EXHIBIT 3

Unidentified Balance Sheets

	A	B	C	D	E
Balance Sheet Percentages					
Cash	7.6%	2.7%	1.4%	7.2%	12.7%
Receivables	31.7	4.7	2.9	60.3	11.5
Inventories	5.3	2.0	23.0	8.7	48.1
Other current assets	1.2	3.0	1.8	7.3	0.0
Property and equipment (net)	30.2	66.6	49.9	4.3	25.0
Other assets	24.0	21.0	21.0	12.2	2.7
Total assets	100.0%	100.0%	100.0%	100.0%	100.0%
Notes payable	38.4%	4.2%	4.6%	50.8%	0.9%
Accounts payable	5.5	3.0	20.0	15.2	21.5
Other current liabilities	1.5	4.7	12.7	5.7	27.4
Long-term debt	17.4	30.0	37.5	22.7	8.1
Other liabilities	26.5	22.9	9.8	1.3	8.1
Owners' equity	10.7	35.2	15.4	4.3	34.0
Total liabilities and equity	100.0%	100.0%	100.0%	100.0%	100.0%
Selected Ratios					
Net profits/Net sales	.04	.14	.02	.01	.05
Net profits/Total assets	.03	.05	.06	.01	.03
Net profits/Owners' equity	.29	.14	.41	.13	.10
Net sales/Total assets	.78	.36	3.2	2.1	.67
Collection period (days)	149	48	3	106	63
Inventory turnover	11	10	10	23	1.1
Total liabilities/Total assets	.89	.65	.85	.96	.66
Long-term debt/Owners' equity	1.6	.85	2.4	5.3	.24
Current assets/Current liabilities	1.0	1.0	.8	1.0	1.4
Quick ratio	.9	.9	.2	.9	.5

General Mills 1994 Annual Report

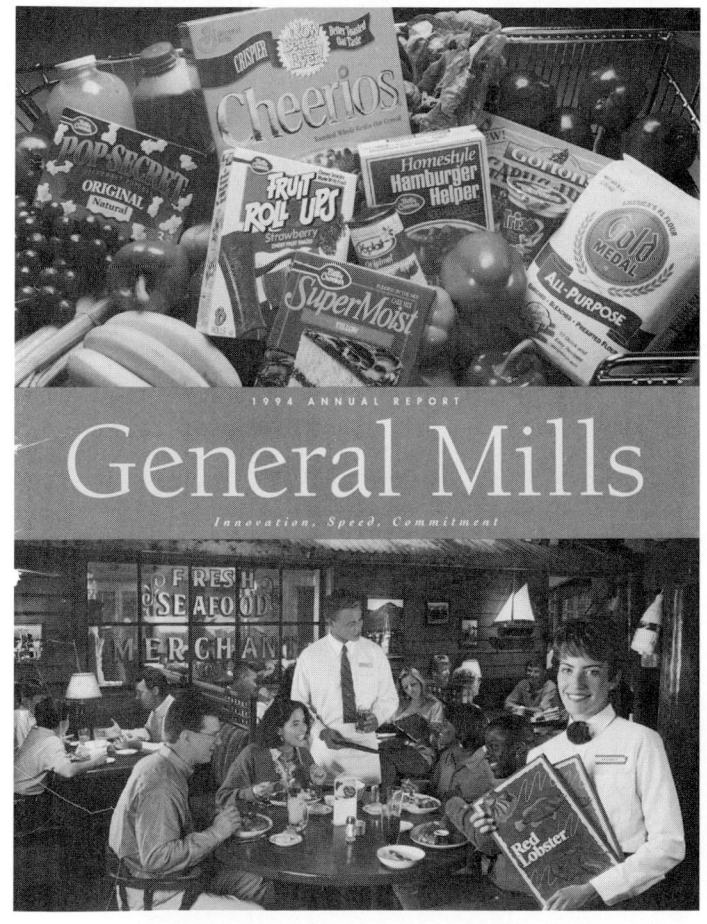

INNOVATION, SPEED, COMMITMENT. These three central values are the keys to General Mills' superior long-term growth record and prospects. Innovation is the principal driver of established business growth and new business development. Speed drives productivity gains. Commitment gives us the persistency to bounce back from disappointment, and drives our ability to deliver financial performance that ranks in the top 10 percent of major U.S. corporations. We have set aggressive goals for the balance of this decade. This report discusses our current position and excellent prospects for achieving our growth goals.

THE YEARS IN BRIEF

	Fiscal Year Ended		
In Millions, Except per Share Data and Percentages	May 29, 1994	May 30, 1993	May 31, 1992
Continuing Operations			
Sales	$8,516.9	$8,134.6	$7,777.8
Earnings after Taxes	469.7	506.1	505.6
Earnings per Share	2.95	3.10	3.05
Return on Average Total Capital	15.8%	18.4%	20.6%
Results After Discontinued Operations			
Discontinued Operations after Taxes	$ -	$ -	$ (10.0)
Accounting Changes	.2	-	-
Net Earnings	469.9	506.1	495.6
Net Earnings per Share	2.95	3.10	2.99
Average Shares Outstanding	159.1	163.1	165.7
Dividends per Share	$ 1.88	$ 1.68	$ 1.48

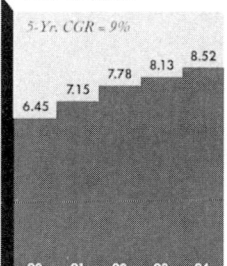

SALES
Dollars in Billions

5-Yr. CGR = 9%

6.45 7.15 7.78 8.13 8.52

90 91 92 93 94

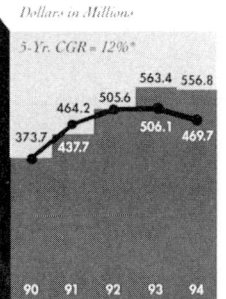

EARNINGS AFTER TAXES
Dollars in Millions

5-Yr. CGR = 12%*

373.7 464.2 505.6 563.4 556.8
437.7 506.1 469.7

90 91 92 93 94

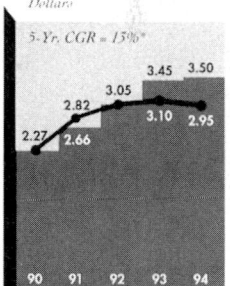

EARNINGS PER SHARE
Dollars

5-Yr. CGR = 15%*

2.27 2.66 2.82 3.05 3.45 3.50
3.10 2.95

90 91 92 93 94

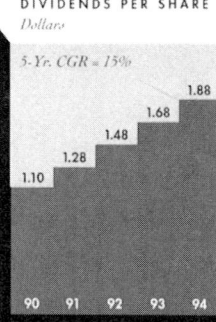

DIVIDENDS PER SHARE
Dollars

5-Yr. CGR = 15%

1.10 1.28 1.48 1.68 1.88

90 91 92 93 94

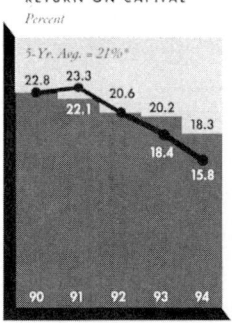

AFTER-TAX RETURN ON CAPITAL
Percent

5-Yr. Avg. = 21%*

22.8 23.3 20.6 20.2 18.3
22.1 18.4 15.8

90 91 92 93 94

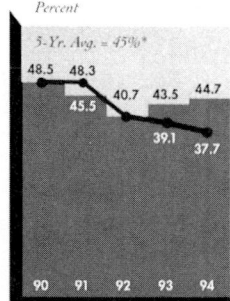

RETURN ON AVERAGE EQUITY
Percent

5-Yr. Avg. = 45%*

48.5 48.3 40.7 43.5 44.7
45.5 39.1 37.7

90 91 92 93 94

■ *Results excluding unusual items*   ■ *Results including unusual items*

*5-Yr. compound growth rates and average returns exclude unusual items

1991 results include an unusual after-tax gain related primarily to disposition of businesses. 1993 results include an unusual after-tax charge related to productivity actions. 1994 results include an unusual after-tax charge related to an improper pesticide substitution by an independent contractor in treating oat supplies. See note two to the consolidated financial statements for further information.

General Mills' financial results in fiscal 1994 were disappointing. These results fell far short of our goal of 12 percent annual growth in earnings per share—a goal the company has met or exceeded consistently since our major restructuring in fiscal 1985. The shortfall was caused by two major problems affecting our Big G cereal business. The balance of the company, excluding Big G, met the company's long-term growth goal. This annual report discusses the two cereal problems and the actions we have taken to deal with them, along with our growth strategies for the balance of the company. Based on these actions and strategies, we believe prospects for achieving our goal of 12 percent average annual earnings-per-share growth over the remainder of this decade are excellent.

Big G Cereals

The first problem affecting Big G was escalating promotional activity by all competitors in the U.S. ready-to-eat cereal market. This activity resulted in reduced profits and little change in market share. It also generated increasing inefficiencies in using coupons and in-store promotions to deliver value to consumers. For instance, 98 percent of cereal coupons issued are thrown away and not redeemed, and roughly half of promotional expenditures do not reach consumers in the form of lower prices. Big G moved decisively to address the promotional escalation by eliminating $175 million annually in inefficient promotional spending and delivering increased value directly to consumers by lowering prices on its largest brands by $110 million. Combined with a focused series of product improvements, promising new products and marketing innovations, these actions are expected to restore Big G's profit growth in 1995. So far, all the signs are positive, as our cereal prices are coming down at retail and promotional activities by industry competitors are scheduled at substantially lower levels. Pages 5 to 7 of this report discuss Big G's action plan in greater detail, along with other initiatives throughout General Mills that demonstrate our commitment to delivering superior long-term financial results.

The second major problem affecting Big G cereals and 1994 results was the improper substitution of an unregistered pesticide during the year by a licensed independent contractor who treated part of the company's raw oat supply. While the substitution did not present any consumer health hazard, it did represent a regulatory violation. We voluntarily halted shipments of affected oat-containing products and did not seek permission to ship affected inventories because the process required to secure regulatory approval proved so lengthy, it would exceed the product age limits we employ to ensure freshness in the market. Production and shipment of our oat cereals was interrupted for a month-long period in June and July. By late July, the company resumed full production and shipment of oat-containing products. Estimated costs associated with this problem, including the disposition of affected inventories, are reflected in an unusual charge to 1994 earnings of 55 cents per share. We are aggressively pursuing insurance recoveries.

Financial Results

Earnings per share before unusual items in 1994 were $3.50, up 1 percent from $3.45 a year earlier. Net earnings per share were $2.95, including the 55-cent unusual charge. Prior-year net earnings per share were $3.10. The year-end market price of General Mills shares was $54.50, down 16 percent. Dividends per share increased 12 percent to $1.88, a payout of 54 percent of earnings before unusual items and the 29th consecutive year of dividend growth. The company remains committed to increasing dividends in line with long-term growth in earnings per share, with a target of paying out 50 percent of earnings.

Innovation, Speed, Commitment

Over the last five years, General Mills' share price has grown at an 11 percent compound rate and dividends have doubled. Thus, total return to shareholders has increased at a 14 percent annual rate over this period, outpacing the 11 percent compound annual return by the S&P 500 stock index.

Performance Review

Despite disappointing cereal results, significant achievements were recorded in the balance of the company.

➤ *Most of General Mills' current businesses demonstrated continued unit and profit growth.* Excluding cereals, Consumer Foods' unit volume was up 5 percent, with growth from established brands and strong volume contributions from innovative new products. Earnings growth exceeded the company's long-term goal. Market shares were increased or sustained in most major categories including cereals.

Red Lobster had an excellent year with very strong profit growth. This performance was driven by the substantial improvements made during the past several years to Red Lobster's menu offerings, service and dining atmosphere. The Olive Garden had a decline in its annual profits. Now 10 years old, The Olive Garden is in the process of going through the same sort of concept updating that Red Lobster has executed so well periodically throughout its history.

➤ *New businesses designed to be major contributors to future growth made continued good progress.* Cereal Partners Worldwide (CPW), the company's joint venture with Nestlé, S.A., posted volume and share gains in existing markets, and entered five

Gaillard, Lee, Atwater, Sanger, Willes

new markets during the year. Snack Ventures Europe, a joint venture with PepsiCo Foods International, also achieved volume gains and expanded beyond its original six European markets into Italy. And China Coast, the company's Chinese dinnerhouse restaurant concept, began its national expansion. Development spending for CPW, China Coast and other ventures totaled $39 million (15 cents per share) in 1994, the same as in 1993. Spending is expected to remain near that level in 1995 and begin declining in 1996.

➤ *General Mills people found ways to improve productivity significantly, benefiting operations throughout the company.* Betty Crocker Products, Gold Medal, Yoplait and Red Lobster were among those divisions whose increasing productivity contributed to margin and earnings growth in 1994. Additional productivity initiatives launched during the year will contribute to earnings growth in future years.

Management Changes

During the year, Steve Sanger was elected president of the company. Charlie Gaillard was elected vice chairman and a member of the board of directors. Jeff O'Hara, president of Red Lobster, and Ron Magruder, president of The Olive Garden, were each named executive vice presidents of the company.

Ted Cushmore, president of Gold Medal, Jon Finley, president of China Coast, Gary Rodkin, president of Yoplait, Jeff Rotsch, president of Betty Crocker Products, and Blaine Sweatt, president of Restaurants New Business Development, were each named General Mills senior vice presidents. Ken Thome was named senior vice president, Financial Operations. He succeeds Tom Nelson, who retired from

LEADING MARKET POSITIONS	1994 Category Sales ($MM)	Market Position	1994 Retail Dollar Share	+/- 1990
Consumer Foods				
RTE Cereals	$9,000	2	29%	+ 2 pts.
Refrigerated Yogurt	1,500	2	25	+ 5
Dessert Mixes	1,100	1	48	+ 5
Frozen Seafood	700	2	22	+ 1
Grain Snacks	625	1	23	+12
Microwave Popcorn	550	2	35	+10
Family Flour	445	1	43	+ 2
Dinner Mixes	410	1	79	+12
Fruit Snacks	410	1	60	+11
Potato Mixes	340	1	54	+ 8
Restaurants				
Full-service Italian	6,200	1	17	+ 7
Full-service Seafood	5,400	1	29	+ 4

General Mills 1994 Annual Report

General Mills in December 1993 after a distinguished 38-year career. Steve Demeritt, senior vice president of General Mills, was named chief executive officer of CPW by the joint venture's board of directors.

Future Outlook

Looking ahead, we believe General Mills' prospects for achieving differential earnings growth with continued high returns remain excellent. As mentioned earlier, our goal for the balance of this decade is to grow earnings per share at a 12 percent compound rate.

1994-2000 EPS GROWTH FACTORS	
EPS Growth Goal	12%
Growth Factors:	
Unit Growth	52%
ROS Improvement	38
Stock Repurchase	10
Total	100%

The key factors necessary to achieve this growth are:
➤ strong unit volume growth in Consumer Foods, averaging 5 percent annually;
➤ combined new unit expansion by Red Lobster, The Olive Garden and China Coast at an average 8 percent annual rate;
➤ the swing to profitability by CPW and China Coast, and accelerating earnings growth by Snack Ventures Europe; and
➤ continued productivity gains in every part of the company, which will help further improve return on sales (ROS) from 6.5 percent before unusual items in 1994 to a targeted minimum of 7.5 percent by the year 2000.

The recently enacted federal corporate tax-rate increase will restrain our growth somewhat, while continued share repurchases will contribute to our earnings per share growth.

We will continue to support the excellent internal growth opportunities our businesses provide with significant levels of fixed-asset investment. Following a period of major expansion in food manufacturing capacity, planned fixed-asset additions will decrease from the $1.88 billion invested from 1992 through 1994 to an estimated $1.57 billion over the next three years. These investments will include productivity initiatives in Consumer Foods along with a minimum of 300 new restau-

rants. The leveling of fixed-asset investment from peak levels increases our ability to use more of our cash flows for our stock repurchase efforts.

General Mills has a long history of dealing decisively, directly and successfully with business problems, which arise virtually every year in one segment of the company or another. Red Lobster, Yoplait and Gold Medal represent businesses that experienced major performance issues at some point in recent years. In each instance, the problems were successfully resolved and all three operations posted excellent results in 1994. We believe our current profit issues will respond to the same type of decisive actions that successfully resolved these earlier problems.

Consequently, we expect our earnings progress to resume in 1995, restoring momentum toward our long-term financial goals. The first quarter will show an earnings decline as compared to last year due to a significant decline in shipments of oat-containing products related to the problems cited earlier, with results improving as the year progresses.

The ultimate basis for our confidence in the company's strong future growth prospects is the collective innovation, speed and commitment of General Mills people. We thank them for their dedication and continuing commitment to superior results.

Sincerely,

H. B. Atwater, Jr.
Chairman and Chief Executive Officer

Stephen W. Sanger
President

Mark H. Willes
Vice Chairman

Joe R. Lee
Vice Chairman

Charles W. Gaillard
Vice Chairman

August 5, 1994

Innovation, Speed, Commitment

COMMITMENT TO RESULTS

General Mills' commitment to shareholders is to deliver financial results that place us in the top 10 percent of major U.S. corporations. Inherent in this commitment are the intensity to innovate continuously and the persistency to bounce back from disappointments when they occur. Outlined below are examples of how the commitment of General Mills people will create differential long-term growth and returns for our shareholders.

Better Value, Better Profits

The company's primary objective is to provide competitively superior products and services that satisfy today's value-conscious consumers. In the current environment, meeting this goal requires strategies that deliver value to consumers as directly as possible.

For example, the Big G cereal division took major steps during the past year to enhance direct consumer value and business profitability. In doing so, Big G broke from the recent industry practice of periodic price increases that were discounted back to the consumer through escalating levels of coupons and promotions. Over the past several years, coupon values of $1 or more became common in the cereal category, and in-store promotions frequently included "buy one, get one free" offers. As a result, roughly 60 percent of cereal purchases last year were made with a coupon or some form of in-store promotion.

Reflecting this escalating promotion, Big G couponing and trade promotion expense grew from 20 percent of sales in 1991 to 28 percent in 1994. But because of the inefficiencies inherent in coupon distribution and price promotions, only

a portion of cereal manufacturers' promotional spending reached consumers.

Big G set a course to deliver greater value directly to consumers. In November 1993, the company added 25 percent more fruit and nut pieces to five popular brands at no change in price. One month later, Big G lowered prices and promotional spending on selected large-size packages of three different cereals. And in April, Big G announced plans to eliminate more than $175 million of inefficient promotional spending, or roughly 30 percent of its 1994 coupon and trade promotion expense, and deliver value directly through price declines on brands representing about 40 percent of annual volume. In all, Big G's actions encompassed more than half of its cereal line. Lower prices have now been reflected by the majority of our major grocery accounts, so better values are available to consumers at every purchase. Big G will also continue to support its product line with coupons and store promotions. Given its new lower prices, the frequency and level of those discounts will be moderated.

By providing more consistent value while reducing the inefficiencies of its couponing and promotional programs, Big G expects to improve its profitability beginning in fiscal 1995. To increase volume and market share, Big G is intensifying its focus on established product improvement, new product innovation and effective marketing. With this renewed focus on the business-building fundamentals, we believe the outlook for Big G and the cereal market is excellent.

General Mills' other food operations have demonstrated the same innovative energy to deliver superior results and more direct consumer value. For example, Betty Crocker has doubled its earnings since 1990 through a 43 percent increase in unit volume, significant productivity gains and virtually no increase in pricing. In 1991, Yoplait reduced prices, moderated promotion spending, and intensified its focus on product innovation, aggressive consumer marketing and continuous productivity improvement. Driven by the combined success of these actions to increase volume and margins, Yoplait's retail volume has increased 49 percent and earnings have more than quadrupled since 1992.

A Superior Dining Experience

General Mills' restaurant operations are committed to delivering a competitively superior dining experience. This requires continuous improvement in all aspects of their food, service and dining atmosphere.

Red Lobster, now in its 27th year of operation, had seen a decline in guest counts and flattening earnings in 1993. In response, Red Lobster took significant actions in 1994 that have refreshed the concept and generated strong profit growth. The updating included a new menu emphasizing quality, freshness and interesting tastes, and a new decor that creates a warm and casual "wharfside" atmosphere. Servers now work in teams that share responsibility for portions of the dining room, resulting in faster service for guests. Servers also handle payments on guest checks, replacing the less-convenient arrangement of separate cashiers. Surveys show guests overwhelmingly view these changes as added value to their dining experience.

Red Lobster is also taking actions to ensure that its food offerings represent good value to guests. Dinner entree prices have not been increased since March 1991, as productivity gains have successfully offset higher ingredient costs. Well-advertised product promotions, such as "Lobster and 18 Shrimp" and *Lobsterfest*, augment both value and variety. In addition, on a regional basis Red Lobster has employed a value menu featuring a strong selection of dinner entrees under $10.

As a result of all these efforts, Red Lobster in 1994 recorded a 23 percent increase in operating profits, driven by growth in

◄ Red Lobster aggressively markets a variety of limited-time promotions that offer value-conscious consumers quality seafood at attractive prices.

➤ Regional consolidation of corrugated packaging purchases with several key suppliers is resulting in increased efficiency for all participants and significant cost savings for the company. Pictured are Sharon Beduhn, General Mills Purchasing, and Ed Murray, senior national accounts manager for Weyerhaeuser Paper Company.

guest counts and average unit sales; increased returns; and a record market share. This strong momentum puts Red Lobster well on track to reach its long-term growth goals.

The Olive Garden Italian restaurant, which experienced its first profit decline in 1994 after six consecutive years of rapid growth, is committed to restoring earnings momentum. In June 1994, The Olive Garden initiated a series of actions to refresh its dining experience and surpass guests' expectations in an increasingly competitive casual dining segment. These actions include a new menu featuring more distinctive foods and greater use of fresh, seasonal ingredients. Additional changes to enhance service and atmosphere, all supported by increased consumer advertising, will be implemented in 1995.

Companywide Productivity Gains

Continued productivity improvement throughout General Mills is key to our ability to deliver product quality and value while increasing earnings. Productivity gains have helped increase our return on sales from 5.6 percent in 1989 to 6.5 percent before unusual items in 1994. Initiatives now under way will support continued improvement in ROS toward our minimum goal of 7.5 percent by 2000.

Consumer Foods has a goal of reducing manufacturing and distribution costs as a percent of sales from 20 percent in 1990 to 17 percent by the year 2000, a pre-tax savings of $250 million. Approximately one-third of this savings has already been achieved.

Our expectations for continued improvement are based in part on our opportunities to maximize utilization of manufacturing capacity added in recent years. This includes new cereal plants in Covington, Ga., and Albuquerque,

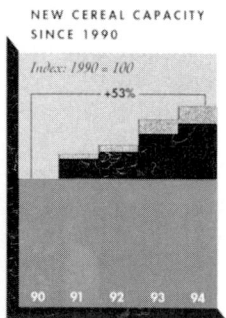

NEW CEREAL CAPACITY
SINCE 1990

Index: 1990 = 100

+53%

90 91 92 93 94

▨ *Productivity Additions*
■ *New Systems*
▨ *1990 Capacity*

N.M., and a new mix plant in Toledo, Ohio. The company also has increased production capacity by adopting high-performance work systems, where teams of self-directed employees share responsibility for all aspects of production. For example, converting to high-performance work methods has increased the capacity of existing cereal lines by more than 10 percent with minimal fixed-asset investment. As Big G fills new capacity with normal growth over the next several years, cereal productivity will increase substantially.

The company is also implementing actions to strengthen supplier partnerships and consolidate purchases of materials, equipment and services across the whole of its Consumer Foods and Restaurant operations. These consolidated purchasing initiatives contributed cost savings of $12 million in 1994, and are projected to contribute over four times that amount by 1996.

Our Restaurant operations have achieved productivity gains by streamlining organizations and adopting management information systems designed to maximize food production and labor-hour efficiency. Eliminating separate cashiers at Red Lobster has simplified operations and will contribute cost savings of $12 million annually. Initiatives like these will allow Restaurants to continue offering exceptional menu value while maintaining or improving returns on sales.

The preceding examples are representative of broad efforts under way in every part of General Mills. Our collective commitment is to innovate relentlessly in all of our markets, to act quickly and decisively when problems arise and to deliver superior long-term results.

CONSUMER FOODS sales grew to $5.55 billion in 1994, a 4 percent increase excluding revenues from European snack businesses no longer consolidated. Domestic packaged foods unit volume increased 3 percent, and market share positions were sustained or increased in most of the company's major food categories. Operating profits before unusual items were restrained by the cereal market promotional escalation and declined 1 percent to $800 million. The major actions taken by Big G to resolve the promotional escalation issue are discussed on pages 5 and 6.

➤ **Big G Cereals** Pound volume for the U.S. ready-to-eat cereal market grew more than 5 percent, driven primarily by

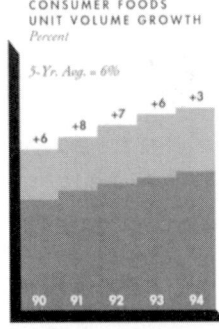

CONSUMER FOODS
UNIT VOLUME GROWTH
Percent

5-Yr. Avg. = 6%

+6 +8 +7 +6 +3

90 91 92 93 94

■ *Products new in last 3 Yrs.*

new product activity. Consumer purchases of Big G cereals also increased 5 percent, nearly matching the market's growth, and the company's dollar market share was 29.1 percent, virtually even with last year's 29.2 percent share. Annual unit volume rose 1 percent as trade inventories declined. ➤ Marketing innovation and continuous product improvement drove volume growth for established cereals. Effective advertising that reinforced *Kix* cereal's appeal to both kids and parents helped the 57-year-old brand achieve a 7 percent volume gain. Significant improvements were made to several brands, including

The Fundamentals of Brand Building

TO GENERATE CONTINUED GROWTH in volume and market share, Big G is intensifying its focus on the fundamentals that build brands: continuous product improvement, new-product innovation and effective marketing. New better-tasting, crispier *Cheerios* and an improved *Wheaties* with a milder whole-grain flavor began arriving on grocers' shelves in late summer, the first of several major product improvements planned in 1995. The company's newest brands, *Reese's Peanut Butter Puffs* and *Sun Crunchers* cereal with sunflower seeds on hearty corn and whole-wheat flakes, represent distinctive new tastes in the cereal aisle. Media spending to support Big G's strong product line-up is being increased in 1995, and effective new advertising has been developed for major brands. These actions are the keys to further differentiating Big G's product line from competitive offerings.

CEREAL PARTNERS WORLDWIDE, the company's joint venture with Nestlé, continues to strengthen its position as the world's No. 2 cereal company outside the United States and Canada. For the 12 months ended March 1994, the period included in General Mills' fiscal-year results, CPW unit volume increased 24 percent and sales grew to nearly $390 million. In the United Kingdom, CP-UK challenged for the No. 2 share position with good performance from its core *Shredded Wheat* and *Shreddies* brands. Original European markets showed continued double-digit growth, although the rates of increase were lower than in recent years. CPW again paced growth and reported share gains in each country. The company completed its first full year of operation in Mexico, Germany and the ASEAN markets in the southwestern Pacific. With operations now expanding to Switzerland, Austria, Belgium, Greece and Chile, CPW competes in markets accounting for 75 percent of cereal consumption outside North America. This represents good progress toward CPW's goal of $1 billion in sales by the year 2000.

CPW ORIGINAL MARKETS					
	1993 Category Volume (Metric Tons in 000's)	Category Growth	Entered Market	1993 Share	Share +/- Year Ago
United Kingdom	332	4%	Jan. 91	16%	+0 pts.
France	72	15	Jan. 91	17	+2
Spain	26	12	Jan. 91	11	+1
Portugal	7	12	Jan. 91	46	+3

MAJOR EXPANSION MARKETS				
	1993 Category Volume (Metric Tons in 000's)	Entered Market	Latest Period Market Share	Share +/- Year Ago
Italy	14	Jan. 92	11%	+1 pts.
Mexico	77	Sept. 92	11	+3
Germany	110	Jan. 93	6	+3

A Growing Worldwide Cereal Business

Lucky Charms and five adult cereals that were enhanced to include 25 percent more fruit and nut pieces. Improvements to *Cheerios, Wheaties* and several other key brands in 1995 will help sustain Big G's established product vitality. ➤ Distinctive cereals introduced in recent years also achieved volume gains. These included *Multi-Grain Cheerios*, the latest addition to the cereal market's leading brand franchise. Two new children's cereals, *Sprinkle Spangles* and *Hidden Treasures*, were introduced during 1994 and both contributed incremental volume. *Fingos* cereal, designed to be eaten dry for breakfasts on the run, did not meet expectations and was discontinued. ➤ Current new product activity is tightly focused on introducing differentiated cereals with strong taste appeal. *Reese's Peanut Butter Puffs* cereal entered distribution in May and initial market performance is strong. *Sun Crunchers*, an innovative entry in the adult cereal segment, will begin entering stores in late August. Additional new products are in development. ➤ Today, cereals are a part of just 30 percent of all breakfast occasions, up from 25 percent a decade earlier. With population growth focused in the child and older adult

segments, where cereal consumption is highest, and with consumers' interest in convenience, nutrition, variety and value increasing, the outlook for both the U.S. cereal market and Big G remains excellent. ➤ **Betty Crocker Products** While competitive activity was high in the dessert, snack and dinner mix markets, Betty Crocker achieved significant productivity gains and recorded another year of excellent earnings growth. Unit volume rose 1 percent, with continued growth from established lines and nearly half of total volume generated by products developed in the last five years. Betty Crocker's strong market positions were maintained or increased in most key categories. ➤ Superior product qual-

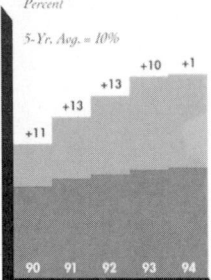

BETTY CROCKER PRODUCTS
UNIT VOLUME GROWTH
Percent

5-Yr. Avg. = 10%

+11   +13   +13   +10   +1

90   91   92   93   94

■ *Products new in last 5 Yrs.*

ity and marketing innovation drove volume growth. *Hamburger Helper* dinner mix volume increased 6 percent on the strength of effective new advertising and good consumer response to hearty *Homestyle* varieties introduced last fall. New *Fruit Roll-Ups Secret Pictures* with press-out cartoon shapes and *Gushers Sour Berry Blast* helped boost volume for these popular fruit snack lines 6 percent. *Nature Valley* granola bar volume grew with the addition of new low-fat varieties. Ongoing actions that will support continued volume growth for established lines include the current introductions of improved *Creamy Deluxe* ready-to-

A Distinguished Record of Product Innovation

BETTY CROCKER has an exceptional record of new product success. Annual unit volume has increased at a 10 percent compound rate since 1989, with new products accounting for an impor-

tant part of that growth each year. Some of these innovations extend existing franchises. For example, new *Creamy Chilled Desserts* represent a distinctive addition to Betty Crocker's dessert line, offering consumers several favorite

refrigerated desserts with the convenience of a prepared mix. *Cheerios* Snack Mix pairs the popular O-shaped cereal with whole wheat squares, cheese crackers and pretzels for a great-tasting new selection in the snack aisle. And *Fruit String Thing* wraps the great taste of *Betty Crocker* fruit snacks into a fun new shape. Other product innovations create entries into new market segments. *Potato Shakers* dry seasoning mixes turn fresh potatoes into oven-browned potatoes. And *Pop Secret Pop Chips* represent a new idea in snacks—made from popcorn,

they are 65 percent lower in fat than regular potato chips. Additional new product activity planned in 1995 should help sustain Betty Crocker's momentum.

![Product photographs of Betty Crocker SuperMoist cake mix, Creamy Deluxe frosting, Homestyle Hamburger Helper, and Cheddar Classics Three Cheese Potatoes, with a prepared Salisbury dinner on a plate]

Continuous Product Improvement Builds Brands

spread frostings and *SuperMoist* layer cakes, innovative new varieties of *Helper* dinner mixes and a four-flavor *Cheddar Classics* line of specialty potatoes. Distinctive additions also are being made to various snack lines, including *Rollerblade* shaped fruit snacks and two cheese varieties of *Pop Secret* microwave popcorn. ➤ **Gold Medal** Annual U.S. per capita flour consumption increased to 143 pounds in calendar 1993. The market's family flour segment declined slightly but bakery flour volume continued its long-term growth, driven by increased away-from-home eating and expansion of in-store bakeries. General Mills' family flour brands achieved 9 percent volume growth and their highest market share in six years by reducing promotional spending and prices while maintaining merchandising effectiveness. Bakery flour operations also had a good year, despite short market supplies of high-quality wheat. ➤ *Bisquick* remained the variety baking mix category's leading brand in 1994 but volume was lower, reflecting aggressive competitive activity. The *Gold Medal* and *Robin Hood Smart Size* pouch baking mix lines posted good volume growth due to expanding distribution and the addition of new varieties. *Bac*Os* volume also grew on the strength of distribution gains. ➤ **Yoplait-Colombo** Volume in the refrigerated yogurt category grew 9 percent, driven by new product activity, a growing children's market segment, and consumers' continued interest in nutrition and value. Yoplait led the market with 21 percent volume

growth, and increased its dollar market share to 22 percent. Continued product innovation from Yoplait and the acquisition of the Colombo refrigerated and frozen yogurt businesses will help sustain momentum. ➤ **Gorton's** Frozen seafood category volume declined 5 percent, but increased new product activity and stable costs are improving the market outlook. Gorton's recorded its third consecutive year of earnings growth on the success of new products such as Garlic and Herb breaded fillets and Value Pack Mini Fish Sticks, improvements to established lines and strong productivity initiatives. ➤ **Foodservice** Unit volume for Foodservice operations rose 4 percent, with double-digit growth in both cereals and snacks. The introduction of *Gold Medal* Dessert Bar Mixes helped Foodservice sustain its leadership position in baking mixes. ➤ **International Foods** Unit volume increased 7 percent for General Mills' Canadian food operations, with cereals, dinner mixes and snack foods each recording gains. Dessert volume matched last year's and key products recorded market share increases. General Mills' export operations focused efforts on broadening dessert mix business in Europe and expanding distribution of snack products. In June 1994, the company sold its 50 percent interest in a flour

Long-familiar Brands, Enjoyed at Home and Away

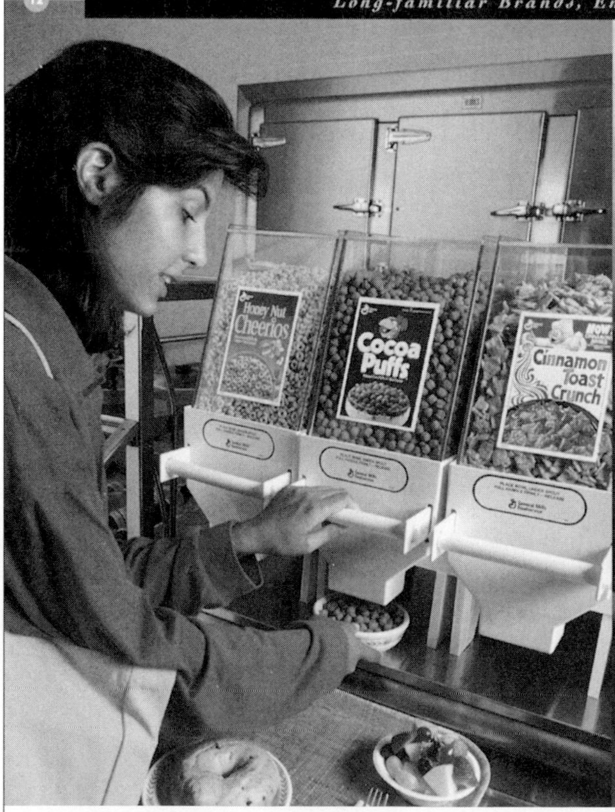

General Mills 1994 Annual Report

REFRIGERATED YOGURT DOLLAR SHARE
Percent

```
                              25
  20    18    19    20
                        22
  90    91    92    93   94
```

■ *Yoplait*   ■ *Colombo*

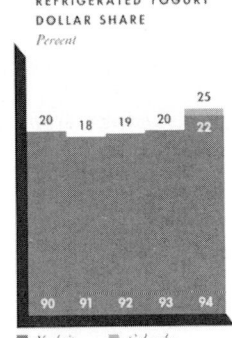

yogurt holds strong share positions in the Northeast, complementing Yoplait's geographic strength in Central and Western markets. In addition, Colombo is a leader in the soft-frozen yogurt category, where combined manufacturers' sales total $400 million. Colombo also holds a strong No. 2 position in the superpremium

YOGURT became a bigger business for General Mills in 1994, as Yoplait achieved excellent growth and the acquisition of Colombo provided strong entries into major new market segments. Yoplait's dollar share of the $1.5 billion refrigerated yogurt market grew to 22 percent. The share gain reflected the impact of

meaningful improvements to established products, including reformulation of *Light Original Yoplait* and the addition of *Light Custard Style*, which boosted total Light volume 25 percent. The success of distinctive new lines such as *Crunch 'n Yogurt* also contributed to Yoplait's share gain. Colombo refrigerated

segment of the $300 million retail market for hard-pack frozen yogurt. Plans call for aggressive efforts to market and grow both of these high-quality yogurt brands.

A Growing Yogurt Business

milling venture in Panama. ➤ **Efficient Consumer Response** General Mills continued to expand efforts supporting Efficient Consumer Response (ECR), the grocery industry's strategy to increase efficiency throughout the supply chain. According to a study sponsored by several industry trade associations, ECR could yield $30 billion in cost savings, $10 billion in the dry grocery segment alone. ECR envisions computer-linked management of information, inventory and invoices between grocery customers, food manufacturers and raw material suppliers. General Mills increased its capabilities for conducting business electronically in 1994, and also installed a powerful new companywide integrated information system. General Mills also expanded its participation in continuous replenishment inventory management. Grocery customers representing 14 percent of annual Consumer Foods volume now provide computer-based inventory and sales records directly to the company, and company sales staff manage product ordering for them. This program, which has resulted in higher sales volumes, lower costs and significantly increased inventory turns in initial tests, is available to all compatible accounts and will include customers representing 30 percent of volume by the end of 1995.

R E S T A U R A N T S sales grew 8 percent to $2.96 billion, and operating profits increased 3 percent to $219 million despite disappointing results at The Olive Garden and unusually harsh winter weather that dampened restaurant traffic in much of the country. Together, Red Lobster, The Olive Garden and China Coast added a net 115 new restaurants during 1994, for a total of 1,158 company-owned units in North America at year end. ➤ **Red Lobster** Red Lobster had an outstanding year with strong profit growth, reflecting the success of strategic actions taken to update the concept. Combined sales in North America rose 5 percent and average unit sales grew 2 percent. U.S. operations posted a 7 percent sales increase, and average unit sales grew to $2.9 million despite the increasing number of small-market restaurants in the chain. Flavorful and distinctive new menu items, improved service, high-value product promotions, and an inviting, new interior decor all contributed to increase Red Lobster's leading share of the seafood dinnerhouse segment from 27 to 29 percent. During 1994, 38 new units opened, for a total of 618 U.S. restaurants at year end, and 75 units were remodeled. In Canada, total sales were lower due to the closing of 13 restaurants in May 1993 as part of the company's restructuring actions, but earnings

Red Lobster Has a Whole New Look

ORIENTAL FOOD is one of America's favorite cuisines, and the Oriental dinnerhouse category is a $6.4 billion market. Today, this market is highly fragmented with no national competition. General Mills' newest restaurant concept, China Coast, has a goal of becoming consumers' favorite

Chinese dinnerhouse by offering food, atmosphere and service that exceed guests' expectations.

China Coast completed 1994 with 25 units located in Florida, Indiana, Texas, Ohio, Michigan and Arizona. Despite variability in individual markets, China Coast's overall results were on pace with expectations.

CHINA COAST MARKET EXPANSION

- *1994 Existing Markets*
- *1995 Expansion Markets*

In 1995, plans call for faster new unit expansion. New restaurants now include a dedicated service area for take-out business, which has performed well in initial units. China Coast is focused on building dinner traffic, and further improving guests' dining experience and store-level operations.

The success of these efforts will help China Coast toward its goal of becoming the third major, national restaurant business for General Mills and an important contributor to earnings growth in the second half of this decade.

China Coast Begins Expansion

General Mills 1994 Annual Report

for the 57 remaining units improved. ➤ Red Lobster is currently testing additional menu, decor and service enhancements to build on the success of its recent updating. In 1995, plans call for remodeling an additional 130 restaurants and opening 40 new units in the United States. ➤ **The Olive Garden** Results for The Olive Garden's North American operations did not meet expectations. Sales grew 12 percent on the strength of continued rapid new unit expansion. However, guest counts and average weekly sales declined 4 percent, reflecting the need to begin updating the dining experience. As a result, operating profits were lower in 1994, following 58 percent compound annual growth over the previous four years. In the United States, the company opened 57 new restaurants for a year-end total of 436 units. Average annual unit sales were $2.6 million. In Canada, where the company opened one new unit for a total of 22 restaurants, performance mirrored U.S. results. ➤ The Olive Garden, leader in the Italian dinnerhouse segment, is taking extensive actions to refresh guests' dining experience. The initial phase of these efforts puts strong focus on offering more distinctive food. A rotation of four seasonal menus will provide guests with increased variety and showcase fresh ingredients. In addition,

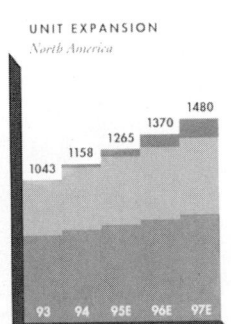

UNIT EXPANSION
North America

1043 1158 1265 1370 1480

93 94 95E 96E 97E

■ *China Coast*
■ *The Olive Garden*
■ *Red Lobster*

specialized training programs that emphasize food preparation and presentation have been developed for restaurant managers. Actions designed to update The Olive Garden's signature *Hospitaliano!* service and interior decor are currently being tested and will be implemented later in 1995. Increased levels of network television advertising will work in combination with local marketing efforts to communicate these enhancements. ➤ In 1995, The Olive Garden expects good profit growth. The company plans to add at least 40 restaurants in the United States, and will expand its test of *The Olive Garden Cafe*. This test explores the opportunities for operating a limited-menu cafe in the food-court settings of regional shopping malls, with units serviced from nearby full-size restaurants. Two test units are open and plans call for adding up to 20 more in 1995. ➤ **Outlook** Growth prospects for General Mills' casual dining restaurants remain excellent. Casual dining is the industry's fastest-growing category, and that good growth is expected to continue with the strong population increase in the 40-to-60-year-old group, the most frequent visitors to casual dining restaurants. In addition, chain restaurants hold just a 22 percent share of the full-service restaurant market, compared to a more than 60 percent share of the fast-food/quick-service segment. This gives strong, expandable concepts like Red Lobster and The Olive Garden opportunity to increase their leading market positions.

16

The Olive Garden's Action Plan

AT THE OLIVE GARDEN, the fresh new ingredients, flavors and recipes represented in their new, seasonal menus are summed up in a single word: *"Freshissimo."* The summer menu introduced in June features distinctive new dishes like Capellini Pomodoro, angel hair pasta topped with fresh Roma tomatoes and fresh basil; or Salad Pizza, a warm three-cheese pizza topped with a crisp, cool Caesar salad. To help foster *"Freshissimo,"* everyone from the managers to the servers and kitchen staff is becoming an expert in the preparation and presentation of these distinctive Italian dishes. Their efforts are being supported by a new television advertising campaign emphasizing all that's new and fresh at The Olive Garden. This enhanced focus on food is just one phase of The Olive Garden's action plan. Tests are now under way to confirm the appeal of a new interior decor and enhanced service programs. Together, these actions are designed to set a new standard for guests' dining experience.

MANAGEMENT DISCUSSION OF RESULTS OF OPERATIONS AND FINANCIAL CONDITION

General Mills' financial goal is to achieve performance that places us in the top 10 percent of major American companies, ranked by the combination of growth in earnings per share and return on capital. Over the past five years, our earnings per share have grown at a 13 percent compound rate and our after-tax return on capital has averaged 21 percent, both before unusual items. Meeting our financial objectives is the key to providing superior returns to shareholders.

In 1994, sales rose 5 percent to $8.52 billion. Earnings per share from continuing operations were $2.95 compared to $3.10 in 1993. After-tax earnings were $469.7 million compared to $506.1 million a year ago. Results for 1994 include an unusual after-tax charge of $87.1 million, or 55 cents per share, to cover estimated costs associated with the actions of an independent licensed contractor who made an improper pesticide substitution in treating some of our oat supplies. See note two to the consolidated financial statements for further discussion. We voluntarily suspended production and shipments of oat-containing products for a period of time during the first quarter of 1995 while resolving this issue; therefore, there will be a negative impact on 1995 first-quarter volume and earnings. There was an unusual net after-tax charge in 1993 of $57.3 million, or 35 cents per share, primarily for restructuring actions at consumer foods manufacturing facilities as well as selected restaurant unit closings.

Segment operating results are summarized in note eighteen to the consolidated financial statements on page 32.

Consumer Foods' sales grew 3 percent in 1994 to $5.55 billion with domestic packaged foods unit volume increasing 3 percent. Operating profits decreased 1 percent excluding unusual items from both years. In 1994, there was an unusual charge of $146.9 million related to the improper pesticide application as noted above. Included in operating profits for 1993 were unusual items totaling $33.4 million for increasing manufacturing productivity, and our share of streamlining and tax-reorganization costs associated with the formation of Snack Ventures Europe (SVE), our joint venture with PepsiCo Foods International. Including the unusual items, operating profits for 1994 decreased to $653.1 million.

Big G's 1994 operating profit decline reflected the year-long cereal market promotional escalation and the fourth-quarter impact of our pricing and promotional actions. In a departure from recent cereal industry practices, the Company announced actions in April 1994 to reduce spending on inefficient cereal couponing and price promotion, and to reduce prices on our largest cereal brands by an average of 11 percent. These actions were designed to deliver consumer value more directly and efficiently, and are anticipated to have positive profit impact in 1995, but are expected to be volume and market share neutral.

Yoplait yogurt, Betty Crocker Products, Gorton's seafood and Canada Foods posted double-digit operating profit gains for the year. SVE showed an excellent increase in operating profits and volume, and expanded beyond its original six European markets to Italy.

CPW, our cereal joint venture with Nestlé, continued to demonstrate progress in existing markets and expanded operations to Belgium, Switzerland, Austria, Greece and Chile during the year. Consumer Foods' operating profits include a loss of $30.3 million in 1994 and $30.6 million in 1993 for General Mills' share of CPW's losses. The developmental spending burden for CPW is expected to moderate as initial operations in European markets approach profitability in 1995.

In 1993, Consumer Foods' sales and operating profits grew 3 percent and 11 percent (excluding unusual items), respectively, led by Betty Crocker Products, Big G cereals, Yoplait yogurt, Foodservice, Gorton's seafood and Canada Foods.

Restaurants' sales grew 8 percent in 1994 to $2.96 billion. An operating profit gain of 3 percent before unusual items in the prior year was achieved despite disappointing results at The Olive Garden and the effects of unprecedented harsh winter weather. A net total of 115 new restaurants were opened in North America. Red Lobster's profits increased strongly as new menu items, improved service and a new decor package favorably influenced results. The Olive Garden's profits were lower, due to a decline in average unit sales that resulted primarily from not updating the successful concept soon enough to meet changing consumer expectations. China Coast commenced broader market expansion in 1994. Twenty new units were opened during the year with plans calling for faster expansion during 1995. Including the unusual items for last year, operating profits increased 21 percent.

In 1993, Restaurants' sales and operating profits before unusual items increased 8 percent and 11 percent, respectively. Results reflected good gains by The Olive Garden and good overall performance by Red Lobster. Together, The Olive Garden and Red Lobster added 112 new units in North America. Results for Canadian restaurants improved versus the prior year, but still trailed expectations. A charge of $30.6 million was recorded in 1993 for closing 31 Red Lobster and The Olive Garden units in the United States and Canada. Including the charge, operating profits decreased 5 percent.

Interest expense in 1994 was $115.6 million, an increase of $27.3 million from the prior year due to borrowing to fund purchases of common shares for treasury. The 1993 interest expense of $88.3 million was $12.4 million greater than 1992 primarily due to funding purchases of common shares for treasury. Interest income of $14.7 million in 1993 was $3.0 million less than the prior year reflecting lower rates.

The effective tax rates in 1994 and 1993 were 37.6 percent and 40.0 percent, respectively. Excluding the unusual items in both years, the rates were 38.1 percent and 38.2 percent in 1994 and 1993, respectively. The federal tax law changes in 1993 did not have a significant impact on 1994, but are expected to have a slight negative impact in the future.

It is management's view that changes in the rate of inflation have not had a significant effect on profitability from continuing operations over the three most recent years. Management attempts to minimize the effects of inflation through appropriate planning and operating practices.

The Financial Accounting Standards Board issued Statement of Financial Accounting Standards No. 115, "Accounting for Certain Investments in Debt and Equity Securities," in May 1993. The American Institute of Certified Public Accountants issued Statement of Position 93-7, "Reporting on Advertising Costs," in December 1993. Neither of these statements will have a significant impact on the Company when adopted.

The Company intends to manage its businesses and financial ratios so as to maintain a strong "A" bond rating, which allows access to financing at reasonable costs. Currently, General Mills' publicly issued long-term debt carries "A1" (Moody's Investors Services, Inc.) and "A+" (Standard & Poor's Corporation) ratings. Our commercial paper has ratings of "P-1" (Moody's) and "A-1" (Standard & Poor's) in the United States and "R-1 (middle)" in Canada from Dominion Bond Rating Service.

General Mills' financial condition remains strong. As important measures of financial strength, the Company focuses on the cash flow to debt and fixed charge coverage ratios, which were 46 percent and 6.2 times, respectively, in 1994. The purchase of 2.4 million shares of common stock for our treasury increased debt and reduced equity by $145.7 million, contributing to a debt to capital ratio of 65 percent.

The composition of the Company's capital structure is shown in the accompanying table.

In Millions	May 29, 1994	May 30, 1993
Notes payable	$ 433.3	$ 339.6
Current portion of long-term debt	115.2	64.3
Long-term debt	1,417.2	1,268.3
Deferred income taxes - tax leases	189.8	195.6
Total debt	2,155.5	1,867.8
Debt adjustments:		
Leases - debt equivalent	434.4	428.8
Domestic cash equivalents	-	(109.4)
Marketable investments	(196.1)	(137.0)
Adjusted debt	2,393.8	2,050.2
Common stock subject to put options	122.0	-
Stockholders' equity	1,151.2	1,218.5
Total capital	$3,667.0	$3,268.7

We selectively use derivatives to hedge financial risks, primarily interest rate volatility and foreign currency fluctuations. The derivatives are generally treated as hedges for accounting purposes. We manage our debt structure through both issuance of fixed and floating-rate debt as well as the use of derivatives. The debt equivalent of our leases and deferred income taxes related to tax leases are both fixed-rate obligations. The table below, when reviewed in conjunction with the capital structure table, shows the composition of our debt structure including the impact of derivatives.

In Millions	May 29, 1994		May 30, 1993	
Floating-rate debt	$ 733.4	31%	$ 534.9	26%
Fixed-rate debt	1,036.2	43	890.9	43
Leases - debt equivalent	434.4	18	428.8	21
Deferred income taxes - tax leases	189.8	8	195.6	10
Total debt	$2,393.8	100%	$2,050.2	100%

Commercial paper has historically been our primary source of short-term financing. Bank credit lines are maintained to ensure availability of short-term funds on an as-needed basis. In June 1994, our fee-paid credit lines were increased from $500.0 million to $650.0 million.

Our shelf registration statement permits issuance of up to $222.1 million net proceeds in unsecured debt securities. The shelf registration authorizes a medium-term note program that provides additional flexibility in accessing the debt markets.

Sources and uses of cash in the past three years are shown in the accompanying table. Operations generated $29.2 million less cash in 1994 than in the previous year primarily due to an increase in inventory levels. We purchased various marketable investments to take advantage of interest rate spreads.

Capital expenditures in 1995 are estimated to be approximately $525 million; an additional $50 million capital investment is anticipated for our joint ventures, principally CPW. In July 1994, the Company purchased 976,000 shares of common stock for $56.4 million as privately placed put options were exercised. The unusual item recorded in 1994 will be substantially included in 1995 as cash outflow. As a result, the Company is anticipating a net cash outflow in 1995 and will borrow either short- or long-term, depending on market conditions.

In Millions	1994	1993	1992
From operations	$ 830.7	$ 859.9	$ 771.6
Fixed assets and other investments-net	(732.1)	(714.4)	(725.7)
From dispositions of businesses	-	-	77.7
Change in marketable investments	(50.1)	(69.7)	-
Increase in outstanding debt-net	287.7	585.7	91.0
Common stock issued	13.3	32.3	39.3
Treasury stock purchases	(145.7)	(420.2)	(40.1)
Dividends paid	(299.4)	(274.8)	(245.2)
Other	(4.2)	(7.4)	(7.9)
Decrease in cash and cash equivalents	$ (99.8)	$ (8.6)	$ (39.3)

REPORT OF MANAGEMENT RESPONSIBILITIES

The management of General Mills, Inc. is responsible for the fairness and accuracy of the consolidated financial statements. The consolidated financial statements have been prepared in accordance with generally accepted accounting principles, using management's best estimates and judgments where appropriate. The financial information throughout this report is consistent with our consolidated financial statements.

Management has established a system of internal controls that provides reasonable assurance that assets are adequately safeguarded, and transactions are recorded accurately, in all material respects, in accordance with management's authorization. We maintain a strong audit program that independently evaluates the adequacy and effectiveness of internal controls. Our internal controls provide for appropriate separation of duties and responsibilities, and there are documented policies regarding utilization of Company assets and proper financial reporting. These formally stated and regularly communicated policies demand high ethical conduct from all employees.

The Audit Committee of the Board of Directors meets regularly to determine that management, internal auditors and independent auditors are properly discharging their duties regarding internal control and financial reporting. The independent auditors, internal auditors and employees have full and free access to the Audit Committee at any time.

KPMG Peat Marwick, independent certified public accountants, are retained to audit the consolidated financial statements. Their report follows.

H. B. Atwater, Jr.
Chairman of the Board and Chief Executive Officer

S. W. Sanger
President

M. H. Willes
Vice Chairman

Innovation, Speed, Commitment

REPORT OF THE AUDIT COMMITTEE

The Audit Committee of the Board of Directors is composed of six outside directors. Its primary function is to oversee the Company's system of internal controls, financial reporting practices and audits to ensure their quality, integrity and objectivity are sufficient to protect stockholder assets.

The Audit Committee met twice during 1994 to review the overall audit scope, plans and results of the internal auditor and independent auditor, the Company's internal controls, emerging accounting issues, officer and director expenses, audit fees, goodwill and other intangible values, and the audits of the pension plans. The Committee also met separately without management present and with the independent auditors to discuss the audit. Acting with the other Board members, the Committee reviewed the Company's annual financial state-ments and approved them before issuance. Audit Committee meeting results were reported to the full Board of Directors. The Audit Committee recommended to the Board that KPMG Peat Marwick be reappointed for 1995, subject to the approval of stockholders at the annual meeting.

The Audit Committee is satisfied that the internal control system is adequate and that the stockholders of General Mills are protected by appropriate accounting and auditing procedures.

M. D. Rose
Chairman, Audit Committee

INDEPENDENT AUDITORS' REPORT

The Stockholders and the Board of Directors
of General Mills, Inc.:

We have audited the accompanying consolidated balance sheets of General Mills, Inc. and subsidiaries as of May 29, 1994 and May 30, 1993, and the related consolidated statements of earnings and cash flows for each of the fiscal years in the three-year period ended May 29, 1994. These consolidated financial statements are the responsibility of the Company's management. Our responsibility is to express an opinion on these consolidated financial statements based on our audits.

We conducted our audits in accordance with generally accepted auditing standards. Those standards require that we plan and perform the audit to obtain reasonable assurance about whether the financial statements are free of material misstatement. An audit includes examining, on a test basis, evidence supporting the amounts and disclosures in the financial statements. An audit also includes assessing the accounting principles used and significant estimates made by management, as well as evaluating the overall financial statement presentation. We believe that our audits provide a reasonable basis for our opinion.

In our opinion, the consolidated financial statements referred to above present fairly, in all material respects, the financial position of General Mills, Inc. and subsidiaries as of May 29, 1994 and May 30, 1993, and the results of their operations and their cash flows for each of the fiscal years in the three-year period ended May 29, 1994 in conformity with generally accepted accounting principles.

As discussed in notes thirteen and fifteen to the consolidated financial statements, the Company adopted the provisions of the Financial Accounting Standards Board's Statements of Financial Accounting Standards No. 112, Employers' Accounting for Postemployment Benefits, and No. 109, Accounting for Income Taxes, in fiscal 1994.

KPMG Peat Marwick

Minneapolis, Minnesota
July 29, 1994

CONSOLIDATED STATEMENTS OF EARNINGS

In Millions, Except per Share Data	Fiscal Year Ended		
	May 29, 1994	May 30, 1993	May 31, 1992
Continuing Operations:			
Sales	$8,516.9	$8,134.6	$7,777.8
Costs and Expenses:			
Cost of sales	4,458.2	4,297.6	4,123.2
Selling, general and administrative	2,755.5	2,578.2	2,516.3
Depreciation and amortization	303.8	274.2	247.4
Interest, net	99.2	73.6	58.2
Unusual expenses (income)	146.9	67.0	(11.8)
Total Costs and Expenses	7,763.6	7,290.6	6,933.3
Earnings from Continuing Operations before Taxes	753.3	844.0	844.5
Income Taxes	283.6	337.9	338.9
Earnings from Continuing Operations	469.7	506.1	505.6
Discontinued Operations after Taxes	-	-	(10.0)
Cumulative Effect to May 31, 1993 of Accounting Changes	.2	-	-
Net Earnings	$ 469.9	$ 506.1	$ 495.6
Earnings per Share:			
Continuing operations	$ 2.95	$ 3.10	$ 3.05
Discontinued operations	-	-	(.06)
Cumulative effect of accounting changes	-	-	-
Net Earnings per Share	$ 2.95	$ 3.10	$ 2.99
Average Number of Common Shares	159.1	163.1	165.7

See accompanying notes to consolidated financial statements.

CONSOLIDATED BALANCE SHEETS

In Millions	May 29, 1994	May 30, 1993
Current Assets:		
Cash and cash equivalents	$ .2	$ 100.0
Receivables, less allowance for doubtful accounts of $4.4 in 1994 and $4.3 in 1993	309.7	287.4
Inventories	488.3	439.0
Prepaid expenses and other current assets	110.6	108.2
Deferred income taxes	220.4	142.3
Total Current Assets	1,129.2	1,076.9
Land, Buildings and Equipment, at cost	3,092.6	2,859.6
Other Assets	976.5	714.3
Total Assets	$5,198.3	$4,650.8
Current Liabilities:		
Accounts payable	$ 650.4	$ 617.0
Current portion of long-term debt	115.2	64.3
Notes payable	433.3	339.6
Accrued taxes	178.3	139.7
Accrued payroll	165.6	158.8
Other current liabilities	289.3	239.4
Total Current Liabilities	1,832.1	1,558.8
Long-term Debt	1,417.2	1,268.3
Deferred Income Taxes	297.4	262.0
Deferred Income Taxes–Tax Leases	189.8	195.6
Other Liabilities	188.6	147.6
Total Liabilities	3,925.1	3,432.3
Common Stock Subject to Put Options	122.0	-
Stockholders' Equity:		
Cumulative preference stock, none issued	-	-
Common stock, 204.2 shares issued	251.0	358.7
Retained earnings	2,457.9	2,284.5
Less common stock in treasury, at cost, shares of 45.7 in 1994 and 43.7 in 1993	(1,334.4)	(1,196.4)
Unearned compensation and other	(160.2)	(167.5)
Cumulative foreign currency adjustment	(63.1)	(60.8)
Total Stockholders' Equity	1,151.2	1,218.5
Total Liabilities and Equity	$5,198.3	$4,650.8

See accompanying notes to consolidated financial statements.

Innovation, Speed, Commitment

CONSOLIDATED STATEMENTS OF CASH FLOWS

	Fiscal Year Ended		
In Millions	May 29, 1994	May 30, 1993	May 31, 1992
Cash Flows - Operating Activities:			
Earnings from continuing operations	$469.9	$506.1	$505.6
Adjustments to reconcile earnings to cash flow:			
Depreciation and amortization	303.8	274.2	247.4
Deferred income taxes	(27.8)	40.8	13.5
Change in current assets and liabilities, net of effects from business acquired	(72.0)	2.5	20.0
Unusual expenses	146.9	57.3	-
Other, net	15.2	(15.0)	3.9
Cash provided by continuing operations	836.0	865.9	790.4
Cash used by discontinued operations	(5.3)	(6.0)	(18.8)
Net Cash Provided by Operating Activities	830.7	859.9	771.6
Cash Flows - Investment Activities:			
Purchases of land, buildings and equipment	(559.5)	(623.8)	(695.3)
Investments in businesses, intangibles and affiliates, net of dividends	(140.8)	(55.8)	(30.6)
Purchases of marketable investments	(83.8)	(82.8)	(6.9)
Proceeds from sale of marketable investments	33.7	13.1	6.9
Proceeds from disposal of land, buildings and equipment	7.2	5.2	8.1
Proceeds from dispositions	-	-	77.7
Other, net	(39.0)	(40.0)	(7.9)
Net Cash Used by Investment Activities	(782.2)	(784.1)	(648.0)
Cash Flows - Financing Activities:			
Increase in notes payable	93.2	207.6	150.3
Issuance of long-term debt	273.6	422.6	188.7
Payment of long-term debt	(79.1)	(44.5)	(248.0)
Common stock issued	13.3	32.3	39.3
Purchases of common stock for treasury	(145.7)	(420.2)	(40.1)
Dividends paid	(299.4)	(274.8)	(245.2)
Other, net	(4.2)	(7.4)	(7.9)
Net Cash Used by Financing Activities	(148.3)	(84.4)	(162.9)
Decrease in Cash and Cash Equivalents	(99.8)	(8.6)	(39.3)
Cash and Cash Equivalents - Beginning of Year	100.0	.5	39.8
Reclassification of Marketable Investment	-	108.1	-
Cash and Cash Equivalents - End of Year	$ .2	$100.0	$ .5
Cash Flow from Changes in Current Assets and Liabilities:			
Receivables	$ (17.3)	$ (44.7)	$ 2.1
Inventories	(111.0)	28.7	.6
Prepaid expenses and other current assets	(5.1)	4.6	(8.9)
Accounts payable	33.2	9.0	54.5
Other current liabilities	28.2	4.9	(28.3)
Change in Current Assets and Liabilities	$ (72.0)	$ 2.5	$ 20.0

See accompanying notes to consolidated financial statements.

NOTES TO CONSOLIDATED FINANCIAL STATEMENTS

A. Principles of Consolidation. The consolidated financial statements include the following domestic and foreign operations: parent company and 100% owned subsidiaries, and General Mills' investment in and share of net earnings or losses of 20-50% owned companies.

Our fiscal year ends on the last Sunday in May. Years 1994 and 1993 each consisted of 52 weeks and 1992 consisted of 53 weeks.

B. Land, Buildings, Equipment and Depreciation. Buildings and equipment are depreciated over estimated useful lives ranging from three to 50 years, primarily using the straight-line method. Accelerated depreciation methods are generally used for income tax purposes.

When an item is sold or retired, the accounts are relieved of its cost and related accumulated depreciation; the resulting gains and losses, if any, are recognized.

C. Inventories. Inventories are valued at the lower of cost or market. Certain domestic inventories are valued using the LIFO method, while other inventories are generally valued using the FIFO method.

D. Intangible Assets. Goodwill represents the difference between purchase prices of acquired companies and the related fair values of net assets acquired and accounted for by the purchase method of accounting. Goodwill acquired after October 1970 is amortized on a straight-line basis over 40 years or less.

Intangible assets include an amount that offsets a minimum liability recorded for a pension plan with assets less than accumulated benefits as required by Financial Accounting Standard No. 87.

The costs of patents, copyrights and other intangible assets are amortized evenly over their estimated useful lives.

The Audit Committee of the Board of Directors annually reviews goodwill and other intangibles. At its meeting on April 25, 1994, the Board of Directors affirmed that the remaining amounts of these assets have continuing value.

E. Research and Development. All expenditures for research and development are charged against earnings in the year incurred. The charges for 1994, 1993 and 1992 were $63.6 million, $60.1 million and $62.1 million, respectively.

F. Earnings per Share. Earnings per share has been determined by dividing the appropriate earnings by the weighted average number of common shares outstanding during the year. Common share equivalents were not material.

G. Foreign Currency Translation. For most foreign operations, local currencies are considered the functional currency. Assets and liabilities are translated using the exchange rates in effect at the balance sheet date. Results of operations are translated using the average exchange rates prevailing throughout the period. Translation effects are accumulated in the foreign currency adjustment in stockholders' equity.

Gains and losses from foreign currency transactions are generally included in net earnings for the period.

H. Interest Rate Swap Agreements. Any interest rate differential on an interest rate swap is recognized as an adjustment of interest expense or income over the term of the agreement. We enter into these agreements with a diversified group of highly-rated financial institutions. We are exposed to credit loss in the event of nonperformance by the other parties to these agreements. However, we do not anticipate any losses.

The fair value of interest rate swaps is the estimated amount we would receive or pay to replace the swap agreements, taking into consideration current interest rates. This estimated amount was immaterial at May 29, 1994.

I. Statements of Cash Flows. For purposes of the statement of cash flows, we consider all investments purchased with a maturity of three months or less to be cash equivalents.

In 1994, we recorded an after-tax charge of $87.1 million ($.55 per share) to cover estimated costs associated with the actions of an independent licensed contractor who made an improper substitution of a pesticide in treating some of our oat supplies, a portion of which were used in production. While the substitution presented no consumer health or safety issues, the pesticide had not been registered for use on oats and thus its application represented a FDA regulatory violation. Due to a lengthy government approval process for registration, the affected finished oat-products inventory would be past the Company's freshness standard dates. Therefore, the charge includes costs associated with disposition of the finished oat products and oats inventory as well as other related expenses. Several consumer class action lawsuits have been filed in connection with this matter. The Company believes these lawsuits are without merit and will not have any material impact on the financial condition of the Company.

We recorded restructuring charges in 1993 related primarily to restaurant closings in the U.S. and Canada, costs for increasing Consumer Foods manufacturing productivity and efficiency, and our share of streamlining and tax reorganization costs associated with the formation of Snack Ventures Europe.

Innovation, Speed, Commitment

These charges resulted in a reduction in net earnings of $57.3 million ($.35 per share). These actions were substantially completed in 1994.

In 1992, we recognized a gain on the sale of the stock of our Spanish frozen food subsidiary, Preparados y Congelados Alimenticios, S.A. (PYCASA) and also recorded charges primarily related to restructuring of Betty Crocker packaged mixes production, European food operations, and Consumer Foods national sales organization, and the call of our 9 3/8% sinking fund debentures. These transactions resulted in no net effect on earnings.

We selectively hedge the potential effect of foreign currency fluctuations related to operating activities and net investments in foreign operations by entering into foreign exchange contracts with major financial institutions. Realized and unrealized gains and losses on contracts that hedge operating activities are recognized currently in net earnings. Realized and unrealized gains and losses on contracts that hedge net investments are recognized in the foreign currency adjustment in stockholders' equity.

The components of our net foreign investment exposure by geographic region are as follows:

In Millions	May 29, 1994	May 30, 1993
Europe	$118.3	$103.9
North/South America	43.3	41.7
Asia	12.1	13.0
Total exposure	173.7	158.6
After-tax hedges	(30.2)	(134.1)
Net exposure	$143.5	$ 24.5

At May 29, 1994, we had forward contracts maturing in 1995 to sell $59.5 million and purchase $7.5 million of foreign currencies. We also had foreign currency put options expiring in 1995 of $26.8 million. The fair value of these contracts is based on third-party quotes and is immaterial at May 29, 1994.

We purchased the Colombo yogurt business for approximately $75.0 million from a U.S. subsidiary of Bongrain S.A. effective December 1993. Colombo has a refrigerated yogurt business in the Northeast and is a leading producer of soft frozen yogurt, as well as premium hard pack frozen yogurt. The transaction did not have any material effect on our 1994 earnings.

During 1994 and 1993, we made capital contributions and advances of $48.3 million and $66.1 million, respectively, to Cereal Partners Worldwide (CPW), our joint venture with Nestlé, S.A.

In 1993, we entered into a joint venture, Snack Ventures Europe (SVE), with PepsiCo Foods International to merge six existing Continental European snack operations (three from each company) into one company to develop, manufacture and market snack foods. We own 40.5 percent of SVE. The merger was effective July 1992. We reclassified the net individual assets and liabilities of our operations to investment in affiliates and excluded the noncash transaction from our statement of cash flows.

The components of inventories are as follows:

In Millions	May 29, 1994	May 30, 1993
Raw materials, work in process and supplies	$245.0	$206.2
Finished goods	249.3	252.6
Grain	47.0	40.5
Reserve for LIFO valuation method	(53.0)	(60.3)
Total inventories	$488.3	$439.0

At May 29, 1994 and May 30, 1993, respectively, inventories of $245.1 million and $244.5 million were valued at LIFO.

The components of certain balance sheet items are as follows:

In Millions	May 29, 1994	May 30, 1993
Land, Buildings and Equipment:		
Land	$ 360.9	$ 302.3
Buildings	1,655.6	1,452.6
Equipment	2,373.8	2,048.1
Construction in progress	299.5	436.5
Total land, buildings and equipment	4,689.8	4,239.5
Less accumulated depreciation	(1,597.2)	(1,379.9)
Net land, buildings and equipment	$3,092.6	$2,859.6
Other Assets:		
Prepaid pension	$ 288.0	$ 257.4
Marketable investments, at cost	196.1	137.0
Investments in and advances to affiliates	188.3	163.9
Intangible assets	157.3	70.6
Miscellaneous	146.8	85.4
Total other assets	$ 976.5	$ 714.3

Based on quoted market prices, the fair value of the marketable investments was $231.4 million at May 29, 1994 and $186.9 million at May 30, 1993.

We have interest rate and currency swap agreements related to marketable investments that convert fixed interest rates to variable interest rates and foreign currencies to U.S. dollars on a notional amount of $81.9 million. These agreements mature from December 1994 to January 2001.

The components of notes payable are as follows:

In Millions	May 29, 1994	May 30, 1993
U.S. commercial paper	$339.2	$255.5
Canadian commercial paper	83.3	75.9
Financial institutions	260.8	208.2
Amount reclassified to long-term debt	(250.0)	(200.0)
Total notes payable	$433.3	$339.6

To ensure availability of funds, we maintain bank credit lines sufficient to cover our outstanding commercial paper. As of May 29, 1994, we had $500.0 million fee-paid lines and $179.4 million uncommitted, no-fee lines available in the U.S. and Canada. In addition, other foreign subsidiaries had unused credit lines of $37.1 million.

We have a revolving credit agreement expiring in 1999 that provides for the fee-paid credit lines. This agreement provides us with the ability to refinance short-term borrowings on a long-term basis, and therefore we have reclassified a portion of our notes payable to long-term debt.

We occasionally enter into swap agreements to lock in interest rates on notes payable that may result in fixed rates higher than short-term rates. At May 29, 1994 we had interest rate swap agreements on a notional amount of $145.0 million that convert an average interest rate of 2.8% to an average interest rate of 5.7%. These agreements mature from June 1994 to August 1994. At May 30, 1993 we had interest rate swap agreements on a notional amount of $169.0 million that converted an average interest rate of 3.3% to an average interest rate of 7.9%.

We purchased and sold interest rate cap agreements, expiring in May 1995, on a notional amount of $200.0 million with strike rates of 5.0% and 6.5%, respectively. These agreements limit our exposure to an increase in short-term interest rates. If rates are between 5.0-6.5%, our rate is limited to 5.0%; if rates are greater than 6.5%, our rate will be 150 basis points less than market rates until the agreements expire.

In Millions	May 29, 1994	May 30, 1993
4.3% to 9.1% medium-term notes, due 1994 to 2033	$1,080.3	$ 918.3
Zero coupon notes, yield 11.1%, $327.0 due August 15, 2013	41.4	47.1
ESOP loan guaranty, variable rate (3.7% at May 29, 1994), due December 31, 2007	50.0	50.0
8.3% ESOP loan guaranty, due through June 30, 2007	78.3	82.0
Zero coupon notes, yield 11.7%, $64.4 due August 15, 2004	20.2	18.0
Notes payable, reclassified	250.0	200.0
Other	12.2	17.2
	1,532.4	1,332.6
Less amounts due within one year	(115.2)	(64.3)
Total long-term debt	$1,417.2	$1,268.3

Our shelf registration statement permits the issuance of up to $222.1 million net proceeds in unsecured debt securities to reduce short-term debt and for other general corporate purposes. This registration includes a medium-term note program that allows us to issue debt quickly for various amounts and at various rates and maturities.

In 1994, we issued $217.9 million of debt under our medium-term note program with maturities from one to 40 years and interest rates from 4.3% to 7.3%. In 1993, $366.7 million of debt was issued under this program with maturities from one to 30 years and interest rates from 3.5% to 8.6%.

We had interest rate swap agreements that convert an average interest rate of 5.5% to an average interest rate of 3.2% on $162.9 million notional amount of medium-term notes. These agreements mature from October 1994 to January 1999. In 1994, we sold a swap option that gives the holder the right, if exercised, to receive a fixed payment of 6.8% and pay a floating rate based on commercial paper on a notional amount of $21.3 million from February 1995 until February 1997. At May 30, 1993 we had interest rate swap agreements that converted an average interest rate of 5.4% to an average interest rate of 2.9% on $120.0 million notional amount of medium-term notes.

In 1992, we called our 9 3/8% sinking fund debentures due March 1, 2009 (see note two). This transaction resulted in a decrease in net earnings of $3.5 million ($.02 per share).

The Company has guaranteed the debt of the Employee Stock Ownership Plans; therefore, the loans are reflected on our consolidated balance sheets as long-term debt with a related offset in stockholders' equity, "Unearned compensation and other."

Based on borrowing rates currently available for debt with similar terms and average maturities, the fair value of our long-term debt, excluding current portion, was $1,476.4 million at May 29, 1994 and $1,413.4 million at May 30, 1993.

The sinking fund and principal payments due on long-term debt are (in millions) $115.2, $72.0, $94.2, $101.0 and $99.7 in years ending 1995, 1996, 1997, 1998 and 1999, respectively. The notes payable that are reclassified under our revolving credit agreement are not included in these principal payments.

Our marketable investments include zero coupon U.S. Treasury securities. These investments are intended to provide the funds for the payment of principal and interest for the zero coupon notes due August 15, 2013 and 2004.

The following table contains information on stock options:

	Shares	Average Option Price per Share
Granted		
1994	4,868,098	$63.22
1993	3,384,144	66.64
1992	2,574,008	58.29
Exercised		
1994	562,714	$31.08
1993	1,962,063	22.90
1992	1,026,760	19.64
Expired		
1994	459,800	$62.56
1993	288,907	61.63
1992	175,804	39.12
Outstanding at year end		
1994	18,009,478	$49.52
1993	14,163,894	44.50
1992	13,030,720	35.88
Exercisable at year end		
1994	10,278,466	$38.73
1993	9,488,948	36.23
1992	8,938,384	28.71

A total of 10,622,403 shares (including 2,535,750 shares for salary replacement options and 321,164 shares for restricted stock) are available for grants of options or restricted stock to employees under our 1990 and 1993 stock plans through October 1, 1998. An additional 3,083,400 shares are available for grants on a one-for-one basis as common stock shares are repurchased by the Company. The options may be granted at a price not less than 100% of fair market value on the date the option is granted. Options now outstanding include some granted under the 1980, 1984 and 1988 option plans, under which no further options or other rights may be granted. All options expire within 10 years plus one month after the date of grant. The plans provide for full vesting of the option in the event there is a change of control.

The 1993 plan permits awards of restricted stock to key employees subject to a restricted period and a purchase price, if any, to be paid by the employee as determined by the Compensation Committee of the Board of Directors. Most of the restricted stock awards require the employee to deposit personally owned shares (on a one-for-one basis) with the Company during the restricted period. In 1994, grants of 95,685 shares of restricted stock were made and on May 29, 1994, there were 188,822 of such shares outstanding.

The 1988 plan also permitted the granting of performance units corresponding to stock options granted. The value of performance units will be determined by return on equity and growth in earnings per share measured against preset goals over three-year performance periods. For seven years after a performance period, holders may elect to receive the value of performance units (with interest) as an alternative to exercising corresponding stock options. On May 29, 1994, there were 2,894,984 outstanding options with corresponding performance units or performance unit accounts.

A total of 52,300 shares are available for grants of options and restricted stock to non-employee directors until September 30, 1995 under a separate 1990 stock plan. Each newly elected non-employee director is granted an option to purchase 2,500 shares at fair market value on the date of grant. Options expire 10 years after the date of grant. Each year 400 shares of restricted stock will be awarded to each non-employee director, restricted until the later of the expiration of one year or completion of service on the Board of Directors.

In Millions, Except per Share Data	$.10 Par Value Common Stock (One Billion Shares Authorized)				Retained Earnings	Unearned Compensation and Other	Cumulative Foreign Currency Adjustment	Total
	Issued		Treasury					
	Shares	Amount	Shares	Amount				
Balance at May 26, 1991	204.2	$320.2	(39.1)	$ (777.4)	$1,795.5	$(177.6)	$(47.2)	$1,113.5
Net earnings					495.6			495.6
Cash dividends declared ($1.48 per share), net of income taxes of $3.1					(242.1)			(242.1)
Stock option, profit sharing and ESOP plans		23.4	1.1	21.5				44.9
Shares purchased on open market			(.7)	(47.0)				(47.0)
Unearned compensation related to restricted stock awards						(4.3)		(4.3)
Earned compensation						9.6		9.6
Translation adjustments, net of income taxes of $.7							(6.7)	(6.7)
Amount charged to gain on sale of foreign operation							7.4	7.4
Balance at May 31, 1992	204.2	343.6	(38.7)	(802.9)	2,049.0	(172.3)	(46.5)	1,370.9
Net earnings					506.1			506.1
Cash dividends declared ($1.68 per share), net of income taxes of $4.2					(270.6)			(270.6)
Stock option, profit sharing and ESOP plans		15.1	1.3	19.7				34.8
Shares purchased on open market			(6.3)	(413.2)				(413.2)
Unearned compensation related to restricted stock awards						(3.2)		(3.2)
Earned compensation						9.6		9.6
Minimum pension liability adjustment						(1.6)		(1.6)
Translation adjustments, net of income tax benefit of $2.0							(14.3)	(14.3)
Balance at May 30, 1993	204.2	358.7	(43.7)	(1,196.4)	2,284.5	(167.5)	(60.8)	1,218.5
Net earnings					469.9			469.9
Cash dividends declared ($1.88 per share), net of income taxes of $2.9					(296.5)			(296.5)
Stock option, profit sharing and ESOP plans		8.0	.4	7.5				15.5
Shares purchased on open market			(2.4)	(145.7)				(145.7)
Put option premium		6.3		.2				6.5
Transfer of put options		(122.0)						(122.0)
Unearned compensation related to restricted stock awards						(3.9)		(3.9)
Earned compensation						9.6		9.6
Minimum pension liability adjustment						1.6		1.6
Translation adjustments, net of income taxes of $4.2							(2.3)	(2.3)
Balance at May 29, 1994	204.2	$251.0	(45.7)	$(1,334.4)	$2,457.9	$(160.2)	$(63.1)	$1,151.2

Cumulative preference stock of 5.0 million shares, without par value, is authorized but unissued.

We have a shareholder rights plan that entitles each outstanding share of common stock to one-fourth of a right. Each right entitles the holder to purchase one one-hundredth of a share of cumulative preference stock (or, in certain circumstances, common stock or other securities), exercisable upon the occurrence of certain events. The rights are not transferable apart from the common stock until a person or group has acquired 20% or more, or makes a tender offer for 20% or more, of the common stock. If the Company is then acquired in a merger or other business combination transaction, each right will entitle the holder (other than the acquiring company) to receive, upon exercise, common stock of either the Company or the acquiring company having a value equal to two times the exercise price of the right. The rights are redeemable by the Board in certain circumstances and expire on March 7, 1996. At May 29, 1994, there were 39.6 million rights issued and outstanding.

The Board of Directors has authorized the repurchase, from time to time, of common stock for our treasury, provided that the number of shares held in treasury shall not exceed 60.0 million.

Through private placements, we issued put options that entitle the holder to sell shares of our common stock to us, at a specified price, if the holder exercises the option. In 1994, we issued put options for 2.6 million shares for $6.5 million in premiums. As of May 29, 1994, put options for 2.2 million shares remain outstanding at strike prices ranging from $50.00

to $59.99 per share with exercise dates from July 1994 to March 1995. The amount related to our potential obligation has been transferred from stockholders' equity to "Common Stock Subject to Put Options."

The components of net interest expense are as follows:

In Millions	Fiscal Year 1994	1993	1992
Interest expense	$121.7	$99.8	$89.5
Capitalized interest	(6.1)	(11.5)	(13.6)
Interest income	(16.4)	(14.7)	(17.7)
Interest expense, net	$ 99.2	$73.6	$58.2

During 1994, 1993 and 1992, we paid interest (net of amount capitalized) of $99.0 million, $77.0 million and $70.7 million, respectively.

We have defined benefit plans covering most employees. Benefits for salaried employees are based on length of service and final average compensation. The hourly plans include various monthly amounts for each year of credited service. Our funding policy is consistent with the funding requirements of federal law and regulations. Our principal plan covering salaried employees has a provision that any excess pension assets would be vested in plan participants if the plan is terminated within five years of a change in control. Plan assets consist principally of listed equity securities and corporate obligations, and U.S. government securities.

Components of net pension income are as follows:

Expense (Income) in Millions	Fiscal Year 1994	1993	1992
Service cost—benefits earned	$ 19.1	$ 14.7	$ 14.2
Interest cost on projected benefit obligation	57.8	52.6	51.2
Actual return on plan assets	(50.5)	(136.6)	(75.0)
Net amortization and deferral	(47.0)	38.3	(26.1)
Net pension expense (income)	$(20.6)	$(31.0)	$(35.7)

The weighted-average discount rate and rate of increase in future compensation levels used in determining the actuarial present value of the benefit obligations were 8.8% and 4.6% in 1994, and 8.5% and 5.1% in 1993, respectively. The expected long-term rate of return on assets was 10.4%.

The funded status of the plans and the amount recognized on the consolidated balance sheets (as determined as of May 31, 1994 and 1993) are as follows:

In Millions	May 29, 1994 Assets Exceed Accumulated Benefits	Accumulated Benefits Exceed Assets	May 30, 1993 Assets Exceed Accumulated Benefits	Accumulated Benefits Exceed Assets
Actuarial present value of benefit obligations:				
Vested benefits	$572.7	$24.1	$545.5	$ 12.1
Nonvested benefits	55.9	3.3	55.0	2.3
Accumulated benefit obligations	628.6	27.4	600.5	14.4
Projected benefit obligation	688.4	30.3	680.9	18.8
Plan assets at fair value	920.8	10.7	921.6	-
Plan assets in excess of (less than) the projected benefit obligation	232.4	(19.6)	240.7	(18.8)
Unrecognized prior service cost	31.4	2.9	40.1	.3
Unrecognized net loss	148.1	10.7	125.3	6.0
Recognition of minimum liability	-	(10.1)	-	(10.7)
Unrecognized transition (asset) liability	(130.6)	6.2	(148.7)	8.8
Prepaid (accrued) pension cost	$281.3	$ (9.9)	$257.4	$(14.4)

We have defined contribution plans covering salaried and non-union employees. Contributions are determined by matching a percentage of employee contributions. Such plans had net assets of $665.3 million at May 31, 1994. Expense recognized in 1994, 1993 and 1992 was $6.7 million, $9.6 million and $12.7 million, respectively.

Within our defined contribution plans we have Employee Stock Ownership Plans (ESOPs). These ESOPs borrowed funds guaranteed by the Company with terms described in the long-term debt footnote, as well as originally borrowed $35.0 million from the Company at a variable interest rate. At May 29, 1994, the interest rate was 4.6% with outstanding amounts of $21.0 million due December 2014 and $7.2 million with sinking fund payments to June 2015. Compensation expense is recognized as contributions are accrued. Our contributions to the plans, plus the dividends accumulated on the common stock held by the ESOPs, are used to pay principal, interest and expenses of the plans. As loan payments are made, common stock is allocated to ESOP participants. In 1994, 1993 and 1992, the ESOPs incurred interest expense of $9.0 million, $9.6 million and $11.3 million, respectively, and used dividends received of $8.9 million, $8.2 million and $7.8 million and contributions received from the Company of $7.4 million, $7.4 million and $7.1 million, respectively, to pay principal and interest on their debt.

We sponsor several plans that provide health care benefits to the majority of our retirees. The salaried plan is contributory with retiree contributions based on years of service.

We fund plans for certain employees and retirees on an annual basis. In 1994, 1993 and 1992 we contributed $38.3 million, $30.6 million and $4.2 million, respectively. Plan assets consist principally of listed equity securities and U.S. government securities.

Components of the postretirement health care expense are as follows:

Expense (Income) in Millions	Fiscal Year		
	1994	1993	1992
Service cost—benefits earned	$ 5.6	$ 3.6	$3.5
Interest cost on accumulated benefit obligation	14.0	11.0	9.7
Actual return on plan assets	(1.5)	(3.9)	(3.0)
Net amortization and deferral	(4.5)	(1.0)	(1.2)
Net postretirement expense	$13.6	$ 9.7	$9.0

The funded status of the plans and the amount recognized on our consolidated balance sheets are as follows:

In Millions	May 29, 1994		May 30, 1993
	Assets Exceed Accumulated Benefits	Accumulated Benefits Exceed Assets	Accumulated Benefits Exceed Assets
Accumulated benefit obligations:			
Retirees	$ 36.3	$ 48.7	$ 80.0
Fully eligible active employees	12.7	8.0	19.3
Other active employees	27.0	48.5	70.4
Accumulated benefit obligations	76.0	105.2	169.7
Plan assets at fair value	89.3	7.4	60.8
Accumulated benefit obligations in excess of (less than) plan assets	(13.3)	97.8	108.9
Unrecognized prior service cost	.1	12.2	14.3
Unrecognized net loss	(28.1)	(27.7)	(51.1)
Accrued (prepaid) postretirement benefits	$(41.3)	$ 82.3	$ 72.1

The discount rates used in determining the actuarial present value of the benefit obligations were 8.8% and 8.5% in 1994 and 1993, respectively. The expected long-term rate of return on assets was 10%.

The health care cost trend rate increase in the per capita charges for benefits ranged from 6.2% to 9.8% for 1995 depending on the medical service category. The rates gradually decrease to 4.4% to 5.7% for 2007 and remain at that level thereafter. If the health care cost trend rate increased by one percentage point in each future year, the aggregate of the service and interest cost components of postretirement expense would increase for 1994 by $3.1 million and the accumulated benefit obligation as of May 29, 1994 would increase by $24.6 million.

In 1994, we adopted Statement of Financial Accounting Standards (SFAS) No. 112, "Employers' Accounting for Postemployment Benefits." The cumulative effect as of May 31, 1993 of changing to the accrual basis for severance and disability costs was a decrease in net earnings of $17.3 million ($.11 per share).

We have profit-sharing plans to provide incentives to key individuals who have the greatest potential to contribute to current earnings and successful future operations. These plans were approved by the Board of Directors upon recommendation of the Compensation Committee. The awards under these plans depend on profit performance in relation to pre-established goals. The plans are administered by the Compensation Committee, which consists solely of outside directors. Profit-sharing expense, including performance unit accruals, was $1.7 million, $7.3 million and $8.8 million in 1994, 1993 and 1992, respectively.

We adopted SFAS No. 109, "Accounting for Income Taxes" as of May 31, 1993. The adoption of SFAS 109 changed our method of accounting for income taxes from the deferred method to the asset and liability method. Deferred income taxes reflect the differences between assets and liabilities recognized for financial reporting purposes and amounts recognized for tax purposes measured using the current enacted tax rates. The cumulative effect of adoption was an increase in net earnings of $17.5 million ($.11 per share).

The components of earnings before income taxes and the income taxes thereon are as follows:

In Millions	Fiscal Year		
	1994	1993	1992
Earnings (loss) before income taxes:			
U.S.	$746.4	$887.2	$818.3
Foreign	6.9	(43.2)	26.2
Total earnings before income taxes	$753.3	$844.0	$844.5
Income taxes:			
Current:			
Federal	$246.5	$243.1	$254.0
State and local	60.9	60.2	55.1
Foreign	4.0	(6.2)	16.3
Total current	311.4	297.1	325.4
Deferred (principally U.S.)	(27.8)	40.8	13.5
Total income taxes	$283.6	$337.9	$338.9

Innovation, Speed, Commitment

During 1994, income tax benefits of $3.5 million were allocated to stockholders' equity. These benefits were attributable to the exercise of employee stock options, dividends paid on unallocated ESOP shares and translation adjustments.

During 1994, 1993 and 1992, we paid income taxes of $273.8 million, $268.3 million and $326.4 million, respectively.

In prior years we purchased certain income tax items from other companies through tax lease transactions. Total current income taxes charged to earnings reflect the amounts attributable to operations and have not been materially affected by these tax leases. Actual current taxes payable on 1994, 1993 and 1992 operations were increased by approximately $10 million, $10 million and $8 million, respectively, due to the effect of tax leases. These tax payments do not affect taxes for statement of earnings purposes since they repay tax benefits realized in prior years. The repayment liability is classified as "Deferred Income Taxes–Tax Leases."

The following table reconciles the U.S. statutory income tax rate with the effective income tax rate:

In Millions	Fiscal Year		
	1994	1993	1992
U.S. statutory rate	35.0%	34.0%	34.0%
State and local income taxes, net of federal tax benefits	5.0	5.2	4.9
Other, net	(2.4)	.8	1.2
Effective income tax rate	37.6%	40.0%	40.1%

The tax effects of temporary differences that give rise to deferred tax assets and liabilities at May 29, 1994 are as follows:

In Millions	
Accrued liabilities	$129.1
Unusual charge for oats	59.8
Compensation and employee benefits	59.6
Disposition liabilities	37.5
Foreign tax loss carryforward	16.2
Other	13.6
Gross deferred tax assets	315.8
Depreciation	219.5
Prepaid pension asset	112.0
Intangible assets	12.7
Other	37.5
Gross deferred tax liabilities	381.7
Valuation allowance	11.1
Net deferred tax liability	$ 77.0

As of May 29, 1994, we have foreign operating loss carryovers for tax purposes of $40.9 million, which will expire as follows if not offset against future taxable income: $11.0 million in 1998, $9.3 million in 1999, $10.9 million in 2000 and $9.7 million in 2001.

We have not recognized a deferred tax liability for unremitted earnings of $60.1 million for our foreign operations because we do not expect those earnings to become taxable to us in the foreseeable future. A determination of the potential liability is not practicable. If a portion were to be remitted, we believe income tax credits would substantially offset any resulting tax liability.

An analysis of rent expense by property leased follows:

In Millions	Fiscal Year		
	1994	1993	1992
Restaurant space	$41.2	$39.5	$33.9
Warehouse space	13.8	13.0	12.6
Equipment	10.6	10.6	8.3
Other	3.9	5.5	5.4
Total rent expense	$69.5	$68.6	$60.2

Some leases require payment of property taxes, insurance and maintenance costs in addition to the rent payments. Contingent and escalation rent in excess of minimum rent payments and sublease income netted in rent expense were insignificant.

Noncancelable future lease commitments are (in millions) $60.6 in 1995, $56.2 in 1996, $52.0 in 1997, $46.9 in 1998, $43.6 in 1999 and $236.5 after 1999, with a cumulative total of $495.8.

We are contingently liable under guarantees and comfort letters for $88.5 million. The guarantees and comfort letters are issued to support borrowing arrangements, primarily for our joint ventures.

We recorded a net after-tax charge related to previously discontinued operations of $10.0 million ($.06 per share) in 1992. This charge primarily related to a lease adjustment with the R. H. Macy Company, which is operating under bankruptcy law protection.

In Millions

	Consumer Foods	Restaurants	Unallocated Corporate Items (a)	Consolidated Total
Sales				
1994	$5,553.9	$2,963.0		$8,516.9
1993	5,397.2	2,737.4		8,134.6
1992	5,233.8	2,544.0		7,777.8
Operating Profits				
1994	653.1(b)	219.4	$(119.2)	753.3
1993	772.6(c)	181.4(c)	(110.0)	844.0
1992	744.3(d)	190.8	(90.6)	844.5
Identifiable Assets				
1994	2,820.8	1,834.9	542.6	5,198.3
1993	2,576.4	1,605.0	469.4	4,650.8
1992	2,481.2	1,419.3	404.5	4,305.0
Capital Expenditures				
1994	207.7	343.3	8.5	559.5
1993	321.6	301.2	1.0	623.8
1992	397.1	297.0	1.2	695.3
Depreciation and Amortization				
1994	176.6	125.4	1.8	303.8
1993	155.8	116.8	1.6	274.2
1992	142.2	101.0	4.2	247.4

	U.S.A.	Foreign	Unallocated Corporate Items (a)	Consolidated Total
Sales				
1994	$8,172.1	$344.8		$8,516.9
1993	7,719.4	415.2		8,134.6
1992	7,039.6	738.2		7,777.8
Operating Profits				
1994	875.6(b)	(3.1)	$(119.2)	753.3
1993	997.1(c)	(43.1)(c)	(110.0)	844.0
1992	896.3(d)	38.8 (d)	(90.6)	844.5
Identifiable Assets				
1994	4,297.6	358.1	542.6	5,198.3
1993	3,828.3	353.1	469.4	4,650.8
1992	3,452.2	448.3	404.5	4,305.0

(a) Corporate expenses reported here include net interest expense and general corporate expenses.
(b) Consumer Foods operating profits include a charge of $146.9 million for unusual items described in note two.
(c) Consumer Foods and Restaurants operating profits include a charge of $33.4 million and $30.6 million, respectively, (U.S.A. $35.5 million; Foreign $28.5 million) for unusual items.
(d) Consumer Foods operating profits include a net gain of $17.5 million (U.S.A. $20.5 million loss; Foreign $38.0 million gain) for unusual items.

Summarized quarterly data for 1994 and 1993 follows:

In Millions, Except per Share and Market Price Amounts	First Quarter 1994	First Quarter 1993	Second Quarter 1994	Second Quarter 1993	Third Quarter 1994	Third Quarter 1993	Fourth Quarter 1994	Fourth Quarter 1993	Total Year 1994	Total Year 1993
Sales	$2,089.8	$2,019.6	$2,182.2	$2,096.9	$2,101.4	$2,010.7	$2,143.5	$2,007.4	$8,516.9	$8,134.6
Gross profit (a)	1,011.7	977.3	1,055.1	1,016.6	994.6	941.4	997.3	901.7	4,058.7	3,837.0
Earnings from operations	165.6	159.6	140.7	138.1	145.0	140.9(b)	18.4(c)	67.5(d)	469.7	506.1
Earnings per share from operations	1.04	.97	.88	.85	.91	.86	.12	.42	2.95	3.10
Cumulative effect of accounting changes	.2	-	-	-	-	-	-	-	.2	-
Net earnings	165.8	159.6	140.7	138.1	145.0	140.9	18.4	67.5	469.9	506.1
Net earnings per share	1.04	.97	.88	.85	.91	.86	.12	.42	2.95	3.10
Dividends per share	.47	.42	.47	.42	.47	.42	.47	.42	1.88	1.68
Market price of common stock:										
High	68 3/4	71 1/8	67 3/4	73 7/8	63	72 1/2	57	74 1/8	68 3/4	74 1/8
Low	56 7/8	62	59 5/8	64 1/2	55 1/2	65	49 7/8	64 1/8	49 7/8	62

(a) Before charges for depreciation.
(b) Includes an after-tax loss of $8.7 million ($.05 per share) for a restructuring charge for SVE.
(c) Includes an after-tax loss of $87.1 million ($.55 per share) related to the improper treatment of oat supplies.
(d) Includes an after-tax loss of $47.0 million ($.29 per share) for restructuring charges related to restaurant closings and Consumer Foods manufacturing costs.

ELEVEN YEAR FINANCIAL SUMMARY AS REPORTED

In Millions, Except per Share Data	May 29, 1994	May 30, 1993	May 31, 1992	May 26, 1991	May 27, 1990	May 28, 1989	May 29, 1988	May 31, 1987	May 25, 1986	May 26, 1985	May 27, 1984
Financial Results											
Earnings (loss) per share (a)	$ 2.95	$ 3.10	$ 2.99	$ 2.87	$ 2.32	$ 2.53	$ 1.63	$ 1.25	$ 1.03	$ (.41)	$ 1.24
Return on average equity	37.7%	39.1%	39.9%	49.2%	49.5%	60.0%	41.1%	31.4%	21.5%	(6.5)%	19.0%
Dividends per share (a)	1.88	1.68	1.48	1.28	1.10	.94	.80	.625	.565	.56	.51
Sales (b)	8,516.9	8,134.6	7,777.8	7,153.2	6,448.3	5,620.6	5,178.8	5,189.3	4,586.6	4,285.2	5,600.8
Costs and expenses:											
Cost of sales (b)	4,458.2	4,297.6	4,123.2	3,722.1	3,485.1	3,114.8	2,847.8	2,834.0	2,563.9	2,474.8	3,165.9
Selling, general											
and administrative (b)	2,902.4	2,645.2	2,504.5	2,386.0	2,138.0	1,808.5	1,710.5	1,757.5	1,547.2	1,443.9	1,841.7
Depreciation and											
amortization (b)	303.8	274.2	247.4	218.4	180.1	152.3	140.0	131.7	113.1	110.4	133.1
Interest (b)(c)	99.2	73.6	58.2	61.1	32.4	27.5	37.7	32.9	38.8	60.2	61.4
Earnings before income taxes (b)	753.3(e)	844.0(f)	844.5	765.6	612.7	517.5	442.8	433.2	323.6	195.9(h)	398.7
Net earnings (loss)	469.9	506.1	495.6	472.7	381.4	414.3(g)	283.1	222.0	183.5	(72.9)(i)	233.4
Net earnings (loss)											
as a percent of sales	5.5%	6.2%	6.4%	6.6%	5.9%	7.4%	5.5%	4.3%	4.0%	(1.7)%	4.2%
Weighted average number of											
common shares (a)	159.1	163.1	165.7	164.5	164.4	163.9	174.0	177.5	178.5	179.0	187.5
Taxes (income, payroll,											
property, etc.) per share (a)(b)	2.98	3.14	3.09	2.77	2.29	1.98	1.66	1.80	1.33	1.00	1.56
Financial Position											
Total assets	5,198.3	4,650.8	4,305.0	3,901.8	3,289.5	2,888.1	2,671.9	2,280.4	2,086.2	2,662.6	2,858.1
Land, buildings and											
equipment, net	3,092.6	2,859.6	2,648.6	2,241.3	1,934.5	1,588.1	1,376.4	1,249.5	1,084.9	956.0	1,229.4
Working capital at year end	(702.9)	(481.9)	(337.1)	(190.1)	(263.1)	(197.1)	(205.5)	(57.1)	41.6	229.4	244.5
Long-term debt, excluding											
current portion	1,417.2	1,268.3	920.5	879.0	688.5	536.3	361.5	285.5	458.3	449.5	362.6
Stockholders' equity	1,151.2	1,218.5	1,370.9	1,113.5	809.7	731.9	648.5	730.4	682.5	1,023.3	1,224.6
Stockholders' equity per share (a)	7.26	7.59	8.28	6.74	4.96	4.54	3.88	4.14	3.81	5.76	6.76
Other Statistics											
Cash provided by operations (b)	836.0	865.9	790.4	548.6	657.1	527.3	329.9	442.9	466.5	150.4	236.1
Total dividends	299.4	274.8	245.2	210.6	180.8	154.4	139.3	110.8	100.9	100.4	96.0
Gross capital expenditures (d)	559.5	623.8	695.3	554.6	540.0	442.4	410.7	329.1	244.9	209.7	282.4
Research and development (b)	63.6	60.1	62.1	57.0	48.2	41.2	40.7	38.3	41.7	38.7	63.5
Advertising media											
expenditures (b)	409.5	395.4	426.8	419.6	394.9	336.5	345.9	330.0	317.0	274.3	349.6
Wages, salaries and											
employee benefits (b)	1,490.0	1,433.2	1,398.5	1,331.6	1,171.5	987.1	911.3	958.6	895.8	860.2	1,121.6
Number of employees (b)	125,670	121,290	111,501	108,077	97,238	83,837	74,453	65,619	62,056	63,162	80,297
Accumulated LIFO reserve	53.0	60.3	67.0	75.9	71.4	65.5	53.0	51.5	45.8	47.5	79.7
Common stock price range (a)	68 3/4	74 1/8	75 7/8	60 7/8	39 5/8	33 7/8	31	28	20	15 1/8	14 1/4
	49 7/8	62	54 1/4	37 7/8	31 3/8	22 3/8	20 3/8	18 1/2	13	11 7/8	10 3/8

(a) Years prior to 1991 have been adjusted for the two-for-one stock splits in November 1990 and 1986.
(b) Includes continuing operations only; years prior to 1989 include the discontinued cafeteria-style restaurant and frozen novelties operations, years prior to 1988 include the discontinued specialty retailing apparel operations, years prior to 1987 include the discontinued furniture operations, and years prior to 1985 include the discontinued toy, fashion and specialty retailing non-apparel operations.
(c) Interest expense is net of interest income; years prior to 1986 are interest expense only with interest income included in selling, general and administrative.
(d) Includes capital expenditures of continuing operations and discontinued operations through the date disposition was authorized.
(e) Includes pretax unusual expense of $146.9 million.
(f) Includes pretax restructuring charge of $67.0 million.
(g) Includes after-tax discontinued operations income of $169.0 million and cumulative effect of accounting change charge of $70.0 million.
(h) Includes pretax restructuring charge of $75.8 million.
(i) Includes after-tax discontinued operations charge of $188.3 million.

FINANCIAL DATA FOR CONTINUING OPERATIONS

| In Millions, Except per Share Data | Fiscal Year Ended | | | | |
	May 29, 1994	May 30, 1993	May 31, 1992	May 26, 1991	May 27, 1990
Sales	$8,516.9	$8,134.6	$7,777.8	$7,153.2	$6,448.3
Earnings after taxes	469.7	506.1	505.6	464.2	373.7
Earnings per share	2.95	3.10	3.05	2.82	2.27

BOARD OF DIRECTORS

H. Brewster Atwater, Jr.
Chairman of the Board and Chief Executive Officer, General Mills, Inc. (1*)
Minneapolis

Richard M. Bressler
Retired Chairman of the Board, El Paso Natural Gas Company (natural resources) (1,2,3*,5)
Seattle, Washington

Livio D. DeSimone
Chairman of the Board and Chief Executive Officer, 3M Company (diversified manufacturer) (1,2,4,6)
St. Paul

William T. Esrey
Chairman and Chief Executive Officer, Sprint Corporation (telecommunications systems) (1,3,5*)
Kansas City, Missouri

Charles W. Gaillard
Vice Chairman, General Mills, Inc.
Minneapolis

Judith Richards Hope
Senior Partner, Paul, Hastings, Janofsky & Walker, Attorneys (2,5,6)
Washington, D.C.

Joe R. Lee
Vice Chairman, General Mills, Inc. (1)
Minneapolis

Kenneth A. Macke
Retired Chairman of the Board, Chief Executive Officer, and Chairman of the Executive Committee,
Dayton Hudson Corporation (retail stores) (2,4,6)
Minneapolis

George Putnam
Chairman of the Board, The Putnam Investment Management Company (1,3,4*,5)
Boston, Massachusetts

Michael D. Rose
Chairman of the Board, The Promus Companies Incorporated (hospitality company) (2*,3,4)
Memphis, Tennessee

Stephen W. Sanger
President, General Mills, Inc.
Minneapolis

A. Michael Spence
Dean of the Graduate School of Business, Stanford University (2,4)
Stanford, California

Mark H. Willes
Vice Chairman, General Mills, Inc. (1)
Minneapolis

C. Angus Wurtele
Chairman of the Board and Chief Executive Officer, The Valspar Corporation (paints and coatings) (3,5,6*)
Minneapolis

Committees of the Board of Directors (1) Executive Committee (2) Audit Committee (3) Compensation Committee (4) Finance Committee (5) Nominating Committee (6) Public Responsibility Committee (*) Denotes Committee Chair

CORPORATE OFFICERS

H. Brewster Atwater, Jr.
Chairman of the Board and Chief Executive Officer

Stephen W. Sanger
President

Mark H. Willes
Vice Chairman

Joe R. Lee
Vice Chairman

Charles W. Gaillard
Vice Chairman

Ronald N. Magruder
Executive Vice President

Jeffrey J. O'Hara
Executive Vice President

Edward K. Bixby
Senior Vice President

Michael E. Cushmore
Senior Vice President

Stephen R. Demeritt
Senior Vice President; Chief Executive Officer, CPW, S.A.

Jon L. Finley
Senior Vice President

Leslie M. Frécon
Senior Vice President, Corporate Finance

Stephen J. Garthwaite
Senior Vice President

David D. Murphy
Senior Vice President

Michael A. Peel
Senior Vice President, Personnel

Gary M. Rodkin
Senior Vice President

Jeffrey J. Rotsch
Senior Vice President

Blaine Sweatt, III
Senior Vice President

Kenneth L. Thome
Senior Vice President, Financial Operations

Stephen H. Warhover
Senior Vice President

Clifford L. Whitehill
Senior Vice President, General Counsel and Secretary

*50/50 joint venture with Nestlé, S.A.

COMPANY OFFICERS

Dean Belbas
Vice President, Director of Investor Relations

Walter W. Faster
Vice President, Director of Corporate Growth and Development

Sandy J. Navin
Vice President, Director of Taxes

Austin P. Sullivan
Vice President, Director of Corporate Communications and Public Affairs

STAFF VICE PRESIDENTS

Ivy S. Bernhardson
Senior Associate Counsel and Assistant Secretary

Edward L. Blood
Director of Strategic Planning and Analysis

Sam A. Catapano
Director of Auditing

Alfred G. Colling
Vice President, Financial Operations

James L. Craig, M.D.
Director of Health and Human Services

James W. Galovan
Director of Personnel-Consumer Foods Marketing

Reatha Clark King
President and Executive Director, General Mills Foundation

D. Russell Norha
Director of Labor Relations

Alan J. Ritchie
Director of Compensation and Benefits

David B. VanBenschoten
Director of Finance–Investments

William A. Van Brunt
General Counsel–Foods

Laurie H. Greeno†
Vice President

† *on leave of absence*

Innovation, Speed, Commitment

CONSUMER FOODS

Betty Crocker Products

Jeffrey J. Rotsch
President

James W. Feil
Vice President, Financial Operations

John O. Hallberg
Vice President, General Manager, Snacks

Christina L. Steiner
*Vice President, General Manager,
Main Meals, Sides Dishes and Beverages*

R. Brooks Gekler
General Manager, Desserts

Big G

Charles W. Gaillard
Vice Chairman

Y. Marc Belton
Vice President, Child/All-Family Cereals

John T. Machuzick
*Vice President, Trade and Promotion
Marketing*

Dorothy J. Muffett
Vice President, Research and Development

Kevin A. Nosbisch
Vice President, Financial Operations

Richard A. Shaeffer
Vice President, Adult Cereals

Christianne L. Strauss
Vice President, New Enterprises

Foodservice

Roger W. Rumble
President

Ronald E. Behm
Director, National Sales

Jerry D. Kaminski
Marketing Director

Gold Medal

Michael E. Cushmore
President

Peter J. Capell
Director, Packaged Products

Richard O. Lund
Vice President, Financial Operations

Robert L. Stretmater
Vice President, Consumer and Bakery Flour

Gorton's

Stephen H. Warhover
President

Mark J. Lamothe
Director, Marketing

Yoplait

Gary M. Rodkin
President

Carol L. Gullstad
Director, Marketing and Sales

Information Systems

Phillip G. Semmer
Vice President

Consumer Foods Sales

Edward K. Bixby
President

James J. Kula
Vice President, Central Zone

David G. Stuckey
Vice President, Western Zone

Jefferson B. Yeakel
Vice President, Eastern Zone

Keith R. Sieck
Vice President, Personnel

David J. McMahon
Director, Trade Relations

Marketing Services

Donald L. Knutzen
Vice President

Technology & Operations

Stephen J. Garthwaite,
*Senior Vice President, Technology
& Operations*

Randy G. Darcy
Vice President, Manufacturing

James R. Getchell
Vice President, Engineering

Thomas J. Lee
Vice President, Procurement

L. Scott Hackett
Vice President, Grain Operations

Joseph R. Mucha
Vice President, Personnel

Sidney F. Sapakie
*Vice President, International Cereal
and Snack Research and Development*

Warren M. Schwecke
*Vice President, Quality and
Regulatory Operations*

John H. Stafford
Vice President, Financial Operations

International Foods

David D. Murphy
*President, General Mills Canada
and International Foods*

Kim S. Leventhal
Vice President, International Foods

General Mills Canada

Barry C. Wolfish
Senior Vice President, Cereals

Scott C. Lutz
Vice President, Betty Crocker Products

CPW, S.A.*

Kendall J. Powell
Vice President, Marketing, CPW

Ian R. Friendly
*Vice President, Director, Business
Development, Latin/South America*

Linda Hipkiss-Mills
Director, Marketing, CP–UK

*50/50 joint venture with Nestlé, S.A.

RESTAURANTS

Red Lobster North America

Jeffrey J. O'Hara
President

Michael Dimopoulos
Executive Vice President, Strategic Planning

Kress T. Muenzmay
Executive Vice President, Operations

Robert W. Mock
*Executive Vice President, General Manager,
Red Lobster Canada*

Kirk L. Spresser
Executive Vice President, Marketing

Linda J. Dimopoulos
Senior Vice President, Financial Operations

Frank E. Ruble
Senior Vice President, Personnel

James E. Salmon
Senior Vice President, Purchasing

Richard J. Walsh
*Vice President, Government and
Community Relations*

U.S. Operations–Senior Vice Presidents

Edward M. Baldwin
Los Angeles

Charles W. Helms
Chicago

David L. Longest
Orlando

Thomas A. Pannullo
New York

Lynn M. Niergarth
Cincinnati

Robert M. Parrotino
Dallas

China Coast

Jon L. Finley
President

Linda R. Sampieri
Senior Vice President, Personnel

David T. Pickens
Senior Vice President, Operations

John E. Murphy, Jr.
Vice President, Financial Operations

New Business Development

Blaine Sweatt, III
President

Roger K. Thompson
Vice President, Strategic Marketing

International

Nobumitsu Kobayashi
President, Red Lobster Japan

The Olive Garden North America

Ronald N. Magruder
President

Bradley D. Blum
Senior Vice President, Marketing

Judith K. Donovan
*Senior Vice President/Division
General Manager*

Richard D. Halterman
Senior Vice President, Development

Daniel M. Lyons
Senior Vice President, Personnel

Jonathan C. Sleik
*Senior Vice President/Division
General Manager*

James D. Smith
Senior Vice President, Chief Financial Officer

George T. Williams
*Senior Vice President,
General Counsel–Restaurants*

Arnym P. Solomon
Vice President, Strategic Planning

U.S. Operations–Regional Vice Presidents

Paul W. Brady
Dallas

Paula M. Dawson
Atlanta

Francis L. Christman
Philadelphia

James R. Hager
Bradenton

Gregory J. MacIsaac
Los Angeles

Philip A. Neal
Chicago

SHAREHOLDER INFORMATION

**Transfer Agent, Registrar, Dividend Payments
and Dividend Reinvestment Plan**
Norwest Stock Transfer
161 North Concord Exchange
P.O. Box 566
South St. Paul, MN 55075-0566
Phone: (800) 670-4763 or
      (612) 450-4084

Address correspondence as appropriate to the attention of:
  Address Changes
  Stock Transfer
  Voluntary Cash (reinvestment plan)
  Shareholder Services

For other stock-related information, call General Mills' Stock
Transfer Department at (800) 245-5703.

Independent Auditor
KPMG Peat Marwick
4200 Norwest Center
90 South 7th Street
Minneapolis, MN 55402-3900
Phone: (612) 341-2222

Form 10-K Report
Company management believes that the financial statements
in this Annual Report to Stockholders include all significant
financial data in the annual report filed on Form 10-K with
the Securities and Exchange Commission. Stockholders may
request a free copy of the Form 10-K and attached schedules
by writing to: Secretary, General Mills, Inc., P.O. Box 1113,
Minneapolis, MN 55440

Shareholder Reports / Investor Inquiries
Shareholders seeking information about General Mills are
invited to contact the Investor Relations Department at (800)
245-5703. Within the 612 area code, call 540-2444. Recorded
summaries of quarterly earnings announcements and other
key company news are available on the toll-free line. Shareholders may also request to receive, free of charge, copies of
quarterly earnings releases.

Notice of Annual Meeting
The annual meeting of stockholders will be held at 11 a.m.,
Central Daylight Time, Monday, Sept. 19, 1994, at the Children's
Theatre Company, 2400 Third Avenue South, Minneapolis.

Corporate Citizenship Report Available
General Mills' 1994 Corporate Citizenship Report details the
company's many community service and philanthropic activ-
ities. The report includes the annual report of the General
Mills Foundation. To receive a copy, write to: General Mills
Community Affairs Department, P.O. Box 1113, Minneapolis,
MN 55440

Holiday Gift Boxes
Shareholders may request a brochure and order form for
General Mills' 1994 Holiday Gift Boxes, which will contain
an assortment of the company's food products and other
items, by writing to: Holiday Gift Box Offer, General Mills,
P.O. Box 1112, Dept. 95, Minneapolis, or by calling (800)
245-5703. Within the 612 area code, call 540-3205.

Markets
New York Stock Exchange
Midwest Stock Exchange

Stock Exchange Symbol: GIS

Company Addresses
General Mills Executive Offices
Number One General Mills Boulevard
Minneapolis, MN 55426
Phone: (612) 540-2311

Mailing Address:
P.O. Box 1113
Minneapolis, MN 55440

♻ *Printed on recycled paper. Cover and pages 1-16 contain 50% recycled fiber
including 10% post-consumer waste. Pages 17-36 contain 50% recycled fiber including
15% post-consumer waste.*

General Mills, Inc.: Appendix of Comparable Company Data

EXHIBIT 1

Financial Ratios for Selected Food and Consumer Products Companies

	Campbell Soup Co. (7/31/94)	Hershey Foods Corp. (12/31/93)	Kellogg Company (12/31/93)	Phillip Morris Companies (12/31/93)	Quaker Oats Company (6/30/94)	Borden, Inc. (12/31/93)	Average of Six Companies
1. Profitability Ratios							
Profit margin	9.4%	8.5%	10.8%	7.1%	3.9%	−01.0%	5.0%
Return on assets	12.6%	10.4%	16.1%	7.0%	7.6%	−01.5%	8.7%
Return on equity	31.7%	21.1%	39.7%	30.7%	19.0%	−23.1%	19.9%
2. Activity Ratios							
Asset turnover	1.35	1.26	1.53	1.00	2.03	1.20	1.4
Days' receivables	33.0	25.0	31.0	29.0	30.0	42.0	31.7
Inventory turnover	4.73	4.16	6.65	3.40	7.45	6.66	5.5
3. Leverage Ratios							
Debt to equity	28.2%	11.7%	30.4%	129.2%	170.4%	504.6%	145.8%
Times interest earned . .	12.6	15.7	26.6	5.2	4.8	.7	10.9
Days' payables	45.9	20.9	41.4	44.5	53.8	41.9	41.4
4. Liquidity Ratios							
Current ratio	.96	1.09	1.03	.87	1.00	.94	1.0
Quick ratio	.40	.38	.52	.28	.52	.32	.4
5. Market Ratios							
Price/earnings ratio	14.7	22.8	19.3	15.8	21.7	NA	18.9
Dividend yield	3.0%	2.3%	2.3%	4.8%	3.0%	5.3%	3.5%

This appendix was prepared by Professor William J. Bruns, Jr.

Copyright © 1996 by the President and Fellows of Harvard College.
Harvard Business School note 197-037.

EXHIBIT 2
Common-Size Balance Sheets for Selected Food and Consumer Products Companies

	Campbell Soup Co. (7/31/94)	Hershey Foods Corp. (12/31/93)	Kellogg Company (12/31/93)	Phillip Morris Companies (12/31/93)	Quaker Oats Company (6/30/94)	Borden, Inc. (12/31/93)	Average of Six Companies
Total current assets	32.1%	31.1%	29.4%	25.0%	41.2%	33.3%	32.0%
Land, buildings, and equipment	48.1	51.2	65.3	21.4	39.9	34.5	43.4
Other assets	19.8	17.7	5.3	53.6	18.9	32.2	24.6
Total assets	100.0%	100.0%	100.0%	100.0%	100.0%	100.0%	100.0%
Total current liabilities	33.4	28.5	28.7	28.7	41.4	35.4	32.7
Long-term debt	11.2	5.8	12.3	29.3	214.9	32.1	19.3
Deferred income taxes	4.2	6.1	4.5	6.0	2.7	1.2	4.1
Other liabilities	11.4	10.1	14.1	13.3	15.8	25.0	15.0
Total liabilities	60.2%	50.5%	59.6%	77.3%	84.8%	93.7%	71.0%
Common stock	3.5	3.5	3.5	1.8	14.3	5.4	5.3
Retained earnings	47.5	50.2	75.9	29.3	34.7	14.7	42.1
Common stock in treasury . .	−12.2	−4.2	−39.0	−8.4	−33.8	−13.8	−18.4
Stockholders' equity	39.8	49.5	40.4	22.7	15.2	6.3	29.0
Total liabilities and stockholders' equity	100.0%	100.0%	100.0%	100.0%	100.0%	100.0%	100.0%
Total assets ($ millions)	$4,922.0	$2,855.1	$4,237.1	$51,205.0	$3,043.3	$3,871.7	$11,688.9

EXHIBIT 3
Common-Size Income Statements for Selected Food and Consumer Products Companies

	Campbell Soup Co. (7/31/94)	Hershey Foods Corp. (12/31/93)	Kellogg Company (12/31/93)	Phillip Morris Companies (12/31/93)	Quaker Oats Company (6/30/94)	Borden, Inc. (12/31/93)	Average of Six Companies
Sales	100.0%	100.0%	100.0%	100.0%	100.0%	100.0%	100.0%
Costs and Expenses							
Cost of sales	56.2	54.3	43.3	50.8	46.3	68.5	53.2
SG&A	24.6	29.7	35.5	29.5	40.7	20.8	30.1
Depreciation and amortization	3.5	2.9	4.2	3.2	2.9	5.3	3.7
Total costs and expenses	84.3	86.9	83.0	83.5	89.9	94.6	87.0
Operating income	15.7	13.1	17.0	16.5	10.1	5.4	13.0
Interest expense	1.3	1.0	.7	2.9	1.7	2.3	1.7
Other income	.4	2.5	0.1	−1.3	−2.1	−3.9	−0.7
Income before taxes	14.8	14.6	16.4	12.3	6.3	−0.8	10.6
Income taxes	5.4	6.1	5.6	5.2	2.4	−0.2	4.1
Income from continuing operations	9.4	8.5	10.8	7.1	3.9	−1.0	6.5
Discontinued operations	0.0	−3.0	0.0	−1.0	0.0	−10.4	−2.4
Net earnings	9.4	5.5	10.8	6.1	3.9	−11.4	4.1
Net sales (millions) . . .	$6,690.0	$3,488.2	$6,295.4	$50,621.0	$5,995.0	$5,506.3	$13,092.7
% of revenue by marketing segment . .	Foods (100%)	Foods (100%)	Foods (100%)	Tobacco (43%) Foods (49%) Beer (7%) Financial services (1%)	Grocery products (100%)	Foods (65%) Nonfood (35%)	

EXHIBIT 4
Income Statements for Selected Food and Consumer Products Companies (millions of dollars)

	Campbell Soup Co. (7/31/94)	Hershey Foods Corp. (12/31/93)	Kellogg Company (12/31/93)	Phillip Morris Companies (12/31/93)	Quaker Oats Company (6/30/94)	Borden, Inc. (12/31/93)
Sales	$6,690.0	$3,488.2	$6,295.4	$50,621.0	$5,955.0	$5,506.3
Costs and Expenses						
Cost of sales	3,759.0	1,895.4	2,723.8	25,729.0	2,755.0	3,770.6
SG&A	1,644.0	1,035.5	2,237.5	14.953.0	2,425.6	1,144.6
Depreciation and amortization	237.0	100.1	265.2	1,611.0	171.2	293.0
Total costs and expenses	5,640.0	3,031.0	5,226.5	42,293.0	5,351.8	5,208.2
Operating Income . . .	1,050.0	457.2	1,068.9	8,328.0	603.2	298.1
Interest expense . . .	85.0	34.9	40.4	1,478.0	99.9	126.2
Other income	23.0	88.5	5.6	−654.0	−124.6	−215.3
Income before taxes	988.0	510.8	1,034.1	6,196.0	378.7	−43.4
Income taxes	358.0	213.6	353.4	2,628.0	147.2	13.5
Income from continuing operations	630.0	297.2	680.7	3,586.0	231.5	−56.9
Discontinued operations	0.0	−103.9	0.0	−477.0	0.0	573.8
Net earnings	$ 630.0	$ 193.3	$ 680.7	$ 3,091.0	$ 231.5	$ −630.7
% of revenue by marketing segment	Foods (100%)	Foods (100%)	Foods (100%)	Tobacco (43%) Foods (49%) Beer (7%) Financial services (1%)	Grocery products (100%)	Foods (65%) Nonfood (35%)

EXHIBIT 5
Balance Sheets for Selected Food and Consumer Products Companies (millions of dollars)

	Campbell Soup Co. (7/31/94)	Hershey Foods Corp. (12/31/93)	Kellogg Company (12/31/93)	Phillip Morris Companies (12/31/93)	Quaker Oats Company (6/30/94)	Borden, Inc. (12/31/93)
Total current assets	$1,601.0	$ 889.0	$1,245.1	$12,808.0	$1,253.6	$1,290.2
Land, buildings, and equipment	2,401.0	1,460.9	2,768.4	10,952.0	1,214.2	1,336.7
Other assets	990.0	505.2	223.6	27,445.0	575.2	1,244.8
Total assets	$4,992.0	$2,855.1	$4,237.1	$51,205.0	$3,043.3	$3,871.7
Total current liabilities	1,665.0	813.9	1,214.6	14,668.0	1,259.1	1,371.5
Long-term debt	560.0	165.8	521.6	15,021.0	759.5	1,240.8
Deferred income taxes	211.0	172.7	188.9	3,067.0	82.2	47.1
Other liabilities	567.0	290.4	598.6	6,822.0	481.4	966.4
Total liabilities	$3,003.0	$1,442.8	$2,523.7	$39,578.0	$2,582.2	$3,625.8
Common stock	175.0	99.6	149.6	935.0	435.3	210.0
Retained earnings	2,373.0	1,431.7	3,216.9	15,007.0	1,054.7	568.5
Common stock in treasury	−559.0	−119.0	−1,653.1	−4,315.0	−1,028.9	−532.6
Total stockholders' equity	1,989.0	1,412.3	1,713.4	11,627.0	461.1	245.9
Total liabilities and stockholders' equity	$ 4992.0	$2,855.1	$4,237.1	$51,205.0	$3,043.3	$3,871.7

Clarkson Lumber Company

After rapid growth in its business during recent years, the Clarkson Lumber Company, in the spring of 1996, anticipated a further substantial increase in sales. Despite good profits, the company had experienced a shortage of cash and had found it necessary to increase its borrowing from the County National Bank to $399,000 in the spring of 1996. The maximum loan that County National would make to any one borrower was $400,000, and Clarkson had been able to stay within this limit only by relying very heavily on trade credit. In addition, County National was now asking that Mr. Clarkson guarantee the loan personally. Keith Clarkson, sole owner and president of the Clarkson Lumber Company, was therefore actively looking elsewhere for a new banking relationship in which he would be able to negotiate a larger loan that did not require a personal guarantee.

Mr. Clarkson had recently been introduced by a friend to Leonard Jackson, an officer of a much larger bank, the Northwestern National Bank. The two men had tentatively discussed the possibility that Northwestern might extend a line of credit to Clarkson Lumber up to a maximum amount of $750,000. Mr. Clarkson thought that a loan of this size would improve profitability by allowing him to take full advantage of trade discounts. Subsequent to this discussion, Mr. Jackson had arranged for the credit department of the Northwestern National Bank to investigate Mr. Clarkson and his company.

The Clarkson Lumber Company had been founded in 1981 as a partnership by Mr. Clarkson and his brother-in-law, Harry Holtz. In 1994, Mr. Clarkson bought out Mr. Holtz's interest for $200,000. Mr. Holtz had taken a note for $200,000, to be paid off in 1995 and 1996, in order to give Mr. Clarkson time to arrange for the necessary financing. This note carried an interest rate of 11% and was repayable in semiannual installments of $50,000, beginning June 30, 1995.

The business was located in a growing suburb of a large city in the Pacific Northwest. The company owned land with access to a railroad siding, and four large storage buildings had been erected on this land. The company's operations were limited to the retail distribution of lumber products in the local area. Typical products included plywood moldings, and sash and door products. Quantity discounts and credit terms of net 30 days on open account were usually offered to customers.

Sales volume had been built up largely on the basis of successful price competition, made possible by careful control of operating expenses and by quantity purchases of materials at substantial discounts. Most of the moldings and sash and door products, which constituted significant items of sales, were used for repair work. About 55% of total sales were made in the six months from April through September. Annual sales of $2,921,000 in 1993, $3,477,000 in 1994, and $4,519,000 in 1995 yielded after-tax profits of $60,000 in 1993, $68,000 in 1994, and $77,000 in 1995. Operating statements for the years 1993–1995 and for the three months ending March 31, 1996, are given in Exhibit 1.

Mr. Clarkson was an energetic man, 49 years of age, who worked long hours on the job. He was helped by an assistant, who in the words of the investigator of the Northwestern National Bank, "has been doing and can do about everything that Mr. Clarkson does in the organization." Other employees numbered 15 in early 1996, 8 of whom worked in the yard and drove trucks, and 7 of whom assisted in the office and in sales.

As part of its customary investigation of prospective borrowers, the Northwestern National Bank sent inquiries concerning Mr. Clarkson to a number of firms that had business dealings with him. The manager of one of his large suppliers, the Bennett Company, wrote in answer:

> The conservative operation of his business appeals to us. He has not wasted his money in disproportionate plant investment. His operating expenses are as low as they could possibly be. He has personal control over every feature of his business, and he possesses sound judgment and a willingness to work harder than anyone I have even known. This, with a good personality, gives him a good turnover; and from my personal experience in watching him work, I know that he keeps close check on his own credits.

All the other trade letters received by the bank bore out this opinion.

In addition to owning the lumber business, which was his major source of income, Mr. Clarkson held jointly with his wife an equity interest in their home. The house had cost $72,000 to build in 1979 and was mortgaged for $38,000. He also held a $70,000 life insurance policy, payable to Mrs. Clarkson. Mrs. Clarkson owned independently a half interest in another house worth about $85,000. Otherwise, they had no sizable personal investments.

The bank gave particular attention to the debt position and current ratio of the business. It noted the ready market for the company's products at all times and the fact that sales prospects were favorable. The bank's investigator reported: "Sales are expected to reach $5.5 million in 1996 and may exceed this level if prices of lumber should rise substantially in the near future." On the other hand, it was recognized that a general economic downturn might slow down the rate of increase in sales. Clarkson Lumber's sales, however, were protected to some degree from fluctuations in new housing construction because of the relatively high proportion of its repair business. Projections beyond 1996 were difficult to make, but the prospects appeared good for continued growth in the volume of Clarkson Lumber's business over the foreseeable future.

The bank also noted the rapid increase in Clarkson Lumber's accounts and notes payable in the recent past, especially in 1995 and in the spring of 1996. The usual terms of purchase in the trade provided for a discount of 2% for payments made within 10 days of the invoice date. Accounts were due in 30 days at the invoice price, but suppliers ordinarily did not object if payments lagged somewhat behind the due date. During the last 2 years, Mr. Clarkson had taken very few purchase discounts because of the shortage of funds arising from his purchase of Mr. Holtz's interest in the business and the additional investments in working capital associated with the company's increasing sales volume. Trade credit was seriously extended in the spring of 1996 as Mr. Clarkson strove to hold his bank borrowing within the $400,000 ceiling imposed by the County National Bank.

Balance sheets at December 31, 1993–1995, and March 31, 1996, are presented in Exhibit 2. Statistics for a sample of lumber outlets are provided in Exhibit 3.

The tentative discussions between Mr. Jackson and Mr. Clarkson had been in terms of a revolving, secured, 90-day note not to exceed $750,000. The specific details of the loan had not been worked out, but Mr. Jackson had explained that the agreement would involve the standard covenants applying to such a loan. He cited as illustrative provisions the requirement that restrictions on additional borrowing would be imposed; that net working capital would have to be maintained at an agreed level; that additional investments in fixed assets could be made only with the prior approval of the bank; and that limitations would be placed on withdrawals of funds from the business by Mr. Clarkson. Interest would be set on a floating-rate basis at 2½ percentage points above the prime rate. Mr. Jackson indicated that the initial rate to be paid would be approximately 11% under conditions in effect in early 1996. Both men also understood that Mr. Clarkson would sever his relationship with the County National Bank if he entered into a loan agreement with the Northwestern National Bank.

EXHIBIT 1

Operating Expenses for Years Ending December 31, 1993–1995, and for First Quarter 1996 (thousands of dollars)

	1993	1994	1995	1st Quarter 1996
Net sales	$2,921	$3,477	$4,519	$1,026[a]
Cost of goods sold				
Beginning inventory	330	337	432	587
Purchases	2,209	2,729	3,579	819
	$2,539	$3,066	$4,011	$1,406
Ending inventory	337	432	587	607
Total cost of goods sold	$2,202	$2,634	$3,424	$ 799
Gross profit	719	843	1,095	263
Operating expenses[b]	622	717	940	244
Earnings before interest and taxes	$ 97	$ 126	$ 155	$ 19
Interest expense	23	42	56	13
Net income before income taxes	$ 74	$ 84	$ 99	$ 6
Provision for income taxes[c]	14	17	22	1
Net income	$ 60	$ 67	$ 77	$ 5

a. In the first quarter of 1995, sales were $903,000 and net income was $7,000.

b. Operating expenses include a cash salary for Mr. Clarkson of $75,000 in 1993; $80,000 in 1994; $85,000 in 1995; and $22,500 in the first quarter of 1996.

c. Clarkson Lumber was required to estimate its income tax liability for the current tax year and pay four quarterly estimated tax installments during that year. The first $50,000 of pre-tax profits were taxed at a 15% rate; the next $25,000 were taxed at a 25% rate; the next $25,000 were taxed at a 34% rate; and profits in excess of $100,000 but less than $335,000 were taxed at a 39% rate.

EXHIBIT 2
Balance Sheets at December 31, 1993–1995, and March 31, 1996 (thousands of dollars)

	1993	1994	1995	1st Quarter 1996
Cash	$ 43	$ 52	$ 56	$ 53
Accounts receivable, net	306	411	606	583
Inventory	337	432	587	607
Current assets	$686	$ 895	$1,249	$1,243
Property, net	233	262	388	384
Total assets	$919	$1,157	$1,637	$1,627
Notes payable, bank[a]	$ —	$ 60	$ 390	$ 399
Note payable to Holtz, current portion[b]	—	100	100	100
Notes payable, trade	—	—	127	123
Accounts payable	213	340	376	364
Accrued expenses	42	45	75	67
Term loan, current portion[c]	20	20	20	20
Current liabilities	$275	$ 565	$1,088	$1,073
Term loan[c]	140	120	100	100
Note payable, Mr. Holtz[b]	—	100	0	0
Total liabilities	$415	$ 785	$1,188	$1,173
Net worth	504	372	449	454
Total liabilities and net worth	$919	$1,157	$1,637	$1,627

a. Interest is computed on the average outstanding loan balance at the rate of prime plus 2½%.

b. Interest is fixed at 11% times the outstanding balance.

c. Interest is fixed at 10% times the outstanding balance; the term loan is secured by the fixed assets and is repayable in semiannual installments of $10,000.

EXHIBIT 3
Selected Statistics on Lumber Outlets

	Low-Profit Outlets[a]	High-Profit Outlets[a]
Percent of sales		
Cost of goods	76.9%	75.1%
Operating expense	22.0	20.6
Cash	1.3	1.1
Accounts receivable	13.7	12.4
Inventory	12.0	11.6
Fixed assets, net	12.1	9.2
Total assets	39.1	34.3
Percent of total assets		
Current liabilities	52.7%	29.2%
Long-term liabilities	34.8	16.0
Equity	12.5	54.8
Current ratio	1.31	2.52
Return on sales	(0.7%)	4.3%
Return on assets	(1.8%)	12.2%
Return on equity	(14.3%)	22.1%

a. Defined as the bottom 25% and as the top 25%, respectively, of all surveyed companies, based on return on sales.

Note on Bank Loans

Bank loans are a versatile source of funding for businesses. For example, these loans can be structured as short- or long-term, fixed- or floating-rate, demand or with a fixed maturity, and secured or unsecured. While each potential borrower's business is unique, reasons to borrow generally include the purchase of assets, including new fixed assets or entire businesses; repayment of obligations; raising of temporary or permanent capital; and the meeting of unexpected needs. Loan repayment generally comes from one of four sources: operations, turnover or liquidation of assets, refinancing, or capital infusion. This note describes traditional bank lending products, the role of the lending officer, credit evaluation, and the structuring of credit facilities and loan agreements. Specialized loan and credit products are described in the Appendix.

Traditional Commercial Bank Lending Products

While increased competition has forced banks to develop innovative credit facilities and financing techniques, traditional products, which include short-term, long-term, and revolving loans, continue to be the mainstay of commercial banking.

Short-Term Loans

Short-term loans, those with maturities of 1 year or less, comprise more than half of all commercial bank loans. Seasonal lines of credit and special-purpose loans are the most common short-term credit facilities. Their primary use is to finance working capital needs resulting from temporary buildups of inventory and receivables. Reflecting their use, repayment of short-term loans typically comes from the routine conversion of current assets to cash. These loans may be either secured or unsecured.

Research Associate Susan L. Roth prepared this note under the supervision of Professor Scott P. Mason and with the assistance of the Citicorp Institute for Global Finance.

A seasonal line of credit is used by companies with seasonal sales cycles to finance periodic increases in current assets, such as inventory. The amount of credit made available is based on the borrower's estimated peak funding requirements. The borrower may draw on the seasonal line of credit as funds are required and repay the line as seasonal sales lead to liquidation of inventories. Interest accrues only on the amount of borrowing outstanding. A bank's commitments under lines of credit may exceed its ability to fund them all simultaneously, though simultaneous demand is unlikely to occur. So as not to have a legal obligation to lend its capital to a borrower in the rare case that demand for funds does exceed supply, the bank may structure this facility with a provision that allows the bank to terminate the facility at its option or provide funding subject to availability.

Businesses use special-purpose loans to finance, on a temporary basis, increases in current assets resulting from unusual or unexpected circumstances. Funding is based on the borrower's estimated needs, with the bank agreeing to fund either all or up to some percentage of the full amount. The credit facility is most likely to require full payment of accrued interest and principal at maturity, that is, a "bullet." The term for such a loan is usually fixed and is determined by approximating the point in time when repayment can be made. The bank's principal risk with a special-purpose loan is default because of a change in the circumstances on which the repayment plan had been based. Therefore, from the bank's perspective, it is important that the source and timing of repayment be clear at the time of funding. Identifying alternatives to routine asset conversion as a source of repayment will further protect the bank.

Long-Term Loans

Introduced in the 1930s, long-term loans, or term loans, are relatively new in banking practice. Providing advantages in its flexibility to adapt to a borrower's special requirements, a term loan has the following characteristics:

- Original maturity of longer than 1 year
- Repayment provided from future earnings or cash flow rather than from short-term liquidation of assets
- Provisions of the loan arrangement detailed in and governed by a signed loan agreement between the borrower and the lender

Term loans are most often used for specific purposes such as purchase of fixed assets, acquisition of another company, or refinancing of existing long-term debt. The term loan may also be used in place of equity or a revolving credit facility to finance permanent working capital needs. The loan's amount and structure will closely match the transaction being financed. A term loan is typically fully funded at its inception, and principal and interest are repaid over a period of years from operating cash flows generated by the borrower. The tenor, or maturity, of term loans ranges from 1 to 10 years, with the average being from 2 to 5 years. Although the lender does not look to liquidation of the acquired assets as the primary source of funds for repayment, a term loan is likely to be secured. Most often, the security will be a claim on the assets purchased with the proceeds of the loan.

Revolving Loans

The revolving credit loan, a variation on the line of credit, has a commitment period often extending beyond 1 year, up to 3 or 4 years, and allows a business to borrow from a bank up to a maximum commitment level at any time over the life of a credit.

The borrower's use of proceeds under a revolving loan tends to be not for an isolated transaction but to fund day-to-day operations, meet seasonal needs, or otherwise provide the borrower with a discretionary range of when and how much to borrow and when to repay the loan. Unlike a line of credit, a revolving loan is often used to finance permanent working capital needs when equity and trade credit are inadequate to support a company's sales volume.

Over the term of a revolving credit facility, the borrower has the right to repay a loan and later reborrow those funds. But this right to reborrow is effective only when the borrower is in compliance with the loan agreement's terms and conditions. The amount of commitment is based upon the value of the assets being funded as well as the borrower's creditworthiness. The borrower pays a commitment fee, based on the total amount of the revolving facility, to secure a formal commitment from the bank. Many revolving loans are structured to convert to term loans or to renew automatically at maturity. The latter structure, called an evergreen facility, automatically renews a revolving credit facility until either the bank or the borrower gives notice of termination. Like other credit facilities, a revolving line of credit may be secured or unsecured.

Role of the Loan Officer

"Banks succeed when the risks they assume are reasonable, controlled, and commensurate with their resources and credit competence. Lending officers, in turn, must accurately identify, measure, and manage risk if their banks are to succeed."[1]

The loan officer must balance two often conflicting responsibilities: those of a marketing officer and those of a credit officer. While budget pressures require the loan officer to develop new banking relationships, credit responsibilities require that these new relationships not sacrifice credit quality for short-term profits. "The costliest mistake that a bank management can make is to book unworthy loans in order to achieve budget goals."[2] The lending institution's credit policy should give loan officers guidelines to enable them to balance loan quality and quantity and achieve the bank's earnings objectives.

The lending institution and its shareholders expect loan officers to understand a credit thoroughly before approving the lending of the bank's capital. The credit proposal memo, described in Exhibit 1, includes the information and analyses used to evaluate a potential borrower's creditworthiness. Every commitment of a lending institution typically requires independent approval and the signatures of at least two senior lending officers, who are held directly accountable for the lending decision. Direct accountability is intended to make them more critical of any exceptions to the bank's credit policy.

Evaluating Creditworthiness

Before a bank agrees to commit its funds to a company, its loan officers analyze the prospective borrower to determine creditworthiness. Loan officers have a responsibility to "grasp the quantitative and qualitative details of each transaction thoroughly, analyze

---

1. P. Henry Mueller, "Lending Officers and Lending," in *Bank Credit*, ed. Herbert V. Prochnow (New York: Harper & Row, 1981), p. 92.

2. P. Henry Mueller, *Perspective on Credit Risk* (Robert Morris Associates, 1988), p. 18.

its variables, and make adequate allowance for their impact."[3] Evaluation of a borrower's ability and willingness to repay a loan at maturity involves financial analysis, including forecasting and sensitivity analysis, a qualitative assessment of management's character and capability, due diligence, and an identification and analysis of risk.

Financial Analysis

A thorough financial analysis requires preparation of the following:

- Year-to-year comparisons of financial statements
- Cash flow statements
- Liquidity analysis
- Capital structure analysis
- Projections and sensitivity analysis
- Estimation of asset values: market value and liquidation value
- Comparison of actual versus budgeted performance

A first step in the financial analysis of a potential borrower is a determination of the quality of earnings and the strength of the balance sheet. To make this determination, the credit officer analyzes financial, operating, and leverage ratios, and trends in revenues and expenses over time, and compares such ratios to industry averages, looking for positive and negative changes in the company's profitability and industry position.

The historical financial condition of a borrower, however, is an incomplete indication of creditworthiness. Because the loan will be approved or denied based, among other essential criteria, on an assessment of a borrower's ability to repay the loan from future cash flow generated by operations, an estimate of a borrower's future financial condition is important to the lending decision.

Pro forma financial and operating statements are prepared so that the lending officer may assess the borrower's potential to generate sufficient free cash flow to make interest and principal payments when due. These projections and the underlying assumptions must be tested under various scenarios to establish the borrower's sensitivity to change. While one cannot possibly test for every possible event, worst-case scenarios will indicate just how poorly the business can perform before the borrower defaults.

Qualitative Assessment

Credit evaluation also requires assessment of the character and capabilities of the persons to whom a loan may be extended, that is, the persons responsible for achieving the goals of the operating and financial plans. Lenders must determine the quality, breadth, and depth of the management team. Assessing its ability to implement operating and financial plans gives the lender insight into the management team's capability. Banks pay a high price for hasty credit decisions. Though gauging the integrity of a new customer takes time, integrity is a critical component of any lending decision. Management's interests should be aligned with the company's and with the bank's interests and expectations. Ownership and compensation systems indicate management's stake in the business.

---

3. Mueller, "Lending Officers and Lending," p. 40.

Due Diligence

Due diligence is the process of going out and "kicking the tires" of the potential borrower. While time-consuming, it is an important aid to understanding better how the prospective borrower does business. Due diligence can include plant tours, trade checks, and interviews with the borrower's competitors, suppliers, customers, and employees. Comprehensive due diligence also includes reviews of employee relations, compensation and benefits, management's planned capital expenditures, other debt obligations, and management information systems and technology. An environmental audit may also be necessary. Due diligence should also uncover any contingent liabilities that may materially affect the borrower's ability to repay the loan at maturity. Unfunded pension liabilities, pending or threatened legal proceedings, and guarantees by the borrower are some examples of contingent liabilities.

Risk Assessment

Risk assessment is another component of the credit evaluation process. The credit officer must identify and analyze the key risks associated with a specific credit. Some risks are associated with the borrower and his or her business; with potential changes in the environment; and with cyclical activity and regulatory or other unanticipated developments. The loan officer must make judgments about future conditions that could affect a borrower's willingness and ability to repay the obligation. Determining potential risks and assessing their level of severity, the probability that they will occur, and the estimated costs associated with their occurrence are critical. The structure of the credit facility and loan agreement attempts to minimize risk.

Determining the Bank's Willingness and Ability to Lend

In addition to conducting a thorough credit evaluation, the loan officer must determine whether approving a loan application is in the bank's best interests and within regulatory capital and operating guidelines. A bank's ability to lend is restricted by banking regulations that limit the amount of loans that may be extended to any one borrower. A bank may also establish an internal limit ("house limit") on the amount lent to a single borrower. What influences a bank's willingness to lend are its earnings targets and portfolio objectives. A bank attempts to maintain diversification in its portfolio of loans and investments to reduce its exposure to risk. These targets and objectives shape a bank's loan origination and acquisition strategy. Thus a potential borrower must not only meet the lending institution's credit standards but also be within its target lending market and legal lending capacity.

Structuring the Credit Facility and Loan Agreement

Once creditworthiness is ascertained and the bank decides it is willing and able to extend credit to a company, the bank and the borrower can begin to structure an appropriate credit facility and loan agreement. The strength and the nature of a credit and the bank's credit policy help to determine the terms and conditions defined in a loan agreement.

Typically, short-term loans are not made pursuant to a loan agreement, or if so, the loan agreement is far less comprehensive than that used for long-term or revolving loans. The loan agreement discussed in this note applies to term and revolving loans and includes the following sections:

- Amount and terms of the credit facility
- Conditions precedent
- Representations and warranties
- Covenants of the borrower
- Events of default

Amount and Terms of the Credit Facility

This first section of a standard loan agreement describes how much and when the borrower may borrow, the interest provisions, repayment terms and additional fees, the intended use of loan proceeds, and any security interest taken by the bank.

The amount of a bank's commitment under a credit facility may be stipulated or based on a formula, for instance, a percentage of accounts receivable. The interest rate charged for use of those committed funds may be based on either a fixed or a floating rate. The use of a fixed or a floating interest rate, the method for determining the floating rate and reset periods, if applicable, and the method for computing accrued interest are negotiable factors. Interest can be computed on the basis of a 360- or a 365-day year. Computation using a 360-day year yields a higher effective rate for the borrower.

Additional fees the bank may charge include commitment and closing fees. The borrower pays a commitment fee to compensate the bank for its use of the bank's capital over the duration of the commitment. This fee typically ranges from .25% to .75% per year. The borrower may also pay a closing fee on the day the loan closes, that is, the date the loan's legal framework is in place. This payment compensates the bank for work done thus far in evaluating the borrower's creditworthiness and setting up a credit facility for it. In a competitive situation, this fee may be .25% to .375%; in a high-risk situation, it can be as much as 2.00% to 2.50% of the amount of the commitment. A penalty or default rate of interest may also be stipulated. Applied in the event that payments are not made when due, this rate is set high enough so that it would not be to the borrower's economic advantage to delay payments.

The option to prepay and the option to reduce the total commitment are provisions negotiated in this section of the loan agreement for term loans and revolving loans, respectively. These provisions distinguish most bank financing from alternative sources of funds. Under a revolving credit facility, the right to reduce the amount of the commitment is valuable to the borrower should the company's financing needs change. Reducing the amount of the commitment will reduce the commitment fee paid by the borrower, since it is based on the total commitment.

In the case of a term loan, the loan agreement may provide for full or partial prepayment of the loan at the borrower's discretion, with or without a premium or upon occurrence of certain events. The option to repay provides a route of escape from covenants that may become overly restrictive. Prepayment also works in favor of the borrower should the cost of other sources of funds decline significantly over the term of the loan, making refinancing more economical. Recognizing the value of this right, a borrower may agree to tighter covenants or a higher rate of interest than if locked in by prepayment restrictions.

A description of the use of loan proceeds is also included in this first section of the loan agreement to assure the bank that the borrower intends to use the loan proceeds in the manner understood by the bank.

An additional provision negotiated in this section of the loan agreement is the taking of collateral or guarantees to secure a loan. A claim on certain assets of the borrower can mitigate the bank's loss should the borrower default. Assets used as collateral are typically those purchased with the loan proceeds; levels of collateral are typically commensurate with the creditworthiness of the borrower. It is often to the bank's advantage to take as much security as possible against a loan.

If the borrower defaults on a secured loan, the bank has the right to take control of and liquidate the pledged assets. Funds from the liquidation are applied against the amount outstanding on the defaulted loan. If default is on an unsecured loan, the bank is only a general creditor of the business, and recovery of the principal is less likely.

Conditions Precedent

The conditions precedent are requirements the borrower must satisfy before the bank has a legal obligation to fund a commitment. These conditions may include any business transactions that must be completed or events that must have occurred. Other standard items in this section are the opinions of counsel, certificate of no defaults, the note, and resolutions of the borrower's board of directors authorizing the transaction. The conditions precedent will also include a material adverse change clause encompassing both balance sheet condition and operations (income statement and prospects). This clause serves an important protective function for the lender in the case that a material adverse change occurs prior to funding and is not yet reflected in the financial statements.

Representations and Warranties

In considering a loan application, the lender relies on certain information furnished by the borrower and has thereupon made assumptions about the borrower's legal status, creditworthiness, and business position. It is upon these assumptions that the bank has agreed to lend money to the borrower. The representations and warranties section documents the information and assumptions relied upon. By executing the loan agreement, the borrower confirms the accuracy and truth of the information provided as of the date of execution. Misrepresentation constitutes an event of default. Principal representations and warranties include:

- Financial statements are correct, and there has been no material adverse change in the financial condition of the borrower
- The borrower is not subject to any litigation, pending or threatened, or party to a contract that could effect a material adverse change in the business position of the borrower
- Other facts pertinent to the credit judgment are correct
- No factual misstatement or omission in information furnished
- Due incorporation
- Continued existence
- The loan agreement will be legal, valid, and binding when signed
- No need for third-party consent
- Corporate authority
- No violation of existing agreements
- No violation of laws
- All tax returns have been filed; all taxes have been paid
- Collateral offered is owned by the borrower and free of liens

The material adverse change clause is designed to cover circumstances in which the borrower's ability to perform obligations under the loan agreement is thrown into doubt. With regard to the financial statements, the material adverse change clause is used to verify that there has been no material adverse change in the borrower's financial condition or operations since the date of the financial statements relied upon for the credit evaluation. This section may also contain a representation as to the accuracy of other information not included in the financial statements, including nonpublic information such as cash flow statements and projections, supplied by the borrower to the bank and fundamental to the credit decision.

The representations and warranties section also contains material adverse change standards with respect to actual or threatened legal proceedings where the outcome could significantly affect the strength of the borrower's credit standing in the eyes of the bank. These standards may also be broadened to include circumstances that may not be reflected immediately in the borrower's financial statements or result in litigation.

Covenants of the Borrower

Covenants are a heavily negotiated part of loan agreements. As representations and warranties verify certain statements by the borrower at the date of execution of the loan agreement, covenants carry forward the representations and warranties, and establish the borrower's ongoing obligation to maintain a certain status for the loan's duration. Covenants set minimum standards for a borrower's future conduct and performance and thereby reduce the risk that the loan will not be repaid. Violation of a covenant creates an event of default and gives the bank the right to refuse to make additional advances.

The use of certain covenants depends upon such factors as the nature of the borrower's business, the financial condition of the borrower, and the term of the loan. If credit risk is high, covenants may be tied directly to detailed financial projections provided by the borrower. If credit risk is low, a few general financial benchmarks may be sufficient. In any case, covenants should be no more restrictive than the policies any prudent manager would follow to maintain or build a solid credit rating, but they should be designed to give early warning of deterioration in the financial condition of the borrower. Covenants should also be drafted to allow for normal seasonal and cyclical variations of the borrower's business so that an event of default is not likely to occur.

Affirmative Covenants.   Affirmative covenants stipulate actions the borrower must take and would normally take even if the loan were not in effect. Generally, they include the following:

- Application of loan proceeds to specified purpose
- Financial covenants
- Reporting requirements
- Compliance with laws
- Preservation of corporate existence
- Rights of inspection
- Maintenance of insurance
- Maintenance of properties
- Maintenance of records and books of account

As in the first section of the loan agreement, the borrower must assure the bank that the proceeds of the loan will be used in the manner the bank understood in its decision to extend credit.

Financial covenants are those based on information contained in the borrower's financial statements and focus on the borrower's financial position and overall operations. Financial covenants establish guidelines for operation of the borrower's business, carry forward the borrower's representations and warranties regarding its financial position, further help the bank to gather information about the borrower, and permit exercise of remedies upon default. Financial covenants establish minimum financial tests with which a borrower must comply. These tests can specify dollar amounts, such as (tangible) net worth and working capital, or ratios such as the current or quick ratios, net worth ratios, leverage ratio, and fixed-charge coverage ratio. Financial covenants should signal financial difficulty and be triggered long before liquidation or bankruptcy filing becomes necessary. They may be used like other affirmative and negative covenants to guide management decisions on an ongoing basis, or serve only as periodic tests.

To keep the bank informed of financial and operating performance, the borrower covenants that he or she will meet certain established reporting requirements and provide such information to the lender in a timely fashion. This information allows the bank's lending officer to monitor the borrower's financial condition and compliance with covenants.

Negative Covenants. The negative covenants tend to be more significant and more heavily negotiated than affirmative covenants because they place clear restrictions upon managerial decisions. These restrictions are intended to prevent management decisions that might impair the borrower's liquidity or solvency, or jeopardize the bank's claim against the borrower's earnings and assets.

Negative covenants typically include the following:

- Restrictions on mortgages, pledges, or other encumbrance of assets (negative pledge)
- Limitation on total indebtedness
- Restrictions on payment of cash dividends
- Restrictions on repurchase of shares
- Restrictions on mergers
- Restrictions on sale of assets
- Restrictions on sale of subsidiaries
- Limitation on capital expenditure
- Restrictions on engaging in other businesses
- Restrictions on voluntary prepayment of other indebtedness
- Limitation on investment of funds
- Limitation on loans and advances
- Limitations on leasing arrangements

The negative pledge covenant is designed to prevent the borrower from creating liens on its assets or earnings for the benefit of other lenders. Its purpose is to provide a pool of assets that will be available for payment of unsecured creditors' claims equally, without preference of one over another in the event of default. The negative pledge is typically given to an unsecured creditor.

Restrictions on total indebtedness apply to a variety of debt instruments and often include capital lease obligations, deferred payment obligations, unfunded vested pension liabilities, guaranteed indebtedness, and indebtedness of others secured by property of the borrower. This restriction is usually stated as a specified amount or in the form of a ratio (total debt to total assets, to working capital, or to [tangible] net worth) and serves to limit the amount of additional indebtedness the borrower may incur over the term of the loan. The restriction may differ for short- and long-term obligations, and exceptions to the limit may be made for certain debt instruments such as subordinated debt.

In restricting the borrower's ability to merge or transfer a substantial part of its assets, the bank is ensuring the survival of the borrower's obligation. With reference to the sale or transfer of assets, those assets or subsidiaries fundamental to the bank's credit analysis should be specified as restricted from sale or transfer. Assets not involving the transfer of the borrower's business in or near its entirety should not be restricted by this covenant.

Restrictions on the use of funds for dividend payments, repurchase of shares, capital expenditures, or otherwise are included so that the bank may be further assured that cash will be available to make interest and principal payments when due. These restrictions and limitations also ensure the borrower's general adherence to its operating plan.

Events of Default

The events of default section describes circumstances in which the bank has the right to terminate the lending relationship. Situations leading to the declaration of an event of default include the following:

- Failure to pay interest or principal when due
- Inaccuracy in representations and warranties
- Failure to abide by a covenant
- Bankruptcy, liquidation, appointment of receiver
- Entry of a judgment in excess of a specified amount
- Impairment of collateral, invalidity of a guaranty or security agreement
- Failure to pay other indebtedness when due or perform under related agreements: cross-default and cross-acceleration
- Change of management or ownership
- Extraordinary circumstances
- Expropriation of assets
- Material adverse change

Upon the occurrence of an event of default, the most common remedy lenders exercise is the renegotiation of the loan agreement. In some cases, usually where the circumstances are considered less significant, the loan agreement provides the borrower a period of time, referred to as a cure or grace period, to correct its breach of a covenant. If the default is cured, the bank is then required to continue providing the loan to the borrower.

In the case where the default is not cured and the loan agreement is not negotiable, the bank may accelerate the loan and terminate the lending relationship. The bank may also set off the borrower's deposits against its obligation to repay the loan and exercise its right to foreclose on security covered under a security agreement.

The cross-default provision gives the bank the right to declare an event of default when the borrower is in default on another obligation. This provision is designed to prevent the bank from being placed at a disadvantage if competition to obtain repayment begins among the borrower's creditors, that is, the borrower has defaulted under another loan agreement and the lender is demanding payment.

Although banks rarely exercise the right to accelerate loan repayment, having this right substantially strengthens a lender's negotiating position with the borrower and other creditors of the borrower if problems are encountered with the loan. Acceleration is used sparingly by banks, since use by one could cause its invocation by other creditors and precipitate a bankruptcy.

Sale of Loans to Third Parties

No longer is the price of a loan set at the discretion of the loan officer guided by the lending institution. With increasing pressure to sell loans to third parties, the market is becoming the most influential factor in setting price.

Certain changes in the regulation of banks and in the business of commercial banking have precipitated increasing sales of loans. Regulatory changes, including new risk-based capital guidelines adopted by the Basle Committee on Banking Regulations and Supervisory Practices on July 11, 1988, require banks to be better capitalized (tangible net worth as a percentage of total assets). This is costly and restricts lending capacity. In addition to the risk-based capital guidelines, regulations and internal bank lending policies restricting the amount of loans a bank can make to one borrower or group of borrowers often force banks to sell off all or a portion of the loans they originate.

Several vehicles facilitate the sale of loans, some allowing an originating bank to maintain partial ownership of the loan or responsibility for its management. Participations, syndications, and asset sales are all examples of underwriting activities undertaken by banks.

Participations

A participation loan is a single loan made to a large borrower by more than one lender. Participation loans are made when the lead lender cannot lend to a large borrower because of legal or internal lending limits restricting the amount of bank capital that can be loaned to one borrower or classification of borrowers. The lead bank originates the transaction and maintains responsibility for servicing the loan.

Many loan participations come about through correspondent banking relationships. A correspondent bank performs services for a bank in a market that is inaccessible to the other. Both banks must evaluate the creditworthiness of the borrower and independently decide to enter into the participation. While credit decisions are made independently, risk may not always be shared equally in participations. Some participations are structured on a last in, first out (LIFO) basis so that the originator, or first in, takes a larger portion of the risk associated with the participation loan.

Syndication

Syndications are similar to loan participations, except that the syndicate members lend directly to the borrower. An originating bank, called the lead bank or manager, arranges a credit facility for a large borrower. The bank then sells off portions of the loan to other lenders.

Syndication has been used increasingly for several reasons, including the ability to spread risk across lenders, to lend to large borrowers when the size of the individual credit is larger than legal or internal standards would allow, and the ability to integrate the borrower's banking relationships. The syndicate members' obligations are separate; one lender is not responsible for the commitment of another; however, the rights and obligations of all the parties (the syndicate members and the borrower) are governed by one agreement, the syndicate loan agreement. Each participant in a syndication shares in the loan's risks and makes its own credit decision.

There are two types of syndicates: best-efforts and firm (or underwritten) commitment. In a best-efforts syndicate, the manager will market the loan under the agreed-upon terms and conditions, but if the syndication is not fully subscribed, the loan will not be made and the manager retains no legal obligation to the borrower. In a firm commitment syndicate, the lead bank agrees to make the loan regardless of its ability to syndicate it completely.

In a syndicate, a borrower pays certain fees in addition to interest on the loan: a commitment fee based on the amount of the credit and the undrawn portion; a management fee paid to the syndicate managers as compensation for assembling the syndicate and servicing the loan; and participation fees to syndicate participants based on the amount of their commitments. Participation fees range from .25% to 1.50% and are used to attract lending institutions to a syndicate. The agency fee paid to the bank servicing the loan can range from $5,000 a year for a routine transaction to $500,000 a year for a more complex transaction.

Asset Sale

A relatively recent development has been the sale of loans to third parties. An asset or loan sale is similar to a syndicate except that the lead bank initially takes the credit on its books and then sells off most or all of the credit, retaining little or nothing for its own portfolio. In this transaction, all risk from the sold portion is eliminated for the originating bank, and the loan is removed from its balance sheet. The bank earns a fee for its efforts in originating the loan. An asset sale typically occurs as a second phase to a syndication.

EXHIBIT 1
The Credit Proposal Memo

The credit proposal memo and presentation typically includes the following information and analyses:

- Company background and relationship with the bank
- Purpose of the credit extension
- Financial statement analysis, cash flow projections, and debt service capacity
- Assessment of management process, strengths, and weaknesses
- Assessment of major risks, including impact of forecasted economic trends and the strength of competitors
- Analysis of repayment sources for all facilities and timing for those with a tenor, or maturity, of greater than 1 year
- Summary of loan structure and repayment terms
- Summary of key covenants and repayment terms of other instruments that might materially affect the position of the bank
- Statement of adherence to credit policy guidelines or explanation of exceptions
- Analysis of collateral
- Listing of noncredit products
- Trade or bank checkings
- Comment on trustee relationships
- Account plans

Source: Citicorp Institute for Global Finance.

Appendix

Specialized Loans and Credit Products

Trade Finance Products

Trade finance products are specialized bank products designed to reduce the risks and uncertainties associated with commercial transactions by substituting the bank's credit risk for that of the purchaser of the goods. Thus, they facilitate trade.

When entering into trade finance credit arrangements, the bank evaluates the obligor's creditworthiness in much the same way it evaluates other short-term credits. The most common trade finance products are letters of credit and banker's acceptances.

Letters of Credit (L/C).   A letter of credit represents a conditional promise to pay and is generally non-negotiable. It substitutes the bank's credit for that of its customers by providing a guarantee of payment to the third party upon the satisfaction of certain conditions. This differs from the banker's acceptance, which, in effect, is payment.

In trade finance, a letter of credit is usually issued by the purchaser's bank, which agrees to pay the purchaser's obligation to a seller upon receiving proof that a specified delivery has been made. The bank has no obligation to delve into the content of the underlying commercial transaction (i.e., the sales agreement between the seller and buyer) except as specifically required by the terms of the L/C. The purchaser agrees to pay the bank the sales amount plus a fee.

The term of an L/C is generally related to the expected amount of time needed to complete the transaction. It may be revocable or irrevocable. A revocable L/C can be withdrawn, without notice to the beneficiary, at any time prior to actual performance of the transaction. An irrevocable L/C cannot be withdrawn before its expiration.

Stand-by letters of credit differ from trade L/Cs in that the issuing bank agrees to pay the L/C beneficiary only if its client defaults on payment to the beneficiary. So, in the above example, the seller would collect from the issuing bank only upon default of the purchaser.

Banker's Acceptances.   A banker's acceptance represents the bank's commitment to pay a specific amount of money on a specific date. This commitment arises when the bank agrees to pay the obligations of a purchaser to enhance its creditworthiness. The commitment is created when a seller prepares a time draft[4] ordering a buyer to pay for goods purchased upon their receipt. Once signed and acknowledged by the purchaser and "accepted" by the purchaser's bank, the draft becomes a banker's acceptance. The liability accepted by the bank is called acceptance liability.

The banker's acceptance is a short-term instrument generally with a duration of six months or less. The purchaser on whose behalf the banker's acceptance was accepted repays the bank under agreed-upon terms from the proceeds on the resale of the purchased goods. Since it is a negotiable instrument, the holder of a banker's acceptance may sell it to a third party or the bank, usually at a discount, to receive payment immediately. Thus, the banker's acceptance can be used as a form of accounts receivable financing.

Factoring

Factoring is a method of accounts receivable financing in which the lender purchases the borrower's receivables. By purchasing a firm's accounts receivable, the bank assumes certain risks and activities it does not have with typical accounts receivable financing, in which a lender lends money to a company based on its accounts receivable balance. Factoring gives the bank legal ownership of the receivables and therefore the risk of accounts receivable defaults. The credit and collection functions formerly handled by the company may be undertaken by the bank. A lender may provide factoring services on a discount or maturity basis.

Discount factoring is a service in which the seller of the receivables receives payment from the bank before their expected maturities. The amount the bank is willing to lend is based on the accounts receivable balance less discounts and estimated returns and bad debts. Interest is charged on the basis of the average daily balances owed.

Maturity factoring differs from discount factoring in that the lender performs the credit and collection functions and pays the borrower on invoice due dates. The factor receives a fee based on handling costs and estimated bad-debt risk.

Asset-Based Lending

Traditional loans may be secured by the assets of the borrower, and repayment is assumed to come from operating cash flow or conversion of current assets to cash. Asset-based loans differ from traditional loans in that the borrower's ability to repay the borrowed funds from operating cash flows is less predictable. A lender making an asset-based loan looks mainly to the value of the assets securing the loan for repay-

---

4. A time draft is one that is due upon presentation and acceptance by the purchaser's bank after a specified period of time, e.g., 30 or 60 days.

ment of the obligation. Asset-based loans are made against accounts receivable, inventory, and equipment.

In lending against accounts receivable, the asset-based lender agrees, after careful analysis, to lend up to a certain percentage of the accounts receivable. The percentage of face value the lender lends against will be based upon the age, quality, and concentration of accounts receivable, keeping in mind the liquidation value should the borrower default. Generally the lender will lend up to 80% of face value of the qualifying receivables amount. Qualifying receivables is the total amount less nonconforming receivables.

The analysis of inventory is similar to the analysis of accounts receivable, where current information and ongoing monitoring are key to successful lending. The lender will identify the percentage of inventory in raw materials, work-in-process, and finished goods inventories that qualifies to be lent against based on their potential liquidation value. The advance rate against inventory is relatively low, sometimes 50% or less. This conservatism reflects the concerns for spoilage, technical obsolescence, and frequent deep discounts in disposing of inventories very quickly.

In lending against equipment, the asset-based lender has little concern for historical cost, fair market value, or replacement value. The lender instead wants to determine the value in a forced liquidation sale after related expenses, for instance, the cost of removing the equipment. Asset-based lenders will typically lend up to 80% of the forced sale value of machinery and equipment.

Kochman, Reidt & Haigh, Inc.

Kochman, Reidt & Haigh, Inc. (KRH) designs, fabricates, and installs high quality, uniquely designed cabinetry. KRH's primary market is residential construction for both new and remodeled homes in the New England region. Most of the residential work is cabinetry for kitchens, bathrooms, studies, and audio/video storage. About 10% of KRH's work involves commercial projects. For example, in 1992 and 1993, KRH made the cabinetry and paneling for the faculty offices and the Aldrich Reading Room in Baker Library at the Harvard Business School.

Drawing from their diverse backgrounds, the partners of KRH had devised a unique operating strategy of producing high-quality custom cabinets at low cost. The low manufacturing costs were achieved through the introduction of automation to the traditionally labor-intensive manufacturing process for custom cabinets. The use of computer-controlled equipment allowed KRH to reduce its labor and other production costs significantly while increasing the efficiency of the manufacturing process. In turn, this enabled the company to offer its customers a wider variety of custom cabinet designs at competitive prices.

To develop its concept fully, KRH needed to fulfill an ambitious capital expenditures program. In the past, the partners of the company had financed their investments with internally generated cash flows. Poor financial performance during the last few years, however, had restricted the amount of cash available for expansion. Finding the company at a crossroads in its development path, KRH's partners felt they needed to clearly define the scope and speed of growth for their business. This type of long-term planning was closely linked to the more immediate need to increase KRH's profitability. Although the limitations of its situation had been the source of some frustration, KRH began to focus on a financial strategy that would support the development of its innovative operating system.

This case was prepared by Professor Richard S. Ruback and Research Associate Roy Burstin.

Copyright © 1993 by the President and Fellows of Harvard College.
Harvard Business School case 294–056.

Background

Kochman, Reidt & Haigh was formed in the 1991 merger of Kochman Woodworking, Inc. and Reidt & Haigh, Inc. Exhibit 1 presents a biographical sketch of the KRH partners. Exhibit 2 presents financial information for Kochman Woodworking, and Exhibit 3 presents financial information for Reidt & Haigh. Prior to the merger, both Kochman Woodworking and Reidt & Haigh specialized in custom cabinetry. Kochman's cabinets were based on simple designs and styles, whereas Reidt & Haigh's cabinetry was characterized by more intricate layouts. Kochman Woodworking had developed an innovative approach to manufacturing custom cabinets that relied heavily on computer-controlled equipment. The automation of a significant portion of the manufacturing process resulted in lower production costs and had the potential for substantial scale economies. Although prior to the merger Reidt & Haigh had also used computer software for the design of its cabinets, the company had not used automation in manufacturing. This was partly because of the higher complexity of Reidt & Haigh's designs. The merger was intended to allow the two companies to pool and improve their knowledge of computer design and automated manufacturing techniques, as well as to broaden their style offerings and expand their customer base.

KRH specialized in uniqueness. Its manufacturing process was designed to produce unique cabinets at a cost comparable to standard-sized stock cabinets of equal quality. As one partner described its operating strategy: "We are reversing the industrial revolution. That was about producing millions of one thing cheaply. We aim to produce millions of things cheaply."

To achieve this goal, KRH sought to automate a wide range of manufacturing processes, beginning with the initial design of the cabinetry. Three of KRH's 33 employees worked directly with customers and architects to produce detailed and comprehensive shop drawings using CAD systems. These designs could incorporate a wide variety of styles, materials, and methods of construction, from traditional face-frame cabinets with insert frames and panel doors to more contemporary European-style cabinets with full overlay doors. The cabinets were designed and fitted to the exact spaces available in each customer's home, and they were therefore free of the limitations of cabinets with prespecified sizes. After the shop drawings were completed, the designs were translated into shop specifications. Using computer models for different types of cabinets, KRH's software would generate a series of machine instructions that controlled the cutting, drilling, and assembling of cabinets. Except for differences in material costs, KRH's cost of manufacturing a cabinet did not depend on its size.

The Industry

KRH's approach to sales and manufacturing was in sharp contrast to standard practice in the $3.2 billion U.S. cabinet industry. As of 1992, stock cabinets comprised about 61% of the market. Custom cabinets, such as those produced by KRH, comprised only 20% of the market in 1992, down from 26% in 1989. Poor economic conditions between 1989 and 1992, the customer's increasing emphasis on value, and the relatively high price for custom cabinets accounted for much of the drop in market share for this segment.

Despite the recent decline, custom cabinetry offered customers many advantages over stock manufacturing. Stock cabinets were produced only in standardized sizes. As a result, the common remodeling/replacement design challenge for customers was to fit the available cabinet sizes in a way that would optimize the usable space in their homes.

Furthermore, standardized products offered limited opportunities for customers to tailor cabinets to their specific tastes and functional requirements. Because of these limitations, KRH's partners believed that the manufacture of custom cabinets at competitive costs (facilitated by automation) would provide an attractive alternative in the market.

KRH sold most of its cabinets directly to consumers. For each of its jobs, KRH developed a working relationship with its client to determine specific needs and tastes, as well as to resolve any potential design problems. By comparison, this type of direct sales method accounted for less than 2% of total industry sales. Cabinet dealers and distributors were the industry's preferred channel to the customer, accounting for 31% and 30% of total industry sales, respectively. For small firms like KRH, with revenues under $5 million, the use of dealers was even more widespread, accounting for approximately 58% of their sales. However, KRH did not sell any of its output through dealers, nor did it use the industry's other preferred channels of sales, such as home improvement centers (19% of industry sales) and builders (18% of industry sales). Furthermore, while it was not uncommon for a small cabinet manufacturer to spend between 1% and 2% of revenues on marketing, KRH's expenditures on marketing were almost nonexistent. The majority of KRH's jobs were the result of client references.

In 1992, small manufacturers like KRH accounted for a modest—and declining—fraction of the cabinet industry. Most firms were much larger. Companies with sales above $15 million accounted for 80% of industry sales, with the 12 largest firms accounting for almost 60% of the total. Leading the industry in 1992 was Masco Corporation, with cabinet sales of $515 million. The concentration of revenues among large manufacturers had been progressing since 1983, when the share of industry revenues of the top 12 firms was only 11%. This trend was partly due to improvements in production efficiencies. In 1992, large firms produced about $120,000 of sales per worker, a gain of 9% over 1991. In contrast, production per employee in medium firms had declined 11% from 1991 levels to $84,000 in 1992. Small firms also experienced a decline in efficiency in 1992, posting an average of $80,000 of revenue per worker, off 2% from 1991.

The outlook for the industry as a whole was favorable. Despite the significant downturn in new-home construction in the early 1990s, the kitchen cabinet industry was buoyed by an increase in home-remodeling activity. Revenues from cabinet unit sales had increased approximately 10% between 1991 and 1992. About 63% of cabinets sold were used in home remodeling. Combined industry sales through the first nine months of 1993 showed another increase of 10% over the same period in 1992. This growth was driven largely by a seasonally adjusted first-quarter jump of 18% in spending for major residential replacements and alterations. Annual sales in this segment were expected to exceed $18 billion in 1993. Sales of stock cabinets benefited the most from this increase, posting an 11% gain. Custom cabinets sales were up a more modest 3%. In the medium term, as the real estate markets embarked on a gradual recovery, growth in expenditures for major residential alterations was expected to be complemented by an increase in residential construction.

Post-Merger Performance

Some of the benefits from the merger of Kochman and Reidt & Haigh were realized quickly. Reidt & Haigh's production was shifted from its Boston facility to Kochman's automated shop in Stoughton, Massachusetts. Sales grew from combining customer bases and styles. Between 1991 and 1992, revenues jumped by about 31% to approximately $1.8 million. Exhibit 4 contains the income statements for KRH on a pro forma basis for 1990, and for the two post-merger years, 1991 and 1992. Exhibit 5 presents KRH's balance sheet for the same periods.

In addition to higher revenues, the merger brought some unanticipated cost increases. The automated manufacturing process developed by Kochman Woodworking could not be easily adapted to the complex styles introduced by Reidt & Haigh. Because a higher percentage of the manufacturing process had to be completed manually, production costs increased substantially. Meanwhile, the significant downturn experienced in residential construction in New England in 1991 limited KRH's ability to raise its prices. As a result, cost of goods sold as a percentage of sales rose dramatically. On a pro forma basis, KRH's cost of goods sold in 1990, the year before the merger, would have been approximately 60% of sales. In 1991, cost of goods sold increased to 67% of sales, and in 1992, the year after the merger, cost of goods sold rose to almost 75% of sales.

The company's financial performance in 1991 and 1992 was, therefore, disappointing. Net income for 1991 was only about $10,000 on sales of almost $1.4 million, a profit margin of less than 1%. In 1992, the significant growth in sales was largely offset by production cost increases. Net income for the year was about $37,000 on sales of approximately $1.8 million, a 2% profit margin. More troubling than its profit margins was KRH's cash flow. Cash after investing and financing activities decreased by $15,298 in 1991 and by $46,955 in 1992. To meet cash requirements during 1992, a partner of KRH made a personal loan of $35,000 to the company. A cash deficit of almost $14,000 at year-end was covered with a bank overdraft. Exhibit 6 sets forth KRH's cash flow statements for 1991 and 1992.

Performance in 1993

In spite of the rise in cost of goods sold, KRH's shop was efficient by industry standards. Average sales for small firms in 1992 had been $79,651 per worker. In 1992, 21 production workers at KRH produced about $84,737 of sales per worker. For 1993, KRH's sales per worker were projected to rise to $102,505, significantly higher than the 1992 industry average of $91,678 per worker. On the basis of revenue dollars per square foot of manufacturing space, KRH also performed above the industry average of $102, posting revenues of $274 per square foot in 1992 and a projected $331 per square foot for 1993. Furthermore, by dealing directly with customers, KRH avoided the 25% distribution cost that traditional cabinet manufactures typically incurred. Instead, two partners and a full-time employee dealt with customer orders.

Given the gradual economic recovery during 1993, the company's partners expected to see significant revenue increases as a result of both higher prices and a larger volume of jobs. While KRH completed approximately 78 jobs in all of 1992, it had already completed 116 jobs in the first 10 months of 1993, a 49% increase. Despite a rise in prices of approximately 10% and the elimination of client discounts during 1993, the average price per job in both of these years (excluding Baker Library and two other large jobs in 1992) was approximately $20,000. As Exhibit 7 shows, the increase in prices and volume of customer orders had a dramatic effect on profits. Through the 10 months ending October 31, 1993, KRH's profits were almost $150,000 and were projected to total about $180,000 for the year. Capital expenditures during the year had amounted to $123,400, for which KRH had incurred $85,700 in debt-bearing interest at 1.5% above the prime rate. Exhibit 8 contains selected financial market data at the end of October 31, 1993. These investments, particularly the purchase of a machine to partially automate the manufacturing of cabinet doors, promised to enhance KRH's production capacity. At the same time, however, the expenditures consumed some of the firm's debt capacity and limited the funds available to finance the remaining items on the company's capital expenditures program.

Capital Expenditures and Future Growth

KRH's partners believed that the high quality of their products justified a small premium in prices over standardized cabinets. In the long term, however, they thought that significant price increases could retard their growth and therefore did not represent a viable path to long-run profitability. Instead, they wanted to focus on cost reductions by continuing to increase the level of automation in the production process. This objective required significant investments in automated woodworking equipment and in the continuous upgrading of their computer software and hardware. Exhibit 9 presents a list of the principal investments KRH was considering.

The major woodworking machinery that KRH sought was an automated finishing system. The partners believed that this investment would improve their finishes, remove a significant health and environmental hazard, and reduce labor costs. Since the size of cabinets varied widely, the finishing system would have to use sophisticated robots with specialized control mechanisms that could generate adequate finishing instructions for each cabinet. As Exhibit 9 shows, KRH also required other investments, including a mezzanine to expand available shop space. To maximize the use of its facility, KRH had adopted a split shift (for which it had to hire an additional supervisor) in 1992. Although this measure provided relief to the crowded conditions on the shop floor, the company needed an adequate storage area for finished jobs. In addition, the woodworking machinery that KRH's partners wanted to acquire required a significant amount of space. A mezzanine would increase the amount of usable workspace by approximately 37%. In total, these enhancements to the company's shop required over $300,000 in capital but would increase production capacity by approximately 50% and save an estimated $170,000 per year in labor costs. Additional benefits would also result from an increase in production efficiency, which would allow the company to shift workers to other areas of the business.

The computer investments that KRH's partners wanted to make involved two important extensions to the automation of their current manufacturing system. The first was the expansion of their existing software to handle the more complex cabinetry that they were now building. The second involved the integration of the CAD systems used to design the cabinetry with the database that generated the list of about 2,500 components that had to be fabricated for a typical kitchen. KRH's partners estimated that they could develop the software necessary for these improvements in-house at a cost of approximately $100,000 over the course of 2 years. In addition, the company expected to continue spending between $25,000–$30,000 per year to keep its computer systems up to date.

To reap the full benefits of these capital expenditures, the company's partners also planned to initiate a marketing effort. They estimated that a brochure and a promotional video for potential clients would probably require around $40,000.

Once its investment program was completed, KRH hoped that it would be able to grow by keeping prices steady and increasing profitability through reduced production costs. However, financing these capital expenditures out of operating cash flows meant delaying the full implementation of this strategy. Furthermore, KRH's partners knew that such a piecemeal approach could potentially have a negative long-term impact on the survival of the firm.

EXHIBIT 1
Biographical Sketch of KRH Partners

Bill Kochman, age 48, was married with two children. After graduating from high school in Scarborough, New York in 1963, Bill moved to California and completed one year at Menlo College in Menlo Park. Bill worked with the Aspen ski patrol for three years before his interest in computers led him to take a year-long course at Control Data Institute. In 1969 this led him to Digital Corporation in Maynard, Massachusetts. His work there consisted of product support and involved traveling to foreign and domestic locations. His work at Digital continued until 1975, when he decided to pursue a lifelong interest in architecture by designing and building a "spec" house in Princeton, Massachusetts, with help from his brother, Jim. In 1976 the proceeds from the sale of the house became the seed money for the inception of Kochman Woodworking. From the beginning of KWW, Bill used his knowledge of computers to take advantage of sophisticated machinery, much of which had, for the most part, remained beyond the grasp of smaller shops.

Jim Kochman, age 43, was married with two children. Jim graduated from Ripon College in Ripon, Wisconsin with a B.A. in Economics. In 1973 he moved to Cape Cod and learned carpentry while working on a construction crew for two years. After moving to Cambridge in 1975, Jim collaborated with his brother in designing and building their "spec" house. During this time, Jim's focus turned more to cabinetry and, in response to local neighborhood demand, led him to set up a small shop in one end of his apartment in the basement of the "Piano Factory" on Boston's Tremont Street. After the sale of the house, he joined his brother in the formation of Kochman Woodworking, where he was finally able to have a shop that was not in his own apartment.

Paul Reidt, age 41, was married with two children. He graduated premed from Hobart College in 1974 and moved to Boston in 1975 to continue graduate school in philosophy at Boston College. After three years and completing all but his dissertation, Paul left Boston College for the Boston Architectural Center, where he studied architecture and interior design for four years. During these years, he supported himself by building cabinets, initially out of his apartment and eventually from a carriage house in Newton. His interest in cabinetmaking grew to the point where it occupied his time completely and took priority over his coursework. By 1980, Paul was building cabinets full-time and had set up a shop in a basement of an old shoe factory in Boston's South End.

Alan Haigh, age 39, was married. His interest in woodworking developed as he worked summers as a carpenter and shipwright on Cape Cod and Martha's Vineyard. He graduated from Clark University in 1978 with a B.A. in comparative literature. After traveling to India and Asia for a year, he returned to Martha's Vineyard and became part of a construction crew that restored and renovated residences. Alan moved to Boston in 1981. To escape working outside during the winter months, he became self-employed as a finish carpenter. While taking classes at the Boston Architectural Center, he met Paul Reidt. He began working for Paul that same year, and two years later, he became a partner in Reidt & Haigh, Inc.

EXHIBIT 2

Historical Financial Information for Kochman Woodworking, Inc. (thousands of dollars)

	Year Ending December 31,			
	1987	*1988*	*1989*	*1990*
Sales	$779	$961	$866	$1,076
Cost of goods sold	579	712	686	711
Gross profit	200	249	180	304
Operating expenses	185	270	276	285
Operating income	15	(21)	(96)	19
Other income (expense)	(1)	5	(3)	(6)
Pretax income	14	(16)	(99)	13
Provision for income taxes	0	0	0	0
Net income	15	(16)	(99)	13
Adjustments to reconcile to cash from operations				
Depreciation	56	63	61	44
Change in working capital[a]	(27)	(35)	43	34
Cash flow from operations	44	12	5	91
Capital expenditures	(73)	(54)	(11)	(45)
Cash flow after investing activities	(30)	(42)	(6)	46
Add back				
Owners' compensation	180	136	130	131
Discretionary expenses[b]	20	143	128	23
Net available cash flow	$171	$237	$252	$ 199

a. Includes accounts receivable, inventories, and accounts payable.

b. Discretionary expenses for 1990 are estimates.

EXHIBIT 3

Historical Financial Information for Reidt & Haigh, Inc. (thousands of dollars)

	Year Ending December 31,			
	1987	1988	1989	1990
Sales	$259	$404	$510	$492
Cost of goods sold	73	103	195	165
Gross profit	186	301	315	327
Operating expenses	172	283	296	344
Operating income	14	18	19	(17)
Other income (expense)	0	0	0	0
Pretax income	14	18	19	(17)
Provision for income taxes	0	0	0	0
Net income	14	18	19	(17)
Adjustments to reconcile to cash from operations				
Depreciation	11	17	24	26
Change in working capital[a]	2	(17)	(15)	(2)
Cash flow from operations	27	18	28	7
Capital expenditures	(24)	0	(26)	(24)
Cash flow after investing activities	(7)	18	(8)	(17)
Add back				
Owners' compensation	40	44	50	62
Discretionary expenses[b]	6	8	13	18
Net available cash flow	$ 39	$ 70	$ 55	$ 63

a. Includes accounts receivable, inventories, and accounts payable.

b. Discretionary expenses for 1990 are estimates.

EXHIBIT 4

Income Statement for Kochman, Reidt & Haigh, Inc.

	Year Ended December 31,		
	1990[a]	1991[b]	1992
Sales	$1,566,924	$1,358,590	$1,779,470
Cost of goods sold	935,994	911,870	1,332,260
Gross profit	630,930	446,720	447,210
SG&A expenses	629,042	456,554	396,808
Income (loss) from operations	1,888	(9,834)	50,402
Other income (expenses)	0	24,738	(1,347)
Gain (loss) on asset sales	0	24,738	(1,347)
Interest income	3,635	3,283	721
Interest expense	(9,782)	(7,717)	(11,511)
Income before taxes	(4,259)	10,470	38,165
Provision for income taxes	456	456	456
Net income	$ (4,714)	$ 10,014	$ 37,709

a. Pro forma results, adjusted to reflect the combined operations of Kochman Woodworking and Reidt & Haigh as if the merger had taken place on January 1, 1990.

b. The merger between Kochman Woodworking and Reidt & Haigh took place on April 8, 1991. Pro forma figures are adjusted to reflect a full year of operating results for Reidt & Haigh.

EXHIBIT 5
Balance Sheets for Kochman, Reidt & Haigh, Inc.

	Year Ended December 31,		
	1990[a]	*1991*	*1992*
Assets			
Current assets			
Cash	$ 48,389	$ 33,091	$ 0
Accounts receivable	80,421	54,593	222,261
Inventories	67,642	95,943	120,195
Current portion of notes receivable	5,000	72	0
Other	1,693	0	0
	203,145	184,349	342,456
Net property and equipment	148,108	174,238	192,118
Notes receivable	48,009	46,720	0
Deposits	0	1,630	1,630
Reorganization costs	0	6,296	6,296
Other	2,000	0	0
	50,009	54,646	7,926
	$401,262	$413,233	$542,500
Liabilities and Shareholders' Equity			
Current liabilities			
Bank overdraft	$ 0	$ 0	$ 13,904
Notes payable	85,184	61,135	63,155
Accounts payable	34,231	51,056	100,005
Payroll withholdings and accruals	6,058	19,651	18,811
Accrued expenses and other	48,400	12,809	12,156
Customer deposits	42,932	48,453	99,210
	216,805	193,104	307,241
Notes payable	39,211	76,503	52,924
Stockholders' equity			
Capital stock	38,530	$ 35,974	36,974
Retained earnings	106,716	107,652	145,361
	145,246	143,626	182,335
	$401,262	$413,233	$542,500

a. Pro forma figures to reflect the pooling interests of Kochman and Reidt & Haigh occurred on January 1, 1990.

EXHIBIT 6
Cash Flow Statement for Kochman, Reidt & Haigh, Inc.

	Year Ended December 31,	
	1991	**1992**
Cash Flow from Operating Activities		
Net income	$ 10,014	$ 37,709
Adjustments to reconcile net earnings (loss) to net cash provided by operating activities		
Depreciation	55,310	45,059
Loss on sale of assets[a]	0	1,347
Compensation paid by note receivable reduction & other	9,260	30,825
Reorganization costs & other	(7,926)	0
Changes in operating assets		
(Increase) decrease in accounts receivable	25,828	(167,668)
(Increase) decrease in inventory	(28,301)	(24,252)
Increase (decrease) in accounts payable	16,825	48,949
Increase (decrease) in accruals	13,593	(840)
Increase (decrease) in expenses	(35,591)	(653)
Increase (decrease) in customer deposits	5,521	50,757
Net cash provided (used) by operating activities	$ 64,533	$ 21,333
Cash Flow from Investing Activities		
Purchase of property and equipment	$(81,440)	$ (56,945)
Proceeds from asset sales	0	5,528
Net cash provided (used in) investing activities	(81,440)	(51,167)
Cash Flow from Financing Activities		
Proceeds from loan repayments	0	1,029
Proceeds from loans	37,292	23,000
Loan repayment	(24,049)	(41,090)
Dividend payments	(11,634)	0
Net cash provided (used in) investment activities	$ 1,609	$ (17,061)
Net Increase (Decrease) in Cash		
Cash and equivalents		
Beginning of period	$(15,298)	$ (46,995)
End of period	48,389	33,091
	$ 33,091	$ (13,904)

a. Loss on sale of assets in 1991 is incorporated into investing activities.

EXHIBIT 7
1993 Actual and Projected Income Statements for KRH, Inc.

	10 Months Ending October 31, 1993	Estimated 1993	% Sales
Sales	$1,793,841	$2,152,609	
Materials expense	479,992	575,990	26.8%
Manufacturing expense			
Staff	421,438	505,726	23.5
Rent	50,000	60,000	2.8
Manufacturing supplies	26,794	32,153	1.5
Utilities	16,379	19,655	0.9
Building maintenance	17,768	21,322	1.0
Other	16,254	19,505	0.9
	$ 549,651	$ 658,361	30.6%
Cost of goods sold	1,029,643	1,234,351	57.4
Gross margin	764,198	918,258	42.6
Sitework expense			
Staff	184,580	221,496	10.3
Other	20,655	24,786	1.2
	$ 205,235	$ 246,282	11.5%
Office expense			
Staff	$ 274,574	$ 329,489	15.3%
Rent	25,000	30,000	1.4
Telephone	13,362	16,034	0.7
Sales	9,595	11,514	0.5
Other	10,212	12,254	0.6
	$ 332,743	$ 399,292	18.5%
Overheads	32,871	39,445	1.8
Profit before depreciation	$ 193,349	$ 232,019	10.8%
Depreciation	37,080	44,496	2.1
Other (income)/expense	7,332	8,798	0.4
Profit before taxes	$ 148,937	$ 178,724	8.3%

EXHIBIT 8
Selected Financial Market Data, October 31, 1993

Treasury note and bond yields	
90 days	3.06%
6 months	3.18
1 year	3.32
5 years	4.82
10 years	5.44
30 years	5.99
Corporate borrowing rates	
Long-term bond yields	
AA	7.16%
A	7.73
BBB	8.18
BB	9.21
B	10.41
Floating rates	
Prime rate	6.00%
Prime commercial paper (6 months)	3.14

Source: Federal Reserve Bulletin; S&P Bond Guide.

EXHIBIT 9
Description of Capital Expenditures Program

Equipment	Estimated Cost	Weekly Labor Savings (Hours)	Yearly Savings ($)
Software development and hardware	$100,000	60	$ 65,000
Finishing robot	120,000	30	54,600
Sanding robot	80,000	40	42,800
Mezzanine	60,000	20	36,400
Edgebander	40,000	5	9,100
	$400,000	155	$207,900

Toy World, Inc.

Early in January 1994, Jack McClintock, president and part owner of Toy World, Inc., was considering a proposal to adopt level monthly production for the coming year. In the past, the company's production schedules had always been highly seasonal, reflecting the seasonality of sales. Mr. McClintock was aware that a marked improvement in production efficiency could result from level production, but he was uncertain what the impact on other phases of the business might be.

Toy World, Inc. was a manufacturer of plastic toys for children. Its product groups included toy cars, trucks, construction equipment, rockets, spaceships and satellites, musical instruments, animals, robots, and action figures. In most of these product categories, the company produced a wide range of designs, colors, and sizes. Dollar sales of a particular product had sometimes varied by 30–35% from one year to the next.

The manufacture of plastic toys was a highly competitive business. The industry was populated by a large number of companies, many of which were short on capital and management talent. Since capital requirements were not large and the technology was relatively simple, it was easy for new competitors to enter the industry. On the other hand, design and price competition was fierce, resulting in short product lives and a relatively high rate of company failures. A company was sometimes able to steal a march on the competition by designing a popular new toy, often of the fad variety. Such items generally commanded very high margins until competitors were able to offer a similar product. For example, Toy World's introduction of a line of super hero action figures in 1991 had contributed importantly to that year's profits. In 1992, however, 11 competitors marketed similar products, and the factory price of the Toy World offering plummeted. In recent years, competitive pressures on smaller firms had also intensified due to an influx of imported toys produced by foreign toy manufacturers with low labor costs.

Company Background

Toy World, Inc. was founded in 1973 by David Dunton after his release from naval service. Before his military service, he had been employed as production manager by a large manufacturer of plastic toys. Mr. Dunton and his former assistant, Jack McClintock, established Toy World, Inc. with their savings in 1973. Originally a partnership, the firm was incorporated in 1974, with Mr. Dunton taking 75% of the capital stock and Mr. McClintock taking 25%. The latter served as production manager, and Mr. Dunton, as president, was responsible for overall direction of the company's affairs. After a series of illnesses, Mr. Dunton's health deteriorated, and he was forced to retire from active participation in the business in 1991. Mr. McClintock assumed the presidency at that time. In 1993, Mr. McClintock hired Dan Hoffman, a recent graduate of a prominent eastern technical institute, as production manager. Mr. Hoffman had worked during summers in the plastics plant of a large diversified chemical company and thus had a basic familiarity with plastics production processes.

Company Growth

Toy World, Inc. had experienced relatively rapid growth since its founding and had enjoyed profitable operations each year since 1976. Sales had been approximately $8 million in 1993, and on the strength of a number of promising new products, sales were projected at $10 million for 1994. Net profits had reached $270,000 in 1993 and were estimated at $351,000 in 1994 under seasonal production. Tables A and B present the latest financial statements for the company. The cost of goods sold had averaged 70% of sales in the past and was expected to maintain roughly that proportion in 1994 under seasonal production. In keeping with the company's experience, operating expenses were likely to be incurred evenly throughout each month of 1994 under either seasonal or level production.

Expanding operations had resulted in a somewhat strained working capital position for Toy World, Inc. The year-end cash balance of $200,000 in 1993 was regarded as the minimum necessary for the operations of the business. The company had periodically borrowed from its primary bank, City Trust Company, on an unsecured line of credit. A loan of $752,000 was outstanding at the end of 1993. Mr. McClintock had been assured that the bank would be willing to extend a credit line of up to $2 million in 1994, with the understanding that the loan would be completely repaid and off the books for at least a 30-day period during the year, and would be secured by the accounts receivable and inventory of Toy World. Interest on the line of credit would be

TABLE A
Condensed Income Statements, 1991–1993 (thousands of dollars)

	1991	*1992*	*1993*
Net sales	$5,213	$6,167	$7,967
Cost of goods sold	3,597	4,440	5,577
Gross profit	$1,616	$1,727	$2,390
Operating expenses	1,199	1,542	1,912
Interest expense	68	75	85
Interest income	20	15	16
Profit before taxes	$ 369	$ 125	$ 409
Federal income taxes	125	43	139
Net profit	$ 244	$ 82	$ 270

TABLE B
Balance Sheet at December 31, 1993 (thousands of dollars)

Cash	$ 200
Accounts receivable	2,905
Inventory	586
Current assets	$3,691
Plant and equipment, net	1,176
Total assets	$4,867
Accounts payable	$ 282
Notes payable, bank	752
Accrued taxes[a]	88
Long-term debt, current portion	50
Current liabilities	$1,172
Long-term debt	400
Shareholders' equity	3,295
Total liabilities and shareholders' equity	$4,867

a. The company was required to make estimated tax payments on the 15th of April, June, September, and December. In 1993 it elected to base its estimated tax payments on the previous year's tax. The balance of $88,000 was due on March 15, 1994.

charged at a rate of 9%, and any advances in excess of $2 million would be subject to further negotiations. Toy World's long-term debt, which had been raised years ago, had a fixed annual rate of interest of 9⅞% and was being amortized by payments of $25,000 in June and December of each year.

The company's sales were highly seasonal. Over 80% of annual dollar volume was usually sold between August and November. Table C shows sales by month for 1993 and projected monthly sales for 1994. Sales were made mainly to large variety store chains and toy brokers. Although the company quoted terms of net 30 days, most customers took 60 days to pay; however, collection experience had been excellent.

The company's production processes were not complex. Plastic molding powder, the principal raw material, was processed by injection molding presses and formed into the shapes desired. The toy sets were then assembled and packaged in cardboard cartons or plastic bags. Typically, all runs begun were completed on the same day, so that there was virtually no work in process at the end of the day. Purchases on net 30-

TABLE C
Monthly Sales Data (thousands of dollars)

	Sales 1993	Projected 1994
January	$ 64	$ 120
February	88	140
March	96	160
April	88	140
May	87	140
June	95	140
July	96	160
August	1,251	1,620
September	1,474	1,840
October	1,723	2,140
November	1,965	2,285
December	940	1,115

day terms were made weekly in amounts necessary for estimated production in the coming week. Total purchases in 1994 were forecast at $3 million. It was the company's policy to retire trade debt promptly as it came due.

Mr. Hoffman, the production manager, believed the company would be able to hold capital expenditures during the next year to an amount equal to depreciation, although he had caution that projected volume for 1994 would approach the full capacity of Toy World's equipment.

Toy World Inc.'s practice was to produce in response to customer orders. This meant only a small fraction of capacity was needed to meet demand for the first seven months of the year. Ordinarily, not more than 25–30% of manufacturing capacity was used at any one time during this period. The first sizable orders for the Christmas business arrived around the middle of August. From August to December the work force was greatly expanded and put on overtime, and all equipment was used 16 hours a day. In 1993 overtime premiums had amounted to $185,000. Whenever possible, shipments were made on the day an order was produced. Hence, production and sales amounts in each month tended to be equal.

As in the past, pro forma balance sheets and income statements based on an assumption of seasonal production had been prepared for 1994 and were presented to Mr. McClintock for his examination. These appear in Exhibits 1 and 2.

The Proposed Change to Level Production

Having experienced one selling season at Toy World, Mr. Hoffman was deeply impressed by the many problems that arose from the company's method of scheduling production. Overtime premiums reduced profits; seasonal expansion and contraction of the work force resulted in recruiting difficulties and high training and quality-control costs. Machinery stood idle for seven-and-a-half months and then was subjected to heavy use. Accelerated production schedules during the peak season resulted in frequent setup changes on the machinery. Seemingly unavoidable confusion in scheduling runs resulted. Short runs and frequent setup changes caused inefficiencies in assembly and packaging as workers encountered difficulty relearning their operations.

For these reasons, Mr. Hoffman had urged Mr. McClintock to adopt a policy of level monthly production in 1994. He pointed out that estimates of sales volume had usually proved to be reliable in the past. Purchase terms would not be affected by the rescheduling of purchases. The elimination of overtime wage premiums would result in substantial savings, estimated at $225,000 in 1994. Moreover, Mr. Hoffman firmly believed that significant additional direct labor savings, amounting to about $265,000, would result from orderly production. But a portion of the savings would be offset by higher storage and handling costs, estimated at $115,000 annually.

Mr. McClintock speculated on the effect that level production might have on the company's funds requirements in 1994. He assumed that except for profits and fluctuations in the levels of inventories, accounts receivable, and accounts payable, funds inflows and outflows would be approximately in balance. To simplify the problem, Mr. McClintock decided to assume that gross margin percentages would not vary significantly by month under either method of production. That is, cost of goods sold would be 70% of sales in each of the 12 months under seasonal production and would be 65.1% of sales in each of the 12 months under level production. The increased storage and handling costs of $115,000 would be included in operating expenses.

EXHIBIT 1
Pro Forma Balance Sheets under Seasonal Production, 1994 (thousands of dollars)

	Actual Dec. 31, 1993	Jan.	Feb.	Mar.	Apr.	May	June	July	Aug.	Sept.	Oct.	Nov.	Dec.
Cash[a]	$ 200	$ 878	$1,526	$1,253	$1,054	$ 915	$ 696	$ 527	$ 200	$ 200	$ 200	$ 200	$ 200
Accounts receivable[b]	2,905	1,060	260	300	300	280	280	300	1,780	3,460	3,980	4,425	3,400
Inventory[c]	586	586	586	586	586	586	586	586	586	586	586	586	586
Current assets	$3,691	$2,524	$2,372	$2,139	$1,940	$1,781	$1,562	$1,413	$2,566	$4,246	$4,766	$5,211	$4,186
Net plant and equipment[d]	1,176	1,176	1,176	1,176	1,176	1,176	1,176	1,176	1,176	1,176	1,176	1,176	1,176
Total assets	$4,867	$3,700	$3,548	$3,315	$3,116	$2,957	$2,738	$2,589	$3,742	$5,422	$5,942	$6,387	$5,362
Accounts payable[e]	$ 282	$ 36	$ 42	$ 48	$ 42	$ 42	$ 42	$ 48	$ 486	$ 552	$ 642	$ 686	$ 334
Notes payable, bank[f]	752	0	0	0	0	0	0	0	433	1,741	1,745	1,677	942
Accrued taxes[g]	88	31	(23)	(162)	(251)	(305)	(394)	(448)	(352)	(271)	(126)	33	40
Long-term debt, current portion	50	50	50	50	50	50	50	50	50	50	50	50	40
Current liabilities	$1,172	$ 117	$ 69	$ (64)	$ (159)	$ (213)	$ (302)	$ (350)	$ 617	$2,072	$2,311	$2,446	$1,366
Long-term debt[h]	400	400	400	400	400	400	375	375	375	375	375	375	350
Shareholders' equity	3,295	3,183	3,079	2,979	2,875	2,770	2,665	2,564	2,750	2,975	3,256	3,566	3,646
Total liabilities and equity	$4,867	$3,700	$3,548	$3,315	$3,116	$2,957	$2,738	$2,589	$3,742	$5,422	$5,942	$6,387	$5,362

a. Assumed maintenance of minimum $200,000 balance; includes excess cash in months when company is out of debt.

b. Assumed 60-day collection period.

c. Assumed inventories maintained at December 31, 1993, level for all of 1994.

d. Assumed equipment purchases equal to depreciation expense.

e. Assumed equal to 30% of the current month's sales and related to material purchases of $3,000,000 for 1994 as against sales of $10 million. This represents a 30-day payment period. Since inventories are level, purchases will follow seasonal production and sales pattern.

f. Plug figure.

g. Taxes payable on 1993 income are due on March 15, 1994. On April 15, June 15, September 15, and December 15, 1994, payments of 25% each of the estimated tax for 1994 are due. In estimating its tax liability for 1994, the company has the option of using the prior year's tax liability ($139,000) for its estimate and making any adjusting tax payments in 1995. Alternatively, the company could estimate its 1994 tax liability directly. Toy World planned to use its prior year's tax liability as its estimate and to pay $35,000 in April, June, September, and December.

h. To be repaid at the rate of $25,000 each June and December.

EXHIBIT 2
Pro Forma Income Statements under Seasonal Production, 1994 (thousands of dollars)

	Jan.	Feb.	Mar.	Apr.	May	June	July	Aug.	Sept.	Oct.	Nov.	Dec.	Total
Net sales	$ 120	$ 140	$ 160	$ 140	$ 140	$ 140	$ 160	$1,620	$1,840	$2,140	$2,285	$1,115	$10,000
Cost of goods sold[a]	84	98	112	98	98	98	112	1,134	1,288	1,498	1,600	780	7,000
Gross profit	$ 36	$ 42	$ 48	$ 42	$ 42	$ 42	$ 48	$ 486	$ 552	$ 642	$ 685	$ 335	$ 3,000
Operating expenses[b]	200	200	200	200	200	200	200	200	200	200	200	200	2,400
Interest expense	7	4	4	4	4	4	3	5	12	17	17	14	95
Interest income[c]	2	4	5	4	3	3	2	1	1	1	1	1	28
Profit (loss) before taxes	$(169)	$(158)	$(151)	$(158)	$(159)	$(159)	$(153)	$ 282	$ 341	$ 426	$ 469	$ 122	$ 533
Income taxes[d]	(57)	(54)	(51)	(54)	(54)	(54)	(52)	96	116	145	159	42	182
Net profit	$(112)	$(104)	$(100)	$(104)	$(105)	$(105)	$(101)	$ 186	$ 225	$ 281	$ 310	$ 80	$ 351

a. Assumed cost of goods sold equal to 70% sales.

b. Assumed to be same for each month throughout the year.

c. Toy World expected to earn a 4% annualized rate of return on average monthly cash balances.

d. Negative figures are tax credits from operating losses, and reduced accrued taxes shown on balance sheet. The federal tax rate on all earnings was 34%.

SureCut Shears, Inc.

On April 28, 1996, Michael Stewart, senior loan officer at the Hudson National Bank of New York, was reviewing the credit file of SureCut Shears, Inc. in preparation for a luncheon meeting with the company's president and treasurer. David Fischer, treasurer of SureCut Shears, had recently informed Mr. Stewart that the company would be unable to liquidate its outstanding seasonal loan as initially anticipated. While agreeing to extend the outstanding $1.15 million loan, Mr. Stewart had suggested that he would like to stop by and discuss the company's recent progress when he was next in the vicinity of Savannah, Georgia, where SureCut Shears's home plant and offices were located.

SureCut Shears manufactured a complete line of household scissors and industrial shears. Its quality lines were distributed through wholesalers to specialty, hardware, and department stores located throughout the country. Cheaper products were sold directly to large variety chains. Although competition was severe, particularly from overseas companies, SureCut Shears had made profits in every year since 1958. Sales and profits had grown fairly steadily, if not dramatically, throughout the period.

Hudson National Bank had been soliciting the SureCut Shears account for several years prior to early 1995. After several unsuccessful calls, Mr. Stewart finally convinced the officers of SureCut Shears that association with a large New York bank offered several advantages not to be found with local banks. He was particularly pleased with the success of his efforts, because SureCut Shears historically held fairly sizable deposit balances in its principal banks.

The company had sufficient capital to cover its permanent requirements over the immediate future. Its short-term borrowings from banks were typically confined to the period July–December of each year, when additional working capital was needed to support a seasonal sales peak. As a matter of policy, the company attempted to produce at an even rate throughout the year, and this accounted in good part for the sizable need for seasonal funds.

In June 1995, Mr. Fischer arranged a line of credit of $3.5 million with the Hudson National Bank to cover requirements for the fall. At the time, he anticipated that the loan would be completely paid off by December 1995. He gave Mr. Stewart a pro forma estimate of the company's fund requirements over the coming 12-month period to support his request. (These estimates are shown in Exhibits 1 and 2.) In addition to these requirements, the forecast showed a need for about $1 million by June 1996. Mr. Fischer attributed this increase in funds requirements (no funds were needed in June 1995) to a plant modernization program. He explained that the program, requiring expenditures of $6 million, was about half completed and would be finished by August 1995. Efficiencies resulting from the modernization program, once completed, were expected to save about $900,000 per year before taxes in manufacturing costs.

Mr. Fischer called Mr. Stewart in early September 1995 to let him know that the company would require $425,000 more than had been initially requested to cover peak seasonal needs. Mr. Fischer explained that the main reason for the larger requirements was higher expenditures for modernization than had initially been estimated. Mr. Stewart informed Mr. Fischer that the bank would be happy to accommodate the additional loan requirements.

In January 1996, Mr. Fischer again contacted Mr. Stewart. He noted that sales had slackened considerably since his previous call. He attributed this decline largely to a retailing downturn then in progress, not to any special conditions affecting his company or the shears industry. Slackening in sales demand had created a need for additional short-term borrowing. Mr. Fischer believed that additional funds would be required until the company could adjust to the new economic conditions. He envisioned that this adjustment would probably not occur until mid-April 1996 or thereabouts. Once more, Mr. Stewart agreed to extend the necessary loan funds to SureCut Shears.

In early April 1996, Mr. Fischer phoned Mr. Stewart a third time to inform him that SureCut Shears would probably not be able to repay its outstanding short-term loan of $1.15 million before the seasonal upturn in funds requirements in June. Mr. Fischer explained that a further sales decline, occasioned by the retailing recession, was largely responsible for the company's inability to liquidate the loan as anticipated. In reply, Mr. Stewart noted that the bank preferred seasonal loans to be "off the books" for at least two months of the year but saw no reason why he would not be willing to renew SureCut Shears's outstanding loan. He nevertheless thought it advisable to explore whether the inability to repay the seasonal loan in 1996 might be caused by a permanent change in the nature of the company's loan needs, such as might be occasioned by the modernization program. Mr. Stewart consequently suggested a meeting for April 29 to discuss the company's recent progress.

In preparing for this meeting, Mr. Stewart carefully examined the various profit and loss statements and balance sheets that Mr. Fischer had submitted to the bank over the course of the previous nine months. (These data are shown in Exhibits 3 and 4.) He hoped this analysis might uncover the reasons for SureCut Shears's inability to repay its loan in accordance with original statements.

EXHIBIT 1

Pro Forma Income Statement, Fiscal 1996 (thousands of dollars)

estimation

	Actual June 30, 1995	1995						1996						Total
		July	Aug.	Sept.	Oct.	Nov.	Dec.	Jan.	Feb.	Mar.	Apr.	May	June	
Sales	$30,135	$2,100	$2,700	$3,300	$4,500	$3,900	$3,300	$2,100	$2,100	$1,800	$1,500	$1,200	$1,500	$30,000
Cost of goods sold														
Materials and labor @ 60% of sales	18,081	1,260	1,620	1,980	2,700	2,340	1,980	1,260	1,260	1,080	900	720	900	18,000
Overhead (including depreciation $130)	3,560	300	300	300	300	300	300	300	300	300	300	300	300	3,600
	21,641	1,560	1,920	2,280	3,000	2,640	2,280	1,560	1,560	1,380	1,200	1,020	1,200	21,600
Gross profit	8,494	540	780	1,020	1,500	1,260	1,020	540	540	420	300	180	300	8,400
Selling and administrative expenses	3,240	270	270	270	270	270	270	270	270	270	270	270	270	3,240
Profit before taxes	5,254	270	510	750	1,230	990	750	270	270	150	30	(90)	30	5,160
Taxes	1,891	97	184	270	443	356	270	97	97	54	11	(32)	11	1,858
Profit after taxes	3,363	173	326	480	787	634	480	173	173	96	19	(58)	19	3,302
Dividends	1,495	0	0	300	0	0	300	0	0	300	0	0	600	1,500
Retained earnings	$ 1,868	$ 173	$ 326	$ 180	$ 787	$ 634	$ 180	$ 173	$ 173	$ (204)	$ 19	$ (58)	$ (581)	$ 1,802
Cumulative retained earnings	—	$ 173	$ 499	$ 679	$1,466	$2,100	$2,280	$2,453	$2,626	$2,422	$2,441	$2,383	$1,802	—

EXHIBIT 2
Pro Forma Balance Sheets, Fiscal 1995 (thousands of dollars)

	Actual June 30, 1995	1995						1996					
		July	Aug.	Sept.	Oct.	Nov.	Dec.	Jan.	Feb.	Mar.	Apr.	May	June
Cash	$ 2,121	$ 736	$ 736	$ 736	$ 736	$ 736	$ 1,139	$ 2,609	$ 3,179	$ 2,413	$ 2,235	$ 1,759	$ 727
Accounts receivable[a]	2,084	2,850	3,750	4,650	6,150	6,150	5,250	3,750	3,150	2,850	2,400	1,950	2,100
Inventories	8,106	8,372	8,312	7,894	6,758	5,981	5,563	5,862	6,161	6,640	7,298	8,135	8,793
Current assets	12,311	11,958	12,798	13,280	13,644	12,867	11,952	12,221	12,490	11,903	11,933	11,844	11,620
Net plant	24,564	26,059	27,554	27,554	27,554	27,554	27,554	27,554	27,554	27,554	27,554	27,554	27,554
Total assets	$36,875	$38,017	$40,352	$40,834	$41,198	$40,421	$39,506	$39,775	$40,044	$39,457	$39,487	$39,398	$39,174
Bank loans payable	$ 0	$ 1,000	$ 2,817	$ 3,253	$ 2,392	$ 628	$ 0	$ 0	$ 0	$ 0	$ 0	$ 0	$ 1,081
Accounts payable[b]	861	744	777	777	777	777	777	777	777	777	777	777	777
Taxes payable[c]	0	80	230	81	497	833	650	742	834	447	458	427	0
Misc. other	270	270	270	270	270	270	270	270	270	270	270	270	270
Current liabilities	1,131	2,094	4,094	4,381	3,936	2,508	1,697	1,789	1,881	1,494	1,505	1,474	2,128
Mortgage 8%	11,960	11,960	11,960	11,960	11,960	11,960	11,661	11,661	11,661	11,661	11,661	11,661	11,362
Common stock	11,500	11,500	11,500	11,500	11,500	11,500	11,500	11,500	11,500	11,500	11,500	11,500	11,500
Earned surplus	12,284	12,463	12,798	12,993	13,802	14,453	14,648	14,825	15,002	14,802	14,821	14,763	14,184
Total liab., net worth	$36,875	$38,017	$40,352	$40,834	$41,198	$40,421	$39,506	$39,775	$40,044	$39,457	$39,487	$39,398	$39,174

a. Assumes collections lag sales by 45 days.

b. Assumes 30-day payment period, in accordance with trade terms.

c. Estimated taxes are paid in four equal installments of $380,000 each in September, December, March, and June based on pro forma earnings calculated the previous June.

(continued)

EXHIBIT 2 *(concluded)*

	1995						1996					
	July	Aug.	Sept.	Oct.	Nov.	Dec.	Jan.	Feb.	Mar.	Apr.	May	June
Raw materials												
Opening balance	$ 810	$ 777	$ 777	$ 777	$ 777	$ 777	$ 777	$ 777	$ 777	$ 777	$ 777	$ 777
Plus: Purchases	744	777	777	777	777	777	777	777	777	777	777	777
Less: Trans. to work in progress	777	777	777	777	777	777	777	777	777	777	777	777
Closing balance	$ 777	$ 777	$ 777	$ 777	$ 777	$ 777	$ 777	$ 777	$ 777	$ 777	$ 777	$ 777
Work in Process												
Opening balance	$3,110	$3,110	$3,110	$3,110	$3,110	$3,110	$3,110	$3,110	$3,110	$3,110	$3,110	$3,110
Plus: Raw materials additions	777	777	777	777	777	777	777	777	777	777	777	777
Plus: Labor additions	778	778	778	778	778	778	778	778	778	778	778	778
Less: Trans. to finished goods	1,555	1,555	1,555	1,555	1,555	1,555	1,555	1,555	1,555	1,555	1,555	1,555
Closing balances	$3,110	$3,110	$3,110	$3,110	$3,110	$3,110	$3,110	$3,110	$3,110	$3,110	$3,110	$3,110
Finished Goods												
Opening balance	$4,186	$4,485	$4,425	$4,007	$2,871	$2,094	$1,676	$1,975	$2,274	$2,753	$3,411	$4,248
Plus: Work in process additions	1,555	1,555	1,555	1,555	1,555	1,555	1,555	1,555	1,555	1,555	1,555	1,555
Loss: Cost of goods sold	1,256	1,615	1,973	2,691	2,332	1,973	1,256	1,256	1,076	897	718	897
Closing balance	$4,485	$4,425	$4,007	$2,871	$2,094	$1,676	$1,975	$2,274	$2,753	$3,411	$4,248	$4,906
Total closing inventory	$8,372	$8,312	$7,894	$6,758	$5,981	$5,563	$5,862	$6,161	$6,640	$7,298	$8,135	$8,793

Actual

EXHIBIT 3
Income Statements, 1995–1996 (thousands of dollars)

	1995						1996		
	July	Aug.	Sept.	Oct.	Nov.	Dec.	Jan.	Feb.	Mar.
Sales	$2,070	$2,605	$3,080	$4,066	$3,373	$2,799	$1,758	$1,738	$1,498
Cost of goods									
Materials and labor	1,304	1,641	1,949	2,440	2,024	1,680	1,056	1,095	960
Overhead (incl. depreciation $130)	296	290	340	310	303	288	293	374[a]	323[a]
	1,600	1,931	2,289	2,750	2,327	1,968	1,349	1,469	1,283
Gross profit	470	674	791	1,316	1,046	831	409	269	215
Selling and administrative expenses	273	273	293	275	275	269	260	258	258
Profit before taxes	197	401	498	1,041	771	562	149	11	(43)
Taxes	67	136	169	354	262	191	51	4	(15)
Profit after taxes	130	265	329	687	509	371	98	7	(28)
Dividends	0	0	300	0	0	300	0	0	300
Retained earnings	$ 130	$ 265	$ 29	$ 687	$ 509	$ 71	$ 98	$ 7	$ (328)
Cumulative retained earnings	$ 130	$ 395	$ 424	$1,111	$1,620	$1,691	$1,789	$1,796	$1,468

[a]Includes special cost for laying off personnel.

EXHIBIT 4
Balance Sheets, 1995–1996 (thousands of dollars)

	1995							1996		
	June	July	Aug.	Sept.	Oct.	Nov.	Dec.	Jan.	Feb.	Mar.
Cash	$ 2,120	$ 957	$ 573	$ 702	$ 696	$ 830	$ 641	$ 1,133	$ 1,076	$ 688
Accounts receivable	2,084	2,837	3,644	4,395	5,651	5,526	5,573	3,958	3,169	2,867
Inventories	8,106	8,378	8,303	7,963	7,179	6,705	6,502	6,925	7,170	7,374
Current assets	12,310	12,172	12,520	13,060	13,526	13,061	12,716	12,016	11,415	10,929
Net plant	24,564	26,103	27,672	27,848	27,858	27,843	27,855	27,843	27,810	27,812
Total assets	$36,874	$38,275	$40,192	$40,908	$41,384	$40,904	$40,601	$39,859	$39,225	$38,741
Bank loans payable	$ 0	$ 1,270	$ 2,758	$ 3,677	$ 3,073	$ 1,879	$ 2,206	$ 1,303	$ 706	$ 1,148
Accounts payable	861	789	774	843	876	834	684	699	658	514
Taxes payable	0	67	204	(64)	290	552	306	357	360	(92)
Misc. other	269	275	317	284	290	275	269	266	260	258
Current liabilities	1,130	2,401	4,053	4,740	4,529	3,540	3,465	2,625	1,984	1,828
Mortgage 8%	11,960	11,960	11,960	11,960	11,960	11,960	11,661	11,661	11,661	11,661
Common stock	11,500	11,500	11,500	11,500	11,500	11,500	11,500	11,500	11,500	11,500
Earned surplus	12,284	12,414	12,679	12,708	13,395	13,904	13,975	14,073	14,080	13,752
Total liab., net worth	$36,874	$38,275	$40,192	$40,908	$41,384	$40,904	$40,601	$39,859	$39,225	$38,741

(continued)

EXHIBIT 4 (*concluded*)

	1995						1996		
	July	*Aug.*	*Sept.*	*Oct.*	*Nov.*	*Dec.*	*Jan.*	*Feb.*	*Mar.*
Raw Materials									
Opening balances	$ 810	$ 814	$ 757	$ 760	$ 793	$ 823	$ 778	$ 762	$ 753
Plus: Purchases	787	777	837	867	802	688	690	652	518
Less: Trans. to work in process	783	834	834	834	772	733	706	661	601
Closing balance	$ 814	$ 757	$ 760	$ 793	$ 823	$ 778	$ 762	$ 753	$ 670
Work in Process									
Opening balance	$3,110	$3,131	$3,196	$3,221	$3,224	$3,139	$3,037	$2,953	$2,781
Plus: Raw materials additions	783	834	834	834	772	733	706	661	601
Plus: Labor additions	789	789	772	789	748	789	789	688	646
Less: Trans. to finished goods	1,551	1,558	1,581	1,620	1,605	1,624	1,579	1,521	1,495
Closing balance	$3,131	$3,196	$3,221	$3,224	$3,139	$3,037	$2,953	$2,781	$2,533
Finished Goods									
Opening balance	$4,186	$4,433	$4,350	$3,982	$3,162	$2,743	$2,687	$3,210	$3,636
Plus: Work in process additions	1,551	1,558	1,581	1,620	1,605	1,624	1,579	1,521	1,495
Less: Cost of goods sold	1,304	1,641	1,949	2,440	2,024	1,680	1,056	1,095	960
Closing balance	$4,433	$4,350	$3,982	$3,162	$2,743	$2,687	$3,210	$3,636	$4,171
Total closing inventory	$8,378	$8,303	$7,963	$7,179	$6,705	$6,502	$6,925	$7,170	$7,374

Hampton Machine Tool Company

On September 14, 1979, Jerry Eckwood, vice president of the St. Louis National Bank, was considering a loan request from a customer located in a nearby city. The company, Hampton Machine Tool Company, had requested renewal of an existing $1 million loan originally due to be repaid on September 30. In addition to the renewal of the existing loan, Hampton was asking for an additional loan of $350,000 for planned equipment purchases in October. Under the terms of the company's request, both loans, totaling $1.35 million, would be repayable at the end of 1979.

Since its establishment in 1915, Hampton Machine Tool Company had successfully weathered the severe cyclical fluctuations characteristic of the machine tool manufacturing business. In the most recent cycle Hampton had experienced record production and profitability during the mid- and late-1960s. Because Hampton's major customers included the military aircraft manufacturers and automobile manufacturers in the St. Louis area, the company's success in the 1960s reflected a strong automobile market and the heavy defense spending associated with the Vietnam War. Hampton rode the 1960s boom into the early 1970s. Hampton, along with the rest of the capital goods industry, experienced a severe decline in sales and profitability in the mid-1970s. Precipitous declines in the production of automobiles in St. Louis facilities reflected the 1973 oil embargo, subsequent increases in the price of gasoline, and the 1974–1975 recession. Massive reductions in defense spending in the post-Vietnam War period had a severe adverse impact on Hampton's other major customer segment, military aircraft manufacturers. Hampton's sales had bottomed out in the mid-1970s, and the several years prior to 1978 had seen a steady rebuilding of sales. Hampton's recovery was due primarily to three factors. First, military aircraft sales had increased substantially, reflecting both an expanding export market and a more benign domestic market. Second, though the automobile manufacturers in the area were not expanding, this segment of Hampton's market had at least stabilized. Finally, the adverse economic conditions in the mid-1970s had taken their toll in the regional capital goods industry. Consequently, Hampton's market share increased as many thinly capitalized competitors had been forced out of the industry. Hampton's recovery had suffered a mild setback, as 1978 sales were far below capacity. However, with a substantial backlog of firm sales orders, Hampton entered 1979 expecting its first year of capacity sales since 1972.

Hampton's conservative financial policies had contributed to its survival and success in the volatile capital goods industry. The company had traditionally maintained a strong working capital position as a buffer against economic uncertainty. As a result, the company had no debt on its balance sheet during the 10 years prior to December 1978. In a meeting in early December 1978, Benjamin G. Cowins, president of Hampton, requested the initial loan of $1 million to facilitate purchasing the stock of several dissident shareholders. While Hampton had some cash in excess of that required for normal operations, excess cash was not sufficient to effect the stock redemption. Therefore, Mr. Cowins had asked Mr. Eckwood for a loan from the St. Louis National Bank. The loan of $1 million was to be taken down at the end of December 1978. Hampton would make monthly interest payments at an interest rate of 1½% per month (approximately 18% on an annual basis) on the principal, which would be due at the end of September 1979. In support of this request, Mr. Cowins had submitted a forecast of monthly shipments for 1979 (see Exhibit 1), a balance sheet dated November 30, 1978 (first column of Exhibit 2), and documentation of Hampton's backlog of sales orders. Mr. Eckwood felt at the time that the documentation provided by Mr. Cowins was sufficient to support favorable action on the request. Furthermore, Hampton had traditionally kept its ample cash balances on deposit at the St. Louis National Bank, and the bank's management knew Mr. Cowins well. Mr. Cowins, then 58 years old, had succeeded his father-in-law as president of Hampton in 1963. He was widely respected in the business community as an energetic and successful executive. In mid-December 1978, Mr. Eckwood had approved the loan to Hampton.

Hampton took down the loan at the end of December 1978. The proceeds of the loan plus $2 million in excess cash were used immediately to repurchase 75,000 shares of Hampton's $10 par value stock from several dissident shareholders at an aggregate cost of $3 million.

After the loan was made, Mr. Cowins regularly sent the bank profit and loss statements and balance sheets documenting Hampton's financial condition. In preparing his analysis of Mr. Cowins's request, Mr. Eckwood focused on the documents presented in Exhibits 1, 2, and 3. In examining Hampton's financial statements, Mr. Eckwood recalled that Hampton's selling terms were 30 days net. Occasionally, a customer placing a large order would make an advance payment to help Hampton finance the construction of the machines ordered. Because Hampton's products were largely made to order, the construction period involved five to six months for some of the larger, more complex types of machines. Upon completion and shipment of orders against which advances had been paid, Hampton deducted the amount of the advance from the amount billed to the customer. Also, Mr. Eckwood understood that the company purchased its materials on terms of net 30 days.

In a letter to Mr. Eckwood, Mr. Cowins had made his request for the extension of the existing Hampton note until the end of the year plus an additional loan of $350,000 to finance equipment purchases. The additional loan would be needed by the end of October and would be payable at the end of the year, with monthly interest payments remaining 1½% of principal. In his letter, Mr. Cowins commented at some length on the company's financial condition, the reasons for the shortfall of actual from projected 1979 shipments, and Hampton's substantial backlog of firm sales orders. In addition,

Mr. Cowins stated that he expected to be able to repay both loans in full by December 31, 1979. Mr. Cowins's letter is presented in full as Exhibit 4. Although Hampton would not need the additional $350,000 loan until the end of October, the maturity date of the existing note was fast approaching. Therefore, Mr. Eckwood needed to decide upon a response to Mr. Cowins's request.

EXHIBIT 1
Shipments at Selling Price (thousands of dollars)

		As Forecast Dec. 1978	Actual	As Forecast Sept. 1979
1979	January	$ 1,302	$ 861	
	February	1,872	672	
	March	1,635	1,866	
	April	1,053	1,566	
	May	1,293	873	
	June	1,479	1,620	
	July	1,488	723	
	August	1,797	507	
Eight months total		$11,919	$8,688	
	September	$ 1,299		$2,163 → shipments.
	October	1,347		1,505
	November	1,311		1,604
	December	2,298		2,265

EXHIBIT 2
Balance Sheets, 1978–1979 (thousands of dollars)

	1978		1979			
	Nov.	Dec.	Mar.	June	July	Aug.
Cash	$2,520	$ 491	$ 505	$1,152	$1,678	$1,559
Accounts receivable, net	1,245	1,863	1,971	1,893	1,269	684
Inventories	2,601	2,478	3,474	3,276	3,624	4,764
Current assets	6,366	4,832	5,950	6,321	6,571	7,007
Gross fixed assets	4,010	4,010	4,010	4,010	4,010	4,010
Accumulated depreciation	2,998	3,010	3,040	3,070	3,080	3,090
Net fixed assets	1,012	1,000	970	940	930	920
Prepaid expenses	62	40	39	24	24	42
Total assets	$7,440	$5,872	$6,959	$7,285	$7,525	$7,969
Notes payable, bank	—	$1,000	$1,000	$1,000	$1,000	$1,000
Accounts payable	$ 348	371	681	399	621	948
Accruals	561	777	849	678	585	552
Taxes payable[a]	150	74	373	354	407	479
Customer advance payments	840	1,040	1,040	1,566	1,566	1,566
Current liabilities	1,899	3,262	3,943	3,997	4,179	4,545
Common stock ($10 par value)	1,178	428	428	428	428	428
Surplus	4,363	2,182	2,588	2,860	2,918	2,996
Net worth	5,541	2,610	3,016	3,288	3,346	3,424
Total liabilities and net worth	$7,440	$5,872	$6,959	$7,285	$7,525	$7,969

a. Tax payments in 1979 include $75,000 due March 15 on underpayment of 1978 taxes and four equal payments of $181,000 due on the 15th of April, June, September, and December for estimated 1979 tax liability, with any underpayment of 1979 taxes due March 15, 1980.

EXHIBIT 3
Income Statements, 1978–1979 (thousands of dollars)

	Fiscal Year Ending 12/31/78	Dec. 1978	1979								Eight Months Ending 8/31/79
			Jan.	Feb.	Mar.	Apr.	May	June	July	Aug.	
Net sales	$7,854	$1,551	$861	$672	$1,866	$1,566	$873	$1,620	$723	$507	$8,688
Cost of sales[a]	5,052	1,122	474	369	1,362	1,137	567	1,197	510	276	5,892
Gross profit	2,802	429	387	303	504	429	306	423	213	231	2,796
Selling and administrative expenses	1,296	248	103	61	205	172	96	130	87	66	920
Interest expense	—	—	15	15	15	15	15	15	15	15	120
Net income before taxes	1,506	181	269	227	284	242	195	278	111	150	1,756
Income taxes	723	87	129	109	136	116	94	133	53	72	842
Net income	$ 783	$ 94	$140	$118	$ 148	$ 126	$101	$ 145	$ 58	$ 78	$ 914
Dividends	$ 50	$ 25	—	—	—	—	—	$ 100	—	—	$ 100

a. Includes depreciation charges of $150,000 in 1978, $12,000 in December 1978, and $10,000 per month in 1979.

EXHIBIT 4

HAMPTON MACHINE TOOL COMPANY
East St. Louis, Illinois

September 12, 1979

Mr. Jerry Eckwood
Vice President
St. Louis National Bank
St. Louis, Missouri

Dear Mr. Eckwood:

I enclose the company's August 31 financial statements. While these statements show our cash balance as $1,559,000, you will note we have an obligation to a customer for cash advances of $1,566,000, and we expect to ship this order over the next three months. With respect to our note for $1,000,000 due September 30, we request that you renew it until the end of 1979. We also wish to borrow an additional $350,000 to be available at the end of October to be repaid by the end of the year with interest at the rate of 1½% per month on the principal. This additional loan is required to purchase certain needed equipment. At the end of the year, as you can see for yourself, we expect to be able to have enough cash on hand to retire our obligations in full.

For the past month or more we have been producing at capacity and expect to continue at this rate through the end of the year and beyond. On August 31, our backlog of unfilled orders amounted to about $16,500,000—approximately 90% of annual capacity. I should stress that these are firm orders from respected customers.

Despite our backlog, our shipment schedule has been upset, particularly the last several months, because we have had to wait on our suppliers for shipment of electronic control mechanisms. On August 31, we had seven machines with an accumulated cost of about $1,320,000 completed except for the installation of these electronic components. The components were finally received last week and will enable us to complete a number of machines in the next few weeks. After this imminent reduction in work in progress of about $1,320,000, the remainder of our work-in-progress inventories will probably remain stable for the foreseeable future because of our capacity rate of production.

We bought raw materials beyond our immediate needs in July and August to be assured of completing our orders scheduled to be shipped by the end of the year. We have accumulated about $420,000 worth of scarcer components above our normal raw materials inventories. The extra $420,000 will be used up by the end of the year, bringing our raw materials inventories back to normal levels for capacity production. Because we bought ahead this way, we expect to cut raw materials purchases to about $600,000 a month in each of the four remaining months of 1979.

Our finished goods inventories are, of course, negligible at all times since we ship machines within a day of completion.

Our revised shipment estimates (at selling price) are as follows:

September	$2,163,000
October	1,505,000
November	1,604,000
December	2,265,000
	$7,537,000

The shipment estimates include the $2,100,000 order for the General Aircraft Corporation. We are now scheduled to ship against this order as follows: September, $840,000; October, $840,000; November, $420,000. Since we obtained a $1,566,000 advance from General Aircraft on this order, we will be due nothing on these shipments until their $1,566,000 credit with us is exhausted.

(continued)

EXHIBIT 4 *(concluded)*

You will note the decline in our accrued expenses. As I mentioned to you last month when you visited us, we have been paying off commissions due to our three principal sales people (who are also large stockholders in the company). Last year when we needed funds to redeem part of our capital stock, these people agreed to defer their commissions until the funds could be more easily spared. In August, we paid off the last of these back commissions. This has been the principal cause of the decline in accruals, which, like prepaid expenses, normally do not change much from month to month. Assuming accruals will stay about the same as on August 31, our monthly outlay for all expenses other than interest and raw materials purchases should be around $400,000 per month.

Due to poor economic conditions and our desire to conserve cash, we have spent very little on new equipment in the last several years, and this has contributed somewhat to the difficulties we have had in maintaining production at a capacity rate this year. We feel that we should not further postpone replacing certain essential equipment if we are to avoid a possible major breakdown at an inconvenient time. Therefore, we think it necessary to purchase additional equipment costing $350,000 in October to maintain production efficiency. The proceeds from the additional loan we have requested will be used at the end of October to pay for this equipment. This equipment has an estimated life of eight years, an estimated net salvage value of zero, and the $350,000 purchase price will be depreciated on a straight-line basis.

Our tax people tell us that the equipment will qualify for a 10% investment tax credit (ITC). However, the tax savings of $35,000 will not affect our scheduled tax payments this year. We are scheduled to pay $181,000 in taxes on September 15 and to make another payment of the same amount on December 15. As I understand it, the ITC savings of $35,000 will reduce both our tax liability and the taxes payable on our balance sheet as well as increase reported earnings. However, the cash-flow impact of this savings will not be felt until March 1980 when we make our final settlement with the government on 1979 taxes.

Despite temporary bottlenecks which reduced shipments, our profits for the year to date have been quite satisfactory. With raw materials and components supply assured and the efficiency provided by the new equipment we plan to purchase, we feel confident we can meet our shipment forecasts for the rest of the year. Furthermore, the business which we expect to ship in the next four months is on our books on profitable terms. While our profit, as you know, varies with the item involved, our engineering estimates indicate that we expect to earn a profit before taxes and interest of about 23% of sales on these shipments. Even after taking into account our tax rate of 48% and the interest we must pay on our notes, 1979 looks like a very good year. Because of these good results and in view of our conservative dividend policy during the last several years of economic uncertainty, we plan to pay a dividend to our stockholders. Our dividend disbursements in 1979 have continued to be quite modest, and we want to be sure that those stockholders who stood by us last December have no cause to regret their action. Under the circumstances, we feel that a dividend of $150,000 payable in December is the least we can do in view of our high earnings and our stockholders' patient support.

If there is anything further you need to know, please do not hesitate to write or phone.

Sincerely yours,
(Signed) B. G. Cowins
President

Science Technology Company (1985)

Early in March 1985, Bill Watson, president of Science Technology Company (STC), was reviewing a 5-year financing plan prepared for the company by Harry Finson, the chief financial officer. Mr. Finson intended to discuss the plan at the forthcoming board meeting. If both the plan and the premises on which it was based were endorsed by the board, the plan would greatly influence the financial policies and the total development of the firm.

After some study, Mr. Watson identified several questions for further consideration and resolution:

1. In view of the uneven growth in sales, inventories and receivables, and earnings in the past, were Mr. Finson's 5-year forecasts useful?
2. What impact would a resurgence of inflation, fueled by massive budget deficits, have on STC?
3. Was the company well positioned to finance the rapid sales growth that was anticipated?

Description of STC

Science Technology Company was a leading manufacturer of computer-controlled automated test equipment (ATE) that was used to monitor and manage quality over the life cycle of electronic products. With 31% market share, the company was the dominant firm in the design and manufacture of testers and test software for printed circuit boards. Its second largest business was its semiconductor test operation, which manufactured complex systems that cost in excess of $1 million and were used to test state-of-the-art very large scale integrated (VLSI) circuits. Other products included a system to test electronic products in the field; systems used to test a product's mechanical and structural integrity under stress; and computer-aided engineering software used to test

Copyright © 1989 by the President and Fellows of Harvard College.
Harvard Business School case 289–040.

and verify designs before they were physically built by creating electronic models and simulating their performance in the software version.

STC was headquartered in Minneapolis, Minnesota, and had plants in Minnesota, Colorado, and Arizona. Customers were supported by a sales and service network with offices and representatives across the United States and more than a dozen countries in North and South America, Europe, Africa, Asia, and Australia. Total sales were $227 million.

STC's Objectives and Strategy

STC's primary objective was to be the recognized international leader in providing integrated quality management systems to manufacturers of electronic devices and equipment. This objective required maintaining its leadership in creating new test technologies and new products for all segments of the design and test markets. This commitment to maintain a fundamental superiority in test expertise required very heavy spending on research and development.

To be viable financially, the company sought to spread the cost of its research and development across a large number of sales. Its strategy was to pursue aggressively most major segments of the semiconductor and electronics manufacturing industries throughout Europe, North America, and the Pacific Basin.

Market for Automated Test Equipment

During the period 1975–1984, computer-related technologies changed swiftly and dramatically. Technological breakthroughs inspired the development of new products that consumers and users eagerly acquired. Examples include personal computers, cordless telephones, video cassette recorders, microprocessor-based home appliances, solar-powered calculators, mainframe computers, automated teller machines, and automated offices and factories. Consumers demanded and could expect products of high quality at low prices. Consequently, electronics manufacturers had critical test requirements at every stage of the product cycle from engineering to manufacturing to service.

So rapidly were new technologies developing that the introduction of a new silicon chip could quickly make the competition obsolete. There was no longer time to follow the traditional product development process of designing, building a prototype, testing, redesigning, building a new prototype, and so forth. It would also have been cost prohibitive to put each design iteration of a complex circuit on a silicon chip. Any change in the design would require making a new chip. STC provided software products that let design engineers know how well a new circuit would work without the costly necessity of building a prototype.

Getting a highly competitive product to market on time, with high quality and within budget, depended on the speed with which a new design was moved into manufacturing. This speed depended on testability. New products could not be made unless they could be tested. The electronic circuitry was contained in small devices mounted on printed circuit boards of varying size and complexity. These devices must work well if a product was to perform well; and cost considerations required electronics manufacturers to be able to sort out good components from bad *before* they were mounted on printed circuit boards, and to spot production problems early.

Automated test equipment was also of increasing importance in the field. High-quality, fast, low-cost repair service must be provided by the electronics manufacturer after the product was sold.

TABLE A
U.S. Factory Shipments, Electronics (billions of dollars)

	1978	*1979*	*1980*	*1981*	*1982*	*1983*	*1984*
Consumer products	$ 9.1	$ 9.4	$ 10.9	$ 12.5	$ 12.5	$ 14.6	$ 17.8
Communications	21.7	25.7	30.8	35.7	39.1	41.4	46.1
Computers	15.1	19.7	24.3	29.1	33.3	37.9	45.0
Industrial	10.6	12.7	14.7	18.1	21.0	20.5	22.6
Components	17.1	21.4	25.6	28.8	29.6	32.9	41.1
Total	$73.6	$88.9	$106.3	$124.2	$135.5	$147.3	$172.6

The growth of the worldwide ATE market was tremendous between 1978 and 1984 (see Table A). Sales increased from $359 million in 1978 to $1.6 billion in 1984. This rapid growth of 28% per year was spurred by the rapid growth of electronic products, powered in part by technological breakthroughs in computers and in miniaturization.

ATE firms were also helped by the steady increase in labor rates, which pushed electronics manufacturers to automate their testing. A second important trend was the move by electronics manufacturers away from the design and manufacture of their own test equipment. In the early 1960s, when the ATE market was just emerging, most ATEs were produced in-house by the electronics manufacturers. One of the main reasons for this was the absence of standard test equipment, especially for testing state-of-the-art semiconductor devices. Later, as semiconductor components increased in number and complexity, most of the major semiconductor and electronics manufacturers found it too difficult and expensive, in view of their limited in-house production volume, to build their own testers. A third trend that spurred the sales of firms specializing in ATEs was the dramatic improvement in testing technology and changes in the devices to be tested. Much of the electronics manufacturers' in-house testing capacity was made obsolete by these forces.

STC's Performance, 1980–1984

With one of the broadest lines in the industry, STC benefited from the strong ATE market. Sales increased by 58%, from $144 million in 1980 to $227 million in 1984, a compound annual growth rate of 12%. Exhibits 1 and 2 show STC's income statements and balance sheets for 1980–1984.

While sales increased each year, profits were erratic. Net profits of $10 million in 1980 were followed by a $3 million loss in 1981. Profitability then improved dramatically to $16.3 million in 1983. With the ATE market strong, management and investors anticipated strong sales and earnings growth. The price of STC shares soared from $10 at the beginning of 1982 to a high of $42 in June 1983. Management responded by selling 1,650,000 shares of common stock at a price of $11½ in June 1982 and another 1,800,000 shares at $26 only nine months later.

The optimism of mid-1983 soon faded. STC's profits were disappointing in 1984, falling to $10 million. Several factors accounted for this poor performance. First, the company increased the number of employees and the amount of plant capacity in anticipation of a stronger sales growth than the 10% realized. Second, market opportunities and competitive pressures required that research and development spending be increased by 32% to a level equal to 16% of sales. Third, the company had significant problems with a new product at the largest division, requiring expensive product recalls and repairs. And finally, the company had major manufacturing problems with a line of very large and complex testers at its semiconductor test division, resulting in divisional losses of $18 million in 1984.

Prospects for the ATE Industry and for STC

Mr. Watson was optimistic about the long-term prospects for the ATE industry. Industry sales were forecast to reach $4 billion in 1988, a compound annual growth rate of 26% from the $1.6 billion level in 1984.

Competition was intensifying, however. There were a large number of competitors, including Teradyne, Zehntel, Takeda Riken, Ando, Marconi, Fairchild, Hewlett-Packard, and LTX. Furthermore, many of these firms were broadening their product lines and the range of markets they served. The VLSI test market was a good example. When STC decided in 1977 to enter, two firms, Fairchild and Tektronix, dominated the market with a combined market share of 80%. After spending approximately $75 million to develop its VLSI testers, STC was faced with a totally different competitive situation in 1985 as the result of the unexpected entry of Teradyne, Takeda Riken, Ando, Megatest, and LTX.

Mr. Watson believed that STC had a number of strengths that would help it during the coming period of intensified competition. It had a large customer base, extensive software, a broad line of testers, a dominant share of the printed circuit board test market, and a fair position in VLSI testing. Quality problems affecting an in-circuit tester that was expected to be a mainstay product over the next few years had been solved; and a high performance new tester, representing a breakthrough in test technology, would be introduced in mid-1986. These two developments were expected to halt the recent decline in STC's share of the printed circuit board segment. The company also was making substantial progress in the VLSI test market and had been selected by the U.S. Department of Defense for a major program.

On the strength of these developments, STC's sales were forecast to reach $295 million in 1985 and $843 million in 1989 (see Exhibit 3).

Financial Pressures

The sale of 3.45 million shares of common stock in 1982 and 1983 raised $66 million and established a strong financial base for the planned growth. STC's financial strength in 1985 matched that of its competitors and seemed sufficient to obviate the need for additional equity issues (see Exhibit 4). Mr. Watson was concerned, however, by the past difficulties in forecasting and by the very substantial increase in debt that Mr. Finson's forecasts assumed.

EXHIBIT 1
Consolidated Income Statements, 1980–1984 (millions of dollars)

	1980	*1981*	*1982*	*1983*	*1984*
Net sales	$144	$154	$171	$206	$227
Cost of goods sold	66	73	79	90	104
Gross profit	78	81	92	116	123
R&D expense	13	19	22	28	37
Selling, general, administrative expenses	42	50	57	65	76
Other expense (income)	—	1	—	(1)	(3)
Interest expense	3	7	3	2	2
Profit before taxes	20	4	10	22	11
Taxes	9	2	3	6	1
Profit after taxes, continuing operations	11	2	7	16	10
Loss from discontinued operations	1	5	—	—	—
Net income	$ 10	$ (3)	$ 7	$ 16	$ 10
Selected Financial Ratios (% of sales)					
Cost of goods sold	46%	47%	46%	44%	46%
R&D expense	9	12	13	14	16
Selling, general, administrative expenses	29	32	33	32	33
Profit after taxes, continuing operations	7.6	1.2	4.1	7.8	4.4

EXHIBIT 2
Consolidated Balance Sheets, 1980–1984 (millions of dollars)

	1980	*1981*	*1982*	*1983*	*1984*
Cash	$ 4	$ 4	$ 4	$ 25	$ 3
Accounts receivable	40	45	46	68	74
Inventories	56	46	49	68	86
Tax claims	1	7	4	5	1
Other	2	5	2	7	10
Current assets	103	107	105	173	174
Net fixed assets	32	32	30	36	62
Other	1	2	2	5	6
Total assets	$136	$141	$137	$214	$242
Notes payable, banks	$ 7	$ 9	$ 5	$ 6	$ 14
Accounts payable	11	9	11	17	13
Accrued taxes	2	1	4	8	1
Accruals	12	14	17	17	18
Current liabilities	32	33	37	48	46
Long-term debt	35	41	7	8	25
Other	1	2	2	4	7
Net worth	68	65	91	154	164
Total liabilities and net worth	$136	$141	$137	$214	$242
Selected Financial Ratios					
Accounts receivables as % of sales	28%	29%	27%	33%	33%
Inventories as % of cost of goods	85	63	62	76	83
Net fixed assets as % of cost of goods	48	44	38	40	60
Accounts payable as % of cost of goods	17	12	14	19	13
Accruals as % of cost of goods	18	19	22	19	17

EXHIBIT 3

Five-Year Capital and Financing Plan

Permanent new capital requirements for Science Technology Company depend almost entirely on sales growth, retained profits, and the efficiency with which corporate assets are employed. Our growth has been moderate–12% per year since 1980. Our net profits have ranged from a deficit (including the loss from discontinued operations) in 1981 to 7.8% of sales in 1983. Profits have not increased our equity rapidly enough to keep up with requirements. However, the absence of any cash dividend and our two share issues, which raised a total of $66 million in new equity, allowed us to avoid excessive debt financing.

At the end of 1984 total assets were $242 million, or 106% of sales. Much of the growth of assets occurred in 1983 and 1984 as: (1) the mix of business shifted toward more complex systems; (2) capacity was expanded to accommodate anticipated strong orders; and (3) production run rates were based on forecasts that proved optimistic in 1984.

	1980–1984 Range	1984	Competitors' 1984 Range
Accounts receivables as % of sales	27–33%	33%	19–39%
Inventories as % of cost of goods	62–85	83	48–50
Net fixed assets as % of cost of goods	38–60	60	67–90
Total assets as % of sales	79–106	106	82–100

The accompanying 5-year financial projection (Table 1 on the next page) shows a 30% annual growth rate for sales, a 7.5% profit margin on sales, and an improvement in the turnover of total assets. The projections are based on the forecasts prepared by the divisional managers and are consistent with the industry sales growth that was discussed during our strategic planning sessions.

From 1985 to 1989 sales are projected to grow from $295 million to $843 million, and net profit from $23 million to $61 million. By 1989 total debt will be 35% of total capital–still in line with the debt levels of competitors. Earnings per share grow from $1.45 in 1985 to $3.84, and the possible market price of the stock reaches $77, assuming a multiple of 20 times.

It is extremely interesting to note the relations among net profit, total debt, and earnings per share.

Net Profit as % of Sales	5-Year Cumulative Profit ($ millions)	Net Worth 1989 ($ millions)	Total Debt 1989 ($ millions)	Total Capital 1989 ($ millions)	Debt as % of Capital 1989	Earnings per Share 1989
5.0%	$133	$297	$265	$562	47%	$2.56
7.5	199	363	199	562	35	3.84
10.0	266	430	132	562	23	5.12

Obviously, the higher the profit rate, the lower the need for additional debt financing and the higher the earnings per share. This demonstrates the importance of our programs to reduce manufacturing costs and to correct the problems at the semiconductor test division.

The price-earnings ratio for the stock seems likely to be influenced by the growth of sales and earnings. The following table, based on a profit margin of 7.5% and an asset-to-sales ratio of .80, considers the implications for stock price of different levels of sales growth. While no one knows with certainty the price-earnings ratio at which a stock will sell 5 years hence, the table does suggest the importance of maintaining a strong sales pattern.

Annual Sales Growth	Earnings per Share 1985	Earnings per Share 1989	Annual % Increase	Price-Earnings Ratio 1989	Stock Price 1989	Debt as % of Capital 1989
10%	$1.18	$1.73	8%	12	$21	0%
20	1.29	2.65	15	15	40	16
30	1.45	3.84	22	20	77	35

(continued)

EXHIBIT 3 *(concluded)*

TABLE 1—Financial Projections, 1985–1989 (millions of dollars)

	1985	*1986*	*1987*	*1988*	*1989*	
Net sales	$295	$385	$499	$648	$843	+30% per year
Cost of goods sold (COGS)	121	157	204	266	345	41% of sales
Gross profit	174	227	295	382	498	
R&D expense	41	54	70	91	118	14% of sales
Selling, general, administrative expenses	91	119	155	201	261	31% of sales
Interest expense	3	4	6	11	17	
Profit before taxes (PBT)	39	50	64	79	102	
Taxes	16	20	26	32	41	40% of PBT
Profit after taxes	$ 23	$ 30	$ 38	$ 47	$ 61	
Cash	$ 2	$ 3	$ 4	$ 5	$ 6	
Accounts receivable	94	123	160	207	270	32% of sales
Inventories	70	91	119	154	200	58% of COGS
Other	4	4	4	4	4	
Current assets	170	221	287	370	480	
Net fixed assets	70	82	106	138	180	
Other	8	8	8	8	8	
Total assets	$248	$311	$401	$516	$668	
Notes payable	$ 1	$ 28	$ 69	$122	$194	Plug
Accounts payable	16	20	27	35	45	13% of COGS
Accruals	21	27	35	46	59	17% of COGS
Current liabilities	38	75	131	203	298	
Long-term debt	21	17	13	9	5	
Other	2	2	2	2	2	
Net worth	187	217	255	302	363	
Total liabilities and net worth	$248	$311	$401	$516	$668	

EXHIBIT 4

Financial Information on Primary Competitors

	Teradyne[a]	Fluke[b]	LTX[a]	STC
Size ($ millions)				
1984 sales	$ 389	$ 208	$ 90	$ 227
1984 assets	350	171	91	242
5-Year Growth				
Sales	+136%	+62%	+186%	+94%
Net income	+280	+97	+299	+67
Earnings per share	+170	+86	+219	+31
Profitability, 1984				
Cost of goods sold as % of sales	45%	44%	46%	46%
R&D expense as % of sales	16	10	15	16
Selling, general, and administrative as % of sales	20	33	27	33
Earnings before interest and taxes (EBIT) as % of sales	19	14	12	6
Net income as % of sales	11	9	7	5
Return on equity	19	18	15	6
Return on capital	15	6	11	6
Financial Condition, 1984				
Current ratio	3.6	3.4	2.5	3.8
Acid ratio	2.0	1.9	1.7	1.9
Total liabilities as % of total assets	35%	39%	52%	33%
Bank and long-term debt as % of equity	28%	27%	61%	24%
EBIT ÷ interest expense	14	8	8	7
Per Share Data, 1984				
Market price	$21–39	$23–31	$14–22	$13–37
Earnings per share	$ 1.87	$ 2.39	$ .86	$ .63
Dividends per share	—	—	—	—
Earnings multiple	16	11	21	40
Book value	$ 10	$ 13	$ 6	$ 11

a. Teradyne and LTX design, manufacture, and sell computer-controlled systems for testing semiconductor integrated circuits and electronic components.

b. Fluke designs, manufactures, and sells commercial electronic test and measurement instruments and systems.

Advanced Medical Technology Corporation

Early in April 1986, Tom Winter, vice president and loan officer of the Western National Bank of San Francisco, California, was reviewing a loan request for $8 million from Peter Haskins, president of Advanced Medical Technology Corporation.

Advanced Medical Technology Corporation (AMT) developed, manufactured, and sold scientific medical instruments, needles, and catheters that allowed rapid and less invasive access to a number of different organs and vessels. These products represented an alternative to traditional surgical procedures and allowed analysis or corrective treatment with less risk and trauma and at lower cost. An example of the products were catheters that could be introduced into a blood vessel and then manipulated through partially closed arteries or into the heart itself.

AMT had experienced extraordinary growth, fueled by heavy spending on research and development and a rapid expansion of its sales force. Its technical staff was very well regarded for developing new products with a wide range of applications. The combination of state-of-the-art products and a rapidly expanding market resulted in sales growth in excess of 30% per year. Mr. Haskins believed that industry sales would continue to grow at this rate and that any failure to maintain AMT's market position would be damaging in terms of competitive position and internal morale.

Sales volume, which had grown continuously from the start, was always large in relation to the available capital. The situation was exacerbated by large operating losses, as AMT entered new markets aggressively.

Management met the financing pressures by heavy reliance on short-term credit, by leasing some manufacturing facilities, and by establishing a connection with Biological Labs, Inc., a leading pharmaceutical firm. Biological Labs had been eager to participate in the large and rapidly expanding medical instrumentation market but had failed in its internal efforts to enter the business. By 1983, Biological Labs had fallen behind in catheter and instrumentation technology. Management abandoned its internal efforts and entered into an agreement with AMT. At the initial closing on June 2, 1983,

AMT received a cash payment of $7 million in exchange for 5% of the outstanding shares and the right to purchase an additional 13% of the outstanding stock over a 5-year period ending June 1988 for $12 million. If Biological Labs purchased the $12 million of additional stock, it would also have the right to require AMT to merge into Biological Labs in 1992. The price would be based on a multiple of average earnings in 1990 and 1991. Subsequent to the agreement, Biological Labs made four purchases of stock, as shown in Table A.

On April 14, 1986, at the suggestion of his public accountant, Mr. Haskins visited the Western National Bank to discuss the possibility of securing a line of credit. He met with Mr. Winter, vice president and loan officer of the bank. Mr. Winter explained that although he was unfamiliar with AMT's products, he had handled the accounts of several similar types of technology companies. Exhibits 1 and 2 present the financial statements that Mr. Haskins brought to the bank.

Mr. Haskins was thoroughly dissatisfied with the company's current loan arrangement with the Sunnyvale Bank, from which it had a credit line of $6 million, with accounts receivable and inventory pledged as security. He thought that Mr. Flint, the loan officer at Sunnyvale, made no effort to understand the company and was constantly making suggestions that seemed inappropriate. He routinely visited AMT once every six months. While the visits were cordial, they were of very little value to Mr. Haskins. Furthermore, Mr. Haskins felt that the bank had been quite arbitrary in selecting the receivables that it would accept as collateral and in setting the percentage of inventory that it would advance as a loan. The restrictive attitude on the bank's part was limiting the company's ability to expand at exactly the time that increased volume seemed to be the key to profitability.

Mr. Haskins was perfectly willing to pledge the company's accounts receivable, inventory, or anything else that the bank thought would be desirable security as long as the arrangement was fair to the company and specific enough so that he could count on having the funds available when he needed them.

Mr. Winter explained that the bank was always interested in sound loan proposals from companies that showed the promise of developing into good accounts. He promised to study the request and said that he hoped to visit the company in the near future.

Before going to the company, Mr. Winter telephoned Mr. Flint, head of Sunnyvale's asset-based lending operation, and learned that his experience with AMT had been thoroughly unsatisfactory. According to Mr. Flint, the company had maintained extremely low balances and on several occasions had overdrawn its account. The pattern of losses, despite excellent products that were well received in the trade, seemed to be the direct result of Mr. Haskins's determination to spend heavily on research and development and on marketing. Lastly, the receivables pledged as security and counted in the borrowing base did not always measure up to the bank's definition of acceptable collateral.

Mr. Flint pointed out that AMT was a familiar name to two other major banks in San Francisco and suggested that Mr. Winter might consider seeking the insights of the loan officers involved. Summaries of their comments are provided in Exhibit 3.

TABLE A
Equity Investments by Biological Labs

April 1985	June 1985	October 1985	May 1985
$4,000,000	$2,000,000	$2,000,000	$4,000,000

Upon visiting the AMT plants, Mr. Winter noted that the production process was primarily an assembly operation, involving several hundred products typically produced in small lots. It took an average of eight weeks to complete the processing of medical instruments. Ten to 12 weeks of finished-goods inventory were maintained to ensure immediate response to orders. However, Mr. Haskins hoped that significant savings in inventory could be realized. A computer-based inventory control system, linking purchasing, production, and sales, had been installed in late 1984. While the pressures to push product development and sales had prevented Mr. Haskins from becoming directly involved, he sensed that important headway was being made.

Sales were made to over 3,000 hospitals, clinics, and doctors. These accounts had been extended open lines of credit on net 30-day terms without investigation. Although Mr. Haskins believed that some of the customers tended to be undercapitalized, collection experience had been excellent. However, slow payment seemed to be a competitive reality. Accounts receivables on AMT's books as of December 31, 1985, included $1.8 million due from foreign customers, representing 27% of the total. An aging of the receivables was as shown in Table B.

Mr. Winter also raised questions over the history of operating losses. Mr. Haskins provided full access to the divisional figures. Two of the three divisions were close to break-even in 1985, with plans to turn profitable in 1986. The third division, which represented a huge growth opportunity, was still incurring major losses as management tried to build a product and market position rapidly. All three divisions had dedicated research, production, sales, and marketing organizations.

When Mr. Winter returned to the bank, he immediately solicited the help of the loan officer who handled the Western National Bank's very substantial relationship with Biological Labs. A meeting was arranged with an executive vice president who assured Mr. Winter that Mr. Haskins was a strong operating manager whose aggressiveness and hard-driving entrepreneurial nature were important in building a major presence in this rapidly evolving industry. Biological Labs was prepared to provide a comfort letter stipulating that it "supported the efforts of AMT for which it had important plans." However, company policy made it impossible to guarantee the debt.

On May 8, 1986, Mr. Haskins returned to the Western National Bank to explain that the Sunnyvale Bank was unwilling to increase the percentages that it would loan against the assets. While Biological Labs had made a final investment of $4 million at the beginning of the month, AMT was rapidly exhausting its $6 million credit line. Mr. Haskins hoped that the Western National Bank would provide an $8 million line, with the agreement that all borrowings from the Sunnyvale Bank would be fully repaid.

Mr. Winter promised to let Mr. Haskins know the bank's decision within a few days.

TABLE B
Aging of Accounts Receivable at December 31, 1985

Month of Shipment	Age (days)	Outstanding Receivables	Sales
December 1985	0–30	$2,598,000	$2,917,000
November	31–60	1,890,000	2,657,000
October	61–90	627,000	2,730,000
Prior	90	881,000	
Total		$5,996,000	

EXHIBIT 1
Income Statements, 1983–1985 (thousands of dollars)

	1983	1984	1985
Net sales	$13,198	$21,624	$30,848
Cost of products sold	6,825	9,682	13,989
Gross profit	6,373	11,942	16,859
General, selling, and administrative expenses	6,299	11,374	14,478
Research and development	1,168	2,839	4,182
Operating earnings	(1,094)	(2,271)	(1,801)
Interest expense	501	611	634
Sale of patents and technology	0	1,370	627
Other income	103	336	321
Earnings before taxes	(1,491)	(1,176)	(1,487)
Income taxes	(202)	0	0
Net earnings	$ (1,289)	$ (1,176)	$ (1,487)

EXHIBIT 2
Balance Sheets at December 31, 1983–1985 (thousands of dollars)

	1983	1984	1985
Cash	$1,243	$ (80)	$ (652)
Accounts receivable	2,549	3,359	5,996
Inventories	3,305	6,782	9,762
Other	520	2,249	2,605
Current assets	7,617	12,310	17,711
Net fixed assets	906	1,494	1,802
Capital leases[a]	321	374	212
Investment[b]	0	1,943	1,049
Other	301	322	303
Total assets	$9,145	$16,443	$21,077
Notes payable to Biological Labs	$ 0	$ 2,260	$ 1,735
Note payable to bank	1,307	5,628	4,900
Note payable to vendor	47	0	0
Accounts payable	725	1,926	1,853
Accrued expenses	740	1,086	1,331
Current portion, long-term debt, capital leases	124	119	90
Other	22	37	33
Current liabilities	2,965	11,056	9,942
Deferred income	0	627	0
Long-term debt	254	0	0
Capital lease obligation	267	277	139
Total liabilities	3,486	11,960	10,081
Net worth	5,659	4,483	10,996
Total liabilities and net worth	$9,145	$16,443	$21,077

a. In addition to the capital leases, the company has entered into noncancellable operating leases in the amount of $2.5 million per year for each of the next 10 years. These leases relate to the company's main manufacturing facilities.

b. Investments represent partial ownership in two small private companies.

EXHIBIT 3
Loan Officers' Comments

Bank of San Francisco (Asset-Based Lending Division)

"Peter Haskins is a very likable, magnetic person who puts you through challenging but enjoyable mental gymnastics during negotiations. He is also a grinder who comes back once a week with a new request. He never lets up when he wants something; just keeps coming at you and grinding away. Peter also tries to get to the highest possible authority, even on mundane issues. He left Bank of San Francisco because of our unwillingness to add to AMT's highly leveraged position. We simply didn't believe that the quality of the assets warranted higher lending limits."

Bank of the West (Technology Lending Group)

"Haskins is extremely honest and made AMT an open book. The bankers were invited to the strategic planning meetings and were kept informed of developments at the company. Haskins is well trained, with an MBA from Wharton, and is a tough, effective operating manager. He is a doer and a shaker. The relationship with Biological Labs is an important plus."

U.S. Bank of Washington

In the fall of 1990, Mal Harding, vice president at the U.S. Bank of Washington, sat down to review a new loan application for the Redhook Ale Brewery. The bank first developed a relationship with Redhook in 1987 when it financed a $750,000 term loan and a $100,000 line of credit. The company had maintained a good relationship with the bank, had met or exceeded financial projections, and had made all payments to the bank in a timely manner.

Redhook had an impressive operating record. Begun in 1981, sales had increased at an average rate of 53% per year since 1984, reaching $2.7 million in 1989. By 1990, Redhook's ales and porters had captured 50% of the growing and increasingly competitive microbrewery market in the Pacific Northwest.

To meet the forecasted increase in demand for its products, Redhook planned to build a new brewery in the Bay Area of northern California. There were also plans to introduce a lager brand, which would require the construction of a second, larger brewery in the Puget Sound region of western Washington. To finance its expansion, Redhook was seeking a $5 million equity infusion from a well-established European brewery with an interest in entering the North American market. In addition, the U.S. Bank of Washington had been approached to provide $6.5 million of new bank financing.

The U.S. Commercial Banking Industry

U.S. commercial banks essentially held loans and securities as assets, which in turn were primarily funded by the issuance of deposit liabilities. By 1989, loans accounted for over 61% of the total assets held by U.S. commercial banks, up from 58.5% in 1985 (see Exhibit 1). The overall expansion of the loan portfolio was the result of the strong growth in real estate loans, coupled with steady growth in consumer loans, more than offsetting the relative decline in commercial and industrial (C&I) loan growth.

This case was prepared by Research Associate Elizabeth R. Lawrence under the supervision of Professor Scott P. Mason.

By the late 1980s, as a result of higher perceived risk in the commercial sector, the composition of banks' real estate portfolios had begun to shift from commercial to residential mortgages. The ability of commercial banks to increase their role in the residential mortgage market was due in large part to the shrinking of the thrift industry. However, problem commercial real estate loans continued to threaten commercial banks. Due primarily to high commercial real estate losses, 1989 witnessed a record 204 federally insured commercial bank failures.

Consumer loans had grown steadily over the 5-year period ending in 1989. In addition, $11 billion of consumer receivables, mostly credit card debt and automobile loans, were securitized in 1989. This, along with the securitization of real estate mortgages, resulted in the growth of bank loan portfolios that understated the actual amount of net new credit being provided to real estate and consumers because the issuance of these securities removed the underlying loans from banks' balance sheets. This removal of loans from banks' balance sheets had the additional effect of lowering the amount of regulatory capital required to support the actual level of banks' lending activities, while still enabling banks to earn fee income from originating and servicing the loans. Consumer loan securitization continued at a heightened pace in 1990. It was motivated in part by the new 1992 risk-based capital standards, which were to phase in beginning at year-end 1990.

The slowed growth in bank C&I loans was significantly affected through the 1980s by the continuing disintermediation of the U.S. banking system (see Table A). Bank borrowers, especially investment-grade corporations, sought to lower their financing costs through the use of nonbank alternatives, most notably commercial paper. Much of this commercial paper was purchased by money market mutual funds, which in turn competed with banks for the business of their deposit customers.

In addition, the growth of the medium-term note market, the high-yield debt market, and sales of C&I loans to nonbanks all contributed to the slowing of the growth of banks' C&I loan portfolios during the 1980s. Finally, in the recessionary climate of 1990, many banks had begun to increase margins for business loans. This, in addition to the tightening of bank credit terms and standards, also helped continue the trend of reduced C&I loan growth.

Bank holdings of securities had been dropping as a percentage of total bank assets since 1987. This was due in large part to the significant decrease in holdings of state and local government debt resulting from the Tax Reform Act of 1986. This legislation repealed the ability of banks to deduct 80% of the interest expense incurred to carry tax-exempt bonds acquired after August 1986. The modest growth in bank holdings of

TABLE A
Comparison of Growth in Bank Loans and Deposits versus Nonbank Alternatives (billions of dollars except growth rate data)

	1979	1984	1989	*Growth Rate 1979–1989*
Bank loans n.e.c.[a]	$409.7	$ 613.4	$ 820.3	7.2%
Commercial paper outstanding	110.9	231.7	519.2	16.7
Bank deposits[b]	986.2	1,551.2	2,172.7	8.2
Money market mutual fund assets	45.2	233.6	428.1	25.2

Source: Federal Reserve Flow of Funds.

a. Bank loans n.e.c. (not elsewhere classified) include C&I loans, foreign loans, loans to financial institutions, farm loans, and other loans.

b. Bank deposits include checkable deposits, small time and saving deposits, and large time deposits.

U.S. government securities was actually the net result of a significant decrease in the relative holdings of U.S. Treasuries securities, combined with an even more significant increase in the relative holdings of government-guaranteed mortgage-backed securities.

Non-interest-earning bank assets included cash and reserves held against deposits at the Federal Reserve Bank in non-interest-bearing accounts.[1] Other non-interest-earning assets included tangible assets, such as premises, furniture and equipment; real estate, including that obtained in satisfaction of loans; and customer's liability on acceptances.[2]

Retail deposits were increasing partly due to consumers transferring funds from thrifts, and partly because banks were acquiring thrift institutions. These deposits helped banks avoid funding asset growth by raising capital in the financial markets, which often proved both difficult and expensive. Bank equity prices were generally down, and new subordinated debt issues were commanding high-risk premiums.

Small time deposits[3] were the dominant retail deposit category and had recently been increasing as a percentage of total assets. These accounts had typically been the main source of funding for thrifts. Demand deposits[4] continued to fall. This was consistent with the growing trend for businesses to pay fees for bank services rather than hold idle balances. Further, higher average interest rates in 1989 increased the incentive for depositors to minimize non-interest-bearing balances. Most banks (approximately 98%) insured their deposits through the Federal Deposit Insurance Corporation (FDIC), for which they paid a small annual premium. Each depositor at an FDIC-insured bank was protected up to $100,000.

In 1989, net income for the banking industry as a whole was down as a percentage of average net assets (see Exhibit 2). This was due primarily to an increase in provisions for losses on nonperforming loans.[5] Further, while gross interest income generated by earning assets was up, the interest cost of deposits and purchased funds increased significantly. This resulted in a lower net interest margin, a key indicator of gross profitability for the industry. Non-interest expenses, which included overhead and operating costs, continued the trend of annual increases as a percentage of total net assets. Non-interest income, which included fees for services, also continued its trend of annual increases.

Retained earnings were a source of capital for banks. However, a decrease in net income combined with the maintenance of dividend payouts resulted in a reduced level of net retained earnings for the industry in 1989 (see Exhibit 2).

---

1. Members of the Federal Reserve System were required to hold vault cash or non-interest-bearing reserves at the Federal Reserve Bank equal to a percentage of their deposits. Since the passage of the Depository Institutions Deregulation and Monetary Control Act (DIDMCA) of 1980, uniform reserve requirements were set for all depository institutions, ranging from 3% to 12% depending on the deposit type and size of the bank's deposits.

2. Customers' liability on acceptances arise generally from international transactions when customers use a bank line of credit to authorize a draft on their account, or when bills of exchange are used to pay for imported goods.

3. Time deposits are typically interest-bearing accounts that require notice for withdrawal of funds. Small time deposits are accounts under $100,000, whereas large time deposits are accounts over $100,000.

4. Demand deposits are typically non-interest-bearing accounts for businesses.

5. Nonperforming assets typically consisted of: (1) loans on which interest was no longer accrued, (2) certain restructured loans for which the rate or terms had been renegotiated so as to be generally unfavorable to the lending institution, and (3) real estate or other fixed assets acquired in satisfaction of loans.

Profit indices for the industry overall were weak in 1989. While small banks continued to book relatively healthy profits, larger banks, particularly the money-center institutions, reported weak earnings. This was due primarily to losses for commercial real estate and domestic business loans. East Coast institutions were particularly hard hit, due in large part to losses in commercial real estate loans. Larger banks (with assets of more than $300 million) experienced an increase in the net charge-off rate of loans, from .75% of average total loans in 1985 growing steadily to 1.21% in 1989. Together, all banks experienced a net charge-off rate of 1.09% in 1989. Overall, the industry's return on assets was just .51%, the second lowest level since 1970, with a return on equity of 7.94% (see Exhibit 3).

U.S. Bancorp

U.S. Bancorp, headquartered in Portland, Oregon, was the parent company of the U.S. Bank of Washington, and the largest financial services holding company headquartered in the Pacific Northwest. Total assets were approximately $17.0 billion at December 31, 1989. Financial statements and summary data are given as Exhibits 4 and 5.

U.S. Bancorp was well diversified in financial services, enabling the corporation to meet many of the financial needs of businesses and individuals. Bank services were provided by different business units. The capital markets group provided services in international banking, merchant banking, and trade financing, and maintained banking relationships with corporate clients with sales exceeding $100 million. The real estate group operated in 10 western states to originate and service commercial and residential real estate loans. Investor services provided trust, asset management, insurance, and brokerage services to bank customers. The leasing group, with 35 sales offices throughout the United States, financed equipment for businesses.

The commercial banking business unit was divided into three groups, one for each state in its primary market. While each was operated as a distinct business, they were all known to the consumer as simply "U.S. Bank." The U.S. Bank of Oregon was the largest bank in the state in 1990, with 193 branches and 42% of the banking deposit market share. In Northern California, the U.S. Bank was the third largest in 1990, with 40 branches and 4% of the banking deposit market share.

The U.S. Bank of Washington was the fourth-largest commercial bank in Washington in 1990, with 14% of the banking deposit market share. The bank had been created as the result of U.S. Bancorp's 1987 acquisition of Old National Bank of Washington in July, and of People's National Bank of Washington in December. In February 1988, U.S. Bancorp merged these two Washington-based banking operations to form the new U.S. Bank of Washington, with combined assets of over $4 billion and over 600,000 accounts.

Overall, U.S. Bancorp was in a generally healthy condition in 1989. Net income for 1989 was $150.8 million, up 22% from $123.9 million in 1988. U.S. Bancorp had also met management's 1989 goal of a 1% return on assets and achieved a 15.12% return on equity.

The company's loan portfolio was 56% concentrated in commercial loans. It was well diversified between Washington and Oregon and between industry segments within these economies. Only a small portion of the loan portfolio was originated outside the bank's primary operating territory. Commercial loans increased in 1989 as a percentage of the total loan portfolio.

Asset quality had been improving, and further reduction of nonperforming assets to 1% of total loans and real estate owned was an important goal for the bank in 1990.

The bank had reduced its level of nonperforming assets to 1.7% of total loans at year-end 1989 from 2.3% at year-end 1988.

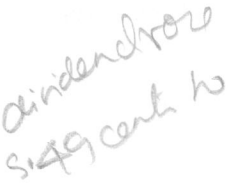

With adequate reserves and improvement in the quality of the loan portfolio, capital was sufficient and met all regulatory guidelines, including the new risk-based capital standards for 1992. However, consistently strong asset growth over the past several years had eroded U.S. Bancorp's capital position expressed as a percent of assets. Further, while retained earnings was an important source of capital for the bank, dividends per share had risen from 49¢ per share in 1985 to 89¢ per share in 1989.

U.S. Bancorp's financial position was in large part influenced by the vitality of the Pacific Northwest, its primary operating territory. Oregon and Washington were national leaders in employment growth in 1989. Washington enjoyed its lowest unemployment rate in over a decade, and population growth rates were over twice the national average. Industrial strength and its location as the gateway to trade with Pacific Rim countries were driving the region's economic growth.

Financing the Redhook Ale Brewery

The Redhook Ale Brewery

In May 1981, Paul Shipman and Gordon Bowker founded Redhook Ale Brewery in Seattle, Washington. While the U.S. brewing industry was dominated by a small number of firms with national marketing scope and large-volume, cost-efficient breweries, some market factors indicated a favorable climate for microbreweries. Most importantly, starting in the early 1970s, sales of imported beer began to grow rapidly, evidencing a shift in the taste of American consumers toward higher-quality products.

Shipman and Bowker's decision to start a regional microbrewery was influenced not only by this promising growth in the national import beer market but also by the fact that local per-capita consumption of draft beer was the highest in the country. This combination of factors indicated to them that the region would be highly receptive to fresh, locally made beers in the European tradition.

The Ballard area of Seattle was chosen as the site of the initial brewery because of its existing light industrial facilities and because the surrounding community still retained strong European traditions. To purchase equipment and provide working capital for operations, $350,000 in equity capital was raised from Seattle-area investors.

Redhook began as a draft-only brewery. On August 11, 1982, the first pint of Redhook Ale was sold. Blackhook Porter was introduced in June 1983. Ballard Bitter, introduced in the spring of 1984, became immensely popular. Demand soon exceeded production capacity, even with the addition of a bottling line in mid-1985.

Management moved the brewery to the old Fremont (Trolley) Car Barn, which once housed the Seattle Electric Railway. The 26,000-square-foot car barn building provided space for expanded brewing capacity, up to 40,000 barrels, as well as a brewpub, which was named the Trolleyman to commemorate the history of the building.

The 110-year-old German company of Anton Steinecker Maschinenfabrik GmbH was chosen to design and build Redhook's state-of-the-art brewing equipment for the Fremont brewery. The acquisition of this new technology positioned Redhook as the most technically advanced craft brewery in North America and ensured product quality and consistency. No other brewery of comparable size had made such an investment in equipment and technology to date. Operations commenced at the Fremont brewery in October 1988.

CEO Paul Shipman's original vision for Redhook was to produce beers that would compete with well-known imported brands from Europe and Canada. Targeting the import drinker, Redhook was committed to producing a quality brew that surpassed imports in freshness and offered consumers a more full-bodied flavor. In addition to imports such as Bass and Fullers, Redhook's ales competed with regional breweries like Anchor Steam and Sierra Nevada; niche microbrewers like Grant's, Hart, and Thousand Oakes; and contract brewers like Samuel Adams.

The company was well positioned as part of a growing market for microbrewery products. In 1975 there was one microbrewery in the United States; by 1989 there were 300, up from 50 in 1985. While the U.S. domestic beer market experienced flat sales growth in 1988 and 1989, microbrewery sales were growing at an estimated 30%–50% per year. This growth came largely at the expense of imports, whose sales declined 7.9% in 1989 and were down 2.7% in the first eight months of 1990. These trends were expected to continue, although a drop in consumption was forecast if legislators were to approve higher beer taxes. Health concerns were also negatively affecting alcohol consumption, although Redhook management believed moderation might encourage the switch to beer—more full-bodied brews in particular.

The Proposed Expansion

Redhook's management believed that increasing profitability and projected growth indicated that the time was right to expand. It also believed that a new lager product would offer significant growth for the company. Shipman saw lagers eventually becoming the company's lead brand, with projected sales of $25 million. This would bring the brewery closer to meeting its ultimate objective: to dominate the regionally produced specialty beer industry in the Pacific Northwest and California.

The consolidation of regional breweries by the large national breweries and the subsequent closing of many smaller facilities created an absence of quality regional lager breweries. Redhook lagers were to fill this void. With Redhook's strong reputation for premium beers, a distribution network in place, heavy advertising, and no domestic competition in their target niche, Redhook management believed it could quickly penetrate the lager market.

The market for lager beer was strong. Lagers, a lighter, more "thirst-quenching" brew, appealed to a much broader population than ales and porters. Ales and porters were a small-niche product, while lagers accounted for the bulk of the malt beverage market. The market size for lager was estimated to be greater than 10 times the size of the ale market. Redhook's new lager product would, however, compete against the higher-priced imported lager beers such as Heineken, Beck's, Corona, and Molson. The size of the high-priced lager market in the Northwest alone was estimated at approximately $145 million. The premium lager market in California was estimated to be over $1 billion.

To introduce its new lager product, Redhook proposed to build a 100,000-barrel brewery with expansion potential to 200,000 barrels in the Puget Sound region of western Washington. This brewery would serve as a back-up source of ale for both the Pacific Northwest and California and would also provide capacity to produce a new lager brand. Redhook also proposed to build another brewery, similar to the Fremont facility, in the Bay Area of northern California to provide local identity to the highly populated California market. The breweries were expected to provide Redhook with sufficient capacity to grow into the late 1990s.

Total investment in property, plant, and equipment was estimated at $15 million. A cash deposit of $1 million would be required on October 1, 1990, and would be applied against the first progress payment due in July 1991. Anton Steinecker Maschinenfabrik GmbH would again design and build the breweries and would require that Redhook secure adequate financing prior to the commencement of its work.

Financing the Deal

Harding carefully reviewed the Redhook Ale Brewery File (see Appendix). He would first have to decide whether to recommend the $6.5 million transaction to the loan committee. Credit relationships of under $3 million could be approved directly by the loan officer in charge of the account in cooperation with an individual assigned from credit administration. Over this ceiling, loans needed the approval of an eight-person loan committee, consisting of the chief credit officer, group heads, and rotating members who had direct credit responsibility. While the loan committee typically approved recommendations, approval was not assured. The committee considered each loan in light of the bank's portfolio, whereas the loan officer looked at each loan as a single transaction; on occasion, these two viewpoints conflicted.

Essential to evaluating Redhook's creditworthiness would be the financials provided by the treasurer and chief financial officer, David Mickelson. In addition to historical financial statements, Mickelson had prepared financial statements that estimated the company's financing needs (see Exhibits A1 and A2). Harding knew he would have to analyze the sensitivity of these projections to changes in the underlying assumptions.

Harding also knew that his recommendation would have to include a pricing structure, including maturity and rate. Mickelson had based his projections on a 7-year term loan, although Harding thought he would be open to a different maturity. Harding expected that the treasury department would fund this loan as part of its portfolio rather than match it on a one-to-one basis, and therefore funding costs would reflect the estimated pooled cost of 7-year money (see Exhibit 6). He would also have to include the costs for servicing overhead, which included insurance, reserves, and closing.

Typically, Harding used a floating rate based on the U.S. Bank of Washington prime lending rate for a deal of this size, although he could also offer a fixed rate. It was also possible for Redhook to pay a higher up-front fee than the typical 1% in order to obtain a lower loan percentage rate. The actual rate finally offered Redhook would include a spread for bank profitability and would reflect Harding's assessment of the company's creditworthiness, the loan collateral, as well as the strengths and weaknesses of the deal.

Finally, the key covenants to be included in the deal would also need to be recommended. Typically, Harding included covenants that set restrictions on the company's leverage and its current ratios. He would also want to protect against spending on future capital improvements and perhaps restrict the salary withdrawal of the CEO and principal owner, Paul Shipman.

Harding had been pleased with his dealings with Redhook in the past. The bank was keen on developing its relationships with strong local businesses and on providing a full range of services to its credit customers. On the other hand, Redhook was entering a new market, and Harding needed to feel confident that the company could meet its projections. Further, the bank was concerned with improving asset quality and was reluctant to fund high-risk projects. While the economy in the Northwest was relatively strong, Harding also knew that the U.S. Bank was not completely insulated from problems in the banking industry and in the national economy.

EXHIBIT 1

Portfolio Composition as a Percentage of Average Consolidated Assets, All Insured Commercial Banks, 1985–1989

	1985	*1986*	*1987*	*1988*	*1989*
Interest-earning assets	86.05%	86.02%	86.62%	87.94%	87.84%
Loans	58.51	57.86	58.36	60.59	61.30
Commercial and industrial	22.26	20.96	20.04	19.55	19.20
Real estate	15.71	16.71	18.69	20.56	22.18
Construction	3.20	3.49	3.87	4.01	4.14
Farmland	.41	.43	.46	.49	.51
One- to four-family residential	7.20	7.31	8.00	9.03	9.94
Multifamily residential	.44	.49	.56	.58	.59
Nonfarm nonresidential	4.00	4.43	5.21	5.77	6.29
Consumer	10.80	11.06	11.10	11.31	11.40
Credit card	2.48	2.75	2.97	3.13	3.26
Installment and other	8.32	8.31	8.13	8.18	8.14
Foreign government	1.56	1.43	1.34	1.23	1.03
Agricultural production	1.51	1.22	1.03	.99	.96
Security	.83	.79	.63	.53	.54
Other	7.19	7.27	6.92	6.42	5.97
Securities	17.58	18.29	18.58	16.84	16.74
U.S. government	9.50	9.26	10.03	10.35	10.78
State and local government	6.99	7.49	6.25	3.69	3.14
Other bonds and stocks	1.08	1.55	2.29	2.80	2.82
Trading account assets	1.24	1.55	1.32	1.26	1.25
Gross federal funds sold and reverse repurchase agreements	4.43	4.72	4.43	4.26	4.20
Interest-bearing deposits	5.53%	5.15%	5.26%	4.99%	4.36%
Deposit liabilities	77.30%	76.72%	76.43%	76.22%	76.01%
In foreign offices	12.61	11.61	11.38	10.85	10.05
In domestic offices	64.69	65.11	65.06	65.37	65.96
Demand deposits	15.63	16.03	15.41	14.34	13.63
Other checkable deposits	4.57	5.21	6.01	6.27	6.16
MMDAs	11.72	12.64	12.32	11.44	10.55
Other savings	4.64	4.79	5.76	6.08	5.81
Small time deposits	16.67	15.68	14.95	16.16	18.15
Large time deposits	11.46	10.76	10.60	11.08	11.66
Gross federal funds purchased and repurchase agreements	7.68	8.25	8.06	7.72	7.95
Other liabilities for borrowed money	3.44	4.02	4.45	4.93	4.87
Other borrowings	5.70%	5.17%	4.90%	3.49%	3.39%
Memo					
Money market liabilities	35.19%	34.63%	34.49%	34.58%	34.53%
Loss reserves	.80	.92	1.36	1.54	1.50
Total equity capital	6.17%	6.21%	6.06%	6.10%	6.27%

Source: Federal Reserve Bulletin, July 1991.

EXHIBIT 2

Income and Expense as a Percentage of Average Net Consolidated Assets, All Insured Commercial Banks, 1985–1989[a]

Item	1985	1986	1987	1988	1989
Gross interest income	9.58%	8.50%	8.34%	8.95%	9.92%
Gross interest expense	6.08	5.11	4.95	5.42	6.41
Net interest margin	3.50	3.39	3.40	3.53	3.51
Non-interest income	1.20	1.28	1.41	1.47	1.55
Loss provisions	.68	.78	1.27	.54	.93
Other non-interest expense	3.17	3.22	3.30	3.33	3.37
Securities gains	.06	.14	.05	.01	.02
Income before tax	.90	.80	.28	1.14	.80
Taxes[b]	.21	.19	.18	.33	.31
Extraordinary items	.01	.01	.01	.03	.01
Net income	.70	.62	.11	.84	.51
Cash dividends declared	.33	.33	.36	.44	.44
Net retained earnings	.37	.29	(.25)	.40	.07

Memo

	1985	1986	1987	1988	1989
Net interest margin, taxable equivalent[c]	3.88%	3.79%	3.61%	3.78%	3.70%

Source: Federal Reserve Bulletin, July 1991.

a. Assets are fully consolidated and net of loss reserves.

b. Includes all taxes estimated to be due on income, extraordinary gains, and security gains.

c. For each bank with profits before tax greater than zero, income from tax-exempt state and local obligations was increased by $[t/(1 - t)]$ times the lesser of profits before tax or interest earned on tax-exempt obligations (t is the marginal federal income-tax rate). This adjustment approximates the equivalent pretax return on tax-exempt obligations.

EXHIBIT 3

Profit Rates, Insured Commercial Banks by Asset Size, 1985–1989 (percent)

Type of Return and Size of Bank[a]	1985	1986	1987	1988	1989
Return on Assets[b]					
	.70%	.62%	.11%	.84%	.51%
Less than $300 million	.74	.58	.63	.74	.88
$300 million to $5 billion	.83	.76	.58	.76	.74
$5 billion or more					
Money-center banks	.45	.46	(.86)	1.06	(.30)
Other	.74%	.68%	(.02)%	.82%	.58%
Return on Equity[c]					
	11.18%	9.97%	1.80%	13.52%	7.94%
Less than $300 million	9.19	7.21	7.76	8.89	10.32
$300 million to $5 billion	12.83	11.52	8.79	11.39	10.93
$5 billion or more					
Money-center banks	9.60	9.50	(19.46)	23.40	(6.17)
Other	13.56%	12.18%	(.28)%	15.16%	10.34%

Source: Federal Reserve Bulletin, July 1991.

a. Size categories are based on year-end fully consolidated assets.

b. Net income as a percentage of average fully consolidated assets net of loss reserves.

c. Net income as a percentage of average equity capital.

EXHIBIT 4
U.S. Bancorp and Subsidiaries Financial Statements:
Consolidated Balance Sheet (thousands of dollars)

	Years Ended December 31,		
	1987	1988	1989
Assets			
Interest-earning assets:			
Money market investments	$ 1,150,894	$ 623,228	$ 484,095
Investment securities (market value 1989–$2,221,124; 1988–$1,541,142)	1,440,600	1,565,887	2,211,898
Trading account securities	—	79,816	121,800
Mortgages held for sale	42,447	78,363	214,048
Loans, net of unearned income[a]	8,668,730	9,676,101	11,409,464
Total interest-earning assets	$11,302,671	$12,023,375	$14,441,305
Allowance for loan losses	(113,387)	(126,227)	(153,557)
Cash and due from banks	1,115,091	1,261,763	1,324,717
Premises, furniture and equipment	270,547	280,596	283,219
Other real estate owned	74,881	64,003	47,892
Customers' liability on acceptances	321,966	371,015	413,039
Other assets	380,917	508,877	618,767
Total assets	$13,352,686	$14,383,402	$16,975,382
Liabilities			
Interest-bearing liabilities:			
Deposits	$ 7,416,651	$ 7,844,640	$ 9,002,799
Federal funds purchased and security repurchase agreements	1,470,232	1,603,546	2,570,281
Commercial paper	284,721	279,989	406,174
Other short-term borrowings	205,134	195,506	278,635
Long-term debt	475,545	624,770	602,975
Total interest-bearing liabilities	$ 9,852,283	$10,548,451	$12,860,864
Non-interest-bearing deposits	2,104,894	2,323,090	2,429,387
Accrued income taxes	97,573	56,861	55,645
Acceptances outstanding	321,966	371,015	413,039
Other liabilities	118,452	140,158	162,706
Total liabiltiies	$12,495,168	$13,439,575	$15,921,641
Shareholders' Equity			
Preferred stock	—	—	—
Common stock	$ 205,888	$ 206,777	$ 249,475
Capital surplus	145,826	148,474	361,447
Retained earnings	321,966	590,720	444,922
Less treasury stock	(2,045)	(2,144)	(2,103)
Total shareholders' equity	$ 857,518	$ 943,827	$ 1,053,741
Total liabiltiies and shareholders' equity	$13,352,686	$14,383,402	$16,975,382

a. U.S. Bancorp's loan portfolio consists of the following loans:

	Years Ended December 31,		
	1987	1988	1989
Commercial	$4,653.1	$5,256.6	$6,371.2
Real estate construct	488.4	630.1	765.2
Real estate mortgage	1,374.8	1,563.2	1,762.5
Consumer	1,867.0	1,944.4	2,117.6
Foreign	16.6	22.6	37.5
Lease financing	$ 268.8	$ 259.2	$ 355.5

(continued)

EXHIBIT 4 *(concluded)*
U.S. Bancorp and Subsidiaries Financial Statements:
Statement of Consolidated Income and Operations Data (thousands of dollars except per share data)

	Years Ended December 31,		
	1987	*1988*	*1989*
Interest income	$976,782	$1,162,964	$1,436,516
Interest expense	529,428	635,483	832,932
Net interest income	$447,354	$ 527,481	$ 603,584
Provision for loan losses	57,430	69,204	83,765
Net interest income after provision for loan losses	$389,924	$ 458,277	$ 519,819
Non-interest revenue	$177,074	$ 217,590	$ 235,517
Non-interest expense	428,739	503,149	544,169
Income before income taxes and accounting changes	$138,259	$ 172,718	$ 211,167
Provision for income taxes	38,621	48,805	60,385
Income before accounting changes	$ 99,638	$ 123,913	$ 150,782
Cumulative effect of accounting changes	8,834	–	–
Net income	$108,472	$ 123,913	$ 150,782
Average number of shares outstanding	49,064	49,237	49,498
Earnings per share			
Before accounting changes	$ 2.03	$ 2.52	$ 3.05
Net income	2.21	2.52	3.05
Dividends per share	.58	.80	.89

	Years Ended December 31,				
	1985	*1986*	*1987*	*1988*	*1989*
Return on average assets	0.81%	0.69%	0.90%	0.92%	1.00%
Return on average equity	11.74	10.12	13.39	13.78	15.12
Equity/Assets	6.65	6.44	6.42	6.56	6.21
Net interest margin	4.80	4.70	4.78	4.87	4.96
Total nonperforming assets as a % of loans outstanding and other real estate owned	3.50	2.60	2.50	2.30	1.70
Allowance for loan losses to year-end loans outstanding	1.13	1.31	1.31	1.30	1.35
Net charge-offs to average loans outstanding	.56%	1.22%	.71%	.64%	.55%

Source: U.S. Bancorp annual reports, 1988 and 1989.

EXHIBIT 5

U.S. Bancorp Average Balances and Tax-Equivalent Net Interest Margin for Years Ending December 31, 1988 and 1989 (millions of dollars)

	1988			1989		
	Average Balance	*Income/ Expense*	*Average Rates Earned/ Paid*	*Average Balance*	*Income/ Expense*	*Average Rates Earned/ Paid*
Interest-Earning Assets						
Money market investments	$ 801.1	$ 61.7	7.70%	$ 437.5	$ 41.5	9.48%
Investments securities	1,436.5	123.8	8.62	1,734.4	157.1	9.06
Trading account securities	84.7	6.8	8.06	134.8	12.1	8.95
Mortgage loans held for sale	49.9	4.9	9.75	115.3	11.4	9.90
Loans, net of unearned income						
Commercial	4,955.2	507.0	10.23	5,696.5	656.1	11.52
Real estate	1,979.3	193.1	9.76	2,373.2	245.4	10.34
Consumer	1,866.0	230.5	12.35	2,062.4	265.4	12.87
Foreign	22.7	2.0	8.95	24.5	3.0	12.41
Lease financing	252.5	20.3	8.04	276.9	25.4	9.16
Total loans	9,075.7	952.9	10.50	10,433.5	1,195.3	11.96
Loan fees		42.4			52.9	
Total loans including fees	9,075.7	995.3	10.97	10,433.5	1,248.2	11.96
Total interest-earning assets/interest income	$11,447.9	$1,192.5	10.42%	$12,855.5	$1,470.3	11.44%
Interest-Bearing Liabilities						
Deposits						
Savings and interest checking	$ 2,142.0	$ 97.2	4.54%	$ 2,197.8	$ 99.7	4.54%
Money market accounts	1,774.7	87.4	4.92	1,493.0	79.2	5.31
Time, $100 thousand or more	1,047.6	76.2	7.27	1,388.4	123.5	8.89
Other time	2,616.9	186.7	7.14	3,329.9	269.8	8.10
Foreign	—	—	—	—	—	—
Total interest-bearing deposits	7,581.2	447.5	5.90	8,409.1	572.2	6.80
Federal funds purchased and security						
repurchase agreements	1,311.6	97.2	7.41	1,642.5	149.3	9.09
Commercial paper	312.3	24.4	7.81	361.2	33.8	9.35
Other short-term borrowings	200.8	15.5	7.72	252.6	22.6	8.96
Long-term debt	556.7	50.9	9.14	587.7	55.0	9.36
Total interest-bearing liabilities/interest expense	$ 9,962.6	$ 635.5	6.38%	$11,253.1	$ 832.9	7.40%
Non-interest-bearing deposits	$ 2,022.5			$ 2,157.8		
Average rate earned on interest-earning assets			10.42%			11.44%
Cost of funds supporting earning assets			5.55			6.48
Net interest income and margin		$ 557.0	4.87%		$ 637.4	4.96%

Source: U.S. Bancorp annual report, 1989.

Note: Loans on nonaccrual status have been included in the computation of average balances; incremental tax rate used is 37.6% in 1989 and 40.5% in 1988.

EXHIBIT 6
Key Money Rates

	8/31/89	8/31/90
Prime rate	10.50%	10.00%
Federal funds[a]	8.875	8.018
3-month T-bills	8.12	7.46
7-year Treasury notes	8.29	8.79
3-month certificates of deposit[a]	8.79	8.04
3-month commercial paper	8.69	7.96
Merrill Lynch money market fund[b]	7.96	7.59

a. Secondary market.

b. Average rate of return after expenses for past 30-day period.

Appendix

The Redhook Ale Brewery File

Summary of Credit Lines/Loans

Line #1

Line #1: $6,500,000. New request.

Purpose: To build a 100,000-barrel brewery in western Washington and a 25,000-barrel brewery in northern California.

Source of payment: Profits/cash flow (see Exhibit A2 for projections).

Fee/rate: To be determined.

Terms of payment: To be determined.

Collateral: (in thousands)

100,000-barrel brewery in western Washington	
Brewhouse:	
Plant	$ 2,500
Installation	350
Filtration	125
	$ 2,975
Equipment:	
Fermentation tanks (20 @ $50,000)	$ 1,000
Malt system	300
Boiler	150
Refrigeration	750
Keg system	1,000
Bottling line	1,300
Hot/Cold water tanks	100
Leasehold improvements	350
	$ 4,950

(continued)

25,000-barrel brewery in northern California

Brewhouse:

Plant	$ 1,250
Installation	250
	$ 1,500

Equipment:

Fermentation tanks (20 @ $50,000)	$ 350
Malt system	110
Boiler	87
Refrigeration	225
Keg system	750
Bottling line	835
Hot/Cold water tanks	60
Leasehold improvements	250
	$ 2,667
Existing equipment, net of depreciation	$ 2,465
Less existing loans	(800)
Total collateral	$13,757

Other costs to build, as estimated by Redhook Management, include:

100,000-barrel brewery in western Washington

Miscellaneous soft costs	$300
Sales tax	650
Contingency	887

25,000-barrel brewery in northern California

Miscellaneous soft costs	$200
Sales tax	392
Contingency	476

Other: Estimated timing of payments for the planned construction:

Date	Brewing Equipment	Furniture and Fixtures	Trucks	Leasehold Improvements
July 1991	$ 2,730,000			
June 1992	2,077,950			$200,000
September 1992	6,660,000			200,000
November 1992		$200,000		
December 1992	2,030,000			200,000
January 1993			$100,000	
April 1993	600,000			
	$14,097,950	$200,000	$100,000	$600,000

Line #2

Line #2: $500,000.

Purpose: Operating line on a transaction basis to supplement cash flow requirements.

Source of payment: Sale of inventory and collection of receivables.

Fee/rate: .25% initiation fee ($250). Interest floating rate tied to U.S. Bank of Washington prime.

Terms of payment: Revolving line note on demand.

Collateral: Supported by perfected security interest in inventory and accounts receivable.

Explanation: This line is expected to have limited usage; it was not used at all in 1989. It will be nonformula based and transactional; used only for special purposes of hops, packaging, glass, or labels; and would be short-term in nature (i.e., 30 to 90 days).

Line #3

Line #3: $805,000.

Purpose: Provided financing to build the Fremont brewing facility and brewpub.

Source of payment: Profits and cash flow.

Fee/rate: Interest floating rate based on U.S. Bank of Washington prime plus 1%, adjusted annually in January (currently 11.5%).

Terms of payment: Interest payable monthly. Amortized over 7 years, with balloon payment at maturity on December 7, 1995. Payments currently $15,635/month.

Collateral: Supported by all of the company's equipment and leasehold improvements.

Other: Requires a debt-to-net-worth ratio of 1.25:1.

Other Important Information

Bank History/Relationship: Redhook has been a customer since 1987. Redhook utilizes depository and bank-card services.

Ownership: Redhook is owned by a group of 30 individuals, holding approximately 34,000 shares. Six individuals, five of whom are on the board of directors, own 65% of the shares.

Key People:

- Paul Shipman, cofounder, president, and CEO. After earning his MBA from the University of Virginia Darden School of Business in 1978, Mr. Shipman went to work as a strategic planner for Chateau Ste. Michelle winery outside of Seattle, Washington.

- Gordon Bowker, secretary, director, and cofounder. Mr. Bowker is an entrepreneur. He has founded multiple companies in the Seattle area. He is the founder and chairman of Starbucks Coffee Company and a director of Sasquatch Publishing.

- Pamela Hinckley, marketing manager. Ms. Hinckley has 11 years of experience in the hospitality and alcoholic beverage industry. This experience includes employment with De Laurenti as a manager for specialty beer and wine procurement.

- David Mickelson, treasurer and CFO. Mr. Mickelson graduated from the University of Washington in 1981 and joined Barclays Bank PLC in Seattle. He began as a credit analyst and was promoted to assistant treasurer and later marketing director. After leaving Barclays in 1985, Mickelson joined Certified Foods, Inc. as its controller.

- Allen Triplett, brewmaster and operations manager. Mr. Triplett's management experience includes working as an oil-drilling supervisor. He has pursued microbiological studies at U.C. Davis' Seibel Institute.

EXHIBIT A1
Redhook Ale Brewery Historical Financial Statements: Profit and Loss

	Year Ended December 31,							
	1982	*1983*	*1984*	*1985*	*1986*	*1987*	*1988*[a]	*1989*
Sales, net of beer taxes	$ 59,345	$259,594	$318,093	$488,151	$702,690	$1,082,589	$1,680,174	$ 2,676,109
Cost of goods sold[b]	67,644	186,962	187,322	250,335	362,766	546,231	1,002,180	1,807,518
Gross profit	(8,299)	72,632	130,771	237,816	339,924	536,358	677,994	868,591
Selling, general, and administrative expenses	150,189	128,222	131,705	168,541	218,234	286,567	520,079	607,148
	(158,488)	(55,590)	(934)	69,275	121,690	249,791	157,915	261,443
Other income (expenses)								
Interest income	9,062	0	18	1,953	505	24,250	14,032	1,724
Interest expense	(699)	(13,155)	(18,526)	(12,502)	(9,054)	(25,646)	(53,863)	(122,211)
Loss on sale of equipment								(9,824)
Other	36	(27)						(7,500)
Income before taxes	(150,089)	(68,772)	(19,442)	58,726	113,141	248,395	118,084	123,632
Income taxes								
Current	0	0	0	0	0	51,018	18,577	46,642
Deferred credit	0	0	0	0	29,132	(6,151)	(12,033)	(27,000)
Net income	$(150,089)	$(68,772)	$(19,442)	$ 58,726	$ 84,009	$ 203,528	$ 111,540	$ 103,990

a. Redhook commenced operations at the Fremont brewery in October 1988. Annual brewing capacity increased from 8,000 to 40,000 barrels.

b. Cost of goods sold includes direct costs, defined as beginning inventory, plus purchases, less ending inventory, and an allocation of fixed expenses. Thus as production volumes neared capacity, total COGS generally increased at a slower rate. COGS can be broken down as follows for 1987–1989:

	1987	*1988*	*1989*
Beginning inventories	$ 28,141	$ 65,419	$ 160,125
Salaries, wages, and taxes	159,084	165,843	282,520
Employee benefits	7,027	13,770	22,700
Professional fees	5,000	5,000	3,903
Rent and common area expense	30,720	94,916	176,891
Real and personal property taxes	5,970	6,392	10,150
Utilities	19,160	39,765	66,746
Insurance	7,734	10,273	16,847
Depreciation	37,127	153,159	252,172
Repairs and maintenance	7,343	7,426	20,581
Purchases	257,795	448,589	717,952
Purchases-promotional items	20,491	29,402	41,029
Brewery supplies and expense	26,058	69,419	90,881
Pub salaries	—	22,982	112,220
Pub operating expenses	—	29,950	102,496
	611,650	1,162,305	2,077,213
Less ending inventories	65,419	160,125	269,695
Cost of goods sold	$546,231	$1,002,180	$1,807,518

(continued)

EXHIBIT A1 (*continued*)
Redhook Ale Brewery Historical Financial Statements: Balance Sheet

					Year Ended December 31,			
	1982	*1983*	*1984*	*1985*	*1986*	*1987*	*1988*b	*1989*
Current assets								
Cash and equivalents	$ 9,151	$ 35,018	$ 28,035	$ 34,583	$ 69,614	$ 192,182	$ 95,220	$ 141,952
Receivables, net	10,866	14,698	14,410	25,781	33,361	57,598	95,157	66,381
Inventories	14,642	13,496	18,565	27,844	28,141	65,419	160,125	269,695
Prepaid expenses	0	0	0	0	1,107	1,591	12,147	4,268
Refundable taxes	0	0	0	0	0	0	15,694	0
Employee advances	0	0	0	0	0	0	1,552	0
Total current assets	$ 34,659	$ 63,212	$ 61,010	$ 88,208	$132,223	$ 316,790	$ 379,895	$ 482,296
Equipment and leasehold improvements, net	248,127	305,412	324,061	348,458	552,873	1,018,673	2,568,011	2,465,374
Other assets	10,386	9,552	8,828	5,864	5,089	565,576a	41,823	16,888
Total assets	$293,172	$378,176	$393,899	$442,530	$690,185	$1,901,039	$2,989,729	$2,964,858
Accounts payable	$ 30,997	$ 8,693	$ 8,552	$ 2,334	$ 19,713	$ 36,932	$ 249,233	$ 116,622
Accrued salaries, wages, and payroll taxes	10,025	5,924	5,408	7,048	13,361	3,722	5,403	6,747
Accrued taxes	3,840	8,430	8,976	12,412	15,226	19,575	46,244	37,525
Deposits on kegs and neons	14,040	50,732	45,917	61,107	71,435	79,914	92,664	97,410
Other deposits	0	0	0	0	0	0	64,920	0
Accrued interest	330	260	375	765	974	1,769	3,949	5,753
Taxes payable	0	0	0	0	0	51,018	0	22,917
Deferred revenue	0	0	0	0	0	1,666	3,067	2,976
Note payable to individual	0	0	0	0	0	0	0	7,500
Current portion of long-term debt	0	32,000	40,750	24,635	40,200	177,624	93,924	104,785
Current portion of capitalized leases	0	0	0	0	0	0	0	5,950
Other	1,208	2,025	2,700	3,375	4,049			
Current liabilities	60,440	108,064	112,678	111,676	164,958	372,220	559,404	408,185
Long-term debt, less current portion	32,000	132,000	66,250	60,532	150,603	35,932	852,519	849,873
Capital lease obligation, less current portion	0	0	0	0	0	0	0	19,561
Deferred rent payable	0	0	0	0	0	0	37,260	53,351
Deferred taxes	10,870	10,123	7,424	4,049	29,132	74,829	10,948	0
Shareholders' Equity								
Common stock, $1.00 par value authorized 50,000 shares, issued and outstanding, 34,904 shares	20,915	21,104	22,904	22,904	22,904	34,904	34,904	34,904
Paid-in capital	365,442	372,152	469,352	469,352	469,352	1,326,390	1,326,390	1,326,390
Retained earnings	(196,495)	(265,267)	(284,709)	(225,983)	(146,764)	56,764	168,304	272,294
	189,862	127,989	207,547	266,273	345,492	1,418,058	1,529,598	1,633,588
	$293,172	$378,176	$393,899	$442,530	$690,185	$1,901,039	$2,989,729	$2,964,558

Note: Redhook currently has no contingent liabilities.

a. Includes $547,768 restricted for equipment acquisitions.

b. Redhook commenced operations at the Fremont brewery in October 1988.

(continued)

EXHIBIT A1 *(concluded)*
Redhook Ale Brewery Historical Financial Statements: Recent Financial Performance

Income Statement[a]

Sales, net of beer taxes	$2,867,442
Cost of goods sold	1,708,961
Gross profit	1,158,481
Selling, general and administrative expense	637,510
Net operating income	520,970
Interest income	9,052
Purchase discounts	2,560
Interest expense	80,406
Income before income taxes	452,177
Income tax expense	153,740
Net income	$ 298,436

Balance Sheet Data[b]

Current assets	$ 782,396
Other assets	106,869
Net equipment and improvements	2,349,311
Total assets	$3,238,576
Current liabilities	$ 490,141
Long-term debt	781,566
Other liabilities	69,044
	1,340,752
Total shareholders' equity	1,897,824
	$3,238,576

a. For the nine months ended September 30, 1990.

b. As of September 30, 1990.

EXHIBIT A2

Redhook Ale Brewery Projected Financial Statements: Profit and Loss

	Year Ended December 31,				
	1990	*1991*	*1992*	*1993*	*1994*
Revenues					
Beer sales					
Draft Ale	$1,233,000	$1,548,900	$1,989,200	$ 2,259,500	$ 2,402,750
Draft Lager				1,205,100	2,166,750
Bottled Ale	2,087,500	3,193,750	4,759,500	5,678,500	6,577,500
Bottled Lager				7,536,000	16,987,400
Trolleyman	480,000	480,000	490,000	490,000	500,000
Gross sales	3,800,500	5,222,650	7,238,700	17,169,100	28,634,400
Less beer taxes	240,793	336,128	461,380	1,328,007	2,174,617
Net sales	3,559,707	4,886,522	6,777,320	15,841,093	26,459,783
Direct cost of goods sold	925,524	1,221,630	1,626,557	3,960,273	6,614,946
Other	1,336,866	1,477,176	1,667,795	4,870,894	5,545,648
Gross profit	$1,297,317	$2,187,716	$3,482,968	$ 7,009,926	$14,299,189
Expenses					
Selling and marketing expense	280,157	381,063	493,250	1,533,086	2,106,150
General and administrative expense	522,601	674,360	834,593	1,371,525	1,863,322
Total operating expenses	$ 802,758	$1,055,423	$1,327,843	$ 2,904,611	$ 3,969,472
Net operating income	494,559	1,132,293	2,155,125	4,105,315	10,329,717
Interest income	306,138	663,561	409,549	4,842	126,742
Earnings before interest and taxes	800,697	1,795,855	2,564,674	4,110,157	10,456,459
Interest expense	110,934	95,079	203,982	771,536	600,332
Income before income taxes	$ 689,763	$1,700,776	$2,360,692	$ 3,338,621	$ 9,856,127
Income taxes	234,519	578,264	802,635	1,135,131	3,351,083
Net income	$ 455,243	$1,122,512	$1,558,057	$ 2,203,490	$ 6,505,044

(continued)

EXHIBIT A2 *(continued)*
Redhook Ale Brewery Projected Financial Statements: Balance Sheet

	Year Ended December 31,				
	1990	*1991*	*1992*	*1993*	*1994*
Assets					
Current assets					
Cash	$ 50,000	$ 50,000	$ 3,057	$ 50,000	$ 50,000
Short-term investments	4,358,209	3,821,464	0	726,327	5,609,474
Accounts receivable, net	214,229	306,788	437,371	1,327,492	2,408,266
Inventory..................	428,457	613,577	874,742	2,084,912	3,567,349
Total current assets	$5,050,895	$4,791,830	$ 1,315,169	$ 4,188,730	$11,635,090
Intangible assets, net	132,159	102,251	72,343	54,435	22,985
Deposits...................	1,000,000	0	0	0	0
Equipment and leasehold improvements	2,989,160	2,989,160	3,789,160	17,987,110	17,987,110
Less accumulated depreciation	823,126	1,122,466	1,431,568	2,896,826	4,214,737
Net equipment and leasehold improvements	2,166,034	1,866,694	2,357,592	15,090,284	13,772,373
Plus construction in progress	0	2,730,000	13,497,950	0	0
Total equipment and leasehold improvements	2,166,034	4,596,694	15,855,542	15,090,284	13,772,373
Total assets	$8,349,088	$9,490,775	$17,243,055	$19,333,450	$25,430,448
Current Liabilities					
Accounts payable	$ 214,229	$ 306,788	$ 437,371	$ 1,042,456	$ 1,783,675
Accrued liabilities	3,880	4,342	4,430	8,730	14,330
Deposits on kegs and neon lights ..	128,160	158,880	201,720	212,940	294,240
Federal income taxes payable	44,799	67,402	69,734	134,451	374,027
Current portion—long-term debt ...	129,669	146,620	158,418	175,740	196,557
Total current liabilities	$ 520,737	$ 684,031	$ 871,673	$ 1,574,317	$ 2,662,829
New term debt	0	0	6,165,000	5,525,000	4,225,000
Other long-term obligations	861,689	732,019	585,400	426,983	251,243
Total long-term debt	861,689	732,019	6,750,400	5,951,983	4,476,243
Less current portion	129,669	146,620	158,418	175,740	196,557
Net long-term debt	732,019	585,400	6,591,981	5,776,243	4,279,686
Other liabilities	7,500	10,000	10,000	10,000	10,000
Stockholders' Equity					
Preferred stock	0	0	0	0	0
Common stock	6,361,294	6,361,294	6,361,294	6,361,294	6,361,294
Retained earnings	727,537	1,850,049	3,408,106	5,611,596	12,116,639
Total equity..................	$7,088,831	$8,211,343	$ 9,769,400	$11,972,890	$18,477,933
Total liabilities and stockholders' equity	$8,349,088	$9,490,775	$17,243,055	$19,333,450	$25,430,448

(continued)

EXHIBIT A2 *(concluded)*
Redhook Ale Brewery Projected Financial Statements

Assumptions

---

1. In recent experience, 12% of sales were generated in cash on the premises of the Trolleyman Pub. Over 25% of sales were earned in a 50-square-mile area around North Seattle and paid for upon delivery in cash or check as required by Washington state law. The remaining sales were paid in cash or became accounts receivable. Accounts receivable turnover averaged 20 days. A 30-day aging of accounts receivable is assumed once lager sales commence.
   A shift in the composition of sales, from the current 45% bottles and 55% draft to 75–80% bottles and the remaining 20–25% in draft, over the next few years was forecast. Bottle sales generated a higher contribution per barrel.
2. Costs were projected to remain relatively stable with gross margins improving as the Fremont brewery reached capacity. Direct costs of goods sold were defined as beginning inventory plus purchases less ending inventory. The remainder of COGS was an allocation of fixed expenses. Thus, as production volume increased and a brewery neared capacity, gross COGS generally increased at a slower rate.
3. Redhook carried on average 40 days' sales as inventory. Raw materials could be converted to finished goods in 10 days and were paid for within 30 days. Accounts payable on average turned over every 20 days.
4. Depreciation charges on brewery equipment, trucks, and leasehold improvements were included in COGS expense. Depreciation of furniture and fixtures was included in selling, general, and administrative expense. No depreciation was expensed until new assets were fully paid for. Projected depreciation expense was $293,640 in 1990 and 1991; $303,402 in 1992; $1,459,557 in 1993; and $1,312,211 in 1994. Projected amortization expense was $21,608 in 1990; $35,608 in 1991 and 1992; $38,608 in 1993; and $37,150 in 1994.
5. On December 31, 1989, the other asset account included net intangible assets as well as an $800 deposit and $8,021 of deferred taxes. Intangible assets include capitalized fees and trademarks. In fiscal year 1990 capitalized fees increased $140,000 and deferred taxes decreased $8,021. The net effect on cash flow in 1990 from the other asset account, including the $1 million equipment deposit paid on October 1, 1990, was a decrease of $1,131,179. It was projected that in 1993, $15,000 was paid to acquire trademarks.
6. Selling and marketing expenses show a dramatic increase in 1993 and 1994, reflecting the rollout of the company's lager product.
7. New Term Debt was expected to have a 7-year term with principal amortization over the term of the loan, with interest expense calculated at 11.5%.
8. Tax payments were figured at a flat 34% rate.
9. The successful placement of $5 million in new common stock is assumed to have taken place in September 1990.

Part II

Long-Term Financing and Liability Management

Continential Carriers, Inc.

In May 1988, Elizabeth Thorp, treasurer of Continental Carriers, Inc. (CCI), was considering the advantages and disadvantages of several alternative methods of financing CCI's acquisition of Midland Freight, Inc. At a recent meeting of the board of directors, there had been substantial disagreement as to the best method of financing the acquisition. After the meeting, Ms. Thorp had been asked by John Evans, president of CCI, to assess the arguments presented by the various directors and to outline a position to be taken by management at the June directors' meeting.

CCI was a regulated general commodities motor carrier whose routes ran the length of the Pacific Coast, from Oregon and California to the industrial Midwest, and from Chicago to several points in Texas. Founded in 1952 by three brothers, the firm had experienced little growth until the mid-1970s. At that point, Mr. Evans joined the firm as president, after many years as an executive of a major eastern carrier. Mr. Evans first concentrated his efforts on expanding CCI's revenues on existing routes through an intensive marketing effort and a renewed emphasis on improving service. In 1982, utilizing the proceeds of CCI's initial public offering of common stock, Mr. Evans began a program designed to reduce operating costs through a combination of extensive computerization of operations and improvement in terminal facilities. As a result of these changes, CCI had become a large and profitable concern, widely respected in the industry for its aggressive management.

By 1988, Mr. Evans and the directors of the firm had concluded that the key to continued expansion in revenues and income was a policy of selected acquisitions. After a study of potential candidates for acquisition, negotiations began with Midland Freight, Inc., a common carrier serving Michigan and Indiana from Chicago. The owners of Midland agreed to sell the firm to CCI for $50 million in cash. Mr. Evans felt that Midland was an outstanding acquisition in that it would expand CCI's route system and seemed well suited for the type of marketing and cost-reduction programs that had fostered CCI's growth. The board had unanimously approved the merger.

CCI's lawyers felt that no difficulty would be encountered in gaining the approval of the Interstate Commerce Commission for the merger, and the closing date for the acquisition was set for October 1, 1988. Mr. Evans realized that the funds for the Midland acquisition would have to be raised from outside sources. Given that Midland would add $8.4 million in earnings before interest and taxes (EBIT) to CCI on an annual basis, he felt that such external financing would not be difficult to obtain.

CCI's management had followed a consistent policy of avoiding long-term debt. The company had met its needs through use of retained earnings supplemented with the proceeds of the 1982 stock offering and infrequent short-term bank loans. As of 1988, CCI's capitalization consisted of common stock and surplus with no fixed debt of any kind. Most of the common stock was held by management. Ownership of the stock was widely distributed, and there was no real dominant interest other than management. The shares were traded infrequently in the over-the-counter market. Discussions with an investment banker led Ms. Thorp to believe that, barring a major market decline, new common stock could be sold to the public at $17.75 per share. After underwriting fees and expenses, the net proceeds to the company would be $16.75 per share. Thus, if common stock were used, the acquisition would require issuance of 3 million new shares.

For the past few years, Ms. Thorp and Mr. Evans had been disappointed in the market performance of CCI's common stock (see Exhibit 1). Thus, they decided to reconsider the firm's policy of avoiding long-term debt (see Exhibit 2). It was felt that such a change might be justified by the anticipated stability of CCI's future earnings. Ms. Thorp had determined that the firm could sell $50 million in bonds to a California insurance company. The interest rate on these bonds would be 10%, and they would mature in 15 years. An annual sinking fund of $2.5 million would be required, leaving $12.5 million outstanding at maturity. Although the bond terms would create a sizable need for cash, Ms. Thorp felt that they were the best that could be obtained.

In addition, Ms. Thorp had calculated that, given the tax deductibility of bond interest and CCI's current marginal tax rate of 40% (34% federal corporate income tax; 9% deductible state and local corporate income taxes), the 10% rate was the equivalent of 6% on an after-tax basis. In contrast, she thought the stock at $16.75 per share and a dividend of $1.50 per share would cost CCI nearly 9%. This cost comparison made the debt alternative seem desirable to Ms. Thorp.

At the May directors' meeting, the Midland acquisition received enthusiastic approval. Ms. Thorp then decided to sound out the board's opinions regarding the possibility of financing the acquisition with long-term debt rather than with common stock. She presented the foregoing cost calculations. To her concern, an acrimonious debate broke out among the directors concerning financing policy.

Ms. Thorp was immediately questioned as to the cost of the debt issue, since her figures did not include the annual payment to the sinking fund. One director argued that this represented 8% of the average size of the bond issue over its 15-year life, and he felt that the stock issue had a smaller cost than the bonds. In addition, he emphasized the cash outlay required by the bond alternative and the $12.5 million maturity, especially in view of CCI's already existing lease commitments. He felt that the use of debt added considerable risk to the company, making the common stock more speculative and causing greater variation in market price.

Another director argued for the issuance of common stock because "simple arithmetic" showed that CCI would net 10%, or $5 million, per year after taxes from the acquisition. Yet, if an additional 3 million shares of common stock were sold, the dividend requirements, at the current rate of $1.50 per share, would be only $4.5

million per year. Since management was not considering raising the dividend rate, she could not see how the sale of the common stock would hurt the interests of present stockholders. Further, if there were any immediate sacrifice by existing shareholders, she argued, it would be overcome as expansion of the firm continued. Under these circumstances, she argued, the bond issue should be rejected, given the cash demands it would place on the firm.

On the other hand, one director became very agitated in arguing that the stock was a "steal" at $17.75 per share. He pointed out that CCI's policy of retaining earnings had built the book value of the firm to $45.00 per share as of December 1987. In addition, he felt that the true value of the company was understated, since the book value of CCI's assets was considerably below current replacement cost. This director was also worried by the substantial dilution of management's voting control of CCI that was implicit in the 3-million-share offering. Thus, he concluded, the sale of common stock at this time would be a "gift" to new shareholders of the substantial value held by current stockholders.

Two directors agreed that sale of stock would dilute the stock's value, but they measured this dilution in terms of earnings per share instead of book or replacement value. These directors anticipated that postacquisition earnings would equal $34 million before interest and taxes. If common stock were sold, earnings per share would be diluted to $2.72. In contrast, they argued, the sole use of debt would increase earnings per share to $3.87. The two directors felt that it was not important that the sinking fund equaled $.56 per share each year.

Finally, a director mentioned some personal observations he had made about financing in the trucking industry. First, he noted that CCI was one of the few major common carriers that had no long-term debt in their capital structures, while CCI's price-earnings ratio was among the lowest in the industry. Second, he wondered whether Ms. Thorp had given consideration to the possibility of issuing preferred stock. This director had determined that CCI could sell 500,000 shares of preferred stock bearing a dividend rate of $10.50 per share and a par value of $100. The director criticized Ms. Thorp for failing to deal with the issues he had raised.

This debate had caused the directors' meeting to run over its scheduled conclusion, and no signs of agreement had developed. Ms. Thorp asked that the discussion of financing alternatives be held over until the June meeting to allow her time to prepare additional material. Now, as the date for the meeting approached, Ms. Thorp once again turned her attention to the issues raised at the board meeting. She realized that a considerable number of issues raised by the directors needed to be considered, and she designed a chart to aid in the comparison of the debt and stock alternatives (Exhibit 3).

EXHIBIT 1

Selected Income and Dividend Data, 1982–1988 (thousands of dollars except per share data)

	Operating Revenue	Income before Taxes	Income after Taxes	Income per Share	Dividends per Share	Market Prices per Share of Common Stock	
						High	Low
1982	$ 630,000	$14,490	$ 7,245	$1.61	$1.00	16¼	11¼
1983	693,750	16,650	8,325	1.85	1.15	19	14¾
1984	737,305	19,170	9,585	2.13	1.25	20⅛	15
1985	858,460	22,320	11,160	2.48	1.25	23¾	17⅜
1986	926,665	25,020	12,510	2.78	1.25	27⅝	22¼
1987	1,028,570	28,800	15,725	3.49	1.50	25	18½
1988 est.[a]	1,080,000	25,600	15,360	3.41	1.50[b]	20[c]	16⅜[c]

a. Excluding the proposed acquisition and its financing.

b. Annual rate.

c. To May 1 (May 1 prices were 18⅞–19⅛).

EXHIBIT 2

Summary Balance Sheet at December 31, 1987
(thousands of dollars)

Cash	$ 19,000
Accounts receivable	38,450
Inventory	8,100
Prepaid expenses	9,100
Current assets	74,650
Carrier operating property (cost)	236,650
Less: Accumulated depreciation	89,100
Net carrier operating property	147,550
Other assets	30,900
Total assets	$253,100
Accounts payable	$ 25,300
Miscellaneous payables and accruals	20,250
Taxes payable	5,050
Current liabilities	50,600
Common stock ($1 par)	4,500
Paid-in surplus	40,000
Retained earnings	158,000
Stockholders' equity	202,500
Total liabilities and stockholders' equity	$253,100

EXHIBIT 3
Analysis of Financial Alternatives

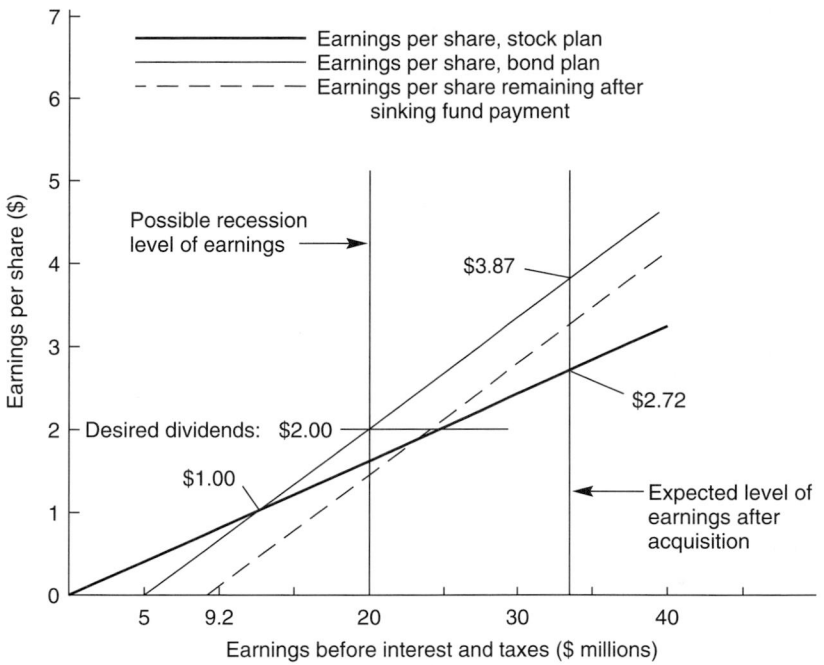

Calculation of Points to Determine Lines (thousands of dollars except per share data)

	Bonds	*Stock*	*Bonds*	*Stock*
EBIT	$12,500	$12,500	$34,000	$34,000
Interest, 1st year	5,000	—	5,000	—
Taxable earnings	7,500	12,500	29,000	34,000
Tax at 40%	3,000	5,000	11,600	13,600
After-tax earnings	4,500	7,500	17,400	20,400
Earnings per share				
÷ 4,500,000	$ 1.00	—	$ 3.87	—
÷ 7,500,000	—	$ 1.00	—	$ 2.72
Annual sinking fund	$ 2,500	—	$ 2,500	—

Note: The effects of leverage and dillution are indicated by the differing slopes of the lines, and can be expressed: "For each million dollar change of EBIT, the bond plan brings a change in earnings per share that is $.0535 greater than the stock plan. Leverage is favorable from EBIT of $12.5 million upward."

E. I. du Pont de Nemours and Company (1983)

In early 1983, the management of E. I. du Pont de Nemours and Company (Du Pont) looked back on two decades of turbulence in the firm's operations. Difficulties in the 1970s and the mega-merger with Conoco had led the company to abandon its long-held policy of an all-equity capital structure. Following the Conoco acquisition in 1981, Du Pont's ratio of debt to total capital had peaked at 42%—the highest in the firm's history. The rapid escalation in financial leverage had cost Du Pont its cherished AAA bond rating. Du Pont had not regained the top rating despite a reduction in debt to 36% of capital by the end of 1982.

The operations of Du Pont had changed dramatically in the past 20 years. With the task of digesting Conoco underway, management faced an important financial policy decision—determining a capital structure policy appropriate for Du Pont in the 1980s. This decision would have implications for Du Pont's financial performance and possibly for its competitive position as well.

E. I. du Pont de Nemours and Company was founded in 1802 to manufacture gunpowder. By 1900, Du Pont had begun to expand rapidly through research and acquisitions. A technological leader in chemicals and fibers, the firm grew to be the largest U.S. chemical manufacturer. At the end of 1980, the firm ranked fifteenth on the Fortune 500 list of U.S. industrials. The 1981 merger with Conoco, Inc., a major oil company, elevated Du Pont to seventh place on the list of U.S. industrials.

Capital Structure Policy, 1965–1982

Historically, Du Pont had been well known for its policy of extreme financial conservatism. The company's low debt ratio was feasible in part because of its success in its product markets. Du Pont's high level of profitability allowed it to finance its needs through internally generated funds (see Exhibits 1 and 2 for selected financial data). In fact, financial leverage was actually negative between 1965 and 1970, since Du Pont's cash balance exceeded its total debt. Du Pont's conservative use of debt combined with its profitability and technological leadership in the chemical industry had made the company one of the few AAA-rated manufacturers. Du Pont's low-debt policy maximized its financial flexibility and insulated its operations from financing constraints.

In the late 1960s, competitive conditions in Du Pont's fibers and plastics businesses began to exert pressure on the firm's financial policy. Between 1965 and 1970, increases in industry capacity outstripped demand growth, resulting in substantial price declines. As a result, Du Pont experienced decreases in gross margins and return on capital. Despite continued sales growth, net income fell by 19% between 1965 and 1970.

Three factors combined to intensify the pressure on Du Pont's financing policy in the mid-1970s. In response to competitive pressures, Du Pont in the early 1970s embarked on a major capital spending program designed to restore its cost position. The escalation of inflation ballooned the cost of the program to more than 50% over budget by 1974. Since capital spending was critical to maintaining and improving its competitive position, Du Pont was reluctant to reduce or postpone these expenditures. Second, the rapid increase in oil prices in 1973 pushed up Du Pont's feedstock costs and increased required inventory investment, while oil shortages disrupted production. Du Pont experienced the full impact of the oil shock in 1974; its revenues rose by 16% and costs jumped by 30%, causing net income to fall by 31%. Finally, the recession in 1975 had a dramatic impact on Du Pont's fiber business. Between the second quarter of 1974 and the second quarter of 1975, Du Pont's fiber shipments dropped by 50% on a volume basis. Net income fell by 33% in 1975. Over the period 1973–1975, Du Pont's net income, return on total capital, and earnings per share all fell by more than 50%.

Severe financing pressures resulted from the combination of inflation's impact on needed capital expenditures, cost increases driven by the escalation in oil prices, and recessionary conditions in the fiber business. The required investment in working capital and capital expenditures increased dramatically at a time when internally generated funds were shrinking. Du Pont responded to the financing shortfall by cutting its dividend in 1974 and 1975 and slashing working capital investment.

Since these measures were insufficient to meet the entire financing requirement, Du Pont turned to debt financing. With no short-term debt outstanding in 1972, the firm's short-term debt rose to $540 million by the end of 1975. In addition, in 1974, Du Pont floated a $350 million 30-year bond issue and a $150 million issue of 7-year notes. The former was Du Pont's first public long-term debt issue in the United States since the 1920s. As a result, Du Pont's debt ratio rose from 7% in 1972 to 27% in 1975, while interest coverage collapsed from 38.4 to 4.6 over the same period. Despite concern that the rapid increase in the company's debt ratio might result in a downgrading, Du Pont retained its AAA bond rating during this period. Had Du Pont abandoned its policy of financial conservatism, or was this a temporary departure from that policy forced by extraordinary financing pressures? In December 1974, Du Pont CEO Irving Shapiro stated, "We expect to use prudent debt financing over the long term."

Nonetheless, Du Pont moved quickly to reduce its debt ratio. Between 1976 and 1979, financing pressures eased. Capital expenditures declined from their 1975 peak as the spending program initiated in the early 1970s neared completion. Net income more than tripled during the period 1975–1979, helped by relatively moderate energy price increases and the economywide recovery from the 1974–1975 recession. Du Pont reduced the dollar value of its total debt in 1977, 1978, and 1979. By the end of 1979, Du Pont's debt had been pared to about 20% of total capital, and interest coverage had rebounded to 11.5 from 4.6 in 1975. Once again, the firm was well within the AAA-rated range. However, it was not apparent that the firm would return to the zero-debt policy of the past. In 1978, Richard Heckert, a Du Pont senior vice president, noted, "While we presently anticipate some further reduction in borrowings, we have considerable borrowing capacity and hence considerable flexibility."

An abrupt departure from maximum financial flexibility occurred in the summer of 1981. In July, Du Pont entered a bidding contest for Conoco, Inc., a major oil company and the fourteenth largest U.S. industrial. After a brief but frenetic battle, Du Pont succeeded in buying Conoco in August 1981. The price of almost $8 billion made the merger the largest in U.S. history and represented a premium of 77% above Conoco's preacquisition market value. With the acquisition, Du Pont virtually doubled its size and significantly increased its orientation toward undifferentiated commodity products. Both Du Pont's stock price and industry analysts responded negatively to the acquisition. Major concerns included the high price Du Pont had paid and the question of how Conoco would contribute to Du Pont's strategic objectives.

To finance the purchase of Conoco, Du Pont issued $3.9 billion in common stock and $3.85 billion in floating-rate debt. In addition, Du Pont assumed $1.9 billion of outstanding Conoco debt. The acquisition propelled Du Pont's debt ratio to nearly 40% from slightly over 20% at the end of 1980. Du Pont's bond rating was downgraded to AA, marking the first time in its history that the firm had fallen below the top rating.

The first year after the merger was a difficult one for Du Pont. Conoco's performance was hampered by declining oil prices in 1982, while an economic recession plagued the chemical industry. Although Du Pont's 1982 revenues were 2½ times 1979 sales, net income in 1982 fell below 1979 results; return on total capital was cut in half during this period, and earnings per share fell by 40%.

As Du Pont's management worked to frame and implement a coherent strategy for the merged company, they also got to work to repair the firm's extended financial condition. To reduce interest rate exposure, Du Pont refunded most of the firm's floating-rate debt with fixed-rate, long-term debt issues. Plans to reduce debt with the proceeds from the sale of $2 billion in Conoco coal and oil assets were frustrated by depressed energy prices. One analyst complained, "Du Pont managed to acquire Conoco at the peak of the oil cycle, and now they are looking at a tremendous glut of coal assets for sale that is going to make it very difficult to sell coal properties." Nevertheless, by the end of 1982, Du Pont had pared its debt ratio to 36% from the postmerger peak of 42%. Poor earnings in 1982 held interest coverage down to a near record low of 4.8. The firm retained its AA bond rating.

The increase in debt ratio accompanying the Conoco merger marked the second time in 10 years that Du Pont departed from its traditional capital structure policy. This, plus the fundamental changes in Du Pont's businesses, mandated the determination of a capital structure policy that would be feasible and appropriate for the years ahead.

Future Capital Structure Policy

Du Pont's financing policy had always been predicated on the notion of maximizing financial flexibility. This ensured that financing constraints did not interfere with the firm's competitive strategy. However, competitors differed widely from Du Pont and each other in their use of financial leverage (see Exhibit 3). Why should not Du Pont, like Dow Chemical and Celanese, reap the benefits of aggressive debt financing even if this resulted in a further reduction in its bond rating? (See Exhibit 4 for bond rating data.) Of course, electric utilities and telephone companies maintained high bond ratings despite aggressive use of debt (see Exhibit 4). While Du Pont's performance was more volatile than a company like AT&T, it was less volatile than many competitors and other industrial firms (see Exhibit 5).

In framing a debt policy, a key concern was how risky Du Pont's businesses were. The degree of business risk would help determine how much debt Du Pont could safely employ in its capital structure without unduly constraining its competitive strategy. The last 20 years had documented the increased volatility of Du Pont's basic businesses. Du Pont's competitive position and profitability had declined in many product lines. In many businesses, products were close to being undifferentiated commodities, and intense competition was common. Excess capacity and the economics of high-fixed-cost businesses pressured prices and profits. Moreover, Conoco competed in a volatile commodity business, a business in which Du Pont's management had little experience. The increased risk of Du Pont's operations argued for a relatively conservative capital structure.

Nonetheless, several factors suggested that the firm could pursue an aggressive debt policy. Du Pont was still the nation's largest chemical manufacturer, and large-scale economies were a common characteristic of chemical production processes. The firm remained the technological leader in the industry, and its success at R&D was second to none. Du Pont was pursuing capital spending programs designed to reduce costs in all business segments. The firm was widely diversified in terms of products and markets. In the past, Du Pont's economic muscle had often been constrained by aggressive antitrust policy, but the near-term future held some promise of a more benign regulatory environment. As for the impact of Conoco on Du Pont's business risk, some analysts thought the major diversification move would dampen the volatility of the firm's earnings. Edward Jefferson, who succeeded Irving Shapiro as Du Pont's chief executive officer, agreed, reasoning that the merger would "reduce the exposure of the combined companies to fluctuations in the price of energy."

Even with a recovery in gross margins, strong sales growth, and successful sales of Conoco assets, Du Pont would be forced to seek external financing each year from 1983 to 1987 (see Exhibit 6 for projections). The major reason was the need for a continued high level of capital expenditures. Capital spending was viewed as critical to Du Pont's future success because it was the key to minimizing the firm's cost position in existing products and launching new products swiftly and efficiently. In view of its importance, capital spending was essentially nondeferrable and often had to be increased rather than cut in bad times in order to redress the causes of poor performance.

Because of its large, nondeferrable financing needs, Du Pont was concerned about the cost and availability of financing (see Exhibit 7 for data on financing costs and volumes). Companies with high debt ratios and low bond ratings appeared to have some difficulty in obtaining debt financing in some years. However, firms rated A and above appeared to have little difficulty in raising funds. But compared with AAA-rated firms, the cost of debt financing was higher for A-rated firms, and the spread between A and AAA rates widened in high-interest-rate environments. In view of the importance and magnitude of Du Pont's projected financing needs, the firm was concerned about how the cost and availability of debt might affect its ability to pursue capital spending programs critical to its competitive position.

Capital Structure Policy Alternatives

One alternative for Du Pont was to restore its historical financial strength and AAA rating. Given Du Pont's substantial projected capital spending requirements, a return to zero debt was infeasible. A target ratio of debt to capital of 25% should be sufficient to ensure a high degree of financial flexibility and insulate Du Pont's competitive strategy from capital market conditions. However, achieving this debt ratio would not be easy (see Exhibit 8 for data on policy alternatives). Reducing the debt ratio from 36% in 1982 to 25% by the end of 1986 would require large equity issues in each year. Maintaining the target of 25% debt in 1987 would require additional large equity infusions. As of the end of 1982, Du Pont's stock price had yet to recover from the market's negative reaction to the Conoco merger, reinforced by the continuing recession. This raised questions concerning the terms and availability of the substantial new equity financing required to achieve a 25% debt ratio (see Exhibit 7 for equity issue data).

Although a conservative capital structure policy had the force of tradition, it was not clear that conservatism was appropriate for Du Pont in the 1980s. The cost of conservatism was clear (see Exhibit 8). Were Du Pont to abandon forever its historical conservatism and maintain a 40% target debt ratio, many measures of financial performance would benefit. For the recovery scenario projected in Exhibits 6 and 8, a high-debt policy generated higher projected earnings per share, dividends per share, and return on equity. No equity issues would be required through 1985. Equity issues in 1986 and 1987 would be much smaller than projected for the low-debt policy and thus might be more easily timed to take advantage of favorable market conditions. However, with higher financial leverage comes higher risk. In a pessimistic scenario (e.g., a recession), earnings per share and return on equity would suffer more severe declines with the high-debt policy. Other concerns were the availability of funds in all economic conditions with the high-debt alternative and the constraints limited availability might place on Du Pont's operations.

The Decision

The two decades drawing to a close in 1982 brought fundamental changes in Du Pont's businesses, culminating in the historic acquisition of Conoco. This acquisition also forced a dramatic departure from Du Pont's long-held capital structure policy. These changes both mandated and provided the opportunity for a fundamental reassessment of Du Pont's financing policy. In view of the escalation in Du Pont's debt ratio, the downgrading of its bond rating, and the negative stock market response to the Conoco merger, there was a considerable degree of uncertainty concerning Du Pont's financial policy. This underscored the importance of determining, committing to, and communicating a capital structure policy in the near future.

EXHIBIT 1

Selected Financial Data, 1965–1982 (millions of dollars except per share data)

	1965	1966	1967	1968	1969	1970	1971	1972
1. Sales	$2,999	$3,159	$3,079	$3,455	$3,632	$3,618	$3,848	$4,366
2. EBIT	767	727	574	764	709	590	644	768
3. Interest	2	4	7	7	10	11	15	20
4. Profit after taxes	407	389	314	372	356	329	356	414
5. Profit after taxes/Sales . . .	13.6%	12.3%	10.2%	10.8%	9.8%	9.1%	9.3%	9.5%
6. After-tax return on total capital[a]	18.5%	16.6%	13.0%	14.2%	12.8%	11.1%	10.9%	12.1%
7. Return on equity	18.6%	16.8%	13.0%	14.6%	13.3%	11.8%	11.5%	12.7%
8. Earnings per share	$ 2.96	$ 2.83	$ 2.24	$ 2.66	$ 2.54	$ 2.29	$ 2.44	$ 2.83
9. Dividends per share	2.00	1.92	1.67	1.83	1.75	1.68	1.67	1.82
10. Average stock price	81.04	80.88	54.42	54.25	44.46	38.29	47.92	54.77
11. Average stock price/ Earnings per share	27.4	28.6	24.3	20.4	17.5	16.7	19.6	19.4
12. Market value/Book value . .	5.40	5.28	3.26	3.07	2.38	1.98	2.40	2.61
13. S&P 400 P/E	16.8	15.2	17.0	17.3	17.5	16.5	18.0	18.0
14. S&P 400 market value/ Book value	2.13	1.96	2.00	2.12	2.07	1.69	1.95	2.10

Sources: Du Pont annual reports; Standard and Poor's Corporation.

a. After-tax return on total capital = (EBIT) (1 − Tax rate)/(All debt + Equity). Average stock price is average of year's high and low values. Per share data restated to be comparable with number of shares outstanding at December 31, 1982.

EXHIBIT 2

Selected Data Related to Funds Needs and Financial Strength, 1965–1982 (millions of dollars)

	1965	1966	1967	1968	1969	1970	1971	1972
Capital expenditures	$ 327	$ 531	$ 454	$ 332	$ 391	$ 471	$ 454	$ 522
Change in working capital[a] . . .	—	(163)	121	102	154	135	(39)	63
Capital structure								
Short-term debt	$ 0	$ 0	$ 31	$ 57	$ 45	$ 56	$ 0	$ 0
	0%	0%	1.2%	2.1%	1.6%	1.9%	0%	0%
Long-term debt	$ 34	$ 58	$ 95	$ 150	$ 141	$ 160	$ 236	$ 240
	1.5%	2.4%	3.7%	5.5%	4.9%	5.3%	7.1%	6.8%
Equity	$2,190	$2,317	$2,409	$2,540	$2,685	$2,790	$3,095	$3,267
	98.5%	97.6%	95.1%	92.4%	93.5%	92.8%	92.9%	93.2%
Total capital	$2,224	$2,375	$2,535	$2,747	$2,871	$3,006	$3,331	$3,507
	100.0%	100.0%	100.0%	100.0%	100.0%	100.0%	100.0%	100.0%
Interest coverage	383.5	181.8	82	109.1	70.9	53.6	42.9	38.4
Bond rating (senior debt)	AAA	AAA	AAA	AAA	AAA	AAA	AAA	AAA

Source: Du Pont annual reports.

a. Working capital investment is defined here as net working capital excluding cash, marketable securities, and short-term debt.

EXHIBIT 1 (*concluded*)

1973	1974	1975	1976	1977	1978	1979	1980	1981	1982
$5,964	$6,910	$7,222	$8,361	$9,435	$10,584	$12,572	$13,652	$22,810	$33,331
1,100	733	574	961	1,141	1,470	1,646	1,209	2,631	3,545
34	62	126	145	169	139	143	111	476	739
586	404	271	459	545	797	965	744	1,081	894
9.8%	5.8%	3.8%	5.5%	5.8%	7.5%	7.7%	5.4%	4.7%	2.7%
15.1%	9.0%	6.6%	9.7%	11.1%	13.7%	15.1%	10.9%	7.5%	6.6%
16.3%	10.7%	7.1%	11.4%	12.6%	16.7%	18.2%	13.1%	10.3%	8.2%
$ 4.01	$ 2.73	$ 1.81	$ 3.30	$ 3.69	$ 5.18	$ 6.23	$ 4.73	$ 5.81	$ 3.75
1.92	1.83	1.42	1.75	1.92	2.42	2.75	2.75	2.75	2.40
58.13	43.92	35.96	46.42	40.04	39.34	42.63	40.32	45.88	37.19
14.5	16.1	19.9	15.0	10.9	7.3	6.6	8.4	10.0	9.8
2.49	1.81	1.46	1.76	1.41	1.26	1.22	1.09	1.04	.83
13.4	9.4	10.8	10.4	9.6	8.2	7.1	8.4	8.5	10.4
1.89	1.34	1.31	1.46	1.33	1.20	1.17	1.26	1.22	1.16

EXHIBIT 2 (*concluded*)

1973	1974	1975	1976	1977	1978	1979	1980	1981	1982
$ 727	$1,008	$1,036	$ 876	$ 704	$ 714	$ 864	$1,297	$ 2,389	$ 3,195
278	561	(122)	20	243	341	438	17	2,046	(987)
$ 169	$ 320	$ 540	$ 259	$ 229	$ 258	$ 230	$ 393	$ 445	$ 319
4.2%	6.5%	10.3%	4.6%	4.0%	4.2%	3.5%	5.5%	2.6%	1.9%
$ 250	$ 793	$ 889	$1,282	$1,236	$1,058	$1,067	$1,068	$ 6,403	$ 5,702
6.2%	16.2%	16.9%	23.0%	21.4%	17.4%	16.1%	14.9%	37.0%	33.8%
$3,593	$3,782	$3,835	$4,032	$4,315	$4,761	$5,312	$5,690	$10,458	$10,850
89.6%	77.3%	72.8%	72.4%	74.6%	78.4%	80.4%	79.6%	60.4%	64.3%
$4,012	$4,895	$5,264	$5,573	$5,780	$6,077	$6,609	$7,151	$17,306	$16,871
100.0%	100.0%	100.0%	100.0%	100.0%	100.0%	100.0%	100.0%	100.0%	100.0%
32.4	11.8	4.6	6.6	6.8	10.6	11.5	10.9	5.5	4.8
AAA	AAA	AAA	AAA	AAA	AAA	AAA	AAA	AA	AA

EXHIBIT 3
Financial Data for Selected Chemical Companies, 1980 and 1982 (millions of dollars)

	Du Pont		Dow Chemical		Monsanto		Celanese	
	1980	1982	1980	1982	1980	1982	1980	1982
Sales	$13,652	$33,331	$10,626	$10,618	$6,574	$6,325	$3,348	$3,062
10-year compound annual sales growth rate	14.2%	22.5%	18.7%	16.0%	12.8%	11.0%	12.4%	7.4%
10-year compound annual EPS growth rate	7.5%	2.9%	19.9%	5.7%	8.3%	9.9%	8.9%	7.3%[a]
Net income	$ 744	$ 894	$ 805	$ 399	$ 149	$ 352	$ 122	$ (34)
Net income/Sales	5.4%	2.7%	7.6%	3.8%	2.3%	5.6%	3.6%	(1.1)%
Return on total capital	10.9%	6.6%	7.2%	7.9%	5.3%	8.3%	9.3%	(.3)%
Return on equity	13.1%	8.2%	18.1%	9.6%	5.5%	10.1%	11.2%	(1.2)%
Dividend payout	58.1%	64.0%	36.2%	101.7%	86.6%	45.2%	42.7%	42.7%[a]
Stock price/EPS[b]	8.4	9.9	7.6	13.7	13.7	8.3	6.3	6.7[a]
Market value/Book value[b]	109%	82.9%	138%	93.4%	72%	84.7%	67%	75.7%
Debt/Total capital	20.4%	35.7%	48.5%	42.7%	33.4%	24.5%	40.7%	42.9%
Interest coverage	10.9	4.8	2.2	1.6	2.8	7.1	4.5	3.8[a]
Bond rating (senior debt)	AAA	AA	A	A	AA	AA	A	BBB

Source: Moody's Investors Service.

a. Celanese 10-year compound annual EPS growth rate, dividend payout ratio, stock price/EPS, and interest coverage use 1981 instead of 1982.
b. Market value/book value and stock price/EPS are based on average of year's high and low stock prices.

EXHIBIT 4
Bond Rating Medians for 1979–1981

	AAA	*AA*	*A*	*BBB*	*BB*	*B*
Industrial Corporation						
Interest coverage	18.25	8.57	6.56	3.82	3.27	1.76
Total debt/Capitalization . .	17.04%	23.70%	30.41%	38.62%	48.07%	58.77%
Electric Utilities						
Interest coverage	>4.00	3.25–4.25	2.50–3.50	<3.00	—	—
Total debt/Capitalization . .	<45%	42–47%	45–55%	>55%	—	—
Telephone Companies						
Interest coverage	>4.50	3.70–4.70	2.80–4.00	<3.00	—	—
Total debt/Capitalization . .	<40%	40–48%	48–58%	58–64%	—	—

Source: Standard and Poor's Corporation.

EXHIBIT 5
Return on Total Capital

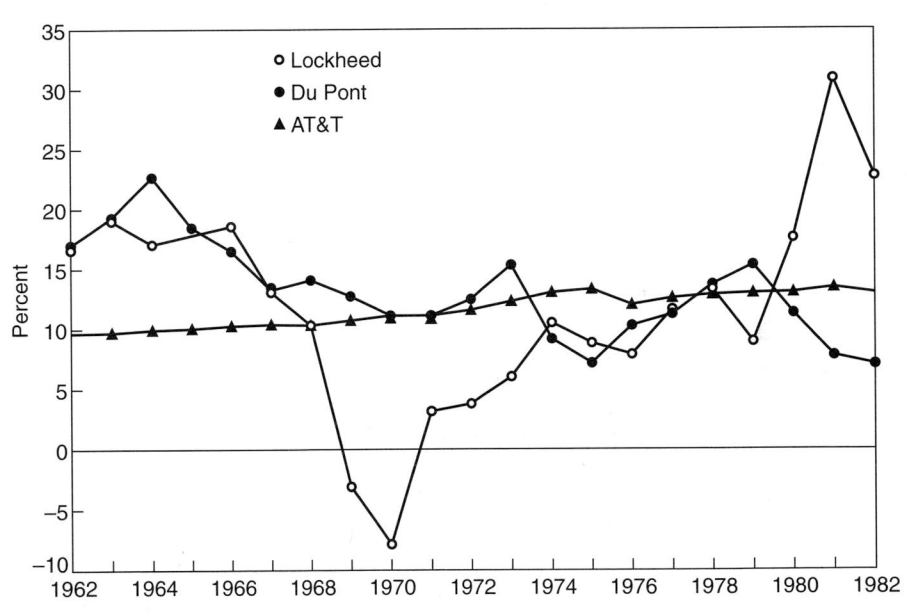

EXHIBIT 6
Financial Projections, 1983–1987 (millions of dollars)

	1983	1984	1985	1986	1987
Sources of Funds					
Net income	$1,009	$1,196	$1,444	$1,591	$1,753
Depreciation	2,101	2,111	2,212	2,396	2,667
Funds from operations	3,110	3,307	3,656	3,987	4,420
Assets sold	600	600	600	0	0
Decrease in cash	199	(200)	(200)	(150)	(150)
Other sources	74	135	135	135	135
Sources before new financing	$3,983	$3,842	$4,191	$3,972	$4,405
Uses of Funds					
Dividends	$ 571	$ 658	$ 794	$ 896	$ 964
Capital expenditures	2,767	3,386	4,039	4,202	4,667
Increase in net working capital[a]	973	414	594	587	650
Other	10	10	10	10	10
Total uses	$4,321	$4,468	$5,437	$5,695	$6,291
Net financing requirement	$ 338	$ 626	$1,246	$1,723	$1,886

Sources: Analysts' forecasts and casewriter's estimates.

Note: Assumptions are as follows: Sales are average of analysts' forecasts; average annual sales growth rate is 10%. EBIT recovers to 8.1% of sales by 1985. Net working capital (excluding cash) equals 13% of sales. Dividend payout ratio is 55%, and no dividend reductions are allowed. Net fixed assets equal 40% of sales. Depreciation is 15% of net fixed assets in the previous year.

a. Net working capital excludes cash, marketable securities, and short-term debt.

EXHIBIT 7
Debt Financing Costs and Volumes, 1970–1982 (millions of dollars)

	1970	1971	1972	1973	1974	1975	1976	1977	1978	1979	1980	1981	1982
Gross New Bond Issues by Industrials													
AAA debt					$1,650	$ 2,875	$ 700	$ 800	$ 275	$ 1,550	$ 1,750	$ 1,852	$ 543
AA debt					2,415	3,310	2,030	1,125	700	1,800	2,900	2,458	3,347
A debt					2,060	5,355	2,205	960	1,310	1,500	4,220	3,887	3,075
BBB debt					440	420	1,010	445	210	0	345	0	1,357
Common and Preferred Stock Issues													
Cash offerings	$9,200	$13,000	$13,100	$11,100	$7,400	$11,900	$13,300	$14,100	$14,600	$17,100	$28,600	$34,400	$38,700
Net[a]	6,800	13,500	13,000	9,100	4,300	10,500	10,300	6,800	(1,400)	(1,900)	18,200	12,000	16,400
Cash offerings by industrials	3,500	3,200	3,100	1,500	1,000	2,400	2,800	2,300	2,900	3,600	10,400	11,900	9,600
Maturity Distribution of New Debt Issues													
Medium-term						43%	30%	16%	21%	30%	44%	55%	62%
Long-term						57	70	84	79	70	56	45	38
Interest Rates													
90-day commercial paper	7.89%	5.12%	4.63%	8.11%	10.06%	6.41%	5.28%	5.45%	7.73%	10.72%	12.37%	15.15%	11.91%
New issue AAA debt	8.39	7.39	7.10	7.42	8.57	8.70	8.15	7.88	8.63	9.39	11.74	14.30	14.14
New issue AAA–AA spread	.26	.12	.10	.10	.20	.27	.17	.09	.14	.22	.44	.50	.38
New issue AAA–BBB spread	1.35	1.07	.71	.75	1.67	2.57	1.44	.79	.81	1.12	1.95	2.09	1.87
S&P 500 price/earnings ratio	16.5	18.0	18.0	13.4	9.4	10.8	10.4	9.6	8.2	7.1	8.4	8.5	10.4

Sources: Salomon Brothers Inc., Bankers Trust Company, and Standard and Poor's Corporation.

a. Stock offerings less stock repurchases.

EXHIBIT 8

Projected Financial Results under Two Financial Policy Alternatives, 1983–1987
(millions of dollars except per share data)

	1983	1984	1985	1986	1987	1987 with 20% Lower EBIT
40% Debt Scenario						
Debt/Total capitalization	36.0%	37.1%	39.7%	40.0%	40.0%	40.0
Interest coverage[a]	3.67	3.88	3.95	3.89	3.86	3.09
Earnings per share	$4.20	$4.98	$ 6.02	$ 6.31	$ 6.62	$ 4.83
Dividends per share	$2.38	$2.74	$ 3.31	$ 3.56	$ 3.64	—
Return on total capital	7.9%	8.6%	9.3%	9.3%	9.2%	7.4%
Return on equity	9.0%	10.1%	11.5%	11.5%	11.4%	8.3%
New equity issues	$ 0	$ 0	$ 0	$ 704	$ 816	$ 816
Millions of shares sold[b]	0	0	0	11.7	13.0	13.0
25% Debt Scenario						
Debt/Total capitalization	33.8%	31.4%	28.2%	25.0%	25.0%	25.0%
Interest coverage[a]	3.91	4.60	5.57	6.23	6.17	4.94
Earnings per share	$4.13	$4.77	$ 5.41	$ 5.46	$ 5.60	$ 4.27
Dividends per share	$2.29	$2.49	$ 2.71	$ 2.72	$ 2.72	—
Return on total capital	7.9%	8.6%	9.3%	9.3%	9.2%	7.4
Return on equity	8.8%	9.8%	10.7%	10.4%	10.2%	7.8%
New equity issues	$ 398	$ 686	$1,306	$1,783	$1,271	$1,271
Millions of shares sold[b]	9.5	14.3	28.8	36.2	25.2	25.2

Sources: Analysts' forecasts and casewriter's estimates, based on assumptions of Exhibit 6.

a. Interest coverage is defined as EBIT/interest.

b. Assumes new shares sold at a price-earnings ratio of 10.

Massey-Ferguson Ltd. (1980)

Massey-Ferguson Ltd. was a multinational producer of farm machinery, industrial machinery, and diesel engines. The company was founded in 1847; by 1980, it had manufacturing and assembly operations in 31 countries throughout the world. Massey-Ferguson was then the West's largest producer of farm tractors and the world's largest supplier of diesel engines to original equipment manufacturers.

In 1978, however, Massey reported an unprecedented year-end loss of US$262.2 million. (Recent and historical financial data are provided in Exhibits 1–4.) The new president, Victor A. Rice, pledged to restore Massey to profitability by the end of its 1979 fiscal year. Massey did show a profit of US$37.0 million in 1979 but reported a loss on continuing operations of US$35.4 million (see Exhibit 2). Sales in the first half of fiscal 1980 were up, but earnings remained severely depressed.

In April 1980 a preferred share issue of Can$300–500 million was postponed indefinitely.[1] The postponement was attributed to Massey's operating problems and to the fact that Argus Corporation, Massey's largest shareholder, refused to take a block of the preferreds as a vote of confidence in Massey.

As 1980 progressed, it became apparent that without an equity infusion, Massey would be in default on several loan covenants before the end of the fiscal year (October 31, 1980). Cross-default provisions made substantially all long- and short-term debts callable if any single default occurred. If Massey's lenders then cut off credit and moved to secure their loans, company operations would quickly come to a halt. Plant shutdowns, further worker layoffs, and a liquidation of corporate assets would follow. Creditors and customers around the world wondered if Massey would make it through the looming financial crisis.

---

1. At the time of this case, the Canadian dollar was trading in the range of US$.80–$.85.

Background

Massey-Ferguson had been called "the one true multinational." Its products—farm equipment, industrial machinery, and diesel engines—were sold throughout the world by dealers, distributors, and company retail outlets. Exhibit 5 shows a breakdown of 1980 sales by national markets. Table A summarizes Massey-Ferguson's sales by product line and geographical area.

Massey's production facilities were also dispersed around the world. Exhibit 5 shows the distribution of Massey-Ferguson's capacity by country. Massey's largest facilities were located in Canada (Brantford and Toronto), France (Marquette), England (Coventry), and Australia (Melbourne). Diesel engine production was concentrated in England (Peterborough).

In certain markets, primarily North America, Massey financed retail sales of farm and industrial machinery through wholly owned finance subsidiaries. In Europe and Australia, Massey's finance subsidiaries were primarily involved in financing sales to distributors, but they sometimes financed dealer receivables in their home markets. In October 1980, Massey's finance subsidiaries had assets totaling US$1,130.6 million and outstanding debts of US$825.6 million. (Massey's finance subsidiaries are not consolidated in the financial statements of Exhibits 1–4.)

Farm and Industrial Machinery

Massey's farm machinery line consisted of tractors, combine harvesters, balers, forage harvesters, cane harvesters, agricultural implements, farmstead equipment, and other equipment for agricultural use. The industrial machinery line consisted of industrial tractors, tractor loaders, tractor-loader-backhoes, rough-terrain fork lifts, skid steer loaders, utility loaders, and log skidders. In 1980, Massey held 17% of the worldwide market for tractors, 14% of the market for combines, and 13% of the market for industrial machinery.

Massey's competition in farm and industrial machinery included both large multinational companies with full product lines and medium-to-small companies conducting business locally with a limited range of products. In the large North American farm equipment market, Massey had traditionally ranked third in sales of farm equipment behind Deere & Co. and International Harvester. However, in 1980, it held first or second position in markets for small (30–90 HP) tractors and combine harvesters. Exhibit 6 compares Massey's sales, operating, and financial data with Deere and Harvester for the years 1976–1980.

Historically, Massey's strength had been in markets outside North America and Western Europe. In less-developed countries, Massey had success in dealing directly with governments or public institutions. During the 1970s, Massey entered into agreements to supply farm equipment or construct manufacturing facilities in Peru, Pakistan, Egypt, Iran, Libya, Mozambique, Turkey, Saudi Arabia, Sri Lanka, and the Sudan. In 1974, Massey obtained a $360 million contract to modernize and expand Poland's tractor and diesel engine industry.

Diesel Engines

Diesel engines were produced in England by the Perkins Engine Group. Perkins produced 60 basic models of multicylinder diesel engines in the 30–300-brake horsepower range. Perkins's engines were used in Massey-Ferguson's equipment and were also sold to manufacturers of a wide variety of agricultural, industrial, and construction

TABLE A
Breakdown of Massey-Ferguson's Sales

	Farm and Industrial Equipment	Diesel Engines
1980 sales ($ millions)	$2,533	$599
Percent North American		
(U.S., Canada, Mexico)	33.2%	
Percent Western Europe	35.6	
Percent rest of world	31.2	
	100.0%	

Source: Massey-Ferguson annual report.

equipment. In 1980, Perkins exported 86% of its product; over 50% of its exports were to Massey-Ferguson's subsidiaries and affiliates.

Because of rising gasoline prices, many auto and equipment manufacturers were expanding research and development in diesel engines. The emerging market for small, high-powered engines used in automobiles and light trucks was particularly promising. Perkins's long-range business plan called for it to maintain and increase its market share in areas such as agriculture vehicles, industrial and construction equipment, and marine craft. Perkins also was engaged in research on the dieselization of gasoline engines and the development of engines capable of operating on a variety of fuels.

Massey's Financial Difficulties

During the 1960s and 1970s, Massey-Ferguson was involved in an ambitious program of acquiring assets and expanding operations. The 1970s were a decade of dramatic growth, which was financed by debt, much of it short-term. By 1978, Massey's debt-to-equity ratio was 2.1 (see Exhibit 4). In that year, Massey lost US$262 million. Management attributed the massive loss to the imposition of credit and monetary restrictions in Argentina and Brazil, which caused sharp declines in farm machinery sales; the decline in North American farm prices and incomes; poor weather in Western Europe; and high interest rates, which raised the cost of carrying excess inventory.

Between 1978 and 1980, Massey reacted to the loss by cutting its labor force from 68,000 to 47,000 and its manufacturing space from 30 million sq. ft. to 20 million sq. ft. The company reduced inventories from US$1,083.2 million to US$988.9 million. Unprofitable operations in the manufacture of office furniture, garden tractors, and construction machinery were eliminated. Twenty-four plants were closed. The divestment program initiated in 1978 resulted in the sale of more than US$300 million in assets by 1980.

Despite these efforts, in fiscal 1979, Massey's loss on continuing operations was US$35.4 million, or US$2.38 per share; losses from discontinued operations amounted to another US$23.0 million. The company showed a positive net income in 1979 only as a result of an extraordinary item reflecting the recovery of previous years' taxes.

In the first three quarters of fiscal 1980, Massey's financial condition deteriorated even further. At the end of the third quarter, year-to-date losses totaled US$62 million, including an unfavorable currency adjustment of $37 million. Preliminary reports indicated that Massey's fourth quarter losses would be as high as those of the three previous quarters combined.

Massey's continuing problems were caused by high interest rates, low demand, lack of alignment between products and markets, and failure to penetrate the North American market.

Interest Rates

The high interest rates of 1979–1980 had a doubly negative impact on Massey's performance. First, the cost of Massey's short-term debt rose dramatically. Second, high interest rates depressed markets for farm and industrial machinery and thus hurt company sales.

Demand

The North American market for farm machinery crashed in the fall of 1980. The decline in demand was attributed to high interest rates, an economic recession, the Soviet grain embargo, and a severe drought during the summer of 1980. Because of the recession, European and Third World markets were also severely depressed.

The recession made 1980 a difficult year for all farm equipment manufacturers. In North America, both Deere and Harvester experienced reduced sales and profits and showed sharp increases in short- and long-term debt. By the end of 1980, International Harvester was in technical violation of debt covenants and was in the process of negotiating a refinancing plan with its bankers.

Product-Market Alignment

Massey's farm equipment production was in rough regional alignment with its sales. At the margin, North America and the United Kingdom were net suppliers to the rest of the world (see Table A and Exhibit 5). Engine production, however, was heavily concentrated in the United Kingdom. In 1980, with the influx of North Sea oil, the British pound rose dramatically relative to currencies in which Massey sold its products. The high price of the pound increased Massey's cost of goods sold, reducing margins and thus hurting the competitiveness of Massey's products.

Lack of alignment between production sites and markets meant that currency fluctuations were a recurring problem for Massey-Ferguson. For example, in 1974, Massey purchased Hanomag, a West German construction equipment manufacturer. The venture was unprofitable, in part because the strong German mark made its exports too costly in world markets. In 1980, the Hanomag subsidiary was sold to IBH Holdings for an undisclosed amount.

Massey-Ferguson's product-market alignment would continue to have an unfavorable impact on profits as long as the British pound was strong and the company's operations concentrated in the United Kingdom. However, political risk argued against matching production and sales on a country-by-country basis. Although successful in negotiating directly with Third World and East Bloc governments, Massey was vulnerable to changing political conditions in these countries. During the 1970s, several governments with whom Massey had dealings, including Iran, Pakistan, Libya, and Poland, were overthrown as a result of coups or civil unrest.

Economies of scale in engine production also made it advisable to concentrate facilities at a few sites. One possibility discussed within Massey was to relocate capacity at the margin in Canada. Concentration of assets in Canada would bring the company closer to North American markets and make its costs similar to those of Deere and Harvester. Massey already had two large Canadian facilities, forming a base on which it could expand.

North American Efforts

In the 1960s, Massey concentrated its marketing and product development efforts overseas. As a result, the company lagged in its development of the high-horsepower tractors and combines desired by farmers in the Canadian and U.S. farm belts.

In 1975, Massey turned its attention to the North American market, introducing a new range of 34–81 HP tractors as well as an improved baler line. In 1978, Massey introduced large, high-horsepower tractors in Europe and North America. Management claimed:[2]

> These new products will make Massey-Ferguson fully competitive in North American and European markets and will demonstrate the company's ability to design, produce, and market large tractors as successfully as tractors in the 40–90 horsepower range.

Unfortunately, Massey's drive into North America coincided with a depressed market and the beginnings of its own financial difficulties. Doubts about the future of the company eroded sales and weakened the distribution network. During 1980, the number of Massey's dealerships in North America fell by 50%, from 3,600 to 1,800.

The Future

Despite these problems, and even though in the fall of 1980 worldwide demand for farm equipment stood at depression levels, management continued to be optimistic about the future. In the 1980 annual report, Mr. Rice reaffirmed that the cost-cutting efforts initiated in 1978 had made Massey a viable company. As evidence, he pointed to a 1% increase in Massey's worldwide tractor sales over the first nine months of 1980, an increase achieved in spite of the collapse of the North American market (see Exhibit 2).

However, in order to take advantage of its long-run opportunities, Massey had to raise capital to finance its investment programs. New funds were needed for: (1) on-going R&D for new product development; (2) repair and replacement of existing facilities; (3) reallocation of facilities from the United Kingdom to Canada; (4) penetration of the North American market; (5) defense of markets in Europe and the rest of the world; (6) further growth in the Third World; and (7) Perkins's prospective entry into the market for small diesel engines. It was not known for sure how much would be needed for each of these programs, but in aggregate they might require US$500–700 million over the next 5 years.

A major unresolved question was the future of the Perkins Engine subsidiary. Perkins was Massey's most valuable salable asset, but at the same time, diesel engines were the company's best hope for profitable future growth. Some thought Massey should seek to cut its foreign exchange losses while concurrently pleasing the governments of Canada and Ontario by setting up diesel engine production in Canada. The possibility of selling Perkins to a third party was also discussed; however, some felt that Perkins's future depended on the existence of a healthy Massey-Ferguson that was able to buy Perkins products.

The most immediate problem, however, was to engineer Massey's survival. By mid-1980, all expenditures except those necessary to continued operations had been suspended in an effort to conserve cash. Despite these efforts, the cash continued to

---

2. Massey-Ferguson annual report (1978).

flow out; by September, bank lines were nearly exhausted and the company's position became daily more precarious.

A major restructuring of claims on Massey-Ferguson was necessary. However, to achieve a restructuring, Massey's lenders and major shareholders had to consent to a refinancing plan. By September 1980, top management knew that a default on Massey's existing debt was practically inevitable at the fiscal year-end. Once Massey defaulted, any lender could potentially trigger a worldwide scramble for assets that would bring company operation to a halt. For this reason, the economic interest of each category of claimant had to be carefully considered to be sure that any refinancing plan proposed would be acceptable to all.

The Players

The Banks

As of late fiscal 1980, Massey-Ferguson had total debt of US$1.6 billion outstanding with more than 100 banks around the world. Exhibits 7 and 8 provide a breakdown of Massey's short-term lines of credit and long-term debt. Most of the borrowing was unsecured. In addition, Massey's finance company subsidiaries owed another US$825 million worldwide. Finance company debt usually was not guaranteed, but Massey had agreed to maintain assets in the subsidiaries in certain specified relations to their indebtedness.

As Exhibits 7 and 8 show, Massey's borrowings were dispersed among lenders in Canada, Great Britain, West Germany, France, Italy, and the United States. Except for a consortium of U.S. banks, which had issued a revolving credit, most lenders operated independently of one another. The numerous covenants related to these loans hampered Massey's free access to the capital markets. For example, before Massey could issue new preferred shares (as it had proposed in April 1980), it had to pay accumulated preferred dividends, which were US$14 million in arrears as of December 1979. But since March 1978, when Massey announced first losses, covenants on certain U.S. loans had caused dividends to both preferred and common shares to be suspended.

The Canadian Imperial Bank of Commerce was Massey's largest lender, with an aggregate exposure estimated at between Can$200 and Can$300 million. Commerce had ties not only to Massey-Ferguson but also to Massey's largest shareholder, Argus Corporation. Conrad Black, Massey's chairman from 1978–1980 and president of Argus from 1978, was made a director of the bank in 1980.

Argus Corporation

Since the 1960s, Argus Corporation, a Canadian holding company, had owned a controlling interest in Massey-Ferguson. Argus's philosophy was to make major investments in a small number of promising enterprises. In 1956, shortly after Massey Harris merged with the Ferguson Company to become Massey-Ferguson, several Argus directors had played a major role in saving the newly formed company from bankruptcy by forcing it to liquidate certain assets and cut its prices on farm equipment. In 1980, Argus held 16.5% of the outstanding shares. Six of the 18 board members were Argus appointees.

In 1978, Conrad Black, age 34, son of one of the founders of Argus, took over as president of Argus and, as a result, became chairman of the board of Massey-Ferguson. Black picked Victor Rice to succeed Albert Thornburgh as Massey's president; 2 years later, in 1980, Mr. Black relinquished the chairmanship of Massey to Mr. Rice.

Argus was considered by the financial community to be a potential source of equity capital for Massey, but Mr. Black's public comments on the company were highly equivocal. In a 1979 interview, he indicated that Argus was "not interested in putting up a lot of money and staying at 16%." He expressed surprise that Massey's lenders kept approaching him for advice when Argus held only 16% of the stock and was therefore much less exposed than the major lenders. There were also perennial rumors that "Conrad Black has been trying to peddle Massey-Ferguson's stock."

In April 1980, a preferred stock issue was postponed, in part because Argus was reluctant to take a block of shares. Chairman Black was quoted as saying: "We could finance the company tomorrow. I'm not going to get panicky. We're good for another year." Mr. Black also maintained that he was willing to contribute Can$100–500 million to Massey-Ferguson "on the right terms."

Other Preferred and Common Shareholders

Massey had two issues of preferred stock outstanding, Series A and B. Each had a liquidation value of $25 per share and was entitled to annual cumulative dividends of $2.50 per share. A total of 1,526,300 shares of Series A preferred had been issued in April 1975, followed by 2,298,500 shares of Series B in March 1976. The purpose of each issue was "to reduce (Massey's) short-term debt." Dividends on the preferred shares were suspended in 1978. Indentures provided that after a failure to pay dividends for eight quarters, each class of preferred stock would have the right to elect two members to Massey's board of directors. Board representation was attained by Series B shareholders in March 1980 and by Series A shareholders in April 1980.

Massey's 18,250,000 shares of common stock were listed on the New York, London, Toronto, Montreal, and Vancouver stock exchanges. From January 1976 through July 31, 1980, Massey lost 16⅞ points per share, or 69% of market value (see Exhibit 9). Over the same period, the New York Stock Exchange composite index gained 30%.

The Governments of Canada, Ontario, and the United Kingdom

Finally, Mr. Rice and Mr. Black had for some time been trying to convince the governments of Canada, Ontario, and the United Kingdom to intervene on Massey's behalf. Massey had approached the Trudeau and Thatcher governments for aid as early as June 1980. The governments were anxious to avoid a loss of jobs (6,700 in Ontario and 17,000 in the combined Massey and Perkins operations in the United Kingdom); but in both Canada and the United Kingdom, there was strong resistance to bailing out a privately owned multinational. Talks with the governments were continuing, but very little progress had been made and time was rapidly running out.

The Situation in the Fourth Quarter of 1980

In August 1980, the international financial press reported that the Canadian governments were considering some form of financial assistance for Massey. It was said that Mr. Rice hoped to make a positive announcement when Massey released its third-quarter results in September. Mr. Black was quoted:

> It's fair to assume that if there isn't any indication of possibility of some equity when third-quarter results are released, the situation could become quite hairy. . . . Either Massey is going to go right under or the company will be restored, not only to its former position, but to a position of strength it hasn't known before.

In September, Massey postponed publication of its third-quarter results as talks continued with the Canadian governments. By October, Massey and its finance subsidiaries had debt of US$2.5 billion outstanding to 150 banks worldwide, and speculation on the probability of Massey's survival was rampant.

Only a few weeks remained before the November 1 deadline when Massey would be technically in default on several loans. Cross-default provisions made substantially all outstanding loans callable if any single default occurred. Suddenly, on October 2, 1980, Argus donated its 16.5% controlling interest to Massey-Ferguson's two pension funds. This move made Massey the world's largest employee-controlled corporation and resulted in a Can$23 million tax write-off for Argus. On the same day, the government of Canada announced it would "work closely" with Massey to achieve a refinancing.

Two weeks later, on October 20, 1980, the governments of Canada and Ontario announced they had reached an agreement in principle with Massey and its major lenders:

> The governments are prepared to guarantee the capital risk of a portion of the new equity investment in Massey, providing various conditions are met, including a satisfactory degree of cooperation from the existing lenders.

The press attributed the governments' actions to the upcoming Ontario provincial election and the need to protect jobs. According to the *Economist:*

> While the federal government is Liberal, Ontario is still Conservative. . . . It needs both the Massey jobs and Mr. Black, a Conservative supporter, who is in favor of more Massey investment in Canada. . . . Meanwhile, the Trudeau government is trying to use Massey to help its constitutional plans.[3]

However, other press reports indicated that the governments had been forced to act, and "in effect [they are] still supplying only inexpensive moral support for the company at this time."

On October 31, Massey-Ferguson closed its books on fiscal year 1980. The loss for the year (subsequently reported) amounted to US$225.2 million, or $12.79 per share. Scheduled principal repayments were suspended in October; interest payments were suspended on December 1, 1980.

Massey-Ferguson began fiscal year 1981 in default on its US$2.5 billion of outstanding debt. The company's future depended on the ability of lenders, the governments of Canada and Ontario, and management to agree on a feasible refinancing plan. In the course of the continuing negotiations, serious questions were raised about Massey's long-term ability to compete in its industry. Persons close to the situation wondered what sort of restructuring would allow the company to survive, and whether Massey would ever regain its status as a self-sufficient corporation.

---

3. The repatriation of the Constitution was a major political issue in Canada in 1980–1981.

EXHIBIT 1

Consolidated Balance Sheets at October 31, 1978–1980 (millions of U.S. dollars)

	1978	1979	1980
Cash	$ 23.4	$ 17.2	$ 56.2
Receivables	531.3	731.1	968.2
Inventories	1,083.8	1,097.6	988.9
Prepaid expenses, other	63.8	89.8	93.0
Current assets	1,702.3	1,935.7	2,106.3
Investments	213.3	217.1	205.8
Fixed assets, net	602.2	568.7	488.2
Other assets and deferred charges	29.3	24.0	27.3
Total assets	$2,547.1	$2,745.5	$2,827.6
Bank borrowings	$ 362.3	$ 511.7	$1,015.1
Long-term debt, current portion	115.0	59.3	60.2
Accounts payable and accrued charges	778.7	907.4	793.8
Other	16.1	31.1	24.5
Current liabilities	1,272.1	1,509.5	1,893.6
Deferred income tax	64.3	13.8	14.3
Long-term debt (less current portion)	651.8	624.8	562.1
Minority interest in subsidiaries	18.4	19.1	4.5
Total liabilities	2,006.6	2,167.2	2,474.5
Redeemable preferred shares	95.8	95.8	95.8
Common (18,250,350 shares)	176.9	176.9	176.9
Retained earnings	267.8	305.6	80.4
Shareholders' equity	540.5	578.3	353.1
Total liabilities and shareholders' equity	$2,547.1	$2,745.5	$2,827.6

EXHIBIT 2

Consolidated Income Statements for Years Ending October 31, 1978–1980
(millions of U.S. dollars)

	1978	1979	1980
Net sales	$2,925.5	$2,973.0	$3,132.1
Cost of goods sold, at average exchange rates for year	$2,371.2	$2,381.8	$2,568.5
Effect of foreign currency exchange rate changes[a]	—	18.6	7.7
	2,371.2	2,400.4	2.576.2
Marketing, general, and administrative	372.0	351.9	404.7
Engineering and product development	66.0	58.2	59.7
Interest on long-term debt	78.6	75.7	71.0
Other interest expenses	108.0[b]	128.8	229.9
Interest income	—	(40.3)	(42.0)
Exchange adjustments	90.9	(24.9)	49.9
Minority interest	(.8)	1.4	.2
Miscellaneous income	(10.6)	(10.3)	(13.5)
Total costs and expenses	$3,075.3	$2,940.9	$3,336.1
Profit (loss) before items shown below	$ (149.8)	$ 32.1	$ (204.0)
Provision for reorganization expense	(116.0)	(95.0)	(28.5)
Income tax recovery	(11.8)	6.3	10.1
Equity in net income of finance subsidiaries	16.3	16.6	22.7
Equity in net income of associate companies	4.6	4.6	—
Income (loss) from continuing operations	(256.7)	(35.4)	(199.7)
Loss from discontinued operations	—	(23.0)	(25.5)
Extraordinary item	—	95.4	—
Net income (loss)	$ (256.7)	$ 37.0	$ (225.2)
Unfavorable (favorable) impact on continuing operations of exchange adjustments and foreign currency exchange rate changes in cost of goods sold	—	$ (6.3)	$ 57.6

a. This item is the difference between costs of goods sold translated to U.S. dollars at average exchange rates and such costs translated at historical rates.

b. Amounts shown are net of interest income.

EXHIBIT 3

Consolidated Statement of Changes in Financial Position for Years Ending October 31, 1978–1980 (millions of U.S. dollars)

	1978	*1979*	*1980*
Source of Funds			
Disposal of investments in associate companies and changes in long-term advances to finance subsidiaries	—	$ 29.1	$ 41.3
Proceeds on disposal of fixed assets	$ 11.3	31.1	34.1
Extraordinary item (less $31.4 in 1979 not affecting working capital)	—	64.0	—
Proceeds from long-term debt issues	169.0	35.8	—
Total sources	$ 180.3	$ 160.0	$ 75.4
Uses of Funds			
Funds used in operations	$ 176.2	$ 30.0	$ 168.4
Reductions in long-term debt	158.6	59.0	67.1
Additions in fixed assets	99.3	76.6	46.2
Other (net)	18.2	(.7)	7.2
Total uses	$ 452.3	$ 164.9	$ 288.9
Working Capital			
Decrease in working caital	$(272.0)	$ (4.9)	$(213.5)
At beginning of year	703.1	431.1	426.2
At end of year	431.1	426.2	212.7
Changes in Elements of Working Capital			
Cash	$ 10.8	$ (6.3)	$ 39.0
Receivables	(19.9)	174.4	237.1
Inventories	(52.1)	13.8	(108.7)
Prepaid expenses, other	(8.4)	26.0	3.2
Current assets	$ (69.6)	$ 207.9	$ 170.6
Bank borrowing and current portion of long-term debt	(132.2)	(93.8)	(504.3)
Accounts payable and accrued charges	55.1	(156.0)	(54.3)
Accrued charges	—	—	59.3
Income, sales, and other taxes payable	(5.4)	33.4	6.0
Advance payments from customers	(9.7)	3.6	.6
Current liabilities	$(202.4)	$(212.8)	$(384.1)
Decrease in working capital	$(272.0)	$ (4.9)	$(213.5)

EXHIBIT 4

Selected Operating Data and Balance Sheets, 1971–1980 (millions of U.S. dollars and percentage of sales or total assets)

	1971		1972		1973		1974		1975		1976		1977		1978		1979		1980	
Selected Operating Data																				
Sales	$1,029	100%	$1,190	100%	$1,497	100%	$1,791	100%	$2,554	100%	$2,772	100%	$2,805	100%	$2,631	100%	$2,973	100%	$3,132	100%
Operating profit[a]	—	—	—	—	—	—	—	—	111	4	126	5	77	3	(133)	(5)	(30)	(1)	(139)	(4)
Net income[b]	—	—	—	—	—	—	—	—	100	4	118	4	32	1	(262)	(10)	37	1	(225)	(7)
Balance Sheets																				
Cash	$ 33	3%	$ 10	1%	$ 8	1%	$ 13	1%	$ 20	1%	$ 7	—	$ 13	—	$ 23	1%	$ 17	1%	$ 56	2%
Receivables	339	33	368	35	417	33	433	27	485	24	558	24%	542	21%	531	21	731	27	968	34
Inventory	335	33	362	34	461	37	711	44	878	44	967	42	1,136	44	1,084	43	1,098	40	989	35
Other	31	3	33	3	53	4	66	4	72	4	83	4	81	3	64	2	90	3	93	3
Current assets	738	72	773	73	939	75	1,223	76	1,455	73	1,615	70	1,772	68	1,702	67	1,936	71	2,106	74
Net P.P.&E.	186	19	180	17	205	16	278	17	401	20	519	23	594	23	602	24	569	21	488	17
Other (investment)	87	9	104	10	105	9	113	7	141	7	171	7	228	9	243	9	241	8	234	9
Total assets	$1,011	100%	$1,057	100%	$1,249	100%	$1,614	100%	$1,997	100%	$2,305	100%	$2,594	100%	$2,547	100%	$2,746	100%	$2,828	100%
Bank borrowings	$ 168	17%	$ 139	13%	$ 81	6%	$ 163	10%	$ 170	9%	$ 113	5%	$ 249	10%	$ 362	14%	$ 512	19%	$1,015	36%
L-T debt, due 1 yr.	10	1	11	1	13	1	16	1	47	2	66	3	96	4	115	5	59	2	60	2
Other	224	22	251	24	406	32	542	34	613	31	704	30	730	28	795	31	938	34	819	29
Current liabilities	402	40	401	38	500	39	721	45	830	42	883	38	1,075	42	1,272	50	1,509	55	1,894	67
Long-term debt	187	18	196	18	244	20	325	20	452	23	529	23	616	24	652	26	625	23	562	20
Other	18	2	16	1	35	3	44	3	63	3	90	4	96	3	82	3	33	1	19	1
Owners' equity	404	40	444	43	470	38	524	32	652	32	803	35	807	31	541	21	579	21	353	12
Tot. liabilities, equity	$1,011	100%	$1,057	100%	$1,249	100%	$1,614	100%	$1,997	100%	$2,305	100%	$2,594	100%	$2,547	100%	$2,746	100%	$2,828	100%

Note: Operating data are shown as percentage of sales, and balance sheet data as percentage of total assets.

a. Operating profit (loss) is defined as total revenue less those recurring expenses that are controllable by management. It excludes extraordinary items, net exchange adjustments, and reorganization expense pertaining to continuing operations.

b. Prior to 1978, results reflect sales and income from construction machinery businesses. After 1978, construction machinery is treated as a discontinued operation.

EXHIBIT 5
Worldwide Sales and Distribution of Capacity by Country

	1980 Sales		Percent Capacity	
	US$ millions	Percent	Farm Equipment	Diesel Engines
North America				
Canada	$ 219	7.0%	27.4%	—
United States	819	26.1	14.6	3.4%
Mexico	75	2.4	—	—
	1,113	35.5	42.0	3.4
Western Europe				
United Kingdom	297	9.5	15.6	76.7
France	227	7.2	10.2	1.0
Italy	211	6.7	8.0	—
West Germany	157	5.0	5.5	—
Spain	8	.3	—	—
Benelux	28	.9	—	—
	928	29.6	39.3	77.7
South America				
Brazil	306	9.8	6.4	17.9
Argentina	44	1.4	1.8	—
	350	11.2	8.2	17.9
Australia	131	4.2	10.5	1.0
Scandinavia	114	3.6	—	—
South Africa	66	2.1	—	—
Iran	31	1.0	—	—
Pakistan	29	.9	—	—
Japan	25	.8	—	—
Turkey	14	.4	—	—
All others	331	10.6	—	—
Totals	$3,132	100.0%	100.0%	100.0%

Note: Percentages may not total to 100% because of rounding.

EXHIBIT 6
Comparative Data on Farm Equipment Producers, 1976–1980 (millions of U.S. dollars)

Company	1976	1977	1978	1979	1980
Massey-Ferguson Limited					
Sales	$2,772	$2,805	$2,631	$2,973	$3,132
Operating profit[a]	126	77	–133	–30	–139
Net income	118	32	–262	37	–225
Assets	2,305	2,594	2,547	2,746	2,828
Short-term debt[b]	180	345	477	571	1,075
Long-term debt	529	469	505	478	415
Equity	803	807	541	578	353
Capital expenditures	175	147	99	77	46
Operating profit/Sales	4.55%	2.74%	–4.55%	–1.01%	–4.44%
Net income/Sales	4.25%	1.17%	–8.77%	1.24%	–7.19%
Short-term debt/Capital[c]	11.89%	21.29%	31.35%	35.09%	58.33%
Total debt/Capital	46.90%	50.24%	64.50%	64.46%	80.85%
Sales/Assets	1.20	1.08	1.15	1.08	1.11
Coverage[d]	2.10	1.42	.14	.82	.46
Market share[e]	33.94%	32.08%	31.03%	27.09%	28.19%
Capital exp. share[f]	47.80%	33.10%	24.69%	17.22%	7.43%
International Harvester					
Sales	$5,488	$5,975	$6,664	$8,392	$6,312
Agricultural sales	2,262	2,334	2,348	3,069	2,507
Operating profit, firm[a]	473	531	610	827	–262
Operating profit, ag.	0	0	288	442	–1
Net income	173	204	187	370	–397
Assets	3,575	3,788	4,316	5,247	5,843
Agricultural assets	0	0	1,385	1,548	1,739
Short-term debt[b]	302	292	380	442	860
Long-term debt	923	926	933	948	1,327
Equity	1,564	1,734	1,876	2,199	1,896
Capital expenditures	158	164	210	285	384
Operating profit/Sales	8.61%	8.89%	9.15%	9.85%	–4.15%
Ag. oper. profit/Ag. sales	—	—	12.25%	14.40%	–.04%
Net income/Sales	3.15%	3.41%	2.80%	4.40%	–6.29%
Short-term debt/Capital[c]	10.84%	9.90%	11.91%	12.31%	21.07%
Total debt/Capital	43.93%	41.28%	41.16%	38.73%	53.56%
Sales/Assets	1.54	1.58	1.54	1.60	1.08
Ag. sales/Ag. assets	—	—	1.70	1.98	1.44
Coverage[d]	3.66	4.11	4.21	4.92	.24
Market share[e]	27.70%	26.70%	24.90%	27.96%	22.57%
Capital exp. share[f]	17.79%	14.43%	18.45%	23.30%	24.62%

(continued)

EXHIBIT 6 *(concluded)*

Company	1976	1977	1978	1979	1980
Deere & Company					
Sales	$3,134	$3,604	$4,155	$4,933	$5,470
Operating profit[a]	438	483	537	564	470
Net income	242	256	265	311	228
Assets.	2,944	3,429	3,892	4,179	5,202
Short-term debt[b]	134	242	137	202	742
Long-term debt	494	482	637	619	702
Equity	1,379	1,571	1,756	1,974	2,141
Capital expenditures	126	233	228	266	421
Operating profit/Sales	13.98%	13.40%	12.92%	11.43%	8.59%
Net income/Sales	7.71%	7.09%	6.37%	6.30%	4.17%
Short-term debt/Capital[c]	6.69%	10.55%	5.43%	7.22%	20.69%
Total debt/Capital	31.31%	31.55%	30.61%	29.36%	40.28%
Sales/Assets	1.06	1.05	1.07	1.18	1.05
Coverage[d]	6.15	6.32	6.38	6.32	3.19
Market share[e]	38.37%	41.22%	44.07%	44.95%	49.24%
Capital exp. share[f]	34.41%	52.47%	56.86%	59.48%	67.96%

a. Casewriter's estimates. Operating profit excludes extraordinary items, foreign exchange gains or losses, and reorganization expense on continuing operations.

b. Short-term debt equals bank borrowing plus long-term debt due in 1 year.

c. Capital equals long- and short-term debt plus equity.

d. Coverage is here defined as operating profit plus interest and lease rental expense divided by interest and lease rental expense plus preferred dividends. No adjustment for taxes was made because of the unstable tax status of these companies in this period. As a result, Deere's actual coverage is understated relative to Massey's in all years and Harvester's in 1980.

e. For each company, market share is calculated as own sales (agricultural only for Harvester) divided by total (three company) agricultural sales.

f. For each company, capital expenditure share is calculated as own capital expenditures divided by total (three company) capital expenditures. Harvester's total capital expenditures are adjusted by the ratio of its agricultural sales to total sales.

EXHIBIT 7
Summary of Long-Term Debt Outstanding at October 31, 1979–1980
(millions of U.S. dollars)

	1979	1980
Bonds, Debentures, Notes, and Loans [a]		
Massey-Ferguson Perkins S.A. (Brazil): Bank loans maturing 1981–1984 repayable in U.S. dollars bearing interest at ¾% to 2½% above Eurodollar interbank rate	$ 30.9	$ 14.3
Massey-Ferguson S.A. (France): Bank loans maturing 1981–1985 bearing interest at 1.95% above base rate	24.4	23.4
Massey-Ferguson S.p.A. (Italy): Bank loans maturing 1981–1982 repayable in U.S. dollars bearing interest at 1.3% above Eurodollar interbank rate	10.0	10.0
Massey-Ferguson Holding Limited (United Kingdom): 7½% loan stock maturing 1986–1992	16.6	19.4
Bank loans maturing 1981–1984 bearing interest at various London bank market rates	38.6	34.5
Massey-Ferguson Inc. (USA): 8.55% promissory notes maturing 1981–1984	26.3	21.6
5⅞% subordinated notes maturing 1981–1984	12.0	10.4
Massey-Ferguson (Delaware) Inc. (USA): 9% senior notes maturing 1983–1997	150.0	150.0
Perkins Diesel Corporation (USA): Capitalized value of property and equipment lease terminating 1993 discounted at 10%	25.5	24.5
General-purpose loans (repayable in U.S. dollars): 9½% sinking fund debentures maturing 1991 [b]	66.0	61.5
9¾% sinking fund debentures maturing 1981–1982	32.0	30.0
Other long-term debt [c]	104.8	75.7
Total unsubordinated long-term debt	$537.1	$475.3
Convertible Subordinated Notes [d]		
Massey-Ferguson (Delaware) Inc. (USA): 10% convertible subordinated notes maturing 1988–1992	147.0	147.0
Total long-term debt	$684.1	$622.3

a. Debts are repayable in currency of country indicated unless otherwise shown. Current maturities are included in this summary; maturity dates are for fiscal years ending October 31. As of September 1980, the company had met all contractual sinking fund requirements. An additional $800,000 in sinking fund payments was due in October 1980. Sinking fund requirements and debt maturities during the next 5 years were as follows: 1981—$60.2 million; 1982—$78.5 million; 1983—$46.3 million; 1984—$54.3 million; 1985—$25.9 million.

b. The company is obligated to purchase for cancellation up to $4.5 million of these debentures each year to 1986 if the market price is below par value during the period March 1 to May 31.

c. Other long-term debt includes long-term loans, each of which is less than $10.0 million.

d. These notes are convertible into common shares of Massey-Ferguson Ltd. at an initial price of US$45.00 per share rising to US$55.00 per share in 1982. There is no dilution of 1980 or 1979 annual results per common share as a result of this convertible feature.

EXHIBIT 8
Short-Term Credit Lines by Bank at June 30, 1980 (millions of U.S. dollars)

				Finance Companies				
	Canada	U.S.	Australia	Germany	Italy	UK	Finag	Total
CIBC	$37.8					$ 27.1		$ 64.9
Barclays						42.5		42.5
Midland						54.3		54.3
Lloyds						42.5		42.5
Citibank		$ 17.5						17.5
Société Générale						9.0		9.0
Deutsche Bank				$ 3.3				3.3
Chase Manhattan		15.0						15.0
Crédit Lyonnais						9.0		9.0
Banque National de Paris			$ 7.8			11.3		19.1
Continental Illinois		21.0			$ 3.8	4.5		29.3
Bank of America		17.5						17.5
Dresdner				3.3				3.3
Commerzbank				3.3				3.3
Bankers Trust		13.0						13.0
FNB Chicago		15.0						15.0
Chemical		13.0						13.0
Allied & Associates						18.5	$45.0	63.5
Banque Francais du Commerce Extérieur								—
Royal Bank of Canada						11.3		11.3
Toronto Dominion						6.8		6.8
Others		78.1	23.4	7.8	81.2	50.8		241.3
Total	$37.8	$190.1	$31.2	$17.7	$85.0	$287.6	$45.0	$694.4

Note: Because of sales seasonality, the maximum use of credit lines usually occurs in June or July. By September 1980, borrowing by manufacturing companies had decreased to approximately US$1.0 billion. Borrowing by finance subsidiaries was down to between US$.8 and $.9 billion.

a. Includes Perkins UK.

b. Includes MF AG, Agrotrac, MF International, and MF Nederland.

EXHIBIT 8 *(concluded)*

					Manufacturing Companies										
Brazil	Argentina	Canada	U.S.	Australia	France	Eicher	GabH	Italy	UK Total[a]	Corporate Companies[b]	France	Brazil	Other	Total	Grand Total
		$222.9			$ 3.6				$ 3.4					$ 229.9	$ 294.8
									133.4					133.4	175.9
									36.2					36.2	90.5
									36.2					36.2	78.7
	$00.5		$ 17.5					$ 3.0	1.1					22.1	39.6
					50.1									50.1	59.1
						$ 5.6	$ 26.6							32.2	35.5
			15.0											15.0	30.0
			3.0		33.0						$ 3.3			39.3	48.3
		15.0			34.6						3.8			53.4	72.5
			21.0											21.0	50.3
			17.5	$ 3.3										20.8	38.3
						3.3	33.3							36.6	39.9
						3.9	27.8							31.7	35.0
			13.0											13.0	26.0
			15.0											15.0	30.0
			13.0					1.2						14.2	27.2
										$ 5.0				5.0	68.5
					18.3						12.2	3.3		33.8	33.8
			15.0								5.0			20.0	31.3
			15.0											15.0	21.8
$31.2	40.1		48.2	25.5	16.1	15.4	28.9	56.3	19.2	51.8	1.0	$7.7	$7.0	348.4	589.7
$31.2	$40.6	$237.9	$193.2	$28.8	$155.7	$28.2	$116.6	$60.5	$229.5	$74.0	$11.4	$7.7	$7.0	$1,222.3	$1,916.7

EXHIBIT 9
Common Stock Price Data: Massey-Ferguson and NYSE Composite Price Index, by Quarters, 1976–1980

	Massey-Ferguson Common Stock		NYSE Composite Price Index
	Quarterly Dividend	Market Price	
1976: March	$.25	$27¾	54.80
June	.25	28¾	55.71
September	.25	22¾	56.23
December	.33	21¾	57.88
1977: March	.25	19⅜	53.53
June	.25	19⅞	55.10
September	.25	17	52.81
December	.25[a]	14½	52.50
1978: March		9	49.85
June		10½	53.66
September		11	57.78
December		8¾	53.62
1979: March		11¾	57.13
June		12⅝	58.38
September		10½	62.24
December		10¼	61.95
1980: March		8⅜	57.65
June		6¾	65.34
September		6½	72.38
December		5½	73.53

Note: Prices as of the last trading day in the month.

a. Dividends were discontinued after December 1977.

American Home Products Corporation

"I just don't like to owe money," said William F. Laporte when asked about his company's almost debt-free balance sheet and growing cash reserves.[1] The exchange took place in 1968, 4 years after Mr. Laporte had taken over as chief executive of American Home Products (AHP). The 13 subsequent years did not improve his opinion of debt financing. During Mr. Laporte's tenure as chief executive, AHP's abstinence from debt continued, while the growth in its cash balance outpaced impressive growth in both sales and earnings. At the end of 1980, AHP had almost no debt and a cash balance equal to 40% of its net worth. In 1981, after 17 years as chief executive, Mr. Laporte was approaching retirement, and analysts speculated on the possibility of a more aggressive capital structure policy.

Description of the Company

AHP's 1981 sales of more than $4 billion were produced by over 1,500 heavily marketed brands in four lines of business: prescription drugs, packaged (i.e., proprietary or over-the-counter) drugs, food products, and housewares and household products. Consumer products included a diversity of well-known brand names, such as Anacin, Preparation H, Sani-Flush, Chef Boy-Ar-Dee, Gulden's Mustard, Woolite, and the Ekco line of housewares. AHP's largest and most profitable business, prescription drugs, included sizable market shares in antihypertensives, tranquilizers, and oral contraceptives. AHP's success in these lines of business was built on marketing expertise. Whether the product was an oral contraceptive or a toilet bowl cleaner, "they sell the hell out of everything they've got," said one competitor.[2]

1. *Forbes,* September 1, 1968, p. 87.

2. *The Wall Street Journal,* December 28, 1981, p. 1.

AHP's Corporate Culture

AHP had a distinctive corporate culture that, in the view of many observers, emanated from its chief executive. This culture had several components. One was reticence. A poll of Wall Street analysts ranked AHP last in corporate communicability among 21 drug companies. A second element of AHP's managerial philosophy was frugality and tight financial control. Reportedly, all expenditures greater than $500 had to be personally approved by Mr. Laporte even if authorized in the corporate budget.

Another important component of AHP's culture was conservatism and risk aversion. AHP consistently avoided much of the risk of new product development and introduction in the volatile drug industry. Most of its new products were acquired or licensed after their development by other firms or were copies of new products introduced by competitors. A substantial portion of AHP's new products were clever extensions of existing products. AHP thus avoided risky gambles on R&D and new product introductions and used its marketing prowess to promote acquired products and product extensions. When truly innovative products were introduced by competitors, AHP responded with "me-too" products and relied on its marketing clout to erode competitors' head starts.

Finally, an integral part of AHP's corporate philosophy was the firm's long-standing policy of centralizing complete authority in the chief executive. The current incumbent was described by a former colleague as a "brilliant marketer and tight-fisted spender."[3] Mr. Laporte's management style was characterized as management from the top, unparalleled in any firm of comparable size. Though reticent in discussing operations, Mr. Laporte was emphatic in stating the objective underlying his use of this authority: "We run the business for the shareholders."[4] The author of a *Business Week* article on the firm commented, "One of the most common business platitudes is that a corporation's primary mission is to make money for its stockholders and to maximize profits by minimizing costs. At American Home, these ideas are a dogmatic way of life."[5]

AHP's Performance

This managerial philosophy produced impressive results. AHP's financial performance was characterized by stable, consistent growth and profitability. The firm had increased sales, earnings, and dividends for 29 consecutive years through 1981. This growth had been consistent and steady, ranging in recent years between 10% and 15% annually (see Exhibit 1 for a 10-year review of AHP's performance). Under Mr. Laporte's stewardship, AHP's return on equity had risen from about 25% in the 1960s to 30% in the 1980s. Because of its passion for parsimony, AHP had been able to finance this growth internally while paying out almost 60% of its annual earnings as dividends.

During Mr. Laporte's reign as chief executive, AHP's price-earnings ratio had fallen by about 60%, reflecting the marketwide collapse of price-earnings ratios of growth companies. Nonetheless, AHP's more than sixfold growth in earnings per share had pushed up the value of its stock by a factor of 3 during his tenure. AHP's stock was widely held by major institutional investors. Its popularity among investors reflected analysts' assessment of AHP's management. In the opinion of one analyst,

---

3. *The Wall Street Journal,* December 28, 1981, p. 6.

4. *HBS Bulletin,* January/February 1981, p. 123.

5. *Business Week,* March 21, 1970, p. 76.

"When you think of American Home Products, you think of the best-managed company in the whole pharmaceutical field."[6] Nevertheless, AHP's excess liquidity and low degree of leverage were criticized by many analysts. Others wondered whether it would be a good idea to tinker with success.

Capital Structure Policy

Many drug firms were relatively unleveraged, but none matched AHP's conservative capital structure. Because of AHP's diversified operations, it was difficult to find a truly comparable firm for comparative analysis. However, Warner-Lambert Company was about the same size as AHP and competed in roughly similar lines of business (see Exhibit 2 for a comparison of AHP and Warner-Lambert). Warner-Lambert had a debt ratio of 32%, and its bond rating was on the borderline between AAA and AA in 1980.

For many years, analysts had speculated on the impact of a more aggressive AHP capital structure policy. An example of a pro forma recapitalization analysis is presented in Exhibit 3. This exhibit shows actual 1981 performance plus pro forma restatements of the 1981 results under three alternative capital structures: 30% debt, 50% debt, and 70% debt. As described in Exhibit 3, these restatements assume that AHP issued debt and used the proceeds plus $233 million of excess cash to repurchase stock in early 1981 at the then prevailing stock price of $30 per share. Though this approach is only one of several ways to achieve a higher debt ratio, it illustrates, in approximate terms, the impact of higher debt on AHP's financial performance.

In view of AHP's firmly rooted financial conservatism, it was premature to consider the details of a realistic recapitalization plan. However, the likely imminent retirement of the firm's strong-willed chief executive fueled speculation concerning an appropriate capital structure policy for AHP and the magnitude of the payoff from such a policy.

---

6. David S. Saks, Wertheim & Co., quoted in *The Wall Street Journal*, January 7, 1981, p. 18.

EXHIBIT 1
Selected Financial Data for American Home Products Corporation, 1972–1981 (millions of dollars except per share data)

	1972	1973	1974	1975	1976	1977	1978	1979	1980	1981
Sales	$1,587.1	$1,784.4	$2,048.7	$2,258.6	$2,471.7	$2,685.1	$3,062.6	$3,406.3	$3,798.5	$4,131.2
Cash	—	—	—	—	358.8	322.9	436.6	493.8	593.3	729.1
Total debt	—	—	—	—	7.8	10.3	13.7	10.3	13.9	16.6
Net worth	—	—	—	—	991.5	1,035.3	1,178.0	1,322.0	1,472.8	1,654.5
Total assets	1,042.0	1,126.0	1,241.6	1,390.7	1,510.9	1,611.3	1,862.2	2,090.7	2,370.3	2,588.5
Net income	172.7	199.2	225.6	250.7	277.9	306.2	348.4	396.0	445.9	497.3
Earnings per share	$ 1.08	$ 1.25	$ 1.42	$ 1.58	$ 1.75	$ 1.94	$ 2.21	$ 2.51	$ 2.84	$ 3.18
Dividends per share	.59	.625	.777	.90	1.00	1.15	1.325	1.50	1.70	1.90
Percentages										
Annual growth in sales	—	12.4%	14.8%	10.2%	9.4%	8.6%	14.1%	11.1%	11.7%	8.8%
Annual growth in EPS	—	15.7	13.6	11.3	10.8	10.9	13.9	13.6	13.1	12.0
Dividend payout	54.6%	50.0	54.7	57.0	57.1	59.3	60.0	59.8	60.0	59.7
After-tax profit margin	10.9	11.2	11.0	11.1	11.2	11.4	11.4	11.6	11.7	12.0
Return on equity	25.9	28.2	28.2	27.9	28.0	29.5	29.6	30.0	30.3	30.1

EXHIBIT 2

1980 Data for American Home Products Corporation and Warner-Lambert Company (millions of dollars except per share data)

	American Home Products Corporation	Warner-Lambert Company
Sales	$3,798.5	$3,479.2
5-year compound annual growth rate	11.0%	9.9%
Profit after taxes	$ 445.9	$ 192.7
5-year compound annual growth rate	12.2%	3.3%
Cash and equivalents	$ 593.3	$ 360.3
Accounts receivable, net	517.3	541.5
Inventory	557.3	645.8
Net property, plant, and equipment	450.5	827.1
Other	251.9	582.5
Total assets	$2,370.3	$2,957.2
Total debt	$ 13.9	$ 710.1
Net worth	1,472.8	1,482.7
Earnings per share	$ 2.84	$ 2.41
5-year compound annual growth rate	12.4%	3.0%
Dividends per share	$ 1.70	$ 1.32
5-year compound annual growth rate	13.6%	8.0%
Stock price (end of 1980)	$ 30	$ 20
Price-earnings ratio	10.6	8.3
Profit margin (Profit after taxes/Sales)	11.7%	5.5%
Return on equity	30.3%	13.0%
Percentage of total debt to total capital	.9%	32.4%
Interest coverage	436.6	5.0
Bond rating	AAA	AAA/AA[a]

a. Warner-Lambert's debt was rated AAA, but analysts felt the firm was close to being downgraded to AA.

EXHIBIT 3
Pro Forma 1981 Results for Alternative Capital Structure (millions of dollars except per share data)

| | Actual 1981 | Pro Forma 1981 for Varying Percentages of Debt to Total Capital | | |
		30%	50%	70%
Sales	$4,131.2	$4,131.2	$4,131.2	$4,131.2
EBIT[a]	954.8	922.2	922.2	922.2
Interest	2.3	52.7	87.8	122.9
Profit before taxes	952.5	869.5	834.4	799.3
Taxes	455.2	417.4	400.5	383.7
Profit after taxes	497.3	452.1	433.9	415.6
Dividends on preferred stock	.4	.4	.4	.4
Earnings available to common shareholders . .	496.9	451.7	433.5	415.2
Dividends on common stock	295.3	271.0	260.1	249.1
Average common shares outstanding	155.5	135.7	127.3	118.9
Earnings per share	$ 3.18	$ 3.33	$ 3.41	$ 3.49
Dividends per share	1.90	2.00	2.04	2.10
Beginning of Year after Recapitalization				
Cash and equivalents	$ 593.3	$ 360.3	$ 360.3	$ 360.3
Total debt	13.9	376.1	626.8	877.6
Net worth	1,472.8	877.6	626.9	376.1
Common stock price	$ 30	—	—	—
Aggregate market value of common stock . . .	$4,665.0	—	—	—

a. EBIT is reduced in pro forma results because of the loss of interest income from the $233 million in excess cash used to repurchase stock.

Detailed Assumptions for Pro Forma Recapitalizations

1. Debt is assumed to be added to the capital structure by issuing debt and using the proceeds to repurchase common stock. All repurchases are assumed to be executed in January 1981.
2. Stock is assumed to be repurchased at a price of $30 per share, which was the prevailing stock price in early January 1981.
3. The minimum cash balance is assumed to be $360.3 million (equal to Warner-Lambert's 1980 cash balance); thus $233 million in excess cash is available for use in repurchasing stock.
4. A tax rate of 48% is used.
5. The common dividend payout ratio is 60%.
6. Interest rate on all debt in all recapitalizations is assumed to be 14% before tax.
7. Interest foregone on excess cash is assumed to be at a rate of 14% before tax, so with recapitalization, EBIT falls by .14 times excess cash of $233 million or $32.6 million.
   Thus, pro forma EBIT is $922.2 million (actual EBIT of $954.8 million minus $32.6 reduction in interest from excess cash).

Details of Recapitalizations (millions of dollars)

	30% Debt	50% Debt	70% Debt
Excess cash	$ 233.0	$ 233.0	$ 233.0
Additional debt	362.2	612.9	863.7
Total repurchase	595.2	845.9	1,096.7
Reduction in common shares outstanding (million shares)	19.8	28.2	36.6

Hospital Corporation of America (A)

In January 1982, Hospital Corporation of America (HCA) faced a complex financial situation. Following a major acquisition in 1981, HCA's ratio of debt to total capital was approaching 70%, well in excess of its well-established target ratio of 60%. Interest coverage had dropped below its target of 3.0 to 2.4, the lowest level experienced since HCA was founded in 1968. Although some investors justified, even welcomed, HCA's more aggressive use of leverage, others were concerned. HCA's capital structure could cost the company its A bond rating. Mounting interest expense on the debt could also result in a decline in HCA's first-quarter earnings per share relative to that for a year ago. If it did, it would be the first such quarter-to-quarter decline in earnings per share in HCA's 13-year history. In light of these developments, HCA's management had to decide what, if anything, should be done about its capital structure and what specific steps should be taken in the near future to achieve the desired mix of debt and equity.

Early Development

Hospital Corporation of America was a proprietary hospital management company. It was founded in Nashville, Tennessee, by two physicians, Thomas F. Frist, Sr., and Thomas F. Frist, Jr., and by Jack C. Massey, a former pharmacist and former owner of Kentucky Fried Chicken. Beginning with only a single 150-bed hospital in 1968, HCA grew to become the nation's largest hospital management company. By 1981, HCA owned or managed 349 hospitals in the United States and overseas and had net operating revenues of $2.1 billion. Since its founding, revenues and earnings had grown at an annual rate of 32.2% and 32.6%, respectively. Pretax profit margins, averaging 9%, were the highest and most consistent among the major proprietary hospital chains. Recent financial statements and a 10-year summary of HCA's operations are presented in Exhibits 1–4.

The Proprietary Hospital Industry

Proprietary hospital management companies—that is, corporations that own and manage chains of hospitals on a for-profit basis—were a relatively new phenomenon in the $118 billion U.S. hospital-care business. The enactment of entitlement programs such as Medicare and Medicaid in 1965 stimulated demand for hospital services and virtually eliminated the tremendous bad-debt burden (i.e., weak accounts receivable) that had traditionally plagued the hospital industry. This created a valuable opportunity for private investors to build or acquire hospitals and operate them profitably. Tight control over costs, and efficiencies in such areas as staffing, purchasing, and hospital design enabled hospital management companies to offer high-quality services at reasonable cost while achieving attractive profit margins.

With the ability to sell equity and other financial securities not generally available to nonprofit hospitals, proprietary hospital management companies expanded rapidly in the 1970s. While the number of hospitals operating in the United States actually declined steadily between 1975 and 1980 from a high of 7,200, the proprietary hospital chains expanded the number of hospitals under their control at a 12.5% annual rate. By 1980, 38 proprietary hospital chains owned or operated 12.4% of the 6,965 hospitals and 7.9% of the 1.37 million licensed hospital beds in the United States. The five largest hospital chains controlled 632 hospitals and 87,502 beds in 1981. A comparison of the major hospital chains is provided in Exhibit 5.

It was expected that revenue growth of the hospital management companies as a group would be approximately 13–14% annually throughout the 1980s. The five major chains, however, were expected to grow at an annual rate of 25% during the first half of the decade. Although still rapid, this expected rate of growth was less than the 35% annual rate they experienced between 1975 and 1980. Shrinkage in the number of attractive acquisitions, along with high costs for construction and acquisition, accounted for the expected slowdown.

Past Growth

HCA's growth during the 1970s was achieved both through acquisition of existing hospitals and construction of new units. Between 1968 and 1981, HCA constructed 70 new and replacement facilities and acquired or leased the rest of its hospitals. Each year HCA evaluated many potential acquisitions and areas for construction and was rather selective in the facilities it acquired. Criteria for selection included the target community's need for health care services, the quality of the target hospital's medical staff and personnel, the population growth pattern in the area served, the facility's suitability for future expansion, and the hospital's overall financial position. Most of HCA's domestic hospitals were located in the Southeast and in the rapidly expanding "sunbelt" area of the United States (see Exhibit 6). This geographic preference reflected, in part, a more favorable regulatory environment in these parts of the United States and, in part, more favorable demographic trends. Roughly 40% of HCA's U.S. facilities were the only hospitals in their areas.

Some of HCA's unit growth had been achieved through the acquisition of other proprietary hospital management companies. A run on other proprietary chains was triggered in 1978 when Humana, Inc. merged with American Medicorp, then the third-largest chain. Following that acquisition, ten other hospital management companies were acquired by the five majors by 1981. HCA accounted for four of these acquisitions. Its most recent one occurred on August 26, 1981, when it purchased Hospital

Affiliates International from INA Corporation, an insurance company, for $425 million cash and common stock valued at $190 million. This acquisition provided HCA with 57 additional owned hospitals and 78 more hospitals under management contract.[1] With revenues of $704 million and earnings of $29 million in 1980, Hospital Affiliates had been the nation's fifth-largest hospital management chain.

Sources of Capital

HCA's operations generated substantial cash that could be used for reinvestment. However, its ambitious construction and acquisition program also required substantial financing from external sources.

Generally, external financing during HCA's early growth period followed a simple pattern: Revolving bank credits were used to fund hospitals under construction, while industrial revenue bonds and privately placed long-term mortgage loans from insurance companies were used to fund completed hospitals and acquisitions. Other sources of capital were difficult to tap at first because of the newness of the proprietary hospital industry, the small size and short track record of HCA itself, and the generally poor image that many investors had of hospital management companies at that time.

However, as the hospital management industry matured and HCA's strong performance became recognized, other types of financing were used beginning in the mid-1970s. In 1975, HCA issued $33 million of 15-year first-mortgage bonds, the first public bond offering undertaken by a hospital management company. Standard and Poor's initially rated the bonds BBB and later upgraded them to A.[2] In an effort to tap sources of funds overseas, HCA also issued $25 million of Eurodollar notes in 1978. In another first for the industry, the company sold $47 million of commercial paper in 1980. The issue was rated A-2 by Standard and Poor's and P-2 by Moody's.

In 1981, HCA added $891 million of debt to its balance sheet. Most of this debt was to mature in less than 7 years, and a substantial portion of it bore fluctuating interest rates that were tied to the prime rate or the London Interbank Offered Rate[3] (a complete schedule of HCA's debt is shown in Exhibit 7). Of this, $425 million was in the form of a revolving bank credit that was used to finance the purchase of Hospital Affiliates. This sudden increase in the level of debt on HCA's books made HCA the highest-leveraged company in the United States with a A bond rating.

HCA had also issued common stock on a number of occasions. It had a public offering of new equity each year from 1969 to 1971 as it built its capital base. Since 1971, HCA had only two public offerings of stock: one in 1976 and the other in 1979, when it sold 2.2 million common shares, receiving net proceeds of $85.8 million, the

---

1. Proprietary hospital management companies frequently managed hospitals for others on a contractual-fee basis. Such management contracts did not require much in the way of capital investment, but neither did they provide as much revenue as owned and operated facilities. They were valuable, however, as a source of potential acquisition candidates and as a means for scouting potential new areas for expansion. In 1981, HCA operated hospitals under management contracts in 38 states throughout the United States.

2. Moody's refused to rate the bonds, claiming that HCA's substantial investment in hospital construction meant that it was actually a real estate company. Because enterprises such as real estate investment trusts (REITs) and hotel chains were performing so poorly at this time, Moody's chose not to rate real estate companies at all. The rating agency eventually changed its mind and gave an A to HCA's $23 million industrial revenue bond issue in 1979.

3. The London Interbank Offered Rate is the interest rate offered for dollar deposits in the London market. It serves as a benchmark interest rate for dollar loans in Europe, much as the prime rate serves as a benchmark for some loans in the United States.

largest stock deal done that year by an industrial company. HCA also issued new common shares in connection with some of its acquisitions.

HCA's management hoped not to have to issue new equity any more frequently than every other year. Nonetheless, they were very careful to maintain close contact with the equity market. They did so through frequent presentations to security analysts and clear and complete disclosure of information in HCA's financial reports.

Future Growth

One of HCA's principal objectives was to realize at least 13% annual growth in earnings per share after removing the effects of inflation. As a practical matter, however, HCA sought annual growth in the 25–30% range (including the effects of inflation) for the foreseeable future. This aggressive rate was sought for several reasons. One was competition from other management companies in the acquisition of hospitals. As Bill McInnes, vice president of finance for HCA, noted:

> There is a feeling here that we must be prepared to strike while the iron is hot. There are only 7,000 hospitals out there and we can't expect to have them all. With, perhaps, three to five good years [of growth by acquisition] left, we will have to move along in an expeditious manner to get our fair share.

Management also recognized that HCA's expected growth rate was a major factor influencing the price of the company's equity. "This is a company in which people check the stock price two or three times a day," Mr. McInnes said.[4] "No one wants to see what will happen [to the stock price] if the growth rate starts to unwind." Management's attention to growth and its impact on equity prices was undoubtedly heightened by security analyst reports on HCA, many of which were predicting 1982 earnings per share of $3.00—a 35% increase over 1981.

Management expected growth to continue in the same basic directions that it had taken since the company's founding—through acquisition, construction of new hospitals, expansion of services, and the signing of new management contracts. Some indication had been given that the company was likely to expand into new areas, but only into other health services such as home health care and outpatient surgery.

As far as future growth by acquisition was concerned, it seemed likely that a somewhat different tack would be taken. Partly for antitrust reasons, many analysts and industry participants believed that the acquisition of other hospital management companies had nearly run its course as a major source of new growth for the large chains in the 1980s. Thereafter, it was believed, growth by acquisition would have to occur primarily through the purchase of nonprofit county, municipal, and religious-order hospitals. Many such hospitals had old buildings in need of renovation, obsolete equipment, and unsophisticated management systems. Because of the unwillingness or inability of their present owners to raise taxes or issue new debt to continue operations, it was likely that many of these units would be put up for sale.

HCA appeared to be well positioned to make inroads into this market. Interestingly, this position had as much to do with HCA's quality image as its financial strength. Among the major hospital management companies, HCA was considered one of the most attractive by which to be acquired because of its industry leadership position, its decentralized management style, and the high quality of its corporate management. Its list of directors read like a page from *Who's Who in Finance and*

---

4. Officers and directors of HCA as a group owned 3.6 million shares of HCA's common stock and 1.8 million options on HCA's common shares.

Industry. The board was chaired by Donald MacNaughton, former chairman and chief executive officer of Prudential Insurance Co. of America, and included other prominent business leaders such as Robert Anderson, chairman and CEO of Rockwell International Corp; Frank Borman, chairman, president, and CEO of Eastern Air Lines; Owen Butler, chairman of Procter & Gamble Co.; John de Butts, retired chairman and CEO of American Telephone and Telegraph; and Irving Shapiro, chairman of the finance committee of E. I. du Pont de Nemours and Co.

HCA's quality image was important when approaching nonprofit hospitals because of the misgivings that some of their owners often had about selling to a profit-oriented management company. Many nonprofit hospitals were directed by politicians, public agents, and other public figures, who sometimes balked at the thought of profits being earned on the care of sick people or who incorrectly believed that past abuses associated with nursing home companies also characterized the proprietary hospital management business. HCA's quality image was often the critical factor in overcoming the doubts of such trustees and convincing them to sell to HCA.

Other Goals

Besides its growth objective, HCA had several other explicitly stated goals and guidelines. A very important one was its 60% target ratio of debt to total capital. This target was in line with the degree of leverage more or less expected by the rating agencies for an A-rated hospital management company. Its origin, however, was somewhat informal. Typically, debt was used to finance real estate development projects on a 75% loan-to-value basis. In HCA's early years management reasoned that, since 15% of its expenditures on hospital projects were for equipment rather than property or plant, it would be conservative and use only 60% debt financing for its hospital construction. Ultimately, this ratio became the standard for the entire proprietary hospital management industry. However, insofar as many hospitals in the 1980s were built and operated on a stand-alone basis with as much as 90% debt financing, a case could be made on comparative grounds for a higher debt ratio for a healthy hospital management company. In fact, several of HCA's managers expressed the belief that HCA could comfortably accommodate as much as 75–85% debt in its capital structure if it so desired.

Return on total capital was expected to be a minimum of 11% after taxes, and return on equity was expected to be at least 17% after taxes. Although very important goals, these target rates of return could be difficult to maintain during periods of rapid growth, especially if that growth were achieved largely through acquisition. The reason was that growth by acquisition often meant the takeover of hospitals that needed to be turned around. This process could take several years and result in the squeezing of profit margins in the meantime.

HCA's other goals included a dividend payout of 15% of net income and the maintenance or improvement of net profit margins as a percent of operating revenues. Sam Brooks, senior vice president of finance and chief financial officer of HCA, had also expressed his desire to keep the average interest cost for all HCA's debt at 15% or lower in the foreseeable future.

Regulatory Change and the Outlook for the Future

The future of the hospital management industry appeared bright in several respects. In the near term, continued growth in revenues and earnings seemed assured as nonprofit hospitals became available for acquisition. In the long run, as growth by acquisition and new construction subsided, the natural expansion and aging of the population could be relied upon to increase occupancy rates, thus providing still further growth. Moreover, because of the high *operating* leverage created by hospitals' fixed costs, much of the growth in revenues due to higher occupancy rates could be expected to translate directly into higher earnings. The provision of additional services and a concentration on further cost containment rather than on geographic expansion could further add to growth in earnings in the long run.

The future was not without its risks, however. The federal government had been exploring ways to reduce hospital and medical costs in order to cut federal expenses for Medicare, VA hospitals, and other government-backed health care programs. Various types of industry deregulation tended to be favored in the political climate of the early 1980s as a means of improving production efficiency and increasing consumer welfare.

Regulatory reform of health care could have potentially far-reaching implications for the hospital management companies. For example, under the present regulatory system, hospital expansion was controlled by local health planning agencies through "certificates of need." New hospital projects would be granted such a certificate only if it could be demonstrated that there existed a genuine need for the new services or expanded capacity being contemplated. Although a bureaucratic headache, this requirement restricted new hospital construction and, in the process, tended to provide existing hospitals with protected franchises. Were certificates of need eliminated, as had been proposed, this form of protection would be removed. This might stimulate rapid expansion by competing hospitals, possibly resulting in the duplication of services, excess bed capacity, and lower occupancy rates than might otherwise be expected. The average occupancy rate for all U.S. hospitals was only 75% in 1979, down from 83% in 1969.

Of equal concern were various proposals to reform the nation's system of health care insurance so that consumers would become more price sensitive and hospitals more cost conscious. Because 90% of all Americans were covered by some form of health insurance, the bulk of hospital revenues came from third-party payers. Consequently, the demand for hospital services by the ultimate consumer was relatively price insensitive. It had been estimated that hospitals could vary prices by as much as 20% up or down without a material effect on patient utilization.[5]

Similarly, because most hospitals receive a substantial part of their reimbursements from government-backed programs such as Medicare and Medicaid, incentives to control costs were diminished. The reason was that such reimbursement programs were "cost-based." That is, hospitals were reimbursed for their costs of providing services to covered patients. Costs allowable under Medicare/Medicaid programs included depreciation and interest but excluded costs of research, losses on bad debts, and expenses for charitable cases. In addition, Medicare allowed a return on equity (excluding non-patient-related assets and liabilities) at a rate equal to 150% of the average annual interest rate on certain debt obligations of the Federal Hospital Insurance Trust Fund. The pretax return on equity allowed was 12.3% in 1978, 13.7% in 1979, 16.5% in 1980, and 20.0% in 1981.

One of the effects of this system of insurance in the United States was to provide hospitals with relatively stable revenue streams that were largely insulated from eco-

---

5. Todd B. Richter, "The Hospital Management Industry: Survival of the Fittest," *Industry Trend Analysis* (Morgan Stanley & Co., Inc., Investment Research), September 30, 1982, p. 11.

nomic cycles, inflation, and other economywide risks. Another was that hospitals tended to compete with one another on the basis of quality and breadth of services, reputation of medical staffs, and advertising rather than on the basis of low prices. Proposals to make consumers bear a greater proportion of their hospital expenses out of their own pockets and to change Medicare and Medicaid to something other than cost-based reimbursement systems could change these characteristics significantly. Some of the proposals being considered included treating health insurance premiums paid by employers as taxable income to employees, increasing the level of out-of-pocket expenses borne by Medicare/Medicaid patients, turning the Medicare program into a voucher system that provided fixed benefits independent of costs, eliminating return-on-equity provisions in Medicare and Medicaid reimbursements, and revising the Medicare/Medicaid programs so that they were *prospective* reimbursement systems. Under a system of prospective reimbursement, hospitals would be paid on the basis of "prospectively" set rates rather than actually realized costs. If a hospital provided services at a lower cost than the established rates, it could earn a profit; if not, it would realize a loss.

Most industry analysts predicted that some form of prospective reimbursement would be implemented some time in the 1980s. What was unclear was the exact composition of hospital costs that would be covered by such a system. One possibility would be a system in which capital costs would be prospectively set along with other costs of providing services. If this were to occur, hospitals would no longer be able to count on recouping the full amount of their allowable interest expense from the federal government. Another possibility was that interest expenses would continue to be paid retrospectively, but the return-on-equity provisions would be dropped altogether. This outcome would place even greater pressure on the private-patient side of a hospital's business to provide an adequate rate on capital. Whatever type of prospective reimbursement system was adopted, it seemed probable that the virtual elimination of losses and the subsidizing of capital costs heretofore provided by the cost-based reimbursement system would be reduced. This would instill greater volatility in hospital revenues and earnings.

Financial Decisions

HCA's growth objective implied capital expenditure outlays of $575 million in 1982. This level could be expected to expand by 20% a year for the next several years. Given these increasing capital requirements, its debt repayment schedule (see Exhibit 7), the future prospects of the hospital care industry, and HCA's other goals, senior management had to determine how best to prepare financially for HCA's future.

The first issue that had to be addressed in this process was HCA's target capital structure. Was its long-standing 60% target ratio of debt to total capital too high, too low, or about right? The rating agencies had made it clear that HCA would have to return to its 60–40 capital structure if it were to retain its A bond rating. In a meeting with the rating agencies, prearranged for the day after the acquisition of Hospital Affiliates was announced, Sam Brooks was "given the distinct impression that we had roughly until the end of the summer of 1982 to do something about our debt ratio." Loss of its A bond rating could make access to the debt markets more difficult for HCA. Historical data on debt issued with various credit ratings are presented in Exhibit 8.

Others, however, saw HCA's high level of debt in a more positive light. One Wall Street analyst was quoted as saying that the acquisition of Hospital Affiliates and the debt burden that accompanied the transaction "removes the stigma, if it is one, that

Hospital Corp. is too conservative. It said for a long time that it would stick to a 60–40 ratio of debt to equity . . . [This] shows they're willing to be flexible when the right move comes along."[6] Although maintaining its high degree of leverage would cost HCA its A bond rating, the loss might not be all that damaging. Du Pont, for example, lost its long-standing AAA bond rating with its acquisition of Conoco in 1981 without a dramatic rise in its cost of debt or a loss of access to the debt market.

Still others argued that even a 60% ratio of debt to total capital could be too high in light of potential changes in the regulatory environment. By increasing the risk surrounding the cash flows of the hospital management companies, such changes might necessitate a capital structure with only 50% debt or less. Reducing leverage to such a level would take time to accomplish and would require corrective action well in advance of the anticipated changes, even if one were beginning at a 60% debt level. As Bill McInnes said, "A $2½ billion capital structure can't be turned around on a dime."

---

6. "Hospital Corp. to Buy INA Unit for $650 Million," *The Wall Street Journal,* April 21, 1981, p. 27.

EXHIBIT 1
Consolidated Income Statements, 1979–1981 (millions of dollars except per share data)

	1979	*1980*	*1981*
Operating revenues	$1,043	$1,429	$2,406
Contractual adj. and doubtful accounts	143	197	343
Net revenues	901	1,232	2,064
Operating expenses	726	998	1,682
Depreciation and amortization	41	53	88
Interest expense	38	50	131
Income from operations	95	130	162
Other income	1	6	22
Income before income taxes	96	136	184
Provision for income taxes			
Current	28	44	49
Deferred	14	11	24
Net income	$ 54	$ 81	$ 111
Average number of common and common equivalent shares (millions)	41	47	50
Earnings per share	$ 1.34	$ 1.73	$ 2.23

Note: Figures may not add exactly because of rounding.

EXHIBIT 2
Consolidated Balance Sheets at December 31, 1979–1981 (millions of dollars)

	1979	*1980*	*1981*
Cash and cash equivalents	$ 30	$ 29	$ 50
Accounts receivable, net	149	214	363
Supplies	29	44	65
Other current assets	10	15	18
Current assets	218	303	498
Net property, plant, and equipment	802	1,187	2,066
Investments and other assets	40	81	188
Intangible assets	18	38	207
Total assets	$1,078	$1,610	$2,958
Accounts payable	$ 38	$ 58	$ 93
Dividends payable	2	3	4
Accrued liabilities	45	80	166
Income taxes payable	56	71	61
Current maturities of long-term debt	19	26	43
Current liabilities	160	238	367
Long-term debt	427	775	1,649
Deferred income taxes	74	85	117
Other liabilities	30	43	58
Total liabilities	691	1,141	2,191
Common stock (issued 52,210,645 shares in 1981; 45,378,375 shares in 1980; 19,456,634 shares in 1979)	19	45	52
Additional paid-in capital	157	144	342
Retained earnings	210	279	374
Shareholders' equity	387	469	768
Total liabilities and shareholders' equity	$1,078	$1,610	$2,958

Note: Figures may not add exactly because of rounding.

EXHIBIT 3

Ten-Year Historical Summary, 1972–1981 (millions of dollars except per share data and percentages)

	1972	1973	1974	1975	1976	1977	1978	1979	1980	1981
Summary of Operations										
Operating revenues	$ 173	$ 223	$ 298	$ 393	$ 506	$ 627	$ 797	$1,043	$1,429	$2,406
Interest expense	6	9	13	17	21	24	32	50	50	131
Income before income taxes	18	23	30	36	47	59	74	96	136	184
Net income	10	12	16	21	27	33	42	54	81	111
Average shares outstanding (millions)[a]	35	34	34	35	38	39	40	41	47	50
Earnings per share[a]	$ .30	$ .35	$ .45	$ .59	$ .71	$ .86	$ 1.05	$ 1.34	$ 1.73	$ 2.23
Cash dividends per share[a]	.02	.04	.05	.06	.09	.12	.17	.22	.27	.34
Dividend payout	6.7%	11.4%	11.1%	10.2%	12.7%	14.0%	16.2%	16.4%	15.6%	15.2%
Financial Position										
Total assets	$ 275	$ 321	$ 417	$ 508	$ 602	$ 709	$ 857	$1,078	$1,610	$2,958
Total debt	155	175	240	298	327	363	427	446	801	1,692
Shareholders' equity	91	107	121	142	186	215	252	387	469	768
Book value per share (year-end)	$ 2.69	$3.12	$3.53	$4.09	$4.89	$5.65	$ 6.57	$ 8.84	$10.33	$14.70
Average price-earnings ratio	33.7	18.1	7.3	8.0	9.2	8.6	10.9	11.8	15.9	18.5
Stock Performance										
High	$12.10	$9.90	$5.10	$7.10	$7.60	$9.00	$15.30	$19.90	$37.00	$50.70
Low	8.10	2.80	1.50	2.30	5.40	5.80	7.50	11.60	17.90	31.70
Selected Ratios										
Current ratio	1.3	1.4	1.2	1.5	1.5	1.4	1.4	1.4	1.3	1.4
Net profit margin	6.0%	5.5%	5.2%	5.3%	5.3%	5.3%	5.2%	5.2%	5.7%	4.6%
Return on beginning assets	5.3%	4.4%	4.9%	5.0%	5.3%	5.5%	5.9%	6.3%	7.5%	6.9%
Return on beginning equity	14.3%	13.4%	14.5%	17.0%	19.0%	17.9%	19.3%	21.5%	20.9%	23.7%
Asset turnover	.89	.81	.93	.94	1.00	1.04	1.12	1.22	1.33	1.50
Total debt/Total capital	63.1%	62.0%	66.4%	67.8%	63.7%	62.7%	62.9%	53.5%	63.1%	68.8%

a. Average share figures include unexercised options. Per share earnings and dividends were computed based on average shares outstanding.

EXHIBIT 4
Key Statistics for HCA's Hospitals, 1972–1981

	1972	1973	1974	1975	1976	1977	1978	1979	1980	1981
Hospitals in Operation										
Owned and leased, U.S.	46	53	56	62	68	72	81	88	144	188
Managed, U.S.	2	4	6	8	15	21	26	45	56	146
Owned and managed, international	–	–	–	2	2	2	5	15	18	15
Total	48	57	62	72	85	95	112	148	188	349
Bed capacity	7,304	8,507	9,280	11,648	13,458	14,465	18,036	22,543	28,204	49,866
Occupancy rate (U.S.-owned only)	na	na	70%	66%	66%	66%	65%	68%	69%	68%
Sources of Revenues by Payer										
Cost-based										
Medicare	27%	27%	29%	30%	32%	33%	35%	36%	37%	38%
Medicaid	4	3	3	4	4	4	4	3	3	5
Blue Cross	8	9	8	7	5	5	5	4	4	3
Total cost-based	39%	39%	40%	41%	41%	42%	44%	43%	44%	46%
Charge-based	61	61	60	59	59	58	56	57	56	54
Total	100%	100%	100%	100%	100%	100%	100%	100%	100%	100%

na=not available.

EXHIBIT 5

Comparative Data on Selected Publicly Held Hospital Management Companies, 1980–1981 (millions of dollars except per share data and percentages)

	Hospital Corporation of America		Humana, Inc.		American Medical International, Inc.		National Medical Enterprises, Inc.		Lifemark	
	1980	1981	1980	1981	1980	1981	1980	1981	1980	1981
Summary of Operations										
Operating revenues	$1,429	$2,406	$1,392	$1,704	$ 766	$1,117	$ 723	$1,044	$ 203	$ 323
Interest expense	50	131	76	60	25	41	26	33	6	12
Income before income taxes	136	184	120	177	66	97	54	96	16	31
Net income	81	111	65	93	33	51	29	52	14	18
Earnings per share, primary	$ 1.73	$ 2.23	$ 1.53	$ 2.33	$ 1.23	$ 1.60	.91	$ 1.24	$ 1.77	$ 1.80
Cash dividends per share	.27	.34	.35	.54	.38	.45	.20	.30	.33	.42
Dividend payout	15.6%	15.2%	22.9%	23.2%	30.9%	28.1%	22.0%	24.2%	18.6%	23.3%
Financial Position										
Total assets	$1,610	$2,958	$1,327	$1,502	$ 663	$ 984	$ 596	$ 867	$ 211	$ 387
Total debt	801	1,692	757	776	312	396	274	299	102	171
Preferred stock	–	–	66	64	–	–	5	5	–	–
Shareholders' equity	469	768	216	297	201	327	200	376	61	135
Book value per share	$10.33	$14.70	$ 5.97	$ 8.01	$ 7.36	$10.20	$ 5.47	$ 8.39	$ 7.56	$13.18
Average price-earnings ratio	15.9	18.5	11.9	16.3	18.3	16.9	8.2	15.6	16.1	10.3
Stock Performance										
High	$37.00	$50.70	$26.20	$46.38	$22.50	$32.50	$10.50	$27.25	$35.80	$28.10
Low	17.90	31.70	10.25	29.75	9.88	21.50	4.38	11.50	21.20	9.10
Bond rating[a]	A	A	NR	B+	Ba	NR	Ba	B+	Ba	BB+
Selected Ratios										
Current ratio	1.3	1.4	1.4	1.4	1.6	1.5	1.8	2.0	1.7	1.2
Net profit margin	5.7%	4.6%	4.6%	5.5%	4.3%	4.5%	4.1%	5.0%	6.9%	5.7%
Return on beginning assets	7.5%	6.9%	5.4%	7.0%	6.5%	7.7%	9.2%	8.7%	11.1%	8.7%
Return on beginning equity	20.9%	23.7%	38.1%	43.1%	21.3%	25.2%	27.0%	25.9%	40.3%	30.3%
Asset turnover	1.3	1.5	1.2	1.3	1.5	1.7	2.3	1.8	1.6	1.5
Total debt/Total capital	63.1%	68.8%	72.8%	68.2%	60.8%	54.8%	57.2%	44.0%	62.7%	55.9%

Hospitals in Operation

Owned/managed	188	349	90	89	61	102	54[c]	57[c]	30	35
Bed capacity	28,204	49,866	16,765	16,431	6,117[b]	9,713[b]	6,593[c]	6,929[c]	3,546	4,563
Occupancy rate	69%[d]	68%[d]	58.9%	61.3%	60.6%[b]	na	na	na	na	na

Sources of Revenues by Payer

Cost-based										
Medicare	37%	38%	39%	40%	45%	45%	42.1%	42.0%	—	—
Medicaid	3	5	5	5	7	7	12.6	12.7	—	—
Blue Cross	4	3	5	5	3	2	4.1	4.5	—	—
Total cost-based	44%	46%	49%	50%	55%	54%	58.8%	59.2%	44%	42%
Charge-based	56	54	51	50	45	46	41.2	40.8	56	58
Total	100%	100%	100%	100%	100%	100%	100%	100%	100%	100%

Growth Rates, 1976–1981

Revenues	35.3%	41.1%	31.2%	47.0%	31.0%
Net income	32.4	54.6	46.1	52.7	40.9
Total assets	34.2	30.0	22.7	34.3	39.7
Hospitals in operation	30.1	6.8	13.4	18.7	11.7

Note: Fiscal year ends August 31 for Humana and American Medical International; December 31 for HCA and Lifemark; May 31 for National Medical Enterprises. NR = not rated; na = not available.

a. Excludes convertibles.

b. For owned hospitals only.

c. Excludes long-term care facilities (i.e., nursing homes).

d. U.S.-owned only.

EXHIBIT 6
HCA's Hospital Locations in the United States

EXHIBIT 7
Schedule of Outstanding Long-Term Debt, 1979–1981 (millions of dollars)

	1979	*1980*	*1981*
Mortgage notes and bonds,			
6%–16½%, due through 1998	$288	$153	$ 176
Revenue bonds, 6¼%–13½%, due through 2011	63	102	134
Notes, debentures, and capitalized leases,			
7%–16½%, due through 1999	75	227	281
Revolving credit and term loan agreements at			
prime or LIBOR, plus ½%–⅝%	–	168	515
Commercial paper and bank financing, 13¼%			
composite effective rate at December 31, 1981[a]	–	125	208
Convertible subordinated debentures:			
8¾%, due 1996, convertible at $43.50 per share	–	–	80
8¾%, due 2006, convertible at $41.17 per share	–	–	125
12%, due 1996, convertible at $62.30 per share	–	–	81
Guaranteed notes, 15½%, due 1988	–	–	50
Total	$427	$775	$1,649

Debt maturing in the next 5 years ($ millions):
1982	$ 34
1983	70
1984	71
1985	117
1986	163

a. In 1980 and 1981 the company entered into revolving credit agreements with a group of banks, aggregating $160 million and $278 million, respectively. The lines were used to support commercial paper and other bank financing during these 2 years. Because of the availability of long-term financing under these agreements, the company classified the commercial paper issue under long-term debt.

EXHIBIT 8
Debt Issued in the U.S. Public Market by Industrial Corporations with Varying Credit Ratings, 1974–1981 (millions of dollars)

Credit Rating	1974		1975		1976		1977		1978		1979		1980		1981	
Aaa	$1,650	25.1%	$ 2,875	24.0%	$ 700	11.7%	$ 800	20.5%	$ 275	8.6%	$1,550	27.4%	$1,750	17.9%	$1,852	20.8%
Aa	2,415	36.7	3,310	27.7	2,030	33.8	1,125	28.9	700	21.8	1,800	31.8	2,900	29.7	2,458	27.7
A	2,060	31.3	5,355	44.7	2,205	36.8	960	24.6	1,310	40.8	1,500	26.5	4,220	43.2	3,887	43.7
Baa	440	6.7	420	3.5	1,010	16.8	445	11.4	210	6.5	0	0	345	3.6	0	0
Other	15	.2	9	.1	53	.9	567	14.6	713	22.3	809	14.3	549	5.6	690	7.8
	$6,580	100.0%	$11,969	100.0%	$5,998	100.0%	$3,897	100.0%	$3,208	100.0%	$5,659	100.0%	$9,764	100.0%	$8,887	100.0%

Source: Salomon Brothers Inc.

Crown Corporation

In February 1969, Walter Bennett, treasurer of Crown Corporation, was considering several financing alternatives. Crown's decision to integrate backward into the production of primary aluminum ingot had resulted in very heavy capital expenditures. Its need for funds for working capital and for completion of a large aluminum plant now outstripped the company's internal cash generation, and it would be necessary to raise $30 million within the next six months to cover capital needs for 1969. Mr. Bennett hoped to develop a financing program that would meet the immediate and the longer-term needs without jeopardizing Crown's 70¢ dividend rate.

Company Description

A series of acquisitions and divestitures during the 1960s had totally transformed Crown Corporation from a mining company into a manufacturer of superalloy castings for aircraft and industrial uses and aluminum products for the building, packaging, and aircraft industries. Sales were evenly divided between castings and aluminum products.

Crown's castings were for the most part designed for operation in the "hot part" of the gas turbine engine. The company worked from designs prepared chiefly by aircraft engine manufacturers. These manufacturers, in their endeavor to obtain greater thrust, designed parts that would function at engine operating temperatures ranging to 2,150 degrees Fahrenheit. The high temperatures required the use of precision castings for blades and vanes. The techniques and know-how involved in casting operations were important, and the commercial success of such an operation was in large measure dependent upon achieving a low ratio of rejects. Crown's constant emphasis on quality and technical excellence had established a high level of confidence among its customers. For adherence to a rigid standard of performance and quality, Crown had been selected to participate in the majority of U.S. jet engine

TABLE A
Consumption, Production, and Sales of Aluminum, 1965–1973

	Actual (millions of pounds)				Estimates (millions of pounds)		
	1965	*1966*	*1967*	*1968*	*1969*	*1970*	*1973*
Consumption of primary aluminum by Crown's fabricating divisions	94	107	116	135	160	185	290
Production of primary aluminum							
Intalco	0	16	69	88	130	130	130
Eastalco	0	0	0	0	0	85	170
Purchases (sales) of primary aluminum by Crown	94	91	47	47	30	(30)	(10)

programs in the past 10 years. (Exhibit 1 provides information on jet engine production in the United States.)

The other half of Crown's sales comprised aluminum products, including a broad product line for the building and construction industry (see Table A). Major efforts had been made to increase the company's captive source of primary aluminum ingot for consumption by its fabricating operations. To ensure a steady and economical source, Crown had become a producer of primary aluminum in 1966 through participation with American Metal Climax, Inc. in a project known as Intalco. Crown's share of Intalco's output was 130 million pounds, roughly 81% of its total need.

In 1967 the decision was made to build a second aluminum ingot plant, named Eastalco, at a cost of $50 million. Eastalco was expected to start operations in mid-1970, providing Crown with additional primary aluminum capacity of 85 million pounds a year and increased net income of $3–4 million. A planned addition of 85 million pounds in 1972 would raise Eastalco's capacity to 170 million pounds and would meet the company's objective to be a fully integrated producer (see Table A).

Company Performance

Crown's sales had risen sharply from $60 million in 1958 to $230 million in 1968 on the strength of 23 acquisitions, strong internal growth, and a firming of aluminum prices.[1] The company's earnings had been considerably more erratic, however, with the volatility largely the result of instability in its aluminum business. After reaching a peak of $1.13 in 1959, earnings per share fell to $.34 in 1963 as overcapacity developed in the aluminum business and prices of fabricated products were eroded. (Crown's operating results are shown in Exhibit 2.) The "great growth potential" of aluminum had encouraged major capacity additions by established producers and entry by new producers during the 1950s. Domestic industry capacity rose by 79% between 1954 and 1960. American producers were also faced with a tremendous buildup in capacity elsewhere in the world. After a decade of generally rising prices, excess capacity began to take its toll in 1958. In April of that year, the producer price for American ingot was lowered from 26 to 24¢ per pound to match a similar reduction initiated by Canadian firms in the world market. By December 1962 the quotation had dropped to 22.5¢ per pound.

---

1. The history of the aluminum industry is drawn in large part from Y. Levy, *Aluminum: Past and Future* (San Francisco. Federal Reserve Bank of San Francisco, 1971).

In the fabricated products market, where the relative ease of entry had brought in many small- and medium-sized independent concerns, competition for the available business was even keener and price erosion more severe. List prices of fabricated products dropped on the average about 20% between late 1961 and late 1963. (Exhibit 3 provides data on aluminum shipments and prices.) The decline in actual market prices undoubtedly was even sharper because of a method of discounting—called commodity pricing—that was undertaken in order to penetrate new markets. This method, most prevalent in sheet, strip, coil, and plate products, involved selling a product for a specific application at a price lower than the published price. The seller then attempted to confine the lower price to specific product areas so as not to reduce revenues. However, in the late 1950s, the whole price structure came tumbling down and profits came tumbling after. Profits of the three major aluminum companies collapsed from $175 million in 1956 to a low of $88 million in 1960.

Demand-supply conditions in the industry finally improved in the early 1960s, and with the improvement came sharply higher earnings for Crown and other aluminum producers. Over the 1961–1966 period, industry shipments of aluminum increased by 14% annually. Despite increases in supply, the price of ingot went up four times between October 1963 and November 1964, from a low of 22.5 to 24.5¢ per pound. But price weakness continued at the fabricating level during this period. The hundreds of small fabricators lowered prices to obtain business for their idle machinery, while consumers increasingly came to disregard published mill prices.

Prices of fabricated products remained weak until 1965, when strike-anticipation hedge buying bolstered demand and pushed up operating rates. Producers raised prices several times early in the year, and then again after a new 3-year labor contract was signed in June. For the next 3 years shipments of aluminum products continued to rise 8–10% annually and prices firmed further. Shortly after a new 3-year labor contract was signed in 1968, producers raised the price of ingot by 4%, to 26¢ per pound, and raised the price of fabricated products by a comparable amount. After a brief period of discounting in the wake of the labor settlement, the new list prices apparently took hold. In January 1969, producers raised the price of ingot from 26 to 27¢ per pound and raised prices on a wide range of mill products by an average of 5%, and further price increases were anticipated.

The strong price situation improved industry profitability dramatically. Profits of the three major aluminum firms rebounded from the 1960 low of $88 million to $230 million in 1966 (see Exhibit 4). Crown's record was no less dramatic. Rising from a low of $.34 per share in 1963, Crown's earnings reached $2.03 per share in 1967. Its stock, which had sold at less than $5 per share in 1963, reached a high of $51 in mid-1968 on the strength of record earnings and an increased dividend rate.

Surpluses of the Seventies?

The improved industry price structure in the late 1960s encouraged aluminum producers to move forward to meet the demands and the opportunities of the 1970s. Throughout the world, producers began to build new smelters and enlarge older ones. In the United States the expansion in capacity contemplated over the next 3 years seemed moderate in terms of past trends in demand. American producers were scheduled to boost their primary production potential from almost 4.2 million tons in 1970 to 5 million tons by 1973, or at a 6.4% annual rate. This rate of expansion, although substantial, was below the 10% rate of growth of domestic aluminum consumption during the 1960s.

In reducing their rate of expansion, U.S. producers recognized that they were facing the strongest counterattack from other materials in their history. Aluminum's success in penetrating the territory staked out by other metals had been phenomenal. Shipments of aluminum ingot and mill products grew at more than twice the rate of durable goods output and construction activity over the 1960s. The industry was successful, through research and development and aggressive marketing techniques, in creating new uses for the metal and in displacing traditional materials in older applications.

The steel industry, the giant of the metal field with 1968 ingot production of 130 million tons as against aluminum's 3 million tons, had initiated a strong fight to ward off the lightweight metal's further advances. In particular, steel was fighting hard to protect its position in the $3.5 billion can market and in the rapid transit market, which could evolve into a $10 billion outlet over the 1970s. The copper industry was also fighting to protect its markets, and the plastics industry was challenging aluminum in each of aluminum's principal markets—construction, transportation, and packaging.

However, the most effective dampening influence on the domestic industry was the huge increase in aluminum capacity abroad. Plans in 1969 called for capacity elsewhere in the non-Communist world to rise at well over double the U.S. rate between 1970 and 1973, as major European and Asian nations built up their own production in an effort to reduce their dependence on imports. With almost 4.4 million tons of new capacity—3.5 millions tons overseas plus .9 million tons in the United States—scheduled to come on stream in the 1970–1973 period, world capacity could rise from about 9.4 million to 13.7 million tons, or at a 14% annual rate.

This expansion in capacity would exceed the anticipated growth in demand, since most industry analysts expected that world aluminum consumption would not exceed the 9% rate of growth registered during the 1960–1968 period. If all the capacity programmed was brought in on schedule, growth in consumption at the 9% level over the next several years could result in as much as 2 million tons of excess capacity by 1973, representing about 15% of the industry's total production capability.

Before jumping to the conclusion that the industry's price structure was in danger of weakening, however, Mr. Bennett realized that the major aluminum producers might stretch out their expansion projects over a longer period, especially where expansion was scheduled through incremental additions to existing plants. Projects not yet started might be postponed or canceled. Furthermore, he did not underestimate the ability of the industry to boost consumption above anticipated levels by imaginative research and development and marketing programs.

Crown's Expected Growth

Mr. Bennett expected that Crown's sales would increase at 6–8% annually, exclusive of acquisitions, over the foreseeable future. No growth was forecast through 1974 in the precision castings business as sharp reductions in defense procurement needs would offset the 15% per year increase in commercial sales. However, sales of aluminum products were expected to rise by 15–20% annually as the company broadened its penetration of major aluminum consuming markets. This sales growth would necessitate heavy spending on aluminum reduction facilities and fabricating capacity. Total capital expenditures, including the Eastalco project, were forecast at $39 million in 1969, $32 million in 1970, $7 million in 1971, and $50 million in 1972. The heavy capital spending would require that Crown raise $30 million in 1969, $22 million in 1970, and $30 million in 1972.

Financing Alternatives

Several alternatives were open to Crown to meet its financing needs in 1969 (see the balance sheets for 1965–1968 shown in Exhibit 5). The company's investment bankers believed that a $30 million common stock issue was possible and pointed to the future financing flexibility afforded by the use of equity financing. On the other hand, the dilution of earnings per share that would result from sale of additional stock was a matter of concern to Mr. Bennett. Crown stock had fallen from $51 per share in May 1968 to a level of $30 per share as investors reacted to disappointing earnings in 1968. (Comparative industry stock price data are provided in Exhibit 6.) Further near-term price weakness seemed likely as earnings per share remained depressed as Crown absorbed heavy start-up costs for the production of the main landing gear for the McDonnell Douglas DC-10 in 1969. Under these conditions, announcement of a large equity issue would drive the stock price down to the low twenties, at which price it would be necessary to sell 1.4 million shares to raise the $30 million net to the company. Mr. Bennett wondered whether equity financing should be deferred until the company resumed its pattern of earnings gains.

As an alternative to equity financing, a consortium of commercial banks had agreed to lend the company up to $30 million at 7¼% interest. The term loan would be repayable at an annual rate of $5 million beginning in 1970 and ending in 1975. Under the provisions of the loan agreement, net working capital must exceed $55 million, dividend payments were restricted to earnings accumulated after the date of the loan agreement, and additional funded debt was limited to $20 million.

It would also be possible to place a $30 million subordinated convertible debenture issue privately with the Northern Life Insurance Company. The debentures would carry a coupon of 6%, with annual debt retirement of $2 million in years 6 through 20. The issue would not be callable for 10 years, except at par for mandatory debt retirement, and would be convertible into common stock at $31.50.

Mr. Bennett was interested in the debt alternatives. Although the company's use of debt had increased sharply and coverage ratios had narrowed, its coverage of interest costs was still considered adequate. On the other hand, the flexibility afforded by use of equity financing could be valuable in future years.

EXHIBIT 1

Aircraft Engine Production, 1946–1968 (number of engines)

		Military			Civil		
	Total	Total Military	Reciprocal	Jet	Total Civil	Reciprocal	Jet
1946	43,407	2,585	1,680	905	40,822	40,822	—
1947	20,912	4,561	2,683	1,878	16,351	16,351	—
1948	14,027	4,988	2,495	2,493	9,039	9,039	—
1949	11,972	7,990	2,981	5,009	3,982	3,982	—
1950	13,675	9,361	3,122	6,239	4,314	4,314	—
1951	20,867	16,287	6,471	9,816	4,580	4,580	—
1952	31,041	25,659	8,731	16,928	5,382	5,382	—
1953	40,263	33,616	13,365	20,251	6,647	6,647	—
1954	26,959	21,440	7,868	13,572	5,519	5,519	—
1955	21,108	13,469	3,875	9,594	7,639	7,639	—
1956	21,348	9,849	2,663	7,186	11,499	11,499	—
1957	21,984	11,087	2,429	8,658	10,897	10,859	38
1958	18,869	8,121	1,452	6,669	10,748	10,233	515
1959	17,162	4,626	661	3,965	12,536	11,152	1,384
1960	16,189	3,673	756	2,917	12,516	10,891	1,625
1961	15,832	5,172	417	4,755	10,660	9,669	991
1962	15,919	5,441	241	5,200	10,478	9,921	557
1963	17,185	5,390	155	5,235	11,795	11,322	473
1964	19,585	5,380	175	5,205	14,205	13,346	859
1965	23,378	5,191	92	5,099	18,187	17,018	1,169
1966	30,810	7,548	45	7,503	23,262	21,324	1,938
1967	28,858	8,046	—	8,046	20,812	18,324	2,488
1968	29,761	8,542	—	8,542	21,219	17,806	3,413

Source: Aerospace Facts and Figures 1973/1974 (New York: Aerospace Industries Association of America, Inc., 1973), p. 48.

EXHIBIT 2

Selected Operating Data, 1963–1968 (millions of dollars except per share data)

	1962	1963	1964	1965	1966	1967	1968
Net sales	$ 110	$ 122	$ 122	$ 141	$ 176	$ 213	$ 230
Operating profit[a]	$ 8.3	$ 4.6	$ 5.5	$ 9.1	$ 18.5	$ 27.8	$ 28.5
Other income (expense)[b]	(.4)	(.6)	(.3)	(.8)	(.1)	(.7)	(1.0)
Income before taxes	7.9	4.0	5.2	8.3	18.4	27.1	27.5
Federal income taxes	3.7	1.5	2.3	3.6	7.6	12.3	13.8
Net income	$ 4.2	$ 2.5	$ 2.9	$ 4.7	$ 10.8	$ 14.8	$ 13.7
Earnings per share	$ .57	$ .34	$ .42	$ .66	$ 1.50	$ 2.03	$ 1.87
Dividends per share	0	.20	.20	.23	.40	.60	.70
Market price							
High	9	7	7	11	27	51	51
Low	5	5	5	6	10	22	32
Price-earnings ratio							
High	16	21	17	17	18	25	27
Low	9	15	12	9	7	11	17

a. After deduction of depreciation expense ($5 million in 1968).

b. Other income and other expenses including interest expense are offset against each other.

EXHIBIT 3
Price Chronology

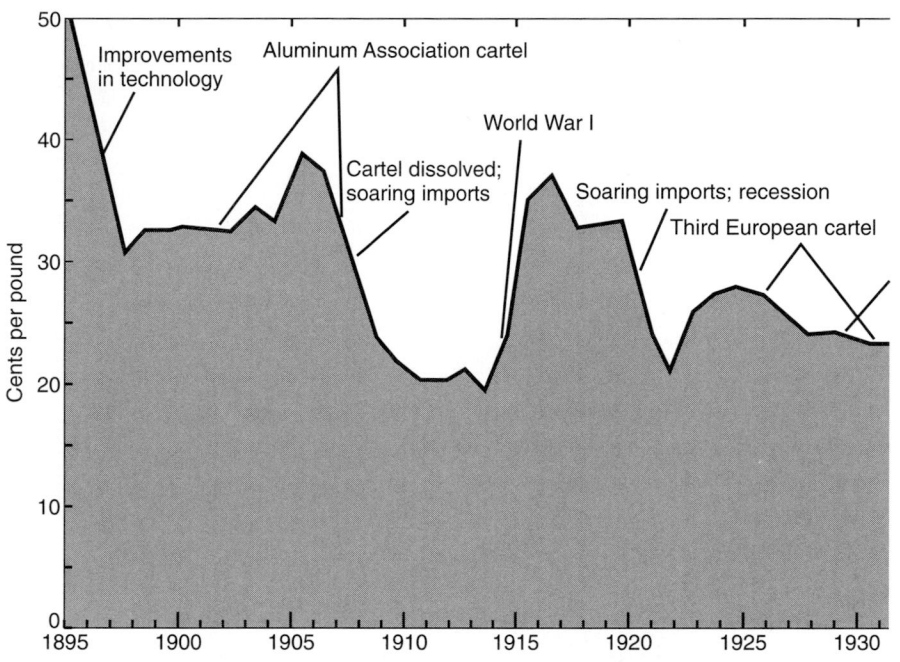

Little over a century ago, aluminum was still a rare metal, costing $545 per pound in 1852. Yet after several decades of technological advance, the price dropped to $8 per pound in 1885. Then, with the development of the electrolytic process for producing aluminum, the metal began to come within the reach of the average consumer. On the eve of World War I, aluminum was selling for 19½¢ per pound, thanks to the growth of a technologically advanced industry in Europe and North America—and despite the efforts of producers' cartels to maintain a high price structure for the metal. As a consequence of this price decline, aluminum markets were no longer confined to speciality items in the cooking, military, and surgical fields but had spread also to tonnage items in the fast-growing electrical and automotive industries. During World War I, prices practically doubled despite the rapid expansion of production facilities. But by the end of 1921, prices were back to prewar levels as producers here and abroad fought to find peacetime markets for wartime-swollen supplies. During the next several decades, aluminum

EXHIBIT 3 *(continued)*

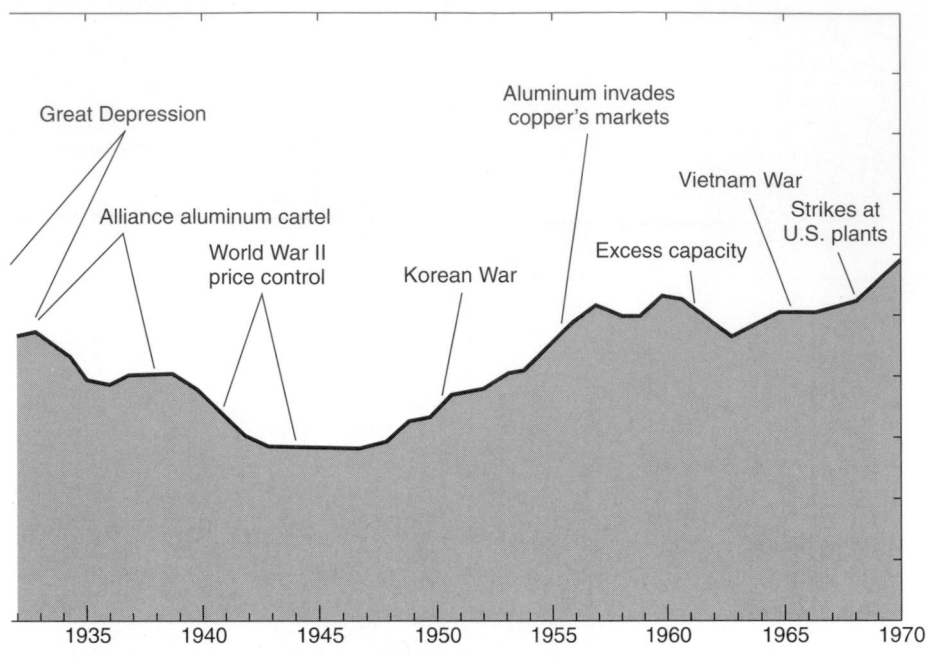

prices trended downwards. In the 1920s and 1930s, industry cartels set prices and imposed output restrictions worldwide in an attempt to manage markets that had been unsettled by lagging demand and increasing capacity. In the 1940s, as the domestic industry expanded rapidly to meet insatiable wartime demands, the government held the price line by setting the ingot price at 14¢ per pound. Prices have generally moved upward since World War II. The surprisingly high level of civilian reconversion demand, plus the heavy Korean War and strategic-stockpile demand, helped push prices from 14 to 25½¢ per pound between 1947 and 1957. But then prices slumped, reaching 22½¢ per pound in 1963, as military and civilian demand turned sluggish in the face of a tremendous buildup in capacity throughout the world. Finally, with the industrial expansion and the war boom of the late 1960s, prices increased again.

Source: Y. Levy, *Aluminum: Past and Future* (San Francisco: Federal Reserve Bank of San Francisco, 1971).

EXHIBIT 3 *(concluded)*

Statistics on Industry Shipments and Prices: Total Aluminum Industry Shipments, 1942–1969 (millions of pounds, net shipments)

	Total	Ingot	Domestic Mill Products	Imported Mill Products
1942	1,452.7	507.4	933.6	11.7
1943	2,217.2	724.6	1,492.4	.2
1944	2,566.4	952.0	1,613.0	1.4
1945	1,866.4	549.2	1,329.8	7.4
1946	1,672.4	529.2	1,140.8	2.4
1947	2,040.1	631.8	1,408.2	.1
1948	2,282.0	629.8	1,640.2	12.0
1949	1,654.1	479.9	1,158.1	16.1
1950	2,460.6	724.6	1,713.4	22.6
1951	2,506.6	709.8	1,756.2	40.6
1952	2,694.5	811.2	1,850.4	32.9
1953	3,276.8	982.9	2,228.2	65.7
1954	3,036.0	920.2	2,086.6	29.2
1955	4,035.1	1,205.4	2,791.8	37.9
1956	4,154.6	1,223.5	2,885.8	45.3
1957	3,880.1	1,161.6	2,677.6	40.9
1958	3,631.2	974.0	2,597.1	60.1
1959	5,061.0	1,575.0	3,386.1	100.1
1960	4,732.5	1,608.6	3,049.1	74.8
1961	4,970.1	1,536.6	3,345.1	88.4
1962	5,772.5	1,858.6	3,811.3	102.7
1963	6,377.0	2,032.6	4,257.2	87.2
1964	7,171.3	2,228.6	4,834.9	107.8
1965	8,150.2	2,337.3	5,679.4	133.5
1966	9,031.6	2,340.1	6,457.5	234.1
1967	8,946.4	2,486.4	6,350.6	109.5
1968	9,977.4	2,694.8	7,167.0	115.6
1969[a]	10,825.0	3,050.0	7,660.0	115.0

Sources: Ingot and mill products, domestic: 1942–1945—Aluminum and Magnesium Division, War Production Board: 1946 to date—U.S. Department of Commerce, Bureau of the Census, Industry Division, and Bureau of Domestic Commerce, Aluminum and Magnesium Industries Operations, Facts for Industry 1946–1959, and Current Industrial Report Series M33–2, 1960 to date.

Mill products, imported: U.S. Department of Commerce, Bureau of the Census, Foreign Trade Division, and CIR Series M33–2.

Note: Details may not add to totals because of rounding.

a. Forecast.

EXHIBIT 4
Charts Showing Improvement in Profits of the Three Major Aluminum Firms in the Late 1960s along with Rising Prices

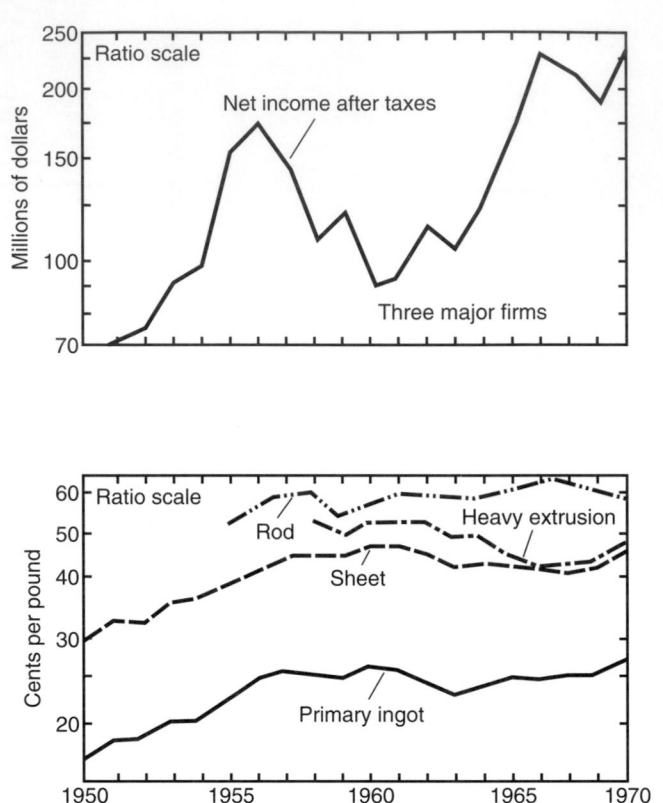

Source: Y. Levy, *Aluminum: Past and Future* (San Francisco: Federal Reserve Bank of San Francisco, 1971).

EXHIBIT 5

Balance Sheets at December 31, 1965–1968 (millions of dollars)

	1965	1966	1967	1968
Cash	$ 3	$ 3	$ 5	$ 4
Marketable securities	7	10	23	6
Accounts receivable	20	23	35	42
Inventories	28	38	45	50
Other	0	0	1	1
Current assets	58	74	109	103
Investments in aluminum plants				
Intalco	32	29	34	36
Eastalco	0	0	0	4
Other net property, plant and equipment	28	31	34	42
Other	3	4	4	4
Total assets	$121	$138	$181	$189
Accounts payable	$ 8	$ 10	$ 13	$ 14
Accrued liabilities	6	7	7	10
Accrued taxes	4	8	8	6
Dividends payable	1	1	1	1
Current maturities—long-term debt	2	2	2	4
Current liabilities	21	28	31	35
Long-term debt[a]	30	28	56	52
Deferred federal taxes	1	2	3	3
Stockholders' equity (7,273,000 shares outstanding at year-end 1968)	69	80	91	99
Total liabilities and net worth	$121	$138	$181	$189

a. Crown Corporation placed a $56 million debt issue directly with several life insurance companies in 1967. Of the proceeds, $26 million represented a refinancing of existing debt and the balance of $30 million represented new money to the company. The debentures have a coupon of 6%, with debt retirement of $4 million annually beginning in 1968 and ending in 1981.

EXHIBIT 6
Comparative Data on Aluminum Companies

	Alcan	Alcoa	Harvey	Crown	Braun[a]	S&P 425 Industrials
Earnings per share						
1962	$ 1.14	$ 2.52	$1.19	$ .57	$1.74	$3.87
1963	1.01	2.27	.90	.34	1.23	4.24
1964	1.57	2.72	.77	.42	1.55	4.83
1965	1.93	3.41	.53	.66	2.14	5.51
1966	2.41	4.83	2.24	1.50	3.30	5.89
1967	1.94	4.93	2.36	2.03	3.00	5.66
1968	2.14	4.75	2.16	1.87	2.81	6.15
1969 est.	2,30	5.40	1.75	1.85[b]	3.00	6.25
Price-earnings ratio						
1962	15–25	18–27	13–25	9–16	14–21	17
1963	20–28	23–31	20–27	15–21	25–34	18
1964	17–21	22–30	22–29	12–19	18–27	18
1965	13–17	18–23	34–44	9–17	13–19	17
1966	10–18	14–20	9–13	7–18	9–16	15
1967	12–17	14–19	11–25	11–25	13–20	18
1968	10–13	13–17	15–25	17–27	15–17	18
Feb. 1969	13	14	20	16	13	18
1968 sales ($ millions)	$1,081	$1,353	$177	$230	$850	—
Book value per share (1968)	$ 23	$ 49	$ 20	$ 13	$ 25	—
Current dividend rate	1.10	1.80	1.20	.70	1.00	3.21
Long-term debt as percent of total capital	46%	39%	41%	34%	55%	—
Times interest earned	5.2	6.6	6.7	9.1	4.8	—
Debt rating						
Senior debt	A	A	—	NR	NR	—
Convertible subordinated debt	—	BBB	BBB	—	—	—

NR = not rated.

a. Affiliated with Braun Industries.

b. Before any new financing.

Valuation and Discounted Cash Flows

1. The Bane & Company pension fund manager has projected a large outflow of funds to pension plan beneficiaries 15 years in the future. To fund this future liability, he has decided to invest in a Guaranteed Investment Contract (GIC) with one of two insurance companies. Bane will make a single $10 million up-front payment in exchange for a GIC that promises a single (larger) maturity payment to Bane in 15 years at a promised interest rate. The GIC options offered to the Bane fund manager are

- Pru-Johntower Life Insurance Company's GIC, promising an annual rate of interest of 10%.
- Tom Paine Mutual Life Insurance Company's GIC, promising a rate of interest of 9.72% per year, compounded monthly.

Compare the effective annual rates of the two GICs; also, compare the future promised payment that Bane will receive in 15 years under each option.

2. Mr. and Mrs. Spirit purchased a $35,000 house 20 years ago. They took a 30-year mortgage for $30,000 at a 3% annual interest rate. They have just made their twentieth annual payment. Their bank, the First Amityville National Bank, has recently offered the Spirits two alternatives by which they could prepay their mortgage:

- The Spirits could prepay their mortgage at a 30% discount from the current principal outstanding. Current 10-year mortgage rates are 12%. Ignore taxes, and assume payments are made at the end of each year (instead of monthly).
- The Spirits' existing mortgage would be replaced with a 5-year zero-interest loan in the amount of their current mortgage's principal outstanding. This new

This case was prepared by Professor Michael E. Edleson.

Copyright © 1991 by the President and Fellows of Harvard College.
Harvard Business School case 291–028.

loan would be repaid in five equal annual payments. The banker pointed out that this option would "save them well over $2,000 in interest."

Which alternative, if either, should the Spirits pursue?

3.   You are considering buying a new $25,000 car. The car dealer offers you a 13.6% loan with 30 equal monthly payments. Upon questioning the dealer, you find that this unusual loan has "add-on" interest, so that an interest charge of $8,500 (13.6% × $25,000 × 2.5 years) is added on to the $25,000, for a total amount to be repaid of $33,500. The payments arc $1,116.67 each month ($33,500 ÷ 30).

What is the approximate effective annual interest rate of this loan?

4.   Ms. Alumm is the portfolio manager for a large insurance company. She is considering investing $1 million to purchase the bonds of Patriot Enterprises, Inc.

a.   All of Patriot's bonds have market prices that imply a yield to maturity of 8% bond-equivalent yield (that is, 4% every six-month period).[1] Each Patriot bond is described here, based on a $1,000 face value (par value), which is the promised payment at maturity.

- Bond A has 5 years until maturity and pays a 9% coupon yield ($45 every six months on a $1,000 face value bond).
- Bond B has 10 years until maturity, pays an 8% coupon yield ($40 semiannual payments), and is being offered in a private placement at par.
- Bond C is a zero-coupon bond that pays no explicit interest but will pay the face amount of $1,000 per bond at maturity in 10 years.

At what price should each bond sell currently?

b.   Ms. Alumm realizes that in addition to determining the current prices of these bonds, she would also like to know how these prices might respond to changing interest rates once her company has purchased them.

If the bonds are purchased at an 8% bond-equivalent yield, *what would happen to the price of each bond, and how much money would the company make, if market yields on Patriot bonds fell to 6%? rose to 10%?*

c.   As an alternative, Ms. Alumm has been invited to invest $1 million in a private placement of a 10-year Eurobond[2] of a second firm, Nationaliste, S.A. Nationaliste bonds are similar in risk to Bond B—they promise an 8% coupon yield for 10 years—but coupons are paid annually, not semiannually. The Nationaliste bonds are priced at a 1% discount from par, or $990 per $1,000 face value.

---

1. Most domestic U.S. bonds pay interest of half the coupon rate semiannually. The bond-equivalent yield to maturity is generally stated in terms of twice the semiannual yield, ignoring the compounding of the midyear coupon payment. Thus, the yield to maturity as commonly stated for semiannual bonds actually understates the true annual effective yield.

2. A common characteristic of many Eurobonds is that they generally pay *annual* coupon payments, as opposed to the semiannual convention for typical domestic U.S. bonds. If one calculates the yield to maturity based on these annual payments, one will obtain an effective annual rate. This differs from the semiannual-based bond-equivalent yield that is the convention for the bond yield quotes in the United States.

What yield to maturity is implied by the Nationaliste Eurobond? Compare this yield to the 8% bond-equivalent of the Patriot semiannual-coupon bond (Bond B). What should Ms. Alumm do?

d. Ms. Alumm receives a call from a Japanese bond dealer who offers to sell her the same Nationaliste bonds, priced at the "Japanese yield to maturity" of 8.16%. In calculating the yield to maturity of a coupon-bearing bond, it is Japanese practice to use the following formula.[3]

$$\text{Yield} = \frac{\text{Annual coupon} + (\text{Par value} - \text{Price})/\text{Years to maturity}}{\text{Price}} \times 100\%$$

Should Ms. Alumm purchase the Nationaliste bonds from the Japanese dealer or in the private placement?

5. You are the chief financial officer of the firm Ponce De Leon Foods. The board has decided to offer an early retirement plan whereby the typical 55-year-old worker can retire now with a small cash severance and draw a pension of $10,000 per year, expected to last for 30 years (the first payment would be made 1 year from now). You plan to set aside sufficient money now to fund the plan, and you have secured guarantees from your insurance company promising you an 8% annual return on all funds deposited by you, to meet these projected payments based on the stated terms and to bear any risk (such as interest rate surprises or longer-than-expected life spans). You expect 100 workers to take advantage of the plan, so you must fund expected pension payouts of $1 million per year for 30 years.

The Amalgamated Paper-or-Plastic Workers Union has objected to the plan, since the pension payments "lose purchasing power" over time because of inflation. It proposes an alternative plan of an $8,000 pension (also beginning in a year) that grows each year at a fixed rate of 5%. It claims that this plan should be attractive to the company, since it needs to pay less money to pensioners ($8,000 versus $10,000) during today's difficult economic times.

How much will it cost you in terms of an up-front payment to fund each plan?[4]

---

3. Basically, this Japanese yield-to-maturity formula takes the *current yield* (Coupon ÷ Price) of the bond and adds to it a simple annual proration of the premium (price over par) or discount (price under par) of the bond.

4. While you could easily solve this on a spreadsheet, you may instead choose to use the following formula for the present value (V) of an initial end-of-year annuity payout of C (growing at g%) per period, with an interest rate of r%, for T periods.

$$V = \frac{C}{r-g}[1 - \left(\frac{1+g}{1+r}\right)^T]$$

Jupiter Management Company

On the morning of May 22, 1991, Win Smith, vice chairman of Jupiter Management Company and president and portfolio manager of Jupiter Venture Fund, was mulling over his options with respect to the impending sale of $100 million principal amount of convertible subordinated debentures by Sensormatic Electronics Corporation. Sensormatic, the leading supplier of electronic antitheft systems to retail stores and other commercial and industrial users, was one of the largest holdings in Jupiter Venture's investment portfolio and one of the best recent performers, having more than doubled in price during its 18 months in the portfolio. The fund now held 353,300 shares with a market value of $6.9 million, making Sensormatic the seventh largest equity position in the portfolio. Jupiter Venture was a small-company growth fund with $376 million of net assets. It was the second largest and fastest growing member of the Jupiter group of mutual funds, a 10-member family of open-end, no-load mutual funds marketed and managed by Jupiter Management.[1,2]

This case was prepared by Professor Ronald W. Moore.
Copyright © 1992 by the President and Fellows of Harvard College.
Harvard Business School case 292–107.

1. Open-end funds continuously sold and redeemed fund shares in response to investor demand. Sales and purchases took place at a price determined by net asset value per share (see note 3) at the close of trading on the date of the transaction. Closed-end funds, in contrast, initially issued a fixed number of shares, generally through an underwritten offering. These shares then changed hands through secondary market trading on one of the stock exchanges.

2. A no-load fund did not charge purchasers of fund shares either a front-end sales commission, known as a load, or a deferred sales commission, known as a 12b-1 fee, which was payable quarterly out of fund assets. Marketing of no-load funds relied heavily upon advertising and direct-mail solicitation by the fund sponsor, coverage by the financial press, and recommendations by financial planners, investment newsletters, and other advisers. Load funds, in contrast, charged purchasers of fund shares a front-end commission. Depending on the fund and, in some instances, on the size of the purchase, loads ranged from 1% to 8.5% of the amount invested, with most load equity funds charging 4.75% to 7.5%. In other words, if an investor put $100 into a fund with a 7.5% load, only $92.50 went into the fund. The balance was divided between the fund sponsor and the organization that actually sold the shares, typically a securities brokerage firm. Funds could also combine a front-end commission with a deferred commission; where there was a deferred commission, there was typically a redemption charge on shares held less than a specified length of time.

Since Smith believed that buying the convertibles of small, less-than-investment-grade companies generally amounted to buying their common stock at a premium price, he rarely considered them for the Jupiter Venture portfolio. In this instance, however, he thought it might make sense to substitute convertibles for some or perhaps all of the fund's Sensormatic common stock. While Smith considered the company's longer-term prospects to be extremely bright, he had some qualms about the near-term earnings outlook.

As he pondered the Sensormatic offering, Smith was mindful that, for the first time in its life of five-plus years, Jupiter Venture's investment results were lagging behind those of direct competitors, as well as stock market indices. Smith attributed the shortfall in 1991 year-to-date results to a heavy influx of new cash into the fund since January 1, the result of growing recognition of Jupiter Venture's exceptional record and a sharp rise in the stock market. With the stock market near an all-time high and the general economy in the third quarter of a recession, Smith simply could not find attractively priced stocks fast enough to absorb the inflows. Cash now comprised 37% of the fund's net assets, and there was no sign that the inflows would soon abate.[3] Smith was reluctant to close the fund. Jupiter Management's revenues were a direct function of net assets under management, and competition among mutual fund groups for investable assets was intense. On the other hand, Jupiter Venture's highly publicized performance figured importantly in the marketing of all of Jupiter Management's investment advisory services.

Earlier in the day, the managing underwriter for the Sensormatic offering had announced that it would be priced that afternoon, after the close of business on the New York Stock Exchange (NYSE) at 4 P.M. Earlier in the week, Smith had placed tentative orders for up to 5% of the offering. In view of strong and increasing investor interest in the offering, he knew he would have to reaffirm or pull those orders before the close.

Mutual Funds

A mutual fund was an investment company (typically a corporation in legal form) that invested on a commingled basis monies derived from the sale of its shares to individual and/or institutional investors. By pooling assets gathered from many investors, a mutual fund could afford its shareholders the benefits of diversification, low operating expenses, and professional investment management otherwise available only to large institutions and the wealthiest individuals. Fund assets (apart from miscellaneous items) consisted of securities held in an investment portfolio that reflected the fund's investment objectives and policies.[4] These varied widely, reflecting the efforts of fund marketers to cater to all significant investor needs and preferences. Broadly speaking, equity funds fell into four categories; in descending order of volatility, these were (1) aggressive growth, (2) long-term growth, (3) growth and income (above average dividend yield plus growth), and (4) equity income (high dividend yield). In addition

---

3. Net assets of a mutual fund were total assets, principally the investment portfolio carried at market value, minus total liabilities, typically only miscellaneous payables and accruals. Net asset value per share (also called net asset value or NAV) was net assets divided by the total number of shares outstanding. NAV was computed and reported daily in the financial press and electronic quotation services.

4. A mutual fund was required to maintain an up-to-date prospectus on file with the Securities and Exchange Commission (SEC) and furnish a copy thereof to existing shareholders annually and to prospective shareholders prior to the sale of shares. Required disclosures included, among other things, information on investment objectives and policies, investment performance, the investment advisor, fees and expenses, and operating results and financial condition, including the composition of the investment portfolio.

to funds that pursued these broad objectives by investing in a wide range of equities, there were funds in each category that focused on a relatively narrow spectrum, such as small-company growth funds, high technology funds, and utilities funds. In addition to domestic funds, which comprised the great majority of equity vehicles, there were global funds and international funds, some of which invested broadly, some in only one region or one country.[5] On the fixed-income side, there were taxable and tax-free funds that specialized in every quality and maturity class, ranging from money market funds to junk bond funds. Finally, there were balanced funds, which invested in a more or less fixed mix of stocks and bonds, and asset allocation funds, which invested in stocks, bonds, and other financial assets in a mix that varied on the basis of the manager's outlook.

From the beginning of 1977, the year in which Jupiter Management entered the mutual fund business, aggregate mutual fund net assets grew explosively, from $51 billion at December 31, 1976, to $1,069 billion at December 31, 1990. Mutual funds, after commercial banks and life insurance companies, were now the third largest intermediary in the U.S. financial system and the fastest growing.[6]

Many factors accounted for this growth. Perhaps the most important were general prosperity and aggressive marketing by fund sponsors who recognized the opportunity to take market share from traditional, high-cost intermediaries such as banks, thrifts, and life insurers. In this regard, the most important development was the money market fund, a convenient, higher-yielding alternative to conventional checking and savings accounts. Other factors were the bull market of the 1980s in all financial assets; the rapid growth in individual retirement accounts and other tax-advantaged, long-term savings plans; and the increasing sophistication of affluent consumers, who had learned in the 1970s about the corrosive effects of inflation on nontradable, fixed-rate capital accumulation vehicles.

At the end of 1990, money market funds, which invested exclusively in short-term taxable or tax-exempt instruments, comprised the largest mutual fund category, with net assets of $498 billion. Taxable and tax-free bond funds held $325 billion. Equity funds held $246 billion, having grown from only $34 billion of aggregate net assets at the end of 1976. No-load funds accounted for about half of the net assets in bond and equity funds and all of those in money market funds. Closed-end bond and equity funds accounted for about $50 billion, or 4.7% of the total, with open-ends accounting for the balance. At the end of 1990, there were 62.6 million mutual fund shareholder accounts with an average balance of about $17,000. Individuals held about two-thirds of total mutual fund net assets. Exhibit 1 presents data on the size, composition, and growth of mutual fund net assets from 1975 through 1990.

To avoid triple taxation of shareholders, which would have made mutual funds infeasible, a fund could elect to be treated as a conduit for income tax purposes, and virtually all publicly available funds did so. To qualify for such treatment, a fund had to meet certain criteria set forth in Subchapter M of the Internal Revenue Code.[7] As a

---

5. International funds invested in non-U.S. securities; global funds invested in U.S. and non-U.S. securities.

6. Source: Investment Company Institute.

7. Subchapter M set forth a number of criteria that an investment company had to meet to qualify to make a Subchapter M election and thus forestall triple taxation of shareholders. The most important were: (1) at least 90% of gross income must come from investments (e.g., interest, dividends, realized capital gains); (2) not more than 30% of gross income could come from capital gains derived from securities held less than 90 days or from short sales; (3) at least 97% of net taxable income (i.e., gross income of the fund less operating expenses) had to be distributed to shareholders annually; and (4) the investment portfolio had to meet certain diversification requirements.

conduit, the fund itself did not incur income tax liability. Instead, fund shareholders incurred such liability on monies distributed by the fund, whether or not the shareholder had elected to have such distributions automatically reinvested in new fund shares. Upon the disposition of fund shares, the investor also realized capital gain or loss measured by the difference between the sale price and the sum of the purchase price plus any reinvested distributions.

Virtually all mutual funds were managed by an external, sponsoring organization. Prominent sponsors included large securities brokerage firms, investment advisory firms, life insurance companies, and large mutual fund complexes. The sponsor organized the fund, established its investment objectives and policies, marketed its shares, and in return for a management fee—generally a percentage of average net assets—furnished investment management services to the fund.[8] It also provided directly or through third parties a variety of administrative functions such as legal services, custodial services, share transfers, SEC and shareholder reporting, record keeping, and the like. The expenses for such services as well as management fees and brokerage commissions were paid out of fund assets.

An investment advisory contract governed the relationship between the fund and the sponsor, and the fund's board of directors, which included unaffiliated members, supervised the sponsor's activities. The investment advisory contract was subject to modification, termination, or transfer by action of the board of directors and, in the case of significant changes, ratification by shareholder vote.

Since a sponsor's revenues were directly linked to net assets under management and its costs were largely fixed and semifixed, its profitability was closely related to the aggregate amount of net assets under management. Fund groups competed for assets on the basis of product line, investment performance, shareholder services, advertising, and distribution. Large mutual fund groups greatly benefited from their ability to offer an integrated package of money management and related services and to amortize capital and operating costs—principally compensation, advertising and promotion, and data processing and telecommunications—over a vast pool of net assets. Exhibit 2 presents summary comparative financial information for three large, publicly traded mutual fund complexes.

Perhaps the exemplar of an aggressive, comprehensive, and integrated approach to the mutual fund business was Fidelity Investments, a closely held, family-controlled organization headquartered in Boston, Massachusetts. With over $115 billion of net assets under management and more than 125 funds, Fidelity was the largest mutual fund complex in the world, the fourth largest asset manager, and a major financial institution by any standard. Besides marketing and managing retail mutual funds, its lines of business comprised discount brokerage, variable life insurance and annuities, institutional money management, and retirement plan administration. In the retail mutual fund business, it sought to address all the investment needs, objectives, and risk preferences of the affluent household, from young adulthood through retirement. Included among its funds were vehicles expressly designed for active traders, for substantial individual investors, for college savings programs, for tax-deferred retirement plans, and for institutions. With more than 125 funds in the family, some Fidelity funds were invariably at or near the top of the quarterly and annual performance rankings, irrespective of market trends and vicissitudes.

---

8. In general, management fees on money funds ranged from .3% to .5% of net assets, on bond funds from .4% to .75%, and on equity funds from .5% to 1%.

The distribution of Fidelity funds encompassed both direct and wholesale channels. No-loads and low-loads (up to 3% sales charge), the great preponderance of the funds, were marketed directly to existing and prospective Fidelity customers. Load funds were marketed through retail securities firms. The direct-marketing effort made heavy use of print and television advertising as well as direct mailings to existing Fidelity fundholders and targeted groups. Since Fidelity Investments was a closely held corporation, the size of its advertising budget was not publicly available. That it was substantial was evidenced by regular television advertising as well as print advertising—frequently in full-page formats and/or multiple inserts—in all issues of a number of leading publications, among them *Barron's, Business Week, Money, The New York Times*, and *The Wall Street Journal*.

The marketing program was supported and reinforced by state-of-the-art shareholder services. Shareholder services, buttressed by sophisticated telecommunications and computer installations, ranged from elaborately detailed consolidated statements to check writing on money funds to extensive 7-day-a-week, 24-hour-a-day telephone facilities. These afforded, among other things, automated lines for obtaining mutual fund quotes and shareholder balances and for exchanging balances among Fidelity funds. Here, as in all facets of Fidelity's operations, the objective was to make it so easy and convenient to invest through Fidelity that once investors had become fundholders, they would maintain and supplement their accounts indefinitely.

Although Fidelity did not publicly report its financial results, it was thought to be an exceptionally profitable financial institution and one of the most aggressive and fastest growing in the world.

Jupiter Management

Jupiter Management, in contrast to Fidelity and the other mutual fund behemoths, was a medium-sized—although rapidly growing and highly profitable—money management firm. Headquartered in New Canaan, Connecticut, it was founded in 1972 by Smith, Alex Beckett, and Jonathan Hill to manage the equity portfolio of a wealthy Connecticut family. Jupiter Management entered the mutual fund business in early 1977 with the introduction of the Jupiter Fund.

Jupiter Management's entry into the mutual fund business proved to be a major success, benefiting from both superior investment results and rapid growth in aggregate mutual fund assets. As of May 1991, the firm had about $7.7 billion of net assets under management, with mutual funds accounting for $5.9 billion of the total. The remainder was divided among institutional accounts, private accounts for individuals and family groups (minimum account size $3 million), and two private limited partnerships, Beckett Partners Fund L.P. I and II, which sought maximum capital appreciation through the use of a variety of aggressive investment techniques such as short selling and buying on margin. The firm employed 40 investment professionals, 25 of whom owned 100% of its equity. Exhibits 3 and 4 present summary income statement and balance sheet data on Jupiter Management.

Jupiter Management did not have the resources to compete with mutual fund giants on the basis of advertising, technology, and product-line extensions. Superior performance in the management of equity portfolios was the cornerstone of its success. The Jupiter Management approach to equity investing emphasized in-house fundamental research (i.e., company-specific security analysis) and bottom-up (i.e., company-by-company) decisions on the purchase and sale of securities. It was premised on the conviction that painstaking and imaginative fundamental research applied to companies with limited research coverage by major brokerage firms could uncover undervalued securities that had both significant appreciation potential and, in a diversified portfolio, less risk than the market as a whole. Heavily researched, large-capitalization companies were generally avoided, based on the perception that whatever was knowable about them was almost always already reflected in their stock prices. Accordingly, the research effort focused on small and medium-sized companies with limited Wall Street research coverage and the potential for significant near- to medium-term price appreciation. The investment approach was eclectic. The catalyst for significant appreciation might be prospects for sustained, superior growth; a significant acceleration or recovery in earning power; prospective disposition or redeployment of underperforming assets; or possible sale of the company as a whole.

Since the founders believed that the future course of the stock market was unknowable, the overall level and outlook for the stock market were not material factors in investment decisions. The objective was to buy a stock only when it was deemed to be substantially undervalued and to sell when it was judged to be fully valued. The results of the Jupiter Management approach are set forth in Exhibit 5.

The Jupiter Family of Funds

Jupiter Management's long-run objective was to create a family of funds that could satisfy all of the investment needs of the high-income household with relatively aggressive investment objectives. As of May 1991, there were five equity funds, two bond funds, and three money market funds: one for short-term, high-quality tax-exempt obligations; one for short-term, high-quality corporate and government obligations; and one for short-term U.S. Treasury obligations. Out of $5.9 billion of mutual fund net assets, equity funds accounted for $2.7 billion. In addition to the Jupiter Fund and Jupiter Venture, these were Jupiter Global, Jupiter Growth and Income, and Jupiter Opportunity, a fund with net assets of $146 million that concentrated its investments in 20–30 stocks deemed to have exceptional capital appreciation potential. Neither the global fund nor the growth and income fund, introduced in late 1990 and early 1991, respectively, had yet accumulated the $50 million of net assets needed for an equity fund to return solid profits to its sponsor.

For all of the funds, the minimum initial investment was $5,000 for individual accounts and $2,000 for individual retirement accounts and other tax-deferred savings plans. Same-day redemptions and exchanges among Jupiter funds were available by telephone from 9 A.M. to 4 P.M., and automated quotes of fund prices and shareholder balances were available by telephone 24 hours a day. Check writing was available on the money funds.

Jupiter Venture

Jupiter Venture was a direct descendent of the Jupiter Fund. Originally a small-company growth stock fund, Jupiter Fund, with over $2 billion of net assets, had gotten too large to invest exclusively in small-capitalization companies and maintain the desired degree of diversification. Jupiter Venture was launched in mid-1985 to fill the specialty niche once occupied by the older fund. Its objective was maximum long-term growth of capital, consistent with the preservation of such capital, primarily from investment in the common stocks of small-capitalization U.S. companies. Current income was neither an objective nor a consideration in investment decisions. In the context of the Jupiter family, Jupiter Venture's risk level was higher than that of the Jupiter Fund but considerably lower than that of Jupiter Opportunity.

Jupiter Venture, managed from its inception by Win Smith, possessed one of the best records in the mutual fund business. In the five years ended 1990, it recorded a compound annual total return of 17.3%, placing it first among the 92 small-company growth funds tracked by the leading mutual fund performance evaluation firm. It was also one of only two mutual funds that had outperformed the S&P 500 in each calendar year of the fund's existence. But for reasons discussed earlier, it appeared that this exemplary relative performance might come to an end in 1991. In the first quarter of the year, the fund had underperformed the S&P 500 by 2% and the mean small-company growth fund by more than 10%.

Sensormatic

Sensormatic, headquartered in Deerfield Beach, Florida, was a rapidly growing, fully integrated manufacturer of electronic security systems. Sensormatic systems were used to deter shoplifting and other theft in retail stores and, increasingly, in nonretail settings. The product line included electronic article surveillance (EAS) systems, including the reusable tags and disposable labels used therewith (78% of revenues); microprocessor-controlled closed-circuit television (CCTV) systems (13% of revenues); and access control systems (6% of revenues). The company also produced a line of point-of-sale scanning devices used in connection with ringing up prices and monitoring inventory at retail checkout counters.

Operations were international in scope, with 37% of revenues coming from non-U.S. sources. Besides being a strong number one in the U.S. market, the company was one of three vying for first place in Europe and to become the leading U.S. supplier to the Far East and Latin America. Exhibits 6, 7, and 8 contain recent operating, balance sheet, and cash flow data.

As of mid-1991, Sensormatic was the recognized world leader in the supply of electronic loss-prevention products to retailers. After an unsuccessful diversification effort in the early 1980s that resulted in significant write-offs and operating losses in 1984 through 1986, Sensormatic completed a sweeping overhaul of operations, reallocated resources to its basic business, and reestablished itself as the dominant factor in its product markets. It now had the broadest product line, the lowest production costs, the most advanced and varied technology, the biggest R&D budget, the strongest financial position, and by far the largest and best-trained sales and service organization. Sensormatic held an estimated market share of 50% of the established domestic market for soft-goods EAS systems, comprising mainly apparel retailers. It held about 40% of the new and burgeoning market for hard-goods EAS systems, which comprised supermarkets, drug stores, home improvements centers, recorded music and video stores, and similar retail outlets. The company was also the largest domestic seller of CCTV systems. Exhibit 9 presents summary comparative data on Sensormatic and its principal competitors.

Retailers accounted for more than 95% of Sensormatic revenues. Use of electronic loss-prevention products was becoming standard practice for larger retailers. Inventory shrinkage was a critical factor in the profitability of retailers—for many, it was the second largest variable expense, exceeded only by payroll—and electronic systems had proven themselves a cost-effective means of containing such losses.

EAS systems consisted of electronic detection units used in conjunction with sensitized reusable tags or disposable labels affixed to the merchandise to be protected. Detection units, housed in pedestals, floor mats, or overhead fixtures, established controlled zones at store exits or other key points in the protected environment. If merchandise passed through a controlled zone without having had its tag or label removed or deactivated at a cashier's station, it was "sighted" by the detection unit, causing alarms to sound or lights to flash.

CCTV systems were used mainly to deter employee and other internal theft. Sensormatic CCTV systems consisted of sophisticated cameras concealed in ceiling domes, and remote-control consoles programmed to monitor and record selected activities such as merchandise and cash handling at point-of-sale stations in retail stores and merchandise handling in storerooms, shipping docks, parking lots, warehouses, and other areas.

In the spring of 1991, Sensormatic's future growth and profitability depended mainly upon how successful it was in continuing to penetrate the burgeoning market for hard-goods EAS systems. The company continued to dominate its traditional soft-goods market, where its gross margins were in excess of 60%. But this market was relatively small and mature; estimated revenues were about $200 million and were expected to grow at about 5%–7% a year. In contrast, the market for hard-goods protection was growing at about 50% a year from a current base of $150 million. It was expected to reach $1–$1.2 billion in annual revenues by the turn of the century.

From 1987 on, Sensormatic's main focus was on penetration of this market with a view toward achieving the same degree of market dominance and profitability it enjoyed in soft goods. Toward this end, R&D spending was stepped up, manufacturing capacity was doubled, and the sales and service organization was greatly enlarged and reorganized along product-market lines. Thanks to superior technology and marketing, Sensormatic achieved sales leadership in the hard-goods market in 1990. In the fiscal year ending May 31, 1991, hard-goods revenues would for the first time exceed those in soft goods. Exhibit 10 presents data on Sensormatic's evolving revenue mix.

But profitability in hard goods was not yet comparable to that in soft goods. Competition for market share was fierce, technology was still evolving, and Sensormatic had not yet fully realized potential volume and learning-curve economies in its new facilities. In the spring of 1991, gross margins on hard-goods EAS systems, although increasing, were about 30%, about half of those on soft goods. The other growing product lines in Sensormatic's revenue mix also had much lower gross margins than soft goods. For example, CCTV systems yielded gross margins in the area of 30%.

On the plus side, Sensormatic's backlog on February 28, 1991, was at a record level, up 40% from the prior year, reflecting mostly the growth in hard goods. Furthermore, since hard-goods systems used disposable labels rather than the reusable plastic tags of the great majority of soft-goods systems, a rapidly increasing percentage of revenues—2% in the third quarter of 1991—was coming from high-margin reorders of disposable labels.

The Sensormatic Offering

The Sensormatic financing was opportunistic in nature (i.e., there was no specific, near-term requirement for external funds). Net proceeds were to be used initially to pay down about $25 million of domestic bank debt and to augment cash reserves. The financing was prompted by the exceptional strength of the market for newly issued convertible securities. Stock market pundits attributed this strength to investors' desires to hedge their bets on a stock market that had advanced almost 20% in the first quarter of 1991 while the general economy was still in recession.

From the perspective of the issuer, it was clear that straight debt financing was relatively unattractive. Sensormatic was a less-than-investment-grade borrower, and the public market for high-yield debt was effectively closed to new issues. A private placement of straight debt, if doable, would have required a coupon of at least 12½%–12¾% and would not have afforded the average maturity or the freedom from burdensome covenants available in the convertible securities market. Exhibit 11 presents a summary of the principal terms of the new Sensormatic convertibles; Exhibit 12 sets forth their impact on the company's capitalization; and Exhibit 13 presents price data on Sensormatic's stock.

Smith's Perspective

With respect to the new Sensormatic issue, the options for Jupiter Venture, as Smith saw them, were: (1) to increase the fund's overall position in Sensormatic securities by purchasing convertibles on the offering; (2) to replace some or all of the existing common stock position with the convertibles; (3) to maintain the current position; or (4) to reduce or eliminate this position.

Smith had tentatively decided against option (4) when the registration statement for the new issue was filed. While the sale of convertibles would involve some near-term earnings dilution, it was considerably less than would have been caused by a common stock offering. Moreover, Smith considered it a significant plus that the sale of convertibles would greatly increase Sensormatic's liquidity and ensure the availability of capital for its ambitious expansion plans.

Based on the underwriter's price talk and input from the Jupiter Management trading desk, Smith expected the Sensormatic convertibles to be priced at par with a coupon of 7% and a conversion price of $23.50, for a conversion premium of 20.5%. (A conversion price of $23.50 meant that each $1,000 convertible subordinated debenture was convertible at any time at the option of the holder into 42.553 shares of common stock. The conversion premium was the difference, expressed in percentage terms, between the conversion price, $23.50, and the current trading price, $19.50, of Sensormatic common stock on the NYSE.)

Smith knew Sensormatic and its management well, and he considered its long-term prospects to be extremely bright. Over the next 5 years, he expected revenues to grow at 20% or more per annum and earnings to grow even faster. In the short run, he thought that Wall Street earnings estimates—$.88 in 1991, $1.10 in 1992, and $1.33 in 1993 versus $.72 in the fiscal year ended May 31, 1990—were not unreasonable. Nevertheless, he was concerned about the possibility of negative surprises in near-term operating results.[9]

The economy was in recession, and a number of Sensormatic's major retailing accounts were in Chapter 11. Further, because of Sensormatic's major bet on the hard-goods market, Smith reckoned that near-term earnings were vulnerable to unquantifiable uncertainties. In view of management's past miscalculations, he also harbored some qualms about the ability of this same management to handle all of the challenges of a rapidly growing and evolving new-product market entirely without missteps or setbacks. In the current stock market environment, any shortfall in earnings versus expectations might trigger an abrupt downward revision in Sensormatic's P/E ratio.

---

9. Per share earnings estimates do not give effect to issuance of the new convertibles.

EXHIBIT 1
Total Mutual Fund Net Assets (billions of dollars)

Year	Equity Funds	Fixed-Income Funds	Money Market Funds	Total
1975	$ 32.4	$ 9.8	$ 3.7	$ 45.9
1976	34.3	13.3	3.7	51.3
1977	30.0	15.0	3.9	48.9
1978	29.0	16.0	10.9	55.9
1979	32.5	16.5	45.5	94.5
1980	41.0	17.4	76.4	134.8
1981	38.4	16.9	186.1	241.4
1982	50.6	26.3	219.2	296.7
1983	73.9	39.7	179.4	293.0
1984	83.1	54.0	233.5	370.6
1985	116.9	134.8	243.8	495.5
1986	161.5	262.6	292.1	716.2
1987	180.7	273.1	316.1	769.9
1988	194.8	277.5	338.0	810.3
1989	249.1	304.8	428.1	982.0
1990	245.8	325.0	498.3	1,069.1

Source: Investment Company Institute.

EXHIBIT 2
Summary Comparative Financial Data for Jupiter Management and Selected Publicly Traded
Investment Management Companies (millions of dollars except as noted)

Company Fiscal Year-End	Jupiter Management 12/31/90	Dreyfus 12/31/90	Franklin Resources 9/30/90	T. Rowe Price 12/31/90
Revenues:				
Advisory and administrative fees	$28.8	$179.2	$222.7	$165.9
Underwriting commissions[a]	—	—	23.0	—
Investment income	10.8	68.9	32.9	4.1
Other	2.1	13.2	9.2	—
Total revenues	$41.7	$261.3	$287.8	$170.0
Operating expenses:				
Compensation	$16.7	$ 59.3	$ n.a	$ 67.6
Advertising and promotion	3.3	53.6	n.a	14.1
General and administrative	9.6	60.0	131.4[c]	44.1
Other	.8	5.1	12.0	6.5
Total operating expenses	$30.4	$178.0	$143.4	$132.3
Operating income:	$11.3	$ 83.3	$144.4	$ 37.7
Other income (expense)[b]	(.5)	—	—	—
Income before taxes	$10.8	$ 83.3	$144.4	$ 37.7
Income taxes	4.0	21.2	55.0	14.3
Income before minority interests	$ 6.8	$ 62.1	$ 89.4	$ 23.4
Minority interests	—	—	—	2.5
Net income	$ 6.8	$ 62.1	$ 89.4	$ 20.9
Net assets under management ($ billions) . . .	$ 7.7	$ 56.9	$ 45.3	$ 29.4
Property and equipment, net	$17.9	$ 50.7	$ 8.5	$ 35.9
Long-term debt	$ 6.0	—	$ 5.4	$ 22.4
Common equity	70.8	742.5	363.3	111.9
Total capital	$76.8	$742.5	$368.7	$134.3

a. Portion of sales load funds retained by fund sponsor.

b. Principally interest expense.

c. Includes compensation, advertising, and promotion expenses.

EXHIBIT 3
Jupiter Management: Summary Income Statement Data (millions of dollars)

Year Ended	12/31/88	12/31/89	12/31/90
Revenues:			
Advisory and administrative fees	$20.3	$27.4	$28.8
Investment income	8.3	13.5	10.8
Other	.9	1.7	2.1
Total revenues	$29.5	$42.6	$41.7
Operating expenses:			
Compensation	$10.3	$17.9	$16.7
Advertising and promotion	2.2	2.5	3.3
General and administrative	8.2	9.1	9.6
Other	1.7	.9	.8
Total operating expenses	$20.4	$30.4	$30.4
Operating income	$ 9.1	$12.2	$11.3
Other income (expense)[a]	.1	(.7)	(.5)
Income before taxes	$ 9.2	$11.5	$10.8
Income taxes	3.4	4.3	4.0
Net income	$ 5.8	$ 7.2	$ 6.8

a. Principally interest expense.

EXHIBIT 4
Jupiter Management: Summary Balance Sheet Data (millions of dollars)

As of:	12/31/90
Assets	
Cash and equivalents	$ 7.7
Receivables, net[a]	6.0
Investments in mutual funds[b]	8.8
Other investments[c]	18.6
Limited partnership interests[c]	22.3
Property and equipment, net	17.9
Other	1.7
Total assets	$83.0
Liabilities and Stockholders' Equity	
Accounts payable and accrued expenses	$ 2.7
Accrued retirement and other compensation expenses	1.9
Income taxes payable	.6
Deferred revenues	1.0
Long-term debt	6.0
Total liabilities	$12.2
Common equity	$70.8
Total liabilities and stockholders' equity	$83.0

a. Principally accrued management fees.
b. Equity holdings in the Jupiter family of funds.
c. Interests in investment real estate, in venture capital investments, and in Beckett Partners Fund, L.P. I and II.

EXHIBIT 5

Comparative Performance Data for Selected Jupiter Funds[a]

Year	Jupiter Fund	Jupiter Opportunity Fund[b]	Jupiter Venture Fund[b]	All Diversified Equity Funds[c]	S&P 500
1981	7.1%	—%	—%	(1.0)%	(5.1)%
1982	30.6	—	—	23.7	21.4
1983	26.1	—	—	21.3	22.5
1984	(0.1)	—	—	(0.5)	6.1
1985	24.6	—	—	27.1	31.8
1986	11.2	12.5	25.4	13.8	18.6
1987	4.2	(11.7)	7.2	0.2	4.9
1988	16.6	19.1	19.6	15.4	16.6
1989	46.3	50.8	38.7	22.7	32.2
1990	(0.7)	0.6	(0.4)	(6.0)	(3.1)
10-year compound growth rate	15.7	—	—	10.4	13.9
Life of fund compound growth rate	18.3	12.4	17.3	N.A.	N.A.

a. All statistics shown are annual total returns assuming reinvestment of all dividends.

b. Record shown from first full year of operations.

c. Column shows average annual total returns for all domestic equity funds classified as maximum capital appreciation (aggressive growth), long-term growth, growth and income, and equity income. Exclusions include sector, gold and precious metals, balanced, and asset allocation funds.

EXHIBIT 6

Sensormatic: Summary Consolidated Operating Results (millions of dollars except per share data)

	Year Ended 5/31					9 Months Ended 2/28	
	1986	1987	1988	1989	1990	1990	1991
Revenues:							
Sales	$ 64.8	$ 74.4	$100.7	$116.5	$153.6	$107.5	$131.4
Rentals	10.3	12.1	10.9	21.7	22.3	16.2	20.6
Other	6.7	8.8	11.3	12.8	15.3	11.0	14.4
Total revenues	$ 81.8	$ 95.3	$122.9	$151.0	$191.2	$134.7	$166.4
Operating costs and expenses	99.6	83.7	104.2	132.7	166.6	117.9	145.8
Operating income (loss)a	$(17.8)	$ 11.6	$ 18.7	$ 18.3	$ 24.6	$ 16.8	$ 20.6
Other incomea	11.2	10.8	5.8	3.1	.4	.2	.1
Income (loss) from continuing operations before income taxes	$ (6.6)	$ 22.4	$ 24.4	$ 21.4	$ 25.0	$ 17.0	$ 20.7
Income taxesb	(1.8)	7.5	5.8	4.4	5.0	3.2	4.4
Equity in income (loss) of affiliates	.8	(.3)	(2.4)	.3	—	—	—
Income (loss) from continuing operations	$ (3.9)	$ 14.6	$ 16.2	$ 16.7	$ 20.0	$ 13.8	$ 16.3
Income (loss) from discontinuing operations	(2.0)	(3.4)	(26.8)	—	—	—	—
Net income (loss)	$ (5.9)	$ 11.2	$ (10.6)	$ 16.7	$ 20.0	$ 13.8	$ 16.3
Income (loss) per common share							
Continuing operations	$ (.14)	$ .51	$ .58	$ .60	$ .72	$ .49	$ .60
Discontinuing operations	(.07)	(.12)	(.96)	—	—	—	—
Net income	$ (.21)	$ .39	$ (.38)	$ .60	$ .72	$ .49	$ .60
Cash dividends per common share	$ .05	$ .05	$ .05	$ .05	$ .185	$ .11	$ .225

a. Composed of mainly interest income net of interest expense.

b. Favorable tax rate results mostly from tax benefits derived from manufacturing principally in Puerto Rico.

EXHIBIT 7
Sensormatic: Summary Balance Sheet Data (millions of dollars)

As of:	5/31/89	5/31/90	2/28/91
Net Tangible Assets			
Cash and equivalents	$ 53.1	$ 26.9	$ 17.9
Receivables, net	76.3	88.8	92.6
Inventories	45.3	44.9	70.4
Total current assets	$174.7	$160.6	$180.9
Short-term debt	—	10.8	23.6
Other current liabilities	42.1	38.8	40.2
Net working capital	$132.6	$111.0	$117.1
Leased equipment, net	19.3	24.8	32.4
PPE, net	21.1	26.4	33.5
Other tangible assets	9.9	15.1	11.5
Total	$182.9	$177.3	$194.5
Net Capitalization			
Long-term debt	$ 15.5	$ 9.2	$ 20.7
Deferred taxes	5.5	6.5	5.7
Common equity	192.0	199.8	221.8
Less: intangibles	(30.1)	(38.2)	(53.7)
Total	$182.9	$177.3	$194.5

EXHIBIT 8
Sensormatic: Summary Cash Flow Data (millions of dollars)

	5/31/89	5/31/90	2/28/91
Operating activities:			
Net income	$ 16.7	$ 20.0	$ 16.3
Depreciation and amortization	10.6	11.3	10.0
Other noncash charges to operations	4.5	4.5	3.4
Increase in net working capital	(19.9)	(22.3)	(18.8)
Other, net	4.3	.8	—
Net cash provided	$ 7.6	$ 14.3	$ 10.9
Investing activities:			
Capital expenses, net	$ (5.8)	$ (8.1)	$ (9.3)
Increase in leased equipment	(9.0)	(5.1)	(11.4)
Net payments for acquisitions	(8.9)	(6.6)	(11.3)
Investments and advances	5.7	(.7)	—
Net proceeds from sale of assets	8.5	—	—
Other, net	3.2	(.1)	8.1
Net cash used	$ (17.6)	$ (20.6)	$ (23.9)
Financing activities:			
Stock repurchases	$ (4.9)	$ (12.8)	$ (3.9)
Net borrowings	.6	4.1	9.9
Cash dividends	(1.4)	(3.7)	(6.0)
Other, net	4.3	(6.3)	3.2
Net cash used	$ (1.4)	$ (18.7)	$ 3.2
Effect of exchange rate changes on cash	$ (.6)	$ .6	$ 1.1
Net decrease in cash	$ 12.0	$ (24.4)	$ 8.7
Beginning cash	56.3	44.3	19.8
Ending cash	$ 44.3	$ 19.8	$ 11.1

EXHIBIT 9
Summary Comparative Data for Sensormatic and Leading Domestic Competitors
(millions of dollars except per share data)

Company Fiscal Year-End	Sensormatic 5/31/90	Checkpoint Systems 12/31/90	Knogo 2/28/91
Revenues			
Latest fiscal year	$191.3	$ 56.7	$ 80.0
3-year growth rate	23.5%	17.0%	19.7%
5-year growth rate	24.1%	15.8%	17.3%
Operating income			
Latest fiscal year	$ 24.6	$ 9.4	$ 10.7
3-year growth rate	14.7%	46.3%	37.7%
5-year growth rate	24.1%	9.3%	0.0%
Net income			
Latest fiscal year	$ 20.0	$ 6.9	$ 1.5
3-year growth rate	13.2%	49.6%	11.9%
5-year growth rate	21.7%	5.0%	(23.7)%
Income per share			
Latest 12 months	$ 0.82	$ 0.63	$ 0.28
Latest fiscal year	$ 0.72	$ 0.72	$ 0.28
3-year growth rate	14.5%	48.5%	20.5%
5-year growth rate	21.7%	4.4%	(25.1)%
Pretax margin			
Latest fiscal year	13.1%	11.8%	2.4%
3-year average	7.4%	9.8%	4.5%
Net margin			
Latest fiscal year	10.5%	12.2%	1.9%
3-year average	4.1%	8.5%	2.8%
Return on equity			
Latest fiscal year	10.4%	18.6%	2.0%
3-year average	3.3%	14.0%	2.5%
Total assets	$265.1	$ 53.1	$139.0
Long-term debt	$ 9.0	$ —	$ 18.0
Common equity	$199.8	$ 41.3	$ 77.9
Long-term debt/Total capital	4.3%	—%	18.8%
Stock price data			
Where traded	NYSE	OTC	NYSE
Beta	.88	1.98	1.13
Current price (5/22/91)	$19½	$9⅜	$7⅞
1991 range[a]	$23⅛–$13⅞	$11⅝–$6⅝	$10½–$6⅜
1990 range[a]	$16⅜–$9⅜	$15⅞–$6⅛	$16¼–$13½
Current price to:			
Latest 12 months' income	23.8X	14.9X	28.1X
Tangible book value	3.0X	2.3X	.5X
Indicated dividend	$ 0.30	Nil	$ 0.30
Yield (5/22/91)	1.5%	—	3.8%
Total market equity (5/22/91)	$525.1[b]	$ 88.4[c]	$ 41.4[d]

a. Calendar year.

b. 26,926,954 common shares outstanding.

c. 9,425,114 common shares outstanding.

d. 5,258,221 common shares outstanding.

EXHIBIT 10
Sensormatic: Revenues by Product Line (millions of dollars)

| | Fiscal Year Ended May 31 | | | | Estimated | |
	1984	1988	1989	1990	1991	1992
Hard Goods	$ 1.9	$ 23.0	$ 38.0	$ 59.0	$ 84.0	$115.0
Soft Goods	87.1	83.0	82.0	87.9	95.0	100.0
CCTV	4.7	14.8	20.5	27.4	30.0	45.0
POS Data[a]	—	2.4	10.6	14.6	14.0	18.0
Access Control	—	—	—	4.4	7.0	10.0
	$ 93.7	$123.2	$151.1	$191.3	$230.0	$288.0
Hard Goods	2.0%	18.7%	25.3%	29.8%	36.5%	39.9%
Soft Goods	93.0	67.5	54.7	45.9	41.3	34.7
CCTV	5.0	12.0	13.7	14.3	13.0	15.6
POS Data[a]	—	2.0	7.1	7.6	6.1	6.3
Access Control	—	—	—	2.3	3.0	3.5
	100.0%	100.0%	100.0%	100.0%	100.0%	100.0%

a. POS Data, a maker of point-of-sale systems, was acquired in midyear 1988.

EXHIBIT 11
Summary of Principal Terms of the Sensormatic Convertible Subordinated Debentures

Issuer:	Sensormatic Electronics Corporation
Amount:	$100,000,000
Listing:	New York Stock Exchange
Ratings (Moody's/S&P):	Ba2/BB-
Use of Proceeds:	Approximately $25 million of estimated net proceeds of $97.3 million to be applied to retirement of short-term debt outstanding under the company's domestic bank facilities. The balance initially to be invested in money market instruments and ultimately to be used for general corporate purposes, including capital expenditures for expansion, working capital to support growth, and potential acquisitions of related businesses.
Coupon:	To be determined; payable semiannually in arrears on May 15 and November 15.
Conversion Price:	To be determined; payable semiannually in arrears on May 15 and November 15.
Maturity:	May 15, 2001
Mandatory Redemption:	Except for a change of control, none prior to May 15, 2001.
Optional Redemption:	Except for a change of control, none prior to June 1, 1994. Thereafter, redeemable in whole or in part at the option of the company at the following prices plus accrued interest: from June 1, 1994, to May 14, 1995, at 104.667% of par; from May 15, 1995, to May 14, 1996, at 103.889% of par; thereafter at prices declining annually and ratably to par at May 15, 2000.
Change of Control:[a]	Upon a change of control, each holder may, at the option of the holder, require the company to redeem for cash all or any part of such holder's debentures at a price of par plus accrued interest.
Subordination:	Subordinate in right of payment to all indebtedness for money borrowed that is not by its terms equal or junior to the debentures in right of payment. Debentures are not subordinate to trade credit or other liabilities not arising from the borrowing of money.
	No payment (interest, principal, redemptions, purchases) to be made with respect to debentures if there exists a payment default on indebtedness to which the debentures are subordinate.
Restrictive Covenants:	No merger, consolidation, sale of substantially all assets or similar transaction, unless (1) the company is the surviving entity; or (2) the surviving entity is a U.S. corporation that assumes all obligations relating to the debentures (except under certain circumstances the conversion rights); and no default on the debentures would exist after the closing of the transaction.
Events of Default:	Bankruptcy: default for 30 days in payment of interest; default in payment of principal when due; default for 90 days with respect to any other covenant or undertaking.
Acceleration:	Bankruptcy: outstanding principal amount of debentures becomes immediately due and payable. Other events of default: the trustee or holders of not less than 25% of the outstanding principal amount of the debentures may declare them immediately due and payable.
Modification and Waiver:	Holders of a majority of the outstanding principal amount of the debentures may change the terms of, or waive defaults relating to, the debentures, except that (1) any change in the interest rate, principal amount, maturity date, or conversion provisions or (2) any waiver of a payment default requires the consent of all holders.

a. In summary, a change of control is defined as: (1) the sale of all or substantially all of the company's assets; (2) a merger, sale of stock, or any other transaction that results in the existing owners (a) having less than 50% of the total voting power in the surviving or resulting entity or (b) otherwise not having control of the company; (3) the acquisition by any person or related group of persons of 50% of the total voting power of company stock; (4) the election to the company's board of directors of a majority of directors nominated by any person or related group of persons other than the board of directors existing prior to such election; or (5) liquidation or dissolution of the company.

Source: Summary of information from Sensormatic prospectus.

EXHIBIT 12

Sensormatic: Capitalization at February 28, 1991, and As Adjusted for Sale of the Convertible Subordinated Debentures (thousands of dollars)

	2/28/91	As Adjusted
Short-term debt:		
Domestic[a,b]	$ 14,814	$ —
Foreign[c]	8,750	8,750
	$ 23,564	$ 8,750
Long-term debt:		
Secured	$ 2,452	$ 2,452
Unsecured	18,201	18,201
Debentures[d]	—	100,000
	$ 20,653	$120,653
Total debt	$ 44,217	$129,403
Common equity[e]	$221,799	$221,799
Total capitalization	$266,016	$351,202

a. About $25 million outstanding as of May 22, 1991.

b. Outstanding under a $25 million bank line of credit, which expires September 30, 1991, and provides for interest payments not higher than the prime rate less 1/2 of 1% and an annual commitment fee of 1/8 of 1% on the average unused amount of the commitment.

c. Outstanding under foreign currency denominated lines of credit made available to foreign subsidiaries of the company by local banks.

d. Does not reflect underwriting discounts and commissions estimated at 2.25% of the principal amount of the debentures or other issuance expenses of the company estimated at $470,000.

e. 26,926,954 common shares issued and outstanding; 60,000,000 common shares authorized.

EXHIBIT 13

Sensormatic: Price Range of Common Stock

| | Fiscal Year Ended May 31 | | | | | |
| | 1989 | | 1990 | | 1991[a] | |
Quarters	High	Low	High	Low	High	Low
First	$ 9⅝	$ 7⅞	$13¾	$11¼	$15⅞	$11¾
Second	10¼	8⅛	13⅞	11½	14⅛	12
Third	11⅛	9	12½	10⅛	18⅛	14¼
Fourth	12⅝	10¼	14¾	11⅞	22⅜	15¾

a. Through May 22, 1991. Trading price on May 22 was $19 1/2.

Anheuser-Busch Company and Campbell Taggart Inc. (Abridged)

In mid-May 1984, Walter Suhre put a yellowing newspaper clipping (see Exhibit 1) back into a folder and closed his case file. The vice president and general counsel of St. Louis-based Anheuser-Busch Company, he believed his company may have suffered losses through insider trading during its acquisition of Campbell Taggart Inc. in 1982. As far as Mr. Suhre could tell, Paul Thayer, who in 1982 was a director of Anheuser-Busch, had leaked confidential information to friends about the impending Campbell Taggart acquisition. Mr. Thayer's friends and others had then purchased shares of Campbell Taggart in the open market (see Exhibits 2, 3, and 4).[1] Mr. Suhre had learned about the details of this insider trading in January 1984, from a legal complaint filed by the Securities and Exchange Commission (SEC) against Mr. Thayer and his friends.

Now, five months later, the SEC complaint was delayed in court. For the moment, Anheuser-Busch and Mr. Thayer had reached a stand-still agreement under which Anheuser-Busch would not sue Mr. Thayer as long as the SEC complaint remained unsettled. This agreement benefited both parties and was terminable by either Anheuser-Busch or Mr. Thayer. Anheuser-Busch gained more time to sue, because the statute of limitations was suspended for the duration of the stand-still. In addition, the company could use any evidence that emerged from the SEC proceedings against Mr. Thayer. Mr. Thayer gained the ability to defend himself against one set of charges at a time. As soon as the stand-still agreement lapsed, the statute of limitations would go back into effect, and Anheuser-Busch would have to file suit within a short time period.

Mr. Suhre realized that he might have to present his recommendations on this matter to Anheuser-Busch senior management. But before he could make a proposal, he wanted to assure himself that the company could demonstrate in court that it had

---

1. In all, 38 insiders and "tippees" purchased a total of 265,000 shares of Campbell Taggart. The figures reported in Exhibit 2 aggregate the trades of all 38 insiders and tippees.

This case was prepared by Professor Erik R. Sirri.

been damaged by the insider trading. On a more basic level, he needed both to confirm the company's stated intention to sue Mr. Thayer and to decide if the company should sue any parties other than Mr. Thayer.

Reasons for the Acquisition

At the time of the acquisition, popular Anheuser-Busch brands such as Budweiser had allowed the company to achieve a dominant 32% share of the market for beer (see Exhibits 5 and 6 for financial statements). Anheuser-Busch's market strength was reflected in its stock performance, which remained good despite a traditionally low dividend yield.[2] Management believed this performance was due to the company's successful growth-based strategy, which stock analysts appreciated and rewarded with consistent "buy" recommendations. However, because management also believed that breweries had little room for continued growth, it was searching for routes to diversify.

The first such effort led to the internal development of Eagle brand snack foods, which were sold through bars, airports, and other distribution channels originally set up for beer sales. By 1982, Anheuser-Busch was considering acquisitions such as Campbell Taggart as well. During this period, Campbell Taggart was regarded as the bakery industry's low-cost producer. Its market share was second only to that of the ITT Continental Baking Company (see Exhibits 5 and 6 for financial statements). Sales were strongest in the rapidly growing southern and southwestern states, where Campbell Taggart breads, rolls, and cakes could be found in most supermarkets. Company stock had performed particularly well in the weeks preceding the merger announcement. In light of the rapid increase in Campbell Taggart's price, Anheuser-Busch made a public statement on August 2, 1982, about its interest in Campbell Taggart.

When the merger proposal was first announced publicly, industry analysts noted that by acquiring a bakery company externally, Anheuser-Busch was taking a new approach to its diversification goals, which previously had been met internally. To justify this shift, Anheuser-Busch looked to the benefits of a distribution network that Campbell Taggart had established at restaurants and supermarkets, where the brewer had been weak.

The Acquisition Process

Anheuser-Busch decided to acquire Campbell Taggart through a negotiated merger. In this type of transaction, also known as a friendly takeover, the acquiring company negotiates a set of merger terms with the target company's board of directors. These terms usually specify the price to be paid for the acquired company and often address operating, employment, and seniority concerns as well. If the negotiations succeed, the board then asks its shareholders to approve the merger in a proxy vote.

An acquiring firm generally offers to pay a premium, or greater-than-market price, for the target's shares. One explanation for this premium is that the bidder must offer existing shareholders an incentive to induce them to sell shares they would normally retain. Another possible explanation is that investors believe the target company will have an intrinsically higher value when and if it falls under control of the new owner. Thus their reservation price, or indifference price, rises in anticipation. In either case, the prospect of receiving a premium for their shares usually causes target shareholders

---

2. The average dividend yield on an S&P 500 stock in 1981 was about 5.1%.

to support merger proposals. It is generally believed that without a reasonable premium, a merger proposal would fail.

The takeover premium that a bidder typically offers ranges from 20% to 40% over the target's premerger stock price.[3] The premium is defined as the percentage increase that the final negotiated offer price represents over the target stock price one month before the merger announcement. Curiously, the price of a target firm often begins to rise before any official announcement of a takeover attempt is made. During the weeks before a merger announcement, the target's price rises an average of 40% of the takeover premium.[4] Although the existence of a takeover premium is fairly consistent for a target stock, a bidding company's stock price tends to remain unchanged or to fall slightly.[5]

Paul Thayer

Throughout his life, Paul Thayer enjoyed being a daredevil and adventurer. In World War II, he was a successful Air Force fighter pilot. After the war, he continued flying, first as a commercial pilot for TWA and later as a test pilot for Chance Vought Aircraft. Not only did he survive this risky career, he advanced rapidly. By 1955, he had become a director of Vought, and after Vought merged with Ling-Temco to become LTV Aerospace, Mr. Thayer was elected chairman, CEO, and president of the new conglomerate. Mr. Thayer's stellar career and personal investment made him a multimillionaire. He began taking positions of civic leadership and sitting on corporate boards, including the Anheuser-Busch board, which he joined in January 1982. In April 1982, he became chairman of the U.S. Chamber of Commerce, where he caused bitter divisions by supporting a controversial tax increase proposed by President Reagan. Later in 1982, President Reagan appointed him Deputy Secretary of Defense, causing Mr. Thayer to resign his position on the Anheuser-Busch board. Once again, Mr. Thayer showed his strong will, this time by spearheading a major campaign to reduce military waste. In his spare time, though he was 62 years old, he continued to scuba dive, ride motorcycles through the Rocky Mountains, and perform death-defying stunts in a vintage World War II fighter plane.[6]

The SEC Complaint

Apparently, Paul Thayer took this taste for adventure too far. According to an SEC complaint filed in January 1984, Mr. Thayer illegally disclosed stock-related information to friends, repeatedly tipping them off about the planned acquisitions, profits, and dividends of the three companies of which he was a director. One of these companies was Anheuser-Busch.

The SEC cited eight friends, the "tippees," in its complaint and claimed that they profited by purchasing shares of stock after hearing the inside information that

---

3. Michael Jensen and Richard Ruback, "The Market for Corporate Control," *Journal of Financial Economics* 2 (1983): 5–50.

4. G. Jarrell and A. Poulson, "Stock Trading Before the Announcement of Tender Offers," *Journal of Law, Economics, and Organization* 5 (1989): 225–248.

5. Jenson and Ruback, "The Market for Corporate Control."

6. Grover Heiman, "The Flier Who Kept a Company from Crashing," *National Business,* June 1982, pp. 54–59.

Mr. Thayer had provided. Later, his friends sold the shares when public announcement of the merger made share prices rise. One tippee, Billy Bob Harris, was the highest paid stockbroker for A. G. Edwards, Inc., a St. Louis-based broker. A second, William Mathis, was a broker for Bear Stearns Companies, Inc., in Atlanta. A third tippee, Sandra Ryno, was a former LTV receptionist who allegedly maintained a "close personal relationship" with Mr. Thayer. The fourth, Julie Williams, an aerobic dance instructor in Dallas, was alleged to have had a similar relationship with Mr. Harris. These four, along with four others, made up what *Time* magazine described as "a small circle of high-living Southerners."[7]

In an example cited by the SEC, Mr. Thayer spent the weekend of June 25, 1982, in Houston with Ms. Ryno, Mr. Harris, and Mr. Williams (see Exhibit 7). On the Monday following the weekend, Mr. Harris "contacted a research analyst at A. G. Edwards and suggested to the analyst that Anheuser-Busch was interested in acquiring Campbell Taggart."[8] That same week, Ms. Ryno purchased 2,000 shares of Campbell Taggart stock at $25¾ and $26⅜ per share (see Exhibit 8). She sold her shares on August 10, after news had come out that Campbell Taggart was targeted in a takeover attempt and the stock price had risen. In its complaint, the SEC accused the defendants of violating rules 10b-5 and 14e-3 of the Securities Exchange Act and stated that the tippees as a group made illegal profits of over $1.9 million from the information that Mr. Thayer had supplied.[9] Mr. Thayer himself did not share in these profits.

Although allegations of insider trading were relatively rare at the time, equivalent SEC charges were often settled out of court with a consent decree, which saved time and money for both sides. In a typical settlement, the defendant would neither deny nor admit guilt but agree instead not to break securities laws in the future. If the defendant was later tried and convicted on a set of charges, the punishment would be more severe because of the violation of the consent decree. However, during negotiations in late 1983, Mr. Thayer refused such a settlement, possibly because it would be tantamount to an admission of guilt.[10] Given his high-profile position, the political embarrassment would be large. In January 1984, Mr. Thayer resigned from the Defense Department in order to avoid further damaging the Reagan Administration and to concentrate fully on defending himself against the SEC charges.

Mr. Thayer claimed that the charges were "entirely without merit." Billy Bob Harris, who gave regular stock reports on Dallas television, said that he had proven his own innocence by passing a lie-detector test.

Mr. Suhre's Decision

Mr. Suhre realized that Anheuser-Busch faced a sticky decision. Filing suit against Mr. Thayer or some other party might cost several million dollars in legal expenses with no guarantee of winning. And even if the company could recover part of the damages, press coverage of the suit could be embarrassing to both sides. To sue a former board director was virtually unprecedented, and Anheuser-Busch had no way to gauge how the rest of corporate America would react. To sue some other party—for example, Mr. Harris, Mr. Mathis, or their employers—had the advantage of increasing the potential

---

7. Evan Thomas, "Life with Paul and Billy Bob," *Time,* January 16, 1984, p. 21.

8. SEC *v.* Thayer et al., U.S.D.C. S.D.N.Y. (January 5, 1984), p. 20.

9. SEC *v.* Thayer et al., p. 8.

10. Ibid.

size of the final settlement. However, Mr. Suhre wondered whether there would be any fallout from suing a major Wall Street firm.

Legal action had drawbacks, but so did inaction. Mr. Suhre felt that Anheuser-Busch had a corporate responsibility to initiate proceedings against Paul Thayer. Also, management was keenly aware of company losses from the merger, resulting both from the insider trading and from disappointing performance of the Campbell Taggart subsidiary during the 2 years following the merger. The SEC had a very strong case against Mr. Thayer. Mr. Suhre was worried that if Anheuser-Busch management did not sue, shareholders might file a derivative action[11] suit against Mr. Thayer or some other party. In any case, not to sue might be seen as tacit forgiveness for the incident.

EXHIBIT 1
News Article, *The Wall Street Journal*, August 10, 1982

ANHEUSER-BUSCH TO BUY CAMPBELL TAGGART INC.
Cash–Stock Offer is Valued at $570 Million

ST. LOUIS—Anheuser-Busch Co. said it agreed in principle to acquire Campbell Taggart Inc., a Dallas-based baked-goods concern, for roughly $570 million in cash and stock.

The brewer, which had disclosed preliminary merger talks last week, said it would pay $36 each for about half of Campbell Taggart's 15 million shares. It would convert the rest into shares of a new Anheuser-Busch convertible preferred stock. Each new share would have a redemption value of $40, bear dividends at a rate of 9% a year, be noncallable for the first 5 years, and be convertible into .645 share of Anheuser-Busch common stock. The value of the new preferred stock is uncertain, but the acquisition would total about $570 million if the stock is assigned its redemption value . . .

Under terms of the acquisition, Campbell Taggart shareholders may choose cash or stock for each share held, subject to proration if required. Anheuser-Busch said the stock swap is intended to be tax-free.

The acquisition requires a definitive agreement and approval of Campbell Taggart shareholders.

Anheuser-Busch said that Campbell Taggart will continue to operate under current management and that its chairman, Bill O. Mead, is expected to be asked to join the Anheuser-Busch board . . .

Stock market response to the plan has been steady, with Campbell Taggart rising to $30.625, up $1, after the announcement last week and closing $1.75 higher yesterday at $31.75 in New York Stock Exchange composite trading. Anheuser-Busch dropped to $49.625 a share, down $4.375, after talks were disclosed and it closed yesterday on the Big Board at $47.50, down 50 cents . . .

Emanuel Goldman of Sanford C. Bernstein & Co. said that the acquisition price was reasonable and that it would lead to a 10% decrease in per-share earnings unless Anheuser-Busch could raise the price of its beer.

---

11. If a corporation sustains significant losses that can be recovered through legal action and management fails to take this action, shareholders have the right to file a derivative suit on behalf of, and over the objections of, the corporation. Management may become a coplaintiff along with the shareholders. The success of such a suit is often interpreted as a failure on the part of management.

EXHIBIT 2
Selected Daily Stock Data, June 1–September 1, 1982

Date	Campbell Taggart Closing Price	Volume (000s)	No. of Insider Trades	Insider Volume (000s)	Anheuser-Busch Closing Price	Volume (000s)	S&P 500 Closing Level	NYSE Volume (millions)
6/01	$23.250	10.3	0	0	$48.750	126.4	111.68	41.65
6/02	23.500	6.9	0	0	49.250	45.0	112.04	49.22
6/03	23.625	4.2	0	0	50.250	89.3	111.86	48.45
6/04	23.250	1.3	0	0	48.750	132.3	110.09	44.11
6/07	23.750	5.1	0	0	49.125	57.1	110.12	44.63
6/08	23.625	1.8	0	0	49.000	124.4	109.63	46.82
6/09	23.000	18.9	0	0	49.000	76.0	108.99	55.77
6/10	23.000	1.4	0	0	49.625	63.6	109.61	50.95
6/11	23.625	3.9	0	0	51.125	101.5	111.24	68.61
6/14	23.875	2.5	0	0	49.875	58.4	109.96	40.10
6/15	23.875	21.3	0	0	50.500	18.4	109.69	44.97
6/16	24.000	16.2	0	0	49.875	48.9	108.87	56.28
6/17	24.500	28.7	0	0	49.875	50.5	107.60	49.23
6/18	24.500	2.2	0	0	50.250	65.7	107.28	53.80
6/21	24.125	1.7	0	0	50.250	31.3	107.20	50.37
6/22	24.375	1.5	0	0	50.375	27.0	108.30	55.29
6/23	24.375	7.4	0	0	51.000	114.3	110.14	62.71
6/24	24.750	38.6	0	0	51.125	127.6	109.83	55.86
6/25	24.625	21.4	0	0	51.375	46.9	109.14	38.74
6/28	24.750	1.0	0	0	52.500	40.6	110.26	40.70
6/29	24.875	6.3	0	0	51.750	59.2	110.21	46.99
6/30	25.750	38.2	1	.1	51.750	46.3	109.61	65.28
7/01	27.000	65.6	9	10.0	51.750	27.4	108.71	47.90
7/02	25.750	46.5	0	0	51.375	27.4	107.65	43.76
7/06	25.875	3.8	0	0	51.125	60.2	107.29	44.35
7/07	25.750	35.2	1	1.5	51.250	17.5	107.22	46.92
7/08	26.000	1.8	0	0	51.125	125.5	107.53	63.27
7/09	25.500	4.7	0	0	52.125	41.6	108.83	65.87
7/12	26.250	28.4	2	1.8	53.625	98.2	109.57	74.69
7/13	26.250	12.2	7	6.9	53.375	50.9	109.45	66.17
7/14	27.000	30.2	3	8.1	53.750	15.6	110.44	58.16
7/15	27.000	10.5	0	0	54.625	94.1	110.47	61.09
7/16	26.750	46.9	0	0	55.750	111.8	111.07	58.74
7/19	26.625	5.2	1	.3	55.125	35.5	110.73	53.03
7/20	26.375	1.8	0	0	55.000	44.8	111.54	61.06
7/21	26.125	18.1	2	5.0	53.625	81.3	111.42	66.77
7/22	26.750	9.1	8	4.8	53.625	40.7	111.47	53.87
7/23	27.000	32.1	8	12.3	53.125	44.5	111.17	47.28
7/26	27.750	25.2	13	17.4	53.500	12.4	110.36	37.74
7/27	28.250	64.0	10	31.7	53.250	43.7	109.43	45.74
7/28	29.125	90.0	13	20.9	53.000	65.8	107.73	53.83
7/29	28.500	154.1	3	8.7	52.875	83.8	107.72	55.68
7/30	29.000	63.9	7	11.3	53.125	39.6	107.09	39.27
8/02	29.625	128.6	5	29.4	54.500	71.3	108.98	53.46
8/03	30.625	219.0	0	0	49.625	394.6	107.83	60.48
8/04	29.500	215.4	0	0	50.000	197.6	106.14	53.44
8/05	30.000	195.7	0	0	49.500	156.5	105.16	54.70
8/06	30.000	134.6	0	0	48.000	93.0	103.71	48.66

(continued)

EXHIBIT 2 *(concluded)*
Selected Daily Stock Data, June 1–September 1, 1982

	Campbell Taggart				Anheuser-Busch			
Date	Closing Price	Volume (000s)	No. of Insider Trades	Insider Volume (000s)	Closing Price	Volume (000s)	S&P 500 Closing Level	NYSE Volume (millions)
8/09	$31.750	360.7	0	0	$47.500	215.7	103.08	54.56
8/10	31.625	204.1	0	0	46.500	126.0	102.84	52.68
8/11	31.625	142.7	0	0	45.500	307.1	102.60	49.04
8/12	31.750	119.8	0	0	46.375	216.5	102.42	50.08
8/13	32.625	132.9	0	0	47.500	93.2	103.85	44.72
8/16	32.750	94.8	0	0	47.750	175.0	104.09	55.42
8/17	33.375	140.2	0	0	49.750	181.5	109.04	92.86
8/18	34.000	238.1	0	0	49.875	300.8	108.53	132.71
8/19	34.000	128.6	0	0	50.000	113.9	109.16	78.27
8/20	34.875	185.9	0	0	52.000	211.0	113.02	95.89
8/23	34.750	34.0	0	0	51.625	115.9	116.11	110.32
8/24	35.125	91.8	0	0	52.750	226.8	115.34	121.76
8/25	35.500	85.2	0	0	54.125	105.4	117.58	106.28
8/26	35.000	262.6	0	0	54.750	155.6	118.55	137.32
8/27	34.625	65.0	0	0	53.500	119.9	117.11	74.41
8/30	35.250	72.8	0	0	54.000	129.4	117.66	59.56
8/31	35.750	89.9	0	0	55.000	106.1	119.51	86.36
9/01	35.000	120.9	0	0	54.875	66.1	118.25	82.83

Note: Short interest is the number of shares investors have "sold short," that is, borrowed and then resold. The mid-month short interest in Campbell Taggart for June, July, August, and September 1982 was 255,969 shares; 255,405 shares; 6,300 shares; and 100 shares, respectively. The mid-month short interest in Anheuser-Busch for June, July, and August 1982 was 78,522 shares; 118,203 shares, and 88,097 shares, respectively.

EXHIBIT 3
Anheuser-Busch: Price and Volume

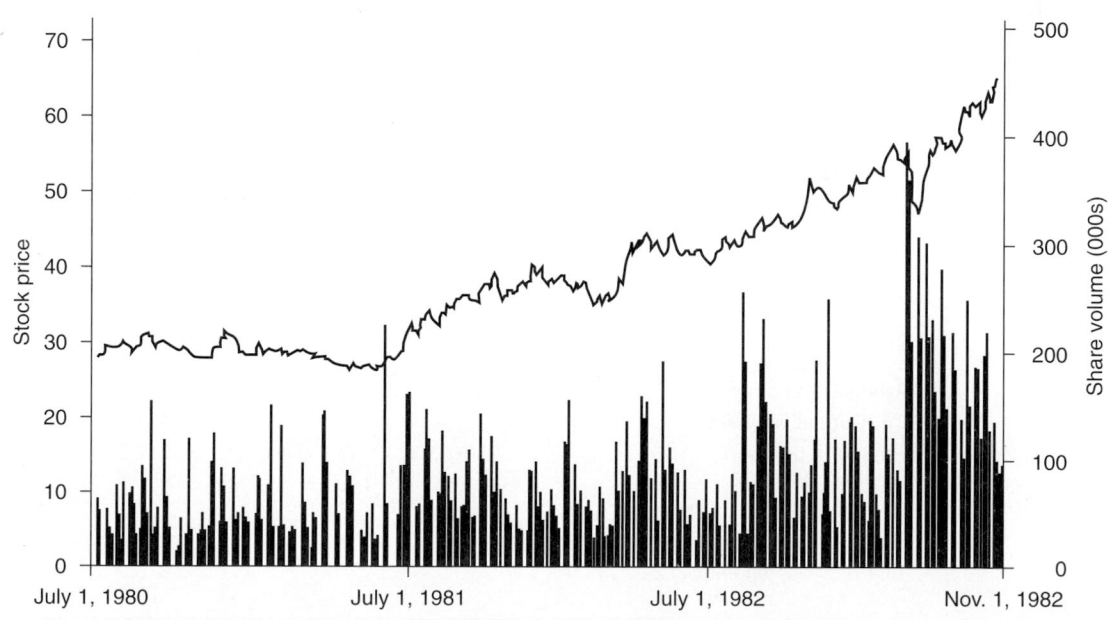

Note: The price data are plotted as a continuous line and should be read off the left-hand axis. The daily volume data are shown as vertical lines rising from the bottom of the plot and should be read off the right-hand axis.

EXHIBIT 4
Campbell Taggart: Price and Volume

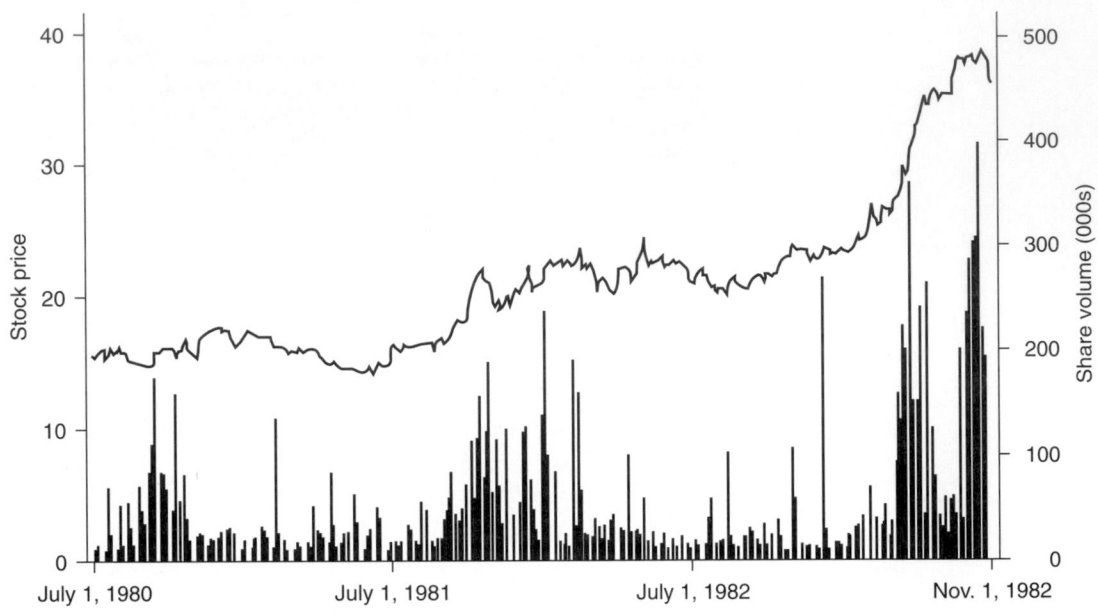

Note: The price data are plotted as a continuous line and should be read off the left-hand axis. The daily volume data are shown as vertical lines rising from the bottom of the plot and should be read off the right-hand axis.

EXHIBIT 5
Consolidated Balance Sheets at December 31, 1981 (millions of dollars)

	Anheuser-Busch	Campbell Taggart
Cash and securities	$ 93.6	$ 20.8
Receivables and inventory	376.1	147.1
Other	69.6	12.7
Current assets	539.3	180.6
Investments and other assets	78.3	42.0
Plant and equipment	2,257.6	292.2
Total assets	$2,875.2	$514.8
Short-term debt	$ 29.5	$ 11.6
Accounts payable	209.8	65.9
Accruals and other	254.1	42.3
Current liabilities	493.4	119.8
Long-term borrowing	817.3	125.5
Deferred taxes	357.7	21.8
Minority interests	.0	22.7
Shareholders equity (issued 45,612,716 shares and 15,974,687 shares, respectively)	1,206.8	225.0
Total liabilities and equity	$2,875.2	$514.8

EXHIBIT 6

Consolidated Income Statements for Year Ending December 31, 1981 (millions of dollars except per share data)

	Anheuser-Busch	Campbell Taggart
Net sales	$3,847.2	$1,257.5
Net cost of goods sold	2,975.5	657.6
Marketing and research	515.0	512.5
Operating income	356.7	87.4
Other income	.0	1.6
Total income	356.7	89.0
Net interest expense	31.5	10.7
Taxes	107.8	36.6
Net income	$ 217.4	$ 41.7
Earnings per share	$ 4.77	$ 2.61
Dividends per share	1.38	.90
Rank in S&P 500 in 1981	139	334

EXHIBIT 7

Chronology of Events

Jan. 5, 1982	Paul Thayer is elected a director of Anheuser-Busch.
June 8, 1982	Anheuser-Busch informs its investment banking firm that it is considering the acquisition of Campbell Taggart.
June 23, 1982	Mr. Thayer attends Anheuser-Busch board meeting at which Campbell Taggart acquisition is considered.
June 25, 1982	Mr. Thayer travels from Dallas to Houston with friends, returning the next day.
June 28, 1982	Mr. Thayer allegedly tells Billy Bob Harris and others about the impending acquisition.
June 28, 1982	Purchases of Campbell Taggart stock by defendants begin.
July 6, 1982	Mr. Thayer telephones chairman of Anheuser-Busch's board of directors, then immediately phones Mr. Harris.
July 28, 1982	Mr. Thayer attends Anheuser-Busch board meeting and telephones Sandra Ryno afterwards.
Aug. 2, 1982	Anheuser-Busch announces merger talks with Campbell Taggart.
Aug. 9, 1982	Anheuser-Busch announces agreement in principle to acquire Campbell Taggart.
Aug. 17, 1982	Boards of both companies approve definitive merger agreement.
Oct. 27, 1982	Campbell Taggart shareholders approve merger agreement.
Nov. 2, 1982	Campbell Taggart becomes a wholly owned subsidiary of Anheuser-Busch.
Dec. 3, 1982	SEC notifies Anheuser-Busch that it is investigating "unusual activity" in Campbell Taggart stock. Anheuser-Busch later cooperates with investigation.
Dec. 6, 1982	President Reagan nominates Mr. Thayer to be Deputy Secretary of Defense. The Senate later confirms the nomination.
Dec. 31, 1982	Mr. Thayer resigns his position on the Anheuser-Busch board.
Jan. 4, 1984	Mr. Thayer resigns as Deputy Secretary of Defense.
Jan. 5, 1984	SEC files a civil complaint against Mr. Thayer, claiming that he leaked corporate takeover plans to eight friends, who made $1.9 million in illegal profits from the information.

EXHIBIT 8
Select Purchases and Sales of Campbell Taggart Stock by Insiders, 1982

Defendant	Purchase Date	No. of Shares	Total Price Paid	Sales Date
Ms. Ryno	June 30	100	$ 2,625	Aug. 10
	July 1	1,900	50,450	
	July 27	4,000	113,827	
Mr. Harris	July 1	3,100[a]	88,200	Aug. 4
	July 27	10,000	284,068	
Mr. Mathis	July 7	1,500	38,745	Aug. 4, Aug. 11, Aug. 24
	July 14	6,200	168,144	
	July 15	3,800	103,094	
	July 21	5,000	130,788	
	July 27	2,000	56,800	
	July 30	2,300	65,895	
	July 30	2,300	65,895	
	Aug. 2	10,000	300,075	
Ms. Williams	July 28	2,000	57,251	Aug. 3
Tippee A	July 28	2,000	57,251	Aug. 3
Tippee B	July 28	13,000	383,195	Aug. 3
	July 30	2,000	58,506	
Other tippees	July 28 and later	31,000	Various	Various

Note: This exhibit describes a subset of the insider trades documented in Exhibit 2.

a. This block of 3,100 shares was purchased for the account of his father and stepmother.

Systems Engineering Laboratories, Inc.

In early 1978, Systems Engineering Laboratories, Inc. was considering how to raise $10–15 million of new capital to finance its rapid growth. Systems was incorporated in 1961. At first, the firm produced components for data acquisition systems. Later, the firm began to produce digital computers for a high-speed acquisition and control of real-time data. The company's sales grew rapidly from $1.0 million in 1962 to $6.2 million by 1966.

In March 1966, Systems first sold stock publicly through an offering of 240,000 shares at $4.50 per share. In a second public offering in November 1967, the firm sold 100,000 shares at $22.00 per share. Two years later, the firm sold stock in a third public offering. The sale of 250,000 shares at a price of $40.25 per share raised approximately $10 million in this public offering.

In the decade following its initial public offering, Systems's financial record was somewhat erratic. The firm's progress was interrupted twice (see Exhibit 1). Sales declines and major losses were sustained in 1971 and again in 1974. In 1971 a soft economy, several disastrous acquisitions, and a significant write-down of obsolete inventory resulted in a sales decline from $21 to $13 million and a loss exceeding $10 million. This loss eliminated almost one half of the firm's net worth.

In 1972, Systems introduced three new major products that helped to rebuild the company's sales. Progress continued until 1974, when sales declined from $17 million to $15 million, and a net loss of $3.8 million was incurred (see Exhibit 1). The loss in 1974 consisted of $2.6 million from operations, $1.2 million from the write-off of obsolete inventory, and $1.3 million from the discontinuation of an obsolete product line. This $5.1 million loss was reduced by a $1.3 million gain on the sale of land.

In 1974, Systems commenced a major new product development effort. This effort was quite successful, and the first models of a newly developed computer series were shipped in October 1975. Shipments of this equipment had a major impact on Systems's sales, profits, and financing requirements (see Exhibit 2).

TABLE A
Market Data (millions of dollars)

	Systems's 1977 Share of Market	Size of Market in 1977	Estimated Size of Market in 1981	Estimated Annual Market Growth 1977–1981
Energy monitoring and control	35%	$ 25	$ 65	27%
Flight-training simulators	25	30	60	19
Laboratory and computation	5	195	300	16

Systems felt that its new products represented a significant improvement in machine performance/price ratios. An improvement of substantial magnitude was usually necessary to prompt users to consider changing their computer vendor, since "computer users characteristically become attached to computer suppliers because of their extensive investments in applications software operable only on the machines for which it is written."[1] In Systems's view, opportunities of the type presented by its new products "do not occur often in the computer industry, and we intend to focus resources to benefit from this situation."[2] In this effort, Systems would be facing some competitors with substantially greater financial resources. Indeed, all of Systems's principal competitors were larger firms. These competitors included Digital Equipment Corporation, Data General Corporation, Prime Computer, Inc., and Perkin-Elmer Corporation (see Exhibit 3).

The bulk of Systems's computer sales were to manufacturers whose products served three markets: (1) energy monitoring and control systems (primarily for electric utilities); (2) flight-training simulators; and (3) laboratory and computation uses. Systems's 1977 share of market and the growth in the computer segment of these markets between 1977 and 1981 were estimated as shown in Table A.

Revolving Credit Financing Arrangement

Through June 1977, Systems had been able to finance its operations through the use of a revolving credit agreement that the firm had established with two banks in 1972. This agreement allowed Systems to borrow (on a fully secured basis) amounts that had, in the past, adequately met the firm's operating needs. Southeast First National Bank of Miami was the lead bank in the credit, and the Chemical Bank joined in the credit with a 50% participation. The revolving credit agreement had been modified many times in the past in order to meet the needs of both Systems and its lenders (see Exhibit 4). By year-end 1977, however, it was clear that Systems would very soon encounter a level of funds needs that would exhaust the desires of the firm's lenders for granting additional credit. The various markets served by Systems had been growing at annual rates of 18–40% in fiscal 1978, a rate somewhat higher than the forecasted longer-run average. These growth rates were not expected to diminish in the immediate future. Systems would thus easily require $10–15 million of new externally supplied capital over the next 2 years to simply keep pace with the growth in its markets, even ignoring the financing requirements associated with Systems's increased market share objective.

---

1. Systems Engineering Laboratories, Inc., annual report (1977), p. 2.

2. Annual report (1977), p. 2.

As the need for additional funds grew, Systems began encountering difficulty meeting the restrictive covenants on its existing debt.

Indeed, Systems had been unable to fulfill the loan restriction relating to the ratio of total liabilities to tangible net worth as of September 23, 1977, and had to obtain a waiver of this restriction from its bankers. At December 23, 1977, Systems was in default of two covenants (i.e., those relating to debt to worth and inventory turnover) and had received waivers. During December 1977, the Chemical Bank dropped out of the credit agreement after declining to increase Systems's line of credit, and the First National Bank of Boston became the lead bank in the loan. The maximum loan limit was raised from $6.5 million to $8.5 million. On March 3, 1978, this loan limit was raised to $10.0 million. By March 24, 1978, Systems was in default of three covenants (i.e., those relating to debt to worth, inventory turnover, and current ratio) and had again received waivers. On May 8, 1978, the Continental Illinois National Bank joined in the credit agreement, raising Systems's maximum credit limit to $12.0 million.

A Need for New Financing

Systems's lenders were endeavoring to assist the firm in achieving its full growth potential. Nonetheless, by 1978, Systems's lenders were insistent that the firm either had to seek new long-term financing or find a way to live within its existing credit limits. The latter choice would require Systems to forgo highly profitable sales, an outcome that the firm was unwilling to accept. Systems simply had to find one or more new sources of financing, and the firm was exploring all available options. By the end of March 1978, it was clear that the sale of two quite different financing instruments was feasible, as were a number of intermediate choices utilizing some variation on the two polar choices.

A Possible Sale of Common Equity

At one extreme, Systems might sell common equity. As shown in Exhibit 5, Systems's stock price had risen sharply in the prior four months, as the firm's improved prospects began to be reflected in reported earnings per share (lines 12 and 13 of Exhibit 2). This increase in stock price for Systems came at a time, however, when the prices of equity securities were declining overall. The weak tone of the broader market for equities added significant risk to a Systems's equity offering that would have to be completed under considerable time pressure. In addition, the market for newly issued securities of small firms was not terribly robust in early 1978. For example, initial public offerings for firms with net worth only slightly below that of Systems had not been well received by the market in recent years (see Exhibit 6). While an equity offering by Systems in early 1978 would have been its fourth registered public offering, the relative receptivity of the equity markets to offerings by small firms over the last decade, as shown by Exhibit 6, was revealing.

A $10 million equity offering would put considerable pressure on Systems's stock price. Indeed, the mere announcement of an offering of such significant size in a declining general market environment might easily wipe away the share-price progress that Systems had achieved over the past several months. It was entirely conceivable that a $10 million transaction might require an offering price of only $8 per share, which, after underwriting discounts and expenses, might produce as little as $7.25 per share for Systems. While net proceeds of $7.25 per share might look quite reasonable in relation to Systems's book value of $4.55 per share, this price looked less attractive

TABLE B
Comparison of Companies at March 31, 1978

	Price/Earnings[a] Ratio of Common Stock	Market Value/Book Value Ratio of Common Stock
Digital Equipment Corp.	11.8	1.9
Data General Corp.	13.4	2.6
Prime Computer, Inc.	17.9	5.0
Perkin-Elmer Corp.	12.5	1.6
Systems Engineering Labs @ $12⅝ per share	16.4	2.8
Systems Engineering Labs @ $7¼ per share	9.4	1.6

a. Calculation based on earnings per share for the 12 months ended March 31, 1978.

in terms of Systems's potential earnings per share in the near future. It also looked less attractive in terms of the price-earnings ratios and market value/book value ratios achieved by Systems's principal competitors (see Table B). Systems did have at least one other, quite different financing alternative, however. That alternative was to issue a high-coupon subordinated debenture.

A Possible Sale of Subordinated Debentures

Systems's size and profit history were such that a large, subordinated debt issue would probably receive an extremely low rating (such as CCC)[3] from bond-rating agencies such as Moody's or Standard & Poor's. Historically, a nonconvertible debt security carrying such a low rating could not be sold for cash. In fact, the volume of publicly traded debt in this rating category was quite small.[4] Most of the debt found in similar rating categories was either convertible debt; had been downgraded from earlier, higher ratings; or was originally issued in exchange for other securities. Starting in late 1976, however, significant quantities of high-coupon, low-rated, nonconvertible debt began to be sold publicly in fairly significant volume. Whereas not a single issue of public debt rated below A was sold by an industrial firm in 1975, net offerings aggregating several hundred million dollars rated BB or lower (two full rating categories below A) were sold in 1977 (see Exhibit 7).

A few investment bankers had begun to specialize in underwriting such debt, and a market for this type of security had developed to the point where at least five mutual funds were specializing in low-rated, high-coupon debt (see Exhibit 8). Some measure of the degree to which investors were beginning to find lower-rated debt attractive can be seen in Exhibit 9. Between January 1977 and March 1978, the yields on Aaa-rated industrials rose 59 basis points from 7.77% to 8.36%. Over this same time period, the yields on Baa industrials rose by only 8 basis points. The yield spreads separating bond rating categories narrowed sharply in 1977 and early 1978. Investors were willing to reach into lower rating categories in order to achieve high yields.

---

3. According to Standard & Poor's: "Bonds rated BB, B, CCC, and CC are regarded, on balance, as predominantly speculative with respect to capacity to pay interest and repay principal in accordance with the terms of the obligation. BB indicates the lowest degree of speculation and CC the highest degree of speculation. While such bonds will likely have some quality and protective characteristics, these are outweighed by large uncertainties or major risk exposures to adverse conditions."

4. Salomon Brothers estimated that 2.6% of all publicly traded debt of industrial firms was rated CCC or lower. Indeed, only 7.2% of all publicly traded debt of industrial firms was rated below BBB.

Systems's investment bankers felt that the climate for low-rated debt was sufficiently attractive in early 1978 that Systems might be able to raise $10 million to $15 million of subordinated debt with an interest coupon of 12.5%.[5] This would represent the highest coupon rate for an industrial borrower in the history of the long-term, public-debt markets. It was thought that such debt could be sold with a 15-year maturity and would require mandatory sinking fund payments equal to 10% of the amount of debt issued. Sinking fund payments would not be required during the first 7 years that the debt was outstanding.[6]

If Systems's sales volume were to expand by 30% per year from the sales rate anticipated for the last fiscal quarter of 1978, Systems's sales, debt ratios, and earnings per share over the period 1978–1981 would be as indicated in Exhibit 10. This exhibit assumes that Systems's capital intensity and operating profit margins would remain at the levels experienced in the most recent fiscal quarters.

In the light of these facts, Systems had to determine promptly the size and form of its next financing. As Systems considered its alternatives, rumors indicated that Prime Computer, Inc., one of Systems's competitors, was preparing to file a registration statement with the SEC indicating its intention to offer $15 million of 15-year, nonconvertible subordinated debentures.

---

5. One other option that Systems could consider was the issuance of a 15-year convertible debenture. Systems's investment bankers felt that if the debenture was made convertible at a 20% premium over the market price on the day of issuance, it might be sold at an 8.5% interest rate. If the debenture was made convertible at a 50% premium over the market on the day of issuance, it might be sold at an 11% interest rate.

6. The issue would be callable at any time at an initial redemption price of 106.75% of the price paid by the public. For a period of 8 years, no redemption would be allowed from money borrowed at an interest cost of less than 12.5%. The debt would be subordinated to all other current and future borrowings, and Systems would be unable to pay a dividend until its net worth reached $18 million.

EXHIBIT 1

Financial History for Fiscal Years Ending June 30, 1968–1978 (thousands of dollars except per share data)

	1968	1969	1970	1971	1972	1973	1974	1975	1976	1977	9 Months Ending 3/31/77	9 Months Ending 3/31/78
1. Revenues	$12,032	$17,298	$21,153	$ 12,773	$15,719	$17,082	$ 14,951	$17,457	$20,003	$30,774	$21,762	$35,368
2. Cost of sales	6,980	9,766	11,592	17,179	9,350	11,404	12,941	11,034	11,832	17,029	12,049	18,750
3. Gross profit	$ 5,052	$ 7,532	$ 9,561	$ (4,406)	$ 6,369	$ 5,678	$ 2,010	$ 6,423	$ 8,171	$13,745	$ 9,713	$16,618
4. Selling, general, and administrative	2,202	3,267	4,639	4,393	3,304	3,699	3,857	4,063	5,186	7,651	5,522	8,672
5. Research and development	969	1,269	1,580	3,523	1,253	1,168	1,894	2,218	2,279	3,737	2,792	3,446
6. Interest	62	173	194	456	631	687	902	513	510	655	512	696
7. Other income (expenses)	—	—	—	—	21	210	(816)	123	(203)	(72)	—	—
8. Income before taxes and extraordinary items	$ 1,819	$ 2,823	$ 3,148	$(12,778)	$ 1,202	$ 334	$ (5,459)	$ (248)	$ (7)	$ 1,630	$ 887	$ 3,804
9. Provision for taxes	830	1,374	1,316	(3,799)	398	39	(270)	199	197	951	479	1,864
10. Income after taxes	$ 989	$ 1,449	$ 1,832	$ (8,979)	$ 804	$ 295	$ (5,189)	$ (447)	$ (204)	$ 679	$ 408	$ 1,940
11. Extraordinary items	—	—	—	(3,464)	308	343	1,336	136	197	870	479	1,551
12. Profit after taxes	$ 989	$ 1,449	$ 1,832	$(12,443)	$ 1,112	$ 638	$ (3,853)	$ (311)	$ (7)	$ 1,549	$ 887	$ 3,491
13. EPS (excluding extraordinary items)	$ .50	$ .69	$ .77	$ (3.50)	$ .31	$ .11	$ (2.01)	$ (.17)	$ (.07)	$ .24	$ .15	$ .68
14. Share price, high	42⅝	53⅞	49⅛	18¼	16⅜	8⅜	2⅞	6¾	10⅜	12	9⅞	13¾
15. Share price, low	23¾	26⅛	10⅛	6¾	6⅞	1⅛	¾	⅞	4⅞	5	5¼	6¼
16. Trading volume in period[b] (000s)	1,096	3,646	6,325	3,124	2,713	1,160	566	1,236	1,815	1,817	754	2,035
17. Beta of common stock												1.72
18. Book value per share	$ 2.47	$ 3.23	$ 7.85[a]	$ 3.78	$ 4.07	$ 4.28	$ 2.90	$ 2.76	$ 2.63	$ 3.19	$ 3.05	$ 4.55
19. Shares outstanding (000s)	2,049	2,091	2,374	2,565	2,620	2,602	2,582	2,582	2,778	2,799	2,727	2,774
20. Total assets	$ 8,760	$15,555	$30,616	$ 21,797	$21,366	$24,232	$ 15,430	$13,662	$17,642	$23,565	$21,144	$35,604
21. Net worth	5,059	6,764	18,684[a]	9,691	10,665	11,146	7,500	7,115	7,294	8,940	8,321	12,623
22. Income after taxes/Net worth	.195	.214	.098	(1.28)	.075	.026	(.692)	(.063)	(.027)	.079		

a. In October 1969, Systems raised $9.4 million via the sale of 250,000 shares of common stock.

b. Calendar year volume data are shown for the fiscal years. Data for nine months cover the period as indicated.

EXHIBIT 2
Quarterly Financial Data, June 1976–June 1978 (millions of dollars except per share data)

	6/25/76	9/24/76	12/24/76	3/25/77	6/24/77	9/23/77	12/23/77	3/24/78	6/30/78
1. Orders	$11.5	$ 8.2	$ 9.8	$ 7.9	$14.7	$14.3	$14.1	$14.3	$15.3
2. Backlog	20.2	22.4	24.3	24.3	30.0	34.6	37.1	37.5	35.2
3. No. of new computer series shipments (units)	—	20	24	31	37	50	59	72	72
4. Revenues	$ 6.3	$ 6.0	$ 7.9	$ 7.8	$ 9.0	$ 9.8	$11.6	$13.9	$17.6
5. Earnings before interest and taxes	.5	.3	.5	.6	.9	1.1	1.6	1.8	2.1
6. Interest	.2	.1	.2	.2	.2	.2	.2	.3	.6
7. Profit before taxes	$ .3	$ .2	$ .3	$ .4	$ .7	$ .9	$ 1.4	$ 1.5	$ 1.5
8. Taxes	.1	.2	.1	.2	.4	.4	.7	.7	.6
9. Profit after taxes (before extraordinary items)	$ .2	$ .0	$ .2	$ .2	$ .3	$ .5	$ .7	$ .8	$ .9
10. Extraordinary items	.1	.1	.1	.2	.4	.4	.5	.6	.6
11. Profit after taxes	$ .3	$ .1	$ .3	$ .4	$ .7	$ .9	$ 1.2	$ 1.4	$ 1.5
12. EPS (before extraordinary items)	$ .02	$ .01	$ .06	$ .07	$ .09	$ .16	$ .25	$ .27	$ .32
13. EPS (after extraordinary items)	.03	.06	.11	.15	.23	.31	.44	.48	.54
14. Cash	$ .7	$ —	$ .7	$ .5	$ .5	$ .2	—	$ 1.2	—
15. Accounts receivable	7.0	8.3	7.8	9.1	9.7	11.7	13.3	16.2	—
16. Inventories	5.8	6.1	6.2	6.3	7.0	7.6	9.5	11.3	—
17. Other current assets	.3	.4	.5	.5	.8	1.1	1.1	1.0	—
18. Total current assets	$13.8	$14.8	$15.2	$16.4	$18.0	$20.6	$23.9	$29.7	—
19. Net equipment leased to others	1.3	1.2	1.0	1.0	1.5	.9	.5	.5	—
20. Net property, plant, and equipment	2.2	2.1	2.1	3.5	3.8	3.9	4.3	5.2	—
21. Other assets	.4	.4	.4	.3	.2	.2	.3	.2	—
22. Total assets	$17.7	$18.5	$18.7	$21.2	$23.5	$25.6	$29.0	$35.6	$44.0
23. Short-term debt, revolving credit[a]	$ 5.8	$ 6.5	$ 6.8	$ 6.5	$ 6.5	$ 6.5	$ 8.5	$10.0	$ —
24. Short-term debt, other	.4	.1	—	.4	.7	.4	—	—	—
25. Accounts payable and accruals	3.2	3.2	3.1	4.4	5.6	6.7	6.9	9.9	—
26. Other current liabilities	.4	.7	.6	.5	.8	1.0	1.0	1.2	—
27. Total current liabilities	$ 9.8	$10.5	$10.5	$11.8	$13.6	$14.6	$16.4	$21.1	—
28. Long-term debt and other liabilities	.6	.6	.4	1.1	1.0	1.2	1.5	1.9	—
29. Total liabilities	$10.4	$11.1	$10.9	$12.9	$14.6	$15.8	$17.9	$23.0	$30.0
30. Net worth	7.3	7.4	7.8	8.3	8.9	9.8	11.1	12.6	14.0[d]
31. Total liabilities and net worth	$17.7	$18.5	$18.7	$21.2	$23.5	$25.6	$29.0	$35.6	$44.0
32. Revenues[b]/Assets	1.95	1.30	1.69	1.47	1.53	1.53	1.60	1.56	1.60
33. Profit after taxes[b]/Revenues	.045	.004	.023	.024	.030	.046	.060	.057	.053
34. Assets/Net worth	2.42	2.50	2.40	2.55	2.64	2.61	2.61	2.83	3.14[d]
35. Profit after taxes[c]/Net worth	.212	.013	.093	.090	.121	.184	.251	.252	.266
36. Earnings before interest and taxes/Revenues	.087	.050	.065	.074	.098	.113	.137	.129	1.20

a. Assumes that all debt under the revolving credit agreement is short-term, even though for some quarters the maturity date was more than 12 months away.

b. Equal to the annualized rate; that is 400% of the results for the quarter.

c. Not including extraordinary credits resulting from the utilization of tax-loss carryforwards.

d. Assuming no new equity raised via sale of stock prior to June 30, 1978.

255

EXHIBIT 3
Key Financial Data for Systems's Principal Competitors, 1974–1977

	1974	*1975*	*1976*	*1977*
Sales ($ millions)				
Digital Equipment	$421.9	$533.8	$736.3	$1,058.6
Data General	93.0	119.6	178.7	254.7
Prime Computer	6.5	11.4	22.8	50.0
Perkin-Elmer Corp.	293.6	323.0	354.7	432.4
Systems Engineering Labs	15.0	17.5	20.0	30.8
Profit after taxes ($ millions)				
Digital Equipment	$ 44.0	$ 46.0	$ 73.4	$ 108.5
Data General	10.1	13.5	20.8	28.6
Prime Computer	(.5)	.7	2.4	3.9
Perkin-Elmer Corp.	19.2	20.5	21.0	26.6
Systems Engineering Labs	(3.9)	(.3)	0.0	1.5
Borrowing ratio[a]				
Digital Equipment	(.12)	(.02)	(.35)	.04
Data General	(.02)	(.79)	(.37)	(.25)
Prime Computer	.59	.53	.59	.39
Perkin-Elmer Corp.	(.09)	(.08)	(.09)	.02
Systems Engineering Labs	.40	.31	.46	.46
Profit after taxes/Net worth				
Digital Equipment	.131	.117	.121	.148
Data General	.216	.151	.181	.196
Prime Computer	(.250)	.250	.453	.255
Perkin-Elmer Corp.	.133	.123	.113	.127
Systems Engineering Labs	(.520)	(.042)	000	.169
Common stock beta				
Digital Equipment	—	—	—	1.21
Data General	—	—	—	1.46
Prime Computer	—	—	—	2.18
Perkin-Elmer Corp.	—	—	—	1.48
Systems Engineering Labs	—	—	—	1.72

Source: Moody's Industrial Manual.

a. The borrowing ratio is defined as debt versus total capitalization, where cash and marketable securities have been removed from both the numerator and the denominator of the ratio. That is, (Borrowed money – Cash – Marketable securities)/(Net worth + Borrowed money – Cash – Marketable securities). This ratio will be negative in those situations where the firm has more cash and marketable securities than it has borrowed money. Under such circumstances, the firm has negative leverage.

EXHIBIT 4
Key Terms and Conditions of Systems's Revolving Credit Agreement, 1972–1978

Date of Agreement	Expiration Date	Maximum Credit ($ millions)	Interest Rate[a]	Loan Participants	Loan Covenants[b]
8/24/72	1/31/75	8.0	1.17 (prime + ½%)	Southeast @ $4.0 Chemical @ $4.0	(1) Tangible net worth ≥ $8.5 million until 6/30/73, after which $9.5 million. (2) Liabilities/net worth ≤ 1.4 times tangible net worth until 6/30/70, after which 1.1 times. (3) Minimum net working capital of at least $3.0 million plus amount of borrowing hereunder. (4) Capital expenditures less than $.8 million per year.
8/27/74	9/30/75	6.0	Same as above	Southeast @ $3.0 Chemical @ $3.0	(1) Tangible net worth ≥ $6.65 million + any profits or equity sales. (2) Liabilities/net worth ≤ 1.3 times. (3) Minimum net working capital of at least $3.0 million. (4) Capital expenditures limited to greater of $250,000 per year or 50% of cumulative profits after tax from date of agreement.
9/9/76	9/30/77	6.5	1.20 (prime + 1%)	Southeast @ $3.25 Chemical @ $3.25	(1) Tangible net worth ≥ $6.5 million to 9/23/76; rising to $8.6 million at 9/30/77. (2) Liabilities/net worth ≤ 1.6 until 12/29/76, and ≤ 1.5 thereafter. (3) Minimum net working capital of at least $3.8 million plus borrowings hereunder until 12/24/76, and at least $4.0 million thereafter. (4) No capital expenditures in excess of $400,000 per year. (5) Equity sales reduce commitment by 100% of the amount issued up to $2.0 million, plus 50% of the amount issued in excess of $2.0 million.

(continued)

EXHIBIT 4 *(concluded)*

Date of Agreement	Expiration Date	Maximum Credit ($ millions)	Interest Rate[a]	Loan Participants	Loan Covenants[b]
12/20/77	12/20/78	8.5	Prime + 1% + compensating balance[c] of 10% of loan + 10% of total commitment	FNB-Boston @ $4.5 Southeast @ $4.0	(1) Tangible net worth ≥ $9.45 million until 12/22/77, after which amounts rising to $13.5 million at 9/29/78. (2) Liabilities/net worth ≤ 1.72 until 12/22/77, after which ratio must decline to 1.20 by 9/29/78. (3) Minimum net working capital ≥ $5.0 million until 12/22/77, after which amount rises to $9.25 million at 6/30/78. (4) Capital expenditures limited to $1.5 million per year. (5) Annualized inventory turnover rate will exceed 2.25x during each quarter. (6) No distributions while tangible net worth less than $20 million. (7) R&D expenditures not to exceed 10% of sales.
3/3/78		10.0	Prime + 1% for $8.5 million; prime + 1½% for balance; + compensating balance[c] of 10% of loan + 10% of commitment	FNB-Boston @ $6.0 Southeast @ $4.0	Same as above except (a) The ratio of liabilities/net worth could decline more slowly in the early period to 1.20 by 9/29/78. (b) Inventory turnover requirement dropped to 2.0 for the quarter ending 3/23/78.
5/8/78		12.0	Same as above[c]	FNB-Boston @ $6.0 Southeast @ $4.0 Continental Ill. @ $2.0	Same as above.

a. The loan terms also included a commitment fee equal to ½% of any unused portion of the maximum credit available.

b. The loan covenants included the condition that essentially all of Systems's assets would be pledged to secure the bank loans, and that the total loan outstanding would not exceed 90% of qualified accounts receivable.

c. Interest equivalent to the lenders' earnings on the compensating balances could be paid in lieu of maintaining these balances.

EXHIBIT 5
Stock Price versus the S&P 500, 1974–1978

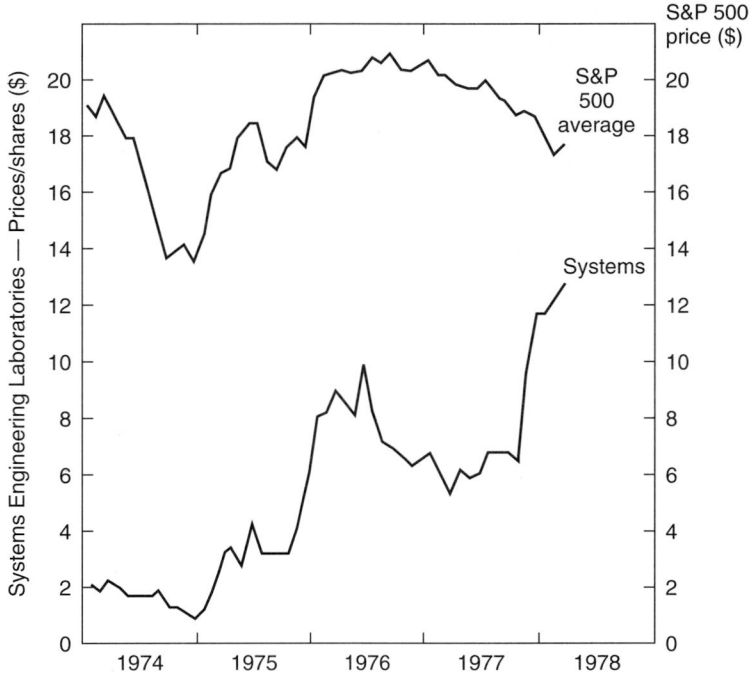

EXHIBIT 6
Underwritten Initial Public Equity Offerings of Small Firms versus the Overall Level of Stock Market Prices, 1968—1977

	Number of Issues Underwritten	Total Size of Offerings ($ millions)	S&P 500 Average
1968	358	$ 745	106.5
1969	698	1,367	91.1
1970	198	375	90.1
1971	248	551	99.2
1972	409	896	117.5
1973	101	205	94.8
1974	9	16	67.1
1975	4	16	88.7
1976	38	168	104.7
1977	29	110	93.8
1978 3 mos	2	12	89.2

Sources: Venture Capital, March 1976, p. 8; January 1977, p. 12; January 1978, p. 7; "Security Price Index Record," *Standard & Poor's Statistical Service,* 1978.

Note: Small firms are defined as those with less than $5 million of net worth prior to their initial public offering through 1975. In 1976 the cutoff point was raised to include all firms with less than $10 million of net worth prior to their initial public offering.

EXHIBIT 7
Public Offerings of Low-Rated, Nonconvertible Debentures

Issuer	*Date*	*Amount ($ millions)*	*Security*	*Rating Moody's/S&P*	*Pro Forma Debt Percent Total Capital*	*Yield to Maturity at Issue Date*	*Lead Manager*	*Underwriting Cost (Percent of Total Issue)*
Western Air Lines	4/76	$ 23.0	10% sub. S.F. notes 1984	Ba/B	57%	10.19%	E. F. Hutton	2.50%
Hospital Affiliates	10/76	12.0	10% sr. debs. 1991	NR/BB+	65	10.00	Goldman Sachs	4.00
City Investing	12/76	125.0	9% S.F. debs. 1996	NR/BB	54	11.02	Blyth Eastman Dillon	2.80
LTV Corp.	2/77	75.0	9¼% S.F. debs. 1997	B/B	75	11.40	Lehman Brothers	3.30
Zapata Corp.	3/77	75.0	10¼% sub. debs. 1997	B/B	68	11.44	Lehman Brothers	3.80
Fuqua Inds.	3/77	60.0	9⅞% sr. sub. debs. 1997	B/B	50	11.27	Lehman Brothers	3.30
Texas International Co.	4/77	30.0	11½% sub. debs. 1997	B/B	52	11.50	Drexel Burnham Lambert	3.00
UV Inds.	4/77	25.0	9¼% sr. sub. notes 1987	Ba/BB–	53	9.25	E. F. Hutton	1.70
APL Corp.	7/77	35.0	10¾% sub. debs. 1997	B/BB	44	10.75	Bear Stearns	2.75
Michigan General Corp.	8/77	27.5	10⅞% sr. S.F. debs. 1992	B/BB	66	10.875	Drexel Burnham Lambert	3.50
Buttes Gas & Oil Co.	8/77	70.0	10¼% sub. debs. 1997	B/B	67	11.10	E. F. Hutton	3.30
U.S. Home Corp.	8/77	50.0	10% notes 1987	NR/BB	52	10.00	White Weld	1.75
City Investing Co.	8/77	100.0	9⅛% S.F. debs. 1997	NR/BB	50	10.43	Blyth Eastman Dillon	2.80
Western Co. of N. Amer.	9/77	32.5	10⅞% sub. debs. 1997	B/B	55	11.29	Smith Barney, Harris Upham	6.40
Loral Corp.	9/77	20.0	10¾% sub. S.F. debs. 1997	B/BB–	48	10.75	Paine Webber	2.50
Action Inds.	9/77	12.0	11% sr. S.F. debs. 1992	B/BB–	55	11.00	Drexel Burnham Lambert	2.50
Gulf Resources & Chem.	10/77	50.0	10⅞% sub. S.F. debs. 1997	B/B	50	10.875	Bear Stearns	2.25
Emerson Radio Corp.	10/77	7.5	11% sr. S.F. debs. 1992	B/B	53	11.49	Drexel Burnham Lambert	4.00
Polychrome Corp.	10/77	20.0	10½% sr. S.F. debs. 1997	Ba/BB	39	10.50	Drexel Burnham Lambert	2.00
Tannetics	12/77	12.5	10½% sr. S.F. debs. 1992	NR/B	46	11.31	Drexel Burnham Lambert	3.75
Cascade Natural Gas	12/77	10.0	10½% sr. sub. debs. 1992	Ba/BB	61	10.50	Hornblower Weeks, Noyes & Trask	3.00
Comdisco	12/77	15.0	11½% sub. debs. 1992	B/B	91	11.50	Drexel Burnham Lambert	3.40
Caesars World	12/77	25.0	11¼% sr. S.F. debs. 1997	NR/B	75	12.29	E. F. Hutton	3.75
Lear Petroleum Corp.	12/77	13.0	11½% sub. debs. 1992	NR/CCC	75	11.50	Bateman Eichler, Hill Richards	4.00
Petro-Lewis Corp.	1/78	25.0	11% sub. debs. 1997	NR/B	70	11.79	Oppenheimer	3.60
Midland Glass Co.	2/78	25.0	10¾% sub. S.F. debs. 1998	B/B	43	10.75	Bear Stearns	2.50
Charter Medical Corp.	2/78	12.0	11% S.F. debs. 1993	NR/B	70	11.00	Drexel Burnham Lambert	3.30
California Life Corp.	3/78	20.0	11% S.F. debs. 1998	NR/BB	48	11.00	First Boston	2.50
A-T-O	3/78	20.0	10⅜% sub. debs. 1998	Ba/B	52	10.375	E. F. Hutton	2.20
Western Co. of N. Amer.	3/78	30.0	10.70% sub. debs. 1998	B/B	58	10.70	Smith Barney, Harris Upham	2.75

Source: Institutional Investor, August 1978, pp. 36–37.

Note: NR = not rated.

EXHIBIT 8

Net Assets of Mutual Funds Specializing in Low-Rated, High-Yield Debt Securities, 1973–1977 (millions of dollars)

	Net Assets				
Fund	*1973*	*1974*	*1975*	*1976*	*1977*
Keystone Custodian Fund, series B-4	$243	$236	$324	$449	$477
First Investors Fund for Income, Inc.	18	43	105	223	363
Lord Abbett Bond-Debenture Fund	99	102	137	175	182
National Bond Fund	40	55	86	120	140
Fidelity Aggressive Income Fund	—	—	—	—	5

Source: Investment Companies 1978, Wiesenberger Investment Company Service.

EXHIBIT 9

Yields on Long-Term Aaa and Baa Industrial Bonds, 90-Day Treasury Bills, and the Commercial Bank Prime Rate, 1st Quarter 1974 to 4th Quarter 1976 and January 1977–March 1978

	Industrial Bond Yields			*90-Day Treasury Bill Rate*	*Commercial Bank Prime Rate*
	Aaa	*Baa*	*Difference*		
Mar. 1974	7.87%	8.42%	.55%	7.99%	9.25%
June	8.34	9.03	.69	8.15	11.75
Sept.	9.12	9.78	.66	8.36	12.00
Dec.	8.74	9.85	1.11	7.18	10.50
Mar. 1975	8.52	10.01	1.49	5.54	7.75
June	8.61	10.39	1.78	5.19	7.00
Sept.	8.68	10.35	1.67	6.38	8.00
Dec.	8.51	10.33	1.82	5.50	7.25
Mar. 1976	8.30	10.07	1.77	5.05	6.75
June	8.40	9.76	1.36	5.44	7.25
Sept.	8.18	9.33	1.15	5.08	7.00
Dec.	7.81	9.03	1.22	4.35	6.25
Jan. 1977	7.77	8.99	1.22	4.60	6.25
Feb.	7.86	9.04	1.18	4.66	6.25
Mar.	7.92	9.04	1.12	4.61	6.25
Apr.	7.86	8.97	1.11	4.54	6.25
May	7.87	8.88	1.01	4.94	6.75
June	7.77	8.80	1.03	5.00	6.75
July	7.78	8.75	.97	5.14	6.75
Aug.	7.82	8.72	.90	5.50	7.00
Sept.	7.76	8.74	.98	5.77	7.25
Oct.	7.88	8.77	.89	6.19	7.75
Nov.	7.93	8.84	.91	6.16	7.75
Dec.	8.04	8.90	.86	6.06	7.75
Jan. 1978	8.31	9.07	.76	6.44	8.00
Feb.	8.37	9.11	.74	6.45	8.00
Mar.	8.36	9.07	.71	6.29	8.00

EXHIBIT 10

Pro Forma Revenues, Profits, Earnings per Share, and Debt/Total Capital Ratios, 1978–1981, under Various Financing Assumptions (millions of dollars except per share data)

	6/30/78	Raise $10 Million Equity in 1978			Raise $10 Million Debt in 1978		
		6/30/79	6/30/80	6/30/81	6/30/79	6/30/80	6/30/81
1. Revenues (quarterly data for fiscal 4th quarter) . . .	$ 17.6	$ 22.9	$ 29.7	$ 38.7	$ 22.9	$ 29.7	$ 38.7
2. Revenues[a]	52.9	81.0	105.2	136.8	81.0	105.2	136.8
3. Earnings before interest and taxes[b]	6.6	10.5	13.7	17.8	10.5	13.7	17.8
4. Interest[c]	1.3	1.3	2.1	3.1	2.7	3.5	4.6
5. Profit before taxes	$ 5.3	$ 9.2	$ 11.6	$ 14.7	$ 7.8	$ 10.2	$ 13.2
6. Taxes	2.4	4.4	5.6	7.1	3.7	4.9	6.3
7. Profit after taxes (before extraordinary items)	$ 2.9	$ 4.8	$ 6.0	$ 7.6	$ 4.1	$ 5.3	$ 6.9
8. Extraordinary items[d]	2.2	.6	—	—	.6	—	—
9. Profit after taxes	$ 5.1	$ 5.4	$ 6.0	$ 7.6	$ 4.7	$ 5.3	$ 6.9
10. Total assets[e]	$ 44.0	$ 57.3	$ 74.3	$ 96.8	$ 57.3	$ 74.3	$ 96.8
11. Liabilities other than borrowed money[f]	$ 13.2	$ 17.2	$ 22.3	$ 29.0	$ 17.2	$ 22.3	$ 29.0
12. Borrowed money	16.8	10.7	16.6	24.8	21.4	28.0	36.9
13. Net worth	14.0[i]	29.4	35.4	43.0	18.7	24.0	30.9
14. Total liabilities and net worth	$ 44.0	$ 57.3	$ 74.3	$ 96.8	$ 57.3	$ 74.3	$ 96.8
15. Shares outstanding[g] (000s)	2,800	4,180	4,180	4,180	2,800	2,800	2,800
16. EPS (before extraordinary items)	$ 1.04	$ 1.15	$ 1.44	$ 1.82	$ 1.46	$ 1.89	$ 2.46
17. Debt/Total capital[h]	.55	.27	.32	.37	.53	.54	.54
18. Senior borrowings/Net worth and subordinated debt	1.20	.36	.47	.58	.40	.53	.66

Source: Casewriter estimates.

a. Assumes revenues in the 4th quarter of each year are 30% higher than the level achieved in the 4th quarter of the prior year, and that sales for the year equal four times the average of the 4th quarter rate of the year in question plus the 4th quarter rate of the prior year.

b. Assumes earnings before interest and taxes equal 13% of revenues per line 36, Exhibit 2.

c. Interest is calculated as 12.5% of year-end borrowed money.

d. Extraordinary items equal to .6 in 1979 represents the utilization of Systems's remaining tax loss carryforward.

e. Assumes that the assets required to support sales at the 4th quarter rate each year would equal (4th quarter revenues) × (4) ÷ 1.6 per line 32, Exhibit 2.

f. Assumes that liabilities other than borrowed money remain at 30% of total assets.

g. Assumes that in order to net $10 million at a share price of $7.25 net to Systems, 1.38 million Systems shares would be sold in an equity offering.

h. Borrowed money/Borrowed money plus net worth.

i. Assumes no new equity raised via sale of stock prior to 6/30/78.

Dividend Policy at FPL Group, Inc. (A)

In the late afternoon of Thursday, May 5, 1994, Kate Stark, the electric utilities analyst at First Equity Securities Corporation, received an investment alert on one of the companies she followed. According to the report, Merrill Lynch's utilities analyst was downgrading FPL Group, Inc., Florida's largest electric utility. The report began:

> We are [lowering] the investment rating for FPL Group . . . due to our expectation that the Directors will choose not to raise the annual dividend from $2.48 at [the annual meeting on] Monday, May 9. FPL's shareholders face the possibility that the dividend is not entirely secure, as we believe FPL may seriously review its dividend policy at this time. . . . Management has suggested that it feels that its dividend payout is inappropriately high (in excess of 90% in 1993) given the increasing risks facing the industry. . . . When asked specifically what might be done about the high dividend payout levels, management suggested that there are two ways to address high payout levels: 1) a company can grow out of a high payout; 2) a company can cut its dividend . . . we expect the company to keep the dividend at the $2.48/share level through 1997.[1]

Although this analyst was predicting the dividend would not change, this was the first time Stark had seen one of her peers suggest the possibility of a dividend cut. Only three weeks earlier, Stark herself had issued a report on FPL Group with a "hold" recommendation based on the assumption that FPL would keep its dividend at $2.48 per share or increase it slightly. What concerned her, however, was the fact that FPL's stock price had fallen by more than 6% that day. While she could not be sure the drop was related to the report, she wondered what, if anything, she should say to her clients regarding FPL's stock and whether she should issue an updated report.

This case was prepared by Research Associate Craig F. Schreiber under the supervision of Professor Benjamin C. Esty. This case was prepared solely on the basis of public information without the participation of FPL Group, Inc.

Copyright © 1995 by the President and Fellows of Harvard College.
Harvard Business School case 295–059.

1. Sanford Cohen and Daniel Ford, "FPL Group: Dividend Policy Review; Lowered Opinion," Merrill Lynch & Co., May 5, 1994, pp. 1, 3.

Electric Utility Industry

One can trace the history of the U.S. electric utility industry back to Thomas Edison's invention of the incandescent lamp in 1878. Electricity quickly became an important part of everyday life because of the ease with which it could be transported from one place to another and converted into other useful forms (mechanical power, light, etc.). Electricity—the flow of electrons—is created by forcing steam or water through a turbine lined with electromagnets, which induces electron movement. Once produced, electricity is transmitted through power lines and distributed to end users.

The concept of a public utility developed in the late nineteenth century to refer to a monopoly supplier of a "vital public service." The vital public service in this case was the generation, transmission, and distribution of electricity. In exchange for the monopoly right to supply electricity, power companies agreed to let government agencies regulate their prices and returns. By 1930, virtually every state had established a regulatory agency. In Florida, the Florida Public Service Commission not only regulated rates, returns, and capacity planning but also determined what nonutility businesses a utility could enter.

The federal government's involvement in electric power began in earnest with the passage of the Federal Power Act in 1935. This act gave the Federal Power Commission (renamed the Federal Energy Regulatory Commission (FERC) in 1977) the authority to oversee wholesale electricity transactions (sales of electricity between utilities rather than to consumers). During that same year, Congress also passed the Public Utilities Holding Company Act (PUHCA), which gave the Securities and Exchange Commission (SEC) the authority to regulate utilities with interstate systems or substantial investments in assets not related to the generation, transmission, and distribution of electricity. To avoid direct SEC supervision, the industry had evolved into a large number of intrastate, and relatively undiversified, utility companies operating under extensive federal and state regulation.

Rise of Deregulation

During the 1970s and 1980s, deregulation eliminated or weakened the monopoly service rights and fixed-price systems common in such industries as trucking, airlines, banking, natural gas, and telecommunications. While the introduction of competition increased economic efficiency, there were often short-term costs in terms of layoffs and business failures. Although the electric utilities industry entered this era of deregulation at roughly the same time as these other industries, deregulation had proceeded at a somewhat slower pace. Nevertheless, regulatory changes had been chipping away at utilities' monopoly franchises in each of the industry's major segments since 1978.

Congress, responding to concerns about U.S. dependence on foreign oil and environmental damage resulting from burning fossil fuels (oil, gas, and coal) to produce electricity, passed the Public Utilities Regulatory Policies Act (PURPA) in 1978. The act encouraged the creation of power plants using renewable or nontraditional fuels such as geothermal, solar, and wind power and authorized FERC to regulate them. As long as these nonutility generators (known as "qualifying facilities," or QFs) met certain efficiency and size standards, the act required local utilities to buy all of their electrical output (see Exhibit 1).

Fourteen years later, Congress introduced competition into the second segment of the industry—transmission—with the passage of the National Energy Policy Act of 1992 (NEPA). This act required utilities to make their transmission systems available to third-party users at the same level of quality and cost enjoyed by the utilities themselves (see Exhibit 1). Prior to NEPA, a generator could sell power into another territory only if another utility agreed to transmit the power; after NEPA, a utility could demand access to another utility's transmission system. Shortly after NEPA took effect, legal disputes arose over transmission access. One of the first cases involved FPL (which controlled over 50% of Florida's transmission lines) and the Florida Municipal Power Agency. The municipal agency sued FPL for charging excessive rates and denying fair access to its transmission system. In October 1993, FERC interceded and ordered the two parties to negotiate a settlement; the negotiations were still going on as of May 1994.

One of the major concerns about the implementation of NEPA was whether there would be sufficient transmission capacity. Analysts generally agreed that existing capacity, combined with construction plans for new transmission lines, would be sufficient through the year 2002. But there was some doubt as to whether certain planned transmission line additions could be constructed due to health concerns regarding high-voltage electromagnetic radiation exposure and opposition to clear-cutting of large swaths of land.

Deregulation of the final segment of the industry—distribution—was just beginning in early 1994. Certain states, including California and Michigan, were either considering or experimenting with competition in the distribution of electricity. For example, on April 20, the California Public Utilities Commission released a proposal (the "blue book") to phase in "retail wheeling" beginning in 1996. California's commissioner said:

> If we ignore . . . the rapid change that is already upon us, we place California utilities and the state's economy at considerable risk. . . . Change isn't coming, it is not on the horizon, it is not around the corner, it is here before you now. . . . [The proposal will be a] godsend, compared to the slow death that utilities surely face if we ignore the change before us.[2]

Under retail wheeling, customers would be allowed to buy power from utilities other than the local monopoly supplier. The local utility would be required to open its transmission and distribution network to outside utilities wishing to sell power in that market (see Exhibit 1). At first, large industrial customers (primarily manufacturing plants) would get the right to choose their electricity suppliers from a range of competitive bids. Over time, the other major customer segments—commercial users (office buildings, retail shops, universities, etc.) and eventually residential users (households)—would also get the right to pick their electricity suppliers. According to the blue book, full retail wheeling would be in place by the year 2002.

In the week following the release of the blue book proposal, California's three largest utilities, Pacific Gas & Electric, Southern California Edison, and San Diego Gas & Electric, together lost over $1.8 billion of market value—an average of 8% each from the day of the announcement. This loss in market value occurred during a week when both the stock market and the S&P Electric Utilities Index were relatively flat.

Responding to the California proposal, a utility executive from Arizona commented: "What happens in California will create a domino effect across the country. . . . [Utility managers will] have to be prepared for competition from new as well as existing players in the market."[3]

---

2. Anonymous, "California PUC Proposes Giving Ratepayers Access to Competitive Electric Market," *Electric Utility Week*, April 25, 1994, p. 6.

3. Brad Altman, "Ratings Climate Just Turned Chillier for Electric Utilities, Agency Raters Say," *The Bond Buyer*, April 26, 1994, p. 5.

While regulators in California were proposing a retail wheeling system, regulators in Michigan were already poised to experiment with such a system. In April 1994, they proposed a plan that would immediately allow several of the state's largest power users, including General Motors and Dow Chemical, to shop for power.[4] In the beginning, utilities with excess generating capacity would compete to serve the largest industrial and commercial customers. Eventually, utilities, or investors, might actually build new, dedicated generating plants to serve these customers.

Company Background

FPL Group's major subsidiary, Florida Power & Light Company (FP&L), was formed in 1925 through the consolidation of numerous electric and gas companies. The company enjoyed steady growth until the 1970s, when rising fuel costs and construction cost overruns—FP&L spent almost $1 billion rebuilding a faulty nuclear plant—reduced its profitability. At the same time, FP&L began experiencing operating problems, which manifested themselves through frequent power outages and increasing customer complaints about service.

To improve FPL Group's profitability, then Chairman Marshall McDonald decided to diversify into higher growth businesses and to establish a holding company structure to manage the new businesses. Over the next several years, FPL made four major acquisitions: Colonial Penn Life Insurance Company (an insurance company purchased for $566 million in 1985); Telesat Cablevision, Inc. (a cable television system purchased for $3.6 million in 1985); CBR Information Group Inc. (an information services company purchased for $54 million in 1986); and Turner Foods Corporation (a Florida citrus producer purchased for $47 million in 1988).[5] Besides the acquisitions, FPL Group established a real estate development subsidiary called Alandco and an alternative energy development subsidiary called ESI Energy.

To address the problems in operations, McDonald instituted a program of Japanese-inspired quality control. Before long, there were 1,700 quality control teams examining every aspect of the business for ways to improve operations. As a result, unscheduled downtime fell from 18% to 4%, and customer complaints fell by 60%.[6] Because of FPL's achievements, the Union of Japanese Scientists and Engineers awarded the company the prestigious Deming Prize for quality in 1989, making it the first non-Japanese company to receive that award. At the time, FPL was viewed as "one of the best-managed U.S. corporations."[7]

Despite the notoriety, the company still had some underlying problems. In 1986 the Nuclear Regulatory Commission (the federal regulator of nuclear power plants) put FPL's Turkey Point nuclear plant on its watch list for safety concerns.[8] Second, demand was growing faster in the late 1980s than expected and was projected to outstrip existing generating capacity in the near future. Third, Colonial Penn had lost more than $250 million since being acquired.[9] And finally, a 1988 survey indicated low employee

---

4. Agis Salpukas, "Electric Utilities Brace for an End to Monopolies," *The New York Times*, August 8, 1994, pp. A1, D5.

5. *Moody's Public Utilities Manual* 1 (1993) 9:1, p. 2709.

6. Robert Chapman Wood, "A Hero Without a Company," *Forbes*, March 18, 1991, p. 113.

7. *International Directory of Company Histories* (Detroit: St. James Press, 1992), p. 624.

8. Wood, "A Hero Without a Company," p. 114.

9. Holt Hackney, "One Turkey Too Many," *Financial World*, May 1, 1990, p. 102.

morale largely due to burdens imposed by the quality management program.[10] As one manager later confided, "We definitely went overboard [with the quality program]."[11]

The Broadhead Era

These problems, combined with the growing prospect of competition, led FPL's board to select an industry outsider, James Broadhead, to succeed McDonald when he retired in 1989. Broadhead came to FPL from GTE, where he had been in charge of the telephone business—another industry that had recently been deregulated. Having seen one industry through deregulation, Broadhead's vision for the electric utility industry was one of full and open competition.

As soon as he arrived, Broadhead began developing a long-range strategic plan. The first step in the process was an "environmental scan." He formed employee teams and asked them to speculate about the industry's future in terms of technological requirements, regulation, and customer needs. From the scan, Broadhead concluded that FPL would need to have a commitment to quality and customer service, increase its focus on the utilities industry, expand capacity, and improve its cost position.

Although he determined that a commitment to quality was essential, he believed the quality program needed to be scaled back. Paperwork had grown exponentially, and managers were spending too much time collecting and analyzing quality reports. Broadhead streamlined the quality process by cutting the number of quality teams, meetings, and reports.

Second, Broadhead wanted to renew FPL's focus on its core business. He said:

> Our long-term success is based on our core utility business. . . . We know a lot about generating, transmitting, distributing, selling, and conserving energy. Why venture away from that with the opportunities for growth that we face today?[12]

To reverse FPL's diversification program, Broadhead made plans to sell several of the nonutility businesses. After writing off $752 million (after-tax) in 1990 for losses at Colonial Penn (the bulk of the losses), Telesat Cablevision, and Alandco, Broadhead sold Colonial Penn in 1991 for an additional after-tax loss of $136 million. By 1994, FPL had written off and was trying to sell both Telesat Cablevision and Alandco.[13] However, FPL still owned three nonutility subsidiaries—ESI Energy, Turner Foods, and Qualtec Quality Services—which contributed 2% of total revenues.

At the same time, Broadhead commenced an aggressive capital expenditure program designed to meet projected demand into the next decade. FPL budgeted $6.6 billion, spread over five years, for the expansion. The various projects included building a new transmission line, refurbishing the oldest generating plant, improving operating efficiency at all plants, and buying a majority share in a coal-burning plant owned by The Southern Company (a utility based in Georgia). By 1994 operating efficiency had improved dramatically: nuclear plant availability had risen to 83% (compared to the industry average of 70%) and fossil fuel plant availability had risen to 89% (compared to

---

10. Wood, "A Hero Without a Company," p. 114.

11. Betsy Wiesendanger, "Deming's Luster Dims at Florida Power & Light," *Journal of Business Strategy*, September/October 1993, p. 61.

12. Hackney, "One Turkey Too Many," p. 102.

13. M. D. Luftig, et al., *FPL Group, Inc.–Company Report*, Kemper Securities Group, Inc., February 2, 1994, p. 3.

83% for the industry).[14] FPL funded this expansion through internal profits and by issuing $3.7 billion of long-term debt and $1.9 billion of common stock (see Exhibit 5).

To reduce costs, Broadhead reengineered the firm's budgeting and procurement procedures, flattened the organization, and reduced headcount by 30%; FPL eliminated 2,300 positions in 1991 (at an after-tax cost of $56 million) and another 1,700 positions in 1993 (at an after-tax cost of $85 million). These efficiency gains lowered operating and maintenance expense from 1.82¢ per kilowatt-hour (kWh) to 1.61¢ between 1990 and 1993.[15]

By early 1994, Broadhead's strategic redirection was showing signs of success. FPL was the largest utility in Florida (and the fourth largest in the country), provided power to 3.4 million customer accounts, and had a service territory covering almost 28,000 square miles (see Exhibit 2). Financially, 1993 had been a record year for FPL; not counting a one-time charge for layoffs related to the cost reduction program, net income was $514 million or $2.75 per share. Exhibits 3, 4a, 4b, and 5 present historical income statements, balance sheets, and cash flow statements for FPL Group.

While 1993 had been a good year, FPL expected 1994 to be even better due to decreasing capital expenditures and increasing sales (see Exhibit 6). Whereas capital expenditures had totaled $5.8 billion during the past five years ($800 million under budget), they were expected to decline by 33% to $3.9 billion over the next five years. FPL's sales growth (measured in kilowatt-hours) had exceeded the national average over the past five years (3.4% annual growth versus 2.0%) and was expected to exceed the national average over the next five years as well (2.7% versus 1.8%).[16]

Recent Events in the Electric Utilities Industry

Several major events that had taken place over the past year had a large impact on the electric utilities industry. Foremost among them was the California proposal on retail wheeling. Although the Florida Public Service Commission was not considering retail wheeling as of May 1994, utility commissions in 23 states were considering various retail wheeling proposals. If and when the Florida regulators authorized retail wheeling, FPL would have many potential competitors. Florida had four major investor-owned utilities (including FPL), accounting for 73% of the state's generating capacity; 20 municipal and rural cooperative generating systems, accounting for about 24% of capacity; and 19 independent power producers (including 18 QF's), accounting for 3% of capacity.[17] In addition, there were several other large investor-owned utilities in neighboring states that might compete for Florida customers (see Exhibit 7).

Because of the changing competitive landscape, Standard & Poor's Ratings Group (S&P) announced a revision of its guidelines for evaluating investor-owned electric utilities in October 1993. Under the new system, S&P would include an evaluation of a utility's competitive position as part of its financial rating. According to the guidelines,

---

14. Antonio N. Fins, "Feeling the Heat at a Florida Utility," *Business Week*, November 12, 1990, p. 94.

15. Excludes expenses for fuel, purchased power, and conservation programs (e.g., free residential energy audits).

16. FPL Group Presentation, EEI Financial Conference, Coronado, California, October 31–November 2, 1994.

17. Casewriter's estimates based on *Statistics of the Florida Electric Utility Industry 1992*, Division of Research & Regulatory Review, Florida Public Service Commission, September 1993, p. 18.

S&P would now consider such factors as the prospects for customer and sales growth, revenue vulnerabilities and dependencies, rates by consumer class relative to competing utilities, adequacy of baseload and peaking capacity, fuel diversity, regulatory environment, and management's financial goals. Based on these criteria, S&P rated FPL's business position above average, placing it in the top 10% of investor-owned utilities.[18] Because of its competitive position and its improving financial performance, S&P had recently upgraded FPL's senior secured debt to "A-plus" and its senior unsecured debt to "single-A."[19]

Despite the improvement in its debt ratings, there was some concern about the company's interest expense given the 140-basis-point increase in long-term interest rates since September 1993 (see Exhibit 8). Historically, bond yields and utility stock prices moved in opposite directions, in part because investors viewed utility stocks with their high-dividend yields as bond surrogates, and in part because utilities had relatively high levels of debt and could not pass through all increases in interest expense to consumers. During this period of rising interest rates and increasing competition (from September 1993 to May 1994), FPL's stock price had fallen by 19.6%, while S&P's Electric Utilities Index had fallen by 22.1%. Compared to the market as a whole, FPL, like most utilities, was a low-beta stock. Over the prior year, its beta was 0.60.

Investment Recommendation on FPL

As Stark sat in her office reviewing her file on FPL and the investment alert from Merrill Lynch, she wondered why FPL might want to cut its dividend. FPL management had stated that the company's payout ratio was too high, particularly given an uncertain and more competitive business environment. While it was true that FPL's payout ratio was at the high end for electric utilities, the industry was known for high payout ratios (see Exhibit 9). More importantly, Stark wondered why FPL would want to break its 47-year streak of dividend increases—a record that placed it first among all utilities and third among all publicly traded companies.

Dividend cuts were not common for utilities except in situations of financial trouble, and even then, they were not well received. She thought back to 1974 when Consolidated Edison Company of New York (Con Ed) surprisingly eliminated its dividend in the face of a hostile regulatory and macroeconomic environment. On the day after the announcement, Con Ed's stock price fell from $18 to $12 per share. More recently, in July 1992, Sierra Pacific Resources, a financially healthy utility in Nevada, cut its dividend by 39% in order to bring its payout ratio below 100%. The cut came during what turned out to be a record year in terms of profitability, not counting certain asset write-downs. The next day, its stock price fell by 23%. Within weeks of the announcement, shareholders filed a class-action suit against the firm for false and misleading financial statements, a suit that was finally settled in April 1994.[20] Given this series of events, Stark looked at the list of FPL's shareholders (see Exhibit 10) and

---

18. Curtis Moulton, "Electric Utility Business Positions Detailed," *Standard & Poor's CreditWeek Reprint*, July 4, 1994, p. 2.

19. Steven Stoll and Judith Waite, "Rating Update," *Standard & Poor's CreditWeek*, April 18, 1994, p. 66.

20. Anonymous, "Sierra Pacific Resources Settles Class-Action Shareholder Lawsuit," *Electric Utility Week*, April 25, 1994, p. 4.

wondered how they would respond to a dividend cut under somewhat similar circumstances. Would they react by suing the company, or would some of them actually prefer a lower dividend?

Because of the negative market reaction that normally accompanied dividend cuts and management's desire not to have to cut the dividend twice, dividend cuts tended to be large when they occurred. One benefit of a large cut, however, was that FPL could show strong dividend growth in the coming years. For example, if FPL were to cut its dividend payout ratio by as much as 30%, thereby putting it at the lower end of the industry in terms of payout ratios (see Exhibit 9), it could increase its dividend in future years faster than without the cut. The issue that puzzled Stark, however, was what FPL would do with the cash it was not paying out as dividends, a sum that might total as much as $150 million per year.

While a dividend cut was possible and would certainly lower the payout ratio quickly, she knew that FPL also had the option of growing out of its high payout ratio. As long as earnings increased at a faster rate than dividends, the payout ratio would fall. According to her numbers, if FPL slowed its dividend growth rate to 1% or so, the payout ratio would fall below 80% by 1998. If FPL kept its dividend at $2.48 per share, the payout ratio would fall below 80% a little sooner, perhaps by 1997.

As she flipped through her FPL file, Stark removed the proxy statement, dated March 22, 1994, for the upcoming annual meeting. At the meeting, shareholders would be asked to vote for directors, to ratify Deloitte and Touche as auditors, and to approve new annual and long-term incentive compensation plans. If approved, incentive compensation would be "based on achieving specific net income goals" rather than a range of financial and operating measures; the maximum bonus payout would be expanded from 100% of an officer's targeted bonus to 160% of the targeted bonus; and bonuses would be paid out in stock and cash in the ratio of 60/40, down from a ratio of 70/30. In addition, shareholders would vote on a proposal to change the voting rules for directors.

Deeper in the file, she came across several research reports put out by other utility analysts, including one that had been issued that day by Prudential Securities:

> We are lowering our rating on . . . FPL Group from a Buy to a Hold . . . We believe that dividend growth . . . will be limited by [FPL's] very high dividend payout ratio . . . We think that the answer for most companies will be to freeze the dividend for the next several years and hope that earnings grow.
>
> —Prudential Securities report, May 5, 1994

> A high dividend payout ratio and increasing competitive forces in the electric utility industry may make it difficult [for FPL] to increase the common dividend . . . Management's comments increase our confidence in our flat dividend expectation.
>
> —Donaldson, Lufkin & Jenrette report, March 24, 1994

> We are upgrading our investment recommendation on the share of FPL Group, Inc. to Buy from Hold . . . The improved outlook for earnings and declining financial pressures would appear to assure continuation of (dividend increases). However, we would not be surprised to see FPL Group reduce the rate of growth in the common dividend.
>
> —Salomon Brothers report, March 16, 1994

It still appeared that everyone, including Sanford Cohen, the author of today's investment alert, was expecting FPL either to increase its dividend slightly or to hold it at $2.48 per share. That morning, Stark had felt comfortable with her recommendation along the same lines. But the day's events made her question her assumptions. She had been watching her monitor to see how other analysts were responding to Cohen's report but had seen little news and no other predictions of a dividend cut.

As Stark sat in her office, she wondered if she should revise her investment recommendation. Given the 6% drop in price, this might be the time to change her recommendation from hold to buy. On the other hand, she might want to change her recommendation to sell if management's concern about the payout ratio stemmed from concerns about future earnings prospects. She knew she had to make a decision quickly—her major clients would likely call her that evening to get her opinion of the day's events in advance of the market's opening the following day.

EXHIBIT 1
The Rise of Deregulation in the U.S. Electric Power Industry

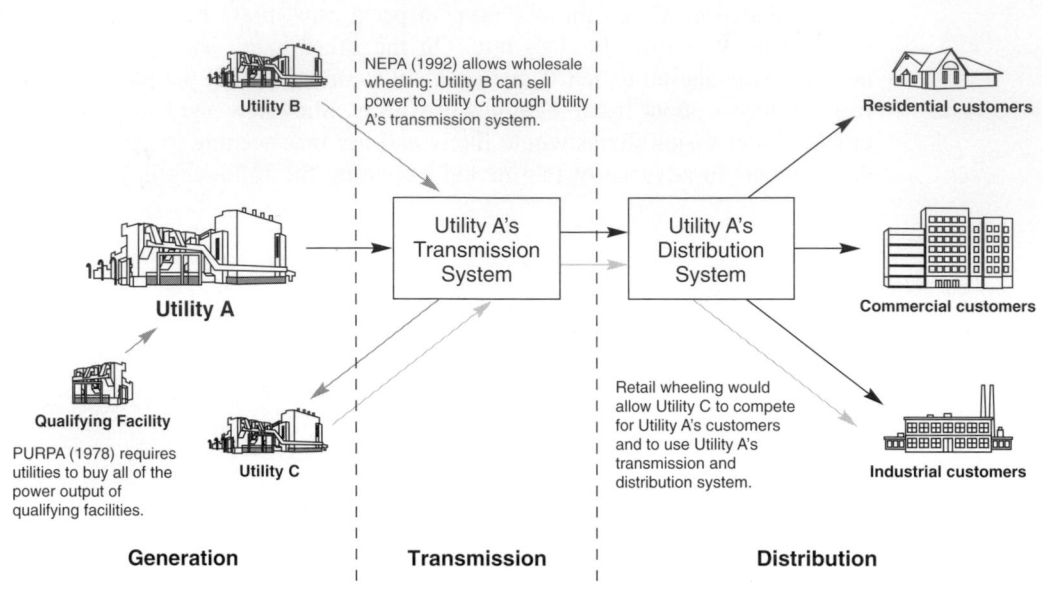

Source: Casewriter's graphic.

EXHIBIT 2
Florida Power & Light's Service Area, Generating Plans, and Bulk Transmission System

FP&L's service area covers 27,650 square miles and contains a population of 6.5 million people. During 1993, FP&L served approximately 3.4 million customer accounts. Florida is the fourth largest state in the United States and continues to experience substantial population growth. This growth is reflected in FP&L's service area, which includes six of the nation's ten fastest growing metropolitan areas—Naples, Fort Myers, Fort Pierce, Melbourne, Daytona Beach, and West Palm Beach.

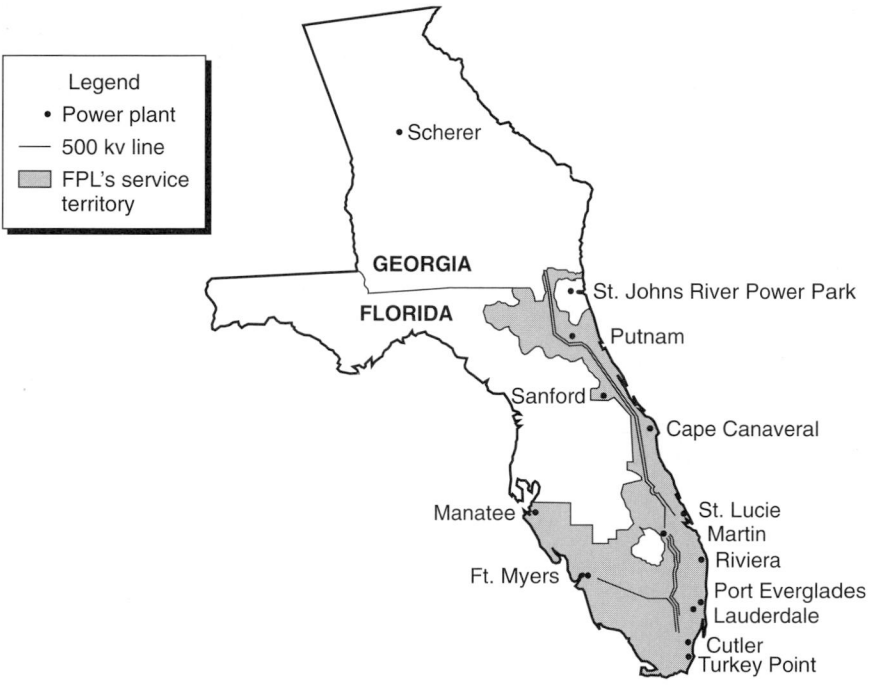

FP&L Capacity Resources

	Name	Units	Capability (megawatts)
1.	Manatee	2	1,566
2.	Ft. Myers	2	504
3.	Turkey Point	4	2,066
4.	Cutler	2	207
5.	Lauderdale	2	274
6.	Port Everglades	4	1,142
7.	Riviera	2	544
8.	Martin	2	1,566
9.	St. Lucie	2	1,553[a]
10.	Cape Canaveral	2	734
11.	Sanford	3	861
12.	Putnam	2	448
13.	St. Johns River	2	250[b]
14.	Scherer	1	150[c]
	Purchased Power		2,598
	Peaking Units		1,892
	Load Management		347
	Total	32	16,702

Source: FPL Group, Inc., 1991 Annual Report, p. 6 (as revised by the casewriter), and FPL Group, Inc., 1992 10-K Report, p. 9.

a. Represents FP&L's ownership of 100% of Unit 1 and 85% of Unit 2.

b. Represents FP&L's 20% ownership of 624 MW units.

c. Represents the first phase of FP&L's purchase of a 76% ownership interest in the 846 MW Scherer Unit 4.

EXHIBIT 3
FPL Group, Inc. Balance Sheet for the Years 1989–1993 (thousands of dollars)

	1989	1990	1991	1992	1993
Assets					
Property, plant, and equipment					
Electric utility plant	$11,488,396	$12,184,176	$12,918,817	$13,534,791	$14,838,160
Construction work in progress	299,705	476,279	597,401	1,158,688	781,435
Other property	378,424	243,185	255,035	278,887	261,125
Less depreciation/amortization	4,087,780	4,481,736	4,690,403	5,106,066	5,591,265
	$ 8,078,745	$ 8,421,904	$ 9,080,850	$ 9,866,300	$10,289,455
Investments					
Utility special use funds	$ 201,217	$ 252,098	$ 291,632	$ 318,798	$ 378,774
Partnerships and joint ventures	0	168,571	236,090	296,593	368,724
Leveraged leases	0	134,174	139,008	144,398	155,449
Insurance/Banking assets	1,878,555	0	0	0	0
Other	287,678	19,060	61,222	62,952	82,045
	$ 2,367,450	$ 573,903	$ 727,952	$ 822,741	$ 984,992
Current assets					
Cash and cash equivalents	$ 61,220	$ 214,164	$ 170,211	$ 78,156	$ 152,014
Marketable securities	0	0	0	75,437	171,988
Receivables:	573,171	492,503	513,937	516,585	504,597
Materials, supplies and fossil fuel	299,567	438,957	374,630	382,080	329,599
Recoverable storm costs	0	197,112	0	72,500	44,945
Other	118,284	43,818	45,419	58,418	48,214
	$ 1,052,242	$ 1,386,554	$ 1,104,197	$ 1,183,176	$ 1,251,357
Deferred debits and other assets					
Unamortized debt reacquisition costs . . .	$ 0	$ 146,841	$ 150,601	$ 175,320	$ 302,561
Deferred litigation items of FPL	125,065	119,371	115,202	110,859	110,859
Deferred pension costs	0	45,918	51,640	0	0
Unamortized insurance policy acquisitions	250,434	0	0	0	0
Other	451,373	107,517	51,343	147,909	138,788
	$ 826,872	$ 419,647	$ 368,786	$ 434,088	$ 552,208
Total assets	$12,325,309	$10,802,008	$11,281,785	$12,306,305	$13,078,012

(continued)

EXHIBIT 3 *(concluded)*

	1989	1990	1991	1992	1993
Capitalization and Liabilities					
Current liabilities					
Notes payable-commercial paper	$ 125,760	$ 48,814	$ 0	$ 0	$ 349,600
Current maturities of long-term debt . . .	15,933	19,572	136,605	164,004	279,680
Accounts payable	335,509	357,904	389,562	411,369	323,282
Customers' deposits	187,875	189,648	201,014	215,435	216,140
Interest accrued	124,022	105,718	109,748	123,735	109,206
Income and other taxes	0	87,517	98,968	90,929	94,880
Deferred clause revenues	0	0	0	175	130,786
Other	0	127,225	171,061	172,069	335,043
	$ 789,099	$ 936,398	$ 1,106,958	$ 1,177,716	$ 1,838,617
Deferred credits/Other liabilities					
Accumulated deferred income taxes . . .	$ 1,516,483	$ 1,538,645	$ 1,507,231	$ 1,718,388	$ 1,512,067
Deferred regular credit-income taxes . . .	0	0	0	0	216,546
Unamortized investment tax credits	430,351	406,251	368,337	345,438	323,791
Capital lease obligations	0	74,887	279,657	324,198	271,498
Insurance/Banking liabilities	1,584,505	0	0	0	0
Other	583,972	319,804	501,216	393,080	517,653
	$ 4,115,311	$ 2,339,587	$ 2,656,441	$ 2,781,104	$ 2,841,555
Capitalization					
Common stock, $.01 par value	$ 1,333	$ 1,610	$ 1,708	$ 1,828	$ 1,901
Additional paid-in capital	1,780,392	2,566,844	2,886,113	3,312,903	3,589,994
Unearned compensation	279	(360,000)	(346,215)	(336,355)	(321,121)
Retained earnings	1,670,152	952,707	812,241	857,613	829,833
	$ 3,452,156	$ 3,161,161	$ 3,353,847	$ 3,835,989	$ 4,100,607
FPL preferred stock					
without sinking fund	$ 346,250	$ 346,250	$ 346,250	$ 421,250	$ 451,250
with sinking fund	173,050	165,950	150,150	130,150	97,000
Long-term debt	3,449,443	3,852,662	3,668,139	3,960,096	3,748,983
	$ 7,420,899	$ 7,526,023	$ 7,518,386	$ 8,347,485	$ 8,397,840
Total capital and liabilities	$12,325,309	$10,802,008	$11,281,785	$12,306,305	$13,078,012

Source: 1989–1993 annual reports for FPL Group, Inc.

EXHIBIT 4a

FPL Group, Inc. Income Statement for the Years 1989–1993 (thousands of dollars)

	1989	1990	1991	1992	1993
Operating revenues					
Utility	$4,946,291	$4,987,690	$5,158,766	$5,100,463	$5,224,299
Nonutility	86,253	98,655	90,670	92,864	91,995
Total operating revenues	$5,032,544	$5,086,345	$5,249,436	$5,193,327	$5,316,294
Operating expenses					
Utility operations:					
Fuel/purchased power	$1,775,557	$1,927,233	$1,932,637	$1,829,908	$1,758,298
Operations and maintenance	1,194,871	1,243,583	1,276,244	1,203,474	1,251,284
Cost reduction program	0	0	90,008	0	138,000
Nonutility operations:	85,101	102,179	69,469	74,195	70,256
Loss on discontinuing businesses	0	99,850	0	0	0
Depreciation and amortization	636,976	501,269	518,068	554,237	598,389
Taxes other than income taxes	408,320	451,494	485,962	497,739	526,109
	$4,100,825	$4,325,608	$4,372,388	$4,159,553	$4,342,336
Operating income	$ 931,719	$ 760,737	$ 877,048	$1,033,774	$ 973,958
Interest expense and other deductions (income)					
Interest and preferred stock dividends	$ 383,375	$ 393,074	$ 411,079	$ 410,152	$ 409,760
Allowance for funds used during construction	(21,623)	(25,424)	(34,044)	(57,782)	(66,238)
Other, net	(32,685)	(26,981)	(47,456)	(46,978)	(48,812)
	$ 329,067	$ 340,669	$ 329,579	$ 305,392	$ 294,710
Income taxes					
Current	$ 183,723	$ 66,632	$ 186,008	$ 147,961	$ 238,557
Deferred	2,086	55,261	(14,687)	113,472	11,942
	$ 185,809	$ 121,893	$ 171,321	$ 261,433	$ 250,499
Income from continuing operations	$ 416,843	$ 298,175	$ 376,148	$ 466,949	$ 428,749
Income (loss) from discontinued operations . . .	16,494	(689,180)	(135,570)	0	0
Net Income (Loss)	$ 433,337	($ 391,005)	$ 240,578	$ 466,949	$ 428,749

Source: 1989–1993 Annual Reports for FPL Group, Inc.

Note: Preferred stock dividends result from intercompany transactions and are not tax deductible.

EXHIBIT 4b

FPL Group, Inc. Earnings and Dividends Per Common Share, 1984–1993

Year	Earnings Per Share	Earnings Per Share before Extraordinary Items	Dividends Per Share	Average Shares Outstanding (in thousands)
1993	$2.30	$2.76	$2.47	186,413
1992	2.65	2.65	2.43	176,207
1991	1.48	2.66	2.39	162,553
1990	(2.86)	2.64	2.34	136,715
1989	3.12	2.99	2.26	131,544
1988	3.42	3.12	2.18	130,932
1987	3.10	2.69	2.10	129.959
1986	2.90	2.90	2.02	126,004
1985	3.11	3.11	1.94	119,696
1984	2.62	2.65	1.77	118,280

Sources: FPL Group, Inc. annual reports, 1989–1993, Value Line, Inc., June 17, 1994.

Note: "Earnings per share before extraordinary items" excludes gains or losses from discontinued operations and charges relating to cost-reduction programs.

EXHIBIT 5

FPL Group, Inc. Cash Flow Statement for the Years 1989–1993 (thousands of dollars)

	1989	*1990*	*1991*	*1992*	*1993*
Cash flows from operating activities					
Net income (loss)	$410,416	($ 391,005)	$ 240,578	$ 466,949	$ 428,749
Depreciation and amortization	636,976	501,269	518,068	554,237	598,389
Increase (decrease) in deferred income taxes	31,325	47,912	(31,414)	211,156	10,225
Provision for refunds	38,650	10,257	0	0	0
(Increase) decrease in recoverable storm costs	0	0	0	(57,130)	12,184
Refund of revenues from tax savings rule	(37,692)	(22,960)	0	0	0
Deferrals under cost recovery clauses	(117,340)	(10,483)	120,772	(102,977)	138,949
Charges for discontinuing businesses	0	99,850	0	0	0
Increase (decrease) in accrued interest and taxes	(42,002)	49,962	15,481	5,948	(10,578)
Loss from discontinued operations	(16,494)	689,180	135,570	0	0
Other	59,129	78,813	194,466	(90,521)	89,058
Net cash provided by operating activities	$962,968	$1,052,795	$1,193,521	$ 987,662	$1,266,976
Cash flows from investing activities					
Capital and nuclear fuel expenditures	($836,493)	($1,038,740)	($1,343,931)	($1,390,930)	($1,247,661)
Sale of Colonial Penn	0	0	128,380	0	0
Net cash provided (used) by discontinued operations	58,488	(92,006)	(49,827)	0	0
Receipts from partnerships and leveraged leases	(90,667)	(96,894)	11,572	17,592	82,462
Other	(107,198)	(55,086)	1,427	(10,013)	34,365
Net cash used in investing activities	($975,870)	($1,282,726)	($1,252,379)	($1,383,351)	($1,130,834)
Cash flow from financing activities					
Unearned ESOP compensation	$ 0	($ 360,000)	$ 0	$ 0	$ 0
Issuance of FPL bonds and other long-term debt	213,542	276,073	265,246	874,633	2,082,993
Issuance of FPL Group capital long-term debt	0	0	0	25,000	125,889
Issuance of preferred stock	0	0	0	125,000	190,000
Proceeds from FPL Group capital borrowings	0	260,000	0	0	0
Retirement of long-term debt and preferred stock	(193,890)	(141,892)	(360,372)	(699,614)	(2,648,170)
Issuance of common stock	73,124	796,491	318,341	422,626	276,287
Dividends on common stock	(297,861)	(323,919)	(392,000)	(430,716)	(461,639)
Sale of nuclear fuel	47,399	75	235,972	0	0
Increase (decrease) in notes payable—commercial paper	107,176	(76,946)	(48,814)	0	349,600
Other	8,478	(7,892)	(3,468)	(13,295)	22,756
Net cash provided (used) in financial activities	($ 42,032)	$ 421,990	$ 14,905	$ 303,634	($ 62,284)
Net increase (decrease) in cash and cash equivalents	($ 54,934)	$ 192,059	($ 43,953)	($ 92,055)	$ 73,858
Cash and cash equivalents at beginning of year	$ 77,039	$ 22,105	$ 214,164	$ 170,211	$ 78,156
Cash and cash equivalents at end of year	$ 22,105	$ 214,164	$ 170,211	$ 78,156	$ 152,014

Source: 1989–1993 annual reports for FPL Group, Inc.

EXHIBIT 6
FPL Group—Financial Projections as of March 1994 (thousands of dollars)

	1992 Actual	1993 Actual	1994 Estimate	1995 Estimate	1996 Estimate	1997 Estimate	1998 Estimate	1993–1998 Annualized Growth
Florida Power & Light Company								
Electric sales (millions of kWh)	$69,290	$72,455	$74,411	$76,420	$78,484	$80,603	$82,779	2.7%
Customer accounts (thousands)	3,281	3,350	3,437	3,526	3,618	3,712	3,809	2.6
Total capacity (owned by FP&L, in megawatts)	16,627	16,697	17,559	17,563	18,030	18,051	18,051	1.6
Net income	$ 467	$ 429	$ 527	$ 557	$ 576	$ 596	$ 615	
Depreciation and amortization	554	598	665	711	741	778	795	
Capital expenditures	$ 1,270	$ 1,337	$ 901	$ 831	$ 743	$ 769	$ 624	
Maturing debt	152	11	2	81	101	4	185	
Preferred dividends	44	43	40	40	40	40	40	
Common dividends	431	461	—	—	—	—	—	
Average shares outstanding (millions)	176.2	186.4	191.5	192.1	192.1	192.1	192.1	
Capitalization ratios								
Long-term debt	48%	46%	46%	46%	45%	44%	44%	
Preferred stock	6	6	6	6	6	6	6	
Equity	46	47	48	48	50	50	50	

Sources: Donaldson, Lufkin & Jenrette Securities Corp., analyst report, May 1994; Salomon Brothers U.S. Equity Research, analyst report, March 16, 1994; Florida Power & Light Company 1994–1998 forecast and 1993 financial and statistical report.

EXHIBIT 7
Investor-Owned Utilities in the Southeast United States in 1993

	FPL Group	Carolina Power	Duke Power	Florida Progress	SCANA Corp.	The Southern Co.	TECO Energy, Inc.
Electric subsidiaries	Florida Power and Light Company	Carolina Power and Light Company	Duke Power Co.	Florida Power Corp.	SC Electric and Gas Company	Alabama Power Co. Georgia Power Co. Gulf Power Co. (FL)	Tampa Electric Co.
Markets and customers							
Major markets	East/South FL	East NC Northeast SC	Central NC Northwest SC	North Central FL	Southwest SC	Northwest FL, GA, and AL	Central FL
Total kWh produced (millions)	72,454.7	45,505.0	76,058.0	28,647.8	16,880.0	119,206.0	13,446.5
Customer mix (percent of sales)							
Residential	56.0%	33.0%	33.0%	47.0%	43.0%	32.0%	44.0%
Commercial	36.0	20.0	24.0	28.0	29.0	26.0	30.0
Industrial	4.0	26.0	28.0	12.0	20.0	27.0	10.0
Utility companies and other	4.0	21.0	15.0	13.0	8.0	15.0	16.0
Capital structure							
Long-term debt/Total capitalization	46.4%	48.2%	39.9%	48.7%	50.2%	45.1%	49.1%
Common stock/Total capitalization	47.3%	49.1%	50.9%	47.5%	47.0%	46.8%	48.3%
Total assets (millions)	$13,078	$8,194	$12,193	$5,639	$4,041	$25,911	$3,128
Profitability							
Return on common stock	12.5%	13.6%	13.2%	10.9%	12.6%	13.0%	14.3%
Earnings per share	$2.75	$2.23	$2.80	$2.26	$3.72	$1.57	$1.30
Cash flow per share	$5.85	$5.09	$5.80	$5.59	$6.02	$3.16	$2.70
Dividend per common share	$2.47	$1.66	$1.84	$1.95	$2.74	$1.14	$0.95
Dividend yield	6%	5%	5%	6%	6%	5%	4%
Payout ratio (all dividends)	91%	74%	68%	87%	74%	75%	73%
Capacity utilization							
Annual load factor[a]	57%	59%	60%	51%	57%	59%	n/a
Capacity margin[b]	8.6%	12.0%	14.3%	11.0%	7.9%	12.1%	13.8%
Percent of power purchased (1993 est.)	30.0%	11.0%	1.0%	15.0%	26.0%	7.0%	3.0%
Costs							
Operation/Maintenance costs/kWh	$0.0075	$0.0103	$0.0072	$0.0070	$0.0051	$0.0059	$0.0049
Busbar cost/kWh[c]	0.0366	0.0403	0.0317	0.0344	0.0293	0.0319	0.0368
Incremental generation cost/kWh[d]	0.0187	0.0154	0.0176	0.0182	0.0186	0.0115	0.0242
Transmission cost/kWh (1987)	0.0019	0.0009	0.0010	0.0010	0.0007	0.0008	0.0006
Rates (average realization per kWh)							
Residential	$0.0811	$0.0828	$0.0732	$0.0792	$0.0713	$0.0732	$0.0813
Commercial	0.0675	0.0694	0.0600	0.0581	0.0562	0.0704	0.0673
Industrial	0.0540	0.0549	0.0431	0.0479	0.0391	0.0451	0.0465

Sources: Value Line; annual reports; North American Utility Almanac (J. C. Bradford & Co., 1993 edition); Goldman Sachs Selected Electric Utility Industry Statistics (November 1994).

a. Annual load factor is the average level of capacity used by the utility.

b. Capacity margin = (Total capacity − Peak load in summer)/Total capacity.

c. Busbar cost is the unit output cost of electric power coming out of a generating plant, before transmission and distribution.

d. Incremental generation cost is the marginal cost to produce an additional kilowatt-hour.

EXHIBIT 8
FPL Group Stock Price and Interest Rates

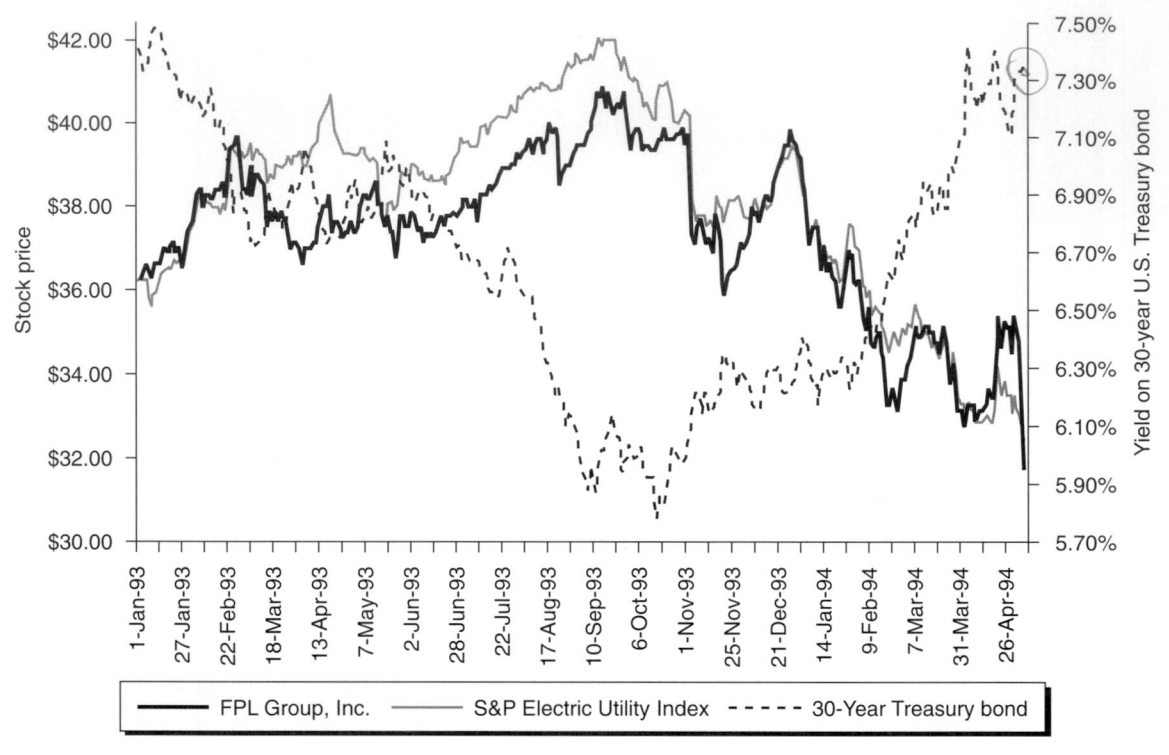

Source: Datastream.

EXHIBIT 9
Dividends by Industry and for Electric Utilities, First Quarter 1994

S&P Industry Groups	Dividend Payout Ratio	Dividend Yield
Health care (drugs)	69.4%	4.1%
Household products	66.9	2.6
Tobacco	65.7	5.2
Publishing (newspapers)	58.0	2.5
Hardware and tools	53.6	2.8
Foods	45.7	2.7
Chemicals (specialty)	39.7	1.8
Cosmetics	39.4	1.9
Telecommunications (long distance)	39.3	2.3
Beverages (soft drinks)	38.2	1.7
Textiles	34.7	2.2
Regional banks	32.6	3.4
Aerospace/Defense	31.0	2.3
Retail (specialty)	29.7	0.9
Shoes	25.5	1.6
Hotel-Motel	25.4	0.9
Entertainment	23.9	0.7
Automobiles	20.6	1.9
Toys	16.0	0.8
Restaurants	15.1	0.8
Computer software/services	10.9	0.4
Electronics (semiconductors)	6.5	0.4
Airlines	deficit	0.1
Steel	deficit	0.9

Sample of Electric Utility Companies

Texas Utilities	106.2%	9.6%
Oklahoma G&E	93.3	8.6
Potomac Electric	92.2	8.7
Houston Industries	90.9	10.0
Delmarva P&L	90.6	8.4
SCE Corp.	88.7	9.9
NY State E&G	88.0	9.3
Central & SW	87.2	7.9
Public Service of CO	87.0	7.7
Commonwealth Edison	84.2	7.1
Northern State Power	81.9	6.6
American Electric	81.4	8.6
Ohio Edison	81.1	9.0
Dominion Resources	79.4	6.5
Consolidated Edison	75.5	7.1
PacificCorp	74.5	6.5
Carolina P&L	72.3	7.1
Southern Company	71.5	6.5
Pacific G&E	71.3	8.5
Entergy	66.7	6.5
General Public Utilities	65.5	6.6
Duke Power	64.8	5.3
Centerior Energy	61.5	7.7
Philadelphia Electric	60.8	5.8

Sources: S&P Analysts' Handbook, September 1994 Monthly Supplement; *Barron's*, May 16, 1994, p. 16.

EXHIBIT 10
FPL Group Ownership Information, First Quarter 1994

Type of Shareholder	Percent of Total Shares		Number of Shareholders
Individuals and other	51.9%		85,442
Institutions (total)	36.9		328
Pension funds/Universities		18.4%	
Mutual funds/Money managers		13.0	
Financial institutions		4.3	
Insurance companies		1.2	
ESOP (Fidelity Management is trustee)	11.1		
Insiders (officers and directors)	0.1		17
Total	100.0%		85,787
Number of shares outstanding at 12/31/93 (millions)	190.1		

Sources: FPL Group 1993 annual report and Proxy Statement (May 4, 1994), CDA/Spectrum, and casewriter estimates.

Note: An ESOP (Employee Stock Ownership Plan) is a program administered by a third-party trustee to encourage employees to purchase stock in the company—often used as a retirement savings vehicle.

Tom Paine Mutual Life Insurance Company (Abridged)

In December 1990, Jack Fuller, an assistant portfolio manager in the Investment and Pension Group (IPG) of Tom Paine Mutual Life Insurance Company, was mulling over what recommendations to make concerning the investment of funds from the sale of a new Guaranteed Investment Contract (GIC) to a large corporate retirement plan. Under the terms of the contract, Tom Paine would receive $109 million on January 15, 1991; it would have to pay $198.5 million on January 15, 1998, that is, $109 million plus accumulated interest calculated at a semiannually compounded rate of 8.75%. Mr. Fuller had been asked to review public and private debt instruments currently available to Tom Paine and to recommend to IPG purchases for the new GIC.

In connection with the assignment, Mr. Fuller had been informed that IPG had already purchased or committed to purchase assets that would absorb $89 million of the January 15 funds inflow. He had also been told that IPG's asset/liability management unit had determined that the remaining assets selected for the new GIC ought to mature approximately 7 years from January 15, 1991.

GIC management involved a number of challenges. Competition for GIC business was intense and focused on price, that is, the yield to maturity guaranteed by the insurer. This, in turn, forced GIC writers to attempt to realize high rates of return on invested assets. To achieve its profitability objectives for the GIC business, Tom Paine needed to invest funds at a gross rate of return approximately 100 basis points above the one guaranteed to the GIC purchaser, while holding credit losses to a minimum.[1]

If badly managed, the GIC business could result in serious direct and indirect losses. In the past 5 years, for example, one of the largest life insurance companies had incurred operating losses of more than $1 billion in the GIC business through overly aggressive guaranteed rate levels, mismanagement of its asset/liability structure, and credit losses on invested assets. That company's ratings had been reduced from AAA

This case was prepared by Professor Ronald W. Moore.

Copyright © 1991 by the President and Fellows of Harvard College.
Harvard Business School case 291–030.

1. A basis point is 1/100 of 1%.

to A, a level that effectively precluded continued participation in the GIC business and seriously hindered efforts to sell other insurance products.

Nevertheless, the GIC business was important for Tom Paine, accounting for 27% of total assets and a rapidly growing proportion of profits.

Background

Tom Paine, headquartered in Boston, Massachusetts, was the thirteenth largest life insurance company in the country. As of December 31, 1989, it had total assets of $26 billion, surplus of $1 billion, and insurance in force of $158 billion.[2] As a mutual company, Tom Paine was owned by its policyholders. Policyholders participated in profits through dividends, which had been paid without interruption since 1878. Exhibits 1 and 2 present recent balance sheets and income statements.

Tom Paine conducted most of its business through three major operating units: Retail Financial Services, Group Benefits, and IPG. Retail Financial Services marketed nationwide a broad array of individual life and health insurance products, mainly through more than 12,000 career agents (company-employed, commission salespeople). Tom Paine sold traditional insurance, such as term life, whole life, and annuities, and newer, investment-oriented products, such as universal life, variable life, and variable annuities.[3] Group Benefits, as the name implies, sold group life and health insurance as well as benefits administration services to employers of all sizes.

IPG invested Tom Paine's investable funds and marketed investment products and services to pension funds and other institutional accounts. In addition to its three main lines of business, Tom Paine was engaged through subsidiaries in a variety of related businesses, among them property and casualty insurance, mutual funds, credit cards, mortgage banking, and consumer finance.

For some time, IPG had taken an increasingly prominent role in Tom Paine's business mix. This reflected, on the one hand, the ongoing decline in the profitability of traditional individual life insurance products and, on the other hand, the rapid expansion of the GIC business. Throughout most of Tom Paine's long history, traditional whole life insurance had been the cornerstone of the company's growth and profitability. Since the mid-1970s, however, many factors, among them high inflation, volatile interest rates, the proliferation of retail investment vehicles, and the growth of employer-sponsored retirement plans, had combined to erode the profitability and salability of traditional whole life. In 1990, Tom Paine would earn on its traditional life insurance business a pretax return on assigned surplus of only about 8–8.5%.

---

2. Surplus in a mutual insurance company is roughly equivalent to equity in an industrial corporation.

3. Term life is pure insurance coverage; premiums go to investment for future death benefits plus administrative expenses, sales commissions, and profits. Traditional whole life combines insurance coverage with a long-term, tax-deferred savings contract. Premiums, typically a multiple of term premiums, go to the same uses and to the policyholder's cash value account, where they earn a contractually fixed rate of return. In addition to pure insurance profits, the insurer earns the spread between its investment returns and the rate paid to the policyholder. Traditional annuities are, in effect, the savings contract component of traditional whole life. In the newer, investment-oriented products, the policyholder earns on the savings component of the premium the full net returns achieved by mutual fund–like pools made available by the insurer. The insurer earns only a competitive management fee on the savings contract, not a spread.

Faced with these problems, senior management had been striving since the mid-1980s to redefine the company, seeking to convert it from a traditional marketer and servicer of insurance products to an institutional investor that gathered funds from a variety of sources, including the sale of traditional and nontraditional insurance products. Toward this end, a number of programs had been initiated to reduce processing and distribution costs and to expand retail and institutional marketing of products emphasizing Tom Paine's investment skills. To date, the one unqualified success had come in guaranteed investment products, particularly GICs.

GICs

The GIC market was large and rapidly growing. Tom Paine management estimated its size at $220 billion and anticipated annual growth of 20–25%. Most defined contribution retirement plans as well as employee thrift and profit-sharing plans included a GIC among the investment options available to plan participants, and 60–70% of the funds in such plans went into GICs.[4] Such plans had grown rapidly during the 1980s and were expected to continue to do so.

A GIC is a contract between a life insurance company and a plan sponsor. Pursuant to this contract, the insurer makes a commitment, fully backed by its general account, to pay on a future date an amount comprising up-front funds received from the plan plus interest thereon at a specified rate. GICs vary greatly in detail but generally take the form of a "bullet" or "window" arrangement. In a bullet contract, the insurer is committed to pay a specified amount on a specified future date in return for one lump-sum, up-front payment. In a typical window deal, the insurer agrees to accept funds up to a specified maximum amount over a specified period (say, 3, 6, or 12 months) and to permit, without penalty, withdrawal of the accumulated balance by plan participants during the life of the contract. In return for providing such flexibility, Tom Paine generally guaranteed a rate 10–20 basis points lower than on a bullet of the same maturity.

The popularity of GICs is easy to understand. They typically yield more than AA corporate bonds (see Exhibit 3) yet are fully guaranteed by an AA or AAA life insurance company. And (as is not the case with direct investment in corporate bonds) the insurer, not the plan beneficiaries, bears all the risk of interest rate changes, early redemptions, bond rating downgrades, and credit losses.

The GIC market was dominated by the largest and most creditworthy life insurers (see Exhibit 4). While price remained a critical factor in getting GIC business, the credit quality of the insurer was also important. Not having an AA rating from at least one rating agency effectively barred an insurer from the GIC business, and an increasing number of sponsors were restricting their business to AAA-rated life insurance companies. In 1990 the many signs of distress in the financial system, for instance, the recent collapse of the junk bond market and the savings and loan system bailout, suggested that concern about the credit quality of GIC writers would continue and probably intensify.

Tom Paine enjoyed the highest claims-paying ability ratings, and senior management considered their maintenance essential to continued success in selling GICs and

---

4. High-grade corporate bonds are those assigned ratings of AAA or AA by the principal credit-rating agencies, Moody's Investors Service and Standard and Poor's Corporation. At the time of the case, high-grade, newly issued intermediate-term industrials were yielding about 40–70 basis points over Treasuries.

other guaranteed investment products. This perception strongly influenced Tom Paine's policies concerning the investment of GIC funds.

Tom Paine's Investment Approach

The profitability of Tom Paine's GIC business depended primarily on the extent to which the company could invest GIC monies at higher rates of return than it contracted to pay. Top management of Tom Paine had mandated a relatively conservative approach to GIC investment. Thus, Tom Paine pursued a spread approach: it sought to lock in a spread, or gross margin, over the cost of its AAA-rated GIC obligations by investing the proceeds in lower-quality assets of similar maturity.

This approach minimized exposure to interest rate movements, which otherwise might significantly enhance or erode GIC returns. Exhibit 5, which shows historical annual returns on a variety of fixed-income instruments, suggests the possible rewards and risks of mismatching the maturities of assets and liabilities.

As to asset quality, senior management had severely limited investment in credit-rated BB or lower, namely, junk bonds. This reflected its assessment of the value of Tom Paine's credit ratings. After profitability, asset quality and surplus adequacy are the most important factors in the determination of these ratings, and significant investment in junk bonds would adversely affect both.

Senior management believed it was possible to earn adequate GIC returns with a nonmismatch, nonjunk investment approach because of Tom Paine's expertise in credit analysis and in the valuation of debt instruments together with its access, as a sizable and active buyer, to most offerings in the private debt markets. These attributes, it was believed, enabled Tom Paine to book relatively high-yielding assets without necessarily bearing commensurate credit risk.

Top management had established a profitability objective for the GIC business of a pretax return on surplus of 15%. The amount of surplus allocated to the GIC business was 2.5% of assets, that is, $2.50 for every $100 of GIC assets. Estimated operating expenses associated with the GIC business currently amounted to about .5–.6% of GIC assets.

In addition, pursuant to regulatory requirements, GIC assets, like all general account debt securities, had to be charged on a current basis for potential credit losses. Tom Paine charged to securities valuation reserves over a 10-year period a total of 1% of the cost of A or better and equivalent unrated credits; 2% of BBB and equivalent credits; and 5% of BB and equivalent credits. With respect to lower-rated securities, 10% of B and equivalent credits had to be charged off over a 5-year period, as did 20% of lower-rated credits. Defaulted securities had to be carried at the lower of cost or estimated net realizable value. Although mortgages were not governed by regulation, Tom Paine charged 2% of mortgages to valuation reserves over a 10-year period. Tom Paine's actual credit experience in recent years had been considerably better than that implied by regulatory requirements.

The Public Debt Market

Mr. Fuller had begun his investigation of public market investment possibilities by preparing a matrix of current new issue interest rate levels. These are shown in Exhibit 6.

Public debt is distinguished from privately placed debt in having been registered with the Securities and Exchange Commission (SEC) prior to issuance.[5] Securities so registered and cleared for sale by the SEC become freely salable to all investors, both upon initial distribution and in subsequent secondary market trading.

Late in December 1990, the domestic public market for nonconvertible corporate debt comprised over 3,500 rated issues, with an aggregate principal amount in excess of $1,500 billion.[6] New-issue volume in 1990 was $106.6 billion and over the preceding 5 years had averaged $125.8 billion.

The public market is almost always the most attractive domestic market for large, creditworthy issuers needing to raise debt of $100 million or more in one transaction. Because public issues are freely tradable and relatively liquid, this market usually affords the lowest all-in borrowing costs, the most flexible redemption and refunding provisions, the least restrictive covenants, and to the extent desired, the longest maturities and average lives.[7]

Based on the data in Exhibit 6 versus the yield requirements of the new GIC, Mr. Fuller had turned his attention to the secondary market. In the secondary market, limited liquidity frequently poses a problem for a buyer seeking to accumulate more than 5–10% of an issue; such purchases can sharply push up prices from quoted levels, and in some instances, sizable amounts are simply unobtainable. On the other hand, Mr. Fuller reasoned, limited liquidity could result in bargain purchase opportunities.

Mr. Fuller had developed a list of outstanding publicly traded bonds that might qualify for purchase. This list contained all nonbank and noninsurance bonds with ratings of A or BBB, $50 million or more of outstanding principal amount, and final maturities within three months of January 15, 1998 (the maturity date of the GIC). Data on these bonds are shown in Exhibit 7.

In connection with his review of secondary market bonds, Mr. Fuller had also examined restrictive covenants contained in a number of indentures. He had concluded that, unlike covenants in private placement note agreements, public issue covenants afforded little or no substantive protection to debtholders.

The Private Placement Market

Privately placed corporate debt securities are not registered and therefore by law are salable only to large, sophisticated investors, those presumed not to need the protection of SEC-regulated disclosure documents. Accordingly, after-market liquidity is minimal. New-issue volume in 1990 was approximately $113.6 billion; in 1989, $168.1 billion; in 1988, $171.2 billion; in 1987, $119.5 billion; in 1986, $105.8 billion.[8]

Large life insurance companies like Tom Paine dominate the buy side of the market. These institutions maintain sizable staffs of private placement specialists, who are trained and experienced in in-depth credit analysis, in structuring complex financing

---

5. Registration entails filing with the SEC and making available to the public a number of documents, including a registration statement describing the issue and prescribed business and financial information on the issuer; it also obligates the issuer to file and make public on an ongoing basis annual and quarterly financial reports and other information.

6. Securities Data Company, Inc.

7. All-in borrowing costs take into account costs of issuance as well as the interest rate.

8. Securities Data Company, Inc.

arrangements, and in tailoring and negotiating terms to meet the needs of both issuer and investor.

The main incentive for a financial institution to participate in the private placement market is the availability of higher yields. Private placement yields generally range from 25 to 35 basis points or more over public levels. This premium represents compensation to the investor for illiquidity and, in many instances, for a superior bargaining position vis-à-vis the borrower. Exhibit 8 sets forth a survey of private placement new-issue rate levels as of late December 1990.

On the issuer side, a wide variety of companies make use of the private placement market. Most important, perhaps, are issuers whose requirements are too small for the public market minimum of $100 million. Such issues, if attempted in the public market, would incur a significant price penalty for illiquidity as well as substantially higher fixed costs of issuance (see Exhibit 9). Other users of the market are borrowers who could not or would not comply with SEC disclosure and reporting requirements (e.g., nonpublic companies, U.S. subsidiaries of foreign companies) and companies with especially complex operations or financing requirements.

Mr. Fuller's review of private placement offerings currently in-house at Tom Paine revealed two possibilities for investment by the new GIC: one was a proposed $40 million, 7-year, senior subordinated debt financing for Sam Adams Financial Corporation; the second was a $25 million refinancing of bank debt for Ginne Enterprises, a family-owned publishing and broadcasting company.

Sam Adams Financial Corporation, a wholly owned subsidiary of a *Fortune 50* corporation, was a major consumer and commercial finance company with related insurance operations. It was a frequent borrower in the public market, raising well over $1 billion annually. Occasionally, it raised in the private placement market relatively small amounts of subordinated debt to comply with certain covenants in the indenture for its 6⅛% senior debentures. Sam Adams's senior ratings were AA by Moody's, A+ by S&P; its senior subordinated ratings were Baal and A, respectively.

Tom Paine already enjoyed an existing credit relationship with Sam Adams Financial Corporation, having bought half ($7.5 million principal amount) of the company's last privately placed senior subordinated debt issue in 1988. The current investment opportunity had resulted from direct discussions between Sam Adams and Tom Paine. Exhibit 10 presents a summary term sheet prepared by Tom Paine. Exhibits 11 and 12 present summary operating and balance sheet data.

The proposed $25 million senior debt financing was for Ginne Enterprises, Inc., a family-owned print and broadcast communications firm based in Stamford, Connecticut. It was run by Jimmy and Sarah Ginne, who had a reputation in their industry as knowledgeable, shrewd, and cautious operators with a knack for acquiring cheap and turning around ailing properties. The purpose of the proposed financing was to refund $25 million of bank debt incurred to acquire a community newspaper in the third quarter of 1990. The proposed financing had been presented to Tom Paine by Ginne's investment banker. Ginne did not have rated debt.

With the acquisition of *The Daily Clarion* in Lakeville, Connecticut, Ginne published daily newspapers in 10 communities in Connecticut, Massachusetts, upstate New York, New Hampshire, and Vermont. Eight of the 10 enjoyed monopoly positions in their markets and commensurate profitability. Ginne also owned and operated two FM stations, located in western Connecticut and western Massachusetts. Although *The Daily Clarion* had not in recent years shown the kind of profitability to which the Ginnes were accustomed, they were confident they could restore circulation and advertising levels and effect significant operating economies by printing at their new state-of-the-art plant in Massachusetts.

Exhibit 13 presents a summary term sheet, prepared by Ginne's investment banker, for the proposed transaction. Exhibits 14 and 15 present summary operating and balance sheet data.

Commercial Mortgage Debt

The commercial mortgage market supplies permanent financing (intermediate- and long-term fixed-rate debt) for office buildings, multifamily housing, shopping centers, hotels and other commercial real estate projects. Financing volume in 1989 was approximately $620 billion; in the preceding 3 years, it had averaged $533 billion.[9]

This market is based on the premise that well-managed, well-located, nonspecialized real property retains its value and, in most instances, appreciates over time. Thus, most financing is nonrecourse; that is, for asset protection and repayment, investors looked to the value and cash flow of the specific property financed rather than to the overall assets and cash flow of the underlying borrower. In addition to a note, the investor takes a lien (mortgage) on the property, which permits foreclosure in the event of a default. In other respects, the market is broadly similar to that for privately placed corporate debt. Large institutions, mainly life insurance companies, dominate, and after-market liquidity is minimal.[10]

Yields, reflecting the undiversified, nonrecourse nature of the credits, are generally somewhat higher than in the private corporate market. A matrix of current interest rates in the commercial mortgage market is presented as Exhibit 16.

At the time of the case, Tom Paine was approaching the mortgage market with particular caution and selectivity. Overbuilding in the 1980s, coupled with the 1990 recession, had resulted in falling property values and a sharp rise in commercial vacancy rates. Certain regional markets were experiencing vacancy rates as high as 27%. At the same time, commercial mortgage delinquencies in life insurance company portfolios were estimated at 3.9% and expected to rise.[11]

In spite of this unpropitious environment, Mr. Fuller had identified one offering that he considered a possibility. This was a $5.5 million, 7-year first mortgage to provide permanent financing on Pali Palms Plaza, a small office complex in the suburbs of Honolulu.

The borrower was Kailua Bay Investors, a California general partnership formed to buy Pali Palms Plaza and owned 50/50 by Tim and Glenda Hurley and Herb Newman. For many years, the Hurleys and Newman had made a success of jointly buying distressed properties at deep discounts from replacement cost, turning them around through a combination of management expertise and financial strength, then operating them as long-term investment properties. Among them, the partners had over 65 years of experience in real estate and an aggregate net worth of more than $100 million.

---

9. Board of Governors of the Federal Reserve System, Flow of Funds Accounts.

10. Liquidity increased in the late 1980s with the development of securitization techniques, whereby diversified packages of mortgages are publicly or privately sold, generally with a limited guarantee by the seller.

11. *Barron's,* December 21, 1990.

Kailua Bay Investors had bought Pali Palms Plaza from Bank of America for $4.2 million in cash in November 1988, following the bank's foreclosure on an $8.8 million construction loan to the original developer. Since that time, the partners had incurred additional costs of $1.3 million for extensive tenant improvements, leasing commissions, and operating deficits.

The property, completed in 1987, consisted of two three-story office buildings and a free-standing restaurant. It contained 58,390 sq ft of net rentable office space, 6,016 ft of restaurant space, and surface and under-building parking for 287 cars. Engineering consultants acceptable to Tom Paine had termed construction sound and free of structural or other discernible defects, and environmental experts had certified the structure as being free of asbestos and other environmental hazards.

Pali Palms Plaza was located 12 miles north of Honolulu in the highly affluent residential suburb of Kailua. It was situated at a major intersection two miles northwest of the town center, directly across the street from a large shopping center and half a mile north of the Kaneohe Marine Corps Air Station.

Vacancy rates in suburban office space varied widely with location, building age and design, and rental levels. The range was zero to as much as 30%, with an overall rate of approximately 8% and a lower rate in the northern and western suburbs. Office vacancy in downtown Honolulu was approximately 11%.

Surburban rents ranged from $1.50 to $2.00 per square foot per month, with operating expense stops, typically, of $.50 per square foot per month.[12] In downtown Honolulu, rental rates for newer space ranged from $1.75 to $2.30, with expense stops of $.65 to $.75 and parking fees of $75 to $115 per month per space.

An appraiser satisfactory to Tom Paine had valued Pali Palms Plaza at $8.9 million. Summary operating data are shown in Exhibit 17. Currently, the property was 89% leased, with 49 tenants paying an average rental of $1.49 per square foot per month. Three leases had been signed in the last quarter at an average rental of $1.60 per square foot per month, and the partners expected to achieve 95% occupancy by mid-1991 on the basis of active discussions with several prospective lessees.

Exhibit 18 presents a summary term sheet for the proposed financing, and Exhibit 19 shows a comparison of the proposed transaction to Tom Paine's internal standards for commercial mortgage loans.

Conclusion

As Mr. Fuller reflected on the options he had identified, he was mindful that the date for the scheduled cash inflow was nearing, and Tom Paine would want to get it fully invested with minimum delay. He was also mindful that Sam Adams had access to many sources of financing and that Ginne Enterprises and Pali Palms Plaza had been offered simultaneously to a number of major private market investors on a first-come, first-served basis. Finally, he was very much aware that as a result of credit problems besetting banks and thrift institutions, Tom Paine, like all the major life insurers, was under increasing scrutiny from regulators and the rating agencies, particularly with respect to asset quality.

---

12. An operating expense stop obligates lessees to bear, on a pro rata square footage or other predetermined basis, operating expenses in excess of the stop.

EXHIBIT 1

Consolidated Balance Sheets, Tom Paine Mutual Life Insurance Company, at December 31, 1988 and 1989 (millions of dollars)

	1988	*1989*
Bonds[a]	$ 8,053.8	$ 8,769.6
Stocks		
Preferred[b]	85.0	81.4
Common[b]	36.7	39.0
Investments in affiliates	351.5	458.7
	473.2	579.1
Mortgage loans on real estate[a]	7,615.4	8.483.5
Real estate[c]		
Company-occupied	154.1	165.8
Investments	1,059.0	971.6
	1,213.1	1,137.4
Policy loans	1,727.7	1,669.2
Cash items		
In banks and offices	80.9	131.9
Temporary investments	352.8	219.9
	433.7	351.8
Premiums due and deferred	308.6	304.7
Investment income accrued	389.2	391.4
Other assets	709.3	793.1
Separate accounts[d]	2,644.6	3,395.4
Total assets	$23,568.6	$25,875.2
Policy reserves	$11,085.2	$11,512.6
Policyholders' and beneficiaries' funds	7,683.2	8.617.4
Dividends payable	317.0	330.8
Policy benefits in process of payment	188.1	171.8
Other policy liabilities	175.6	170.3
Mandatory securities and other asset valuation reserves[e]	326.2	381.2
Accrued taxes	134.1	144.4
Other liabilities	89.0	134.2
Separate accounts[f]	2,623.1	3,371.1
Total liabilities	22,621.4	24,833.8
Special surplus	101.1	105.1
Unassigned surplus	846.1	936.3
Total surplus	947.2	1,041.4
Total liabilities and surplus	$23,568.6	$25,875.2

Note: Includes the accounts of U.S.-domiciled life insurance operations. Investments in other affiliates are included on the equity method.

a. Generally carried at amortized cost.

b. Sinking fund preferred stocks generally carried at cost; other stocks carried at market.

c. Carried at depreciated cost, less encumbrances.

d. Refers to third-party assets under management, mainly related to variable life and annuity and similar products and mainly comprising stock, bond, and real estate commingled funds. These funds are carried at market and also appear on the liability side of the balance sheet.

e. A reserve to cover the potential for default risk on debt securities.

f. See note (d). These funds are carried at market and also appear on the asset side of the balance sheet.

EXHIBIT 2

Consoldiated Summary of Operations and Changes in Surplus, Tom Paine Mutual Life Insurance Company, for Years Ending December 31, 1988 and 1989 (millions of dollars)

	1988	*1989*
Premiums, annuity considerations, and pension fund contributions	$4,243.5	$5,094.1
Investment income	1,932.4	2,093.8
Separate account capital gains	147.0	304.6
Other, net	32.8	68.1
Total income	6,355.7	7,560.6
Death benefits	565.8	546.1
Accident and health benefits	443.1	412.5
Annuity benefits	599.5	642.9
Surrender benefits and annuity fund withdrawals	2,736.1	2,702.6
Matured endowments	18.2	16.6
Payments to policyholders, beneficiaries	4,362.7	4,320.7
Additions to reserves	952.3	2,141.2
General and adminstrative expenses		
Field sales	248.8	247.8
Home office and general	289.8	317.8
State premiums, payroll and misc. taxes	57.5	58.6
Total benefits and expenses	5,911.1	7.086.1
Gain from operations	444.6	474.5
Dividends paid to policyholders	293.5	313.4
Federal income taxes	19.0	1.4
Gain from operations before net realized capital gains	132.1	159.7
Net realized capital gains	4.6	25.8
Net income	136.7	185.5
Other changes in surplus		
Net unrealized capital losses, other adjustments	(56.7)	(66.7)
Valuation reserve changes	(5.8)	13.9
Prior years' federal income taxes	6.5	(16.8)
Other adjustments	(15.3)	(2.6)
Net increase in surplus	$ 65.4	$ 113.3

EXHIBIT 3

Representative GIC Rates, December 1990

Rates	*3 Years*	*5 Years*	*7 Years*
High	8.41%	8.93%	9.25%
Average	7.98	8.52	8.82
Low	7.60	8.12	8.25
Treasury notes	7.48	7.84	8.08
Number of GIC vendors	34	36	30

Source: Barron's, December 21, 1990.

EXHIBIT 4
Largest GIC Providers as of January 1, 1990 (billions of dollars)

	GIC Amounts	Total Assets	Claims-Paying Ability Ratings		
			Best's[a]	Moody's[b]	S&P[c]
Prudential Insurance	$21.2	$164.0	A+	Aaa	AAA
Metropolitan Life	17.1	98.9	A+	Aaa	AAA
Aetna Life & Casualty	13.2	87.1	A+	Aaa	AAA
Equitable Life	11.1	61.7	A	A1	A
Travelers	9.2	56.5	A+	A1	A+[d]
John Hancock	8.4	32.3	A+	Aaa	AAA
New York Life	7.9	46.7	A+	Aaa	AAA
Tom Paine	7.0	25.9	A+	Aaa	AAA
Principal Financial	6.9	25.3	A+	Aaa	AAA
Provident National	5.7	11.9	A+	Aa1	A+
Massachusetts Mutual	4.2	24.8	A	Aaa	AAA
Continental Assurance	3.7	8.9	A+	Aa1	A+
Connecticut Mutual	2.8	11.2	A+	Aa2	AA−
State Mutual	2.7	7.2	A+	Aa1	AAA
Crown Life	2.6	7.2	A+	A1	AA
Pacific Mutual	2.6	8.6	A+	Aa2	AAA

Source: Pension and Investment Age.

a. Ratings range from A+ to C−.

b. Ratings range from Aaa to C.

c. Ratings range from AAA to D.

d. On "credit watch" with negative implications.

EXHIBIT 5
Historical Annual Returns on Selected Fixed-Income Instruments, 1975–1989

	Long-Term Corporate Bonds	U.S. Treasury Securities		
		Bills	Intermediate-Term Bonds	Long-Term Bonds
1975	14.64%	5.80%	7.83%	9.19%
1976	18.65	5.08	12.87	16.75
1977	1.71	5.12	1.40	(.67)
1978	(.70)	7.18	3.48	(1.16)
1979	(4.18)	10.38	4.09	(1.22)
1980	(2.62)	11.24	3.91	(3.95)
1981	(.96)	14.71	9.45	1.85
1982	43.79	10.54	29.10	40.35
1983	4.70	8.80	7.41	.68
1984	16.39	9.85	14.02	15.43
1985	30.90	7.72	20.33	30.97
1986	19.85	6.16	15.14	24.44
1987	(.27)	5.47	2.90	(2.69)
1988	10.70	6.35	6.10	9.67
1989	16.23	8.37	13.29	18.10

Source: Ibbotson Associates.

Note: Returns represent interest income plus change in market value.

EXHIBIT 6

Indicative New Issue Levels for Publicly Offered Debt Securities: Reoffering Spreads over Treasury Securities, December 1990 (basis points)

Issuer	Ratings Moody's/S&P	Years to Final Maturity					
		2	3	5	7	10	30
U.S. agencies							
FNMA	NR/NR	17	19	27	30	35	120[a]
TVA	Aaa/AAA	20	20	25	35	41	109[a]
Industrials							
IBM	Aaa/AAA	25	30	35	40	45	65
Du Pont	Aa2/AA	40	50	60	70	75	100
Pepsico	A1/A	60	65	70	80	90	110
ConAgra	Baa1/BBB	110	120	130	140	150	165
Utilities							
SoCal Edison	Aa2/AA	60	70	75	80	85	135[b]
Alabama Power	A1/A	75	85	90	95	100	150[b]
Cincinnati Gas &							
Electric	Baa1/BBB+	90	100	105	115	125	190[b]
Finance							
IBM Credit	Aaa/AAA	35	45	50	55	60	na
Amex Credit	Aa2/AA	90	100	110	120	130	na
CIT	A1/A+	135	155	165	175	190	na
Banks[c]							
Morgan Guaranty Trust	Aaa/AAA	60	60	65	75	85	na
Bankers Trust	Aa2/AA	70	85	105	125	140	na
Bank of America	Aa3/A	80	95	115	135	155	na
U.S. Treasury Securities[d]		7.28%	7.48%	7.84%	8.08%	8.18%	8.30%

Note: All indications for noncall life instruments unless otherwise indicated.

NR=not rated; na=not available.

a. Nonredeemable for 5 years, thereafter redeemable at declining premiums over par.

b. Nonrefundable for 5 years, thereafter refundable at declining premiums over par.

c. For issuance of bank level, not holding company.

d. Actual prevailing yields, not new issue indications.

EXHIBIT 7
Price Data Relating to Selected Publicly Traded Debt Securities

Issuer	Ratings Moody's/S&P	Issue Date	Outstand. Amount ($ mills.)	Coupon	Maturity	Sinking Fund		Approx. Avg. Life (years)	Call		Current Price
						Begins	Retires[a]		Begins	Price	
Cabot Corp.	Baa1/BBB+	1987	$ 100	10¼%	12/15/97	—	—	7.0	—	—	$101½
Capital Cities/ABC	A1/A+	1985	200	10½	9/1/97	—	—	6.8	9/1/92	$100.00	104⅜
Commercial Credit	A2/A	1988	100	8½	2/15/98	—	—	7.2	—	—	98⅜
Commonwealth Edison[b]	Baa1/BBB+	1968	50	6¼	2/1/98	—	—	7.2	Current	101.67	84¾
Consumers Power[b]	Baa3/BBB–	1988	250	8¾	2/15/98	—	—	7.2	—	—	98
Dillard Dept. Stores	A2/A	1988	50	9½	1/15/98	—	—	7.0	—	—	101
Eastman Kodak	A2/A–	1988	1,100	9⅛	3/1/98	—	—	7.2	3/1/95	100.00	98⅝
Hertz Corp.	A3/BBB	1988	75	9.70	9/15/97	—	—	6.7	—	—	99⅜
Household Finance	A2/A+	1989	100	8¼	3/1/98	—	—	7.2	3/1/94	100.00	93⅜
ITT Financial	A1/A+	1988	100	8½	1/15/98	—	—	7.0	—	—	98⅞
Marriott Corp.	Baa2/BBB	1987	150	9⅞	11/1/97	—	—	6.9	11/1/94	100.00	89¼
Morgan Stanley	A1/A+	1988	100	9.80	1/15/98	—	—	7.0	6/15/95	100.00	103⅛
New York Telephone	A1/A	1960	60	4⅝	10/1/97	—	—	6.8	Current	100.33	79½
Ohio Power[b]	A2/A–	1988	100	9⅞	1/1/98	Current	1%	6.8	5/31/93[e]	102.83	103⅛
Penn Central[c]	Baa1/BBB–	1987	134	11	12/15/97	—	—	7.0	Current	102.00	101⅝
J.C. Penney	A1/A+	1990	250	10	10/1/97	—	—	6.8	—	—	101⅜
J.C. Penney	A1/A+	1988	200	9⅜	2/1/98	—	—	7.2	2/1/95	100.00	98⅝
Pennsylvania Power & Light[b]	A2/A–	1988	125	9¼	3/1/98	Current	1	7.1	2/28/93	102.56	99⅞
Philadelphia Electric[b]	Baa3/BBB	1967	75	6⅛	10/1/97	—	—	6.8	Current	101.40	83½
Phillips Petroleum	Baa1/BBB	1990	300	9½	11/1/97	—	—	7.0	—	—	99⅞
Ryder System	A3/A–	1988	100	9⅜	1/15/98	—	—	7.0	1/15/95	100.00	97
Scott Paper	A3/BBB+	1990	200	9¾	10/1/97	—	—	6.8	—	—	101¼
Southern California Gas[b]	A1/A+	1988	100	9⅜	1/15/98	Current	1	6.8	6/14/93	102.45	101¼
Stanley Works	A2/A	1988	50	9	2/1/98	—	—	7.2	—	—	99⅜
Texas Eastern Corp[d]	Ba1/BBB–	1987	100	10½	12/15/97	—	—	7.0	12/15/94	100.00	100⅝
Union Pacific Corp.	A2/A	1988	200	8⅞	3/1/98	—	—	7.2	3/1/95	100.00	100⅛

a. Indicates amount to be retired annually.

b. Debt secured by a first mortgage on certain properties.

c. Subordinated debt.

d. Issuer has first mortgage debt outstanding.

e. Bonds are nonrefundable prior to this date; that is, issuer is prohibited from redeeming the bonds directly or indirectly with money borrowed at a lower cost than the effective interest rate incurred on these bonds at date of issuance.

EXHIBIT 8

Indicative New Issue Levels for Privately Placed Debt Securities: Purchase Spreads over Treasury Securities, December 1990 (basis points)

Ratings[a]	No. of Investors[b]	3 Years		5 Years		7 Years		10 Years		15 Years	
		Low	High	Low	High	Low	High	Low	High	Low	High
A+	1	110	—	115	—	120	—	130	—	—	—
A	9	100	130	105	145	110	245	120	175	130	200
A−	3	100	115	105	125	105	135	115	160	150	—
BBB+	6	100	175	110	175	130	180	150	195	190	200
BBB	10	100	180	100	185	125	195	145	200	150	240
BBB−	15	150	260	165	300	180	340	195	385	250	255
BB+	3	200	375	205	425	215	455	220	485	370	380

Note: Indications given by major insurance companies to a major investment banking firm between November 12, 1990, and December 12, 1990.

a. Investors not distinguishing within the A or BBB categories are shown here as indicating A or BBB.

b. Number of investors indicating interest in private placement purchases in the rating and maturity categories shown. Ratings shown are those indicated by such investors.

EXHIBIT 9

Comparison of Approximate Estimated Public and Private Issuance Costs for a $100 Million Intermediate-Term Debt Issue (thousands of dollars)

	Public	Private
Accounting fees[a]	$ 50	—
Legal fees[a]	150	$ 50
New York Stock Exchange listing fee[b]	23	—
Printing[a]	100	—
Rating agency fees[b]	60	—
SEC registration fee[b]	25	—
Trustee[a]	50	—
Underwriting or agent commission[b]	625	375
Other (engraving and printing of certificates, postage, etc.)[a]	25	—
Total	$1,108	$425
Approximate cost in basis points	23	9

a. Wholly or largely independent of issue size.

b. Wholly or largely dependent on issue size.

EXHIBIT 10
Summary of Proposed Terms of Senior Subordinated Notes, Sam Adams Financial Corporation

Issuer: Sam Adams Financial Corporation.

Amount: $40 million.

Maturity: Seven years from date of closing.

Interest rate: 9.7%, payable semiannually in arrears.

Issue price: 100%.

Closing: The legal documents will be executed and delivered as soon as practicable.

Takedown: At closing.

Mandatory prepayments: None.

Optional prepayments: None.

Seniority: These notes will be junior in right of payment to all indebtedness for borrowed money that is not expressly by its terms *parri passu* with or junior in right of payment to these notes.

All other terms: To be indentical to those contained in the company's note agreement, dated June 30, 1988, relating to the 9.2% senior subordinated notes due June 15, 1998. (This agreement limits the company's ability to engage in businesses other than consumer finance and commercial finance, to create liens against finance receivables without equally and ratably securing these notes, and to merge or sell all or substantially all of its assets without assumption of these notes by the successor entity. It provides for modification of nonmoney terms and acceleration by vote of 51% of holders of the notes.)

EXHIBIT 11
Summary Operating Data, Sam Adams Financial Corporation, for Years Ending December 31,1985–1989 (millions of dollars)

Operating Revenues

1985	$1,164.1
1986	1,285.5
1987	1,283.3
1988	1,461.9
1989	1,780.0

Interest Expense[a]

1985	$ 467.5
1986	492.9
1987	489.3
1988	586.6
1989	761.7

Provision for Credit Losses

1985	$ 133.8
1986	185.6
1987	248.3
1988	190.3
1989	288.7

Pretax Income and Margins

1985	$ 140.5	12.1%
1986	152.6	11.9
1987	118.2	9.2
1988	182.8	12.5
1989	184.3	10.4

Net Income and Margins

1985	$ 111.2	9.6%
1986	134.8	10.5
1987	101.4	7.9
1988	138.9	9.5
1989	155.9	8.8

Net Charge-Offs (Percent of Average Net Receivables)[b]

1985	2.10%
1986	2.79
1987	3.89
1988	2.31
1989	3.23

Delinquencies (Year-End Net Receivables)[c]

1985	5.16%
1986	4.99
1987	3.58
1988	4.62
1989	5.69

a. Includes interest factor attributable to rentals.

b. Earlier of when account is deemed uncollectible or is 181 days past due.

c. 61 days or more past due.

EXHIBIT 12

Summary Balance Sheet Data, Sam Adams Financial Corporation, at December 31, 1989

Finance receivables net	$ 8,563.8
Investment securities[a]	1,709.4
Other assets	316.0
Total assets	$10,589.2
Commercial paper and other short-term debt[b]	$ 4,587.4
Deposits and certificates[c]	390.7
Insurance reserves	407.5
Funded debt	
Senior	2,763.3
Senior subordinated	394.3
Junior subordinated	197.2
	3,354.8
Other liabilities	665.8
Total liabilities	4,020.6
Common equity	1,183.0
Total liabilities and net worth	$10,589.2

a. Related to insurance subsidiaries; carried at amortized cost.

b. Includes $467.3 million in current maturities of funded debt.

c. Related to Newport Beach Savings and Loan Association, a wholly owned subsidiary.

EXHIBIT 13

Summary of Proposed Terms of Privately Placed Senior Notes, Ginne Enterprises, Inc.

Issuer: Ginne Enterprises, Inc.

Amount: $25 million.

Maturity: Eight years from date of closing.

Interest rate: 9.90%, payable semiannually in arrears.

Issue price: 100%.

Closing: The legal documents will be executed and delivered as soon as practicable.

Takedown: At closing.

Mandatory prepayments: Beginning at the end of the sixth year, the company will make two equal annual payments of 33⅓% of the initial principal amount, leaving 33⅓% due at maturity. The resulting average life will be 7.0 years.

Optional prepayments: None.

Use of proceeds: The company will use the proceeds from the sale of the notes to retire existing short-term bank indebtedness.

Restriction on incurrence of additional funded debt: None permitted.

Limitation on short-term debt: Short-term debt not permitted for at least 30 consecutive days in every calendar year.

Limitation on liens: With certain exceptions, e.g., liens relating to performance bonds, governmental contracts and the like, none permitted without equally and ratably securing these notes.

Limitation on sale and leasebacks: Not permitted unless the net proceeds of such sales are applied to the retirement of funded debt.

Restricted payments: The company and its subsidiaries will not (a) pay dividends other than stock dividends; (b) purchase or otherwise acquire for value any shares of the company's capital stock; or (c) make loans or advances to, or investments, in the securities of entities other than subsidiaries, unless, after giving effect to such action, the aggregate of (a), (b), and (c) will not thereby exceed 50% of consolidated net income accumulated after closing plus $2.5 million.

Merger and sale of substantially all assets: Not permitted, unless the company is the survivor or the successor corporation is a U.S. corporation, assumes all obligations under the note agreement. There would be no default, and the company could incur $1.00 of additional funded debt.

Sale of a substantial part of assets: Except as provided under "Merger and Sale of Substantially All Assets," not permitted to exceed in any one fiscal year 10% of consolidated net tangible assets.

Restriction on subsidiary debt: None permitted.

Modification: Terms may be amended, modified, or waived with the consent of holders of not less than 66⅔% of the principal amount of the notes, except that no change may be made in the payment terms, e.g., coupon, principal amount, interest, and principal payment dates, without the consent of all holders.

Events of default: (a) Default for more than five days in payment of interest when due; (b) default in payment of principal when due; (c) default for more than 30 days in compliance with any other covenant in the note agreement.

Acceleration: In case of an event of default under this note agreement or under any other loan agreement, note agreement, indenture, or other evidence of indebtedness under which the company or any subsidiary is obligated, holders of not less than 25% of the principal amount of the notes may declare the principal and all accrued and unpaid interest to be due and payable.

EXHIBIT 14
Summary Operating Data, Ginne Enterprises, Inc., 1980–1990 (thousands of dollars)

Operating Revenues

1980	$ 68,479
1983	86,279
1986	103,319
1987	110,462
1988	118,628
1989	126,269
1990	134,732

Operating Income and Margins[a]

1980	$ 18,275	26.7%
1983	20,549	23.8
1986	23,560	22.8
1987	25,772	23.3
1988	25,586	21.6
1989	25,254	20.0
1990	27,290	20.3

Interest Expense

1980	$ 4,633
1983	1,208
1986	1,231
1987	2,717
1988	3,747
1989	6,924
1990	7,866

Pretax Income and Margins[a]

1980	$ 13,642	19.9%
1983	19,341	22.4
1986	22,329	21.6
1987	23,055	20.9
1988	21,839	18.4
1989	18,330	14.5
1990	19,424	14.4

Net Income and Margins[a]

1980	$ 7,452	10.9%
1983	10,108	11.7
1986	12,098	11.7
1987	12,612	11.4
1988	12,386	10.4
1989	12,407	9.8
1990	13,148	9.8

Operating Cash Flow[a]

1980	$ 9,315
1983	12,533
1986	15,243
1987	16,017
1988	15,359
1989	15,903
1990	16,435

a. Excludes gains on sales of properties as follows: 1980, $4.7 million; 1986, $7.3 million; 1988, $9.1 million.

EXHIBIT 15

Summary Balance Sheet Data, Ginne Enterprises, Inc., at September 30, 1990 (thousands of dollars).

Current assets	$ 64,688
Less: Short-term debt	30,888
Less: Other current liabilities	29,008
Net working capital	4,792
Property, net	131,223
Other tangible assets[a]	25,191
Net tangible assets	$161,206
Funded debt[b]	$ 71,014
Deferred items[c]	14,706
Common equity	141,524
Less: Intangibles	66,038
Net tangible liabilities	$161,206

a. Primarily equity investments in associated companies.

b. Average interest rate of 9.75% with annual maturities as follows: 1991, $3.6 million; 1992, $7.3 million; 1993, $6.5 million; 1994, $18.5 million.

c. Primarily related to retirement and deferred compensation plans.

EXHIBIT 16

Indicative Rates for Immediate Takedown Fixed-Rate Commercial Mortgages

Maturity	Amortization	Rate[a,b]		Number of Investors[c]	U.S. Treasury Securities
		Low	High		
First mortgages					
3 years	—	9.25%	9.85%	9	7.48%
5 years	—	9.50	10.25	18	7.84
7 years	—	9.75	10.50	18	8.08
10 years	25–30 years	10.05	11.05	20	8.18
30 years	30 years	10.40	10.85	2	8.30
Second mortgages					
3 years	—	9.70	—	1	7.48
5 years	—	10.75	—	1	7.84
7 years	—	11.50	—	1	8.08
10 years	—	11.75	—	1	8.81

Note: Commercial and industrial properties only. Does not include apartment buildings, for instance.

a. Semiannual equivalent of monthly pay interest rates.

b. Includes the effect of front-end fees where applicable.

c. Number of investors indicating interest in each maturity. Rates shown are those indicated by such investors.

EXHIBIT 17

Summary Operating Data for Pali Palms Plaza, Kailua Bay Investors (thousands of dollars)

	Operating Results	
	Latest 12 months	Projected
Base rent		
Office[a]	$ 929.2[a]	$ 996.5
Restaurant	108.7	108.7
Percentage rent, restaurant	53.7	55.0
C.A.M. recoveries[b]	53.5	55.0
Other income	4.2	5.0
Total income	1.149.3	1.220.2
Operating expenses	329.3	350.0
Miscellaneous	11.5	12.5
Total expenses	340.8	362.5
Net operating income	$ 808.5	$ 857.7

Lease Expirations (percent of space)	
1991	10%
1992	6
1993	15
1994	12
1995	20
After	12

a. Current vacancy rate is 11%. Projected results assume reduction in vacancies from 11% to 5% with new rentals at $1.60 per square foot per month.

b. Common area maintenance expenses, such as for lobbies and elevators, passed through to tenants.

EXHIBIT 18
Summary of Proposed Terms of First Mortgage Loan, Kailua Bay Investors

Issuer: Kailua Bay Investors, a California general partnership whose sole operating asset is Pali Palms Plaza.

Amount: $5.5 million.

Maturity: Seven years from date of closing.

Interest rate: 10.50% (semiannual equivalent), payable monthly in arrears.

Issue price: 100%.

Closing: The legal documents will be executed and delivered as soon as practicable.

Takedown: At closing.

Mandatory prepayments: None. The resulting average life will be 7 years.

Optional prepayments: None, except in the event of sale of the property. In that event, the investor must prepay the notes at a price equal to the greater of (a) par plus accrued interest, or (b) the present value of all remaining interest and principal payments, such present value to be determined using a discount rate equal to .25% plus the yield on U.S. Treasury obligations having a maturity date corresponding with the remaining average life of the notes.

Use of proceeds: Permanent financing of earlier acquired property, which will serve as security for this loan.

Security: These notes will be secured by a first mortgage against the land and buildings of Pali Palms Plaza, located at 970 North Kalaheo Avenue, Kailua, Hawaii.

Recourse: None.

Second mortgage financing: None permitted.

Other restrictive covenants: None.

Undertakings: Issuer will pay all property and other taxes when due, maintain adequate insurance, etc.

Events of default: (a) Default in payment of interest when due plus five days; (b) default in payment of principal when due; (c) failure to perform for 30 days any other terms of provisions of these notes.

EXHIBIT 19
Summary Comparison of Proposed Kailua Bay Investors Financing to Tom Paine's Commercial Mortgage Investment Standards

	Standard	Pali Palms Plaza
Debt service coverage[a]	1.25	1.40
Loan to appraised value	75%	61.8%
Interest rate (semiannual equivalent minimum rate for 7 years)	10.25%	10.50%
Amortization	30 years	None
Break-even occupancy	85%	76.6%
Put or maturity	10 years or less	7 years
Elevators: up to a three-story building with 15,000 sq ft per floor or less	Minimum of 1	Yes
Parking ratio (cars per 1,000 sq ft)	3	4.2
Efficiency minimum[b]	80%	83%
Lavatories	1 set per floor	Yes
Net rentable space on leases of 3 years or more	80%	73%
Full expense stop or CPI adjustment	Required	Expense stop

a. Annual net operating income divided by pro forma annual interest and principal payments.

b. Usable square feet as a percent of gross square feet.

Introduction to Derivative Instruments

A derivative is a financial instrument, or contract, between two parties that derives its value from some other underlying asset or underlying reference price, interest rate, or index. Common derivatives include options, forward contracts, futures contracts, and swaps. Common underlying assets include interest rates, exchange rates, commodities, stocks, stock indices, bonds, and bond indices. Derivatives are created and traded in two interlinked markets—organized exchanges at the national and regional level, and an international network of dealers and end-users in which transactions are executed privately, that is, "over the counter" (OTC).

Over recent decades, financial markets have been marked by increased volatility. As foreign exchange rates, interest rates, and commodity prices continue to experience sharp and unexpected movements, it has become increasingly important that corporations exposed to these risks be equipped to manage them effectively. Rick management, the managerial process that is used to control such price volatility, has consequently risen to the top of financial agendas. And in the hot spot are these so-called derivatives. Furthermore, as these instruments have become more readily available, their application has extended beyond traditional risk management to the more opportunistic realm of speculation. In both applications, derivatives represent powerful tools by which institutions and individuals alike can significantly affect their financial security and viability.

Derivatives are used by a variety of entities such as corporations, commercial banks, and individual and institutional investors to reduce or "lay off" various risks, including the aforementioned interest rate risk, foreign currency risk, commodity price risk, and investment risk. Exhibit 1 provides results of a survey on the uses of derivatives by chief financial officers. For example, a chief financial officer (CFO) of a company heavily exposed to foreign exchange fluctuations often exploits the foreign exchange forward market to shield the company's balance sheet from currency depre-

This case was prepared by Research Associate Kendall Backstrand under the supervision of Professor W. Carl Kester.

ciation. Similarly, a grain producer might use a forward contract to hedge against price depreciation in, say, wheat or soybeans. Through the use of a put option, an investor can establish a limit on the potential loss on an investment. On the other end of the application spectrum, an entity can trade derivatives for purely speculative purposes. Broadly, holders of derivatives securities, as well as their counterparties, can achieve goals ranging from risk management to speculation. The derivatives themselves help allocate economic risks efficiently by transferring risks between parties such that each holds the risks it is better able or more willing to bear.

This note provides a conceptual basis for understanding the fundamental properties and applications of common derivative products that give rise to their use in financial management. Each of three major families of derivative instruments—options, forwards and futures, and swaps—is discussed in the separate sections that follow.

Options

Common Terminology

Options are derivative instruments that can be used as a means of speculation or investment as well as hedging or risk management. Options written on both financial and physical assets have been traded for many years in dealer markets. However, it was not until 1973, when the Chicago Board of Trade formed the Chicago Board Options Exchange (CBOE), that organized public markets for options began to appear. Exchanges were then established to trade options written on assets such as individual stocks, stock indices, commodities, foreign currencies, and Treasury bonds.

An option is a contract between the buyer (or holder) of the option and the seller (or writer) of the option. This contract gives the buyer of the option the *right* to buy (or sell) an asset from (to) the seller of the option. The seller, on the other hand, is *obligated* under the terms of the option contract to perform. Plainly stated, an option contract defines the rights of the buyer and the obligations of the seller. The option to buy an asset is known as a *call* option, and the option to sell an asset is known as a *put* option. An example of a call and put option written on a particular company's common stock, that of Microsoft Corporation, is provided in Table A.

The specified asset involved in the option contract is referred to as the *underlying asset* on which the option is written. The specified price at which the asset may be bought or sold in the future is known as the *exercise*, or *strike, price*. Purchasing or selling the asset in the future through the option contract is referred to as *exercising* the option, and the specified date on or before which the option may be exercised is called the *expiration date*, or *maturity date*. So-called *American*-style options are contracts that may be exercised at any time prior to maturity, whereas *European*-style options are contracts that may be exercised only at maturity.

The options on Microsoft's stock shown in Table A were American options. A holder of the call option could have purchased Microsoft's stock at $60 per share by

TABLE A
Options Traded on Microsoft's Stock, November 30, 1994 (dollars per share)

Stock (asset) price	$64.125
Exercise price	$60
Maturity date	April 15, 1995
Call option price (premium)	$7.50
Put option price (premium)	$2.125

exercising the call option on or before April 15, 1995. Likewise, a holder of the put option could have sold Microsoft's stock at $60 per share by exercising the put option on or before April 15, 1995.

Option contracts have a *market*, or *premium, value*, and an *intrinsic value*. The market value of the option contract is simply the price at which a buyer and seller are willing to enter into an option contract. More specifically, it is the up-front cash premiums that the buyer must pay the seller in order to claim the rights of that particular option contract. As shown in Table A, the market value of the call option on Microsoft's stock was $7.50 per option as of the end of trading on November 30, 1994. Likewise, the market value of the put option on Microsoft's stock was $2.125. Because standard option contracts are contracts to buy or sell 100 shares at a time, an investor would actually have had to pay $750.00 to buy a standard call option contract on Microsoft's stock, and $212.50 to buy a standard put contract.

The intrinsic value of an option can be thought of as the price a rational investor would pay for an option if it were about to mature instantly. Because an option contract gives the holder the right to exercise but not the obligation, the intrinsic value of an option can never be less than zero. This is true because if the option is never exercised by the holder, it simply expires worthless.

If, for instance, the price of Microsoft's stock had fallen to $55 per share, the owner of the call option described in Table A would not have elected to exercise the option to buy at $60 per share. An investor wishing to own Microsoft's stock, in this case, would have been better off buying it directly on the stock exchange at $55 per share. Thus, at a stock price of $55 per share, the intrinsic value of a call option with an exercise price of $60 would have been zero, representing a worthless position for the holder of the call.

In general, the intrinsic value of a call option is always the greater of zero and the difference between the current market price of the underlying asset and the option's exercise price. In the case of a call option, this intrinsic value will be positive when the market price of the asset exceeds the exercise price of the option, and zero otherwise. At $64.125 per share, the call option on Microsoft's stock had a positive intrinsic value of $64.125 less $60, or $4.125. The call option holder could have bought Microsoft's stock for less than its actual market value. The opposite is true in the case of a put option: Sensible investors would not sell a put option's underlying asset at the put's exercise price unless that exercise price were above the asset's market value. Thus, the intrinsic value of a put option is always the greater of zero and the difference between the put's exercise price and the current market price of the underlying asset.

An option is said to be *in-the-money* when its intrinsic value is positive and *out-of-the-money* when it is zero. That is, a call option is in-the-money when its underlying asset's market price is above the exercise price; it is out-of-the-money when the opposite occurs. The converse is true for a put option: When the exercise price is above (below) the underlying asset's market price at maturity, the put is considered in-the-money (out-of-the-money). As the term suggests, an *at-the-money* option describes an option when its exercise price exactly equals the underlying asset's market price. Again using the Microsoft example, the terms described in Table A constitute an in-the-money call option and an out-of-the-money put option. If the exercise price were $64.125, or the stock price were $60, both options would be at-the-money. If the market price of an underlying asset is far above (below) the exercise price of a call (put) option, then the option is said to be *deep-in-the-money*. If the opposite is true, it is said to be *deep-out-of-the-money*. A deep-in-the-money position at maturity is the most desirable outcome for either a call or put option.

FIGURE A
Payoff Diagrams

Total Payoff on a Call Option

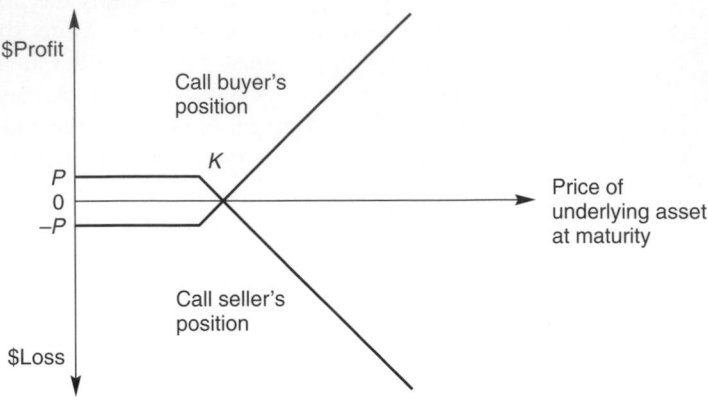

Total Payoff on a Put Option

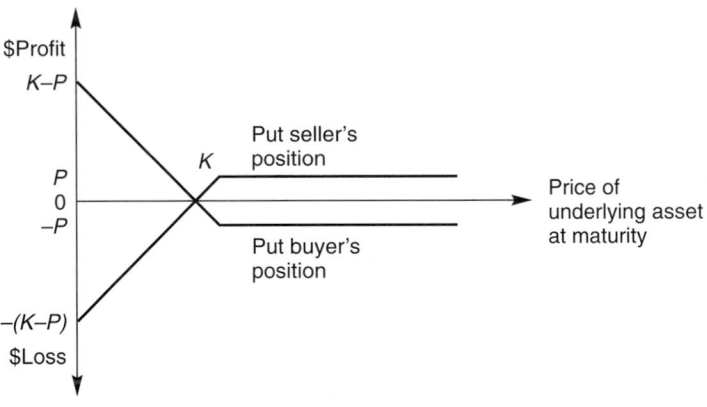

Graphical representation of an option's intrinsic value is useful to illustrate its total payoff. Payoff diagrams for both put and call options written on the same underlying asset with the same exercise price are provided in Figure A, where K = Exercise price, and P = Premium.

Determinants of Option Value

Notice in Table A that each option's market value is greater than its intrinsic value. This will always be true for options that have some time remaining before maturity. A graph of a call option's market, or premium, value relative to intrinsic value is shown in Figure B, where

K = Exercise price

FIGURE B
Call Option Premium in Relation to Intrinsic Value

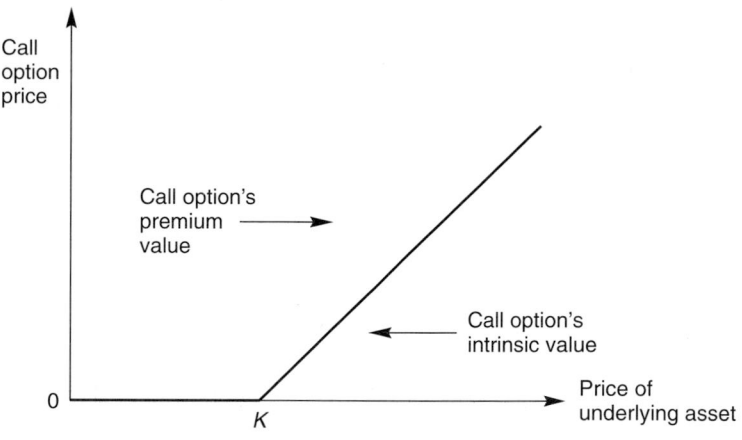

How much greater the premium value is over the intrinsic value depends on several factors. In general, for generic American-style call and put options, the premium value depends upon the following six determinants: underlying asset price, exercise price, the risk-free rate of return, volatility of the asset price, time to expiration, and expected cash distributions, if any. Their respective effects on option value are briefly described below.

Asset Price. For an American or European call option, the higher the price of the underlying asset, the greater the option's intrinsic value and the more likely it will remain above the option's exercise price at expiration. Hence, the higher the asset price, the greater will be the call option's premium, other things held constant. The opposite is true for American and European put options: the higher the value of the underlying asset, the lower the put option's intrinsic value and premium, other things held constant.

Exercise Price. An increase in a call option's exercise price *decreases* both the intrinsic value of the option and the likelihood that the option will be worth anything at maturity. Consequently, the higher an American or European call option's exercise price, the lower its premium value will be, other things held constant. Again, the opposite is true of a put option: A higher exercise price *increases* the put option's intrinsic value, other things held constant, and would be reflected in a higher premium.

Interest Rates. Because buyers of options do not pay or receive the option's exercise price until later, if ever, interest rates play a role in the determination of option premium value. Specifically, an increase in the interest rate lowers the present value of the cash exercise price expected to be paid or received in the future. For a call option, a rise in interest rates means the future cash payment of its exercise price is worth less in present value terms, implying greater option value for the holder. Hence, the value of an American or European call option increases as interest rates rise, holding other factors constant. In contrast, a rise in interest rates lowers the present value of the cash that a put option holder might receive in the future upon exercising the put. Consequently, American and European put option premiums decline as interest rates rise, other things being equal.

Volatility of the Asset Price.   Other factors held constant, the more volatile the underlying asset price, the more valuable the option. Again, this is true because of the asymmetrical construct between an option's potential upside gains and downside losses (see Figure A). The holder of a call option experiences unlimited potential gains as the price of the asset increases. At the same time, however, the call option holder effectively limits loss by simply not exercising the option if the asset's price falls below the option's exercise price. The holder of a put, although only experiencing limited potential gains (the maximum gain being obtained when the asset price is zero upon maturity, implying an intrinsic value exactly equal to the option's exercise price), can also limit loss by simply not exercising the put if the asset's price rises above the put's exercise price. In short, the more volatile the asset price, the greater the chance the holder of either a put or call option has of realizing a gain without equally increasing the chance of incurring a large loss. Thus, higher expected volatility in the underlying asset's price enhances both American and European option values, other things being equal.

Time to Expiration.   American and European call options increase in value when the time remaining to expiration is further away. This positive influence derives from two sources. First, in connection with the interest rate effect, the longer the time before expiration when the exercise payment will be made, the lower the discounted present value of that cash payment. Second, in connection with the volatility effect, the more time there is before expiration, the more likely it is that a large price change will occur and dramatically increase the value of the option. Consequently, so long as there is time remaining before expiration, an option's premium will exceed its intrinsic value. Provided there are no cash distributions to owners of a call option's underlying asset (see below), it follows that a call option should not be exercised before maturity, because doing so would sacrifice the value attributable to time.

American put option value is also positively affected by time to expiration. Because of the asymmetry between potential gains and losses from holding a put option, more time before expiration increases the chance that the put will mature in the money. Although the proceeds to be received from the future exercise of the put will have a lower present value as time to expiration increases, other things constant, this negative influence will not generally outweigh the positive influence associated with price volatility unless interest rates are high. When this is so, American put option holders might find it in their best interests to exercise their puts prematurely and reinvest the cash proceeds.

For European put options, the time to expiration can have either a positive or negative influence on prices depending on which of two effects dominate. When a European put is in the money, a longer time to expiration will tend to have a negative influence on premium value because the expected receipt of cash proceeds from exercising the put is farther in the future. However, if the European put is deep-out-of-the-money, a long time to expiration will tend to enhance option value. This is because more time provides a greater opportunity for the stock price to drop far enough to make the put valuable at expiration. Of course, the stock price could rise as well, but as in the case of call options, losses on the downside can be limited by simply not exercising the put.

Cash Distributions.   Some assets, notably many common stocks, have cash distributions associated with them. A cash dividend paid on an underlying stock decreases the value of a call option, other things held constant. The reason is that cash dividends reduce the market price of the stock on the day the stock goes *ex dividend* (i.e., begins to trade without rights to any cash dividends previously declared on the stock; shareholders of record just prior to the ex dividend date are entitled to the cash dividends, but holders of call options on that stock are not). As the price of a stock declines when it goes ex dividend, so too will the value of a call option on the stock, other things remaining constant. The opposite is true for a put option: the holder of the put option, as well as the owner of the stock, benefit from cash dividends in that the stock owner receives a cash payout and the put holder obtains increased option value when the stock's price declines upon going ex dividend.

A summary of the effect each of the preceding factors has on American option value is illustrated in Table B.

TABLE B
Summary of Factors Determining American Option Value[a]

	Call Option	Put Option
Asset price	+	−
Exercise price	−	+
Interest rates	+	−
Volatility of the asset price	+	+
Time to maturity	+	+[b]
Cash distributions	−	+

a. The + and − signs indicate the nature of the effect each factor has on the value of the option.

b. As discussed above, time to maturity could have either a positive or negative influence on European put option value.

Put-Call Parity

Consider again the Microsoft put and call options described in Table A. Notice that, in addition to being written on the same stock, these options had identical exercise prices and maturity dates. Given their similar characteristics, it seems logical that the market values of the call and put would have been related to one another in a predictable way. That is, as the price of Microsoft's stock changed, the prices of the options should also have changed, but in such a way that an astute investor could not have bought one and sold another so as to lock in a virtually riskless profit. Should such an *arbitrage* opportunity develop, the very act of exploiting it ought to set buy and sell transactions in motion that will ultimately ensure a kind of parity between put and call prices.

This is, in fact, the case. A condition known as *put-call parity* describes the relationship that a put and call option written on the same stock with the same exercise price and maturity date must sustain if there are to be no riskless arbitrage opportunities.[1] Specifically, put-call parity states that the difference in price between a call

---

1. Strictly speaking, put-call parity as described above applies only to European options because, unlike American options, they cannot be exercised prior to the expiration date.

option and a put option with the same terms should equal the price of the underlying asset less the present discounted value of the exercise price. This relationship can be described as follows:

$$V_c - V_p = P_a - X$$

where

V_c = the price of a call option
V_p = the price of a put option
P_a = the price of the underlying asset
X = present discounted value of the underlying asset's exercise price

Another way to interpret this relationship is to say that someone owning a call option while having simultaneously written (sold) a comparable put option on the same asset should, at all times, be in a position equivalent to someone who purchased the underlying asset with a pure-discount (i.e., zero-coupon) loan having a face value equal to the option's exercise price and maturing at the option's expiration date. The value of these two options must be equal because each investor would realize identical payoffs at the time of maturity. You can demonstrate this to yourself by constructing payoff diagrams such as those shown in Figure A for each of these two positions. As you will observe, the payoff in both cases is equivalent to owning stock purchased on "margin" (that is, purchased partly with borrowed proceeds).

Consider what could be done if this relationship were not true. For illustrative purposes, assume that the options on Microsoft's stock shown in Table A were European options. Suppose further that the call option on Microsoft's stock shown in Table A actually sold for $8.50 instead of $7.50. At the time, short-term interest rates were about 6% annually (equivalent to a compound daily rate of 1.6 basis points, or 0.016%). Under these conditions, strict put-call parity would *not* have held:

$$(\$8.50 - \$2.125) > (\$64.125 - \$58.709)$$

$$\$6.375 > \$5.414$$

where

$8.50   = assumed market value of the call option
$2.125 = market value of the put option
$64.125 = market value of Microsoft's stock
$58.709 = current value of a pure-discount loan maturing on April 15 at a value of 60

Upon observing such a discrepancy, an astute trader would have executed the following transactions:

November 30, 1994	**Per share cash proceeds**
1. Write (sell) a call option on Microsoft's stock	$8.50
2. Buy a put option on Microsoft's stock	(2.125)
3. Borrow $58.709 at a daily compound rate of interest of 0.016%	58.709
4. Purchase Microsoft's stock at $64.125	(64.125)
Net proceeds	$0.959

April 15, 1995

a. If Microsoft's stock was worth more than $60 per share, then:

   1. Deliver the stock to the call option owner . . . .   —
   2. Receive $60 from the call option owner $60.00
   3. Use the proceeds from the exercise of the call option
       to repay the loan . . . .   (60.00)
          Net proceeds $0.00

b. If Microsoft's stock was worth less than $60 per share, then:

   1. Exercise the put by delivering the stock to the
       put writer . . . .   —
   2. Receive $60 from the put writer $60.00
   3. Use the proceeds from exercising the put to repay
       the loan . . . .   (60.00)
          Net proceeds $0.00

Notice that regardless of what happened to the price of Microsoft's stock, the trader would have received $60 on April 15, 1995, which is exactly sufficient to repay the loan with interest. Thus, the residual net proceeds of $0.959 per share from the November 30, 1994, transactions represent an immediate, riskless profit involving no commitment of the trader's own capital. Notice too that such an arbitrage profit would have been virtually immaterial at the call option's actual price of $7.50. If call or put option prices deviated substantially from levels dictated by the put-call parity relationship, transactions similar to those described above would drive prices up or down until the arbitrage opportunity was eliminated.

Applications

Options can be used to insure against various risks as well as to bet on various market movements. Risk management, or insurance, is often achieved through, for example, the purchase of put options. Assume a company expects to receive some foreign currency and is concerned that the currency will depreciate against its home currency. To limit its losses, the company might elect to purchase an at-the-money put option written on the exposed currency. Buying such a put option would, in effect, limit the company's loss associated with currency depreciation to the amount of the put premium. In effect, by buying a put option, the company buys insurance against currency depreciation. The cost of this insurance is the put premium. By insuring against loss in this way, however, the company also gives up some of the potential gains it might realize from currency appreciation in that it must pay a cash premium to buy the put.

Speculative positions can also be achieved by using options. A directional position is taken when a company or individual uses options to bet on a belief that the underlying asset price will move in one particular direction. If an entity believes that the British pound will appreciate, for example, then it could buy a call option written on the pound (i.e., go "long" British pounds). Because the currency could easily move in the "wrong" direction, (i.e., contrary to one's prior beliefs), buying currency call options does not secure a profit, nor does this transaction cover an already exposed position. But still, because of the inherent asymmetry of potential upside gains and downside losses, the holder stands to gain quite a bit, while potentially losing only the amount of the premium paid for the call option. This would be a more powerful way to speculate on the pound's movement than simply buying the currency in the spot market because, for a given amount of dollars, considerably more currency can be controlled through the purchase of relatively inexpensive option contracts than can be done by buying pounds outright on the spot foreign exchange market (a standard option contract on British pounds would provide an investor with a call option on £62,500 for a price in the vicinity of $1500; the same amount of currency might cost $95,000 to $100,000 on the spot market).

Forwards and Futures

Forwards and futures, like options, are derivative securities that can be used as a means of hedging or risk management, as well as to speculate. Predating any other derivative instrument, the privately traded forward contract serves as the foundation for its more standardized exchange-traded variant, the futures contract. While these two contracts are viewed and traded quite differently, they both operate under the same essential framework. Specifically, both the forward and the futures contract are defined by an obligation of the buyer and the seller both to perform under the specified terms of the contract. In this respect, forward and futures contracts differ fundamentally from option contracts. Because options give the owner the right but not the obligation to exercise the option, option contracts provide owners with asymmetric payoff patterns that are well suited to insuring against loss under certain circumstances. Because forwards and futures provide an obligation to transact at a prespecified future price, they are better suited for true "hedging" activities in which transacting parties wish to lock in future prices without risk. Figure C provides a payoff diagram of a generic forward contract to illustrate and distinguish these particular forms of derivative securities from options. (Note that F = Forward price.)

FIGURE C
Total Payoff on a Forward Contract

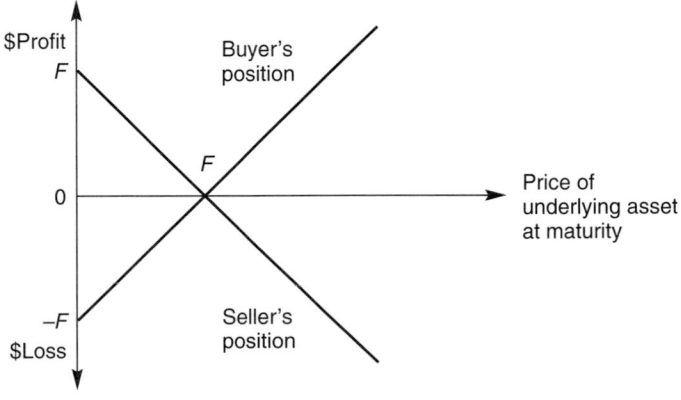

Forward Contracts

In contrast to exchange-traded derivatives, forward contracts are not standardized products. Instead, forward contracts are OTC derivatives that can be tailored to meet specific user needs. The underlying assets of these contracts include traditional agricultural or physical commodities, currencies (referred to as foreign exchange forwards), and interest rates (referred to as forward rate agreements or FRAs). A forward transaction typically involves a contract, most often with a bank, under which both the buyer (or holder) of the contract and the seller (or writer) of the contract are obligated to execute a transaction at a prespecified price on a prespecified date. That is, the seller is *obligated* to deliver a specified asset to the buyer on a specified date in the future. Likewise, the buyer is *obligated* to pay the seller a specified price (the forward price) upon delivery. If, at maturity, the actual spot market price is higher than the forward contract's exercise price, the contract holder makes a profit and the seller suffers a loss; if the spot price is lower, the contract seller makes a profit and the buyer suffers a loss. In any event, one party's gain is the other party's loss.

Normally, a forward contract's exercise price is fixed at inception at a level that makes the contract's value zero in the eyes of both the buyer and the seller. That is, ignoring risk aversion, both sides of the transaction would be roughly indifferent between entering into the contract at the specified exercise price or remaining unhedged. However, as the value of the underlying asset changes throughout the life of the contract, the value of the forward contract as seen by the buyer and the seller also changes. Specifically, the value changes for the benefit of one party and at the expense of the other. This property of the forward contract makes it a "zero-sum game" for the buyer and the seller.

To illustrate this zero-sum characteristic, consider a forward contract written on some specified asset with a forward exercise price for the asset of $50. Now imagine how a sudden upswing in the asset's price to $55 will affect both parties' views of the value of the contract. The party on the sell side of the forward contract views the contract to have lost value because the price at which he or she is obligated to sell the asset ($50) is now below that which could be received in the spot market ($55). In contrast, the party on the buy side of the contract sees this change as positive because, as the spot price of the asset increases, there is a better chance that the forward exercise price will be below the prevailing spot market price in the future when the forward contract matures and the asset is to be delivered. If this market condition persists until the specified delivery date, the seller's loss of $5 ($55–$50) equals the buyer's gain.

To summarize, both the buyer and the seller of a forward contract view their positions as having zero initial value. The agreed-upon forward price for the underlying asset is the contract price that fulfills this initial condition; that is, the forward price is determined so as to eliminate any initial value for either party. Subsequent changes in the spot market price of the underlying asset will lead to equal but opposite gains on the part of the buyer and seller.

Cost of Carry, Arbitrage, and Forward Prices. To understand how the correct forward price is determined, one must first appreciate the concepts of *cost of carry* and, again, *arbitrage*. Simply stated, the cost of carry is the opportunity cost that would be borne by an investor if the asset underlying a forward contract were actually bought and held rather than the forward contract itself. In the simplest possible case, this would essentially be the cost of money; that is, the opportunity cost of tying up one's money in the asset in question, thereby foregoing its use in other investments. For some underlying assets, however, ownership requires storage and the incurrence of *storage costs* (e.g., rental of space in a grain silo, rental of vault space, insurance costs). Storage costs, if any, add to the cost of carry.

Offsetting some of the cost of carry are cash payouts on the underlying asset (e.g., cash interest payments on debt securities or cash dividend payments on shares of stock) and so-called *convenience yields*. A convenience yield is the value that might be associated with actually owning, and therefore being able to use, the asset in question rather than simply having a future claim on that asset. A manufacturer that uses a lot of copper, for example, might wish to own a fairly sizable inventory of copper to assure that shortages are not experienced as demand for output fluctuates. Likewise, heavy users of fuel oil will often prefer to own oil itself rather than oil futures to safeguard against unanticipated interruptions in supply.

Consider now an asset such as gold, which provides no cash payouts, and capital market conditions in which the 1-year yield on Treasury bills is 10%. For simplicity, assume further that under current market conditions, the convenience yield on gold equals storage costs. Under these simplified conditions, the cost of carry on gold is simply the cost of money. If someone were to purchase gold with cash in the spot market for \$375 per ounce and hold it for a year, money would be tied up for a year, thereby imposing an opportunity cost on the investors of 10%, or \$37.50—resulting in a total cost of \$412.50 per ounce of gold by the time it is used or sold 1 year later.

This opportunity cost could be avoided if the investor elected instead to enter into a forward contract that would oblige him or her to pay cash for gold a year later, but not before. What would be a fair price to agree to pay 1 year later? In principle, the investor should be happy to pay any price less than or equal to \$412.50, for at such prices, the investor should be no worse off, and possibly better off, than buying gold and holding it for a year. Similarly, the party writing the forward contract should be happy to sell the contract at any price equal to or greater than \$412.50, for such prices would permit the writer to buy and hold gold for a year, thus eliminating the risk of future price changes in the spot market, while also at least covering his or her cost of carry. The interests of both the buyer and the seller can be met at their mutual break-even price of \$412.50 = \$375 × (1 + .10).

This pricing equilibrium implies the following simple formula for determining the forward price of an asset:

$$F_n = S(1 + c)^n$$

where

F_n = the forward price of an asset n years into the future
S = the current spot price for the asset
c = the annual cost of carry, expressed as a fraction of the asset's spot price (e.g., .01, .05, etc.)
n = years to maturity

Because c is composed of several different costs and yields, the forward price can also be expressed more fully as

$$F = S(1 + r_f + s - i - v)^n$$

where

r_f = the riskless rate of return
s = storage costs
i = cash yield
v = convenience yield

All are expressed as annual costs or yields as a fraction of the spot price.

Forward contracts in which the forward price is established at inception, according to the above formula, will have an initial value of zero. Notice that any other forward price would lead to a potential arbitrage opportunity. Suppose, for example, that a forward contract on gold such as that described above was struck at a below-market forward price of $400 per ounce. This being the case, and assuming ample supplies of gold in storage, arbitrageurs could lock in a riskless profit by simultaneously buying that which is relatively "cheap" (gold in the forward market) and selling that which is relatively "expensive" (gold in the spot market).

Specifically, an arbitrageur would:

	Per ounce cash proceeds
1. Borrow some gold and sell it (i.e., "short" gold)	$375.00
2. Invest the proceeds of the sale for 1 year at 10%	(375.00)
3. Enter into a 1-year forward contract to purchase gold at $400.00/oz.	—
Net proceeds	$0.00

One year later, the same arbitrageur would:

	Per ounce cash proceeds
1. Collect the proceeds from the 1-year investment	$412.50
2. Use the proceeds to execute the forward agreement to buy gold at $400/oz.	(400.00)
3. Deliver the gold to the party from whom it was originally borrowed	—
Net proceeds	$12.50

In effect, market arbitrageurs would make a riskless profit of $12.50 per ounce of gold on zero net investment. This arbitrage opportunity arises because the forward price is too low given the current spot price and the cost of carry. To eliminate this arbitrage opportunity, forward and/or spot prices for gold must adjust until the forward price formula shown above is satisfied.

Notice that if a forward contract's underlying asset does not have a significant cash payout relative to the cost of money, and/or if storage costs significantly exceed convenience yields, the cost of carry will be positive and the current forward price will be greater than the spot price. This premium of the forward price over the spot price is known as *contango*. Typical examples of assets with low or no cash payouts are stock indices and foreign exchange.[2] The opposite will be true if there are large cash payouts

---

2. In the particular case of foreign exchange, the forward price must take account of two interest rates because two currencies are involved. "Shorting" one currency implies borrowing it at prevailing interest rates in that currency, while investment in the other currency will take place at that other currency's prevailing interest rates. The formula for determining the forward exchange rate between a domestic currency (d) and a foreign currency (f) is as follows:

$$F = S \times (1 + R^d)/(1 + R^f)$$

where

F = forward rate of exchange, expressed as units of domestic currency per unit of foreign
S = spot market rate of exchange, expressed as units of domestic currency per units of foreign
R^d = domestic interest rate
R^f = foreign interest rate

or when the convenience yield is especially high (a common occurrence for many commodities when supply conditions in the spot market become quite tight). Under these conditions, the forward price will be below the spot price, a condition known as *backwardation*. Notice too that, regardless of how high or low the forward price is relative to the spot price at the time the forward contract is established, the forward price eventually converges with the spot price as the time to delivery shortens to zero. This is because the cost of carry in an asset necessarily becomes less as the time to delivery approaches.

Futures Contracts

Futures contracts, unlike forwards, trade on organized exchanges. They are traded in three primary areas: agricultural commodities, metals and petroleum, and financial assets. While commodity futures have been traded since the 1860s, financial futures were first traded in 1972 with the advent of the foreign currency future. Since then, financial futures have been established for various debt instruments, stock market indices, and foreign currencies.

The basic form of the futures contract mirrors that of the forward contract: Both parties are obligated under the terms of the contract to deliver a specified asset or pay the specified price of the asset on the contract maturity date. In addition, the futures contract entails the following two obligations, both of which help to minimize the default (or credit) risk inherent in forward contracts.

1. The value of the futures contract is "settled" (i.e., paid or received) at the end of each trading day. In the language of the futures markets, the futures contract is *cash settled*, or *marked-to-market*, daily. The marked-to-market provision effectively reduces the performance period of the contract to a day, thereby minimizing the risk of default.
2. Both buyers and sellers are required to post a performance bond called *margin*. At the end of each trading day, gains and losses are added to and taken away from the margin account, respectively. The margin account must remain above an agreed-upon minimum or the account will be closed. The margin provision prevents the depletion of accounts, which, in turn, largely eliminates the risk of default.

With these additional features in mind, a futures contract can be thought of as a connected series of 1-day forward contracts in which the forwards are settled and restruck daily until the specified maturity date. By definition, a futures contract is an agreement between the seller of the contract and the buyer of the contract in which the seller is obligated to deliver a specified asset to the buyer on a specified date in the future and the buyer is obligated to pay the seller the then prevailing futures price upon delivery. The nature of marked-to-market defines the "then prevailing futures price" simply as the then prevailing spot price. Therefore, upon final settlement of a futures contract that has reached maturity, the only profit and loss incurred is that associated with the last day's market movement.

Applications

The two generic uses for forwards and futures are speculation and hedging. As an example of forward market speculation assume an investor expects the dollar price of the Japanese yen to fall dramatically over the next 90 days. Foreign currency markets allow such an investor to bet on his or her expectations. First, the investor sells yen forward at the prevailing forward spot rate. After 90 days, assuming the yen depreciated as expected, the investor then purchases yen in the spot market for delivery on the forward contract. If all goes well, the forward price at which the investor sells yen will exceed the future spot price a which he or she buys, and a profit will result from the difference. Of course, if the opposite is true and the yen strengthens against the dollar, the investor will lose the difference between the future spot rate and the forward price.

Hedging, unlike speculation, is a tactic used to avoid or limit risk. Forward and futures contracts are commonly used for this purpose. For example, assume an investor will hold some specified asset for 1 year and is fearful of price depreciation over the holding period. To hedge against price depreciation by locking in a known value today, the investor could sell a forward contract written on the asset; that is, he could sell the asset forward, just as the investor in the previous speculation example sold the yen forward. In doing so, the investor covers his or her "long" position in the asset with a "short" position (the forward sale). Losses that might occur on the long position will be offset by gains on the short position, and vice versa. In this way, uncertainty about the future market value of the asset in question can be eliminated.

Swaps

A swap is any agreement to a future exchange of one asset for another, one liability for another, or more specifically, one stream of cash flows for another. The most common swaps include currency swaps, in which one currency is exchanged for another at prespecified terms on one or more prespecified future dates, and interest rate swaps, in which one type of interest payment (e.g., interest payments that float with LIBOR[3]) is exchanged for another (e.g., fixed interest payments) at one or more prespecified future dates. Like other derivative securities, these swaps (as well as more sophisticated swaps not addressed in this note) are used by various entities such as corporations, banks, and investors to hedge risk or to speculate in the expectation of making a profit. As a tool of risk management, swaps offer considerable flexibility and cost savings to their users. The boom in swaps transactions since the early 1980s is testament to the growing demand for flexible and standardized risk management products.

Although its origins can be traced back to the 1970s, the swap market did not publicly exist until 1981 when currency swaps were first introduced. U.S. interest rate swaps followed in 1982 as rising interest rate volatility necessitated a flexible means by which companies with floating interest rate exposures could hedge such risk. As swap markets grew, swaps became common adjuncts to financings, particularly cross-border financings, as a way to help companies lower their funding costs. They did so by enabling companies to source capital in whatever market or currency it was found to be cheapest (e.g., floating-rate Swiss francs), and then to convert the resulting liability into whatever form made most sense (e.g., fixed-rate dollars). Today it is a common practice of major borrowers to analyze funding opportunities in light of relative pricings for new debt issues and swaps across global markets.

Like a forward or futures contract, a swap is a private agreement between two parties in which both parties are *obligated* to exchange some specified cash flows at periodic intervals for a fixed period of time. In contrast to a forward or futures contract, a swap agreement generally involves multiple future points of exchange. The

---

3. LIBOR stands for the London Interbank Offered Rate. It is the interest rate offered by banks for dollar deposits in the London market. It is frequently used as a base interest rate for dollar loans.

cash flows of a swap may be fixed in advance, or adjusted for each settlement date by reference to some specified interest rate, such as LIBOR, or other market yield. Although it is convenient to describe swaps as involving an outright exchange of cash flows at the so-called *settlement dates*, in practice, it is generally the case that a *difference check* is simply paid by whichever party in the swap is obligated to pay more cash than is to be received at that settlement date. For example, consider a fixed-for-floating interest rate swap agreement that requires one party to pay a fixed rate of interest of 9% a year on $100 million of principal in exchange for receiving from a counterparty interest equal to LIBOR plus ½% on $100 million. If, at the first settlement date, LIBOR is equal to 7.5%, the party paying a fixed rate would owe the floating-rate counterparty a net payment of $1 million: $[.09 - (.075 + .005)] \times \$100$ million. If, at the next settlement date, LIBOR had risen to 9%, the fixed-rate party would receive a net cash payment of $.5 million from the floating rate counterparty: $[.09 - (.09 + .005)] \times \$100$ million. All of these settlements would be carried out by a financial intermediary such as an investment or commercial bank.

Also, like forward or futures contracts, swaps are priced so as to have zero value at inception. As interest rates or exchange rates change, the swap agreement then takes on positive value for whichever party becomes a net recipient of cash, and negative value for the counterparty that is the net payer of cash. In a sense, a swap agreement can be thought of as a prepackaged bundle of forward contracts, and its cash flows can be decomposed into the equivalent cash flows of these individual forward contracts.

Currency Swaps

In its simplest form, a currency swap is an agreement between two parties to exchange a given amount of one currency for another and to repay these currencies with interest in the future. As an example, consider one party, Global Enterprises, Inc. (Global) that has borrowed 200 million Swiss francs (SF) at 6% and wishes to transform this liability into dollars. At the same time, the World Financial Institution (WFI), which actively manages the currency mix of its debt portfolio in light of changing economic conditions, wishes to convert a $100 million obligation bearing 8% interest into a Swiss franc liability. Both companies' obligations have a 4-year maturity and are rated AAA. The prevailing spot exchange rate between the Swiss franc and the U.S. dollar is SF 2.00/$1.

Given these "matching," or opposite, hedging needs, a mutually satisfactory swap could be arranged in which Global agrees to pay 8% dollar interest to WFI for 4 years plus $100 million at maturity, and WFI agrees to pay Global 6% Swiss franc interest for 4 years plus SF 200 million at maturity. In this way, each borrower would have its debt service to its respective lender exactly covered, and each would be left with a payment stream in the currency of its choice. Figure D illustrates this arrangement and the cash flows entailed.

In practice, one party in a swap agreement seldom makes payments directly to the counterparty. When parties to a swap are matched directly, a financial institution usually intermediates the agreement, guaranteeing each party that payments in the needed currency will continue uninterrupted even if the counterparty defaults. The intermediary is paid a fee for acting as guarantor.

The most common swap arrangement is one in which the intermediary itself acts as the swap counterparty to its corporate clients. Major international banks make a market in currency swaps by quoting bid and offer rates for payments in various currencies for various maturities. The bid rate and the offer rate are the fixed rates of

FIGURE D
FX Swap Illustration

Swap Diagram

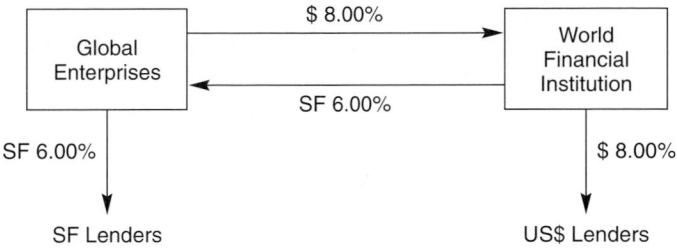

Swap Cash Flow Diagram (millions)

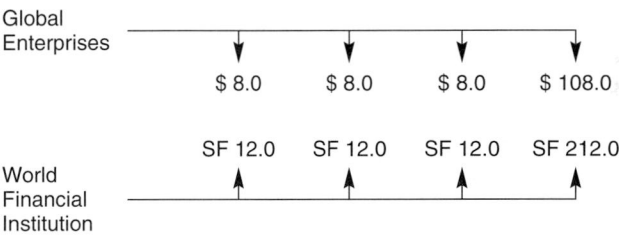

return in a specified currency that a bank is willing to pay a corporate client in exchange for receiving six-month dollar LIBOR, or to receive from a corporate client in exchange for paying six-month dollar LIBOR. For example, foreign currency swap rates being quoted by Morgan Guaranty, Ltd. in London on December 16, 1985, are shown in Table C.

The bank earns a profit on swap transactions by realizing the spread between its bid and offer rates on six-month dollar LIBOR. Notice that by relating any two quotes to dollar LIBOR, fixed swap rates can be quoted between any two currencies. For instance, using the quotes in Table C, the bank would be willing to pay yen for 3 years

TABLE C
Selected Swap Rates, December 16, 1985[a]

	3 Years		5 Years	
	Pay	**Receive**	**Pay**	**Receive**
U.S. dollars	8.79%	8.97%	9.42%	9.58%
British sterling	11.49	11.70	11.45	11.66
Japanese yen	7.12	7.28	7.02	7.17
Swiss francs	5.10	5.35	5.35	5.60
Deutsche marks	5.80	6.10	6.45	6.75

a. All quotes are fixed annual rates against six-month dollar LIBOR, and quoted from the swap dealer's perspective. That is, the bank is willing to pay British sterling at a fixed annual rate of 11.49% in exchange for receiving six-month dollar LIBOR, and to receive British sterling at a fixed annual rate of 11.70% in exchange for paying six-month dollar LIBOR.

at a fixed annual rate of 7.12% in exchange for receiving deutsche marks for 3 years at a fixed annual rate of 6.10%, and to receive yen at a fixed annual rate of 7.28% in exchange for paying deutsche marks at a fixed annual rate of 5.80%.

Applications

Currency swaps, like other derivative instruments, are often used by corporations, banks, and government entities to hedge foreign exchange risk on both assets and liabilities. In this capacity, a currency swap functions much like a series of long-dated forward foreign exchange contracts.

One of the most common applications of currency swaps is their use in conjunction with debt issues. Companies sometimes find that they can source capital especially cheaply by selling debt denominated in a foreign currency. At the same time, however, they may wish to avoid the exchange rate risk associated with such foreign currency debt. A currency swap allows such companies to capture the low-cost capital while avoiding exchange rate risk. In effect, currency swaps allow corporate financial officers to uncouple the market in which financial execution takes place from the currency of the liability that they ultimately incur. In addition to transforming new debt, swaps are also flexible tools for companies to transform the currency denomination of existing debt. To cite a well-known example of such an application, the World Bank pursues a swap program to fine-tune its liability structure by actively swapping into and out of different currencies to achieve the lowest possible debt costs.

Interest Rate Swaps

An interest rate swap is a derivative transaction in which an asset or liability with a floating rate of interest can be converted into a fixed-rate instrument, or vice versa. Like a currency swap, an interest rate swap is a counterparty transaction in which the respective positions of two counterparties with equal but opposite needs are exchanged.

Principal payments are not exchanged in interest rate swaps. This is because the dollar value of the principal remains the same throughout the contract for both the fixed-rate asset or liability and the floating-rate asset or liability. The agreed "notional" principal is only used as a basis for calculating the fixed- and floating-rate payment streams. These payments are made, or more commonly netted by the use of a difference check, on specified periodic settlement dates. While the fixed rate of interest is set for the life of the contract, the floating interest rate is set at the beginning of each interval and typically based on three- or six-month LIBOR.

An example of a typical U.S. dollar-denominated interest rate swap might involve a company that wants to convert a portion of its fixed-rate debt to floating rate, perhaps because it has acquired some assets generating cash flows that will vary directly with short-term interest rates. To achieve this conversion, the company's treasurer could call a swap dealer at a major bank to obtain quotes on interest rate swaps. As with currency swaps, dealers in interest rate swaps typically make a market in six-month LIBOR. That is, swap dealers quote a bid rate, which is the fixed rate of interest the bank will pay in exchange for receiving six-month LIBOR (i.e., the "price" at which the bank stands ready to "buy" six-month LIBOR), and an offer rate, which is the fixed rate of interest the bank is willing to accept as payment in exchange for paying six-month LIBOR (i.e., the "price" at which the bank stands ready to "sell" six-month LIBOR).

TABLE D
Interest Rate Swap Quotes[a]

Years	Bid	Offer
3	8.79%	8.97%
5	9.21	9.36
7	9.48	9.63

a. Rates are quoted from the bank's perspective. Thus, the bank is willing to pay a fixed rate of interest of 8.79% in exchange for receiving six-month LIBOR for 3 years, and to receive 8.97% in exchange for paying six-month LIBOR for 3 years.

Swap rate quotes made in London by Morgan Guaranty, Ltd. on December 16, 1985, are shown in Table D.

Given these quotes, a company wishing to get out of fixed-rate debt into floating-rate debt for, say, 5 years could do so by agreeing to pay the bank six-month LIBOR in exchange for receiving fixed-rate payments of 9.21%, which could then be used to cover a portion of the interest on its outstanding fixed-rate debt obligations.[4]

Applications

Interest rate risk is the leading reason that corporations use swaps. They are typically used to insure against loss in value of existing corporate liabilities and assets due to unexpected changes in interest rates. For example, a corporation that has recently taken on a substantial amount of debt might want to adjust the duration of its debt to match better the duration of its expected cash inflows, thereby reducing the exposure of the corporation's market value to interest rate risk.

In addition to hedging, corporations often use interest rate swaps to reduce debt costs. There are three principal ways by which these swaps might provide cost savings: (1) speculating on market movements, (2) exploiting arbitrage opportunities, and (3) reducing transactions costs. A corporation can speculate on the direction of interest rates by swapping in and out of fixed- and floating-rate agreements in hopes of achieving lower borrowing rates. Of course, this sort of speculation can result in higher borrowing costs if interest rates move in an adverse direction.

A corporation might also reduce borrowing costs by exploiting arbitrage opportunities arising from an ability to source either fixed- or floating-rate debt at particularly attractive rates in one market compared to another. A company wishing to issue fixed-rate debt might, for example, discover that it can command unusually low rates in the Eurodollar floating-rate note market. The company can exploit this opportunity by issuing the floating-rate notes, thus securing the low-cost funds, and then entering into an interest rate swap that would convert the floating-rate debt to fixed rate. In this respect, like currency swaps, interest rate swaps enable corporate treasurers to uncouple the market in which they source funds from the desired interest rate structure of their debt obligations. In the early days of the swap market, funding could be obtained at savings of as much as 50 basis points given the significant arbitrage opportunities that were then available. Today, due to more integrated capital markets, arbitrage savings are rarer and more commonly below 20 basis points.

---

4. In practice, the bid rate by the bank may not cover precisely the fixed rate of interest that the company must pay to its debt holders. When this occurs, an adjustment is made by adding or subtracting an appropriate number of basis points to the fixed rate paid and six-month LIBOR received.

Finally, transaction costs of an interest rate swap are relatively lower than those of its predecessor, the interest rate forward contract (forward rate agreements), due to the standardized nature of the swap market. Thus, interest rate swaps represent an attractive risk management and cost-savings tool for an increasingly wide range of market participants.

Basis Rate Swaps

A basis rate swap is essentially an interest rate swap in which both interest rates are floating. In effect, a basis rate swap allows a borrower or investor to exchange cash flows determined by one floating interest rate for cash flows determined by another floating interest rate. For example, a corporation could transform a loan based on six-month LIBOR to the same loan based on one-month commercial paper rates.

A basis rate swap can be thought of as two interest rate swaps paired together. One of the pair would be a floating-for-fixed swap, and the other would be an exchange of the fixed rate with another floating rate. For example, a company could swap a six-month LIBOR obligation for a fixed rate, and then swap the fixed rate with another counterparty for another floating-rate obligation based upon commercial paper rates. The basis rate swap conveniently rolls into one transaction what would otherwise be two using conventional fixed-for-floating interest rate swaps.

EXHIBIT 1
Survey of the Use of Derivatives by CFOs

A. Percent of affirmative answers to the question: What kind of derivatives, if any, does your company use?

Foreign exchange forwards	64.2%
Interest rate swaps	78.9
Foreign exchange options	40.4
Oil and energy-linked swaps	11.9
Other commodity-linked swaps	14.7
Exchange-traded interest rate futures and options	29.4
Exchange-traded foreign exchange futures and options	11.0
Exchange-traded equity futures and options	10.1
OTC interest rate futures and options	13.8
Equity-linked swaps	4.6
Equity swaps	2.8

B. Percent of affirmative answers to the question: For what purpose does your company use derivatives?

To hedge floating rate debt	52.7%
To hedge commercial paper issuance	23.2
To create synthetic floating-rate debt at a lower cost	35.7
To create synthetic fixed-rate debt at a lower cost	43.8
To access capital markets globally	15.2
To hedge investments overseas	36.6
To achieve strategic liability management	40.2

Source: Institutional Investor, CFO forum, February 1993.

Glossary

American option   See **Option**.

Arbitrage   Profiting from price differences on the same security, currency, or commodity traded in two or more markets.

At-the-money   Term used to describe an option contract that has an exercise price equal to the current market price of the underlying asset.

Backwardation   Pricing situation in which forward and futures prices are higher for those contracts expiring in the near future than those expiring farther out.

Bid/ask spread   Difference between the bid price (the highest price a prospective buyer is prepared to pay for a particular security) and the ask price (the lowest price a prospective seller is willing to accept for the same security).

Call option   See **Option**.

Contango   Pricing situation in which forward and futures prices get progressively higher as maturities get progressively longer.

Cost of carry   Out-of-pocket costs incurred while an investor has an investment position.

Deep-in/out-of-the-money   Call option whose exercise price is well below the current market price of the underlying asset (**deep-in-the-money**) or well above the current market price of the underlying asset (**deep-out-of-the-money**). The situation would be exactly opposite for a put option.

Default (credit) risk   Financial risk that a debtor will fail to make timely payments of interest and principal as they come due, or to meet some other provision of a financial agreement.

Derivative instrument   Financial instrument whose value is based on that of another underlying security.

Difference check   Form of direct, one-way payment upon settlement of a financial contract.

European option   See **Option**.

Ex-dividend   The absence of the right to receive a cash dividend payment already declared on a stock.

Exercise price   Price at which some security underlying a derivative instrument can be purchased or sold on or before the contract's maturity date.

Expiration date   See **Maturity date**.

Forward contract   Privately traded contract to buy or sell a specific amount of some underlying asset at a specified price on a specified future date.

Futures contract   Standardized exchange-traded contract to buy or sell a specific amount of some underlying asset at a specified price on a specified future date.

Guarantor   Entity that takes on a contingent liability by assuming the responsibility for payment of a debt or perfor-

mance of some obligation if the party primarily liable fails to perform.

Hedging   The reduction of risk by eliminating the possibility of future gains or losses (e.g., by buying or selling forward and futures contracts).

Insurance   The reduction of risk by the purchase of contingent claims (e.g., put options, call options, guarantees, insurance policies) that offset future losses by paying off under those circumstances in which losses are expected to be incurred.

In-the-money   Term used to describe an option contract that has an exercise price below the current market price of an underlying asset in the case of a call option, and above the current market price of the underlying asset in the case of a put option.

Intrinsic value   For call options, the greater of zero and the difference between the market value of the call's underlying asset and its exercise price. For put options, the greater of zero and the difference between the put's exercise price and the market value of its underlying asset.

London Interbank Offered Rate (LIBOR)   Rate that the most creditworthy international banks dealing in Eurodollars charge each other for large loans.

Margin   Amount of cash an investor deposits with a broker when borrowing from the broker to buy securities. If the price of the security purchased "on margin" falls, the broker will require the investor to put up more "margin" by making additional cash deposits.

Mark-to-market   Adjust the recorded value of a security or portfolio to reflect actual current market values.

Market value (or price)   The price at which willing buyers and sellers trade similar items in a free and open market.

Maturity date   Date on which payment on some financial contract becomes due and payable. In the case of options, the maturity date is the final date on which the option owner can buy or sell the underlying asset.

Option   The right, but not the obligation, to buy or sell some specified underlying asset for a specified price on (or before) a specified date.

- **Call option**   Gives its buyer the right to buy some underlying asset at a fixed price on or before a specified date in the future.

- **Put option**   Gives its buyer the right to sell some underlying asset at a fixed price on or before a specified date in the future.

- **American option**   Option that can be exercised on or before the expiration date.

- **European option**   Option that can be exercised only on the expiration date.

Option premium   Price an option buyer must pay an option seller for an option contract.

Out-of-the-money   Term used to describe an option contract that has an exercise price above the current market price of the underlying asset in the case of a call option, and below the current price of the underlying asset in the case of a put option.

Over-the-counter (OTC)   Market in which securities transactions are conducted through a telephone and computer network connecting dealers in stocks and bonds, rather than on the floor of an organized exchange.

Put-call parity   Relationship between put and call option prices that, if held in parity, prevents arbitrage opportunities.

Put option   See **Option**.

Settlement date   Date by which an executed order must be settled, either by a buyer paying for the securities with cash or by a seller delivering the securities and receiving the proceeds of the sale for them.

Speculation   Assumption of risk in anticipation of gain, but often implying a higher than average possibility of loss.

Spot price   Current delivery price of some physical commodity or financial asset traded in the spot market.

Strike price   See **Exercise price**.

Swap   Exchange of one asset or liability with particular terms and conditions for another asset or liability with different terms and conditions for a specified period of time.

Transaction costs   Cost of buying or selling a security, which consists mainly of the brokerage commission, the dealer markdown or markup, or fee (as would be charged by a bank).

Zero-coupon security   Security that makes no periodic interest payments but instead is sold at a deep discount from its face value.

The Keller Fund's Option Investment Strategies

The Keller All-Star Growth Fund (the Keller Fund) was a medium-sized closed-end investment company with approximately $300 million invested primarily in publicly traded common stocks. Shares in the fund were owned by a large number of individual investors and were themselves listed and traded on a public stock exchange.

The Keller Fund's investment objective was to provide long-term capital appreciation. While some of its investments did yield dividends, income was not an important consideration in its selection of stocks. Since its inception in 1985, the fund sought to achieve this objective by investing in a diversified portfolio of common stocks with above average potential for growth in revenues and earnings. High technology stocks tended to dominate its portfolio. In most years, the fund's return performance equaled or exceeded that of the Standard & Poor's composite index of 500 common stocks, though its net asset value experienced greater volatility than that of the market as a whole.

A Proposal to Initiate Option Trading Strategies

At a recent board meeting, one of the fund's trustees proposed that the board consider using put and call options as a means of enhancing the fund's performance. The fund's charter permitted it to engage in options trading, though it had not yet made use of this privilege. The trustee suggested that intelligent trading in options on a regular basis might be able to improve the fund's returns, while possibly lowering its volatility. If the board did approve the initiation of an options trading policy, the fund's charter would permit the following investment strategies:

1. Buying the stock of a listed company.
2. Buying a call option on a listed stock.

This case was prepared by Professor W. Carl Kester.

Copyright © 1995 by the President and Fellows of Harvard College.
Harvard Business School case 295–096.

3. Writing (i.e., selling) a call option on a listed stock.

4. Buying a put option on a listed stock.

5. Selling a put option on a listed stock.

6. Various combinations of the above strategies.

Without committing the fund to pursue option trading, the board agreed that studying the concept would be in order. To prepare for their discussion at the next meeting, the trustees requested that a pilot study of the profits or losses resulting from selected option trading be conducted. As a first step, the fund officer assigned to oversee the pilot study decided to collect some information about option contracts on the common stock of AT&T Corporation and Lotus Development Corporation. These stocks were both being considered by the fund for possible purchase in the near future.

Option Prices

On Tuesday, January 18, 1994, the stock of both AT&T and Lotus closed at exactly $55 per share. Various put and call options for each of these stocks traded on the Chicago Board Options Exchange. As shown in Exhibit 1, the maturity of these options ranged from a few days to 2 years in the case of AT&T options (options with maturities longer than 1 year were called LEAPS). All of these contracts were so-called American options in that they could be exercised by the holder any time on or before maturity.[1]

The quoted option prices shown in Exhibit 1 were in dollars per share. Each option, however, represented a contract to buy or sell 100 shares. Thus, a call option contract quoted at, say, 5 (see the Lotus April 55 call option) would actually cost $500 per contract and would give the buyer the right to purchase 100 shares of Lotus's common stock.

Background information about AT&T and Lotus is provided in Exhibits 2 and 3, respectively.

---

1. An alternative type of option contract is a European option, which can be exercised only at the point of expiration.

EXHIBIT 1
Selected Closing Option Prices, January 18, 1994

A. Options on AT&T Corp.'s Stock[a]

Calls

Stock's Closing Price	Exercise Price	1994 Jan.	Feb.	April	July	1995 Jan.	1996 Jan.
55	30	25.0	—	—	—	—	—
55	50	5.0	—	—	6.375	7.875	10.25
55	55	0.5	1.375	2.3125	3.5	5.25	8.0
55	60	0.0625	—	—	—	—	—
55	65	—	—	—	—	1.5	—

Puts

Exercise Price	1994 Jan.	Feb.	April	July	1995 Jan.	1996 Jan.
30	—	—	—	—	—	—
50	—	—	—	—	2.0	3.25
55	0.5	1.125	2.0625	2.75	4.375	5.5
60	4.75	—	—	—	—	—
65	—	—	—	—	—	—

B. Options on Lotus Development Corporation's Stock[a]

Calls

Stock's Closing Price	Exercise Price	1994 Jan.	Feb.	April
55	55	1.375	2.875	5.0
55	60	0.0625	1.75	—

Puts

Exercise Price	1994 Jan.	Feb.	April	1996 Jan.
55	0.75	2.625	5.0	60
4.0	5.5	—	—	

a. Expiration dates are as follows: January 22, 1994; February 19, 1994; April 16, 1994; July 16, 1994; January 21, 1995; and January 20, 1996.

EXHIBIT 2
Background Information on AT&T Corp. (millions of dollars except per share data)

AT&T Corp. is the largest U.S. provider of long-distance and cellular telephone services. It is also a major supplier of telecommunications equipment, computers, information management services, and leasing and financial services. In 1993 telecommunications provided 59% of its total revenues. AT&T's stock is listed on the New York Stock Exchange.

| | | | | Per Share | | | | |
| | | | | | | Stock Price | | |
Year	Revenues	Operating Income	Net Income	Earnings	Dividends	High	Low	P/E Ratio
1989	50,976	7,634	2,697	2.50	1.20	47⅜	28⅛	19-11
1990	51,321	7,821	2,735	2.51	1.32	46⅝	29	19-12
1991	63,089	9,451	522	0.40	1.32	40⅜	29	NM
1992	64,089	9,941	3,807	2.86	1.32	53⅛	36⅝	19-13
1993	67,156	9,864	3,974	2.94	1.32	65	50⅛	22-17

AT&T Corp.'s Daily Stock Price Returns, 1993

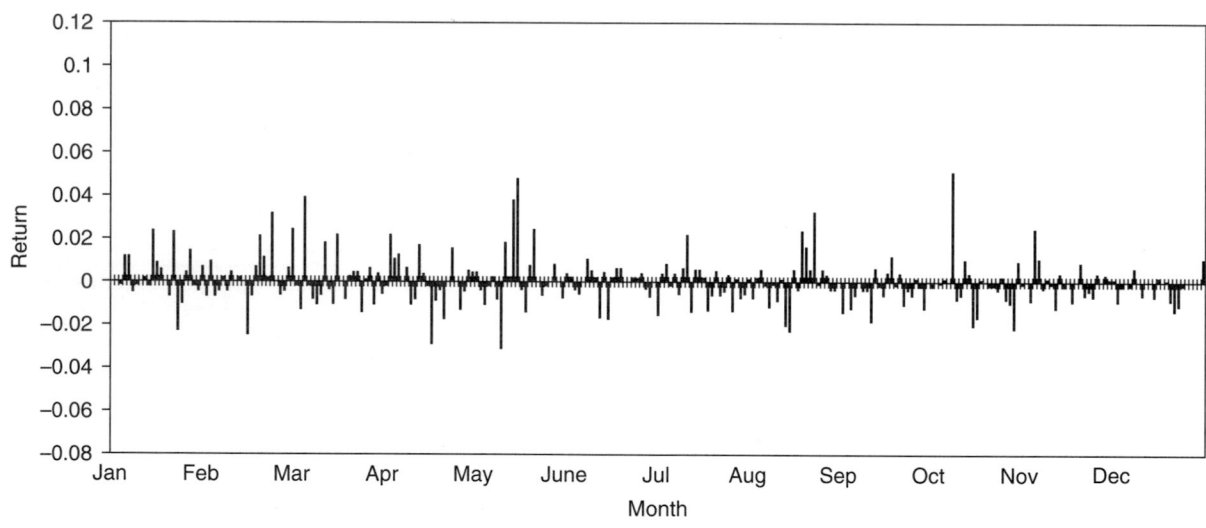

EXHIBIT 3
Background Information on Lotus Development Corporation (millions of dollars except per share data)

Lotus Development Corporation is a leading developer, producer, and vendor of applications software and information services. Its major desktop applications include spreadsheet and word-processing programs, and communications products and services, including groupware and electronic mail offerings. Lotus's stock is traded over the counter on the National Association of Securities Dealers Automated Quotation (NASDAQ) system.

| | | | | Per Share | | | | |
| | | | | | | Stock Price | | |
Year	Revenues	Operating Income	Net Income	Earnings	Dividends	High	Low	P/E Ratio
1989	556	106	68.0	1.61	Nil	33½	18	21-11
1990	692	147	23.3	0.54	Nil	39¼	12½	73-23
1991	829	154	43.1	0.98	Nil	40¾	14¾	42-15
1992	900	151	80.4	1.87	Nil	38¾	14¾	21-8
1993	981	181	55.5	1.24	Nil	58¾	18¾	47-15

Lotus Development Corporation's Daily Stock Price Returns, 1993

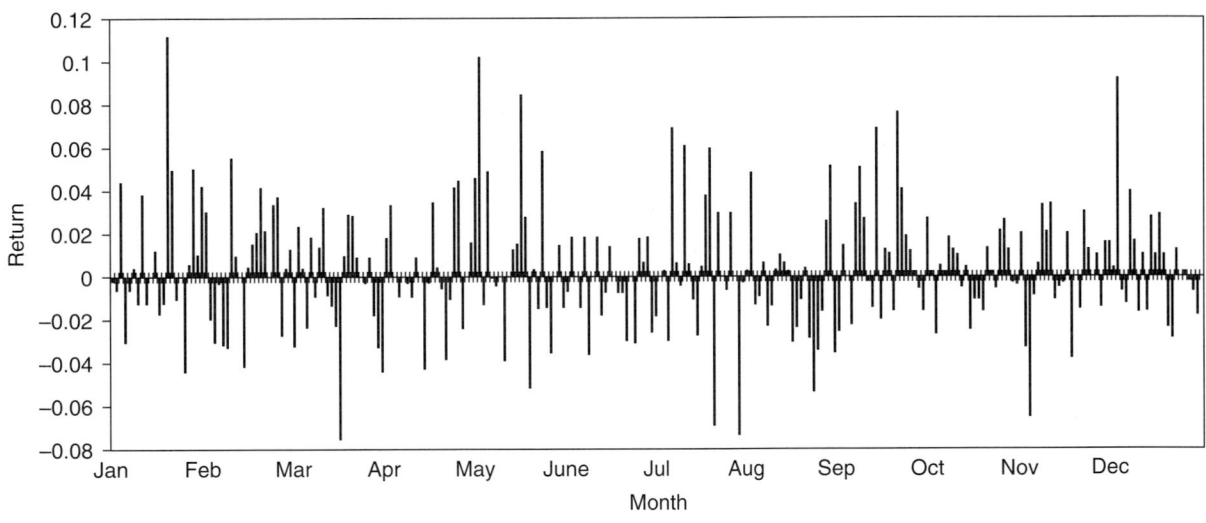

Phelps Dodge Corporation

Nineteen eighty-four had been a painful year for Phelps Dodge. As it closed its books on 1984's third quarter, the largest independent U.S. copper producer faced the inevitability of having to report annual losses for the third consecutive year. Once debt free with ample cash balances, the company's debt-to-net-worth ratio had climbed to 70%. Although the entire U.S. copper industry had been "in the pits" since the copper market collapsed in 1981, Phelps Dodge was particularly vulnerable to weak copper prices because of its present financial situation, coupled with its heavy dependence on copper. The few years following the initial downturn in copper prices had been marked by high capital expenditure needs in the face of very tight cash flow. The prospect of history repeating itself, with copper prices rebounding relatively quickly after a downturn, seemed unlikely. In fact, a market study conducted by Douglas C. Yearley, then senior vice president, had concluded that copper prices were likely to remain depressed for several years to come. Posting losses of about $25 million a quarter, it was evident that the company could not afford to wait out such a long down cycle.

In response, a five-member senior management team, including Yearley, engineered a corporate restructuring plan to present to the board of directors in November 1984. The plan called for a commitment to two critical initiatives: (1) cutting costs of its core copper business, and (2) strengthening the balance sheet. Both of these initiatives were crucial in bringing Phelps Dodge back to life in the short term.

In addition to the restructuring plan, the issue of diversification was also high on the agenda of the company's November board of directors meeting. Phelps Dodge had diversified itself somewhat during the past decade but reversed this move after noncopper ventures produced mixed results. After 3 consecutive years of net losses, a stretch unmatched by the company even during the Great Depression, the nation's largest independent copper producer wondered if diversification as a tool to achieve long-term financial health and stability was not a bad idea after all.

This case was prepared by Research Associate Kendall Backstrand under the supervision of Professor W. Carl Kester.

Company Background

Phelps Dodge Corporation, incorporated under the laws of New York in 1885, had consistently ranked among the leading North American producers of copper. As an independent producer that depended almost entirely on fluctuating copper prices, Phelps Dodge had become an anomaly in the world copper industry by 1984. In an average year, Phelps Dodge mined about 20% of the copper produced in the United States. In 1983, it produced approximately 260,000 tons of copper, about 80% of normal capacity, up from 150,000 tons in 1982.

Over nearly a century, Phelps Dodge never strayed from its original vision to be the top independent copper producer worldwide. The company's core business remained the production of copper, although it had expanded to include the production of copper rod and magnet wire as well. In 1984, Phelps Dodge consisted of two business segments: (1) primary metal and (2) manufacturing. Primary metal included copper mining, smelting and refining, copper rod production, and ancillary activities related to mining and smelting operations. The majority of Phelps Dodge's copper concentrate production took place in the southwestern United States, where it owned three open-pit copper mines (the Morenci mine at Morenci, Arizona; the New Cornelia mine at Ajo, Arizona; and the Tyrone mine at Tyrone, New Mexico). Copper precipitates were also produced at Morenci and Tyrone. These concentrates and precipitates were then smelted at the company's four copper smelters (at Morenci, Ajo, and Douglas, Arizona, and at the Hidalgo smelter at Playas, New Mexico). Of mining operations, Morenci accounted for 65% of total capacity, followed by Tyrone at about 25%. Most of the copper from these facilities was then cast into rod. A major source of revenue for the primary metal division came from its production of copper, which was primarily sold in the form of rod to outside wire and cable manufacturers. In addition, primary metal included the production of other metals such as silver, gold, and molybdenum; copper chemicals (produced principally as by-products); and sulfuric acid from air-quality-control facilities. These peripheral operations generally contributed only minimally to the division's total revenue. In total, primary metals accounted for 53% of the company's revenues and all of its operating losses.

The manufacturing division accounted for about 47% of Phelps Dodge's total sales. Included in this division was Phelps Dodge Magnet Wire, which produced magnet wire and bare and stranded wire. Also included in this division was Phelps Dodge International Corporation (PDIC), another subsidiary that managed various interests in companies that produced wire and cable in 14 foreign countries.

In 1984, Phelps Dodge's principal investments included a 16.25% interest in Southern Peru Copper Corporation; a 44.6% interest in Black Mountain Mineral Development Company (Pty.) Limited, which operated a lead-silver-zinc-copper mine in South Africa; and a 100% interest in Western Nuclear, Inc., a subsidiary that produced uranium oxide for sale to the nuclear power industry. All three of these investments had consistently fallen short of their anticipated financial goals.

In the first three quarters of 1984, Phelps Dodge had lost a total of $51 million on sales of $692 million. By comparison, it had earned $61 million on sales of $1,094 million by the end of the third quarter in 1981, the last fairly representative year for the copper industry before the copper crash. The third quarter of 1984 continued a losing streak for Phelps Dodge stretching back ten straight quarters. Total losses since 1981 amounted to $188 million, or $8.65 per share. Relevant financial statements for Phelps Dodge are provided in Exhibits 1 and 2, and a 5-year performance summary is provided in Exhibit 3.

The Changing Copper Industry

During the decades leading up to 1984, the world copper industry had been transformed from one in which demand drove prices and production to one in which supply seemed insensitive to demand and prices. The reason for this transformation was largely due to a gradual change in the industry's ownership structure. In the 1950s, the copper production capacity was almost entirely owned by independent copper companies like Phelps Dodge. By the early 1980s, it was estimated that approximately 40% of the world's copper supply was controlled by governments, primarily among developing nations. Another 35% was owned by noncopper companies, the majority of them being oil companies. Last in the order of control were independent copper companies, such as Phelps Dodge, Asarco Incorporated, and Newmont Mining Corporation, which owned about 25% of the industry's capacity (a comparison of the major independent U.S. producers appears in Exhibit 4).

In the 1960s, governments such as Chile and Peru became focused on copper production as a means of providing jobs and accumulating hard currency. As the growth rate of refined copper consumption (4%) remained slightly above the growth rate of mine capacity (3.8%) from 1960 to 1973, these state-owned producers entered the market without creating serious ripples. However, since 1974, consumption had remained relatively flat, while supply had increased by a total of 22%. With generally lower-cost mines and richer ore bodies, state-owned producers flooded global markets with cut-rate copper, despite weakening demand. In Chile, for example, state-owned Codelco turned out refined copper at a cost of about 45¢ per pound, while Phelps Dodge's lowest-cost operations were producing at costs barely under 70¢ per pound. The result was structural overcapacity followed by dismal market prices.

In the wake of mounting pressure on profit margins and cash flow, many independent copper producers fell prey to acquisition-oriented oil giants that sought to expand their natural-resource bases. Anaconda, for example, sold out to Arco in 1977. A few years later in 1981, Kennecott was acquired by Sohio for $1.8 billion. At the time, oil companies were flush with cash and, consequently, were able to provide copper companies the financial support needed to continue producing even while prices were temporarily below cost. This exacerbated the copper industry's problems, as more productive facilities owned by independent producers closed down during low-price periods, while less efficient mines remained in operation.

The Copper Crisis and Phelps Dodge's Plight

As a result of ownership changes and falling copper demand, the copper market collapsed in 1981. The price of copper per pound quoted on the COMEX (Commodity Exchange) fell from a high of about $1.40 in 1980 to the mid-70¢ range by the end of 1981. Once thought of as a cyclical yet buoyant market in which a sharp downturn was quickly followed by a healthy recovery in anticipation of stronger demand, the saturated copper market of the early 1980s was not expected to be as resilient. This proved, in fact, to be an understatement. In 1984 copper prices dipped even further to hover just above 60¢ per pound despite a rebound in consumption followed by shrinking stockpiles (see Exhibit 5 for a history of copper price cyclicality).

Phelps Dodge's past earnings record was reflective of this cyclicality. Earnings plunged from $122 million to $18 million from 1974–1977, soared back up to $111 million by 1979, and then turned down again in 1980 and 1981. Phelps Dodge reported losses of $74 million and $64 million in 1982 and 1983, respectively. Unlike previous downturns, such as those experienced during the 1970s, the present situation gave no signs of a sizable recovery in the near future.

To cover operating losses that reached nearly $1 million per day in early 1982, Phelps Dodge more than doubled its short-term debt, which reached a total of $98 million in the first quarter of 1982. Then, to curb this surge in short-term debt, the company took several cost-cutting steps. First, management halted production at the Ajo and Tyrone mines and at the Douglas smelter. This led to laying off 3,800 blue-collar and salaried employees. The pay and bonuses of the remaining 4,500 salaried jobs were reduced by as much as 25%. The company's dividend payment on its common shares was first slashed by 75%, down to 10¢, and then cut entirely. Despite the need for substantial capital expenditures to pay for development and expansion projects, as well as to comply with environmental standards at its Morenci, Arizona, smelter, Phelps Dodge reduced capital expenditures from $150 million in 1981 to $100 million in 1982.

The following year was marked by similar cost-cutting and debt-reduction efforts. Labor costs were capped after Phelps Dodge ended an acrimonious year-long labor strike with its Arizona workers, whose union had demanded new higher-wage contracts. From an asset restructuring program that was launched in 1983, Phelps Dodge expected to recover more than $150 million. This program called for the sale of the company's brass foundry, tube mill, and telephone cable plants and related businesses in 1983, and the subsequent sale of its power cable and building wire operations in 1984. Phelps Dodge planned to use the proceeds to reduce debt and enhance production efficiencies. Despite these strenuous measures, Phelps Dodge was still losing money in 1984.

The 1984 Restructuring Plan

In response to the financial crisis brought about by the prolonged period of low copper prices, Douglas Yearley took the initiative to execute a long-term study of the copper market as a basis for preparing a comprehensive plan for restoring Phelps Dodge to profitability. In developing this plan, Yearley and the restructuring committee assumed an average realized copper price of 65¢ for the ensuing 3 years. To achieve a turn-around in the face of such persistently weak copper prices, the committee's plan embodied a new approach toward financial management in the copper industry. Instead of the traditional tendency to wait out the downturns, the plan demanded a more proactive approach. It defined several new initiatives that would enable Phelps Dodge to operate profitably and meet its financial obligations.

First, the committee recommended a further restructuring of copper operations to produce significant gross profits that would eventually total more than $50 million per year, even at a 65¢ price per pound. Among other actions, the plan called for the Tyrone and Morenci mining and milling facilities to be operated on a continuous basis. It also concluded that the Morenci smelter and the Ajo mine and smelter were unprofitable given the 65¢ price and called for their indefinite closure. A joint venture was recommended for the Morenci operations to enable it to keep operating at capacity. Such an arrangement would improve Phelps Dodge's financial situation by providing an immediate infusion of cash, as well as by allowing the company to avoid nearly $11 million of capital expenditures requested in the 1985 budget for the underperforming Ajo operations and Morenci smelter.

The plan also called for a 1984 write-down of assets totaling $230 million, and for a $21.2 million reduction in total overhead. The paring of overhead costs included the reduction of corporate and western office overheads by 40% from 1984's budgeted levels (achieved largely by shrinking the New York headquarters staff from 178 to 71) and a reduction of the western office staff from 149 to 52. It was also suggested that the New York headquarters be moved from Manhattan to another less costly location. In addition to the reduction of the company's primary overhead costs, the plan proposed substantial cutbacks in Phelps Dodge Mining and Wire's overhead, as well as in exploration and research and development. Capital expenditures, which were expected to reach $74.4 million by the end of 1984, would be reduced to $19 million in 1985 and to $14 million in each of the next two years.

Even with all of these major overhead reductions, the committee concluded that the operating cash flow would not cover all of the cash needs of the company. However, the committee proposed that the sale of several assets not essential to the company's core business would raise enough cash to put Phelps Dodge in a net positive cash flow position. These sales included Black Mountain, PDIC Far Eastern operations, Western Nuclear, and a 40% interest in the Morenci operations. In total, Phelps Dodge could expect to recover in excess of $250 million from these sales, including a few smaller asset sales from 1984. Regarding the company's other major assets, the plan recommended that the balance of PDIC investments and the equity in Southern Peru be sold at the earliest date at which appropriate values could be realized.

Overall, the plan forecasted a reduction in the unit costs of mining copper to less than 40¢ per pound. Shipping, smelting, refining, and freight would raise the total unit costs of production to approximately 62¢ per pound. At these levels, the plan projected a modest net profit of $2.6 million in 1985, $10 million in 1986, and $8.9 million in 1987. As Phelps Dodge was currently losing about $10 million per month, the committee emphasized in its report that immediate implementation was the key to achieving the plan's objectives.

Diversification

In addition to the particular cost-cutting initiatives set forth in the restructuring committee's plan, the subject of diversification was also an important issue to be considered at the November board meeting. While formal, detailed diversification plans had not yet been developed, diversification into noncopper businesses was an issue that top management felt deserved careful discussion. Diversification was seen by some as a means by which Phelps Dodge could receive earnings from other sources during troughs in the copper cycle. As such, diversification would help smooth earnings and cash flow for an independent copper company that was highly exposed to a deeply cyclical market. However, in light of only moderately successful diversification attempts in the past, it was not entirely clear how, if at all, such an initiative would benefit Phelps Dodge and its shareholders.

Phelps Dodge's Diversification History

The few attempts Phelps Dodge had made to diversify into noncopper areas had not generated a unanimous consensus that such a move was appropriate for the future. In 1970 the company entered into an aluminum partnership with Swiss Aluminum that, over the years, proved to be only a marginally profitable investment. By 1980 it was clear that the partnership would need a substantial amount of new capital, prompting Phelps Dodge to sell its 40% interest at an $18 million profit. Also in 1970, Phelps Dodge tried to diversify away from copper by acquiring a uranium company, Western

Nuclear. This investment also fell short of expectations, after the 1979 Three Mile Island accident pushed uranium prices down from about $40 per pound to $15 per pound virtually overnight.[1] The company's more recent venture, a 45% interest in Black Mountain in South Africa, required additional capital funds that Phelps Dodge desperately needed to use to fund domestic efforts.

In general, Phelps Dodge had been down the diversification road before, only to be met with mixed results. By the time copper-price disaster struck in 1981, Phelps Dodge had shifted gears to concentrate almost entirely on copper once again. Over the next few years, Phelps Dodge stripped even further down to its copper core in an attempt to recover significant operating losses. The strategy of the early 1980s, while providing immediate sources of badly needed cash, left the company's bottom line highly exposed to copper-price volatility. The potentially harmful consequences of such a strategy had caused critics both inside and outside the company to second-guess management's decision to refocus on copper.

Alternatives to Diversification

From time to time, Phelps Dodge had relied upon futures contracts to manage its copper inventories. Futures contracts committed buyers (sellers) to the purchase (delivery) of copper at some future date at a fixed, predetermined price. Futures contracts on copper were bought and sold on the COMEX. Copper futures contracts were for 25,000 pounds and ranged in maturity from 1 to 24 months. In 1984 the average daily trading volume of copper futures was about 10,000 contracts per day, implying an annual volume of approximately 2.5 million contracts. Less than 2% of these contracts were settled by actual delivery of copper metal. Copper futures prices in October 1984 are shown in Exhibit 6. As of 1984, option contracts on copper were not available, although the already well-established silver and gold options on the COMEX implied copper option's pending arrival.

The Board Meeting

Members of Phelps Dodge's board of directors convened in November to consider both the restructuring committee's plan and the diversification question. Clearly, the proposed cost-cutting and debt-reduction initiatives, both of which demanded immediate implementation if benefits were to be realized, were top priorities. The issue of diversification, though not as pressing in the short term, was viewed by many as a critical long-term priority. At the heart of this issue was the question of how an almost pure play in a volatile market such as copper could best meet its objective of creating the most value for its shareholders.[2]

---

1. The Three Mile Island incident involved a valve failure at the Three Mile Island nuclear power plant in Pennsylvania. As a result of the valve failure, cooling water stopped flowing, resulting in a meltdown of the reactor's uranium and the release of unknown quantities of radioactive gas.

2. In 1984 it was estimated that between 50% and 60% of Phelps Dodge's equity was owned by institutional investors. Officers and directors of the company beneficially owned 0.85% of outstanding common shares. All other shares were widely held by individual investors.

EXHIBIT 1
Consolidated Income Statements (thousands of dollars except per share data)

	December 31,	
	1982	*1983*
Sales and other operating revenues.	$ 957,795	$ 977,383
Operating costs and expenses		
Cost of products sold	925,844	910,044
Depreciation, depletion, and amortization.	56,609	67,531
Selling and general administrative expense	54,584	46,857
Exploration and research expense	25,313	20,357
	1,062,350	1,044,789
Operating income (loss)	(104,555)	(67,406)
Equity earnings (losses)	(9,875)	2,803
Earnings (losses) from operations	(114,430)	(64,603)
Interest expense	(52,022)	(45,724)
Interest and miscellaneous income	59,612	7,130
Income (loss) before taxes	(106,840)	(103,197)
Provision for taxes	32,544	39,700
Net income (loss)	(74,296)	(63,497)
Net income (loss) per common share after preferred dividend requirements	$ (3.59)	$ (2.76)
Average number of shares outstanding	21,742,298	24,273,229

EXHIBIT 2
Consolidated Balance Sheets (thousands of dollars except per share data)

	December 31,	
	1982	*1983*
Assets		
Current assets		
Cash and short-term investments, at cost	$ 18,758	$ 25,629
Receivables	133,367	143,332
Inventories	103,819	92,699
Supplies	90,078	87,957
Prepaid expenses	2,005	8,332
Deferred income tax charges	7,879	—
Current assets	355,906	357,949
Investments and long-term receivables	137,184	117,971
Property, plant, and equipment	1,513,301	1,454,046
Deferred charges	7,506	6,153
	$2,013,897	$1,936,119
Liabilities		
Current liabilities		
Short-term borrowings	$ 28	$ —
Current portion of long-term debt	8,381	13,972
Accounts payable and accrued expenses	144,640	179,909
Income taxes	39,865	31,632
Current liabilities	192,914	225,513
Long-term debt	667,212	600,263
Deferred income taxes	88,092	45,932
Other liabilities and deferred credits	39,398	36,092
	987,616	907,800
Minority interest in subsidiary	—	6,000
Redeemable preferred shares	48,290	41,290
Common shareholders' equity		
Common shares	136,004	154,018
Capital in excess of par value	45,595	110,758
Cumulative translation adjustments	(26,847)	(39,990)
Retained earnings	823,239	756,243
	977,991	981,029
	$2,013,897	$1,936,119

EXHIBIT 3
Five-Year Financial Summary, 1979–1983 (millions of dollars except per share data)

	1979	1980	1981	1982	1983
Sales and other operating revenues	$1,280.8	$1,440.1	$1,438.6	$ 957.8	$ 977.4
Earnings before interest, taxes, and					
miscellaneous items	174.7	123.9	74.5	(114.4)	(64.6)
Interest expense	(40.1)	(43.8)	(41.9)	(52.0)	(45.7)
Profit after taxes	110.8	91.3	69.3	(74.3)	(63.5)
Dividends per common share	1.20	1.55	1.60	.30	—
Earnings per share	5.06	4.20	3.12	(3.59)	(2.76)
Capital expenditures^a	106.8	126.7	147.7	100.1	59.2
Depreciation, depletion, and amortization	67.3	70.4	77.4	56.6	67.5
Total current assets	462.2	525.1	473.4	355.9	357.9
Cash and short-term investments	12.0	19.6	15.4	18.8	25.6
Total assets	2,000.2	2,112.1	2,144.4	2,013.9	1,936.1
Total current liabilities	246.5	285.5	290.8	192.9	225.5
Short-term debt	—	40.3	42.0	—	—
Long-term debt	605.6	626.7	579.5	667.2	600.3
Total liabilities	956.4	1,034.4	1,007.1	987.6	907.8
Net worth	$1,043.8	$1,077.7	$1,137.3	$1,026.3	$1,028.3
Stock price (per common share)					
High	$ 32.00	$ 48.25	$ 48.50	$ 34.00	$ 34.00
Low	20.875	25.00	31.13	18.25	22.50
Close	$ 30.875	$ 37.625	$ 33.625	$ 28.125	$ 25.25
P/E ratio	6.1	9.0	10.8	—	—
Stock beta (β)	.85	—	—	—	1.45
Standard & Poor's 500 Index	103.01	118.78	128.05	119.71	160.41

a. Includes capitalized mine development expenses.

EXHIBIT 4
Comparative Information on Major Independent U.S. Copper Producers, 1983 (millions of dollars except per share data and ratios)

A. Financial Data			
	Phelps Dodge	**Asarco**	**Newmont**
Sales	$ 997.4	$1,512.2	$ 720.9
Earnings before interest and taxes	(64.6)	38.4	20.6
Interest expense	(45.7)	(47.6)	(23.7)
Profit after taxes	(63.5)	58.3	52.9
Dividends per common share	—	.40	1.00
Earnings per share	(2.76)	1.54	1.75
Capital expenditures	59.2	105.2	147.6
Depreciation, depletion, and amortization	67.5	55.0	(56.4)
Total assets	1,936.1	2,227.1	2,091.2
Total liabilities	907.8	1,062.5	613.9
Net worth	$1,028.3	$1,164.6	$1,477.3
Debt/total capital	.37	.32	.12
Common stock price (close)	$ 25.25	$ 30.00	$ 50.75
P/E ratio	—	19.5	29
Beta	1.45	1.45	1.25

B. Lines of Business		
		Percent of Total Sales
Phelps Dodge		
Primary metals (chiefly copper)		53%
Wire and cable		47
Copper	20	
Other	80	
Asarco		
Primary metals		82%
Silver	36	
Copper	35	
Lead, zinc, gold, services, and other	29	
Asbestos		7
Recycling		6
Coal		2
Other		3
Newmont		
Gold		15%
Nonferrous metals		44
Copper	84	
Lead, zinc, nickel, and cobalt	16	
Energy		10
Other		31%

EXHIBIT 5

Copper Spot Prices on the COMEX, January 1975–October 1984 (cents per pound)

Years	High	Low	Close
1975	62.60¢	50.90¢	n.a.
1976	77.30	53.40	62.40¢
1977	71.80	51.90	n.a.
1978	69.20	54.70	69.60
1979	117.00	78.10	103.50
1980	143.10	77.05	83.75
1981	88.40	70.40	73.90
1982	74.00	54.30	68.35
1983	80.90	61.45	65.75
1984	71.10¢	54.95¢	59.45¢

EXHIBIT 6

Copper (CMX) Futures Prices for October 31, 1984 (cents per pound; 25,000 pounds per contract)

Maturity Dates	Closing Prices	Open Interest
1984		
Nov.	59.45¢	1
Dec.	59.95	39,355
1985		
Jan.	60.50	247
Mar.	61.60	26,962
May	62.75	7,956
July	63.85	4,386
Sept.	64.90	4,217
Dec.	66.40	2,659
1986		
Mar.	67.90	563
May	68.95	274
July	70.00	257

Tiffany & Company (1993)

In July 1993, Tiffany & Company concluded an agreement with its Japanese distributor, Mitsukoshi Ltd. that would fundamentally change its business in Japan. Under the new agreement, Tiffany's wholly owned subsidiary, Tiffany & Company Japan Inc. (Tiffany–Japan), assumed management responsibilities in the operation of 29 Tiffany & Company boutiques previously operated by Mitsukoshi in its stores and other locations in Japan. Tiffany looked forward to the new arrangement, as it was now responsible for millions of dollars in inventory that it previously sold wholesale to Mitsukoshi, resulting in enhanced revenues in Japan derived from higher retail prices. It was also apparent, however, that fluctuations in the yen/dollar exchange rate would now affect the dollar value of its Japanese sales, which would be realized in yen. Since Japanese sales were large and still growing, it seemed evident such fluctuations could have a substantial impact on Tiffany's future financial performance.

Company Background

Founded in New York in 1837, Tiffany & Company was an internationally renowned retailer, designer, manufacturer, and distributor of luxury goods. The famous blue-box company found its initial success in fine jewelry, most notably diamonds, but had since expanded its product line to include timepieces, china, crystal, silverware, and other luxury accessories. In the fiscal year ending January 31, 1993 (FY 1992), Tiffany earned $15.7 million on revenues of $486.4 million and had total assets of $419.4 million. Recent financial statements are provided in Exhibits 1 and 2. An historical summary of operations is provided in Exhibit 3.

After more than a century of independence, Tiffany was acquired by Avon Products, Inc. in 1979. For the next several years, Avon, a nationwide door-to-door cosmetics marketer, worked to expand Tiffany's product line to reach beyond its traditional

This case was prepared by Research Associate Kendall Backstrand under the supervision of Professor W. Carl Kester.

Copyright © 1994 by the President and Fellows of Harvard College.
Harvard Business School case 295–047.

affluent customer base to the larger middle market. While this diversification strategy resulted in enhanced sales for Tiffany from $84 million in 1979 to $124 million in 1983, operating expenses as a percentage of sales grew inordinately from 34% to 43% in 1978 and 1983, respectively. Avon soon realized that Tiffany's traditional market niche was substantially different than its own and, in 1984, decided to put the company up for sale. The most attractive offer came from Tiffany's own management, who agreed to buy back Tiffany's equity and the Fifth Avenue store building for a total of $135.5 million. In what ultimately took the form of a leveraged buyout (LBO), the terms of the deal distributed virtually all of the equity shares to three key investor groups. Management ended up with 20% of total equity shares. Investcorp, the Bahrain- and London-based merchant bank that backed management in the deal, received 49.8% of total equity shares. The third player, General Electric Credit Corporation (GECC), ended up with 25.7% of total equity shares. It was through an $85 million credit arrangement with GECC that management was able to refinance a substantial portion of the purchase price.[1]

The aftermath of the LBO was marked by very tight free cash flow coupled with significant growth potential on the horizon. After the company had once again become profitable and realizing that the company's growth prospects demanded more cash than could be generated internally, in 1987, management offered Tiffany stock to the public at approximately $15 a share (adjusted for a subsequent stock split). In 1989, Mitsukoshi purchased 1.5 million shares of Tiffany's common stock from GECC.[2] As of January 31, 1993, Mitsukoshi owned approximately 14% of Tiffany stock, the largest percentage of any single institutional investor. Three other institutional investors collectively owned approximately 26% of the stock, followed by all Tiffany executive officers and directors as a group at 4.9%.

In 1993, Tiffany was organized into three distribution channels: U.S. retail, direct marketing, and international retail. U.S. retail included retail sales in Tiffany-operated stores in the United States and wholesale sales to independent retailers in North America. The 16 stores in this channel accounted for 50% of total sales in FY 1992. Direct marketing, representing the smallest channel of distribution, consisted of corporate and catalog sales. In FY 1992, its sales represented 18% of Tiffany's total sales. International retail, which included retail sales through Tiffany-operated stores and boutiques, corporate sales, and wholesale sales to independent retailers and distributors, primarily in the Far East and Europe, accounted for 32% of total sales in FY 1992. Jewelry sales from all three channels accounted for 65% of 1993 sales, making jewelry the most significant product line. Exhibit 4 provides financial results of Tiffany's domestic and foreign operations.

The past several years for Tiffany were marked by a trend of international expansion, beginning in 1986 when it opened a flagship retail store in London. Additional flagship stores were then opened in Munich and Zurich in 1987 and 1988, respectively. In 1990, the Zurich store was expanded. Stores were opened in Hong Kong at the Peninsula Hotel and at the Landmark Center in August 1988 and March 1989, respectively. Taipei saw the opening of a store in 1990, as did Singapore (at the Raffles

---

1. This included a $75 million secured revolving credit facility; a $10 million, 16% subordinated note due in 1992; and common stock warrants to purchase approximately 25% of the company's equity on a fully diluted basis.

2. Prior to Mitsukoshi's purchase of Tiffany's common stock from GECC, Tiffany and Mitsukoshi entered into an agreement by which Mitsukoshi agreed not to purchase in excess of 19.99% of Tiffany's issued and outstanding common shares. This agreement would expire on September 31, 1994.

Hotel), Frankfurt, and Toronto in 1991. Also in 1991, the London store was expanded. In 1992, Tiffany opened five new boutiques in Japan, and two new boutiques were opened by an independent retailer in Korea. Early 1993 saw continued international growth, with the opening of two more boutiques in Japan, a second store in Singapore's Ngee Ann City, two boutiques by independent retailers in Saipan and the Philippines, and the expansion of the Peninsula Hotel store in Hong Kong.

Exhibit 5 shows the growth in the number of Tiffany stores and boutiques around the world from 31 to 79, implying a 250% increase from 1987 to 1993. These 79 retail locations included 16 stores in the United States, 56 stores in the Far East, 6 stores in Europe, and 1 store in Canada, all of which ranged in size from 700 to 13,000 gross square feet, with a total of approximately 127,000 gross square feet devoted to retail purposes.

Tiffany's worldwide capital expenditures were $22.8 million in FY 1992, compared with $41.4 million in FY 1991. These expenditures were primarily for the opening of new stores and boutiques and the expansion of existing stores. Management anticipated capital expenditures to drop further to $18.0 million in FY 1993 before rebounding to approximately $25.0 million in FY 1994. Management also expected to open four or five new stores per year in the foreseeable future.[3] To support future expansion plans, and fluctuations in seasonal working capital needs, management planned to rely upon internally generated funds and a $100 million noncollateralized revolving credit facility available at interest rates based upon Eurodollar rates, a prime rate, certificate of deposit rates, or money market rates.[4] As in the past, cash dividends were expected to be maintained at a relatively moderate level, which would permit the company to retain a majority of its earnings.

Impetus for Change in the Japanese Operations

While Tiffany found new market potential across the globe, nowhere was it as promising as in Japan, where Tiffany's sales accounted for only 1% of the $20 billion Japanese jewelry market. The thriving Japanese economy of the late 1980s and very early 1990s stimulated a booming demand for certain types of expensive and glamorous Western goods. Among these were Tiffany products, principally those of the fine jewelry line marketed toward older women. However, as the Japanese economy finally slowed and Japanese consumers became more cautious in their spending, the demand for Tiffany's luxury items also slumped. In response to soft consumer demand in Japan, Mitsukoshi cut back on Tiffany inventory levels. Mitsukoshi's wholesale purchases from Tiffany-Japan declined from 23% of Tiffany's total sales in FY 1991 to 15% in FY 1992. Declining wholesale shipments were also accompanied by a small decline in gross margin from 49.4% in FY 1991 to 48.7% in FY 1992. Despite lackluster consumer demand in the first half of FY 1993, however, Tiffany continued to believe that Japanese sales had attractive long-run growth potential. It was for this reason that Tiffany sought greater control over its future in Japan and ultimately decided to restructure its Japanese operations.

---

3. Due to the significant number of Tiffany boutiques already operating in Japan, future openings there were expected to occur only at a very modest rate, if at all, in the near-term future.

4. Tiffany's business was seasonal in nature, with the fourth quarter typically representing a proportionally greater percentage of annual sales, income from operations, and net income. In FY 1992, net sales totaled $107,238,000, $120,830,000, $105,897,000, and $152,431,000 for the first, second, third, and fourth quarters, respectively. Management expected this pattern to continue in the future.

From 1972 through July 1993, Mitsukoshi acted as the principal retailer of Tiffany products in Japan, purchasing selected goods from Tiffany-Japan on a wholesale basis. Mitsukoshi sold the products on a retail basis to the Japanese consumer, realizing profits in the form of relatively higher retail prices. Since the wholesale transactions were denominated entirely in dollars, fluctuations in the yen/dollar exchange rate did not represent a source of volatility for Tiffany's expected cash flows. Instead, Mitsukoshi bore the risk of any exchange rate fluctuations that took place between the time it purchased the inventory from Tiffany and when it finally made cash settlement. Typically, Tiffany merchandise sold by Mitsukoshi was priced at a substantial premium (100% in some cases) over the domestic U.S. retail price for such merchandise.[5]

The new agreement between the two companies, however, fundamentally changed both companies' financial situations. In repurchasing the merchandise previously sold by Tiffany to Mitsukoshi, Tiffany-Japan assumed new responsibility for establishing yen retail prices, holding inventory in Japan for sale, managing and funding local advertising and publicity programs, and controlling local Japanese management.[6] Mitsukoshi, on the other hand, would no longer be an independent retailer of Tiffany products but would still receive fees equaling 27% of net retail sales in compensation for providing boutique facilities, sales staff, collection of receivables, and security for store inventory.[7]

With greater control over retail sales in its Japanese operations, Tiffany looked forward to long-run improvement in its performance in Japan despite continuing weak local economic conditions. However, increased sales and profits were not the only changes that Tiffany could anticipate as a result of the new agreement. Tiffany now faced the risk of foreign currency fluctuations previously borne by Mitsukoshi. Past history warned Tiffany that the yen/dollar exchange rate could be quite volatile on a year-to-year, and even month-to-month, basis. Exhibit 6 illustrates the significant strengthening of the yen against the dollar during the 10 years ending in 1993. While a continuation of this strengthening would enhance the dollar value of Tiffany's yen-denominated cash inflows, there was the distinct possibility that the yen might eventually become overvalued and crash suddenly, just as the U.S. dollar did in 1985. Indeed, there was some evidence that the yen was overvalued against the dollar in 1993 (see Exhibit 7).

---

5. Tiffany management believed that a retail price reduction in Japan of 20% to 25% would likely result in a substantial increase in unit volume of jewelry sales.

6. The repurchase of inventory by Tiffany necessitated the reversal of $115 million in sales and related gross profit previously recognized on merchandise sold to Mitsukoshi. Accordingly, Tiffany recorded a $57.5 million reserve to provide for product returns, which reduced the second fiscal quarter's (ended July 31, 1993) net income by approximately $32.7 million, or $2.07 per share. Of the $115 million of sales being reversed, only $52.5 million of inventory held in Mitsukoshi boutiques was actually repurchased during the month of July 1993 (Mitsukoshi agreed to accept a deferred payment on $25 million of this repurchased boutique inventory, which was to be repaid in yen on a quarterly basis with interest of 6% per annum over the next 4 1/2 years). Approximately $62.5 million of Tiffany & Company inventory maintained in Mitsukoshi warehouses would be repurchased throughout the period ending February 28, 1998. Payment for this warehouse inventory was to be made in yen 40 days following actual receipt of the inventory.

7. Fees were reduced to 5% on certain high-value jewelry items repurchased from Mitsukoshi. Tiffany-Japan would also pay Mitsukoshi incentive fees equal to 5% of the amount by which boutique sales increase year-to-year, calculated on a per-boutique basis. In Tokyo, Tiffany boutiques could be established only in Mitsukoshi's stores, and Tiffany-brand jewelry could be sold only in such boutiques (though Tiffany-Japan reserved the right to open a single flagship store in Tokyo).

Hedging to Manage Foreign Exchange Risk

The possibility of sharp, unexpected movements in the yen/dollar exchange rate had prompted Tiffany's management to study the desirability of engaging in a program to manage exchange rate risk. To reduce exchange rate risk on its yen cash flows, Tiffany had two basic alternatives available to it. One was to enter into forward agreements to sell yen for dollars at a predetermined price in the future. The other was to purchase yen put options. The terms at which Tiffany could purchase forward contracts and put options, along with other financial market data, are shown in Exhibit 8.

Before committing Tiffany to a hedging program, management wanted to be sure it understood what the potential risks and rewards were for each of these so-called "derivative" instruments. Perhaps more importantly, it was essential to determine whether or not a risk management program was appropriate for Tiffany, what its objectives should be, and how much, if any, exposure should be covered.

EXHIBIT 1
Consolidated Income Statements (thousands of dollars)

Annual Income Statements

	Years ended January 31,	
	1992	*1993*
Net sales	$491,906	$486,396
Cost of goods sold	248,897	249,363
Gross profit	243,009	237,033
Selling, general, and administrative expenses	180,939	209,140
Provision for uncollectible accounts	1,042	1,152
Income/(loss) from operations	61,028	26,741
Interest expense and financing costs	6,337	7,231
Other income	375	415
Income/(loss) before income taxes	55,066	19,925
(Benefit)/provision for income taxes	23,261	4,213
Net income/(loss)	$ 25,470	$ 15,712

Second Quarter Income Statements (thousands of dollars)

	Six months ended July 31,	
	1992	*1993[a]*
Net sales	$228,068	$223,714
Product return for Japan realignment	0	(115,000)
	228,068	108,714
Cost of goods sold	119,481	117,486
Cost related to product return for Japan realignment	0	(57,500)
Gross profit	108,587	48,728
Selling, general, and administrative expenses	92,578	99,792
Provision for uncollectible accounts	458	906
Income/(loss) from operations	15,551	(51,970)
Other expenses, net	3,453	3,410
Income/(loss) before income taxes	12,098	(55,380)
(Benefit)/provision for income taxes	5,106	(23,867)
Net income/(loss)	$ 6,992	$ (31,513)

a. Data reflect the loss in net income for the second fiscal quarter ending July 31, 1993, due to the repurchase.

EXHIBIT 2
Consolidated Balance Sheets (thousands of dollars)

	July 31, 1993	Years ended January 31, 1992	Years ended January 31, 1993
Assets			
Current Assets			
Cash and short-term investments	$ 6,665	$ 3,972	$ 6,672
Accounts receivable, less allowances			
of $4,170 and $7,293	51,432	51,687	51,378
Income tax receivable	10,630	—	—
Inventories	247,891	213,435	224,151
Prepaid expenses	14,058	12,777	10,107
Total current assets	$330,676	$281,871	$293,408
Property and equipment, net	$ 96,320	$ 88,975	$ 94,454
Deferred income taxes	21,205	5,047	5,723
Other assets, net	26,204	18,989	25,770
Total assets	$474,405	$394,882	$418,255
Liabilities and Stockholders' Equity			
Current Liabilities			
Short-term borrowings	$ 24,235	$ 43,566	$ 22,458
Accounts payable and accrued liabilities	98,497	66,781	61,919
Income taxes payable	0	7,371	2,679
Merchandise and other customer credits	6,029	4,687	5,318
Total current liabilities	$128,761	$122,405	$ 92,374
Long-term trade payable	$ 26,472	—	—
Reserve for product return	31,768	—	—
Long-term debt	101,500	50,000	101,500
Deferred income taxes	0	7,957	3,858
Postretirement benefit obligation	14,510	11,960	13,560
Other long-term liabilities	$ 1,921	$ 2,521	$ 2,157
Shareholders' Equity			
Common stock, $.01 par value; authorized 30,000			
shares, issued 15,660 and 15,620	$ 157	$ 159	$ 156
Additional paid-in capital	69,969	67,927	69,553
Retained earnings	107,002	129,364	140,705
Foreign currency translation adjustments[a]	(7,655)	2,680	(5,608)
Total stockholders' equity	$169,473	$200,039	$204,806
Total liabilities and shareholders' equity	$474,405	$394,882	$418,255

a. The accounting for foreign exchange translation gains and losses is governed by the Statement of Financial Accounting Standards #52 (FASB #52). Under this accounting method, all foreign assets and liabilities are translated at the exchange rate prevailing on the balance sheet date. Equity accounts are translated at historical rates. Income statement items are translated either at the prevailing rate on the date that a sale or purchase occurred, or a weighted average of exchange rates for the appropriate period. An important provision in FASB #52 is that translation gains and losses are *not* flowed through the income statement. Instead, they are booked directly to a separate equity account such as "Foreign Currency Translation Adjustments" or "Cumulative Translation Adjustment." Only if and when an asset is sold or liquidated does the realized translation gain or loss move from the translation adjustment account to flow through the income statement.

EXHIBIT 3
Historical Summary (thousands of dollars except per share amounts)

	January 31,					
	1988	*1989*	*1990*	*1991*	*1992*	*1993*
Summary of operations						
Net sales	$230,488	$290,344	$383,964	$455,712	$491,906	$486,396
Income/(loss) from operations	33,691	44,193	60,977	67,806	61,028	26,741
Interest expense and financing costs . .	2,174	826	2,578	4,475	6,337	7,231
Income/(loss) before income taxes . . .	31,194	43,032	58,387	63,475	55,066	19,925
Net income/(loss)	$ 16,176	$ 24,901	$ 33,305	$ 36,661	$ 25,470	$ 15,712
Capital expenditures	$ 1,895	$ 9,680	$ 14,040	$ 24,835	$ 41,385	$ 22,754
Depreciation and amortization	1,118	1,634	3,455	5,487	8,134	11,425
Common shares outstanding	12,570	15,370	15,560	15,670	15,870	15,620
Income/(loss) per share	$ 1.17	$ 1.62	$ 2.13	$ 2.34	$ 20.1	$ 1.00
Cash dividends per share	—	$ 0.10	$ 0.18	$ 0.26	$ 0.28	$ 0.28
Dividend payout (%)	0.0%	6.0%	8.0%	11.0%	14.0%	28.0%
Financial position						
Net working capital[a]	$ 66,772	$ 89,082	$127,074	$162,265	$203,032	$220,813
Inventories	70,778	103,771	142,545	173,964	213,435	224,151
Total assets	126,669	162,648	237,061	307,268	394,882	419,355
Total debt	—	7,253	32,565	49,272	93,566	123,958
Shareholders' equity	71,621	99,193	135,568	176,183	200,039	204,806
Book value per share	$ 5.70	$ 6.29	$ 8.71	$ 11.24	$ 12.61	$ 13.11
Average annual P/E	14.5	14.3	19.8	16.9	24.2	34.0
Stock price						
High	$ 27.30	$ 29.70	$ 61.30	$ 53.80	$ 57.50	$ 52.90
Low	$ 9.70	$ 14.00	$ 26.00	$ 27.50	$ 32.60	$ 23.00
Equity beta (β)						1.35
Selected ratios						
Current ratio	2.4	2.5	2.5	2.3	2.3	3.2
Net profit margin (%)	7.3%	8.6%	8.7%	8.0%	6.5%	3.2%
Return on assets (%)	13.0%	15.0%	14.0%	12.0%	8.0%	4.0%
Return on equity (%)	23.0%	25.0%	25.0%	21.0%	16.0%	8.0%
Asset turnover	1.82	1.79	1.62	1.48	1.25	1.16
Total debt/total capital (%)	0.0%	4.0%	14.0%	16.0%	24.0%	30.0%

a. Excluding short-term borrowings.

EXHIBIT 4
Domestic and Foreign Operations (thousands of dollars)

	Years ended January 31,	
	1992	*1993*
Domestic		
Net sales	$439,055	$414,558
U.S.	316,282	326,828
Export	122,773	87,730
Income/(loss) from operations	98,229	73,559
Identifiable assets	278,730	287,127
Foreign		
Net sales	52,851	71,838
Income/(loss) from operations	3,888	2,381
Identifiable assets	116,152	132,228

EXHIBIT 5
Worldwide Retail Locations

| End of Fiscal Year | Tiffany's Subsidiary Companies | | | | | Independent | | Total |
| | North America and Europe | | | Pacific Rim | | | | |
	U.S.	Canada	Europe	Japan	Elsewhere	Mitsukoshi	Others	
1987	8	0	2	0	0	21	0	31
1988	9	0	3	0	1	21	0	34
1989	9	0	5	0	2	24	0	40
1990	12	0	5	0	3	27	0	47
1991	13	1	7	0	4	38	2	65
1992	16	1	7	7	4	36	4	75
1993	16	1	6	37	5	8	6	79

EXHIBIT 6
Yen/Dollar Exchange Rates (end of period)

Year/Month	Yen/Dollar	Year/Month	Yen/Dollar
1983	231.70	1992	
1984	251.60	January	125.55
1985	200.25	February	129.15
1986	158.30	March	132.92
1987	121.25	April	133.30
1988	125.05	May	127.75
1989	143.80	June	125.87
1990	135.75	July	127.20
1991		August	123.08
January	131.45	September	120.07
February	132.95	October	123.45
March	140.60	November	124.75
April	136.38	December	124.86
May	138.45	1993	
June	137.90	January	124.80
July	137.42	February	118.00
August	136.85	March	116.65
September	132.85	April	111.60
October	130.60	May	107.25
November	130.08	June	106.35
December	124.90		

End-of-Year Exchange Rates

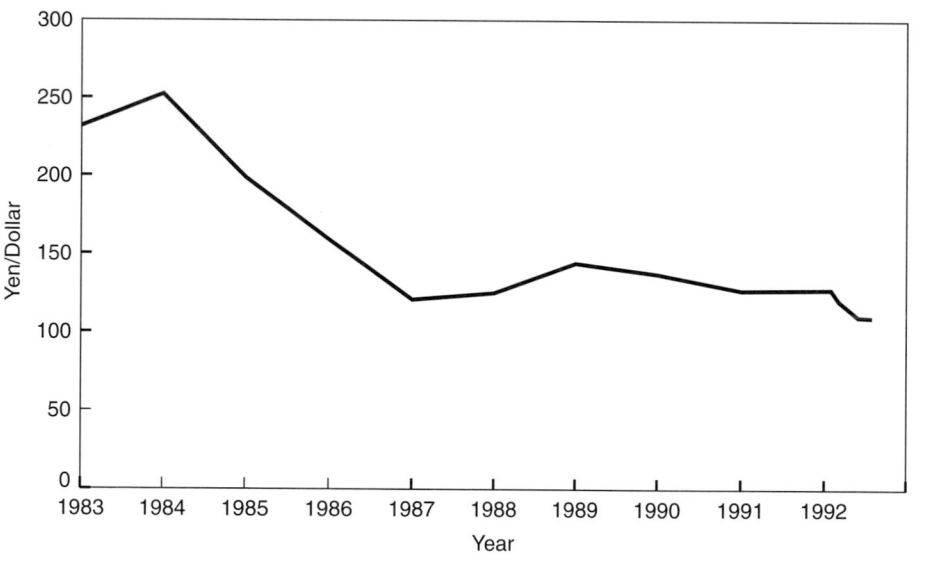

EXHIBIT 7
Japanese Yen: Percent Over-/Under-Valued versus U.S. Dollar[a]

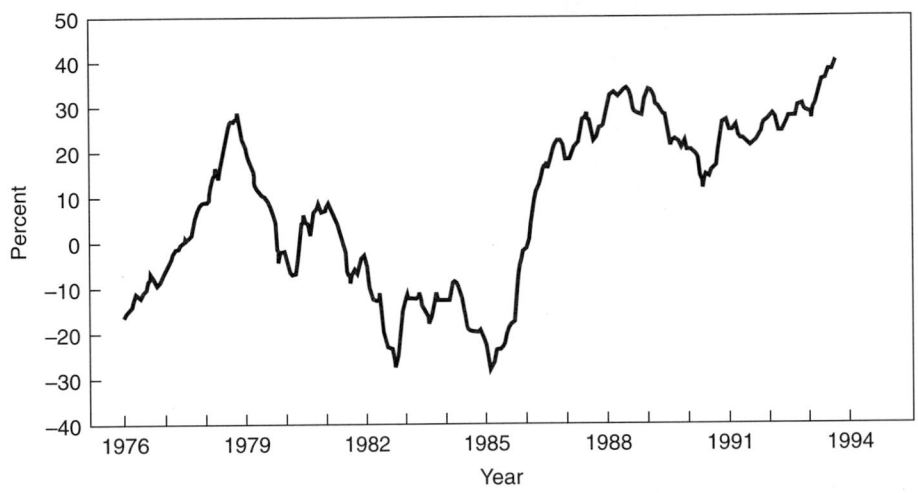

Source: Currency and Bond Market Trends (Merrill Lynch, October 1994), p. 22.

a. Estimates of over- and under-valued percentages are based on long-run purchasing power parity estimates. The Purchasing Power Parity (PPP) theory of exchange rate determination holds that long-run trends in exchange rates are determined by cumulative differences in national inflation rates. Specifically, PPP maintains that $S = P_F/P_D$, where S is the spot exchange rate expressed as foreign currency per unit of domestic currency, P_F is the foreign national price level, and P_D is the domestic national price level. Relative PPP stipulates that $\dot{s} = \dot{p}_f - \dot{p}_d$, where $\dot{s}$ is the rate of change in the exchange rate, and $\dot{p}_f$ and $\dot{p}_d$ are the national rates of inflation in the foreign and domestic currencies, respectively. Currencies that weaken faster (or strengthen more slowly) than the rate justified by the difference in national inflation rates are said to be depreciating in *real* terms. Likewise, currencies that strengthen faster (or weaken more slowly) than the rate justified by the inflation rate difference are said to be appreciating in *real* terms.

EXHIBIT 8
Selected Financial Market Data (end of month)

A. Interest Rates

1993 Eurodollar Interest Rates (percentage)

	One Month	Three Months	Six Months	One Year
January	3.1250	3.2500	3.3750	3.6875
February	3.1250	3.1250	3.2500	3.5000
March	3.1250	3.1875	3.3125	3.5625
April	3.0625	3.1250	3.2500	3.5000
May	3.1875	3.3125	3.4375	3.8125
June	3.1250	3.2500	3.5000	3.6875

1993 Euroyen Interest Rates (percentage)

	One Month	Three Months	Six Months	One Year
January	3.5000	3.4375	3.3750	3.3125
February	3.2188	3.2813	3.2188	3.2188
March	3.5313	3.4063	3.4063	3.4063
April	3.2188	3.2188	3.2813	3.3125
May	3.2500	3.2500	3.3438	3.4375
June	3.1875	3.1875	3.1876	3.2501

B. 1993 Yen/Dollar Exchange Rates (yen per dollar)

	Spot	Forward	
		One Month	Three Months
January	124.800	124.845	124.865
February	118.000	118.015	118.025
March	116.650	116.665	116.675
April	111.600	111.605	111.605
May	107.250	107.255	107.230
June	106.350	106.355	106.330

(continued)

EXHIBIT 8 *(concluded)*

C. June 1993 Yen/Dollar Foreign Currency Option Prices (100ths of a cent per yen; each option contract is for ¥6,250,000

Strike Price	Month of Maturity			Strike Price	Month of Maturity		
	July	August	September		July	August	September
Calls				*Puts*			
87.0				87.0			0.36
89.0				89.0			0.54
90.0				90.0	0.25	0.50	0.92
91.0			3.32	91.0			1.04
91.5				91.5		0.85	
92.0	1.54		2.52	92.0	0.57	1.07	1.44
92.5				92.5	0.94	1.12	1.63
93.0	1.02			93.0	1.16		
93.5			2.22	93.5	1.22		2.06
94.0	0.94	1.46	1.99	94.0	1.26		
94.5	0.66	1.15		94.5			
95.0	0.59	1.21	1.33	95.0			
96.0		0.70	0.93	96.0			
97.0		0.55	0.78	97.0			
98.0			0.59	98.0			

The B.F. Goodrich–Rabobank Interest Rate Swap

On Monday, March 7, 1983, B.F. Goodrich and Rabobank simultaneously executed two financings and an interest rate swap, the net effect of which was: (1) to provide U.S. investors with an attractive and unique LIBOR-based floating-rate note; (2) to provide Eurobond market investors with an attractive AAA fixed-rate bond; (3) to raise $50 million of floating-rate Eurodollar financing for Rabobank; and (4) to raise $50 million of fixed-rate, 8-year financing for Goodrich. It was apparently one of those rare and satisfying financial arrangements in which everyone believed he or she had emerged a clear winner.

The Company

B.F. Goodrich was a diversified manufacturer of tires and related rubber products, chemicals and plastics, and a wide variety of industrial products, components, and systems. Among other businesses, it was the fourth-largest U.S. producer of tires and the largest U.S. producer of polyvinyl chloride (PVC) resins and compounds.

The steep recession of 1982 had caused significant financial difficulties for Goodrich, as it had for most other companies in comparable businesses. Exhibits 1 and 2 show relevant balance sheets and income statements for the company. Goodrich's earnings and cash flow had been adversely affected, its credit rating had been downgraded from BBB to BBB-, and it was about to announce the $33 million loss for 1982 shown in Exhibit 2.

The Financing Problem

Early in 1983, Goodrich needed $50 million to fund its ongoing financial needs. In theory, it could have merely borrowed $50 million more from its committed bank lines, with a borrowing cost slightly above the prime rate (plus compensating balances). But

This case was prepared by Professor Jay O. Light.

Copyright © 1984 by the President and Fellows of Harvard College.
Harvard Business School case 284–080.

Goodrich was reluctant to consume a substantial part of its remaining short-term availability under those lines or, for that matter, to compromise its future flexibility by borrowing in the short- to intermediate-term (2–5 years) range. It wanted to borrow longer term, in either the 8–10-year range or perhaps in the 30-year range, and it wanted fixed-rate money. The problem was clear, though. With the general level of interest rates quite high and with its lowered credit rating, long-term fixed-rate money would be quite expensive. For example, with 30-year U.S. Treasuries yielding around 10.30% in the current market, Goodrich believed it would have to pay around 13% for a 30-year corporate debenture.

The Financing Opportunity

Salomon Brothers, however, had come to Goodrich with another suggestion. As Salomon explained the idea, Goodrich could borrow in the U.S. public debt market with a floating-rate debt issue tied to LIBOR (the London interbank offering rate) and then swap interest payments with a Euromarket bank that had raised funds in the fixed-rate Eurobond market. While there had never been a public debt security tied to LIBOR in the U.S. domestic market before, Salomon Brothers was confident it could be done. In fact, Salomon thought that many U.S. thrift institutions would be eager potential buyers of such a security. As Salomon explained, the recent deregulation of deposit markets had allowed deposit institutions (both commercial banks and thrift institutions) to offer new variable-rate money market deposit accounts and super now accounts, and this had caused an interesting set of circumstances in the domestic floating-rate markets. Large thrift institutions, and particularly the large mutual savings banks in eastern cities like New York, had been aggressively pricing their new deposit accounts in early 1983 and successfully recapturing flows of funds from the money market funds, broker-sponsored cash management accounts, and the open-market instruments that had disintermediated them in recent years. These huge new inflows of deposits had to be invested, however, and the dangers of their traditional investments, 30-year fixed-rate residential mortgages, were clear to the savings bankers. Alternatively, they could invest in short-term Treasury bills, the large CDs of commercial banks (domestic or Euro CDs), or perhaps the floating-rate notes of major U.S. banks whose yields were tied to Treasury bill notes. Or alternatively, as Salomon Brothers explained, they might be interested in buying Goodrich floating-rate notes with a yield tied to LIBOR.

The Rabobank Nederland

The Rabobank was a major Dutch banking organization, one of the world's 50 largest, with assets exceeding 110 billion Dutch guilders (approximately $42 billion). The organization consisted of more than 1,000 agricultural cooperative banks (Rabobanks), which had a network of 3,100 local offices in the Netherlands. The banks traditionally serviced the agricultural sector and smaller communities, acting as savings banks and lenders to Dutch farmers. They were all connected through a central cooperative bank, the Centrale Rabobank, which operated on behalf of the individual banks in the domestic and international money markets. Not only was Rabobank a dominant factor in the agricultural sector, providing about 90% of all loans to farming and agribusiness, but the organization had also moved into commercial lending and other traditional banking activities in more recent years. It was believed to have relations with one-third of all Dutch companies and to hold 40% of all Dutch savings as deposits. Even the central Rabobank, however, was not particularly well known outside the Netherlands. Though it was rated AAA, it had never borrowed in the Eurobond market before. It conducted only a small amount of dollar-based business, and most of the dollar-denominated assets were loans whose rates floated with LIBOR. It was able to fund those assets through interbank deposits at LIBOR or prime Eurodollar CDs. Though it has a small branch office in New York City, few American investors had ever heard of Rabobank.

The London branch of a major U.S. bank had approached the central Rabobank and proposed to syndicate a large fixed-rate Eurobond issue with the ultimate intention of swapping interest payments with a U.S. corporation. Rabobank agreed, in principle, to explore the transaction. As its willingness to swap became known, quite a few offers from potential counterparties came pouring into Rabobank. From these offers, Rabobank and their U.S. bank (the potential syndicator of the Eurobond issue) selected Salomon Brothers' Goodrich proposal.

The Swap

While agreed to in principle, the swap was still a difficult piece of financial innovation to effect. Its relative attractiveness was critically dependent upon the fluctuating spreads between interest rates, in particular the relation between domestic U.S. and Euro rates. Moreover, two public debt issues had to be sold in completely separate markets as close to simultaneously as possible.

On the first Friday of March, the relation between relative interest rates seemed favorable, and commitments were made over the weekend such that, by Monday, the overall transaction was ready to be completed. There were, in fact, three separate and virtually simultaneous parts of the swap.

As the first part of the transaction, Salomon Brothers underwrote and sold a B.F. Goodrich 8-year floating-rate note in the U.S. bond market. It was generally believed that most of the note issue was sold to a number of mutual savings banks located in major metropolitan regions. The terms of the note were as follows:

Issuer:	B.F. Goodrich
Credit rating:	BBB
Amount:	$50 million
Maturity:	8 years (noncallable)
Coupons:	The notes will bear interest, payable semiannually, at an annual rate equal to the future prevailing three-month Eurodollar London interbank rate (LIBOR) + .50%.

On the same Monday, the Rabobank-Nederland issued an 8-year fixed-rate bond in the Eurobond market. The terms were as follows:

Issuer:	Rabobank-Nederland (the central organization)
Credit rating:	AAA
Amount:	$50 million U.S. dollars
Maturity:	8 years, noncallable
Coupon:	An annual coupon, fixed at 11%

The two issuers then executed a pair of bilateral swap agreements with the Morgan Guaranty Bank as an intermediary guarantor. In particular, one swap agreement included these provisions:

- B.F. Goodrich agreed to pay the Morgan bank $5.5 million once each year for 8 years to cover the 11% fixed annual coupon.
- The Morgan bank agreed to pay to B.F. Goodrich 8 years of semiannual payments, each equal to one-half (because they were semiannual) of $50 million times a floating rate. The floating rate would be set equal to the future prevailing three-month London interbank rate minus a discount (LIBOR − x), where the size of this discount was undisclosed.

And similarly, the other swap agreement included an identical set of provisions:

- The Morgan bank agreed to pay the Rabobank $5.5 million once each year for 8 years.
- The Rabobank agreed to pay the Morgan bank the 8 years of semiannual payments at three-month LIBOR − x.

As the structure of the provisions suggests, Morgan Guaranty was merely agreeing to serve as a passive conduit for the swap payments between the two principals, assuming there would be no default. In the event of a default by one party, however, Morgan would continue its agreement with the other party.[1] In effect, by entering into separate bilateral agreements with each party, Morgan was guaranteeing each party's role in the swap to the other. Because of Morgan's AAA rating and international reputation, this guarantee effectively lowered whatever credit risk might have otherwise been present in the swap agreement to acceptable levels for Rabobank. In exchange for assuming this role, Morgan Guaranty received from Goodrich a one-time initial fee of $125,000 and an undisclosed annual fee for each of the next 8 years.[2]

Exhibit 3 displays the level of market interest rates on Monday, March 7. Exhibits 4, 5, and 6 display the recent history of various short-term interest rates. At the time, other issuers, investment bankers, and commercial bankers were quite intrigued with this entire swap transaction. As one commercial banker put it, "There is no way Goodrich could have gotten that pricing from their banks. It's almost off the market, it's so good."[3]

---

1. Also, if Goodrich defaulted under its bilateral obligation to pay the fixed-rate stream to Morgan, it could not collect the floating-rate stream from Morgan. The swap was strictly a two-way or no-way transaction. The same was true of the bilateral agreement between Rabobank and Morgan.

2. While the annual fee on this particular deal was undisclosed, it was reasonably well known that during the most recent six months the going rate for these fees in the swap market had ranged from as low as 8 or 10 to as high as 37.5 basis points times the principal amount. There was, however, some considerable controversy, both among and within financial institutions, as to what really was an appropriate fee for these guarantees.

3. *Institutional Investor*, July 1983, p. 39.

EXHIBIT 1
Balance Sheets at December 31, 1979–1982 (millions of dollars)

	1979	*1980*	*1981*	*1982*
Cash and marketable securities	$ 67	$ 40	$ 212	$ 45
Accounts receivable	438	515	512	371
Inventory	467	522	464	400
Property, plant, and equipment	851	925	1,333	1,341
Other	258	214	200	214
Total assets	$2,081	$2,216	$2,721	$2,371
Short-term bank debt	$ 35	$ 49	$ 12	$ 17
Accounts payable	467	447	487	445
Other	45	35	142	67
Short-term liabilities	547	531	641	529
Long-term debt	376	475	644	503
Capitalized lease obligations	63	58	101	99
Deferred taxes and other accruals	148	163	208	187
Total liabilities	1,134	1,227	1,594	1,318
Net worth	947	989	1,127	1,053
Total liabilities and net worth	$2,081	$2,216	$2,721	$2,371

EXHIBIT 2
Income Statements for Years Ending December 31, 1979–1982 (millions of dollars)

	1979	*1980*	*1981*	*1982*
Sales	$2,988	$3,080	$3,185	$3,005
Costs of products sold	2,279	2,367	2,455	2,311
Sales, general, and administrative expenses	548	587	631	643
Operating profit	161	126	99	51
Interest expense	44	56	60	84
	117	70	39	(33)
Income from sales of tax benefits	—	—	73	9
Gain on sale of subsidiary companies and disposition of operations	2	8	41	(27)
Equity in earnings of foreign associate companies	5	10	14	(14)
Other income	8	2	(4)	(2)
Income	131	89	162	(68)
Less provision for income taxes	45	25	68	(38)
Less minority interests	3	3	2	3
Plus extraordinary gain	—	—	18	—
Net income	$ 83	$ 62	$ 110	$ (33)

EXHIBIT 3
Market Interest Rates, March 7, 1983

Domestic Markets		*Eurodollar Markets*	
Federal funds rate (interbank rate):	8.05%		
Prime rate:	10 5/8%		
3-Month Maturities			
Treasury bills	8.07%	Prime Eurodollar CDs	8.50%
Prime domestic CDs	8.40%	LIBOR	8.75%
Yankee CDs	8.55%		
		7–10-Year Fixed-Rate Eurobonds[a]	
7–10-Year Fixed-Rate Bonds		*(U.S. dollar obligations)*	
Treasuries	10.10%	AAA Eurobonds	10.71%
Federal agencies	10.40		
AAA industrials	10.50		
AA industrials	10.70		
BBB industrials	12–12.5%		
7–10-Year Floating-Rate Notes[a,b]		*7–10-Year Floating-Rate Notes[a]*	
AAA bank holding cos.	T-bills + 1.00%	Foreign gov't guaranteed	LIBOR + 1/4
AA bank holding cos.	T-bills + 1.25%	AAA banks	LIBOR + 1/4 − 3/8%
30-Year Fixed-Rate Obligation			
Long-term bonds			
Treasuries	10.30%		
AAA Industrial	11 1/4–11 1/2%		
BBB Industrial	12 3/4–13%		
Residential mortgages			
FHA insured	12 1/2–13%		
Conventional	13–13 1/2%		

a. All of these rates are quoted here on a semiannual equivalent yield basis, the conventional yield to maturity basis used in the domestic U.S. bond markets. In the Eurobond markets, bonds typically pay interest annually, not semiannually as in the United States. An 11% Eurobond (with annual coupons) would have a semiannual equivalent yield to maturity of 10.71%, not 11% $[(1.11)^{.5} − 1] \times 200$.

b. This is a thin market where almost all notes have been issues by high credit quality bank holding companies. It is difficult, therefore, to estimate market rates other than for these AAA and AA bank notes.

EXHIBIT 4
Short-Term (three-month) Yields, January 1980–February 1983

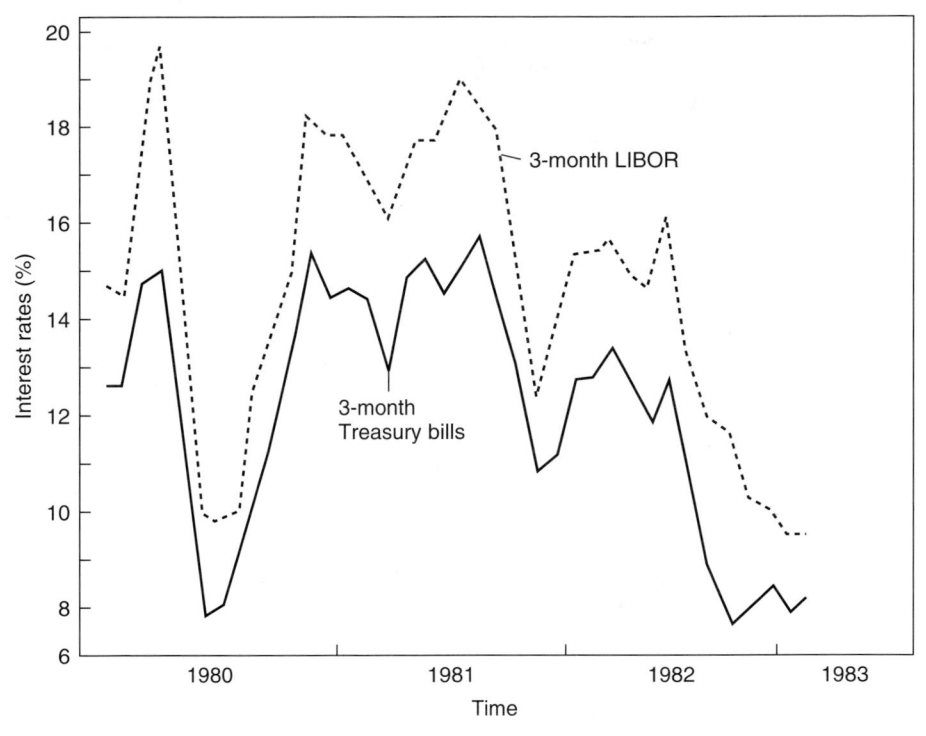

EXHIBIT 5
Three-Month Yield Spreads Relative to U.S. Treasury Bills, January 1980–February 1983

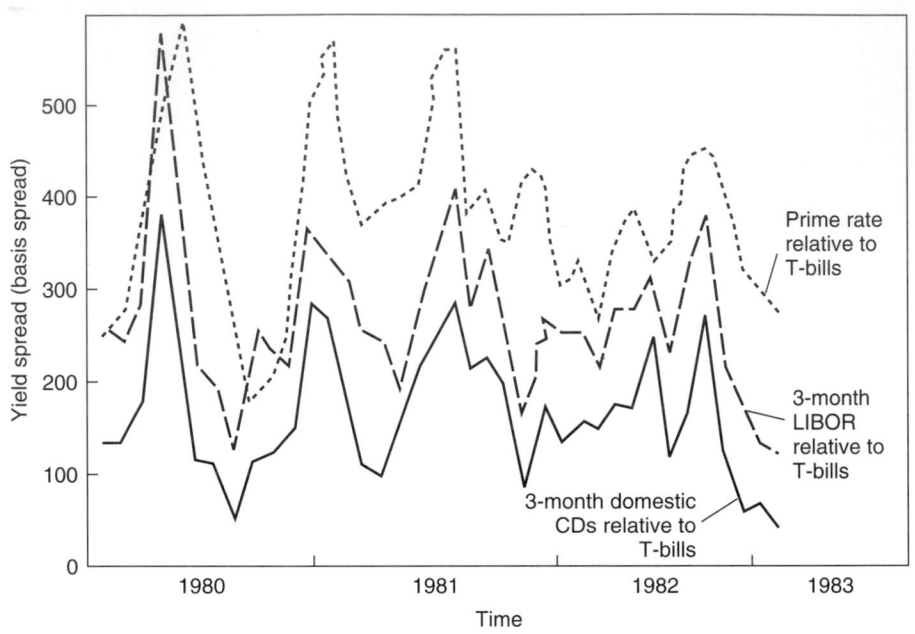

EXHIBIT 6
Yields and Yield Spreads, 1975–1983

Year	Average 3-Month Treasury Bill Yield	Average Gross Spreads versus the 3-Month Treasury Bill		
		3-Month CDs	Commercial Paper	3-Month LIBOR
1975 .... 5.85		.76	.56	1.36
1976 .... 5.03		.27	.25	.58
1977 .... 5.17		.37	.27	.75
1978 .... 7.12		.92	.61	1.48
1979 .... 9.84		1.18	.88	1.93
1980 ....11.25		1.72	1.12	2.81
1981 ....13.99		1.92	1.17	2.83
1982 ....10.75		1.66	1.16	2.68
1983[a] 8.00		.59	.30	1.29

Note: Average of 12 monthly observations for each year.

a. Yields and yield spreads averaged over January and February 1983 *only*.

Financial Execution

MCI Communications Corporation (1983)

In April 1983, Wayne English, chief financial officer of MCI Communications Corporation, faced the problem of setting financial policy in an environment characterized by a large potential demand for external funding and great uncertainty concerning MCI's future. MCI, which provided long-distance telecommunications services in competition with AT&T, had seen its revenues grow from almost nothing in FY1974 (ending March 31, 1974) to more than $1 billion in FY1983. During that period, the company climbed from a loss of $38.7 million in FY1975 to a profit of $170.8 million in FY1983. In the last 2 years, its stock price had increased more than fivefold.

Nevertheless, the antitrust settlement between AT&T and the U.S. Department of Justice in January 1982 had significantly altered the economic landscape for MCI. The settlement, providing for the breakup of AT&T by early 1984, would affect MCI in two important ways. On the one hand, it offered the opportunity for greatly increased growth, since AT&T would be required, for the first time, to compete on equal quality-of-service terms with MCI. On the other hand, the settlement posed new uncertainties, since it promised to eliminate certain MCI cost advantages and to increase AT&T's competitive flexibility.

Even in the face of intensifying competition from AT&T, however, MCI was committed to extending the reach and capacity of its network. According to Brian Thompson, senior vice president for corporate development: "Economies of scale and scope are everything in this business. In the long term, the strategic high ground lies in owning your own facilities for basic call services and then leveraging off this to provide value-added services."

Company Background

MCI was organized in August 1968 under the leadership of William McGowan as the Federal Communications Commission (FCC) appeared willing to allow increased competition with AT&T in the long-distance market. In June 1971, the FCC formally adopted a policy of allowing qualified new companies to enter the market for specialized long-distance services, which consisted chiefly of *private line* (i.e., dedicated telephone line) services for large telephone users. By June 1972, MCI was ready to begin construction of its telecommunications network.

To provide the necessary funds, MCI sold 6 million shares of common stock to the public at $5 per share.[1] Net proceeds after expenses and commissions were $27.1 million. MCI also obtained a $64 million line of credit from a group of four banks headed by the First National Bank of Chicago and further loan promises of $6.45 million from private investors in the form of 7½% subordinated notes (with attached warrants) of up to 5-year maturities. The bank loans carried an interest rate of 3¾% above prime, plus a commitment fee of ½% per annum on the unborrowed balance.

By March 31, 1974, the MCI communications system had grown to 2,280 route-miles of transmission circuits, linking 15 major metropolitan areas. Still, this was far short of the 11,600 route-mile system originally planned in 1972. MCI had to rely on AT&T facilities to carry calls from its subscribers to MCI transmission centers in each metropolitan area. Since AT&T had successfully resisted providing a full range of these interconnection services, MCI was unable to generate significant subscriber revenues. Late in 1973, MCI suspended all construction activity as it pursued legal and regulatory remedies. As part of this process, it filed an antitrust suit against AT&T in March 1974 (Exhibit 1 presents this sequence of events schematically). The FCC ordered AT&T to provide MCI with the full range of interconnection facilities as of May 1974; MCI then resumed construction of its network.

In FY1975, MCI had revenues of $6.8 million but losses of $38.7 million. By September 1975, despite a network consisting of 5,100 route-miles connecting 30 major metropolitan areas, MCI had a negative net worth of $27.5 million, an accumulated operating deficit of $87.3 million, and a stock market price just below $1 per share (see Exhibit 2 for MCI's financial and operating history). MCI had exhausted its line of credit from the banks, had been forced to renegotiate the previous credit agreement to defer interest payments, and was in technical default of many provisions of the revised credit agreement. In the midst of this crisis, MCI managed a public sale of 9.6 million shares of common stock in December 1975, each share having an associated 5-year warrant with an exercise price of $1.25. The net proceeds of this offering, which amounted to $8.2 million (or about $.85 per share-plus-warrant, compared with a then prevailing market price of $.875 per share), enabled MCI to survive.

MCI reached a turning point in 1976. "Execunet" service, which had been introduced in the winter of 1974, began to yield substantial revenues and changed the nature of the company. Execunet provided a service comparable to standard long-distance calling, with customers having random access to MCI's transmission lines. This enabled MCI to attract small business subscribers who could not afford the expense of dedicated private lines between particular cities (private line customers tended to be large corporations with large call volumes). Partly as a result, revenues increased to $28.4 million in FY1976 and $62.8 million in FY1977 (about half of which came from Execunet). Interest payments to the consortium of lending banks, which had been previously suspended, were resumed in August 1976. Just as MCI made its first profit of $100,000 in September 1976, the FCC won a court order that restricted Execunet to existing subscribers; this order was not lifted completely until May 1978.

---

1. This and subsequent prices and numbers of shares have been adjusted for all stock splits on or before April 1, 1983.

The order restricting Execunet slowed, but did not halt, MCI's progress. Revenue growth slowed to 18% between FY1977 and FY1978 but quickly returned to annual rates of more than 50% once the order was lifted. The number of employees tripled from 605 in March 1977 to 1,980 in March 1981; plant grew from $136.6 million to $410.0 million over the same period. More important, MCI's profitability improved rapidly. After-tax earnings from continuing operations rose from a loss of $1.7 million for FY1977 to a profit of $21.1 million in FY1981 (see Exhibit 2). As a result, MCI had exhausted its tax loss carry-forward by the end of FY1981, and stockholders' equity was a positive $148 million.

This record paled, however, in comparison to MCI's growth in subsequent years. In March 1980, MCI offered Execunet service to residential customers (hitherto it had been available exclusively to businesses) on a trial basis in Denver, Colorado. The results were so striking that within a week plans were made to offer Execunet to households nationwide. MCI's growth was then constrained only by a lack of investment capital, which soon became available in substantial quantities (see Exhibit 3). Revenues more than doubled to $506 million in FY1982 and, with the acquisition of Western Union International from Xerox for $195.1 million in June 1982, revenues doubled again to $1,078 million in FY1983. Income from operations was $295.1 million, with net earnings of $170.8 million. A range of new products such as MCI Mail (an electronic mail service) and the results of AT&T's settlement with the Department of Justice offered dramatic opportunities for further growth. (Income statements and balance sheets for MCI for 1981–1983 are presented in Exhibits 4 and 5.)

Financial Policy

Until 1976 the need to obtain funds to continue operations dominated MCI's financial policy. The court's 1976 order preventing the extension of Execunet service to new customers restricted opportunities for growth and consequently reduced the need for investment funds. At the same time, restrictive covenants associated with the bank loans from the syndicate headed by the First National Bank of Chicago severely limited MCI's ability to raise new capital for expansion. Between 1976 and the summer of 1978, lease financing of new fixed investment was the only substantial source of funds available. This went largely into expanding capacity in MCI's existing markets.

Withdrawal of the court's Execunet order in May 1978 opened the way for accelerated growth if the required investment funds could be obtained. Wayne English, who had arrived as chief financial officer in February 1976, spent the summer of 1978 preparing to do this. First, he obtained agreement from the majority of the lending banks to a public offering of securities whose proceeds would retire their loans. Second, he arranged for the loans of those banks that refused this accommodation to be bought out by private investors. Finally, he bought up or converted a number of outstanding warrants and loans held by earlier investors. Consequently, in December 1978, MCI was able to enter the public capital markets for the first time since the equity issue of December 1975, with an offering of convertible preferred stock which raised $25.8 million—net of all issue expenses (see Exhibit 6). A second convertible preferred offering in September 1979 raised $63.1 million and a third in October 1980 netted $46.7 million.

The choice of convertible preferred stock was dictated on the one hand by the need for some form of equity capital, and on the other hand by the fact, as expressed by Mr. English, that "it was always our conviction that issuing more common would knock the props out from under the stock." As it was, the conversion price on the preferred stock rose with each offering, from $2.1875 in December 1978 to $5 in September 1979 to $9 in October 1980. In addition, the dividend on the preferred stock would be 85% tax-deductible to corporate purchasers without costing MCI a significant loss of tax benefits, since MCI's earnings were still sheltered by the carry-forward of past losses.

An additional feature of these preferred issues was a *call* provision that enabled MCI to force investors to convert to common stock, thus eliminating the drain of preferred dividends on cash flow. This provision typically specified that if the market price of MCI's common stock exceeded the conversion price by more than a stated margin (e.g., 25%) for 30 consecutive trading days, MCI could call the unconverted preferred shares in question for redemption at 110% of their issue value. Owners of preferred stock would, of course, voluntarily exchange their shares for common at the conversion price rather than allow them to be repurchased. A steadily rising stock price enabled MCI to use this mechanism to convert all three preferred issues to common stock by November 1981.

Proceeds from these preferred offerings allowed MCI to retire its short-to-intermediate term bank debt and to issue longer-term debt. Leasing activity decreased and, in July 1980, MCI raised $50.5 million through the public sale of 20-year subordinated debentures.

In FY1981, as the demand for investment funds intensified, the direction of MCI's financial policy shifted slightly from offerings of convertible preferreds to convertible debt. After obtaining $102.1 million in April 1981 through a straight subordinated debenture issue, MCI raised $98.2 million in August 1981 and $245.9 million in May 1982 with convertible debentures.

These convertible debentures carried forced conversion (i.e., *call*) provisions similar to those of the earlier preferred stock issues. As a result, MCI was able to force conversion of the May 1982 issue in December 1982 and of the August 1981 issue in February 1983. The consequent additions to common equity enabled MCI to take on a still greater debt burden. Thus, a straight debenture issue in September 1982 yielded $209.9 million, and a further convertible debenture in March 1983 produced almost $400 million.

In all, MCI raised about $1,050 million from the public sale of securities in FY1982 and FY1983. As with all MCI offerings, the initial issues were oversubscribed. Interest costs were relatively high (see Exhibit 7), but in the words of Mr. English, "Availability of funds [was] the paramount consideration"; cost was "secondary." Moreover, since profitability was increasing more rapidly than interest expense, interest coverage actually increased during this time. Considering the situation in 1975, and in comparison to other companies (see Exhibit 8), this was a remarkable achievement.

However, as details of the FCC's response to the AT&T antitrust settlement began to emerge, the resulting uncertainty cast doubt on MCI's continued ability to raise funds in these amounts. MCI would have to proceed with care, agility, and imagination.

The AT&T Antitrust Settlement and Other Developments

Historically, AT&T provided a necessary part of the MCI system—and its most serious competition. One part of AT&T—the local telephone operating companies (e.g., Illinois Bell, New England Telephone)—supplied MCI with connections to subscribers through their local telephone networks. MCI paid for these services at a rate negotiated in 1978, under the FCC's supervision, between MCI and the local telephone companies (predominantly AT&T subsidiaries). This charge was about $230 per month per access line, or $172.7 million a year by FY1983. MCI also used AT&T and other long-distance facilities to enable its customers to reach areas not already served by the MCI network. In FY1983, MCI paid at the standard commercial rate $137.2 million for these services.

MCI's principal competitor in the market for interstate long-distance services was AT&T's Long Lines division, with about 95% of the market in March 1983. AT&T Long Lines also reimbursed local operating companies for access lines, but at a rate about three times that charged MCI and the other competing carriers, such as GTE, Sprint, and ITT. This discrepancy was justified by the fact that MCI customers usually had to dial 20 digits to reach a long-distance number, compared with 11 digits (1, plus area code, plus 7-digit number) for an AT&T customer. Thus, AT&T Long Lines was expected to pay more for "superior access."

The settlement of the antitrust suit between AT&T and the Justice Department in January 1982 would separate AT&T from its local operating subsidiaries. AT&T would retain the Long Lines division and the intrastate long-distance facilities of the local companies. After separation occurred in January 1984, the long-distance operations would be consolidated in a new AT&T subsidiary named AT&T Communications. AT&T Communications would eventually compete on a more or less equal basis with MCI and the other long-distance companies (GTE, ITT, and so on). To ensure this result, the settlement required that by 1986 the newly independent local telephone companies provide *equal* quality of *access* to all competing long-distance providers. To implement equal access, a series of elections would be held in communities nation-wide in which consumers would be asked to select a long-distance provider. Simulta-neously, an FCC plan would phase out the differential in access charges between AT&T and its competitors by increasing the fees paid by MCI and others. Although equal access would be phased in over 2 to 3 years, the FCC plan in its original form called for an initial increase of about 80% in MCI access charges in 1984. Thus, on the one hand, MCI would eventually gain by acquiring equal access but, on the other hand, would immediately lose much of its existing cost advantage over AT&T.

The value of equal access to MCI was difficult to measure precisely. Some cus-tomers already enjoyed effectively equal access, since electronic switchboards had features that would automatically route calls via MCI lines whenever the usual 10- or 11-digit long-distance number was dialed. However, these tended to be large business customers who made up only a small fraction of MCI's revenue. A trial of equal access in part of Iowa led to an almost immediate increase in MCI's share of the long-distance market, from less than 5% to about 20%. In this case, however, competition from MCI's non-AT&T competitors was not severe, and AT&T still paid more in access fees.

The impact of equalized access charges on market share was also difficult to judge. Under the FCC plan, AT&T's access pricing flexibility was expected to increase as deregulation of the long-distance market—the FCC's ultimate goal—proceeded. In principle, therefore, AT&T would be able to reduce its prices to prevent further erosion of its market share. In practice, however, it would make little economic sense for AT&T, with 95% of the market, to cut prices for the sake of preventing anything less than massive losses of market share to MCI and its other competitors. The outcome would depend on the direction taken by AT&T's management, which had been surpris-ingly aggressive in the past.

In the face of these uncertainties, it was difficult to predict MCI's growth in revenues and earnings in FY1984 and beyond. Forecasting the need for fixed and working capital was equally difficult; nevertheless, a consensus forecast is presented in Exhibit 9. Against these contingencies, MCI held about $550 million in cash in the spring of 1983. At the beginning of April 1983, its stock price stood at $47, and long-term interest rates had declined dramatically.

EXHIBIT 1
Chronology of Significant Events, 1971–1984

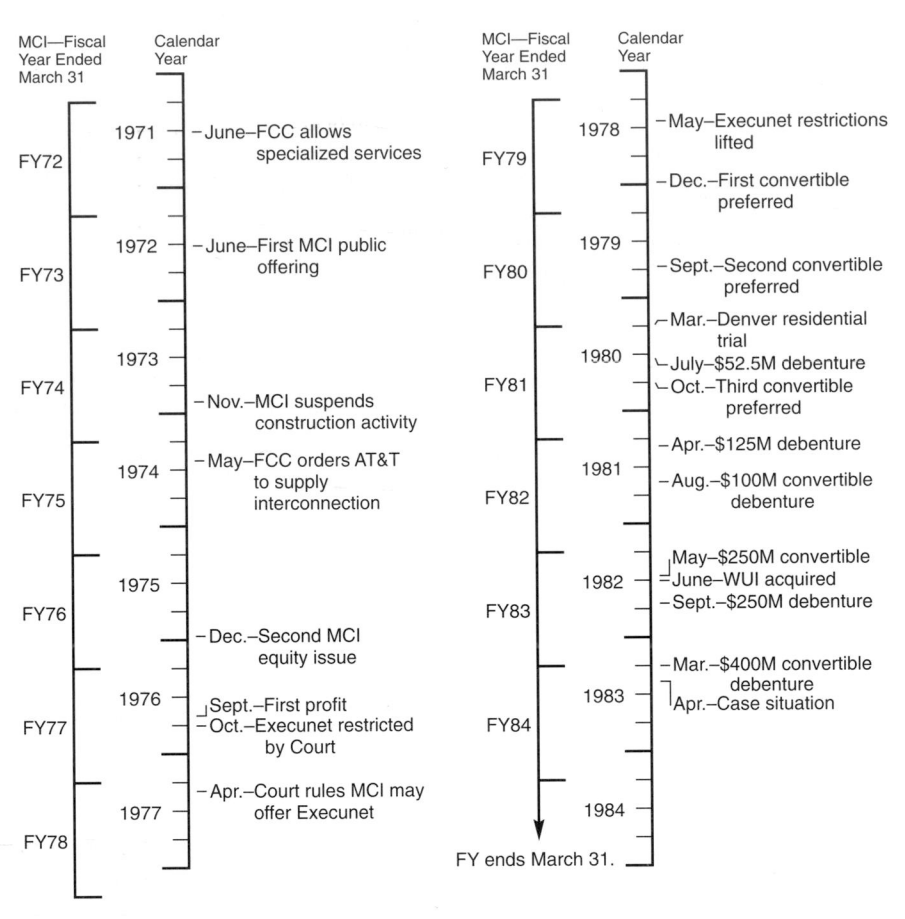

MCI—Fiscal Year Ended March 31	Calendar Year	Event
FY72	1971	June–FCC allows specialized services
FY73	1972	June–First MCI public offering
FY74	1973	Nov.–MCI suspends construction activity
FY75	1974	May–FCC orders AT&T to supply interconnection
FY76	1975	
FY77	1976	Dec.–Second MCI equity issue; Sept.–First profit; Oct.–Execunet restricted by Court
FY78	1977	Apr.–Court rules MCI may offer Execunet
FY79	1978	May–Execunet restrictions lifted; Dec.–First convertible preferred
FY80	1979	Sept.–Second convertible preferred
FY81	1980	Mar.–Denver residential trial; July–$52.5M debenture; Oct.–Third convertible preferred
FY82	1981	Apr.–$125M debenture; Aug.–$100M convertible debenture
FY83	1982	May–$250M convertible; June–WUI acquired; Sept.–$250M debenture
FY84	1983	Mar.–$400M convertible debenture; Apr.–Case situation
	1984	FY ends March 31.

EXHIBIT 2
MCI Operating History for Years Ending March 31, 1974–1983 (millions of dollars except per share data)

	1974	1975	1976	1977	1978	1979	1980	1981	1982	1983
Revenues	$ .7	$ 6.8	$ 28.4	$ 62.8	$ 74.0	$ 95.2	$144.3	$234.2	$506.4	$1,073.2
Operating income	(15.0)	(17.3)	(10.6)	17.7	25.0	30.6	37.2	51.3	167.0	295.1
Net interest	3.8	11.6	15.5	18.4	20.5	23.1	24.1	27.4	35.1	54.1
Net after-tax earnings	(20.1)	(38.7)	(27.2)	(1.7)	5.2	7.1	13.3	21.1	86.5	170.8
Cash, cash equivalents	1.2	1.4	3.7	2.8	4.3	10.3	7.9	12.7	144.8	542.0
Working capital[a]	.3	(7.4)	(12.7)	(18.3)	(21.7)	(26.9)	(34.1)	(24.8)	42.5	391.8
Plant, equipment	60.0	81.0	120.8	136.6	148.9	188.9	282.0	410.0	619.5	1,324.2
Total assets	71.8	90.1	131.2	147.7	161.2	209.5	309.8	466.9	860.4	2,070.5
Short-term debt[b]	1.2	4.0	9.8	17.0	20.2	25.8	31.6	39.9	40.3	48.0
Long-term debt	48.4	95.2	144.3	149.7	152.8	153.3	172.9	242.7	400.0	895.9
Stockholders' equity	19.1	(14.4)	(29.1)	(32.2)	(22.7)	11.5	78.8	148.0	240.8	765.6
Million shares outstanding[c]	27	30.6	41	40.2	40.6	43.4	65.8	75.6	97.4	117.2
Earnings per share[d]	$ (.74)	$ (1.42)	$ (.81)	$ (.06)	$ .05	$ .04	$ (.01)	$ .09	$ .91	$ 1.69
Price range—common stock	1½–4½	½–2½	½–2½	1–2	1–2½	1½–3½	2–4½	2½–7	7–18	16–47

Sources: MCI annual reports; 10-K reports; and prospectuses.

a. Current assets less current liabilities (current assets include cash, cash equivalents).
b. Includes long-term debt payable within 1 year.
c. At year-end. MCI has never paid any dividend on its common stock.
d. Earnings per common share after preferred dividends, before extraordinary items.

EXHIBIT 3

Sources and Uses of Funds for Years Ending March 31, 1978–1983 (millions of dollars)

	1978	*1979*	*1980*	*1981*	*1982*	*1983*
Sources of Funds						
Funds from operations						
Retained earnings[a]	$ 2.5	$ 1.6	$ (1.1)	$ 7.2	$ 83.1	$ 170.8
Depreciation	11.2	13.6	18.3	27.2	60.8	108.6
Other[b]	2.7	3.5	7.0	6.1	35.2	57.1
Total	16.4	18.7	24.2	40.5	179.1	336.5
Funds from external financing						
Net increase in lease obligations	10.2	35.0	65.4	47.7	(5.0)	(18.3)
Other net borrowing, sale of securities	(4.6)	(.8)	19.3	85.1	158.8	842.2
Total	5.6	34.2	84.7	132.8	163.8	823.9
Total sources	$22.0	$52.9	$108.9	$173.3	$342.9	$1,160.4
Uses of Funds						
Investment in plant, equipment	$22.2	$52.5	$110.3	$155.7	$271.5	$ 623.0
Acquisitions	—	—	—	—	—	195.1
Increase in adjusted working capital[c]	(1.7)	(5.6)	1.0	12.8	(60.4)	(55.2)[d]
Change in cash holdings	1.5	6.0	(2.4)	4.8	131.8	397.5
Total uses	$22.0	$52.9	$108.9	$173.3	$342.9	$1,160.4

Sources: MCI annual reports; 10-K reports.

Note: Numbers may not add exactly because of rounding.

a. Net income less preferred dividends.

b. Deferred taxes, employee stock purchase plan.

c. Working capital excluding cash and short-term debt.

d. Not including working capital of WUI.

EXHIBIT 4

MCI Income Statements for Years Ending March 31, 1981–1983 (millions of dollars)

	1981	*1982*	*1983*
Revenues	$234	$506	$1,073
Operating expenses (excluding depreciation)	157	283	674
Depreciation	26	56	104
	183	339	778
Operating income	51	167	295
Interest expense	28	54	75
Interest income (less other expense)	1	16	21
	27	38	54
Profit before taxes	24	129	241
Provision for income taxes	5	43	70
Net income	19	86	171
Extraordinary item	2	0	0
Adjusted net income	21	86	171
Preferred dividends	11	3	0
Income available for common stock	$ 10	$ 83	$ 171

EXHIBIT 5

MCI Balance Sheets at March 31, 1981–1983 (millions of dollars)

	1981	1982	1983
Cash, cash equivalents	$ 13	$144	$ 542
Accounts receivable	32	79	162
Other	4	5	9
Current assets	49	228	713
Plant, equipment (net)	410	619	1,324
Other	8	13	33
Total assets	$467	$860	$2,070
Accounts payable, accrued liabilities	$ 34	$137	$ 251
Accrued taxes	0	8	22
Debt due within 1 year	40	40	48
Current liabilities	74	185	321
Long-term debt	243	400	896
Deferred income taxes	2	34	88
Total liabilities	319	619	1,305
Preferred stock (par value)	1	0	0
Common stock (par value)	4	5	12
Surplus capital paid in	220	230	576
Retained earnings (deficit)	(77)	6	177
Total liabilities and net worth	$467	$860	$2,070

EXHIBIT 6
Public Sales of Securities by MCI, 1972–1983

Date	Instrument	MCI Price on Issue Date	Amount/Price	Net Proceeds	Date Called for Conversion
June 1972	Common stock	IPO	6,000,000 shares @$5	$ 27,070,000	na
Nov. 1975	Common stock plus 5-year warrant attached (exercise price—$1.25)	$ 7/8	9,600,000 units @$1	$ 8,165,000	na
Dec. 1978	$2.64 convertible cumulative preferred stock (conversion price—$2.1875 per share of common)	$ 1⅞	1,120,000 shares @$25	$ 25,760,000	Mar. 1980
Sept. 1979	$1.80 senior convertible cumulative preferred stock (conversion price—$5 per share of common)	$ 3¼	4,500,000 shares @$15	$ 63,125,000	May 1981
July 1980	15% subordinated debentures due August 1, 2000	—	$52,500,000 @100% of face value	$ 50,545,000	na
Oct. 1980	$1.84 cumulative convertible preferred stock (conversion price—$9 per share of common)	$ 6¹/₁₆	3,300,000 shares @$15	$ 46,725,000	Nov. 1981
Apr. 1981	14⅛% subordinated debenture due April 1, 2001	—	$125,000,000 @84.71% of face value	$102,055,000	na
Aug. 1981	10¼% convertible subordinate debenture due August 15, 2001 (conversion price—$12.825 per share of common)	$10⅞	$100,000,000 @100% of face value	$ 98,200,000	Feb. 1983
May 1982	10% convertible subordinated debenture due May 15, 2002 (conversion price—$22.50 per share of common)	$18⅝	$250,000,000 @100% of face value	$245,925,000	Dec. 1982
Sept. 1982	12⅞% subordinated debenture due October 1, 2002	—	$250,000,000 @85.625% of face value	$209,922,500	na
Mar. 1983	7¾% convertible subordinated debenture due March 15, 2003 (conversion price—$52.125 per share)	$43⅜	$400,000,000 @100%	$393,675,000	—

Source: MCI prospectuses.

Note: All prices and share figures adjusted for subsequent stock split. Amounts are initial offering levels. In each case, the offerings were oversubscribed and additional funds were raised.
na = not available.

EXHIBIT 7
Comparative Interest Rates, 1978–1983

	Industrials				Utilities			
	Bonds[a]		Preferred Stock[b]		Bonds[a]		Preferred Stock[b]	MCI[c] Bonds, Preferred
Issue Date	A	BBB	Medium	Speculative	A	BBB	Medium	Stock at Issue
Dec. 1978	9.17%	9.76%	9.45%	10.34%	9.50%	9.78%	10.48%	PS 10.56%
Sept. 1979	9.74	10.41	9.76	11.53	10.05	10.51	10.97	PS 12.00
July 1980	11.35	11.74	10.56	10.91	11.54	12.60	12.32	D 15.00
Oct. 1980	12.92	13.03	11.43	11.98	12.79	14.14	14.32	PS 12.27
Apr. 1981	13.29	14.18	13.19	13.65	14.01	15.17	15.12	D 16.80
Aug. 1981	16.25	17.25	13.46	14.99	17.50	18.00	15.85	CD 10.25
May 1982	15.50	16.50	13.16	14.62	16.25	17.00	14.93	CD 10.00
Sept. 1982	13.75	14.63	13.21	14.49	14.00	15.13	14.11	D 15.17
Mar. 1983	12.50	13.00	11.36	12.67	12.75	13.25	12.51	CD 7.75

PS = convertible preferred stock; D = straight debenture; CD = convertible debenture.

a. Standard and Poor's rating.

b. Rates are for nonconvertible preferred stock.

c. MCI bonds are nonrated for most of this period.

EXHIBIT 8
Comparison of Companies, 1983 (billions of dollars)

	MCI[a]	AT&T	GTE	IBM	ITT
Revenues	$ 1.1	$ 65.1	$ 12.1	$ 34.4	$16.0
Net income	.17	6.99	.90	4.41	.70
Assets	2.1	148.2	21.9	32.5	14.1
Return on					
Sales	15.9%	10.7%	7.4%	12.8%	4.4%
Assets	11.0	8.6	4.1	14.1	4.8
Equity	32.4	12.2	15.6	22.9	12.7
Payout ratio	0	67	61	47	54
Debt ratio[b]	55	43	57	14	38
Current ratio	2.2	.9	1.0	1.6	1.3
Interest coverage	4.2	3.6	2.4	18	2.5
Bond rating	NR	Aaa	Baa	Aaa	A
Price-earnings range	8–27	6–8	6–10	8–13	5–7

Source: Standard and Poor's reports; Moody's.

NR = not rated.

a. Fiscal year ending March 31.

b. Total debt to capital.

EXHIBIT 9
Baseline Forecast of Anticipated MCI Operating Characteristics for Years Ending March 31, 1983–1990 (millions of dollars)

	1983	1984	1985	1986	1987	1988	1989	1990
1. Interstate long-distance market	$27,000	$29,800	$32,800	$36,000	$39,700	$43,600	$48,000	$52,800
2. MCI market share[a]	4.0%	6.2%	9.6%	13.5%	18.6%	19.8%	20.0%	20.0%
3. MCI revenues [(1) × (2)]	$ 1,073	$ 1,850	$ 3,160	$ 4,870	$ 7,380	$ 8,660	$ 9,600	$10,560
4. Access charges (% of sales)	16%	23%	29.5%	29.5%	29.5%	28.5%	27.5%	26.5%
5. Operating margin[b]	27.5%	20.5%	12.0%	12.0%	12.0%	13.0%	14.0%	15.0%
6. Operating earnings (EBIT) [(3) × (5)]	$ 295	$ 380	$ 390	$ 590	$ 890	$ 1,125	$ 1,345	$ 1,580
7. Interest paid	$ 75	$ 100	$ 100	$ 100	$ 100	$ 100	$ 100	$ 100
8. Other income	$ 21	$ 13	$ 3	$ 4	$ 4	$ 5	$ 5	$ 5
9. Provision for taxes	$ 70	$ 83	$ 58	$ 123	$ 206	$ 299	$ 400	$ 475
10. After-tax net income [(6) − (7) + (8) − (9)]	$ 171	$ 210	$ 235	$ 371	$ 588	$ 731	$ 850	$ 1,010
11. Increase in deferred taxes	$ 53	$ 65	$ 88	$ 106	$ 120	$ 140	$ 146	$ 140
12. Incremental investment factor	1.15	1.15	1.12	1.10	1.08	1.06	1.04	1.0
13. Capital expenditures for new capacity [Change in (3) × (12)]	$ 623	$ 890	$ 1,467	$ 1,881	$ 2,710	$ 1,357	$ 980	$ 960
14. Capital expenditures for replacement		—	—	$ 50	$ 50	$ 100	$ 100	$ 100
15. Total capital expenditures [(13) + (14)]	$ 623	$ 890	$ 1,467	$ 1,931	$ 2,760	$ 1,457	$ 1,080	$ 1,060
16. Depreciation	$ 104	$ 173	$ 272	$ 412	$ 601	$ 749	$ 800	$ 826
17. Net plant, equipment (end of year)	$ 1,324	$ 2,041	$ 3,236	$ 4,755	$ 6,914	$ 7,622	$ 7,902	$ 8,136
18. Additional working capital required	0	0	0	0	0	0	0	0

Source: Casewriter's estimate based on security analysts' forecasts.

a. This is total MCI revenue as a fraction of long-distance revenues and includes non-long-distance revenues. MCI's actual share of the interstate long-distance market would be slightly lower.

b. Includes depreciation as a cost.

(continued)

EXHIBIT 9 *(concluded)*
Assumptions Underlying the Forecasts

1. The interstate long-distance market, which amounted to about $27 billion in FY1983, would grow at 10% per year through FY1990.
2. MCI's revenues would increase from 4% of total long-distance revenues in FY1983 to 20% in FY1990. The increase would be rapid in the years immediately following the advent of *equal access,* but would subsequently slow down as AT&T began to defend its reduced share of the market, other competitors developed their networks, and the market itself adapted to the shock of competition. This pattern is shown on line 2. In each year, 10% of MCI revenues would come from other than long-distance growth. Thus, in FY1990, MCI was projected to hold 18% of the long-distance market. MCI's management was believed to be committed to a growth program of the dimensions shown on line 3 and would, if necessary, sacrifice profit margins to achieve it.
3. Access charges paid by MCI would almost double between FY1983 and FY1985. They would then taper off to about 26.5% of total revenues in FY1990. This was consistent with announced FCC intentions at the end of March 1983. However, there was a great deal of uncertainty in this area. AT&T currently paid access charges amounting to more than 50% of revenues, and reductions to the levels on line 4 would depend on the imposition of *direct access* charges on households and businesses. Legislation in Congress with a reasonable chance of passage forbade the imposition of such direct access charges.
4. MCI's operating margin (operating earnings as a fraction of revenues) would shrink under the dual pressure of higher access charges and increased competition from both AT&T and other long-distance suppliers. Ultimately, however, as access charges fell and the market stabilized, margins were expected to recover to a level of about 15%. Anticipated yearly margins are shown on line 5. However, as noted, these were subject to substantial uncertainty. In the best case, favorable regulatory and legislative action, coupled with restrained competitor behavior, might increase margins by as much as 7% (up to 22% of sales) from these levels. In an unfavorable situation, severe competition and high access charges could reduce margins by an equal amount.
5. Interest payments on MCI's outstanding debt were running at an annual rate of about $100 million at the end of FY1983 (for the year as a whole, interest payments were only $75 million because the debt level increased during the year) and, with no net change in indebtedness, would remain stable at this level through FY1990.
6. Other income, shown on line 8, represents interest on holdings of cash equivalents. As *excess* cash is used up, this figure is expected to decline to $3 million and then grow roughly with sales. This projection does not include interest on the proceeds of any future security offerings that are added temporarily to cash.
7. Provision for taxes, shown on line 9, amounts in 1984 to 25% of net income, which is below the 46% base rate because of investment tax credits and other special credits. As growth and investment slow in later years and reduce the available credits, taxes as a percentage of net income should increase.
8. Increases in deferred taxes, shown on line 11, accumulate at a rate related to present and past capital expenditures. As growth slows, so does the rate of accumulation of deferred tax credits.
9. In March 1983 each extra dollar of revenue required about $1.15 worth of investment in fixed plant and equipment. This factor was expected to fall to about $1.00 by FY1990, as improved electronic technology reduced equipment costs. The expected yearly pattern is shown on line 12. It was possible, however, that in the latter part of the period (post-FY1987) this factor would fall substantially below $1.00.
10. Replacement of older equipment would require the investments described on line 13.
11. Depreciation would be charged at an annual rate equal to 9.8% of the value of plant and equipment in place at the beginning of each year plus 4.9% of the value of total new investment.
12. No additions to working capital would be required throughout the period and any cash on hand at the end of FY1983 could be devoted to investment programs.
13. MCI would not penetrate the intrastate toll market.

Intel Corporation (1992)

In late December 1991, Intel Corporation's cofounder and chairman of the board, Gordon Moore, was rethinking the company's capital-structure and cash-disbursement policies. The company had just completed an extremely successful 5-year period during which annual revenues had grown almost fourfold. Now the firm found itself with cash balances (net of long-term debt) of $2.4 billion—well over one-third of total assets of $6.3 billion. With a market capitalization of almost $9 billion, Intel had become one of the largest firms in the United States never to have paid a dividend.[1] Moore wondered whether the firm he founded in 1968 had grown sufficiently mature to begin returning some of its cash to investors, perhaps by beginning to pay dividends or repurchasing shares of stock.

While returning cash was a worthwhile goal, Moore recognized that cash availability was an essential component of the firm's overall strategy and that future cash needs were very uncertain. He knew that the company faced considerable competitive pressure over the next few years. Imitations of Intel's proprietary microprocessor products had recently obtained substantial market share. Furthermore, the production and development of new Intel products required ever-larger up-front expenditures. In 1992 alone, Intel was expecting to spend over $700 million on research and development (R&D) and approximately $1.2 billion on new plant and equipment. The rapid rate of innovation in Intel's business meant that it would be extremely costly—perhaps even fatal—to delay or scrimp on these expenditures.

Moore was also concerned with the stock market's response to recent competitive pressures. Over the last few weeks, Intel's stock had been trading at a price of $42.50 per share—a price-earnings (P/E) ratio of under 11, far below the P/E of about 20 for the Standard and Poor's 500. Some outside analysts seemed to be pessimistic about

---

1. The largest firm in all of U.S. history never to have paid a dividend was Digital Equipment Corporation (DEC), which in 1987 had a market capitalization as high as $26.6 billion. However, by December 1991, DEC's market capitalization had fallen below Intel's, to $6.7 billion.

This case was prepared by Professor Kenneth A. Froot.

Copyright © 1992 by the President and Fellows of Harvard College.
Harvard Business School case 292–106.

Intel's ability to keep its profits high. Notwithstanding these concerns, Moore asked Intel's chief financial officer, Harold Hughes, and treasurer, Arvind Sodhani, to determine whether Intel's current capital structure was appropriate. Moore also wanted to know what alternatives might be available for disbursing cash to shareholders.

Company Background

Intel was founded in 1968 by Moore and the recently deceased Robert Noyce (coinventor of the integrated circuit and vice chairman of Intel until 1988). The company quickly established a reputation as a leading innovator in the design, development, and manufacture of semiconductors. In 1969, Intel produced the world's first static random access memory (SRAM). This was followed by the 1024-bit dynamic random access memory (DRAM) in 1970. Intel DRAMs, which rapidly grew in capacity, quickly became the industry standard and were by 1972 the largest-selling semiconductor components in the world. In addition, Intel introduced in 1971 the first erasable programmable read-only memory (EPROM) chip. This was an important innovation because it created a versatile and inexpensive data-storage medium. Intel soon was the leading supplier of successive generations of EPROMs.

Intel's most important early breakthrough, however, came in the early 1970s. That breakthrough was the microprocessor, a logic product that ultimately would become the "computer inside the personal computer." Upon its development, Intel proclaimed that microprocessor chips would "usher in a new era of integrated electronics." Yet the innovation came years ahead of the development of its most popular end-use product—the personal computer. Indeed, Intel underestimated the importance of its technology, missing the opportunity to commercialize its early stand-alone personal computer to compete with Apple, whose first 8-bit machine was introduced in 1978.

Throughout the 1970s, Intel continued to innovate, creating a second generation of microprocessors, the i8088™ and i8086™. In 1980, the i8088 was chosen as the computational centerpiece of IBM's first microcomputer, the PC. Later, IBM decided to base its more advanced AT computer on Intel's i80286™ and its even more advanced PS/2 on Intel's i80386DX™. IBM's sheer size and open-architecture policy quickly made its PC and AT important standards, in turn propelling Intel's microprocessors into a position of dominance.

During its first 15 years, Intel's record of innovation had been impressive. According to one observer, Intel was responsible for 16 of the 22 major breakthroughs in microelectronics between 1971 and 1981. The pace of the firm's technological innovation was exemplified by "Moore's Law," which had become an industrywide benchmark. The law held that the number of components on a chip doubled every 2 years. To fund this continuing innovation, Intel's strategy had been to withdraw from product segments that had matured and to redirect resources toward new products, which sold at premium prices.

However, the focus on rapidly developing product markets with steep learning curves created risks. A major mistake or delay in a product could result in Intel falling permanently behind its competitors. In one example, Intel's failure to produce a viable 256K DRAM product in the mid-1980s, after being the world leader in DRAMs in the 1970s, led to its permanent withdrawal from DRAM design and production activities.

In spite of such lapses, by 1991, Intel had become the world's second-largest manufacturer of integrated circuits, with estimated 1991 integrated-circuit revenues of almost $4.1 billion, and the world's largest metal-oxide-silicon (MOS) manufacturer.[2] Exhibit 1 reports revenue data on Intel's largest competitors. Although based in the United States, Intel operated 40 major manufacturing and development facilities on 3 continents and had 90 sales offices in over 21 nations. Gordon Moore, with his gentle and deferential manner, had become perhaps the most-respected figure in the semiconductor industry (in addition to one of its richest, with holdings of about 7% of Intel's stock). Exhibits 2 and 3 provide important financial information on Intel.

Products

In 1991, Intel's mission was to be the leading "building-block supplier to the new computer industry." To fulfill this mission, management believed the firm had to invest in the design, development, and manufacture of a variety of advanced microcomputer components and related products at various levels of integration. Exhibit 4 gives details on sales and operating margins for Intel's various product lines.

Memory (10% of Sales)

Intel supplied a broad line of memory components, including EPROMs, DRAMs, and SRAMs (both produced in recent years by subcontractors for Intel), and flash memories (introduced by Intel in 1988). Flash memories were easier and faster to update than EPROMs because they could be reprogrammed after installation.

Microprocessors and Coprocessors (52% of Sales)

Processor and logic products performed the central and peripheral data-processing functions for microcomputers. Intel produced several families of processors for personal computers (see Exhibit 5). The higher-performance microprocessors in the 32-bit i386 and i486 families were also powerful enough to be used in minicomputers, parallel-processing systems, and engineering workstations. The most recent addition to the i386 family was Intel's i386SL, a microprocessor designed for portable computers that was introduced in 1990. It incorporated a power management unit that extended battery life up to ten hours. The high-performance i486 family was introduced in 1989. Intel was also developing two even more advanced processors, the P5 (referred to by analysts as the i586) and the P6. These chips were expected to include networking and digital-video-interface circuitry directly on the microprocessor and were scheduled to become available in mid-1992 and late 1993, respectively.

In addition to these processors, in 1989, Intel introduced the i860 microprocessor, which was designed for high-speed multiprocessing systems and technical workstations. Intel also made coprocessors for various applications: graphics, disk drives, keyboards, printers, networks, and high-speed mathematical calculations.

Microcontrollers, Peripherals, and Systems (38% of Sales)

Microcontrollers were designed to be embedded within an application and to be programmed to control the operation of that application. They typically integrated a central processing unit (CPU), memory, and other features on a single chip and were used in computer and communications systems, automobile-control applications, robotics, electronic instrumentations, home video machines, and other applications.

---

2. MOS was the newer and more efficient of two processes for making integrated circuits.

Intel's technological leadership in microprocessors gave it certain competitive advantages in designing and marketing integrated microcomputer systems based on Intel products. Intel microprocessors were also at the heart of the company's design and development of parallel-processing supercomputers, which began in 1986.

Intel's Microprocessor Competitors

In the late 1970s, before a standard microprocessor technology had emerged, semiconductor producers typically cross-licensed products with competing companies. Intel's sales contracts often stipulated that Intel facilitate the development of second sources for its i8088, i8086, and i80286 microprocessors. The company therefore licensed the i8088 and i8086 to 12 competitors, and it licensed the i80286 to 4. These competing producers commanded a substantial fraction of industry microprocessor sales. Indeed, by the end of 1990, Intel had garnered only 19% of i8088 unit sales (against 51% by Advanced Micro Devices (AMD) and 13% by Siemens); 23% of i8086 family unit sales (against 23% by AMD and 37% by NEC); and 41% of i80286 unit sales (against 37% by AMD and 10% by Siemens).

Meanwhile, the design, development, and production costs of successive generations of microprocessors were rising rapidly. In just a few years, Intel's development expenses went from $100 million for the i386, to $300 million for the i486, to an estimated $500 million for the P5, and to perhaps $600 million for the P6. The costs of building state-of-the-art fabrication facilities (fabs) and equipment capable of producing 32-bit (and beyond) processors were increasing even more rapidly. Intel's capital spending on plant and equipment rose from $422 million in 1989, to $680 million in 1990, to an estimated $948 million in 1991, and to an expected $1.2 billion in 1992 (see Exhibit 3). These setup costs also represented an ever-increasing fraction of total production costs. For example, analysts estimated that Intel's marginal costs for the i486 would fall from about $75 per unit in 1990 to about $6 per unit by 1993 as more sophisticated fabs were employed and learning-by-doing effects made existing processes more efficient. Such dramatic declines in marginal costs were very common for new microprocessor products.

The economics of microprocessor production combined with the emergence of the X86 family as the dominant industry standard gave Intel the strategic leverage it needed to change its licensing policies. Beginning with the i386 family, which was introduced in 1986, the company refused to grant second-source contracts to customers other than IBM, which retained the right to manufacture the i386 for some of its own machines. Demand for Intel's i386 microprocessors seemed to be less price sensitive than that for earlier processors because there were no competing suppliers. Partly as a result, Intel's operating margins for microprocessors began to rise beginning in 1987, as the i386 product cycle moved into its "ramp-up" phase (see Exhibit 4). Net income increased from a loss of $203 million in 1986 to an expected $819 million in 1991.

Intel's decision to produce its newer microprocessors exclusively raised competitive challenges. One source of competition came from imitations (commonly, but inaccurately, called clones) of Intel's products. Intel had already seen imitations of its mathematics coprocessors take considerable market power and market share away. In general, imitations were much less expensive to develop than the original processor and tended to appear after demand for the original had already ramped up. This timing allowed imitators to avoid the costly development and market-acceptance phases of the life cycle and to align their product features with more recent changes in demand. Exhibit 6 depicts the time profile of a typical microprocessor life cycle. (Industry analysts believe that life cycles for newer processors are considerably shorter than that shown in Exhibit 6.) In Intel's experience, imitators tended to enter when (and if) the product reached the "growth" or ramp-up phase. Exhibit 7 presents time-series data on both shipments and the installed base of various microprocessors.

In one example of a late-entry imitation, AMD began shipping its i386SX and i386DX compatibles in December 1990, almost 5 years after Intel introduced the originals. By that time, the i386 family was roughly between the growth and maturity phases of the life cycle (see Exhibit 6), with Intel's i386 sales having reached an annual rate of about $1.2 billion on volume of about 12 million units. AMD's chips, however, had somewhat higher operating speeds and better power usage than comparable Intel processors. With a selling price slightly below Intel's, AMD's share of monthly i386 shipments had shot up to about 30% at the end of 12 months' time. AMD sold approximately $145 million worth of imitation i386s in the last quarter of 1991 alone (about 27.5% of the last quarter's market of $2.1 billion in annualized sales). See Exhibit 7 for data on the industrywide number of units shipped. Late entry into successful markets was the strategy of W. J. Sanders, AMD's flamboyant chairman and chief executive officer (CEO). He kept AMD focused on high-volume products and well behind the cutting edge.

By the end of 1991, the number of companies that sold imitation products had grown dramatically. Chips and Technologies had recently announced a group of chips that mimicked the functions of the i386, and Cyrix was expected to do the same in the near future. AMD and NexGen Microsystems were expected to introduce i486-compatible processors during 1992. Imitating an existing processor's functions was less expensive and time consuming than designing the original; analysts reported that Chips and Technologies created its imitation i386 for about $50 million, which was reportedly what AMD needed to spend on each of its i386 and i486 compatibles. Exhibit 8 reports general financial information as well as data on net cash assets for several of Intel's competitors.

Another competitive threat was posed by alternative CPUs that did not attempt compatibility with Intel's products. Motorola's 68000 family of CPUs, used principally on Apple machines, had for several years been a potentially threatening alternative. Furthermore, several high-performance reduced-instruction-set-computing (RISC) processors had recently been introduced: the ACE consortium would use a product of NEC and Siemens, the MIPS chip; Fujitsu had built the SPARC chip for Sun Microsystems; and a recent Apple/IBM alliance would use the Motorola-built, IBM-designed RS6000 series as a platform. Some informed observers believed that these processors might have performance advantages over Intel's X86 microprocessors. There was also concern that the large Japanese companies might price their RISC processors very aggressively in order to gain market share.

Intel's response to these competitive challenges was fourfold. First, Intel used the legal system to defend vigorously what it believed to be infringements of its intellectual property rights. In early 1991, Intel sued AMD for illegal use of Intel's microcode in its processors. The case was originally to come to trial in February 1992, although AMD had filed for a continuance to delay the trial until April 1992. In January 1991, Intel had also filed a preliminary injunction in the U.S. District Court in Sherman, Texas, against Cyrix Corporation, a Texas-headquartered firm. Intel sought to prohibit Cyrix from shipping its cloned math coprocessors and claimed that Cyrix was infringing on Intel's patents. The case was not expected to go to trial until 1993. Intel was also pursuing actions against several companies, such as USLI and Cyrix, that had allegedly copied patented Intel circuits in their microprocessors and were not licensed by Intel to do so. These companies argued that they could employ Intel circuits without violating the patent law, provided that they used fabs owned by companies that *were* licensed by Intel. Court decisions in these cases were expected soon.

Second, Intel responded to the "me-too" competitors with a major advertising thrust (see Exhibit 2 for advertising expense data). The "Intel Inside" campaign, which would cost almost $100 million per year, attempted to gain better premium-brand recognition. In addition, Intel tried to exploit its continuity as a producer of microprocessors in its "pull" campaign. This was intended to attract consumers to the i486's easy upgradeability feature—a feature that no other supplier currently offered.

Intel's third competitive response was to speed up the product cycle by switching consumers to its "second-wave" 32-bit microprocessors, the i386SL and i486 family. Analysts anticipated that the newer i386SL, with its advanced power-management circuitry, would displace a substantial portion of the demand for first-wave i386 imitations. First-wave 386 processors were increasingly used in the large and rapidly growing portable- and laptop-computer market, where power-management features were crucial. However, due to a certain software bug, demand for Intel's i386SL had thus far been disappointing. Intel also began to encourage vendors and OEM manufacturers to switch from 386 processors to Intel's new 1.2 million transistor i486 family through price cuts and greater availability. Demand for i486 processors had begun to accelerate but was hampered by some observers' skepticism about the chips' performance. (See Exhibit 7 for data on shipments.) In spite of these delays, one analyst expected shipments of the i386SL to rise from a negligible number of units in 1990 to 1.8 million in 1992, and those of the i486 family to rise from 0.3 million units in 1990 to 3.7 million in 1992. In addition to accelerating the life cycle for existing processors, Intel had moved up the introduction date of the P5 and P6, further shortening future life cycles. Intel's forecast of microprocessor sales by type is reported in Exhibit 9. It predicted a rapid decline in shipments of 8- and 16-bit processors.

Intel attempted to counter the competitive threat from RISC-based chips by emphasizing performance and portability. It was believed that high-speed i486 and P5 chips would at least match the performance of recently introduced RISC products. Furthermore, Intel had an advantage over other microprocessor platforms in the sheer size of the previously installed based—85 million existing X86-based PCs, with more than 50,000 software applications and $40 billion invested in software. Exhibit 10 shows that, as of 1991, all major operating systems for microcomputers ran (or were soon to run) on Intel designs. No other type of microprocessor had more than two operating systems designed for it. The result was that Intel architecture had become the "port of choice," according to Andrew Grove, Intel's CEO.

Intel's final strategy for confronting potential competitors was its aggressive spending on R&D, equipment, and fabs to produce its chips. The company wanted to be strong in process technology and production capacity, and it wanted to use those strengths, together with its design capability, as competitive weapons.

In spite of Intel's responses, many informed observers worried about the company's ability to continue its rapid growth and sustain its generous margins. Analysts argued that if AMD could successfully clone the i486, others could and would do so as well. Rumors were already circulating that AMD would announce its 486-compatible chip earlier than expected and soon thereafter would raise substantial outside money for additional fabs. Even if AMD failed to build its own facilities, suitable state-of-the-art fabs could be rented from companies that produced less profitable semiconductors such as DRAMs and EPROMs. Analysts also knew that although the best known names in the PC business—Compaq, IBM, Dell, NEC, and Toshiba (together representing about 30% of microcomputer sales)—had thus far purchased microprocessors only from Intel, it was not clear that they would continue to do so.

The stock market seemed to treat the competitive threats to Intel with increasing seriousness. From the time of the announcement of the i386 in early 1986 until the recognition that AMD was successfully shipping its imitation in mid-1991, Intel's stock price rose from approximately $13 to $59 per share. By the fall of 1991, however, the stock had fallen to the low $40s. (See Exhibit 11 for information on stock prices.) Given 1991 anticipated earnings of $819 million, Intel's P/E was less than 11. Intel's management had become concerned about the market's increasingly negative view of Intel's competitive positioning.

Financial History

Intel had become a public corporation in 1971, the year it recorded its first net profit. Even at that time, Intel carried almost no debt on its books. As of December 31, 1971, Intel's net worth and total assets were $13,456,344 and $14,839,755, respectively. The firm's policy was to issue debt only when and if the terms were attractive. For example, in the fall of 1983, Intel issued $110 million of 20-year, adjustable-rate industrial revenue bonds, with an average interest rate of just under 8%.[3] In connection with those bonds, Intel was obliged to spend $110 million to finance expansion in Puerto Rico. To ensure that adequate debt financing would be available if suddenly needed, the company and its subsidiaries kept bank credit lines in place, currently allowing for over $900 million in borrowing capacity.

Intel's debt issues often contained equity-linked components. For example, in August 1980, the firm issued $150 million in 20-year, 7% convertible subordinated debentures. These debentures were called on September 14, 1983, and one month later, the bonds were converted into 5 million shares at approximately $30 per share. Intel also issued 10-year notes in May 1985 and April 1987 ($236.5 million of zero-coupon, 11.75% notes and $110 million of 8.125% notes, respectively). Both sets of notes were sold with detachable warrants, which yielded an additional $27.1 and $90.4 million in cash, respectively. The warrants from the note issues were exercised in 1990, resulting in the issuance of 14.15 million shares at an average price of $27.80 per share.

Intel had also issued stock during the last decade, although never publicly. On February 7, 1983, IBM purchased 12.5 million newly issued shares in Intel (equivalent to approximately 13% of previously outstanding shares) for $250 million. IBM, which accounted for 8.6% of Intel revenues in 1983, had clear incentives to strengthen Intel's balance sheet. In June 1987, however, IBM was persuaded to terminate its investment in Intel, and Intel repurchased and retired 13,350,000 shares from IBM for $361.6 million, or about $27 per share. In August 1987, Intel also issued 9 million 1-year warrants for $63.3 million. In August 1988, the warrants were exercised at a price of $30 per share, yielding Intel another $268.6 million in cash net of fees. Exhibit 11 shows the timing of these equity-linked transactions.

The company also maintained several liberal stock option plans, which generated cash through the exercise of employee options and direct-share purchases. During 1990—not an atypical year—options were exercised on 2.9 million shares, generating approximately $42 million in cash. In that year, employees also purchased an

---

3. During that year, the average U.S. Treasury medium- and long-term bond yields were 10.45% and 11.11%, respectively.

additional 1.4 million shares under Intel's stock participation plan, resulting in an additional inflow of $39.3 million.

In an effort to offset the steady dilution from the stock purchase and option plans, in August 1990, management authorized the repurchase of up to 20 million shares. Repurchases would be performed by the treasurer and would take place in the open market or in privately negotiated transactions. After consulting with Moore and others, Arvind Sodhani soon executed the repurchase of approximately 3.2 million shares at a total cost of $102.4 million. However, as management was hesitant to buy back shares at a price much above $40 per share, the repurchase activity soon came to a halt. With the stock price stalled in the low $40s, some analysts began to interpret Intel's reluctance to repurchase as a negative signal about the firm's future prospects.

Although Sodhani did not repurchase additional shares directly, he did perform a "conditional" repurchase in November 1991. That is, Intel privately sold about 3.5 million tradeable put warrants to some of its institutional investors for approximately $14 million. Each warrant gave its holder the right to sell one share of common stock back to Intel at $40 per share in 1 year's time. The repurchase was considered conditional because investors would not rationally elect the repurchase unless the stock price was below $40 per share on the warrants' expiration date.

In April 1989, Intel undertook several steps to strengthen its independence and to protect itself from potential hostile acquirers. Specifically, Intel issued to its existing stockholders a set of common-stock purchase rights, which would trade in a one-to-one ratio with existing shares of common stock. The rights could be exercised or traded separately from the shares of stock they represented only if certain events occurred. For example, under one of the rights' provisions, at any time after an entity acquired more than 20% but less than 50% of Intel's stock, Intel had the option to exchange the rights (other than those held by the acquirer) for shares of common stock, with an exchange ratio of one to one.[4] This gave Intel the ability to dilute substantially a potential acquirer's holdings and therefore create a large disincentive to attempt a hostile takeover.

During the 1980s, Intel's net cash position grew steadily. Between 1980 and 1982, the ratio of long-term debt to total assets stood at approximately 20%, and the firm's cash position was negligible. After IBM's stock purchase and the 1985 issuance of 10-year notes, Intel's cash and equivalents plus long-term investments (which consisted of liquid investments in bonds rated AA or higher) less long-term debt rose to approximately 15% of total assets in December 1986. By December 1991, this ratio had grown to approximately 38%. This was in spite of the fact that, during the 1986–1991 period, Intel had experienced very rapid growth, with revenues increasing at a compound annual rate of over 30%. Intel's competitors kept proportionately much smaller cash balances (see Exhibit 9), although several large firms in the industry, such as IBM, held larger absolute amounts.

The Decision

As Moore contemplated these developments, he wondered whether Intel's cash balances had grown unnecessarily large. At $2.4 billion, the firm could fund its planned investment expenditures out of cash for almost 2½ years without using any cash flow

---

4. The statuary and case law pertaining to such rights issues was highly developed in the State of Delaware, where Intel was incorporated beginning in mid-1989.

from operations. Although there remained great uncertainty about the level of these flows, earnings estimates from analysts suggested that operations would continue to generate cash—indeed, perhaps in substantial amounts. Exhibit 12 presents cash flow forecasts based on several analysts' expectations of future earnings.

Harold Hughes and Arvind Sodhani weighed the arguments for and against a change in cash disbursement policies. Both believed that Intel's cash was an important competitive weapon and that, with the economy in recession, "cash was king." It seemed to Hughes and Sodhani that the costs of holding cash were small, especially in view of the high returns Intel's treasury had earned on its cash balances. For several years, Hughes and Sodhani had posted returns of approximately 170 basis points over U.S. Treasury bills without investing in securities rated below AA (see Exhibit 2). This excess after-tax income in 1990 alone came to about $18 million. Nonetheless, Hughes and Sodhani started to explore several cash disbursement options that were open to Intel.

First, Intel could continue or expand its market-repurchase program. In practice, however, open-market repurchases were executed only when management could agree that the stock price was unduly low. Hughes and Sodhani knew that such consensus was difficult to achieve. One alternative was to undertake a formal fixed-price tender offer, in which Intel would publicly announce an offer to buy back shares at a given price. Another repurchase possibility was a Dutch auction, in which shareholders submitted schedules that reported the number of shares they would tender at each price across a range of prices. Intel would then choose the number of shares it wanted to repurchase by picking a single price at which to buy.

A second alterative was for Intel to declare a 40¢-per-share ($84 million total) annual dividend on its common stock. Dividends were controversial within Intel. While some favored dividends, others, such as Hughes and Sodhani, opposed them because dividends were a tax-disadvantaged means of disbursing corporate cash and represented an ongoing commitment that could be potentially difficult to maintain. Indeed, Hughes and Sodhani speculated that the market might react negatively to a dividend, perhaps pushing the stock price down even further. Nevertheless, dividends would give shareholders income on their holdings without their having to sell shares.

A final alternative was a package of two less conventional securities. For the first, Intel would distribute to shareholders a 2-year put warrant, one warrant for each share of stock. Each warrant would be tradeable and give its holder the right to sell 0.1 shares of stock back to Intel at the end of 2 years' time at a price of $50 per share. Thus, for example, if Intel's stock price was $40 per share in 2 years, Intel would be obliged to buy back 208.99/10 = 20.9 million shares at $50 each (or a total of $1 billion) from those who held the warrants. Investors who were not interested in holding the warrants could sell them in the open market at an expected price of about 60¢ per warrant. The second security in the package was $1 billion of 10-year convertible subordinated debentures with a 5% coupon. The bonds would be convertible at the end of 2 years into 13.3 million shares of Intel common stock at a conversion price of $75 per share.

Moore wondered about the implications of these measures for the company's future competitive position and for shareholder value.

EXHIBIT 1
Top Integrated Circuit Manufacturers, Worldwide Revenues (millions of dollars)

1976	Revenues	1981	Revenues	1987	Revenues	1991	Revenues
TI	$135	Intel	$491	NEC	$2,006	NEC	$4,742
Intel	132	NEC	438	Toshiba	1,566	Intel	4,059
NEC	74	Motorola	372	Intel	1,473	Toshiba	3,910
Gen'l Inst.	68	TI	350	Hitachi	1,236	Hitachi	3,587
National	67	Hitachi	288	Fujitsu	1,014	Motorola	3,096
Hitachi	63	National	255	Motorola	986	TI	2,667
AMI	59	Toshiba	250	Mitsubishi	811	Mitsubishi	2,121
Mostek	56	Fujitsu	218	TI	784	AMD	1,185
Motorola	55	Mostek	210	Matsushita	593	VLSI Tech.	165
Rockwell	50	Gen'l Inst.	141	OKI	566	Chips & Tech.	158

Source: Dataquest, 1992.

EXHIBIT 2
Annual Income Statements, 1980–1991 (millions of dollars)

	December 1980	December 1981	December 1982	December 1983	December 1984	December 1985	December 1986	December 1987	December 1988	December 1989	December 1990	December 1991(E)
Sales	$855	$789	$900	$1,122	$1,629	$1,365	$1,265	$1,907	$2,875	$3,127	$3,921	$4,779
Cost of goods sold	350	395	467	539	774	784	687	872	1,295	1,440	1,638	1,898
	504	393	432	583	855	581	578	1,035	1,580	1,687	2,283	2,881
SG & A	272	301	329	359	496	482	540	618	775	849	1,133	1,383
R&D	96	116	131	142	180	195	228	260	318	365	517	618
Advertising expense	12	14	14	16	24	30	28	28	55	55	94	121
Operating income before depreciation	232	93	103	224	359	99	38	417	805	838	1,151	1,498
Depreciation, depletion, and amortization	49	63	75	85	109	159	174	171	211	237	292	418
Operating profit	183	30	28	139	250	(60)	(135)	246	594	601	858	1,080
Interest expense	8	15	17	17	15	26	39	66	78	102	102	105
Interest income	9	21	18	46	57	53	42	61	102	154	203	194
Other nonoperating income	0	5	2	10	6	27	(42)	46	11	(70)	27	26
Pretax income	185	40	30	178	298	(5)	(175)	288	629	583	986	1,195
Total income taxes	89	13	0	62	100	(7)	9	112	176	192	336	376
Income before extraordinary items and discontinued operations	185	40	30	116	198	2	(183)	176	453	391	650	819
Extraordinary items	0	0	0	0	0	0	10	73	0	0	0	0
Net income	$ 97	$ 27	$ 30	$ 116	$ 198	$ 2	$ (173)	$ 248	$ 453	$ 391	$ 650	$ 819
Earnings per share (fully diluted)	0.74	0.20	0.22	0.70	1.13	0.01	–0.99	1.38	2.51	2.06	3.19	3.62
Common shares outstanding	128.21	131.30	136.09	167.55	170.75	174.12	176.66	168.33	180.54	184.52	199.65	208.99
Book value per share	3.38	3.72	4.06	6.60	7.97	8.16	7.22	7.76	11.52	13.81	17.99	21.14
Market-to-book ratio (end of year)	3.97	2.02	3.19	4.18	2.34	2.39	1.94	3.41	2.06	2.50	2.14	2.01

Source: Intel Corporation 1991 figures include casewriter estimates.

EXHIBIT 3

Annual Balance Sheet (millions of dollars)

	December 1980	December 1981	December 1982	December 1983	December 1984	December 1985	December 1986	December 1987	December 1988	December 1989	December 1990	December 1991(E)
Assets												
Cash and equivalents	$128	$115	$ 85	$ 389	$ 231	$ 361	$ 373	$ 619	$ 971	$1,090	$1,785	$2,277
Net receivables	196	180	221	303	354	364	298	439	506	569	710	698
Inventories	91	97	122	152	219	171	198	236	366	347	415	422
Other current assets	32	67	100	89	154	128	154	138	126	157	209	207
Total current assets	447	460	528	933	958	1,024	1,024	1,431	1,970	2,163	3,119	3,604
Gross PP&E	447	591	697	801	1,165	1,338	1,364	1,536	1,898	2,249	2,814	3,723
Accumulated depreciation	126	179	236	297	386	490	585	645	775	965	1,156	1,560
Net PP&E	321	412	462	504	778	848	779	891	1,122	1,284	1,658	2,163
Long-term investments[a]	0	0	51	217	272	267	264	262	422	508	561	480
Other assets	0	0	16	26	21	12	13	13	36	39	38	46
Total assets	$767	$872	$1,056	$1,680	$2,029	$2,152	$2,080	$2,597	$3,550	$3,994	$5,276	$6,292
Liabilities												
Long-term debt: current portion	$ 0	$ 0	$ 0	$ 0	$ 0	$ 4	$ 0	$ 117	$ 0	$ 16	$ 86	$ 0
Notes payable	12	32	75	81	66	84	112	335	217	140	193	173
Accounts payable	12	32	39	79	80	57	62	115	153	165	209	245
Taxes payable	4	0	0	18	40	3	15	25	156	167	241	152
Accrued expenses	55	46	56	73	117	85	118	206	308	337	464	536
Deferred income on shipment to distributors	46	53	52	74	88	72	67	83	100	96	121	122
Total current liabilities	147	172	223	326	390	307	374	882	934	921	1,314	1,228
Long-term debt	150	150	197	128	146	271	287	298	479	412	345	363
Deferred taxes	23	44	68	89	113	134	132	105	56	111	126	144
Investment tax credit	14	18	17	15	20	19	12	6	0	0	0	0
Equity												
Common stock + capital surplus[b]	128	143	177	631	671	730	757	540	861	1,011	1,404	1,411
Retained earnings[b]	305	345	375	491	689	691	518	766	1,219	1,538	2,188	3,007
Common equity	433	488	552	1,122	1,360	1,421	1,275	1,306	2,080	2,549	3,592	4,418
Put warrants	0	0	0	0	0	0	0	0	0	0	0	140
Total equity	433	488	552	1,122	1,360	1,421	1,275	1,306	2,080	2,549	3,592	4,558
Total liabilities and equity	$767	$872	$1,056	$1,680	$2,029	$2,152	$2,080	$2,597	$3,550	$3,994	$5,376	$6,292
Capital expenditures	156	157	138	145	388	236	155	302	362	422	680	948
Cash + Long-term investments – Long-term debt/Assets	−0.03	−0.04	−0.06	0.28	0.18	0.17	0.17	0.22	0.26	0.30	0.37	0.38

Source: Intel Corporation 1991 figures include casewriter estimates.

a. Long-term investments are held almost exclusively in investment-grade bonds.

b. Surplus on common stock and retained earnings accounts are restated from company reports in order that the retained earnings account above be consistent with the income statement in Exhibit 2.

EXHIBIT 4
Analyst Estimates of Market Segments, 1987–1991 (millions of dollars)

	1987	1988	1989	1990	1991
Segment Sales					
EPROMS	$ 130	$ 220	$ 265	$ 252	$ 228
SRAM	103	180	140	116	113
Other	102	137	120	133	131
Memory	335	537	525	501	472
8086 Family	69	39	29	18	12
80286	275	202	98	63	41
80386	210	538	822	1,084	1,361
80486	0	0	22	338	713
80586	0	0	0	0	0
i860	0	0	18	70	65
Coprocessors	81	175	163	233	255
Other	37	35	22	48	54
Microprocessors	672	989	1,174	1,854	2,501
8-bit microcontrollers	200	255	245	223	195
16-bit microcontrollers	67	110	120	143	177
Microcontrollers	267	365	365	366	372
Processor support	94	145	160	159	222
Graphics/Disk controllers	58	73	80	79	122
Communications	53	84	75	63	117
Peripherals	205	302	315	301	461
OEM PC	0	0	45	175	295
Other systems	428	682	702	723	723
Systems	428	682	747	898	1,018
Total	$1,907	$2,875	$3,126	$3,920	$4,824
Operating Profit					
Memory	$ 41	$ 81	$ 50	$ 57	$ 51
Microprocessors	97	275	262	500	776
Microcontrollers	25	71	68	62	46
Peripherals	23	50	61	65	91
Systems	60	117	116	174	123
Total	$ 246	$ 594	$ 557	$ 858	$1,087
Operating Margin					
Memory	12%	15%	10%	11%	11%
Microprocessors	14	28	22	27	31
Microcontrollers	9	19	19	17	12
Peripherals	11	17	19	22	20
Systems	14	17	16	19	12
Total	13%	21%	18%	22%	23%

Source: Analyst estimates, Morgan Stanley.

EXHIBIT 5
Intel Microprocessor Product Line

Chip Name	Introduction Date	Clock Speed	Mips	Price per Chip[a]	Internal Bus	External Bus	Number of Transistors	Typical Use
i8086	June 1978	5MHz	0.33	$ 5.50	16-bit	16-bit	29,000	Portable computing
		8MHz	0.66	6.00				
		10MHz	0.75	16.00				
i8088	June 1979	5MHz	0.33	3.00	16-bit	8-bit	29,000	Portable computing
		8MHz	0.66	4.00				
i286	February 1982	8MHz	1.20	8.00	16-bit	16-bit	130,000	Portable computing
		10MHz	1.50	8.00				
		12MHz	2.66	8.00				
i386DX	October 1985	16MHz	6.00	156.00	32-bit	32-bit	275,000	Desktop computing
	February 1987	20MHz	7.00	156.00				
	April 1988	25MHz	8.50	156.00				
	April 1989	33MHz	11.40	195.00				
i386SX	June 1988	16MHz	2.50	57.00	32-bit	16-bit	275,000	Entry-level desktop and portable computing
	January 1989	20MHz	4.20	85.50				
i386SL	October 1990	20MHz	4.21	135.00	32-bit	16-bit	855,000	Portable computing
	September 1991	25MHz	5.30	189.00				
i486DX	April 1989	25MHz	20.00	428.00[b]	32-bit	32-bit	1,200,000	Desktop computing and servers
	May 1990	33MHz	27.00	428.00				
	June 1991	50MHz	40.70	644.00				
i486SX	September 1991	16MHz	13.00	214.00[c]	32-bit	32-bit	1,185,000	Desktop computing
	April 1991	20MHz	16.50	242.00[d]				
	September 1991	25MHz	20.00	333.00[e]				

Source: Intel Corporation and *PC Week* (November 1981).

a. Based on purchase of 1,000 chips.

b. Low-power version costs $471.00.

c. Low-power version costs $235.00.

d. Low-power version costs $266.00.

e. Low-power version costs $366.00.

EXHIBIT 6
Microprocessor Product Life Cycle

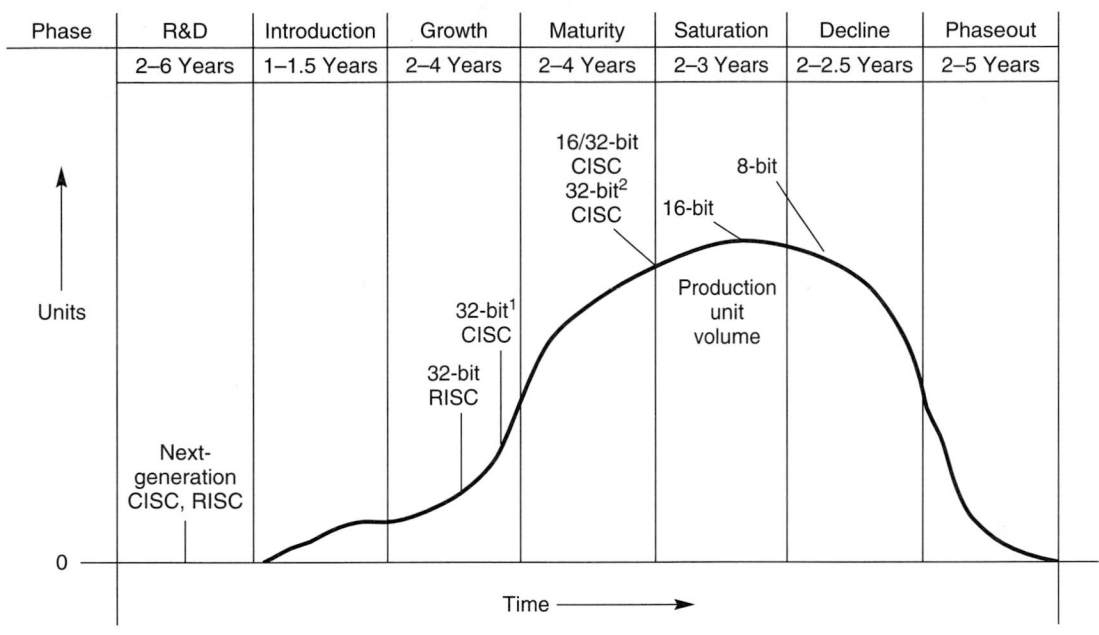

Source: Dataquest and case writer estimates.

Note: 16/32-bit CISC includes i386SX, 32-bit[2] CISC includes i386DX, 32-bit[1] CISC includes i386SL and i486 family, and next-generation CISC includes Intel's P6 microprocessor.

EXHIBIT 7

Shipments and Installed Base of Various Microprocessors, 1981–1991 (millions of units)

	1981	*1982*	*1983*	*1984*	*1985*	*1986*	*1987*	*1988*	*1989*	*1990*	*1991*
Intel micro-based											
Units shipped	0.0	0.2	1.0	2.6	4.6	6.1	8.8	11.9	15.7	18.6	20.7
Installed base	0.0	0.2	1.2	3.7	9.2	15.1	23.5	34.4	47.8	62.6	77.7
8088, 8086											
Units shipped	0.0	0.2	0.9	2.4	4.1	4.5	5.1	5.0	4.7	3.4	2.3
Installed base	0.0	0.2	1.1	3.5	8.7	13.1	17.9	22.0	24.7	24.7	22.8
80286											
Units shipped	0.0	0.0	0.0	0.1	0.4	1.6	3.3	5.7	7.6	7.2	6.8
Installed base	0.0	0.0	0.0	0.1	0.5	2.0	5.2	10.9	18.4	25.3	31.2
80386											
Units shipped	0.0	0.0	0.0	0.0	0.0	0.0	0.4	1.2	3.3	7.8	10.3
Installed base	0.0	0.0	0.0	0.0	0.0	0.0	0.4	1.5	4.7	5.5	12.5
80486											
Units shipped	0.0	0.0	0.0	0.0	0.0	0.0	0.0	0.0	0.0	0.1	1.3
Installed base	0.0	0.0	0.0	0.0	0.0	0.0	0.0	0.0	0.0	0.1	1.3
Motorola micro-based											
Units shipped	0.0	0.0	0.0	0.5	0.7	0.9	1.2	1.6	1.8	2.6	3.0
Installed base	0.0	0.0	0.1	0.5	1.3	2.2	3.4	5.0	6.4	8.4	10.7
RISC											
Units shipped	0.0	0.0	0.0	0.0	0.0	0.0	0.0	0.0	0.0	0.2	0.3
Installed base	0.0	0.0	0.0	0.0	0.0	0.0	0.0	0.0	0.1	0.3	0.6

Source: Infocorp (1992).

EXHIBIT 8
Selected Financial Data, 1987–1991 (millions of dollars)

Advanced Micro Devices

	1987	1988	1989	1990	1991(E)
Sales	$ 997	$ 1,126	$ 1,105	$ 1,059	$ 1,175
Net income	(48)	19	46	(54)	(59)
Cash flow	105	173	182	75	188
Capital expenditures	138	132	159	304	142
Cash	235	287	279	115	128
Total assets	1,114	1,081	1,122	1,112	—
Long-term debt	$ 136	$ 130	$ 126	$ 131	$ 155
(Long-term debt – Cash)/Market value of equity (%)	-0.13	-0.23	-0.24	0.04	—
Years of cash[a]	0.7	1.2	1.0	-0.1	-0.2
Return on equity (%)	-7.3	3.0	6.7	-8.4	
Cash dividend	$ 0	$ 0	$ 0	$ 0	$ 0
High price	$ 24.88	$ 16.88	$ 10.50	$ 11.38	—
Low price	$ 7.50	$ 7.13	$ 7.13	$ 3.63	—
Book/share	$ 6.21	$ 5.91	$ 6.39	$ 5.63	$ 6.70
P/E ratio	—	78	18	—	—
Market value	$ 775	$ 690	$ 639	$ 401	
Shares (millions)	78.51	79.95	81.14	82.34	83.60
Beta	1.96	1.90	1.94	1.69	1.92

Chips and Technologies

	1987	1988	1989	1990	1991
Sales	$ 80	$ 141	$ 218	$ 293	$ 225
Net income	13	22	33	29	(10)
Cash flow	14	24	38	29	2
Capital expenditures	2	7	5	14	9
Cash	30	48	59	72	38
Total assets	51	95	141	202	159
Long-term debt	$ 1	$ 3	$ 6	$ 9	$ 7
(Long-term debt – Cash)/Market value of equity (%)	-1.09	-0.17	-0.16	-0.21	-0.30
Years of cash[a]	18.5	6.8	10.8	4.7	3.6
Return on equity (%)	48.8	33.2	31.4	1.9	-8.4
Cash dividend	$ 0	$ 0	$ 0	$ 0	$ 0
High price	$ 37.75	$ 21.25	$ 26.25	$ 23.50	$ 13.25
Low price	$ 8.25	$ 10.75	$ 13.25	$ 5.25	$ 6.00
Book/share	$ 2.03	$ 4.79	$ 7.30	$ 9.31	$ 8.51
P/E ratio	14	8	7	10	
Market value	$ 322	$ 261	$ 339	$ 306	$ 103
Shares (millions)	13.01	13.92	14.44	14.39	13.44
Beta	—	—	2.13	1.92	2.12

Intel

	1987	1988	1989	1990	1991(E)
Sales	$ 1,907	$ 2,875	$ 3,127	$ 3,921	$ 4,779
Net income	248	453	391	650	819
Cash flow	347	664	628	943	1,215
Capital expenditures	302	477	422	680	873
Cash[b]	881	1,393	1,598	2,346	2,757
Total assets	2,597	3,550	3,994	5,376	6,292
Long-term debt	$ 298	$ 479	$ 412	$ 345	$ 363
(Long-term debt – Cash)/Market value of equity (%)	-0.13	-0.21	-0.19	-0.26	-0.49
Years of cash[a]	1.9	1.9	2.8	2.9	2.7
Return on equity (%)	13.4	21.8	15.3	18.1	22.8
Cash dividend	$ 0	$ 0	$ 0	$ 0	$ 0
High price	$ 41.83	$ 37.25	$ 36.00	$ 52.00	$ 59.00
Low price	$ 13.83	$ 19.25	$ 22.88	$ 28.00	$ 37.00
Book/share	7.76	11.52	13.81	17.99	21.14
P/E ratio	19	9	17	12	11
Market value	$ 4,461	$ 4,288	$ 6,366	$ 7,687	$ 8,882
Shares (millions)	168.33	180.54	184.52	199.65	208.99
Beta	1.67	1.74	1.68	1.70	1.75

IBM

	1987	1988	1989	1990	1991
Sales	$54,217	$59,681	$62,710	$69,018	$64,700
Net income	5,258	5,806	3,758	5,020	2,425
Cash flow	8,785	9,362	7,998	10,237	8,696
Capital expenditures	4,304	5,390	6,414	6,509	6,580
Cash	6,967	6,123	4,961	4,551	4,700
Total assets	63,688	73,037	77,734	87,568	—
Long-term debt	$ 3,858	$ 8,518	$10,825	$11,943	$11,991
(Long-term debt – Cash)/Market value of equity (%)	-0.05	0.03	0.11	0.11	
Years of cash[a]	0.7	-0.4	-0.9	-1.1	1.1
Return on equity (%)	13.7	13.9	9.8	14.1	
Cash dividend	$ 2,654	$ 2,609	$ 2,752	$ 2,774	$ 2,803
High price	$175.88	$129.50	$130.88	$123.13	—
Low price	$102.00	$104.25	$ 93.38	$ 94.50	—
Book/share	64.09	66.99	67.01	74.96	74.60
P/E ratio	13	13	15	11	—
Market value	$68,960	$71,875	$54,094	$64,567	—
Shares (millions)	597.05	589.74	574.70	571.39	572.14
Beta	0.75	0.81	0.85	0.75	0.74

a. Years of cash reports the number of years of current investment expenditures that can be funded by net cash balances: (Cash – Long-term debt)/Capital expenditures.
b. Cash balances for Intel include long-term investments.

(continued)

EXHIBIT 8 (concluded)

LSI Logic Corp.

	1987	1988	1989	1990	1991
Sales	$ 262	$ 379	$ 547	$ 655	—
Net income	11	25	(25)	(33)	—
Cash flow	50	77	63	67	—
Capital expenditures	174	101	114	62	—
Cash	267	204	153	159	—
Total assets	699	787	765	784	—
Long-term debt	$ 188	$ 192	$ 204	$ 190	—
(Long-term debt – Cash)/Market value of equity (%)	-0.20	-0.03	0.18	0.12	—
Years of cash[a]	0.5	0.1	-0.4	-0.5	—
Return on equity (%)	3.5	7.2	-8.4	-12.3	—
Cash dividend	$ 0	$ 0	$ 0	$ 0	—
High price	$17.25	$13.63	$12.38	$13.00	—
Low price	$ 6.50	$ 7.25	$ 6.25	$ 5.13	—
Book/share	$ 7.70	$ 8.20	$ 7.24	$ 6.55	—
P/E ratio	37	19	—	—	—
Market value	$ 395	$ 435	$ 293	$ 263	—
Shares (millions)	40.05	40.46	41.07	42.06	—
Beta	2.30	1.95	1.76	1.48	1.71

Motorola, Inc.

	1987	1988	1989	1990	1991(E)
Sales	$ 6,707	$ 8,250	$ 9,620	$10,885	$11,400
Net income	308	445	498	499	450
Cash flow	802	988	1,148	1,289	1,267
Capital expenditures	689	873	1,094	1,256	1,128
Cash	258	340	433	577	627
Total assets	5,321	6,710	7,686	8,742	—
Long-term debt	$ 344	$ 343	$ 755	$ 792	$ 794
(Long-term debt – Cash)/Market value of equity (%)	0.01	0.00	0.04	0.03	—
Years of cash[a]	-0.1	-0.0	-0.3	-0.2	-0.1
Return on equity (%)	10.2	13.2	13.1	11.7	—
Cash dividend	$ 83	$ 87	$ 99	$ 100	$ 100
High price	$ 74.00	$ 54.63	$ 62.50	$ 88.38	—
Low price	$ 34.50	$ 35.88	$ 39.50	$ 49.13	—
Book/share	$ 23.26	$ 26.02	$ 28.16	$ 32.32	$ 35.05
P/E ratio	21	12	15	14	—
Market value	$ 6,433	$ 5,447	$ 7,612	$ 6,898	—
Shares (millions)	129.30	129.70	130.40	131.70	131.95
Beta	1.47	1.49	1.55	1.48	1.49

Texas Instruments

	1987	1988	1989	1990	1991
Sales	$5,594	$6,295	$6,522	$6,567	$6,600
Net income	309	366	292	(39)	(170)
Cash flow	637	756	745	502	398
Capital expenditures	463	628	863	909	500
Cash	663	780	637	412	416
Total assets	4,256	4,427	4,804	5,048	—
Long-term debt	$ 487	$ 624	$ 618	$ 715	$ 950
(Long-term debt – Cash)/Market value of equity (%)	-0.04	-0.05	-0.01	0.10	—
Years of cash[a]	0.4	0.2	0.0	-0.3	-1.0
Return on equity (%)	14.9	21.3	14.9	-2.1	—
Cash dividend	$ 55	$ 58	$ 59	$ 59	$ 59
High price	$80.25	$60.00	$46.75	$44.00	—
Low price	$36.25	$34.50	$28.13	$22.50	—
Book/share	$21.95	$21.36	$24.10	$22.46	$17.10
P/E ratio	15	10	12	—	—
Market value	$4,383	$3,306	$2,924	$3,108	—
Shares (millions)	78.62	80.65	81.50	81.78	81.99
Beta	1.09	1.31	1.50	1.43	1.58

VLSI Technology

	1987	1988	1989	1990	1991
Sales	$ 172	$ 221	$ 288	$ 325	$ 410
Net income	8	7	1	(13)	9.5
Cash flow	32	36	38	36	57
Capital expenditures	50	55	39	35	50
Cash	103	75	55	35	41
Total assets	271	303	318	327	—
Long-term debt	$ 81	$ 84	$ 85	$ 89	$ 100
(Long-term debt – Cash)/Market value of equity (%)	-0.09	0.04	0.17	0.48	—
Years of cash[a]	0.4	-0.2	-0.8	-1.5	-1.2
Return on equity (%)	5.7	4.5	0.3	-8.7	—
Cash dividend	$ 0	$ 0	$ 0	$ 0	$ 0
High price	$20.25	$11.38	$10.13	$12.25	—
Low price	$ 7.13	$ 5.88	$ 6.38	$ 3.00	—
Book/share	$ 6.15	$ 6.40	$ 6.42	$ 5.86	$ 6.30
P/E ratio	36	29	369	@NM	—
Market value	$ 246	$ 200	$ 178	$ 113	—
Shares (millions)	22.86	23.48	24.17	25.11	25.81
Beta	2.11	1.84	1.69	1.63	1.99

Source: Value Line and Standard and Poor's.

a. Years of cash reports the number of years of current investment expenditures that can be funded by net cash balances: (Cash – Long-term debt)/Capital expenditures.

b. Cash balances for Intel include long-term investments.

EXHIBIT 9
Intel X86 Family Sales

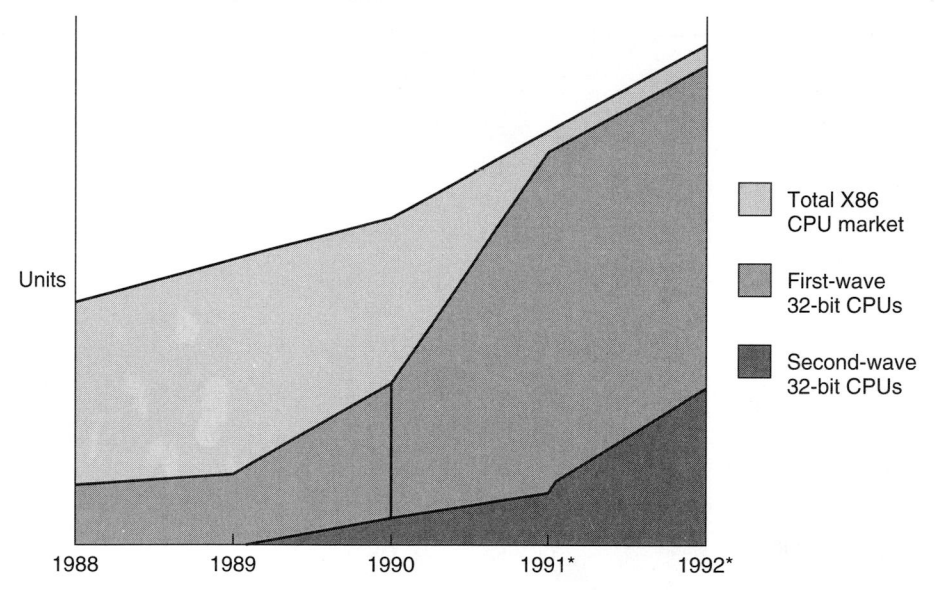

Source: Intel Corporation.

*Projected.

Note: First-wave 32-bit CPUs include i386DX and i3865SX; second-wave 32-bit CPUs include i386SL and the i486 family.

EXHIBIT 10
Portability of Various Microprocessor Platforms

	Microprocessor Platform				
Operating System Software	*X86*	*68000*	*MIPS*	*SPARC*	*RS/6000*
DOS	x				
Windows	x				
32-bit OS/2	x				
UNIX	x	x	x	x	x
Microsoft Windows NT#	x		x		
Apple/IBM New OS#	x	x			x
Sunsoft Solaris 2.0#	x			x	

Source: Intel Corporation.

Note: # = Software under design.

EXHIBIT 11
Stock Price History and Recent End-of-Month Stock Prices

Intel Stock Price History

Recent End-of-Month Stock Prices

	Intel	AMD	Chips & Technology
31-Dec-90	$38.500	$ 4.875	$ 7.250
31-Jan-91	45.750	7.250	10.125
28-Feb-91	47.750	8.125	11.250
29-Mar-91	46.750	10.500	10.750
30-Apr-91	49.250	12.250	10.000
31-May-91	55.750	13.500	9.750
28-Jun-91	46.500	12.000	7.625
31-Jul-91	47.000	11.125	8.000
30-Aug-91	49.500	12.375	8.875
30-Sep-91	42.250	9.375	9.125
31-Oct-91	40.625	12.750	8.125
29-Nov-91	41.000	14.375	8.000
20-Dec-91	42.500	17.000	7.750

EXHIBIT 12
Estimates of Future Cash Flows

Depreciation Worksheet	*1991*	*1992*	*1993*	*1994*	*1995*
Earnings estimates from analysts					
Average	819	862	1,028	1,166	1,339
Pessimistic	819	485	595	700	900
Capital expenditures	(948)	(1,200)	(1,380)	(1,587)	(1,746)
Land and buildings	(237)	(240)	(276)	(317)	(349)
Machinery and equipment	(711)	(960)	(1,104)	(1,270)	(1,397)
Depreciation expense	418	666	971	1,044	1,235
Net additions to PPE	(530)	(534)	(409)	(543)	(511)
Decrease in net working capital	(58)	(11)	(42)	(35)	(43)
Shares issued, @$40, 3M/yr	120	120	120	120	120
Put warrants issued	14	0	0	0	0
Paydown of long-term debt to 0	0	(91)	(91)	(91)	(90)
Annual change in cash[a]					
Average	365	346	606	617	815
% of estimated revenues	8%	9%	12%	11%	12%
Pessimistic	365	1	198	221	426
% of estimated revenues	8%	0%	2%	3%	4%
Cash balance plus long-term investments less long-term debt					
Average	2,394	2,740	3,346	3,964	4,779
Pessimistic	2,394	2,395	2,593	2,815	3,241
Total assets	6,292	7,169	8,309	9,335	10,694
Total cash/Total assets					
Average	38%	38%	40%	42%	45%
Pessimistic	38%	33%	31%	30%	30%

Source: Intel Corporation, and casewriter and analyst estimates.

Notes:

Capital expenditures are assumed to grow at 15% per year.

Depreciation is calculated straight line over 3.5 years for machinery and equipment and 25 years for plant and property.

Capital spending is also depreciated for six months in the year made. Net working capital is calculated as Current assets – Current liabilities – Cash and cash equivalents. In 1990 and 1991, net working capital was 28% and 24% of earnings, respectively. Estimates for 1992–1995 assume that net working capital remains at 25% of average estimated earnings.

a. Annual change in cash is equal to Estimated earnings and net additions to PP&E + Decrease in net working capital + Proceeds from shares and warrants issued + Cost of paying down long-term debt.

R.J. Reynolds International Financing

In August 1985, Earl Hall, the director of corporate finance at R.J. Reynolds Industries, Inc. (RJR), had requested from the company's various bankers proposals for financing a portion of its recent $4.9 billion acquisition of Nabisco Brands, Inc. As part of the acquisition agreement, RJR would issue $1.2 billion of 12-year notes and $1.2 billion of preferred stock in the U.S. domestic markets within the next few weeks. It had already funded $1.5 billion of the Nabisco acquisition, leaving $1 billion more to finance.

Responding to this request, a financing team at Morgan Guaranty Trust Company in New York, along with their colleagues at Morgan Guaranty Ltd. (the merchant banking affiliate) in London, had spent the last few weeks analyzing the terms of potential deals RJR could issue in the Eurobond market. One interesting idea was a 5-year, yen/dollar dual-currency Eurobond. The New York team had been told by London that Reynolds could issue ¥25 billion of noncallable bonds at a price of 101.50% of par, with an annual coupon of 7¾% paid in yen and fees of 1⅞%. However, the final principal payment would be $115.956 million rather than the ¥25 billion face amount. RJR might want some 5-year debt, and the coupon seemed attractive. However, the team was concerned about the foreign exchange risks presented by such a hybrid structure and whether this transaction made sense for RJR. Thus, the team would also need to consider ways to hedge the dual-currency bond.

Furthermore, the group in New York thought it was appropriate to evaluate the costs of this structure in light of the terms on other potential deals mentioned by London. One alternative would be 5-year Eurodollar bonds, and another was 5-year Euroyen bonds. The team realized that it would also need to evaluate the Eurodollar bonds in terms of the all-in cost of hedging or swapping the Euroyen bonds into a dollar liability.

This case was prepared by Research Associate William B. Allen, Jr. under the supervision of Professor W. Carl Kester.

Harvard Business School case 287–057.

R.J. Reynolds

R.J. Reynolds Industries, Inc., a major international consumer products company based in Winston-Salem, North Carolina, operated tobacco products and food and beverage businesses throughout the world. RJR sold tobacco products to more than 160 markets around the world. Popular cigarette brands in the United States included Camel, Winston, Salem, and Vantage, all four of which ranked among the top ten best-selling domestic brands in 1984. Food and beverage operations were conducted through Del Monte, Heublein, and Kentucky Fried Chicken subsidiaries. Del Monte was the largest canner of fruits and vegetables in the world; its other product lines included Canada Dry and Hawaiian Punch beverages, Sunkist soft drinks, Morton frozen foods, and Chun-King oriental-style foods. Heublein was the largest producer of vodka and pre-mixed cocktails in the United States and one of the nation's largest producers of wine. Kentucky Fried Chicken was the largest chicken chain in the United States and ranked second in worldwide fast-food sales.

RJR's strategy was to focus on high-margin consumer-related businesses with a dominant or leading position in their respective industries. This led to an active program of acquisitions and divestitures, which began with the purchase of Del Monte in 1979, followed by the purchase of Heublein in 1982. During 1983, RJR acquired Canada Dry and Sunkist as part of its Del Monte subsidiary. This consumer focus was further refined in 1984 with the spin-off of Sea-Land, the world's largest container shipping company, and the sale for cash of Aminoil, the second-largest independent oil and gas exploration company in the United States. The acquisition of Nabisco in mid-1985 fit neatly within the company's overall strategic plan.

RJR, which ranked 23rd in 1984 on the *Fortune 500* list of companies, had sales of almost $13 billion and net income of $1.2 billion for that year (see Exhibit 1). Tobacco-related sales accounted for 58% of revenues and 75% of income, with food and beverage sales accounting for another 36% of revenue and 22% of income. Although tobacco products sales had grown at an annual rate of approximately 8% over the last few years, food and beverage sales had grown at an annual rate of 22%.

Total assets were $9.3 billion at the end of 1984 (see Exhibit 2). With the sale of its energy operations, cash and short-term investments more than tripled to $1.3 billion in 1984 from $363 million in 1983. Total long-term debt of $1.3 billion was 14% of total assets—a slight decrease compared to 15% in 1983. In November 1984, RJR purchased and retired 10 million shares of its common stock at an aggregate cost of $738 million. In May 1985 common stock was split 2.5 for 1. By August 1985, RJR had repurchased an additional 7.9 million of its common shares at an aggregate cost of $248 million. As of mid-1985, the stock was selling for around $27 per share, and RJR was in the process of listing its shares on several major foreign stock markets.

The majority of RJR's sales and manufacturing was in the United States, although Europe, Canada, Australia, and parts of Asia were important markets (see Exhibit 3). RJR's various foreign subsidiaries hedged nondollar operating cash flows through its Swiss banking subsidiary, which, in turn, selectively hedged the global currency exposure of RJR. Foreign subsidiaries with substantial manufacturing operations, such as Germany, financed these assets in part by borrowing in local markets. RJR's Japanese operations consisted primarily of its Kentucky Fried Chicken chain. Fixed assets were minimal, and yen cash flows were used to support expansion within Japan.

The Nabisco Acquisition

In June 1985, RJR announced the acquisition of Nabisco Brands, Inc. for $4.9 billion. Nabisco, one of the largest food companies in the United States, manufactured and sold cookies, crackers, nuts and snacks, confectionery desserts, margarines, hot cereals, pet snacks, and consumer yeast. Nabisco products were also produced and marketed in Canada, the United Kingdom, Continental Europe, Latin America, and the Asia/Pacific region.

Nabisco's sales grew 5% to $6.3 billion during 1984, while net income decreased to $309 million from $323 million (see Exhibit 4). Total assets at the end of 1984 were $3.8 billion, and the balance sheet showed little change from the previous year (see Exhibit 5). Over 60% of sales and 75% of earnings were in the United States (see Exhibit 6). Assets in the United States, including corporate headquarters, represented about 60% of the consolidated total. Significant foreign operations were located in both Europe (including the United Kingdom) and Canada. In 1984 European sales and earnings were 18% and 10%, respectively, of the consolidated total. Products marketed in Europe were primarily brand-name biscuits, crackers, and desserts. Identifiable assets in Europe of $373 million represented 21% of the world total. In Canada, manufacturing plants in various provinces supported sales of brand-name cookies, crackers, and other food products. Sales in Canada were 12% and earnings 10% of the consolidated total.

The first step of the acquisition was a tender offer for 51% of Nabisco's stock for $2.5 billion in cash. The remaining 49% of the outstanding stock, valued at an additional $2.4 billion, would be acquired in a few weeks by an exchange of both RJR preferred stock and 12-year U.S. domestic notes, each with a value of $1.2 billion at the time of the exchange.

The $2.5 billion cash paid at the conclusion of the tender offer was obtained from $500 million of cash on hand and $2 billion of bank borrowings and commercial paper. RJR decided to retain only $500 million of this amount as short-term, floating-rate debt and to seek alternative funding for the remaining $1.5 billion. The company analyzed the maturity spectrum of its existing debt and targeted amounts for various maturities ranging from 4 to 30 years. The entire financing operation was further complicated by the fact that RJR's debt had been downgraded to single A following the announcement of the acquisition. The company was not sure how this decision would affect its financing operation.

By the end of July, RJR saw windows in the domestic bond market and quickly issued $500 million of bonds: $250 million of 30-year debentures and $250 million of 8-year notes. The all-in costs of these issues were 11.857%, or Treasuries plus 99 basis points, for the 30-year debentures, and 10.90%, or Treasuries plus 54 basis points, for the 8-year notes. Sourcing the remaining $1 billion remained problematic, however. RJR did not wish to jeopardize the reception of either the $1.2 billion of domestic 12-year notes or the $1.2 billion of preferred stock that it was committed to exchange for the remaining portion of Nabisco stock.

Dual-Currency Bonds

Dual-currency bonds were denominated and paid interest in one currency but were redeemable in another. Typically, the denominations and interest payments were in low-interest-rate foreign currencies, such as Swiss francs or Japanese yen, while redemption was in U.S. dollars. The coupons were usually set above the yields prevailing in the foreign currency but below the rates on dollar bonds. Also, the implied exchange rate at redemption, determined by dividing the foreign currency denomination amount by the dollar redemption amount, provided for some appreciation of the foreign currency against the dollar.

The first dual currency bonds were launched by American Medical International N.V. in the Swiss market in 1982. This was followed by a slow but steady stream of Swiss franc/U.S. dollar dual-currency issues over the following years. By mid-1985 there were just over 20 dual-currency bonds listed on the Zurich stock exchange, totaling almost SFr 2 billion. Most of these bonds had 8–10-year maturities, although some of the earlier issues had 12- and 15-year maturities. The coupons were typically 7–7½%—perhaps 100–200 basis points higher than comparable regular Swiss franc bonds. However, the implied exchange rate at maturity was often SFr 1.60–1.90 per U.S. dollar compared to spot rates that averaged above SFr 2.00 from 1982 to 1985. With a favorable exchange rate at redemption relative to prevailing spot rates, Swiss franc dual-currency bonds were targeted to small retail investors to provide a convenient way to speculate in future SFr/U.S.$ exchange rates.

Although there had been some interest in dual-currency bonds in other currencies, the real growth potential in the market appeared to be in yen/U.S. dollar bonds. With the liberalization in May 1985 of the Euroyen market, several yen/U.S. dollar issues had been launched during the summer of 1985. The standard for these issues was set by the Ford Motor Credit yen/U.S. dollar dual-currency bonds launched in July 1985. This 10-year, ¥25 billion issue was offered at a price of $100^{11}/_{16}\%$ of par, with a coupon of 8% and an effective redemption exchange rate of ¥208. Coupons on comparable Euroyen bonds were 100 to 150 basis points lower than this, and new 10-year Japanese government bonds had coupons of only 6.2%.

The yen/U.S. dollar dual-currency bonds were targeted primarily at Japanese institutions that wished to lock in high coupon yields and were willing to assume the foreign exchange risk at redemption. Many Japanese investment funds, such as those managed by the life insurance companies, were evaluated in light of current yields, while foreign exchange and capital gains and losses were booked to reserve accounts. These and other institutions wanted to replace the substantial amounts of maturing 10-year Japanese government bonds, issued in the turbulent years following the oil crisis in 1974–1975, which bore coupons of 8% or more.

An important part of many of these deals was the attractive foreign exchange forward rates Japanese banks would often offer to borrowers. A host of U.S. corporations and some European sovereigns and corporations were able to hedge the yen liabilities into other currencies—primarily U.S. dollars—at extremely favorable rates. Market participants wondered if these off-market forward rates were economical deals for the Japanese banks, perhaps offset by the likes of Japanese oil importers who needed to buy dollars forward to pay for future oil supplies, or whether they were ambitious attempts to buy into the Eurobond business by winning the attention of prestigious borrowers.

Despite their popularity with borrowers, yen/U.S. dollar dual-currency bonds were not without their critics. Many investors, noting the exchange rates indicated in the long-dated forward exchange market, believed that either the coupon was too low for the implied redemption exchange rate, or the redemption exchange rate did not allow enough appreciation of the yen against the dollar. Other market participants compared these bonds to private placements because they were usually presold to Japanese financial institutions. Although many of these deals were arranged by non-Japanese investment banks, it was primarily the Japanese banks that had strong placing power with investors. In some cases, the non-Japanese bank underwriter who arranged the deal was a colead manager in name only and took no allocation of bonds to sell. Yen/U.S. dollar dual-currency bonds typically disappeared from dealers' screens just a few days after they were launched, and there was virtually no secondary market trading.

Neither the stipulation by the Japanese Ministry of Finance (MOF) that no more than 10% of a Japanese firm's assets be held in foreign securities nor the requirement that Eurobonds be held for 180 days outside Japan prevented most of these bonds from ultimately finding their way back to Japan. Many observers believed that the offshore subsidiaries of cash-rich Japanese life insurance and trust companies warehoused these bonds for six months until they could be sold in Japan. During the summer of 1985, suspected hedging activities associated with temporarily warehousing the large rush of issues caused the yen/U.S. dollar six-month forward foreign exchange market virtually to dry up. With such apparent disregard for the guidelines, many market participants wondered if the MOF would soon crack down.

Analyzing the Yen/Dollar Dual-Currency Eurobonds

Before making a proposal to Mr. Hall at RJR, the Morgan team in New York wanted to consider carefully the terms of the various deals supplied by its colleagues at Morgan Guaranty Ltd. (MGL) in London. Based on its close relationships with various Japanese financial institutions, MGL felt confident that it could arrange a ¥25 billion issue of 5-year, noncallable yen/U.S. dollar dual-currency Eurobonds at 101.50% of par. The annual coupons of 7¾% would be paid in yen, but the final principal repayment would be $115.956 million rather than the yen face amount. (See Exhibit 7 for a summary of financing terms for various structures available to RJR.) The team realized that dual-currency bonds might present RJR with additional foreign exchange exposure risks and, therefore, would require careful analysis. Furthermore, it wanted to be prepared for questions about the relative cost of this issue and how the markets would receive this structure.

The team would first need to determine whether it made sense for RJR to take on a yen liability. If so, it would then need to determine whether RJR would be better off leaving the cash flows of the dual-currency bond as proposed, thus exposing RJR only to the annual yen coupons, or modifying the cash flow structure. The yen/U.S. dollar dual-currency Eurobond could, for example, be converted into a regular yen liability by buying dollars for 5-year forward delivery against the yen in the interbank foreign exchange (FX) forward market. If a yen liability did not make sense, a regular dollar liability could be created by buying yen forward against dollars to cover the annual yen coupons over the next 5 years. The group in New York was aware that MGL had negotiated special yen/U.S. dollar FX forward rates for RJR (see Exhibit 8) through Nikko Securities Ltd., which would likely participate in the management group for this deal. These forwards might make the all-in dollar cost of this alternative quite attractive.

The all-in costs of the modified yen/U.S. dollar dual-currency bonds could then be compared with the all-in costs of other potential deals. With $1.2 billion of 12-year notes scheduled to be launched in the domestic debt market in just a few weeks, it seemed prudent to restrict other financing choices to the offshore markets. One relatively straightforward alternative would be to issue 5-year Eurodollar bonds. RJR could issue $100 million of 5-year, noncallable Eurodollar bonds at 100.125% of par, with an annual coupon of 10⅛% and fees of 1⅞%. The all-in cost of this deal would provide a benchmark spread over comparable Treasury securities that could be used in comparing the various financing alternatives under consideration. Five-year U.S. Treasuries were trading at a yield of 9.88%.

RJR could also issue ¥25 billion 5-year noncallable Euroyen bonds at a price of 100.25% of par, with an annual coupon of 6⅜% and fees of 1⅞%. The team wondered how the all-in yen cost of this deal would compare to the yen/U.S. dollar dual-currency bond completely hedged into yen. It also wondered how the all-in *dollar* costs of the Euroyen bonds (either hedged or swapped into a dollar liability) compared to the all-in cost of the straight Eurodollar bonds. The Euroyen bonds could be hedged into dollars using FX forwards in a manner similar to that used to hedge the yen/U.S. dollar dual-currency bonds into dollars.

As an alternative to using FX forwards, RJR could convert a Euroyen liability to a dollar liability with a currency swap. MGL indicated that it could arrange swaps in which it would pay to RJR fixed yen cash flows with an annual internal rate of return of 7.10% in exchange for receiving from RJR six-month dollar LIBOR. Similarly, MGL would agree to pay six-month dollar LIBOR to RJR in exchange for receiving from RJR fixed dollar cash flows with an annual internal rate of return of 10.92% (see Exhibit 9). Since the LIBOR payments and receipts offset each other, RJR could effectively contract to receive from MGL fixed yen cash flows in exchange for paying fixed dollar cash flows.

To calculate the all-in dollar costs of the Euroyen bond swapped into dollars, the quoted yen swap rate would be adjusted to make it equal the all-in cost of the Euroyen bond. The team suspected that the 7.10% quoted yen swap rate paid to RJR would exceed the all-in cost of the Euroyen bonds; thus, there would be extra yen basis points left on the table. These extra yen basis points could be converted to dollar basis points. The equivalent amount of dollar basis points would then be subtracted from the dollar swap rate in order to determine the all-in cost of the dollar cash flows from the swap. Before making the calculations, the team drew a simple swap diagram to illustrate the all-in costs of the various cash flows from the Euroyen bond and the currency swap (see Exhibit 10).

The team also wanted to be prepared to discuss the best way to structure the cash flows of the swap transaction. MGL was willing to make future yen swap payments to RJR that perfectly coincided with the yen coupon and principal payments in order to eliminate any yen exposure. The initial yen payment from RJR would be the present value of these future yen swap payments to RJR discounted at the swap rate. One way to structure the dollar swap flows was to "scale" the initial dollar swap "principal" RJR would receive using a negotiated spot exchange rate and calculate RJR's future annual dollar payments by multiplying the dollar swap rate times this principal. In the final year, the total dollar payment made by RJR would consist of both the annual payment plus the repayment of the swap principal.

As it began its evaluation of the dual-currency structure, the Morgan team realized the complexity of the analysis it would need to make. Furthermore, like most Eurobond proposals, the terms were probably good for a few hours only. Given RJR's tremendous need for financing, it certainly did not want to miss a potentially attractive opportunity.

EXHIBIT 1

Consolidated Statements of Earnings and Earnings Retained (millions of dollars except per share amounts)

	1982	*1983*	*1984*
Net sales	$10,160	$12,312	$12,974
Costs and expenses			
Cost of products sold	6,719	8,226	8,282
Selling, advertising, administrative, and general expenses	2,219	2,689	3,073
Earnings from continuing operations	1,222	1,397	1,619
Interest and debt expense (net of capitalized amounts of $29, $9, and $4 respectively)	(186)	(196)	(187)
Other income (expense), net	61	87	120
Earnings from continuing operations before provisions for income taxes	1,097	1,288	1,552
Provision for income taxes	513	586	709
Earnings after taxes	584	702	843
Extraordinary items	250	117	311
Net earnings applicable to common stock	834	819	1,154
Earnings retained at beginning of year	3,457	3,987	4,461
Less			
Cash dividends on common stock	304	345	360
Distribution of Sea-Land stock	—	—	540
Retirement of common stock	—	—	681
Earnings retained at end of year	$ 3,987	$ 4,461	$ 4,034
Net earnings per common share			
Continuing operations	$ 5.14	$ 5.66	$ 7.00
Discontinued operations	2.68	1.59	3.27
	$ 7.82	$ 7.25	$ 10.27
Average number of common shares outstanding (in thousands)	106,706	112,997	112,375

EXHIBIT 2
Consolidated Balance Sheets (millions of dollars)

	December 31,	
	1983	*1984*
Assets		
Current assets		
Cash and short-term investments	$ 363	$1,323
Accounts and notes receivable (net)	1,344	1,226
Inventories	2,690	2,493
Prepaid expenses	64	72
Total current assets	$4,461	$5,114
Property, plant, and equipment—at cost	$3,001	$3,760
Less depreciation and amortization	(794)	(944)
Net property, plant, and equipment	2,207	2,816
Other assets	2,549	1,342
Total assets	$9,217	$9,272
Liabilities and Stockholders' Equity		
Current liabilities		
Notes payable	$ 132	$ 101
Accounts payable and accrued accounts	1,205	1,459
Current maturities of long-term debt	38	227
Income taxes accrued	124	463
Total current liabilities	$1,499	$2,250
Long-term debt (less current maturities)	1,420	1,257
Other noncurrent liabilities	168	265
Deferred income taxes	276	523
Redeemable preferred stocks	631	499
Common stockholders' equity		
Common stock	280	255
Paid-in capital	585	344
Cumulative translation adjustments	(103)	(155)
Earnings retained	4,461	4,034
Total common stockholders' equity	5,223	4,478
Total liabilities and stockholders' equity	$9,217	$9,272

EXHIBIT 3

R.J. Reynolds Geographic Data (millions of dollars)

	1982	1983	1984
Net sales			
United States	$ 7,753	$ 9,584	$10,216
Canada	548	566	628
Europe	1,146	1,383	1,336
Other geographic areas	1,038	1,117	1,194
Less transfer between geographic areas	(325)	(338)	(400)
Consolidated net sales	$10,160	$12,312	$12,974
Earnings from continuing operations			
United States	$ 1,172	$ 1,297	$ 1,464
Canada	44	44	53
Europe	32	37	46
Other geographic areas	50	110	150
Other (principally corporate expense)	(76)	(91)	(94)
Consolidated earnings from continuing operations	$ 1,222	$ 1,397	$ 1,619
Assets			
United States	$ 4,641	$ 4,443	$ 5,203
Canada	304	337	399
Europe	413	451	511
Other geographic areas	515	560	594
Corporate	1,517	1,977	2,565
Net assets of discontinued operations	1,850	1,449	—
Consolidated assets	$ 9,240	$ 9,217	$ 9,272
Liabilities of company's continuing operations located in foreign countries	$ 729	$ 844	$ 832

EXHIBIT 4

Consolidated Statement of Income for Nabisco Brands, Inc. (millions of dollars except per share data)

	1982	1983	1984
Net sales	$5,871	$5,985	$6,253
Cost of sales	3,700	3,730	3,939
Gross profit	2,171	2,255	2,314
Selling, general, and administrative expenses	1,597	1,627	1,735
Operating income	574	628	579
Interest expense	90	77	77
Miscellaneous (income) expense, net	(39)	(15)	(27)
Income before income taxes	523	566	529
Income taxes			
Current			
United States	75	90	86
Foreign	74	78	75
State and local	20	13	19
Deferred	39	62	40
Total income taxes	208	243	220
Net income	$ 315	$ 323	$ 309
Net income per common share	$ 4.84	$ 4.87	$ 5.03
Dividends declared per common share	$ 2.05	$ 2.28	$ 2.48
Average common shares outstanding (in thousands)	65,026	66,310	61,486

411

EXHIBIT 5
Consolidated Balance Sheet for Nabisco Brands, Inc. (millions of dollars)

	December 31,	
	1983	*1984*
Assets		
Current assets		
Cash and short-term investments	$ 251	$ 268
Accounts receivable (net)	621	604
Inventories	766	766
Prepaid expenses	25	29
Total current assets	$1,663	$1,667
Property, plant, and equipment	2,376	2,459
Less depreciation	(868)	(913)
Other assets (net)	455	548
	$3,626	$3,761
Liabilities and Stockholders' Equity		
Current liabilities		
Notes payable	$ 39	$ 27
Accounts payable and accrued expenses	924	923
Current maturities of long-term debt	42	33
Income taxes accrued	74	54
Total current liabilities	$1,079	$1,037
Long-term debt	$ 482	$ 682
Other liabilities and minority interests	110	205
Deferred income taxes	244	292
Redeemable preferred stocks	2	2
Common stockholders' equity		
Common stock	139	139
Paid-in capital	276	277
Cumulative translation adjustments	1,680	1,837
Earnings retained	(151)	(215)
Less treasury stock at cost	(235)	(495)
Total common stockholders' equity	$1,709	$1,543
	$3,626	$3,761

EXHIBIT 6
Nabisco Geographic Data (millions of dollars)

	1982	*1983*	*1984*
Net sales			
United States	$3,491	$3,622	$3,950
Canada	639	732	721
Europe	782	1,138	1,102
Latin America	374	298	290
Asia/Pacific	178	195	190
Other			407
Consolidated net sales	$5,871	$5,985	$6,253
Earnings from continuing operations			
United States	$ 438	$ 475	$ 451
Canada	60	67	61
Europe	67	81	78
Latin America	57	58	53
Asia/Pacific	12	13	10
Other (principally corporate expense)	(60)	(66)	(63)
Consolidated earnings from continuing operations	$ 574	$ 628	$ 590
Assets			
United States	$1,541	$1,659	$1,730
Canada	415	376	373
Europe	819	822	791
Latin America	259	191	197
Asia/Pacific	120	136	119
Corporate	770	442	551
Consolidated assets	$3,924	$3,626	$3,761

EXHIBIT 7
Summary of 5-Year Eurobond Terms Available to R.J. Reynolds

	Dollar Eurobonds	*Yen Eurobonds*	*Yen/U.S. Dollar Dual-Currency Eurobonds*
Face value	$100 million	¥25 billion	¥25 billion
Price	100.125%	100.250%	101.500%
Fees	1.875%	1.875%	1.875%
Coupon (paid annually)	10.125%	6.375%	7.750%
Final redemption	Par	Par	$115.956 million

EXHIBIT 8
Long-Dated Yen/U.S. Dollar Forward Exchange Rates

	Outright Rates	
Year	Bid	Offer
0	. . . . .236.80[a]	236.90
1	. . . . .231.30	231.70
2	. . . . .223.90	225.90
3	. . . . .215.60	218.70
4	. . . . .207.10	211.20
5	. . . . .197.60	202.70

Note: Forwards arranged by Nikko Securities.

a. Bid and offer rates are quoted from the perspective of the market-making dealer. For example, a dealer bank would buy a dollar from a corporation in exchange for selling to it 236.80 yen. Similarly, the bank would sell a dollar to a corporation in exchange for buying from it 236.90 yen.

EXHIBIT 9
Currency and Interest Rate Swap Indications

	Semiannual Quotations		Benchmark U.S. Treasury	Semiannual Fixed Rates Against 6-Month Dollar LIBOR		Annual Fixed Rates Against 6-Month Dollar LIBOR	
	Pay	Receive		Pay[a]	Receive	Pay	Receive
5-year dollar rates[b] . .	T+60	T+76	9.88%	10.48%	10.64%	10.75%	10.92%
5-year yen rates				6.98%	7.22%	7.10%	7.35%

Note: All rates are against six-month dollar LIBOR.

a. All rates are quoted from the perspective of the bank offering the swap; that is, a bank would agree to pay semiannual fixed dollars at 10.48% against receiving semiannual six-month dollar LIBOR. Similarly, the bank would agree to receive semiannual fixed dollars at 10.64% against paying semiannual six-month dollar LIBOR.

b. *T* represents the semiannual yield on 5-year U.S. Treasury securities.

EXHIBIT 10
Annual All-In Costs on Cash Flows from 5-Year Euroyen Bond with Yen/U.S. Dollar Swap

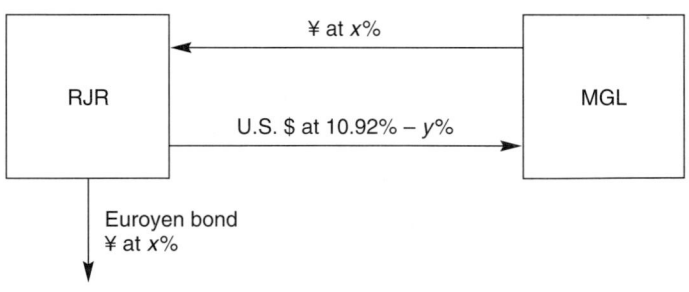

Note: The internal rate of return of the yen cash flows from both the Euroyen bond and the yen swap is represented by *x* and the dollar equivalent of the excess yen basis points is represented by *y*.

Compañia de Teléfonos de Chile

In April 1990, Claudio Garcia, the newly appointed senior executive vice president for finance and administration for Compañia de Teléfonos de Chile (CTC), found the telephone company in the middle of a challenging financial dilemma. CTC had embarked upon an aggressive expansion program that required substantial capital resources. The expansion program had been approved under Alan Bond, an Australian entrepreneur. The plan included reducing substantially the time needed to install telephone service and expanding capabilities to provide some of the latest high-tech capabilities that telecommunications had to offer.

However, because of significant personal financial difficulties, Mr. Bond sold his stake in the telephone company in April 1990. CTC was currently looking for new investors who could provide the necessary operating capital to continue its expansion. In seeking these investors, CTC had several options, but all had their drawbacks.

CTC could try to raise money from the local stock market. However, there were questions about whether there was sufficient capital in the market to finance fully CTC's needs. It could try to raise money from Chilean banks, but the small size of these banks and the legal restrictions they faced in being exposed to any one credit risk could prove problematic. Foreign commercial bankers had the necessary capital, but they shied away from making investments in Latin America—a region in which they faced massive loan write-offs from the debt crisis of the 1980s. Finally, CTC could also try to raise equity overseas through the listing of American Depository Receipts (ADRs), a step that likely would put its stock on the New York Stock Exchange. But this alternative also presented some substantial hurdles.

These, and many other questions, preoccupied Sr. Garcia as he considered how CTC's management might relax the financial constraints retarding CTC's growth.

This case was prepared by Charles M. La Follette (MBA '92) under the supervision of Professors W. Carl Kester of Harvard Business School (Boston, MA, USA) and Enrique Ostale of Universidad Adolfo Ibañez (Santiago, Chile).

Chile

The Country

In 1990, Chile was a country with a population of 12.9 million. Geographically, it was a long, thin country bounded by the Pacific Ocean on its west and the Andes Mountains along its east. These features made an extensive and reliable telephone network essential to the promotion of commerce within the country.

Since 1973, Chile had been ruled by Augusto Pinochet, a military general who had come to power in a coup over Salvador Allende, an elected Marxist leader who had ruled since 1970. In 1989, Pinochet put his continued leadership to a vote in a plebiscite—a vote that he lost. Though he promised an orderly transition of power, some observers questioned his sincerity. His long years in power, his vast control of the government through civil service appointments, and his complete dominance of the military forces made him a potent political force. Many wondered whether, once officially out of power, Pinochet might not continue to intervene in the governmental affairs of the country, or even stage another coup.

The Chilean Economy

The Chilean economy was largely based upon raw materials. The country was the world's largest exporter of copper and its third-largest producer (see Exhibit 1). Unlike its neighbors—Argentina, Bolivia, and Peru—Chile enjoyed a relatively stable economy. Inflation averaged 20.2% from 1984 to 1989.

Chile's history of debt payment was good. Unlike most of the Latin American region, Chile had never accumulated interest arrears on its $18 billion debt. Nevertheless, its image suffered in the financial community from being associated with Latin American economies in general. Throughout the 1980s, the total debt of Latin America had increased 76.9%. Interest arrears of the region had boomed 22-fold since 1983 (see Exhibit 2).

During the early 1980s, the debt-to-export ratio of the continent steadily increased from approximately 2-to-1 to nearly 4-to-1 by 1986. To many in the world's financial centers, it seemed that the region would never be able to earn its way out of financial distress. Exchange rates and other economic data for Chile are provided in Exhibit 3. Economic data on selected other Latin American countries are provided in Exhibit 4.

Company Background

CTC's Privatization

By the late 1980s, Chile did not have a broad telecommunications network. In fact, the country ranked only 12th out of 24 Latin American and Caribbean nations in the extensiveness of its telephone network (see Exhibit 5). Though it was a state-owned enterprise, CTC suffered from a mediocre record in servicing customer needs. Hundreds of thousands of potential customers had been on the waiting list for service for several years (see Exhibit 6).

In 1987 the government decided to address the country's telecommunications problems by privatizing CTC. It put the firm up to bid on the stipulation that the winning bidder would expand, modernize, and improve the telecommunications network, as well as provide some initial financial security to employees who might be let go in a reorganization.

Several firms made bids for the telephone network, including BellSouth, Bond Company, Alcatel Althsom N.V., Nippon Telegraph & Telephone Corp., Chase Manhattan, and Communicaciones Chile. Several of the bidders offered distressed Chilean debt securities as payment, seeking to perform a debt-for-equity swap for the company. But in the end, Alan Bond's firm won the day. Though lower in total value, Bond Company's all-cash bid of $114.8 million for 151 million shares (approximately 35% of total shares) of CTC was deemed more attractive than other, more creative financing bid structures. Bond Company subsequently acquired more shares that raised its ownership of CTC's stock to 49.5% by the end of 1988.

Bond Company immediately went to work on expanding the firm's operations. Soon after the acquisition, CTC embarked on an aggressive expansion mode to add 600,000 lines of service by the end of the 1992. In addition, Bond Company's management began to implement a variety of other tactics that would further develop the company and make it one of the most modern telephone networks in South America. Among these goals were proposals to install a cellular service, implement new services such as paging and mobile radiocommunications, develop a high-speed data transmission network, advance towards full digitization of the network, improve the network maintenance and replacement program, introduce new value-added services, and operate a nationwide network of fiber optic and satellite transmission links.

Initial Setbacks

Unfortunately, the expansion and modernization program soon hit substantial difficulties. Many of these problems stemmed from the financial distress that began to afflict the Bond empire soon after its acquisition of CTC. Investors spanning the spectrum from American banks to local Chilean institutions began to shy away from CTC as an investment vehicle. By the late 1980s, the Bond Company found itself increasingly under pressure to sell substantial stakes in its holdings in order to meet debt obligations.

On April 11, 1990, Bond Company sold its stake of 365.5 million shares in CTC (along with an option to buy an additional 9.1 million shares) to Telefónica de España, S.A., the Spanish telephone company, for $392 million. Nevertheless, even after Alan Bond had sold his stake in CTC, investors continued for a while to associate the company with Bond's difficult financial situation.

In addition, Claudio Garcia—who had joined the firm in September 1989—soon learned that the development program might not meet its targets. In hiring an international telephone operating company as an outside consultant in December 1989, CTC's administration acknowledged that substantial changes needed to be made in the management of the expansion plan.

Financial Concerns

In light of CTC's pressing financial and operating problems, Telefónica chose to cut its dividend. Both as a state-owned enterprise and under Bond's ownership, CTC had paid cash dividends in the amount of 100% of its net income. In 1990, CTC lowered its dividend to 80% of net income for the year. Within each fiscal year, CTC had historically maintained a policy that required it to pay out 60% of each quarter's earnings to the shareholders through a dividend. (When paying out 100% of its earnings, the fraction paid out each quarter was 75% of that quarter's earnings.) This meant that it had a particularly large final dividend payout to make at the end of each year. Relevant financial statements for CTC are provided in Exhibits 7 and 8. CTC's dividend history is provided in Exhibit 9.

The lowered dividend did not solve all of CTC's financial problems, however. The company still faced an uphill struggle in sourcing capital externally to meet its substantial capital expenditure budget. Following Telefónica's takeover, this budget increased as a consequence of the decision to extend CTC's line expansion target to 1.7 million by 1996 (see Exhibit 10 for capital expenditures projected through 1996). In particular, there were well-voiced concerns at CTC about whether the company would be able to raise substantial funds from its home country.

The Local Stock Market

The local Chilean stock market was thinly capitalized. At a market capitalization of $11.6 billion as of March 31, 1990, the Chilean stock market was less than one third of 1% the size of the U.S. market, which had an estimated capitalization of $2.9 trillion. Chile's market was not even big by developing country standards. Its market ranked only 11th among the world's 32 developing country stock markets in market capitalization (see Exhibit 11).

Chile's stock market was open only between 10:30 AM and 11:15 AM, and again between 11:45 AM and 12:30 PM each business day. Odd lots of stock were traded only once a week by auction. Average daily trading in the market was only about $7–$8 million. Analysts estimated that a large Chilean company could expect to raise only about 1% of the total market capitalization of the market in any new offering. Trading data for CTC's stock is provided in Exhibit 12.

Chilean Banks

Commercial banks might also be constrained from providing CTC with the necessary capital. Chile's banking community was not particularly large. Only 3 of the world's 1000 largest banks were based in Chile. Even by Latin American standards, Chile had a small banking community—ranking fifth out of the nine largest bank centers in Latin America in terms of total assets (see Exhibit 13).

Under Chilean law, commercial banks could lend up to 25% of their capital and reserves to a single company if the loans were adequately secured by tangible assets. However, because covenants on CTC's outstanding debentures prohibited it from pledging assets to secure new debt without the approval of a majority of the debenture holders, Chilean banks were constrained to lend no more than 5% of their total capital and reserves to CTC. It was possible that CTC's financial needs would quickly top this limit.

Chilean Pension Funds

One of the most rapidly growing domestic pools of capital in Chile was private pension funds. However, regulations constrained the types of investments these funds could make. Although CTC's equity would normally have been an eligible investment for Chilean pension funds, the funds were prevented from investing in any company in which a single investor (other than the Chilean government) owned 45% of the stock or more. Thus, in April 1990, CTC was not an eligible investment for private Chilean pension funds.

The Overseas Capital Markets

American depository receipts, or ADRs, represented a new potential option for raising additional capital. ADRs are receipts traded in the United States that represent the shares of foreign companies. They allow U.S. investors to invest in foreign markets through securities denominated in dollars and traded on American exchanges. Though the actual shares are deposited in a custodian bank located in the issuer's home country, the instruments have proven to be convenient and trustworthy.

ADRs grew in popularity throughout the 1980s as institutional investors sought to diversify their portfolio risk across international boundaries. Their ADR holdings increased substantially during this period. Since 1987, the annual ADR trading volume on U.S. exchanges increased by an average of 23.8%, while trading of U.S. stocks grew by only 4.2%. In 1989 foreign companies raised $2.5 billion in new equity through ADRs. Exhibit 14 shows the growth of ADRs as a financial vehicle. Exhibit 15 shows the major institutional purchasers of ADRs.

Several different ADR programs were available. They differed primarily in the degree of financial reporting that a firm was willing to make to U.S. regulatory bodies. Level I ADRs provided the simplest method of accessing the U.S. capital markets. Level I ADRs were unlisted and traded by dealers in the over-the-counter market; the foreign company did not have to comply with U.S. generally accepted accounting principles (GAAP) or full Securities and Exchange Commission (SEC) disclosure requirements. In fact, Level I ADRs allowed non-U.S. companies to enjoy the benefits of a publicly traded U.S. security without having to alter their current reporting procedures at all.[1]

To list securities on U.S. exchanges, foreign issuers had to use sponsored Level II or Level III ADRs. Each level required different degrees of SEC registration and reporting, and adherence to U.S. GAAP.[2] A brief summary of the different requirements by level is shown in Exhibit 16. Level III ADRs provided the most comprehensive (and expensive) means of entering the U.S. equity markets. Level III ADRs required full reporting of corporate data on a quarterly basis according to U.S. GAAP. In effect, in sponsoring a Level III ADR, foreign firms agreed to all of the reporting requirements with which listed domestic U.S. firms must comply.

Raising funds by issuing ADRs raised numerous problems for CTC. First, there was the potential problem that significant quantities of CTC's stock might flow back to the home market during market downturns—thereby causing disruptions, even suspensions, of trading in CTC stock on the Santiago Stock Exchange. Backflow could drive the price of the stock down and could lead to lower valuations in future stock offerings the company might pursue.

In addition, most ADRs came from companies domiciled in developed economies, not from companies in Latin America (see Exhibit 17). The appetite of U.S. investors for ADRs listed by a Latin American corporation had not been tested. Though there had recently been stock offerings for foreign telecommunication companies like Telefónica de España; Hongkong Telecommunications, Ltd.; Cable & Wireless Public Ltd., Co. (a U.K. company); and Telecom Corporation of New Zealand, Ltd., there

---

1. Private Placement 144a ADRs was another method for entering the U.S. equity markets. In private placement ADRs, a private company could raise capital by placing ADRs with large institutional investors, again without registering with the SEC. However, this rule was not expected to become effective before June 1990.

2. The Bank of New York, "American Depository Receipts and Privatizations," 1991, p. 5.

might be perceptions of differences between the political risk of those countries and a country like Chile. In fact, there was no precedent to guide American institutional investors in evaluating a Chilean company, for there were no Chilean companies listed on the New York Stock Exchange.[3] In addition, given the recent questions about CTC's development program raised by an independent—and American—telephone company, there were some concerns about whether CTC could withstand the scrutiny of skeptical analysts in road shows across the United States.

Finally, there were questions about whether CTC could satisfy the arduous reporting requirements of a Level III ADR. Would it be worth paying for the increased administrative cost of fulfilling those reporting requirements? Where would it obtain the necessary skills to satisfy these requirements?

There were no easy answers to any of these questions. Nevertheless, it was imperative that Sr. Garcia devise a strategy to finance CTC's ambitious program of investment and growth, analyze the financing alternatives, and submit a plan soon to CTC's board of directors.

EXHIBIT 1

Copper Production and Export (thousands of tons)

Top 5 Producers, 1988		*Top 5 Exporters, 1988*	
U. S.	1,857	Chile	976
USSR	1,380	Zambia	424
Chile	1,013	Canada	262
Japan	955	Zaire	198
Canada	529	Peru	147

Source: Economist Pocket World in Figures (London: Hutchinson Business Books, 1990), p. 35.

EXHIBIT 2

Total Latin American Debt and Interest Arrears (millions of dollars)

Year	*Total Debt*	*Interest Arrears*
1980	$242,535	$ 8
1983	360,999	1,198
1984	377,531	3,108
1985	389,974	2,463
1986	409,708	3,285
1987	445,122	8,393
1988	427,597	8,944
1989	422,188	16,722

Source: "External Debt of Developing Countries," in *World Debt Tables, 1990–1991* (Washington, D.C.: The World Bank, 1991), p. 142.

---

3. Also, there was no tax treaty in force between Chile and the United States. Chilean tax law provided for a 35% withholding tax on dividends paid to foreign shareholders. The 10% corporate tax on income from which dividends were paid was available to shareholders as a credit against the withholding tax, but that credit increased the base on which the withholding tax was imposed (thus, on CP 100 of dividends, foreign shareholders would pay a net withholding tax of CP 27.78 = .35 × CP 111.11 − .10 × CP 111.11).

EXHIBIT 3
Chilean Peso Exchange Rates and Economic Indicators

Chilean Peso/U.S. $ Exchange Rate

Year Ended December 31	Year-End Rate	Average Rate[a]	High Rate	Low Rate
1985	183.86	163.03	183.86	129.43
1986	204.73	194.15	204.73	185.70
1987	238.14	221.09	238.14	205.18
1988	247.20	245.48	248.24	240.90
1989	297.37	297.34	297.37	245.84
1990	296.98[b]	na	na	na

Note: na = Not available.

a. The average rate is calculated on the basis of month-end exchange rates.

b. End of March 1990.

Selected Macroeconomic Indicators

Item	1979	1980	1981	1982	1983	1984	1985	1986	1987	1988	1989
GDP growth[a] (%)	8.3	7.8	5.5	−14.1	−0.7	6.3	2.4	5.7	5.7	7.4	10.0
Increase in Consumer Price Index (%)	38.9	31.2	9.5	20.7	23.1	23.0	26.4	17.4	21.5	12.7	21.40
Population (millions)[b] . .	10.9	11.1	11.3	11.3	11.7	11.9	12.1	12.3	12.5	12.7	12.90
Exports ($ millions) . . .	3,835	4,705	3,837	3,706	3,831	3,651	3,804	4,199	5,224	7,052	8,190.40
Imports ($ millions) . . .	4,191	5,469	6,513	3,643	2,845	3,288	2,956	3,099	3,994	4,833	
Current account surplus/ deficit ($ millions) . . .	−1,189	−1,971	−4,733	−2,304	−1,117	−2,111	−1,329	−1,137	−808	−167	−740
Total external debt ($ billions)	8.5	11.1	15.5	17.2	17.4	18.9	19.4	19.5	19.2	17.6	16.25
Debt service ratio to GDP[c] (%)	7.41	7.78	7.75	12.11	10.15	11.73	12.84	12.13	8.95	6.82	5.75
Exchange rate (pesos per $)[d]	38.00	39.00	39.00	73.57	87.07	128.24	183.66	204.73	238.14	247.20	297.37
Unemployment rate (%)	13.6	10.4	11.3	19.6	14.8	13.9	12.0	8.8	7.9	8.3	5.30

Source: Central Bank of Chile.

a. Adjusted for inflation.

b. Estimated as of June of each year.

c. Includes mandatory amortization and interest payments on medium- and long-term debt and interest on short-term debt.

d. Observed exchange rate as of December 31 of each year.

EXHIBIT 4

Comparison of Macroeconomic Indicators for Selected Latin American Countries

	1985	1986	1987	1988	1989
Increase in Consumer Price Index					
Argentina	672.20%	90.00%	131.58%	342.73%	3,079.16%
Brazil	226.90	145.00	229.80	670.42	1,309.19
Colombia	24.00	18.90	23.30	26.10	25.65
Peru	163.40	78.00	85.96	666.16	3,398.50
Venezuela	11.40	11.50	28.16	29.46	84.27
Exports ($ millions)					
Argentina	$ 8,396.1	$ 6,852.2	$ 6,360.2	$ 9,134.8	$ 9,579.3
Brazil	25,639.0	22,349.0	26,224.0	33,789.0	34,383.0
Colombia	3,551.6	5,101.6	4,642.6	5,037.0	5,716.5
Peru	2,978.5	2,530.6	2,660.8	2,701.0	3,488.0
Venezuela	$ 14,438.0	$ 8,660.0	$ 10,577.0	$ 10,239.0	$ 13,310.0
Imports ($ millions)					
Argentina	$ 3,814.2	$ 4,724.1	$ 5,817.8	$ 5,321.6	$ 4,203.2
Brazil	14,332.0	15,557.0	16,581.0	16,055.0	20,016.0
Colombia	4,140.9	3,861.6	4,321.9	5,001.8	5,004.1
Peru	1,835.0	2,908.8	3,562.3	3,348.0	2,749.2
Venezuela	$ 8,106.0	$ 8,504.0	$ 9,659.0	$ 12,726.0	$ 7,803.0
Current Account Surplus/Deficit ($ millions)					
Argentina	$ (952)	$ (2,859)	$ (4,235)	$ (1,572)	$ (1,305)
Brazil	(273)	(5,304)	(1,450)	4,159	1,025
Colombia	(1,809)	383	336	(216)	(195)
Peru	135	(1,077)	(1,481)	(1,091)	324
Venezuela	$ (3,334)	$ (2,693)	$ (2,709)	$ (4,302)	na
Total External Debt ($ millions)					
Argentina	$ 49,148.7	$ 51,422.0	$ 58,324.0	$ 58,803.0	$ 63,314.0
Brazil	106,472.8	111,045.0	121,174.0	113,469.0	115,096.0
Colombia	14,237.4	14,987.0	15,663.0	16,434.0	16,013.0
Peru	14,136.9	14,477.0	15,373.0	16,493.0	16,827.0
Venezuela	$ 34,692.8	$ 33,839.0	$ 34,833.0	$ 34,684.0	$ 33,194.0
GNP Growth (%)					
Argentina	−4.50%	5.60%	2.50%	−2.50%	−4.50%
Brazil	8.30	7.50	3.60	0.00	3.31
Colombia	3.10	5.80	5.40	4.10	3.40
Peru	2.40	9.17	8.26	−8.34	−11.65
Venezuela	1.30	6.34	4.51	6.11	−7.83
Population (millions)					
Argentina	30.33	30.74	31.14	31.53	31.93
Brazil	135.56	138.49	141.45	144.43	147.40
Colombia	28.62	29.19	29.73	30.24	32.53
Peru	19.70	20.21	20.73	21.26	21.79
Venezuela	17.32	17.79	18.27	18.76	19.25

Source: International Financial Statistics (Washington, D.C.: International Monetary Fund, April 1992).

Note: na = Not available.

EXHIBIT 5

Population per Telephone Line in 1986 for Latin American and Caribbean Nations (persons per line)

Argentina	9.7
Bahamas	2.2
Barbados	3.3
Bolivia	41.4
Brazil	11.3
Chile	15.5
Colombia	13.0
Costa Rica	7.9
Cuba	18.9
Ecuador	27.4
El Salvador	38.1
Guatemala	62.0
Guyana	23.0
Honduras	86.6
Jamaica	205.0
Mexico	10.4
Neth. Antilles	4.0
Nicaragua	63.4
Panama	9.4
Paraguay	41.1
Peru	32.8
Trinidad and Tobago	11.0
Uruguay	7.6
Venezuela	11.3

Source: Economist Pocket World in Statistics (London: Hutchinson Business Books, 1990), p. 125.

EXHIBIT 6

CTC's Lines in Service and Waiting List

	December 31,				
	1986	*1987*	*1988*	*1989*	*1990*[a]
Number of telephones	749,110	770,199	820,260	894,824	1,096,056
Telephones per 100 inhabitants	6.6	6.7	7.0	7.4	8.9
Number of lines installed	584,829	614,884	634,327	799,917	1,018,568
Lines in service	527,789	548,359	591,565	645,863	811,811
Applications pending	219,265	230,452	236,349	283,919	307,843
Digitalization (%)[b]	36.8	36.0	37.9	51.1	64.0
Automation (%)[c]	96.1	98.0	98.5	99.3	99.6
Local calls (millions)[d, e]	1,095	1,146	1,231	1,341	1,524
Local calls per line in service[e, f]	2,667	2,686	2,778	2,610	2,587

Source: Corporate documents.

a. Estimated.

b. Percentage of lines installed and connected to digital exchanges.

c. Percentage of lines installed and connected to automatic exchanges.

d. Does not include calls made under CTC's "flat fee" charge system, or calls made from public telephones.

e. Reflects information for the period ending the date indicated.

f. Lines in service do not include lines that provide service on the "flat fee" charge system or that provide service from public telephones. Totals were calculated for each year on the basis of the monthly average of the number of lines in service during each year.

EXHIBIT 7

Consolidated Balance Sheets (Adjusted for general price-level changes and expressed in millions of *constant* 1990 Chilean pesos [CP], except number of shares)

	1989	1988
Assets		
Current assets		
Cash and cash equivalents	CP 29,782	CP 27,770
Marketable securities	7,829	5,377
Accounts and notes receivable	31,094	16,722
Inventories	6,824	2,726
Other	743	1,587
Total current assets	76,272	54,182
Property, plant, equipment, net	295,440	216,796
Other assets	12,634	24,867
Total assets	CP 384,346	CP 295,845
Liabilities and shareholders' equity		
Current liabilities		
Bank borrowings	CP 11,232	CP 9,462
Current maturities of long-term debt	10,570	78
Accounts payable and accrued	46,012	28,029
Due to ENTEL	3,546	—
Other	3,481	159
Total current liabilities	74,841	37,728
Long-term liabilities		
Long-term debt	80,710	50,526
Accrued severance indem.	4,971	5,142
Deferred income taxes	—	156
Total long-term liabilities	85,681	55,824
Shareholders' equity		
Common stock	200,560	195,694
Retained earnings	23,264	6,599
Total shareholders' equity	223,824	202,293
Total liabilities and shareholders' equity	CP 384,346	CP 295,845

Source: Corporate documents.

EXHIBIT 8
Consolidated Statements of Income (adjusted for general price-level changes and expressed in millions of *constant* 1990 Chilean pesos [CP], except number of shares)

	1988	1989
Operating revenues		
Tariff regulated services	CP 68,498	CP 82,676
Other	13,342	20,859
Total operating revenues	81,840	103,535
Operating costs and expense		
Oper. salaries and related	16,770	18,101
Depreciation and amort.	12,088	13,868
Cost of ENTEL services	199	975
Other operating costs	11,339	16,031
Admin. and selling costs	9,836	11,371
Total operating costs and expenses	50,232	60,346
Operating income	31,608	43,189
Other income (expenses)		
Interest income	1,651	4,967
Net interest expense[a]	(3,961)	(2,226)
Purchasing power gain[b]	5,517	7,098
Other	(7,013)	(10,042)
Total other income, net	(3,806)	(203)
Income before income tax	27,802	42,986
Income tax[c]		
Current	1,479	(298)
Deferred	1,317	(3,322)
Net income	CP 25,006	CP 46,606

Source: Corporate documents.

a. Capitalized interest expense was CP 5,081 million in 1989 and CP 1,656 million in 1988, which gave rise to total (i.e., capitalized and noncapitalized) interest expense of CP 7,307 million and CP 5,617 million in 1989 and 1988, respectively.

b. Purchasing power gains are noncash sources of earnings that reflect the effect of Chilean inflation on the monetary liabilities owed by CTC during each year, net of the loss resulting from the effect of inflation on monetary assets held.

c. On January 14, 1989, the Chilean income tax was substantially changed. Among other changes, corporations were not subject to income tax beginning on January 1, 1989. Income taxes were payable by the shareholders on dividends received. In light of this change, the net liability for deferred taxes shown on the balance sheet as of December 31, 1988, was credited to income in 1989.

Subsequent Chilean legislation passed in the first half of 1990 introduced a corporate tax rate of 10% on income earned after January 1, 1990, with an increase in the rate to 15% for 1991, 1992, and 1993, and a decrease to 10% for the years 1994 and beyond.

EXHIBIT 9
CTC's Cash Dividend History[a] (Chilean pesos per share)

	Interim	Final[b]	Total
1986	35.93	—	35.93
1987	17.14	25.56	42.70
1988	38.17	16.75	54.92
1989	46.02	9.06	55.08

Source: Public documents.

a. Chilean pesos are reflected at historical values, not at constant 1990 purchasing power values.

b. The final dividend for each year is declared (and hence accrued) in April of each subsequent year.

EXHIBIT 10

CTC's Actual and Projected Capital Expenditures (millions of Chilean pesos)

	Actual	
	1988	*1989*
For tariff-regulated services	CP 41,719	CP 79,325
For services not currently subject to tariff regulation	4,377	11,520
For new services requiring new concessions		6,422
Total	CP 46,096	CP 97,267

	Projected			
	1990	*1991*	*1992*	*1993–1996*
For tariff-regulated services	CP 100,602	CP 95,042	CP 77,458	CP 243,735
For services not currently subject to tariff regulation	4,963	4,380	3,413	10,880
For new services requiring new concessions	15,187	15,441	8,468	14,658
Total	CP 120,752	CP 114,863	CP 89,339	CP 269,273

Source: Corporate documents.

EXHIBIT 11

World Stock Exchanges: Market Capitalization of Emerging Markets (millions of dollars)

	1989
Argentina	$ 4,225
Bangladesh	476
Brazil	44,368
Chile	9,587
Cote D'Ivoire	437
Colombia.....................	1,136
Egypt	1,760
Greece	6,376
India	27,316
Indonesia	2,514
Jamaica	957
Jordan	2,162
Kenya	474
South Korea	140,946
Kuwait	9,932
Malaysia	39,842
Mexico	22,550
Morocco	621
Nigeria	1,005
Pakistan	2,457
Philippines...................	11,965
Portugal	10,618
Sri Lanka	471
Taiwan	237,012
Thailand	25,648
Trinidad and Tobago	411
Turkey	6,783
Uruguay	24
Venezuela	1,816
Zimbabwe	1,067

Source: Economist Book of Vital World Statistics (London: Random Century House, 1991), p. 146.

EXHIBIT 12
Trading Data for CTC's Stock[a]

	Per Share (CP)[b]		Average Daily Number of Shares Traded (000s)[c]
	High	**Low**	
1989			
First quarter	188	149.5	135
Second quarter	207	172.5	342
Third quarter	206	173.75	202
Fourth quarter	200	169	383
1990			
First quarter	255	190	467

Source: Public documents.

a. Reported figures are for Series A shares only. CTC's capital is represented by no-par-value shares divided into two series (Series A and B). The rights of both series of shares are identical, except that the Series A shareholders as a class appoint six directors and the Series B shareholders as a class appoint one director. On December 31, 1989, there were 634,527,896 Series A shares issued and outstanding, and 67,552,376 Series B shares issued and outstanding.

b. Chilean pesos are reflected at historical values; not at constant 1990 purchasing power values.

c. Series A shares are traded principally on the Bolsa de Comercio de Santiago (the Santiago Stock Exchange). The shares are also listed on the Bolsa de Comercia do Valparaíso (the Valparaíso Stock Exchange) and are tradeable in a nascent electronic over-the-counter trading system. However, the Santiago Stock Exchange accounts for approximately 95% of the trading volume of CTC's shares in Chile.

EXHIBIT 13
Banking in Latin America

	Number of Banks in Top 1,000	Total Capital ($ millions)
Argentina	7	$ 3,159
Brazil	17	10,914
Chile	3	878
Colombia	1	94
Mexico	5	2,226
Panama	1	89
Peru	1	170
Uruguay	1	822
Venezuela	5	934

Source: Economist Book of Vital World Statistics (London: Random Century House, 1991), p. 148.

EXHIBIT 14
Selected Data on ADR Programs

	1983	1984	1985	1986	1987	1988	1989
Total number of ADR programs	585	625	683	700	754	782	804
Number of ADR offerings	10	9	2	8	19	8	20
Total capital raised with ADRs ($ millions) . .	617	608	28	696	4,586	1,275	2,614

Source: Philip Maher, "ADR Market Continued Growth in 1990, Riding Global Trend," *Investment Dealers' Digest,* February 1991, p. 12.

EXHIBIT 15
Top Institutional Holders of ADRs (July 1989)

	Amount ($ millions)
CIGNA	$980
Delaware Management	738
FMR	522
Manufacturers International	501
Capital Guardian	413
Wellington	386
California Public Management	369
INVESCO	239
Alliance Capital	232
IDS Financial	227
American Capital	206
Lazard Freres	198
J. P. Morgan	198
Scudder, Stevens	197
Dreman Value	182
Merrill Lynch Asset Management	181
Templeton	169
Pioneering Management	167
Newbold's Asset Management	143
Rosenberg Institute	143

Source: Investment Dealers' Digest, October 16, 1989.

EXHIBIT 16
Comparison of ADR Facilities

Type of Program	Registration Requirements[a]	Disclosure Requirements	Type of U.S. Equity Offering[b]	Listing Possibilities	Typical Cost to Company
Unsponsored[c]	Form F–6 / Rule 12g3–2(b)	None / None	Rule 144A private placement	OTC/pinks / Bulletin board	None / None
Private placement	Rule 12g3–2(b)	Eurostyle	Rule 144A private placement	Various	$100,000 to $300,000
Sponsored					
Level I	Form F–6 / Rule 12g3–2 (b)	None / None	Rule 144A private placement	OTC/pinks / Bulletin board	$5,000 to $20,000
Level II	Form F–6 / 20–F	None / Detailed	Rule 144A private placement	NYSE / AMEX / NASDAQ	$200,000 to $400,000
Level III	F–1 / 20–F	Rigorous / Detailed	Public offering	NYSE / AMEX / NASDAQ	$400,000 to $800,000

Sources: The Bank of New York, "American Depository Receipts and Privatizations," 1991; and J.P. Morgan, "American Depository Receipts for Chilean Companies: Benefitting from the U.S. Capital Markets," unpublished presentation materials.

a. The Securities Act of 1933 requires public securities to be registered with the Securities and Exchange Commission (SEC). Filing a Form F–6 registration statement complies with this requirement without substantial disclosure of information. Form F–1 requires financial information that is less than six months old and conforms to U.S. GAAP.

The Securities Exchange Act of 1934 requires companies listed on a major exchange to make regular filings of interim and annual reports to the SEC. A 20–F report requires detailed disclosure by foreign companies equivalent to a 10K report by domestic U.S. companies. Rule 12g3–2(b) of the 1934 Act permits exemption from such detailed disclosure by allowing foreign companies to file, on an ongoing basis, only that information that it is required to disclose in its country of domicile or that it distributes to any security holders outside the United States.

b. Rule 144A permits restricted or nonpublic securities issued by foreign investors to be placed and traded privately among large, sophisticated institutional investors.

c. No unsponsored programs have been initiated since 1983.

EXHIBIT 17
ADR Programs by Country of Origin (July 1989)

Percentage of Total ADR Programs by Country

	Number	*Percentage*
United Kingdom	197	23.0%
Australia	179	20.9
Japan	144	16.8
South Africa	91	10.6
Hong Kong	30	3.5
France	24	2.8
Germany	24	2.8
Netherlands	21	2.5
Italy	20	2.3
Other	127	14.8
Total	857	100.0%

Percentage of Sponsored ADR Programs by Country

	Number	*Percentage*
United Kingdom	148	38.3%
Australia	80	20.7
Japan	19	4.9
Netherlands	18	4.7
France	14	3.6
Sweden	13	3.4
Norway	12	3.1
Mexico	11	2.9
Spain	8	2.1
Other	63	16.3
Total	386	100.0%

Source: Investment Dealers' Digest, October 16, 1989.

Part III

Valuation and Investment

Investment Analysis and Lockheed Tri Star

1. Rainbow Products is considering the purchase of a paint-mixing machine to reduce labor costs. The savings are expected to result in additional cash flows to Rainbow of $5,000 per year. The machine costs $35,000 and is expected to last for 15 years. Rainbow has determined that the cost of capital for such an investment is 12%.

    a. Compute the payback, net present value (NPV), and internal rate of return (IRR) for this machine. Assume that all cash flows (except the initial purchase) occur at the end of each year, and do not consider taxes.
    Should Rainbow purchase the machine?

    b. For a $500-per-year additional expenditure, Rainbow can get a "good as new" service contract that essentially keeps the machine in new condition forever. Net of the cost of the service contract, the machine would then produce cash flows of $4,500 per year in perpetuity.
    Should Rainbow purchase the machine with the service contract?

    c. Instead of the service contract, Rainbow engineers have devised a different option to preserve and actually enhance the capability of the machine over time. By reinvesting 20% of the annual cost savings back into new machine parts, the engineers can increase the cost savings at a 4% annual rate. For example, at the end of year 1, 20% of the $5,000 cost savings ($1,000) is reinvested in the machine; the net cash flow is thus $4,000. The next year, the cash flow from cost savings grows by 4%, to $5,200 gross or $4,160 net of the 20% reinvestment. As long as the 20% reinvestment continues, the cash flows continue to grow at 4% in perpetuity. The formula for the present

This case was prepared by Professor Michael E. Edleson.

value (V) of an initial end-of-year perpetuity payout of $\$C$ (growing at $g\%$) per period, with a discount rate of $k\%$, is

$$V = \frac{C}{k - g}$$

when k and g are expressed as decimal fractions (e.g., .12 and .04).

What should Rainbow do?

2. Suppose you own a concession stand that sells hot dogs, peanuts, popcorn, and beer at a ball park. You have 3 years left on the contract with the ball park, and you do not expect it to be renewed. Long lines limit sales and profits. You have developed four different proposals to reduce the lines and increase profits:

- The first proposal is to renovate by adding another window.
- The second is to update the equipment at the existing windows.

These two renovation projects are not mutually exclusive; you could take on both projects. The third and fourth proposals involve abandoning the existing stand.

- The third proposal is to build a new stand.
- The fourth proposal is to rent a larger stand in the ball park. This option would require a $1,000 up-front investment for new signs and equipment installation; the incremental cash flows shown for later years are net of lease payments.

You have decided that a 15% discount rate is appropriate for this type of investment. The incremental cash flows associated with each of the proposals are as follows:

INCREMENTAL CASH FLOWS

Project	Investment	Year 1	Year 2	Year 3
Add a new window	−$ 75,000	$44,000	$44,000	$44,000
Update existing equipment	−50,000	23,000	23,000	23,000
Build a new stand	−125,000	70,000	70,000	70,000
Rent a larger stand	−1,000	12,000	13,000	14,000

Using the internal rate of return (IRR) rule, which proposal(s) do you recommend?

Using the net present value (NPV) rule, which proposal(s) do you recommend?

How do you explain any differences between the IRR and NPV rankings? Which rule is better?

3. MBATech, Inc. is negotiating with the Mayor of Bean City to start a manufacturing plant in an abandoned building. The cash flows for MBAT's proposed plant are as follows:

Year 0	−$1,000,000
Year 1	371,739
Year 2	371,739
Year 3	371,739
Year 4	371,739

The city has agreed to subsidize MBAT. The form and timing of the subsidy have not been determined and depend on which investment criterion is used by MBAT. In preliminary discussions MBAT suggested four alternatives:

- Subsidize the project to bring its IRR to 25%.
- Subsidize the project to provide a 2-year payback.
- Subsidize the project to provide an NPV of $75,000 when cash flows are discounted at 20%.
- Subsidize the project to provide an accounting rate of return (ARR) of 40%. This is defined as

$$ARR = \frac{\text{Average annual cash flow} - (\text{Investment/No. of years})}{\text{Investment/2}}$$

You have been hired by Bean City to recommend a subsidy that minimizes the costs to the city. Subsidy payments need not occur right away; they may be scheduled in later years if appropriate.

How much of a subsidy would you recommend for each year under each alternative suggested by MBAT?

Which of the four subsidy plans would you recommend to the city if the appropriate discount rate is 20%?

4. You are the CEO of Valu-Added Industries, Inc. (VAI). Your firm has 10,000 shares of common stock outstanding, and the current price of the stock is $100 per share. There is no debt; thus, the "market value" balance sheet of VAI is as follows:

Assets . . . $1,000,000   Equity . . . $1,000,000

You then discover an opportunity to invest in a new project that produces positive cash flows with a present value of $210,000. Your total initial costs for investing and developing this project are only $110,000. You will raise the necessary capital for this investment by issuing new equity. All potential purchasers of your common stock will be fully aware of the project's value and cost, and they will be willing to pay "fair value" for the new shares of VAI common.

What is the net present value (NPV) of this project?

How many shares of common stock must be issued (at what price) to raise the required capital?

What is the effect of this new project on the value of the stock of the existing shareholders, if any?

Lockheed Tri Star and Capital Budgeting[1]

In 1971 the American firm Lockheed found itself in congressional hearings seeking a $250 million federal guarantee to secure bank credit required for the completion of the L-1011 Tri Star program. The L-1011 Tri Star Airbus is a wide-bodied commercial jet aircraft with a capacity of up to 400 passengers; it competes with the DC-10 trijet and the A-300B airbus.

---

1. Facts and situations concerning the Lockheed Tri Star program are taken from U. E. Reinhardt, "Break-Even Analysis for Lockheed's Tri Star: An Application of Financial Theory," *Journal of Finance* 27 (1972), pp. 821–838; and from House and Senate testimony.

Spokespersons for Lockheed claimed that the Tri Star program was economically sound and that their problem was merely a liquidity crisis caused by some unrelated military contracts. Opposing the guarantee, other parties argued that the Tri Star program had been economically unsound and doomed to financial failure from the very beginning.

The debate over the viability of the program focused on estimated break-even sales—the number of jets that would need to be sold for total revenue to cover all accumulated costs. Lockheed's CEO, in his July 1971 testimony before Congress, asserted that this break-even point would be reached at sales of between 195 and 205 aircraft. At that point, Lockheed had secured only 103 firm orders, plus 75 options-to-buy, but company representatives testified that sales would eventually exceed the break-even point and that the project would thus become "a commercially viable endeavor."

Costs

The preproduction phases of the Tri Star project began at the end of 1967 and lasted 4 years, after running about six months behind schedule. Various estimates of the up-front costs ranged between $800 million and $1 billion. A reasonable approximation of these cash outflows would be $900 million, occurring as shown in Table A.

According to Lockheed testimony, the production phase was to run from the end of 1971 to the end of 1977, with about 210 Tri Stars as the planned output. At that production rate, the average unit production cost[2] would be about $14 million per aircraft. The inventory-intensive production costs would be relatively front-loaded, so that the $490 million ($14 million per plane, 35 planes per year) annual production costs could be assumed to occur in six equal increments at the end of years 1971 through 1976 ($t = 4$ through $t = 9$).

Revenues

In 1968 the expected price to be received from the L-1011 Tri Star was about $16 million per aircraft. These revenue flows would be characterized by a lag of 1 year to the production cost outflows; annual revenues of $560 million can be assumed to occur in six equal increments at the end of each year from 1972 through 1977 ($t = 5$ through $t = 10$). Inflation-escalation terms in the contracts ensured that any future inflation-based cost and revenue increases would virtually offset each other nearly exactly, thus providing no incremental net cash flows.

Deposits toward future deliveries were received from Lockheed customers. Roughly one quarter of the price of the aircraft was actually received 2 years early. For example, for a single Tri Star delivered at the end of 1972, $4 million of the price was received at the end of 1970, leaving $12 million of the $16 million price as cash flow at the end of 1972. So, for the 35 planes built (and presumably sold) in a year, $140 million of the $560 million in total annual revenue is actually received as a cash inflow 2 years earlier.

Discount Rate

Experts estimated that the cost of capital applicable to Lockheed's assets (prior to Tri Star) was in the 9–10% range. As the Tri Star project was quite a bit riskier (by any measure) than the typical Lockheed operation, the appropriate discount rate was almost certainly higher than that. Using 10% should give a reasonable (although possibly generous) estimate of the project's value.

---

2. Excluding preproduction cost allocations. That is, the $14 million cost figure is totally separate from the $900 million of preproduction costs shown in Table A.

TABLE A
Cash Flows

Year-End	Time Index	Cash Flow ($ millions)
1967	$t = 0$	–$100
1968	$t = 1$	–200
1969	$t = 2$	–200
1970	$t = 3$	–200
1971	$t = 4$	–200

Break-Even Revisited

In an August 1972 *Time* magazine article, Lockheed (after receiving government loan guarantees) revised its break-even sales volume: "[Lockheed] claims that it can get back its development costs [about $960 million] and start making a profit by selling 275 Tri Stars."[3] Industry analysts had predicted this (actually, they had estimated 300 units break-even volume) even prior to the congressional hearings.[4] Based on a "learning curve" effect, production costs at these levels would average only about $12.5 million per unit instead of $14 million as indicated earlier. Had Lockheed been able to produce and sell as many as 500 aircraft, this average cost figure may have been even as low as $11 million per aircraft.

Lockheed had testified that it had originally hoped to capture 35–40% of the total free-world market of 775 wide bodies over the next decade (270–310 aircraft). This market estimate had been based on a wildly optimistic assumption of 10% annual growth in air travel; at a more moderate 5% growth rate, the total world market would have been only 323 aircraft. The Tri Star's actual sales performance never approached Lockheed's high expectations. Lockheed's share price plummeted from a high of about $70 to around $3 during this period. There were approximately 11.3 million shares of Lockheed common outstanding during this period. Exhibit 1 contains additional information on Lockheed's common stock.

Value Added?

As concerns the economic viability of the Tri Star program, there are several interesting points to consider:[5]

- At planned production levels (210 units), what was the true value of the Tri Star program?
- At a break-even production of roughly 300 units, did Lockheed really break even in value terms?
- At what sales volume would the Tri Star program reach true economic (as opposed to accounting) break-even?
- Was the decision to pursue the Tri Star program a reasonable one? What were the economic effects of this project on Lockheed shareholders?

---

3. *Time,* August 21, 1972, p. 62.

4. Mitchell Gordon, "Hitched to the Tri Star—Disaster at Lockheed Would Cut a Wide Swathe," *Barron's,* March 15, 1971, pp. 5–14.

5. Ignore taxes and depreciation tax shields here. In cases near the break-even volume, these would tend to offset each other nearly completely.

EXHIBIT 1
Monthly Prices of Lockheed Common Stock, January 1967–1974

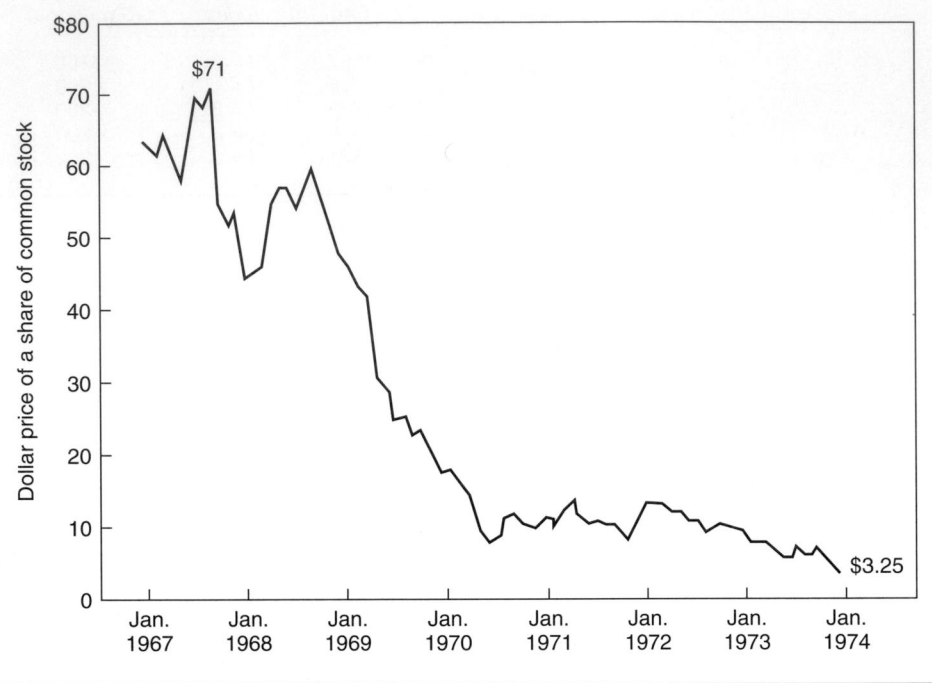

The Super Project

In March 1967, Crosby Sanberg, a financial analysis manager at General Foods Corporation, told a casewriter, "What I learned about incremental analysis at the Business School doesn't always work." He was convinced that under some circumstances sunk costs were relevant to capital project evaluations. He was also concerned that financial and accounting systems did not provide an accurate estimate of incremental costs and revenues, and that this was one of the most difficult problems in measuring the value of capital investment proposals. Mr. Sanberg used the Super project as an example.[1]

Super was a new instant dessert, based on a flavored, water-soluble, agglomerated powder.[2] Although four flavors would be offered, it was estimated that chocolate would account for 80% of total sales.

General Foods was organized along product lines in the United States, with foreign operations under a separate division. Major U.S. product divisions included Post, Kool-Aid, Maxwell House, Jell-O, and Birds Eye. Financial data for General Foods are given in Exhibits 1, 2, and 3.

The $200,000 capital investment project request for Super involved $80,000 for building modifications and $120,000 for machinery and equipment. Modifications would be made to an existing building, where Jell-O was manufactured. Since available capacity of a Jell-O agglomerator would be used in the manufacture of Super, no cost for the key machine was included in the project. The $120,000 machinery and equipment item represented packaging machinery.

1. The name and nature of this new product have been disguised to avoid the disclosure of confidential information.

2. Agglomeration is a process by which the processed powder is passed through a steam bath and then dried. This fluffs up the powder particles and increases solubility.

The Market

A Nielsen survey indicated that powdered desserts constituted a significant and growing segment of the total dessert market, as shown in Table A. On the basis of test market experience, General Foods expected Super to capture a 10% share of the total dessert market. Eighty percent of this expected Super volume would come from growth in total market share or growth in the powders segment, and 20% would come from erosion of Jell-O sales.

Production Facilities

Test market volume was packaged on an existing line, inadequate to handle long-run requirements. Filling and packaging equipment to be purchased had a capacity of 1.9 million units on a two-shift, five-day workweek basis. This represented considerable excess capacity, since 1968 requirements were expected to reach 1.1 million units, and the national potential was regarded as 1.6 million units. However, the extra capacity resulted from purchasing standard equipment, and a more economical alternative did not exist.

Capital Budgeting Procedure

The General Foods Accounting and Financial Manual identified four categories of capital investment project proposals: (1) safety and convenience; (2) quality; (3) increased profit; and (4) other. Proposal procedures and criteria for accepting projects varied according to category (Exhibit 4). In discussing these criteria, Mr. Sanberg noted that the payback and return guidelines were not used as cutoff measures and added:

> Payback and return on investment are rarely the only measures of acceptability. Criteria vary significantly by type of project. A relatively high return might be required for a new product in a new business category. On the other hand, a much lower return might be acceptable for a new product entry which represented a continuing effort to maintain leadership in an existing business by, for example, filling out the product line.

Super fell into the third category, as a profit-increasing project. Estimates of payback and return on funds employed were required for each such project requiring $50,000 or more of new capital funds and expense before taxes. The payback period was the length of time required for the project to repay the investment from the date

TABLE A
Dessert Market, August–September 1966 Compared with August–September 1965

Desserts	Market Share Aug.–Sept. 1966	Change from Aug.–Sept. 1965	
		Share Points	Volume (%)
Jell-O	19.0%	3.6	40.0
Tasty	4.0	4.0	(new)
Total powders	25.3	7.6	62.0
Pie fillings and cake mixes	32.0	–3.9	(no change)
Ice cream	42.7	–3.4	5.0
Total market	100.0%		13.0

the project became operational. In calculating the repayment period, only incremental income and expenses related to the project were used.

Return on funds employed (ROFE) was calculated by dividing 10-year average profit before taxes by the 10-year average funds employed. Funds employed included incremental net fixed assets plus or minus related working capital. Start-up costs and any profits or losses incurred before the project became operational were included in the first profit and loss period in the financial evaluation calculation.

Capital Budgeting Atmosphere

A General Foods accounting executive commented on the atmosphere within which capital projects were reviewed:

> Our problem is not one of capital rationing. Our problem is to find enough good solid projects to employ capital at an attractive return on investment. Of course, the rate of capital inputs must be balanced against a steady growth in earnings per share. The short-term impact of capital investments is usually an increase in the capital base without an immediate realization of profit potential. This is particularly true in the case of new products.
>
> The food industry should show a continuous growth. A cyclical industry can afford to let its profits vary. We want to expand faster than the gross national product. The key to our capital budgeting is to integrate the plans of our eight divisions into a balanced company plan which meets our overall growth objectives. Most new products show a loss in the first two or three years, but our divisions are big enough to introduce new products without showing a loss.

Documentation for the Super Project

Exhibits 5 and 6 document the financial evaluation of the Super project. Exhibit 5 is the summary appropriation request prepared to justify the project to management and to secure management's authorization to expend funds on a capital project. Exhibit 6 presents the backup detail. Cost of the market test was included as "Other" expense in the first period, because a new product had to pay for its test market expense, even though this might be a sunk cost at the time capital funds were requested. The "Adjustments" item represented erosion of the Jell-O market and was calculated by multiplying the volume of erosion times a variable profit contribution. In the preparation of this financial evaluation form, costs of acquiring packaging machinery were included, but no cost was attributed to Jell-O agglomerator capacity to be used for the Super project, because the General Foods Accounting and Financial Manual specified that capital project requests be prepared on an incremental basis:

> The incremental concept requires that project requests, profit projections, and funds-employed statements include only items of income and expense and investment in assets which will be realized, incurred, or made directly as a result of, or are attributed to, the new project.

Exchange of Memos on the Super Project

After receiving the paperwork on the Super project, Mr. Sanberg studied the situation and wrote a memorandum arguing that the incremental approach advocated by the manual should not be applied to the Super project. His superior agreed with the memorandum and forwarded it to the corporate controller with the covering note contained in Appendix A. The controller's reply is given in Appendix B.

Appendix A
Memos to Controller

To: J. C. Kresslin, Corporate Controller

From: J. E. Hooting, Director, Corporate Budgets and Analysis

March 2, 1967

Super Project

At the time we reviewed the Super project, I indicated to you that the return on investment looked significantly different if an allocation of the agglomerator and building, originally justified as a Jell-O project, were included in the Super investment. The pro rata allocation of these facilities, based on the share of capacity used, triples the initial gross investment in Super facilities from $200,000 to about $672,000.

I am forwarding a memorandum from Crosby Sanberg summarizing the results of three analyses evaluating the project on an

1. Incremental basis
2. Facilities-used basis
3. Fully allocated facilities and costs basis

Crosby has calculated a 10-year average ROFE using these techniques. Please read Crosby's memo before continuing with my note.

*   *   *

Crosby concludes that the fully allocated basis, or some variation of it, is necessary to understand the long-range potential of the project.

I agree. We launch a new project because of its potential to increase our sales and earning power for many years into the future. We must be mindful of short-term consequences, as indicated by an incremental analysis, but we must also have a long-range frame of reference if we are to really understand what we are committing ourselves to. This long-range frame of reference is best approximated by looking at fully allocated investment and "accounted" profits, which recognize fully allocated costs, because in fact, over the long run all costs are variable unless some major change occurs in the structure of the business.

Our current GF preoccupation with only the incremental costs and investment causes some real anomalies that confuse our decision making. Super is a good example. On an incremental basis the project looks particularly attractive because, by using a share of the excess capacity built on the coattails of the lucrative Jell-O project, the incremental investment in Super is low. If the excess Jell-O capacity did not exist, would the project be any less attractive? In the short term, perhaps yes because it would entail higher initial risk; but in the long term, it is not a better project just because it fits a facility that is temporarily unused.

Looking at this point from a different angle, if the project exceeded our investment hurdle rate on a short-term basis but fell below it on a long-term basis (and Super comes close to doing this), should we reject the project? I say yes, because over the long run, as "fixed" costs become variable and as we have to commit new capital to support the business, the continuing ROFE will go under water.

In sum, we have to look at new project proposals from both the long-range and the short-term point of view. We plan to refine our techniques of using a fully allocated basis as a long-term point of reference and will hammer out a policy recommendation for your consideration. We would appreciate any comments you may have.

To: J. E. Hooting, Director, Corporate Budgets and Analysis

From: C. Sanberg, Manager, Financial Analysis

February 17, 1967

Super Project: A Case Example of Investment Evaluation Techniques

This will review the merits of alternative techniques of evaluating capital investment decisions using the Super project as an example. The purpose of the review is to provide an illustration of the problems and limitations inherent in using incremental ROFE and payback, and thereby provide a rationale for adopting new techniques.

Alternative Techniques

The alternative techniques to be reviewed are differentiated by the level of revenue and investment charged to the Super project in figuring a payback and ROFE, starting with incremental revenues and investment. Data related to the alternative techniques are summarized at the end of this memo.

Alternative 1. Incremental Basis

Method.   The Super project as originally evaluated considered only incremental revenue and investment, which could be directly identified with the decision to produce Super. Incremental fixed capital ($200M) basically included packaging equipment.

Result.   On this basis, the project paid back in 7 years with a ROFE of 63%.

Discussion.   Although it is General Foods' current policy to evaluate capital projects on an incremental basis, this technique does not apply to the Super project. The reason is that Super extensively utilizes existing facilities, which are readily adaptable to known future alternative uses.

Super should be charged with the "opportunity loss" of agglomerating capacity and building space. Because of Super, the opportunity is lost to use a portion of agglomerating capacity for Jell-O and other products that could potentially be agglomerated. In addition, the opportunity is lost to use the building space for existing or new product volume expansion. To the extent there is an opportunity loss of existing facilities, new facilities must be built to accommodate future expansion. In other words, because the business is expanding, Super utilizes facilities that are adaptable to predictable alternative uses.

Alternative 2. Facilities-Used Basis

Method.   Recognizing that Super will use half of an existing agglomerator and two thirds of an existing building, which were justified earlier in the Jell-O project, we added Super's pro rata share of these facilities ($453M) to the incremental capital. Overhead costs directly related to these existing facilities were also subtracted from incremental revenue on a shared basis.

Result.   A ROFE of 34% results.

Discussion.   Although the existing facilities utilized by Super are not incremental to this project, they are relevant to the evaluation of the project because, potentially, they can be put to alternative uses. Despite a high return on an incremental basis, if the ROFE on a project were unattractive after consideration of the shared use of existing facilities, the project would be questionable. Under these circumstances, we might look for a more profitable product for the facilities.

In summary, the facilities-used basis is a useful way of putting various projects on a common ground for purposes of *relative* evaluation. One product using existing capacity should not necessarily be judged to be more attractive than another practically identical product that necessitates an investment in additional facilities.

Alternative 3. Fully Allocated Basis

Method.   Further recognizing that individual decisions to expand inevitably add to a higher overhead base, we increased the costs and investment base developed in Alternative 2 by a provision for overhead expenses and overhead capital. These increases were made in year 5 of the 10-year evaluation period, on the theory that, at this point, a number of decisions would result in more fixed costs and facilities. Overhead expenses included manufacturing costs, plus selling and general and administrative costs on a per unit basis equivalent to Jell-O. Overhead capital included a share of the distribution system assets ($40M).

Result.   A ROFE of 25% results.

Discussion.   Charging Super with an overhead burden recognizes that overhead costs in the long run increase in proportion to the level of business activity, even though decisions to spend more overhead dollars are made separately from decisions to increase volume and provide the incremental facilities to support the higher volume level. To illustrate, the Division-F1968 Financial Plan budgets about a 75% increase in headquarters' overhead spending in F1968 over F1964. A contributing factor was the decision to increase the sales force by 50% to meet the demands of a growing and increasingly complex business. To illustrate further, about half of the capital projects in the F1968 3-year Financial Plan are in the "nonpayback" category. This group of projects comprised largely "overhead facilities" (warehouses, utilities, etc.), which are not directly related to the manufacture of products but are necessary components of the total business activity as a result of the cumulative effect of many decisions taken in the past.

The Super project is a significant decision that will most likely add to more overhead dollars, as illustrated above. Super volume doubles the powdered dessert business category; it increases the Division businesses by 10%. Furthermore, Super requires a new production technology: agglomeration and packaging on a high-speed line.

Conclusions

1. The incremental basis for evaluating a project is an inadequate measure of a project's worth when existing facilities with a known future use will be utilized extensively.

2. A fully allocated basis of reviewing major new product proposals recognizes that overheads increase in proportion to the size and complexity of the business and provides the best long-range projection of the financial consequences.

Alternative Evaluations of Super Project (thousands of dollars)

	1. Incremental Basis	2. Facilities- Used Basis	3. Fully Allocated Basis
Investment			
Working capital	$267	$267	$267
Fixed capital			
Gross	200	653	672
Net	113	358	367
Total net investment	380	625	634
Profit before taxes[a]	239	211	157
ROFE	63%	34%	25%
Jell-O Project			
Building	$200 × ⅔ = $133		
Agglomerator	640 × ½ = 320		
	$453		

Note: Figures based on 10-year averages.

a. Assumes 20% of Super volume will replace existing Jell-O business.

Appendix B
Controller's Reply

To: Mr. J. E. Hooting, Director, Corporate Budgets and Analysis

From: Mr. J. C. Kresslin, Corporate Controller

Subject: Super Project

March 7, 1967

On March 2 you sent me a note describing Crosby Sanberg's and your thoughts about evaluating the Super project. In this memo you suggest that the project should be appraised on the basis of fully allocated facilities and production costs.

In order to continue the dialogue, I am raising a couple of questions below.

It seems to me that in a situation such as you describe for Super, the real question is a *management decision* as to whether to go ahead with the Super project or not go ahead. Or to put it another way, on the basis of our current knowledge, are we or are we not better off in the aggregate if we use half of the agglomerator and two thirds of an existing building for Super?

It might be assumed that, for example, half of the agglomerator is being used and half is not and that a minimum economically sized agglomerator was necessary for Jell-O and, consequently, should be justified by the Jell-O project itself. If we find a way to utilize it sooner by producing Super on it, aren't we better off in the aggregate, thus rendering the different ROFE figure for the Super project by itself somewhat irrelevant? A similar point of view might be applied to the portion of the building. Or if we charge the Super project with half an agglomerator and two thirds of an existing building, should we then go back and relieve the Jell-O projects of these costs in evaluating the management's original proposal?

To put it another way, since we are faced with making decisions at a certain point in time on the basis of what we know, I see very little value in looking at the Super project all by itself. Better we should look at the total situation before and after to see how we fare.

As to allocated production costs, the point is not so clear. Undoubtedly, over the long haul, the selling prices will need to be determined on the basis of a satisfactory margin over fully allocated costs. Perhaps this should be an additional requirement in the course of evaluating capital projects, as we seem to have been surprised at the low margins for "Tasty" after allocating all costs to the product.

I look forward to discussing this subject with you and with Crosby at some length.

EXHIBIT 1
Consolidated Balance Sheet of General Foods Corporation at April 1, 1967
(millions of dollars)

Cash	$ 20
Marketable securities	89
Receivables	180
Inventories	261
Prepaid expenses	14
Current assets	564
Land, buildings, equipment (at cost, less depreciation)	332
Long-term receivables and sundry assets	7
Goodwill	26
Total assets	$929
Notes payable	$ 22
Accounts payable	86
Accrued liabilities	73
Accrued income taxes	57
Current liabilities	238
Long-term notes	39
3⅜% debentures	22
Other noncurrent liabilities	10
Deferred investment tax credit	9
Total liabilities	318
Common stock issued	164
Retained earnings	449
Common stock held in treasury, at cost	(2)
Stockholders' equity	611
Total liabilities and stockholders' equity	$929
Common stock—no. of shares outstanding at year-end	25,127,007

EXHIBIT 2
Common Stock Prices of General Foods Corporation, 1958–1967

	Low	*High*
1958	$24	$ 39¾
1959	37⅛	53⅞
1960	49⅛	75½
1961	68⅝	107¾
1962	57¾	96
1963	77⅝	90½
1964	78¼	93¼
1965	77½	89⅞
1966	62¾	83
1967	65¼	81¾

EXHIBIT 3

Summary of Statistical Data of General Foods Corporation, Fiscal Years 1958–1967 (millions of dollars except assets per employee and figures on a share basis)

	1958	1959	1960	1961	1962	1963	1964	1965	1966	1967
Earnings										
Sales to customers (net)	$1,009	$1,053	$1,087	$1,160	$1,189	$1,216	$1,338	$1,478	$1,555	$1,652
Cost of sales	724	734	725	764	769	769	838	937	965	1,012
Marketing, admin, and general expenses	181	205	236	261	267	274	322	362	406	449
Earnings before income taxes	105	115	130	138	156	170	179	177	185	193
Taxes on income	57	61	69	71	84	91	95	91	91	94
Net earnings	$ 48	$ 54	$ 61	$ 67	$ 72	$ 79	$ 84	$ 86	$ 94	$ 99
Dividends on common shares	24	28	32	35	40	45	50	50	53	55
Retained earnings—current year	24	26	29	32	32	34	34	36	41	44
Net earnings per common share[a]	$ 1.99	$ 2.21	$ 2.48	$ 2.69	$ 2.90	$ 3.14	$ 3.33	$ 3.44	$ 3.73	$ 3.93
Dividends per common share[a]	1.00	1.15	1.30	1.40	1.60	1.80	2.00	2.00	2.10	2.20
Assets, Liabilities, and Stockholders' Equity										
Inventories	$ 169	$ 149	$ 157	$ 189	$ 183	$ 205	$ 256	$ 214	$ 261	$ 261
Other current assets	144	180	200	171	204	206	180	230	266	303
Current liabilities	107	107	126	123	142	162	202	173	219	238
Working capital	$ 206	$ 222	$ 230	$ 237	$ 245	$ 249	$ 234	$ 271	$ 308	$ 326
Land, buildings, equipment, gross	203	221	247	289	328	375	436	477	517	569
Land, buildings, equipment, net	125	132	148	173	193	233	264	283	308	332
Long-term debt	49	44	40	37	35	34	23	37	54	61
Stockholders' equity	287	315	347	384	419	454	490	527	569	611
Stockholders' equity per common share[a]	$11.78	$12.87	$14.07	$15.46	$16.80	$18.17	$19.53	$20.99	$22.64	$24.32
Capital Program										
Capital additions	$ 28	$ 24	$ 35	$ 40	$ 42	$ 57	$ 70	$ 54	$ 65	$ 59
Depreciation	11	14	15	18	21	24	26	29	32	34
Employment Data										
Wages, salaries, and benefits	$ 128	$ 138	$ 147	$ 162	$ 171	$ 180	$ 195	$ 204	$ 218	$ 237
Number of employees (000s)	21	22	22	25	28	28	30	30	30	32
Assets per employee ($ 000s)	21	22	23	22	22	23	24	25	29	29

Note: Column totals may not add exactly because of rounding.

a. Per share figures calculated on shares outstanding at year-end and adjusted for 2-for-1 stock split in August 1960.

EXHIBIT 4
Criteria for Evaluating Projects by General Foods Corporation

The basic criteria to be applied in evaluating projects within each of the classifications are set forth in the following schedule:

Purpose of Project	*Payback and ROFE Criteria*
a. Safety and Convenience: 1. Projects required for reasons of safety, sanitation, health, public convenience, or other overriding reason with no reasonable alternatives. Examples: Sprinkler systems, elevators, fire escapes, smoke control, waste disposal, treatment of water pollution, etc.	Payback—return on funds projections not required but the request must clearly demonstrate the *immediate* need for the project and the lack or inadequacy of alternative solutions.
2. Additional nonproductive space requirements for which there are no financial criteria. Examples: Office space, laboratories, service areas (kitchens, rest rooms, etc.)	Requests for nonproductive facilities, such as warehouses, laboratories, and offices should indicate the advantages of owning rather than leasing, unless no possibility to lease exists. In those cases where the company owns a group of integrated facilities and wherein the introduction of rented or leased properties might complicate the long-range planning or development of the area, owning rather than leasing is recommended. If the project is designed to improve customer service (such as market-centered warehouses), this factor is to be noted on the project request.
b. Quality: Projects designed primarily to improve quality.	If payback and ROFE cannot be computed, it must be clearly demonstrated that the improvement is identifiable and desirable.
c. Increased Profit: 1. Projects justified primarily by reduced costs.	Projects with a payback period *up to ten years* and a ten-year return *on* funds as *low as 20%* PBT are considered worthy of consideration, provided (1) the end product involved is believed to be a reasonably permanent part of our line or (2) the facilities involved are so flexible that they may be usable for successor products.
2. Projects designed primarily to increase production capacity for an existing product.	Projects for a proven product where the risk of mortality is small, such as coffee, Jell-O gelatin, and cereals, should assure a payback in *no more than ten years* and a ten-year PBT return on funds of *no less* than 20%.
3. Projects designed to provide facilities to manufacture and distribute a new product or product line.	Because of the greater risk involved, such projects should show a high potential return on funds (not less than a ten-year PBT return of 40%). The payback period, however, might be as much as *ten years* because of losses incurred during the market development period.*
d. Other This category includes projects which by definition are excluded from the three preceding categories. Examples: standby facilities intended to insure uninterrupted production, additional equipment not expected to improve profits or product quality and not required for reasons of safety and convenience, equipment to satisfy marketing requirements, etc.	While standards of return may be difficult to set, some calculation of financial benefits should be made where possible.

Source: The General Foods Accounting and Financial Manual.

*These criteria apply to the United States and Canada only. Profit-increasing capital projects in other areas in categories c1 and c2 should offer at least a ten-year PBT return of 24% to compensate for the greater risk involved. Likewise, foreign operation projects in the c3 category should offer a ten-year PBT return of at least 48%.

EXHIBIT 5

Capital Project Request Form of General Foods Corporation

NY 1292-C 10-64
PTD. In USA

"Super" Facilities   66-42
Division & Location

Jell-O Division   —   St. Louis
Division & Location

December 23, 1966
Date

New Request [X]   Supplement [ ]

Expansion-New Product   [X] A
Purpose
                                          [ ] R

Project Description

To provide facilities for production of Super, chocolate dessert. This project included finishing a packing room in addition to filling and packaging equipment.

Summary of Investment	
New Capital Funds Required	$200M
Expense Before Taxes	– –
Less: Trade-In or Salvage, If Any	– –
Total This Request	$200M
Previously Appropriated	– –
Total Project Cost	$200M

Financial Justification	
ROFE (PBT Basis) - 10 Yr. Average	62.9
Payback Period	6.83 Yrs.
Not Required	[ ]
* Based on Total Project Cost and Working Fund of	$510M

Estimated Expenditure Rate	
Quarter Ending Mar. F19 67	$160M
Quarter Ending June F19 68	40M
Quarter Ending F19	
Quarter Ending F19	
Remainder	

Other Information	
Major [ ] Specific [ ] Blanket [ ] Ordinary	
Included in Annual program Yes [ ] No [ ]	
Per cent of Engineering Completed	80%
Estimated Start-Up Cost	$15M
Estimated Start-Up Date	April

Level of Approval Required
[ ] Board   [ ] Chairman   [ ] Exec. V.P.   [ ] Gen. Mgr.

For Division Use—Signatures		
Name & Title		Date

Signatures		
Director Corp. Eng.		Date
Director B&A		
General Manager		
Exec. Vice President		
President		
Chairman		

(continued)

EXHIBIT 5 *(concluded)*

INSTRUCTIONS FOR CAPITAL PROJECT REQUEST FORM NY 1292-A

The purpose of this form is to secure management's authorization to commit or expend funds on a capital project. Refer to Accounting and Financial Manual Statement No. 19 for information regarding projects to which this form applies.

NEW REQUEST–SUPPLEMENT—Check the appropriate box.

PURPOSE—Identify the primary purpose of the project in accordance with the classifications established in Accounting and Financial Statement No. 19, i.e., Sanitation, Health and Public Convenience, Non-Productive Space, Safety, Quality, Reduce Cost, Expansion—Existing Products, Expansion—New Products, Other (specify). Also indicate in the appropriate box whether the equipment represents an addition or a replacement.

PROJECT DESCRIPTION—Comments should be in sufficient detail to enable Corporate Management to appraise the benefits of the project. Where necessary, supplemental data should be attached to provide complete background for project evaluation.

SUMMARY OF INVESTMENT

New Capital Funds Required—Show gross cost of assets to be acquired.

Expense Before Taxes—Show incremental expense resulting from project.

Trade-In or Salvage—Show the amount expected to be realized on trade-in or sale of a replaced asset.

Previously Appropriated—When requesting a supplement to an approved project, show the amount previously appropriated even though authorization was given in a prior year.

FINANCIAL JUSTIFICATION

ROFE—Show the return on funds employed (PBT basis) as calculated on Financial Evaluation Form NY 1292-C or 1292-F. The appropriate Financial Evaluation Form is to be attached to this form.

Not Required—Where financial benefits are not applicable or required or are not expected, check the box provided. The nonfinancial benefits should be explained in the comments.

In the space provided, show the sum of The Total Project Cost plus Total Working Funds (line 20, Form NY 1292-C, or line 5, Form NY 1292-F) in either of the first three periods, whichever is higher.

ESTIMATED EXPENDITURE RATE—Expenditures are to be reported in accordance with accounting treatment of the asset and related expense portion of the project. Insert estimated quarterly expenditures beginning with the quarter in which the first expenditure will be made. The balance of authorized funds unspent after the fourth quarter should be reported in total.

OTHER INFORMATION—Check whether the project is a major, specific ordinary, or blanket, and whether or not the project was included in the Annual Program. Show estimated percentage of engineering completed; this is intended to give management an indication of the degree of reliability of the funds requested. Indicate the estimated start-up costs as shown on line 32 of Financial Evaluation Form NY 1292-C. Insert anticipated start-up date for the project; if start-up is to be staggered, explain in comments.

LEVEL OF APPROVAL REQUIRED—Check the appropriate box.

Source: General Foods.

EXHIBIT 6
Financial Evaluation Form of General Foods Corporation (thousands of dollars)

NY 1292-C 10-64
PTD. In USA

									Date	

Jell-O		St. Louis			The Super Project			67-89		Supplement No.
Division		Location			Project Title			Project No.		

Project Request Detail	1st Per.	2nd Per.	___ Per.	___ Per.	___ Per.	Return of New Funds Employed—10-Yr. Avg.			
								PBT (C ÷ A)	PBT (B ÷ A)
1. Land	$					A - New Funds Employed (Line 21)		$380	$380
2. Buildings	80					B - Profit Before Taxes (Line 35)			$239
3. Machinery & Equipment	120					C - Net Profit (Line 37)		$115	
4. Engineering						D - Calculated Return		30.2%	62.0%
5. Other (Explain)									
6. Expense Portion (Before Tax)									
7. Sub Total	$200								
8. Less: Salvage Value (Old Asset)						Part Year Calculation for First Period			
9. Total Project Cost*	$200					Part Year Calculation for First Period			– Yrs.
10. Less: Taxes on Exp. Portion						Number of Full Years to Pay Back			6.00 Yrs.
11. Net Project Cost	$200					Part Year Calculation for Last Period			0.83 Yrs.
*Same as Project Request						Total Years to Pay Back			6.83 Yrs.

Funds Employed	1st Per. F 68	2nd Per. F 69	3rd Per. F 70	4th Per. F 71	5th Per. F 72	6th Per. F 73	7th Per. F 74	8th Per. F 75	9th Per. F 76	10th Per. F 77	11th Per. ___	10-Yr. Avg.
12. Net Project Cost (Line 11)	$200	200	200	200	200	200	200	200	200	200		
13. Deduct Depreciation (Cum.)	19	37	54	70	85	98	110	121	131	140		
14. Capital Funds Employed	$181	163	146	130	115	102	90	79	69	60		113
15. Cash												
16. Receivables	124	134	142	157	160	160	169	169	178	178		157
17. Inventories	207	222	237	251	266	266	281	281	296	296		260
18. Prepaid & Deferred Exp.												
19. Less Current Liabilities	(2)	(82)	(108)	(138)	(185)	(184)	(195)	(195)	(207)	(207)		(150)
20. Total Working Funds (15 Thru 19)	329	274	271	264	241	242	255	255	267	267		267
21. Total New Funds Employed (14 + 20)	$510	437	417	394	356	344	345	334	336	327		380
Profit and Loss												
22. Unit Volume (in thousands)	1100	1200	1300	1400	1500	1500	1600	1600	1700	1700		1460
23. Gross sales	$2200	2400	2600	2800	3000	3000	3200	3200	3400	3400		2920
24. Deductions	88	96	104	112	120	120	128	128	136	136		117
25. Net Sales	2112	2304	2496	2668	2880	2880	3072	3072	3264	3264		2803
26. Cost of Goods Sold	1100	1200	1300	1400	1500	1500	1600	1600	1700	1700		1460
27. Gross Profit	1012	1104	1196	1288	1380	1380	1472	1472	1564	1564		1343
Gross Profit % Net Sales												
28. Advertising Expense	1100	1050	1000	900	700	700	730	730	750	750		841
29. Selling Expense												
30. Gen. and Admin. Cost												
31. Research Expense												
32. Start-Up Costs	15											2
33. Other (Explain) Test Mkt.	360											36
34. Adjustments (Explain) Erosion	180	200	210	220	230	230	240	240	250	250		250
35. Profit Before Taxes	$(643)	(146)	(14)	168	450	450	502	502	564	564		239
36. Taxes	(334)	(76)	(7)	87	234	234	261	261	293	293		125
36A. Add: Investment Credit	(1)	(1)	(1)	(1)	(1)	(1)	(1)	(1)	–	–		(1)
37. Net Profit	(308)	(69)	(6)	82	217	217	242	242	271	271		115
38. Cumulative Net Profit	$(308)	(377)	(383)	(301)	(84)	133	375	617	888	1159		
39. New Funds to Repay (21 less 38)	$818	814	800	695	440	211	(30)	(283)	(552)	(832)		

See Accounting & Financial Manual Policy No. 19 for Instructions.

(continued)

EXHIBIT 6 *(continued)*

INSTRUCTIONS FOR PREPARATION OF FORM NY 1292-C
FINANCIAL EVALUATION

This form is to be submitted to Corporate Budget and Analysis with each profit-increasing capital project request requiring $50,000 or more of capital funds and expense before taxes.

Note that the ten-year term has been divided into eleven periods. The first period is to end on the March 31st following the operational date of the project, and the P & L projection may thereby encompass any number of months from one to twelve, e.g., if the project becomes operational on November 1, 1964, the first period for P & L purposes would be 5 months (November 1, 1964 through March 31, 1965). The next nine periods would be fiscal years (F'66, F'67, etc.) and the eleventh period would be 7 months (April 1, 1974 through October 30, 1974). This has been done primarily to facilitate reporting of projected and actual P & L data by providing for fiscal years. See categorized instructions below for more specific details.

PROJECT REQUEST DETAIL—*Lines 1 through 11* show the breakdown of the Net Project Cost to be used in the financial evaluation. *Line 8* is to show the amount expected to be realized on trade-in or sale of a replaced asset. *Line 9* should be the same as the "Total Project Cost" shown on Form NY 1292-A, Capital Project Request. Space has been provided for capital expenditures related to this project which are projected to take place subsequent to the first period. Indicate in such space the additional costs only; do not accumulate them.

FUNDS EMPLOYED

Capital Funds Employed—*Line 12* will show the net project cost appearing on *line 11* as a constant for the first ten periods except in any period in which additional expenditures are incurred; in that event show the accumulated amounts of *line 11* in such period and in all future periods.

Deduct cumulative depreciation on *line 13*. Depreciation is to be computed on an incremental basis, i.e., the net increase in depreciation over present depreciation on assets being replaced. In the first period depreciation will be computed at one half of the first year's annual rate; no depreciation is to be taken in the eleventh period. Depreciation rates are to be the same as those used for accounting purposes. *Exception:* When the depreciation rate used for accounting purposes differs materially from the rate for tax purposes, the higher rate should be used. A variation will be considered material when the first full year's depreciation on a book basis varies 20% or more from the first full year's depreciation on a tax basis.

The ten-year average of Capital Funds Employed shall be computed by adding *line 14* in each of the first ten periods and dividing the total by ten.

Total Working Funds—Refer to Financial Policy No. 21 as a guide in computing new working fund requirements. Items which are not on a formula basis and which are normally computed on a five-quarter average shall be handled proportionately in the first period. For example, since the period involved may be less than 12 months, the average would be computed on the number of quarters involved. Generally, the balances should be approximately the same as they would be if the first period were a full year.

Cash, based on formula which theorizes a two weeks' supply (2/52nds), should follow the same theory. If the first period is for three months, two-thirteenths (2/13ths) should be used; if it is for 5 months, two-twenty-firsts (2/21sts) should be used, and so forth.

Current liabilities are to include one half of the tax expense as the tax liability. The ten-year averages of Working Funds shall be computed by adding each line across for the first ten periods and dividing each total by ten.

PROFIT AND LOSS PROJECTION

P & L Categories (Lines 22–34)—Reflect only the incremental amounts which will result from the proposed project; exclude all allocated charges. Include the P & L results expected in the individual periods comprising the first ten years of the life of the project. Refer to the second paragraph of these instructions regarding the fractional years' calculations during the first and eleventh periods.

Any loss or gain on the sale of a replaced asset (see *line 8*) shall be included in *line 33*.

As indicated in the caption Capital Funds Employed, no depreciation is to be taken in the eleventh period.

The ten-year averages of the P & L items shall be computed by adding each line across for the eleven periods (10 full years from the operational data) and dividing the total by ten.

Adjustments (Line 34)—Show the adjustment necessary, on a before-tax basis, to indicate any adverse or favorable incremental effect the proposed project will have on any other products currently being produced by the corporation.

Investment Credit is to be included on *line 36-A*. The Investment Credit will be spread over 8 years, or fractions thereof, as an addition to PAT.

(continued)

EXHIBIT 6 *(concluded)*

RETURN ON NEW FUNDS EMPLOYED—Ten-year average returns are to be calculated for PAT (projects requiring Board approval only) and PBT. The PAT return is calculated by dividing average PAT *(line 37)* by average new funds employed *(line 21);* the PBT return is derived by dividing average PBT *(line 35)* by average new funds employed *(line 21).*

PAYBACK YEARS FROM OPERATIONAL DATE

Part Year Calculation for First Period—Divide number of months in the first period by twelve. If five months are involved, the calculation is 5/12 = .4 years.

Number of Full Years to Payback—Determined by the last period, excluding the first period, in which an amount is shown on *line 39.*

Part Year Calculation for Last Period—Divide amount still to be repaid at the end of the last full period *(line 39)* by net profit plus the *annual* depreciation in the following year when payback is completed.

Total Years to Payback—Sum of full and part years.

Source: General Foods.

Economy Shipping Company (Abridged)

In the spring of 1950 the controller of Economy Shipping Company, located near Pittsburgh, was preparing a report for the executive committee regarding the feasibility of repairing one of the company's steam riverboats or of replacing the steamboat with a new diesel-powered boat.

The Economy Shipping Company was engaged mainly in the transportation of coal from the nearby mines to the steel mills, public utilities, and other industries in the Pittsburgh area. Occasionally, the company's several steamboats also carried cargoes to places as far away as New Orleans. The boats owned by Economy Shipping were all steam powered. All were at least 10 years old, and the majority of them were between 15 and 30 years old.

The steamboat the controller was concerned about, the *Conway*, was 23 years old and required immediate rehabilitation or replacement. It was estimated that the *Conway* had a useful life of another 20 years provided that adequate repairs and maintenance were made. The book value of the *Conway* was $39,500, but the controller believed that if the company sold the boat in 1950, it would bring only around $25,000. The immediate rehabilitation costs for the *Conway* were estimated to be $115,000. The controller estimated that these general rehabilitation expenditures would extend the useful life of the *Conway* for about 20 years.

New spare parts from another boat, which had been retired in 1948, were available for use in the rehabilitation of the *Conway*. If these parts were used on the *Conway*, an estimate of their fair value was $43,500, which was their book value. Use of these parts would, in effect, decrease the immediate rehabilitation costs from $115,000 to $71,500. It was believed that if these parts were sold on the market they would bring only around $30,000. They could not be used on any of the other Economy Shipping steamboats.

Currently, the *Conway* was operated by a crew of 20. Annual operating costs for the 20-person crew are shown in Table A.

TABLE A
Annual Operating Costs for the *Conway* and Its Crew

Wages	$110,200
Vacation and sickness benefits	1,880
Social security payments	2,400
Life insurance	1,800
Commissary supplies	15,420
Repairs and maintenance	24,400
Fuel	34,500
Miscellaneous service and supplies	12,550
Total	$203,150

The controller estimated that the cost of dismantling and scrapping the *Conway* at the end of its useful life after the overhaul would be offset by the value of the scrap and used parts taken off the boat.

An alternative to rehabilitating the steamboat was the purchase of a diesel-powered boat. The Quapelle Company, a local boat manufacturer, quoted the price of $325,000 for a diesel boat. An additional $75,000 for a basic parts inventory would be necessary to service a diesel boat, and such an inventory would be sufficient to service up to three diesel boats. If four or more diesels were purchased, however, it was estimated that additional spare parts inventory would be necessary.

The useful life of a diesel-powered boat was estimated to be 25 years; at the end of that time the boat would be scrapped or completely rehabilitated at a cost approximately equal to that of a new boat. The controller did not contemplate the possibility of diesel engine replacement during the 25-year life, because information from other companies having limited experience with diesel-powered riverboats did not indicate that such costs needed to be anticipated. A general overhaul of the engines, costing $60,000 at current prices, would, however, be expected every 10 years.

After consulting the Quapelle Company and other companies operating diesel-powered boats, the controller estimated that the annual operating costs of such a boat would total $156,640 (see Table B).

Although the Economy Shipping controller had not considered the matter, at the end of the twentieth year, the diesel boat would have a realizable value of $32,500 and the inventory of parts, $37,500.

Another factor the controller was considering at this time was alternative uses of funds. In the spring of 1950, Economy had sufficient funds to buy four diesel-powered boats; however, there were alternative uses for these funds. The other projects that

TABLE B
Annual Operating Costs for a Diesel-Powered Boat

Wages for a 13-person crew	$ 77,300
Vacation and sickness benefits	1,320
Social security payments	1,680
Life insurance	1,170
Commissary supplies	10,020
Repairs and maintenance[a]	21,700
Fuel	28,800
Miscellaneous service and supplies	14,650
Total	$156,640

a. Excluding possible major overhaul of diesel engines.

management was considering at this time had an estimated return of at least 10% after taxes. The income tax rate at the time was $48%.

Questions

What are the relevant cash flows associated with each alternative, and in what years do they occur? To simplify the calculations, use the straight-line method of depreciation. Also, make the following assumptions:

1. The diesel boat, if acquired, would be sold at the end of the twentieth year.
2. The inventory of parts for the diesel boat can be depreciated for tax purposes over a 25-year period.
3. The hull of the diesel boat ($265,000) would be depreciated over a 25-year period for tax purposes, and the engines over a 10-year period.
4. The book cost of the *Conway,* including rehabilitation costs, would be depreciated over a 20-year period if rehabilitation were chosen.
5. The $32,500 residual value for the diesel boat in year 20 assumes no overhaul of the engines in year 20.

Pressco, Inc. (1985)

In November 1985, Jane Rogers, a marketing representative for Pressco, Inc., was preparing a financial presentation designed to help close the sale of mechanical drying equipment to Paperco, Inc. The equipment that Ms. Rogers hoped to sell to Paperco at a price of $2.9 million would replace less efficient facilities that had been placed in service late in December 1979 by Paperco. The cost savings (exclusive of depreciation charges) that Ms. Rogers felt certain Paperco would realize from the proposed new equipment installation amounted to $560,000 per year. Of this amount, $360,000 in savings was expected to come from more efficient fuel utilization.

One year earlier, Rogers had been unsuccessful in interesting Paperco's management in this cost-reduction opportunity. The customer viewed the proposed investment as moderately attractive but easily postponable at little cost to Paperco, and was originally unwilling to commit to the purchase for this reason. But since Rogers's earlier presentation, new tax legislation had been rumored that would (1) eliminate the investment tax credit for new equipment;[1] (2) extend depreciation lives for new equipment; and (3) reduce the corporate tax rate from 46% to 34% beginning in 1986.

While the prospects for passage of the rumored tax legislation were uncertain, Pressco's senior management was concerned that the basic thrust of the legislation might hurt the firm's sales of mechanical drying equipment. Rogers found this concern somewhat curious because she had experienced an unprecedented surge in customer inquiries following the announcement of the new tax initiative. Indeed, Paperco's management suddenly expressed significant interest in moving forward with the purchase of the mechanical drying equipment and seemed anxious to sign a binding contract.

In preparing the economic analysis to support her sales presentation to Paperco, Rogers recalled that Paperco had utilized double-declining-balance (DDB) deprecia-

---

1. Exhibit 1 presents a chronology of changes in the tax law regarding investment tax credits from 1975 to 1985 as well as the change *anticipated* but not yet *enacted* for 1986.

tion for assets acquired before January 1, 1981, and was using accelerated cost recovery system (ACRS) depreciation for assets acquired on or after that date (see Exhibit 2). To be consistent with these assumptions, Rogers prepared the relevant depreciation schedules for old and new equipment as indicated in Exhibits 3 and 4.

In the event that new tax legislation were passed prior to the signing of a binding sales contract with Paperco, Rogers also prepared a depreciation schedule utilizing the terms of the rumored new tax legislation (see Exhibit 5). She was mindful of the fact that, to reduce the economic uncertainty surrounding long-term capital investments, Congress normally grandfathered more favorable depreciation and investment tax credit schedules for projects entered into via binding contracts before new (and less favorable) tax legislation was passed. Rogers thought this fact might have something to do with the sense of urgency shown by potential customers like Paperco.

The remaining assumptions that Rogers planned to utilize in her presentation of the investment opportunity to Paperco's management are outlined below:

1. Equipment cost: $2,100,000

2. Start-up of facility: December 1986, 12 months after receipt of order, which was anticipated in December 1985

3. Equipment payment terms: 50% ($1,050,000) with order, December 1985; 50% ($1,050,000) upon start-up of facility, December 1986

4. Installation cost: $800,000; 100% upon start-up of facility, December 1986

5. Paperco cost of capital: 12%

6. Depreciable life and estimated salvage value (see Table A)

7. Physical life of new facility (after start-up): 10 years

8. Facility to be replaced:

Original equipment cost	$500,000
Original installation cost	$500,000
Estimated market value of equipment if sold in 12 months (when displaced)	$150,000
Estimated remaining physical life as of December 1985	11 years

9. Because the existing facility would remain in service for virtually all of 1986, Paperco would be able to recognize total depreciation charges on the old equipment as a 1986 expense, as shown in the schedule provided in Exhibit 4.

TABLE A
Depreciable Life and Estimated Salvage Value

Tax Reports	Facility to Be Replaced	New Facility (Existing Tax Legislation)	New Facility (Rumored New Tax Legislation)
Equipment depreciation period	10 years, DDB[a]	5 years (ACRS)	7 years (MACRS)[b]
Installation depreciation period	8 years, DDB[a]	5 years (ACRS)	7 years (MACRS)
Estimated salvage value at end of life	$60,000	$250,000	$250,000

a. The IRS permitted taxpayers to switch from the DDB method of depreciation to the straight-line method of depreciation whenever the switch became advantageous. A switch to straight-line depreciation at the most advantageous time is incorporated in the data presented in Exhibit 4.

b. MACRS is the anticipated new depreciation system.

10. Investment tax credits, if any, would be determined on the basis of both equipment *and* installation costs. The credits would be taken in the year in which the equipment was put in service.

11. Paperco currently paid federal income taxes at the rate of 46%. If the rumored tax legislation were passed, this rate would be 34% beginning in 1986.

EXHIBIT 1
Investment Tax Credit (ITC)

IRS regulations allow a credit against tax for investment in certain depreciable property. The amount of the credit is shown in the following table:

	Depreciable Life (Years)	ITC Rate (%)
Property placed in service	3–4	3⅓
after Jan. 21, 1975 but	5–6	6⅔
before Jan. 1, 1981	7 and over	10
Property placed in service on or after Jan. 1, 1981	3	6
but before Jan. 1, 1983	5	8
Property placed in service	3	4
on or after Jan. 1, 1983	5	8
Anticipated new tax legislation for 1986	All lives	0

If the equipment upon which an ITC was taken is retired before the end of its depreciable life, some portion of the ITC is recaptured by the IRS. While the entire amount of the anticipated ITC is deducted from a firm's taxes as soon as the equipment is placed in service, in fact, this ITC is "earned" in the sense that it cannot be recaptured by the IRS according to the following schedule:

	Cumulative ITC Earned	
Minimum Number of Months Property Must Be Held to Earn Credit	Property Placed in Service between Jan. 21, 1975, and Dec. 31, 1980	Property Placed in Service on or after Jan. 1, 1981
12	0 %	20%
24	0	40
36	33⅓	60
48	33⅓	80
60	66⅔	100
72	66⅔	100
84	100	100

EXHIBIT 2

Depreciation Rates Permitted for Tax Purposes for Machinery and Equipment of the Type Purchased by Paperco

Year	Percent of Cost to Be Depreciated in Year for Property Placed in Service			
	Tax Legislation in Effect Prior to 1980		Tax Legislation in Effect 1980–1985	Rumored New Tax Legislation
	10-year life property	8-year life property	5-year life[a] property	7-year life[b] property
1	20.00%	25.00%	15.00%	14.29%
2	16.00	18.75	25.50	24.29
3	12.80	14.06	17.85	17.49
4	10.24	10.55	16.66	12.49
5	8.19	7.91	16.66	8.93
6	6.55	7.91	8.33	8.92
7	6.56	7.91	—	8.93
8	6.55	7.91	—	4.46
9	6.56	—	—	—
10	6.55	—	—	—
	100.00%	100.00%	100.00%	100.00%

(handwritten annotation: lines drawn from 16.66 (year 4) and 16.66 (year 5) to 12.49 and 8.93, marked "Year 4" and "Year 5")

a. Under the tax laws in effect in late 1985, no residual value was deducted from the amount to be depreciated. Under this law a half-year of depreciation was allowed for all equipment placed in service during a year regardless of the specific date the equipment was actually placed in service. This depreciation table is based on the 150% declining-balance depreciation method with switch to straight-line in year 3.

b. The rumored tax legislation was expected to extend the depreciation life of equipment similar to that sold by Pressco from 5 to 7 years but permit a 200% declining-balance depreciation method with switch to straight-line in year 4.

EXHIBIT 3

Depreciation Expense: *New* Equipment and Installation with *No Change* in Tax Legislation or with *Grandfathering* Because of a Binding Contract (thousands of dollars)

	Accelerated Cost Recovery System (ACRS)		
	Equipment	Installation	Total
1986	$ 315	$120	$ 435
1987	535	204	739
1988	375	143	518
1989	350	133	483
1990	350	133	483
1991	175	67	242
1992	—	—	—
1993	—	—	—
1994	—	—	—
1995	—	—	—
	$2,100	$800	$2,900

Note: Assumes installation date of December 1986 for new equipment and disposal date of December 1986 for old equipment.

EXHIBIT 4

Depreciation Expense: *Replaced* Equipment and Installation (thousands of dollars)

	Double-Declining-Balance Method[a]		
	Equipment	Installation	Total
1979	$100	$125	$ 225
1980	80	93	173
1981	64	70	134
1982	51	52	103
1983	41	40	81
1984	33	40	73
1985	33	40	73
1986	33	40	73 → 1986.
1987	33	0	33
1988	32	0	32
1989	0	0	0
	$500	$500	$1,000

a. See Table A, note a, regarding the switch to straight-line depreciation in the first year that this switch becomes advantageous.

EXHIBIT 5

Depreciation Expense: *New* Equipment and Installation with *Rumored* Tax Legislation and Contract Signed Too Late to Qualify for *Grandfathering*[a] (thousands of dollars)

	Anticipated New Depreciation System (MACRS)		
	Equipment	Installation	Total
1986	$ 300	$114	$ 414
1987	514	196	710
1988	367	140	507
1989	262	100	362
1990	188	72	260
1991	188	71	259
1992	188	71	259
1993	93	36	129
1994	—	—	—
1995	—	—	—
	$2,100	$800	$2,900

a. Assumes installation date of December 1986 and that the anticipated tax legislation is passed *before* Paperco signs a binding contract. Paperco would thus lose the 8% ITC and the 5-year ACRS depreciation schedule.

MSDI—Alcala de Henares, Spain

On June 24, 1987, John Verniero, financial analyst at Merck & Co., Inc., was reviewing an investment proposal from Merck Sharp and Dohme International (MSDI). The proposal called for the purchase and installation of new automatic inspection equipment for the filling of glass ampules with liquid pharmaceutical products. The equipment was to be installed in a facility operated by MSDI in Alcala de Henares, a suburb of Madrid, Spain. The new machinery was manufactured by Brevetti Cea, s.p.a., an Italian firm, and was expected to result in significant savings of labor and materials. Fully installed, the machinery would cost 61.525 million pesetas (Pts), or nearly $500,000. For investments of this size, Merck required a discounted cash flow analysis and approval from corporate headquarters in Rahway, New Jersey.

Merck & Co., Inc.

Merck is a large multinational producer of pharmaceuticals for human and animal health care. Sales for 1987 were projected to be about $5 billion. For the year ended December 31, 1986, the company reported earnings of $676 million on sales of $4,129 million. Exhibit 1 presents selected consolidated financial data for Merck.

The company's extensive international operations are conducted primarily through subsidiaries grouped within its MSDI division. These include manufacturing facilities, research laboratories, and experimental farms in 20 countries, and sales and marketing subsidiaries in many more. In 1986 subsidiaries outside the United States recorded about half of Merck's sales and slightly less than 40% of pretax income.

Operations at Alcala de Henares

The manufacturing facility at Alcala de Henares began operating in 1969 and was located near a research laboratory and an experimental farm that were also owned by Merck. The factory produced, among other things, ampules of liquid Lidocaine, a local anesthetic used as a diluent for certain antibiotic powders. Manufacturing inputs were sourced locally, and the finished product was sold primarily to Spanish customers. Lidocaine was one of Merck's older products, and sales of the drug in Spain were expected to decline gradually over the next decade.

One of the primary production processes at Alcala de Henares consisted of washing, filling, inspecting, and sealing the ampules of Lidocaine. Ampules are small glass containers, about 0.25 to 0.50 inches in diameter, with conical tops. These were purchased from local suppliers and subjected to vigorous washing and sterilization by automated machinery. Washing and sterilization had to conform to stringent quality-control guidelines, and a number of ampules were inevitably chipped or broken in this process.

Once washed, the ampules were filled by automated machinery with liquid Lidocaine. The filled ampules then proceeded to an inspection station. This was essentially a viewing box that illuminated and magnified the ampules. Particles larger than 50 microns,[1] primarily fragments of glass from the washing process, were then visible, and workers pulled the contaminated ampules off the line. Ampules that passed inspection had their conical tops flame-sealed and were then ready for packaging and shipping.

In the spring of 1987, the inspection station at Alcala de Henares was running at 200% of planned capacity. An added shift of ten workers was needed to sustain this level of production. Each required two to three months of training to become proficient with the semiautomatic inspection equipment. MSDI's investment proposal called for replacing this semiautomatic inspection process with photoelectric-sensing machinery that would measure electronically the number and size of particles in the ampules. The high-speed equipment manufactured by Brevetti Cea had a rated capacity of nearly 6 million ampules per year, or about 25% more volume than MSDI anticipated in 1988. Inspection criteria and rejection thresholds were easily adjusted by the user, and the machinery did not require specially trained operators.

Cost Savings from the Proposed New Equipment

The new equipment could process MSDI's projected volume using four employees rather than ten, resulting in savings of both direct labor and training costs. Under very favorable circumstances, only three workers would be required. It would also eliminate human performance variability, which currently caused many good ampules to be rejected. Tests of the new equipment indicated that the rejection rate would drop from 11% of all ampules tested to about 3%. Thus, MSDI expected savings in materials as well. Exhibit 2 compares projected operating data for the existing semiautomatic inspection process and the proposed automatic photoelectric process. The projections in Exhibit 2 assume a constant inflation rate in Spain of 8% over the life of the project.

The new equipment would have a useful life of 10 years and would be depreciated under the straight-line method for both tax and financial reporting purposes. The equipment being replaced had a book value and tax basis of Pts 1,605,000, and 3 years of straight-line depreciation remaining. Its market value was thought to be about Pts 950,000. After considering Merck's consolidated tax position, Verniero determined that his analysis would use the local tax rate of 35%.

The issue that remained unresolved was whether the discounted cash flow analysis should be performed in dollars or pesetas, or indeed, whether it mattered which cur-

---

1. One micron equals one millionth of one meter.

rency was used. Certainly, borrowing costs in the two currencies were different: U.S. banks' prime rate for dollar loans was 8.50%, while the rate in Spain on short-term peseta loans had recently risen to about 18%. MSDI could obtain longer-term (peseta) funds at 15%. The spot exchange rate on July 27 was Pts 127.00/US$. One- and three-month forward rates were Pts 125.85/US$ and Pts 123.70/US$, respectively.

Many analysts were predicting a real appreciation of the peseta against the dollar over the next 5 years. They pointed to recent improvements in the performance of the Spanish economy as the reason for their bullish view of the peseta. Spain's real economic growth was running higher, and inflation lower, in 1987 than in 1986. Still, economists' 5-year forecasts for the peseta/dollar exchange rate covered a wide range, from a low of Pts 80/US$ to a high of Pts 170/US$. Selected financial and macroeconomic data are presented in Exhibits 3 and 4.

EXHIBIT 1

Merck & Co., Inc.—Selected Consolidated Financial Data[a] (millions of US$ except as noted)

					Years Ending December 31					
	1977	1978	1979	1980	1981	1982	1983	1984	1985	1986
Sales	$1,724.4	$1,981.4	$2,384.6	$2,734.0	$2,929.5	$3,063.0	$3,246.1	$3,559.7	$3,547.5	$4,128.9
Net income	277.5	307.5	381.8	415.4	398.3	415.1	450.9	493.0	539.9	675.7
Total assets	1,993.4	2,278.1	2,649.1	2,907.7	3,317.2	3,655.4	4,214.7	4,590.6	4,902.2	5,105.2
Long-term debt	213.8	211.4	213.7	211.4	241.0	337.3	385.5	179.1	170.8	167.5
Equity	1,260.2	1,436.3	1,645.0	1,841.6	1,978.2	2,180.2	2,409.9	2,518.6	2,607.7	2,541.2
Earnings/share ($)	1.84	2.03	2.53	2.77	2.68	2.81	3.05	3.36	3.79	4.85
Dividend/share ($)	.75	.85	.95	1.15	1.30	1.40	1.40	1.50	1.60	1.90
Return on sales (%)	16.1 %	15.5 %	16.0 %	15.2 %	13.6 %	13.6 %	13.9 %	13.8 %	15.2 %	16.4 %
Return on beginning equity (%)	25.2 %	24.4 %	26.6 %	25.3 %	21.6 %	21.0 %	20.7 %	20.5 %	21.4 %	25.9 %
Capital expenditures	$ 177.2	$ 155.9	$ 170.1	$ 256.5	$ 322.8	$ 295.1	$ 272.8	$ 274.4	$ 237.6	$ 210.6
Depreciation	65.8	74.3	80.6	91.3	105.0	121.1	135.2	151.6	163.6	167.2
R&D expenditures	144.9	161.4	188.1	233.9	274.2	320.2	356.0	393.1	426.3	479.8

a. As reported in the Merck & Co., Inc. 1987 annual report.

EXHIBIT 2

Comparison of Projected Operating Data for Different Inspection Processes (thousands of pesetas unless noted)

	Years Ending December 31									
	1988	1989	1990	1991	1992	1993	1994	1995	1996	1997
Projected ampule volume (000)	4,590	4,258	4,166	4,020	3,854	3,702	3,566	3,443	3,335	3,240
Projected Operating Costs,										
Semiautomatic Equipment[a]										
Materials	14,872	14,900	15,744	16,407	16,988	17,624	18,334	19,118	20,000	20,985
Direct labor	29,376	29,431	31,099	32,410	33,557	34,812	36,216	37,764	39,506	41,451
Overhead[b]	44,248	44,331	46,843	48,817	50,546	52,436	54,551	56,883	59,506	62,436
Total	88,496	88,662	93,686	97,634	101,091	104,872	109,101	113,765	119,012	124,872
Projected Operating Costs,										
New Photoelectric Equipment[a]										
Materials	13,678	13,704	14,480	15,091	15,625	16,210	16,863	17,584	18,395	19,301
Direct labor	11,750	11,773	12,440	12,964	13,423	13,925	14,487	15,106	15,803	16,581
Overhead[b]	44,248	44,331	46,843	48,817	50,546	52,436	54,551	56,883	59,506	62,436
Total	69,676	69,808	73,763	76,872	79,594	82,571	85,901	89,573	93,704	98,318

a. Projections reflect 8% annual inflation in per-ampule costs.

b. Does not include depreciation.

469

EXHIBIT 3

Selected Spanish Financial and Macroeconomic Data

Date	Average Daily Interbank Rate (Pts %)	6–12 Month Deposit Rate (Pts %)	Short-Term Commercial Lending Rate (Pts %)	Consumer Prices Inflation (Pts %)	Real Growth in GDP (%)
1980	18.6%	13.1%	16.9%	10.2%	1.5%
1981	18.7	11.4	15.3	11.5	0.2
1982	20.3	12.3	15.0	14.7	1.2
1983	16.4	12.3	15.0	12.2	1.8
1984					
I	14.8	12.5	20.0		
II	11.9	12.6	17.2		
III	12.5	12.4	15.0		
IV	12.2	11.7	14.0	11.3	1.9
1985					
I	12.1	11.1	13.7		
II	14.0	10.7	14.0		
III	11.1	10.5	14.3		
IV	9.9	9.9	12.0	8.8	2.2
1986					
I	11.3	9.4	11.6		
II	12.0	9.2	12.4		
III	11.6	8.9	12.5		
IV	11.8	8.7	12.3	8.8	3.3
1987					
I	14.4	8.6	13.1		
II	18.1	8.8	17.9		

EXHIBIT 4

Selected U.S. Financial and Macroeconomic Data

Date	Average Yield on 3-Month T-Bills (US$ %)	Average Yield on 10-Year T-Bills (US$ %)	Average Yield on 6-Month Commercial Paper (US$ %)	Prime Commercial Lending Rate (US$ %)	Consumer Price Inflation (US$ %)	Real Growth in GDP (%)
1980	11.50%	11.46%	12.29%	15.27%	13.5%	−0.2%
1981	14.03	13.91	14.76	18.87	10.4	1.9
1982	10.69	13.00	11.89	14.86	6.1	−2.5
1983	8.63	11.10	8.89	10.79	3.2	3.6
1984						
I	9.13	11.94	9.45	11.25		
II	9.84	13.20	10.77	12.75		
III	10.34	12.87	11.15	12.75		
IV	8.97	11.74	9.26	11.00	4.3	6.8
1985						
I	8.18	11.58	8.69	10.50		
II	7.52	10.81	7.91	9.75		
III	7.10	10.34	7.72	9.50		
IV	7.15	8.76	7.70	9.50	3.6	3.0
1986						
I	6.89	8.56	7.41	9.25		
II	6.13	7.60	6.54	8.50		
III	5.53	7.31	5.89	7.50		
IV	5.34	7.26	5.73	7.50	1.9	2.9
1987						
I	5.53	7.19	5.95	7.50		
II	5.73	8.34	6.85	8.50		

Note on Fundamental Parity Conditions

For modern firms and investors alike, an appreciation of the forces underlying exchange rate movements is important because of the impact such changes can have on the value of investments and investment opportunities. This note discusses the basic building blocks for characterizing exchange rates and expected exchange rate movements. The framework is founded upon assumptions of rational economic behavior and the ability to transact freely at no cost in the markets for goods and credit as well as the market for foreign exchange. A handful of fundamental parity and market equilibrium conditions describe the connections among these international markets.

The empirical evidence supporting each individual parity condition is mixed. But collectively, they constitute a useful way of ordering one's thinking about the economic forces governing exchange rate movements. Their usefulness is less as accurate descriptors of international financial markets and more as a unified framework for focusing attention on relevant issues and questions as far as exchange rate movements are concerned.

Purchasing Power Parity

One of the simplest and most widely discussed parity conditions is purchasing power parity (PPP). In its simplest form, PPP can be cast as the Law of One Price (LOP). This condition states that the same good in different countries should sell for the same price when expressed in a common currency. For example, according to the LOP, the dollar cost of ball bearings purchased in Japan should be the same as the dollar cost of ball bearings purchased in the United States. Naturally, the same is true for the yen cost of ball bearings in the United States and Japan. If we take Japan to be the domestic economy and the United States to be the foreign, then the LOP implies

This note was prepared by Research Associate Richard P. Melnick and Professor W. Carl Kester, and revised by Professor Kenneth A. Froot.

$P_D = S^{D/F} \times P_F$, where P_D is the price of the good in domestic currency (e.g., yen), P_F is the price in foreign currency (e.g., dollars), and $S^{D/F}$ is the spot exchange rate expressed as units of domestic currency per unit of foreign currency (e.g., 100 yen per dollar).

Clearly, the LOP can be enforced by commodity arbitrageurs who buy and sell across borders to exploit differences in commodity prices not justified by transportation or other transaction costs. Their actions, it is often argued, equilibrate common-currency commodity prices around the world. Even without direct arbitrage, of course, the LOP can prevail over the long run due to the forces of supply and demand. Sellers of high-price ball bearings will find that, over time, demand is lost to lower-price producers if customers view the products as close substitutes.

The more general version of the LOP is called absolute PPP. It states that national price levels—not just individual goods' prices—are equal when expressed in a common currency. For absolute PPP, $P_D = S^{D/F} \times P_F$ implies that P_D and P_F represent prices of domestic and foreign *baskets* of goods. For example, PPP implies that the cost of living, as represented by, say, the consumer price index (CPI) in the foreign and domestic economies should be equated by the current spot exchange rate, $S^{D/F}$. Any number of baskets of goods can (and are) used in place of the CPI—producer price indexes, unit labor costs, and so forth.

Of course, the forces of supply and demand that help to enforce the LOP are likely to be weaker for such baskets. Consider, for example, absolute PPP applied to Japanese and U.S. CPIs. CPIs include goods such as haircuts and apartments, which are non-traded goods. Nontraded goods, such as haircuts and apartments in Tokyo, are not close substitutes for haircuts and apartments in New York. The presence of nontraded goods reduces the scope for arbitrage or trade substitution to equalize the price of broad price-level measures. Absolute PPP may therefore apply better to producer price indexes (PPIs), whose components are more tradable internationally. In any case, one might expect absolute PPP to hold less tightly than the LOP.

By converting the price levels into inflation rates and currency levels into rates of depreciation, one converts absolute PPP into relative PPP. In its relative form, PPP states that a currency's exchange rate depreciates over time at a rate equal to the difference in inflation rates in the two countries. The condition can be expressed notationally as[1]

$$(1 + \dot{s}) = \frac{(1 + \dot{p}_D)}{(1 + \dot{p}_F)} \tag{1}$$

where

$\dot{s}^{D/F}$ = the rate of change in the spot exchange rate (domestic currency per unit of foreign currency) over some relevant time interval, expressed as a decimal fraction (e.g., .05 for a 5% rate of change)

$\dot{p}_F$ = the rate of foreign price inflation over the same time interval, expressed as a decimal fraction

---

1. It is assumed here and throughout the rest of this note that exchange rates are expressed in units of domestic currency per unit of foreign currency. For exchange rates where this is not the convention (e.g., British sterling viewed from a non-United Kingdom perspective), the parity equations should be modified appropriately by inverting ratios on the side of the equation opposite the exchange rates.

$\dot{p}_D$ = the rate of domestic price inflation over the same time interval, expressed as a decimal fraction[2]

Notice that equation (1) follows from absolute PPP. Notice further that if equation (1) holds in fact, then it should also hold in expectation. That is, relative PPP can be construed as saying that *expected* currency depreciation is equal to the relative (domestic compared with foreign) *expected* rates of inflation.

Covered Interest Parity

Covered interest parity (CIP) stipulates that the forward premium or discount for one currency relative to another should be equal to the ratio of nominal interest rates on securities of equal risk denominated in the two currencies in question. Notationally, the relationship can be expressed as[3]

$$\frac{F}{S} = \frac{(1 + R_D)}{(1 + R_F)}$$

or alternatively,

$$F = S \frac{(1 + R_D)}{(1 + R_F)} \tag{2}$$

where

S = the current spot exchange rate, expressed in units of domestic currency per unit of foreign currency

F = the forward exchange rate for a given time interval, in units of domestic currency per unit of foreign currency

R_D = the nominal interest rate on a security of equivalent maturity and denominated in the domestic currency, expressed as a decimal fraction

R_F = the nominal interest rate on a security with a maturity equal to that of the forward exchange rate and denominated in a foreign currency, expressed as a decimal fraction

If this condition does not hold, then it will be possible to engage in covered interest arbitrage: a series of transactions that will provide a riskless profit. For example, if the yield on 1-year deutsche mark government bonds is 4% and the yield on 1-year U.S. Treasury notes is 8%, the deutsche mark should be trading at a 1-year

---

2. A common alternative expression for relative PPP is: $\dot{p}_D - \dot{p}_F = \dot{s}$. This is a correct expression whenever rates of change are expressed on a continuously compounding basis (continuously compounding rates of change can be calculated by taking the natural log of 1 plus the discrete-time rate of change, e.g., $\ln(1.10)$ = .095). Both relative PPP formulations will give approximately equivalent results when the relevant rates of inflation are very close to each other. However, when rates of inflation in the two economies are widely divergent, merely taking the simple difference of discrete time changes rather than the ratio as shown in equation (1) can lead to large errors.

3. Expressing interest rates on a continuously compounded basis, let $r_D = \ln(1 + R_D)$ and $R_F = \ln(1 + R_F)$. Similarly, if we express the forward premium as a continuously compounded rate, we have $f - s = \ln(F/S) = \ln(F) - \ln(S)$. Using these expressions, under continuous compounding, CIP can be written as

$$f - s = r_D - r_F$$

This says that the forward premium or discount on a currency should equal the interest differential.

forward premium to the dollar of $3.7\% = [(1.04/1.08) - 1] \times 100$. Suppose the deutsche mark/dollar spot exchange rate was 1.8000. CIP would imply a 1-year forward rate of $1.7333 = 1.8[1.04/1.08]$. If, instead, the deutsche mark were trading in the 1-year forward market at 1.75, a riskless profit could be earned by buying what was cheap and selling what was dear, all the time remaining in a "square" position (i.e., being neither long nor short of deutsche marks or dollars). The arbitrage would work as follows:

1. Borrow deutsche marks today for one year at 4%;
2. Convert the borrowed deutsche marks to dollars in the spot market at an exchange rate of DM 1.8/\$1;
3. Invest the dollars for 1 year at 8%; and
4. Buy deutsche marks forward 1 year at DM 1.75/\$1.

If an arbitrageur borrowed, say, DM 10 million in step one, received \$5,555,556 upon immediate conversion in the spot market and \$6,000,000 after investing the dollars for 1 year at 8%, his future profit would be \$57,143, regardless of what happened to the deutsche mark/dollar exchange rate during the intervening year. This can be determined by calculating the dollar size of the forward contract the arbitrageur would have to execute in order to repay the borrowed deutsche mark principal plus interest 1 year later: DM 10,400,000/1.75 = \$5,942,857. The difference between this sized forward contract and the \$6 million proceeds from the dollar investment yields the riskless profit of \$57,143. Note that the arbitrageur could achieve this without taking on any risk. As many arbitrageurs can and will act to exploit this opportunity if it should arise, exchange rates and interest rates should conform well to CIP.

Uncovered Interest Parity

A related parity condition is called uncovered interest parity (UIP). UIP simply says that one can replace the forward rate in equation (2) with the spot exchange rate expected to prevail when the forward contract matures, $E(S_{t+1})$, where E implies the expected future value of the variable within the parentheses, and the $t + 1$ subscript indicates the date in the future when the forward contract expires. When this expression is substituted into equation (2), the resulting expression says that the expected rate of change in the spot exchange rate equals the ratio of nominal interest rates in the two countries:

$$\frac{E(S)}{(S)} = \frac{(1 + R_D)}{(1 + R_F)}$$

or alternatively,

$$E(S) = S \frac{(1 + R_D)}{(1 + R_F)} \tag{3}$$

Thus, returning to the deutsche mark/dollar example used above, UIP would imply that the market expects the deutsche mark to appreciate against the U.S. dollar over the next year by 3.7%. In effect, UIP says that equilibrium can be maintained in global capital markets only if German investors in U.S. dollar securities will be compensated for the expected decline of the dollar against the deutsche mark by means of higher nominal dollar interest rates (alternatively, it can be said that U.S. investors in deutsche mark securities must be compensated for lower German interest rates by means of an appreciating deutsche mark). Notice that equation (2) implies that, under UIP, the expected returns on domestic and foreign interest-bearing notes are equal when expressed in a common currency. This suggests that, when UIP holds, investors view domestic and foreign interest-bearing notes as nearly perfect substitutes, in spite of the fact that foreign currency notes are riskier from the domestic investor's perspective.

Uncovered interest parity is not a riskless arbitrage condition as is CIP. It holds only if investors aggressively push rates of return toward levels that exactly offset expected currency changes. Given the difference in currency risk between domestic and foreign notes, investors may not always aggressively enforce UIP with their actions. As a result, UIP is more of a useful benchmark for market expectations than it is a strict arbitrage condition.

Note that UIP and CIP together imply that the forward rate is equal to the market's expectation of the future spot rate, $F = E(S_{t+1})$. This does *not* say that the forward rate or the interest differential are perfectly accurate predictors of the actual future spot rate. In fact, as will be shown later, forward rates and interest differentials are often poor predictors. If expectations are fairly rational, UIP merely states that on average, forward rates and interest differentials neither systematically over- nor underestimate the future spot rate. Put differently, deviations of the actual future spot rate from the forward rate average about zero when observed over a long span of time. Thus, an implication of UIP combined with CIP is that an investor cannot hope to profit systematically by speculating on differences between the forward rate and the subsequent spot rate prevailing at the time a forward contract matures.

Finally, note that if UIP and relative PPP are combined, we have that expected inflation differentials are equal to nominal interest differentials. This means that (expected) *real* interest rates in different countries are equal. To see this, note that UIP (in equation (3)) and PPP (in equation (1)) together imply

$$\frac{1 + \dot{p}_D}{1 + \dot{p}_F} = \frac{1 + R_D}{1 + R_F} \tag{4}$$

Equation (5) implies that real interest rates are equal in each country:

$$\frac{1 + R_F}{1 + \dot{p}_F} = \frac{1 + R_D}{1 + \dot{p}_D} \tag{5}$$

That is, the real rate in each currency is equal to (1 plus) that currency's nominal interest rate divided by (1 plus) that currency's inflation rate.

The equality of real interest rates around the world is sometimes referred to as the International Fisher Effect (IFE), named after the economist Irving Fisher. The disciplinary force behind IFE comes from investors who have in mind a real rate of return that they expect to earn when investing money overseas, where the real rate is figured relative to the foreign inflation rate. If investors behave in this way, they will demand higher returns in inflationary environments to compensate for the erosion of foreign currency purchasing power they expect. Thus, if investors sought a real return of 3% during a year in which inflation was expected to be 5%, an 8.15 % = {[(1.03)(1.05) − 1] × 100} nominal yield would be necessary to offset the effects of inflation.

Empirical Evidence

The major parity and market equilibrium conditions discussed so far are summarized in Exhibit 1 (definitions of variables are the same as those used in this note's main text). If all these conditions held precisely at every point in time, and assuming freely and efficiently operating capital markets, life would be fairly simple. Simultaneous satisfaction of all the parity conditions would ensure that (1) no one could profit systematically from foreign exchange transactions (over and above returns just adequate to compensate for risk); (2) various methods of covering foreign exchange exposure would have equal expected costs (e.g., forward contracting and money market hedges); and (3) covering oneself would have zero expected losses or gains relative to remaining uncovered. In other words, a policy of proactively covering all transaction exposures would be expected to produce the same gains or losses, on average, over the long run, as would a passive policy of simply executing all transactions at the then prevailing future spot rates. Furthermore, there would appear to be no net advantage to financing in different currencies or markets. The real cost of capital measured in one's home currency would be equivalent no matter what the source and currency of the capital raised.

Unfortunately, though not surprisingly, the bulk of empirical evidence does not support PPP or UIP, suggesting, therefore, that the IFE also fails. The earliest studied and least well supported of these is PPP.[4] Many empirical tests involving major currencies and covering different time spans fail to support relative PPP in the short run and even medium run. Absolute PPP fails even more clearly at any given moment. However, there is some evidence that PPP holds better over the long run. Furthermore, even those studies that reject absolute PPP do find a strong proportional relationship between inflation rates in two economies and the rate of change in the exchange rate between their two currencies; that is, these studies suggest that relative PPP holds well. The usual rule for deviations from absolute PPP is that, on average, deviations die away with a half-life of about 4 years.

As suggested above, CIP seems to hold much better. An illustration of this sort of result is provided by Exhibit 2, which shows the pattern of potential covered interest arbitrage opportunities between the yen and the dollar from January 1976 to November 1985. Panel A of Exhibit 2 plots forward premia and discounts on the yen against the national differences in interest rates; note the close conformity. Panel B, however, magnifies the difference between these two plots. Spikes above and below the zero baseline in panel B represent deviations of the yen–dollar interest rate differential from the yen's forward dollar premium or discount.

At first glance, numerous profit opportunities would appear to exist, suggesting a breakdown of CIP between the yen and the dollar. However, one must recognize that, in practice, an arbitrageur must execute four transactions to exploit a covered interest arbitrage opportunity. Specifically, the arbitrageur must borrow at the offer rate in one currency, convert to another currency on one side of the spot dealer's spread, lend in that currency at the bid rate, and then cover forward on the other side of the forward dealer's spread. Thus, there are two spreads to be spanned, as well as the possibility of other transactions costs such as brokerage frees, transmission costs, and transaction taxes. These costs, which evidence indicates to be about 25 basis points during this time period, are represented by a band above and below the zero baseline.[5] (The band is drawn as two fixed, horizontal lines for convenience only. In fact, transactions costs could, and probably did, vary over time, with the band widening during volatile

---

4. For reviews of the large literature testing purchasing power parity, see, K.A. Froot and K. Rogoff, "Perspectives on PPP and Long Run Real Exchange Rates," in *Handbook of International Economics,* (North Holland, 1995): 1647–1688; and L.H. Officer, "The Purchasing-Power-Parity Theory of Exchange Rates: A Review Article," IMF Staff Papers 23 (March 1976): 1–60.

5. See W.C. Kester and T. Leuhrman, *Japan and the World Economy* 1, no. 3 (1989): 1–23.

periods in the exchange market and narrowing during relatively calm periods.) Truly profitable covered interest arbitrage opportunities are really presented only in those instances where the spikes extend above or below the band. While a number of such opportunities appear to remain, they are fewer in number and less dramatic in size. Indeed, the remaining opportunities could be more apparent than real, resulting from flawed data observations rather than true market opportunities.

This sort of result is typical for most of the world's major currencies: few truly profitable deviations from CIP are found to exist after transaction costs are considered, and most of those will be fairly short-lived. Indeed, only professionals that watch the market closely are likely to be in a position to exploit such opportunities when they arise, and they will do so in large volume. This very action on their part serves to eliminate the arbitrage opportunity fairly quickly. The same is not likely to be true for less actively traded currencies, or currencies in which credit is severely restricted. In these cases, arbitrageurs may not be able to construct their hedges properly due to an inability to borrow, lend, or cover forward in size.

Evidence on the empirical validity of UIP is poorer. While some studies found evidence in favor of UIP,[6] other studies claim to have detected a "forward bias" that is suggestive of failure of UIP.[7] These latter studies find that forward rates (and interest differentials) have differed systematically from subsequent future spot rates at the end of the contract date. These deviations could be due to market imperfections (e.g., expectations of the imposition of exchange or credit controls), to faulty statistical inferences, to irrational investors, or to systematic risk associated with certain currencies. Systematic currency risk premia can arise whenever exchange rate movements are correlated with returns on other assets. Since risks of this nature cannot be diversified away, a risk premium would be required to induce investors to bear them. Still, much of the bias appears to be short-term in nature. Over longer periods, UIP may perform somewhat better.

Managerial Implications

The inconclusive evidence regarding some parity conditions is no great surprise. Despite the increased efficiency and integration of global markets—particularly goods markets— there are still sufficient imperfections to make it unlikely that parity will hold at all points in time. As a consequence, one conclusion is that investing in foreign countries (versus domestically) need not be a sterile exercise generating no expected gain or loss for shareholders. Genuine opportunities to create or destroy value for the corporation may present themselves from time to time. It may also be possible to borrow at low real interest rates in some countries, or set up particularly low-cost hedges.

Given the highly uneven track record of the parity conditions as accurate descriptions of market behavior, their real value to managers lies in their role as a conceptual

---

6. See R.Z. Aliber, *A Short Guide to International Finance* (1977); J.A. Frenkel, "A Monetary Approach to the Balance of Payments; Doctrinal Aspects and Empirical Evidence," *Scandinavian Journal of Economics,* May 1976, pp. 200–204; I. Giddy, "An Integrated Theory of Foreign Exchange Equilibrium," *Journal of Financial and Quantitative Analysis,* December 1976, pp. 863–892; S.W. Kohlagen, "The Forward Rate as an Unbiased Predictor of the Future Spot Rate," *Columbia Journal of World Business,* Winter 1979, pp. 77–85; and S.P. Magee, "The Empirical Evidence of the Monetary Approach of the Balance of Payments and Exchange Rates," *American Economic Review: Proceedings,* May 1976.

7. For an overview of forward-rate bias and the apparent failures of UIP, see K.A. Froot and R. Thaler, "Anomalies: Foreign Exchange," *Journal of Economic Perspectives,* Summer 1990, pp. 179–192.

framework. They offer, in other words, a useful starting point for analyses involving foreign exchange movements. Predictions of future exchange rates derived from one or more of the parity conditions (e.g., PPP, UIP, or IFE) may not be especially accurate, but on average, they are likely to perform no worse than those arising from more complex economic models.

Ultimately, the parity conditions are most useful as a means of organizing and disciplining one's thinking about exchange rate determination. Even if markets do not operate perfectly efficiently, one should maintain a healthy skepticism of "free lunches." When presented with a scheme for making money in foreign exchange markets, or for covering an exposure at exceptionally low cost, a grasp of the fundamental parity conditions can help one pinpoint the inefficiency being exploited and formulate the relevant questions to pose to those sponsoring the idea. In this way, one can be more certain that a viable economic rationale, not merely a quick sales pitch, underlies the scheme's promised returns.

EXHIBIT 1
Summary of Major Parity and Market Equilibrium Conditions

1. Law of One Price (LOP):

$$P_D = S^{D/F} \times P_F$$

2. Purchasing Power Parity (PPP):

   a. Absolute:

$$P_D = S^{D/F} \times P_F$$

   b. Relative:

$$(1 + \dot{s}) = \frac{(1 + \dot{p}_D)}{(1 + \dot{p}_F)}$$

3. Covered Interest Parity (CIP):

$$\frac{F}{S} = \frac{(1 + R_D)}{(1 + R_F)}$$

4. Uncovered Interest Parity (UIP):

$$\frac{E(S)}{S} = \frac{(1 + R_D)}{(1 + R_F)}$$

5. International Fisher Effect (IFE)

$$\frac{1 + R_F}{1 + \dot{p}_F} = \frac{1 + R_D}{1 + \dot{p}_D}$$

EXHIBIT 2
Hypothetical Covered Interest Arbitrage Opportunities Between the Yen and the Dollar,
1976–1985

A. Comparison of FX Forward Premia/Discounts to Interest Rate Difference

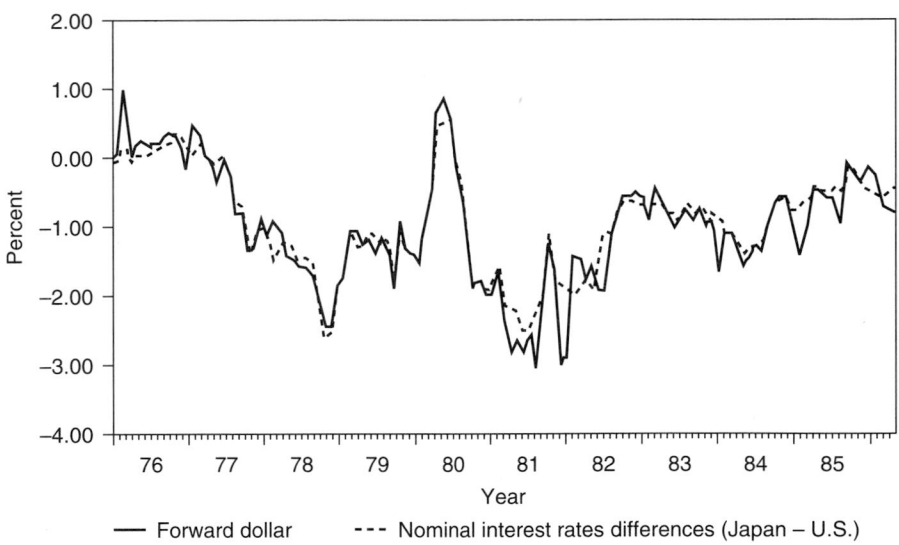

B. Covered Interest Arbitrage Opportunities

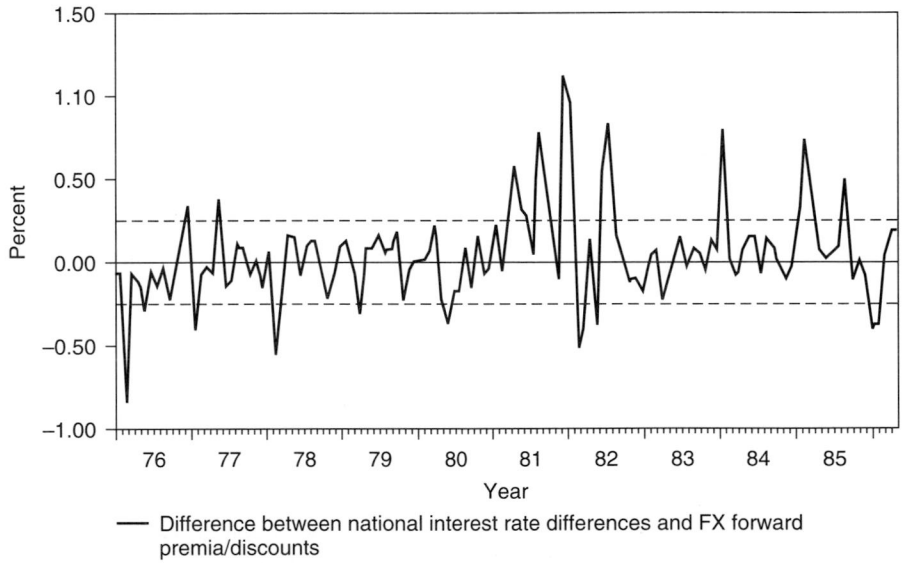

Note: Graphs are constructed using monthly observations of 90-day Eurodollar and Euroyen yields and three-month forward rates for the yen. All data were obtained from the IMF's *International Financial Statistics* computer tapes.

Acid Rain: The Southern Company (A)

Early in 1992 managers at the Southern Company were reexamining their strategy for complying with the acid rain provisions of the 1990 amendments to the Clean Air Act. The Southern Company was a holding company; its operating units were electric utilities in Georgia, Alabama, Mississippi, and Florida. The largest Southern subsidiaries, Georgia Power and Alabama Power, provided most of the electricity in their respective states.

Dozens of Southern Company executives had worked on compliance strategies since the Clean Air Act's passage in November 1990, but the time for analysis was just about over. Because of long lead times in installing pollution-control equipment, the final decisions on compliance strategy would have to be made in 1992 in order to meet the act's 1995 effective date.

The choices that the company faced at Georgia Power's Bowen coal-fired plant were representative of the dilemmas the Clean Air Act posed for the Southern Company as a whole. The Bowen plant sat on the banks of the Etowah River near Taylorsville, Georgia, northwest of the city of Atlanta. Completed in 1975, it was capable, when all four of its generators were running at capacity, of producing enough power to serve the residential, commercial, and industrial demands of 1 million people.

The Bowen plant was an unusually large, but otherwise fairly typical, coal-fired steam electric plant. Coal was burned in massive vessels. Steam, traveling through pipes that ran through these vessels, was heated by the energy from the burning coal. Adjacent turbines converted the energy in the steam to mechanical energy, which was then converted to electrical energy in the plant's generators. Large coal-fired plants like Bowen had high fixed costs but relatively low variable costs and were designed to operate continuously. Utilities used them for baseload generation, supplementing the energy from the coal plants with power from oil- or gas-fired plants to meet peak demands.

This case was prepared by Professor Forest Reinhardt.

Copyright © 1992 by the President and Fellows of Harvard College.
Harvard Business School case 792–060.

Running the Bowen plant was an operation of vast scale. Hundreds of railroad cars carrying coal from southeastern Kentucky arrived at the plant each day, contributing to a pile of inventory that weighed over 1 million tons. During 1990, Bowen's generators consumed 8.338 million tons of coal (952 tons of coal every hour) and generated 21,551 million kilowatt-hours of electricity. The value of this electricity varied substantially across markets, but in 1990 the Southern Company realized an average of 5.6¢ per kilowatt-hour in revenues.

Also during 1990, over 30 tons of sulfur dioxide left the stacks of the Bowen plant each hour. This pollutant was an important precursor of acid deposition, or acid rain, which had been implicated in damage to lakes, forest ecosystems, and manmade materials like metals and paints. New legislation aimed at controlling acid rain, passed by Congress and signed by President Bush in November 1990, would regulate these emissions starting in 1995.

Most previous regulations for air pollution control had specified a particular quantity of pollution that a facility could emit. A firm faced fines or other sanctions if its emissions exceeded the permitted level, but it had no incentive to reduce its emissions below the level specified in the permit. The new acid rain law, by contrast, allowed firms to choose their own emissions levels. They would be granted allowances to emit a certain amount of sulfur dioxide based on the amount of electricity they had generated in the past. Starting in 1995 (in "Phase One" of the law), each of about 100 large coal-fired utility plants across the country, including Bowen, would receive allowances to emit 2.5 pounds of sulfur dioxide per million British thermal units (MMBtu) of coal consumed. In the year 2000 ("Phase Two"), all coal-fired utility plants, including those regulated in Phase One, would get allowances worth 1.2 pounds per MMBtu of coal.

If they wished, utilities could reduce their emissions below the amount for which they had been given allowances and sell the extra allowances to other utilities. Alternatively, they could purchase additional allowances from other firms, which would permit them to release larger quantities of sulfur dioxide.

Compared to other plants that would be regulated in Phase One, Bowen was fairly clean; many other utility plants, including some in the Southern Company system, were emitting sulfur dioxide in quantities up to two times higher than Phase One levels. Nevertheless, Bowen would have to reduce its emissions by 1995, or purchase allowances, in order to comply with the law. Further reductions or increased purchases of allowances would be necessary beginning in the year 2000.

The Clean Air Act amendments specified the quantity of allowances Bowen would receive. The plant would receive allowances for 254,580 tons of sulfur dioxide in each of the 5 years beginning in 1995. Starting in the year 2000, it would receive allowances worth 122,198 tons per year.

There were several options for complying with the new law. First, the company could continue to operate Bowen as it had in the past, burning high-sulfur Kentucky coal without scrubbing the exhaust gases. If it did, its emissions would exceed the amounts for which it would receive allowances. Each year beginning in 1995, Bowen would purchase allowances from other Southern Company plants or on the open market to make up the difference.

Second, the company could install scrubbers at the Bowen plant that would remove sulfur dioxide from the exhaust gases of the generators. The scrubbers could be installed from 1992 to 1994 so they would be on line during Phase One; in that case, Bowen would generate excess allowances that could be sold to other utilities or to other Southern Company plants. Alternatively, the company could delay the installation of the scrubbers until 1997 through 1999, in which case they would begin working in the year 2000; in that case, Bowen would generate excess allowances starting in 2000, but it would need to buy allowances from other plants during 1995 through 1999.

The company's last option was to switch the Bowen plant to low-sulfur coal from Kentucky or West Virginia. This strategy would bring Bowen's emissions below the amount of its Phase One permits. In Phase Two, the Bowen plant would need to buy allowances. (Nothing prevented the Southern Company from switching fuels and also installing scrubbers, but this option made little sense economically. If a plant burned low-sulfur coal, the gases leaving its boilers would be sufficiently low in sulfur that scrubbers could not remove enough additional sulfur to pay for themselves.)

Under any of the options, the Bowen plant would continue to generate electricity at its 1990 levels through the year 2016. In 2016, Bowen was likely to be retired as new, more efficient plants came on stream, and its salvage value would be negligible.

Company planners expected the price of electricity to remain constant during the period Bowen was in operation. They also figured that operating costs exclusive of fuel and pollution-control expenditures, which had averaged 0.00281 dollars per kilowatt-hour in recent years, would stay about the same until the plant was retired.

The prices the Southern Company could charge for its electricity in Georgia were determined by the Public Service Commission, a body of five officials elected statewide. The utility customarily applied for rate increases to recover the costs of new construction or to pass on increases in operating costs. The Southern Company's government relations personnel were uncertain whether the commission would approve rate increases to cover the total costs of compliance with the Clean Air Act. The commission might force the company's shareholders to bear some of the costs of compliance rather than pass them on to its ratepayers. A second possibility was that the company might be allowed to recover its costs only if it could show that it had complied in the least costly manner. In either case, company executives felt that they should search for the most cost-minimizing method of complying with the Act.

Numerous government agencies and private firms had developed predictions of the prices of allowances in Phase One and Phase Two. As a working estimate, company planners felt that the price of allowances would probably be $250 per ton of sulfur dioxide in 1995, the first year of Phase One, and that the price would rise at 10% per year through the year 2010. Thereafter, the allowances were expected to stay at their 2010 price. Allowances could be bought or sold on the open market, and a multiplant firm like the Southern Company could also move allowances from one of its plants to another in an internal transaction. From an economic standpoint, it was irrelevant whether allowances were traded within the firm or externally, since the value of an allowance—and hence the appropriate internal transfer price—would be determined in the external market.

In Georgia, the Southern Company paid federal and state income taxes at a combined effective rate of 37.7%. The company customarily used an after-tax discount rate of 10% in evaluating investment opportunities.

Option 1: Burn High-Sulfur Coal without Scrubbers; Purchase Allowances

Aside from capital costs, costs of fuel were the largest single expense at Bowen. Coals varied widely both in delivered price per ton and in heat content per pound, so prices were usually expressed in dollars per ton and in dollars per MMBtu.

The high-sulfur Kentucky coal burned at Bowen cost, on average, $41.46 per ton delivered to the plant. Starting in 1996, the price was expected to fall to $29.82 per ton, delivered. Bowen's generators required coal with a total heat content of 202.3 million MMBtu; the heat content of the coal was 24.262 MMBtu per ton, so Bowen needed 202,300,000/24.262, or 8.338 million, tons of that sort of coal per year.

The coal currently burned at Bowen contained an average of 1.6% sulfur by weight. Burning 8.338 million tons of this coal without installing additional pollution-control equipment would generate 266,550 tons of sulfur dioxide emissions.

Option 2: Burn High-Sulfur Coal with Scrubbers; Sell Allowances

In order to reduce emissions of sulfur dioxide at Bowen, the Southern Company could install wet-limestone flue gas desulfurization (FGD) equipment, commonly known as scrubbers. The gases from the generator already went through one pollution-control device, called an electrostatic precipitator, before release to the atmosphere; the precipitator eliminated most of the ash and particles from the gas. If scrubbers were installed, the gases, after leaving the precipitator, would enter another large chamber, where they would be mixed with a slurry of water and limestone. The limestone would react with the sulfur dioxide, forming a sludge that could be landfilled. The gases, with 90% of the sulfur dioxide removed, would then be vented to the air.

Scrubbers were enormous, as large as the generators themselves; they were also expensive. To install them at Bowen in time to reduce emissions in 1995 would require outlays of $143.85 million in 1992, $503.61 million in 1993, and $71.97 million in 1994. Once installed, the scrubbers would add 0.13¢ per kilowatt-hour to the operating costs of the Bowen plant, primarily for the purchase of limestone and the disposal of the sludge. They would also consume 2% of the total amount of electricity generated at the plant once they were turned on. This would, in effect, reduce revenues by 2%.

The capital costs of the scrubbers could be depreciated over 20 years beginning in the first year of operation (i.e., beginning in 1995 if the scrubbers were installed to meet Phase One deadlines). In each of the first 5 years of the depreciation schedule, 14% of the capital costs could be depreciated; for the next 15 years, the company could depreciate 2% of the capital costs. These capital costs would include the capitalized interest (at 10% per year) on the scrubbers during the period when the devices were being installed. The scrubbers were not expected to have an appreciable salvage value.

The Southern Company could also wait to begin installing the scrubbers until 1997, bringing them on line in time for the more stringent Phase Two requirements. This strategy would delay the capital outlays of installing the scrubbers by 5 years, but in Phase One, Bowen would have to buy allowances or burn lower-sulfur coal.

Option 3: Burn Low-Sulfur Coal

Instead of installing the FGD equipment, the Southern Company could switch to low-sulfur coal from Kentucky or West Virginia. If Bowen chose to switch to this type of coal, it would wait until the beginning of 1996 to do so, since the utility's take-or-pay contract with its current supplier would expire at the end of 1995. The low-sulfur coal contained 1% sulfur by weight. It cost less than the company was currently paying for the coal burned at Bowen, but its cost was greater than the expected 1996 cost of high-sulfur coal. Its use, without scrubbers, would generate extra allowances under Phase

One of the Clean Air Act. During Phase Two, Bowen would have to purchase some allowances.

Most coal was purchased and transported under contracts lasting from 5 to 20 years. The Southern Company could write contracts with mining companies and the railroads that would move the coal to Georgia for any length of time it chose.

Low-sulfur coal with a heat content of 24.110 MMBtu per ton could be delivered to Bowen starting in 1996 for $30.37 per ton. Starting in 2000, however, its price was expected to rise to $34.92 per ton as the tighter controls in Phase Two drove up demand. It would take 8.391 million tons of this low-sulfur coal per year to generate electricity at Bowen at historic levels, and this coal would generate 167,650 tons of sulfur dioxide per year if burned without scrubbers.

Switching to low-sulfur coal would require changes in the electrostatic precipitators used to control airborne particulate matter (fly ash) at Bowen, because the equipment currently in place was designed to operate with high-sulfur coal. These investments would cost $22.1 million and would be depreciated like the investments in scrubbers.

Other Considerations

If the Southern Company installed scrubbers at Bowen, it would have to make modest investments in working capital, primarily to maintain an inventory of limestone. If it switched to low-sulfur coal for Phase One, it would burn its two-month inventory of high-sulfur coal at the beginning of 1996, so that 1996 emissions would be somewhat higher than emissions in 1997 and subsequent years. The effects of such changes were small, however, and did not materially alter the company's appraisal of its options. A summary of each option's major features, and of assumptions common to all options, is provided in Exhibits 1–4.

EXHIBIT 1

Projected Operating Data for the Bowen Plant: Assumptions Common to All Options

Output	21,551 million kilowatt-hours
Revenue	$0.056 per kilowatt-hour
Input required	202.3 million MMBtu[a]
Sulfur dioxide allowances	
1995–1999	254,580 tons
2000–2016	122,198
Operating cost (excluding fuel and pollution allowances)	$0.00281 per kilowatt-hour
Tax rate	37.7%
Discount rate (after tax)	10%

a. Coal tonnage depends on heat content of coal.

EXHIBIT 2
Projected Operating Data for the Bowen Plant: High-Sulfur Coal Without Scrubbers

Fuel

Cost of coal per ton
  1992–1995 . . . . $41.46
  1996–2016 . . . . 29.82

Tons of coal to meet input requirements (per year) . . . . 8.338 million

Pollution

Sulfur dioxide emitted per year . . . . 266,550 tons

Additional Costs 0

EXHIBIT 3
Projected Operating Data for the Bowen Plant: High-Sulfur Coal with Scrubbers

Fuel

Cost of coal per ton
  1992–1995 . . . . $41.46
  1996–2016 . . . . 29.82

Tons of coal to meet input requirements (per year) . . . . 8.338 million

Pollution

Sulfur dioxide emitted per year
  Before scrubbers are installed . . . . 266,550 tons
  Once scrubbers are operational 26,655

Additional Costs

Investment
  In Year 0 . . . . $143.85 million
  In Year 1 . . . . 503.61 million
  In Year 2 . . . . 71.97 million

Additional operating costs ($/kWh) $0.0013

Energy consumption (% of revenue) 2%

EXHIBIT 4
Projected Operating Data for the Bowen Plant: Low-Sulfur Coal without Scrubbers

Fuel

Cost of coal per ton
  1992–1995 (high-sulfur) $41.46
  1996–1999 . . . . 30.37
  2000–2016 . . . . 34.92

Tons of coal to meet input requirements
  High sulfur . . . . 8.338 million
  Low sulfur . . . . 8.391 million

Pollution

Sulfur dioxide emitted per year:
  Before switching . . . . 266,550 tons
  After switching 167,650

Additional Costs

Investment in year switch occurs . . . . $22.1 million

Trading the Right to Pollute: Developing the Market for Pollution Allowances

From 1970, when the U.S. Environmental Protection Agency (EPA) was formed, to 1990, the costs of cleaning up the nation's environmental problems escalated dramatically. The EPA found itself chronically overstretched and underfunded as Congress set ever more far-reaching environmental goals (see Exhibit 1). By the time George Bush was sworn in as the new "environmental" president, it was clear that radical, new solutions were needed to tackle the nation's cleanup problems. Increasingly, the government turned to the private sector for support in achieving its environmental objectives.

The Clean Air Act: 1990 Amendment

In the early 1990s, pressure to tackle air pollution was rising both at home and abroad. Global warming and ozone depletion were recognized as serious issues by the scientific community. Complaints about damage from U.S. acid rain were mounting, smog had become a chronic problem in many leading U.S. cities, and research had begun to link airborne hazardous emissions to cancer and other health risks.

A few gases—particularly CO_2, SO_2, and NO_x—were significant contributors to many of these air pollution problems. These gases were mainly produced by burning fossil fuels, and thus energy-intensive industries—particularly electric utilities and transportation—came under increasing scrutiny by the EPA and environmental groups (see Exhibit 2). The 1990 amendments to the Clean Air Act therefore held significant implications for these industries.

Title IV of the act introduced a radically new mechanism: tradeable pollution allowances. Policymakers and environmentalists alike hoped that a system of tradeable pollution rights would enable the United States to harness market forces to achieve its environmental objectives while minimizing its compliance costs.

This case was prepared by Sue Hall, Charles M. Williams fellow, and Professor Carliss Y. Baldwin.

Acid Rain

From 1940 through 1970, the level of U.S. air emissions had been climbing inexorably (see Exhibit 3). The Clean Air Act of 1970 tackled the problem by setting strict emissions standards for key air pollutants. However, the emissions were monitored at ground level, and thus some firms found it expedient to build tall smokestacks, which enabled sulfur and nitrogen oxides to be carried long distances and deposited beyond state boundaries as acid rain.

Acid rain is a mixture of dilute acids, which are formed when sulfur dioxide (SO_2) and nitrogen oxides (NO_x) are emitted into the earth's atmosphere. Around 30% of SO_2/NO_x emissions fall back to earth as "dry" deposits within the local area; the other 70% are carried into the upper atmosphere and react with hydrogen peroxide to form sulfuric and nitric acids. These acids eventually fall to earth, sometimes thousands of miles away. SO_2 accounts for around two-thirds of acid rain formation; NO_x accounts for the remaining one-third.

Within the United States in 1988, the electric utility industry accounted for around 70% of SO_2 emissions and one-third of NO_x emissions (see Exhibit 2). Coal-burning plants—particularly those burning high-sulfur coal, which are most prevalent in the Midwest—were the strongest polluters; in 1988 coal-burning utilities accounted for over 63% of total U.S. SO_2 output.[1] Acid rain therefore fell from the Midwest to the East Coast and in Canada (see Exhibit 4).

Although the pattern of acid rain in the United States was well established, there was still controversy over its impact on the natural environment. A 10-year congressional research program, the National Acid Precipitation Assessment Program (NAPAP), commented that "whilst acid rain was suspected to have negative effects on surface waters, crops, forests, building materials, visibility and human health . . . fortunately the research has shown that the damage from current and historical levels of acid rain has ranged from negligible (e.g., for crops) to modest (e.g., on lakes and streams)."[2] By contrast, one of the most respected environmental research groups, the WorldWatch Institute, concluded that "extensive investigations in the seventies revealed that acid deposition was indeed acidifying water and killing fish. In the early eighties . . . concern spread to forests . . . and crops. Multibillion-dollar price tags have been suggested for building corrosion damage in the United States" (see Exhibit 5). NAPAP considered the overall cost of acid rain to be "small at best, not exceeding $100 million for the recovery of U.S. lakes to fishable status—the most definable benefit." By contrast, again, WorldWatch estimated some $5.4 billion for crop damage alone.[3]

Title IV: Clean Air Act

Despite such uncertainties, Title IV of the 1990 amendment to the Clean Air Act sought to reduce the levels of SO_2 and NO_x in the atmosphere by setting new emissions limits for these gases (see Exhibit 6). It also outlined a radically new approach by which industry should achieve these goals. A system of tradeable pollution permits was designed to give companies flexibility in deciding how to reduce their emissions most efficiently.

---

1. National Coal Association, *Facts About Coal* (Washington, D.C.: 1991), p. 39.

2. Lawrence Kulp, "Acid Rain: Causes, Effects and Control," *Regulation*, Winter 1990; drawn from NAPAP 1987 Interim Assessment (Kulp was director of NAPAP).

3. Kulp, "Acid Rain: Causes, Effects and Control;" and Worldwatch Institute, "Clearing the Air," *State of the World 1990.*

As a pilot project, Title IV established a tradeable allowance system for SO_2 emissions within the electric utilities industry. Title IV adopted a two-phase approach. First, over a period of 5 years from 1995 on (Phase I), it required a reduction in utility SO_2 emissions of 10 million tons, from a 1980 baseline of 18.9 million tons. Second, from the year 2000 (Phase II), it established a cap on SO_2 emissions of 8.9 million tons (see Exhibit 7). Other sections of Title IV also set guidelines for NO_x and industrial SO_2 emissions.[4]

In Phase I, from 1995 to 2000, each of 111 large, mostly coal-burning utilities would be allocated 2.5 pounds of SO_2 per year for every million Btus (British thermal units) of energy that it had consumed annually during the period from 1985 to 1987. In Phase II, this allocation would be reduced to 1.2 pounds per million Btus.[5] To simplify the accounting, allowances were to be issued in units equivalent to one ton of SO_2 emission.

The law required that, at the end of each year, a utility's "stock" of tradeable allowances should at least equal its SO_2 emissions for the year. If its allocation was insufficient to meet requirements, a utility could buy allowances from other utilities with below-average emissions that had allowances to sell, or from a small fund of allowances that the EPA would auction each year (see Exhibit 8). The month of January was a grace period in which utilities could buy and sell allowances to bring their books into balance. Penalties would be applied if a utility's emissions exceeded its January 31 allowance balance: It would be fined $2,000 per ton of SO_2 emitted in excess of allowances and would be required to reduce the following year's emissions by an amount equal to its current year's excess.

Under this new scheme, each utility could thus trade-off the price of allowances in the open market against the cost of reducing emissions internally. Plants with below-average compliance costs had incentives to reduce their emissions in order to sell surplus allowances on the open market.[6] In turn, higher-cost plants could purchase allowances instead of physically reducing their emissions. Thus, the scheme sought to minimize the total cost of reducing U.S. SO_2 emissions. Annual cost savings from allowing trade in emission rights were originally estimated to be $3 billion—a 50% savings over conventional "command and control" approaches.[7] More recent estimates suggested more modest savings of $300 million a year.[8]

Utility Strategies

Unlike earlier legislation, Title IV gave utilities considerable leeway in deciding how to comply with emissions guidelines. Whereas the 1977 Clean Air Act Amendment had effectively required all new plants to fit scrubber units in order to reduce SO_2

---

4. Title IV set a Phase II cap on industrial emissions of 5.6 million tons, a small decrease from actual emission levels of 5.9 million tons in 1988. See the Congressional Research Service, "Implementing Acid Rain Legislation," April 23, 1991. It also required reductions in NO_x emissions of 2 million tons from 1980 levels of around 7 million for the utility industry and 22 million tons for the United States as a whole. These NO_x and industrial SO_2 reductions were largely to be achieved using traditional regulatory techniques, although industrial polluters could decide to opt into the SO_2 allowances system.

5. Phase I restrictions applied to utilities producing more than 100 megawatts; Phase II applied to those producing more than 25 megawatts.

6. Indeed, although not specifically implicated by the act, industrial plants with similarly low cost positions could also elect to opt into the scheme; they could receive allowances equal to any new reductions in SO_2 emissions they chose to make, which they could also sell on the open market at a profit.

7. Rob Stavins, "Project 88: Harnessing Market Forces to Protect Our Environment," Washington, 1988.

8. Torrens, Platt, et al., *Annual Review of Energy*, 1992.

emissions by the required 70–90%, Title IV did not indicate any one technology choice or mandate unit-specific reductions in emissions. This flexibility, however, meant that utilities had to decide how best to manage their compliance both technically and financially. Potential strategies spanned traditional "end-of-pipe" solutions to more innovative "front-end" options (see Exhibit 9).

Industry Overview

In 1992 the U.S. electric utility industry was a set of regional monopolies regulated by local Public Utility Commissions (PUCs). The PUCs carefully scrutinized utilities' strategic plans and operations and could allow or disallow electricity rate increases. In effect, they could approve or disapprove both a utility's operating strategy and its tradeable pollution permit strategy. On the operations side, a PUC's motives could often conflict with a utility's, particularly if the latter operated in more than one state. For example, a PUC might favor a strategy that protected local coal-mining jobs, whereas a utility might prefer a different option to optimize operations across its different regional plant locations. It was feared that such conflicts could result in long, drawn-out approval processes that could force utilities to implement their plans without full PUC approval in order to meet the 1995 deadline. These utilities then ran the risk of not being able to fund their investment decisions through electricity price increases if PUCs refused rate increases in a "post-hoc" fashion. Multistate utilities also ran other risks: If one PUC refused to approve plans for plants in one state, this threatened to throw a utility's plans for all of its plants in other states into disarray.

PUCs also held considerable power over utilities' allowance-trading strategies. For example, a PUC could determine how far a utility could go "long" or "short" on its inventory of tradeable permits, and how large a risk it could incur on its position. Furthermore, a utility might not be able to sell one of its allowances until its PUC gave formal approval for the sale, potentially creating two kinds of allowances: those with and those without formal PUC approval. PUCs had very limited experience of capital market instruments, and since few had explicitly welcomed the new trading scheme, it was unclear whether they would allow free trade in allowances. In fact, in 1992, some PUCs were already seeking to restrict trade to within state boundaries.

The U.S. electric utility industry relied more on coal for its basic energy requirements than did many other countries; in 1988 coal supplied 57% of basic needs, compared to 41% on average in Organization for Economic Cooperation and Development (OECD) countries (see Exhibit 10). The use of coal tended to increase utilities' SO_2 emissions, since alternative fuels like natural gas gave off less SO_2 per unit of electricity.

Emissions had remained relatively stable over time, gradually declining since 1984. Individual plants also exhibited fairly steady rates of emission over each annual accounting period, although there could be variations within a given year. Thus, although Title IV potentially gave industries the power to hedge their compliance position against variances in their emission levels, this would not be a great benefit to this particular industry, for SO_2 emissions seemed less volatile than other pollutants.[9]

However, electric utilities could benefit from the ability to hedge uncertainties associated with investments in new pollution-control technologies. For example, if an

---

9. Significant changes in output could be anticipated well in advance since lead times for increased capacity, application of scrubber units, or technology innovations were long. Only the weather could seriously affect SO_2 output, as energy demands fluctuated with changes in temperature.

innovative technology failed to deliver the emission reduction expected, the utility could still buy allowances to cover their out-of-compliance position more cheaply than incurring violation penalties.

In 1992 utilities faced two basic decisions. First, what operating strategy should they pursue to control their SO_2 emissions? Should they invest in pollution-control technologies, consider switching to less polluting fuels, or adopt alternative approaches such as managing consumers' demand for electricity? Second, what tradeable pollution allowance strategy should they adopt to complement their choice of operating strategy?

Operating Strategy

Overall, utilities faced three basic strategic choices. First, they could fit scrubber units onto existing plants in time to comply with either the 1995 or 2000 requirements and sell any surplus allowances. Second, they could switch to low-sulfur fuel. Last, they could do nothing and rely upon purchasing allowances in the open market.

Scrubbers were very large cleaning units that stripped SO_2 from the gases in plants' flue pipes. Although they could reduce SO_2 emissions by up to 90%, they created a myriad of other problems. They reduced the efficiency of energy conversion by around 2%, from 36% to 34%; produced waste that had to be disposed of separately; and increased emissions of CO_2—a principal contributor to global warming not yet covered under the Federal Clean Air Act.[10] The scrubbers were also very expensive, costing in the range of $200 million to $600 million[11] in capital outlays alone, and required long construction lead times. However, they were a proven technology, albeit (in the words of one environmentalist) "the gold-plated Cadillac solution" to SO_2 emissions.

Utilities could also consider switching to low-sulfur coal. While utilities would need to factor in increases of 50–100%[12] in coal costs per ton, compared to high-sulfur coal, low-sulfur reserves were considered adequate to meet switching requirements.[13]

In the longer term, utilities had other options. They could invest in innovative repowering technologies, which altered the physical combustion process itself to reduce emissions (rather than relying on scrubbers to strip the SO_2 out once combustion had taken place). These technologies simultaneously improved energy efficiency and reduced SO_2 emissions, but they could not always be retrofitted to existing plants. Many were still in the development stage, and most were relatively costly.

Utilities could also consider switching from coal to other less polluting raw materials like natural gas (see Exhibit 11). However, U.S. production could only supply about 30% of current requirements; thus, a wholesale switchover could make the nation vulnerable to supply shocks such as the energy crisis of 1974.

Finally, utilities could seek to manage consumers' demand for electricity through energy-efficiency programs. Such schemes had enjoyed some success on the West Coast and represented the only solution that actually tackled the root of the problem of

---

10. CO_2 emissions would increase 4% if a scrubber were fitted.

11. For a 2,000-megawatt plant, at between $150 and $250 per kw capacity; plant capacities could range from 50 to 3,500 megawatts.

12. Increases were estimated in the $10–$18 per ton range, compared to high-sulfur coal costs of $20–$25 per ton.

13. *Clear Air Response: A Guidebook to Strategies.* (Permission to cite granted by EPRI.) Very low-sulfur coal reserves were estimated to be at best 2.3 billion tons, versus future demand levels in the region of 100 million tons per year.

SO_2 emissions: the high level of energy consumption itself. However, it was unclear whether this option could achieve large enough reductions for many utilities to rely on it extensively.

A complex set of tradeoffs therefore faced utilities as they considered the strategies they should adopt. They needed to consider several factors: the price of their raw material inputs and likely fluctuations over time; the cost implications of any new emissions technology, both capital and operating; the impact on emissions—of SO_2, NO_x, and CO_2—of each of the technology options; and the implications for thermal efficiency of each option. Data to evaluate these tradeoffs were scant, although some indications could be gleaned from a summary of leading research findings (see Exhibit 12). Lastly, utilities had to give some consideration to likely changes in legislation over the next decades, for the equipment they would be investing in had life expectancies of between 20 and 40 years and would need to conform to future emissions requirements for air toxics such as CO_2.

To complicate life further, utilities also had to consider some bonus allowances that Title IV offered as incentives to persuade utilities to adopt strategies that they considered environmentally superior. Bonuses were of two types. First, if a utility adopted a technology that could reduce a unit's emission by at least 90%, it could be awarded extra allowances during 1995 and 1996 to cover the extra emissions it might incur while the new device was being installed. The extra allowances would be taken from a pool of 3.5 million on a first-come, first-served basis. Second, if a utility initiated a consumer demand management program or employed renewable energy generation technologies like solar, biomass, and wind, bonuses could be drawn from another pool of 300,000 allowances. On a first-come, first-served basis, utilities could draw down a bonus equal to the SO_2 emissions its conservation programs were estimated to have saved.[14]

Tradeable Allowance Strategies

In deciding how to construct its tradeable allowance strategy, a utility had several instruments to consider, each of which could be deployed in a number of ways. Title IV defined two kinds of allowances: (1) a "spot" allowance issued each year to utilities on the basis of their baseline qualification, and (2) a "forward" allowance that, purchased today, would permit an SO_2 emission in 7 years' time. The spot allowance could be used in the current year, banked for future use, or sold on the open market. Forward allowances could be purchased through the EPA auction and sales system and were designed to enable utilities to cover any increase in SO_2 emissions that would result from future capacity expansions.

The Chicago Board of Trade (CBT) was also proposing to establish a series of futures contracts based on the spot allowance market.[15] These instruments might begin trading in early 1993 and would provide utilities with the ability to hedge against fluctuations in the price of their allowances in future years. The contracts would thus enable utilities to construct quite sophisticated risk management techniques to cover their positions. These positions could be significant: some utilities had estimated that, during the 1995–2005 period, they would accumulate surplus allowances with values

---

14. This section draws on an EPA paper, "Allowance System: Proposed Acid Rain Rule," October 1991.

15. The CBT had approved the proposal to establish this market. In July 1991 it was still seeking approval from the Commodity Futures Trading Commission.

comparable to a whole year's revenues. Future contracts might also be attractive to speculators if sufficient volatility developed in the market.

There was considerable uncertainty as to the price that tradeable allowances and futures might sell for in the market. Estimates for allowance prices had ranged from $300 to $2000,[16] and futures prices estimates ranged between $400 and $2000.[17]

Some Practical Considerations

Under Title IV, each utility or trading unit needed to appoint a designated representative to register any allowance transaction with the EPA so that the sale or purchase could count towards end-of-year emissions requirements. Information about the status of a utility's account would be held in the EPA's electronic Allowance Tracking System (ATS). Although trades need not be registered on this system immediately, registration was required before the transaction was considered official for compliance purposes. It was therefore likely that purchasers of allowances would seek to register sales promptly.

EPA records were public by law, so it was theoretically possible for utilities to gain insight into each others' future compliance plans by scanning the ATS register. This practice would essentially provide an X-ray of players' net positions. Some utilities had begun to wonder whether their competitive position might be compromised by such visibility. While earlier EPA legislation had given the U.S. public the right to know detailed information about a company's compliance position, some feared this practice could undermine the development of a strong trading base within the market. In effect, the mechanics of operating a market might conflict with the EPA's priorities and the public interest.

Other practical considerations associated with operating the market raised similar concerns. For example, should names of trading partners be disclosed? Should individual trades be logged using ID numbers for each allowance permit to facilitate inspection for fraud? Or should accounts reflect only the net purchases and sales of each trader? Should the price of each trade be recorded and made public? These questions held significant implications for both utilities and the EPA, as well as potential speculators and market makers.

Important questions about compliance were also unanswered. Unlike other trading markets, there was no physical good to which trades could ultimately be traced, the way an oil trade is tied to a physical consignment.[18] Instead, Title IV required the EPA to establish Continuous Emissions Monitoring systems (CEMs), which would record the level of emissions in flue gases at each site at fixed time intervals (e.g., every 15 minutes). However, CEMs were costly to install (costing around $1 million[19]) and subject to inaccuracies—up to 40% according to one report.[20] Since the whole tradeable allowance system rested upon such measurements, this variability was cause for concern.

The legal status of allowances was also questionable. An allowance permitted its owner to emit one ton of SO_2 at some specified date and thus appeared to be a property

---

16. *Crain's Chicago Business*, July 22, 1991.

17. *American Metal Market*, July 22, 1991.

18. Oil trades are allocated a specific lifting number to correspond to particular barrels of oil in set locations within the hold.

19. EPRI interviews. Operating costs were estimated at $100,000 per year.

20. *Scientific American*, May 1991, quoting Henry Beal, vice president of Cottrell Companies.

right. However, Congress had come under intense pressure from some environmental groups for seemingly granting companies a "right to pollute," and as a result, Title IV stated that the allowances could be rescinded by Congress at will. Therefore, although it was in the EPA's interest to help establish a tradeable allowance system in which the market *perceived* the permits as property rights, technically speaking, this was not the case.

Finally, a whole category of trades was threatened by a tax ruling that the IRS was expected to apply to allowance sales. If the IRS decided to treat utilities' sales as subject to a capital gains tax, then incentives to trade on quite closely matched deals might be significantly compromised.

However, beyond such relatively sophisticated concerns, all utilities were asking themselves one basic question: Would the tradeable allowance system work? Would people trade? In other words, could a utility rely upon buying and selling allowances sufficiently to incorporate this assumption into their strategies going forward? Title IV had hardly touched on how the trading environment would be structured. Utilities understood that unless a market forum could be constructed to meet their trading needs, the benefits of tradeable pollution allowances would not materialize.

The Structure of the Tradeable Allowance Market

In 1991 the EPA began to conduct research on how to structure a tradeable allowance market. It recognized that buyers and sellers needed to have confidence that the contracts would be honored. It also recognized that some kind of clearinghouse through which to conduct these trades was necessary in order to disclose and accept offers to buy and sell; to register and publicly publish prices; and to track trades and account for participants' inventory positions.

Seven separate market structures were analyzed, ranging from very decentralized, informal trading between small groups of utilities to highly centralized electronic trading systems within official exchange markets such as the CBT. The basic options for the market's structure included:

1. Internal company trades between generating units.
2. Informal, one-to-one trades between selected, reliable partners, to reduce trading risks or match unusual allowance requirements.
3. Trading through specialized brokers, whose role would be to match the unique requirements of buyers and sellers in a market with little homogeneity of contract.
4. Trading through an informal, self-policing network of dealers, as in the Brent crude oil market. Dealers would themselves keep track of trades and maintain records of players' net positions.
5. Trading through an electronic, interlinked, real-time trading system like NASDAQ, which could provide different layers of information to brokers and to companies.
6. Trading through one or more market makers, who would also provide clearinghouse services. The market makers might be self-selected or licensed by the EPA.
7. Trading through a formal exchange like the CBT, on its pit floor, through its upstairs brokers, or on a new electronic trading system that the CBT wanted to introduce. The new system was specifically designed to handle trading in low-volume instruments, such as the allowances were expected to become.

Each of these alternative market structures offered different costs and benefits. Thus, the EPA and the utilities needed to consider several questions and make some complex tradeoffs. For example, the success of the market would depend on transaction costs. Commissions varied widely: from 6% to 10% for specialized unique transactions to less than 1% for trading on a major high-volume exchange. What kind of transaction costs could this market stand?

Generally speaking, the more formal markets were lower cost, provided more privacy and security, but required homogeneous contracts. Traditionally, they had also been the more innovative markets and possessed electronic systems to trade and publish prices in real time. However, not all of these qualities were necessary—or even desirable—in an allowance market in its early stages.

As other markets had developed, they often progressed from more informal to more formal market structures over time. However, the EPA felt it did not have the expertise to run a sophisticated trading market and execute trades. Pressure was therefore building to privatize the system to a body that could act as the EPA's agent and thus be held accountable. The CBT was an obvious candidate for such a role. However, this need for the expertise that a centralized exchange could offer ran somewhat counter to some utilities' initial preferences to develop the market along more informal lines.

Under each of these options, procedures through which trades would be cleared and the EPA notified had to be established. While the CBT had its own clearing systems, settlement procedures and surveillance programs would need to be developed for the other market options. Clearly, it was easier to investigate clearing/trading errors or disputes in the more formal exchanges. For example, on NASDAQ, brokers covered their clients in the case of payment defaults and the market's clearinghouse, the National Stock Clearing Corporation (NSCC), assumed all financial responsibility associated with clearing mistakes once they had declared a trade matched. Since each allowance could potentially be worth around $400 and an average utility could be allocated 250,000 allowances each year, trading could involve sums on the order of $100 million, a figure not insignificant compared to annual revenues of $1 billion and net income of around $100 million.[21]

Constituency Group Interests

The EPA, the electric utilities themselves, and the CBT each had different interests and goals in setting up an allowance market. The concerns of these three key interest groups would strongly influence the kind of market that would develop.

The EPA sought to develop a market that would meet the needs of the utility companies, but it was also committed to privatizing the market and preferred an agent that could be held accountable.

The utilities tended to prefer a relatively limited, simple approach, at least initially. Although the CBT had estimated the initial tradeable allowance market to total $8.5 million annually, many utilities were hesitant to trade at all.[22] One survey in September 1991 found that only 18% of the utilities were "looking into trading,"[23] while around

---

21. EEI, "Electric Power Annual 1990," from a composite income statement for selected investor-owned utilities.

22. *Crain's Business Review*, July 22, 1991.

23. *Scientific American*, May 1991. Survey conducted by John Palmisano of AER*X, a Washington emissions brokerage.

5% of designated allowances were expected to be actually traded.[24] Other experts indicated that utilities were considering only banking or selling the allowances; generally speaking, utilities did not want to rely on buying allowances in order to comply.[25] Thus, utilities were essentially wary of the CBT scheme. One environmental manager remarked, "It is an interesting concept, but we most likely would deal directly with other large utilities."[26] Indeed, some utilities had put forward the concept of pooling their allowances to facilitate trading among a limited group of players. This idea appealed to utilities, since they used a similar scheme to swap electricity-generating capacity to match shortfalls and surpluses in their requirements.

In contrast, the CBT had already decided to launch a futures contract, the first in what it hoped would become a family of pollution contracts. The CBT saw an emerging market in such commodities. As one director put it: "Air and water are the biggest commodities in the world. Given that they're now scarce, they will have to be valued, and if they're valued, they will be traded."[27]

First-mover advantage was an important factor in gaining share within the commodities exchange industry; CBT hoped to use the SO_2 contracts as a beachhead from which to build its leadership in this field. Indeed, discussions were even underway to investigate the possibility of launching an international CO_2 tradeable allowance and futures system, which the CBT was proposing to host.[28] Furthermore, its facilities could be used to trade both the spot and future EPA allowances. The CBT had therefore made a strong bid to the EPA to be designated the marketplace for pollution allowances. Discussion were also underway to determine whether the CBT could also run the EPA's auctions and sales. Finally, CBT had invested in a new electronic trading system for low-volume instruments, which it wanted to test using the SO_2 allowances.

A Complex Challenge

In January 1992 electric utility companies faced considerable uncertainties in how they should best develop their technology and tradeable allowance strategies. Each utility needed to assess the viability of the tradeable allowance market. Previous small pilot projects had failed to yield either the promised cost savings or, indeed, any significant volume of trade (see Exhibit 13). Would the new trading system that the Clean Air Act sought to create become a reality? Would it perform efficiently? How far should a utility actually rely upon being able to trade allowances in the future to achieve its compliance position? And what price/cost should it assign to allowances in its capital investment analyses going forward?

---

24. Interview, Jeremy Platt, EPRI.

25. Interview, Dan Dudek, EDF.

26. Michael Hertel, manager Environmental Affairs, Southern California Edison Co., in the *LA Times*, July 19, 1991.

27. Richard Sandor, director of CBT, in *Crain's Chicago Business*, July 22, 1991.

28. Knight-Ridder Financial Information, January 31, 1992.

EXHIBIT 1
U.S. Environmental Legislation since 1970, EPA Budget, and EPA Staff Headcount

	Major New Regulations	*EPA Budget ($ billions)*	*Total EPA Staff*
1970	Clean Air amendments . . . . Water Quality Improvement Act Resource Recovery Act	1,004	3,860
1971	. . . .	1,289	7,198
1972	Marine Protection, Research & Sanctuaries Act	2,448	8,050
1973	. . . .	2,377	8,858
1974	Safe Drinking Water Act	518	9,203
1975	. . . .	699	9,203
1976	Resource Recovery & Conservation Act . . . . Toxic Substances Control Act	772	9,550
1977	Clear Air Act amendments . . . . Clear Water Act	2,764	10,150
1978	Federal Pesticide Act	5,499	10,224
1979	. . . .	5,003	10,698
1980	Acid Precipitation Act . . . . Solid Waste Disposal Act Comprehensive Environmental Response, Compensation & Liability Act	4,669	11,004
1981	. . . .	3,031	13,130
1982	. . . .	3,678	12,161
1983	. . . .	3,689	11,025
1984	. . . .	4,067	11,598
1985	. . . .	4,354	12,626
1986	Superfund amendments & Reauthorization Act . . . . Water Resources Development Act Safe Drinking Water amendments	3,651	13,461
1987	Water Quality Act	5,339	14,268
1988	Ocean Dumping Ban Act . . . . Lead Contamination Control Act Radon Program Development Act	5,060	14,450
1989	. . . .	5,166	14,720
1990	Clean Air Act amendments . . . . Superfund extension Food, Agriculture Conservation & Trade Act	5,558	15,840

Source: EPA, Budget Division.

EXHIBIT 2
Overview of Key Contributors to Air Pollution

	SO_2	NO_x	CO/CO_2	Other
Acid rain	65%	30%		5%
Smog	LO	LO	HI	
Ozone depletion				HI[a]
Hazardous emissions				HI[b]
1980 U.S. emissions (million tons)	25.8	22.8		HI
Index of manmade contribution relative to natural baseline	1.4	0.4	.25	
Principal contributors (to manmade emissions)				
Industry	85%	12%	75%	
Manufacturing	13	Small	7	
Agriculture	1	80	15	
Traditional energy	5	8	3	
Fossil fuel contribution	80	"most"	75[c]	
Industry breakdown				
Utilities	69%	32%		
Transportation	4	43		
Manufacturing[d]	13	5		
Combustion				
Industrial	11	16		
Other	3	4		
Utility breakdown				
Coal	88%			
Other	12			

Sources: Scientific American, September 1990; *McGraw-Hill Encyclopedia of Science and Technology*; EPA, "Proposed Acid Rain Rules," October 1990.

a. Primarily particulates.

b. Primarily CFCs and halons.

c. Industry contribution (of 75%) is almost entirely due to fossil-fuel burning (*Scientific American*, September 1990).

d. Industrial/manufacturing processes.

EXHIBIT 3
Air Pollutant Nationwide Emissions 1940–1970 (million short tons/year)

	1940	*1950*	*1960*	*1970*
SO_x	19.4	21.8	21.7	31.2
NO_x	7.5	10.3	14.1	20.1
CO	89.9	94.9	97.1	110.4
Particulates	25.5	27.4	23.8	20.4
Volatile organic compounds	20.0	22.3	24.9	28.9

Source: Portney, "Air Pollution Policy."

EXHIBIT 4
Map of Average Rainfall pH in United States

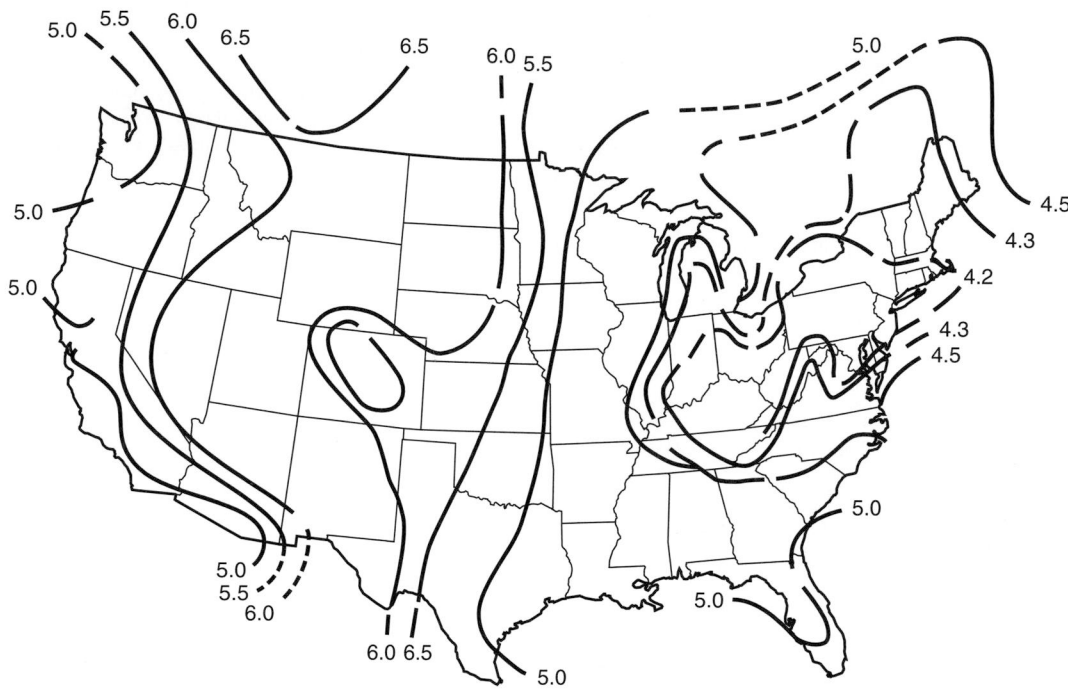

Acidity of rain is measured in terms of pH, a logarithmic scale running from 1 to 14. A pH of 7 is neutral; a pH of 1 is most acidic; and a decrease of 1 pH denotes a tenfold increase in acidity.

Theoretically, the natural acidity of precipitation corresponds to a pH of 5.6, which represents the pH of pure water in equilibrium with atmospheric concentrations of carbon dioxide. The presence of naturally occurring SO_2, NO_x, ammonia, and windblown dust results in an actual pH between 4.9 and 6.5 for most natural precipitation. The distribution and magnitude of precipitation pH in the United States therefore suggest the impact of manmade rather than natural causes.

Source: McGraw-Hill Encyclopedia of Science and Technology, 6th edition.

EXHIBIT 5
Comparison of Research Findings on the Impact of Acid Rain

Areas of Disagreement

Health Impact

"SO_2, transformed into fine sulphate particles that mix with water and become aerosols . . . may be responsible for as many as 50,000 deaths in the United States every year—2% of annual mortality."

"We need more research to establish how acidic aerosols may affect human lungs, but the available data suggest that the effect is not very significant."

Water/Health

"In portions of the United States . . . elevated levels of certain metals have been found in (drinking) water supplies of areas receiving acid precipitation."

"Where metal concentrations in untreated drinking water have exceeded water standards, these concentrations have not been traceable to differential acidity in rainfall."

Forest Degradation

"It's plain," says plant pathologist Robert Bruck, who has been studying damage (to the red spruce and Fraser fir in North Carolina) for years, "that no one has proved or ever will that air pollution has been killing the trees up here. But, far more quickly than we ever expected, we've ended up with a highly correlated bunch of data—high levels of air pollution correlated to the decline we're watching in progress."

"Researchers have been unable to find that acid rain caused direct foliar damage or soil-mediated effects on red spruce."

Crops

"Air pollution threatens crops. Ozone is of primary concern, although SO_2, nitrogen oxides, and sulfates and nitrates are also thought to be potentially harmful."

"Experiments have demonstrated that there is no significant effect on growth (of crops) even at ten times the acidity now observed in the Eastern United States. Current concentrations of acidity in rain observed in agricultural areas do not retard growth."

Buildings

"In the United States, (many of the) nation's historical monuments are under threat . . . . (Overall), studies have suggested a multibillion-dollar price tag."

"Building materials are affected by many factors: solar radiation, ozone, thermal cycling, moisture cycling . . . it's difficult to determine the incremental corrosion of these materials due to ambient levels of acid rain. Acid rain, at worst, appears to make only a secondary contribution."

Areas of Relative Agreement

Lakes and Streams

"The area in the United States most affected by acid rain is the Adirondack Park of New York, where 10% of the fishable lake area has a pH of less than 6. This corresponds fairly well to the fraction of the lake area with substandard fish populations. Although some of these acidic lakes may have developed their acidity from natural causes, researchers generally believe that the most common cause is acid rain."

Visibility

"Sulfuric acid . . . combined with other particles . . . produces haze, especially at high levels of humidity. This effect is particularly evident in the relatively clean air areas of the western states. In many of the national park areas the sulfate create 50% to 60% of the degradation in visibility. In the East, it is closer to 70%, and the total haze is much greater."

Sources: Worldwatch Institute, "Clearing the Air," *State of the World 1990*; Lawrence J. Kulp, "Acid Rain: Causes, Effects, and Control," *Regulation*, Winter 1990.

EXHIBIT 6
Historic and Projected Levels of SO₂ and NOₓ

Historical Trend of Sulfur Dioxide Emissions

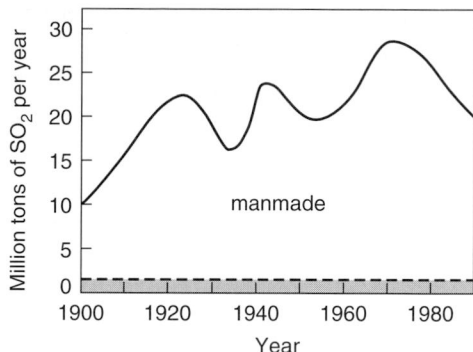

Emissions of Selected Pollutants in the United States, 1950–1987

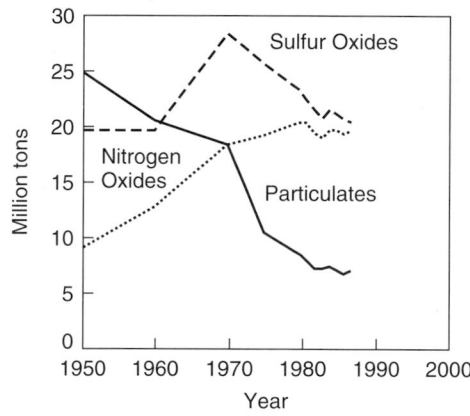

Source: EPA.

Future Emissions of Sulfur Dioxide

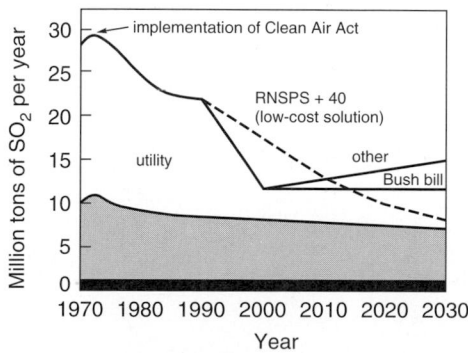

Sources: "Acid Rain," *Cato Review of Business and Government*, Winter 1990; Worldwatch Institute, "Clearing the Air," *State of the World 1990*.

EXHIBIT 7
Title IV SO₂ Emissions Requirements by Source

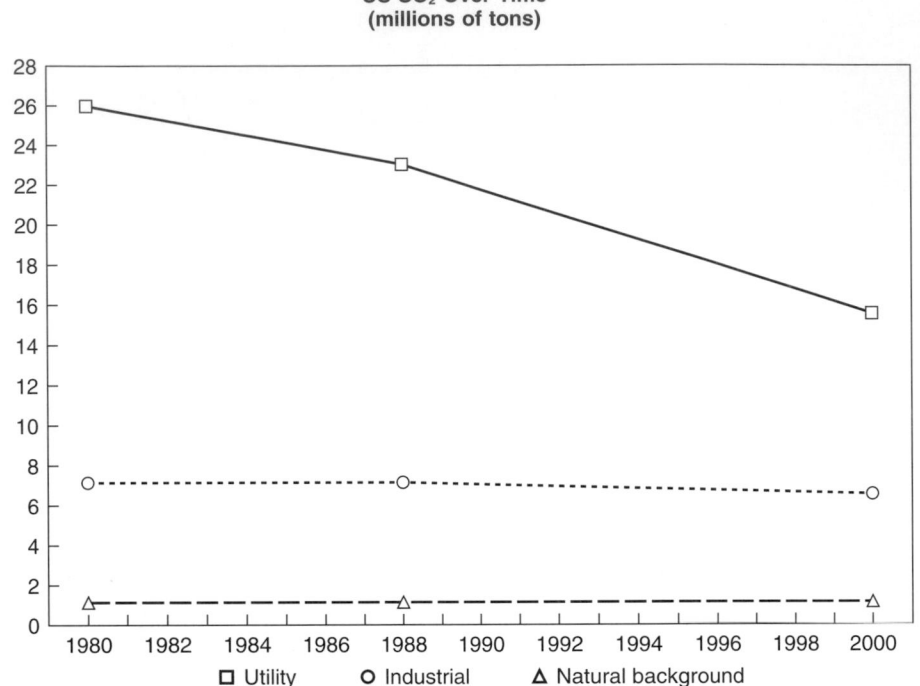

**US SO$_2$ Over Time
(millions of tons)**

	1980	*1988*	*1992*	*1995*	*2000*
Utility	18.9	15.9	17.5	NA	8.9
Industrial	5.9	5.9	NA	NA	5.6
Background	1.0	1.0	1.0	1.0	1.0
Total	25.8	22.8	NA	NA	15.5[a]

Source: Congressional Research Service, "Implementing Acid Rain Legislation," 1991.

a. Required by EPA caps.

EXHIBIT 8
Profile of EPA Auctions and Sales

EPA's Auction and Sales Programs

To stimulate the market in allowance trading and establish a market price for allowances early on, EPA will set aside a Special Allowance Reserve for public auction and sales. This reserve will consist of 2.8% of the total annual allowances that would otherwise be allocated to existing units. Allowances offered for auction or sale will be divided between spot allowances, which can be used in the year they are bought (except for allowances purchased in spot auctions before 1995, which cannot be used for compliance until 1995), and advance allowances, which cannot be used until 7 years after they are bought.

EPA will hold spot and advance auctions for allowances starting no later than March 31 of each year. To participate in the auction, bidders will send EPA sealed bids specifying the number of allowances they would like to buy and their stated price. There will be no minimum price. After all of the allowances in the EPA reserve have been auctioned off, private allowance holders may offer their allowances for sale. These private holders must have their allowances recorded by EPA prior to the auction. Private holders may specify a minimum price. The auction results will be published in the *Federal Register* and the *Commerce Business Daily*.

EPA will begin spot and advance sales no later than June 1 of each year and will continue until January 30 following that year, the last day on which allowances may be transferred. Spot sales will begin in 2000, and advance sales will begin in 1993 for use beginning in 2000. EPA will sell 25,000 allowances each year in advance sales from 1993 through 1999 and 50,000 allowances per year split among spot and advance sales beginning in 2000. The allowance will be sold on a first-come, first-served basis at $1,500 per allowance, with the price adjusted annually for inflation using the Consumer Price Index (CPI).

Anyone can buy allowances in the direct sale, but independent power producers (IPPs) can obtain written guarantees from EPA stating that they will have first priority. These guarantees, which will be awarded on a first-come, first-served basis, secure the option for qualified IPPs to purchase a yearly amount of allowances for the life of a new unit. This provision enables IPPs to ensure lenders that they will have access to allowances they need to build new units. To continue to hold a guarantee, however, an IPP must certify a continuing need. EPA may also terminate the guarantee if certain requirements are not fulfilled.

Source: EPA, "Allowance System: Proposed Acid Rain Rule," October 1991.

EXHIBIT 9
Overview of Utilities' Potential Strategies

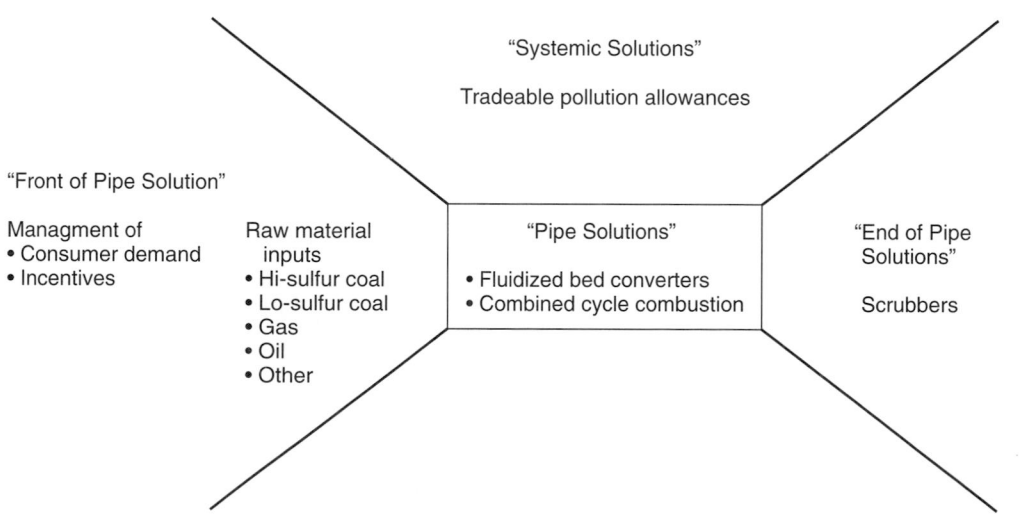

"Systemic Solutions"

Tradeable pollution allowances

"Front of Pipe Solution"

Managment of	Raw material	"Pipe Solutions"	"End of Pipe
• Consumer demand	inputs		Solutions"
• Incentives	• Hi-sulfur coal	• Fluidized bed converters	
	• Lo-sulfur coal	• Combined cycle combustion	Scrubbers
	• Gas		
	• Oil		
	• Other		

EXHIBIT 10
U.S. versus OECD Electricity Industry Energy Profile[a]

			Reserves (Number of Years' Capacity Remaining at Current Consumption Rates)	
Source of Raw Material	United States	OECD	United States	Worldwide
Coal	57%	41%	312	344
Natural gas	9	9	9	55
Oil	6	10	4	42
Other	28	40	N/A	N/A

Sources: Edison Electric Institute, *Statistical Yearbook of the Electric Utility Industry*, 1988; *Economist*, September 6, 1991; *International Energy Annual*, February 1991.

a. OECD stands for Organization for Economic Cooperation and Development.

EXHIBIT 11
Global Energy Used by Source over Time

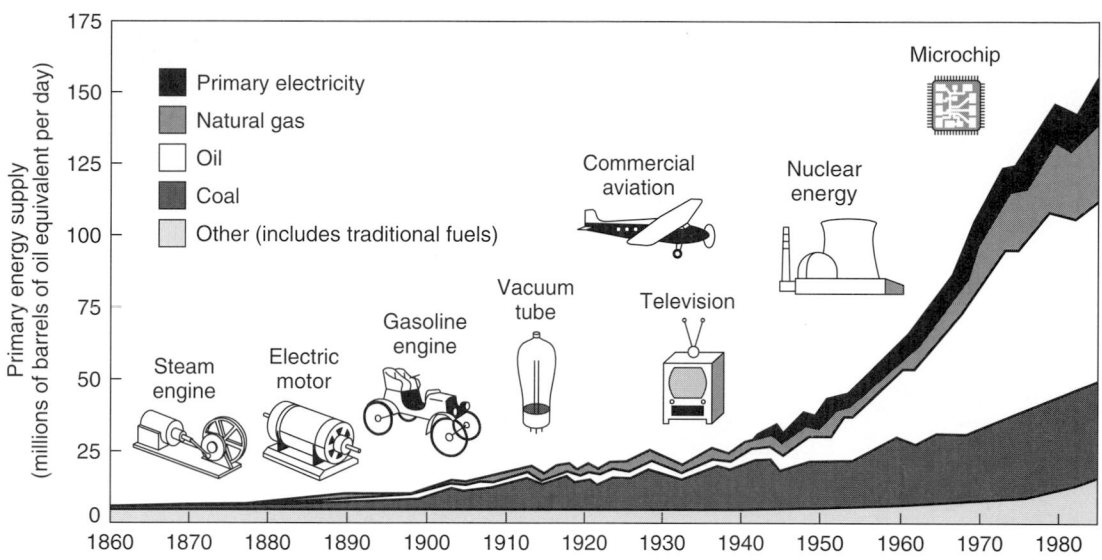

Historical Price Fluctuations

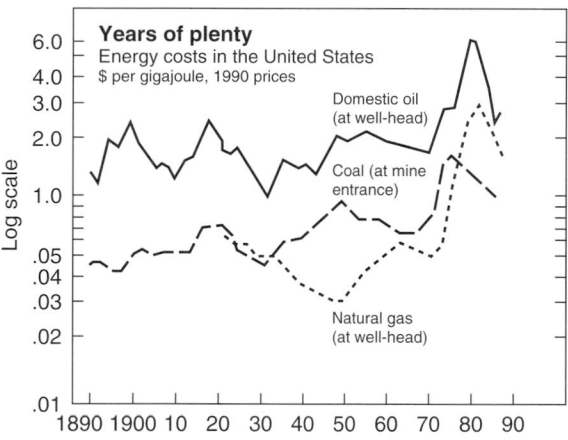

Source: Economist, August 31, 1991 (data from *Scientific American*).

Current and Projected Market Shares for Energy Input to Electric Utilities in the United States

	1960	*1970*	*1980*	*1990*	*2000*	*2010*
Coal	52%	44%	50%	56%	50%	50%
Natural gas	22	25	15	9	27	29
Oil	7	13	11	4	6	7

Sources: State Energy Data Report, May 1991; *Electric Power Annual*, 1990.

EXHIBIT 12

Relative Costs and Benefits of Different Technology Strategies

Current Plant Cost Breakdown	
Capital	43%
Fuel	27
Operations and maintenance	30

Source: Electric Power Annual, 1990.

Projected Changes in Plant Costs	Capital: $/kw Capacity	Operating Cost Increase/ (Decrease)
Coal		
Unscrubbed		0%
Scrubbed		
Retrofit to existing plant	150–250	5–20[b]
New plant[a]	1,600	5–20[b]
Low sulfur	50–450	Low
Combined cycle combustion[c]	1,700	(25–30)
Fluidized bed converter[c]	1,200[d]	(25–30)
Gas	760	

a. Includes plant capital costs as well as scrubbed capital costs.

b. Primarily due to changes in thermal efficiency.

c. Estimates for new plant construction; cannot be retrofitted.

d. Approximation: very few pilot schemes worldwide.

Projected Raw Material Costs ($ per million Btu)[a]	1990	1995	2000	2005
Unscrubbed coal	1.47	1.59	1.74	1.82
Gas	2.26	2.51	2.37	4.39
Oil	2.49	3.84	4.76	5.43

a. 1990 dollars.

(continued)

EXHIBIT 12 *(continued)*

Current Emission Levels by Energy Source and New Requirements

	SO_2	NO_x	CO_2
Total emissions (million short tons/years)	16.5	7.1	1976
Breakdown by energy source (pounds per million Btu)			
Coal	1.0–8.0[a]	0.65–1.0[b]	
		0.7–1.4[c]	
Gas	0.018	0.16	
Oil	0.6	0.35	
Title IV requirements (pounds per million Btu)	2.5 (Phase I)	0.45[b]	
	1.2 (Phase II)	0.5[c]	

a. Depending on the sulfur content of the fuel used.

b. Tangential-fired boilers.

c. Dry-bottom wall-fired boilers.

Projected Utility Emissions Levels and Energy Efficiencies Using Different Technologies

	% Reduction in:		**Actual Emissions:**		
	SO_2	NO_x	NO_x *(mg per million joules of electricity)*	CO_2 *(kg per carbon per kWh)*	*Thermal Energy Efficiency*
Coal					
Unscrubbed	0%	0%		<.25	36%
Scrubbed	50–90	Low	300	.25	34
Low sulfur	30				
Combined cycle[b]	99	>50	25	.20	42[a]
Fluidized bed					
converters[b]	85–95	>50	60	.19	42
Gas[c]					
Conventional	99	80	180	.14	36[d]
Combined cycle	[e]	>80%	0	0.00	47[f]

Sources: McGraw-Hill Encyclopedia of Science and Technology; Electric Power Annual, 1990; Scientific American, September 1990; *Economist,* September 6, 1991; Worldwatch Institute, "Clearing the Air"; David Newbery, "Acid Rain," *Economic Policy* (October 1990). Interviews at The McIlvaine Company.

a. Other sources indicate up to 49%.

b. Cannot be retrofitted; applies to new plant capacity only.

c. Reduction in SO_2/NO_x emissions relative to unscrubbed coal alternatives.

d. Other U.K. sources indicated up to 55% potentially.

e. Denotes traced emissions only.

f. Other sources estimate this could rise as high as 80–90%.

(continued)

EXHIBIT 12 *(concluded)*

Estimates of Costs of Reducing SO₂ by Various Means

Source	Action	Cost ($1989) per Ton of SO_2 Removed
A	Moving to low sulphur gas oil	2,560
A	Moving to low sulphur fuel oil	640
A	Fluidized bed combusters (FBC)	
	New boilers	96
	Existing plant	2,240
B	Drax FGD new plant (scrubber)[a]	350
C	FGD retrofit 2,000 MW plant	400–750
D	60% reduction from 40 GW CEGB coal capacity	600
E	FGD 90% removal	600
E	FGD marginal cost of next 5% removal	1,600
F	U.S. coal generators, coal switching, avg. cost	400
F	U.S. coal generators, no coal switching, avg. cost	460
G	East Germany, Wellman-Lord FGD, net of S sales	300
H	Move from 2.15% to 1% sulphur heavy fuel oil	380
H	Move from 1% to 0.7% sulphur heavy fuel oil	825

Sources:

A: Environmental Resources Limited (1983), p. 137, uprated by 1.28 to 1989 dollars.

B: Based on Layfield (1987), and Jeffrey (1988).

C: Longhurst et al. (1987).

D: Dudley, et al. (1985), p. 121.

E: Brackley (1987).

F: Congressional Budget Office (1986); Dowlatabadi and Harrington (1989). These are average costs; marginal costs might be twice average cost.

G: *Acid News*, No. 3, July 1989, p. 9.

H: Alfsen et al. (1986); David Newbery, "Acid Rain," *Economic Policy* (October 1990).

a. Flue Gas Desulfurization unit, known as a "scrubber."

EXHIBIT 13
Results of Other Tradeable Pollution Permit Systems

Emissions in the Fox River, Wisconsin

- Firms were allowed to trade the rights to pollute the river.
- Resulting cost savings were minimal.
- The results were considered unsurprising since the main sources of the pollution were regulated municipal utilities and oligopolistic paper and pulp manufacturers.

Lead Content in Gasoline—the most successful example in the United States

- Refineries were able to buy or sell rights to lead levels in gasoline, based upon an existing standard per gallon.
- About 15% of total lead rights used were traded with an active spot market and an intertemporal market via "banking." The system appears to have worked well because it is easy to monitor and there was widespread agreement about the objectives of the program.

Source: David Newbery, "Acid Rain," *Economic Policy* (October 1990), quoting original research by Robert Hahn, 1989.

Arundel Partners: The Sequel Project

In April 1992, David A. Davis, a movie industry analyst at Paul Kagan Associates, Inc. in Los Angeles, was asked to look at and comment on an unusual business idea. The idea was to create an investment group, Arundel Partners, that would purchase the sequel rights associated with films produced by one or more major U.S. movie studios. As owner of the rights, Arundel would judge the success of a movie and then decide whether or not to produce a second film based on the story or characters of the first.

The proposal was innovative in several respects. First, Arundel would purchase sequel rights before the first films were even made, let alone released. Second, the investor group would not make artistic judgments or attempt to select the rights for particular movies based on predictions of a possible sequel's success. Instead, Arundel would contract to purchase *all* of the sequel rights for a studio's entire production during a specified period (1–2 years) or, alternatively, for a specified number of major films (15–30). Third, Arundel's advance cash payments for the rights, at an agreed-upon price per film, would help finance production of the initial films.

The idea was intended to capitalize on a few specific characteristics of the movie industry. Producing and distributing motion pictures was a risky business, and predicting the success of any one film was extremely difficult, if not altogether impossible. Moreover, studios' production decisions were driven by both creative and business considerations, which often conflicted. The combination of uncertainty and conflict sometimes strained the financial resources of even the largest studios. Arundel could expect to avoid the conflict between art and commerce and, at the same time, escape (for a price) much of the risk associated with the unpredictability of moviegoers' tastes. The idea was expected to appeal to studios because Arundel would offer cash when it was needed most, during an initial film's production. Since Arundel would seek to purchase the rights to many films, the total payments by Arundel could be substantial and would help reduce individual studio borrowing.

This case was prepared by William A. Teichner, Charles M. Williams Fellow, under the supervision of Professor Timothy A. Luehrman.

Whether Arundel could expect to make money depended heavily on how much it had to pay to purchase a portfolio of sequel rights. In 1992 the major studios did not usually sell sequel rights, nor did they explicitly assign them a value when deciding to put a project into production. However, casual inquiries suggested that studios would find the idea tempting at a price of $2 million or more per movie. At prices below $1 million per movie, they probably would not even discuss it. Paul Kagan Associates, Inc. had expertise in analyzing the film business, and it had assembled certain proprietary data on industry cash flows. Hence, Mr. Davis was asked how much the sequel rights were worth.

The Movie Business

To reach the public, a movie went through three stages: production, distribution, and exhibition. Production involved creating the film negative. Distribution consisted of advertising the film, making prints, shipping prints to theaters, reproducing the film onto videocassettes, and licensing the film to pay and nonpay television and other outlets. Finally, exhibition traditionally consisted of projecting films in theaters, but it increasingly included other viewing media, such as home video.

In 1992 the major movie companies (and ultimate parent companies, if different) involved in U.S. production and distribution were MCA Universal (Matsushita Electric Industrial Co., Ltd.); Metro-Goldwyn-Mayer, Inc. (Credit Lyonnais Bank Nederland N.V.); Orion Pictures Corp.; Paramount Pictures Corp. (Paramount Communications, Inc.); Sony Pictures Entertainment, Inc. (Sony Corp.);[1] The Walt Disney Company;[2] Twentieth Century Fox Film Corp. (The News Corporation, Ltd.); and Warner Brothers, Inc. (Time Warner, Inc.).

These companies, or studios, were all engaged in both production and distribution, and in some cases, exhibition as well. Several of the parent companies or their subsidiaries owned movie theater chains, pay TV channels, and/or TV stations.

In 1991 the major studios and smaller distributors released 150 and 274 films, respectively, in the United States. While the major studios distributed just 35% of all films released in the United States, they accounted for 93% of all revenues received from U.S. movie theaters. These revenues were known as film rentals because the distributor essentially rented prints of the film to theaters for a specified period of time. The top U.S. rental film of 1991, Tri-Star's *Terminator 2*, represented approximately 5% of total U.S. industry rentals. The top five films accounted for 16% of total rentals and the top ten films accounted for 26%. The industry's market share leader (in rentals) changed from year to year according to which studio's releases were most successful. Exhibit 1 presents selected data from 1980–1991 for U.S. film distributors.

Production

Most movies were based on existing literary properties, and producers who planned to adapt a property into a movie normally had to acquire its film rights.[3] Sometimes, literary agents introduced properties to producers. Other times, large talent agencies

---

1. Sony Pictures owned Columbia Pictures and Tri-Star Pictures. Both were involved in production and distribution.

2. The Walt Disney Company owned three film studios: Walt Disney, Touchstone, and Hollywood Pictures, and distributed its films through Buena Vista Pictures Distribution, Inc., a wholly owned subsidiary.

3. The term *producer* was used in a variety of ways in the motion picture industry. Here, it refers to the individuals or companies that owned the rights to produce a film.

presented producers with packages consisting of a script, director, and principal actors. Producers sometimes discovered or created properties on their own. Producers frequently purchased options on the film rights to literary properties. However, most such options were never exercised—the likelihood that a movie would be made from an optioned property was very small.

Production costs were incurred in each of three primary stages: preproduction, principal photography, and postproduction. Costs for preproduction included expenditures for script development, set design, casting of actors, film crew selection, costume design, location scouting, and budget planning. The costs associated with principal photography included fixed salaries of actors, directors, and other personnel.[4] They also included rent, wages, and other expenses for soundstages, set construction, lighting, transportation (for location shooting), costume making, special effects, and miscellaneous items. Finally, postproduction costs consisted of expenses for film editing, the laying down of sound effects and music, and the addition of titles and credits. On average, the entire production cycle required 1 year from the time a project was put into production until the finished film was released to theaters.[5]

The total cost of production, including fixed expenses for story acquisition, was called the negative cost, the cost to create the film's completed negative, from which positive prints could be made.[6] The negative cost excluded advertising and other distribution expenses. While the negative cost included fixed salaries to actors and others, it did not include future compensation that was linked to either the film's revenues or its earnings. Exhibit 2 presents a breakdown of items normally included in a film's negative cost.

In 1991 the average negative cost, excluding interest, for a major new movie was approximately $20 million. This cost had to be financed somehow. Some producers (such as wealthy individuals, producer partnerships, and movie studios) financed their own projects. In some cases, the rights to certain revenues, such as from the home video or non-U.S. theater markets, were presold to raise cash for production. In other cases, independent producers obtained financing from major studios. When a studio financed an independent production, it frequently supplied personnel, facilities, supervision, and equipment.

It was very common for a project to be rejected by one or more studios before it finally received financial support. Furthermore, studios often backed out of projects after investing initial time or money but before beginning principal photography.

Distribution

Typically, the studio that produced or financed a particular movie also distributed it. When producers financed negative costs without help from studios, they often engaged studios simply to pick up, or distribute, their films once they were completed. In their capacity as film distributors, the studios managed the circulation of movies to theaters,

---

4. It also included the costs of line producers who were hired by the financiers or producers of a movie. Line producers managed the day-to-day physical production of the movie, from pre- to postproduction. They also oversaw production costs and hired and fired personnel. Their screen credits included executive producer, producer, and associate producer.

5. While it took about a year to complete most production, a script might hibernate in preproduction development for several months or even years before the beginning of principal photography if a producer could not easily arrange financing or if a studio was not very interested in the project.

6. Interest charges on loans to finance production were sometimes included in negative costs. Here, interest charges are excluded from negative costs.

the licensing of films to pay and nonpay TV, and the duplication and distribution of videocassettes. They handled advertising, publicity, and promotion for the films they distributed, and they also collected proceeds from theaters and ancillary revenue sources.

The traditional contract between the distributor and the producer allowed the distributor to charge distribution expenses and distribution fees, which were deducted from the revenue the distributor collected from theaters and ancillary markets. Distribution expenses included the direct costs of distributing the film; distribution fees were charged to cover the distributor's overhead and profit.

Distribution Expenses.   These expenses primarily represented the costs of advertising in newspapers and on television, of making prints of the film for theaters, and of duplicating videocassettes. Advertising costs were ordinarily the largest single distribution expense by a wide margin and occasionally exceeded a film's negative cost. They varied with the length of time a movie played in theaters. In 1991 the average U.S. advertising cost for a major film was $10 million. The cost of prints and videocassette duplication varied with the number of theaters in which a movie played and the number of videocassettes sold, respectively. Other smaller distribution expenses were shipping costs, insurance costs, and miscellaneous fees, duties, and taxes.

Distribution Fees.   Distributors traditionally charged a fixed percentage of the proceeds they received from the various theatrical and ancillary markets to cover their overhead and profit. Because distribution fees were often calculated as a fixed percentage, they could be more or less than the overhead expenses actually incurred by the distributor.[7] In its role as a distributor, the studio generally charged lower fees when an independent producer (rather than the studio) financed the negative. In addition, fees varied by ancillary market and country. For example, fees were usually higher on non-U.S. proceeds than on U.S. proceeds.

For independently financed films distributed by a studio, a common distribution fee was 22.5% of U.S. rentals and 32.5% of most non-U.S. rentals. However, if the movie was financed by the studio, the fee was generally 30% of U.S. rentals and 40% of most non-U.S. rentals.[8] Fees on home video and pay television revenues were often the same as those on theater rentals. U.S. network TV fees were sometimes several percentage points lower, while U.S. syndicated TV and non-U.S. TV fees were several percentage points higher.

Exhibition

Exhibition usually referred to projection of movies in theaters, but defined broadly, it encompassed ancillary markets as well. Films were released to the various markets in stages that spanned 7 or more years from the date of initial release. U.S. films were typically released first to U.S. movie theaters, about 1 year after going into production. Revenues from ticket sales in movie theaters were known as gross box office proceeds.

---

7. The distribution fee percentage was sometimes lowered once certain predetermined dollar amounts were reached.

8. Under both scenarios, fees on U.K. and Canadian rentals were typically lower than for other countries. In addition, distribution fees were generally lower when independent producers helped finance distribution expenses.

During 1991, for each dollar of gross box office proceeds, about 50¢ were remitted to the distributor as film rentals.[9]

Films were released to non-U.S. theaters about two months after their release in the United states. About eight months after theatrical release, videocassettes were sold in the United States; they were sold soon thereafter in non-U.S. markets. Movies normally appeared on pay TV in the beginning of the second year after release and shortly afterwards on non-U.S. pay TV. In the third year, films aired on U.S. networks and non-U.S. TV. Finally, films might be licensed to independent television stations around the world 6 to 8 years after their theatrical release. Exhibit 3 illustrates the sequence of releases to various markets.

Calculation of Net Profits

After distribution expenses, distribution fees, the negative cost, and any other expenses were subtracted from all revenue, what remained were net profits.

For an independently financed film distributed by a studio, the studio collected proceeds from the various revenue sources, subtracted distribution expenses and fees, and remitted the balance to the producer.[10] After subtracting the cost of the film's negative, the independent producer was left with the film's net profits.[11] See Exhibit 2 for the calculation of net profits for a typical movie.

For movies financed by a studio, the studio—rather than the producer—subtracted out the negative cost. Again, what remained was the film's net profits. For taking on the risk of financing the film, the studio often kept 50% or more of the net profits and remitted what was left to the producer. If there were zero or negative net profits, the studio remitted nothing and bore any loss itself.

Sequels and Arundel Partners

More than 60 films produced since 1970 had one or more sequels. Not all commercially successful first films were followed by sequels, but practically all sequels followed successful films. Many of the most profitable movies of the past 20 years spawned one or more sequels. These included, for example, *Airport, Back to the Future, Beverly Hills Cop, Friday the 13th, Ghostbusters, The Godfather, Jaws, Police Academy, Raiders of the Lost Ark, Rocky, Star Trek, Star Wars, Superman, Teenage Mutant Ninja Turtles,* and *Terminator.* The long-running James Bond film series, which began in 1962 with *Dr. No*, included 16 sequels.

---

9. A common arrangement between the distributor and the theater exhibitor provided that the distributor would receive the greater of: (1) 70% of the gross box office proceeds in the first two weeks (60% for the following two; 50% for the next two; 40% for the next two; and 35% for the remainder of the run) or (2) 90% of the gross box office proceeds after subtracting out a reasonable, predetermined amount of cash to cover the costs of operating the theater.

10. Occasionally, a major actor's contract specified that he or she would receive a percentage of the film's revenues. In that case, these gross participations were often paid out of the distributor's proceeds before fees and expenses.

11. Sometimes creative talent received net profit participations, or percentages of any positive net profits the film made. The arrangement described in the text, wherein fees were deducted by the distributor, was fairly standard in the industry and was called a distribution fee deal or net deal. In the 1980s, two other kinds of deals became common. These were the gross percentage deal and adjusted gross percentage deal. In the gross percentage deal, the producer received a fixed percentage of the film's proceeds received by the distributor. In the adjusted gross percentage deal, the producer received a fixed percentage of the distributor's proceeds after certain items were first subtracted.

Sequels were based on characters or situations portrayed in the initial movies. Scripts for sequels were usually written after the first film's release and, in some cases, were worked on by individuals other than those who had created the original. The median release date for a sequel was 3 years after the first film's release; most sequels were released within 1 to 5 years.

The average negative cost for a sequel was higher than for the first film. For sequels made after 1970, the inflation-adjusted negative cost was about 120% of the first film's negative cost, according to one estimate. This was partly because the commercial success of the first film enhanced the bargaining power of key creative talent, who demanded higher compensation for the sequel.

A similar analysis showed that the average sequel produced only 70% of the inflation-adjusted (real) rentals that the initial film had earned. Exhibit 4 displays comparative inflation-adjusted cost and revenue data for a sample of first films and their sequels. Exhibit 5 shows rental data for a small number of films that spawned more than one sequel. For most such film series, rentals declined with each additional installment in the series.

The Sequel Project

Arundel Partners would be interested in purchasing the sequel rights for one or more studios' entire production over an extended period of not less than 1 year. If a particular film was a hit and Arundel thought a sequel would be profitable, it would exercise its rights by producing the sequel itself or hiring professionals to do so. Alternatively, it could sell the rights to the highest bidder. Inevitably, most first films would not justify sequels; for those films, the sequel rights would simply not be exercised. As a practical matter, for most movies, it would be very clear after their first few weeks in U.S. theaters whether or not a sequel would be economical.

It would be critically important to Arundel that a number of films and a price per film be agreed upon *before* either Arundel or the studio knew which films would be produced. Once production started, the studio would gradually, but inevitably, form an opinion about the movie, and Arundel would not want to have to bargain over individual projects about which it knew less than the studio.

Otherwise, many details of a potential contract between Arundel and the prospective studio still needed to be worked out. For example, in addition to the price of the rights, a satisfactory method of payment had to be agreed upon. The simplest approach would be for Arundel to make payments to an escrow account when a first film went into production. These payments could then be disbursed to a studio as the movie progressed through production. Certain films might have to be excluded from the arrangement if the studio itself did not already own their sequel rights. To keep the studio committed to the success of possible sequels, it would probably be desirable to have the studio retain an interest in the revenues or the net profits of the sequel, or to have rights for subsequent sequels—that is, third, fourth, and other future films—revert to the studio.

For tax purposes, it might be desirable to fix an expiration date for the sequel rights, perhaps 3 years from the first film's release, by which time Arundel would have to declare its intentions or forfeit the rights. This would allow Arundel enough time to make a decision about making a sequel and enable it to write off more quickly its investment in rights it chose not to exercise. If the studio were interested, Arundel could grant it a right of first refusal on any rights it planned to sell. The contract also could provide that Arundel would use the original studio for distribution, assuming its distribution fees and expenses were competitive.

Available Movie Data

The value of the sequel rights depended heavily on the statistical distribution that characterized the returns earned by first films. Actual data on realized returns for a large sample of first films were not publicly available, although rough estimates could be made for hundreds of films based on public information. Further, Paul Kagan Associates, Inc. had assembled a proprietary database on which even more reliable estimates could be based for an even larger sample of recent movies.

Estimates of the financial performance of all first films released by six major studios during 1989 are presented in Exhibit 6.[12] These estimates were used to compute the discounted cash flows presented in Exhibit 7, under the assumptions described in the Appendix. The discounted costs and revenues were used to compute simple 1-year returns for each film. As Exhibit 7 shows, returns were highly variable, ranging from 1,224% for Tri-Star's *Look Who's Talking* to −91% for Paramount's *We're No Angels*.

Exhibit 6 and 7 also estimate costs, revenues, and 1-year returns for hypothetical sequels for each first film, according to the assumptions outlined in the Appendix. Essentially, these figures are projections of how a sequel would perform, assuming it were made and assuming it were "typical." For example, Warner Brothers' *Batman* was expected to result in a successful sequel, with a projected return of 225%. Not surprisingly, however, most movies' hypothetical sequels performed poorly and undoubtedly would not be produced. Exhibit 8 presents histograms of the one-year returns tabulated in Exhibit 7 for first films and sequels. Exhibit 9 summarizes some characteristics of the distribution of hypothetical sequel returns for a sample of first films released in 1987 and 1988 that had negative costs of at least $14 million.

Because Arundel's tax situation might be exceedingly complex, David Davis was asked to estimate the value of the sequel rights on a pretax basis. He had access to data such as that in Exhibits 6–9, as well as the larger, more detailed dataset at Paul Kagan Associates. There were two obvious ways to begin analyzing the data. One was to use the projected financial performances of all the 1989 hypothetical sequels to decide which ones should be produced. It would then be possible to estimate how much money they would make in total, and hence, how much per 1989 first film. The other approach would be to apply a simple option pricing model to the parameters of the distribution of sequel returns or sequel net present values and so estimate directly the value of sequel rights for a random film in the available sample. Each approach would require some simplifying assumptions. Davis wondered what biases might be generated by the various assumptions, which methodology would give the more useful result, and whether either result was reliable enough to justify an investment of millions of dollars.

---

12. Exhibits 6–9 exclude releases from Orion and Metro-Goldwyn-Mayer, both of which were experiencing severe financial problems in 1992. Orion was in Chapter 11 bankruptcy proceedings in April 1992.

EXHIBIT 1
Selected Motion Picture Industry Data, 1980–1991

	North American Theatrical Film Rental Shares of Major Film Distributors[a,b]								
	Sony[c]	*20th Century Fox*	*Metro-Goldwyn-Mayer*	*Paramount*	*MCA Universal*	*Warner Brothers*	*Buena Vista[d]*	*Orion*	*Total Majors*
1980	14%	16%	7%	16%	20%	14%	4%	2%	93%
1981	13	13	9	15	14	18	3	1	86
1982	10	14	11	14	30	10	4	3	96
1983	14	21	10	14	13	17	3	4	96
1984	21	10	7	21	8	19	4	5	95
1985	20	11	9	10	16	18	3	5	92
1986	16	8	4	22	9	12	10	7	88
1987	9	9	4	20	8	13	14	10	87
1988	10	12	10	15	10	11	19	7	94
1989	16	7	6	14	17	17	14	4	95
1990	14	13	3	15	13	13	16	6	93
1991	20	12	2	12	11	14	14	9	93

	Number of Films Released in the U.S. by Major and Independent Distributors[e]		*Aggregate Box Office Data*		
	Major Releases	*Independent Releases*	*U.S. and Canada Gross Box Office (millions)*	*U.S. Rentals[f] (millions)*	*U.S. Average Theater Ticket Price*
1980	134	NA	$2,749	$1,235	$2.69
1981	145	NA	2,967	1,335	2.78
1982	150	211	3,453	1,555	2.94
1983	166	230	3,766	1,700	3.15
1984	152	256	4,031	1,800	3.36
1985	138	251	3,749	1,635	3.55
1986	133	286	3,778	1,650	3.71
1987	122	365	4,253	1,830	3.91
1988	153	319	4,458	1,920	4.11
1989	157	292	5,033	2,165	4.45
1990	158	221	5,022	2,260	4.75
1991	150	274	4,803	2,160	4.89

Sources: Goldman Sachs Investment Research, *Movie Industry Update 1992*; MPAA, *1991 U.S. Economic Review*; and industry sources.

a. Several companies have undergone various transformations since 1980. The chart shows the company's current name.

b. Includes rereleases of films that were first released in earlier years.

c. Includes films distributed by Columbia and Tri-Star. Tri-Star began operations in 1984.

d. Buena Vista distributes films by The Walt Disney Company; data include films produced by the Disney, Touchstone, and Hollywood Pictures studios.

e. Excludes rereleases of films first issued in prior years.

f. Excludes independent films.

EXHIBIT 2

Revenue and Cost Estimates for Typical Film Distributed by a Major Studio[a,b] (millions of 1991 dollars)

		Percent of U.S. Theatrical Rentals	Percent of Total Revenue
Revenue Collected by Distributor			
U.S. theater rentals	$10.0	100%	22%
Non-U.S. theater rentals	9.0	90	19
Worldwide home video	15.0	150	32
Worldwide pay TV	5.5	55	12
Worldwide TV[c]	7.0	70	15
Total	$46.5	465%	100%
Distribution Fees			
Worldwide theater	$ 5.0	50%	11%
Worldwide home video	4.0	40	9
Worldwide pay TV	1.5	15	3
Worldwide TV	2.0	20	4
Total	$12.5	125%	27%
Distribution Expenses			
Worldwide theater	$12.0	120%	26%
Worldwide home video	3.5	35	8
Worldwide pay TV	—	—	—
Worldwide TV	—	—	—
Total	$15.5	155%	33%
Negative Cost[d]			
Story rights/script development	$ 0.5		
Actors/director	6.0		
Production management	1.0		
Production crew	1.0		
Set design/construction	2.0		
Transportation/locations	1.5		
Wardrobe/makeup/hair	0.5		
Extras/props	0.5		
Lighting	0.3		
Special effects	0.3		
Other principal photography	1.0		
Film editing	0.7		
Music	0.4		
Other postproduction	0.8		
All other	1.5		
Total negative cost	$18.0		
Pretax net profits[e]	$ 0.5		

a. The figures represent estimates of a typical film, not the average film.

b. Fee structure assumes film is independently financed.

c. In this chart, worldwide TV includes U.S. network, U.S. syndicated, and non-U.S. television.

d. The negative cost breakdown is shown for illustrative purposes only and provides one possible breakdown of a film's cost.

e. Excludes interest charges. Assumes no gross participation.

EXHIBIT 3
Typical Beginning Dates for Film Production and Release

						Year											
	0.0	0.5	1.0	1.5	2.0	2.5	3.0	3.5	4.0	4.5	5.0	5.5	6.0	6.5	7.0	7.5	8.0
Film production	X						S[a]										
Release schedule																	
U.S. movie theaters			X														
Non-U.S. movie theaters			X														
U.S. home video				X													
Non-U.S. home video				X													
U.S. pay per view					X												
U.S. pay TV					X												
Non-U.S. pay TV					X												
U.S. network TV							X										
Non-U.S. TV							X										
U.S. syndicated TV																	X
Non-U.S. TV, second run																	X

a. S = A possible sequel's most likely beginning date of production. The rest of the pattern for a sequel was expected to be similar to that of the first film.

EXHIBIT 4
Comparative Cost and Revenue Data of First Films and Their Sequels

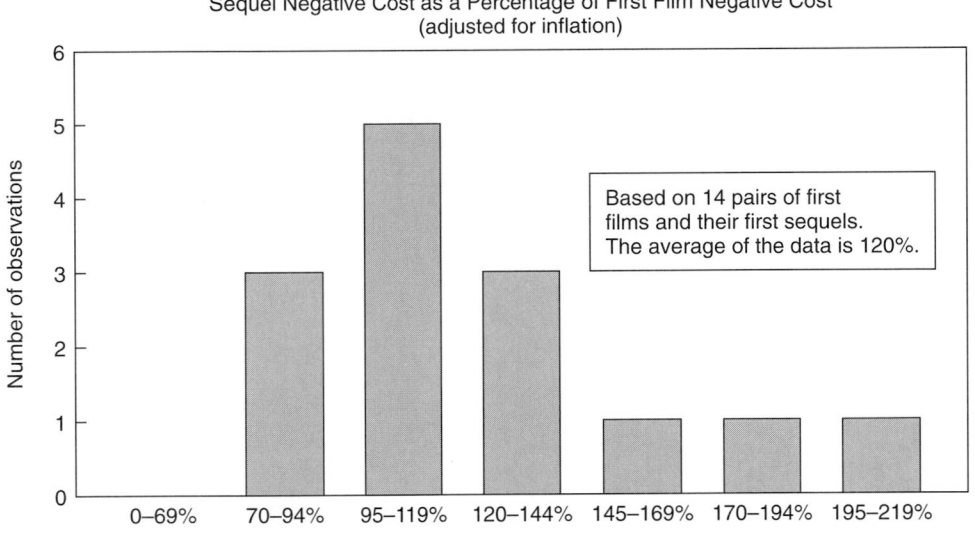

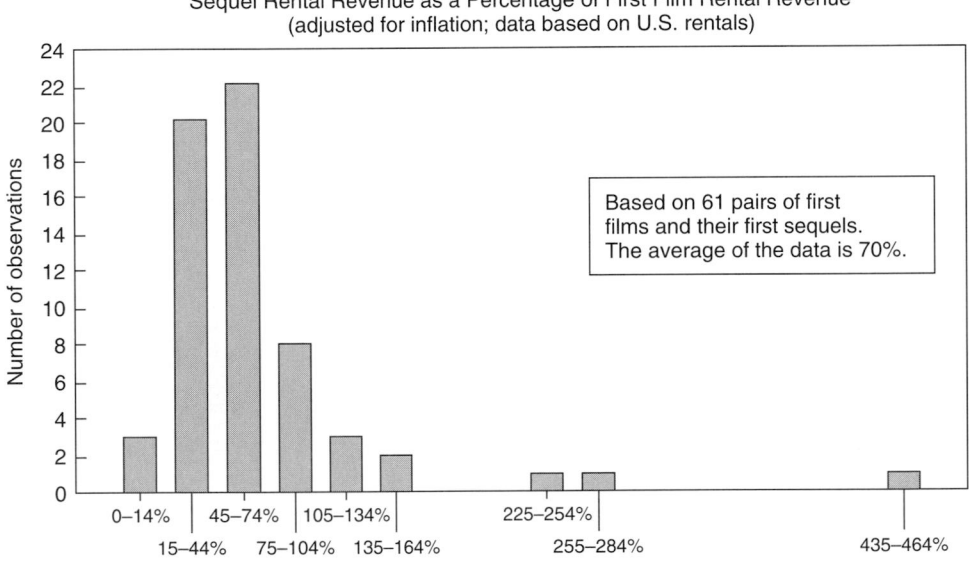

EXHIBIT 5
U.S. Theater Rental Data for Several Films Having More Than One Sequel

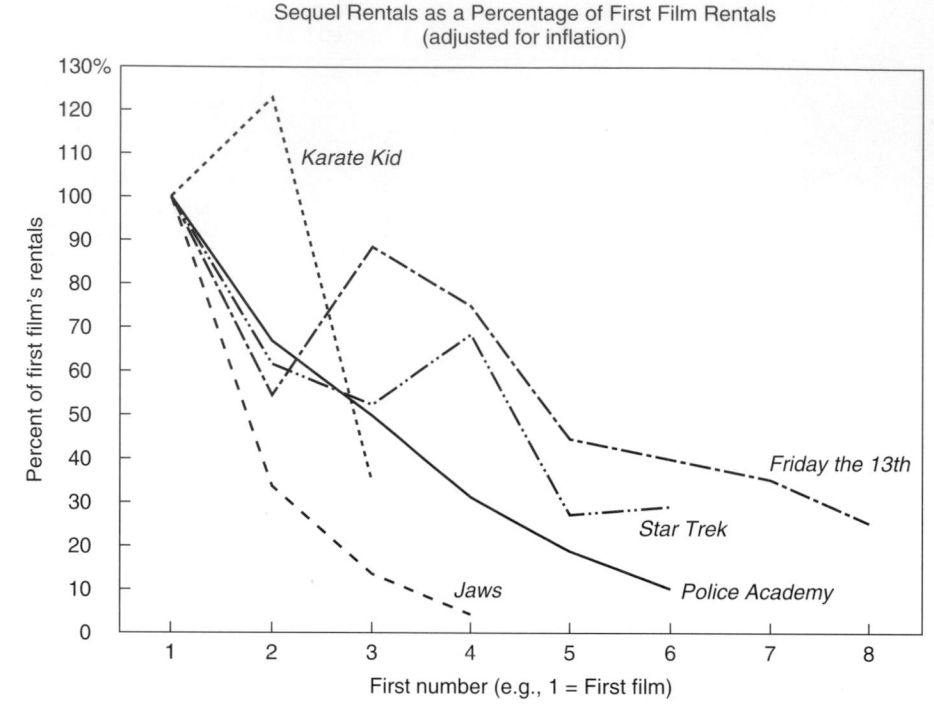

Sequel Rentals as a Percentage of First Film Rentals
(adjusted for inflation)

EXHIBIT 6
Estimated Revenues and Costs for Films Released in 1989 by Six Major Studios and Their Hypothetical Sequels[a] (millions of dollars)

Studio/Movie Title	First Film					Hypothetical Sequel				
	U.S. Theater Rentals	Other Revenue	Distribution Fees	Distribution Expense	Negative Cost	U.S. Theater Rentals	Other Revenue	Distribution Fees	Distribution Expense	Negative Cost
MCA Universal										
1 Parenthood	$55.0	$146.1	$53.6	$43.1	$22.0	$38.5	$106.1	$38.5	$32.6	$26.4
2 Born on the Fourth of July	40.5	110.9	40.3	33.1	19.8	28.4	81.4	29.2	26.0	23.7
3 Field of Dreams	33.6	94.1	34.0	31.6	17.6	23.5	69.7	24.8	22.9	21.1
4 Uncle Buck	33.3	93.6	33.8	30.2	16.5	23.3	69.3	24.7	22.8	19.8
5 Sea of Love	31.5	89.0	32.1	32.0	27.5	22.0	66.1	23.5	22.0	33.0
6 Always	22.0	66.1	23.4	28.0	34.1	15.4	50.1	17.4	17.7	40.9
7 K-9	20.5	62.3	22.0	20.9	13.2	14.3	47.5	16.4	17.0	15.8
8 The 'Burbs	19.0	58.9	20.7	22.9	18.7	13.3	45.0	15.5	16.4	22.4
9 The Dream Team	15.8	51.1	17.8	19.0	16.5	11.1	39.6	13.5	14.9	19.8
10 Do the Right Thing	14.6	48.2	16.7	14.6	7.7	10.2	37.6	12.7	14.4	9.2
11 Dad	11.9	41.5	14.2	20.0	20.9	8.3	32.9	11.0	13.1	25.0
12 Shocker	8.3	32.7	10.9	14.6	6.6	5.8	26.7	8.6	11.5	7.9
13 The Wizard	5.5	26.1	8.4	9.5	8.8	3.9	22.1	6.9	10.3	10.5
14 Renegades	4.6	23.9	7.6	13.1	13.2	3.2	20.6	6.3	9.9	15.8
Paramount Pictures										
15 Harlem Nights	$36.3	$100.8	$36.5	$41.7	$33.0	$25.4	$74.4	$26.6	$24.1	$39.5
16 Pet Sematary	29.1	83.2	29.9	27.1	12.1	20.3	62.0	21.9	20.9	14.5
17 Black Rain	27.5	79.4	28.5	31.6	33.0	19.3	59.4	20.9	20.2	39.5
18 Major League	23.7	70.1	25.0	26.1	13.2	16.6	52.9	18.5	18.4	15.8
19 Cousins	11.0	39.4	13.4	14.4	14.3	7.7	31.4	10.4	12.8	17.1
20 We're No Angels	5.5	26.1	8.4	19.9	24.2	3.9	22.1	6.9	10.3	29.0
21 Let It Ride	2.3	18.3	5.5	10.8	19.8	1.6	16.7	4.8	8.8	23.7
22 Shirley Valentine	2.3	18.3	5.5	5.6	8.8	1.6	16.7	4.8	8.8	10.5
23 Fat Man and Little Boy	1.5	16.5	4.8	9.2	20.9	1.1	15.3	4.3	8.5	25.0
24 The Experts	0.0	12.7	3.4	0.8	13.2	0.0	12.7	3.4	7.8	15.8
Sony Pictures Entertainment[b]										
25 Look Who's Talking (TS)	$75.8	$196.5	$72.6	$51.7	$11.0	$53.1	$141.4	$51.8	$41.9	$13.2
26 When Harry Met Sally (C)	46.1	124.5	45.4	38.1	20.9	32.3	91.0	32.8	28.5	25.0
27 Steel Magnolias (TS)	44.0	119.4	43.5	35.9	24.2	30.8	87.4	31.5	27.6	29.0
28 See No Evil; Hear No Evil (TS)	22.5	67.1	23.8	23.1	19.8	15.7	50.8	17.7	17.9	23.7
29 The Bear (TS)	14.9	48.7	16.9	22.5	23.1	10.4	37.9	12.8	14.5	27.7
30 Glory (TS)	14.3	47.4	16.4	14.5	23.1	10.0	37.0	12.5	14.2	27.7
31 Look Up (TS)	8.8	34.1	11.4	16.1	18.7	6.2	27.7	9.0	11.8	22.4
32 Casualties of War (C)	8.1	32.5	10.8	17.1	27.5	5.7	26.6	8.6	11.5	33.0
33 Chances Are (TS)	7.2	30.1	9.9	15.4	19.8	5.0	24.9	7.9	11.0	23.7

(continued)

EXHIBIT 6 (concluded)

Studio/Movie Title	First Film					Hypothetical Sequel				
	U.S. Theater Rentals	Other Revenue	Distribution Fees	Distribution Expense	Negative Cost	U.S. Theater Rentals	Other Revenue	Distribution Fees	Distribution Expense	Negative Cost
34 Family Business (TS)	$ 6.6	$ 28.7	$ 9.4	$ 16.5	$19.8	$ 4.6	$ 23.9	$ 7.6	$10.8	$23.7
35 She's Out of Control (C)	5.7	26.6	8.6	12.2	16.5	4.0	22.4	7.0	10.4	19.8
36 Who's Harry Crumb? (TS)	5.0	24.7	7.9	13.2	15.4	3.5	21.1	6.5	10.0	18.5
37 Adventures of Baron Munchausen (C)	4.3	23.1	7.3	7.8	57.1	3.0	20.0	6.1	9.7	68.5
38 True Believer (C)	4.1	22.6	7.1	12.8	15.4	2.9	19.6	6.0	9.6	18.5
39 Troop Beverly Hills (C)	4.0	22.3	7.0	11.5	19.8	2.8	19.5	5.9	9.6	23.7
40 Tap (TS)	3.9	22.1	6.9	11.4	16.5	2.7	19.3	5.8	9.5	19.8
41 Deepstar Six (TS)	3.4	21.0	6.5	10.0	8.8	2.4	18.5	5.5	9.3	10.5
42 Johnny Handsome (TS)	2.9	19.7	6.0	9.7	22.0	2.0	17.6	5.2	9.1	26.4
43 Music Box (TS)	2.8	19.4	5.9	8.4	19.8	1.9	17.4	5.1	9.0	23.7
44 Immediate Family (C)	2.3	18.3	5.5	12.1	15.4	1.6	16.7	4.8	8.8	18.5
45 Listen to Me (C)	2.0	17.5	5.2	12.0	16.5	1.4	16.1	4.6	8.7	19.8
46 Physical Evidence (C)	1.7	16.7	4.9	9.2	18.7	1.2	15.5	4.4	8.5	22.4
47 Old Gringo (C)	1.5	16.5	4.8	6.6	37.3	1.1	15.3	4.3	8.5	44.8
48 Loverboy (TS)	1.5	16.5	4.8	10.5	11.0	1.1	15.3	4.3	8.5	13.2
49 Sing (TS)	1.0	15.1	4.3	9.0	15.4	0.7	14.4	4.0	8.2	18.5
50 Winter People (C)	0.8	14.6	4.1	6.3	17.6	0.5	14.0	3.8	8.1	21.1
51 Welcome Home (C)	0.4	13.8	3.8	4.9	15.4	0.3	13.5	3.6	8.0	18.5
52 Adventures of Milo and Otis (C)	0.1	13.0	3.5	6.0	8.8	0.1	12.9	3.4	7.8	10.5
53 The Big Picture (C)	0.1	13.0	3.5	0.8	8.8	0.1	12.9	3.4	7.8	10.5
54 Slaves of New York (TS)	0.1	13.0	3.5	1.5	6.6	0.1	12.9	3.4	7.8	7.9
55 Eat a Bowl of Tea (C)	0.1	13.0	3.5	0.8	2.2	0.1	12.9	3.4	7.8	2.6
56 To Kill a Priest (C)	0.0	12.7	3.4	0.8	11.0	0.0	12.7	3.4	7.8	13.2
57 Me and Him (C)	0.0	12.7	3.4	0.8	8.8	0.0	12.7	3.4	7.8	10.5
58 Bloodhounds of Broadway(C)	0.0	12.7	3.4	0.8	3.3	0.0	12.7	3.4	7.8	4.0
Twentieth Century Fox										
59 The War of the Roses	$ 45.6	$123.2	$ 44.9	$ 39.1	$27.5	$ 31.9	$ 90.0	$ 32.5	$28.3	$33.0
60 The Abyss	31.6	89.3	32.2	37.2	49.4	22.1	66.3	23.5	22.0	59.3
61 Weekend at Bernie's	15.4	50.1	17.4	16.3	11.0	10.8	38.9	13.2	14.7	13.2
62 Say Anything	9.8	36.5	12.3	15.2	14.3	6.9	29.4	9.6	12.2	17.1
63 Skin Deep	9.4	35.4	11.9	15.0	11.0	6.5	28.6	9.3	12.0	13.2
64 The Fabulous Baker Boys	8.8	34.1	11.4	16.1	14.3	6.2	27.7	9.0	11.8	17.1
65 Millennium	2.6	19.1	5.8	7.1	16.5	1.8	17.2	5.0	9.0	19.8
66 Worth Winning	1.7	16.7	4.9	10.5	14.3	1.2	15.5	4.4	8.5	17.1
67 Gleaming the Cube	1.2	15.7	4.5	6.5	12.1	0.8	14.8	4.1	8.3	14.5
68 How I Got into College	0.6	14.1	3.9	8.8	13.2	0.4	13.7	3.7	8.0	15.8
69 When the Whales Came	0.0	12.7	3.4	1.4	4.4	0.0	12.7	3.4	7.8	5.3

Warner Brothers

70 Batman	$165.6	$414.2	$154.5	$102.0	$54.9	$115.9	$293.7	$109.2	$82.3	$65.9
71 Driving Miss Daisy	55.6	147.4	54.1	43.3	8.8	38.9	107.0	38.9	32.8	10.5
72 Tango & Cash	33.1	93.0	33.6	40.4	60.4	23.2	68.9	24.5	22.7	72.5
73 Lean on Me	15.8	51.1	17.8	17.7	16.5	11.1	39.6	13.5	14.9	19.8
74 Her Alibi	10.1	37.3	12.6	16.6	22.0	7.1	29.9	9.8	12.4	26.4
75 Next of Kin	7.7	31.4	10.4	14.3	13.2	5.4	25.8	8.3	11.3	15.8
76 Pink Cadillac	7.5	30.9	10.2	16.8	20.9	5.2	25.4	8.1	11.2	25.0
77 Young Einstein	6.6	28.7	9.4	11.3	4.4	4.6	23.9	7.6	10.8	5.3
78 Dead-Bang	3.9	22.1	6.9	11.4	15.4	2.7	19.3	5.8	9.5	18.5
79 Dead Calm	3.6	21.5	6.7	10.1	9.9	2.5	18.9	5.7	9.4	11.9
80 Second Sight	2.8	19.4	5.9	9.7	11.0	1.9	17.4	5.1	9.0	13.2
81 See You in the Morning	2.4	18.6	5.6	9.6	18.7	1.7	16.8	4.9	8.9	22.4
82 In Country	1.8	17.0	5.0	9.3	19.8	1.2	15.7	4.5	8.6	23.7
83 Cookie	1.1	15.4	4.4	5.1	14.3	0.8	14.6	4.1	8.3	17.1
84 How to Get Ahead in Advertising	0.2	13.3	3.6	0.9	5.5	0.2	13.1	3.5	7.9	6.6
85 Powwow Highway	0.1	13.0	3.5	0.8	4.4	0.1	12.9	3.4	7.8	5.3
86 Bert Rigby, You're a Fool	0.0	12.7	3.4	1.4	14.3	0.0	12.7	3.4	7.8	17.1
87 Penn & Teller Get Killed	0.0	12.7	3.4	0.8	8.8	0.0	12.7	3.4	7.8	10.5
88 Checking Out	0.0	12.7	3.4	0.8	5.5	0.0	12.7	3.4	7.8	6.6
Averages	$ 14.9	$ 48.8	$ 16.9	$ 17.4	$17.6	$ 10.4	$ 38.0	$ 12.9	$14.5	$21.2

The Walt Disney Company

89 Honey, I Shrunk the Kids (W)	$ 80.0	$206.7	$ 76.4	$ 58.6	$24.2	$ 56.0	$148.5	$ 54.5	$43.8	$29.0
90 Dead Poets Society (T)	53.3	141.8	52.0	46.2	22.0	37.3	103.1	37.4	31.8	26.4
91 The Little Mermaid (W)	44.2	120.0	43.7	38.6	22.0	31.0	87.8	31.6	27.7	26.4
92 Turner & Hooch (T)	38.8	106.9	38.8	32.5	19.8	27.2	78.6	28.2	25.3	23.7
93 Three Fugitives (T)	20.4	62.1	21.9	22.2	18.7	14.3	47.3	16.4	17.0	22.4
94 An Innocent Man (T)	11.6	40.7	13.9	17.2	18.7	8.1	32.3	10.7	13.0	22.4
95 Blaze (T)	9.9	36.7	12.4	17.8	19.8	6.9	29.5	9.7	12.3	23.7
96 New York Stories (T)	5.2	25.3	8.1	10.7	20.9	3.6	21.5	6.7	10.1	25.0
97 Gross Anatomy (T)	5.1	25.0	8.0	13.2	13.2	3.5	21.3	6.6	10.1	15.8
98 Disorganized Crime (T)	4.4	23.4	7.4	11.7	12.1	3.1	20.2	6.2	9.8	14.5
99 Cheetah (W)	4.4	23.4	7.4	10.4	7.7	3.1	20.2	6.2	9.8	9.2

a. Metro-Goldwyn-Mayer and Orion are excluded. Fees assume films were financed by an independent producer. Costs exclude gross participations and interest charges.

b. C = Columbia Pictures; TS = Tri-Star; W = Walt Disney; T = Touchstone.

EXHIBIT 7
Estimated Expected Present Values and 1-Year Holding Period Returns Based on Data in Exhibit 6 (millions of dollars)

Studio/Movie or Title	First Film			Hypothetical Sequel		
	PV of Net Inflows at Year 1[a]	PV of Negative Cost at Year 0	1-Year Return[b]	PV of Net Inflows at Year 4[a]	PV of Negative Cost at Year 3	1-Year Return[b]
MCA Universal						
1 Parenthood	$100.1	$21.5	$ 3.65	$ 76.8	$28.2	$ 1.72
2 Born on the Fourth of July	74.5	19.4	2.85	56.8	25.4	1.24
3 Field of Dreams	59.1	17.2	2.44	47.3	22.6	1.10
4 Uncle Buck	60.0	16.1	2.72	47.0	21.2	1.22
5 Sea of Love	53.5	26.9	0.99	44.4	35.3	0.26
6 Always	34.3	33.3	0.03	31.4	43.7	(0.28)
7 K-9	37.8	12.9	1.93	29.3	16.9	0.73
8 The 'Burbs	32.2	18.3	0.76	27.3	24.0	0.14
9 The Dream Team	28.4	16.1	0.76	22.9	21.2	0.08
10 Do the Right Thing	30.0	7.5	2.98	21.2	9.9	1.15
11 Dad	17.7	20.4	(0.13)	17.4	26.8	(0.35)
12 Shocker	14.3	6.5	1.22	12.4	8.5	0.47
13 The Wizard	12.7	8.6	0.48	8.7	11.3	(0.23)
14 Renegades	6.9	12.9	(0.46)	7.4	16.9	(0.56)
Paramount Pictures						
15 Harlem Nights	$ 55.4	$32.3	0.72	$ 51.1	$42.3	0.21
16 Pet Sematary	52.6	11.8	3.45	41.1	15.5	1.65
17 Black Rain	44.1	32.3	0.37	39.0	42.3	(0.08)
18 Major League	40.3	12.9	2.12	33.7	16.9	0.99
19 Cousins	21.2	14.0	0.52	16.2	18.3	(0.11)
20 We're No Angels	2.1	23.7	(0.91)	8.7	31.0	(0.72)
21 Let It Ride	3.6	19.4	(0.82)	4.3	25.4	(0.83)
22 Shirley Valentine	8.9	8.6	0.04	4.3	11.3	(0.62)
23 Fat Man and Little Boy	3.3	20.4	(0.84)	3.2	26.8	(0.88)
24 The Experts	8.2	12.9	(0.36)	1.1	16.9	(0.94)
Sony Pictures Entertainment[c]						
25 Look Who's Talking (TS)	$142.3	$10.8	12.24	$105.5	$14.1	6.48
26 When Harry Met Sally (C)	83.3	20.4	3.08	64.6	26.8	1.41
27 Steel Magnolias (TS)	80.4	23.7	2.40	61.7	31.0	0.99
28 See No Evil; Hear No Evil (TS)	40.5	19.4	1.09	32.0	25.4	0.26
29 The Bear (TS)	22.4	22.6	(0.01)	21.5	29.6	(0.27)
30 Glory (TS)	29.3	22.6	0.30	20.8	29.6	(0.30)
31 Look Up (TS)	14.1	18.3	(0.23)	13.2	24.0	(0.45)
32 Casualties of War (C)	11.4	26.9	(0.57)	12.3	35.3	(0.65)
33 Chances Are (TS)	10.8	19.4	(0.44)	10.9	25.4	(0.57)
34 Family Business (TS)	8.3	19.4	(0.57)	10.2	25.4	(0.60)
35 She's Out of Control (C)	10.5	16.1	(0.35)	9.0	21.2	(0.58)
36 Who's Harry Crumb? (TS)	7.6	15.1	(0.49)	7.9	19.7	(0.60)
37 Adventures of Baron Munchausen (C)	11.6	55.9	(0.79)	7.0	73.4	(0.90)
38 True Believer (C)	5.8	15.1	(0.61)	6.7	19.7	(0.66)
39 Troop Beverly Hills (C)	6.9	19.4	(0.64)	6.5	25.4	(0.74)
40 Tap (TS)	6.7	16.1	(0.58)	6.4	21.2	(0.70)
41 Deepstar Six (TS)	7.1	8.6	(0.17)	5.8	11.3	(0.49)
42 Johnny Handsome (TS)	6.0	21.5	(0.72)	5.0	28.2	(0.82)
43 Music Box (TS)	7.1	19.4	(0.63)	4.9	25.4	(0.81)
44 Immediate Family (C)	2.2	15.1	(0.85)	4.3	19.7	(0.78)
45 Listen to Me (C)	1.6	16.1	(0.90)	3.8	21.2	(0.82)
46 Physical Evidence (C)	3.6	18.3	(0.80)	3.4	24.0	(0.86)
47 Old Gringo (C)	6.0	36.6	(0.84)	3.2	48.0	(0.93)
48 Loverboy (TS)	2.0	10.8	(0.81)	3.2	14.1	(0.77)
49 Sing (TS)	2.2	15.1	(0.85)	2.4	19.7	(0.88)
50 Winter People (C)	4.4	17.2	(0.74)	2.1	22.6	(0.91)
51 Welcome Home (C)	5.1	15.1	(0.66)	1.7	19.7	(0.91)
52 Adventures of Milo and Otis (C)	3.1	8.6	(0.64)	1.2	11.3	(0.89)
53 The Big Picture (C)	8.4	8.6	(0.02)	1.2	11.3	(0.89)

(continued)

EXHIBIT 7 *(concluded)*

Studio/Movie or Title	First Film			Hypothetical Sequel		
	PV of Net Inflows at Year 1[a]	PV of Negative Cost at Year 0	1-Year Return[b]	PV of Net Inflows at Year 4[a]	PV of Negative Cost at Year 3	1-Year Return[b]
54 *Slaves of New York* (TS)	$ 7.8	$ 6.5	$ 0.20	$ 1.2	$ 8.5	$(0.85)
55 *Eat a Bowl of Tea* (C)	8.4	2.2	2.92	1.2	2.8	(0.56)
56 *To Kill a Priest* (C)	8.2	10.8	(0.24)	1.1	14.1	(0.92)
57 *Me and Him* (C)	8.2	8.6	(0.05)	1.1	11.3	(0.90)
58 *Bloodhounds of Broadway* (C)	8.2	3.2	1.54	1.1	4.2	(0.74)
Twentieth Century Fox						
59 *The War of the Roses*	$ 80.8	$26.9	$ 2.01	$ 63.8	$35.3	$ 0.81
60 *The Abyss*	48.4	48.4	0.00	44.6	63.5	(0.30)
61 *Weekend at Bernie's*	30.2	10.8	1.81	22.3	14.1	0.58
62 *Say Anything*	17.5	14.0	0.25	14.6	18.3	(0.21)
63 *Skin Deep*	16.6	10.8	0.54	14.0	14.1	(0.01)
64 *The Fabulous Baker Boys*	14.1	14.0	0.01	13.2	18.3	(0.28)
65 *Millennium*	8.2	16.1	(0.49)	4.7	21.2	(0.78)
66 *Worth Winning*	2.2	14.0	(0.84)	3.4	18.3	(0.82)
67 *Gleaming the Cube*	5.3	11.8	(0.55)	2.7	15.5	(0.82)
68 *How I Got into College*	1.3	12.9	(0.90)	1.8	16.9	(0.89)
69 *When the Whales Came*	7.5	4.3	0.75	1.1	5.6	(0.81)
Warner Brothers						
70 *Batman*	$311.5	$53.8	$ 4.80	$229.1	$70.5	$ 2.25
71 *Driving Miss Daisy*	101.2	8.6	10.76	77.6	11.3	5.87
72 *Tango & Cash*	48.9	59.1	(0.17)	46.7	77.6	(0.40)
73 *Lean on Me*	29.8	16.1	0.85	22.9	21.2	0.08
74 *Her Alibi*	16.8	21.5	(0.22)	15.0	28.2	(0.47)
75 *Next of Kin*	13.2	12.9	0.02	11.7	16.9	(0.31)
76 *Pink Cadillac*	10.1	20.4	(0.51)	11.4	26.8	(0.58)
77 *Young Einstein*	13.6	4.3	2.17	10.2	5.6	0.80
78 *Dead-Bang*	6.7	15.1	(0.55)	6.4	19.7	(0.68)
79 *Dead Calm*	7.6	9.7	(0.22)	6.1	12.7	(0.52)
80 *Second Sight*	5.8	10.8	(0.46)	4.9	14.1	(0.65)
81 *See You in the Morning*	5.1	18.3	(0.72)	4.4	24.0	(0.82)
82 *In Country*	3.8	19.4	(0.80)	3.5	25.4	(0.86)
83 *Cookie*	6.4	14.0	(0.54)	2.6	18.3	(0.86)
84 *How to Get Ahead in Advertising*	8.6	5.4	0.61	1.4	7.1	(0.80)
85 *Powwow Highway*	8.4	4.3	0.96	1.2	5.6	(0.78)
86 *Bert Rigby, You're a Fool*	7.5	14.0	(0.46)	1.1	18.3	(0.94)
87 *Penn & Teller Get Killed*	8.2	8.6	(0.05)	1.1	11.3	(0.90)
88 *Checking Out*	8.2	5.4	0.53	1.1	7.1	(0.85)
The Walt Disney Company						
89 *Honey, I Shrunk the Kids* (W)	$145.5	$23.7	$ 5.15	$111.2	$31.0	$ 2.58
90 *Dead Poets Society* (T)	92.5	21.5	3.30	74.4	28.2	1.64
91 *The Little Mermaid* (W)	78.1	21.5	2.63	62.0	28.2	1.20
92 *Turner & Hootch* (T)	71.2	19.4	2.68	54.6	25.4	1.15
93 *Three Fugitives* (T)	36.3	18.3	0.98	29.1	24.0	0.21
94 *An Innocent Man* (T)	19.7	18.3	0.08	17.0	24.0	(0.29)
95 *Blaze* (T)	15.0	19.4	(0.22)	14.7	25.4	(0.42)
96 *New York Stories* (T)	10.7	20.4	(0.47)	8.2	26.8	(0.69)
97 *Gross Anatomy* (T)	7.8	12.9	(0.39)	8.1	16.9	(0.52)
98 *Disorganized Crime* (T)	7.8	11.8	(0.34)	7.1	15.5	(0.54)
99 *Cheetah* (W)	9.2	7.5	0.22	7.1	9.9	(0.28)
Average	$ 27.7	$17.3	$ 0.67	$ 21.6	$22.6	$(0.08)
Median	$ 10.5	$16.1	$(0.02)	$ 8.7	$21.2	$(0.54)
Standard deviation	$ 41.4	$10.1	$ 2.07	$ 31.5	$13.3	$ 1.21
Interquartile range	$ 6.9	$10.8	$(0.55)	$ 3.4	$14.1	$(0.82)
	to	to	to	to	to	to
	$ 34.3	$20.4	$ 0.99	$ 29.1	$26.8	$ 0.21

a. Net inflows consist of all revenues minus associated distribution fees and expenses.

b. One-year return is defined as: (PV of net inflows − PV of negative cost) ÷ (PV of negative cost).

c. C = Columbia Pictures; TS = Tri-Star; W = Walt Disney; T = Touchstone.

EXHIBIT 8

Histograms of 1-Year Returns for First Films and Hypothetical Sequels (Based on data calculated in Exhibit 7)

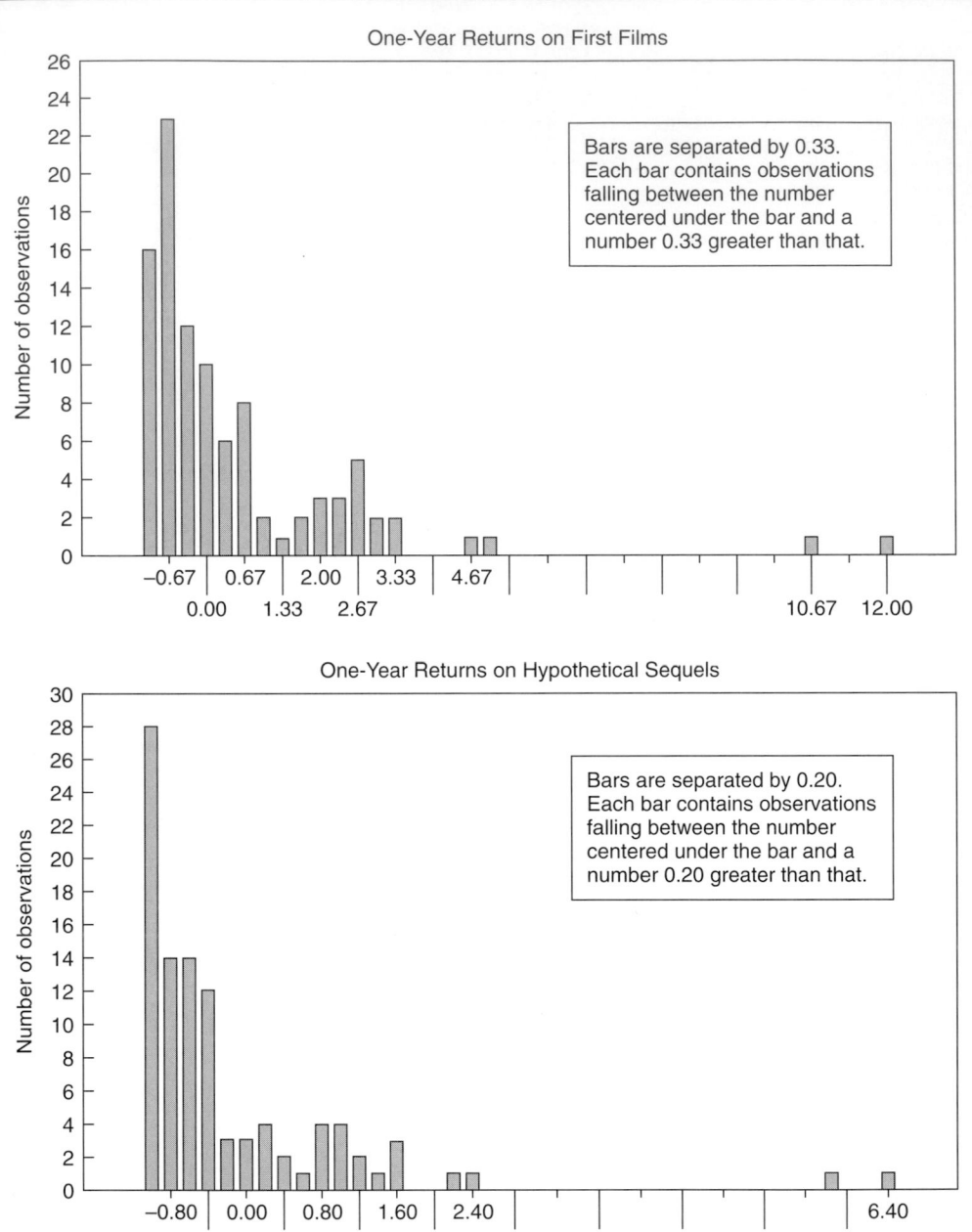

EXHIBIT 9
Summary Statistics for Samples of Films Released in 1987 and 1988[a] (millions of dollars)

1987 Data

(in 1991 dollars)	First Film					Hypothetical Sequel				
	U.S. Theater Rentals	Other Revenue	Distribution Fees	Distribution Expense	Negative Cost	U.S. Theater Rentals	Other Revenue	Distribution Fees	Distribution Expense	Negative Cost
Average	$21.3	$64.4	$22.8	$21.5	$26.3	$14.9	$48.9	$17.0	$17.4	$31.6

	First Film			Hypothetical Sequel		
	PV of Net Inflows at Year 1	1-Year Return[a]	PV of Negative Cost at Year 0	PV of Net Inflows at Year 4	1-Year Return[a]	PV of Negative Cost at Year 3
Average	$39.4	$0.71	$25.8	$30.4	$0.01	$33.8
Median	$30.9	0.04	$22.3	$24.0	(0.39)	$29.3
Standard deviation	$38.4	2.05	$ 9.4	$29.4	1.20	$12.3
Interquartile range	$11.1 to $52.1	$(0.60) to $1.22	$18.8 to $29.3	$ 8.8 to $40.2	$(0.75) to $0.31	$24.6 to $38.5

1988 Data

(in 1991 dollars)	First Film					Hypothetical Sequel				
	U.S. Theater Rentals	Other Revenue	Distribution Fees	Distribution Expense	Negative Cost	U.S. Theater Rentals	Other Revenue	Distribution Fees	Distribution Expense	Negative Cost
Average	$19.7	$60.5	$21.3	$20.5	$24.4	$13.8	$46.1	$15.9	$16.7	$29.2

	First Film			Hypothetical Sequel		
	PV of Net Inflows at Year 1	1-Year Return[a]	PV of Negative Cost at Year 0	PV of Net Inflows at Year 4	1-Year Return[a]	PV of Negative Cost at Year 3
Average	$36.4	$0.48	$23.8	$28.2	$(0.13)	$31.3
Median	$22.4	0.01	$20.3	$17.5	(0.40)	$26.6
Standard deviation	$38.2	1.37	$11.4	$29.3	0.80	$14.9
Interquartile range	$ 9.3 to $42.1	$(0.48) to $0.93	$16.9 to $24.8	$ 7.5 to $32.5	$(0.69) to $0.14	$22.2 to $32.5

a. One-year return is defined as: (PV of net inflows − PV of negative cost) ÷ (PV of negative cost).

Appendix

This appendix describes how the estimates of first films' and hypothetical sequels' financial performance were produced for Exhibits 6 and 7. (Exhibit 9 is exactly analogous.)

Description of Exhibit 6: Revenues and Costs in 1991 Dollars

Exhibit 6 presents estimates for the major categories of revenues and costs for first films released by six major studios in 1989, and corresponding estimates for a hypothetical sequel based on each. These are estimates of how each film would perform if independently financed (Arundel would finance its own productions). Figures in Exhibit 6 are based on film-by-film estimates of negative costs, U.S. rentals, and U.S. print and advertising costs published by the trade periodical *Variety* between 1990 and 1992. Estimates of ancillary market revenues, distribution fees, and distribution expenses are based on expected relationships between each of these variables and one or more items of the *Variety* data. All items in Exhibit 6 are expressed in 1991 dollars to facilitate the use of expected relationships between real variables, as derived from various datasets.

Revenues for each of the ten ancillary markets listed in Exhibit 3 are projected from estimated U.S. rentals according to relationships derived from a large sample of films. Distribution fees are computed as a fixed percentage of the revenue from each source, assuming independent financing. Distribution expenses for the U.S. theatrical run are grossed up from *Variety*'s estimates of U.S. print and advertising costs; distribution expenses for other, ancillary markets are based on expected relationships between a given market and its associated expenses. Negative costs are equal to *Variety*'s estimates, inflated to 1991 dollars.

Estimates of the performance of a hypothetical sequel for each first film were developed similarly. The sequel's estimated negative cost and U.S. theater rentals are 120% and 70%, respectively, of the corresponding items for the first film, per Exhibit 4. However, ancillary market revenues and distribution fees and expenses are not 70% of the corresponding figures for first films, but only because the underlying relationship between ancillary revenues and U.S. theater rentals is not a fixed percentage.

Description of Exhibit 7: Discounted Values and the Distribution of Returns

Exhibit 7 uses data from Exhibit 6 to compute nominal cash flows; distribute them over time; discount them; and estimate 1-year returns. In effect, Exhibit 7 treats film production as a 1-year investment. For both first films and sequels, the producer invests the present value of the negative cost; 1 year later, he or she receives the discounted value of all future net cash flows.

Films' future net cash flows consist of all ancillary revenues minus associated distribution fees and expenses, each inflated to nominal dollars (at 1.5% semiannually) and arrayed in time according to Exhibit 3. Negative costs are spread evenly over the year in which production occurs, and are partly inflated. Nominal negative costs are discounted (at 6% semiannually) to the point at which the production decision is made. Future net cash flows are discounted to a point 1 year later, at the assumed U.S. theatrical release date. The return on this 1-year investment is computed simply as net cash flow minus cost, divided by cost. Sample statistics in Exhibit 7 are based on the sample of 99 films and corresponding sequels.

Capital Projects as Real Options: An Introduction

This note introduces an approach to capital budgeting that relies on option pricing theory to analyze and evaluate capital projects. The approach is intended to supplement, not replace, capital budgeting analyses and investment criteria based on standard discounted cash flow (DCF) methodologies. For a wide range of corporate investments, insights from an options-based analysis can improve estimates of project value and, perhaps more important, enhance project management.

Motivation

Why treat a corporate investment proposal as a call option, as suggested here, rather than as a bond or an unlevered equity? The latter are easier to understand and value, and the associated analyses are easier to communicate and defend within a large organization. However, many corporate investment proposals, particularly "strategic" ones, bear a stronger resemblance to a call option than to a stock or a bond. Ignoring the optionlike features of such projects can lead to poor decisions. The most likely mistakes are (1) failing to invest in a valuable project because imbedded options are overlooked—this will make the corporation appear shortsighted; and (2) not getting the timing right, that is, committing funds earlier or later than would be ideal.

Asset-in-Place versus Options

Standard DCF valuation methodologies treat projects as follows: managers make a decision to invest (or not) and then wait to see what happens (see Figure A). For some projects this is an adequate representation of reality, but for others, it is backwards. Sometimes managers can wait and see what happens (at least some uncertainty is resolved) and *then* make a decision to invest or not (see Figure B). These two are obviously quite different. The latter is an option and the former is not. An

This note was prepared by Professor Timothy A. Luehrman.

FIGURE A
An Irreversible Commitment to Invest

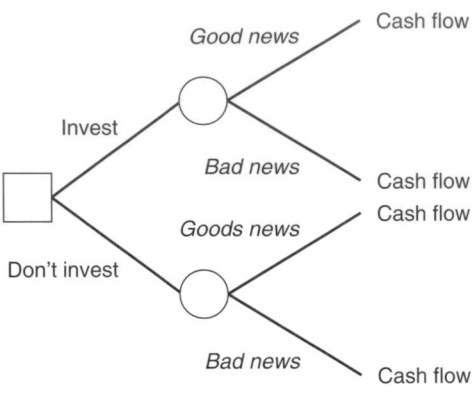

FIGURE B
An Option to Invest

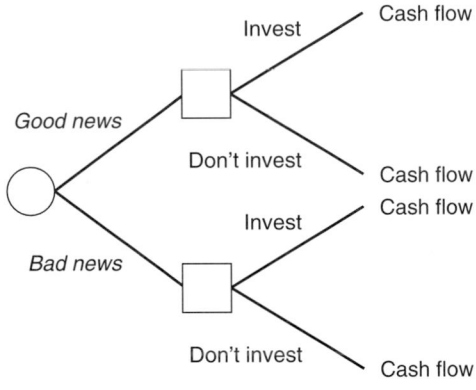

efficient capital market would not place the same value on both, and neither should a corporation.

A great many corporate investment proposals are complex and fit neither of these examples exactly. More often, they contain elements of both. An R&D program, for example, may create both a cash-producing new product and opportunities for further R&D aimed at yet more new products. Investing in a new market may lead to both immediate cash flow and future expansion opportunities. Creating a brand identity may simultaneously create future brand-extension possibilities. Replacing a first-generation technology with a second makes it possible eventually to replace the second with a third, and so forth. All of these examples contain both *assets-in-place* (cash-producing assets that can be evaluated with DCF methodologies) and *growth options* (opportunities to make future investments, which require an option-pricing methodology). Growth options and a few other decision opportunities are known, collectively, as "real" options to distinguish them from "financial" options such as exchange-traded puts and calls. Projects with high option content are likely to be misevaluated by DCF techniques: either the options will be ignored (resulting in undervaluation and under-investment), or they will be poorly approximated (resulting in either under- or over-investment in addition to poor timing and management).

A sensible solution is to separate a project's assets-in-place from its growth options and to analyze each part accordingly. Unfortunately, this is often difficult, first because a neat separation may not be possible, and second, because estimating the option valuation for a capital project is usually a difficult analytical task. This note is aimed at the second problem. It explains (1) how to set up a mapping between the simplified project and a call option; (2) how to perform an option valuation and relate it to a DCF valuation; and (3) how to extract some managerial insights from the option-pricing framework.

Preliminaries

As a starting point, this note presumes a working knowledge of basic option pricing and basic capital budgeting (see Figure C). Readers should be acquainted with puts and calls, position diagrams, determinants of call option value, option deltas, and comparative statics. This body of material is covered in most graduate-level corporate finance texts.[1] Readers also need to be familiar with incremental cash flows, time value, opportunity cost, value additivity, net present value, and the NPV rule.[2]

From this knowledge base, it is possible to construct a mapping between a corporate investment project and a call option and to see the relationship between a project's NPV and the value of an analogous call option.

Projects as Call Options

An opportunity to invest in a corporate project bears an obvious similarity to an option to invest in a corporation's stock. Both involve the right, but not the obligation, to acquire an asset by paying a certain sum of money on or before a certain time. The right to buy the stock is known as a call option. European calls are exercisable only at expiration, whereas an American call may be exercised at any time prior to expiration.

FIGURE C
Preliminaries

	Basic Option Pricing	*Basic Capital Budgeting*

To get started analyzing corporate projects as real options, you need to know:	Basic definitions
	Position diagrams
	Determinants of value
	Comparative statics
	Put-call parity
	Complications:
	   Dividends
	   Early exercise
		Incremental cash flows
		Opportunity cost
		Basic discounting:
		   Time value
		   Risk
		NPV rule

1. See, for example, Brealey and Myers, *Principles of Corporate Finance,* 4th ed. (New York: McGraw-Hill, Inc., 1991), chapter 20, pp. 483–510.

2. Ibid, Chapters 2–6, pp. 11–128.

FIGURE D
Mapping Project Characteristics Onto Call Option Variables

Project	Variable	Call Option
Expenditures required to acquire the assets	X	Exercise price
Value of the operating assets to be acquired	S	Stock price
Length of time decision may be deferred	t	Time of expiration
Riskiness of the underlying operating assets	σ^2	Variance of returns on stock
Time value of money	r	Risk-free rate of return

Obviously, an American call must be at least as valuable as an otherwise-identical European call. The Black-Scholes option pricing model gives the value of a European call on a tradable stock that pays no dividends as a function of five variables: the stock price, S; the exercise price, X; the time to expiration, t; the risk-free rate of return, r; and the standard deviation of returns on the stock, σ.

By establishing a mapping between project characteristics and the determinants of call-option value, a corporate project can be valued in the same way (see Figure D). Most projects involve making an expenditure to buy or build a productive asset. This is analogous to exercising an option: the amount expended is the exercise price (X), and the value of the asset built or acquired is the stock price (S). The length of time the company can wait without losing the opportunity is the time to expiration (t), and the riskiness of the project is reflected in the standard deviation of returns on the asset (σ). Time value is still given by the risk-free rate (r).

Relating DCF Valuation to Option Valuation

To see how option valuation is related to traditional DCF-based capital budgeting, begin by considering the typical project's NPV. NPV is simply a measure of the difference between how much an asset is worth and what it costs. When it is worth more than it costs, the project has a positive NPV and the corporation goes ahead and invests. Put another way, NPV = PV(expected net cash flows) − PV(capital expenditure), and the decision rule is "invest if NPV > 0."

Notice that NPV can be expressed as a quotient rather than a difference: Define $NPV_q \equiv$ PV(expected net cash flows) ÷ PV(capital expenditure). And similarly, the decision rule can be restated as "invest if $NPV_q > 1$." Figure E shows a line on which projects can be arrayed according to NPV_q. Those for which $NPV_q > 1$ are accepted; those for which $NPV_q < 1$ are rejected.

Figure E can be used in the same way to decide whether to exercise a call option *at expiration*. A call option should be exercised if, at expiration, the stock price exceeds the exercise price (the call is "in the money"). Here, the stock price, S, corresponds to PV(expected net cash flows) and the exercise price, X, corresponds to PV(capital expenditure). Thus, for a call option, $NPV_q = S/PV(X)$. If this quotient exceeds 1, the option should be exercised. If $NPV_q < 1$, the option is "out of the

FIGURE E
Expressing NPV as a Quotient Rather Than a Difference

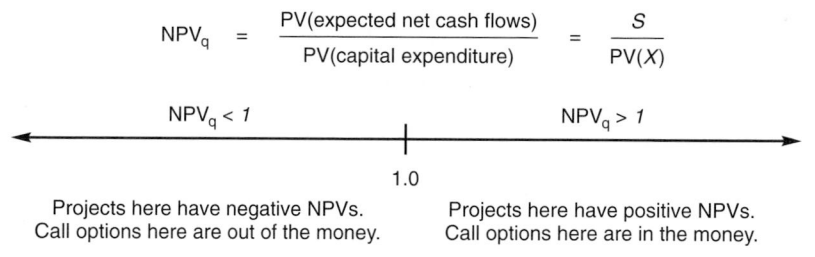

money" and should not be exercised. In effect, the traditional approach to deciding whether to invest in a project is identical to deciding whether to exercise a call option at expiration. Notice that NPV_q combines four of the five determinants of option value: $S; X; r;$ and t.[3] Note further that call option value is an increasing function of NPV_q: the higher NPV_q, the higher the call value.

When a decision cannot be delayed, the call option and the project can *both* be evaluated using simple DCF tools and rules—reality is pretty well represented by Figure A. But when the decision can be delayed, the project is like an option that has not yet expired—reality is better represented by Figure B. In this case, NPV_q still matters, but so does the riskiness of the project, which is reflected in the remaining option-pricing variable, σ.

The variability, per unit of time, of returns on the project is measured by the variance of returns, σ^2. Multiplying the variance per unit of time by the amount of time remaining gives cumulative variance, $\sigma^2 t$. Cumulative variance is a measure of how much things could change before time runs out and a decision must be made. The more cumulative variance, the more valuable the option. It may be helpful to think of a collection of balls, each with a number on it, that has been placed in an urn. Variance is the amount of variability in the set of numbers written on the balls, and t is the number of draws to be made from the urn. Cumulative variance is simply the variance for each draw times the number of draws.

Cumulative variance and NPV_q together are sufficient to value a European call option. Figure F expands Figure E to include an extra dimension for $\sigma\sqrt{t}$, which is simply the square root of cumulative variance. Options (or projects) for which either σ or t is zero have no cumulative variance and can be evaluated with standard discounted cash flow techniques, that is, with NPV or NPV_q alone. When both σ and t are nonzero, however, a DCF analysis will certainly give the wrong value and may lead to the wrong exercise (or investment) decision: in other words, Figure F should be used rather than Figure E.

The Black-Scholes model, with values for the five variables as inputs, will give a dollar value for a European call option. Some financial calculators and spreadsheet applications come preprogrammed with the Black-Scholes formula. Alternatively, Ex-

---

3. The variables r and t come into NPV_q because X is being discounted to present value. In the Black-Scholes model, discounting is performed on a continuously compounded basis, so the present value of X is actually given by $X(e^{-rt})$. Note, though, that at expiration, $t = 0$, therefore the present value of X is simply X and NPV_q is simply S/X as stated in the text. Prior to expiration, however, $X(e^{-rt}) < X$ so, all else equal, $NPV_q > S/X$.

FIGURE F
Pricing Call Options: NPV_q and Cumulative Variance

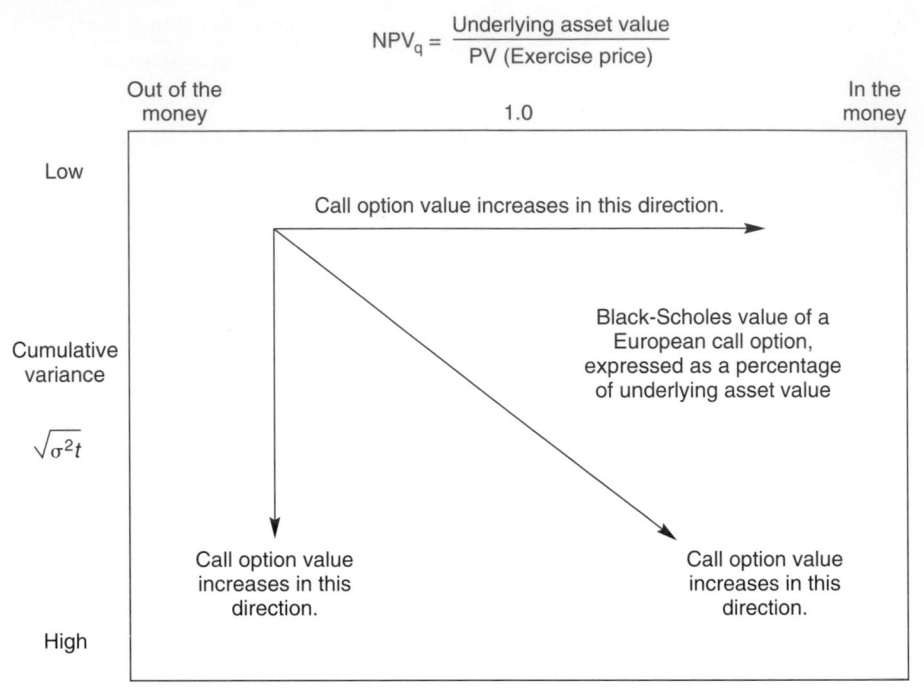

$$NPV_q = \frac{\text{Underlying asset value}}{\text{PV (Exercise price)}}$$

Out of the money

1.0

In the money

Low

Call option value increases in this direction.

Cumulative variance

$\sqrt{\sigma^2 t}$

Black-Scholes value of a European call option, expressed as a percentage of underlying asset value

Call option value increases in this direction.

Call option value increases in this direction.

High

hibit 1 tabulates European call option value as a percentage of the underlying asset value (S) for combinations of NPV_q and $\sigma\sqrt{t}$. The value of a European call can simply be looked up, without a formula or a computer.

To illustrate, consider a simple project that requires an investment of $100, in return for which the company would receive an asset that is currently worth $90. However, the asset is risky and its value is likely to change; returns on the asset have a standard deviation of about 40% per year. Moreover, the company can wait for up to 3 years before deciding to invest. Finally, suppose the risk-free rate is 5%. Viewed conventionally, this project's NPV is $90 − $100 = −$10. Clearly though, having the opportunity to wait 3 years and see what happens is valuable. In effect, the company owns a 3-year European call with an exercise price of $100 on underlying assets worth $90. NPV_q for this option is $90 ÷ [$100/(1.05)^3] = 1.04.[4] Cumulative variance is 0.40 times $\sqrt{3}$, or 0.69. Exhibit 1 shows that an option with these characteristics is worth 28.4% of the value of the underlying asset, or .284($90) = $25.56.

Managerial Decisions: Optimal Exercise

The simple project just examined had an NPV of −$10 but an option value of more than $25. Are these contradictory? What should the company do? In fact, the NPV and the option value do not contradict one another. The company should not invest in the

---

4. The difference between discrete and continuous compounding to compute the present value of X is negligible in this case.

project now. If it does, it will both forfeit the option and waste $10. But neither should it discard the project. It should wait, watch, and actively cultivate the project over the next 3 years. Although NPV < 0, the project is very promising because $NPV_q > 1$. That is to say, although $X > S$, these two variables are relatively close to one another because $S > PV(X)$. They are separated only by time value. Over time, we expect the market value of the asset, S, to increase at some rate greater than r (no one would be willing to hold the asset otherwise).[5] By the end of 3 years, there is a good chance that the NPV will exceed zero and the option will be exercised. In any event, at expiration, the option will be worth the greater of zero or $S - X$. In the meantime, the option on the project really is worth $25, not −$10, provided the company does not exercise it (invest) now.

The difference between NPV and NPV_q contains a useful managerial insight. As time runs out, these two must converge to some agreement: at expiration, they will be either greater than 0 and 1, respectively, or less than these values. But prior to expiration, NPV_q may be positive even when NPV is negative (just as in the preceding example). Figure G shows this diagrammatically. All options that fall in the right half of Figure G have $NPV_q > 1$. But not all of these are in the money; that is, the NPV of an "exercise-now" strategy is positive for some and negative for others. The locus of points that corresponds to NPV(exercise now) = 0 is a curve that starts at the top,

FIGURE G
Mapping Projects into Call-Option Space

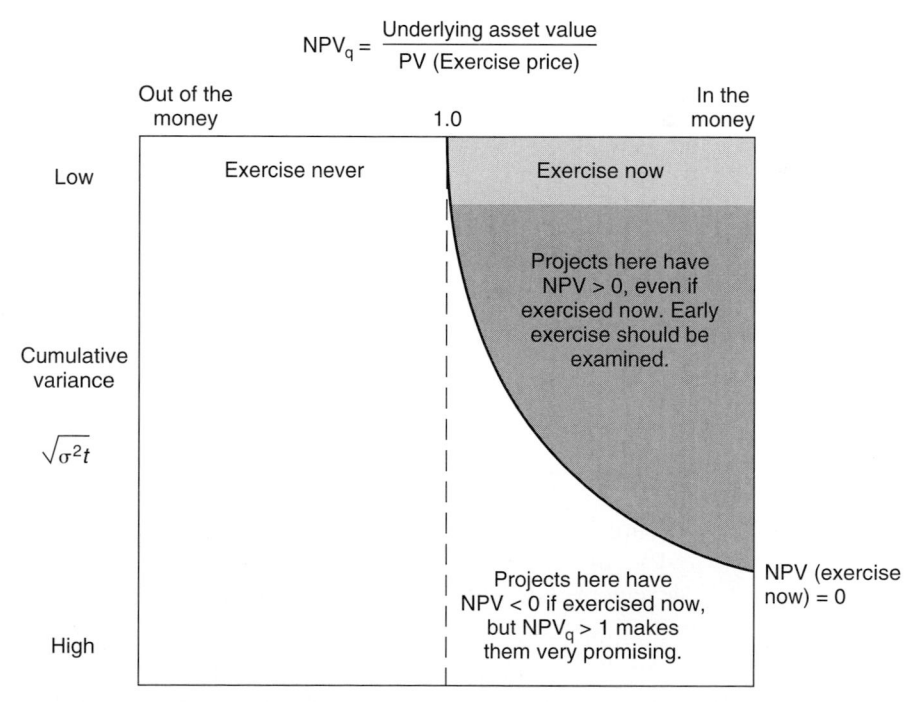

---

5. This argument assumes that the asset is like a stock that pays no dividends. The exception to this case is quite important and is treated below.

where cumulative variance is zero and $NPV_q = 1$, and runs down and to the right.[6] Options that fall above this curve have both $NPV > 0$ and $NPV_q > 1$; they are in the money. Those below the curve have $NPV_q > 1$ but $NPV < 0$; they are out of the money.

We can now generate three different managerial prescriptions for options with $NPV_q > 1$, each corresponding to a different region in the right half of Figure G. At the very top right (light shading) are options with no cumulative variance—either time has run out or there is no variance. These options are in the money ($NPV > 0$) and should be exercised immediately—there is no value in waiting.

Just below these (darker shading) are options that are in the money, but for which there is still some cumulative variance. The company should wait, if possible, to exercise these options. Early exercise may be desirable when the underlying asset is "wasting." If, for example, its value is subject to erosion due to competitors' actions, or if it is already paying out cash, then it is analogous to a dividend-paying stock. Holders of American call options on a dividend-paying stock sometimes will find it optimal to exercise early, prior to expiration. This is a way to capture the cash being paid out or prevent the value erosion. However, by exercising early, the holder of an American call option foregoes the interest on the exercise price. Hence, a tradeoff must be evaluated in order to determine the better course of action. The distinction between American and European calls is very important for real options. Real options typically can be exercised early, and often, the value of the underlying asset is subject to erosion by competitors' actions or technical or demographic changes.[7]

Finally, at the bottom of the right half of Figure G (no shading) are options like the simple example presented above; they are very promising because $NPV_q > 1$ even though $NPV < 0$. If, as time runs out, neither S nor X changes, then NPV_q will fall and these options will expire unexercised. But among a large sample of such projects, we should expect many to end up in the money, especially if they receive active attention and management.

A Stylized Map: The "Tomato Garden"

Pushing the logic of Figure G a bit further, we can divide the call-option space roughly into six regions, each corresponding to a different managerial prescription as shown in Figure H. The right side of Figure H is divided into regions I, II, and III, in all of which $NPV_q > 1$. These correspond to the three regions in the right half of Figure G just described. The left half of Figure H is divided symmetrically, into regions IV, V, and VI, in all of which $NPV_q < 1$. In region VI at the top, cumulative variance is zero, so these options are never exercised. Region V contains relatively unpromising options. For them, NPV_q and/or $\sigma\sqrt{t}$ is low. Not many of these projects will make it, regardless of the attention they may receive. In region IV are options for which either NPV_q or $\sigma\sqrt{t}$ is reasonably high, but the other is low. These projects require active development to end up in the money. In general, projects will tend to move upward in

---

6. The location of this curve varies with r and σ. The curve is located by holding r and σ constant as t varies, and solving for the NPV_q that corresponds to $NPV = 0$. Note that in the extreme case of $r = 0$, the curve is a vertical line passing through $NPV_q = 1$. As r increases, the slope of the curve decreases, bending to the right, as shown in Figure G.

7. For more on American calls and dividend-paying stocks, see Brealey and Myers, *Principles of Corporate Finance,* 4th ed. (New York: McGraw-Hill, Inc., 1991), chapter 21, pp. 526–529.

FIGURE H
A Stylized Mapping of Projects into Call-Option Space

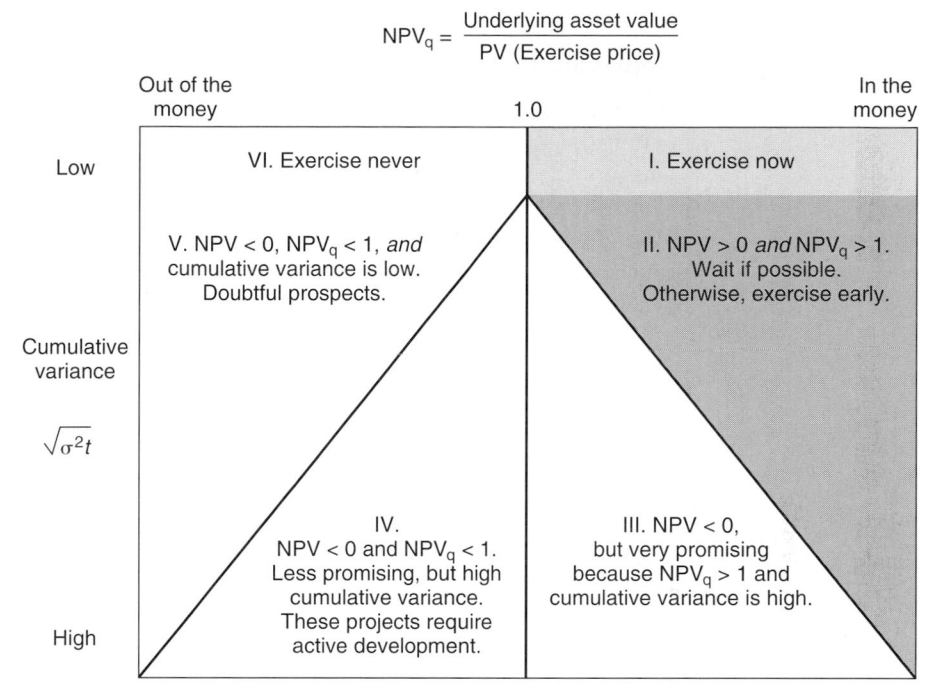

$$NPV_q = \frac{\text{Underlying asset value}}{\text{PV (Exercise price)}}$$

Figure H as time passes, because time runs out and uncertainty is resolved. Managers have two jobs: (1) to try to move projects to the right before time runs out, and (2) to avoid making mistakes in their exercise (investment) decisions in the meantime.

The analogy of a tomato garden located in an unpredictable climate may be a helpful memory cue. Managers are the gardeners; they do the cultivating and eventually decide which tomatoes to pick. At one extreme are perfect, ripe tomatoes (region I of Figure H), which should be picked and eaten immediately. At the other extreme are rotten tomatoes (region VI), which should never be picked. In between are many different tomatoes with varying prospects. Those in region II are edible and could be picked, but they would improve with more time on the vine. The gardener will pick them early only if competitors (e.g., squirrels) are likely to get them otherwise. Tomatoes in region III are not edible and should not be picked regardless of competitors. Over time, however, many in region III will ripen and eventually be picked. Region IV contains fruit that is less promising and may not ripen before the season is over. Nevertheless, with more sun or water, fewer weeds, or just good luck, some of these tomatoes may become edible. Finally, region V contains late blossoms and small green tomatoes that have not much chance of growing and ripening before the season ends.

Practical Issues

Using option pricing models to analyze capital projects presents some practical problems. Comparatively few of these have completely satisfactory solutions; on the other hand, some insight is gained just from formulating and articulating the problems. Still more, perhaps, is available from approximations. To interpret an analysis, it helps to remain aware of whether it represents an exact answer to an approximated (simplified) problem, or an approximate answer to an exact problem. Either may be useful.

Simplifying Complex Projects

Real corporate projects, especially long-horizon ones, are complex. They are most often combinations of assets-in-place and options. Further, the options are nested; that is, managers face a *sequence* of serially dependent choices. It helps to simplify such problems, not only for formal analytical purposes, but also to make them understandable and discussible within the group of responsible managers. Further, an unsimplified problem may be unique (and practically insoluble), whereas a simplified problem may fit into a larger class of problems, which will provide hints or boundaries for a solution.

Most real option problems can either be abstracted as fairly simple call options, or broken into pieces, each one of which is a fairly simple call option. A useful guide in simplifying is to search for the primary uncertainty against which managers select. That is, by waiting and watching, what is the main thing a manger learns, and how will he or she exploit the learning? Some projects have optionlike characteristics (e.g., the project is risky and managers clearly have a choice about whether to undertake it), but as long as the company does nothing, it learns nothing. For such projects, a DCF approach may be appropriate; in effect, the company has to make the investment in order to resolve the uncertainty (such projects resemble Figure A). However, for many other projects, the resolution of a small set of uncertainties determines the outcome, and at least some can be resolved without making the entire investment. Such projects resemble Figure B, and identifying the key uncertainties is the first step toward a useful simplification.

Another useful approach is to construct simplifications such that the simplified project is both priceable and either dominating or dominated, compared to the real project. A dominated project is one that is clearly less valuable than the real project. If it also can be priced, then its value provides a lower bound for the project value. For example, a simple European call is clearly dominated by a (more realistic) American call on an asset exposed to erosion by competitors' investments. Dominating simplifications similarly provide an upper bound for project value. Sometimes it is possible to construct and compute both upper and lower bounds.

Estimating Volatility

The option-pricing input managers are least accustomed to estimating is variance, or standard deviation. For a real option, σ cannot be looked up in a table or newspaper, and most people do not have highly developed intuition about, for example, the annual variance of returns on assets associated with entering a new market. Nevertheless, estimating σ is not a completely hopeless task. There are at least three reasonable approaches:

1. *Take a guess.* Systematic risk (β) and total risk (σ) are positively correlated in large samples of operating assets; those with high asset betas are likelier to have higher standard deviations. What is a high standard deviation? Returns on broad-based U.S. stock market indices had a standard deviation of about 20% per year for much of 1986–1994, with exceptions (upward spikes) associated with events like the 1987 market crash and the 1990–1991 Persian Gulf crisis. Individual projects will have higher volatilities than a diversified portfolio of

the same projects. Volatility of 20–30% per year is not remarkably high for a single project.

2. *Gather some data.* Volatility can be estimated for some businesses using historical data on investment returns in certain industries. Alternatively, implied volatilities can be computed from quoted option prices for a very large number of traded equities. The length, breadth, and quality of such data have improved greatly in recent years and should continue to do so. These data do require some adjustment, however. Equity returns are levered and are therefore more volatile than underlying asset returns.

3. *Simulate σ.* Spreadsheet-based projections of a project's future cash flows, together with Monte Carlo simulation techniques, can be used to synthesize a probability distribution for project returns. Inputs include estimated volatilities for specific items, such as commodity prices or exchange rates. Using these inputs, a computer simulates the project and, in the process, synthesizes a probability distribution for desired output variables, such as project returns. From the synthesized probability distribution, σ can be estimated.[8] Simulation software for desktop computers is commercially available and designed to work as an add-in with popular spreadsheet applications.

Some insight is available from Figure H even without precise estimates of σ. Simply knowing whether cumulative variance is high or low is enough to locate a project in one part or another of Figure H and, with some knowledge of NPV_q, to suggest a managerial course of action.

Checking Models and Distributions

All formal option pricing models, including Black-Scholes, assume that the riskiness of an asset can be expressed as a probability distribution for returns (or prices or payouts) for the asset. Some of the assumed distributions are elegantly simple, such as the lognormal distribution assumed by Black-Scholes. But corporate data for some real projects are inelegant and may be inconsistent with, for example, a lognormal distribution. One approach to this problem is to figure out in which direction a simplified distribution biases the analysis and then interpret the output accordingly, as an upper or lower bound for the actual project's value. Another is to choose a model, if one exists, based on a more appropriate distribution. Many models have been constructed and solved, though most are mathematically sophisticated and unwieldy for use with real options.[9]

More fundamental than the particular distribution assumed by a given model is the type of world being modeled. The Black-Scholes world, for example, is one in which underlying assets are securities that are traded continuously. Real options involve underlying assets that are not traded continuously or, in some cases, not traded at all. For such assets, the five variables (six, if dividends are allowed) of the Black-Scholes model are not sufficient to characterize and price a call option. Whether one model or another remains useful as a way to price a simplified version of the project is a

---

8. Skillful simulation requires knowledge of probability and statistics, including the forms of distributions, elementary sampling theory, differences between time series and cross-sectional analyses, and so forth. A useful reference is Kelton and Law, *Simulation Modeling and Analysis* (New York: McGraw-Hill, Inc., 1991).

9. A bibliography of sophisticated models is given in Merton, *Continuous-Time Finance* (Cambridge, Mass.: Basil Blackwell, Inc., 1990). A more narrowly focused reference is Wilmott, Dewynne, and Howison, *Option Pricing: Mathematical Models and Computation* (Oxford: Oxford Financial Press, 1993).

judgment the analyst must make. One alternative to such modeling is brute force, in the form of computing power. High-speed computers and advanced spreadsheet software make it possible to simulate some projects as a complicated decision tree. Decision-tree analysis is not, formally speaking, option pricing, but if well executed, it provides a better treatment of uncertainty and of managers' scope for decision making than conventional DCF analysis alone.

Interpreting Results

To execute a useful analysis, simplification is essential. To interpret the results, some sophistication is equally essential. This typically involves layering complexity back into the problem, in the form of sensitivity analyses and the conditioning or qualifying of inferences. To arrive at Figure H, we first took a complicated project and simplified it enough to regard it as a European call option. Then, drawing on an understanding of option pricing and capital budgeting, we further simplified the analysis by combining five variables into two. But now, after valuing a project and locating it in Figure H, we should put some of the complexity back in and begin looking at sensitivity analyses. This will help us understand which of a project's characteristics cause it to fall where it does on the map. For example, in region III, is cumulative variance high primarily because of σ or t? Which of the elements of NPV_q is most readily managed—net cash inflows (S) or capital expenditures (X)? And so forth. The process is iterative. The results of one analysis suggest a further one until the process converges on an understanding, in both financial and managerial terms, of the project.

EXHIBIT 1

Option-Pricing Table: Black-Scholes Value of a European Call Option, Expressed as a Percentage of Underlying Asset Value

NPV_q = (Underlying asset value)/PV(Exercise price)

Rows: Cumulative variance: $\sigma[sqrt(t)]$

	0.30	0.35	0.40	0.45	0.50	0.55	0.60	0.65	0.70	0.75	0.80	0.82	0.84	0.86	0.88	0.90	0.92	0.94	0.96	0.98	1.00	1.02	1.04	1.06	1.08	1.10	1.12	1.14	1.16	1.18	1.20	1.25	1.30	1.35	1.40	1.45	1.50	1.75	2.00	2.50	
0.05	0.0	0.0	0.0	0.0	0.0	0.0	0.0	0.0	0.0	0.0	0.0	0.0	0.0	0.0	0.0	0.0	0.1	0.3	0.6	1.2	2.0	3.1	4.5	6.0	7.5	9.1	10.7	12.3	13.8	15.3	16.7	20.0	23.1	25.9	28.6	31.0	33.3	42.9	50.0	60.0	0.05
0.10	0.0	0.0	0.0	0.0	0.0	0.0	0.0	0.0	0.0	0.0	0.0	0.1	0.2	0.3	0.5	0.8	1.2	1.7	2.3	3.1	4.0	5.0	6.1	7.3	8.6	10.0	11.3	12.7	14.1	15.4	16.8	20.0	23.1	25.9	28.6	31.0	33.3	42.9	50.0	60.0	0.10
0.15	0.0	0.0	0.0	0.0	0.0	0.0	0.0	0.0	0.1	0.2	0.5	0.7	1.0	1.3	1.7	2.2	2.8	3.5	4.2	5.1	6.0	7.0	8.0	9.1	10.2	11.4	12.6	13.8	15.0	16.2	17.4	20.4	23.3	26.0	28.6	31.1	33.3	42.9	50.0	60.0	0.15
0.20	0.0	0.0	0.0	0.0	0.0	0.0	0.0	0.1	0.4	0.8	1.5	1.9	2.3	2.8	3.4	4.0	4.7	5.4	6.2	7.1	8.0	8.9	9.9	10.9	11.9	13.0	14.1	15.2	16.3	17.4	18.5	21.2	23.9	26.4	28.9	31.2	33.5	42.9	50.0	60.0	0.20
0.25	0.0	0.0	0.0	0.0	0.0	0.1	0.2	0.5	1.0	1.8	2.8	3.3	3.9	4.5	5.2	5.9	6.6	7.4	8.2	9.1	9.9	10.9	11.8	12.8	13.7	14.7	15.7	16.7	17.7	18.7	19.8	22.3	24.7	27.1	29.4	31.7	33.8	42.9	50.0	60.0	0.25
0.30	0.0	0.0	0.0	0.1	0.1	0.3	0.7	1.2	2.0	3.1	4.4	5.0	5.7	6.3	7.0	7.8	8.6	9.4	10.2	11.1	11.9	12.8	13.7	14.6	15.6	16.5	17.4	18.4	19.3	20.3	21.2	23.5	25.8	28.1	30.2	32.3	34.3	43.1	50.1	60.0	0.30
0.35	0.0	0.0	0.1	0.2	0.4	0.8	1.4	2.3	3.3	4.6	6.2	6.8	7.5	8.2	9.0	9.8	10.6	11.4	12.2	13.0	13.9	14.8	15.6	16.5	17.4	18.3	19.2	20.1	21.0	21.9	22.7	24.9	27.1	29.2	31.2	33.2	35.1	43.5	50.2	60.0	0.35
0.40	0.0	0.1	0.2	0.5	0.9	1.6	2.4	3.5	4.8	6.3	8.0	8.7	9.4	10.2	11.0	11.7	12.5	13.4	14.2	15.0	15.9	16.7	17.5	18.4	19.2	20.1	20.9	21.8	22.6	23.5	24.3	26.4	28.4	30.4	32.3	34.2	36.0	44.0	50.5	60.1	0.40
0.45	0.1	0.2	0.5	1.0	1.7	2.6	3.7	5.0	6.5	8.1	9.9	10.6	11.4	12.2	12.9	13.7	14.5	15.3	16.2	17.0	17.8	18.6	19.4	20.3	21.1	21.9	22.7	23.5	24.3	25.1	25.9	27.9	29.8	31.7	33.5	35.3	37.0	44.6	50.8	60.2	0.45
0.50	0.2	0.5	1.0	1.7	2.6	3.7	5.1	6.6	8.2	10.0	11.8	12.6	13.4	14.2	14.9	15.7	16.5	17.3	18.1	18.9	19.7	20.5	21.3	22.1	22.9	23.7	24.5	25.3	26.1	26.8	27.6	29.5	31.3	33.1	34.8	36.4	38.1	45.3	51.3	60.4	0.50
0.55	0.5	1.0	1.7	2.6	3.8	5.1	6.6	8.3	10.0	11.9	13.8	14.6	15.4	16.1	16.9	17.7	18.5	19.3	20.1	20.9	21.7	22.4	23.2	24.0	24.8	25.5	26.3	27.0	27.8	28.5	29.2	31.0	32.8	34.5	36.1	37.7	39.2	46.1	51.9	60.7	0.55
0.60	0.9	1.6	2.5	3.7	5.1	6.6	8.3	10.1	11.9	13.8	15.8	16.6	17.4	18.1	18.9	19.7	20.5	21.3	22.0	22.8	23.6	24.3	25.1	25.8	26.6	27.3	28.1	28.8	29.5	30.2	30.9	32.6	34.3	35.9	37.5	39.0	40.4	47.0	52.5	61.0	0.60
0.65	1.4	2.4	3.6	4.9	6.5	8.2	10.0	11.9	13.8	15.8	17.8	18.6	19.3	20.1	20.9	21.7	22.5	23.2	24.0	24.7	25.5	26.2	27.0	27.7	28.4	29.1	29.8	30.5	31.2	31.9	32.6	34.2	35.8	37.4	38.9	40.3	41.7	48.0	53.3	61.4	0.65
0.70	2.1	3.3	4.7	6.3	8.1	9.9	11.9	13.8	15.8	17.8	19.8	20.6	21.3	22.1	22.9	23.6	24.4	25.2	25.9	26.6	27.4	28.1	28.8	29.5	30.2	30.9	31.6	32.3	32.9	33.6	34.2	35.8	37.3	38.8	40.3	41.6	43.0	49.0	54.0	61.9	0.70
0.75	3.0	4.4	6.1	7.9	9.8	11.7	13.7	15.8	17.8	19.8	21.8	22.5	23.3	24.1	24.8	25.6	26.3	27.1	27.8	28.5	29.2	29.9	30.6	31.3	32.0	32.7	33.3	34.0	34.6	35.3	35.9	37.4	38.9	40.3	41.7	43.0	44.3	50.0	54.9	62.4	0.75
0.80	4.0	5.7	7.5	9.5	11.5	13.6	15.7	17.7	19.8	21.8	23.7	24.5	25.3	26.0	26.8	27.5	28.3	29.0	29.7	30.4	31.1	31.8	32.4	33.1	33.8	34.4	35.1	35.7	36.3	36.9	37.5	39.0	40.4	41.8	43.1	44.4	45.6	51.1	55.8	63.0	0.80
0.85	5.1	7.1	9.1	11.2	13.3	15.5	17.6	19.7	21.8	23.8	25.7	26.5	27.2	28.0	28.7	29.4	30.2	30.9	31.6	32.2	32.9	33.6	34.2	34.9	35.5	36.2	36.8	37.4	38.0	38.6	39.2	40.6	41.9	43.3	44.5	45.8	46.9	52.2	56.7	63.6	0.85
0.90	6.4	8.5	10.7	13.0	15.2	17.4	19.6	21.7	23.8	25.8	27.7	28.4	29.2	29.9	30.6	31.3	32.0	32.7	33.4	34.1	34.7	35.4	36.0	36.6	37.3	37.9	38.5	39.1	39.6	40.2	40.8	42.1	43.5	44.7	46.0	47.1	48.3	53.3	57.6	64.3	0.90
0.95	7.8	10.1	12.5	14.8	17.1	19.4	21.6	23.7	25.7	27.7	29.6	30.4	31.1	31.8	32.5	33.2	33.9	34.6	35.2	35.9	36.5	37.2	37.8	38.4	39.0	39.6	40.1	40.7	41.3	41.8	42.4	43.7	45.0	46.2	47.4	48.5	49.6	54.5	58.6	65.0	0.95
1.00	9.3	11.8	14.3	16.7	19.1	21.4	23.6	25.7	27.7	29.7	31.6	32.3	33.0	33.7	34.4	35.1	35.7	36.4	37.0	37.7	38.3	38.9	39.5	40.1	40.7	41.2	41.8	42.4	42.9	43.4	44.0	45.2	46.5	47.6	48.8	49.9	50.9	55.6	59.5	65.7	1.00
1.05	10.9	13.6	16.1	18.6	21.0	23.3	25.6	27.7	29.7	31.6	33.5	34.2	34.9	35.6	36.2	36.9	37.6	38.2	38.8	39.4	40.0	40.6	41.2	41.8	42.4	42.9	43.5	44.0	44.5	45.0	45.5	46.8	48.0	49.1	50.2	51.2	52.2	56.7	60.5	66.5	1.05
1.10	12.6	15.4	18.0	20.6	23.0	25.3	27.5	29.6	31.6	33.5	35.4	36.1	36.7	37.4	38.1	38.7	39.3	40.0	40.6	41.2	41.8	42.3	42.9	43.5	44.0	44.5	45.1	45.6	46.1	46.6	47.1	48.3	49.4	50.5	51.6	52.6	53.5	57.9	61.5	67.2	1.10
1.15	14.4	17.2	20.0	22.5	25.0	27.3	29.5	31.6	33.6	35.4	37.2	37.9	38.6	39.2	39.9	40.5	41.1	41.7	42.3	42.9	43.5	44.0	44.6	45.1	45.6	46.2	46.7	47.2	47.7	48.2	48.6	49.8	50.9	51.9	52.9	53.9	54.9	59.0	62.5	68.0	1.15
1.20	16.2	19.1	21.9	24.5	27.0	29.3	31.5	33.6	35.5	37.3	39.1	39.7	40.4	41.0	41.7	42.3	42.9	43.5	44.0	44.6	45.1	45.7	46.2	46.7	47.3	47.8	48.3	48.7	49.2	49.7	50.1	51.3	52.3	53.3	54.3	55.2	56.1	60.2	63.5	68.8	1.20
1.25	18.1	21.1	23.9	26.5	29.0	31.3	33.5	35.5	37.4	39.2	40.9	41.5	42.2	42.8	43.4	44.0	44.6	45.2	45.7	46.3	46.8	47.3	47.8	48.4	48.8	49.3	49.8	50.3	50.7	51.2	51.6	52.7	53.7	54.7	55.7	56.6	57.4	61.3	64.5	69.6	1.25
1.30	20.0	23.0	25.9	28.5	31.0	33.3	35.4	37.4	39.3	41.0	42.7	43.3	43.9	44.5	45.1	45.7	46.3	46.8	47.4	47.9	48.4	48.9	49.4	49.9	50.4	50.9	51.3	51.8	52.2	52.7	53.1	54.1	55.1	56.1	57.0	57.9	58.7	62.4	65.5	70.4	1.30
1.35	21.9	25.0	27.9	30.5	33.0	35.2	37.3	39.3	41.1	42.8	44.4	45.1	45.7	46.3	46.8	47.4	47.9	48.5	49.0	49.5	50.0	50.5	51.0	51.5	52.0	52.4	52.9	53.3	53.7	54.1	54.6	55.6	56.5	57.4	58.3	59.1	59.9	63.5	66.5	71.1	1.35
1.40	23.9	27.0	29.9	32.5	34.9	37.1	39.2	41.1	42.9	44.6	46.2	46.8	47.4	47.9	48.5	49.0	49.6	50.1	50.6	51.1	51.6	52.1	52.6	53.0	53.5	53.9	54.3	54.8	55.2	55.6	56.0	56.9	57.9	58.7	59.6	60.4	61.2	64.6	67.5	71.9	1.40
1.45	25.8	29.0	31.9	34.5	36.9	39.1	41.1	43.0	44.7	46.4	47.9	48.5	49.0	49.6	50.1	50.7	51.2	51.7	52.2	52.7	53.2	53.6	54.1	54.5	55.0	55.4	55.8	56.2	56.6	57.0	57.4	58.3	59.2	60.0	60.9	61.6	62.4	65.7	68.4	72.7	1.45
1.50	27.8	31.0	33.8	36.4	38.8	40.9	42.9	44.8	46.5	48.1	49.6	50.1	50.7	51.2	51.8	52.3	52.8	53.3	53.7	54.2	54.7	55.1	55.6	56.0	56.4	56.8	57.2	57.6	58.0	58.4	58.8	59.7	60.5	61.3	62.1	62.9	63.6	66.8	69.4	73.5	1.50
1.55	29.8	33.0	35.8	38.4	40.7	42.8	44.8	46.6	48.2	49.8	51.2	51.8	52.3	52.8	53.3	53.8	54.3	54.8	55.3	55.7	56.2	56.6	57.0	57.4	57.8	58.2	58.6	59.0	59.4	59.7	60.1	61.0	61.8	62.6	63.3	64.1	64.7	67.8	70.3	74.3	1.55
1.60	31.8	35.0	37.8	40.3	42.6	44.6	46.5	48.3	49.9	51.4	52.8	53.4	53.9	54.4	54.9	55.4	55.9	56.3	56.8	57.2	57.6	58.0	58.5	58.9	59.2	59.6	60.0	60.4	60.7	61.1	61.4	62.3	63.1	63.8	64.5	65.2	65.9	68.8	71.3	75.1	1.60
1.65	33.8	36.9	39.7	42.2	44.4	46.4	48.3	50.0	51.6	53.1	54.4	54.9	55.4	55.9	56.4	56.9	57.3	57.8	58.2	58.6	59.1	59.5	59.9	60.2	60.6	61.0	61.4	61.7	62.1	62.4	62.7	63.5	64.3	65.0	65.7	66.4	67.0	69.9	72.2	75.9	1.65
1.70	35.8	38.9	41.6	44.0	46.2	48.2	50.0	51.7	53.2	54.7	56.0	56.5	57.0	57.5	57.9	58.4	58.8	59.2	59.7	60.1	60.5	60.9	61.2	61.6	62.0	62.3	62.7	63.0	63.4	63.7	64.0	64.8	65.5	66.2	66.9	67.5	68.2	70.9	73.1	76.6	1.70
1.75	37.7	40.8	43.5	45.9	48.0	50.0	51.7	53.4	54.8	56.2	57.5	58.0	58.5	58.9	59.4	59.8	60.2	60.7	61.1	61.5	61.8	62.2	62.6	62.9	63.3	63.6	64.0	64.3	64.6	64.9	65.3	66.0	66.7	67.4	68.0	68.7	69.2	71.9	74.0	77.4	1.75
2.00	47.3	50.1	52.5	54.6	56.5	58.2	59.7	61.1	62.4	63.6	64.6	65.0	65.4	65.8	66.2	66.6	66.9	67.3	67.6	67.9	68.3	68.6	68.9	69.2	69.5	69.8	70.0	70.3	70.6	70.8	71.1	71.7	72.3	72.9	73.4	73.9	74.4	76.5	78.3	81.0	2.00
2.25	56.1	58.6	60.7	62.5	64.1	65.6	66.8	68.0	69.1	70.0	70.9	71.3	71.6	71.9	72.2	72.5	72.8	73.1	73.4	73.7	73.9	74.2	74.4	74.7	74.9	75.2	75.4	75.6	75.8	76.0	76.3	76.8	77.2	77.7	78.1	78.5	78.9	80.6	82.1	84.3	2.25
2.50	64.0	66.1	67.9	69.4	70.8	72.0	73.1	74.0	74.9	75.7	76.4	76.7	77.0	77.2	77.5	77.7	78.0	78.2	78.4	78.7	78.9	79.1	79.3	79.5	79.7	79.9	80.0	80.2	80.4	80.6	80.7	81.1	81.5	81.9	82.2	82.6	82.9	84.3	85.4	87.2	2.50
2.75	70.9	72.7	74.2	75.4	76.6	77.5	78.4	79.2	79.9	80.5	81.1	81.4	81.6	81.8	82.0	82.2	82.4	82.6	82.7	82.9	83.1	83.3	83.4	83.6	83.7	83.9	84.0	84.2	84.3	84.4	84.6	84.9	85.2	85.5	85.8	86.0	86.3	87.4	88.3	89.7	2.75
3.00	76.9	78.3	79.5	80.5	81.4	82.2	82.9	83.5	84.1	84.6	85.1	85.3	85.4	85.6	85.8	85.9	86.1	86.2	86.4	86.5	86.6	86.8	86.9	87.0	87.1	87.3	87.4	87.5	87.6	87.7	87.8	88.1	88.3	88.5	88.8	89.0	89.2	90.0	90.7	91.8	3.00
3.50	86.0	86.9	87.6	88.3	88.8	89.3	89.7	90.1	90.5	90.8	91.1	91.2	91.3	91.4	91.5	91.6	91.6	91.7	91.8	91.9	92.0	92.1	92.1	92.2	92.3	92.4	92.4	92.5	92.6	92.6	92.7	92.8	93.0	93.1	93.3	93.4	93.5	94.0	94.4	95.1	3.50
4.00	92.0	92.5	92.9	93.3	93.6	93.9	94.2	94.4	94.6	94.8	94.9	95.0	95.0	95.1	95.2	95.2	95.3	95.3	95.4	95.4	95.4	95.5	95.5	95.6	95.6	95.7	95.7	95.7	95.8	95.8	95.8	95.9	96.0	96.1	96.2	96.2	96.3	96.6	96.8	97.2	4.00
4.50	95.7	96.0	96.2	96.4	96.6	96.7	96.9	97.0	97.1	97.2	97.3	97.3	97.3	97.4	97.4	97.4	97.5	97.5	97.5	97.5	97.6	97.6	97.6	97.6	97.6	97.7	97.7	97.7	97.7	97.8	97.8	97.8	97.9	97.9	97.9	98.0	98.0	98.2	98.3	98.5	4.50
5.00	97.8	97.9	98.1	98.2	98.3	98.3	98.4	98.5	98.5	98.6	98.6	98.6	98.6	98.7	98.7	98.7	98.7	98.7	98.7	98.7	98.8	98.8	98.8	98.8	98.8	98.8	98.8	98.8	98.8	98.9	98.9	98.9	98.9	98.9	99.0	99.0	99.0	99.1	99.1	99.2	5.00
6.00	99.5	99.5	99.6	99.6	99.6	99.6	99.7	99.7	99.7	99.7	99.7	99.7	99.7	99.7	99.7	99.7	99.7	99.7	99.7	99.7	99.7	99.7	99.7	99.7	99.7	99.7	99.7	99.7	99.7	99.8	99.8	99.8	99.8	99.8	99.8	99.8	99.8	99.8	99.8	99.8	6.00

Note: Values in the table represent percentages of underlying asset values: e.g., 39.3 denotes a call option worth 39.3% of the underlying asset value.

Values in the table were computed from the Black-Scholes option pricing model.

Source: The format of the table was adapted from Brealy and Myers, *Principles of Corporate Finance,* 4th edition (New York: McGraw-Hill, Inc., 1991), Appendix Table 6, pp. AP12–13.

Pioneer Petroleum Corporation

One of the critical problems confronting management and the board of Pioneer Petroleum Corporation in July 1991 was the determination of a minimum acceptable rate of return on new capital investments. The company's basic capital budgeting approach was to accept all proposed investments with a positive net present value when discounted at the appropriate cost of capital. At issue was how the appropriate discount rate would be determined.

The company was weighing two alternative approaches for determining a minimum rate of return: (1) a single cutoff rate based on the company's overall weighted average cost of capital, and (2) a system of multiple cutoff rates that reflected the risk-profit characteristics of the several businesses or economic sectors in which the company's subsidiaries operated. The issue had assumed increased importance because of management's decision to extend the use of the cutoff rate to the evaluation of existing operations and investments. It was planned to evaluate divisional managers on the basis of their net profits after the deduction of a charge for capital employed by the division.

Pioneer Petroleum had been formed in 1924 through the merger of several formerly independent firms operating in the oil refining, pipeline transportation, and industrial chemicals fields. Over the next 60 years, the company integrated vertically into exploration and production of crude oil and marketing refined petroleum products, and horizontally into plastics, agricultural chemicals, and real estate development. It was restructured in 1985 as a hydrocarbons-based company, concentrating on oil, gas, coal, and petrochemicals. Pioneer was one of the primary producers of Alaskan crude, and in 1990, Alaska provided 60% of Pioneer's domestic petroleum liquids production. Pioneer was also one of the lowest-cost refiners on the West Coast and had an extensive West Coast marketing network. Pioneer's Alaskan crude production provided all of the crude oil for its West Coast refining and marketing operations. This integration required collaboration and coordination among divisions to optimize overall performance and to decrease overall risk.

In 1990 total revenues exceeded $15.6 billion and net income was over $1.5 billion. (See Exhibit 1 for a financial summary of recent operations.) Volatile oil prices were a major concern for Pioneer. In 1990, for example, the price of West Texas Intermediate crude during the first quarter was $21.80 per barrel, and it reached a low of about $15.50 in mid-June. With the Iraqi invasion of Kuwait, crude prices rose to more than $40 per barrel, but they fell to about $25 per barrel as the year ended. The average price of West Texas Intermediate crude during 1990 was about $24.50 per barrel. The management of Pioneer emphasized the importance of operational and financial flexibility to respond to these price swings.

Pioneer spent about $3.1 billion on capital expenditures in 1990 and forecasted capital expenditures of almost $4.5 billion in 1991. Some of these expenditures, like the addition of a sulfur recovery facility and the improvement of a coker, allowed the refineries to process the heavy Alaskan crude oil more efficiently. These types of investments had provided good returns, and the light product yield in Pioneer's refineries was substantially higher than the industry average. Pioneer also invested in exploration and development, as it replaced all its 1990 production with new reserves. Most of this exploration was in the lower 48 states and the Gulf of Mexico. Investments were also directed to environmental projects, and Pioneer anticipated spending an additional $3 billion in the next 5 years to meet the new standards of the 1990 Clean Air Act amendments and the California Air Resources Board's regulations. These environmental regulations also provided opportunities for Pioneer to capitalize on its strengths. Pioneer's gasolines were among the cleanest burning in the industry, and its chemical unit produced about one-third of the world's supply of methyl tertiary butyl ether (MTBE), which was used to make cleaner-burning gasolines. The market for MTBE had been growing, and the new regulations were expected to lead to even higher growth. Also, Pioneer's SMOGMAN service centers specialized in state-required smog checks and related repairs.

Weighted Average Cost of Capital

The company's weighted average cost of capital was calculated in three steps: first, the expected future target proportions of debt and equity in the company's capital structure were estimated; second, costs were assigned to each of these capital components; third, a weighted average cost of capital was calculated on the basis of these proportions and costs (see Table A).

There was a general consensus in management on the future mix of debt and equity in Pioneer's capital structure. A firm policy had been adopted that debt should represent approximately 50% of total capital (defined as total debt plus book equity) to balance the competing objectives of enhancing the returns to shareholders and maintaining financial flexibility. The company was committed to using its dividend and

TABLE A
1990 Weighted Average Cost of Capital Calculation

Source	Target Proportion of Future Capital Components	Estimated Future After-Tax Cost	Weighted Cost
Debt	.50	7.9%	4.0%
Equity	.50	10.0	5.0
			9.0%

stock repurchase program to maintain appropriate financial leverage. Cash dividends increased by 10% in both 1990 and 1991. Its debt was A rated.

Assigning an after-tax cost to debt was straightforward. Pioneer's investment bankers, Steven, Mitchell, O'Hara, forecasted early in 1990 that the company's future debt issues would require a coupon of 12%, assuming continuation of its debt policy and A rating. At a 34% tax rate, this represented a 7.9% after-tax cost.

The cost of equity had been more difficult to conceptualize or to estimate. After prolonged debate, Pioneer decided to use the current earnings yield on the stock as the cost of both new equity and retained earnings. Advocates pointed out that no dilution of earnings per share would occur if the company earned at least this return on new equity. With earnings per share estimated at $6.15 in 1990 and a market price of $63, cost of equity had been set at 10%.

Divisional Costs of Capital

The alternative proposed by the supporters of multiple cutoff rates in lieu of a single companywide rate involved determining the cost of capital for each division. The divisional rate would reflect the risks inherent in each of the economic sectors or industries in which the company's principal operating subsidiaries worked. For example, the divisional cost of capital for production and exploration was 20%, and the divisional cost of capital for transportation was 10%. All the other divisional rates fell within this range. The suggestion was that these multiple cutoff rates determined the minimum acceptable rate of return on proposed capital investments in each of the main operating areas of the company and represented the rate charged to each of the various profit centers for capital employed. However, there were still areas of ambiguity. For example, it was unclear whether all environmental projects would have the same discount rate or the discount rate corresponding to the division.

The divisional cost of capital would be calculated using a weighted average cost of capital approach for each operating sector. The calculations would follow three steps: first, an estimate would be made of the usual debt and equity proportions of independently financed firms operating in each sector. Several such independents competed against each of the company's affiliates. Second, the costs of debt and equity given these proportions and sectors would be estimated in accordance with the concepts followed by the company in estimating its own cost of capital. Third, these costs and proportions would be combined to determine the weighted average cost of capital, or minimum acceptable rate of return, for net present value discounting purposes in each sector.

These multiple hurdle or discount rates had been calculated for several periods in the past, and it invariably turned out that their weighted average, when weighted according to the company's relative investment in each sector, exceeded the company's actual overall average cost of capital. The difference was attributed to the fact that the divisional cost of capital overlooked the risk diversification benefits of many investments undertaken by Pioneer Petroleum. As compared to nonintegrated enterprises operating in any given branch, a vertically and horizontally integrated firm such as Pioneer Petroleum enjoyed some built-in asset diversification and important captive markets between certain of its vertically integrated parts. For example, the risks associated with a refinery investment by an integrated company like Pioneer Petroleum were much less than for an identical investment made by an independent. It was proposed that this diversification premium be allocated back and deducted from the multiple subsidiary discount rates as calculated previously in proportion to the relation between the investment in each subsidiary and the company's total assets.

The Management Discussion

As management and the board of Pioneer Petroleum began their latest review of the alternatives of using single or multiple minimum acceptable cutoff rates, the officers of the operating subsidiaries were asked to restate their positions.

Those supporting the use of a single target rate contended that the stockholders of Pioneer Petroleum expected the company to invest their funds in the highest return projects available. They suggested that, without exception, the affiliates backing multiple rates were those that were unable to compete effectively for new funds when measured against the corporate group's actual cost of capital. Furthermore, it was not obvious that the categories suggested by the advocates of multiple rates were very helpful in grouping projects according to their riskiness. For example, recent experience in tankers had been disastrous for many companies, and yet tanker investments would be initiated by the transportation division and would therefore be subjected to an unrealistically low hurdle rate.

The proponents of multiple divisional hurdle rates argued that a single company-wide cost of capital subsidized the higher-risk divisions at the expense of the lower-risk divisions. Because the cost of capital was too high for the low-risk divisions, too few low-risk investments were made. In the high-risk divisions too much investment occurred because the hurdle rate was too low. As evidence, proponents of multiple rates noted that Pioneer was the only major company that continued to invest heavily in exploration and development, and that it lagged behind its competitors in marketing and transportation investment. The proponents also argued that the companywide cost of capital was too low, and that investments should be required to earn at least as much as an investment in common stocks. The average return since 1980 on the S&P index of common stocks of 16.25% substantially exceeded the 9% companywide cost of capital (see Exhibit 2). If Pioneer was serious about competing over the long run in industries with such disparate risk-profit characteristics, it was absolutely essential to relate internal target rates of return to the individual businesses.

EXHIBIT 1
Financial Summary, 1983–1990

	1983	1984	1985	1986	1987	1988	1989	1990
Sales ($ millions)	$20,397	$20,268	$18,594	$12,687	$14,182	$15,259	$13,417	$15,646
Net income ($ millions)	1,133	326	(297)	428	923	1,211	1,542	1,555
Earnings per share	$ 3.38	$ 2.27	$ .86	$ 1.65	$ 3.41	$ 4.43	$ 5.59	$ 6.15
Dividends per share	1.75	1.50	1.20	2.00	2.00	2.00	2.20	2.45
Return on book equity	15.9%	13%	4.8%	11.4%	19.6%	21.2%	26.3%	25%
Beta								.8

EXHIBIT 2
Information on U.S. Capital Markets, 1980–1990

	1980	1981	1982	1983	1984	1985	1986	1987	1988	1989	1990
Yields on newly issued Aa industrials	11.8%	14.0%	13.4%	11.9%	12.9%	11.4%	9.4%	9.7%	9.9%	9.5%	9.4%
Yields on 90-day T-bills	11.2	14.7	10.5	8.8	9.9	7.7	6.2	5.5	6.4	3.4	7.8
Realized returns on S&P 500 index of common stocks	32.4	–4.9	21.4	22.5	6.3	32.2	18.5	5.3	16.8	31.5	–3.2

Diversification, the Capital Asset Pricing Model, and the Cost of Equity Capital

Risk as Variability in Return

The rate of return an investor receives from holding a stock for a given period of time is equal to the dividends received plus the capital gains in the period divided by the initial market value of the security:

$$R = \frac{\text{Dividends} + (\text{Ending price} - \text{Beginning price})}{\text{Beginning price}}$$

Alternatively, return can be viewed as the dividend yield plus the percentage capital appreciation:

$$R = \text{Dividend yield} + \text{Percentage capital appreciation}$$

Suppose an investor buys one common share of Du Pont for $100 on January 1. Over the year, he or she receives $4 in dividends and sells the share for $108 on December 31. The return on this investment is 12%:

$$R_{\text{Du Pont}} = \frac{\$4 + (\$108 - \$100)}{\$100} = \frac{\$12}{\$100} = .12$$

or

$$R_{\text{Du Pont}} = 4\% \text{ dividend yield} + 8\% \text{ appreciation} = 12\%$$

If the ending price is $85, the return is −11%.

The return on any security can be viewed as the cash the security holder receives (including liquidation at the end of the period) divided by the initial investment. Investing in a savings account that offers a 5% interest rate results in an annual return of 5%:

$$R_{\text{Savings account}} = \frac{\$5 + (\$100 - \$100)}{\$100} = .05$$

There is an important difference, however, between investing in a savings account and investing in common stocks. The investor knows before committing any funds that the savings account will earn a return of 5%. The actual return will not differ from the expected return of 5%. Thus, savings accounts are considered a safe, or risk-free, security.

On the other hand, an investor who expects a return of 12% on Du Pont's common shares may be disappointed or pleasantly surprised. The actual return on Du Pont may be less than or greater than 12%, since (1) Du Pont may change its dividend and, more important, (2) the market price at the end of the period may differ from the anticipated

FIGURE A
Risk as Variability in Return

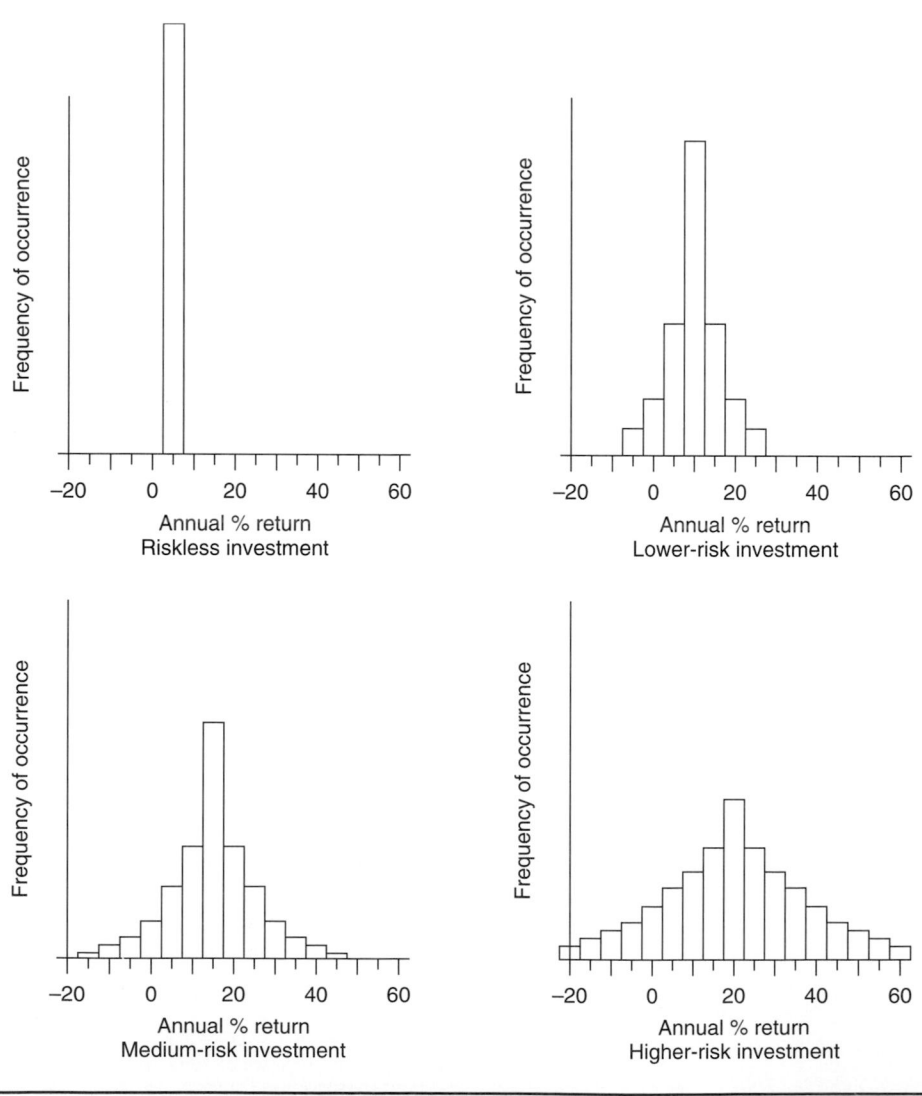

price. Actual returns on common stock vary widely from year to year. An investor committing funds at the beginning of any period cannot be confident of receiving the average or expected return.

In general, an investment with actual returns that are not likely to depart from the expected or average return is considered a low-risk investment. One with quite volatile returns from year to year is said to be risky. Thus, risk can be viewed as variability in return (see Figure A).

Risk Reduction through Diversification

Risky stocks can be combined in such a way that the combination of securities, called a portfolio of securities, is less risky than any one of the component individual stocks. Consider the example outlined in Table A. Suppose we have two firms located on an isolated Caribbean island. The chief industry on the island is tourism. Company A manufactures and sells suntan lotion. Its sales, earnings, and cash flows are highest during sunny years. Thus, its stock does well in sunny years and poorly in rainy years. Company B manufactures and sells disposable umbrellas. Returns on its stock reflect its higher earnings in rainy years. In purchasing stock in either A or B, an investor is subject to considerable risk or variability in return. For instance, the investor's return on the stock of company B will vary from 33% to −9%, depending on weather conditions.

Suppose, however, that instead of buying only one security, the investor puts half of his or her funds in stock A and half in stock B. The possible returns on this portfolio of securities are calculated in Table A. If a recession occurs, a $50 investment in stock A loses $4.50, while $50 invested in stock B returns $16.50. The total return on $100 invested in the portfolio is 12%:

$$\frac{-\$4.50 + \$16.50}{\$100}$$

TABLE A
Example of Risk Reduction through Diversification

	Weather Conditions	Return on Stock A = R_A
Company A: Suntan lotion manufacturer	Sunny year Normal year Rainy year	33% 12 −9

	Weather Conditions	Return on Stock B = R_B
Company B: Disposable umbrella manufacturer	Sunny year Normal year Rainy year	−9% 12 33

Returns on a Portfolio (R_p) Consisting of 50% Invested in Stock A and 50% in Stock B:
$R_p = .50\ (R_A) + .50\ (R_B)$

	Weather Conditions	Return on the Portfolio = R_p
Portfolio containing A and B	Sunny year Normal year Rainy year	.50 (33%) + .50 (−9%) = 12% .50 (12%) + .50 (12%) = 12% .50 (−9%) + .50 (33%) = 12%

Note that the return on this portfolio is 12% regardless of which weather condition prevails.

Combining these two risky securities yields a portfolio with a certain return. Since we are sure of earning 12% on the portfolio, it is a very low-risk investment, comparable to a risk-free security such as a savings account. This example demonstrates risk reduction through diversification. By diversifying the investment over both firms, the investor creates a portfolio that is less risky than its two component stocks.

Total risk elimination is possible in this example because there is a perfect negative relation between the returns on stock A and B. In practice, such a perfect relation is very rare. Most firms' securities tend to move together, and therefore complete elimination of risk is not possible. However, as long as there is some lack of parallelism in the returns of securities, diversification will always reduce risk. Since companies' fortunes, and therefore their stocks' returns, do not move completely in parallel, investment in a diversified portfolio composed of many securities is less risky than investment in a few individual stocks.

Systematic and Unsystematic Risk

Combining securities into portfolios reduces risk. When combined with other securities, a portion of a stock's variability in return is canceled by complementary variations in the returns of other securities. Some firms represented in the portfolio may experience unanticipated adverse conditions (e.g., a wildcat strike). However, this may well be offset by the unexpected good fortune of other firms in the portfolio. Nevertheless, since to some extent stock price (and returns) tend to move in concert, not all variability can be eliminated through diversification. Even investors holding diversified portfolios are exposed to the risk inherent in the overall performance of the stock market (for instance, the stock market crash of October 1987). Thus, it is convenient to divide a security's total risk into that portion that is peculiar to a specific firm and can be diversified away (called unsystematic risk) and that portion that is market-related and nondiversifiable (called systematic risk):

$$\text{Total risk} = \text{Unsystematic risk} + \text{Systematic risk}$$
$$\text{(diversifiable risk,} \quad \text{(nondiversifiable risk,}$$
$$\text{firm-specific)} \quad \text{market-related)}$$

Figure B illustrates the reduction of total risk as securities are added to a portfolio. Unsystematic risk is virtually eliminated in portfolios of 30 or 40 securities drawn from industries that are not closely related. Because the remaining systematic risk is market related, diversified portfolios tend to move in tandem with the market. The popular market indices (the Dow Jones Industrial Average, the S&P 500, and the New York Stock Exchange Index, for instance) are themselves diversified portfolios and tend to move in parallel. Thus, there is a close correspondence between swings in the returns of any diversified portfolio and in the returns on market indices such as the Dow. Examples of systematic and unsystematic risk factors are listed in Table B.

Risk, Return, and Market Equilibrium

Investors are risk-averse and must be compensated for taking risk. Thus, risky securities are priced by the market to yield a higher expected return than low-risk securities. This extra reward, called the risk premium, is necessary to induce risk-averse investors to hold risky securities. In a market dominated by risk-averse investors, there must be a

FIGURE B
Elimination of Unsystematic Risk through Diversification

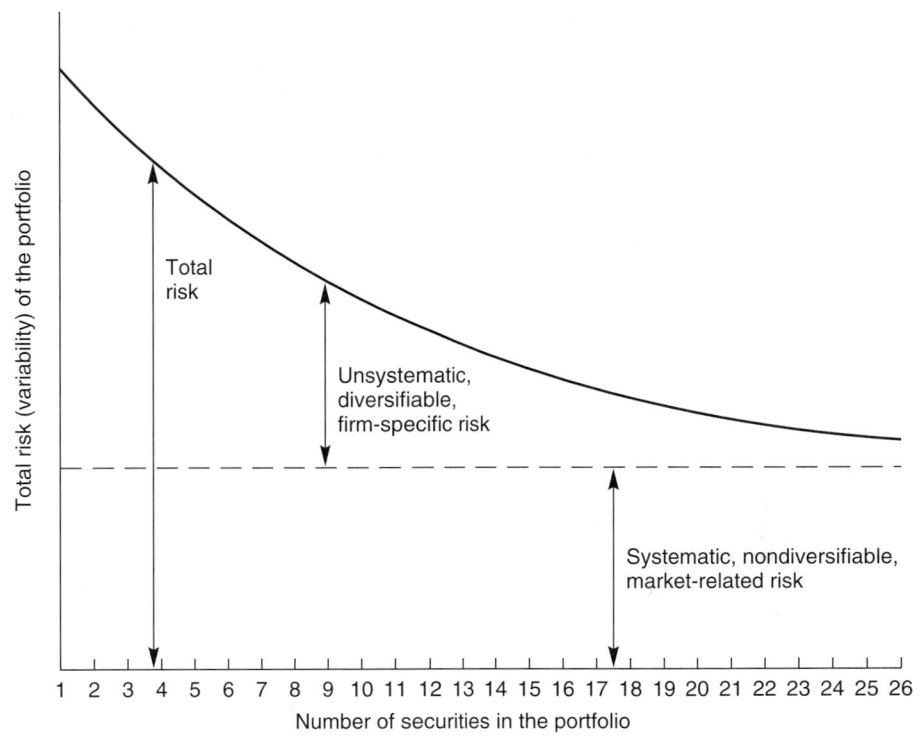

TABLE B
Systematic and Unsystematic Risk Factors

Examples of Unsystematic Risk Factors

A firm's technical wizard is killed in an auto accident.
A wildcat strike is declared.
A lower-cost foreign competitor unexpectedly enters a firm's product market.
Oil is discovered on a firm's property.

Examples of Systematic Risk Factors

Oil-producing countries institute a boycott.
Congress votes for a massive tax cut.
The Federal Reserve follows a restrictive monetary policy.
There is a precipitous rise in long-term interest rates.

positive relation between risk and expected return to achieve equilibrium. The expected return on a risk-free security (such as a Treasury bill) is the risk-free rate. The expected return on risky securities can be thought of as this risk-free rate plus a premium for risk:

$$R_S = R_F + \text{Risk premium}$$

The market's risk/return trade-off is illustrated in Figure C.

FIGURE C
Market's Risk/Expected Return Trade-Off in Equilibrium

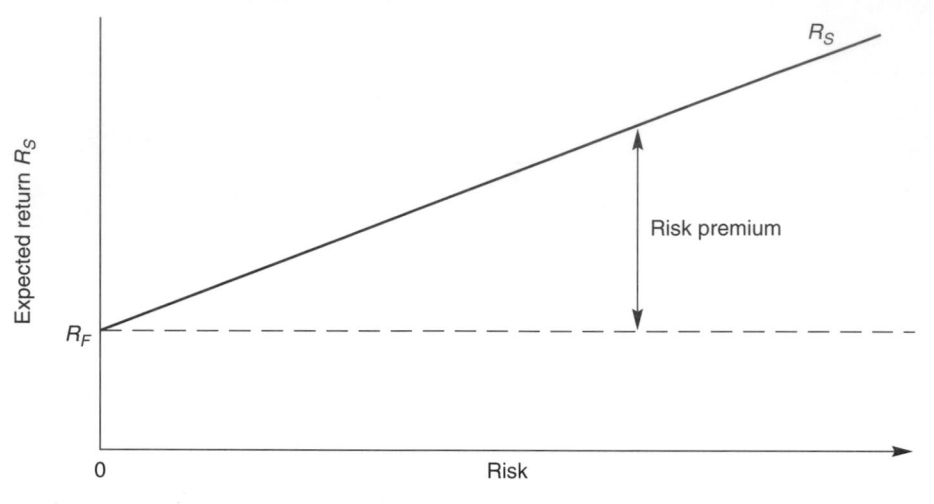

The Capital Asset Pricing Model (CAPM)

The capital asset pricing model (CAPM) represents an idealized view of how the market prices securities and determines expected returns. It provides a measure of the risk premium and a method for estimating the market's risk/expected return curve.

In the CAPM, investors hold diversified portfolios to minimize risk. Because they hold portfolios consisting of many securities, events peculiar to specific firms (i.e., unsystematic risk) have a negligible impact on their overall return. Only a small fraction of an investor's funds are invested in each security. Furthermore, variations in returns from one security will, as likely as not, be canceled by complementary variations in the returns of other securities. Therefore, the only risk to which investors are sensitive is systematic, or market-related, risk.

Since unsystematic risk can be eliminated simply by holding large portfolios, investors are not compensated for bearing unsystematic risk. Investors holding diversified portfolios are exposed only to systematic, market-related risk. Therefore, the relevant risk in the market's risk/expected return trade-off is systematic risk, not total risk. The investor is rewarded with a higher expected return for bearing systematic, market-related risks. Only systematic risk is relevant in determining the premiums for bearing risk. Thus, the model predicts that a security's return is related to that portion of risk that cannot be eliminated by portfolio combination.

An individual investor who invests in only one stock is still exposed to both systematic and unsystematic risk. However, he or she is rewarded in terms of a higher expected return only for the systematic risk he or she bears. There is no reward for bearing unsystematic risk, since it can be eliminated by adequate diversification.

The CAPM provides a convenient measure of systematic risk. This measure, called beta (β), gauges the tendency of a security's return to move in parallel with the overall market's return (e.g., the return on the S&P 500). A stock with a beta of 1 tends to rise and fall the same percentage as the market (i.e., the S&P 500 index). Thus, $\beta = 1$ indicates an average level of systematic risk. Stocks with $\beta > 1$ tend to rise and fall by a greater percentage than the market. They have a high level of systematic risk and are very sensitive to market changes. Similarly, stocks with $\beta < 1$ have a low level of systematic risk and are less sensitive to market swings.

These results determine the risk/expected return trade-off under the CAPM. In general,

$$R_S = R_F + \text{Risk premium}$$

If the CAPM correctly describes market behavior,

$$R_S = R_F + \beta_S(R_M - R_F)$$

The expected return on a security (R_S) is equal to the risk-free rate plus a risk premium. With the CAPM, the risk premium is β multiplied by the return on the market (R_M) minus the risk-free rate. Alternatively, the relation can be expressed in terms of the risk premium (i.e., the return over and above the risk-free rate):

$$R_S - R_F = \beta_S(R_M - R_F)$$
$$= \text{Risk premium for security } S$$

Thus, the risk premium on a stock (or portfolio or any security) varies directly with the level of systematic risk, β. This risk/expected return trade-off with the CAPM is called the security market line (SML) and is illustrated graphically in Figure D.

One perhaps counterintuitive aspect of the determination of expected returns with the CAPM can be illustrated with a simple example. Consider a firm engaged in oil exploration. The return (denoted R_A) to the shareholders in such a firm is very variable. If oil is found, the return is very high. If no oil is discovered, shareholders lose their entire investment and the return is negative. The stock's total risk level is very high. However, much of the variability in return is generated by factors independent of the returns on other stocks (i.e., the return on the market). This risk is unique to the firm and is therefore unsystematic risk. Since the stock's return is not closely related to the return on the market as a whole, it contributes little to the variability of a diversified

FIGURE D
Security Market Line: The Risk/Expected Return Trade-Off with the CAPM

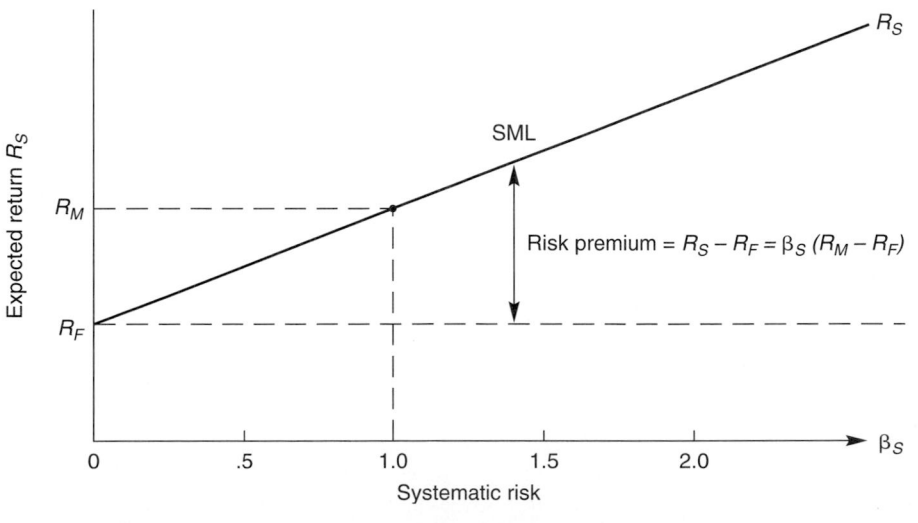

portfolio. Its unsystematic risk can be diversified away by holding large portfolios. Nevertheless, the costs of exploration and the price of oil are related to the general level of economic activity. As a result, the stock does contain some systematic, market-related risk. Most of its total risk is unsystematic risk, however, associated with the chances of finding oil.

Although the firm's stock is very risky in terms of total risk, it has a low level of systematic risk. Its beta might be .8. The market will therefore price this stock to yield a relatively low expected return. From the viewpoint of investors holding large portfolios, it is a low-risk security. Its expected return is denoted R_A in Figure E. Note that the return on this stock (R_A) is less than the return on the average stock in the market (R_M).

In contrast, consider a firm that manufactures computers. As a large stable firm, its total variability in return might be less than that of the oil exploration firm. However, its sales, earnings, and therefore stock returns are closely related to changes in overall economic activity. The return on its stock is very sensitive to changes in the return on the market as a whole. Therefore, its risk cannot be eliminated by diversification. When combined with other securities in a diversified portfolio, changes in its return tend to reinforce swings in the returns of the other securities. It has a relatively high level of systematic risk and a beta of perhaps 1.2. Viewed as an individual security, it appears less risky (in terms of total risk) than the oil exploration firm. Nevertheless, because of its high level of nondiversifiable risk, the market considers it the riskier security. Therefore, it is priced to yield a high expected return. Its return is labeled R_B in Figure E. Such counterintuitive examples are rare, however. Most firms with high total risk also have high betas (and vice versa).

In summary, if the CAPM correctly describes market behavior, the relevant measure of a security's risk is its market-related or systematic risk (measured by beta). If a security's return has a strong positive relation with the return on the market (i.e., has a high beta), it will be priced to yield a high expected return (and vice versa). Since unsystematic risk can be easily eliminated through diversification, it does not increase

FIGURE E
Example of Determining Expected Returns with the CAPM

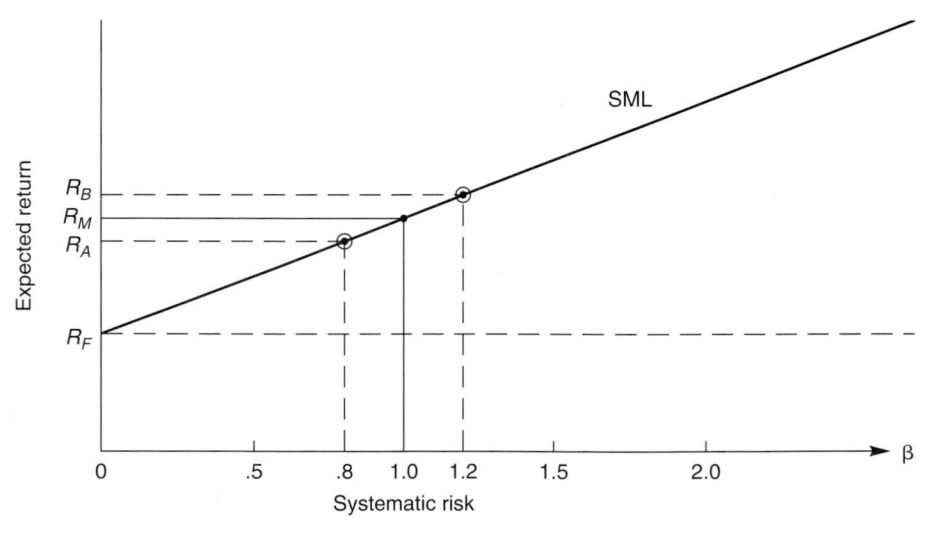

TABLE C
Summary of the Determination of Expected Returns with the CAPM

1. Total risk is defined as variability in return.
2. The investor can reduce risk by holding a diversified portfolio.
3. The total risk of a security can be divided into unsystematic and systematic risk.
   a. Risk that can be eliminated through diversification is called unsystematic risk. It is associated with events unique to the firm and independent of other firms.
   b. The risk remaining in a diversified portfolio is called systematic risk. It is associated with the movement of other securities and the market as a whole.
4. If the CAPM correctly describes market behavior, investors hold diversified portfolios to minimize risk.
5. Since investors hold diversified portfolios with the CAPM, they are exposed only to systematic risk. In such a market, investors are rewarded in terms of a higher expected return only for bearing systematic, market-related risk. There is no reward associated with unsystematic risk because it can be eliminated through diversification. Thus, relevant risk is systematic or market-related risk, and it is measured by beta.
6. The risk/expected return trade-off with the CAPM is called the security market line (SML). Securities are priced such that:

$$R_S = R_F + Risk\ premium,\ or\ R_S = R_F + \beta_S(R_M - R_F)$$

Thus, the SML gives us an estimate of the expected return on any security, R_S.

---

a security's expected return. The market cares only about systematic risk. These results are summarized in Table C.

Application of the CAPM to Corporate Finance: Estimating the Cost of Equity Capital

The CAPM provides insight into the market's pricing of securities and the determination of expected returns. It has clear applications in investment management and in corporate finance. The cost of equity capital, k_E, is the expected (or required) return on a firm's common stock. The firm must be expected to earn k_E on the equity-financed portion of investments to keep the price of its stock from falling. If the firm cannot expect to earn at least k_E, funds should be returned to the shareholders, who can earn k_E on marketable securities of the same risk level. Since k_E involves the market's expectations, it is difficult to measure. The CAPM can be used by financial managers to obtain an estimate of k_E.

The CAPM provides a conceptual framework for determining the expected return on common stocks, and it can be used to estimate firms' cost of capital. If the CAPM correctly describes market behavior, the market's expected return on a common stock is given by the security market line (SML):

$$R_S = R_F + \beta_S(R_M - R_F)$$

The expected return on a firm's stock is, by definition, its cost of equity capital. Therefore, in terms of cost of capital, the SML is

$$k_E = R_F + \beta_S(k_M - R_F)$$

where

$k_E = R_S =$ Firm's cost of equity capital
$k_M = R_M =$ Cost of equity for the market as a whole (or for an average firm in the market)
$\beta_S =$ Beta of the firm's stock

Thus, to estimate k_E we need estimates of R_F, the risk-free rate; $k_M = R_M$, the expected return on the market as a whole; and β_S, the level of systematic risk associated with the firm's stock.

R_F can be estimated as the average or expected rate of return on Treasury bills in the future. In recent years, this rate has ranged between 3% and 9%. A reasonable estimate might be 6% per year.

The market risk premium is the difference between the return on the market, k_M, and the risk-free rate, R_F. The expected risk premium in the future is difficult to estimate. A common approach is to assume that investors expect returns in the future to be about the same as returns in the past. The average annual market risk premium (large company equities versus long-term Treasury bonds) was 7.4% in the period 1926–1995.[1]

The stock's beta, β_S, can be estimated by linear regression.[2] Betas are also available from many brokerage firms and investment advisory services. Furthermore, one can get an intuitive estimate simply by observing the stock's reaction to swings in the market as a whole. Finally, a rough guess at beta can be made by noting the tendency of the firm's earnings and cash flows to move in parallel with the earnings and cash flows of other firms in the economy.

Betas for selected firms in four industries are presented in Table D. Despite relatively high degrees of operating and financial leverage, electric utilities have very stable earnings streams. Swings in the earnings and stock returns of utilities are modest relative to swings in the earnings and returns of most firms in the economy. Therefore, electric utilities have a low level of systematic risk and low betas.

At the other extreme, airline revenues are closely tied to passenger miles, which are in turn very sensitive to changes in economic activity. This basic variability in revenues is amplified by high operating and financial leverage. The result is earnings and returns that show wide variations relative to swings in the earnings and returns of most firms. Thus, airlines have high betas.

Estimates of the cost of equity capital for four firms are presented in Table E. Plugging the assumed values of R_F, k_M, and β into the SML generates estimates of k_E.

TABLE D
Betas for Selected Firms in Four Industries

Electric Utilities		Airlines		Computer Hardware		Computer Software	
Company	β	Company	β	Company	β	Company	β
American Electric Power	.75	AMR Corp.	1.25	AST Research	1.50	Adobe Systems	1.80
Baltimore Gas & Electric	.80	Delta	1.20	Apple Comp.	1.10	Borland International	1.60
Consolidated Edison	.75	Northwest	1.75	Compaq	1.25	Computer Assoc.	1.55
Duke Power	.75	UAL	1.60	Digital Equip.	1.05	Intuit	1.85
FPL Group	.75	US Air Group	1.55	Hewlett-Packard	1.10	Microsoft	1.20
Niagara Mohawk	.80			IBM	.90	Novell Inc.	1.40
Ohio Edison	.80					Oracle	1.45
Pacific Gas & Electric	.75						

1. *Stocks, Bonds, Bills, and Inflation—1996 Yearbook: Market Results for 1926–1995* (Chicago: Ibbotson Associates, 1996).

2. The estimated regression equation is $R_S - R_F = \alpha + \beta_S(R_M - R_F) + e$. Given past values of R_F, R_S, and R_M, the regression yields estimates of alpha, α (which should be zero), and the stock's beta, β_S.

TABLE E
Examples of Estimating the Cost of Equity Capital Using the CAPM

Assumptions	*SML*
R_E = .09 = risk-free rate	$k_E = R_F + \beta(k_M - R_F)$
$R_M - R_F$ = .08	= .09 + β(.08)

Consolidated Edison	**Delta Airlines**	**Digital Equipment**	**Adobe**
$\beta_{Consolidated}$ = .75	β_{Delta} = 1.20	β_{DEC} = 1.05	β_{Adobe} = 1.80
k_E = .06 + .75(.07) .11	k_E = .06 + 1.20(.07) = .14	k_E = .06 + 1.05(.07) = .13	k_E = .06 + 1.80(.07) = .19

As expected, the low-risk utility has an estimated cost of equity below that of the other three firms.

The assumed value of k_M represents a major potential source of error in these estimates. High and low estimates of k_M can be used to generate a reasonable range of estimates of k_E. The estimation of β also introduces error into the estimate of k_E.

The CAPM and Risk-Adjusted Discount Rates

The CAPM provides a conceptual framework for determining the k_E appropriate for a subsidiary's capital budgeting decisions. Assume that the holding company described in Figure F has no debt outstanding. The parent company owns all the equity in its subsidiaries, and the holding company's stock is publicly traded.[3] Such a firm can be viewed as a portfolio of assets. Its stock's beta is a weighted average of the betas associated with the riskiness of each subsidiary industry. Suppose that the parent

FIGURE F
Corporate Structure of a Holding Company with Three Subsidiaries

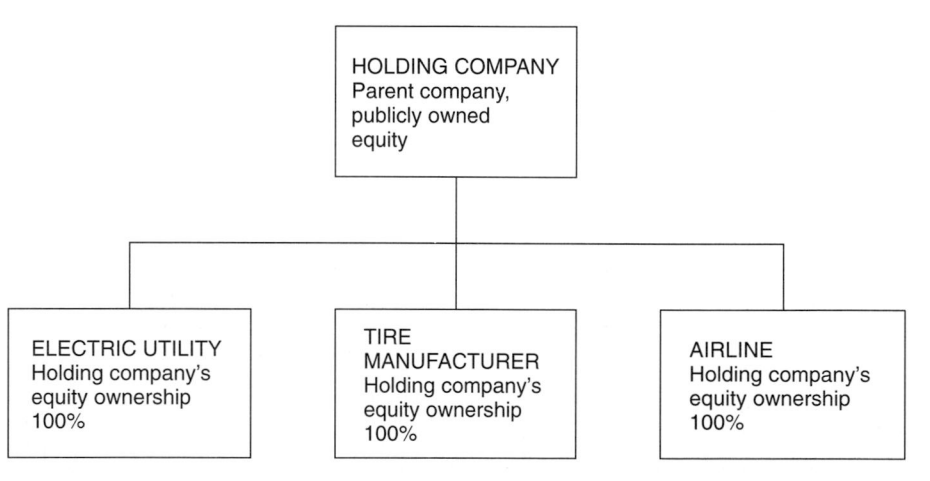

---

3. The cost of equity is appropriate to evaluate capital investment only when the firm is all equity-financed. The note "Leveraged Betas and the Cost of Equity" explains how to estimate the cost of capital for firms that are financed with debt.

company's beta is 1. However, the appropriate cost of equity capital for capital budgeting purposes is not the k_E derived from the beta of the holding company's stock. The cost of equity capital used to evaluate investment proposals for a subsidiary should reflect the risk associated with the industry in which that subsidiary operates. Thus, while the holding company's beta of 1 yields a k_E of 13%, investments in the utility subsidiary should be evaluated using a lower k_E, since the utility industry is less risky than the other subsidiary industries. Therefore, the market's expected (or required) return is lower for investments in the utility subsidiary. Since the airline industry is risky, a higher k_E should be used in capital budgeting for an airline subsidiary.

Application of the firm's overall k_E to the individual subsidiaries would result in poor decisions. Good projects in the utility subsidiary would be rejected, while poor projects in the airline subsidiary would be accepted. When the cost of equity capital used in a subsidiary's capital budgeting decisions reflects the risk associated with that subsidiary's line of business, this ensures that project returns are measured against the returns shareholders would expect to receive on alternative investments of corresponding risk.

How can we estimate the beta appropriate for a subsidiary? An obvious approach is to use the beta on similar independent firms operating in the same industry. The resulting estimates of k_E reflect the risk level of the industry and are therefore appropriate for investment decisions concerning a subsidiary operating in the same industry. If there are no independent firms in the industry, an intuitive estimate of beta can be made. This estimate would reflect the degree to which the subsidiary's earnings and cash flows tend to move in concert with other firm's earnings and cash flows.

Conclusion and Caveats

The CAPM is widely applied in investment management and corporate financial management. Although some of the model's assumptions are clearly unrealistic, empirical tests demonstrate that there is a strong relation between returns and risk as measured by beta. However, the nature and stability of the relations predicted by the SML are not fully supported by these tests. Furthermore, application of the CAPM requires estimating $k_M - R_F$, the market risk premium, and R_F, the risk-free rate. The estimates of beta are also subject to error. Thus, the CAPM should not be relied upon as the sole answer to cost-of-capital determination.

Nevertheless, the model has much to say about the way returns are determined in the securities market. The cost of equity capital is inherently difficult to measure. The shortcomings of the CAPM appear less severe than those of alternative methods of estimating the cost of equity capital (for instance, the dividend growth model). Though imperfect, the CAPM represents an important approach to this difficult task. Using the CAPM in conjunction with more traditional approaches, corporate financial managers can develop realistic, useful estimates of the cost of equity capital.

Beta Management Company

In early January 1991, Sarah Wolfe was in her office considering new goals and directions for her company for the coming year. Ms. Wolfe was the founder and chief executive officer of the Beta Management Group, a small investment management company based in a Boston suburb. She dealt with a growing number of high-net-worth individual clients and had $25 million in assets under management. Beta's investment success during the past year had brought in a steady stream of new clients and additional money from existing clients. At the same time, Ms. Wolfe had inquiries from some small institutions, and she was hoping to expand her business in 1991.

Beta Management Company was founded in 1988. A wealthy couple had become fed up with their investment losses stemming from the October 1987 crash and had asked their friend, Ms. Wolfe, to manage a portion of their money. While business was slow at first, she gradually developed a client base through good performance and word of mouth. Ms. Wolfe considered herself a market strategist, and Beta Management's stated goals were to enhance returns but reduce risks for clients via market timing. Given the small size of her accounts, the easiest way for Ms. Wolfe to maintain and adjust equity market exposure was to "index." She would keep a majority of Beta's funds in no-load, low-expense index funds (with the remainder in money market instruments), adjusting the level of market exposure between 50% and 99% of Beta's funds in an attempt to "time the market." She had toyed with using a few different index funds at first, but she soon settled on exclusive use of Vanguard's Index 500 Trust due to its extremely low expense ratio and its success at closely matching the return on the S&P 500 Index.

While Beta's performance had lagged market returns in 1989, Ms. Wolfe had been quite successful in 1990. She had reduced Beta's equity position to 50% in June, partially missing a large two-month market decline (see Exhibit 1). After nervously waiting out August and September, she began moving money back into the index fund. The report in front of her showed that as of January 4, 1991, Beta Management had

---

This case was prepared by Professor Michael E. Edleson.

Copyright © 1992 by the President and Fellows of Harvard College.
Harvard Business School case 292–122.

79.2% of its $25 million invested in the Vanguard fund; Beta had also made money for its clients during a down market year.

This success had brought in enough new money to double the size of Beta in under six months, allowing Ms. Wolfe to finally make the move to work full time managing money. But she had lost some potential new clients who had thought it unusual that Beta Management used only an index mutual fund and picked none of its own stocks. Ms. Wolfe had felt this same resistance in conversations with a few of the potential institutional clients she was courting. As a result, one of her New Year's resolutions had been to begin looking at some individual stocks for possible purchase for Beta's equity portfolio. She would focus on smaller stocks because she did not want to compete with larger, analyst-staffed funds on their own turf, and because she already had exposure to the S&P 500 stocks through investment in the index fund. She also decided to increase the proportion of Beta's assets in equities because she felt the market was still a good value and that 1991 would be a good year.

As a first step toward both of these goals, Ms. Wolfe was considering immediately increasing her equity exposure to 80% with the purchase of one of two stocks recommended by her newly hired analyst. Both were small NYSE-listed companies whose stock prices had eroded over the past 2 years (see Exhibit 1) to levels that seemed unreasonably low.

California REIT was a real estate investment trust that made equity and mortgage investments in income-producing properties (retail buildings, 57%; industrial, 17%; offices, 15%; and apartments, 11%) in Arizona (51%), California (30%), and Washington (19%). Its investments and stock price had been badly damaged by the "World Series" earthquake of 1989 and the downturn in California real estate values (see Exhibit 1). Ms Wolfe viewed California REIT as a good value but noticed that it was an extremely volatile stock (see Exhibit 2). Its stock price closed at $2.25 per share on January 4, 1991.

Brown Group, Inc. was one of the largest manufacturers and retailers of branded footwear and had been undergoing a major restructuring program since 1989. Earnings dropped in 1989 but had stayed positive and steady; the stock price had dropped substantially in late 1989 and late 1990 (see Exhibit 1). Ms. Wolfe knew that some of Brown's many brand names—including Jordache, Naturalizer, and Buster Brown—would wear well during the current recession, and she liked the steady cash flow and earnings. She noted, however, that Brown's stock price seemed quite variable and somewhat sensitive to movements in the stock market (see Exhibit 3). Still, she felt it was an attractive opportunity at its January 4 price of $24.

Ms. Wolfe felt that now was the right time to begin her program of adding individual stock investments and increasing her equity position. A $200,000 purchase of one of these stocks would increase her total equity exposure to $20 million. Still, she had some doubts. She was quite worried about the variability in individual stocks in general, and in these stocks in particular. After all, she had always promised her clients reasonable returns with a focus on keeping their exposure to risk under control. She noticed that these stocks both seemed to bounce around in price much more than the market (or the index fund), and she wondered if exposing her clients to these new risks was the right thing to do.

EXHIBIT 1
Investment Return Data (percentages)

Month	Vanguard Index 500 Trust	California REIT	Brown Group
1989			
January	7.32%	−28.26%	9.16%
February	−2.47	−3.03	0.73
March	2.26	8.75	−0.29
April	5.18	−1.47	2.21
May	4.04	−1.49	−1.08
June	−0.59	−9.09	−0.65
July	9.01	10.67	2.22
August	1.86	−9.38	0.00
September	−0.40	10.34	1.88
October	−2.34	−14.38	−7.55
November	2.04	−14.81	−12.84
December	2.38	−4.35	−1.70
1990			
January	−6.72	−5.45	−15.21
February	1.27	5.00	7.61
March	2.61	9.52	1.11
April	−2.50	−0.87	−0.51
May	9.69	0.00	12.71
June	−0.69	4.55	3.32
July	−0.32	3.48	3.17
August	−9.03	0.00	−14.72
September	−4.89	−13.04	−1.91
October	−0.41	0.00	−12.50
November	6.44	1.50	17.26
December	2.72	−2.56	−8.53

EXHIBIT 2
Monthly Returns of California REIT versus S&P 500 Index Fund

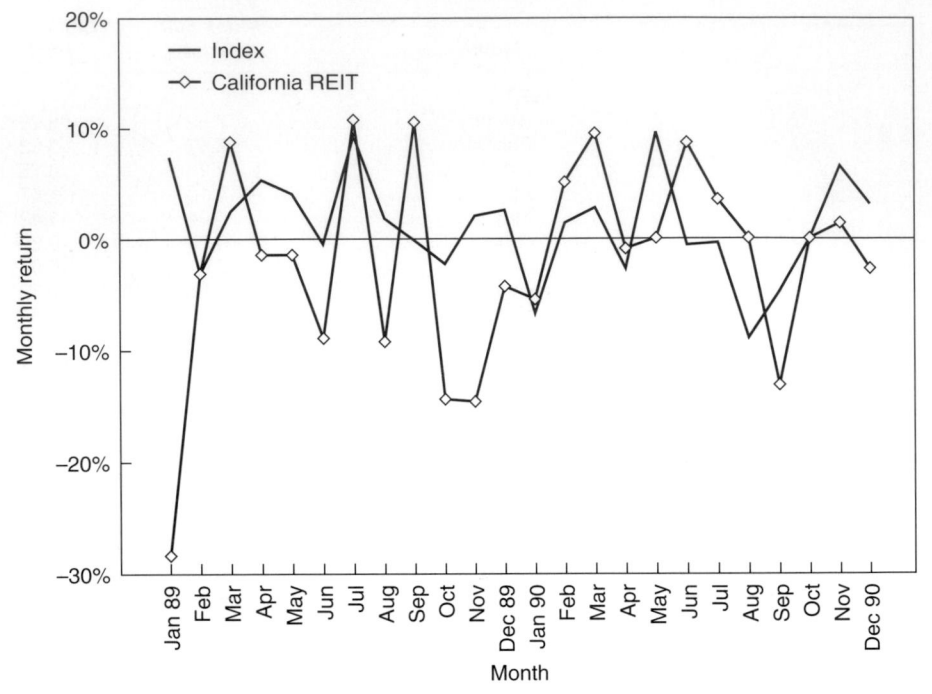

EXHIBIT 3
Monthly Returns of Brown Group, Inc. versus S&P 500 Index Fund

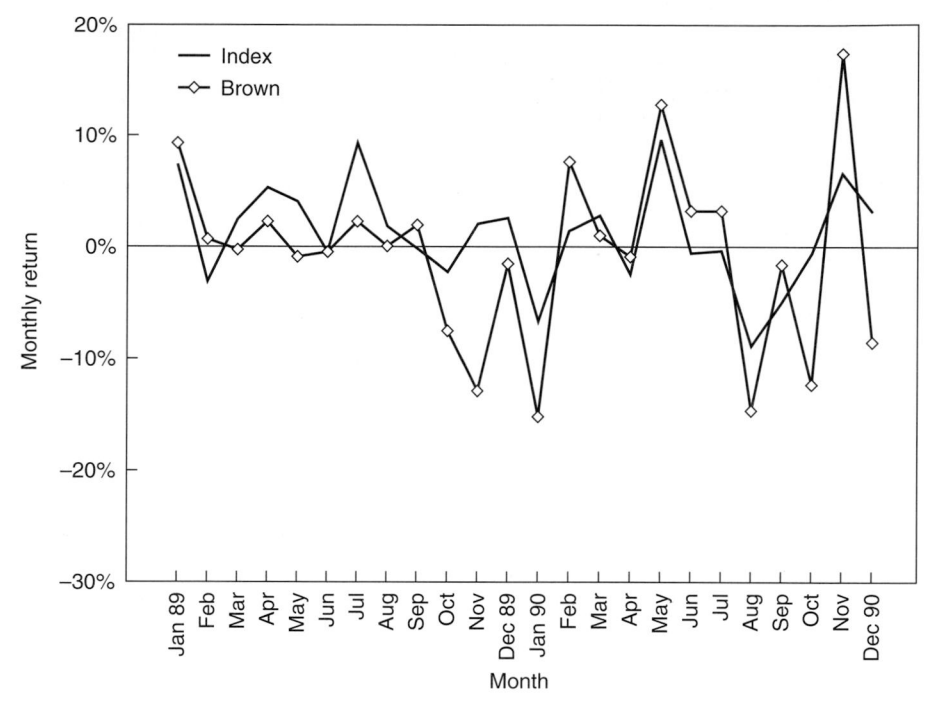

Leveraged Betas and the Cost of Equity

A stock's expected return, its dividend yield plus expected price appreciation, is related to risk. Risk-averse investors must be compensated with higher expected returns for bearing risk. One source of risk is the financial risk incurred by shareholders in a firm that has debt in its capital structure. The objective of this note is to delineate a methodology for measuring the risk associated with financial leverage and estimating its impact on the cost of equity capital.

Financial Leverage and Risk

The presence of debt in a firm's capital structure has an impact on the risk borne by its shareholders. In the absence of debt, shareholders are subjected only to basic business or operating risk. This business risk is determined by factors such as the volatility of a firm's sales and its level of operating leverage. As compensation for incurring business risk, investors require a premium in excess of the return they could earn on a riskless security such as a Treasury bill. Thus, in the absence of financial leverage, a stock's expected return can be thought of as the risk-free rate plus a premium for business risk.

The addition of debt to a firm's capital structure increases the risk borne by its shareholders. One course of additional risk is the increased risk of financial distress (e.g., bankruptcy). A second source is the effect of financial leverage on the volatility of shareholders' returns. The fixed obligations associated with debt amplify the variations in a firm's operating cash flows. The result is a more volatile stream of shareholders' returns. For investors to hold the shares of firms with debt in their capital structures, they must be compensated for the additional risk generated by financial leverage. The additional risk premium associated with the presence of debt in a firm's capital structure is the financial risk premium.

The expected return on a firm's stock is the risk-free rate plus a premium for risk:

$$\text{Expected return} = \text{Risk-free rate} + \text{Risk premium}$$

The risk premium consists of a premium for business risk and a premium for financial risk:

$$\text{Expected return} = \frac{\text{Risk-free}}{\text{rate}} + \frac{\text{Business risk}}{\text{premium}} + \frac{\text{Financial risk}}{\text{premium}}$$

This relation can be expressed in symbols:

$$R_S = R_F + BRP + FRP$$

Thus, the expected return on a firm's stock can be decomposed into three components. These components are: (1) the return on a riskless security, R_F; (2) a premium reflecting the firm's basic business (or operating) risk in the absence of financial leverage, *BRP*; and (3) a premium for the additional risk created by the existence of debt in a firm's capital structure, *FRP*. This relation is illustrated graphically in Exhibit 1. The capital asset pricing model (CAPM) provides a methodology for measuring these risk premiums and estimating the impact of financial leverage on expected returns.

The Effect of Financial Leverage on Beta

The CAPM is an idealized representation of the manner in which capital markets price securities and thereby determine expected returns.[1] Since the CAPM models the risk/expected return trade-off in the capital markets, it can be used to examine the impact of financial leverage on expected returns.

In the CAPM, systematic (or market-related) risk is the only risk relevant in the pricing of securities and the determination of expected returns. Systematic risk is measured by beta (β). The CAPM provides a measure of a stock's risk premium employing beta, which facilitates the estimation of the stock's expected return. In general,

$$R_S = R_F + \text{Risk premium}$$

If the CAPM correctly describes market behavior,

$$R_S = R_F + \beta(R_M - R_F)$$

A stock's expected return is equal to the risk-free rate, R_F, plus a premium for risk. With the CAPM, the risk premium is beta times the expected return on the market, R_M, minus the risk-free rate. This basic CAPM expression is known as the security market line, the SML.

If a firm has no debt in its capital structure, the stock's risk premium consists solely of a business risk premium. The stock's beta therefore reflects the systematic risk inherent in the firm's basic business operations. With no financial leverage, this beta is the stock's unlevered beta, β^U. This unlevered beta is the beta the stock would have if the firm had no debt in its capital structure.

The presence of debt in a firm's capital structure results in additional risk. The systematic risk inherent in the firm's basic business operations is amplified by financial leverage. With financial leverage, the beta on a firm's stock reflects both business and financial risk. This beta is called a levered beta, β^L. Employing a levered beta in the CAPM expression, the SML measures both the business risk premium and the finan-

---

1. For a more complete description of the CAPM, see the note "Diversification, the Capital Asset Pricing Model, and the Cost of Equity Capital."

cial risk premium. The beta published by various investment advisory services reflects *both* the business and the financial risk experienced during the time period over which the beta was determined.

Under the assumptions of the CAPM there is a simple relation between levered and unlevered betas:

$$\beta^L = \beta^U(1 + D/E)$$

Alternatively,

$$\beta^U = \frac{\beta^L}{1 + D/E}$$

A stock's levered beta is equal to its unlevered beta multiplied by a factor that includes the firm's ratio of debt to equity, *D/E*. Therefore, a stock's beta (and its expected return) increases as its debt ratio increases. The increase in beta reflects the additional systematic risk generated by financial leverage. The resulting increase in expected return reflects the increase in the financial risk premium required by investors as compensation for additional risk.[2]

These results can be employed to estimate the impact on expected return of a change in a firm's capital structure. The approach is illustrated in Exhibit 2. Assuming the firm currently employs debt in its capital structure, its observed beta will be the levered beta associated with its current ratio of debt to equity. The beta the stock would have if the firm changed its debt ratio can be estimated by a two-step procedure. The first step involves unlevering the stock's beta. Given its current debt ratio, *D/E,* and its current beta, β^L, its unlevered beta, β^U, can be calculated from the foregoing equation. The second step consists of relevering the stock's beta to reflect a change in capital structure. Given β^U and the new hypothetical debt ratio, *D/E,* the other equation presented can be used to calculate the stock's new levered beta, β^L. This levered beta is an estimate of the beta the stock would have if the debt ratio changed to that employed in the second stage of the procedure. The resulting estimate of beta can then be plugged into the familiar CAPM expression presented earlier, the security market line, to estimate the stock's expected return associated with the proposed debt ratio.

An example of levering and unlevering beta and expected return is presented in Exhibit 3 for General Electric (GE). An increase in GE's ratio of debt to equity from approximately .05 to .33 would result in an increase in its beta from 1.15 to 1.46. The increase in financial risk would result in an increase in the financial risk premium required by investors. Therefore, the estimated expected return on GE's stock rises from about 14% to roughly 16%. Similarly, a decrease in GE's debt ratio would decrease its beta and expected return.

The Decomposition of Expected Return into the Risk-Free Rate, Business Risk Premium, and Financial Risk Premium

The CAPM can be employed to decompose a stock's expected return into its basic components. This can be accomplished by combining the equation relating levered and unlevered beta and the basic CAPM expression, the SML. The general and CAPM versions of this decomposition are

2. This relation is only valid when the firm's debt does not have any systematic risk. It would be inappropriate to use this approach when the firm has risky debt outstanding.

$$\text{Expected return} = \frac{\text{Risk-free}}{\text{rate}} + \frac{\text{Business risk}}{\text{premium}} + \frac{\text{Financial risk}}{\text{premium}}$$

$$R_S = R_F + \beta^U(R_M - R_F) + \beta^U(D/E)(R_M - R_F)$$

Alternatively,

$$R_S = R_F + \beta^U(R_M - R_F) + (\beta^L - \beta^U)(R_M - R_F)$$

Thus, the expected return on a stock can be decomposed into (1) the risk-free rate, (2) a business risk premium present with no debt in the firm's capital structure (i.e., $D/E = 0$), and (3) the additional risk premium created by the existence of debt in the capital structure. With no debt in a firm's capital structure, the expected return on its stock consists only of the first two components. The effects of financial leverage are captured entirely in the third component. With the CAPM, this third component, the financial risk premium, is simply the increase in its beta, $\beta^L - \beta^U$, caused by financial leverage, multiplied by the risk premium on the market as a whole, $R_M - R_F$. Additional debt amplifies the systematic risk inherent in a firm's basic business operations and drives up the beta and expected return on its stock.

The example presented in Exhibit 4 demonstrates the use of these concepts to decompose the expected returns on two stocks, Procter & Gamble (P&G) and Colgate-Palmolive. P&G's business (or operating) risk is somewhat greater than Colgate's. Colgate's unlevered beta is .88, versus .92 for P&G, leading to a business risk premium of 6.16% for Colgate compared with 6.44% for P&G. Colgate's basic business risk is amplified by the higher level of debt in its capital structure, however, resulting in a financial risk premium which is roughly .70 percentage points more than P&G's. Thus, Colgate's overall risk premium—business risk premium plus financial risk premium—is actually larger than P&G's. Consequently, Colgate's levered beta and the expected return on its stock reflect its higher level of business and financial risk relative to P&G.

An example of the decomposition of the expected return on GE's stock at different debt ratios is presented in Exhibit 5. Note that changing the firm's debt ratio affects only its financial risk premium. As expected, the financial risk premium, the levered beta, and the expected return on GE's stock all increase with additional financial leverage.

Application to Corporate Finance

The CAPM facilitates the examination of the impact of financial leverage on expected returns. It therefore has an important application to corporate finance. A firm's cost of equity capital, k_E, is the expected (or required) return on the firm's stock. If the firm cannot expect to earn at least k_E on the equity-financed portion of its investments, funds should be returned to its shareholders, who can earn k_E on other securities of the same risk level in the financial marketplace. The CAPM can be used by financial managers to obtain an estimate of k_E and to examine the impact on k_E of financial leverage.

A firm's cost of equity capital is by definition the expected return on its stock. Since the basic CAPM expression, the security market line, yields estimates of expected returns, it can also be used to estimate costs of equity capital. Similarly, the CAPM concepts and techniques relating expected returns and financial leverage can be applied in examining the impact of financial leverage on the cost of equity capital. *The* *results presented earlier can be applied directly simply by recognizing that R_S, a stock's expected return, is equal to k_E, its cost of equity capital.*

To apply these concepts requires as inputs the risk-free rate, R_F, the expected return on the market as a whole, R_M, the stock's beta, and the ratio of debt to equity, D/E. As with any CAPM application, R_F can be estimated as the return on Treasury bills or bonds, and R_M can be estimated as the expected return on the Standard and Poor's Index of 500 Stocks. Betas can be estimated by linear regression and are also published by various investment advisory services. In estimating the debt ratio, the CAPM approach assumes that market values of debt and equity are employed. By definition, market values reflect the current values of debt and equity. In contrast, book values represent values prevailing in the past when the securities were issued. In addition, betas are themselves market-determined variables. Nevertheless, for convenience, book value debt ratios are often used in practice.

To examine the relation between the cost of equity capital and financial leverage, the estimated inputs are simply plugged into the equations presented earlier. The resulting expected returns are, by definition, costs of equity capital. The approach demonstrates that a firm's cost of equity is positively related to the level of debt in its capital structure, and the increment to the cost of equity generated by financial leverage can be estimated in the manner described earlier.

Conclusion

The capital asset pricing model is based upon extremely simple and clearly unrealistic assumptions. Empirical studies demonstrate that, consistent with the CAPM, there is a strong relation between stock returns and risk as measured by beta. Studies also generally support the relation between returns and financial leverage posited by the CAPM. However, these studies are by no means conclusive in establishing the validity of the CAPM. The application of the CAPM is also limited by problems associated with the model's inputs. Use of the model requires ad hoc estimates of several inputs, and the betas employed are subject to substantial estimation errors.

Thus, the CAPM should not be viewed as a wholly reliable method of estimating the cost of equity and examining the impact of financial leverage. However, in view of the deficiencies in alternative approaches, the CAPM represents a useful tool that managers may apply to an inherently difficult area of corporate finance. Finally, an alternative approach relating expected returns and financial leverage is outlined briefly in the Appendix.

Appendix

The CAPM methodology described in this note incorporates the implicit assumption that the firm's cost of debt is equal to the risk-free rate. An alternative approach that relaxes this restrictive assumption is presented in this Appendix. This more general approach examines the relation between the cost of equity capital and financial leverage. This relation expressed in cost of equity terms is

$$k_E^L = k_E^U + (k_E^U - k_D)\ D/E$$

where

k_E^L = levered cost of equity capital
k_E^U = unlevered cost of equity
k_D = cost of debt
D/E = ratio of debt to equity

In this equation k_E^U is the cost of equity if the firm has no debt in its capital structure. Therefore, k_E^U reflects the risk-free rate and a premium for business risk. The second term on the right-hand side of the equation captures the impact of financial leverage—the financial risk premium. With additional debt, the increase in the levered cost of equity is related to the difference between the unlevered cost of equity and the cost of debt. Solving for k_E^U, the equation becomes

$$k_E^U = \frac{k_E^L + k_D(D/E)}{1 + D/E}$$

Thus, given estimates of k_E^L, k_D, and D/E, the firm's unlevered cost of equity, k_E^U, can be calculated. The value of k_D will change with the degree of leverage in the firm's capital structure. Thus, the schedule of debt cost versus leverage must be known to estimate a new equity capital cost at a new debt ratio. To estimate the levered cost of equity associated with some new debt ratio, k_E^U, the new k_D, and the proposed D/E can be used as inputs in the previous equation.

This alternative approach can be employed in a manner analogous to that described previously. The equations can be manipulated to yield estimates of the cost of equity associated with various debt ratios and to decompose the cost of equity into its components. The advantage of this approach is that it is not tied exclusively to the assumptions of the CAPM. Specifically, it avoids the assumption that the firm's cost of debt is the risk-free rate. The advantage of the CAPM approach is the simple methodology it provides for levering and unlevering betas.

EXHIBIT 1
The Relation between a Firm's Financial Leverage and the Expected Return on Its Stock

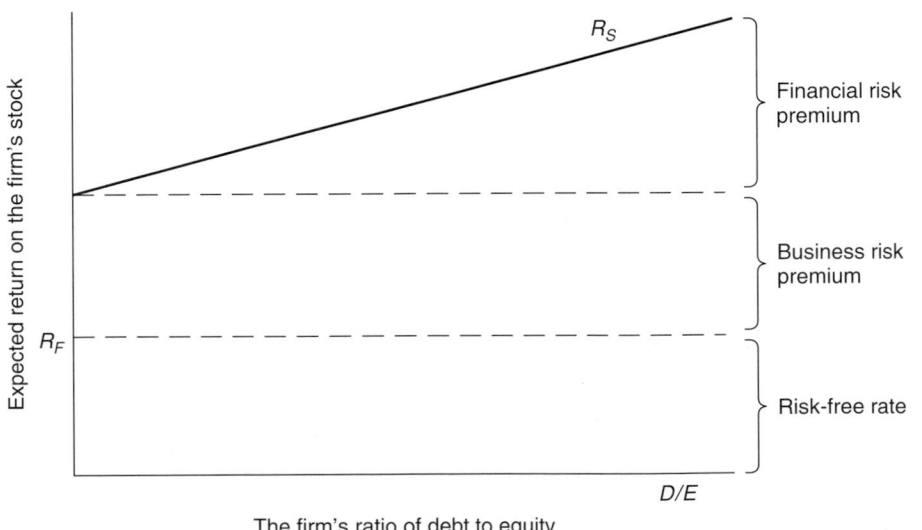

The firm's ratio of debt to equity

EXHIBIT 2
The Relation of Expected Return and Financial Leverage with the CAPM

Definitions:

R_S = stock's expected return
R_M = expected return on the market
D/E = firm's ratio of debt to equity
β^L = (levered) beta on the stock of a firm if $D/E > 0$
β^U = (unlevered) beta on the stock of the same firm if $D/E = 0$

CAPM equations:

Security market line (SML): $R_S = R_F + \beta(R_M - R_F)$
Levering beta: $\beta^L = \beta^U(1 + D/E)$

Unlevering beta: $\beta^U = \dfrac{\beta^L}{1 + D/E}$

To estimate the impact of a change in capital structure:

Step 1: Estimate the unlevered beta.
Given: current D/E and current estimated β^L.

Unlever the beta by solving: $\beta^U = \dfrac{\beta^L}{1 + D/E}$

Step 2: Estimate the levered beta associated with the new D/E.
Given: β^U from Step 1 and the new D/E.
Lever the beta by solving: $\beta^L = \beta^U(1 + D/E)$

The estimated beta for the new debt ratio is then used in the SML equation to estimate the expected return associated with the new D/E.

EXHIBIT 3
Sample Analysis of the Impact on Expected Return of Financial Leverage with the CAPM, General Electric Company

Assumptions:

$R_M = 13\%$; $R_F = 6\%$
GE's current $D/E = .05$
Current $\beta^L_{GE} = 1.15$

Unlevering GE's beta:

$$\beta^U_{GE} = \frac{\beta^L_{GE}}{1 + D/E} = \frac{1.15}{1 + .05} = 1.10$$

CAPM:

	Levering Beta	Security Market Line (SML)
Equations:	$\beta^L_{GE} = \beta^U_{GE}(1 + D/E)$	$R_S = R_F + \beta_{GE}(R_M - R_F)$
Example:		
Proposed $D/E = 0.50$	$\beta^L_{GE} = 1.10(1 + .50) = 1.65$	$R_S = 6\% + 1.65(13\% - 6\%) = 17.6\%$

Summary results:

Debt Ratio	GE's Beta	GE's Expected Return, R_S
Currently, $D/E = .05$	1.15	14.0%
Unlevered, $D/E = 0$	1.10	13.7%
Proposed, $D/E = .33$	1.46	16.2%
Proposed, $D/E = .50$	1.65	17.6%

EXHIBIT 4
Sample Decomposition of Expected Return, Procter & Gamble Company and Colgate-Palmolive Company

	Procter & Gamble	**Colgate-Palmolive**
Unlevering betas:		
Debt ratio	$D/E = .14$	$D/E = .31$
Levered beta	$\beta^L_{PG} = 1.05$	$\beta^L_{CG} = 1.15$
To unlever beta	$$\beta^U = \frac{\beta^L}{1 + D/E}$$	
Unlevered beta	$\beta^U_{PG} = .92$	$\beta^U_{CP} = .88$

Expected return calculation and decomposition:

Assumptions: $R_M = 13\%$; $R_F = 6\%$

Definitions: BRP = business risk premium; FRP = financial risk premium

Procter & Gamble

Expected return decomposition:	$R_{PG} = R_F + \beta^U_{PG}(R_M - R_F)$	$+ (\beta^L_{PG} - \beta^U_{PG})(R_M - R_F)$
Substituting assumed values:	$R_{PG} = 6\% + .92(13\% - 6\%)$	$+ (1.05 - .92)(13\% - 6\%)$
Results:	$13.35\% = 6\% + 6.44\%$	$+ .91$
	$R_{PG} = R_F + BRP_{PG}$	$+ FRP_{PG}$

Colgate-Palmolive

$R_{CP} = R_F + \beta^U_{CP}(R_M - R_F)$	$+ (\beta^L_{CP} - \beta^U_{CP})(R_M - R_F)$
$R_{CP} = 6\% + .88(13\% - 6\%)$	$+ (1.15 - .88)(13\% - 6\%)$
$14.05\% = 6\% + 6.16\%$	$+ 1.89\%$
$R_{CP} = R_F + BRP_{CP}$	$+ FRP_{CP}$

EXHIBIT 5
Sample Decomposition of Expected Return at Various Debt Ratios,
General Electric Company

| | *From Exhibit 3:* | |
| | *Debt Ratio* | *GE's Beta* |

Assumptions:

$R_M = 13\%$ Currently, $D/E = .05$ $\beta_{GE}^{L} = 1.15$

$R_F = 6\%$ Unlevered, $D/E = 0$ $\beta_{GE}^{U} = 1.10$

Proposed, $D/E = .33$ $\beta_{GE}^{L} = 1.46$

Proposed, $D/E = .50$ $\beta_{GE}^{L} = 1.65$

Expected return decomposition:

$$R_{GE} = R_F + BRP_{GE} \qquad + FRP_{GE}$$

$$R_{GE} = R_F + \beta_{GE}^{U}(R_M - R_F) \qquad + (\beta_{GE}^{L} - \beta_{GE}^{U})(R_M - R_F)$$

Example:
Proposed
$D/E = .50$

$$R_{GE} = 6\% + 1.10(13\% - 6\%) + (1.65 - 1.10)(13\% - 6\%)$$

$$17.55\% = 6\% + 7.70\% \qquad + 3.85\%$$

Summary results:

Debt Ratio	$R_{GE} = R_F + BRP_{GE} + FRP_{GE}$
Currently, $D/E = .05$	$14.05\% = 6\% + 7.70\% + .35\%$
Unlevered, $D/E = 0$	$13.70\% = 6\% + 7.70\% + 0\%$
Proposed, $D/E = .33$	$16.22\% = 6\% + 7.70\% + 2.52\%$
Proposed, $D/E = .50$	$17.55\% = 6\% + 7.70\% + 3.85$

Marriott Corporation: The Cost of Capital (Abridged)

In April 1988, Dan Cohrs, vice president of project finance at the Marriott Corporation, was preparing his annual recommendations for the hurdle rates at each of the firm's three divisions. Investment projects at Marriott were selected by discounting the appropriate cash flows by the appropriate hurdle rate for each division.

In 1987, Marriott's sales grew by 24% and its return on equity (ROE) stood at 22%. Sales and earnings per share had doubled over the previous 4 years, and the operating strategy was aimed at continuing this trend. Marriott's 1987 annual report stated:

> We intend to remain a premier growth company. This means aggressively developing appropriate opportunities within our chosen lines of business—lodging, contract services, and related businesses. In each of these areas, our goal is to be the preferred employer, the preferred provider, and the most profitable company.

Cohrs recognized that the divisional hurdle rates at Marriott would have a significant impact on the firm's financial and operating strategies. As a rule of thumb, increasing the hurdle rate by 1% (for example, from 12% to 12.12%), decreased the present value of project inflows by 1%. Because costs remained roughly fixed, these changes in the value of inflows translated into changes in the net present value of projects. Figure A shows the substantial impact of hurdle rates on the anticipated net present value of projects. If hurdle rates increased, Marriott's growth would be reduced, as once profitable projects would no longer meet the hurdle rates. Conversely, if hurdle rates decreased, Marriott's growth would accelerate.

Marriott also considered using the hurdle rates to determine incentive compensation. Annual incentive compensation constituted a significant portion of total compensation, ranging from 30% to 50% of base pay. Criteria for bonus awards depended on specific job responsibilities but often included the earnings level, the ability of managers to meet budgets, and overall corporate performance. There was some interest,

This case was prepared by Professor Richard S. Ruback.

Copyright © 1989 by the President and Fellows of Harvard College.
Harvard Business School case 289–047.

FIGURE A
Typical Hotel Profit and Hurdle Rates

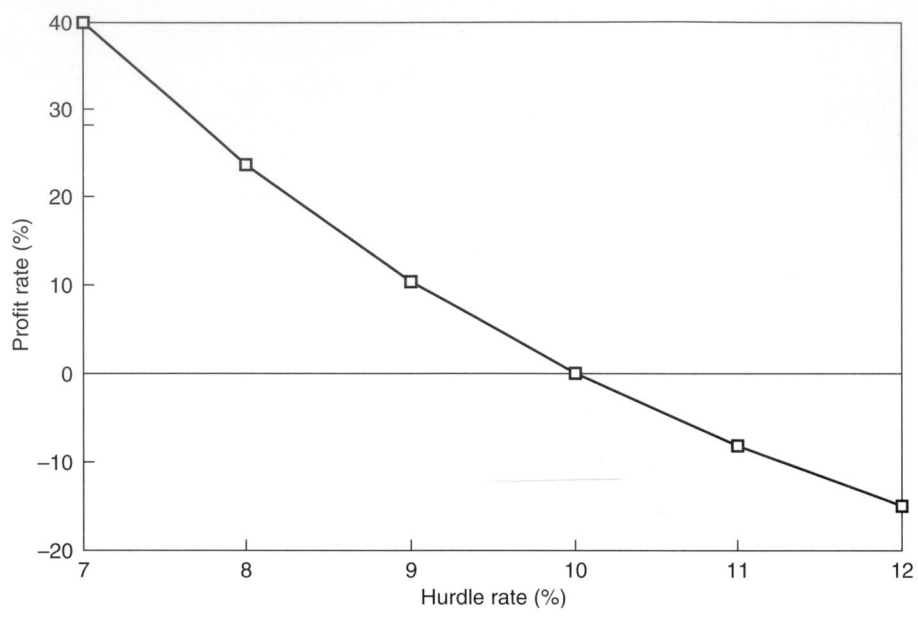

Source: Casewriter's estimates.

Note: Profit rate for a hotel is its net present value divided by its cost.

however, in basing the incentive compensation, in part, on a comparison of the divisional return on net assets and the market-based divisional hurdle rate. The compensation plan would then reflect hurdle rates, making managers more sensitive to Marriott's financial strategy and capital market conditions.

Company Background

Marriott Corporation began in 1927 with J. Willard Marriott's root beer stand. Over the next 60 years, the business grew into one of the leading lodging and food service companies in the United States. Marriott's 1987 profits were $223 million on sales of $6.5 billion. See Exhibit 1 for a summary of Marriott's financial history.

Marriott had three major lines of business: lodging, contract services, and restaurants. Exhibit 2 summarizes its line-of-business data. Lodging operations included 361 hotels, with more than 100,000 rooms in total. Hotels ranged from the full-service, high-quality Marriott hotels and suites to the moderately priced Fairfield Inn. Lodging generated 41% of 1987 sales and 51% of profits.

Contract services provided food and services management to health-care and educational institutions and corporations. It also provided airline catering and airline services through its Marriott In-Flite Services and Host International operations. Contract services generated 46% of 1987 sales and 33% of profits.

Marriott's restaurants included Bob's Big Boy, Roy Rogers, and Hot Shoppes. Restaurants provided 13% of 1987 sales and 16% of profits.

Financial Strategy

The four key elements of Marriott's financial strategy were:

- Manage rather than own hotel assets.
- Invest in projects that increase shareholder value.
- Optimize the use of debt in the capital structure.
- Repurchase undervalued shares.

Manage Rather Than Own Hotel Assets

In 1987, Marriott developed more than $1 billion worth of hotel properties, making it one of the ten largest commercial real estate developers in the United States. With a fully integrated development process, Marriott identified markets, created development plans, designed projects, and evaluated potential profitability.

After development, the company sold the hotel assets to limited partners, while retaining operating control as the general partner under a long-term management contract. Management fees typically equaled 3% of revenues plus 20% of the profits before depreciation and debt service. The 3% of revenues usually covered the overhead cost of managing the hotel. Marriott's 20% of profits before depreciation and debt service often required it to stand aside until investors earned a prespecified return. Marriott also guaranteed a portion of the partnership's debt. During 1987, 3 Marriott hotels and 70 Courtyard hotels were syndicated for $890 million. In total, the company operated about $7 billion worth of syndicated hotels.

Invest in Projects That Increase Shareholder Value

The company used discounted cash flow techniques to evaluate potential investments. The hurdle rate assigned to a specific project was based on market interest rates, project risk, and estimates of risk premiums. Cash flow forecasts incorporated standard companywide assumptions that instilled some consistency across projects. As one Marriott executive put it:

> Our projects are like a lot of similar little boxes. This similarity disciplines the pro forma analysis. There are corporate macro data on inflation, margins, project lives, terminal values, percent of sales required to remodel, and so on. Projects are audited throughout their lives to check and update these standard pro forma template assumptions. Divisional managers still have discretion over unit-specific assumptions, but they must conform to the corporate templates.

Optimize the Use of Debt in the Capital Structure

Marriott determined the amount of debt in its capital structure by focusing on its ability to service its debt. It used an interest-coverage target instead of a target debt-to-equity ratio. In 1987, Marriott had about $2.5 billion of debt, 59% of its total capital.

Repurchase Undervalued Shares

Marriott regularly calculated a "warranted equity value" for its common shares and was committed to repurchasing its stock whenever its market price fell substantially below that value. The warranted equity value was calculated by discounting the firm's equity cash flows by its equity cost of capital. It was checked by comparing Marriott's stock price with that of comparable companies using price/earnings ratios for each business and by valuing each business under alternative ownership structures, such as a leveraged buyout. Marriott had more confidence in its measure of warranted value than in the day-to-day market price of its stock. A gap between warranted value and market price, therefore, usually triggered repurchases instead of a revision in the warranted value by, for example, revising the hurdle rate. Furthermore, the company believed that repurchases of shares below warranted equity value were a better use of its cash flow and debt capacity than acquisitions or owning real estate. In 1987, Marriott repurchased 13.6 million shares of its common stock for $429 million.

The Cost of Capital

Marriott measured the opportunity cost of capital for investments of similar risk using the weighted average cost of capital (WACC):

$$\text{WACC} = (1 - \tau)\bar{r}_D(D/V) + \bar{r}_E(E/V)$$

where D and E are the market value of the debt and equity, respectively, $\bar{r}_D$ is the pretax cost of debt, $\bar{r}_E$ is the after-tax cost of equity, and V is the value of the firm. ($V = D + E$), and τ is the corporate tax rate. Marriott used this approach to determine the cost of capital for the corporation as a whole and for each division.

To determine the opportunity cost of capital, Marriott required three inputs: debt capacity, debt cost, and equity cost consistent with the amount of debt. The cost of capital varied across the three divisions because all three of the cost-of-capital inputs could differ for each division. The cost of capital for each division was updated annually.

Debt Capacity and the Cost of Debt

Marriott applied its coverage-based financing policy to each of its divisions. It also determined for each division the fraction of debt that should be floating-rate debt based on the sensitivity of the division's cash flows to interest rate changes. The interest rate on floating-rate debt changed as interest rates changed. If cash flows increased as the interest rate increased, using floating-rate debt expanded debt capacity.

In April 1988, Marriott's unsecured debt was A rated. As a high-quality corporate risk, Marriott could expect to pay a spread above the current government bond rates. It based the debt cost for each division on an estimate of the division's debt cost as an independent company. The spread between the debt rate and the government bond rate varied by division because of differences in risk. Table A provides the market-value target leverage rates, the fraction of the debt at floating rate, the fraction at fixed rates, and the credit spread for Marriott as a whole and for each division. The credit spread was the debt rate premium above the government rate required to induce investors to lend money to Marriott.

TABLE A
Market-Value Target Leverage Ratios and Credit Spreads for Marriott and Its Divisions

	Debt Percentage in Capital	Fraction of Debt at Floating	Fraction of Debt at Fixed	Debt Rate Premium Above Government
Marriott	60%	40%	60%	1.30%
Lodging	74	50	50	1.10
Contract services . . .	40	40	60	1.40
Restaurants	42	25	75	1.80

TABLE B
U.S. Government Interest Rates, April 1988

Maturity	Rate
30-year	8.95%
10-year	8.72
1-year	6.90

[handwritten: — longterm → short ti.]

Because lodging assets, like hotels, had long useful lives, Marriott used the cost of long-term debt for its lodging cost-of-capital calculations. It used shorter-term debt as the cost of debt for its restaurant and contract services divisions because those assets had shorter useful lives.

Table B lists the interest rates on fixed-rate U.S. government securities in April 1988.

The Cost of Equity

Marriott recognized that meeting its financial strategy of embarking only on projects that increased shareholder values meant that it had to use its shareholders' measure of equity costs. Marriott used the capital asset pricing model (CAPM) to estimate the cost of equity. The CAPM, originally developed by John Lintner and William Sharpe in the early 1960s, had gained wide acceptance among financial professionals. According to the CAPM, the cost of equity, or equivalently, the expected return for equity, was determined as

$$\text{Expected return} = R = \text{Risk-free rate} + \beta \times (\text{Risk premium})$$

where the risk premium is the difference between the expected return on the market portfolio and the riskless rate.

The key insight in the CAPM was that risk should be measured relative to a fully diversified portfolio of risky assets such as common stocks. The simple adage "Don't put all your eggs in one basket" dictated that investors could minimize their risks by holding assets in fully diversified portfolios. An asset's risk was not measured as its individual risk. Instead, the asset's contribution to the risk of a fully diversified or market portfolio was what mattered. This risk, usually called systematic risk, was measured by the beta coefficient (β).

Betas could be calculated from historical data on common stock returns using simple linear regression analysis. Marriott's beta, calculated using monthly stock returns during the 1983–1987 period, was 1.11.

Two problems limited the use of the historical estimates of beta in calculating the hurdle rates for projects. First, corporations generally had multiple lines of business. A company's beta, therefore, was a weighted average of the betas of its different lines of business. Second, leverage affected beta. Adding debt to a firm increased its equity beta even if the riskiness of the firm's assets remained unchanged, because the safest cash flows went to the debt holders. As debt increased, the cash flows remaining for stockholders became more risky. The historical beta of a firm, therefore, had to be interpreted and adjusted before it could be used as a project's beta, unless the project had the same risk and the same leverage as the firm overall.

Exhibit 3 contains the beta, leverage, and other related information for Marriott and comparable companies in the lodging and restaurant businesses.

To select the appropriate risk premium to use in the hurdle rate calculations, Mr. Cohrs examined a variety of data on the stock and bond markets. Exhibit 4 provides historical information on the holding-period returns on government and corporate bonds and the S&P 500 Composite Index of common stocks. Holding-period returns were the returns realized by the security holder, including any cash payment (e.g., dividends for common stocks, coupons for bonds) received by the holder plus any capital gain or loss on the security. As examples, the 5.23% holding-period return for the S&P 500 Composite Index of common stocks in 1987 was the sum of the dividend yield of 3.20% and the capital gain of 2.03%. The −2.69% holding-period return for the index of long-term U.S. government bonds in 1987 was the sum of the coupon yield of 7.96% and a capital gain of −10.65%.[1]

Exhibit 5 provides statistics on the spread between the S&P 500 Composite returns and the holding-period returns on Treasury bills, U.S. government bonds, and high-grade, long-term corporate bonds.

Mr. Cohrs was concerned about the correct time interval to measure these averages, especially given the high returns and volatility of the bond markets shown in Exhibits 4 and 5.

---

1. Cash payments are assumed to be invested in the respective securities monthly.

EXHIBIT 1
Financial History of Marriott Corporation (millions of dollars except per share amounts)

	1978	1979	1980	1981	1982	1983	1984	1985	1986	1987
Summary of Operations										
Sales	$1,174.1	$1,426.0	$1,633.9	$1,905.7	$2,458.9	$2,950.5	$3,524.9	$4,241.7	$5,266.5	$6,522.2
Earnings before interest expense and income taxes	107.1	133.5	150.3	173.3	205.5	247.9	297.7	371.3	420.5	489.4
Interest expense	23.7	27.8	46.8	52.0	71.8	62.8	61.6	75.6	60.3	90.5
Income before income taxes	83.5	105.6	103.5	121.3	133.7	185.1	236.1	295.7	360.2	398.9
Income taxes	35.4	43.8	40.6	45.2	50.2	76.7	100.8	128.3	168.5	175.9
Income from continuing operations[a]	48.1	61.8	62.9	76.1	83.5	108.4	135.3	167.4	191.7	223.0
Net income	54.3	71.0	72.0	86.1	94.3	115.2	139.8	167.4	191.7	223.0
Funds provided from cont. operations[b]	101.2	117.5	125.8	160.8	203.6	272.7	322.5	372.3	430.3	472.8
Capitalization and Returns										
Total assets	$1,000.3	$1,080.4	$1,214.3	$1,454.9	$2,062.6	$2,501.4	$2,904.7	$3,663.8	$4,579.3	$5,370.5
Total capital[c]	826.9	891.9	977.7	1,167.5	1,634.5	2,007.5	2,330.7	2,861.4	3,561.8	4,247.8
Long-term debt	309.9	365.3	536.6	607.7	889.3	1,071.6	1,115.3	1,192.3	1,662.8	2,498.8
Percent to total capital	37.5%	41.0%	54.9%	52.1%	54.4%	53.4%	47.9%	41.7%	46.7%	58.8%
Shareholders' equity	418.7	413.5	311.5	421.7	516.0	628.2	675.6	848.5	991.0	810.8
Per Share and Other Data										
Earnings per share										
Continuing operations[a]	$ .25	$ .34	$ .45	$ .57	$ .61	$ .78	$1.00	$1.24	$1.40	$1.67
Net income	.29	.39	.52	.64	.69	.83	1.04	1.24	1.40	1.67
Cash dividends	.026	.034	.042	.051	.063	.076	.093	.113	.136	.17
Shareholders' equity	2.28	2.58	2.49	3.22	3.89	4.67	5.25	6.48	7.59	6.82
Market price at year-end	2.43	3.48	6.35	7.18	11.70	14.25	14.70	21.58	29.75	30.00
Shares outstanding (in millions)	183.6	160.5	125.3	130.8	132.8	134.4	128.8	131.0	130.6	118.8
Return on avg. shareholders' equity	13.9%	17.0%	23.8%	23.4%	20.0%	20.0%	22.1%	22.1%	20.6%	22.2%

Source: Company reports.

a. The company's theme park operations were discontinued in 1984.

b. Funds provided from continuing operations consist of income from continuing operations plus depreciation, deferred income taxes, and other items not currently affecting working capital.

c. Total capital represents total assets less current liabilities.

don't take th book value

EXHIBIT 2
Financial Summary by Business Segment, 1982–1987 (millions of dollars)

	1982	1983	1984	1985	1986	1987
Lodging						
Sales	$1,091.7	$1,320.5	$1,640.8	$1,898.4	$2,233.1	$2,673.3
Operating profit	132.6	139.7	161.2	185.8	215.7	263.9
Identifiable assets	909.7	1,264.6	1,786.3	2,108.9	2,236.7	2,777.4
Depreciation	22.7	27.4	31.3	32.4	37.1	43.9
Capital expenditures	371.5	377.2	366.4	808.3	966.6	1,241.9
Contract Services						
Sales	$ 819.8	$ 950.6	$1,111.3	$1,586.3	$2,236.1	$2,969.0
Operating profit	51.0	71.1	86.8	118.6	154.9	170.6
Identifiable assets	373.3	391.6	403.9	624.4	1,070.2	1,237.7
Depreciation	22.9	26.1	28.9	40.2	61.1	75.3
Capital expenditures	127.7	43.8	55.6	125.9	448.7	112.7
Restaurants						
Sales	$ 547.4	$ 679.4	$ 707.0	$ 757.0	$ 797.3	$ 879.9
Operating profit	48.5	63.8	79.7	78.2	79.1	82.4
Identifiable assets	452.2	483.0	496.7	582.6	562.3	467.6
Depreciation	25.1	31.8	35.5	34.8	38.1	42.1
Capital expenditures	199.6	65.0	72.3	128.4	64.0	79.6

Source: Company reports.

Max - operating profit → lodging.

C. s %.

capital expenditures keep increasing.

EXHIBIT 3

Information on Comparable Hotel and Restaurant Companies

Company and Nature of Business	Arithmetic Average Return[a]	Equity Beta[b]	Market Leverage[c]	1987 Revenues ($ billions)
Marriott Corporation .... (Owns, operates, and manages hotels, restaurants, and airline and institutional food services)	10.57%	1.11	41%	6.52
Hotels				
Hilton Hotels Corporation .... (Owns, manages, and licenses hotels; operates casinos)	17.16	0.76	14	0.77
Holiday Corporation.............. (Owns, manages, and licenses hotels and restaurants; operates casinos)	32.89	1.35	79	1.66
La Quinta Motor Inns .... (Owns, operates, and licenses motor inns)	−5.19	0.89	69	0.17
Ramada Inns, Inc................ (Owns and operates hotels and restaurants)	10.57	1.36	65	0.75
Restaurants				
Church's Fried Chicken .... (Owns and franchises restaurants and gaming businesses)	1.79	1.45	4	0.39
Collins Foods International .... (Operates Kentucky Fried Chicken franchise and moderately priced restaurants)	24.32	1.45	10	0.57
Frisch's Restaurants .... (Operates and franchises restaurants)	45.83	0.57	6	0.14
Luby's Cafeterias .... (Operates cafeterias)	15.50	0.76	1	0.23
McDonald's .... (Operates, franchises, and services restaurants)	23.93	0.94	23	4.89
Wendy's International .... (Operates, franchises, and services restaurants)	7.76	1.32	21	1.05

Source: Casewriter estimates.

a. Calculated over the period 1983–1987.

b. Estimated using 5 years of monthly data over the 1983–1987 period.

c. Book value of debt divided by the sum of the book value of debt plus the market value of equity.

Total

EXHIBIT 4
Annual Holding-Period Returns for Selected Securities and Market Indexes, 1926–1987

Years	Arithmetic Average	Standard Deviation
Short-Term Treasury Bills		
1926–1987	3.54%	0.94%
1926–1950	1.01	0.40
1951–1975	3.67	0.56
1976–1980	7.80	0.83
1981–1985	10.32	0.75
1986	6.16	0.19
1987	5.46	0.22
Long-Term U.S. Government Bond Returns		
1926–1987	4.58%	7.58%
1926–1950	4.14	4.17
1951–1975	2.39	6.45
1976–1980	1.95	11.15
1980–1985	17.85	14.26
1986	24.44	17.30
1987	−2.69	10.28
Long-Term, High-Grade Corporate Bond Returns		
1926–1987	5.24%	6.97%
1926–1950	4.82	3.45
1951–1975	3.05	6.04
1976–1980	2.70	10.87
1981–1985	18.96	14.17
1986	19.85	8.19
1987	−0.27	9.64
Standard and Poor's 500 Composite Stock Index Returns		
1926–1987	12.01	20.55
1926–1950	10.90	27.18
1951–1975	11.87	13.57
1976–1980	14.81	14.60
1981–1985	15.49	13.92
1986	18.47	17.94
1987	5.23	30.50

Source: Casewriter estimates based on data from the University of Chicago's Center for Research in Security Prices.

EXHIBIT 5
Spreads between S&P 500 Composite Returns and Bond Rates, 1926–1987

Years	Arithmetic Average	Standard Deviation
Spread between S&P 500 Composite Returns and Short-Term U.S. Treasury Bill Returns		
1926–1987	8.47%	20.60%
1926–1950	9.89	27.18
1951–1975	8.20	13.71
1976–1980	7.01	14.60
1981–1985	5.17	14.15
1986	12.31	17.92
1987	−0.23	30.61
Spread between S&P 500 Composite Returns and Long-Term U.S. Government Bond Returns		
1926–1987	7.43%	20.78%
1926–1950	6.76	26.94
1951–1975	9.48	14.35
1976–1980	12.86	15.58
1981–1985	−2.36	13.70
1986	−5.97	14.76
1987	7.92	35.35
Spread between S&P 500 Composite Returns and Long-Term, High-Grade Corporate Bonds		
1926–1987	6.77%	20.31%
1926–1950	6.06	26.70
1951–1975	8.82	13.15
1976–1980	12.11	15.84
1981–1985	−3.47	13.59
1986	−1.38	14.72
1987	5.50	34.06

Source: Casewriter estimates based on data from the University of Chicago's Center for Research in Security Prices.

American Chemical Corporation

In June 1979, American Chemical Corporation announced a tender offer for any and all shares of the Universal Paper Corporation. American was one of the largest diversified chemical companies in the United States (see Exhibit 1). Universal was a large paper and pulp company (see Exhibit 2).

Universal's management opposed the takeover and, among other things, sued in federal court to have the tender offer blocked on grounds that American's acquisition of Universal would violate the Clayton Act of the U.S. antitrust laws. Both firms engaged in the production of sodium chlorate. Universal alleged that its acquisition by American would substantially reduce competition in the sodium chlorate business, particularly in the southeastern U.S. market, where the two firms were competitors. The U.S. government joined Universal in seeking a preliminary injunction to stop American's tender offer. Though it denied the allegations, American prevented a preliminary injunction by agreeing to divest its sodium chlorate plant located near Collinsville, Alabama, in the event it acquired Universal. American subsequently was successful in acquiring over 91% of Universal's shares.

In October 1979, American began looking for a buyer for the Collinsville plant. A number of potential buyers were approached, including the Dixon Corporation, a specialty chemicals company. After lengthy negotiations. Dixon agreed to purchase the net assets of the Collinsville plant from American for $12 million, subject to approval by its board of directors.

The Market for Sodium Chlorate

Sodium chlorate ($NaClO_3$) was a chemical produced by the electrolytic decomposition of salt ($NaCl$) according to the chemical formula

$$NaCl + 3H_2O + energy \rightarrow NaClO_3 + 3H_2$$

Sodium chlorate was sold either as a white crystalline solid or in a 25% water solution.

Approximately 85% of the sodium chlorate produced in the United States was sold to the paper and pulp industries, where it was used in the bleaching of pulp. Sodium chlorate was reacted with salt (NaCl) and sulfuric acid (H_2SO_4) to produce a bleaching agent, chloride dioxide (ClO_2), according to the formula

$$NaClO_3 + NaCl + H_2SO_4 \rightarrow \tfrac{1}{2}Cl_2 + ClO_2 + Na_2SO_4 + H_2O$$

Chloride dioxide was the active ingredient actually used by paper and pulp producers to bleach pulp. The remaining 15% of the sodium chlorate produced in the United States was used in soil sterilants, in oxidizers for use in uranium mining, and in producing various chemicals, including sodium chlorite, potassium chlorate, and ammonium perchlorate.

Sales of sodium chlorate had grown rapidly during the 1970s, from 220,000 tons in 1970 to an expected 435,000 tons in 1979 (see Exhibit 3). Sales increased by approximately 8.6% per year during the period 1970–1974 but then declined 12% in 1975 when pulp production decreased during the recession. Demand improved during the subsequent recovery, and sales grew by more than 10% per year between 1975 and 1979.

Demand for sodium chlorate from pulp producers was expected to continue increasing at 8–10% per year. While pulp production was projected to increase at a slower annual rate of about 3–4%, pulp producers' use of sodium chlorate was expected to grow more rapidly because use of sodium chlorate (and the active ingredient chloride dioxide) helped solve their plant effluent problems. Other uses of sodium chlorate also were expected to grow at about 8–10% per year.

Capacity additions had not kept pace with sales growth during the 1970s (see Exhibit 3). Though sales had increased by over 95% between 1970 and 1979, capacity had increased by less than 70% during this period. The resulting tight markets in 1973–1974 and 1977–1978 caused a substantial improvement in profit margins between 1970 and 1979, even though production costs also increased greatly during this period. These tight markets and cost increases had caused prices for sodium chlorate to increase rapidly beginning in 1973 (see Exhibit 3).

In late 1979, there were a dozen domestic producers of sodium chlorate (see Exhibits 4 and 5). The market was dominated by large diversified chemical companies (Hooker, Pennwalt, American, and Kerr-McGee). However, a number of paper and pulp companies (Georgia-Pacific and Universal) had integrated backward into the production of sodium chlorate. In addition, two firms (Brunswick and Southern) specialized in producing sodium chlorate. The three largest producers accounted for over 55% of domestic capacity.

The majority of sodium chlorate plants were located in the southeastern United States (see Exhibit 4), where approximately two-thirds of the product was consumed due to the high regional concentration of pulp and paper mills. Freight costs represented a significant portion of delivered sodium chlorate costs, and plants tended therefore to be located within 800 miles of their principal markets. Market concentration was slightly higher in the southeastern market than in the total U.S. market. The three largest producers accounted for approximately 59% of the southeastern market.

In addition to existing producers, two firms had announced plans to enter the sodium chlorate business in 1980. Union Chemicals Corporation was constructing a 40,000-ton plant in Gainsville, Georgia, and Louisiana Paper Company was building a 35,000-ton plant in Greenville, Mississippi. This increase in industry capacity was expected to reduce margins and decrease capacity utilization during 1980 and 1981. However, as sales and productive capacity achieved a closer balance, prices and margins were expected to improve once again. It should be noted that the selling price necessary to obtain a 15% return on investment on a newly constructed 40,000-ton sodium chlorate plant was estimated to be $420 per ton in 1979.

The Collinsville Plant

American's plant in Collinsville, Alabama, had the capacity to produce 40,000 tons of sodium chlorate per year. Sodium chlorate was produced by the electrolysis of sodium chloride brine in electrolytic cells called D cells, which used graphite electrodes. The facility consisted of 20 cell tanks (or groups of cells) that were operated batchwise. They were filled with saturated brine and then electrolized to an endpoint. Graphite was consumed in the process. The resulting fluid was chemically treated to precipitate impurities, which were discarded. The remaining sodium chlorate solution was either shipped as a fluid or crystallized to a white solid.

The plant had been consistently profitable during the period 1974–1979 (see Exhibit 6). Operating profits had ranged from a low of $817,000 in 1975 to a high of $4,845,000 in 1978. Net assets had grown from $4,619,000 in 1974 to $5,414,000 in 1979. Though the ratio of operating profits to net assets had dropped to 16.9% in 1975, it equaled 90.0% in 1978 and averaged 54.3% during the 1974–1979 period.

The major cost of production was electric power. The Collinsville facility needed approximately 7,000 kilowatt-hours (kWh) to produce a ton of sodium chlorate, and power costs accounted for 55–60% of manufacturing costs. Salt, graphite, and other variable costs typically represented another 20%, and labor and maintenance costs accounted for the remaining 20% of manufacturing costs.

Electric power was purchased from the Tennessee Valley Authority (TVA), whose hydroelectric power plants historically had been a source of cheap electric power. During the early 1970s, TVA's rates had been as much as 50% less than the rates of other electric utilities. However, as the region's power demands grew, TVA was finding it necessary to supplement its hydroelectric power plants with more expensive fossil fuel plants. TVA also was facing increasing pressure from consumer groups to allocate the more expensive power of fossil fuel plants to industrial users instead of residential users. As a result, the Collinsville plant's cost of power had increased from $.019 per kWh in 1977 to $.025 per kWh in 1979.

Capital expenditures at the Collinsville plant had ranged from $200,000 to $500,000 per year between 1973 and 1979 and were primarily for maintenance and pollution control. In late 1979, the plant was basically in compliance with all environmental regulations. Future capital expenditures were expected to range from $475,000 to $600,000 per year.

American had supported a research and development program that was expected to reduce costs at its sodium chlorate plants. New sodium chlorate plants increasingly were using metal electrodes (instead of graphite electrodes), which eliminated graphite costs and also reduced power needs by approximately 30%. However, the graphite electrodes at American's plants at Collinsville and Wenatchee, Washington, were not convertible at an acceptable cost to commercially available metal electrodes. American's research group therefore was working on a permanent laminate (or coating) that could be applied to the graphite electrodes in American's plants. Use of this laminate would eliminate graphite costs and was expected to reduce power needs by 15–20%. Development was approximately 40% complete, and scale-up to a pilot plant was scheduled for March 1980. American expected that the laminate could be installed at the Collinsville plant at a one-time cost of about $2.25 million, which could be depreciated over a period of 10 years. Installation at Collinsville was scheduled for December 1980.

Proposed Sale of the Collinsville Plant to the Dixon Corporation

The Dixon Corporation was a specialty chemicals company that produced a number of chemicals for sale primarily to the paper and pulp industry. Its principal products included sulfuric acid, aluminum sulfate, and liquid sulfur dioxide. As described earlier, sulfuric acid was used together with sodium chlorate to produce chloride dioxide, which was the active ingredient used to bleach pulp. Sulfuric acid also was used in the manufacture of other chemicals, steels, rayon, and detergents and in oil refining. Aluminum sulfate was used as a coagulant and purifying agent in the treatment of industrial and municipal waste. Dixon sold liquid sulfur dioxide to the paper and pulp industry for use in bleaching pulp, though it also was used to produce hydrosulfites for use in textile dyeing. The firm's principal plant was located in Calhoun, Georgia, and its sales were concentrated in the southeastern United States. Dixon's sales had grown rapidly and the firm had been consistently profitable (see Exhibit 7).

Acquisition of the Collinsville plant fit well with Dixon's strategy of supplying chemicals to the paper and pulp industry. Sodium chlorate would complement Dixon's existing product lines. Dixon already did business with some of the Collinsville plant's major customers. Sodium chlorate, therefore, could be marketed largely through Dixon's existing sales group.

In evaluating the plant's purchase, Dixon prepared the pro forma financial statements shown in Exhibit 8. These figures analyzed the plant's future profitability given its unlaminated graphite electrodes and in the absence of the operating economies that might be realized from installing laminated electrodes. Industry overcapacity was expected to push margins down in the short run. However, Dixon expected that sodium chlorate prices would increase on average at 8% per year. Power costs (per kWh) were projected to increase more rapidly, at 12% per year. Selling expenses could be reduced by marketing sodium chlorate through Dixon's existing sales force. Dixon also expected to write up the value of the Collinsville plant, which would increase its depreciation charges.[1]

As part of the sale agreement, American agreed to provide ongoing technical support to the Collinsville plant. American would keep Dixon informed concerning development of the laminated electrodes and make this technology available to Dixon. However, Dixon would have to pay for all costs associated with installation of the laminated electrodes.

The $12 million purchase price was to be financed entirely with debt capital. It was to be financed in part by privately placing $8 million in 15-year mortgage bonds with two insurance companies. These bonds would carry an 11.25% interest rate. The sinking fund provision on these bonds would retire $800,000 of bonds each year

---

1. Net working capital accounted for $1.4 million of the $12 million purchase price (Exhibit 6). Dixon planned to allocate the $10.6 million balance of the $12 million purchase price to the Collinsville plant. The plant would be depreciated over 10 years on the straight-line method of depreciation to a zero residual value. This relatively short life was permitted for tax purposes because it corresponded to the anticipated remaining physical life of the plant.

beginning the sixth year. The remainder of the $12 million purchase price was to be financed by having Dixon issue American a $4 million note to be paid off in equal amounts over 5 years. The note also carried an 11.25% interest rate.[2]

This financing package would temporarily increase Dixon's debt-to-total-capital ratio to approximately 47%. Though the firm had almost no debt immediately prior to the proposed acquisition, Dixon had relied more heavily on debt capital in the past. However, use of this much debt would initially raise the debt ratio above the firm's target debt ratio of about 35%.

---

2. Market interest rates were as follows:

Short-term Treasury bills:	10.5%
Long-term Treasury bonds:	9.5%
Long-term AA corporate bonds:	10.25%
Long-term A corporate bonds:	10.75%
Long-term BBB corporate bonds:	11.25%

EXHIBIT 1
Financial Statements for American Chemical and Other Selected Large Chemical Companies, 1974–1978 (millions of dollars except per share data)

American Chemical

	1974	1975	1976	1977	1978
Sales	$4,828	$4,671	$4,805	$5,235	$5,490
Net income	323	198	212	251	349
Earnings per share	$ 7.60	$ 4.66	$ 4.98	$ 5.91	$ 8.20
Dividends per share	1.00	1.25	1.50	1.65	1.80
Dividend yield	5.3%	5.7%	4.3%	5.0%	4.1%
Common stock prices					
High	$ 23	$ 30	$ 36	$ 46	$ 48
Low	10	17	21	30	32
Closing	19	22	35	33	44
Closing P/E ratio	2.5	4.7	7.0	5.6	5.4
Total capitalization	$2,014	$2,109	$2,198	$2,465	$2,527
% debt	44%	37%	37%	29%	39%
% preferred stock	—	—	—	—	20%
% common stock	56%	63%	63%	71%	41%
Beta			1.20		
Interest coverage[a]	6.3	3.9	4.1	4.3	6.7
Bond rating[b]			BBB/A		

Allied Chemical

	1974	1975	1976	1977	1978
Sales	$2,216	$2,333	$2,630	$2,923	$3,268
Net income	151	116	117	135	120
Earnings per share	$ 5.43	$ 4.17	$ 4.52	$ 4.93	$ 4.25
Dividends per share	1.53	1.80	1.80	1.85	2.00
Dividend yield	6.3%	5.4%	4.5%	4.5%	7.1%
Common stock prices					
High	$ 54	$ 42	$ 45	$ 51	$ 45
Low	23	27	33	39	28
Closing	28	33	40	44	28
Closing P/E ratio	5.2	7.9	8.8	8.9	6.6
Total capitalization	$1,550	$1,839	$1,959	$2,279	$2,467
% debt	28%	34%	33%	36%	38%
% preferred stock	—	—	—	—	—
% common stock	72%	66%	67%	64%	62%
Beta			1.43		
Interest coverage[a]	9.2	5.7	5.2	5.4	4.9
Bond rating[b]			A/A		

Dow Chemical

	1974	1975	1976	1977	1978
Sales	$4,938	$4,888	$5,652	$6,234	$6,888
Net income	558	616	613	566	575
Earnings per share	$ 3.18	$ 3.33	$ 3.30	$ 3.01	$ 3.16
Dividends per share	.60	.75	.95	1.15	1.30
Dividend yield	2.5%	1.7%	2.3%	4.5%	5.6%
Common stock prices					
High	$ 35	$ 48	$ 57	$ 44	$ 31
Low	25	27	38	25	22
Closing	28	46	43	27	25
Closing P/E ratio	8.8	13.8	13.0	9.0	7.9
Total capitalization	$3,498	$4,316	$5,118	$5,889	$6,793
% debt	37%	36%	37%	40%	43%
% preferred stock	—	—	—	—	—
% common stock	63%	64%	63%	60%	57%
Beta			1.25		
Interest coverage[a]	10.6	8.2	6.5	4.9	4.4
Bond rating[b]			A/Aa		

Du Pont

	1974	1975	1976	1977	1978
Sales	$6,910	$7,221	$8,361	$9,435	$10,584
Net income	404	272	459	545	787
Earnings per share	$ 2.74	$ 1.81	$ 3.10	$ 3.69	$ 5.39
Dividends per share	1.83	1.42	1.75	1.92	2.42
Dividend yield	6.0%	3.2%	3.7%	4.8%	5.8%
Common stock prices					
High	$ 60	$ 45	$ 54	$ 45	$ 46
Low	28	29	39	35	33
Closing	31	42	45	40	42
Closing P/E ratio	11.3	23.2	14.5	10.8	7.8
Total capitalization	$4,874	$5,085	$5,772	$6,127	$ 6,394
% debt	16%	17%	22%	21%	17%
% preferred stock	5%	5%	4%	4%	4%
% common stock	79%	78%	74%	75%	79%
Beta			1.22		
Interest coverage[a]	9.5	4.1	6.0	6.1	9.5
Bond rating[b]			AAA/Aaa		

Monsanto

	1974	1975	1976	1977	1978
Sales	$3,498	$3,625	$4,270	$4,595	$5,019
Net income	323	306	366	276	303
Earnings per share	$ 9.35	$ 8.63	$10.05	$ 7.46	$ 8.29
Dividends per share	2.30	2.55	2.75	3.03	3.18
Dividend yield	5.9%	3.4%	3.2%	5.4%	6.8%
Common stock prices					
High	$ 70	$ 81	$ 100	$ 89	$ 60
Low	39	41	76	52	44
Closing	41	76	88	58	47
Closing P/E ratio	4.4	8.8	8.8	7.8	5.7
Total capitalization	$2,396	$2,942	$3,349	$3,668	$4,115
% debt	25%	29%	27%	28%	30%
% preferred stock	—	—	—	—	—
% common stock	75%	71%	73%	72%	70%
Beta			1.43		
Interest coverage[a]	11.4	9.1	8.4	7.0	6.5
Bond rating[b]			AA/Aa		

Union Carbide

	1974	1975	1976	1977	1978
Sales	$5,320	$5,665	$6,346	$7,036	$7,870
Net income	530	382	441	385	394
Earnings per share	$ 8.69	$ 6.23	$ 7.15	$ 6.05	$ 6.09
Dividends per share	2.18	2.40	2.50	2.80	2.80
Dividend yield	5.3%	3.9%	4.0%	6.8%	8.2%
Common stock prices					
High	$ 46	$ 67	$ 77	$ 62	$ 43
Low	32	40	56	40	34
Closing	41	61	62	41	34
Closing P/E ratio	4.7	9.8	8.7	6.8	5.6
Total capitalization	$3,752	$4,485	$5,212	$5,750	$5,997
% debt	26%	30%	32%	30%	28%
% preferred stock	—	—	—	—	—
% common stock	74%	70%	68%	70%	72%
Beta			1.05		
Interest coverage[a]	14.0	8.4	7.0	5.0	4.9
Bond rating[b]			A/Aa		

a. Defined as EBIT/interest.

b. Standard and Poor's rating/Moody's rating.

EXHIBIT 2

Financial Statements for Universal Paper and Other Selected Large Paper Companies, 1974–1978 (millions of dollars except per share data)

Universal Paper

	1974	1975	1976	1977	1978
Sales	$1,867	$1,902	$2,136	$2,248	$2,525
Net income	149	109	154	168	191
Earnings per share	$ 3.60	$ 2.63	$ 3.72	$ 4.06	$ 4.61
Dividends per share	.75	.75	.75	.85	1.00
Dividend yield	6.3%	3.9%	2.5%	2.8%	3.6%
Common stock price					
High	$ 17	$ 21	$ 34	$ 36	$ 38
Low	10	12	18	24	26
Closing	12	19	30	30	28
Closing P/E ratio	3.4	7.1	8.1	7.4	6.0
Total capitalization	$1,349	$1,620	$1,787	$1,938	$2,018
% debt	30%	29%	32%	32%	33%
% preferred stock	—	—	—	—	—
% common stock	70%	71%	68%	68%	67%
Beta			1.52		
Interest coverage[a]	6.8	5.0	6.8	7.4	8.2
Bond rating[b]			A/Aa		

Crown Zellerbach

	1974	1975	1976	1977	1978
Sales	$1,172	$1,767	$2,136	$2,318	$2,467
Net income	125	75	98	109	112
Earnings per share	$ 5.06	$ 3.01	$ 3.88	$ 4.34	$ 4.39
Dividends per share	1.75	1.80	1.80	1.83	1.90
Dividend yield	7.5%	5.1%	4.0%	5.6%	6.2%
Common stock price					
High	$ 40	$ 41	$ 49	$ 45	$ 38
Low	20	24	36	32	29
Closing	24	36	43	34	31
Closing P/E ratio	4.7	12.0	11.6	7.8	7.1
Total capitalization	$1,220	$1,290	$1,345	$1,446	$1,647
% debt	33%	33%	31%	30%	34%
% preferred stock	1%	1%	1%	1%	1%
% common stock	66%	66%	68%	69%	65%
Beta			1.03		
Interest coverage[a]	8.1	4.5	5.3	5.7	4.7
Bond rating[b]			A/A		

International Paper

	1974	1975	1976	1977	1978
Sales	$3,042	$3,081	$3,541	$3,669	$4,150
Net income	263	218	254	234	234
Earnings per share	$ 5.95	$ 4.93	$ 5.60	$ 4.98	$ 4.94
Dividends per share	1.75	2.00	2.00	2.00	2.00
Dividend yield	5.6%	3.5%	2.9%	4.6%	5.5%
Common stock price					
High	$ 56	$ 62	$ 80	$ 70	$ 49
Low	32	35	58	39	35
Closing	36	58	69	44	37
Closing P/E ratio	6.1	11.8	12.3	8.8	7.5
Total capitalization	$2,207	$2,801	$3,093	$3,303	$3,407
% debt	33%	41%	34%	32%	28%
% preferred stock	—	—	—	—	—
% common stock	67%	59%	66%	68%	72%
Beta			1.43		
Interest coverage[a]	11.1	5.4	5.1	4.7	5.3
Bond rating[b]			AA/Aa		

Mead Corporation

	1974	1975	1976	1977	1978
Sales	$1,526	$1,245	$1,599	$1,822	$2,322
Net income	82	53	89	98	121
Earnings per share	$ 3.27	$ 2.05	$ 3.61	$ 4.10	$ 5.12
Dividends per share	.60	.80	.89	.98	1.21
Dividend yield	9.2%	6.6%	4.4%	4.7%	6.8%
Common stock price					
High	$ 13	$ 13	$ 23	$ 24	$ 34
Low	8	9	12	18	17
Closing	9	12	21	22	23
Closing P/E ratio	2.8	5.9	5.8	5.4	4.5
Total capitalization	$ 826	$ 880	$ 965	$1,071	$1,171
% debt	34%	35%	33%	38%	36%
% preferred stock	6%	6%	5%	4%	1%
% common stock	60%	59%	62%	58%	63%
Beta			2.16		
Interest coverage[a]	4.6	2.9	4.5	4.7	5.3
Bond rating[b]			A/A		

Kimberly-Clark

	1974	1975	1976	1977	1978
Sales	$1,439	$1,484	$1,585	$1,726	$1,911
Net income	95	103	121	131	149
Earnings per share	$ 4.10	$ 4.41	$ 5.21	$ 5.60	$ 6.36
Dividends per share	1.48	1.60	1.80	2.20	2.60
Dividend yield	6.5%	4.4%	4.1%	5.1%	6.4%
Common stock price					
High	$ 35	$ 37	$ 47	$ 48	$ 50
Low	19	24	36	37	39
Closing	25	37	44	43	41
Closing P/E ratio	6.1	3.4	8.4	7.7	6.4
Total capitalization	$1,030	$1,086	$1,196	$1,347	$1,435
% debt	24%	21%	20%	20%	19%
% preferred stock	—	—	—	—	—
% common stock	76%	79%	80%	80%	81%
Beta			.99		
Interest coverage[a]	9.1	8.3	10.0	10.1	10.5
Bond rating[b]			AA/Aa		

St. Regis Paper

	1974	1975	1976	1977	1978
Sales	$1,471	$1,395	$1,642	$1,996	$2,300
Net income	105	96	91	107	127
Earnings per share	$ 4.76	$ 4.27	$ 3.82	$ 3.36	$ 3.94
Dividends per share	1.25	1.43	1.55	1.66	1.74
Dividend yield	7.3%	4.5%	4.2%	5.6%	6.4%
Common stock price					
High	$ 37	$ 35	$ 31	$ 39	$ 35
Low	18	20	34	29	26
Closing	19	34	39	31	28
Closing P/E ratio	4.0	8.0	10.2	9.2	7.1
Total capitalization	$1,127	$1,189	$1,296	$1,694	$1,791
% debt	33%	29%	26%	31%	30%
% preferred stock	—	—	—	—	—
% common stock	67%	71%	74%	69%	70%
Beta			1.14		
Interest coverage[a]	7.6	7.2	6.1	5.6	5.9
Bond rating[b]			NR		

a. Defined as EBIT/interest.

b. Standard and Poor's rating/Moody's rating; NR = not rated.

EXHIBIT 3

Sales and Capacity of Sodium Chlorate Producers in the United States, 1970–1979

	Sales of Sodium Chlorate (tons)	Domestic Capacity (tons)	Average Price (dollars/ton)
1970	220,000	270,000	$129
1971	260,000	300,000	136
1972	280,000	300,000	144
1973	300,000	320,000	152
1974	310,000	335,000	188
1975	270,000	355,000	243
1976	345,000	370,000	295
1977	380,000	385,000	367
1978	410,000	420,000	392
1979	435,000[a]	455,000	413[a]

a. Expected.

EXHIBIT 4

Domestic Producers of Sodium Chlorate

Producer	Capacity (tons)	Plants	Capacity (tons)
Hooker Chemical Corporation	114,000	Columbus, Miss.[a]	65,000
		Taft, La.[a]	40,000
		Niagara Falls, N.Y.	9,000
Pennwalt Corporation	72,000	Calvert City, Ky.[a]	37,000
		Portland, Ore.	26,000
		Tacoma, Wash.	9,000
American Chemical Corporation	65,000	Collinsville, Ala.[a]	40,000
		Wenatchee, Wash.	25,000
Kerr-McGee Corporation	63,000	Hamilton, Miss.[a]	33,000
		Henderson, Nev.	30,000
International Minerals & Chemicals Corporation	40,000	Orrington, Me.	40,000
Olin Corporation	20,000	McIntosh, Ala.[a]	20,000
ERCO Corporation	20,000	Monroe, La.[a]	20,000
Universal Paper Corporation	20,000	Rome, Ga.[a]	20,000
Georgia-Pacific Corporation	15,000	Plaquemine, La.[a]	15,000
Brunswick Chemical Company	11,000	Brunswick, Ga.[a]	11,000
Southern Chemicals Corporation	10,000	Reigelwood, N.C.[a]	6,000
		Butler, Ala.[a]	4,000
Pacific Eng. and Prod. Co. of Nevada	5,000	Henderson, Nev.	5,000
U.S. total	455,000		455,000
Southeastern U.S. total			311,000

a. Plants serving the southeastern U.S. market.

EXHIBIT 5

Financial Statements of Selected Sodium Chlorate Producers, 1974–1978 (millions of dollars except per share data)

Pennwalt

	1974	1975	1976	1977	1978
Sales	$ 641	$ 714	$ 777	$ 835	$ 921
Net income	27	33	35	42	45
Earnings per share	$ 2.81	$ 3.25	$ 3.56	$ 4.23	$ 4.54
Dividends per share	1.24	1.36	1.54	2.25	2.05
Dividend yield	7.4%	4.6%	4.9%	5.2%	6.7%
Common stock prices					
High	$ 26	$ 30	$ 38	$ 39	$ 43
Low	15	17	27	32	32
Closing	17	28	33	39	33
Closing P/E ratio	6.0	8.6	9.3	9.2	7.3
Total capitalization	$ 371	$ 441	$ 469	$ 500	$ 524
% debt	28%	34%	33%	34%	31%
% preferred stock	—	—	—	—	—
% common stock	72%	66%	67%	66%	69%
Beta			1.33		
Interest coverage[b]	2.9	3.3	3.8	4.1	4.2
Bond rating[c]			A/A		

Kerr-McGee

	1974	1975	1976	1977	1978
Sales	$1,550	$1,799	$1,955	$2,165	$2,072
Net income	116	131	134	119	118
Earnings per share	$ 4.64	$ 5.15	$ 5.19	$ 4.61	$ 4.57
Dividends per share	.85	1.00	1.19	1.25	1.25
Dividend yield	1.4%	1.4%	1.8%	2.7%	2.6%
Common stock prices					
High	$ 93	$ 95	$ 83	$ 75	$ 53
Low	47	60	61	45	40
Closing	72	70	68	47	48
Closing P/E ratio	15.5	13.6	13.1	10.2	10.5
Total capitalization	$ 851	$1,091	$1,325	$1,433	$1,533
% debt	19%	20%	24%	21%	17%
% preferred stock	—	—	—	—	—
% common stock	81%	80%	76%	79%	83%
Beta			1.06		
Interest coverage[b]	19.4	17.1	10.8	8.4	6.4
Bond rating[c]			AA/Aa		

Inter. Minerals & Chemicals

	1974	1975	1976	1977	1978
Sales	$ 859	$1,303	$1,260	$1,280	$1,364
Net income	70	166	135	108	120
Earnings per share	$ 3.59	$ 9.91	$ 7.73	$ 6.09	$ 6.61
Dividends per share	.57	1.38	2.10	2.45	2.60
Dividend yield	1.9%	5.3%	5.9%	6.4%	7.4%
Common stock prices					
High	$ 41	$ 49	$ 42	$ 44	$ 44
Low	21	31	33	35	34
Closing	39	38	41	41	35
Closing P/E ratio	10.9	3.8	5.3	6.7	5.3
Total capitalization	$ 577	$ 781	$ 990	$1,083	$1,161
% debt	42%	38%	37%	36%	32%
% preferred stock	10%	4%	2%	1%	1%
% common stock	48%	58%	61%	63%	67%
Beta			.81		
Interest coverage[b]	5.5	11.6	8.4	5.5	6.3
Bond rating[c]			NR/A		

Georgia-Pacific

	1974	1975	1976	1977	1978
Sales	$2,432	$2,359	$3,038	$3,675	$4,403
Net income	164	148	215	262	302
Earnings per share	$ 1.74	$ 1.54	$ 2.12	$ 2.54	$ 2.93
Dividends per share	.47	.49	.70	.83	1.03
Dividend yield	3.1%	1.9%	2.1%	3.5%	4.5%
Common stock prices					
High	$ 27	$ 30	$ 37	$ 37	$ 33
Low	13	16	26	25	24
Closing	15	26	37	28	24
Closing P/E ratio	8.6	16.9	17.4	11.0	8.2
Total capitalization	$1,935	$2,150	$2,045	$2,541	$2,878
% debt	45%	42%	22%	29%	29%
% preferred stock	—	—	—	—	—
% common stock	55%	58%	78%	71%	71%
Beta			1.50		
Interest coverage[b]	4.3	4.4	8.1	9.9	9.3
Bond rating[c]			AA/Aa		

Brunswick Chemical

	1974	1975	1976	1977	1978
Sales	$ 1.9	$ 2.1	$ 3.0	$ 4.0	$ 4.3
Net income	.20	.15	.37	.71	.79
Earnings per share	$ .40	$ .30	$ .74	$ 1.42	$ 1.58
Dividends per share	.10	.10	.15	.35	.40
Dividend yield	a	a	a	2.9%	3.5%
Common stock prices					
High	a	a	a	$ 13	$ 14¼
Low	a	a	a	7½	9
Closing	a	a	a	12	11½
Closing P/E ratio	a	a	a	8.5	7.3
Total capitalization	$ 1.8	$ 1.9	$ 2.1	$ 2.6	$ 3.2
% debt	33%	30%	25%	19%	15%
% preferred stock					
% common stock	67%	70%	75%	81%	85%
Beta				1.10	
Interest coverage[b]	6.7	5.0	12.3	47	53
Bond rating[c]			NR		

Southern Chemicals

	1974	1975	1976	1977	1978
Sales	$ 1.7	$ 2.0	$ 2.7	$ 3.6	$ 3.9
Net income	.10	(.05)	.28	.74	.73
Earnings per share	$ .61	$ (.24)	$ 1.38	$ 3.69	$ 3.66
Dividends per share	—	—	—	.30	.30
Dividend yield	a	—	—	1.2%	1.3%
Common stock prices					
High	a	a	a	$ 28	$ 31
Low	a	a	a	11	20
Closing	a	a	a	25	23
Closing P/E ratio	a	a	a	6.7	6.4
Total capitalization	$ 1.6	$ 1.5	$ 1.8	$ 2.4	$ 3.0
% debt	50%	50%	41%	28%	21%
% preferred stock	a	—	—	—	—
% common stock	50%	50%	59%	72%	79%
Beta				1.20	
Interest coverage[b]	3.5	.4	9.0	22	24
Bond rating[c]			NR		

a. Stock not publicly traded.

b. Defined as EBIT/interest.

c. Standard and Poor's rating/Moody's rating; NR = not rated.

EXHIBIT 6

Financial Statements for the Collinsville Plant, 1974–1979 (thousands of dollars)

	1974	1975	1976	1977	1978	1979[a]
Operating Data						
Sales (tons)	36,899	30,819	37,464	40,076	39,790	38,507
Average price ($/ton)	$ 188	$ 243	$ 295	$ 367	$ 392	$ 413
Sales	$ 6,937	$ 7,489	$11,052	$14,708	$15,598	$15,903
Variable costs						
Power	2,935	3,395	4,631	5,530	6,173	6,759
Graphite	354	369	545	653	689	714
Salt and other	693	800	1,047	1,274	1,307	1,385
Total variable costs	3,982	4,564	6,223	7,457	8,169	8,858
Fixed costs						
Labor	590	608	646	739	924	1,072
Maintenance	143	201	220	272	235	237
Other	474	659	902	1,063	509	1,107
Total fixed costs	1,207	1,468	1,768	2,074	1,668	2,416
Total manufacturing costs	5,189	6,032	7,991	9,531	9,837	11,274
Depreciation	433	394	402	391	384	399
Selling	114	92	126	155	181	204
R&D	105	154	207	274	351	429
Total other costs	652	640	735	820	916	1,032
Operating profit	$ 1,096	$ 817	$ 2,326	$ 4,357	$ 4,845	$ 3,597
Percent of Sales Ratios						
Power costs	42.3%	45.3%	41.9%	37.6%	39.6%	42.5%
Variable costs	57.4	60.9	56.3	50.7	52.4	55.7
Fixed costs	17.4	19.6	16.0	14.1	10.7	15.2
Manufacturing costs	74.8	80.5	72.3	64.8	63.1	70.9
Operating profit	15.8	10.9	21.0	29.6	31.1	22.6
Accounts receivable	10.1	10.4	10.2	9.9	10.1	10.2
Inventories	3.7	7.3	6.2	4.4	4.1	4.1
Accounts payable	5.8	6.3	5.6	5.3	5.1	5.5
Net assets	66.6	64.5	47.0	35.2	34.5	34.0
Asset Data						
Accounts receivable	$ 701	$ 779	$ 1,128	$ 1,456	$ 1,575	$ 1,622
Inventories	254	544	681	647	639	651
Net property, plant, and equipment	4,066	3,978	4,003	3,853	3,964	4,014
Total assets	5,021	6,301	5,812	6,956	6,178	6,287
Accounts payable	402	472	619	780	795	873
Net assets	$ 4,619	$ 4,829	$ 5,193	$ 5,176	$ 5,383	$ 5,414
Operating profit/net assets	23.7%	16.9%	44.8%	84.2%	90.0%	66.4%

a. Expected.

EXHIBIT 7
Financial Statements for Dixon Corporation, 1975–1979 (thousands of dollars except per share data)

	1975	*1976*	*1977*	*1978*	*1979*[a]
Income Statements					
Sales	$19,128	$23,830	$28,348	$34,770	$42,259
Cost of goods sold	14,085	16,889	19,950	24,467	29,185
Selling and administrative	1,952	2,308	2,824	3,291	4,436
Research	325	388	593	682	716
Interest	400	320	240	160	80
Taxes	1,125	1,878	2,285	2,932	3,818
Profit after taxes	$ 1,241	$ 2,047	$ 2,456	$ 3,238	$ 4,024
Earnings per share	$ 1.13	$ 1.86	$ 2.23	$ 2.94	$ 3.66
Dividends per share	.20	.30	.40	.40	.50
Balance Sheets					
Cash and marketable securities	$ 385	$ 357	$ 556	$ 1,273	$ 2,996
Other current assets	4,208	5,016	5,939	7,267	8,917
Property, plant, and equipment	7,436	7,895	8,354	8,842	8,918
Total assets	$12,029	$13,268	$14,849	17,382	$20,831
Current liabilities	$ 2,314	$ 2,836	$ 3,402	$ 4,138	$ 5,113
Debt (including current maturity)	5,000	4,000	3,000	2,000	1,000
Stockholders' equity	4,715	6,432	8,447	11,244	14,718
Total liabilities and equity	$12,029	$13,268	$14,849	$17,382	$20,831
Stock price range	$ 7–14	$ 8–22	$ 19–30	$ 25–40	$ 35–45
Closing stock price	9	20	27	38	40[b]
Beta			1.06		
Bond rating			NR		

NR = not rated.

a. Expected.

b. October 30, 1979.

EXHIBIT 8
Pro Forma Financial Statements for the Collinsville Plant, 1979–1984 (thousands of dollars)

	1979[a]	1980	1981	1982	1983	1984
Operating Data						
Sales (tons)		32,000	35,000	38,000	38,000	38,000
Average price ($/ton)		$ 415	$ 480	$ 520	$ 562	$ 606
Sales		$13,280	$16,800	$19,760	$21,356	$23,028
Variable costs						
Power		6,304	7,735	9,386	10,526	11,780
Graphite		645	791	875	940	992
Salt and other		1,285	1,621	1,753	1,836	1,956
Total variable costs		8,234	10,147	12,014	13,302	14,728
Fixed costs						
Labor		1,180	1,297	1,427	1,580	1,738
Maintenance		256	277	299	322	354
Other		1,154	1,148	1,179	1,113	1,153
Total fixed costs		2,590	2,722	2,905	3,015	3,245
Total manufacturing costs		10,824	12,869	14,919	16,317	17,973
Selling		112	125	138	152	168
R&D		451	478	508	543	591
Depreciation		1,060	1,110	1,160	1,210	1,270
Total other costs		1,623	1,713	1,806	1,905	2,029
Operating profit		$ 833	$ 2,218	$ 3,035	$ 3,134	$ 3,026
Percent of Sales Ratios						
Power costs		47.5%	46.0%	47.5%	49.3%	51.2%
Variable costs		62.0	60.4	60.8	62.3	64.0
Fixed costs		19.5	16.2	14.7	14.1	14.1
Manufacturing costs		81.5	76.6	75.5	76.4	78.0
Operating profit		6.3	13.2	15.4	14.7	13.1
Accounts receivable		10.0	10.0	10.0	10.0	10.0
Inventories		4.5	4.5	4.5	4.5	4.5
Accounts payable		5.5	5.5	5.5	5.5	5.5
Net assets		84.5	65.2	53.7	47.5	41.8
Asset Data						
Accounts receivable	$ 1,622	$ 1,328	$ 1,680	$ 1,976	$ 2,136	$ 2,303
Inventories	651	598	756	889	961	1,036
Net property, plant, and equipment . . .	10,600	10,025	9,440	8,840	8,230	7,560
Total assets	12,873	11,951	11,876	11,705	11,327	10,899
Accounts payable	873	730	924	1,087	1,175	1,267
Net assets	$12,000	$11,221	$10,952	$10,618	$10,152	$ 9,632
Operating profit/Net assets		7.4%	20.3%	28.6%	30.9%	31.4%

Note: These pro forma financial statements were based on the following assumptions: (1) Continued use of *unlaminated* graphite electrodes. (2) Though excess industry capacity would hold price increases to less than an 8% annual rate in 1980, by 1984 the average annual price increase over the period 1979–1984 was assumed to equal 8%. (3) Power costs per kWh would increase 12% per year. (4) Depreciation would increase because Dixon would have written up the value of the Collinsville plant to $10.6 million.

a. Expected.

Cooper Industries, Inc.

In May 1972, Robert Cizik, executive vice president of Cooper Industries, Inc., was reviewing acquisition candidates for his company's diversification program. One of the companies, Nicholson File Company, had been approached by Cooper Industries 3 years earlier but had rejected all overtures. Now, however, Nicholson was in the middle of a takeover fight that might provide Cooper with a chance to gain control.

Cooper Industries

Cooper Industries was organized in 1919 as a manufacturer of heavy machinery and equipment. By the mid-1950s, the company was a leading producer of engines and massive compressors used to force natural gas through pipelines and oil out of wells. Management was concerned, however, over its heavy dependence on sales to the oil and gas industries and the violent fluctuation of earnings caused by the cyclical nature of heavy machinery and equipment sales. Although the company's long-term sales and earnings growth had been above average, its cyclicality had substantially dampened Wall Street's interest in the stock. (Cooper's historical operating results and financial condition are summarized in Exhibits 1 and 2.)

Initial efforts to lessen the earnings volatility were not successful. Between 1959 and 1966, Cooper acquired (1) a supplier of portable industrial power tools, (2) a manufacturer of small industrial air and process compressors, (3) a maker of small pumps and compressors for oil field applications, and (4) a producer of tire-changing tools for the automotive market. The acquisitions broadened Cooper's markets but left it still highly sensitive to general economic conditions.

A full review of Cooper's acquisition strategy was initiated in 1966 by the company. After several months of study, three criteria were established for all acquisitions. First, the industry should be one in which Cooper could become a major factor. This requirement was in line with management's goal of leadership within a few distinct areas of business. Second, the industry should be fairly stable, with a broad market for the products and a product line of "small-ticket" items. This product definition was intended to eliminate any company that had undue profit dependence upon a single customer or several large sales per year. Finally, it was decided to acquire only leading companies in their respective market segments.

The new strategy was initially implemented with the acquisition in 1967 of the Lufkin Rule Company, the world's largest manufacturer of measuring rules and tapes. Cooper acquired a quality product line, an established distribution system of 35,000 retail hardware stores throughout the United States, and plants in the United States, Canada, and Mexico. It also gained the services of William Rector, president of Lufkin, and Hal Stevens, vice president of sales. Both were extremely knowledgeable in the hand tool business and had worked together effectively for years. Their goal was to build through acquisition a hand tool company with a full product line that would use a common sales and distribution system and joint advertising. To do this, they needed Cooper's financial strength.

Lufkin provided a solid base to which two other companies were added. In 1969 the Crescent Niagara Corporation was acquired. The company had been highly profitable in the early 1960s but had suffered in recent years under the mismanagement of some investor-entrepreneurs who had gained control in 1963. A series of acquisitions of weak companies with poor product lines eroded the company's overall profitability until, in 1967, a small loss was reported. Discouraged, the investors wanted to get out, and Cooper—eager to add Crescent's well-known and high-quality wrenches, pliers, and screwdrivers to its line—was interested. It was clear that some of Crescent's lines would have to be dropped and inefficient plants would have to be closed, but the wrenches, pliers, and screwdrivers were an important part of Cooper's product policy.

In 1970, Cooper further expanded into hand tools with the acquisition of the Weller Electric Corporation. Weller was the world's leading supplier of soldering tools to the industrial, electronic, and consumer markets. It provided Cooper with a new, high-quality product line and production capacity in England, West Germany, and Mexico. (Information on the three acquisitions is provided in Exhibit 3.)

Cooper was less successful in its approach to a fourth company in the hand tool business, the Nicholson File Company. Nicholson was on the original "shopping list" of acceptable acquisition candidates that Mr. Cizik and Mr. Rector had developed, but several attempts to interest Nicholson in exploring merger possibilities had failed. The Nicholson family had controlled and managed the company since its founding in 1864, and Paul Nicholson, chairman of the board, had no interest in joining forces with anyone.

Nicholson File Company

But Nicholson was too inviting a takeover target to be overlooked or ignored for long. A relatively poor sales and profit performance in recent years, conservative accounting and financial policies, and a low percentage of outstanding stock held by the Nicholson family and management all contributed to its vulnerability. Annual sales growth of 2% was far behind the industry growth rate of 6% per year, and profit margins had slipped to only one-third those of other hand tool manufacturers. In 1971, Nicholson common stock was trading near its lowest point in many years and well below its book value of $51.25. Lack of investor interest in the stock was reflected in its low price-earnings ratio of 10–14, which compared with 14–17 times earnings for other leading hand tool companies. The stock was clearly selling on the basis of its dividend yield, with only limited hopes for capital appreciation. (Exhibits 4 and 5 show Nicholson's operating results and balance sheets.)

What made Nicholson so attractive was its basic competitive strength—strengths that the family-dominated management had not translated into earnings. The company was one of the largest domestic manufacturers of hand tools and was a leader in its two main product areas. Nicholson held a 50% share of the $50 million market for files and rasps, where it offered a broad, high-quality line with a very strong brand name. Its second product line, hand saws and saw blades, also had an excellent reputation for quality and held a 9% share of this $200 million market. Only Sears, Roebuck and Company and Disston, Inc., had larger market shares.

Nicholson's greatest asset, however, was its distribution system. Forty-eight direct salesmen and 28 file and saw engineers marketed its file, rasp, and saw products to 2,100 hardware wholesalers in the United States and Canada. These wholesalers in turn sold to 53,000 retail outlets. Their efforts were supported by heavy advertising and promotional programs. Overseas, the company's products were sold in 137 countries through 140 local sales representatives. The company seemed to have all the necessary strengths to share fully in the 6–7% annual sales growth forecast for the industry.

The Raid by H. K. Porter Company

Cooper was not alone in its interest in Nicholson. H. K. Porter Company, a conglomerate with wide-ranging interests in electrical equipment, tools, nonferrous metals, and rubber products, had acquired 44,000 shares of Nicholson stock in 1967 and had been an attentive stockholder ever since. On March 3, 1972, Porter informed Nicholson management of its plan to tender immediately for 437,000 of Nicholson's 584,000 outstanding shares at $42 per share in cash. The offer would terminate on April 4 unless extended by Porter; and the company was unwilling to acquire fewer shares than would constitute a majority.

Nicholson management was alarmed by both the proposal and the proposer. The company would contribute less than one-sixth of the combined sales and would clearly be just another operating division of Porter. It was feared that Porter's quest for higher profits might lead to aggressive cost cutting and the elimination of marginal product lines. Nicholson's Atkins Saw Division seemed especially vulnerable in view of its low profitability.

Loss of control seemed both painful and likely. The $42 cash offer represented a $12 premium over the most recent price of the stock and threatened to create considerable stockholder interest. The disappointing performance of the stock in recent years would undoubtedly increase the attractiveness of the $42 offer to Nicholson's 4,000 stockholders. And the Nicholson family and management owned only 20% of the outstanding shares—too few to ensure continued control.

Immediately after learning of the Porter tender offer, Mr. Cizik and Mr. Rector approached the Nicholson management with an offer of help. It was clear that Nicholson had to move immediately and forcefully; the first ten days of a tender offer are critical. Messrs. Cizik and Rector stressed that Nicholson must find a better offer and find it fast. Indeed, Cooper would be willing to make such an offer if Nicholson's management and directors would commit themselves to it—now.

Nicholson was not ready for such decisive action, however, and three days passed without any decision. With each day the odds of a successful counteroffer diminished. Finally, the Cooper officers decided the risks were too great and that Porter would learn of Cooper's offer of help and might retaliate. Cooper's stock was depressed, and it was possible that an angry Porter management might strike for control of Cooper. The offer was withdrawn.

By late March, the situation was increasing in seriousness. Management of Nicholson moved to block the raid. It personally talked with the large shareholders and made a strong public statement recommending against the offer. But announcements by Porter indicated that a substantial number of Nicholson shares were being tendered. It was no longer a matter of whether or not to be acquired. The issue was, by whom!

Management sought to find an alternative merger that would ensure continuity of Nicholson management and operating independence. Several companies had communicated with Nicholson in the wake of the Porter announcement, but no one other than Cooper had made a specific proposal. This was largely due to their reluctance to compete at the price levels being discussed or to enter into a fight with Porter.

Finally, on April 3, agreement was reached with VLN Corporation on the terms of a merger with VLN. VLN was a broadly diversified company with major interests in original and replacement automotive equipment and in publishing. Under the VLN merger terms, one share of new VLN cumulative convertible preferred stock would be exchanged for each share of Nicholson common stock. The VLN preferred stock would pay an annual dividend of $1.60 and would be convertible into five shares of VLN common stock during the first year following the merger, scaling down to four shares after the fourth year. The preferred stock would be callable at $50 per share after the fifth year and would have liquidating rights of $50 per share. (See Exhibit 6 for a financial summary of VLN.)

Nicholson management, assured of continued operating independence, supported the VLN offer actively. In a letter to the stockholders, Paul Nicholson pointed out that (1) the exchange would be a tax-free transaction, (2) the $1.60 preferred dividend equaled the current rate on the Nicholson common stock, and (3) a preferred share was worth a minimum of $53.10 (VLN common stock had closed at $10.62 on the day prior to the offer). He felt confident that the necessary majority of the outstanding common stock would be voted in favor of the proposed merger when it was brought to a vote in the fall. (Under Rhode Island law, a simple majority was sufficient to authorize the merger.[1])

Porter quickly counterattacked by pointing out to Nicholson stockholders that VLN common stock had recently sold for as low as $4⅝, which would put a value in the first year of only $23.12 on the VLN preferred stock. Furthermore, anyone who converted into VLN common stock would suffer a sharp income loss, since VLN had paid no common dividends since 1970.

Nicholson's stockholders were thus presented with two very contradictory appraisals of the VLN offer. Each company based its argument on some stock price, either the highest or the lowest, that would make the converted preferred stock compare favorably or not with the $42 cash offer.

---

1. Nicholson File was incorporated in Rhode Island. Under Rhode Island corporation law, a merger can be voted by shareholders holding a majority of the common stock outstanding. For reasons specific both to the laws of Rhode Island and to the Nicholson situation, dissenting stockholders of Nicholson would not be entitled to exercise the rights of dissent and would be forced to accept the exchange offer.

Opportunity for Cooper?

Mr. Cizik and his staff were still attracted by the potential profits to be realized from Nicholson. It was felt that Nicholson's efforts to sell to every market segment resulted in an excessive number of products, which held down manufacturing efficiency and ballooned inventories. Cooper estimated that Nicholson's cost of goods sold could be reduced from 69% of sales to 65%.

The other major area of cost reduction was Nicholson's selling expenses. There was a substantial overlap of Nicholson's sales force and that established by Cooper for its Lufkin-Weller-Crescent hand tool lines. Elimination of the sales and advertising duplications would lower selling, general, and administrative expenses from 22% of sales to 19%.

There were other possible sources of earnings, but they were more difficult to quantify. For instance, 75% of Nicholson's sales were to the industrial market and only 25% to the consumer market. In contrast, sales by Cooper's hand tool group were distributed between the two markets in virtually the exact opposite proportions. Thus, sales increases could be expected from Nicholson's "pulling" more Cooper products into the industrial markets and vice versa for the consumer market. Also, Cooper was eager to use Nicholson's strong European distribution system to sell its other hand tool lines.

The battle between Porter and VLN seemed to provide Cooper with an unexpected, second opportunity to gain control of Nicholson. Porter had ended up with just 133,000 shares tendered in response to its offer—far short of the 249,000 shares needed to give it majority control.[2] Its slate of directors had been defeated by Nicholson management at the Nicholson annual meeting on April 21. Tom Evans, president of Porter, now feared that Nicholson might consummate the merger with VLN and that Porter would be faced with the unhappy prospect of receiving VLN preferred stock for its 177,000 shares of Nicholson stock. Mr. Evans knew that the VLN stock had been a lackluster performer and might not show any significant growth in the near term. Furthermore, the $1.60 dividend rate seemed low in relation to current market yields of 7% on straight preferred stocks and 6.5% on intermediate-term U.S. Treasury bonds. Finally, he feared that it would be difficult to sell a large holding of VLN stock, which traded in small volume on the American Stock Exchange.

On the other hand, a merger of Cooper and Nicholson would allow Mr. Evans to convert his Nicholson shares into either common stock or convertible preferred stock of Cooper. This was a much more attractive alternative, assuming that an acceptable exchange rate could be set. Mr. Evans anticipated that earnings should rebound sharply from the cyclical downturn in 1971 and felt that Cooper stock would show significant price appreciation. Furthermore, Cooper stock was traded on the New York Exchange, which provided substantial liquidity. At a private meeting in late April, Mr. Evans tentatively agreed to support a Cooper–Nicholson merger on the condition that he receive Cooper common or convertible securities in a tax-free exchange worth at least $50 for each Nicholson share he held.

Mr. Cizik was now faced with the critical decision of whether to move for control. Cooper had acquired 29,000 shares of Nicholson stock during the preceding month in the open market—in part to build some bargaining power but largely to keep the loose

---

2. Porter needed 292,584 shares to hold 50.1% majority control. It already owned 43,806 shares and needed, therefore, an additional 248,778 shares.

shares out of the hands of Porter. Still uncommitted, however, were an estimated 50,000–100,000 shares that had been bought by speculators in the hope of an escalation of acquisition offers. Another 150,000–200,000 shares were unaccounted for, although Mr. Cizik suspected that a considerable number would go with the recommendation of Nicholson management. (Exhibit 7 shows Mr. Cizik's best estimate of the distribution of Nicholson stock in early May.) His hopes for gaining 50.1% of the Nicholson shares outstanding depended upon his gaining support of at least 86,000 of the shares still either uncommitted or unaccounted for.

If he decided to seek control, it would be necessary to establish both the price and the form of the offer. Clearly, the terms would have to be sufficiently attractive to secure the shares needed to gain majority control.

Mr. Cizik also felt that the terms should be acceptable to the Nicholson management. Once the merger was complete, Cooper would need to work with the Nicholson family and management. He did not want them to feel that they and other Nicholson stockholders were cheated by the merger. As a matter of policy, Cooper had never made an "unfriendly" acquisition, and this one was to be no exception. The offer should be one that would be supported by the great majority of the stockholders.

However, the price and the form of the payment had to be consistent with Cooper's concern that the acquisition earn a satisfactory long-term return and improve the trend of Cooper's earnings per share over the next 5 years. (A forecast of Cooper's earnings per share is shown in Exhibit 8.) The company anticipated making additional acquisitions, possibly on an exchange of stock basis, and maintenance of a strong earnings pattern and stock price was therefore important. On May 3, the common stock of Cooper and Nicholson closed at $24 and $44, respectively.

EXHIBIT 1
Condensed Operating and Stockholder Information, Cooper Industries, Inc., 1967–1971
(millions of dollars except per share data)

	1967	1968	1969	1970	1971
Operations					
Net sales	$ 198	$ 206	$ 212	$ 226	$ 208
Cost of goods sold	141	145	154	164	161
Depreciation	4	5	4	4	4
Selling and administrative expenses	23	25	29	29	29
Interest expense	1	2	3	4	3
Income before taxes and extraordinary items	29	29	22	24	11
Income taxes	14	15	11	12	5
Income before extraordinary items	15.2	13.9	10.6	12.4	5.6
Preferred dividend	1.0	.9	.9	.9	.9
Net income applicable to common stock	$ 14.2	$ 13.0	$ 9.7	$ 11.5	$ 4.7
Common Stock					
Earnings per share before extraordinary items	$ 3.34	$ 3.07	$ 2.33	$ 2.75	$ 1.12
Dividends per share	1.20	1.25	1.40	1.40	1.40
Book value per share	16.43	17.26	18.28	19.68	18.72
Market price	23–59	36–57	22–50	22–35	18–38
Price-earnings ratio	7–18	12–19	9–22	8–13	16–34

EXHIBIT 2
Balance Sheet at December 31, 1971, Cooper Industries, Inc. (millions of dollars)

Cash	$ 9	Accounts payable	$ 30
Accounts receivable	49	Accrued taxes	3
Inventories	57	Long-term debt due	5
Other	2	Current liabilities	38
Current assets	117	Long-term debt[a]	34
Net plant and equipment	47	Deferred taxes	4
Other	8	Preferred stock	11
		Common equity (4,218,691 shares outstanding)	85
Total assets	$172	Total liabilities and net worth	$172

a. Maturities of long-term debt are $5.5 million, $6 million, $4 million, $2 million, and $2 million in the years 1972 through 1975, respectively.

EXHIBIT 3
Summary of Cooper Industries' Recent Acquisitions (millions of dollars)

	Year Preceding Acquisition by Cooper				
	Sales	Net Income	Book Value	Acquisition Price Paid	Form of Transaction
Lufkin Rule Company	$22	$1.4	$15	$20.6	Convertible preferred
Crescent Niagara Corporation	16	(.04)	4.9	12.5	Cash
Weller Electric Corporation	10	.9	4.4	14.6	Common stock

EXHIBIT 4

Condensed Operating and Stockholder Information, Nicholson File Company, 1967–1971 (millions of dollars except per share data)

	1967	1968	1969	1970	1971
Operations					
Net sales	$ 48.5	$ 49.1	$ 53.7	$ 54.8	$ 55.3
Cost of goods sold	32.6	33.1	35.9	37.2	37.9
Selling, general, and administrative					
expenses	10.7	11.1	11.5	11.9	12.3
Depreciation expense	2.0	2.3	2.4	2.3	2.1
Interest expense	.4	.7	.8	.8	.8
Other deductions	.3	.1	.2	.2	.2
Income before taxes	2.53	1.85	2.97	2.42	2.02
Taxes[a]	.60	.84	1.31	.88	.67
Net income	$ 1.93	$ 1.01	$ 1.66	$ 1.54	$ 1.35
Percentage of Sales					
Cost of goods sold	67%	67%	67%	68%	69%
Selling, general, and administrative					
expenses	22	23	21	22	22
Income before taxes	5.2	3.8	5.5	4.4	3.7
Stockholder Information					
Earnings per share	$ 3.19	$ 1.65	$ 2.88	$ 2.64	$ 2.32
Dividends per share	1.60	1.60	1.60	1.60	1.60
Book value per share	45.66	48.03	49.31	50.20	51.25
Market price	33–46	35–48	29–41	25–33	23–32
Price-earnings ratio	10–14	21–30	10–14	9–13	10–14

a. The ratio of income taxes to income before taxes has been reduced primarily by the investment tax credit and by the inclusion in income of equity in net income of partially owned foreign companies, the taxes for which are provided for in the accounts of such companies and not in the tax provision of Nicholson. It was estimated that the average tax rate would be 40% in future years.

EXHIBIT 5

Balance Sheet at December 31, 1971, Nicholson File Company (millions of dollars)

Cash	$ 1	Accounts payable	$ 2
Accounts receivable	8	Other	2
Inventories[a]	18	Current liabilities	4
Other	1	Long-term debt	12
Current assets	28	Common stock	31
Investment in subsidiaries	3	Total liabilities and net worth	$47
Net plant and equipment	16		
Total assets	$47		

a. Inventories in the amount of $11.8 million are priced at cost on the last-in, first-out method. The estimated replacement cost exceeds the carrying amounts by $9.2 million. The remaining inventories are priced at the lower of cost on the first-in, first-out method or market.

EXHIBIT 6
Condensed Operating and Stockholder Information, VLN Corporation, 1967–1971 (millions of dollars except per share data)

	1967	1968	1969	1970	1971
Operations					
Net sales	$ 45	$ 97	$ 99	$ 98	$ 100
Net income	1.97	3.20	3.20	1.13	2.98
Financial Position					
Current assets	$ 25	$ 46	$ 49	$ 41	$ 46
Current liabilities	6	11	15	10	13
Net working capital	19	35	34	31	33
Long-term debt	10	18	16	15	17
Shareholders' equity	21	36	40	39	41
Stockholder Information					
Earnings per share	$ .78	$ .61	$ .53	$ .27	$ .54
Dividends per share	—	—	—	.20	—
Shareholders' equity per share	8.23	9.64	10.00	9.24	9.69
Market price range	6–17	10–18	7–18	4–10	5–8
Price-earnings ratio	8–22	16–30	13–34	15–37	9–15

EXHIBIT 7
Estimated Distribution of Nicholson File Company Stock

Shares supporting Cooper		
H. K. Porter	177,000	
Cooper Industries	29,000	206,000
Shares supporting VLN		
Nicholson family and management	117,000	
Owned by VLN	14,000	131,000
Shares owned by speculators		50,000–100,000
Shares unaccounted for		197,000–147,000
Total Nicholson shares outstanding		584,000

EXHIBIT 8
Five-Year Forecast of Cooper Industries' Earnings, Excluding Nicholson File Company, 1972–1976

	1972	1973	1974	1975	1976
Net income available to common stockholders ($ millions)	$11.0	$11.9	$12.8	$13.8	$15.0
Number of shares outstanding (millions)	4.21	4.21	4.21	4.21	4.21
Primary earnings per share	$2.61	$2.83	$3.04	$3.27	$3.56

Note: Forecasts are casewriter's estimates.

Interco

On August 8, 1988, Interco's board of directors met to discuss, among other matters, a merger proposal from City Capital Associates Limited Partnership. City Capital had offered $64 per common share of Interco on July 28, 1988, and had raised that offer to $70 per share on the morning of August 8. At this board meeting, Interco's financial advisors, Wasserstein, Perella & Co., established a valuation range of $68–$80 per common share of Interco and presented its evaluation of the offer. Given its valuation, Wasserstein Perella advised the Interco board (see Exhibit 1) that the $70 per share offer was inadequate and not in the best interests of the company and its shareholders. The board of directors voted to reject the City Capital offer.

The Company

Founded in December 1911, the International Shoe Company was established as a footwear manufacturing concern and remained so until the early 1960s. In 1966 the company was renamed Interco to reflect the changing character of its business. It had grown into a major manufacturer and retailer of a wide variety of consumer products and services. Among the most well known of the Interco brands were Converse and Florsheim shoes, Ethan Allen furniture, and London Fog rain gear.

Interco's various operations were substantially autonomous and were supported by a corporate management staff in St. Louis, Missouri. The company's philosophy had historically been to acquire companies in related fields and to provide their existing management teams with the incentives to expand their businesses, while relieving them of such routine support functions as financial and legal requirements. Nearly half of Interco's growth had come through acquisition. The company continually sought entities that would complement the existing Interco companies. Additional criteria used in screening and selecting acquisition candidates included the presence of highly

This case was prepared by Research Associate Susan L. Roth under the supervision of Professor Scott P. Mason.

Copyright © 1991 by the President and Fellows of Harvard College.
Harvard Business School case 291–033.

skilled managers, and products that had established leadership positions in their respective markets.

Equity analysts viewed Interco as a conservative company that was finally "overcapitalized." With a current ratio of 3.6 to 1 and a debt-to-capitalization ratio, including capitalized leases, of 19.3% on February 29, 1988, Interco had ample financial flexibility. This flexibility had allowed the company to repurchase its common shares and make acquisitions as opportunities arose.

Operating Divisions

Interco was organized in four major operating divisions:

- Apparel Manufacturing
- General Retail Merchandising
- Footwear Manufacturing and Retailing
- Furniture and Home Furnishings

As listed in Exhibit 2, there were numerous independent companies within these four operating divisions.

Apparel Manufacturing. This group consisted of 11 apparel companies that designed, manufactured, and distributed a full range of branded and private-label sportswear, casual apparel, outer garments, and headwear for men and women. Apparel brands included Le Tigre, Sergio Valente, and Abe Schrader. Distribution was national in scope to department stores, specialty shops, and other retail units, including discount chains.

General Retail Merchandising. This group operated 201 retail locations in 15 states. General retailing included large do-it-yourself home improvement centers, general merchandise discount stores, men's specialty apparel shops, and specialty department stores. Over the prior few years, general retail had been greatly scaled back; it was now dominated largely by Central Hardware, a do-it-yourself home improvement chain that emphasized customer service and a broad selection of products.

Footwear Manufacturing and Retailing. This division designed, manufactured, and distributed men's and women's footwear principally in the United States, Australia, Canada, and Mexico. The group operated 778 retail shoe stores and leased shoe departments in 42 states and in Australia. Interco's two major footwear operations, Converse Inc. and the Florsheim Shoe Co., commanded leading positions in their respective markets: athletic shoes and men's traditional footwear.

Furniture and Home Furnishings. This group manufactured, distributed, and retailed quality wood and upholstered furniture and home furnishings. Furniture brands included Broyhill, Lane, Ethan Allen, and Hickory Chair. In recent years, furniture had expanded through acquisitions and increasing profitability to dominate Interco's net income. At the end of fiscal year 1988, Interco was the largest furniture manufacturer in the world.

Strategic Repositioning Program

Interco's goals included long-term sales and earnings growth, increased return on corporate assets, and most important, improved return on shareholders' equity. To achieve these goals, Interco took a four-pronged approach that included (1) improving

TABLE A
Percent of Sales by Operating Group, 1988 and 1984

	1988	1984
Apparel	24%	33%
General retail	16	26
Footwear	27	21
Furniture	33	20

Source: Interco annual report, February 29, 1988.

the profitability of existing operations, (2) divesting underperforming assets, (3) making acquisitions that had the potential for better-than-average returns and growth, and (4) employing opportunistic financial strategies such as share repurchases and the prudent use of borrowing capacity.

With these goals established, Interco began a strategic repositioning program in 1984 aimed at improving overall corporate performance, As part of this initiative, Interco accelerated its efforts to divest underperforming assets and reposition itself in markets offering superior growth opportunities and profitability. The program resulted in a substantial change in Interco's mix of sales, as shown in Table A. In fiscal 1988 the furniture and footwear groups together accounted for 60% of corporate sales, with apparel and general retail accounting for the rest. This was a reversal of the sales distribution in fiscal 1984.

Recent Financial Performance

Overall corporate performance for fiscal year 1988 was positive, with sales and net income increasing 13.4% and 15.4%, respectively, over 1987 levels. This performance was attributable largely to the contributions of the furniture and home furnishings and footwear groups, as well as a decrease in Interco's effective tax rate. Due to the Tax Reform Act of 1986, the company's effective tax rate in 1988 was 42.8%, versus 47.1% in fiscal 1987. Growth in earnings moved Interco further toward its goal of a 14–15% return on equity; 1988's ROE of 11.7% was up from 9.7% in fiscal 1987.

The furniture and home furnishings group had an outstanding year in 1988, earning an operating profit of $149.1 million, versus $123.8 million in fiscal 1987, and achieving sales of $1.11 billion, compared to $967.4 million in 1987. Favorable demographic trends in family formations made the outlook for this group positive despite its exposure to cyclical fluctuations in housing starts and interest rates.

Showing the largest percentage gains for fiscal year 1988, sales for the footwear group increased 34.2%, and operating profits soared nearly 77%. These earnings were supported by the performance of Converse, acquired in September 1986, which had a record year in sales and earnings in 1988.

Despite multiple restructuring efforts, including divestiture of underperforming assets, the apparel manufacturing and general retail divisions remained ongoing problems, due largely to a change in the nature of these businesses. In calendar year 1987, a variety of problems continued to plague the U.S. apparel manufacturing industry. Consumer spending was lower than anticipated, imports from countries with lower labor costs continued to flow into the United States, and department stores increasingly emphasized private-label goods at the expense of manufacturers of branded apparel. In response to an intensely competitive retailing industry and a drop-off in consumer spending, retailers implemented heavy promotion and deep-discounting programs in

1987 and into 1988. As a result, sales had been advancing at a moderate pace, with earnings declining at a more rapid rate. Industry experts were forecasting moderate industry growth in the absence of any significant economic downturn.

Interco's general retail merchandising and apparel manufacturing groups turned in less than stellar performances in fiscal 1988. The former group's operating profits fell 3.7% on a modest increase in sales over the comparable 1987 period. The latter group earned operating profits of $20.2 million after an $11.6 million restructuring charge, compared to $47.3 million in 1987, on sales that slipped only slightly from 1987 levels.

The Takeover Bid

Interco management and Wall Street analysts believed that the apparel group's performance would continue to weaken Interco's overall operations and cause the equity markets to undervalue its common stock. Exhibits 3 and 4 give the history of Interco's common stock price. After the stock market crash of October 1987, Interco had accelerated its share repurchase program with the board of directors' authorization to buy back up to 5 million shares. By the end of fiscal year 1988, more than 4 million shares of common stock had been repurchased at a total cost of $152.3 million.

Given that Interco was widely viewed in the investment community as a potential takeover target, Harvey Saligman, Interco's chairman and CEO, contacted Wasserstein, Perella & Co. to discuss potential defensive measures aimed at maintaining Interco's independence. To deter any unwanted third-party acquisition, the board voted on July 11, 1988, to amend Interco's shareholder rights plan, making any hostile takeover of the company prohibitively expensive. Exhibit 5 describes Interco's shareholder rights plan in more detail.

Determined to improve the return on shareholders' investment and to deter a third-party acquisition further, on July 15, 1988, Interco announced plans to restructure. The apparel group's performance for the quarter ended May 31, 1988, continued to be poor, with a 13.4% decline in sales from the comparable 1987 quarter. The proposed restructuring would involve the sale of the apparel segment, a special dividend, and/or a stock repurchase. Interco retained two investment banking firms, Goldman, Sachs & Co. and Wasserstein, Perella & Co., to explore strategic alternatives and to sell the apparel manufacturing division and possibly other assets. Saligman's restructuring plan was aimed at "narrow[ing] the focus of Interco's business and improv[ing] the price of its shares."[1]

But a takeover attempt could not be avoided. City Capital had already accumulated 8.7% of Interco's common stock, and on July 27, 1988, it proposed a merger with Interco. Pursuant to this proposal, City Capital offered to buy all of Interco's common shares that it did not already own at a price of $64 per share. City Capital also advised the board of its willingness to negotiate the terms of the proposal, including price. In response, the Interco board expanded Wasserstein, Perella's mandate as financial advisor. Its advisory services would now include delivering an opinion on the fairness of City Capital's offer and valuing and recommending other alternatives.[2] How much

1. Francine Schwade, "Interco Receives Bid from Rales Group for Takeover Value at $2.26 Billion," *The Wall Street Journal,* July 29, 1988, p. 4.

2. Interco had retained Wasserstein, Perella pursuant to a unique compensation contract that offered a substantial contingency fee of $3.7 million payable to Wasserstein, Perella once City Capital rescinded its

Interco was worth was a question its board of directors would have to consider in evaluating alternatives to a merger with City Capital.

City Capital Associates Limited Partnership

City Capital Associates Limited Partnership was led by two Washington, D.C., businessmen, Steven M. Rales and his brother Mitchell. The Rales brothers had been involved in multiple acquisitions, either through Danaher Corporation, a publicly owned company they controlled, or through one of their other partnerships. These acquisitions had included Western Pacific Industries, Inc., Chicago Pneumatic Tool Co., Mohawk Rubber Co., and Master Shield, Inc. The brothers' acquisition focus had been on undervalued targets with strong market niches. With the completion of eight medium-sized acquisitions, Danaher had grown since 1981 from a small real estate trust into a diversified conglomerate of manufacturing companies. Due in part to the acquisitions and the use of tax loss carryforwards, Danaher Corp.'s earnings had increased sixfold, from $2.9 million in 1984 to $19 million in 1987.

The Rales brothers had formed City Capital with the sole purpose of acquiring Interco. As disclosed in a Securities and Exchange Commission filing, it was their intention, after completing the acquisition, to sell Interco's apparel businesses and to consider selling parts of the footwear and general retailing businesses. In this same filing, the Rales brothers indicated that they would consider paying more than $64 per common share for Interco.

On the morning of August 8, 1988, City Capital raised its offer for Interco to $70 per share and stated its willingness to increase the price per share further should a review of more-detailed company information so warrant. Under the assumption of 37.5 million fully diluted shares outstanding, the offer had an indicated value of over $2.6 billion. The offer was conditional upon, among other things, the board's redemption of the newly amended rights plan or the invalidation of those rights pursuant to the proposed merger. Before raising the value of its offer for Interco, City Capital had arranged the required $2.5 billion in financing. Drexel Burnham Lambert, Inc., City Capital's financial advisor, had stated that it was "highly confident" it could raise up to $1.375 billion of debt and/or equity for the $70-per-share proposal. Additional bank financing, including a $1.1 billion credit facility arranged by Chase Manhattan Corp., would provide the remainder of the necessary funding.

Evaluation of the Takeover Bid

The original agenda for Interco's board meeting on August 8, 1988, largely focused on a previously announced restructuring plan that included selling the company's faltering apparel group, paying a special dividend, and/or repurchasing shares of common stock. However, with City Capital already owning a sizable portion of Interco's stock, Saligman and the board of directors recognized the urgency of responding to the Rales brothers' offer. To arrive at a conclusion, the board members would spend much of the August 8 board meeting discussing Wasserstein, Perella's evaluation of the $64-per-share City Capital offer and other proposed alternatives. The two key alternatives consisted of a friendly merger and a restructuring of the company. Under both scenar-

---

offer and only if a recapitalization was completed. Wasserstein, Perella would receive $1.8 million for its services with or without this contingency fee. See George Anders and Francine Schwadel, "Wall Streeters Helped Interco Defeat Raiders But at a Heavy Price," *The Wall Street Journal,* July 7, 1990, p. A1.

ios, it was assumed that key managers, including Saligman, would remain with the company. Before any decision could be made on City Capital's offer or any of the strategic alternatives, however, it was important for the board to assess Interco's value as determined by Wasserstein, Perella. Historical financial statements are provided in Exhibits 6 and 7. Business segment information is given in Exhibit 8.

As the financial advisor to Interco, Wasserstein, Perella prepared a number of analyses that resulted in a valuation range for the company of $68–80 per share. Specifically, discounted cash flow analysis, comparable transaction analysis, and premiums paid analysis were used to determine that City Capital's offer of $70 per share was inadequate and not in the best interests of Interco and its shareholders. Exhibits 9–13 provide significant assumptions that Wasserstein, Perella relied on in determining its expert opinion on Interco's value. Exhibit 14 gives then-current market interest rates.

At Interco's board meeting on August 8, 1988, Wasserstein, Perella informed the board of its analysis of City Capital's offer. Interco's board of directors voted to reject the $70-per-share bid the same day.

EXHIBIT 1
Board of Directors as of May 16, 1988

Harvey Saligman	Chairman of the board and chief executive officer (CEO) of Interco
Harry M. Krogh	President and chief operating officer (COO) of Interco
Ronald L. Aylward	Vice chairman of the board of Interco
R. Stuart Moore	Vice president of Interco; president of The Lane Company, Inc., a subsidiary of Interco
Mark H. Lieberman	Vice president of Interco; president of Londontown, a division of Interco
Richard B. Loynd	Vice president of Interco; chairman of the board of Converse, Inc., a subsidiary of Interco
Charles J. Rothschild, Jr.	Vice president of Interco; chairman of the board of Megastar Apparel Group, a division of Interco
Zane E. Barnes	Chairman of the board, president, CEO, and director of Southwestern Bell Corporation, engaged in the general telecommunications business
Donald E. Lasater	Chairman of the board, CEO, and director of Mercantile Bancorporation, Inc., a bank holding company, and chairman of the board and director of Mercantile Bank National Association
Lee M. Liberman	Chairman of the board, president, CEO, and director of Laclede Gas Company, a gas public utility
Robert H. Quenon	President, CEO, and director of Peabody Holding Company, Inc., which is engaged in coal mining and sales
William E. Cornelius	President, CEO, and director of Union Electric Company, an electric public utility
Marilyn S. Lewis	Civil leader and volunteer
Thomas H. O'Leary	Vice chairman of the board and director of Burlington Northern, Inc., a holding company with transportation, energy, and natural resources concerns

As of April 15, 1988, all directors, nominees, and officers of Interco as a group (24 persons) beneficially owned 1.14% of the outstanding shares of Interco's common stock.

Source: Notice and proxy statement, May 16, 1988.

EXHIBIT 2
Subsidiaries

Abe Schrader Corp.	Golde's Department Stores, Inc.
Big Yank Corp.	Grand Entry Hat Corp.
Bowen Shoe Co., Inc.	Highland House, Inc.
Broyhill Furniture Industries, Inc.	Highland Transport, Inc.
Campco Holdings, S.A.	Hy-Test, Inc.
Campus Pacific, Ltd.	Interco Subsidiary, Inc.
Central Hardware Co.	Keith O'Brien Investment Co.
Clayton Operations, S.A.	Lane Co., Inc.
College-Town, Inc.	Lease Management, Inc.
Converse, Inc.	Julius Marlow Holdings, Ltd.
Delmar Sportswear, Inc.	L. J. O'Neill Shoe Co.
Ethan Allen, Inc.	ORC Financial Ag
Factory Outlet Co.	Patriot Investment Co.
Fine's Men's Shops, Inc.	Queen Casuals, Inc.
Florsheim, Inc.	Senack Shoes, Inc.
Florsheim Shoe Store Co. of Hawaii	Sky City Stores, Inc.
Florsheim Shoe Store Co.—Midwest	Stuffed Shirt, Inc.
Florsheim Shoe Store Co.—Northwest	United Shirt Distributors, Inc.
Florsheim Shoe Store Co.—South	Walton Road Management Co.
Florsheim Shoe Store Co.—West	

Source: Lotus One Source.

EXHIBIT 3
Common Stock Price History (monthly)

Month-End Prices (adjusted for stock splits)	
1986	
31-Jan-86	$35.125
28-Feb-86	39.000
31-Mar-86	39.250
30-Apr-86	39.625
30-May-86	43.500
30-Jun-86	47.188
31-Jul-86	41.375
29-Aug-86	43.750
30-Sep-86	40.000
31-Oct-86	43.750
28-Nov-86	44.125
31-Dec-86	36.875
1987	
30-Jan-87	39.750
27-Feb-87	42.625
31-Mar-87	44.125
30-Apr-87	39,625
29-May-87	40.125
30-Jun-87	45.375
31-Jul-87	51.250
31-Aug-87	53.250
30-Sep-87	47.500
30-Oct-87	36.000
30-Nov-87	30.000
31-Dec-87	32.250
1988	
29-Jan-88	37.125
29-Feb-88	42.000
31-Mar-88	42.000
29-Apr-88	41.125
31-May-88	43.875
30-Jun-88	44.750
29-Jul-88	68.500

Source: Interactive Data Corporation.

EXHIBIT 4
Common Stock Price History (Daily)

Daily Closing Prices

02-May-88	$40.250	21-Jun-88	43.125
03-May-88	41.500	22-Jun-88	43.750
04-May-88	41.000	23-Jun-88	43.625
05-May-88	41.625	24-Jun-88	43.500
06-May-88	40.625	27-Jun-88	43.625
09-May-88	40.875	28-Jun-88	44.000
10-May-88	41.750	29-Jun-88	44.000
11-May-88	41.625	30-Jun-88	44.750
12-May-88	42.000	01-Jul-88	44.625
13-May-88	42.125	04-Jul-88	N.A.
16-May-88	42.250	05-Jul-88	45.375
17-May-88	42.000	06-Jul-88	44.500
18-May-88	41.500	07-Jul-88	44.625
19-May-88	40.625	08-Jul-88	45.000
20-May-88	40.625	11-Jul-88	45.250
23-May-88	40.375	12-Jul-88	45.375
24-May-88	41.500	13-Jul-88	46.375
25-May-88	42.500	14-Jul-88	49.000
26-May-88	42.625	15-Jul-88	54.375
27-May-88	41.250	18-Jul-88	54.500
30-May-88	N.A.	19-Jul-88	58.375
31-May-88	43.875	20-Jul-88	58.125
01-Jun-88	43.500	21-Jul-88	57.875
02-Jun-88	42.875	22-Jul-88	57.250
03-Jun-88	44.125	25-Jul-88	58.000
06-Jun-88	43.250	26-Jul-88	58.875
07-Jun-88	42.000	27-Jul-88	59.375
08-Jun-88	43.875	28-Jul-88	67.750
09-Jun-88	43.375	29-Jul-88	68.500
10-Jun-88	43.375	01-Aug-88	68.875
13-Jun-88	43.500	02-Aug-88	67.625
14-Jun-88	43.625	03-Aug-88	67.000
15-Jun-88	42.500	04-Aug-88	67.375
16-Jun-88	42.875	05-Aug-88	68.250
17-Jun-88	43.625	08-Aug-88	72.500
20-Jun-88	43.250		

Source: Interactive Data Corporation.

EXHIBIT 5
Shareholder Rights Plan

On September 23, 1985, Interco's board of directors adopted a shareholder rights plan designed to deter unsolicited takeover bids by creating the threat of substantial dilution for any person or group attempting an unfriendly merger with Interco.

The original plan was amended on July 11, 1988, by the board of directors. At that time, the directors were aware that Interco's common stock was under accumulation and were suspicious of a third-party acquisition offer for the company.[a] Changes in the purchase price per share and certain triggering provisions, otherwise known as poison pill shareholder rights, made the takeover defense more onerous. Specifically, the amended rights plan declared that it would issue a dividend of one share purchase right per share of common stock. The amended rights plan also gave the board sole discretion to lower certain triggering percentages such that the massive dilutive effects of the plan would come into play when a person or group acquired as little as 15% of the shares of Interco's stock.

At Interco's board meeting on August 8, 1988, the board approved "golden parachute" severance agreements for Interco's senior executives, to be triggered upon an acquisition by a third party, including City Capital. According to an SEC filing, the golden parachute severance agreements were valued at $16.3 million and covered 17 top executives at Interco. Lump-sum payments, including $2.2 million to Harvey Saligman, would be made under certain conditions if the company was taken over.

a. As claimed in Civil Action No. 10111, the Second Amended and Consolidated Class Action Complaint, as filed in the Court of Chancery of the State of Delaware in and for New Castle County, p. 16.

EXHIBIT 6

Interco's Consolidated Balance Sheets (thousands of dollars except per share data)

	February 28,			May 31,	
	1986	*1987*	*1988*[a]	*1987*	*1988*
Current assets					
Cash	$ 16,856	$ 16,631	$ 20,849	$ 29,700	$ 19,622
Marketable securities	127,341	63,747	11,033	57,789	16,366
Receivable, net	402,225	446,755	486,657	431,743	460,759
Inventories	647,116	733,907	805,095	786,792	872,135
Prepaid expenses and other current assets	22,547	25,614	35,665	25,622	44,959
Total current assets	$1,215,815	$1,286,654	$1,359,299	$1,331,646	$1,413,840
Property, plant, and equipment					
Land	26,770	32,266	32,525	—	—
Buildings and improvements	437,812	465,811	471,787	—	—
Machinery and equipment	320,256	364,499	380,402	—	—
	784,838	862,576	884,714	868,670	890,887
Less accumulated depreciation	343,018	377,226	405,215	386,762	412,332
Net property, plant, and equipment	441,820	485,350	479,499	481,908	478,555
Other assets	99,238	153,383	146,788	149,170	146,878
Total assets	$1,756,893	$1,925,387	$1,985,586	$1,962,724	$2,039,273
Current liabilities					
Notes payable	$ —	$ 68,840	$ 70,517	$ 97,297	$ 146,016
Current maturities of long-term debt and capital lease obligations	9,647	11,915	8,172	9,288	8,900
Accounts payable and accrued expenses	184,032	216,365	239,513	278,847	292,051
Income taxes	12,699	17,327	4,402	15,294	5,463
Total current liabilities	$ 249,587	$ 358,226	$ 373,343	$ 400,726	$ 452,430
Long-term debt, less current maturities	127,409	135,019	257,327	133,403	255,279
Obligations under capital leases, less current maturities	56,495	50,546	41,813	49,270	40,032
Other long-term liabilities	43,249	55,381	61,766	56,410	63,484
Shareholders' equity					
Preferred stock, no par value	66,027	61,795	57,113	61,285	36,721
Common stock, $3.75 stated value	163,765	163,643	155,088	155,088	155,088
Capital surplus (41,356,847 shares issued)	104,205	98,246	44,539	49,149	32,117
Retained earnings	1,027,895	1,099,006	1,179,964	1,111,527	1,194,884
	1,361,892	1,422,690	1,436,704	1,377,049	1,418,810
Less 5,173,811 treasury shares	81,739	96,475	185,367	54,134	190,762
Total shareholders' equity	1,280,153	1,326,215	1,251,337	1,322,915	1,228,048
Total liabilities and net worth	$1,756,893	$1,925,387	$1,985,586	$1,962,724	$2,039,273

Source: Annual reports and 10-Q reports.

a. February 29, 1988.

EXHIBIT 7

Interco's Consolidated Statement of Earnings (thousands of dollars)

	Years Ended February 28,			First Quarter Ended May 31,	
	1986	*1987*	*1888*[a]	*1987*	*1988*
Income:					
Net sales.	$2,832,384	$2,946,902	$3,341,423	$781,421	$778,107
Other income	36,140	32,175	29,237	6,293	6,864
	2,868,524	2,979,077	3,370,660	787,714	784,971
Costs and expenses:					
Cost of sales	1,932,258	2,000,423	2,284,640	522,759	522,942
Selling, general, and					
administrative expenses	681,886	712,861	799,025	199,145	201,129
Interest expense.	25,523	28,082	33,535	7,351	9,179
	2,639,667	2,741,366	3,117,200	735,438	733,067
Earnings before income taxes	228,857	237,711	253,460	52,276	51,904
Income taxes	109,008	111,937	108,457	25,276	25,762
Net earnings	$ 119,849	$ 125,774	$ 145,003	$ 26,514	$ 30,689
Operating income[b]	218,240	233,618	257,758	53,334	54,219
Operating cash flow[c]	267,756	287,133	319,275	—	—

Source: Annual reports and 10-Q reports.

a. For the year ended February 29, 1988.

b. Operating income equal to the sum of earning before income taxes and interest expense less other income.

c. Operating cash flow equal to the sum of operating income and depreciation expense.

EXHIBIT 8
Business Segment Information

	Years Ended February 28,			First Quarter Ended May 31,	
	1986	*1987*	*1988*	*1987*	*1988*
Net sales to unaffiliated customers					
Apparel	$ 907,833	$ 817,660	$ 813,198	$160,339	$138,836
General retail	461,785	498,324	532,251	148,138	149,209
Footwear	558,286	663,521	890,411	209,535	226,672
Furniture	904,480	967,397	1,105,563	263,409	263,390
Total	$2,832,384	$2,946,902	$3,341,423	$781,421	$778,107
Operating earnings					
Apparel	$ 66,716	$ 47,269	$ 20,240	$ (670)	$ (247)
General retail	32,085	40,610	39,101	14,136	12,498
Footwear	48,475	52,136	92,204	15,777	19,700
Furniture	105,111	123,766	149,090	38,319	32,196
Total	$ 252,387	$ 263,781	$ 300,635	$ 67,562	$ 64,147
Other income	$ 36,140	$ 32,175	$ 29,237	$ 6,293	$ 6,864
Corporate expense	(34,147)	(30,163)	(42,877)	(14,228)	(9,928)
Earnings before interest and taxes	254,380	265,793	286,995	59,627	61,083
Interest expense	(25,523)	(28,082)	(33,535)	(7,351)	(9,179)
Earnings before income taxes	$ 228,857	$ 237,711	$ 253,460	$ 52,276	$ 51,904
Identifiable assets at year end					
Apparel	$ 456,972	$ 465,601	$ 425,350		
General retail	234,004	248,639	252,195		
Footwear	291,292	497,706	595,861		
Furniture	618,980	640,106	688,853		
	$1,601,248	$1,852,052	$1,962,259		
Corporate assets	155,645	73,335	23,327		
Total	$1,756,893	$1,925,387	$1,985,586		
Depreciation expense					
Apparel	$ 11,965	$ 12,123	$ 12,521		
General retail	8,294	9,079	9,681		
Footwear	8,286	10,638	13,107		
Furniture	20,971	21,675	26,208		
Capital expenditures					
Apparel	$ 13,433	$ 8,869	$ 9,220		
General retail	6,169	8,167	10,735		
Footwear	8,114	7,486	9,236		
Furniture	27,278	24,720	36,188		

Source: Annual reports and 10-Q reports.

EXHIBIT 9
Summary of the Takeover Offer

City Capital Associates, L.P. Offer	
Date	August 8, 1988
Price per share	$70.00
Premium to stock one-day prior[a]	17.9%
Premium to stock one-month prior	59.1%
Premium to 52-week low	137.3%
Premium to 52-week high	17.2%
Value of equity	$2,622.8MM
Net debt	318.5MM
Value of firm	$2,941.3MM

	Value of Firm as a Multiple of:			Value of Equity as a Multiple of:	
	Sales	Operating Cash Flow	Operating Income	Net Income	Book Value
Year ending 2/29/88	0.9x	9.2x	11.4x	18.1x	2.2x
Estimate of year ending 2/28/89	0.9	8.8	10.7	17.0	2.2

Source: Adapted with minor modifications in terminology from Wasserstein, Perella & Co. presentation to the Interco Board of Directors, August 8, 1988. Civil Action No. 10111, filed in the Court of Chancery of the State of Delaware in and for New Castle County, Exhibit 23.

a. Premiums based on stock prices as of July 27, 1988.

EXHIBIT 10
Premiums Paid Analysis

	# Deals[a]	Average Premium Paid over Stock Price			
		1 Day	4 Weeks	52-Week Low	52-Week High
1st Quarter 1988	19	62.3%	95.5%	159.5%	16.7%
2nd Quarter 1988	9	68.6	91.3	182.8	31.5
3rd Quarter 1988[b]	12	36.5	49.9	181.3	2.6
1988	40	56.0	80.9	171.3	15.8
Rales		17.9	59.1	137.3	17.2

Source: Wasserstein, Perella & Co. presentation to the Interco Board of Directors, August 8, 1988. Civil Action No. 10111, filed in the Court of Chancery of the State of Delaware in and for New Castle County, Exhibit 23.

a. Wasserstein, Perella & Co. selected tender offers.

b. Selected tender offers from the months of July and August.

EXHIBIT 11
Comparable Transaction Analysis

Purchase Price Multiples by Business Segment

Furniture Manufacturing Companies

Announcement Date	Acquiror/Target	Aggregate Price ($MM)[a]	Purchase Price Multiples[a]				
			Net Income	Book Value[b]	Sales	Operating Income	Operating Cash Flow
12/14/87	La-Z-Boy/Kincaid	$ 63.5	22.0x	2.1x	0.8x	11.7x	8.1x
11/17/86	INTERCO/Lane	523.7	19.3	2.8	1.6	11.1	9.6
08/12/86	Chicago Pacific/General Mills Furniture	89.3	14.1	1.8	1.0	12.0	9.9
06/03/86	Masco/Henredon	260.9	31.6	2.6	2.1	20.3	15.8
08/08/88	Rales Proposal	$2,941.3	18.1	2.2	0.9	11.4	9.2

Source: Wasserstein, Perella & Co. presentation to the Interco Board of Directors, August 8, 1988. Civil Action No. 10111, filed in the Court of Chancery of the State of Delaware in and for New Castle County, Exhibit 23.

a. Sales, operating income, and operating cash flow multiples adjusted for the value of net debt outstanding.

b. Book value adjusted for intangibles.

Footwear Manufacturing Companies

Announcement Date	Acquiror/Target	Aggregate Price ($MM)[a]	Purchase Price Multiples[a]				
			Net Income	Book Value[b]	Sales	Operating Income	Operating Cash Flow
04/25/88	NIKE/Cole Haan	$ 95.0	36.2x	N.M.	1.5x	14.1	12.2
06/03/87	Moacq/Morse Shoe	312.5	2.5	1.8	0.5	13.0	9.2
03/10/87	Reebok/AVIA	191.0	40.6	6.7	2.1	24.6	23.3
09/18/86	Reebok/Rockport	146.1	30.7	N.M.	1.7	26.0	23.9
07/31/86	INTERCO/Converse	202.7	37.1	1.8	0.9	24.7	18.2
08/08/88	Rales Proposal	$2,941.3	18.1	2.2	0.9	11.4	9.2

Source: Wasserstein, Perella & Co. presentation to the Interco Board of Directors, August 8, 1988. Civil Action No. 10111, filed in the Court of Chancery of the State of Delaware in and for New Castle County, Exhibit 23.

a. Sales, operating income, and operating cash flow multiples adjusted for the value of net debt outstanding.

b. Book value adjusted for intangibles.

(continued)

EXHIBIT 11 *(continued)*

Apparel Companies

Announcement Date	Acquiror/Target	Aggregate Price ($MM)[a]	Purchase Price Multiples[a]				
			Net Income	Book Value[b]	Sales	Operating Income	Operating Cash Flow
04/28/88	Wesray/William Carter	$ 157.4	N.M.	1.6x	0.8x	24.0x	13.7x
02/02/88	Salant/Manhattan Indus.	129.7	N.M.	1.4	0.4	N.M.	N.M.
03/17/86	W Acquisition/Warnco	504.7	21.0x	2.5	0.9	10.6	9.2
11/04/85	West Point Pepperall/Cluett, Peabody	551.9	19.6	1.5	0.6	10.6	9.2
08/08/88	Rales Proposal	$2,941.3	18.1	2.2	0.9	11.4	9.2

Source: Wasserstein, Perella & Co. presentation to the Interco Board of Directors, August 8, 1988. Civil Action No. 10111, filed in the Court of Chancery of the State of Delaware in and for New Castle County, Exhibit 23.

a. Sales, operating income, and operating cash flow multiples adjusted for the value of net debt outstanding.

b. Book value adjusted for intangibles.

Central Hardware Division

Announcement Date	Acquiror/Target	Aggregate Price ($MM)[a]	Purchase Price Multiples[a]				
			Net Income	Book Value[b]	Sales	Operating Income	Operating Cash Flow
06/24/88	Management Group/Payless Cashways	$1,189.4	22.0x	2.3x	0.6x	13.1x	9.2x
08/08/88	Rales Proposal	$2,941.3	18.1	2.2	0.9	11.4	9.2

Source: Wasserstein, Perella & Co. presentation to the Interco Board of Directors, August 8, 1988. Civil Action No. 10111, filed in the Court of Chancery of the State of Delaware in and for New Castle County, Exhibit 23.

a. Sales, operating income, and operating cash flow multiples adjusted for the value of net debt outstanding.

b. Book value adjusted for intangibles.

(continued)

EXHIBIT 11 *(concluded)*

Value Ranges by Business Segment

Business Segment	1988 Sales	Multiple Range	Value Range	Median Value
Apparel	$ 813.2	.4– .9	$ 325.3–$ 731.9	$ 569.2
General retail	532.3	.6– .6	319.4– 319.4	319.4
Footwear	890.4	.5– 2.1	445.2– 1,869.8	1,335.6
Furniture	$1,105.6	.8– 2.1	884.5– 2,321.8	1,437.3
			$1,974.4–$5,242.9	$3,661.5

Business Segment	1988 Operating Income	Multiple Range	Value Range	Median Value
Apparel	$ 20.2	10.6–24.0	$ 214.1–$ 484.8	$ 214.1
General retail	39.1	13.1–13.1	512.2– 512.2	512.2
Footwear	92.2	13.0–26.0	1,198.6– 2,397.2	2,268.1
Furniture	$ 149.1	11.1–20.3	1,655.0– 3,026.7	1,766.8
			$3,579.9–$6,420.9	$4,761.2

Business Segment	1988 Operating Cash Flow	Multiple Range	Value Range	Median Value
Apparel	$ 32.7	9.2–13.7	$ 300.8–$ 448.0	$ 300.8
General retail	48.8	9.2– 9.2	448.9– 448.9	448.9
Footwear	105.3	9.2–23.9	968.8– 2,516.7	970.7
Furniture	$ 175.3	8.1–15.8	1,419.9– 2,769.7	1,709.2
			$3,138.4–$6,183.3	$3,429.6

Source: Wasserstein, Perella & Co. presentation to the Interco Board of Directors, August 8, 1988. Civil Action No. 10111, filed in the Court of Chancery of the State of Delaware in and for New Castle County, Exhibit 23.

EXHIBIT 12
Discounted Cash Flow Analysis

Assumptions	Furniture Group	Footwear Group	Apparel Group	Retail Group	Total
Sales growth[a]	7.7%	6.3%	7.1%	7.6%	7.2%
Operating margin range[b]	13.1%–14.1%	9.1%–10.4%	6.4%–7.0%	6.5%–7.5%	9.2%–10.1%
Capital expenditures[c]	1x	1x	1x	1x	1x
Increase in working investment[d]	12.5%	12.5%	12.5%	7.5%	11.6%
Tax rate					41.0%

	Multiple of Cash Flow in Year 10		
	14.0x	15.0x	16.0x
Terminal value ($millions)	$4,746.0	$5,085.0	$5,424.0
Implied stock price Discount rate			
10.0%	$ 80.00	$ 84.00	$ 88.00
11.0	74.00	77.00	81.00
12.0	68.00	72.00	75.00
13.0	63.00	66.00	69.00

Source: Adapted with minor modifications in terminology from Wasserstein, Perella & Co., presentation to the Interco Board of Directors, August 8, 1988. Civil Action No. 1011, filed in the Court of Chancery of the State of Delaware in and for New Castle County, Exhibit 23.

a. 10-year annual compound growth rate.

b. Projected operating margin in 1989 and in 1998.

c. As a multiple of depreciation.

d. As a percent of the change in sales in 1994 forward.

EXHIBIT 13
Reference Range—Retain Core Companies Case (millions of dollars except per share data)

Segment	Range
Furniture group	$1,525 – $1,750
Footwear group	775 – 900
Total	2,300 – 2,650
After-tax divestiture proceeds	588 – 639
Net corporate adjustments[a]	(335)– (273)
Range	2,553 – 3,016
Per share range[b]	68.00 – 80.00+

Source: Wasserstein, Perella & Co. presentation to the Interco Board of Directors, August 8, 1988. Civil Action No. 1011, filed in the Court of Chancery of the State of Delaware in and for New Castle County, Exhibit 23.

a. Accounts for net debt, overfunded pension, and miscellaneous other assets that include real estate, which could be understated.

b. Based on 37.5 million fully diluted shares outstanding.

EXHIBIT 14

Indexes of Monthly Adjusted Closing Prices 1980–1988; Actual Daily Closing Prices, July–August 1988; and Market Interest Rates, August 1988

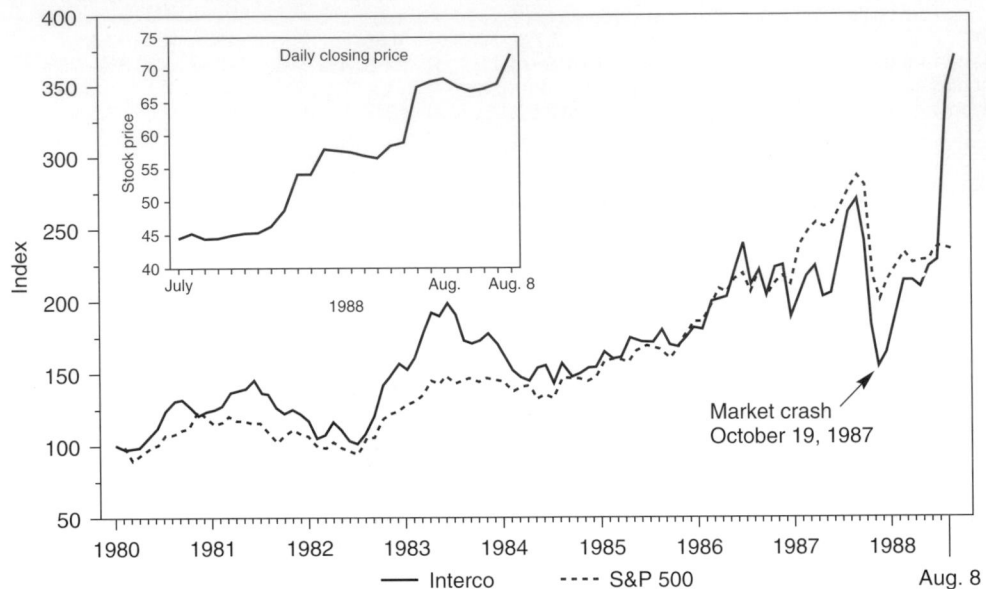

Source: Interactive Data Corp.

Market Interest Rates

Yield curve at August 4, 1988

1-year Treasury bills	7.83%
7-year Treasury bonds	8.87
10-year Treasury bonds	9.01
30-year Treasury bonds	9.10

Corporate bond rates at August 5, 1988 (industrial companies)

10-year AAA	9.50%
10-year AA	9.65
10-year A	9.80
10-year BBB	10.10

Source: Salomon Brothers, Inc.

Eskimo Pie Corporation

In early 1991, Reynolds Metals, the makers of Aluminum Foil and other aluminum products, decided to sell its holding of Eskimo Pie, a marketer of branded frozen novelties. Reynolds had few interests outside its aluminum and packaging business, and the Eskimo Pie Corporation, with roughly $47 million in sales, accounted for less than 1% of Reynolds revenues. Reynolds planned to use the proceeds from the sale of Eskimo Pie to fund investments in its core aluminum business. Eskimo Pie was 84% owned by Reynolds Metals and 4% owned by the Reynolds Foundation. The remaining 12% of Eskimo Pie was held by various Reynolds family members and a small group of outside investors.

Goldman Sachs, a New York investment banking firm, was retained to assist with the sale of Eskimo Pie. Goldman estimated that the sale price of Eskimo Pie would be about 1.2 times 1990 sales, or about $57 million. In 1990, Nestle Foods paid a comparable multiple for Drumstick, another ice cream novelty company. Goldman organized an auction for Eskimo Pie, and Nestle was the highest of six bidders, with a price of $61 million.

Mr. David Clark, president of Eskimo Pie Corporation, recognized that the sale of Eskimo Pie to Nestle would mean the end of its independence. Nestle was likely to consolidate its ice cream novelty businesses by eliminating Eskimo Pie's headquarters and management staff. Clark had struggled to find a way to keep the company independent since he first learned of the sale, but he had been unable to raise sufficient funds to purchase Eskimo Pie in a leveraged buyout (LBO), and the sale to Nestle seemed inevitable.

This case was prepared by Professor Richard S. Ruback and Research Assistant Dean Mihas (MBA '92).

The Eskimo Pie Corporation

Background

Eskimo Pie, a chocolate-covered bar of vanilla ice cream, was the first ice cream novelty. Its history appears on the Eskimo Pie box:

> Genuine Eskimo Pie . . .
>
> One day [while] working in a confectionery store to supplement his teaching income, Christian K. Nelson became puzzled by a little boy's indecision between a chocolate candy bar and a scoop of ice cream. When questioned, the freckle-faced boy replied, "I want 'em both but I only got a nickel."
>
> With a clever hunch and a little ingenuity, Mr. Nelson found a way to combine the two ingredients in what would become America's first chocolate-covered ice cream bar. The little boy got his wish and Mr. Nelson founded a corporation on the success of the Eskimo Pie product.

Christian Nelson, age 27, began trying to make chocolate stick to ice cream in 1920 while operating an ice cream and confectionery store in Iowa. After months of experimentation, Nelson discovered that cocoa butter made the chocolate adhere to the ice cream. He introduced his product as the "I-Scream-Bar" in 1921. One year later, Mr. Nelson formed a partnership with Russell Stover, and the product was renamed Eskimo Pie.

Because the lack of refrigeration made centralized production and distribution impossible, Eskimo Pie licensed rights to make and distribute the Eskimo Pie bar according to Mr. Nelson's recipe. By the spring of 1922, licenses had been sold to 2,700 manufacturers across the country. Sales were averaging 1 million Eskimo Pies a day and soared to 2 million a day by early summer. Russell Stover, Nelson's business partner, designed a tin foil wrapper that added to the product's glamour and provided a mechanism to collect royalties. U.S. Foil Company, which was later renamed Reynolds Metal Company, manufactured the printed wrappers around the clock to satisfy demand.

In spite of the popularity of Eskimo Pies, the Eskimo Pie Corporation was not financially successful. Eskimo Pie had difficulty collecting royalties both because the company lacked a reliable accounting system and because of patent infringers. By the summer of 1923, it was estimated that over 1 billion Eskimo Pies had been sold, and yet the firm could not pay its debt of $100,000. Nelson sold Eskimo Pie to the U.S. Foil Company, and in 1924, Eskimo Pie Corporation became a subsidiary of U.S. Foil Company.[1] Nelson was paid a small fraction of a cent in royalties on every Eskimo Pie sold thereafter.

1991 Operations

Eskimo Pie had two lines of business in 1991. The first was the licensing of the Eskimo Pie brand products and the sublicensing of Welch's and Heath brand products. The second was a manufacturing operation that produced and distributed ingredients

---

1. Stover sold his share for $30,000 in 1923. Stover went on to develop a nationwide candy business. After the sale of Eskimo Pie to U.S. Foil, Nelson was employed by Eskimo Pie and retired as a vice president in 1961. His signficiant inventions include the use of dry ice to store ice cream and machinery that automated the production of ice cream novelties. Mr. Nelson died on March 8, 1992, at the age of 98.

TABLE A
Sales by Business Line

	Year Ended December 31,		
Business	1989	1990	1991
Licensing			
Eskimo Pie	58%	59%	56%
Welch's and Heath[a]	14	14	24
Flavors, packaging, and other	28	27	20

a. Heath products included only in 1991.

and packaging for the dairy industry. Table A presents the sales breakdown of these businesses. The company was also engaged in intensive research and product development efforts to extend its product lines. Eskimo Pie had a total of 130 employees.

Exhibit 1 presents historical financial information for Eskimo Pie from 1987 to 1990, and Exhibit 2 contains a summary of cash flows from 1989 and 1990.

Licensing

Eskimo Pie granted exclusive territorial licenses for the manufacture, distribution, and sale of Eskimo Pie brand products through a national network of about 20 dairy product manufacturers. Eskimo's licensees agreed to maintain the company's strict quality standards, and Eskimo maintained the right to inspect all premises used for the manufacture and handling of Eskimo products. The licensees were Eskimo Pie's direct customers, and the top 10 licensees accounted for over 75% of revenues. Carnation was Eskimo Pie's largest licensee and manufacturer, with territorial licenses to 11 western states.

Payment to Eskimo Pie by licensees was embedded in the price paid for ingredients and packaging supplied by Eskimo Pie rather than as a royalty payment based on units sold. If a licensee elected to use outside parties for certain ingredients and packaging, the licensee then paid Eskimo Pie a trademark license fee.

Eskimo Pie also sublicensed the manufacture and distribution of frozen novelties under established brand names of other food companies. Sublicensing had been an important component of Eskimo Pies's strategy since 1975 when it developed the Nestle Crunch Bar and sublicensed its manufacture and distribution. In 1986, shortly after it acquired Carnation, Nestle terminated the sublicensing arrangement.

In 1991, Eskimo Pie licensed frozen novelties for Welch's and Leaf Incorporated, who owned the Heath brand name. Under the arrangements, Eskimo Pie had the exclusive authority to grant sublicenses for the manufacture and sale of these products similar to the way it did for its own Eskimo Pie brand products. Eskimo Pie purchased the base ingredients from the food companies and resold them, along with packaging, to sublicensees. Approximately 80% of the Eskimo Pie brand licensees were also licensees for Welch's and/or Heath products.

Eskimo Pie provided centralized marketing for Eskimo Pie, Welch's, and Heath brand products. The majority of marketing expenses were spent on retail advertising and promotions; the balance went to regional consumer promotions using television and coupon campaigns. One or more of the company's Eskimo Pie brand products were found in 98% of all U.S. grocery stores, and Eskimo Pie enjoyed one of the highest consumer brand name recognition levels in the industry. Exhibit 3 shows the distribution and market share of Eskimo Pie products (including Heath and Welch's) during the 1987–1991 period.

Manufacturing

Eskimo Pie operated three plants in the United States. These plants manufactured key ingredients and packaging used by licensees, such as the proprietary chocolate coating, Midnite Sun, that gave Eskimo Pie products their distinctive flavor. The plants also produced generic ingredients and packaging sold both to licensees and nonlicensees in the dairy industry. The plants employed a total of 46 hourly workers at an average hourly wage of $10.06. The plants also employed 18 salaried employees.

Product Innovation

Eskimo Pie's new product program was successful: ten products introduced since 1987 were being actively marketed and sold in 1991. Eskimo Pie was the first to market a sugar-free frozen dairy novelty bar made with NutraSweet, and it held a patent on that product's coating. The introduction of Sugar Freedom Eskimo Pie products in 1987 was largely responsible for the growth of Eskimo Pie's unit market share from 2.3% in 1987 to 5.3% in 1991. As of 1991, the Sugar Freedom Eskimo Pie products were leading the Eskimo Pie line. The company was also the first to introduce a fat-free frozen novelty product made with Simplesse, a patented fat substitute. By the end of 1991, Eskimo Pie was test marketing a fat-free ice cream sandwich and expected to introduce a Fat Freedom Eskimo Pie line in the spring of 1992.

The Frozen Novelty Industry

The frozen novelty industry in 1991 was highly fragmented, with over 400 brands representing sales of $1.3 billion. During the 1980s, major food companies such as General Foods, Mars, and Coca Cola entered the frozen novelties business. This transformed the industry's structure of low growth, little advertising, and few participants into a rapidly growing industry. Industry revenues went from $590 million in 1980 to $1.5 billion by 1987. The number of ice cream novelty brands, 100 in 1980, expanded to over 500 by 1987. Advertising expenditures increased from less than $2 million to $75 million per year during this period. Exhibit 4 presents the frozen novelties sales trends.

By the late 1980s, the industry began to consolidate, with many of the larger companies exiting or significantly reducing their commitment to the frozen novelty business. By 1991 advertising expenditures had been reduced to about $25 million, and the market growth had slowed significantly. Table B shows the top five frozen novelties as ranked by unit market share in 1991.

TABLE B
1991 Leading Frozen Novelty Brands

Brand	Company	Unit Share
Popsicle	Unilever	7.6%
Klondike	Empire of Carolina	5.4
Eskimo Pie	Eskimo Pie	5.3
Snickers	Mars	4.8
Weight Watchers	H.J. Heinz	4.3

Nestle's Offer

Reynolds retained Goldman Sachs to sell Eskimo Pie because of its long-standing relationship with Reynolds and because it represented Nestle in its Drumstick acquisition. David Clark was directed to work with the Goldman Sachs team that arrived in April 1991 to prepare a sales strategy and the documentation required by buyers. Clark and his staff cooperated reluctantly, recognizing that Eskimo Pie would be unlikely to continue its 70-year history of operating as a stand-alone company in Richmond and that its corporate staff would be unlikely to retain their positions. Exhibit 6 presents the projected income statements that Goldman collected.

Eskimo Pie's management and Wheat First Securities, a Richmond, Virginia, investment banking firm, formed a group to attempt a private buyout. This group obtained $20 million in credit and contributed another $15 million in equity, but the bid was rejected early on when higher offers came in. The buyout proposal could not secure additional financing because of the generally tight credit environment and the unpopularity of high-yield, debt-financed LBOs. Also, Eskimo Pie could not use secured borrowing because the business was not asset intensive.

Goldman contacted several potential buyers. Many expressed interest but were concerned that Eskimo Pie's licensing approach to the business diverged from the more traditional integrated manufacturing and marketing approach. Reynolds received six offers for Eskimo Pie. Nestle Foods was the highest bidder at $61 million, and Reynolds began negotiating the specifics of the sale in mid-1991.

Negotiations between Reynolds and Nestle progressed slowly because of two complications. First, Nestle, a Swiss company, wanted to tailor the transaction to take advantage of its tax conditions. Second, Eskimo Pie discovered in the third quarter of 1991 that a small quantity of cleanup solvents, inks, and oils were disposed of at its New Jersey plant. The company contacted the regulatory authorities and conducted testing to determine the extent of any contamination. Although Eskimo Pie did not expect cleanup costs to exceed $300,000, Nestle remained cautious.

The Proposed Initial Public Offering

As the end of fiscal year 1991 approached, it was becoming apparent that Eskimo Pie was going to have a record year. Sales were higher than anticipated, and operating margins had improved. In addition, Eskimo Pie had also accumulated a $13 million cash reserve. David Clark contacted Wheat First again, searching for an alternative to the Nestle acquisition that would keep Eskimo Pie independent. Any solution would have to provide Reynolds with as much cash as the proposed acquisition.

Wheat First proposed the initial public offering (IPO) of Reynolds' shares. Reynolds had dismissed this possibility early on, at the advice of Goldman Sachs. Goldman argued that a public offering would be worth less than a private sale because of the potential for synergies with an acquiring firm. The fact that Nestle, with its potential synergies in its Carnation and Drumstick units, had submitted the highest bid seemed to confirm Goldman's reasoning. Wheat First, however, had two reasons to think that its IPO might yield more than the sale to Nestle. First, as Exhibit 5 shows, the new issues market was hot, and the number of new issues and their dollar values soared. Second, Wheat First was working with an updated forecast, and it projected a more promising outlook. The forecasted 1991 net income in Exhibit 6 was $2,893,000; actual results were going to be closer to $4,000,000. And forecasted sales in 1991 were projected at about $57 million; actual sales would be about $61 million. Capital expenditures were expected to be less than $1 million in 1992.

Wheat First proposed a two-step transaction. First, Eskimo Pie would pay out a $15 million, or $4.52 per share, special dividend. The $15 million dividend would be funded by the $13 million in cash that Eskimo Pie had accumulated and another $2 million in debt. The second step of the transaction was an IPO of up to 100% of the existing Eskimo Pie common shares. Wheat First suggested offering 3.3 million secondary shares with the option to offer 10–15% more shares. The "green shoe" clause[2] would provide cash to pay off the $2 million loan and provide over $2 million in working capital.

Wheat First estimated that the offering price would be between $14 and $16 a share. Exhibit 7 shows the proceeds from the IPOs at the two offering prices. At $16 a share, the firm and Reynolds obtained more from the IPO than from the Nestle bid of $61 million. Furthermore, even at an offering price of $14, the IPO equaled the Nestle offer, without the complications and conditions that Nestle wanted to attach to its purchase of Eskimo Pie. Exhibit 8 shows that price/earnings ratios for comparable companies such as Ben & Jerry's and Dreyer's Grand Ice Cream, were 24x and 24.2x, respectively. The S&P 500 was trading at 25x earnings at the time.

Wheat First had not done business with Reynolds, and Goldman Sachs advised Reynolds Metals against the IPO. Goldman argued that a deal with Nestle was more certain, and they remained skeptical that an IPO could yield as much as the private sale. The sale to Nestle was likely to be closed soon, especially in light of the potential public offering. An IPO would take several months to complete, and Reynolds would risk changes in market conditions that would cool off the IPO market. Furthermore, an offering the size of the proposed Eskimo Pie deal would be one of Wheat First's largest. Wheat First and the management of Eskimo Pie stressed that with a public offering, the sale of Eskimo Pie by Reynolds would be made much easier, without complicated negotiations and compromises. In addition, an independent Eskimo Pie would stay in Richmond, allowing Reynolds to get liquidity while saving a local company and local jobs.

---

2. A "green shoe" clause in an underwriting agreement provides the issuer the opportunity to issue additional shares for distribution.

EXHIBIT 1

Historical Financial Information (thousands of dollars except per share data)

	Year Ended December 31,			
	1987	*1988*	*1989*	*1990*
Income Statement Data				
Net sales[a]	$30,769	$36,695	$46,709	$47,198
Cost of goods sold	21,650	25,635	31,957	31,780
Gross profit[a]	9,119	11,060	14,752	15,418
Advertising and sales promotions	4,742	4,241	5,030	5,130
General and administrative	6,068	5,403	6,394	7,063
Operating income (loss)	(1,691)	1,416	3,328	3,225
Interest income	308	550	801	1,004
Interest expense	(88)	(107)	(88)	(67)
Other income (expense), net[b]	1,738	(77)	(108)	(20)
Income taxes	96	729	1,511	2,362
Net income	$ 171	$ 1,053	$ 2,422	$ 2,526
Balance Sheet Data				
Cash	$ 5,550	$ 8,109	$10,723	$13,191
Working capital	9,342	11,107	10,830	11,735
Total assets	20,857	23,006	26,159	29,518
Total debt	1,269	1,094	919	744
Stockholders' equity	16,162	17,215	18,215	19,496
Per Share Data				
Weighted average number of common shares outstanding	3,316	3,316	3,316	3,316
Net income per share	$ 0.05	$ 0.32	$ 0.73	$ 0.76
Cash dividend per share	—	—	$ 0.40	$ 0.40

Source: Eskimo Pie Prospectus, p. 10.

a. Beginning in 1991, the company increased prices for products and assumed responsibility for advertising and sales promotion costs previously shared with licensees. This change in business practice accounts for approximately one-half of the increase in net sales for 1991, with a similar impact on 1991 gross profit.

b. Includes the gain on the sale of buildings of approximately $1,700,000 in 1987.

EXHIBIT 2
Cash Flow Summary (thousands of dollars)

	Year Ended December 31,	
	1989	*1990*
Operating Activities		
Net income	$ 2,422	$ 2,526
Depreciation	1,006	1,352
Amortization	175	118
Deferred income taxes	250	(58)
Pension liability and other	(154)	(156)
Decrease (increase) in receivables	1,212	(734)
Decrease (increase) in inventories and prepaid expenses	(524)	(51)
Increase (decrease) in payables to parent	2,054	(621)
Increase (decrease) in accounts payable and accrued expenses	143	3,006
Net cash provided by operating activities	6,595	5,382
Investing Activities		
Capital expenditures[a]	(2,358)	(1,311)
Other	(121)	(101)
Net cash used in investing activities	(1,379)	(1,412)
Financing Activities		
Cash dividends	(1,327)	(1,327)
Principal payments on long-term debt	(175)	(175)
Net cash used in financing activities	(1,502)	(1,502)
Increase (decrease) in cash and cash equivalents	2,614	2,468
Cash and cash equivalents at beginning of year	8,109	10,723
Cash and cash equivalents at end of year	$10,723	$13,191

Source: Eskimo Pie Prospectus, p. F–4.

a. Capital expenditures in 1989 are principally related to equipment acquired for use by licensees and, in 1990, an expansion of an ingredient's manufacturing facility.

EXHIBIT 3
Distribution and Market Share of Eskimo Pie, Heath, and Welch's Frozen Novelties

	1987	*1988*	*1989*	*1990*	*1991*
Distribution of at least one Eskimo product at U.S. grocery stores	76.3%	78.1%	91.2%	95.6%	97.9%
Unit market share of Eskimo products	3.3	3.9	5.7	6.8	7.5

Source: Eskimo Pie prospectus.

EXHIBIT 4
Industry Information for Frozen Novelties

Year	Industry Revenues (millions)	Units Sold (millions)	% Change in Sales	Average Price	Advertising Spending (millions)
1980	$ 590	N/A	N/A	N/A	$ 2
1981	680	N/A	15.3%	N/A	4
1982	770	457	13.2	$1.69	17
1983	940	525	22.1	1.79	23
1984	1,100	577	17.0	1.90	32
1985	1,300	643	18.2	2.02	44
1986	1,400	681	7.7	2.06	77
1987	1,500	717	7.1	2.09	38
1988	1,355	637	−9.7	2.13	26
1989	1,332	623	−1.7	2.19	40
1990	1,321	590	−0.8	2.24	21

Source: 1980–1987 Nieldsen; 1988–1990 IRI.

EXHIBIT 5
Initial Public Offerings (volume in billions of dollars by quarter)

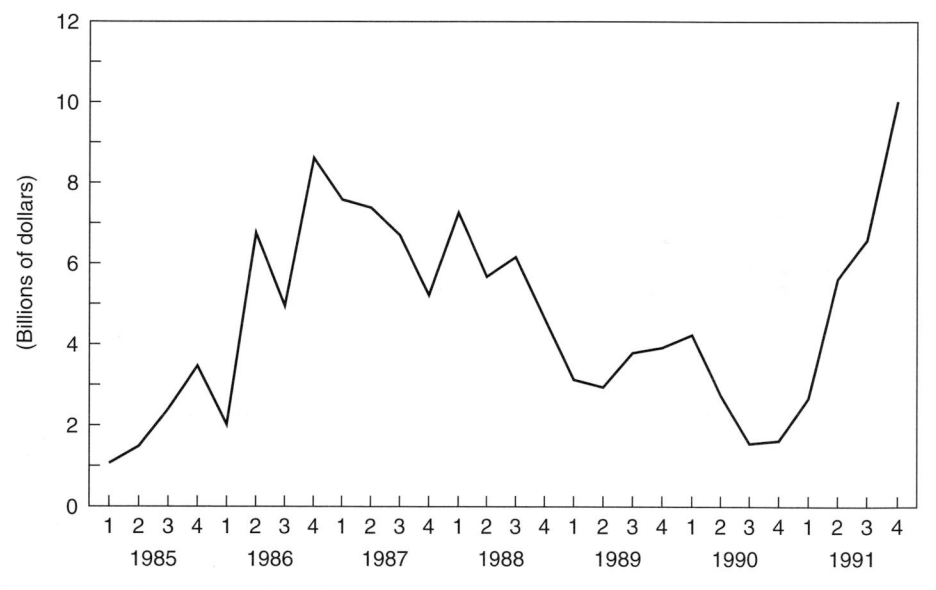

Source: Securities Data Corp.

EXHIBIT 6
Goldman Sachs's Projected Income Statements (thousands of dollars except per share data)

	Year Ended December 31,		
	1991	*1992*	*1993*
Net sales	$55,655	$59,228	$59,961
Operating expenses	52,610	54,755	55,337
Operating income	4,045	4,473	4,624
Interest income	828	890	1,058
Interest expense	52.5	38.5	24.5
Pretax income	4,821	5,324	5,657
Income taxes	1,928	2,130	2,263
Tax rate	40.00%	40.00%	40.00%
Net income	$ 2,893	$ 3,195	$ 3,394
Margin	5.1%	5.4%	5.7%
Earning per share	$ 2.18	$ 2.41	$ 2.58
Average shares outstanding	1,326.6	1,326.6	1,326.6

Source: Goldman Sachs.

EXHIBIT 7
Hypothetical Proceeds from an Initial Public Offering

Total for Firm		
Offer price	$ 14.00	$ 16.00
Special dividend	4.52	4.52
Total per share	$ 18.52	$ 20.52
Shares outstanding	3,316	3,316
Equity value	$46,431	$53,064
Dividend	14,990	14,990
Total	$61,421	$68,054
1991 net income	$ 3,749	$ 3,749
Implied P/E multiple	12.38	14.15
Reynolds's Proceeds		
Shares owned	2,789	2,789
Per share proceeds		
Stock price	$ 14.00	$ 16.00
Special dividend	4.52	4.52
Total per share	$ 18.52	$ 20.52
Total for holdings	$51,645	$57,222

Source: Casewriter estimates.

EXHIBIT 8
Financial Information about Comparable Companies (millions of dollars)

Company	Sales	Cash Flow	Operating Income[a]	Net Income	Book Value of Equity	Market Value of Equity	Total Debt	Beta
Ben & Jerry's	$ 97.0	$ 6.7	$ 10.2	$ 3.7	$ 26.3	$ 110.1	$ 2.8	1.2
Dreyer's Grand Ice Cream	354.9	24.1	37.0	15.9	113.1	534.0	44.3	1.4
Empire of Carolina, Inc.	243.1	16.8	37.4	8.8	45.1	51.4	89.8	0.3
Steve's Homemade Ice Cream	35.1	2.7	3.9	1.8	11.1	37.4	3.1	2.5
Hershey Foods Corp.	2,899.2	292.3	463.0	219.5	1,335.3	4,002.5	282.9	1.0
Tootsie Roll Inds.	207.9	32.5	47.2	25.5	152.8	728.8	0.0	1.0

Source: Standard & Poor's; Compustat; and casewriter estimates.

a. Before extraordinary items.

EXHIBIT 9
Selected Financial Market Data, November 1991

Treasury Yields

90 day	4.56%
6 months	4.61
1 year	4.64
5 years	6.62
10 years	7.42
30 years	7.92

Corporate Borrowing Rates

Long-term bond yields

AA	8.74%
A	9.27
BBB	9.56
BB	11.44
B	14.68

Floating rates

Prime rate	7.50%
Prime commercial paper (6 months)	4.76

Source: Federal Reserve Bulletin; S&P Bond Guide.

Netscape's Initial Public Offering

August 8, 1995, had taken an unexpected turn for Netscape Communications Corporation's board of directors. Earlier that morning, the day before the company's scheduled initial public offering (IPO), Netscape's lead underwriters proposed to the board a 100% increase in the original offering price, from $14 to $28 per share. This recommendation came in response to the remarkable oversubscription for Netscape's shares, which had already prompted the underwriters to increase the number of shares to be offered from 3.5 million to 5 million. Under the current proposal, a company with a net book value of just over $16 million that had yet to turn a profit was suddenly valued at over $1 billion.

The board faced a pricing dilemma within the context of an extremely unpredictable industry. While its members wanted to be responsive to Wall Street's current zeal, they also wanted to make sure that the fundamentals of Netscape justified such a dramatic increase in valuation.

Netscape Communications

Founded in April 1994, Netscape Communications Corporation provided a comprehensive line of client, server, and integrated applications software for communications and commerce on the Internet and private Internet Protocol (IP) networks. These products enabled the growing network of servers on the World Wide Web to communicate through multimedia, including graphics, video, and sound. Designed with enhanced security code, these software products provided the confidentiality required to execute financial transactions and to sell advertisements on the Internet and private IP networks.

The company's most popular product, Netscape Navigator, was the leading client software program that allowed individual personal computer (PC) users to exchange

This case was prepared by Research Associate Kendall H. Backstrand under the supervision of Professor W. Carl Kester.

Copyright © 1996 by the President and Fellows of Harvard College.
Harvard Business School case 296–088.

information and conduct commerce on the Internet. Navigator featured a click-and-point graphical user interface that enabled users to navigate the Internet by manipulating icons and windows rather than by using text commands. With the user-friendly interface as a guide, Navigator offered a variety of Internet functions, including Web browsing, file transfers, news group communications, and e-mail. Initially shipped in December 1994, Netscape Navigator generated 49% and 65% of total revenues for the quarters ended March 31, 1995, and June 30, 1995, respectively.

Netscape's server software provided enterprises with the basic capabilities necessary for creating and operating Web server "sites," or places on the Web where browsers could visit. Incorporating both browser and server functions, the company's integrated applications software programs were designed to provide enterprises with the capability to manage large-scale commercial sites on the Internet. Such applications enabled these enterprises to conduct full-scale electronic commerce through a seamless system. Together, server and integrated applications software accounted for 36% of total revenues in the first quarter of 1995, and 28% of total revenues in the second. Of these revenues, the majority were generated by one of Netscape's three server products, Netscape Commerce Server.[1] Revenues from Netscape's server and integrated applications products were expected to increase as a percentage of overall revenues in the future.

In addition to product revenues, Netscape generated service revenues, which were attributable to fees from consulting, maintenance, and support services. These revenues amounted to approximately 5% and 7% of total revenues for the quarters ended March 31, 1995, and June 30, 1995, respectively.

Financial Performance

Netscape had incurred total losses of $4.3 million on total revenues of $16.6 million for its first two operating quarters ending June 30, 1995. The company expected to continue to operate at a loss for the foreseeable future. Exhibits 1 and 2 provide Netscape's financial statements since its incorporation in April 1994.

Operating activities for the six months ended June 30, 1995, had generated $7.3 million in cash. Cash flows from financing activities of $20.5 million were primarily attributable to the net proceeds of $17.3 million from the issuance of Series C Preferred Stock and borrowings of $2.2 million under a debt facility agreement. Cash used in investment activities of $22.1 million related to $16.6 in short-term investments and $5 million in capital expenditures. At the end of the second quarter of 1995, Netscape's principal sources of liquidity were $8.9 million in cash and the $16.6 million in short-term investments. The company expected total capital expenditures for 1995 of approximately $12 million.

Industry Background

The demand for Netscape's products had evolved out of the development of the Internet in the late 1960s. The Internet was a global network designed to facilitate communication between some 35,000 computer networks using the enabling code termed Internet Protocol. According to International Data Corporation (IDC), in mid-1995 there were approximately 57 million Internet users. Of those 57 million users,

---

1. Bundled packages of Netscape Navigator and Netscape Commerce Server accounted for about 10% of total revenues in the first quarter, while their contribution in the second quarter was immaterial.

IDC estimated that approximately 8 million were accessing information on the World Wide Web.

Engineered in the early 1990s, the Web was a technology that linked one bit of information on the Internet with another so that users could share "webs" of ideas. The Web consisted of a network of Web servers, which posted information in a common format described by the Hypertext Markup Language (HTML). Internet users were able to access information on the Web by implementing the appropriate Hypertext Transfer Protocol (HTTP). Because it necessitated complex coding, the Web had remained largely undiscovered by nontechnical users who simply wanted to browse, a popular pastime that came to be dubbed "surfing the Net."

Netscape's Entrance

Meanwhile, at the University of Illinois at Urbana-Champaign, a group of computer science students working at the National Center for Supercomputing Applications (NCSA) developed the graphical software program that gave rise to the notion of "surfing." Named NCSA Mosaic, the software program enabled nontechnical users to access and retrieve information on the Web. The Mosaic code organized Web information into neat collections of graphical electronic menus on which users could simply click-and-point to browse their contents.

In April 1993, the founders of Mosaic, under the leadership of then senior Marc Andreessen, began distributing the software for free to anyone who had the technical means to retrieve it electronically. The superb results of this strategy—2 million Mosaic users within 1 year—made for more than cocktail conversation among high-tech gurus in California's Silicon Valley. Jim Clark, the founder of Silicon Graphics, Inc. (known for its workstations that turned data into 3-D computer images), was among those who were impressed not only by Mosaic itself but by the broader vision of its creator, Andreessen.

After hearing that Andreessen had moved to Silicon Valley in early 1994, Clark sent him an e-mail asking if they might meet to discuss the future of Mosaic. This exchange and subsequent discussions formed the launching pad for Mosaic Communications, which was shortly renamed Netscape Communications Corporation. In addition to dropping the Mosaic name, Netscape paid Spyglass (the company that had engaged in an exclusive licensing arrangement with the University of Illinois) a one-time $2.4 million fee for the rights to certain Mosaic code. With the original code, Clark's management experience and $3 million in seed money, and Andreessen's vision and technical expertise, Netscape made its entrance into the highly dynamic Internet market.

Netscape entered the broad Internet market via the Web browser market, where it faced two challenges: (1) it had to set a new industry standard, and (2) it had to make money. The former challenge was the immediate concern. To set a new standard, Netscape had to create a program that would destroy Mosaic, which in 1994 wielded 60% of the Web browser market. The rival program was initially named Mozilla and then renamed Netscape Navigator at the time of its debut in December 1994. Using the same "give away today and make money tomorrow" strategy that Andreessen's team had used to popularize Mosaic, Netscape had succeeded in capturing 75% of the Web browser market by the spring of 1995. Mosaic, under the guise of Spyglass, trailed far behind with 5% of the market. Having set the industry standard, Netscape was poised to make money by selling server software to companies that wanted marketing access to potential consumers.

The Competitors

Netscape was the indisputable leader of its kind. As the Internet community and its demands continued to increase, however, so did the multitude of competitors. Netscape faced potential competition from PC and UNIX software vendors and on-line service providers, which were new entrants in the Web browser, server, and service markets. Financial information on the following competitors is provided in Exhibit 3.

Spyglass, Inc., with its Enhanced Mosaic Web browser technology, was Netscape's nearest competitor. However, while Spyglass marketed the only current rival product to Netscape's Navigator, it did so to a distinctly different market. Instead of focusing on the commercial browser market dominated by Netscape, by mid-1995, Spyglass had honed its strategy on the code market. As a code vendor, Spyglass produced the code and then sold it to other software companies wanting to incorporate it into their own programs. Spyglass also sold the computer code for creating server software. By employing this strategy, Spyglass attempted to capture the corporate market, which would ultimately compete with Netscape on the end-user front. Microsoft, for example, was among Spyglass' licensees and a rising competitor for Netscape.

As the de facto gatekeeper of computing, Microsoft was perhaps the most formidable of Netscape's competitors in the long term. In August 1995, the powerful PC software company was only weeks away from releasing its long-awaited Windows 95 operating system, which included a rival browser it had created from Spyglass code. The Microsoft browser would allow Windows users to access Microsoft Network, the company's proprietary on-line service, and would also offer broader Internet access. Further, Microsoft was scheduled to release its server software in mid-1996.

The on-line computer service providers also had made strides recently to move into Netscape's market. For example, both America Online and Prodigy had created independent browsers. Compuserve had licensed Spyglass software code for its recently released Web browser software. In mid-1995, these three on-line services had a total of approximately 8–9 million subscribers. As the on-line market became increasingly threatened by the rising popularity of the Web and its access providers, it was imperative that these companies compete for Netscape's market if they hoped to participate in the unfolding future of on-line commerce and communication.

Initial Public Offerings (IPOs)

Young, rapidly growing companies facing intense competition typically raise equity capital in two broad ways. One way is through a private equity transaction, and the other is through a public offering of stock. A private transaction involves direct negotiations with various financial or nonfinancial institutions. In such a case, a company raises money from these various entities, which then own a portion of that company in the form of its privately held shares of stock or other securities convertible into stock. Given the absence of a liquid market, these private investors must negotiate the terms of the sale with known buyers to whom they wish to sell their stakes in the company.

A public issue entails the sale of a company's equity to the public at large. The stock trades on public markets (either organized exchanges such as the New York Stock Exchange or over-the-counter markets such as the NASDAQ), provided that the issue has been registered with the Securities and Exchange Commission (SEC). An example of a public issue is an initial public offering (IPO), in which a company issues a portion of its stock to the public for the first time. Companies find it desirable to "go public" when their equity capital needs increase to the point where the opportunity cost of remaining private and compensating investors for the lack of liquidity becomes too great relative to the lower cost of capital derived from liquid public markets.

While the monetary benefits of going public are potentially sizable, so too are the associated costs. The total costs are comprised of ongoing costs associated with being a publicly traded company and one-time costs associated with the IPO itself. Specifically, ongoing costs result from the need to report timely information to investors and regulators. One-time costs, which are attributable to direct costs (legal, auditing, and underwriting fees) and indirect costs (management time invested in the process, and the dilution associated with selling shares at an offering price that is, on average, below the price prevailing in the market shortly after the IPO), reflect the time and financial commitments associated with the IPO process.

The human capital resources involved in the process of an initial public offering include the company's founders and senior management, the underwriters, and institutional investors. If the company had received venture capital in the early stages of its development, a characteristic referred to as "venture-backed," the venture capitalists are often intimately involved in the IPO process as well as the company's operations. By creating liquidity and market-determined prices for the stock, going public creates the potential for substantial financial rewards for all of the parties involved.

The "Going Public" Process

In the United States, companies issuing stock to the public for the first time typically use what is known as a "firm commitment contract."[2] This contract describes the relationship between the issuing firm and the investment bankers underwriting the offering. Specifically under the contract, the underwriters first commit to bear the risk of the issue by purchasing the shares offered, less an underwriting discount. The underwriters then guarantee to deliver the proceeds of the sale (net of commission) to the issuing company, whether or not the offer is fully subscribed. In the event of weak demand or undersubscription, the underwriters are allowed to sell the remaining shares at a lower price. Such action is referred to as "breaking the syndicate," as the syndicate of underwriters is originally formed to stabilize the market price immediately following the offering. On the other hand, in the event of strong demand or oversubscription at the time of the offering, the underwriters can sell additional shares, called an overallotment option or "greenshoe," amounting to as much as 15% of the total shares offered.

At times, the IPO market is characterized as a "hot issue" market because of the high returns earned by initial buyers of the shares. Such desirable returns occur as a result of either underpricing or oversubscription of a company's shares. This was the experience of Boston Chicken, which saw heavy initial demand and an unprecedented increase of 143% in the company's stock price after its IPO in November 1993. In Boston Chicken's case, this value increase was sustained over time. Not all companies experience a similar result, however. Snapple, for example, saw its stock price explode in after-market trading following its December 1992 IPO, only to lose this premium

---

2. Another type of contract between the issuer and the underwriters is known as a "best efforts" contract. Unlike a firm commitment, in which the underwriters assume risk, a best efforts contract only requires the investment bankers to make their best efforts to sell the minimum number of shares. In the event there is insufficient demand to fully subscribe the minimum number of shares, the issue is withdrawn. This type of contract is typically used in smaller, more speculative offerings.

value over time. In yet another recent IPO, that of PixTech in July 1995, the company's stock price fell nearly 15% after the first day of trading following the offering. Clearly, not all companies have the good fortune of offering their stocks to the public during hot issue markets as indicated by such disparate outcomes.

Netscape's IPO

In response to its growing capital needs, in early 1995, Netscape began to explore the option of raising money through an initial public offering. The IPO market in the first half of 1995 had generated proceeds totaling nearly $12 billion for some 300 companies, which saw their stock prices increase on the first day of trading by an average of 20%. This outstanding momentum was largely attributable to venture-backed high-technology stock offerings (which recently represented well over half of all venture-backed IPOs), particularly those related to the Internet. (A 5-year history of the IPO market is illustrated in Exhibit 4; a chart illustrating IPO waves for the past 25 years is shown in Exhibit 5; and information on several recent Internet-related IPOs is provided in Exhibit 6.) In the spring of 1995, Netscape decided that the time was right to initiate an initial offering of its stock, despite its limited track record. The principal reasons for going public were to fund expected future growth, to stockpile cash reserves for potential acquisitions, and to gain visibility and credibility within the industry.

Netscape's Financing History

Since Clark's initial investment, Netscape had been injected with various forms of investment capital. Clark himself contributed an additional $1.1 million in the fall of 1994. At the same time, the Silicon Valley venture capital firm of Kleiner, Perkins, Caufield & Byers invested $5 million. The third and largest round of financing came in April 1995 from Adobe Systems and five other media companies. This final private placement of stock totaled $18 million and was orchestrated by Morgan Stanley. At the time of the IPO, Clark, Kleiner Perkins, and the group of media companies owned the largest stakes of Netscape's equity at 24%, 11%, and 11%, respectively. The company's president and CEO, James Barksdale, held shares amounting to 10% of total equity.

The IPO Team

The principal parties involved in the IPO of Netscape included the founders and the senior management team; the venture capitalists at Kleiner Perkins; and the investment bankers at Morgan Stanley and Hambrecht & Quist (H&Q), the co-underwriters of the IPO. In addition to the lead underwriters, there were 26 other investment banks in the syndicate to help create a market for Netscape's shares. They all had agreed to pay the final offering price, less underwriting fees, to Netscape in the event investors withdrew their orders. Auditors, lawyers, and insurers also provided necessary services.

Netscape's cofounders and senior management were intimately involved in the IPO process, both from a practical and financial perspective. Since Netscape was not generating profits, the lure for Netscape's recently formed senior management team was not high salaries but rather preferred stock that could be converted into shares of common stock when Netscape went public. Clark and Barksdale, as well as others on the management team, including the vice president of technology, Andresseen, stood to gain millions on paper in the face of a highly oversubscribed IPO within a "hot issue" market.

The lead underwriters were engaged in the IPO process from the very beginning. The investment bankers from these firms were responsible for everything from doing the initial "due diligence" to issuing the final prospectus, which stipulated the final offering price of the shares. If the proposed $28-per-share price was approved by the board, the underwriters would earn $9.8 million, or a 7% sales commission on every share sold to initial investors.[3]

Going Public

On July 17, 1995, Morgan Stanley and H&Q issued a preliminary prospectus, or an offering circular, suggesting it might offer 3.5 million Netscape shares priced at $12 to $14 per share. This preliminary offering price was based on the future business prospects of Netscape and the Internet industry in general, financial and operating information of Netscape, and stock price-related data and other financial and operating information of competitors.

The next and final step before the offering was the "road show," in which management and underwriters made presentations to potential major investors throughout the world. The purpose of a road show was largely to stimulate interest among institutional investors. Clark and Barksdale joined the underwriters for a two-week road show, which entailed traveling to 20 cities and talking to about 2,000 institutional investors. A road show also enabled underwriters to gauge the interest of institutional investors for purposes of determining the final offering price. Upon returning from the road show, the Morgan Stanley underwriters called some of the investors they had previously visited to assess their current interest in terms of price and quantity of shares. The response was overwhelmingly favorable, yet only indicated potential demand. Such potential would not be realized until the orders in the "book" were translated into purchase orders when trading began on the day of the offering. Despite this uncertainty, however, the investment bankers from Morgan Stanley and H&Q felt confident enough to recommend doubling the offering price proposed in the preliminary prospectus.

The Board Decision

The time had come when Clark and the other Netscape board members had to approve or reject their underwriters' vote of high confidence. In going over the new valuation of the company, the board struggled to disregard the wild speculation surrounding what had been called the hottest IPO of the year. Indeed, Netscape had commercialized the young world of cyberspace, causing a flood of enthusiasm on Wall Street greater than that experienced by the biotech industry in the 1980s and early 1990s. Much like the then unchartered biotech industry, however, the future commercial size of cyberspace was unknown. Perhaps most unavoidable in the minds of the board members, the subscription for such a hot stock had the potential of reaching many times 5 million shares by the time of the offering the next morning. Still, Netscape had a negative

---

3. This commission value does not account for the potential exercise of the overallotment option. At 750,000 shares, this option would generate an additional $1,470,000 at $1.96 per share. Clearly, the underwriters would benefit from any demand for shares in excess of the original 5 million being considered.

bottom line and parents who had watched the Regenerons of the IPO world make painful mistakes.[4] Perhaps the investment community would react similarly to Netscape's decision to raise the price, interpreting such an increase as unjustifiably opportunistic. The board's responsibility was thus to determine the appropriateness of the proposed increase in price after balancing the potential risks and rewards that might accompany such a move.

EXHIBIT 1
Consolidated Income Statements for Netscape Communications Corporation

	Inception (April 4 to December 31, 1994)	Six Months Ended June 30, 1995
Revenues		
Product revenues	$ 378,490	$15,580,258
Service revenues	317,381	1,045,133
Total revenues	695,871	16,625,391
Cost of revenues		
Cost of product revenues	114,777	1,222,045
Cost of service revenues	104,313	513,767
Total cost of revenues	219,090	1,735,812
Gross profit	476,781	14,889,579
Operating expenses		
Research and development	2,031,986	6,115,152
Sales and marketing	2,813,689	9,256,066
General and administrative	1,669,193	3,693,005
Property rights agreement and related charges	2,486,688	500,000
Total operating expenses	9,001,566	19,564,223
Operating loss	(8,524,775)	(4,674,644)
Interest income	55,238	495,583
Interest expense	(308)	(128,655)
Net loss	$(8,469,845)	$ (4,307,716)
Net loss per share	$ (0.26)	$ (0.13)
Shares used in computing net loss per share	32,256,307	33,000,751

---

4. Regeneron Pharmaceuticals, Inc., a pharmaceutical company developing treatments for diseases of the central nervous system, had raised its offering price and the number of shares to be sold subsequent to its successful road show, only to be met with a discounted stock price after disappointed investors withdrew their orders. In addition to being negative publicity for Regeneron itself, the Regeneron experience was thought to have been a catalyst for the subsequent closing of the window for biotech IPOs at large.

EXHIBIT 2
Consolidated Balance Sheets for Netscape Communications Corporation

	December 31, 1994	June 30, 1995
Assets		
Cash and short-term equivalents	$3,243,510	$ 8,868,436
Short-term investments	—	16,567,300
Accounts receivable	701,649	8,277,869
Other current assets	67,284	804,971
Total current assets	4,012,443	34,518,576
Property and equipment, net	2,447,098	6,761,045
Deposits and other assets	699,100	1,251,582
Total assets	$7,158,641	$42,531,203
Liabilities and Stockholders' Equity		
Accounts payable	$ 855,068	$ 4,607,174
Accrued compensation and related liabilities	527,340	1,075,066
Other accrued liabilities	667,503	1,897,819
Deferred revenues	2,575,145	14,963,843
Current portion of long-term obligations	725,000	725,000
Installment notes payable	—	551,449
Total current liabilities	5,350,056	23,820,351
Long-term obligations	725,000	725,000
Installment notes payable	—	1,511,331
Total liabilities	6,075,056	26,056,682
Preferred stock, $0.0001 par value	701	901
Common stock, $0.0001 par value	451	1,514
Additional paid-in capital	9,552,278	39,683,666
Notes receivable from stockholders	—	(638,065)
Deferred compensation	—	(9,812,151)
Accumulated deficit	(8,469,845)	(12,777,561)
Accumulated translation adjustment	—	16,217
Total stockholders' equity	1,083,585	16,474,521
Total liabilities and stockholders' equity	$7,158,641	$42,531,203

EXHIBIT 3

Comparative Information on Potential Competitors (for year ended June 30, 1995; thousands of dollars except per share data)

	Netscape[a]	America Online, Inc.	Microsoft Corp.	Spyglass, Inc.
Net revenues	$17,321	$394,290	$5,937,000	$ 9,084
Operating expenses	30,521	413,584	3,899,000	6,745
Operating income (loss)	(13,200)	(19,294)	2,038,000	2,339
Interest expense	(129)	—	—	—
Net income (loss)	(12,778)	(33,647)	1,453,000	1,509
Earnings per share	(0.39)	(0.99)	2.32	0.41
Weighted average shares outstanding	33,001	33,986	627,000	3,788
Capital expenditures	7,618	57,751	495,000	824,609
Depreciation, depletion, and amortization	918	11,136	269,000	161,303
Current assets	34,519	132,856	5,620,000	37,372
Cash and short-term investments	25,436	64,050	4,750,000	34,556
Total assets	42,531	406,464	7,210,000	39,963
Current liabilities	23,820	133,312	1,347,000	2,718
Total liabilities	26,057	188,520	1,877,000	4,368
Net worth	$16,475	$217,944	$5,333,000	$35,595
Current ratio	1.45	1.00	4.17	13.75
Debt/total capital	0.18	0.08	—	—
Common stock price (close)	N/A	22.00	90.38	14.31
P/E ratio	N/A	N/A	39.00	34.90
Equity beta[b]	N/A	0.73	0.72	N/A

a. Netscape's financial data reflects the company's performance since inception in April 1994. Netscape did not begin to ship products or earn significant product revenues until December 1994.

b. Bloomberg estimates based on weekly data for the year ended June 30, 1995.

EXHIBIT 4

Historical Data of the IPO Market

	1990	1991	1992	1993	1994
All IPOs					
Number of companies	166	352	477	604	510
Total dollar amount offered (in $ billions)	$ 4.75	$16.01	$22.76	$30.74	$17.98
Average % gain after first day of trading	10.3%	11.6%	9.4%	11.7%	8.1%
Venture-Backed IPOs					
Number of companies	42	122	152	165	136
Average age of companies	6	6	6	7	7
Total dollar amount offered (in $ billions)	$ 1.19	$ 3.90	$ 4.58	$ 4.86	$ 3.35
Average offering size (in $ millions)	28.3	32.0	29.1	29.6	24.8
Average offering valuation (in $ millions)	$109.3	$118.5	$101.7	$100.5	$ 86.8

EXHIBIT 5
Total Number of IPOs, 1970–1994

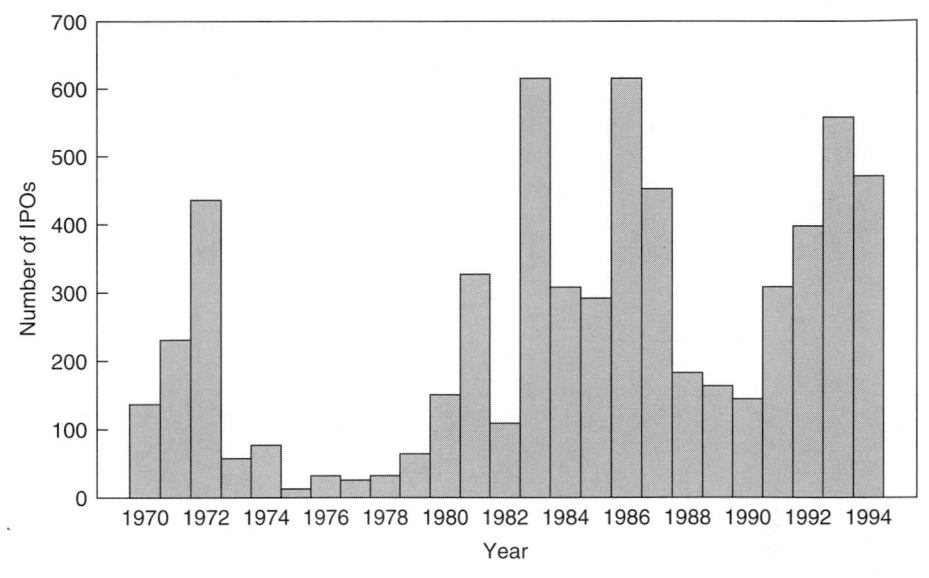

EXHIBIT 6

Information on Internet-Related IPOs (for the respective fiscal year preceding the IPO)

	Netcom Online Communication Services, Inc. (year ended 12/31/93)	Performance Systems International, Inc. (year ended 12/31/94)	Spyglass, Inc. (year ended 9/30/94)	Uunet Technologies Inc. (year ended 12/31/94)
Financial Data				
Net revenues	$2,411,600	$15,214,000	$3,629,392	$12,413,863
Operating costs and expenses	2,169,600	19,876,000	2,272,662	19,387,821
Operating income	242,000	(4,662,000)	751,520	(6,973,958)
Interest expense	(3,400)	(731,000)	—	(76,232)
Net income	227,300	(5,342,000)	1,331,262	(6,948,759)
Earnings per share	$ 0.04	$ (0.26)	$ 0.39	$ (0.35)
Weighted average shares outstanding	6,300,600	20,395,000	3,448,952	20,029,824
Capital expenditures	1,027,600	2,536,000	208,567	5,897,309
Depreciation, depletion, and amortization	156,900	3,183,000	68,034	1,010,027
Current assets	235,500	5,564,000	3,254,562	6,192,629
Cash and short-term investments	75,500	3,358,000	1,450,651	4,649,737
Total assets	1,347,000	17,055,000	5,296,727	12,024,575
Current liabilities	789,300	7,118,000	1,406,727	5,755,418
Total liabilities	802,300	11,721,000	3,056,727	6,422,085
Net worth	$ 544,700	$ 5,334,000	$2,240,000	$ 5,602,490
IPO Data				
Date of IPO	12/14/94	5/8/95	6/27/95	5/25/95
Price per share offered	$ 13.00	$ 12.00	$ 17.00	$ 14.00
Number of shares offered	1,850,000	4,370,000	2,000,000	4,725,000
% of total equity sold	28%	17%	40%	17%
% change in stock price after first day of trading	+31%	+27%	+60%	+96%
Price per share on August 8, 1995	$ 36.375	$ 22.00	$ 49.25	$ 46.25

Gulf Oil Corporation—Takeover

On the morning of March 5, 1984, George Keller of the Standard Oil Company of California (Socal) still had not made up his mind about how much to bid. The stakes were high. For sale was Gulf Oil Corporation, the most doddering of the seven sisters. But the price was high as well. Determined to depart in dignity, Gulf management made clear that it would not consider any bid below $70 per share, a considerable premium over the $43 price at which Gulf had traded during the close of 1983, when the sale of Gulf was a remote possibility.

Bidding against Mr. Keller were some who were willing to pay $70 and more. Included in the confidential auction in Pittsburgh with Standard Oil of California were members of the Atlantic Richfield Company (ARCO) and bankers from Kohlberg, Kravis, Roberts & Co., specialists in leveraged buyouts.

Mr. Keller felt the bid from Kohlberg, Kravis was the one to beat, since it came essentially from Gulf itself. This proposal allowed Gulf to become a private firm by tendering for the shares of its public stock. The undeniable attraction of the offer lay in its preservation of the name, the assets, and the jobs of Gulf Oil, until management found a long-term solution.

The challenge from ARCO was far less threatening. If ARCO offered more than $75 per share, its debt-to-total-capital ratio would exceed 60%, an uncomfortably high level. Socal, in contrast, had a debt-to-total-capital ratio that was so low that the banks were queuing up to lend money to it. The banks were so anxious to lend Socal $14 billion that the potential loan was oversubscribed by 30%.

The profusion of bank credit meant that Mr. Keller could safely bid $79, $80, or even higher. The opportunities created by the acquisition were enormous, but so were the risks of betting the whole company on them. With one stroke, Socal could ensure itself access to vast quantities of high-quality light oil. Overnight, Socal could virtually double its reserves and give the next generation of management something with which to work.

An appraisal of the value of the opportunities offered by the Gulf deal required, of course, an idea of how the two companies (Exhibit 1) would perform as a unit. A pro forma balance sheet (Exhibit 2) showed that the combined firm would have a considerable amount of financial leverage. While manageable in the short run, the debt would have to be reduced over the next few years.

The most direct way of accomplishing this reduction was to sell some of Gulf's assets. Another way, Mr. Keller felt, was to make use of funds Gulf currently spent on exploration and development.[1] These funds amounted to over $2 billion in 1983 (Exhibit 3). The only question was whether, by using funds that had been earmarked for the search for more oil, the long-run viability of the new enterprise would be sacrificed at the expense of financial expediency. After all, if investing in new sources of oil were worthwhile before Gulf's acquisition, it would be just as worthwhile afterwards. An opposite point of view, however, was that if Socal purchased Gulf, its reserves would be so large that Gulf's contribution to the exploratory effort could safely be discontinued.

Aside from the question of how to reduce the takeover debt, there was the issue of the tax cost of the acquisition. Although the tax considerations were complex,[2] it was felt that the tax benefits and costs nearly offset each other.[3] The decision, therefore, of how much to bid depended solely upon the economic benefits of the acquisition. At times, those benefits seemed almost incalculable. As Mr. Keller said, "But it's like a 100-year mining project. A straight rate of return analysis would prevent you from doing it. The decision has to be a little glandular."[4]

The Takeover

While the seeds for Gulf's demise were sown over the course of a decade, the event that precipitated the emergency meeting in Pittsburgh on March 5, 1984, was far more recent. The decision to sell the company was made in response to a takeover attempt by Boone Pickens, Jr., the chief executive officer of Mesa Petroleum Company.

Boone Pickens had a long string of successes in targeting undervalued oil companies, beginning in 1969. In 1982, the year prior to its attempt on Gulf, Mesa tendered for two companies: Cities Service, and General American Oil of Texas. In both cases, Mesa failed to gain control but made a substantial profit in reaching an accommodation with the target. In the case of Cities Service, Mesa sold back the stock it acquired

---

1. Exploration and development is a time-consuming effort. For an on-shore site, it generally takes 4 years between the time the lease is acquired until the field comes on-stream. Having been developed, the field is productive for another 7–10 years.

2. Advice concerning the tax aspects of this transaction was provided by the law firm of Simpson Thacher & Bartlett.

3. It was expected that the acquisition would be structured as a liquidating sale of Gulf's assets. Under the Tax Equity and Fiscal Responsibility Act of 1982 (TEFRA), the treatment of such a sale held both benefits and drawbacks for the acquiring company. On the positive side, no gain was recognized by the acquired company on the sale of its assets. More important, the acquiring company was allowed to step up the assets to their fair market value, thereby realizing future tax benefits through higher depreciation and depletion deductions. On the negative side, certain tax deductions taken in the past by the acquired company became recaptured and had to be repaid immediately upon liquidation. For example, since Gulf used the LIFO (last in, first out) method to account for petroleum inventories, the difference between the FIFO (first in, first out) and LIFO valuations had to be treated as ordinary income and taxes paid accordingly. Also recaptured and treated as ordinary income was any depreciation in excess of the straight-line amount on real property and certain accelerated drilling costs.

4. *Fortune,* April 2, 1984, p. 22.

through the tender offer for a gain of $31.5 million. In the case of General American, Mesa received $15 million for withdrawing its tender offer and another $42.4 million when it sold the shares accumulated in open market purchases to a higher bidder.

On August 11, 1983, Mr. Pickens and a consortium of experienced investors began purchasing shares of Gulf Oil for $39. Two months later, the Gulf Investors' Group, as the consortium called itself, had spent $638 million and had acquired about 9% of all the Gulf shares outstanding at an average cost of approximately $43 per share.

The share purchases were totally unexpected. Mesa Petroleum was a small company compared to Gulf. If Mr. Pickens intended to acquire control of Gulf, the deal would require borrowing at least $10 billion, many times the magnitude of Mesa's net worth. To put the effort in perspective, 4 years before, the largest takeover was $1 billion, and that involved the conglomerate United Technologies. What Mr. Pickens was attempting was as audacious as it was unprecedented.

What contributed to the surprise was the opinion of many that the time for oil mega-mergers had passed. Within a few years, Occidental Petroleum had acquired Cities Service; U.S. Steel had bought Marathon Oil; Du Pont had taken over Conoco; and Elf Aquitane had gained control of Texasgulf. The political sentiment was that these takeovers, costing tens of billions of dollars, were not in the public interest. Senator Bennett Johnston (D, La.) put the principle forcefully: "When a few merge, it's one thing, but when a whole industry is consolidating, it's a very different matter. One's a glass of wine with Christmas dinner; the other, a six-month binge."[5]

After the shock subsided, Gulf's response to the investors' group was one of indignation and outrage. The chairman of Gulf, James Lee, described the group led by Mr. Pickens as "corporate raiders" who were "cannibalizing" the company. Harold Hammer, the chief administrative officer of Gulf, said, "We've got to roll up our sleeves and hit him where it really smarts."[6] In the meantime, the investors' group raised its share in Gulf to 13.2%.

Mr. Pickens stated that his immediate objective was to put himself on the board of directors, where he could effect changes in Gulf policy. He said he was particularly interested in forcing Gulf to spin off its domestic oil and gas properties into a royalty trust, a device he popularized and perfected at Mesa.[7] To thwart this, Gulf sought to move its corporate charter from Pennsylvania to Delaware, where Mr. Pickens would need a majority vote of the shareholders to elect alternative directors. This move, which occurred on January 18, 1984, followed a long and acrimonious proxy battle over the reincorporation. Gulf won that battle with 53% of the vote in its favor. In that contest, Gulf was heavily supported by individual investors, most of whom were personally lobbied by Gulf executives (Exhibit 4). After winning the proxy contest, Gulf felt confident that the reincorporation would deny the investors' group, with limited capital at its disposal, its only means of access to the boardroom.

On February 22, 1984, Mr. Pickens announced a partial tender offer at $65 per share. This price was within the range that the Gulf Investors' Group estimated the

---

5. Ibid.

6. *New York Times,* November 5, 1983.

7. The principal advantage of a trust was the elimination of a second layer of taxation on distributed earnings and the tax savings from the step-up in the basis of the properties. However, some past tax deductions were recaptured in the process, and the shareholders had to pay capital gains rates on the difference between the trading value of the trust units and their basis in the corporation's stock. The arrangement worked well if the corporation had a high dividend payout ratio and stockholders had a high tax basis.

royalty trust shares would trade if the proposed reorganization took place, according to its December 30 presentation to the Gulf board of directors. The offer price represented a significant premium over price levels of the recent past (Exhibit 5) and the closing price of $52⅝ on the day before. To make the offer, Mr. Pickens had to borrow $300 million from Penn Central Corp., using securities of Mesa Petroleum as collateral. Even with this capital infusion, the investors' group could only afford to purchase 13.5 million shares, which would leave it far short of a majority, with 21.3% of the stock. The Pickens group, however, hoped that this show of strength would enable it to attract further financial backing.

The motives of the Pickens group were widely impugned by those sympathetic to Gulf's management. On the day of the tender offer, for instance, a local Pittsburgh paper editorialized: "Mesa chairman T. Boone Pickens, Jr., expects primarily to cash in on Gulf's golden eggs, which are in the form of vast amounts of oil and gas. After obtaining the revenue there, he plans to slaughter the goose."[8]

The tender offer precipitated a crisis at Gulf. Seeming to sense the inevitability of the outcome, Gulf decided to seek a liquidation on its own terms. James Murdy, an executive vice president of Gulf, said in a retrospective interview:[9]

> Now all of this attention put enormous speculative pressure on our stock. We saw that, and we knew we had to do the best job for all shareholders while at the same time saving as much as possible for employees and others with a stake in Gulf. So when Mesa finally launched its unfair partial tender offer, our board was willing to consider selling the company to a strong merger partner rather than see Mesa steal the company.

Having made the decision to liquidate, Gulf contacted several firms—including Allied, ARCO, Socal, Sohio, and Unocal—and invited them to Pittsburgh for an unprecedented sale.

Recent History

In 1975, Gulf lost a large portion of its reserves when Kuwait and Venezuela canceled Gulf's oil concession. In the years that followed, total reserves declined, reaching a record low in 1981. In that year, James Lee became chairman. Mr. Lee enunciated a clear strategy to reverse the decline in Gulf's competitive position. His strategy was twofold. First, he would concentrate Gulf's efforts on oil. In the past, Gulf had developed into an energy conglomerate through acquisitions of coal mines, uranium mines, and synthetic fuel plants. In the future, Gulf intended to de-emphasize these ventures, which were not notably successful. The second part of the strategy arose naturally from the first. In keeping with the renewed emphasis on oil, Mr. Lee continued to increase expenditures on exploration and development. As a result of this policy, outlays for exploration more than doubled between 1978 and 1982, and the long decline in reserves was finally arrested and reversed. He was quite explicit about his policy. In this own words, "Gulf's number one priority is to replace our domestic reserves of hydrocarbons through discoveries and acquisitions."[10]

A key phrase in this statement of purpose is "discoveries *and* acquisitions." In 1982, Gulf made an effort to acquire Cities Service. Ironically, Gulf's attempted acqui-

---

8. *Pittsburgh Post Gazette,* February 23, 1984.

9. *Energy Bureau Seminar,* October 3, 1984.

10. Gulf Oil Corporation, Annual Report (1981), p. 3.

sition of Cities Service involved a confrontation with Mesa Petroleum, which almost cost Mesa its corporate life. The takeover of Cities Service collapsed at the last minute, however, when the Federal Trade Commission raised several objections and Gulf withdrew its offer, causing many arbitrageurs to lose heavily.

Mr. Lee's business plan underwent a midcourse correction as a result of developments in the oil markets. Beginning in 1982 and continuing throughout 1983, the real price of oil and natural gas declined (Exhibit 6). As 1984 began, almost all experts were in agreement that, in constant dollars, the price of oil would not change for the next 10 years. Even the oil ministers of Saudi Arabia and Qatar shared this opinion.

In response to these changing fundamentals, Mr. Lee trimmed exploration expenditures significantly in 1983.[11] Even at this reduced level, however, spending for exploration in real terms equaled or exceeded that of every year before his arrival except one (Exhibit 3).

In addition to investing in discovering new sources of oil and gas, Gulf management began using the company's sizable cash flow to repurchase shares. From mid-1981 to March 1983, Gulf purchased 30 million shares of the 195 million outstanding. At that point, Mr. Lee said, "I have no philosophical problem with another bite if everything is as it is now and if our stock is as good a buy as it is now."[12]

Mr. Keller's Decision

Mr. Keller was as aware as Mr. Lee of Gulf's lackluster showing on most measures of financial performance (Exhibit 7). Indeed, Gulf's sluggish returns and weak earnings were the chief attraction, since they suggested great opportunities for improvement. The only uncertainty facing Mr. Keller on the morning of March 5 was not whether to bid but how much to bid to be sure the opportunities did not get away.

EXHIBIT 1

Results of 1983 Operations, Oil and Gas Producing Activities Only (millions of dollars)

	Gulf	*Socal*
Revenues, oil and gas production only	$6,503	$5,742
Less: Costs		
Lifting costs		
Production	911	1,454
Wellhead taxes	792	504
Exploration expense	594	758
Depreciation, etc.	1,000	646
Other operating expenses	358	116
Income taxes[a]	1,933	1,368
Results of operations after income taxes	$ 915	$ 896

a. Gulf's effective marginal tax rate was approximately 50%.

(continued)

---

11. See Exhibit 8 for a discussion of accounting policies relating to exploration and development.

12. Quoted in *Gulf Oil Corporation Appraisal* (John S. Herold, Inc., 1983), p. 349.

EXHIBIT 1 *(concluded)*
Comparison of 1983 Balance Sheets for Total Corporation (millions of dollars)

	Gulf	Socal
Current assets	$ 5,653	$ 7,328
Net properties	14,090	14,222
Investments in affiliates	608	2,319
Deferred charges and other assets	613	141
Total assets	$20,964	$24,010
Current liabilities	$ 4,756	$ 5,117
Long-term debt and capital leases	2,291	1,896
Deferred taxes	2,651	1,960
Deferred credits	—	852
Other liabilities	355	79
Minority interests	783	—
Total liabilities	10,836	9,904
Common stock	165	1,026
Paid-in capital	1,095	871
Retained earnings	8,868	12,209
Stockholders' equity	10,128	14,106
Total liabilities and stockholders' equity	$20,964	$24,010
Beta of common stock	1.15	1.15

EXHIBIT 2
Pro Forma Balance Sheet, Gulf and Socal Combined (millions of dollars)

	Offer Price of Socal for All Outstanding Gulf Shares[a]		
	$70/Share	$80/Share	$90/Share
Current assets	$12,751	$12,751	$12,751
Net properties	29,768	31,421	33,075
Other assets	3,901	3,901	3,903
Total assets	$46,420	$48,073	$49,727
Current liabilities	$ 9,873	$ 9,873	$ 9,873
Long-term debt and capital leases	15,761	17,414	19,068
Deferred items	5,463	5,463	5,463
Other liabilities and minority interests	1,217	1,217	1,217
Total liabilities	32,314	33,967	35,621
Stockholders' equity	14,106	14,106	14,106
Total liabilities and stockholders' equity	$46,420	$48,073	$49,727

a. Gulf had 165.3 million shares outstanding.

EXHIBIT 3
Exploration Cost and Reserve Data for Gulf and Socal, 1976–1983

Gulf

	Exploration Cost ($ millions)			Reserve Data (millions of composite bbls)			
	Expensed	+ Capitalized	= Total	Begin	+ Add'ns	– Prod'n	= End
1976	$343	$ 645	$ 988	3,672	280	365	3,257[a]
1977	457	1,175	1,632	3,257	326	338	3,333[b]
1978	367	905	1,272	3,333	392	334	3,392
1979	389	1,223	1,612	3,392	127	367	3,152
1980	561	1,524	2,085	3,152	198	342	3,008
1981	688	2,008	2,696	3,008	266	323	2,951
1982	727	1,919	2,646	2,951	314	296	2,969
1983	594	1,595	2,189	2,969	359	290	3,038[c]

Socal

	Exploration Cost ($ millions)			Reserve Data (millions of composite bbls)			
	Expensed	+ Capitalized	= Total	Begin	+ Add'ns	– Prod'n	= End
1976	$256	$ 518	$ 774	3,263	115	260	3,118
1977	250	640	890	3,118	180	255	3,043
1978	371	792	1,163	3,043	129	252	2,920
1979	409	1,194	1,603	2,920	345	261	3,004
1980	629	1,601	2,230	3,004	246	262	2,988
1981	862	2,700	3,562	2,988	162	259	2,891
1982	939	1,851	2,790	2,891	198	257	2,832
1983	758	1,332	2,090	2,832	240	261	2,811

a. Reduced by 330 million bbls expropriated by Ecuador.

b. Includes 88 million bbls acquired from Kewanee Industries, Inc.

c. J. S. Herold estimates that 725 million bbls in West Africa are not recoverable because of expropriation, which reduces the recoverable reserves to 2,313 million bbls.

EXHIBIT 4
Results of Proxy Vote on Reincorporation Proposal

	Voting by Shares (millions)			
	For	Against	Abstain[a]	Subtotal
Individuals	71.1	9.2	12.0	92.3
Gulf Investors' Group	—	21.7	—	21.7
Institutions	16.0	23.2	12.1	51.3
Total	87.1	54.1	24.1	165.3
	(52.7%)	(32.7%)	(14.6%)	(100%)

	Percentage Voting by Category			
	For	Against	Abstain[a]	Subtotal
Individuals	77%	10%	13%	100%
Gulf Investors' Group	—	100	—	100
Institutions	31	45	24	100

a. An abstention is essentially a vote against the proposal.

EXHIBIT 5
Trading Prices and Volumes, Gulf and Socal, 1983–1984

	Gulf		*Socal*	
	Price	*Volume*[a]	*Price*	*Volume*[a]
Aug. 5, 1983	$37⅜	16,633	$35⅝	21,473
Aug. 12	39	23,955		
Aug. 19	42⅝	49,186		
Aug. 26	41½	13,737		
Sept. 2	41½	8,942	37¼	11,452
Sept. 9	41½	23,020		
Sept. 16	41½	26,515		
Sept. 23	44½	31,475		
Sept. 30	42⅛	14,590		
Oct. 7	44⅛	39,708	35⅜	17,384
Oct. 14	47	71,629		
Oct. 21	46½	91,278		
Oct. 28	47½	19,415		
Nov. 4	44½	39,761	35⅜	18,269
Nov. 11	45⅛	26,660		
Nov. 18	42¼	56,685		
Nov. 25	43¾	43,358		
Dec. 2	45⅛	65,168	34⅛	14,356
Dec. 9	43	15,568		
Dec. 16	42¾	13,879		
Dec. 23	42⅝	5,210		
Dec. 30	43⅛	10,301		
Jan. 6, 1984	46⅝	34,790	34⅞	9,959
Jan. 13	49¼	51,756	35⅝	15,098
Jan. 20	47	23,003	35⅞	16,351
Jan. 27	53⅛	39,693	35½	15,687
Feb. 3	55½	62,309	36½	16,680
Feb. 10	57	48,409	33⅞	19,866
Feb. 17	54	70,678	35⅞	13,798
Feb. 24	62⅝	96,862	36⅝	12,775
Mar. 2	69½	175,126	35¾	20,691
Mar. 9	65⅛	153,597	34½	23,149

a. Total volume for week in hundreds of shares. All dates shown are Fridays.

EXHIBIT 6
Selected Market Prices, 1976–1983

| | | | | Avg. Stock Price, | Gulf | | Socal | |
	S&P 500[a]	*Oil Price per Composite Bbl*[b]	*Consumer Price Index*	*Seven Majors*[c]	*Closing Price*	*Dividend/ Share*	*Closing Price*	*Dividend/ Share*
1976	107.46	$ 5.76	170.5	$56.21	$29	$1.73	$21	$1.06
1977	95.10	7.22	181.5	45.92	27	1.83	19	1.18
1978	96.73	8.35	195.4	43.20	24	1.90	23	1.28
1979	105.76	10.63	217.4	51.89	35	2.06	28	1.45
1980	136.34	16.92	246.8	70.00	44	2.37	50	1.80
1981	122.74	22.88	272.4	51.55	35	2.65	43	2.20
1982	138.34	22.21	289.1	44.48	30	2.80	32	2.40
1983	164.90	22.42	298.4	53.03	43	2.85	35	2.40

a. End of year.

b. Composite amounts represent crude oil, natural gas liquids, and natural gas on a per barrel basis. Natural gas volumes are converted to crude oil equivalent barrels using a conversion ratio of 5.7 thousand cubic feet per barrel.

c. Exxon, Gulf, Mobil, Shell, Standard Oil California, Standard Oil Indiana, and Texaco.

EXHIBIT 7
Comparison of Gulf with Industry (Seven Major Producers), 1972–1982

| | *Production*[a] | | *Earnings/ Share*[b] | *Return on Equity* | | *Return on Assets* | |
	Oil	*Gas*		*Gulf*	*Industry*	*Gulf*	*Industry*
1972	5.3%	4.4%	49%	10%	14%	4.8%	6.0%
1973	5.0	4.0	56	13	15	8.0	8.5
1974	4.8	3.7	56	14	16	8.5	9.0
1975	4.6	3.6	52	10	12	5.6	6.5
1976	4.4	3.4	54	12	14	6.1	7.0
1977	4.3	3.5	48	11	14	5.3	6.0
1978	4.0	3.6	49	11	14	5.3	6.0
1979	3.9	3.5	44	16	21	7.7	9.0
1980	3.6	3.3	39	15	24	7.5	9.0
1981	3.2	3.1	38	13	20	6.0	8.0
1982	3.0	2.8	40	9	11	4.4	5.5

Note: The seven major producers are Exxon, Gulf, Mobil, Shell, Standard Oil California, Standard Oil Indiana, and Texaco.

a. Gulf's U.S. production as percent of U.S. production of seven majors.

b. As percent of seven-company average.

EXHIBIT 8
Summary of Accounting Policies

Exploration and Development

The most significant accounting policy in the petroleum industry relates to the method of accounting for the exploration and development of oil and gas reserves. Gulf follows the "successful efforts" concept, which requires that all exploratory drilling and equipment costs be capitalized pending determination of whether the drilling is unsuccessful or successful; if unsuccessful, these costs are expensed. All other exploratory costs, including geological and geophysical costs, are charged against income as incurred. All development drilling and equipment costs are capitalized whether successful or unsuccessful.

Depreciation and depletion expenses for all capitalized costs of oil- and gas-producing properties are determined on a unit-of-production method as the reserves are produced.

Philip Morris Companies and Kraft, Inc.

John M. Richman, the chairman and chief executive officer of Kraft, Inc., concluded his October 23, 1988, letter to shareholders as follows:

> We deeply regret the dislocation and hardships that the [restructuring] plan we contemplate will cause, and we will seek to ameliorate these hardships as much as possible. We know that our shareholders, employees, customers, suppliers and communities recognize that today's situation is not of our making. Rather it is the product of current era investment policies and financial attitudes that favor short-term financial gratification over steady, long-term growth and the need to provide a sound economy for future generations.
>
> It will take several years, but with the history and traditions of Kraft and the dedication of Kraft people, we are confident that we will rebuild Kraft to the leading position it occupies today.

The letter announced a radical restructuring of Kraft in response to a hostile tender offer by Philip Morris Companies: $90 per share in cash for all of Kraft's outstanding common stock. The offer had been announced just five days earlier, on October 18, 1988.

Kraft, Inc.

In 1987, Kraft was known for such brand names as Miracle Whip, Seven Seas, and Kraft salad dressings; Kraft mayonnaise; Velveeta cheese; Parkay and Chiffon margarines; Lender's Bagels; and Breyers ice cream. Net sales from continuing operations were $9.9 billion in 1987, an increase of 27% over 1986. Net income from continuing operations rose 11%, to $435 million. Exhibit 1 presents operating and stockholder information for Kraft from 1982 through 1987. Exhibit 2 presents balance sheet information for 1986 and 1987.

Kraft's strategy was focused on food. Its 1987 annual report stated:

> The food industry offers such diverse and rewarding opportunities that we see no purpose in running the risk of diluting our efforts or our focus with other lines of business.

This all-food strategy was in sharp contrast to its earlier diversification program. Most of the diversification occurred when Mr. Richman engineered the September 1980 merger between Kraft and Dart Industries, a $2.4 billion consumer products manufacturer. Mr. Richman, who had been promoted to chairman and CEO less than 1 year before the merger, noted that the merger brought "diversification in one fell swoop to Kraft." Dart's products included Tupperware containers, Duracell batteries, and West Bend appliances. The merger was accomplished by exchanging one share of the merged company, Dart & Kraft, for each outstanding share of the two preexisting companies. Dart & Kraft was the twenty-seventh-largest company in the United States at the time of the merger. Six months later, in March 1981, Dart & Kraft acquired Hobart Corporation, the manufacturer of KitchenAid and other food-related equipment, for $460 million.

Mr. Richman reversed direction and began pursuing the all-food strategy in 1986. Kraft spun off most of its nonfood businesses acquired in the Dart & Kraft merger into Premark International, Inc., on October 31, 1986. Each shareholder of Dart & Kraft received one share of Kraft common stock and a quarter share of Premark. Kraft, with sales of about $9.9 billion after the spin-off, retained its food businesses and Duracell batteries. Premark's share of Dart & Kraft included Tupperware and Hobart food service equipment, with combined sales of $1.8 billion.[1]

Kraft sold its last nonfood asset, Duracell, to Kohlberg, Kravis, Roberts & Co., a leveraged buyout firm, for $1.8 billion in June 1988. According to Kraft's 1987 annual report, the proceeds of the sale were to be used to repurchase shares and to repay debt obligations. In October 1987, Kraft authorized the repurchase of 10 million shares, and 6 million were repurchased under the authorization by year-end.

In 1987, Kraft was organized into three business segments: U.S. Consumer Food, U.S. Commercial Food, and International Food. In 1987, U.S. Consumer Food had sales of $4.5 billion and an operating profit of $593 million. U.S. Commercial Food, which included Kraft Foodservice, the second-largest U.S. food service distributor, had sales of $3 billion and an operating profit of $86.4 million. International Food had sales of $2.3 billion and an operating profit of $229.8 million. Exhibit 3 presents a financial summary of Kraft by business segment.

The Philip Morris $90-per-Share Tender Offer

On the evening of October 18, 1988, Philip Morris offered to purchase all Kraft common stock at $90 per share in cash. The offer represented a 50% premium over the $60.125 closing price on October 18. At $11 billion in total value the bid, if successful, would have been the second-largest acquisition ever completed, exceeded only by Chevron Corporation's $13.3 billion acquisition of Gulf Oil Corporation in 1984.[2]

Most Philip Morris sales and profits came from its Marlboro, Benson & Hedges, and Virginia Slims cigarettes. The company's tobacco sales increased by 15%, to $14.6 billion, in 1987. Philip Morris increased its domestic share of the cigarette market to 38% in 1987, from 37% in 1986, and 1987 operating profits were $3.3 billion. Nevertheless, consumption of cigarettes in the United States had been declining from its 1981 peak of 640 billion cigarettes. Estimated U.S. consumption for 1988

---

1. KitchenAid had been sold in February 1986 for $150 million.

2. Kraft had 119,285,155 shares outstanding and outstanding employee stock options on 2,396,808 shares. The total number of Kraft shares purchased under the offer was therefore 121,681,963.

was 563 billion cigarettes. Increases in exports offset the decline in U.S. consumption, as new markets were entered, especially Japan and Taiwan. Overall, cigarette exports were predicted to increase by 15%, to 115 billion cigarettes in 1988.

Philip Morris had been pursuing a strategy of diversifying out of the tobacco business since 1969, when it acquired 53% of the Miller Brewing Company's common shares, the remainder of which it acquired in 1970. With brands like Miller, Lite, and Matilda Bay Wine Coolers, the brewing division generated sales of $3.1 billion in 1987. Philip Morris also purchased Seven-Up Company in May 1978 for $520 million. Its largest food acquisition by far was General Foods, which Philip Morris purchased in 1985 for $5.6 billion. Like Kraft, General Foods was based on brand-name products such as Maxwell House coffee, Birds Eye frozen foods, Jell-O, Oscar Mayer meats, Ronzoni pasta, and Post cereals. It had 1987 sales of $10 billion.

Philip Morris's acquisitions had mixed results. See Exhibit 4 for operating and stockholder information from 1982 through 1987. Exhibit 5 presents balance sheet information for 1986 and 1987. Exhibit 6 presents the consolidated changes in financial position, and Exhibit 7 reports line-of-business information.

Philip Morris sold its Seven-Up operations in 1986 for about book value after a $50 million write-off in 1985. General Foods' operating profit declined from $624 million in 1986 to $605 million in 1987. The 1987 operating profit represented a 9.3% return on Philip Morris's $6.5 billion investment in the food industry, including additional postacquisition investments of $868 million. Speculation was that Philip Morris might use Kraft's management team to revitalize General Foods, which had been without a chief executive officer since July 1988, when Philip L. Smith left to become chairman of Pillsbury.[3] Smith, a 22-year veteran of General Foods, had been president and chief operating officer before its merger with Philip Morris.

The acquisition of Kraft would have made Philip Morris the world's largest food company, and it would have been a major step in the firm's strategy of reducing its dependence on tobacco and moving into the food business. As Hamish Maxwell, the chairman and CEO of Philip Morris, said in his October 21, 1988, letter to John Richman:

> Our goal is to have Kraft combine with Philip Morris to create the leading international food company. . . . Our intention is to keep Kraft's present businesses intact and for the company to be managed by Kraft executives, using your present headquarters and facilities.

Exhibit 8 contains excerpts from the letters between the two companies throughout the takeover contest.

Philip Morris proposed to finance the acquisition with $1.5 billion in excess cash and its available bank credit lines of up to $12 billion.

Kraft's Response

On October 23, 1988, Kraft's board of directors rejected the Philip Morris bid:

> We strongly believe the $90 takeover bid . . . undervalues Kraft, for these important reasons: first, after careful analysis, our investment banker, Goldman, Sachs & Co., has advised us that the bid is inadequate; and second, our stock has been trading above the $90 offer, a clear signal that investors see the bid as low.

---

3. The combination also would have increased leverage with grocery stores and advertisers. In 1987, Philip Morris spent $1.5 billion and Kraft $400 million on advertising.

Kraft's response occurred when the food industry was undergoing a major restructuring and revaluation. Grand Metropolitan PLC began a hostile tender offer for Pillsbury on October 4, 1988. Grand Met was a diversified British company that brewed and distributed beer, ale, and lager; produced and distributed alcoholic beverages; and owned and operated pubs and restaurants. Pillsbury was a diversified food and restaurant company, with popular brands such as Pillsbury Doughboy bakery items, Green Giant vegetables, and Häagen-Dazs ice cream in its food business, and Burger King in its restaurant group. Like Kraft, Pillsbury had just completed a major restructuring that focused the company on the food business. The $5.2 billion Grand Met bid was a 53% premium over the previous market price—about 25 times Pillsbury's net earnings and about four times the book value of common equity.[4] Pillsbury opposed the bid, and its outcome was uncertain.

The developments at RJR Nabisco were more startling. Management, in partnership with the investment banking firm of Shearson Lehman Hutton, had proposed a $17 billion leveraged buyout of RJR Nabisco on October 20, 1988. Like Philip Morris, RJR Nabisco was a tobacco and food company, with brand names such as Winston and Salem cigarettes, Oreo cookies, Ritz crackers, Planters nuts, LifeSavers candies, Royal gelatin, and Del Monte fruit and vegetables. At $75 per share, the buyout offer was a 34% premium over the previous market price of RJR Nabisco, $55.875. The $75 offer was about 16 times RJR Nabisco's 1987 earnings per share of $4.70 and about three times the book value of common equity. Analysts speculated that a higher offer for RJR Nabisco was likely: its stock closed above the offer price.

Taken together, the Philip Morris bid for Kraft, Grand Metropolitan's bid for Pillsbury, and the RJR Nabisco leveraged buyout attempt by its management involved about $34 billion—an amount unprecedented in the history of the industry. Exhibit 9 examines this history, with statistics on mergers and acquisitions for food and beverage firms as well as a listing of transactions of more than $1 billion. Exhibit 10 contains historical stock prices and return-on-equity information for the food and tobacco industries.

Kraft proposed a restructuring plan as an alternative to the Philip Morris tender offer. For each share of common stock, shareholders would receive a cash dividend of $84 and a high-yield debt valued at $14, and they would retain their now highly leveraged equity interest. Kraft valued the postrestructuring stock at $12 per share and the total restructuring package at $110 per share.

Under the plan Kraft would sell some businesses for cash proceeds of about $2.1 billion after taxes. The businesses to be sold represented 45% of estimated 1988 revenues and 19% of estimated 1988 operating profits. Kraft would also reduce operating expenses. It would finance the $10.2 billion in dividend payments to shareholders with $6.8 billion in bank borrowings at a 12% annual interest rate and the $3 billion in debt with rates ranging from 12.5% to 14.75%. The $2.1 billion from asset sales would be used to pay down the bank debt.

The company planned to retain $904 million of existing debt at an average annual interest rate of 8.65%.

The debt received by shareholders would accrue interest at a 15.25% annual rate (paid semiannually), with no cash payments in the first 5 years. Interest would be paid

---

4. Pillsbury's 1988 net earnings per share were $2.45, excluding unusual items, and $.81, including unusual items. The difference was due to a restructuring charge of $1.64 per share. Its 1987 net earnings per share were $2.24, excluding unusual items, and $2.10, including unusual items.

in cash at the 15.25% semiannual rate after the fifth year. Exhibit 11 presents pre-bid sales and profit forecasts for Kraft through 1989. Exhibit 12 presents earnings and cash flow forecasts for the restructuring plan proposed by Kraft's management.

The Stock Market Response

The price of Kraft common stock rose $10 per share, to $102, in response to the restructuring announcement. Philip Morris criticized the restructuring plan and reiterated its offer to negotiate with Kraft, which responded that "if Philip Morris or another company truly wishes to negotiate with Kraft, a simple phone call proposing a price of more than $110 is all that is necessary." Philip Morris did not increase its bid.

Uncertainty about the market value of food assets grew as Kohlberg, Kravis, Roberts entered the bidding for RJR Nabisco, with a $20.6 billion offer on October 24, 1988.

On Thursday, October 27, Kraft's common stock closed at $94.50. On Friday, October 28, Kraft's stock rose $2, closing at $96.50. Exhibit 13 contains the closing stock prices for Kraft and Philip Morris throughout the takeover contest.

EXHIBIT 1

Condensed Operating and Stockholder Information for Kraft, 1982–1987 (millions of dollars except per share data)

	1982	1983	1984	1985	1986	1987
Revenues	$7,041	$6,660	$6,831	$7,065	$7,780	$9,876
Cost of goods sold[a]	5,350	4,928	4,969	4,963	5,393	6,912
Depreciation	103	80	74	74	79	103
Delivery, sales, and administrative expenses	1,183	1,157	1,238	1,391	1,620	2,068
Interest, net	24	(8)	22	26	31	91
Other income (expense)[b]	(38)	23	43	37	37	86
Income from continuing operations before taxes	343	526	571	648	694	788
Income taxes	164	225	252	286	300	353
Income from continuing operations	179	301	319	362	394	435
Income from discontinued operations[c]	171	134	137	104	19	54
Net income	$ 350	$ 435	$ 456	$ 466	$ 413	$ 489
Earnings per share	$ 2.13	$ 2.65	$ 3.17	$ 3.24	$ 3.06	$ 3.73
Dividends per share	1.20	1.28	1.38	1.52	1.68	1.84
Closing stock price[d, e]	22.83	22.21	28.04	43.38	49.38	48.25
Price-earnings ratio[e]	11	8	9	13	16	13
Number of shares (millions)[e]	164	164	144	144	135	131
Beta[f]	.72	.55	.69	1.12	1.18	.74

Sources: Company reports and casewriter's estimates.

a. Cost of goods sold does not include annual depreciation.

b. Includes the cumulative effect of a change in method of accounting for income taxes of $45 million in 1987 and a nonoperating item of –$91 million in 1982.

c. Discontinued operations include Duracell, the sale of which was announced in 1987, and the business of Premark International, which was spun off on October 31, 1986. Also included in discontinued operations is a $41 million gain on the sale of KitchenAid in 1986.

d. Adjusted for a 3-for-1 stock split in 1985.

e. Year-end.

f. Calculated by ordinary least-squares regression using daily stock price data.

EXHIBIT 2
Consolidated Balance Sheets for Kraft, 1986–1987 (millions of dollars)

	1986	1987
Cash	$ 321.5	$ 189.0
Accounts receivable	637.6	763.6
Inventories	1,061.1	1,283.4
Investments and long-term receivables	236.2	178.3
Prepaid and deferred items	127.5	161.5
Property, plant, equipment, net	1,087.7	1,424.2
Intangibles	419.0	888.3
Net assets of discontinued operations	600.7	598.4
Total assets	$4,491.3	$5,486.7
Accounts payable	$ 492.1	$ 544.8
Short-term borrowings	596.4	645.9
Accrued compensation	148.9	151.2
Accrued advertising and promotions	113.7	132.8
Other accrued liabilities	188.4	245.4
Accrued income taxes	335.3	399.3
Current portion of long-term debt	108.5	37.2
Current liabilities	1,983.3	2,156.6
Long-term debt	237.7	895.3
Deferred income taxes	286.4	282.7
Other liabilities	185.9	253.7
Total liabilities	2,693.3	3,588.3
Shareholders' equity	2,798.0	1,898.4
Total liabilities and net worth	$4,491.3	$5,486.7

Source: Company reports.

EXHIBIT 3

Financial Summary for Kraft by Business Segment, 1983–1987 (millions of dollars)

	1983	*1984*	*1985*	*1986*	*1987*
U.S. Consumer Food[a]					
Sales	$3,718.0	$3,781.2	$3,911.3	$4,016.1	$4,518.9
Operating profit	388.1	446.0	527.3	545.9	593.3
Identifiable assets	1,450.9	1,615.4	1,309.1	1,807.6	2,509.3
Depreciation	54.0	50.0	37.6	36.6	47.4
Capital expenditures	58.0	71.7	63.1	93.7	151.2
Operating profits/Identifiable assets . . .	26.75%	27.61%	40.28%	30.20%	23.64%
U.S. Commercial Food					
Sales	$1,172.7	$1,349.3	$1,421.0	$1,755.8	$3,022.0
Operating profit	na	na	61.7	79.5	86.4
Identifiable assets	na	na	291.4	558.9	914.6
Depreciation	na	na	7.6	8.0	15.3
Capital expenditures	na	na	5.2	17.6	33.7
Operating profits/Identifiable assets . . .	na	na	21.17%	14.22%	9.45%
International Food					
Sales	$1,769.7	$1,707.2	$1,733.0	$2,007.7	$2,334.8
Operating profit	165.4	169.4	145.9	182.8	229.8
Identifiable assets	680.9	701.1	793.7	861.1	1,000.5
Depreciation	19.2	18.9	20.6	27.5	34.0
Capital expenditures	37.3	36.2	39.2	41.7	48.3
Operating profits/Identifiable assets . . .	24.29%	24.16%	18.38%	21.23%	22.97%
Direct Selling[b]					
Sales	$ 825.1	$ 776.9	—	—	—
Operating profit	189.3	138.8	—	—	—
Identifiable assets	462.7	488.0	—	—	—
Depreciation	36.0	28.9	—	—	—
Capital expenditures	40.7	62.8	—	—	—
Operating profits/Identifiable assets . . .	40.91%	28.44%	—	—	—
Consumer Products[c]					
Sales	$1,181.0	$1,244.8	$ 962.5	—	—
Operating profit	104.7	118.4	66.9	—	—
Identifiable assets	828.0	958.8	849.6	—	—
Depreciation	26.9	42.9	34.2	—	—
Capital expenditures	43.0	67.9	47.4	—	—
Operating profits/Identifiable assetes . .	12.64%	12.35%	7.87%	—	—
Commercial Products[d]					
Sales	$1,047.5	$ 899.3	—	—	—
Operating profit	104.8	101.0	—	—	—
Identifiable assets	727.6	556.9	—	—	—
Depreciation	30.4	23.9	—	—	—
Capital expenditures	25.4	28.1	—	—	—
Operating profits/Identifiable assets . . .	14.40%	18.14%	—	—	—

Source: Company reports.

na = not available.

a. Figures for 1983 and 1984 include both U.S. consumer foods and U.S. commercial foods.

b. Includes Tupperware, which was spun off to Premark International in 1988.

c. Includes Duracell, West Bend, Health Care, and KitchenAid. All assets except Duracell were sold or spun off to Premark International in 1986.

d. Includes Hobart, which was spun off to Premark International in 1986.

EXHIBIT 4

Condensed Operating and Stockholder Information for Philip Morris, 1982–1987 (millions of dollars except per share data)

	1982	*1983*	*1984*	*1985*[c]	*1986*	*1987*
Revenues	$11,586	$12,976	$13,814	$15,964	$25,409	$27,695
Cost of goods sold[a]	5,046	5,028	5,170	5,926	10,495	10,664
Excise taxes	2,615	3,510	3,676	3,815	4,728	5,416
Depreciation and amortization . . .	281	327	375	424	655	704
Selling, administrative, and research expenses[b]	2,125	2,377	2,467	3,244	6,061	7,004
Equity in net earnings of unconsolidated subsidiaries . . .	71	83	54	82	111	126
Interest	246	230	273	308	770	685
Other expense	44	—	300	—	—	—
Income before taxes	1,300	1,587	1,607	2,329	2,811	3,348
Income taxes	518	681	718	1,074	1,333	1,506
Net income	$ 782	$ 906	$ 889	$ 1,255	$ 1,478	$ 1,842
Earnings per share	$ 3.11	$ 3.58	$ 3.62	$ 5.24	$ 6.20	$ 7.75
Dividends per share	1.20	1.45	1.70	2.00	2.48	3.15
Closing stock price[d]	30	35.875	40.375	44.125	71.875	85.375
Price-earnings ratio[d]	9	10	11	8	11	11
Number of shares (millions)[d]	252	250	243	239	238	237
Beta[e]	1.04	.77	.94	.88	1.24	.88

Sources: Company reports and casewriter's estimates.

a. Cost of goods sold does not include annual depreciation.

b. Selling, administrative, and research cost includes corporate expenses.

c. General Foods was acquired on November 1, 1985.

d. Year-end.

e. Calculated by ordinary least-squares regression using daily stock price data.

EXHIBIT 5
Consolidated Balance Sheets for Philip Morris, 1986–1987 (millions of dollars)

	1986	1987
Cash	$ 73	$ 189
Receivables	1,878	2,083
Inventories	3,836	4,154
Other current assets	127	146
Property, plant, equipment, net	6,237	6,582
Investments in unconsolidated subsidiaries and affiliates	1,067	1,244
Goodwill and other intangibles	3,988	4,052
Other assets	436	695
Total assets	$17,642	$19,145
Notes payable	$ 864	$ 691
Accounts payable	813	803
Current portion of long-term debt	103	465
Accrued liabilities	1,967	2,277
Income taxes payable	557	727
Dividends payable	178	213
Current liabilities	4,482	5,176
Long-term debt	5,945	5,222
Deferred income taxes	994	1,288
Other liabilities	566	636
Total liabilities	11,987	12,322
Stockholders' equity	5,655	6,823
Total liabilities and net worth	$17,642	$19,145

Source: Company reports.

EXHIBIT 6
Consolidated Statements of Changes in Financial Position for Philip Morris, 1985–1987
(millions of dollars)

	1985	*1986*	*1987*
Funds Provided by			
Net earnings	$ 1,255	$ 1,478	$ 1,842
Depreciation and amortization	424	655	704
Deferred income taxes	159	133	338
Equity in undistributed net earnings of unconsolidated subsidiaries and affiliates	(63)	(52)	(95)
Total funds from operations	1,775	2,214	2,789
Increase in accrued liabilities and other payments	1,467	226	505
Working capital from sales of operations	169	487	20
Currency translation adjustments affecting working capital	18	77	139
Other, net	211	210	—
Total funds provided	$ 3,640	$ 3,214	$ 3,453
Funds Used for			
Increase (decrease) in			
Cash and receivables	$ 1,005	$ (2)	$ 321
Inventories	1,174	9	318
Other current assets	74	14	19
Capital expenditures	347	678	718
Dividends declared	479	590	749
Increase in property, plant, and equipment from income tax election	—	508	—
Investment in General Foods Corp. exclusive of $718 million working capital acquired	4,864	—	—
Other, net	—	—	301
Total funds used	$ 7,943	$ 1,797	$ 2,426
Net funds provided (used)	$(4,303)	$ 1,417	$ 1,027
Financing Activities			
Increase in current notes payable	$ 149	$ 289	$ 189
Long-term debt financing	4,666	1,788	492
Reduction of long-term debt	(326)	(3,385)	(1,534)
Purchase of treasury stock	(216)	(140)	(200)
Issuance of shares	30	31	26
Funds (used for) provided from financing activities	$ 4,303	$(1,417)	$(1,027)
Increase (decrease) in working capital	$ 637	$ (494)	$ (36)
Working capital (year-end)	1,926	1,432	1,396

Source: Company reports.

EXHIBIT 7
Financial Summary for Philip Morris by Business Segment, 1982–1987 (millions of dollars)

	1982	1983	1984	1985	1986	1987
Tobacco						
Sales	$7,821.8	$9,094.9	$9,802.0	$10,539.0	$12,691.0	$14,644.0
Operating profit	1,475.7	1,647.0	2,141.0	2,441.0	2,827.0	3,273.0
Identifiable assets	5,070.7	5,114.3	5,149.0	5,622.0	5,808.0	6,467.0
Depreciation	97.7	124.7	151.0	166.0	200.0	214.0
Capital expenditures	498.0	319.9	163.0	151.0	191.0	256.0
Operating profit/Identifiable assets	29.10%	32.20%	41.58%	43.42%	48.67%	50.61%
Food Products						
Sales	—	—	—	$ 1,632.0	$ 9,664.0	$ 9,946.0
Operating profit	—	—	—	95.0	624.0	605.0
Identifiable assets	—	—	—	7,974.0	8,629.0	9,129.0
Depreciation	—	—	—	29.0	167.0	201.0
Capital expenditures	—	—	—	71.0	395.0	402.0
Operating profit/Identifiable assets	—	—	—	1.19%	7.23%	6.63%
Beer						
Sales	$2,935.5	$2,935.5	$2,940.0	$ 2,925.0	$ 3,054.0	$ 3,105.0
Operating profit	159.0	227.1	116.0	136.0	154.0	170.0
Identifiable assets	2,113.7	2,138.9	1,892.0	1,779.0	1,736.0	1,680.0
Depreciation	122.3	130.5	144.0	134.0	136.0	137.0
Capital expenditures	286.3	174.6	94.0	87.0	80.0	57.0
Operating profit/Identifiable assets	7.52%	10.62%	6.13%	7.64%	8.87%	10.12%
Other[a]						
Sales	$ 822.9	$ 945.5	$1,072.0	$ 868.0	—	—
Operating profit (loss)	(2.4)	(10.9)	23.0	14.0	$ (9.0)	$ 19.0
Identifiable assets	979.4	1,007.3	1,018.0	643.0	—	—
Depreciation	—	—	—	—	—	—
Capital expenditures	—	—	—	—	—	—
Operating profit/Identifiable assets	−.25%	−1.08%	2.26%	2.18%	—	—

Source: Company reports.

a. Includes the Seven-Up Company, which was sold in 1986.

EXHIBIT 8
Correspondence During Takeover Bid Between Kraft and Philip Morris, October 1988

October 20, 1988

Mr. Hamish Maxwell
Chairman and Chief Executive Officer
Philip Morris Companies Inc.
120 Park Avenue
New York, NY 10017

Dear Hamish:

In addition to your letter requesting "negotiations" following your commencing, on Monday, a tender offer without talking to me beforehand, your lawyers and investment bankers have been barraging our advisers with similar requests. You did not see fit to discuss your takeover attempt when we were together at the Grocery Manufacturers of America meeting last Wednesday and Thursday, nor did you see fit to tell me that you were planning on filing a bizarre and baseless law suit against me and our Board of Directors on Monday.

You must have been planning your takeover bid for a long time. We intend to take our time and study the situation very carefully. We have a fiduciary duty to our shareholders and an obligation to our employees, customers, suppliers, and communities to do so. Following our study, the Board of Directors will consider the situation and determine Kraft's response. If at that time there is a purpose to be served by our meeting, we will so advise you.

Sincerely,
JOHN M. RICHMAN
Chairman and Chief Executive Officer
Kraft, Inc.

October 21, 1988

Mr. John M. Richman
Chairman and Chief Executive Officer
Kraft, Inc.
Kraft Court
Glenview, IL 60025

Dear John:

I understand and sympathize with your reaction to the events of this week. I would have preferred to discuss our offer with you prior to taking the actions we commenced. However, in the current legal environment in which we live, I accepted the advice to proceed as we did as a business decision. Our actions were designed to minimize uncertainties and delays in addressing the main issue—the economic benefits and other factors favoring the merger of Kraft with Philip Morris.

I hope you understand that any discussion of our interest in Kraft would have been premature and inappropriate when we saw each other last week at the Grocery Manufacturers of America meeting. At that time we had made no final decision to proceed with an offer and our Board had not yet approved our actions. In any event, I am hopeful you and we can now move forward in a positive and constructive manner.

I quite appreciate your need to study our offer carefully before responding to it. We have, however, seen press reports that Kraft may consider other possibilities including highly leveraged transactions that could encumber the company, operationally and financially, and which also might lead to the dismemberment of Kraft. From what I know of you and some public statements you have made, I feel sure that this is not the route you would prefer to take.

(continued)

EXHIBIT 8 *(continued)*

As we have said, our goal is to have Kraft combine with Philip Morris to create the leading international food company. I repeat that our intention is to keep Kraft's present businesses intact and for the company to be managed by Kraft executives, using your present headquarters and facilities.

I believe it to be in the best interests of your shareholders and other constituencies that we avoid a prolonged struggle that could disrupt Kraft's business without adding to the value that would be realized by your shareholders.

I also believe that a meeting between us could only be helpful to you in understanding our purposes and positive thoughts concerning a combination of our two companies. . . . I want to emphasize that we are prepared to discuss all aspects of our offer.

I would be available to meet with you in Chicago at any time on short notice. I can be reached through my office if, as I hope, you see the benefits of such a meeting.

Yours sincerely,
HAMISH MAXWELL
Chairman and Chief Executive Officer
Philip Morris Companies Inc.

October 23, 1988

To: Shareholders of Kraft, Inc.

Dear Shareholder:

Kraft has an outstanding record of profitability and growth. It is a great company with great traditions, great brands, a great future, and great people who have devoted their lives to making your company what it is today.

Kraft's record of success—an increase in shareholder value, without regard to recent events, at a compound annual rate of more than 20% over the past 5 years—has been based on a strategy of balancing significant short-term returns and continued investment for long-term growth. This strategy has been working, but—frustratingly—the stock market has long been undervaluing companies which, like Kraft, sacrifice short-term profit in order to invest in long-term growth.

Last Monday, Philip Morris Companies, seeking to take advantage of this undervaluation, announced an unsolicited tender offer for Kraft at $90 per share.

We strongly believe the $90 takeover bid also undervalues Kraft, for these important reasons: first, after careful analysis, our investment banker, Goldman, Sachs & Co., has advised us that the bid is inadequate; and second, our stock has been trading above the $90 offer, a clear signal that investors see the bid as low.

Your Board of Directors has unanimously rejected the offer, and we strongly recommend that you do not tender your Kraft shares to Philip Morris.

At the same time, both your Board and company management recognize that, as a practical matter, the Philip Morris bid makes it impossible for us to go back to the situation that existed prior to the bid. Under the circumstances, your Board believes that we should take action to maximize shareholder value rather than accept an inadequate offer. Together with Goldman, Sachs we are developing a potential recapitalization plan that we believe will have a value of significantly more than $90 per share.

(continued)

EXHIBIT 8 *(continued)*

The plan we are working on is intended to result in a total value estimated to be in excess of $110 per share, with a distribution in cash and securities totaling approximately $98 per share and the retention of your common stock interest, the price of which will be adjusted by the market to reflect the cash and securities distribution. Under the plan, you will receive a cash distribution and new securities, and retain your Kraft common stock. Most shareholders will have less tax to pay as a result of the distribution than if Kraft were to be acquired by Philip Morris (or anyone else) at a price that is equal to the value of the restructuring plan.

Your Board believes that this plan will enable you as a shareholder to realize present value for your shares and also continue to participate in the future of Kraft, including some exciting new product lines we have been developing.

The plan will involve the sale of some of our businesses, bank borrowings of more than $6.8 billion, and the sale of $3.0 billion of debt. We have already begun to implement some of these transactions. Goldman, Sachs has advised us that it is highly confident with respect to the placement of the debt under current market conditions. We will retain our core businesses, together with the key brands which have provided Kraft's historic strength and currently account for approximately 80% of its profitability.

Because the restructured Kraft will have more than $12.4 billion in debt and require herculean efforts by our employees, the plan will replicate the structure currently in use in sponsored leveraged buyouts by providing significant equity incentives for employees in the form of stock options and an employee stock ownership plan. This very important link between employee compensation and company performance will, we believe, ensure the enormous efforts required to make the recapitalization a complete success.

We expect that the plan will be fully developed and our Board will be able to approve it in the very near future, at which time we will announce the details. Because the plan involves very significant restructuring of our businesses and financial structure, the Board also believes you should have the opportunity to vote upon it at a special meeting of shareholders.

For your further information, on Friday, October 21, there was a series of communications with Philip Morris. Philip Morris renewed their request for immediate negotiation, stating that all aspects of their offer, including price, are open for discussion. Philip Morris said that there would be real value to them if they could conclude the agreement with us over the weekend and asked for a meeting on Saturday. We responded that if Philip Morris were prepared to offer a realistic price, we would meet on Saturday. We told Philip Morris that their $90 bid is substantially below our valuation and Goldman, Sachs's valuation and that there would be no purpose served by a meeting unless Philip Morris were prepared to start the negotiations from a price substantially greater than $90. We asked Philip Morris to tell us where they stood and told Philip Morris that if they were in the range of value that we and Goldman, Sachs believe is obtainable, we would meet with them on Saturday. Philip Morris replied that they completely disagree with our opinion of their $90 price, that they believe $90 represents full value, and they would not tell us what price they are prepared to offer. Given this attitude on the part of Philip Morris, it was clear that a meeting would not have served any purpose of Kraft and its shareholders, and we so advised Philip Morris. We also advised Philip Morris that we were not foreclosing negotiations and that if they were to offer a price that reflects the full value of Kraft, we would negotiate with them.

Since we believe that the restructuring plan will create greater shareholder value and opportunity than the Philip Morris bid or any other known alternative, it is our intention to proceed with the restructuring on an exclusive basis. However, if someone comes forward with a transaction that would be more desirable than the restructuring plan, we will negotiate and your Board will give full consideration to such a transaction.

We deeply regret the dislocation and hardships that the plan we contemplate will cause, and we will seek to ameliorate these hardships as much as possible. We know that our shareholders, employees,

---

(continued)

EXHIBIT 8 *(continued)*

customers, suppliers, and communities recognize that today's situation is not of our making. Rather it is the product of current era investment policies and financial attitudes that favor short-term financial gratification over steady, long-term growth and the need to provide a sound economy for future generations.

It will take several years, but with the history and traditions of Kraft and the dedication of Kraft people, we are confident that we will rebuild Kraft to the leading position it occupies today.

On behalf of the Board of Directors,
JOHN M. RICHMAN
Chairman

October 24, 1988

Calvin J. Collier, Esq.
Senior Vice President and General Counsel
Kraft, Inc.
Kraft Court
Glenview, IL 60025

Dear Mr. Collier:

In light of the announcement yesterday of Kraft, Inc.'s proposed recapitalization plan, Philip Morris believes that Kraft is required to take all necessary steps to ensure that Philip Morris is given an opportunity to analyze fully Kraft's contemplated recapitalization transaction and any other proposed transaction for the sale of Kraft or any of its assets to a third party. . . .

We have a number of questions that bear on the feasibility and value to Kraft's shareholders of the announced recapitalization plan. . . .

We request that Kraft immediately supply to us specific information concerning the details of Kraft's recapitalization plan, all information concerning Kraft which may assist us in evaluating the company, and any information supplied to other third parties with respect to the sale of the company or any parts of the company.

We also request that, consistent with the responsibilities of your Board of Directors to your shareholders, Kraft not enter into, or agree to enter into, any extraordinary transaction, including a recapitalization plan, a sale of assets or securities of Kraft, or a sale of the company, or take any steps to implement any of the foregoing, until Philip Morris is given a full and fair opportunity to develop its response, and that Kraft not take any action which may diminish the value of Kraft. To that end we are today filing a motion in the Federal District Court.

Philip Morris continues to believe that, if our companies work together, a transaction can be negotiated which will achieve maximum value for Kraft's shareholders speedily and without the extraordinary disruptions to Kraft's businesses which Kraft acknowledges would be inherent in the contemplated restructuring plan.

Sincerely,
MURRAY H. BRING
Senior Vice President and General Counsel
Philip Morris Companies Inc.

(continued)

EXHIBIT 8 *(concluded)*

October 25, 1988

Mr. Hamish Maxwell
Chairman and Chief Executive Officer
Philip Morris Companies Inc.
120 Park Avenue
New York, NY 10017

Dear Hamish:

I have previously advised Philip Morris of Kraft's position on your tender offer. The letter your general counsel sent to our general counsel yesterday, and the papers your lawyer filed in court yesterday, indicate that Philip Morris does not understand what Kraft is doing—or more likely, Philip Morris is pretending not to understand in order to increase its pressure tactics. Obviously it is in your interest to try to pressure Kraft and the Kraft shareholders into a transaction that benefits you at their expense. Kraft will not permit this.

Let me again make clear Kraft's position.

Kraft was not "for sale" and is not "for sale." This is no "auction" of Kraft. Philip Morris made a unilateral tender offer for Kraft. The Kraft Board of Directors rejected your tender offer. Your price is too low. Kraft has a recapitalization plan that creates far greater value for the Kraft shareholders than your inadequate offer. Kraft is submitting the recapitalization plan to Kraft shareholders for their consideration. The recapitalization will take place only if our shareholders approve it. Kraft will not pressure its shareholders, nor will Kraft permit you to stampede them. The Kraft Board is not taking action to "entrench" itself. Just the opposite, it is proceeding expeditiously to provide Kraft shareholders with a choice between your inadequate $90 bid and a better than $110 recapitalization.

As frequently happens—witness the RJR Nabisco situation—new bidders appear and old bidders raise their bids. The Kraft Board recognizes that another company or Philip Morris may offer more than $110 per share to acquire Kraft. Accordingly, the Kraft Board said that Kraft would negotiate with that company, or you, and if it, or your company, has a better transaction than the recapitalization plan, Kraft will enter into that transaction.

In other words, if Philip Morris or another company truly wishes to negotiate with Kraft, a simple phone call proposing a price of more than $110 is all that is necessary.

Please give a copy of this letter to your general counsel as our answer to his letter, and ask him to give copies to your other lawyers and financial advisers, and instruct them to stop mischaracterizing our position.

Sincerely,
JOHN M. RICHMAN
Chairman and Chief Executive Officer
Kraft, Inc.

EXHIBIT 9
Mergers and Acquisitions in the Food Processing and Beverage Industries, 1981–1987

	Number and Dollar Value of Mergers in the Food and Beverage Industry	
	Number of Transactions	*Amount Paid ($ billions)*
1981	88	$ 4.55
1982	83	4.96
1983	85	2.71
1984	79	7.95
1985	105	12.86
1986	127	8.43
1987	97	7.75

Mergers in the Food and Beverage Industry over $1 Billion ($ millions)

Bidder	Target	Year	Target's Sales	Amount Paid	Premium Percent	Price-Earnings Ratio	Multiple to Book
Philip Morris	General Foods	1985	$9,022.4	$5,627.5	35.2%	18.7	3.5
RJ Reynolds	Nabisco Brands	1985	5,985.0	4,906.4	31.5	16.7	4.1
Nestlé S.A.	Carnation Co.	1984	3,370.0	2,885.4	9.9	14.4	2.7
Beatrice Foods	Esmark Inc.	1984	4,120.0	2,508.6	39.5	15.7	2.5
RJ Reynolds	Heublein, Inc.	1982	2,140.0	1,302.6	36.5	13.1	2.7
Bond Corporate Holdings Ltd.	G. Heileman Brewing Co.	1987	1,173.8	1,083.6	21.6	23.0	3.2

Source: W. T. Grimm and Co., *Mergerstat Review,* 1981–1987.

EXHIBIT 10
Stock Price Indexes and Returns on Equity, 1982–1987

	1982	*1983*	*1984*	*1985*	*1986*	*1987*
Stock price index (1981 = 100)						
Kraft	144.1	148.5	200.6	321.2	397.3	409.3
Philip Morris	128.8	161.2	190.0	218.3	368.7	453.0
RJR Nabisco	114.8	144.8	192.2	220.1	357.4	337.0
Pillsbury	133.0	202.1	256.4	365.4	413.5	440.8
Food index	132.9	161.1	186.9	297.6	387.4	398.8
Tobacco index	117.7	142.4	165.7	179.2	279.7	299.0
S&P 500 index	114.7	134.5	136.4	172.3	197.6	201.5
Return on equity (ROE)						
Kraft	12.6%	14.9%	17.6%	16.2%	23.0%	25.8%
Philip Morris	21.3	22.4	21.7	26.5	26.1	27.0
RJR Nabisco	20.8	17.1	22.3	20.8	20.0	22.8
Pillsbury	16.6	15.0	17.0	17.3	16.8	13.5
Food index	14.3	17.0	17.9	18.0	12.0	12.5
Tobacco index	19.0	18.2	19.4	21.6	20.0	20.3
S&P 500 index	10.9	11.7	13.1	11.0	10.5	11.8

EXHIBIT 11
Pre-Bid Sales and Profit Forecasts for Kraft, 1988–1989 (millions of dollars)

	1987	Est. 1988	Est. 1989
Revenues	$9,876	$11,200	$12,500
Earnings before interest and taxes	834	950	1,050
Interest, net	91	95	108
Income from continuing operations before taxes	743	855	942
Income taxes	353	333	368
Accounting change	45	—	—
Income from continuing operations	435	522	574
Income from discontinued operations[a]	54	658	—
Net income	$ 489	$ 1,180	$ 574

Source: Analysts' estimates.

a. Duracell was sold to Kohlberg, Kravis, Roberts & Co. for $1.8 billion on June 24, 1988. Duracell's 1987 after-tax income was $54 million, and Kraft's 1988 gain on its sale was $658 million.

EXHIBIT 12
Projections for Kraft's Restructuring Plan, 1989–1998 (millions of dollars)

	1989	1990	1991	1992	1993	1994	1995	1996	1997	1998
Sales	$ 6,515	$ 6,804	$7,125	$7,481	$7,855	$8,248	$8,660	$9,093	$9,548	$10,025
Earnings before interest and taxes	1,280	1,487	1,671	1,755	1,842	1,935	2,031	2,133	2,239	2,351
Interest	1,380	1,270	1,310	1,286	1,278	1,257	1,212	1,155	1,086	1,010
Taxes	(39)	89	148	192	231	278	336	401	473	550
Profit (loss) after taxes from continuing operations	(61)	128	213	277	333	400	483	577	680	791
Cash flow available for capital payments[a]	2,481[b]	496	636	630	742	334	411	500	597	728
Principal payments										
Preexisting debt	111	33	57	287	100	100	100	100	16	0
Bank debt	2,370	463	579	343	642	234	311	400	581	728
Year-end book values										
Preexisting debt	793	759	703	416	316	216	116	16	0	0
Bank debt	4,430	3,968	3,389	3,046	2,404	2,170	1,859	1,459	878	150
High-yield debt	3,000	3,000	3,000	3,000	3,000	3,000	3,000	3,000	3,000	3,000
Cram-down debt	1,974	2,286	2,648	3,067	3,553	3,553	3,553	3,553	3,553	3,553
Total	$10,197	$10,013	$9,740	$9,529	$9,273	$8,939	$8,528	$8,028	$7,431	$ 6,703

Sources: Kraft and casewriter's estimates.

a. Cash flow available for capital payments = Net income + Depreciation, amortization, deferred taxes – Capital expenditures – Change in working capital + Net proceeds from asset sales.

b. Includes the $2,146 million in cash proceeds from the sale of businesses in 1989.

EXHIBIT 13
Stock Prices and Market Index, October 1988

Date	Philip Morris	Kraft	S&P 500	Event
Oct. 3	$ 97.000	$ 60.000	638.710	
4	98.000	58.500	637.010	Grand Metropolitan bids for Pillsbury Company.
5	97.375	59.375	640.020	
6	96.875	59.375	641.360	
7	100.875	60.625	654.830	
10	101.125	60.750	655.320	
11	100.750	60.375	654.680	
12	98.875	59.500	645.470	
13	99.250	59.250	648.480	
14	98.625	59.500	649.230	
17	100.000	60.125	651.460	
18	95.500	88.250	658.560	Philip Morris bids $90 per share for Kraft.
19	94.000	90.375	652.970	
20	99.000	90.250	666.990	RJR Nabisco management proposes a $17 billion leveraged buyout.
21	97.375	92.000	668.920	
24	97.500	102.000	665.760	Kraft proposes its restructuring plan and Kohlberg, Kravis, Roberts
25	95.875	99.000	666.090	announces its bid for RJR Nabisco.
26	95.500	97.500	663.820	
27	95.000	94.500	654.240	
28	94.750	96.500	657.280	

Time, Inc.'s Entry into the Entertainment Industry (A)

On June 7, 1989, Time, Inc.'s chairman and chief executive officer, Richard Munro, called an emergency meeting of the board of directors for the next day. Munro had just received a letter from Martin S. Davis, chairman and chief executive officer of Paramount Communications, Inc.:

> We have today commenced a cash tender offer for all of Time's outstanding shares at $175 per share. This price represents a premium of more than 60 percent over the price of Time's shares at the time you announced your proposed transaction with Warner. We believe our offer provides extraordinary value to all of your shareholders as well as to our own.
>
> Together, we will be a communications company rich in resources and with unparalleled range and depth. We will be strongly positioned for global growth through the next decade and into the next century. No other company will be as significant a force in entertainment and publishing with operations in quality magazine and book publishing, as well as in motion picture and television production and distribution, cable systems and cable programming. The fit is superb.[1]

Paramount had conditioned its bid on cancellation of Time's plans to merge with Warner Communications. Time had announced the plans on March 4, 1989, after careful consideration of a comprehensive list of possible partners, including Paramount. The board endorsed Munro's decision to merge with Warner because the two firms held a wide range of complementary assets. Munro wondered how Time should respond to Paramount's hostile bid and what specific course of action he should recommend to the board at its emergency session.

This case was prepared by Professor Lisa K. Meulbroek with the assistance of Research Associates Carolyn Hart and Jane Katz.

Copyright © 1993 by the President and Fellows of Harvard College.
Harvard Business School case 293–117.

1. *Paramount Communications Inc. v. Time Inc.,* Civil Action No. 10670, Delaware Chancery Court, Finkelstein deposition, Exhibit 12.

Time, Inc.

Time, Inc. was formed in 1924 when Henry Luce and Briton Hadden resigned their reporting jobs at the *Baltimore News* to publish their new magazine *Time.* During the next 35 years, Luce and Hadden grew their firm by introducing new magazines, including *Life,* and by acquiring established publications. A series of acquisitions in the late 1970s and 1980s had both strengthened the firm's presence in its established markets and diversified its activities outside the publishing industry (See Exhibit 1). By 1989 the firm had refocused on its core publishing business and renewed its commitment to leadership as an originator of news and entertainment for consumers around the world. Time published magazines and books, distributed cable television programming, and operated local cable television franchises. Exhibits 2 and 3 show financial results by line of business.

Magazines (42% of revenues)

Time was the largest publisher of general circulation magazines in the United States, with 15 titles, including *Sports Illustrated, People, Fortune,* and *Money,* as well as *Time* and *Life.* Time's magazines accounted for more than 20% of advertising in U.S. consumer magazines each year. Foreign editions of *Time* and *Fortune* were published through joint ventures.

Books (15% of revenues)

Time distributed books through five publishing organizations. Time-Life Books was the largest direct-mail publisher of general interest books in series, and Book-of-the-Month Club operated the largest general-circulation book club and several other book clubs. Little, Brown and Company published trade and professional books, and Oxmoor House published how-to and illustrated books on a variety of subjects. In 1986, Time acquired Scott, Foresman and Company, publisher and distributor of elementary, high school, and college textbooks.

Cable Television Programming (17% of revenues)

In a move hailed as visionary, Time invested in a cable television network in 1972. Analysts predicted that cable television would become a dominant vehicle for distributing news and entertainment to the general public by the beginning of the twenty-first century. In 1989, Time operated both the Home Box Office (HBO) and Cinemax networks. Only consumers with hookups to local cable franchises were eligible to subscribe to these networks. Subscribers paid monthly fees for access to programming on HBO or Cinemax.

HBO's programming included feature-length films, sporting events, special entertainment events, and movies commissioned by HBO. Cinemax offered a broad range of movies and special entertainment events. Experience had shown that consumers did not often cancel their subscriptions to cable-television networks. Most programming on HBO and Cinemax consisted of recently released feature-length films. HBO acquired programming through licensing agreements with film producers and film distributors. HBO Video distributed films and other programming on home videocassettes in the United States and Canada. Time also had a 14% ownership interest in Turner Broadcasting System, Inc., a broadcast network.

Local Cable Television Franchises (25% of revenues)

American Television and Communications Corporation (ATC), an 82%-owned subsidiary of Time, was the second-largest cable television franchise in the United States, with 3.9 million subscribers. Local municipalities awarded franchises an exclusive license to distribute cable programming, such as HBO, to subscribers' television sets through a network of cables.

Industry and Competitive Dynamics

At the beginning of the 1980s, the film, television, and publishing industries had been largely independent of each other. By 1989 a series of related trends had blurred their boundaries. Figure A depicts several of the relationships that had emerged.

Several major film producers, including Paramount, MCA, and Warner (profiled below), had integrated vertically. To ensure access to outlets for their products, their activities included exhibition (movie-theater ownership) in addition to film production and distribution. Deregulation also spurred vertical integration: regulations preventing television and film producers from owning television stations were relaxed, and court decisions allowed film producers to own theaters. Exhibit 4 shows the extent in 1988 of vertical integration.

The average cost of producing a feature film had escalated from $2.5 million in 1975 to more than $2 million by 1987. During the same period, the number of feature films offered on the market had increased, elevating the competitive stakes in film production and reducing the chances of a hit. The risk of failure at the box office had

FIGURE A
The Film, Television, and Publishing Industries in the Late 1980s

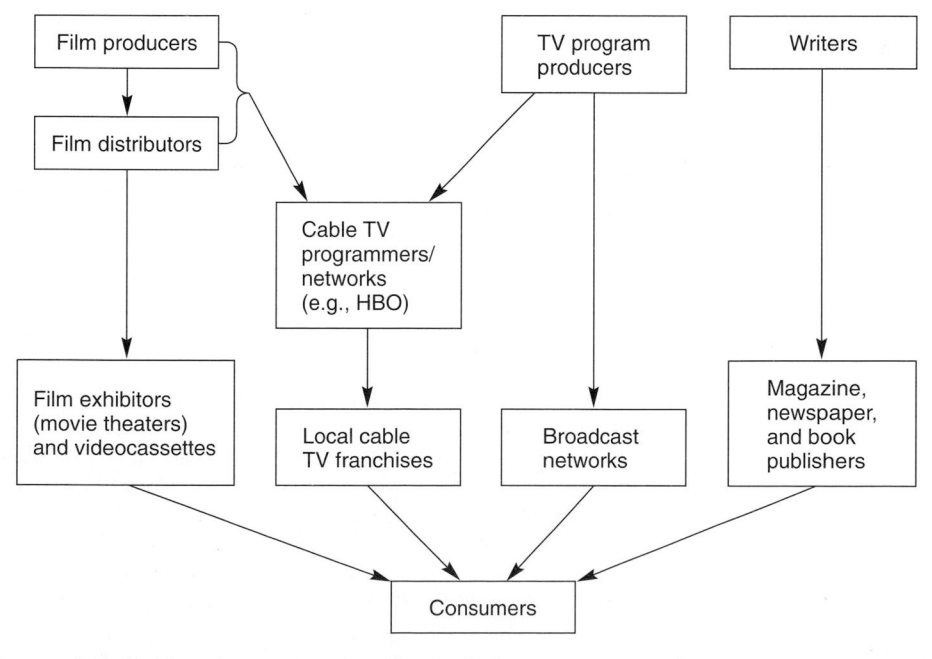

prompted entry into production of television programs, which required less investment than major motion pictures.

At the same time, the proliferation of cable networks had dramatically increased demand for high-quality programming. These networks sold their products directly to consumers through local cable television franchises. Some networks recouped by charging consumers access fees, and others obtained revenue by selling advertising. By 1989 cable programmers were competing directly with broadcast networks for access to feature films, original television productions, advertising space, as well as for other means of attracting consumers' attention.

Time's Strategy for the 1990s

As early as 1983 and 1984, Time's executive board and management began to review its long-term goals. According to one press report, Time's top management felt that its magazine business, though profitable, was not growing fast enough. Munro stated, "We have two huge engines that drive that division, *People* and *Sports Illustrated.* So I would say that growth there is a little limited."[2] Instead, HBO and the cable side of the business had become the largest and fastest-growing component of profit, contributing almost half of Time's earnings. Nonetheless, Time had to pay increasingly high prices for the programs it carried, making potential ownership of the production and associated copyrights attractive. Moreover, the presence of HBO's guaranteed distribution channels would presumably reduce the risk of producing the programs:

> The $35 million price tag of a movie like *Batman* looks less chancy when a company knows it can get its money back by showing the movie in the United States, then showing it abroad, selling the videocassette, selling the soundtrack on records, compact discs and tapes, showing it on pay-TV, and perhaps selling related books or producing related TV programs, all using the company's own resources.[3]

In the spring of 1988, Time senior management held a meeting on long-term strategy at Lyford Cay. They concluded that

> if we want to remain the preeminent source of information and entertainment, we must acknowledge the increasing dominance of video as the medium of choice worldwide. This conclusion reaffirms our view that Time, Inc. must expand its position in the ownership and creation of video programming.[4]

Munro and N.J. Nicholas Jr., Time's president and chief operating officer (Harvard Business School MBA 1964), described Time's goals in their 1988 Letter to Shareholders, issued after the Time-Warner merger announcement:

> Every smart player in the media and entertainment business will try to compete in the new global marketplace. To do so and achieve the necessary economies of scale, companies will have to grow dramatically. In the media and entertainment business of the future, the winners will own the copyrights to creative products, as well as avenues of distribution. We intend to increase our ownership of both.[5]

---

2. Bill Saporito, "The Inside Story of Time Warner," *Fortune,* November 20, 1989, p. 165.

3. Ibid., p. 166.

4. Memo to board of directors from Dick Munro, June 20, 1988; Temple deposition, Exhibit 1.

5. Time, Inc. 1988 annual report, pp. 1–13.

Size, created through vertical integration, would allow Time to " . . . create, market and disseminate [its] products worldwide . . . and amortize the costs across as many distribution outlets as possible."[6]

Possible Merger Partners

At a July 1988 meeting, Time's investment bankers, Shearson Lehman Hutton and Wasserstein, Perella and Co., presented the board of directors with potential merger partners to implement its long-term strategy: Warner, Paramount, Columbia, Disney, Twentieth Century-Fox, and MCA (see Exhibit 4 for additional information on these companies).

Columbia Pictures International operated primarily in the movie (44% of revenues), television (41% of revenues), and exhibition (13% of revenues) businesses. Columbia's major presence in filmed entertainment was attractive, but it lacked local cable franchise assets.

Disney was a diversified international company engaged in the family entertainment business, with operations in theme parks and resort (64% of revenue), filmed entertainment (30% of revenue), and consumer products (6% of revenue). The investment bankers reminded the board that Disney lacked major cable TV franchise assets and that its resorts accounted for 71% of its operating profits.

Twentieth Century-Fox, a wholly owned subsidiary of News Corp., was in the filmed entertainment business, producing and distributing movies and television programming. Its film library was extensive (2,500 titles), but it, too, lacked major cable franchises.

MCA had seven major business segments: filmed entertainment (51% of revenue), music entertainment (18% of revenue), retail and mail order (12% of revenue), book publishing (6% of revenue), toy products (4% of revenue), broadcasting (3% of revenue), and other operations (4% of revenue). Shearson's presentation to the board noted that an acquisition of MCA would not provide major cable franchise assets and that real estate assets provided a significant proportion of MCA's value. On the positive side, MCA possessed a major presence in filmed and music entertainment.

At the July board meeting, two additional candidates stood out.

Warner Communications

Warner Communications (Warner) was primarily in the communications and entertainment business through operations in filmed entertainment (40% of revenue), recorded music and music publishing (45% of revenue), cable and broadcasting (11% of revenue), and publishing and related distribution (4% of revenue). Through its Warner Brothers subsidiary, Warner produced, financed, and distributed to theaters feature motion pictures; distributed feature films to television stations, networks, and pay television systems; and distributed prerecorded videocassettes and videodiscs. Shearson and Wasserstein indicated that Warner was one of the top three studios for 15 years, and that the consistency of its operating income was tied to the consistency of its studio performance. Exhibit 5 details Warner's historical performance.

Warner Brothers also produced and distributed made-for-television movies, program series, and miniseries for television (e.g., "Murphy Brown" and "The Bugs Bunny/Tweety Show"); in 1989 it had acquired Lorimar Telepictures, one of the

---

6. Ibid.

leading suppliers of original network and first-run syndicated television programming in the United States (e.g., "Dallas" and "People's Court").

Warner Brothers operated a worldwide theatrical distribution organization through which it distributed its own films, as well as films produced by others. The Warner Home Video subsidiary distributed prerecorded videocassettes and videodiscs, containing Warner Brothers films and those of others, to the home video market. Warner Home Video was an industry leader (ranking third), benefiting from wide distribution from large retailers such as Kmart and Sears. Sixty percent of its sales were international.

Warner's recorded music business was conducted primarily through its Warner Brothers Records, Atlantic Recording Corp., WEA, Inc., and Elektra/Asylum/Nonesuch Records subsidiaries, including performers such as Madonna, Randy Travis, and U2. WEA manufactured and distributed compact discs, cassette tapes, and vinyl records domestically and internationally. Warner shared its leadership position in records with CBS-Sony.

Another Warner subsidiary, Warner Cable, operated its cable television business, which comprised primarily the distribution of broadcast television signals and satellite programming to television receivers of subscribers. Warner Cable's franchise included the boroughs of Queens and Brooklyn in the city of New York. With 1.4 million subscribers, Warner was the sixth-largest cable operator.

Warner Publishing published comic books (e.g., "Superman" and "Batman"), and mass market, trade paperback, and hardcover books, and distributed magazines and books through wholesalers in the United States and Canada.

The investment bankers' presentation to the board emphasized Warner's outstanding expertise in operating management; its leadership position in film, records, home video, TV programming, and cable operations; its substantial international business in records and film; and its significant debt capacity. They also outlined potential difficulties with acquiring Warner: Warner's cultural differences and management coordination issues.

Paramount

Paramount (formerly Gulf and Western) had three lines of business: entertainment (39% of revenue), publishing/information (23% of revenue), and consumer/commercial finance (38% of revenue). Exhibit 6 shows Paramount's historical performance by line of business.

The entertainment operations (Paramount Pictures; Famous Players, the company's Canadian theater chain; Cinamerica, the company's 50%-owned domestic theater chain; and Madison Square Garden) produced, financed, and distributed motion pictures, television programming, and prerecorded videocassettes, and operated movie theaters in the United States and Canada. Paramount and MCA jointly owned USA Network, a national advertiser-supported basic cable television network—one of the largest of its kind in the United States.

Paramount also produced and distributed series (e.g., "Cheers" and the original "Star Trek"), specials, and made-for-television movies for network television, first-run syndication, pay and basic cable, and videocassettes. In addition to distributing its own product, Paramount distributed television products acquired from independent producers to the foreign market.

Paramount sold videocassettes for the home video market featuring its movie and television program library, as well as programs made by others. It owned and operated movie theaters in the United States and Canada, and jointly owned theaters in eight other countries, including Australia. It was expanding in the United Kingdom and Ireland.

Paramount's publishing/information line (Simon & Schuster and Prentice-Hall) published hardcover and paperback books for the general public (e.g., the *Harlequin/ Silhouette* romance lines, and trade books such as *The Closing of the American Mind*); published textbooks for elementary schools, high schools, and colleges; and provided information services for business and professions.

Paramount's subsidiary, Associates Corporation of North America, provided consumer finance (including direct installment and revolving credit loans and other consumer finance services), specialized commercial finance (including transportation and industrial equipment financing), and related insurance services in the United States, Canada, the United Kingdom, and Japan. Associates Corp. was the third-largest independent finance company in the United States.

Shearson and Wasserstein viewed Paramount's extensive presence in filmed entertainment and its extensive library and major publishing interests as assets but noted that Paramount would not provide major cable assets and that the finance subsidiary, which represented 41% of total operating profit, did not fit with Time's entertainment strategy.

Management's Decision

Munro thought that Warner was the most attractive merger candidate because of its successful movie studio, Warner Brothers; its existing cable operations, which could combine easily with Time's; its prominent music business (where Time had no presence); and its international distribution assets and capability.[7] The board supported Munro's conclusion that Warner fit best with Time's strategic objectives, although a few directors had some initial reservations. (Exhibit 7 lists Time's directors.) Henry R. Luce III, son of Time's founder, objected to the high compensation of Warner's chief executive officer (CEO), Steven J. Ross. Along with another Time director, Arthur Temple, Luce opposed the new employment contracts and generous compensation terms granted to Time's managers under the terms of the merger. Luce wanted to pursue McGraw-Hill, a major publishing firm. Other directors expressed concerns about the probability of completing the merger and its effect on Time's culture, if successful.[8]

Time's investment bankers valued Warner at $65 to $73 per share. Exhibits 8 through 10 show their discounted cash flow analysis. For comparison purposes, the investment bankers prepared a similar analysis of Time, which they valued at $189 to $212 per share.

Time and Warner opened merger discussions in July 1988. The major issue they needed to resolve was management succession. The majority of Time's outside directors thought that Time's senior management should control Time-Warner. Control of the joint entity was important to the Time board because, first, they wanted Time to remain an independent company in charge of its own destiny, and second, they wanted to preserve the editorial independence of Time's magazines.

---

7. *Paramount Communications v. Time Inc.,* Civil Action Nos. 10866, 10670, and 10935 (consolidated), Delaware Chancery Court, Fed. Sec. L. Rep. (CCH), p. 12.

8. From *Paramount Communications v. Time Inc.,* Civil Action No. 10670, Temple deposition, Exhibits 9 and 4.

TABLE A
Executive Succession Plan for Time-Warner, Inc.

	Steven Ross	*Richard Munro*	*N. J. Nicholas*
1989–1990	Co-CEO Co-Chairman	Co-CEO Co-Chairman	President
1990–1994	Co-CEO	Chairman of Executive Committee	President and Co-CEO
1994–1999	Chairman	Chairman of Executive Committee or Advisor	President and CEO

Sources: Compiled from *Paramount Communications v. Time, Inc.,* Nicholas deposition, Exhibit 6; and summary opinion of Judge William T. Allen, Delaware Chancery Court, C.A. Nos. 10866 and 10670.

Note: Munro and Nicholas received new employment contracts at substantial increases. Munro, for example, would get a $7 million increase over 10 years. Munro had long planned a 1990 retirement but would get an employment contract to serve as chairman of the executive committee. Nicholas would have his current contract, set to expire in 7 years, extended an additional 3 years.

On March 3, 1989, the boards of both companies unanimously approved the transaction (see Exhibit 11 for transaction details). The new company would be named Time-Warner, Inc. and have a board of directors consisting of 24 members, 12 from Time and 12 from Warner. Table A shows how the companies resolved the management succession issue. The merger would be structured as a stock swap; that is, Warner shareholders would receive Time shares in return for Warner shares. The advantage of structuring the deal as a stock swap was that Time would not have to incur any debt to accomplish the merger as it would have if it had made a cash tender offer for Warner shares. In fact, Munro viewed the strength of Time's balance sheet as one of its strategic strengths. A stock merger would ensure that Time would have the financial capacity to take advantage of future opportunities.[9] In addition, Warner insisted on a stock swap in order to preserve its shareholders' ownership in the new corporation. Finally, because the transaction was a stock swap, the accounting treatment of the merger would involve no goodwill and instead be a tax-free merger of equals using "pooling of interest" accounting.

The disadvantage of a stock swap was the amount of time needed to complete the deal. Delay occurred because a stock merger required approval by both Time and Warner shareholders. The Time board scheduled the shareholder vote on the proposed merger for June 23, 1989, the date of the annual shareholders' meeting.

The market reaction to the March 4 merger announcement was mixed. Time's stock price closed at $109.125 on March 3, prior to the merger announcement. The next trading day, the stock price fell to a low of $106.500 but, on speculation of a hostile tender offer, rebounded to close at $107.500. Warner's stock price closed at $45.875 on March 3 and increased to $48.25 on the following trading day.

Analysts reacted positively to the merger announcement. A Shearson Lehman analyst wrote:

> It is my opinion that the major communications companies in the United States must be allowed to combine and vertically integrate in order to compete effectively with their foreign competition. Moreover, it would also appear that combinations via stock transactions that leave the combined company with a stronger balance sheet and greater ability to

---

9. *Paramount Communications v. Time Inc.,* Civil Action No. 10866, Delaware Chancery Court, 1989, Nicholas deposition, Exhibit 6.

expand globally are preferable to leveraged buy-outs, due to the possibility that a cold spell at the box office could result in insufficient cash flow to service the debt.[10]

A Bear Stearns analyst concluded that

> the merger strengthens Time's distribution franchises (ATC, HBO, and Cinemax) immeasurably because of their new association with Warner Bros., one of the world's most successful producers of programming. We don't think the combined company's size and diversification will necessarily make it a more viable global competitor . . . it will, however, have tremendous resources to draw upon—both financial and creative—and we believe there is much untapped opportunity abroad.[11]

Paramount's Offer

Following the March 4 announcement of the Time-Warner merger, several investment banking firms, including Paramount's advisor Morgan Stanley, began recruiting potential hostile bidders for Time. (Exhibit 12 shows market interest rates during that period, March 1989.) Several major companies, including General Electric, Cablevision Systems Corp., Robert M. Bass Group, and Capital Cities/ABC, were rumored to be interested in Time. Time's stock price increased steadily in response to these hostile merger rumors (see Exhibit 13). On June 6, 1989, its stock price closed at $126.000.

Paramount, already in the process of recasting itself as a global entertainment and media business, began the preparations for a hostile bid for Time. Paramount CEO Martin S. Davis's previous transformation of the former Gulf and Western from a "motley conglomerate of manufacturing businesses into a streamlined entertainment and communications concern . . . won praise on Wall Street."[12] In April 1989, Paramount announced plans to sell the Associates Corp., its financial services unit, for $4–5 billion.

On June 7, 1989, following Time's distribution of proxy materials in late May to its shareholders for the required shareholder vote on the proposed Time-Warner merger, Paramount launched its cash bid for Time for $175 a share and indicated its willingness to negotiate all aspects of the offer. Time's stock price immediately increased $44.00, to $170.000 per share, Warner's increased $1.75, to $53.50, and Paramount's rose $0.75, to $54.75.

Paramount conditioned its tender offer on the termination of the Time-Warner merger agreement and share-exchange agreement, receipt of all approvals and franchise transfers relative to Time's programming and cable TV business, financing of the offer, and a majority of shareholders' tendering their shares (see Exhibit 14 for details of Paramount's offer).

Davis, aware that Time's board was concerned about the editorial independence of its magazines, stated that Paramount's educational and consumer publishing units had

---

10. Statement by Alan Kassam, Shearson Lehman Hutton, in *Hearing before the Subcommittee on Economic and Commercial Law of the Committee on the Judiciary House of Representatives,* March 14, 1989, p. 99.

11. Kukowski, of Bear Stearns & Company, March 10, 1989, "Time, Inc. and Warner Communications—Company Report."

12. "Paramount Makes $10.7 Billion Bid for Time, Threatening Warner Communications Merger," *The Wall Street Journal,* June 7, 1989, p. A22.

"a strong record of respecting editorial integrity, [which] has always been the corner-stone to the Time Inc. tradition."[13]

Paramount's offer stunned Munro; he thought that Davis had previously given him "explicit assurances" that Paramount would not make an offer.[14] Munro considered Time's options: it could accept Paramount's bid, go ahead with the Warner merger (subject to shareholder approval), or acquire Warner for cash or a cash and stock combination (such a merger would not require shareholder approval). In preparation for the emergency board meeting, Munro directed his staff to revisit the Warner valuation prepared by the investment bankers. He realized that he would feel more comfortable accepting the Paramount bid if it exceeded the combined value of Time and Warner. If, however, Time should choose instead to continue with the Warner merger, Munro wondered what protection the "business judgment rule"[15] would afford Time in charting its own course.

EXHIBIT 1
History of Selected Acquisitions of Time, Inc.

Date Announced	Company Acquired	Business	Price	Time's Stock Price Near the Acquisition Announcement	
				Day Before	Day After
5/22/78	Inland Container Corp.	Maker of containerboards, corrugated containers	$272 million	$ 47.750	$ 44.875
6/18/82	Great American Reserve Insurance Co.	Life and health insurance; spun off with Inland Container in 1984	$76 million	$ 29.125	$ 28.625
2/21/85	Southern Progress Corp.	Magazine publisher, book marketer	$480 million	$ 49.625	$ 48.500
12/09/85	Group W Cable, Inc.	Cable TV system; Time and Tele-Communications own 25%–35% each	Cash and assumption of debt; total of $1.75 billion	$ 61.250	$ 59.625
10/14/86	Scott, Foresman & Co.	Textbook publisher	$520 million	$ 76.625	$ 73.500
10/20/88	Whittle Communications	Magazine publishing, advertiser-supported TV	$185 million	$118.750	$116.875

Sources: Compiled from *Moody's Industrial Manual, The New York Times, The Wall Street Journal, The Washington Post, Investment Dealers Digest, Inc., Interactive Data Corp.,* and CRSP daily stock files.

---

13. Ibid., p. A22.

14. Ibid.

15. Historically, the business judgment rule provided managers protection from shareholder intervention in corporate decision making. A ruling by the Delaware Supreme Court, however, limited managerial discretion in takeover situations,

> The Revlon court held that when sale or breakup of a target corporation becomes "inevitable" the directors must act as auctioneers whose primary responsibility is to realize the best sale price for the benefit of stockholders. The directors must deal fairly and equally with competing bidders and must not close off active bidding without significant gain to shareholders. [Steven G. Bradbury, "Corporate Auctions and Directors' Fiduciary Duties: A Third-Generation Business Judgment Rule," *Michigan Law Review,* October 1988, p. 111.]

Munro wondered whether this ruling would obligate Time to auction itself to the highest bidder.

EXHIBIT 2
Time's Income Statement (millions of dollars)

	For Years Ended December 31,				
	1984	*1985*	*1986*	*1987*	*1988*
Magazines[a]					
Revenues	$1,321	$1,482	$1,576	$1,621	$1,752
Operating income	180	155	153	276	279
Identifiable assets	212	582	663	694	923
ROIA (operating income/identifiable assets)	0.85	0.27	0.23	0.40	0.30
ROS (operating income/revenues)	0.14	0.10	0.10	0.17	0.16
Books					
Revenues	$ 491	$ 552	$ 663	$ 954	$ 891
Operating income	60	83	73	85	100
Identifiable assets	278	468	1,151	1,156	1,225
ROIA (operating income/identifiable assets)	0.22	0.18	0.06	0.07	0.08
ROS (operating income/revenues)	0.12	0.15	0.11	0.09	0.11
Programming					
Revenues	$ 810	$ 854	$ 952	$ 971	$1,122
Operating income	124	115	99	116	136
Identifiable assets	481	665	824	1,054	1,095
ROIA (operating income/identifiable assets)	0.26	0.17	0.12	0.11	0.12
ROS (operating income/revenues)	0.15	0.13	0.10	0.12	0.12
Cable Television					
Revenues	$ 510	$ 584	$ 637	$ 714	$ 812
Operating income	86	100	130	162	180
Identifiable assets	976	1,024	1,107	1,195	1,505
ROIA (operating income/identifiable assets)	0.09	0.10	0.12	0.11	0.12
ROS (operating income/revenues)	0.17	0.17	0.20	0.18	0.22
Consolidated					
Revenues[b]	$3,067	$3,404	$3,762	$4,193	$4,507
Operating income[c]	391	388	308	582	653
Identifiable assets	2,615	3,072	4,230	4,424	4,913
ROIA (operating income/identifiable assets)	0.15	0.13	0.07	0.13	0.13
ROS (operating income/revenues)	0.13	0.11	0.08	0.14	0.14

Sources: Compiled from SEC filings (Time, Inc. 10-Ks) and Time, Inc. annual reports.

a. Segment operating income = Segment revenue – Operating expenses – Depreciation – Amortization.

b. Consolidated revenue does not include intersegment sales from the programming segment to the cable TV segment.

c. Consolidated operating income = Σ segment operating income – Corporate expense.

EXHIBIT 3
Consolidated Balance Sheet as of December 31, 1988

	Time ($ millions)	Warner ($ millions)	Paramount ($ millions)
Assets			
Current assets			
Cash and equivalents	$ 121	$ 229	$ 616
Receivables	506	940	668
Inventories	299	459	416
Prepaid programming	190	na	na
Prepaid promotion	205	na	na
Other	na	141	447
Total current assets	$1,321	$1,769	$2,147
Investments	740	na	na
Net property, plant, and equipment	1,399	999	414
Goodwill and intangible assets	986	na	na
Deferred charges and other assets	na	688	na
Programming and other assets	467	1,143	2,817
Total assets	$4,913	$4,599	$5,378
Liabilities and Shareholders' Equity			
Accounts payable and accrued expenses	$ 734	$1,489	$ 964
Other	171	44	117
Total current liabilities	$ 905	$1,533	$1,081
Unearned portion of paid subscriptions	424	na	na
Long-term debt	1,485	721	1,390
Deferred income taxes	511	na	na
Other liabilities	229	na	641
Accounts payable due after one year	na	552	na
Total shareholders' equity	$1,359	$1,793	$2,266
Total liabilities and shareholders' equity	$4,913	$4,599	$5,378

Source: Compiled from SEC filings (10-Ks) and company annual reports.

Consolidated Operating and Shareholder Information

	Time	Warner	Paramount
Times interest earned[a]	8.5	29.0	7.3
Debt ratio[b]	0.17	0.07	0.18
Market-to-book[c]	5.3	5.2	2.8
Market value of equity[d]	7250	9579	6332
Stock price			
June 6, 1989	126	51¾	54
52 weeks	135½–93	52¾–32⅜	56½–37⅛
Beta	1.1	1.2	1.1
Debt rating	Aa3	A3	A2

Sources: Compiled from *Value Line, Moody's Industrial Manual,* CRSP, 10-Ks, and annual reports.

a. (EBIT + Depreciation)/(Net interest expense) for fiscal year 1988.

b. Long-term debt/(Long-term debt + Market equity); Debt from fiscal year 1988, market equity as of June 6, 1989.

c. (Stock price June 6, 1989)/(Book value of equity per share 1988).

d. Market value of equity = Number of common shares outstanding × June 6, 1989, stock price.

EXHIBIT 4
Attributes of Major Companies Involved in Entertainment Industry

Company	Film and TV Production	Size of Film Library	Cable Programming	Film Distribution	Theaters	Home Video	TV Stations	Cable Systems	Other	Entertainment Revenue FY 1988	Market Value Debt + Equity (year-end 1988)
Time			HBO TBS 14% Cinemax, Movietime 22%					ATC 82% 3.9 million subscribers	Magazines, book publishing	$1,934	$ 8,081
Warner	Yes	1,400	TBS 11%	Worldwide	Cinamerica 50%	Yes	BHC 42.5%	Warner Cable 1.5 million subscribers	Recorded music, book publishing, comics	$4,067	$ 7,752
Paramount	Yes	820	USA 50% MSG	Domestic; international through United International Pictures, 33%	Cinamerica 50% Cinema International Corp. 50%	Yes	5 TV stations		Book publishing Financial services	$1,862	$ 6,749
MCA	Yes	3,000+	USA 50%	Domestic; international through United International Pictures 33%	Cineplex Odeon 50% Cinema International Corp. 49%	Yes	WWOR-NY		Theme parks, publishing, recorded music	$2,290	$ 5,274
Columbia Pictures	Yes	2,700		Worldwide	Loews, USA	RCA/ Columbia				$1,146	$ 3,054
Disney	Yes	610	Disney Sky 50%	Worldwide			KHJ-TV in Los Angeles		Theme parks, consumer products	$3,438	$10,608

(continued)

EXHIBIT 4 *(concluded)*

Company	Film and TV Production	Size of Film Library	Cable Programming	Film Distribution	Theaters	Home Video	TV Stations	Cable Systems	Other	Entertainment Revenue FY 1988	Market Value Debt + Equity (year-end 1988)
News Corp	20th Century Fox	2,500	Sky 50%	Worldwide		Yes	7 TV stations Fox Network		Books, magazines, and newspapers	$1,265	$ 6,579
MGM/UA	Yes	1,034		Domestic; international through United International Pictures 33%		Yes			Aircraft Finance Co. 49%	$ 675	$ 1,516
GE	TV only		CNBC 50% after 4/89				NBC 7 affiliates			$3,638	$44,121
Capital Cities/ABC	TV only		ESPN other interests				ABC 8 affiliates			$3,750	$ 7,770
CBS, Inc.	TV only						CBS 5 affiliates			$2,778	$ 4,997
Tele-Communications, Inc.			Interests		Yes			8 million subscribers		$2,143	$10,085
Orion Pictures	Yes	Large								$ 395	$ 680
Turner Broadcasting	No	Owns MGM library	CNN, TBS TNT				WTBS			$ 807	$ 3,384
Viacom			NTV, Nick, other interests	Large in TV distribution	Yes		4	Large		$1,259	$ 4,813

Source: Compiled from analyst reports (Baliz and Zorn, Inc., Report on Time, Inc., November 21, 1988; Wertheim Schroder & Co. Industry Report, March 1, 1989; Drexel Industry Report, October 17, 1989; S.E.C. filings (10-Ks).

EXHIBIT 5
Warner Communications' Income Statement (millions of dollars)

	For Years Ended December 31,				
	1984	*1985*	*1986*	*1987*	*1988*
Filmed Entertainment					
Revenues	$1,090	$1,201	$1,251	$1,355	$1,571
Operating income	150	160	172	176	207
Identifiable assets	779	950	1077	1193	1536
ROIA (Operating income/Identifiable assets)	0.19	0.17	0.16	0.15	0.13
ROS (Operating income/Revenue)	0.14	0.13	0.14	0.13	0.13
Music					
Revenues	$ 818	$ 912	$1,139	$1,530	$2,040
Operating income	90	112	151	213	319
Identifiable assets	384	398	453	998	1,290
ROIA (Operating income/Identifiable assets)	0.23	0.28	0.33	0.21	0.25
ROS (Operating income/Revenue)	0.11	0.12	0.13	0.14	0.16
Cable TV					
Revenues	$ 363	$ 296	$ 326	$ 387	$ 456
Operating income	(106)	(9)	16	42	72
Identifiable assets	213	300	753	794	994
ROIA (Operating income/Identifiable assets)	−0.50	−0.03	0.02	0.05	0.07
ROS (Operating income/Revenue)	−0.29	−0.03	0.05	0.11	0.16
Publishing					
Revenues	$ 115	$ 122	$ 133	$ 130	$ 139
Operating income	11	14	12	11	11
Identifiable assets	27	50	55	59	98
ROIA (Operating income/Identifiable assets)	0.41	0.28	0.22	0.19	0.11
ROS (Operating income/Revenue)	0.10	0.11	0.09	0.08	0.08
Lorimar[a]					
Revenues	$ 334	$ 466	$ 571	$ 637	$ 525
Operating income	150	67	36	(39)	(362)
ROS (Operating income/Revenue)	0.45	0.14	.06	(.06)	(.69)
Consolidated[b]					
Revenues	$2,023	$2,235	$2,848	$3,404	$4,206
EBIT	208	252	312	399	531
Interest expense, net	139	59	55	20	26
Gain on sale of subsidiaries	(611)	208	62	40	35
Profit before tax	69	401	319	419	541
Profit after tax	(590)	195	252	328	423

Source: Compiled from SEC filings (Warner Communication's 10-Ks); annual reports; and *Paramount Communications, Inc. and KDS Acquisition Corp. v. Time, Inc.* Civil Action No. 10670, Finkelstein deposition, Exhibit 7.

a. Warner acquired Lorimar-Telepictures in January 1989; "We anticipate that in the near future, Lorimar in particular will make major earnings contributions . . . as the demand for worldwide TV programming increases dramatically." (Warner 1988 annual report.)

b. Does not include Lorimar.

EXHIBIT 6
Paramount Communications'[a] Income Statement (millions of dollars)

	For Years Ended December 31,				
	1984	*1985*	*1986*	*1987*	*1988*
Entertainment					
Revenues	$1,266	$1,063	$1,154	$1,850	$1,862
Operating income	109	69	129	297	252
ROS (Operating income/Revenue)	0.09	0.06	0.11	0.16	0.14
Publishing/Information					
Revenues	$ 317	$ 798	$ 949	$1.074	$1,194
Operating income	44	104	141	162	180
ROS (Operating income/Revenue)	0.14	0.13	0.15	0.15	0.15
Consumer/Commercial Finance					
Revenues	$1,236	$1,460	$1,687	$1,778	$2,052
Operating income	188	251	290	324	372
ROS (Operating income/Revenue)	0.15	0.17	0.17	0.18	0.18
Consolidated					
Revenues	$2,819	$3,321	$3,790	$4,702	$5,108
Operating income	283	358	496	722	748
Interest and other	(68)	(122)	(110)	(114)	(107)
Earnings before income taxes	215	236	386	608	641
Provision for income tax	76	84	158	253	256
Earnings before extraordinary items	139	152	228	355	385
Extraordinary items	0	0	39	0	0
Earnings from discounted operations	99	96	0	0	0
Net earnings	$ 238	$ 248	$ 267	$ 355	$ 385
ROS (Operating income/Revenue)	0.10	0.11	0.13	0.15	0.15
Identifiable assets	4,203	4,064	4,243	4,928	5,378
ROIA (Operating income/Identifiable assets)	0.07	0.09	0.12	0.15	0.14

Sources: Compiled from SEC filings (Gulf & Western 10-Ks) and annual reports.

a. Formerly Gulf and Western.

EXHIBIT 7
Board of Directors, Time, Inc., 1989

Name and Year Appointed	Background	Comments
James F. Beré (1979)	Chairman of the board and chief executive officer (CEO) of Borg-Warner Corporation	Also director of Temple-Inland.
Michael D. Dingman (1978)	Chairman and CEO of the Henley Group, Inc.	Also director of Ford.
Edward S. Finkelstein (1984)	Chairman and CEO of Macy and Co., Inc.	Also director of Chase Manhattan.
Henry C. Goodrich (1978)	Former chairman of Sonat Inc. (diversified natural resources company)	Also director of Temple-Inland. Not nominated to Time-Warner board. Resigned June 11, 1989.
Clifford J. Grum (1980)	President, CEO, and director of Temple-Inland Inc.	Not nominated to Time-Warner board. Resigned June 11. 1989.
Matina Horner (1975)	Former president of Radcliffe College	
David T. Kearns (1978)	Chairman and CEO of Xerox Corporation	Also director of Chase Manhattan.
Gerald M. Levin (1988)[a]	Vice chairman of the board; previously executive vice president of Time, Inc. for corporate strategy, planning, and administration	
Henry R. Luce III (1967)	President of The Henry Luce Foundation, Inc. and son of the founder of Time, Inc.	Controlled 4.2% of outstanding Time stock.
Jason D. McManus (1988)[a]	Editor-in-chief of Time, Inc.	
J. Richard Munro (1978)[a]	Chairman and CEO of Time, Inc.	Also director of Genentech, IBM, and Mobil.
N.J. Nicholas Jr. (1963)[a]	President and chief operating officer (COO) of Time, Inc.	Also director of Bankers Trust and Xerox.
John R. Opel (1984)	Former chairman and CEO of IBM Corporation	Also director of IBM and Xerox.
Donald S. Perkins (1979)	Former chairman of Jewel Companies, Inc. (a diversified retailer)	Also director of Temple-Inland.
Arthur Temple (1973)	Chairman of Temple-Inland Inc.	Resigned following Warner merger vote in March 1989. Controlled 1.1% of outstanding Time stock.
Clifton R. Wharton Jr. (1982)	Chairman and CEO of Teachers Insurance and Annuity Association–College Retirement Equities Fund	Also director of Ford and NYSE. Not nominated to Time-Warner board. Resigned June 11, 1989.

Sources: Compiled from S.E.C. filings (Time, Inc. Proxy, May 22, 1989; Time, Inc. 10-K, for fiscal year ending December 31, 1989); and *Who's Who in Business.*

a. Also an officer of Time, Inc.

EXHIBIT 8

Warner Pro Forma Free Cash Flow by Segment (millions of dollars)[a]

	1989	1990	1991	1992	1993	1994	1995	1996	1997	1998
Filmed entertainment ..	$104.00	$118.60	$139.70	$164.80	$180.10	$ 196.20	$ 213.70	$ 232.90	$ 253.80	$ 276.50
Music/music publishing	307.50	307.60	324.20	343.20	354.40	392.70	432.50	475.10	522.00	573.50
Cable TV	42.10	151.50	181.50	205.80	233.70	266.70	298.80	327.60	355.70	386.00
Publishing	15.20	8.80	8.90	9.50	10.10	10.80	11.60	12.40	13.30	14.20
Lorimar........	14.00	67.50	85.00	124.70	137.20	137.40	96.50	106.20	116.80	128.50
Total	$482.80	$654.00	$739.30	$848.00	$915.50	$1,003.80	$1,053.10	$1,154.20	$1,261.60	$1,378.70

a. Free cash flow = Sales − Operating expenses − Taxes + Depreciation and amortization + Deferred taxes − Capital expenditures − Increase in film inventory − Increase in working capital.

Discounted Cash Flow Valuation of Warner Communications (millions of dollars)

	Terminal EBIT Multiples[b]				
Discount Rate	**9x**	**10x**	**11x**	**12x**	
10%	$ 5,934	$ 5,934	$ 5,934	$ 5,934	Present value of cash flows[a]
	8,408	9,342	10,276	11,210	Present value of terminal value
	$14,342	$15,276	$16,210	$17,144	
11%	5,696	5,696	5,696	5,696	Present value of cash flows
	7,680	8,533	10,276	10,240	Present value of terminal value
	$13,376	$14,230	$15,972	$15,936	
12%	5,473	5,473	5,473	5,473	Present value of cash flows
	7,021	7,801	8,582	9,362	Present value of terminal value
	$12,495	$13,275	$14,055	$14,835	
13%	5,265	5,265	5,265	5,265	Present value of cash flows
	6,424	7,138	7,852	8,565	Present value of terminal value
	$11,689	$12,402	$13,116	$13,830	

Sources: Compiled from Wasserstein, Perella & Co, Inc. and Shearson Lehman Hutton, Inc. presentation at the March 3, 1989, Time board of directors meeting.

Presentation obtained from *Paramount Communications, Inc. and KDS Acquisition Corp. v. Time, Inc.* Civil Action No. 10670, Finkelstein deposition, Exhibit 7.

a. Casewriter's note: Present value of free cash flows shown in above table.

b. Casewriter's note: Terminal value apparently based on multiples of 1988 EBIT, not 1988 free cash flow.

EXHIBIT 9
Discounted Cash Flow Valuation of Warner Communications (millions of dollars)

Value of the firm[a]	$11,689–$13,116
Adjustments	
Add	
Investments	1,337.5
Cash and equivalents	320.3
Overfunded pensions	26.3
Less	
Short-term debt	32.2
Long-term debt	1,230.3
Corporate overhead	350
Total net adjustments	71.6
Value of equity	$11,760–$13,188
Share of outstanding (fully diluted)	183.5MM
Value per share	$64.08–$71.86

Source: Compiled from Wasserstein, Perella & Co, Inc. and Shearson Lehman Hutton, Inc. presentation at the March 3, 1989, Time board of directors meeting.

Presentation obtained from Finkelstein, *Paramount Communications, Inc. and KDS Acquisition Corp. v. Time, Inc.* Civil Action No. 10670, Exhibit 7.

a. Casewriter's note: based on 13% discount rate.

EXHIBIT 10
Comparable Transaction Acquisition Analysis: Premiums Paid in Recent Acquisitions by Industry[a]

Industry	Number of Acquisitions	Average EBIT Multiple Paid
Cable programming 1		
Film 5		19
Music 1		10
Book publishing 9		15
Magazine publishing 9		13

Source: Compiled from Wasserstein, Perella & Co., Inc. and Shearson Lehman Hutton, Inc. presentation at the March 3, 1989, Time board of directors meeting.

Presentation obtained from *Paramount Communications, Inc. and KDS Acquisition Corp. v. Time, Inc.* Civil Action No. 10670, Finkelstein deposition, Exhibit 7.

a. Cable systems typically valued as multiple of number of subscribers instead of EBIT. In 1989 the average value was $2,209 per subscriber.

EXHIBIT 11
Initial Terms of Time-Warner Merger Agreement, March 3, 1989

Time, Inc. agreed to exchange .465 of a share of its common stock for each share of Warner common stock and exchange, for Warner's convertible preferred stock, securities having the same characteristics as those of Warner's preferred stock. Time had 57 million shares of common stock outstanding on March 31, 1989; Warner had 178.3 million shares. Therefore, Warner shareholders would receive 82.9 million shares in Time-Warner in exchange for their 178.3 million Warner shares. Following the merger, a total of 139.9 million shares of new Time-Warner stock would exist.

	Shares Outstanding (March 1989)	Number of Time-Warner Shares Issued in Exchange for Warner Shares	Share Ownership in New Time-Warner (#)	(%)
Time	57.0mm	82.9mm	57.0mm	41
Warner	178.3mm	—	82.9mm	59

To protect against the threat of a hostile bidder, the merger plan called for a Share Exchange Agreement. The Share Exchange Agreement was a type of poison pill where the companies agreed to exchange 7.1 million shares of Time common stock for 17.3 million shares of Warner common stock. This provision would be triggered if a hostile bidder sought more than 25% of Time before the merger was completed. The merger agreement also stated that "Time may not solicit or encourage or take any other action to facilitate any inquiries on the making of any proposal which constitutes or may . . . lead to, any takeover proposal." The only exception to such provision would occur if a hostile tender offer for 25% or more of Time's stock was announced (or 10% of its stock was purchased), at which time, Time could, after consultation with Warner, communicate with the offeror (or stockholder). Such an occurrence would not excuse Time's performance under the merger agreement, but would give Warner a way out.

Time, Inc. had obtained written assurances from a group of banks that, if necessary, the banks were prepared to arrange up to $5 billion in financing for Time, Inc., with the specific terms and conditions subject to negotiation.

The merger required shareholder approval by both corporations. The Time shareholders were scheduled to vote on the merger agreement at a meeting on June 23, 1989. Proxy information in advance of the meeting was dated May 22, 1989, and released on May 23, 1989.

EXHIBIT 12
Market Interest Rates

Yield Curve March 1989

1-year Treasury Bills	9.43%
7-year Treasury Bonds	9.30
10-year Treasury Bonds	8.91
30-year Treasury Bonds	8.91

Corporate Bond Rates March 1989 (industrial average)

10-year AAA	9.81%
10-year AA	10.18
10-year A	10.59
10-year BBB	10.96
10-year B	12.01
10-year B	12.79

Sources: Compiled from S&P Security Price Record (aka S&P Statistical Service), 1992; and Interactive Data Service.

EXHIBIT 13
Time, Inc. and Warner Communications: Daily Stock Price, 1989

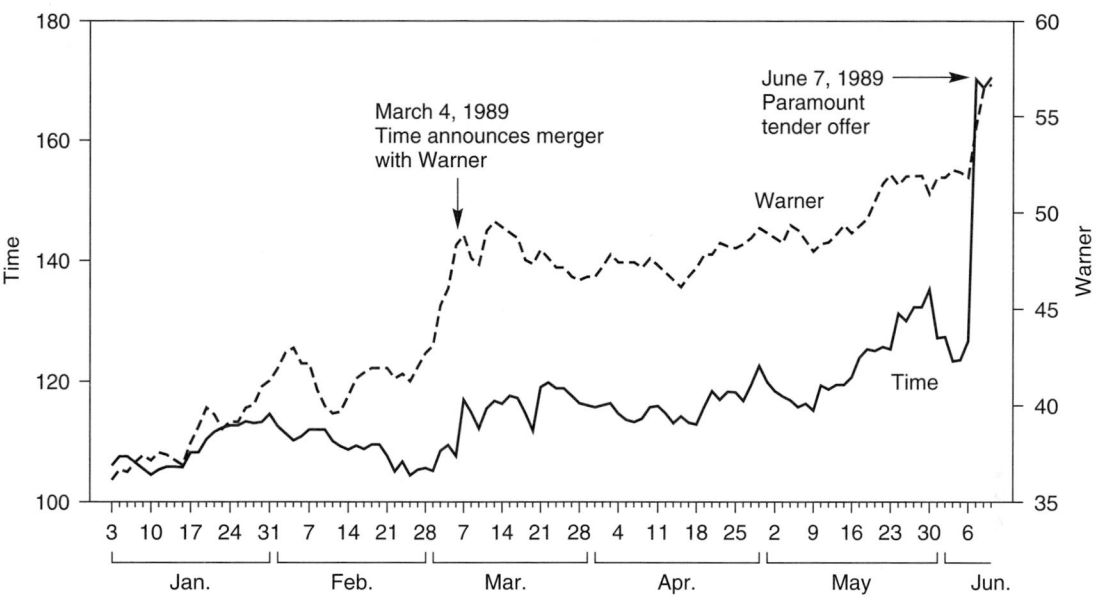

Source: Interactive Data Corp.

EXHIBIT 14
Terms of Paramount Communications' Offer for Time, Inc., June 7, 1989

On June 7, 1989, KDS Acquisition Corporation, an indirect, wholly owned subsidiary of Paramount Communications, Inc. offered to purchase all outstanding shares of Time, Inc. common stock at a price of $175 in cash per share.

Paramount conditioned its offer on the following:

1. A minimum number of shares tendered.
2. Termination of the Time-Warner merger agreement, or allowing the agreement to be subject to shareholder approval, where Paramount controlled a sufficient number of shares to deny such approval.
3. Termination or invalidation of the Share Exchange Agreement without Time's incurring any liabilities, and removal of Time's poison pill (i.e., its Share Exchange Agreement).
4. Obtaining approvals from cities and towns for the transfer of cable licenses from Time to Paramount, as well as on obtaining license transfers from the Federal Communications Commission for such privileges as microwave relays and radio operating permits associated with cable transmission. Because this transfer might be lengthy, Paramount established a voting trust to hold Time shares until it was completed. The trust would pay Time shareholders immediately.

Citibank, which would provide $1 billion of senior bank debt financing for the offer, stated it was highly confident of its ability to arrange for a syndicate of lenders to provide the balance on a senior-debt basis.

	Paramount						
	Before Acquisition		**Payment in Acquisition**	**After Acquisition**		**After Debt Reduction from Asset Sales**[a]	
	($ bil.)	*(%)*	*($ bil.)*	*($ bil.)*	*(%)*	*($ bil.)*	*(%)*
All borrowed money . . .	$1.7	43%	$10.7	$12.4	84%	$ 8.9	79%
Owners' equity	2.3	57%		2.3	16%	2.3	21%
	$4.0			$14.7		$11.2	

Sources: Compiled from *WSJ Index;* Paramount SEC filings; and Time/Warner/Paramount Battle, a company report by E.A. Fruelich, June 22, 1989.

a. Assumes sale of The Associates for 3.5 billion, net of taxes.

John M. Case Company

In March 1985, Anthony W. Johnson was working on a proposal to purchase his employer's firm, the John M. Case Company. The Case Company, with corporate headquarters in Dover, Delaware, was a leading manufacturer of commercial desk calendars. Mr. Johnson, vice president of finance and administration, considered the company an excellent acquisition opportunity, provided the owner's asking price was acceptable and satisfactory financing for the transaction could be arranged.

Background

A few weeks earlier, John M. Case, board chairman, president, and sole owner of the company, had informed his senior management group that he intended to retire from business and was about to initiate a campaign to sell the company. For several years, his physician had been urging him to avoid all stress and strain; now Mr. Case had decided to sever his business connections and devote his time to travel and a developing interest in art history and collection.

On the basis of previous offers for the company, Mr. Case had decided to ask for $20 million, with a minimum of $16 million immediately payable in cash. He thought acquisitive corporations should find this price attractive, and he believed it would be easy to dispose of the business.

Mr. Case had assured the management group that its jobs and benefits would be well protected by the terms of any sale contract that he might negotiate. Despite his faith in Mr. Case's good intentions, Mr. Johnson had been quite apprehensive about the prospect of having his career placed in the hands of an unknown outsider. However, after some reflection, Mr. Johnson had concluded that the sale decision should be viewed as an opportunity to acquire control of a highly profitable enterprise. Purchase of the Case Company would not only ensure career continuity but also provide a chance to turn a profit in the company's equity. Mr. Johnson had realized that his

Copyright © 1990 by the President and Fellows of Harvard College.
Harvard Business School case 291–008.

personal financial resources were far too limited to allow him to bid alone for control of the company. Consequently, he had persuaded August Haffenreffer, vice president–marketing; William Wright, vice president–manufacturing; and Richard Bennink, the controller, to join him in trying to buy the company, rather than standing by while control passed to an outsider. In response to Mr. Johnson's request, Mr. Case had agreed to defer all steps to merchandise the company until he had accepted or rejected a purchase proposal from the management group, provided this proposal was submitted within six weeks.

Because of his background in finance and his role in initiating the project, Mr. Johnson had assumed primary responsibility for assessing the profit potential of the opportunity and for structuring a workable financial plan for the acquisition. Since Mr. Case had not yet solicited bids from other potential purchasers, Mr. Johnson believed that it would be most realistic to regard Mr. Case's stated sale terms as fixed and nonnegotiable.

Mr. Johnson, then, needed to determine whether he could meet the asking price and still realize a profit commensurate with the risk in this purchase. Moreover, he needed to figure out how the management group, with roughly $500,000 among them, could finance the purchase and at the same time obtain voting control of the company.

Thus far Mr. Johnson had managed to obtain a tentative commitment for a $6 million unsecured bank term loan, and he had persuaded Mr. Case to accept unsecured notes for the noncash portion of the purchase price. He was still faced with the problem of raising close to $10 million on an equity base of $500,000 without giving up control to outsiders.

Mr. Johnson now had three weeks in which to come up with a workable financial plan or lose the deal. He was acutely aware that his own life savings and those of his associates would ride on his judgment and ingenuity.

Description of the Company

The John M. Case Company was the leading producer of business calendars in the United States. The company was established in 1920 by Robert Case (Mr. Case's paternal grandfather) to do contract printing of commercial calendars. Mr. Case had joined the organization in 1946 upon graduation from college, and in 1951 he had inherited the company.

Under Mr. Case's leadership, primary emphasis was placed on controlled expansion in the established line of business. By 1984 the company, with an estimated 60–65% share of its market, had been for a decade the largest company in a small but lucrative industry. Operations had been profitable every year since 1932, and sales had increased every year since 1955. In 1984, the most recently completed fiscal year, earnings had amounted to $1,966,000 on sales of approximately $15.3 million. The return on average invested capital in 1984 was about 20%. Over the past 5 years, sales had increased at a 7% compound rate, while earnings, benefiting from substantial cost reductions, had more than doubled. Exhibits 1–3 present recent financial figures for the company.

Products

As noted, the Case Company's principal products were commercial desk calendars. The company designed and manufactured disposable-page and flipover-page desk calendar pads in a variety of sizes. The company also sold desk calendar bases, which were purchased from outside suppliers who manufactured to Case's specifications. In 1984 standard desk calendar pads had contributed approximately 80% of net sales and 90% of earnings before taxes. Bases accounted for 10% of sales, and miscellaneous merchandise, chiefly wall calendars, accounted for the rest.

Sales were highly seasonal. Most final consumers did not start using calendars for the forthcoming year until November or December of the current year. Consequently, about 90% of Case's total shipments typically took place between June and December, with about 60% of shipments concentrated in the third quarter and 25% in the fourth quarter. Since calendar pads were dated, any merchandise remaining in stock at the end of the selling season was subject to rapid obsolescence.

Manufacturing

The production process was relatively simple, employing widely available skills and technology. High-speed offset presses were used to print appropriate dates on paper purchased in bulk from outside suppliers; the printed sheets were then trimmed to the required sizes and stored for shipment. The entire process was highly automated and was characterized by high fixed costs, high setup costs, and low variable costs.

In spite of highly seasonal sales, the Case Company operated on level production schedules. Since the product lines were for all practical purposes undifferentiated from competing lines and the relevant production technology was well known, the capacity to sell on the basis of price, while achieving a good return on invested capital, was regarded by management as a critical success factor in the industry. Minimum production costs were therefore imperative.

Level production enabled the company to take advantage of extremely long production runs and thus to minimize down time, the investment in equipment, expensive setups, and the use of transient labor. Level production, in conjunction with the company's dominant market share, provided scale economies well beyond the reach of any competitor.

The combination of seasonal sales and level production resulted in the accumulation of large seasonal stocks. However, by concentrating the sales effort in the middle six months of the year, the Case Company was able to circumvent most of the risk usually associated with level production in a seasonal company in return for modest purchase discounts. Since customers could easily predict their needs for Case products as their budgets for the forthcoming year took shape, they were willing to place their orders well in advance of shipment. As a result, Case could manufacture against a firm backlog in the last few months of the year and thus circumvent the risk of overproducing and ending the year with large stocks of outdated finished goods.

The company maintained production facilities in nearby Wilmington, Delaware, and, through a wholly owned subsidiary, in Puerto Rico. Earnings of the Puerto Rican subsidiary, which sold all its output to the U.S. parent, were entirely exempt from U.S. taxes and until 1992 would be exempt from all Puerto Rican taxes. The tax exemption on Puerto Rican production accounted for Case's unusually low income tax rate. All Case plants and equipment were modern and excellently maintained. A major capital expenditures program, completed in 1983, had resulted in the company's having the most modern facilities in the industry. At the predicted rate of future sales growth, Mr. Wright, the chief production officer, did not anticipate any need for substantial capital expenditures for at least 5 or 6 years.

None of the company's work force was represented by labor unions.

Marketing

As its products were nondifferentiable, Case's marketing program concentrated on providing high-quality customer service and a uniformly high-quality product. Case products were sold nationwide. Geographically, the company was strongest in the Northeast, the Southwest, and the far West. Large accounts were handled by the company's five salespeople, and smaller accounts were serviced by office supply wholesalers. Roughly 10% of sales had historically gone to the federal government.

Even though the product was undifferentiated, Mr. Haffenreffer, the marketing vice president, believed that it did have some significant advantages from a marketing viewpoint. Selling costs were extremely low, as consumption of the product over the course of a year automatically generated a large replacement demand without any effort on the part of Case. About 95% of total sales generally consisted of reorders from the existing customer base, with only 5% of sales going to new customers. Historically, over 98% of the customer base annually reordered Case pads and, as needed, additional Case bases. By dealing with only one source of supply, the customer was able to take maximum advantage of discounts for volume purchases. As the product was virtually immune to malfunction and the resultant customer dissatisfaction, once Case bases had been installed, the typical buyer never had any incentive to spend time and money on a search for alternative sources. Consumption of Case products was, in addition, extremely insensitive to budget cuts, economy drives, consumer whims, and the like. The desk calendar was a small-ticket but high-priority item. It was an essential in the work routines of most of its users, and it was not expensive enough to yield a meaningful reward in savings to would-be cutters. As a dated product, the desk calendar, unlike many other office products, represented a nondeferrable purchase.

Finances

Mr. Case had been greatly influenced by his father's memories of the Great Depression, and he steadfastly refused to consider leveraging his equity in the company. Accordingly, the company operated with an all-equity capitalization. The size of the capital budget was determined by the volume of internally generated funds in conjunction with Mr. Case's decision on how much to withdraw in the form of dividends. Dividend payments had sometimes been sharply contracted to accommodate capital investment opportunities. Over the past 3 years, however, internally generated funds had been plentiful, and dividends had averaged 70% of net earnings.

Like the capital budget, the seasonal accumulation of inventories and receivables was financed from internal sources. To minimize warehousing expenses for finished goods, Case provided generous credit terms to customers who accepted early shipments. Payments for June–October shipments were not due until the end of November, although substantial discounts were offered for earlier payment. The collection period averaged 60 days. Credit experience was excellent, and generous credit terms were considered a key factor in the company's competitive success.

Although the company had not resorted to seasonal borrowing in nearly 10 years, it maintained for emergency purposes two $2 million lines of credit at major Eastern banks. Exhibit 4 shows 1984 working capital balances by month.

The Case Company's credit with suppliers was excellent. All trade obligations were promptly paid when due.

Management

The senior management team consisted of Mr. Case plus the four individuals interested in buying the company. Transfer of ownership to the latter would not occasion much change in the de facto management of the organization. Although Mr. Case continued to exercise the final authority on all major issues of policy and strategy, over the past few years he had gradually withdrawn from day-to-day affairs and now spent much of his time in Europe and Puerto Rico. As Mr. Case had relaxed his grip on the company's affairs, he had increasingly delegated the general management of the firm to Mr. Johnson.

Compensation was generous at the senior executive level. Mr. Case drew an annual salary of $400,000; his four key subordinates received an average salary of $90,000. In addition, the four senior executives received annual bonuses which aggregated 10% of earnings before taxes and bonuses.

The members of the purchasing group were all in their thirties and early forties and among them represented close to 50 years' experience in the business. A graduate of a leading school of business administration, Mr. Johnson, aged 40, had worked for 5 years in the venture capital department of a large Eastern bank and for 2 years in his own management consulting firm before joining the Case Company.

Company Prospects

The overall prospect was for continued growth at a steady, though unspectacular, pace. The rate of Case sales growth, management believed, was closely correlated with the rate of growth in the size of the domestic white-collar work force. Given expectations of a continuing shift of labor out of agricultural and blue-collar and into white-collar occupations, this suggested that the company should grow somewhat faster than the economy as a whole. Assuming no material changes in product lines or market share, management thought sales growth would average about 5–6% per year in the foreseeable future. Profit margins were expected to improve somewhat over the next few years, as volume expanded and an increasing proportion of new production was directed to the tax-exempt Puerto Rican facility.

Competition

Although the commercial desk calendar industry was profitable indeed for its leading participant, it was not, in the opinion of Case management, an attractive area for potential new competitors. At that time, the industry was divided between Case, with roughly a 60–65% share of market, and the Watts Corporation, a privately held company, with an estimated 20–25% share. Watt's strength was concentrated in the Midwest and Southeast. The remainder of industry sales was fragmented among a host of small, financially weak printing shops. Case management found it difficult to imagine how a potential competitor could arrive at an economically justifiable decision to enter their market. Price was the only conceivable basis on which a new entrant could compete, but lacking the scale economies available to Case, a new entrant would necessarily be a high-cost competitor. Mr. Haffenreffer estimated that it would take a new entrant at least 3–5 years to reach break-even, assuming no retaliatory price cuts by Case. Furthermore, entering this market would necessitate a minimum capital investment of $2–4 million plus the working capital needed to support seasonal sales. On balance, it seemed unlikely that a potential competitor would brave these obstacles in the hope of grabbing a share of a $25–30 million industry with mediocre growth prospects.

Mr. Case judged that the company's financial strength, relative cost advantages, and entrenched distribution system had served to deter Watts from trying to invade any of Case's prime market areas. Similarly, he thought Case could not take away a substantial market share from Watts without risking a price war that might seriously impair margins for a protracted period.

Unexploited Opportunities

The business plan finally approved by Mr. Case had not incorporated a diversification scheme vigorously advanced by the other members of senior management. The vice president had contended that the company could significantly boost both the rate of growth and level of earnings by using its cash flow and its production and distribution strengths to expand into related product lines. The proposal had called for expansion into other dated products, such as appointment books, planning books, and the like, imprinted with the name, logo, or other message of the customer, and into desk calendars similarly imprinted. Mr. Johnson had estimated that this project would require an initial capital investment of $200,000 and special product development and merchandising expenses of $900,000 spread over the first 2 years of the undertaking. It had been estimated that the new line should yield sales of approximately $1 million in the first full year of operation, with a growth rate of about 40% per year in years 2–4, as the line achieved nationwide distribution and recognition. A 12–15% growth rate was anticipated in subsequent years. It was thought that this type of product line would have a profit margin before taxes of about 6%. The management group believed that the proposed line could serve as a profitable first step toward developing a full line of desktop products for commercial, industrial, and government markets.

Mr. Case had rejected the proposal on several grounds. He had observed that the proposal advocated entering a riskier line of business in which none of the management group had experience. In the proposed line of business the customer could choose among a variety of competing designs, and manufacturers had to actively generate repeat sales. He had also pointed out that the project would require a substantial investment in working capital for seasonal sales, if the new line grew as predicted. Finally, he had stated, he was quite content with his present income and, at his age, unwilling to reinvest earnings in the hope of achieving a strong position in a more competitive and less profitable business than the present one.

With Mr. Case out of the picture, the management group would have the freedom to pursue its growth program. Mr. Johnson believed that over a period of years, the Case Company's growth rate could be improved significantly if earnings were reinvested in related businesses rather than disbursed as dividends. The higher growth rate would be translated into profits for management if, for instance, the faster growth allowed them to take the company public at a relatively high price-earnings ratio.

The Purchase Proposal

Mr. Johnson recognized that a successful proposal would have to blend and reconcile the interests and goals of all parties to the transaction: the seller, the buyers, and external suppliers of finance.

The management group had determined that among them they could raise at most about $500,000 for investment in Case. Raising this amount would necessitate drawing down savings accounts, refinancing home mortgages, and liquidating positions in the stock market. Mr. Johnson was prepared to commit $160,000, Mr. Haffenreffer $140,000, and Messrs. Wright and Bennink $100,000 apiece. It had been tentatively agreed that all members of the management group would buy stock at the same price. It had also been tentatively concluded that the group would not accept a proposal that left them with less than 51% of the shares. With less than 51% of the stock, the management group might not achieve the autonomy to establish corporate policy or to dispose of the company where and as it chose.

Valuation

As mentioned previously, Mr. Johnson believed that Mr. Case's asking terms of $20 million with a minimum of $16 million in cash would remain fixed, at least until the company had been shown to a number of prospective buyers. In the past year Mr. Case had held discussions with two companies that had made unsolicited bids to purchase the company. The first offer, $15 million in cash, had come from a medium-sized firm with a diversified line of office products. It had been rejected by Mr. Case on the basis of price. The second offer had come from a highly diversified, medium-sized company sporting a price-earnings ratio of more than 20 and seeking to establish a position in office products through a series of acquisitions. The final offer had come to $32 million in letter stock of the acquirer.[1] Mr. Case had found this bid extremely tempting but had been unwilling to tie up his wealth in unmarketable shares of a company with which he was not intimately familiar. The acquirer, lacking excess debt capacity and unwilling to float new stock to raise cash, had backed out of the discussions.

Mr. Johnson had, in addition, assembled financial figures on the publicly traded companies he thought most comparable to the Case Company. These data are presented in Exhibit 5.

Financing

In terms of the mechanics of the transaction, Mr. Johnson planned to effect the purchase through a new corporation in which the management group would buy 500,000 common shares at $1.00 per share. Given the management group's $500,000 versus the $20 million asking price, the biggest problem facing Mr. Johnson was how to fund the new company at all, not to mention the objective of keeping control in the management group. Mr. Johnson had managed to obtain tentative commitments for $10.5 million, including the management group's $500,000. Prior to submitting a purchase proposal to Mr. Case, however, he would have to line up commitments for the entire $20 million funds needed.

It was clear that the noncash component of the purchase price would have to be met by issuing notes with a market value of $4 million to Mr. Case. In order to maintain the maximum amount of flexibility and borrowing capacity for raising financing from outsiders, Mr. Johnson had proposed that Mr. Case take 4%, junior subordinated, nonamortizing notes. After some negotiation, Mr. Case had expressed his willingness to accept a $6 million nonamortizing, 4% 5-year note that would be junior

---

1. Letter stock is unregistered stock. Such stock may not be sold to the public without registration under the Securities Act of 1933, a costly and time-consuming process. Because letter stock is restricted in its transferability, it represents a relatively illiquid investment and generally sells at a discount below the price that registered stock would command in the public securities markets. When letter stock is issued in an acquisition, the acquirer generally specifies that the stock cannot be registered for a certain period of time.

to all other debt obligations of the newly formed corporation. The members of the management group, as well as the corporate acquirer, would have to endorse the note. It was agreed that covenants on the note would include: (1) no additional debt or leases except debt incurred in the acquisition of the Case Company, short-term seasonal borrowings, or debt incurred to retire the 5-year note; (2) no dividends and maintenance of at least $3 million in working capital; (3) no changes in management or increase in management compensation; and (4) no sale of Case shares by Messrs. Johnson, Haffenreffer, Wright, or Bennink as long as the 5-year note was outstanding. If the borrower should default on any terms of this note or of any other indebtedness, the junior subordinated notes would become immediately due and payable. If not promptly paid, ownership of the shares held by the management group would revert to Mr. Case. The note could be retired before maturity in whole or in part in accord with the following schedule of discounts:

Year	Percent of Face Value
1	58%
2	71
3	81
4	96
5	100

In his efforts to line up financing from outside sources, Mr. Johnson had succeeded in obtaining a tentative commitment for a $6 million term loan from a large Philadelphia bank known for its aggressive lending policies. This loan would be amortized over a maximum period of 6 years through annual installments. The rate would be two points above floating prime, and the borrower would have to maintain average compensating balances of 10% of the outstanding principal amount of the loan. The amount of $6 million was the maximum the bank would commit on a term basis. Lending officers of the bank had emphasized that any additional term indebtedness incurred in the acquisition of Case would have to be effectively subordinated to this loan. Exhibit 6 presents an abstract of the provisions that the bank term loan would bear. Exhibit 7 presents Mr. Johnson's forecast of Case's cash flows over the next 6 years.

Having negotiated the bank commitment, Mr. Johnson was still left with the problem of raising an additional $9.5 million. He thought that he would have to turn to venture capital sources to raise the rest of the funds needed. Based on his experience in venture finance, Mr. Johnson knew that a venture capitalist would expect to earn about 20–25% on funds. He also knew that most venture capitalists preferred to place their funds in the form of debt securities rather than common stock. The venture capitalist could generally exercise more effective control over investment through the covenants on a debt obligation than through the voting power on stock. Principal repayment on debt also provided a mechanism for a tax-free recovery of capital; this might not be possible with stock until the company had gone public. Mr. Johnson expected to have to pay an 8–9% coupon rate on any debt funds obtained from a venture capital source. The venture capitalist would probably attempt to realize the rest of the return by taking warrants to buy shares in the new corporation at $1.00, the same price initially paid by the management group. The venture capitalist would probably insist on having the option of exercising the warrants in either cash or Case debentures.

EXHIBIT 1
Consolidated Income Statements, 1980–1984 (thousands of dollars)

	1980	1981	1982	1983	1984
Net sales	$9,740	$10,044	$11,948	$13,970	$15,260
Cost of sales	5,836	5,648	6,994	8,304	9,298
Gross profit on sales	3,904	4,396	4,954	5,666	5,962
Selling and administrative expenses	2,216	2,072	2,470	3,022	3,274
Other income, net	40	108	70	128	120
Profit before income taxes	1,728	2,432	2,554	2,772	2,808
Federal income taxes	816	972	920	942	842
Net profit	$ 912	$ 1,460	$ 1,634	$ 1,830	$ 1,966

EXHIBIT 2
Consolidated Balance Sheet at December 31, 1984 (thousands of dollars)

Cash and marketable securities	$ 5,762	Accounts payable	$ 654
Accounts receivable	2,540	Accrued expenses	366
Inventories at lower of cost or market	588	Accrued income taxes	246
Prepaid expenses	108	Current liabilities	1,266
Current assets	8,998	Common stock ($1.00 par value)	200
Property, plant, equipment, net	2,110	Retained profits	9,716
Miscellaneous assets	74	Shareholders' equity	9,916
Total assets	$11,182	Total liabilities and shareholders' equity	$11,182

EXHIBIT 3
Ten-Year Summary of Operations, 1975–1984 (thousands of dollars except per share data)

	1975	1976	1977	1978	1979	1980	1981	1982	1983	1984
Net sales	$7,688	$8,356	$8,526	$8,790	$9,350	$9,740	$10,044	$11,948	$13,970	$15,260
Net profit	638	668	742	748	758	912	1,460	1,634	1,830	1,966
Dividends	600	200	280	280	440	440	480	1,220	1,374	1,480
Earnings per share	$ 3.19	$ 3.34	$ 3.71	$ 3.74	$ 3.79	$ 4.56	$ 7.30	$ 8.17	$ 9.15	$ 9.83
Net profit margin	8.3%	8.0%	8.7%	8.5%	8.1%	9.4%	14.5%	13.7%	13.1%	12.9%

EXHIBIT 4
Monthly Working Capital Balances, 1984 (thousands of dollars)

	Jan.	Feb.	Mar.	Apr.	May	June	July	Aug.	Sept.	Oct.	Nov.	Dec.
Cash	$5,536	$5,714	$5,396	$4,784	$4,328	$4,098	$2,354	$ 766	$2,050	$3,830	$5,734	$5,762
Accounts receivable	1,480	760	734	804	718	604	3,432	6,104	6,164	4,322	2,398	2,540
Inventories	1,124	1,666	2,210	2,752	3,294	3,838	2,754	1,670	526	588	608	588
Current liabilities	(1,186)	(1,220)	(1,242)	(1,146)	(1,422)	(1,344)	(1,072)	(1,216)	(1,174)	(1,384)	(1,340)	(1,266)
Net working capital	$6,954	$6,920	$7,098	$7,194	$6,918	$7,196	$7,468	$7,324	$7,566	$7,356	$7,400	$7,624

EXHIBIT 5
Comparative Data on Selected Companies in Related Lines of Business

	S&P Publishing Averages	S&P 425 Industrial Stocks	DeLuther[a]	Wakefield Co.[b]	Officomp[c]	Case Co.
Trading market			OTC	OTC	OTC	—
Current market price			$22¼	$14¾	$29¼	—
Indicated dividend yield			5.5%	8.7%	3.7%	—
Price-earnings ratio						
1984	14.6	9.9	8.7	7.2	10.5	—
1983	19.6	11.8	6.4	5.0	10.2	—
1982	14.4	10.4	10.8	11.9	13.8	—
Price range						
1984			$24⅝–16¼	$14⅞–8⅛	$33⅛–26½	—
1983			18½–12⅛	11½–5⅛	19¾–12⅞	—
Earnings per share (E) and index (I)						
1984			(E) $2.48 / (I) 110	(E) $1.62 / (I) 82	(E) $2.98 / (I) 177	(E) $9.83 / (I) 216
1980			2.26 / 100	1.97 / 100	1.68 / 100	4.56 / 100
Sales (S) ($000s) and index (I)						
1984			(S) $16,427 / (I) 142	(S) $12,223 / (I) 108	(S) $18,608 / (I) 160	(S) $15,260 / (I) 157
1980			11,568 / 100	11,317 / 100	11,630 / 100	9,740 / 100
Net earnings (N) ($000s) and index (I)						
1984			(N) $1,051 / (I) 117	(N) $501 / (I) 84	(N) $1,656 / (I) 178	(N) $1,966 / (I) 216
1980			902 / 100	600 / 100	930 / 100	912 / 100
Net profit margins						
1984			6.4%	4.1%	8.9%	12.9%
1980			7.8	5.3	8.0	9.4
Profit/Net worth						
1984			16.6%	6.0%	16.9%	19.8%
1983			14.2	5.7	15.0	19.0
1982			15.4	8.8	14.7	19.2
Book capitalization[d] ($000s)						
Long-term debt			$ 3,995 / 38.7%	$ 1,822 / 18.0%	$ 4,173 / 29.9%	— / —
Common stock and surplus			6,318 / 61.3	8,298 / 82.0	9,783 / 70.1	9,916 / 100.0%
Total			$10,313 / 100.0%	$10,120 / 100.0%	$13,956 / 100.0%	$ 9,916 / 100.0%
Total market value ($000s)			$ 9,456	$ 4,573	$16,234	$ 9,916
Shares outstanding (000s)			425	310	555	200

a. Producer of desk-top accessories, advertising specialty calendars, office stationery.
b. Producer of advertising specialty calendars.
c. Producer of broad line of office paper products and desk accessories.
d. All companies, December 31, 1984.

EXHIBIT 6
Excerpts from Summary of Loan Agreement for Bank Term Loan

Description of the Loan

Amount. $6 million.

Rate. Prime rate plus 2%, floating.[a]

Term. 6 years.

Repayment. Annual payments equal to the greater of $1 million or the sum of net profit plus amortization of goodwill and debt discounts less $200,000.

Prepayment. Permitted in whole or in part at any time without penalty. All prepayments to be applied to the outstanding principal balance of the loan in inverse order of maturity.

Compensating balances. Borrower must maintain average annual deposit balances equal to at least 10% of the outstanding principal amount of the loan.

Conditions Precedent

Prior to the making of the loan described above, borrower must have satisfied the following terms and conditions:

Incorporation. Borrower must be a duly incorporated corporation authorized to undertake this borrowing and all other transactions associated with this borrowing.

Purchase agreement. Borrower must have entered a contract to purchase 100% of the John Case Company.

Financing. Borrower must have arranged firm commitments for the financing of this transaction in a manner consistent with the terms of this loan agreement.

Equity purchase. Messrs. Johnson, Haffenreffer, Wright, and Bennink must have committed not less than $500,000 to the purchase of common stock in the newly formed corporation that will purchase the John Case Company.

Affirmative Covenants

During the life of this loan, borrower will adhere to the following terms and conditions:

Financial statements. Quarterly financial statements must be provided within 60 days of the end of the first three quarters. Audited financial statements bearing an unqualified opinion from a public accounting firm must be provided within 90 days of the end of borrower's fiscal year.

Accounting changes. Borrower will make no changes in its method of accounting.

Negative Covenants

During the life of this loan, borrower will not do any of the following without written consent of the lender:

Continuation of management. No changes in management. Aggregate compensation to Messrs. Johnson, Haffenreffer, Wright, and Bennink not to be increased by more than 5% in any year. Present compensation to serve as a base for this computation.

Negative pledge. No assets to be pledged or otherwise used as collateral for any indebtedness.

Sales of assets. No sale of a substantial portion of the assets of the borrower. Borrower will not merge with or be acquired by any other entity.

Acquisitions. Borrower will not acquire any other entity.

Capital expenditures. Not to exceed $300,000 in any one year.

Dividends. In any one year restricted to after-tax profits minus all principal repayments on outstanding indebtedness.

(continued)

EXHIBIT 6 *(concluded)*

Working capital. Not to decline below $3 million.

Additional indebtedness. No additional debt (including leases) with a term exceeding 1 year, unless subordinated to this loan. Any short-term debt must be retired for a period of at least 30 consecutive days in every year.

Senior debt. Senior debt, including all short-term indebtedness, may not exceed $10 million plus all earnings retained in the business after Dec. 31, 1985.

Events of Default

In the event of default, this loan plus accrued interest will become immediately due and payable. The following will constitute events of default:

Failure to pay interest or principal when due.
Violation of any affirmative or negative covenant on this loan.
Bankruptcy, reorganization, receivership, liquidation.
Commission of an event of default on any other indebtedness.

a. At the time of the case, the prime rate was 10.00%.

EXHIBIT 7
Cash Flow Forecasts, 1985–1990 (thousands of dollars)

	1985	*1986*	*1987*	*1988*	*1989*	*1990*
Net sales	$16,024	$16,844	$17,686	$18,570	$19,498	$20,472
Earnings before interest and taxes[a]	3,433	3,640	3,757	3,608	3,788	3,976
Interest expense[b]	1,675	1,538	1,369	908	800	800
Profit before taxes	1,758	2,102	2,388	2,700	2,988	3,176
Taxes	274	364	440	556	660	714
Profit after taxes	1,484	1,738	1,948	2,114	2,328	2,462
Add back: Noncash charges	240	260	284	300	310	340
Cash flow from operations	1,724	1,998	2,232	2,444	2,638	2,802
Less: Increase in working capital	156	162	170	180	190	200
Less: Capital expenditures	120	134	142	150	466	600
Available for debt retirement	$ 1,448	$ 1,702	$ 1,920	$ 2,114	$ 1,982	$ 2,002
Planned debt retirement						
Bank loan	$ 1,448	$ 1,702	$ 1,920	$ 930	$ 0	$ 2,002
Mr. Case's note	0	0	0	1,184	4,766[c]	0
Subordinated loan	0	0	0	0	0	0
Debt as percent of total capital	89%	80%	70%	58%	47%	35%

a. Reflects elimination of Mr. Case's salary.

b. 9% coupon on subordinated loan of $6 million; 4% coupon on seller's note of $6 million; 12% rate on bank term loan; 10% rate on seasonal loan.

c. Mr. Case's note is retired from cash flow and a $2.8 million new bank term loan in 1989.

Congoleum Corporation (Abridged)

In the summer of 1979, Thomas Cassidy, Arthur Nagle, and Anthony Grassi, officers of First Boston Corporation, were discussing with David Koester and John Uecker of Prudential Insurance Company the proposed terms for participation in the largest leveraged buyout (LBO) in history. The subject of these discussions was Congoleum Corporation, a diversified firm competing in resilient flooring, shipbuilding, and automotive accessories.

Messrs. Cassidy and Nagle first approached Prudential in May 1979 to solicit interest in the concept of the LBO. The participation of Prudential, the largest institutional investor in the United States, was considered crucial to the development of a deal. Prudential did express interest. On July 16, 1979, First Boston formally proposed the purchase of Congoleum by private and institutional investors at $38 per common share. The preceding trading day, Congoleum common closed at $25.375 per share. Given 12.2 million shares outstanding, this implied an aggregate premium of $154 million. The directors of Congoleum agreed to discuss this offer and to provide some confidential information necessary to value the firm.

The next step was to agree in principle to merge Congoleum into a new holding company. This included arranging the terms and commitments for financing.

Description of Congoleum Corporation

In 1978, Congoleum had earnings of $42 million on revenues of $576 million (see Exhibits 1 and 2). Its base of total assets was $323 million (see Exhibit 3). The firm was active in three product market segments (see Exhibit 4): home furnishings, shipbuilding, and automotive and industrial distribution. Congoleum had no material intersegment sales.

Home furnishings products included resilient flooring targeted to the home remodeling market, and furniture and bedding for sale to the mobile home industry. The firm was one of the four largest producers of resilient flooring. The principal elements of competition were product styling, price, product performance, and service. Because of the importance of style, Congoleum produced and sold a large number of different designs and colors and introduced many new designs each year. The process for manufacturing resilient flooring was developed and patented by Congoleum. The foreign and domestic patents covering this process were due to expire from 1980 to 1987, although most would expire by 1984. The firm successfully defended its patents against infringement by three competitors, which in one case resulted in a $35 million out-of-court settlement paid by Armstrong Cork Company in 1976. Congoleum granted royalty-bearing licenses under these patents to other manufacturers, generating royalties of $17.2 million in 1978 and $13.2 million in 1977. Research and development expenditures were approximately $5 million in both 1978 and 1977.

Congoleum's shipbuilding subsidiary, Bath Iron Works (BIW), built and refurbished naval and civilian vessels. It held an excellent reputation for quality work completed within budget and on schedule. BIW had between 10 and 15 domestic competitors, most of whom were substantially larger and had poorer performances despite government support. The backlog at December 31, 1978, of $445 million included $413 million for naval ships and overhauls and $32 million for commercial ships and industrial work. This compared with a backlog of $453 million for 1977. BIW expected to fill about $225 million of its backlog in 1979. In April 1979, BIW was awarded $209 million in more naval contracts.[1] The contracts for merchant ships were fixed-price but contained escalation provisions. Naval ships were built under fixed-priced incentive contracts also containing escalation provisions. Naval contracts were subject to termination at the convenience of the government, in which case the government would pay costs incurred, termination costs, and a portion of the profit. In the last 10 years, none of BIW's contracts was terminated in this manner.

The third segment of Congoleum's business was the distribution of automotive and industrial maintenance parts. This business segment was created from Curtis Noll Corporation, which was acquired in October 1977. The products distributed were purchased from numerous suppliers. Congoleum owned patents for a code key cutter and duplicator, which it considered significant to the business of this segment. In 1978 this segment provided revenues of $115 million and operating income of $10 million (see Exhibit 4).

Officers and directors owned beneficially 3.8% of the equity of Congoleum on a fully diluted basis. A portion of these shares was represented by stock options exercisable at an average price of $13.07 (see Exhibit 5). It was planned that the chairman, vice chairman, and other officers would remain with the firm after the transaction (Exhibit 5). Byron C. Radaker, chairman and chief executive officer, and Eddy G. Nicholson, vice chairman and chief operating officer, had managed Congoleum since 1975 and were credited for the company's improved performance. This was accomplished by an internal reorganization, the divestment of less profitable businesses, and the turnaround of other businesses.

Valuation by Lazard Frères & Co.

The firm of Lazard Frères & Co. was retained by Congoleum's directors to render an opinion as to the $38 per share offer. Lazard concluded, "We are of the opinion that the proposed offer of $38 per share of Congoleum is fair to the shareholders of Congoleum from a financial point of view." This analysis was based on a comparison

---

1. First Boston's offering circular noted: "Bath Iron Works does not anticipate being able to deliver any new commercial business until at least 1985 because of capacity limitations and its expectations for continued involvement in the [Navy's] FFG program."

of Congoleum's operations with its competitors, premiums paid in other recent acquisitions (see Exhibit 6), and values obtainable on liquidation (see Exhibit 7). Lazard relied on a method of valuation based on price-earnings multiples. Other information of significance in the valuation is presented in Exhibits 8 and 9.

Description of Prudential

The Prudential Insurance Company of America was the largest institutional investor in the United States, with assets of $21 billion invested in fixed-income securities. It was regarded as the leader in privately placed investments. Of Prudential's $6 billion annual cash flow, about 60% was invested through its corporate finance department in fixed-income securities (debt securities and preferred stocks). The department's portfolio consisted of investments in more than 1,400 companies in all major industries. Loan proposals were typically analyzed by teams of three officers and approved by the senior vice president in charge of the department and by the finance committee of the board of directors.

Prudential's private lending included LBOs. The term of most of its private loans typically ranged from 12 to 20 years. Loan size varied from $500,000 to $250 million. The majority of the loans carried a fixed interest rate and were unsecured. Prudential's literature stated:

> On leveraged buyouts or credits for other borrowers with higher risk characteristics, our loans may include profit participation, warrants, or convertible securities in addition to a fixed interest rate.

John T. Uecker, vice president and member of the team considering First Boston's proposal, commented on financing of leveraged buyouts:

> These investments fit with our long-term portfolio strategy. We're more risk-oriented than our competitors. But we structure the deals so that the reward is consistent with the risk we take. We always compare the terms with other buyouts we may be considering at the same time, as well as other investment alternatives we have. And we analyze the company's earnings and cash flow projections—modified by the probability of meeting them. Furthermore, we value each segment of a company on its own. Finally, we compare the returns on each type of security with those available in the market [Exhibits 10 and 11]. This is done by individual securities and then as a package. The senior debt and common stock are relatively easy to value; the junior debt is more difficult. Given the huge proportion of debt in these deals, we can view the junior notes as equity and seek an equity-type return. The alternative is to compare them to B-rated securities and look for some premium over their returns. But obtaining a high yield on junior debt is inevitably constrained by what the company can service. In these cases, we look for an equity kicker (through warrants, convertibles, and common stock) to achieve the required rate of return. In the final analysis, we're more concerned about getting an appropriate return on the total package rather than how that return gets divided up between the various securities, though we would like to see each security able to stand on its own.

About 50% of Prudential's private placement financing was proposed by investment bankers.

Description of First Boston

First Boston Corporation was a special bracket investment banking firm. Although the firm had originated no leveraged buyouts previously, it had considerable experience with aspects of the deal: private placement financing, firm valuation, acquisitions, and so forth. The three officers, Thomas L. Cassidy and Arthur Nagle, both managing directors, and Anthony Grassi, vice president, developed the proposed deal. James Harpel, president of Century Capital Corporation, originally identified Congoleum as an LBO candidate and proposed that First Boston lead the negotiations. But Century Capital remained as one of the prospective equity participants. Thomas Cassidy said:

> The ability to deal effectively with people having diverse interests is extremely important in a transaction as complex as this. It may appear relatively simple after the fact. But actually it is fragile up until closing. At the beginning the interest among the participants was understandably tentative. Our first conversations with the Pru were of a conceptual nature, and the initial reaction of Congoleum management—whose involvement was very important—was "We're open to the idea, assuming you can put together the rest of the pieces and assuming the end result is in the best interests of our stockholders. . . . " The final form of the deal evolved out of a series of negotiations. Originally it was to have been a purchase of stock; it eventually evolved into a purchase of assets. Our "strip" concept was very helpful in keeping all of the institutions together. Closing the deal requires a fair amount of corporate finance capability, ingenuity, determination, and patience.

Terms of the Proposal

Cassidy, Nagle, and Grassi proposed that a holding company be formed to buy Congoleum for an amount equivalent to about $38 per share. The buyout actually consisted of a two-step merger and sale. First, the stock of Bath Iron Works would be purchased for $92.3 million. BIW would then be merged into the buying company. Second, the remaining net assets of Congoleum (including about $95.1 million of excess cash and the Congoleum Corporation name) would be purchased for approximately $371.3 million. The "old Congoleum" would settle its remaining liabilities and pay a liquidating dividend of $38 per share.

The purchasers would adopt the name Congoleum Corporation and proceed as a privately held firm. The assets of BIW and Congoleum would have a tax basis equal to the amounts paid for the stock and assets, respectively, plus any liabilities assumed. Accordingly, the tax basis of the new firm would exceed its present tax basis by several hundred million dollars. This increase in tax basis could result in reduced taxable income because of increased deductions for (a) the amortization of the value of patents and patent-licensing agreements, (b) depreciation, and (c) cost of goods sold due to the write-up of shipbuilding backlog and inventories. This increase in tax basis would be available only in the event of a taxable acquisition and could not be achieved by the current stockholders. Exhibit 12 describes the allocation of the purchase premium in more detail.

The proposal provided financing of $379.6 million for the purchase in the form of bank borrowings, debt securities, and preferred and common stock. The distinctive feature of prior LBOs was that debt as a percent of total capital ranged up to 80%. Since banks typically would not allow all of that to be senior financing, the layering of the claims usually was one of the more delicate points of negotiation. David Koester, senior member of Prudential's team, said:

> We wanted all the players to share the same incentives in order to reduce any intramural warfare if trouble developed. So we insisted that the institutional investors purchase "strips," or units, containing a mixture of senior notes, subordinated notes, preferred stock, and common stock. This made First Boston's job more difficult. Previously, no leveraged buyouts had been financed in this manner. First Boston did an outstanding job assembling the players for a financing of this type and size.

Also it was proposed that First Boston, Century Capital, and the management of the new firm purchase common stock. The purchase of stock by management in the new firm was typical of LBOs. In summary, the proposed amounts to be financed by each investor and type of security were as shown in Table A.

The Decision

At this stage of negotiation, the central issues under consideration were valuation and the appropriateness of the offering price of $38 per share.[2] Exhibit 13 shows the financial forecast on which the valuation of Congoleum was based. Exhibits 14–16 provide supporting material for the Exhibit 13 forecast.

TABLE A
Sources of Acquisition Financing (millions of dollars)

Bank borrowings		$125.0
Insurance company investor "strips"		
11¼% senior notes, principal amount $115,000,000 (due 1995)	$113.6	
12¼% subordinated notes, principal amount $92,000,000 (due 2000)	89.8	
($11.00) cumulative preferred stock (322,000 shares)	26.2	
Common stock	16.5	
		246.1
First Boston and Century Capital		4.5
Congoleum management		4.0
		$379.6

---

2. In the cases of First Boston, Century Capital, and Congoleum management, it was also possible to augment common stock returns with other forms of compensation, such as consulting fees, stock options, and salaries guaranteed by employment contracts. As investment banker in this transaction, First Boston would be paid a fee.

EXHIBIT 1
Ten-Year Historical Financial Data, 1969–1978 (millions of dollars except per share data)

	1969	1970	1971	1972	1973	1974	1975	1976	1977	1978
Net sales	$189.9	$187.7	$250.6	$345.2	$385.7	$377.1	$395.9	$294.8	$388.6	$575.8
Royalty revenues (incl. in net sales)	—	—	—	—	4.0	5.5	7.0	10.1	13.2	17.2
Net income	7.6	7.0	12.1	23.4	22.2	.5	9.6	15.7	24.7	41.7
Earnings per share	$ .70	$ .65	$ 1.07	$ 1.67	$ 1.89	$ .05	$ .83	$ 1.36	$ 2.13	$ 3.58
Dividends per share	—	.02	.09	.13	.20	.27	.27	.33	.40	.67
Stock price										
High	17.5	11.6	24.0	30.9	24.6	14.9	9.2	12.9	14.6	26.3
Low	7.5	3.9	10.1	20.7	8.5	2.4	3.0	8.0	8.8	12.0
Working capital	$ 35.2	$ 49.0	$ 53.5	$ 69.6	$ 88.1	$ 92.8	$ 81.1	$ 76.8	$ 78.0	$110.1
Long-term debt	31.7	42.6	40.0	42.1	59.3	74.6	52.3	16.6	16.1	14.9
Net worth	58.9	59.1	73.3	99.5	116.3	113.8	120.3	132.6	153.1	187.5

Note: Congoleum acquired Curtis Noll Corporation October 31, 1977, on a purchase basis. Its performance is consolidated with Congoleum after October 31, 1977. Certain operations were discontinued in 1976. Results for 1969 to 1975 have not been adjusted for discontinued operations.

EXHIBIT 2

Historical Income Statements for Years Ending December 31, 1976–1978 (thousands of dollars except per share data)

	1976	1977	1978
Net sales	$284,735	$375,466	$558,633
Royalties[a]	10,080	13,163	17,197
Total revenues	294,815	388,629	575,830
Cost of sales	224,028	285,770	385,851
Selling and administrative expenses	37,805	55,023	108,648
Operating income	32,982	47,836	81,331
Interest expense	(2,064)	(1,734)	(1,266)
Miscellaneous income	3,821	3,538	4,281
Total other income and expense	1,757	1,804	3,015
Income from continuing operations before income taxes	34,739	49,640	84,346
Provision for income taxes	17,400	24,900	42,600
Income from continuing operations	17,339	24,740	41,746
Loss from discontinued operations	(19,500)	—	—
Patent infringement settlement	17,885	—	—
Net income	$ 15,724	$ 24,740	$ 41,746
Per Share			
Income from continuing operations . . . . $	1.50	$ 2.13	$ 3.58
Loss from discontinued operations	(1.69)	—	—
Patent infringement settlement	1.55	—	—
Net income . . . . $	1.36	$ 2.13	$ 3.58

Note: These statements reflect the addition of Curtis Noll Corporation only after October 31, 1977, the date of acquisition. The acquisition was accounted for as a purchase. Restating the results of 1977 and 1976 as if Noll were included yields the following:

	1976	1977
Total revenues	$416,000	$497,300
Income from continuing operations	19,592	27,725
Net income	17,977	27,725
Earnings per share . . . . $	1.56	$ 2.39

a. Royalties are from licenses of the company's resilient flooring patents as well as license agreements for know-how. These patents expire from 1980 through 1987, although most expire by 1984.

EXHIBIT 3

Consolidated Balance Sheets at December 31, 1977–1978 (thousands of dollars)

	1977	1978
Cash and temporary investments	$ 12,369	$ 77,254
Receivables	55,053	40,424
Shipbuilding contracts in progress	18,936	24,058
Inventories	73,318	75,258[a]
Other	5,679	3,511
Current assets	165,355	220,505[b]
Property, plant, and equipment	131,621	135,627[c]
Less: Accumulated depreciation and amortization	60,472	64,850[d]
Net	71,149	70,777[e]
Goodwill	18,520	18,520
Other	11,356	13,250
Total assets	$266,380	$323,052[f]
Current maturities of long-term debt	$ 2,055	$ 460
Accounts payable	38,391	41,578
Accrued liabilities	28,928	30,102
Income taxes	17,985	38,257
Current liabilities	87,359	110,397
Long-term debt	16,067	14,949
Deferred income taxes and other liabilities	9,886	10,221
Common stock	5,859	5,859
Surplus	11,846	11,345
Retained earnings	137,256	171,229
Treasury stock	(1,893)	(948)
Net worth	153,068	187,485
Total liabilities and net worth	$266,380	$323,052

Replacement cost data:

a. $79,518.	d. $188,281.
b. $224,765.	e. $93,986.
c. $282,267.	f. $352,710.

EXHIBIT 4
Product Line Data, 1974–1979 (millions of dollars)

	Year Ended December 31					9 Months	
	1974	*1975*	*1976*	*1977*	*1978*	*1978*	*1979*
Revenues by segment							
Home furnishings	$143	$153	$180	$198	$225	$170	$177
Shipbuilding	107	126	115	167	211	158	181
Automotive and industrial distribution	79	85	95	105	115	86	89
	$329	$364	$390	$470	$551	$414	$447
Operating income (loss) by segment[a]							
Home furnishings	$ 22	$ 27	$ 34	$ 42	$ 58	$ 43	$ 40
Shipbuilding	(11)	1	2	10	19	13	28
Automotive and industrial distribution[b]	6	7	8	9	10	7	8
	$ 17	$ 35	$ 44	$ 61	$ 87	$ 63	$ 76
Identifiable assets by segment							
Home furnishings	$ 93	$ 93	$ 97	$ 92	$ 93	na	na
Shipbuilding	37	38	42	54	59	na	na
Automotive and industrial distribution	48	52	56	62	64	na	na
	$178	$183	$195	$208	$216	na	na

na = not available.

a. Operating income does not include an allocation of interest income or expense, miscellaneous and other unallocable expenses, corporate office expenses, or provisions for income taxes.

b. The pro forma amounts for the automotive and industrial distribution segment include the results of Curtis Noll Corporation.

EXHIBIT 5
Management Stock and Option Ownership in Congoleum Corporation, Autumn 1979

	Number of Shares Subject to Options and Stock Appreciation Rights	*Weighted Average Exercise Price*	*Number of Other Shares Beneficially Owned*	*Total Number of Shares Beneficially Owned*
Byron C. Radaker (Chairman, CEO)	47,250	$11.87	12,750	60,000
Eddy G. Nicholson (Vice Chairman, COO)	27,750	11.31	11,250	39,000
Harry F. Pearson (Executive Vice Pres.)	7,000	15.38	47,492	64,492
All directors and officers as a group	164,699	13.07	293,023	457,722

Note: Officers of Congoleum expected to assume equivalent positions in the new firm.

It was proposed that Radaker and Nicholson be allowed to purchase 7% and 5%, respectively, of the new firm's equity, subject to the right of the firm to repurchase the equity if their employment is terminated before 1984. Stock in the new venture was also reserved for other key employees.

Radaker and Nicholson would be employed under 5-year contracts, which specified a base salary, incentive compensation, and entitlements in the event of termination. Current and proposed compensation compared as follows:

	Radaker	*Nicholson*
1979 compensation	$370,000	$295,000
1980 compensation per contract		
Maximum	500,000	380,000
Minimum	375,000	290,000

EXHIBIT 6
Data on Comparable Leveraged Buyouts and Other Acquisitions

Company Acquired	Date	Acquisition of Stock or Assets	Premium/Price One Day Prior to Announcement	Offer as a Multiple of Net Income	Offer as a Multiple of Book Value	Senior Debt/ Total Debt	Sub. Debt/ Total Debt	Senior Debt/ Total Cap.	Sub. Debt/ Total Cap.
Houdaille Industries	10/28/78	S	93%	13.9	2.0	65.5%	34.5%	56%	29.6%
Bliss & Laughlin	8/10/79	A	23	8.7	1.7				
Carrier Corp.	9/16/78	A	39	10.2	1.6				
Gardner-Denver	1/22/79	A	46	12.2	2.1				
Washington Steel	3/12/79	A	34	7.3	1.3				
Eltra Corp.	6/29/79	A	25	11.6	1.5				
Studebaker-Worthington	7/25/79	A	17	10.7	1.4				
Marathon Manufacturing	8/13/79	A	13	11.4	2.1				
Congoleum		A/S	50	9.4	2.4	68.6	31.4	60.4	27.6

EXHIBIT 7

Valuation Based on a Breakup Price Estimated by Lazard Frères for Each Component (millions of dollars except per share data)

	1979 Estimated Results by Segment			
	Home Furnishings Segment	*Bath Iron Works*	*Automotive and Industrial Distribution*	*Total Corporate Consolidated*
Operating income[a]	$56.1	$29.0	$11.9	$97.0
Corporate office and other[b]	1.1	1.3	.7	3.1
Pre-tax income	55.0	27.7	11.2	93.9
Taxes (48%)	26.4	13.3	5.4	45.1
Net income	$28.6	$14.4	$ 5.8	$48.8

	Valuation Based on Assumed Price-Earnings Ratio							
	Low	*High*	*Low*	*High*	*Low*	*High*	*Low*	*High*
Assumed price-earnings ratio	9.0	10.0	5.0	6.0	10.0	11.0		
Derived valuation	$257.4	$286.0	$72.0	$86.4	$58.0	$63.8	$387.4	$436.2
Plus: Estimated excess cash on 12/31/79[c]							95.1	95.1
Less: Estimated long-term debt and current maturity of long-term debt on 12/31/79							15.6	15.6
Less: Unfunded vested pension liabilities (as of 12/31/78)							34.5	34.5
Net breakup value							$432.4	$481.2
Net breakup value per share (based on 12,201,000 shares)							$35.44	$39.43

a. From Congoleum's internal reporting of quarterly operating income and performance report. Operating income for the Home Furnishings segment was reduced by $2.7 million attributable to the Kinder Division. This operation has been assumed to be sold for $10 million by the end of 1979.

b. Allocated based on 1979 estimated sales (excluding $36.0 million attributable to Kinder and excluding royalty payments).

c. Total cash at year-end estimated at $103.1 million minus $8 million. Excess cash is therefore estimated at $95.1 million.

EXHIBIT 8

Forecast of Congoleum Operations, 1979–1981 (millions of dollars except per share data)

	1979	*1980*	*1981*
For Year Ended December 31			
Revenues	$ 596	$ 680	$ 737
Operating income	86	97	112
Net income	45	51	60
Net income per share	$3.80	$4.35	$5.00
Dividends per share	.90	1.10	1.30
At December 31			
Cash and temporary investments	$ 93	$ 136	$ 182
Working capital	140	169	209
Long-term debt	15	14	14
Stockholders' investment	220	259	304

Note: These data are from an internal forecast by Congoleum prepared in the summer of 1978 and subsequently made available to First Boston Corp.

EXHIBIT 9

Financial Data on Market Segment Competitors

	Five-Year Expected Growth	P/E	β[a]	LT Debt % Cap.	1979 ROE	1982–1984 Expected Div. Yield
Home furnishings						
Armstrong Cork	17.5%	5.8	1.00	18.2%	11.6%	3.2%
GAF Corp.	14.0	6.0	1.15	35.0	10.4	2.6
Shipbuilding						
Todd Shipyards	21.0	5.3	1.00	69.0	22.0	2.0
Automotive and industrial distribution						
Genuine Parts	16.0	10.4	.95	5.0	19.2	2.5
General Automotive Parts	16.0	9.6	.75	7.0	19.0	2.4
Barnes Group	12.5	5.1	.85	18.0	20.6	2.7
Congoleum	22.5	7.9	1.25	7.0	23.0	3.0

a. The risk-free rate was assumed to be 9.5% and the market premium 8.6%.

EXHIBIT 10

Average or Comparable Debt Yields by Quality, September 1979

S&P Rating	Yield	Firm Name	Debt/Total Capital
AAA	9.35%		
AA	9.54	Average in category	
A	9.78		
BBB	10.49		
BB	13.76	Action Industries	56.9%
	11.06	Control Data	21.1
	11.86	Sun Chemical	47.6
	10.59	Talley Industries	43.0
B	13.32	APL Corp.	57.9
	12.70	Arrow Electronics	49.7
	11.98	Charter Company	50.4
	12.46	Columbia Pictures	41.3
	12.87	Texas International Airlines	51.0
CCC	16.11	Altec Corp.	70.8
	13.32	General Host	74.4
	17.22	Grolier, Inc.	na
	14.26	LTV Corp.	73.8
	15.02	Rapid American Corp.	75.7

na = not available.

EXHIBIT 11
Average or Comparable Preferred Stock Dividend Yields by Quality, September 1979

S&P Rating	*Yield*	*Firm Name*	*Debt/Total Capital*
Moody's Rating			
Aaa	NR		
Aa	9.6%	Average in category	
A	10.3		
Baa	10.5		
S&P Rating			
BB	10.0	Control Data	21.1%
	10.8	Evans Products	36.8
	10.0	Fairmont Foods	39.0
	11.5	Flexi-Van Corp.	64.0
B	12.1	Eastern Airlines	68.1
	11.5	Humana, Inc.	72.1
	12.5	Norin Corp.	49.5
	12.6	Petro-Lewis	67.2
CCC	18.2	Chrysler Corp.	33.8
	11.9	Continental Copper Steel	45.0
	14.0	Susquehanna Corp.	25.3
	15.0	United Brands	33.3
	14.0	Warnaco	35.0
	13.0	Wheeling Pittsburgh Steel	33.7

NR = not rated.

EXHIBIT 12
Sources and Allocation of Purchase Premium (millions of dollars)

Cost of stock ($38 × 12.2 million shares)	$463.6	
Expenses	7.0	
Purchase price		$470.6
Stockholders' investment, 12/31/78	$187.5	
Claim settlement	3.5	
Proceeds from exercise of stock options	5.0	
Estimated 1979 additions to retained earnings	37.7	
Stockholders' investment, 12/31/79	233.7	
Less: Unfunded pension liabilities	34.5	
Adjusted stockholders' investment, 12/31/79		199.2
Purchase premium		$271.4
Inventory write-up from recapture of LIFO reserve	$ 4.2	
Fixed assets	83.4	
Patents	150.0	
Goodwill	33.8	
Purchase premium		$271.4

Note: After the July 16, 1979, bid First Boston retained American Appraisal Company to render a "comfort level" opinion of the fair market value of inventories as of June 30, 1979, and the shipbuilding contract backlog and patents and patent licensing agreements at December 31, 1979. Its report concluded that the net realizable value of the inventories was $83,633,000, of the backlog was $73,500,000, and of the patents and patent licensing agreements was $174,000,000. The book value of inventories at June 30, 1979, was $50,000,000. Shipbuilding contract backlog and patents and patent licensing agreements had been carried on the books at nominal values.

EXHIBIT 13

Income and Cash Flow Forecast for Congoleum Reflecting the Terms of the Proposed Leveraged Buyout, 1978–1984 (millions of dollars)

	Actual 1978	Projected						Total 1980–1984
		1979	1980	1981	1982	1983	1984	
1. Operating income (Exhibit 15)	$95.5	$105.9	$111.5	$132.2	$158.7	$175.9	$ 166.1	
2. Less: Corporate expenses	7.5	8.6	4.3	5.1	5.9	6.8	7.6	
3. Less: Depreciation and amortization	6.7	7.5	35.51	36.26	37.07	37.95	21.23	
4. Earnings before interest and taxes	81.3	89.8	71.69	90.84	115.73	131.15	137.27	
5. Less: Interest expense, net[a]	(3.0)	(5.7)	42.92	40.55	37.33	34.12	29.87	
6. Profit before taxes	$84.3	$ 95.5	$28.77	$50.19	$78.40	$97.03	$107.40	
7. Less: Tax (@ 48%)		45.8	13.80	24.09	37.63	46.57	51.55	
8. Profit after taxes		$ 49.7	$14.97	$26.10	$40.77	$50.46	$ 55.85	$188.2
Adjustments								
9. Add back: Depreciation and Amortization[b]			$35.51	$36.26	$37.07	$37.95	$ 21.23	$168.0
10. Less: Capital expenditures			15.0	16.2	17.5	18.9	20.4	88.0
11. Less: Investment in working capital			2.0	14.0	23.3	11.2	12.8	63.3
12. Less: Preferred dividends			3.5	3.5	3.5	3.5	3.5	17.5
13. Less: Principal repayments			17.14	24.75	24.52	36.75	24.55	127.7
14. Free cash flow (to common stock)[c] . .			12.84	3.91	9.02	18.06	15.83	59.7
15. Add: Dividends, interest, and principal			63.56	68.80	65.35	74.37	57.96	330.0
16. Free cash flow (to all capital)			76.40	72.71	74.37	92.43	73.79	389.7
17. Less: Bank and preexisting interest and principal			35.85	33.46	30.86	40.74	25.28	166.2
18. Free cash flow to buyout participants			$40.55	$39.25	$43.51	$51.69	$ 48.51	$223.5
19. Net working capital		$120.0	$122.0	$136.0	$159.3	$170.5	$ 183.3	
20. Change in net working capital			2.0	14.0	23.3	11.2	12.8	

a. With no leveraged buyout, Congoleum's net interest expenses were expected to be, in millions of dollars, $(2.0), $(2.0), $(2.1), $(2.1), and $(3.0) over the years 1980–1984.

b. With no leveraged buyout, Congoleum's depreciation and amortization expenses were expected to be, in millions of dollars, $7.5, $8.3, $9.0, $9.9, and $10.9 over the years 1980–1984.

c. Because of covenants prohibiting dividends, these free cash flows would be reinvested (presumably in cash and marketable securities), reducing financial risk and increasing the free cash flow. Does not reflect income from the reinvestment of surplus cash.

EXHIBIT 14
Assumptions for Financial Projections

Corporate Expenses

$8.6 million in 1979, growing at 8% thereafter from 1980 to 1984. A savings of $5 million annually is assumed as a result of Congoleum's being a private company.

Depreciation and Amortization

The amortization of patents was proposed as follows. Amortization of patents will be the same for book and tax purposes.

	Value *($ millions)*	*Remaining Life* *(years)*
Chemical embossing process	$ 40	4
Code key cutter	40	10
Future value of U.S. royalties	30	4
Future value of foreign royalties	40	10
Total	$150	

Depreciation of Plant and Equipment

For tax purposes, the fixed asset base will be $200.2 million. Of this, 50% is assumed to relate to plant and will be depreciated over 20 years. The other 50%, related to equipment, will be depreciated over 7 years. All subsequent capital expenditures will be depreciated over 20 years. For book purposes, the fixed asset base will be $154.0 million. The other policies above will apply.

Interest Expense and Principal Repayments

Bank debt. Assume 14% interest on principal of $120 million. Principal is to be amortized at $16.666 million annually starting in 1980.

Senior notes. 11¼% interest on principal of $115 million, amortized at $7,636,000 per year starting on January 30, 1981.

Subordinated notes. 12¼% interest on principal of $92 million, amortized at $7,636,000 per year starting on January 30, 1989.

Covenants. Prohibit the payment of dividends on other than the preferred stock.

Taxes. The corporate income tax rate is assumed to be 48%.

Capital expenditures. Assumed to be $15 million in 1980 and increasing 8% annually thereafter.

Minimum working capital. 20% of nonroyalty sales. Net working capital immediately following the buyout is projected to be $120 million.

Required cash. Assumed to be 2.5% of nonroyalty sales.

Note. By 1980 a pattern of leveraged buyouts had emerged such that the firms were taken public again within a few years, usually when the various value-creating effects were diminished. The end of 1984 was one such horizon for Congoleum.

EXHIBIT 15

Projected Segment Revenue and Operating Income for Congoleum, 1979–1984 (millions of dollars)

	Actual 1978	Projected 1979	1980	1981	1982	1983	1984
Revenues							
Home furnishings, net	$207.9	$234.9	$217.9	$241.9	$273.3	$308.8	$349.0
Home furnishings royalties	17.2	20.6	24.8	29.7	35.7	42.8	21.4
Total home furnishings	225.1	255.5	242.7	271.6	309.0	351.6	370.4
Shipbuilding	211.0	230.4	247.9	279.2	345.1	345.1	345.1
Automotive, expediter	78.8	90.6	104.2	119.8	137.8	158.5	182.3
Automotive, conventional	45.0	45.0	40.0	40.0	40.0	40.0	40.0
Total automotive	123.8	135.6	144.2	159.8	177.8	198.5	222.3
Total revenues	$559.9	$621.5	$634.8	$710.6	$831.9	$895.2	$937.8
Operating Income							
Home furnishings, net	$ 43.7	$ 42.0	$ 39.2	$ 48.4	$ 57.4	$ 64.8	$ 73.3
Home furnishings royalties	17.2	20.6	24.8	29.7	35.7	42.8	21.4
Total home furnishings	60.9	62.6	64.0	78.1	93.1	107.6	94.7
Shipbuilding	21.7	31.5	33.9	38.5	47.7	47.7	47.7
Automotive, expediter	na	11.8	13.6	15.6	17.9	20.6	23.7
Automotive, conventional	na	0	0	0	0	0	0
Total automotive	12.9	11.8	13.6	15.6	17.9	20.6	23.7
Total operating income	$ 95.5	$105.9	$111.5	$132.2	$158.7	$175.9	$166.1

Note: These data are from projections made by First Boston Corporation, and assume the buyout is completed. Neither depreciation nor corporate-level expenses are reflected in operating income, nor is income from the reinvestment of surplus cash.

na = not available.

EXHIBIT 16
Capital Structure and Debt Repayment Schedule for Congoleum, 1979–1984 (millions of dollars)

			Projected as of December 31			
	1979	1980	1981	1982	1983	1984
Old Debt						
1. 7½% subordinated debentures due 1983	$ 12.2	$ 12.2	$ 12.2	$ 12.2	$ 0	$ 0
2. Other long-term debt	4.24	3.77	3.32	3.11	2.86	2.61
New Debt						
3. Bank term notes	$125.0	$108.33	$91.67	$75.00	$58.34	$41.67
4. 11¼% senior notes due 1995	113.6	113.6	106.0	98.3	90.7	83.1
5. 12¼% subordinated notes due 2000	89.8	89.8	89.8	89.8	89.8	89.8
6. Preferred stock $11.00 (322,000 shares)	26.2	26.2	26.2	26.2	26.2	—
Common Stock						
7. Par value .10 (1,000,000 shares)	$ .1	$ .1	$ .1	$ .1	$ .1	$ .1
8. Paid-in surplus	24.9	24.9	24.9	24.9	24.9	24.9
Interest						
9. 7½% subordinated debentures ⎫ (assumed in acquisition)		$ .92	$ .92	$ .92	$ .92	$ —
10. Other long-term debt ⎭		.30	.26	.23	.22	.20
11. Bank term notes @ 14%		17.50	15.17	12.83	10.50	8.17
12. 11¼% senior notes		12.94	12.94	12.08	11.22	10.23
13. 12¼% subordinated notes		11.27	11.27	11.27	11.27	11.27
14. Total interest payments		$ 42.92	$40.56	$37.33	$34.12	$29.87
15. Preferred dividend		3.54	3.54	3.54	3.54	3.54
Amortization						
16. 7½% subordinated debentures ⎫ (assumed in acquisition)	$ .46	$ —	$ —	$ —	$ —	$ —
17. Other long-term debt ⎭		.47	.45	.21	.24	.25[a]
18. Bank term notes		16.67	16.67	16.67	16.67	16.67
19. 11¼% senior notes		—	7.67	7.67	7.68	7.67
20. 12¼% subordinated notes		—	—	—	—	—
21. Total: Interest, principal, dividends		63.60	68.85	65.39	74.41	57.96

Note: Totals may not add exactly due to rounding.

a. Includes anticipated repayments as well as required repayments.

RJR Nabisco

On October 20, 1988, Charles E. Hugel, chairman of RJR Nabisco, was appointed chairman of the Special Committee. The Special Committee (Exhibit 1) was formed to consider a proposal to purchase the company for $17 billion by a group (the Management Group) consisting of F. Ross Johnson, president and chief executive officer of RJR Nabisco; Edward A. Horrigan, vice chairman of RJR Nabisco and chief executive officer of RJ Reynolds Tobacco Company; and the investment banking firm of Shearson Lehman Hutton. At $75 per share, the buyout offer was 34% above the pre-offer price of $55.875. No details about the form of the offer were immediately available.[1] Within four days, Kohlberg, Kravis, Roberts & Co. (KKR), a firm specializing in leveraged buyouts, announced a competing tender offer for RJR Nabisco. The KKR bid was for $90 per share, or about $20.3 billion in total.

Company Background

RJR Nabisco began as a tobacco company in 1875 and remained primarily a tobacco company until the RJR Foods subsidiary was formed after a series of acquisitions in 1967. By 1987 the company's sales had grown to $15.8 billion (Exhibit 2), and assets stood at $16.9 billion (Exhibit 3). The tobacco business included established brand-name cigarettes such as Winston, Salem, Camel, and Vantage, and also products such as Planters nuts and LifeSavers candies. The business segment data in Exhibit 4 show that the tobacco business had sales of $6.3 billion and operating income of $1.8 billion in 1987.

The food products initially included Hawaiian Punch beverages, Chun King oriental foods, My-T-Fine puddings, Davis baking powder, Vermont Maid syrup, and Patio Mexican dinners. Del Monte, which was acquired in 1979, added canned goods and

This case was prepared by Professor Richard S. Ruback.

Copyright © 1989 by the President and Fellows of Harvard College.
Harvard Business School case 289–056.

1. The directors of RJR Nabisco viewed Mr. Johnson's consideration of a buyout as material information and disclosed the buyout proposal when it was discussed by the board.

fresh bananas and pineapples. RJR Nabisco's food businesses expanded substantially with the 1985 acquisition of Nabisco Brands, Inc., which added brand names like Oreo, Fig and Fruit Newtons, and Chips Ahoy! cookies; Ritz, American Classic, and Quakers crackers; Nabisco Shredded Wheat cereal; Fleischmann's margarine; A-1 Steak Sauce; Ortega Mexican foods; and Milk-Bone dog biscuits. In 1987 the food business had sales of $9.4 billion and an operating income of $915 million.

RJR Nabisco had also entered and exited several lines of business. Sea-Land, a container-shipping company, was acquired in 1969 and divested in 1984. Heublein, Inc., a producer of alcoholic beverages and the owner of Kentucky Fried Chicken, was acquired in 1982. Kentucky Fried Chicken was sold in 1986, and the wine and spirits business of Heublein was sold in 1987. The company entered the energy business with the acquisition of American Independent Oil Company in 1970 and the U.S. subsidiaries of Burmah Oil Company in 1976. It exited the energy business by selling these assets in 1984.

Exhibit 5 contains projections for RJR Nabisco, assuming that it continued under its pre-offer operating plans. A total of nearly $10 billion in capital expenditures was projected for 1989 through 1998. The major investment in the tobacco business was extending development and test marketing of Premier, a smokeless cigarette. The company had already spent $300 million on Premier, and substantial costs would be associated with manufacturing and marketing the product. It had also approved plans to spend about $2.8 billion to modernize Nabisco's bakeries. The plans included constructing two new bakeries for $600 million each, spending $1.6 billion on the complete retrofittings of four plants, and closing five others.

The Management Group Bid

The Management Group's strategy was to sell off RJR Nabisco's food businesses and retain its tobacco business. The strategy was based on the view that the market undervalued the strong cash flow from the tobacco business and did not fully value its food businesses because of its association with tobacco. Selling RJR Nabisco's food assets and taking the tobacco business private would eliminate the undervaluation and generate substantial gains.

F. Ross Johnson had experience selling food assets. He was CEO of Standard Brands when Nabisco acquired it to form Nabisco Brands in 1981. And he was CEO of Nabisco Brands when RJ Reynolds acquired it in 1985 to form RJR Nabisco. Furthermore, the Management Group bid occurred when the food industry was undergoing a major restructuring and revaluation. Both Pillsbury and Kraft were in the midst of takeover contests.

Grand Metropolitan PLC began a hostile tender offer for Pillsbury on October 4, 1988. Grand Met was a diversified British company that brewed and distributed beer, ale, and lager; produced and distributed alcoholic beverages; and owned and operated pubs and restaurants. Pillsbury was a diversified food and restaurant company, with popular brands such as Pillsbury Doughboy bakery items, Green Giant vegetables, and Häagen-Dazs ice cream in its food business, and Burger King in its restaurant group. The $5.2 billion Grand Met bid was a 53% premium over the previous market price—about 25 times Pillsbury's net earnings and about four times the book value of common equity.[2] Pillsbury opposed the bid, and its outcome was uncertain.

---

2. Pillsbury's 1988 net earnings per share were $2.45, excluding unusual items, and $.81, including unusual items. The difference was due to a restructuring charge of $1.64 per share. Its 1987 net earnings per share were $2.24, excluding unusual items, and $2.10, including unusual items.

Philip Morris offered to purchase all Kraft common stock at $90 per share in cash on October 18, 1988. Like RJR Nabisco, Philip Morris earned most of its profits from tobacco: its Marlboro, Benson & Hedges, and Virginia Slims cigarettes had 1987 sales of $14.6 billion and operating profits of $3.3 billion. And, also like RJR Nabisco, Philip Morris acquired most of its food assets in 1985. Philip Morris acquired General Foods, which had brand-name products such as Maxwell House coffee, Birds Eye frozen foods, Jell-O, Oscar Mayer meats, Ronzoni pasta, and Post cereals. Philip Morris also had brewing interests, with brands like Miller, Miller Lite, and Matilda Bay Wine Coolers. Kraft was known for such brand names as Miracle Whip, Seven Seas, and Kraft salad dressings; Kraft mayonnaise; Velveeta cheese; Parkay and Chiffon margarines; Lender's Bagels; and Breyers ice cream. The $11 billion Philip Morris offer for Kraft was a 50% premium over the pre-offer stock price and about 21 times Kraft's net earnings.[3]

Based on the prices bid for Pillsbury and Kraft, analysts estimated the value of RJR Nabisco's food businesses as follows (billions of dollars):

Nabisco	$	8–9.5
Del Monte	$	3–4
Planters	$	1.5–2
Total	$	12.5–15.5

Exhibit 6 contains projections for RJR Nabisco under the Management Group plan.

The KKR Bid

Henry Kravis, a general partner of KKR, first expressed interest in organizing a leveraged buyout of RJR Nabisco at a September 1987 dinner meeting with F. Ross Johnson. KKR had been organized in 1976 by three former executives of Bear Stearns Companies, Inc.: Jerome Kohlberg, Henry Kravis, and George Roberts. Since then, KKR had acquired more than 35 companies, paying more than $38 billion in total. KKR also completed the $6.2 billion leveraged buyout of Beatrice foods in 1986, at the time the largest completed leveraged buyout.

KKR offered to purchase up to 87% of RJR Nabisco common stock for $90 per share in cash. The remaining shares would receive securities with a value of $90 per share and terms to be negotiated by KKR and the Special Committee. KKR's $20.7 billion bid also offered $108 per share for the preferred stock of RJR Nabisco.[4] The KKR bid was conditional on approval of the merger by RJR Nabisco's board of directors.

KKR's strategy for managing RJR Nabisco contrasted sharply with the Management Group's proposal to sell all of the company's food assets. According to KKR's letter to the Special Committee:

> We do not contemplate the dismemberment of the company's operations. . . . Our present intention is to retain all of the tobacco businesses and to continue their important presence in Winston-Salem, North Carolina. We also expect to retain a significant portion of the food

---

3. Kraft's forecasted 1988 net income from continuing operations was $522 million. It also had income of $658 million from the sale of its Duracell battery business to KKR in 1988.

4. RJR Nabisco had 225,336,442 shares of common stock outstanding and outstanding employee stock options to purchase 3,628,414 common shares. There were 1,308,760 shares of preferred stock outstanding.

operations. Moreover, our financing plan does not require, nor do we intend, any presales of parts of the company.

Exhibit 7 contains projections for RJR Nabisco under the KKR operating plan.

KKR did not present specific details on financing for its offer. It had raised a $5.6 billion pool of equity capital for investments in leveraged buyouts. Also, KKR retained Morgan Stanley Group, Inc., Wasserstein, Perella & Co., Drexel Burnham Lambert Inc., and Merrill Lynch Capital Markets to assist in financing the cash portion of the buyout.

Following its bid, KKR entered into a confidentiality agreement with RJR Nabisco, giving KKR access to nonpublic material information about the company. The agreement also gave KKR the opportunity to meet with RJR Nabisco's management. Meeting them was especially important to KKR because its rival, the Management Group, had access to such information because of its position within the firm. In return for access to the information, KKR agreed not to purchase any RJR Nabisco securities, participate in a proxy contest, or advise or influence any participant in such a contest for 2 years unless it obtained approval of RJR Nabisco's board of directors.

KKR invited the Management Group to join with it in a joint bid. However, the two parties could not agree on a joint bid and abandoned the attempt on October 26, 1987. A second attempt to form a joint bid also failed, on November 3, and later that same day the Management Group announced a revised proposal to acquire RJR Nabisco. The revised bid was for $92 per share, or $21.1 billion in total, and included $84 per share in cash and $8 per share in securities. Like the KKR bid, no details on the financing for the offer or the terms of the securities were available.

In addition to the bids by the Management Group and KKR, a third bid for RJR Nabisco by groups led by Forstmann, Little & Co. and First Boston Corporation was being considered. The Forstmann, Little group had entered into a confidentiality agreement much like KKR's agreement with RJR Nabisco.

The Auction

On November 7, the Special Committee adopted a set of rules and procedures "to determine which alternative would best serve the interests of [RJR Nabisco's] shareholders." Although not a commitment to recommend selling the company, the rules were "intended to constitute a single round of bidding. Any proposal should reflect the potential purchaser's highest offer." All bids were due by 5 P.M. on Friday, November 18. Any bid that did not conform to these rules would be considered hostile by the Special Committee.[5] The rules for bids included the following:

- Proposals should not be conditional on the sale of any assets of RJR Nabisco.
- Proposals should provide RJR Nabisco shareholders with a "substantial common-stock-related interest."
- Proposals should include details on financing arrangements, including commitment agreements and details of any noncash component of the offer.
- Proposals should be approved by the bidding firm's board of directors.

---

5. RJR Nabisco had a variety of antitakeover provisions that could be used to oppose a hostile offer, including a supermajority provision (requiring a two-thirds vote of disinterested shareholders to approve a merger), a poison pill rights plan (which forces an acquiring firm to purchase preferred stock at a substantial premium), and Section 203 of Delaware Law (which prevents a merger within 3 years of acquiring 15% or more of a target firm).

The board of directors and the Special Committee reserved the right to amend or terminate any of the rules, to terminate discussions with any bidder, and to reject any or all proposals.

The Bids

On a per share basis, KKR's bid was $75 cash, $11 for pay-in-kind preferred stock, and $6 principal amount of pay-in-kind converting debt, which KKR valued at $8.[6] The debt would convert to common stock at the end of 1 year unless the holder decided to retain it. If all debt was converted into common stock, it would represent 25% of the outstanding common stock of RJR Nabisco. The cash portion of the bid would be financed by $1.5 billion in equity, $3.5 billion in subordinated debt, and $12.4 billion in bank debt. KKR also planned on assuming the $5.2 billion of preexisting debt.

On a per share basis, the Management Group's bid was $90 cash, $6 of pay-in-kind preferred stock, and $4 of convertible preferred stock. The convertible preferred stock, as a class, could be converted into about 15% of the surviving company's equity, but it was callable by the company at any time for the face value and accumulated dividends. The cash portion of the bid would be financed by $2.5 billion in equity, $3 billion in subordinated debt, and $15 billion in bank debt. Like KKR, the Management Group planned on assuming the $5.2 billion of outstanding debt.

The First Boston group's offer involved the purchase of RJR Nabisco's tobacco business by the First Boston group and the sale of the food businesses. The food businesses would be sold for a $13 billion installment note before December 31, 1988, and a right to 80% of the net proceeds of the subsequent sale of the food business in excess of the installment note. RJR Nabisco shareholders would receive the proceeds from the sale of the food business. First Boston would purchase the tobacco business for $15.75 billion, plus warrants (valued at $2–3 per RJR Nabisco share) to acquire up to 20% of the equity of the tobacco business. On a per share basis, RJR Nabisco shareholders would receive a cash payment ranging from $98 to $110, securities valued at $5, and warrants worth $2–3. Unlike the bids by KKR and the Management Group, the First Boston proposal did not include information about its financing.

---

6. Pay-in-kind securities pay dividends and coupons with additional units of the security instead of cash.

EXHIBIT 1

Composition of the Special Committee of the RJR Nabisco Board of Directors to Consider Offers for the Company

Committee Member	Biographical Sketch	Common Stock Ownership (shares)
Charles E. Hugel, Chairman	Age 60; chairman of RJR Nabisco; president and chief executive officer of Combustion Engineering, Inc.	750
John D. Macomber, Vice Chairman	Age 60; chairman of Lasertechnics; retired chairman and chief executive officer of Celanese Corporation	16,425
Martin S. Davis	Age 61; chairman and chief executive officer of Gulf and Western, Inc.	1,000
William S. Anderson	Age 69; retired chairman and chief executive officer of the executive committee of NCR Corporation	1,500
Albert L. Butler, Jr.	Age 70; president of Arista Company; chairman of RJR Nabisco's organization, compensation, and nominating committee	9,465

Investment Bankers	Legal Counsel
Dillon, Read & Co.	Skadden, Arps, Slate, Meagher and Flom
Lazard Frères, Inc.	Young, Conaway, Stargatt and Taylor

EXHIBIT 2

Condensed Operating and Stockholder Information, 1982–1987 (millions of dollars except per share data)

	1982	1983	1984	1985	1986	1987
Revenues	$7,323	$7,565	$8,200	$11,622	$15,102	$15,766
Operating income	1,142	1,205	1,412	1,949	2,340	2,304
Interest and debt expense	180	177	166	337	565	489
Income before income taxes	1,012	1,110	1,353	1,663	1,782	1,816
Income from continuing operations	548	626	747	917	1,025	1,081
Income from discontinued operations[a]	322	255	463	84	39	128
Net income	$ 870	$ 881	$1,210	$ 1,001	$ 1,064	$ 1,209
Earnings per share	$ 3.13	$ 2.90	$ 4.11	$ 3.60	$ 3.83	$ 4.70
Dividends per share	1.14	1.22	1.30	1.41	1.51	1.76
Closing stock price[b]	20.40	24.30	28.80	31.38	49.25	45.00
Price-earnings ratio[b]	6.5	8.38	7.01	8.72	12.86	9.57
Numbers of shares (millions)[b, c]	281.5	283.2	258.4	250.6	250.4	247.4
Beta[d]	.80	.70	.74	1.21	1.24	.67

Sources: Company reports and casewriter's estimates.

a. Divestitures and acquisitions for 1982–1987 are as follows:

    1982   Heublein acquired for $1.36 billion.
    1983   Energy division sold for after-tax gain of $275 million.
    1984   Divestiture of transportation division completed by spinning off common stock to Sea-Land Corp. (transportation accounted for as a discontinued operation since 1983).
    1985   Nabisco Brands acquired at a total cost of $4.9 billion.
    1986   Kentucky Fried Chicken sold at after-tax loss of $39 million.
    1987   Heublein sold for after-tax gain of $215 million.

b. Year-end.

c. Figures include a 2.5-for-1 stock split effective May 17, 1985.

d. Calculated by ordinary least-squares regression using daily stock price data.

EXHIBIT 3
Consolidated Balance Sheets, 1986–1987 (millions of dollars)

	1986	*1987*
Cash	$ 827	$ 1,088
Net receivables	1,675	1,745
Inventories	2,620	2,678
Other current assets	273	329
Property, plant, and equipment, net	5,343	5,847
Goodwill and other intangibles	4,603	4,525
Net assets of discontinued operations	716	—
Other assets	644	649
Total assets	$16,701	$16,861
Notes payable	$ 518	$ 442
Accounts payable	2,923	3,187
Current portion of long-term debt	423	162
Income taxes payable	202	332
Current liabilities	4,066	4,123
Long-term debt	4,833	3,884
Deferred income taxes	751	846
Redeemable preferred stock	291	173
Other liabilities	1,448	1,797
Total liabilities	11,389	10,823
Stockholders' equity	5,312	6,038
Total liabilities and net worth	$16,701	$16,861

Source: Company reports.

EXHIBIT 4
Financial Summary by Business Segment, 1982–1987 (millions of dollars)

	1982	1983	1984	1985	1986	1987
Tobacco						
Sales	$4,822	$4,807	$5,178	$5,422	$5,866	$6,346
Operating profit	1,187	1,150	1,305	1,483	1,659	1,821
Identifiable assets	3,219	3,378	3,812	4,496	4,822	5,208
Depreciation	81	78	108	146	205	244
Capital expenditures	238	383	527	647	613	433
Restructuring expense	—	—	—	—	—	(261)
Operating profit/identifiable assets	36.9%	34.0%	34.2%	33.0%	34.0%	35.0%
Food Products						
Sales	$2,501	$2,758	$3,022	$6,200	$9,236	$9,420
Operating profit	21	129	181	549	820	915
Identifiable assets	1,710	1,761	2.211	9,598	9,822	10,117
Depreciation	51	56	68	195	376	380
Capital expenditures	84	94	86	279	344	445
Restructuring expense	—	—	—	—	—	18
Operating profit/Identifiable assets	1.2%	7.3%	8.2%	6.0%	8.0%	9.0%
Spirits and Wines						
Sales	$ 392	$ 746	$ 703	$ 766	$ 876	—
Operating profit	53	113	122	131	138	—
Identifiable assets	1,084	740	815	895	991	—
Depreciation	14	24	22	24	30	—
Capital expenditures	11	13	13	26	25	—
Restructuring expense	—	—	—	—	—	—
Operating profit/Identifiable assets	4.9%	15.,3%	15.0%	14.6%	14.0%	—
Other (Including Corporate)[a]						
Sales	—	—	—	—	—	—
Operating profit (loss)	$ (66)	$ (74)	$ (74)	($ 83)	$ (139)	$ (182)
Identifiable assets	3,106	3,197	2,257	1,684	1,319	1,536
Depreciation	11	16	16	13	24	28
Capital expenditures	16	15	29	20	65	58
Restructuring expense	—	—	—	—	—	(7)
Operating profit/Identifiable assets	−2.1%	−2.3%	−3.3%	−5.0%	−10.5%	−11.9%

Source: Company reports.

a. Includes earnings on cash and short-term investments and miscellaneous discontinued operations.

EXHIBIT 5
Cash Flow Projections under Pre-Bid Strategy, 1988–1998 (millions of dollars)

	1988	1989	1990	1991	1992	1993	1994	1995	1996	1997	1998
Tobacco sales	$7,061	$ 7,650	$ 8,293	$ 8,893	$ 9,731	$10,540	$11,418	$12,368	$13,397	$14,514	$15,723
Food sales	9,889	10,438	11,383	12,092	12,847	13,651	14,507	15,420	16,393	17,428	18,533
Total	16,950	18,088	19,676	21,075	22,578	24,191	25,925	27,788	29,790	31,942	34,256
Operating income (expense)											
Tobacco	1,924	2,022	2,360	2,786	3,071	3,386	3,733	4,115	4,534	4,998	5,508
Food	1,079	1,163	1,255	1,348	1,459	1,581	1,713	1,855	2,011	2,178	2,361
Corporate	(350)	(287)	(279)	(296)	(314)	(333)	(353)	(374)	(396)	(420)	(445)
Total	2,653	2,898	3,336	3,838	4,216	4,634	5,093	5,596	6,149	6,756	7,424
Interest expense	551	582	662	693	690	658	594	458	410	259	−21
Net income	1,360	1,498	1,730	2,023	2,259	2,536	2,858	3,251	3,625	4,094	4,625
Depreciation, amortization, deferred taxes	730	807	791	819	849	866	867	867	867	867	861
Capital expenditures	1,142	1,708	1,462	1,345	930	738	735	735	735	735	735
Change in working capital	—	80	111	98	105	113	121	130	140	151	162
Cash flow available for capital payments[a]	—	$ 517	$ 948	$ 1,399	$ 2,073	$ 2,551	$ 2,869	$ 3,253	$ 3,617	$ 4,075	$ 4,589

a. Cash flow available for capital payments = Net income + Depreciation, amortization, deferred taxes − Capital expenditures − Change in working capital.

EXHIBIT 6
Cash Flow and Capital Structure Projections under the Management Group Strategy, 1989–1998 (millions of dollars)

	1989	1990	1991	1992	1993	1994	1995	1996	1997	1998
Operating Information										
Sales	$7,650	$8,293	$8,983	$9,731	$10,540	$11,418	$12,368	$13,397	$14,514	$15,723
Operating income	1,917	2,385	2,814	3,266	3,589	3,945	4,337	4,768	5,243	5,766
Interest expense	2,792	1,353	1,286	1,183	1,037	850	624	351	0	0
Amortization[a]	388	388	388	388	388	388	388	388	388	388
After-tax income	(965)	293	621	987	1,297	1,655	2,063	2,527	3,073	3,418
Depreciation, amortization, deferred taxes	777	725	726	735	749	754	758	763	769	774
Capital expenditures	432	381	380	389	396	402	412	422	432	442
Change in working capital	41	45	48	52	57	61	67	72	78	85
Net proceeds from asset sales	12,680	0	0	0	0	0	0	0	0	0
Cash flow available for capital payments[b]	$12,018	$ 593	$ 919	$1,282	$ 1,594	$ 1,946	$ 2,344	$ 2,797	$ 3,332	$ 3,666
Capital Structure										
Principal payments										
Assumed debt	$ 310	$ 375	$ 721	$ 816	$ 400	$ 728	$ 1,854	$ 0	$ 0	$ 0
Bank debt	11,708	218	198	466	1,194	1,217	0	0	0	0
Subordinated debt	0	0	0	0	0	0	490	2,510	0	0
Preferred stock	0	0	0	0	0	0	0	287	3,332	3,327
Convertible preferred stock	0	0	0	0	0	0	0	0	0	339
Total	$12,018	$ 593	$ 919	$1,282	$ 1,594	$ 1,946	$ 2,344	$ 2,797	$ 3,332	$ 3,666
Year-end book values										
Assumed debt	4,894	4,519	3,798	2,982	2,582	1,854	0	0	0	0
Bank debt	3,292	3,075	2,877	2,411	1,217	0	0	0	0	0
Subordinated debt	3,000	3,000	3,000	3,000	3,000	3,000	2,510	0	0	0
Total	$11,186	$10,594	$9,675	$8,393	$ 6,799	$ 4,854	$ 2,510	$ 0	$ 0	$ 0
Preferred stock	1,632	1,938	2,303	2,736	3,250	3,861	4,587	5,162	2,801	0
Convertible preferred stock	1,035	1,229	1,460	1,735	2,061	2,448	2,909	3,455	4,105	4,538
Common stock	1,535	1,828	2,449	3,436	4,733	6,388	8,451	10,978	14,051	17,469
Total	$ 4,202	$ 4,995	$6,212	$7,907	$10,044	$12,697	$15,947	$19,595	$20,957	$22,007

Note: Figures may not add exactly because of rounding.

a. The amortization of goodwill of $338 million per year is from the proposed acquisition of RJR Nabisco at $22.9 billion, which had the book value of $7.4 billion at the end of 1988. The difference between the purchase price and book value is amortized over 40 years using the straight-line method.

b. Cash flow available for capital payments = Net income + Depreciation, amortization, deferred taxes – Capital expenditures – Change in working capital + Net proceeds from asset sales.

EXHIBIT 7

Cash Flow and Capital Structure Projections under KKR's Strategy, 1989–1998 (millions of dollars)

	1989	1990	1991	1992	1993	1994	1995	1996	1997	1998
Operating Information										
Tobacco sales	$ 7,650	$ 8,293	$ 3,983	$ 9,731	$10,540	$11,418	$12,368	$13,397	$14,514	$15,723
Food sales	8,540	6,930	7,485	8,084	8,730	9,428	10,183	10,997	11,877	12,827
Total	16,190	15,223	16,468	17,815	19,270	20,846	22,551	24,394	26,391	28,550
Operating income (expense)										
Tobacco	2,022	2,360	2,786	3,071	3,386	3,733	4,115	4,534	4,998	5,508
Food	1,060	1,026	1,191	1,245	1,307	1,367	1,430	1,494	1,561	1,630
Corporate	(219)	(158)	(167)	(176)	(185)	(194)	(203)	(213)	(224)	(235)
Total	2,862	3,228	3,811	4,140	4,508	4,906	5,341	5,815	6,335	6,902
Interest expense	2,754	2,341	1,997	1,888	1,321	1,088	806	487	21	0
Amortization[a]	388	388	388	388	388	388	388	388	388	388
After-tax income	(281)	233	845	1,134	1,751	2,168	2,641	3,164	3,814	4,203
Depreciation, amortization, deferred taxes	1,159	991	899	907	920	924	928	933	939	945
Capital expenditures	774	556	555	572	586	598	618	638	658	678
Change in working capital	79	84	87	94	102	110	119	129	140	151
Noncash interest expense	206	237	312	366	0	0	0	0	0	0
Net proceeds from asset sales	3,500	2,700	0	0	0	0	0	0	0	0
Cash flow available for capital payments[b]	$ 3,732	$ 3,521	$ 1,414	$ 1,740	$ 1,983	$ 2,383	$ 2,832	$ 3,330	$ 3,956	$ 4,319
Capital Structure										
Principal payments										
Assumed debt	$ 310	$ 375	$ 721	$ 816	$ 400	$ 400	$ 2,182	$ 0	$ 0	$ 0
Bank debt	3,422	3,146	693	924	1,583	1,983	629	0	0	0
Subordinated debt	0	0	0	0	0	0	21	3,330	149	0
Preferred stock	0	0	0	0	0	0	0	0	3,806	4,319
Total	$ 3,732	$ 3,521	$ 1,414	$ 1,740	$ 1,983	$ 2,383	$ 2,832	$ 3,330	$ 3,956	$ 4,319
Year-end book values										
Assumed debt	4,894	4,519	3,798	2,982	2,582	2,182	0	0	0	0
Bank debt	8,958	5,812	5,119	4,195	2,612	629	0	0	0	0
Subordinated debt	3,500	3,500	3,500	3,500	3,500	3,500	3,470	149	0	0
Converting debt[c]	1,580	1,817	2,129	2,495	0	0	0	0	0	0
Total	18,932	15,648	14,546	13,172	8,694	6,311	3,470	149	0	0
Preferred stock	2,896	3,331	3,958	4,702	5,586	6,636	7,883	9,365	7,320	4,377
Common stock	1,219	1,452	2,297	3,430	7,676	9,844	12,485	15,648	19,463	23,666
Total	$ 4,115	$ 4,783	$ 6,255	$ 8,132	$13,262	$16,480	$20,368	$25,013	$26,783	$28,043

Note: Figures may not add exactly because of rounding.

a. The amortization of goodwill of $338 million per year is from the proposed acquisition of RJR Nabisco at $22.9 billion, which had the book value of $7.4 billion at the end of 1988. The difference between the purchase price and the book value is amortized over 40 years using the straight-line method.

b. Cash flow available for capital payments = Net income + Depreciation, amortization, deferred taxes − Capital expenditures − Change in working capital + Noncash interest expense + Net proceeds from asset sales.

c. Assumes converting to equity in 1993.

Marriott Corporation (A)

Over the next few years we will place special emphasis on enhancing our strong customer preference, increasing operating cash flow and reducing debt.

—Chairman's letter to shareholders,
Marriott Corporation *1990 Annual Report,* p. 3

Priorities for the next few years: Reduce our long-term debt to about $2 billion by the end of 1994, by maximizing cash flow and selling assets.

—Chairman's letter to shareholders,
Marriott Corporation *1991 Annual Report,* p. 5
[Third in a list of four priorities.]

J.W. Marriott, Jr., chairman of the board and president of Marriott Corporation (MC), had weathered difficult times in the last few years. The company his father had founded in 1927 had grown explosively during the 1980s, developing hotel properties around the world and selling them to outside investors while retaining lucrative long-term management contracts. However, the economic slowdown in the late 1980s and the 1990 real estate market crash left MC owning many newly developed properties for which there were no buyers, together with a massive burden of debt. As Marriott had promised in successive annual reports in recent years, the company was working to sell properties and reduce that burden, but progress was slow. Looking ahead to the end of 1992, three months away, financial results promised to be only slightly better than for 1991, although still a significant improvement over the low point reached in 1990. For the foreseeable future, MC's ability to raise funds in the capital markets would be severely limited.

This case was prepared by Research Associate Charles A. Nichols III under the supervision of Professor Lynn Sharp Paine.

Copyright © 1993 by the President and Fellows of Harvard College.
Harvard Business School case 394–085.

But Marriott now faced a decision that had the potential to change this situation completely. He was considering a radical restructuring of the company proposed by Stephen Bollenbach, the new chief financial officer (CFO), under which the bulk of MC's service businesses would be split off from its property holdings—and debt. A new company would be created for the service businesses, with existing shareowners of MC receiving a share of stock in the new company to match each share they owned in the old one. The new company would have the financial strength to raise capital to take advantage of investment opportunities. The old one, valued for the chance of appreciation in its property holdings when the real estate market recovered, and not on the basis of earnings, would be under less pressure to sell properties at depressed prices.

Bollenbach had served as treasurer of MC in the early 1980s at the beginning of its period of rapid growth. After leaving in the middle of the decade, he had built a reputation for creating innovative financial structures in the hotel industry with the 1987 recapitalization of Holiday Corporation (later named Promus Companies, Inc.), and then with his rescue of Donald Trump's heavily indebted real estate holdings. Bollenbach returned to MC as CFO in February 1992. His proposed restructuring, called Project Chariot, reflected the imaginative and innovative thinking characteristic of the financial advisors who had contributed so much to MC's growth in the 1980s.

Project Chariot seemed like the perfect solution to the company's problems. Was it the right step to take now? MC's board of directors would be meeting soon, and Marriott needed to decide what to recommend.

Company and Industry Background[1]

Founding and Early Years

With 202,000 employees at the end of 1991, MC was ranked as the twelfth-largest employer in the United States.[2] The company traced its beginnings to 1927, when J.W. Marriott Sr. opened a small root beer stand in Washington, D.C. The business soon began to sell food and was renamed the Hot Shoppe restaurant. Working with his wife, Alice, Marriott Sr. saw the business grow throughout the 1930s and 1940s into a family-owned chain of 45 restaurants in nine states. The Marriotts also acquired contracts to run cafeterias and company kitchens, as well as to supply food to the airline industry. Growth and success were based upon a policy of careful attention to details and centralized and standardized operating procedures.

Initial Public Offering

MC went public in 1953, selling one-third of its shares. Although the company continued to sell stock to the public over the years, in 1992 the Marriott family still owned 25% of the company. In the first 5 years after the initial stock offering, it had doubled in size. In 1956 it opened its first hotel, in Washington, and in the next 8 years had grown to 120 Hot Shoppes and 12 hotels. J.W. Marriott Sr. resigned the position of president in 1964, passing it to his son J.W. Marriott Jr., then only 32. Under the son's leadership, MC abandoned the father's conservative financial policies. It turned to major borrowing to finance expansion that would maintain its historical 20% annual

---

1. Much of the material in this section is based upon Keith F. Girard's, "What the Hell Happened to Marriott?" *Regardies,* April–May 1991, pp. 71–91.

2. *Dun's Business Rankings,* 1993.

revenue growth rate. In the 1970s, MC began to use bank credit and unsecured debt instead of mortgages to finance development. According to new financial thinking developing in the company, borrowing was acceptable as long as cash flow was maintained at a sufficient multiple of interest charges. The company acquired restaurant chains and entered new businesses, such as theme park development and operation.

Joint Ventures

In 1978, MC embarked upon its first joint venture, constructing a group of hotels and then selling them to the Equitable Life Assurance Society, a major insurance company. Thus began a powerful growth strategy in which the company would plan and develop hotels, sell the properties to investors, and retain long-term management contracts. By 1980, following a 5-year period of 30% annual growth, 70% of MC's hotel rooms were owned by outside investors. MC possessed an enviable reputation for quality and reliability in service, and together with careful site selection procedures and hotel sizing, this reputation translated into occupancy rates 4–6% above industry averages. This gap had widened to more than 10% by 1992; when the industry average was only around 65%, MC's rate was 76–80%.[3]

The Economic Recovery Tax Act of 1981 created new incentives for the ownership of real estate, which further fueled MC's hotel-developing activities. Its first real estate limited partnership, offered in that year, gave investors $9 in tax writeoffs for every $1 invested. Beginning in 1983, MC also branched out into the mid-price lodging market with "Courtyard" hotels, which were bundled into groups of 50 or more for limited partnership offerings. In 1985 scaled-down but full-service "compact hotels" for smaller city markets, as well as all-suite hotels and longer-term residence inns were introduced; MC entered the budget hotel market with "Fairfield Inns" in 1987. MC also continued to acquire restaurant chains, including Gino's in 1982 and Howard Johnson's in 1985, although its success in establishing a national business in this area was limited. In 1984 the company discontinued its theme park operations.

End of the Boom

In 1986 the Tax Reform Act ended most of the tax incentives for real estate investment, but MC, relying on the strong economy and its own reputation, continued its high-paced development activities. However, the market for its limited partnerships was drying up, and in 1989 the company experienced a sharp drop in income. It froze capital expenditures, which had increased threefold over the previous 6 years, sold off its airline in-flight catering business, and discontinued its restaurant operations. In 1990 the real estate market collapsed. MC's income plummeted and its year-end stock price fell by more than two-thirds, a drop of over $2 billion in market capitalization. For the first time, investor-owned Marriott hotels went bankrupt.

MC was saddled with large interest payments on properties it was unable to sell. Industry excess capacity led to low occupancy rates and deep discounting on room rates, resulting in large losses for many of MC's competitors and even bankruptcies in some cases. In 1991, MC intensified its focus on contract and management opportunities that required less capital outlay. These included captive food service markets such as hospitals, office buildings, and turnpike service plazas, as well as management of golf courses. The development and management of "life-care" community facilities

---

3. Joseph J. Doyle, CFA, *Marriott Corporation,* Smithy Barney Research Report (released December 18, 1992).

TABLE A
Market Statistics on Marriott Corporation, September 1992

Recent market price	$16.00
Estimated earnings per share	.75
Stock beta	1.30
Price/earnings ratio	
Marriott Corporation	21.30
S&P 500 Industrials (close of 3Q1992)	26.00
S&P Hotel/Motel (close of 3Q1992)	22.70

Sources: Value Line reports (September 4, 1992); MC annual statement; *S&P Analysts' Handbook.*

for senior citizens was also a high-growth market that MC had entered, but capital constraints forced it to cut back on planned new construction.

Thus, the MC of September 1992 was a far cry from the real estate development engine of the 1980s. Capital spending had been reduced to an annual level of $350 million, only the amount necessary to maintain and refurbish the existing properties. While the company had improved its position from the low point in 1990, investors still regarded it at best as a company beset by the problems of a severely depressed industry, with several years of slow recovery ahead before it could begin to grow again. (See Table A for market statistics on MC.)

Corporate Culture

However, MC remained a company with many strengths, not least of which was a unique corporate culture built around the personality and values of the Marriott family, and especially of J.W. Marriott Sr., the founder. In every Marriott hotel lobby hung a painting of the two J.W. Marriotts; every Marriott hotel room contained a Gideon Bible, the Book of Mormon, and an authorized biography of J.W. Marriott Sr., a book commissioned and written in the 1970s and published in 1977.[4] The biography detailed the life of the founder, beginning with his roots in the Mormon frontier communities in Utah, his childhood and early struggles in difficult economic circumstances, and his work for several years as a missionary for his church. It described the source of his lifelong aversion to borrowing: the burden of debt on his family's sheep farm in Utah and the resulting foreclosure during the depression following World War I. The book closed with the picture of a wealthy and respected man, a leader in his church and active in politics and philanthropy.

In describing the growth of the MC, the book stressed the themes of careful attention to detail and organization, and above all of service to customers. But the organization itself was focused on the employees. On his retirement in 1964, in a letter to his son and successor, J.W. Marriott Sr. listed a number of "guideposts" in his management philosophy, including the principle that "People are No. 1—their development, loyalty, interest, team spirit."[5] And 9 years later, in introducing J.W. Marriott Sr. as a speaker to the employees at the opening of the Los Angeles Marriott, a company senior executive remarked, "Marriott believes that the customer is great, but you come first. Mr. Marriott knows that if he takes care of his employees, they'll take care of the customers."[6]

---

4. Robert O'Brien, *Marriott: The J. Willard Marriott Story* (Salt Lake City: Desert Book Company, 1977).

5. Ibid., p. 266.

6. Ibid., p. 8.

Project Chariot[7]

Under Project Chariot, MC would become two separate companies. The division would be effected by a special stock dividend, giving stockholders of MC a share of stock in the new company to match each share they held of MC. The new company, to be called Marriott International, Inc. (MII), would comprise MC's lodging, food, and facilities management businesses, as well as the management of its life-care facilities. Food management had become a major segment of MC's business. With nearly 3,000 accounts, it included as clients some of the largest corporations and educational institutions in the United States. The existing company, to be renamed Host Marriott Corporation (HMC), would retain MC's real estate holdings and its concessions on tollroads and in airports (see Exhibit 1 for details). The transaction would be conditioned upon a ruling from the International Revenue Service that the special dividend would be tax free to shareholders, and upon ratification by a majority of MC stockholders. The plan called for the distribution of the dividend by mid-1993.

Under the plan, MII and HMC would have separate management teams. J.W. Marriott Jr. would be chairman, president, and chief executive officer of MII; his brother Richard Marriott (currently vice chairman of MC) would be chairman of HMC; and Stephen Bollenbach (the current MC chief financial officer) would be HMC's president and chief executive officer. The two companies would also have separate boards of directors, except that the two brothers would each serve on both boards. MII would have an ongoing contractual relationship with HMC similar to the current relationship between MC and owners of hotel properties managed by MC. Such contracts typically involved the payment by the property owners of an annual management fee of 2–3% of revenues. Similarly, MII would have the right to lease and operate the senior living facilities owned by HMC.

Under the spin-off, MII would have the right to purchase up to 20% of HMC's voting stock at market value in the event of a change in control of HMC. MII would also have right of first refusal if HMC offered its toll road and airport concessions for sale.

In the past several years, MC had reduced its work force significantly in response to its difficult economic situation. It was not expected that Project Chariot would lead to further cuts in the work force. After the division, MII would have 182,000 employees, and in 1992, on a projected pro forma basis, would have had $7.9 billion in sales and operating cash flow before corporate expenses, interest expense, and taxes of $408 million. HMC would have 23,000 employees, and 1992 projected pro forma sales of $1.8 billion, with operating cash flow before corporate expenses, interest expense, and taxes of $363 million. Under the plan, HMC would retain nearly all of MC's long-term debt of nearly $3 billion, although it would have access to a revolving line of credit of $600 million from MII through December 1997. However, MII itself would have very little long-term debt (see Exhibit 1).

Management Perspectives

Pure Plays. Dividing MC into two companies was consistent with the company's general strategy of separating property ownership from management operations. The theory was that added value came from finding investment opportunities and develop-

---

7. Much of the material in this section is taken from Marriott Corporation Press Release, October 5, 1992, and from Mitch Hara, James Kirby, and Renee Noto, "Analysis of the Marriott Restructuring," a paper dated May 5, 1993, and written for the Harvard Business School class on Corporate Restructuring.

ing and managing hotels, not from the ownership of real estate. MC management had long felt that the financial markets undervalued the company's stock because of the difficulty investors had in distinguishing and separately valuing property ownership and management. Project Chariot offered investors the opportunity to participate in "pure plays" in the hotel management business and in hotel real estate investment business for longer-term appreciation.

Career Opportunities.   In many ways, Project Chariot would offer attractive possibilities to Marriott's management. In the downsizing of the previous few years, many executive positions had been lost. MC had also seen the departure of fast-track executives who decided that their chances of rapid ascent in the organization and wealth accumulation were not as good as elsewhere. With two separate companies, there would now be twice as many top-level positions, and with MII poised for rapid growth, ambitious managers would be more likely to stay. Managers with stock holdings and options would also benefit personally from the expected increase in the value of the company's stock after the Project Chariot restructuring.[8]

Opportunities for HMC and MII.   Because HMC would be valued more on the basis of the chance of appreciation in its property holdings than on expected income, the company would be under less pressure from investors to sell off hotels at distress prices. To the extent that HMC operated at a loss, the combined after-tax earnings of the two separate companies would be smaller than that of MC as a single entity, for HMC's losses would no longer offset MII's positive earnings. On the other hand, unburdened by debt, MII would have the ability to raise additional capital to finance growth, perhaps to participate in the consolidation of the hotel industry by purchasing the assets of competitors in financial difficulty. These new acquisitions would strengthen MII from a customer-service point of view.

Implications for Bondholders

While Project Chariot would very likely benefit stockholders in MC, the situation was quite different for bondholders. (See Exhibit 2 for a summary of MC's long-term debt.) Although MC management was confident that HMC would have the financial strength to make all payments of interest and principal on long-term obligations when due, the separation of the two companies would affect the security of MC debt holders. Bond rating agencies such as Moody's Investors Services (Moody's) and Standard and Poor's Corporation (S&P) were likely to lower the ratings on MC's long-term bonds to a level below investment grade. (See the Appendix for a discussion of bond ratings.) This development could force some institutional holders of MC debt to sell their holdings, since banks, insurance companies, and pension funds often operated under legal restrictions that limited the amount of non-investment-grade securities they could own. Fiduciaries managing such funds were also typically required by law to follow the "prudent person" rule in making investment decisions.

---

8. According to the MC March 1992 proxy statement, the Marriott family was deemed to control 25.75% (approximately 25.6 million shares) of common stock of MC. The holdings of all other directors, nominees, and executive officers amounted to approximately 300,000 shares. An additional 800,000 shares were set aside for executive officers under a restricted stock plan and deferred stock agreements, as well as approximately 2.8 million stock options (of which 1.1 million were currently exercisable) under a stock option plan.

Legal Considerations

Covenants.   MC's debt indentures contained the usual provisions but lacked so-called "event-risk" covenants that would have blocked the Project Chariot restructuring or required any measures to protect bondholders from its potentially adverse effects. Event-risk covenants had emerged in the 1980s when transactions such as leveraged buyouts (LBOs) had provided stockholders with large profits from tender offers at premium prices while creating large losses for bondholders in the reduced market value of their newly speculative investments. In response, bondholders began to insist on new covenants to protect them against the risk of the occurrence of such transactions.

These covenants provided that, on the occurrence of certain "triggering events," such as a merger or consolidation, a change in ownership, or a major distribution of cash or securities, the company might be required to redeem immediately all or a specified proportion of the debt, provide collateral, or increase the interest rate to market levels. Research revealed that in 1989, 30% of bonds issued included such covenants, with the securities of companies expected to be targets of takeovers more likely to be so protected.[9]

While event-risk covenants protected bondholders, they often did so at the cost of lower interest rates. With the collapse of the junk bond market in the early 1990s and the slowing of takeover and LBO activity, the use of such covenants decreased. None of MC's long-term debt indentures contained event-risk covenants, including the indentures under which MC issued $400 million of long-term bonds in April and May of 1992 (see Exhibit 2). These were now selling at 110, reflecting a general decline in market interest rates during 1992.

Fraudulent Conveyance[10].   Several LBOs that became insolvent were attacked by creditors using the legal theory of "fraudulent conveyance." The doctrine of fraudulent conveyance, which dated to a sixteenth-century English statute, protected creditors from debtors who tried to shelter their wealth or avoid their debts by conveying their property to others. In some cases of failed LBOs, unsecured creditors attempted to recover funds from those benefiting from the LBO transaction, such as shareholders or advisors to the transaction. Because it was often difficult to prove intentional fraud by these parties, most LBO-related fraudulent conveyance actions were brought under the constructive fraud provisions of statutes such as the Federal Bankruptcy Code, the Uniform Fraudulent Conveyance Act, or the Uniform Fraudulent Transfers Act. According to section 548(a)(2) of the Bankruptcy Code, constructive fraud could be established when the debtor

1. received less than reasonably equivalent value for the property transferred; *and*
2. either
   a. was insolvent or became insolvent as a result of the transfer,
   b. retained unreasonably small capital after the transfer, or
   c. made the transfer with the intent or belief that it would incur debts beyond its ability to pay.

---

9. Kenneth Lehn and Annette B. Poulsen, "Contractual Resolution of Bondholder–Stockholder Conflicts in Leveraged Buyouts," *Journal of Law and Economics* 24 (October 1991): 645–673.

10. Material in this paragraph is taken from Timothy A Luehrman and Lance L. Hirt, "Highly Leveraged Transactions and Fraudulent Conveyance Law," *The Continental Bank Journal of Applied Corporate Finance* 6, no. 1 (Spring 1993): 104–105.

In the LBO situation, the tests of solvency and capitalization were the critical factors in determining constructive fraud.[11] Since courts excluded from consideration both intangible value created by a transaction and tangible value received by anyone other than the debtor (the corporation), LBOs failed the "reasonably equivalent value test" by their very nature.

LBO lawsuits were rarely successful. In large cases, plaintiffs almost always agreed to settlements averaging less than ten cents for each dollar of their claims.[12] A review of two dozen decisions found only five with a verdict for the plaintiffs, and federal appeals courts ruled for the defendants in virtually every key case considered between 1986 and 1992. Among the most favored defendants were "public shareholders who received most of the funds, but did not control the deal."[13]

Duties to Bondholders. U.S. courts had held that corporations have no responsibilities to safeguard the interests of bondholders other than those spelled out by the terms of the bond indenture. For example, in 1986 the Delaware Court of Chancery stated in *Katz v. Oak Industries:*

> Arrangements among a corporation, the underwriters of its debt, trustees under its indentures, and sometimes ultimate investors, are typically thoroughly negotiated and massively documented. The rights and obligations of the various parties are, or should be, spelled out in that documentation. The terms of the contractual relationship agreed to, and not broad concepts such as fairness, define the corporation's duty to bondholders.[14]

However, a more recent Delaware Chancery Court decision took the position that the duties of corporate boards of directors toward holders of corporate debt could be more extensive than simply to observe indenture provisions, particularly when the corporation was facing serious economic difficulties or bankruptcy. In such cases, very risky courses of action could be beneficial to stockholders yet injurious to the interests of debt holders. In *Credit Lyonnais Bank N.V. v. Pathe Communications* (1991 WL 277613), the court imposed a duty on the board to respect "the community of interest that sustained the corporation, to exercise judgment in an informed, good faith effort to maximize the corporation's long-term wealth creating capacity."[15] A commentator noted that this decision altered the traditional approach in which "the board's duties to the company ran primarily to the stockholders, unless the company became insolvent, in which case the board's duty in some sense 'flipped' to creditors." In contrast, the new decision

> recognizes that there is no magic point at which duties should shift from stockholders to creditors. Instead, there is a continuum approaching insolvency in which the board's incentives become increasingly distorted and the creditor-stockholder conflict increases.[16]

The Delaware Chancery Court's decision in the *Credit Lyonnais* case was not based upon completely novel ideas about the legal responsibility of corporate leaders.

---

11. Ibid., pp. 106–107.

12. Jack Friedman, "LBO Lawsuits Don't Pick Deep Pockets," *The Wall Street Journal,* January 27, 1993.

13. Ibid.

14. Cited in Lehn and Poulsen, p. 646.

15. Richard P. Swanson, Esq., "Directors' Duties to Creditors," p. 16.

16. Ibid., p. 16.

As far back as 1932, E. Merrick Dodd Jr., in an article in the *Harvard Law Review,* noted that

> Despite many attempts to dissolve the corporation into an aggregate of stockholders, our legal tradition is rather in favor of treating it as an institution directed by persons who are primarily fiduciaries for the institution rather than for its members.[17]

However, Professor Dodd's view was far from the orthodox position of most financial economists and lawyers in 1990, who regarded managers as agents for the shareholders with responsibility primarily to protect and promote shareholders' interests.

Social and Economic Climate

As the junk bond market collapsed and many of its high-risk issues headed towards bankruptcy or renegotiation, public opinion regarding the acceptability of massive wealth transfers through financial engineering shifted. Although there were still defenders of such transactions, they were viewed with suspicion by large segments of the public who condemned them as paper transactions that contributed no real value to the economy. Junk bonds and real estate investments had left many financial intermediaries, such as commercial banks, pension funds, and life insurance companies, in financially shaky positions. Although commercial bank profits were starting to improve, the real estate market continued to languish as financial institutions shed nonperforming real estate loans, and residual fears dampened the enthusiasm of potential investors.

The Decision

Marriott wondered what he should recommend to the board of directors regarding Project Chariot. (See Exhibits 3–7 for relevant financial data.) He had been assured by legal counsel that the corporation was within its rights as a debtor to restructure itself in this way. Investment advisors had given him an opinion that the transaction was in the best interests of shareholders. His CFO, Bollenbach, was convinced that cash flows for HMC were more than adequate to cover debt service requirements. And surely, if public reaction were extremely negative, or if other difficulties arose, Project Chariot could be abandoned without significant loss. But with this transaction the company was entering new territory.

The board would be meeting soon, and Marriott needed to decide.

---

17. E. Merrick Dodd, Jr., "For Whom are Corporate Managers Trustees?" *Harvard Law Review* XLV, no. 7 (May 8, 1932): 1162–1163.

EXHIBIT 1

Project Chariot: Division of Marriott Corporation into Marriott International, Inc. and Host Marriott Corporation (amounts are projected)

Marriott Corporation

Project Chariot

Marriott International

Trademarks, reservation system
Franchise system, trade names
Land leased to affiliates
All management and franchise
    contracts on hotels, inns, suites,
    resorts
Marriott Management Services
Marriott Sr. Living Services
Marriott Distribution Services

Host Marriott Corp.

Owned real estate
    resorts, inns, suites, hotels
    retirement communities
Undeveloped land
Partnership interests in
    unconsolidated affiliates
Host/Travel Plazas

1992 Statistics[a]

	Marriott International	*Host Marriott Corp.*
EBIT	$259	$123
Interest	25	210
Net income	134	(49)
Preferred dividend	0	$ 17
Net income, common	$134	($66)
EPS	1.40	($0.69)
Total assets	$2,600	$4,600
Debt	400	2,000
Preferred stock	0	200
Common equity	800	600
Times interest	10.4	.59
Debt % book capital	67%	76%

a. Millions of dollars, except per share data.

EXHIBIT 2
Marriott Corporation Long-Term Debt (millions of dollars)

	1990	1991	Moody's	S&P
Secured notes, with an average rate of 8.6% at January 3, 1992, maturing through 2010	$ 175	$ 527	Baa3	BBB
Unsecured debt				
Senior notes, with an average rate of 9.3% at January 3, 1992, maturing through 2001[a]	1,198	1,323	Baa3[c]	BBB[c]
Debentures, 9.4%, due 2007	250	250	Baa3	BBB
Revolving loans, with an average rate of 5.3% at January 3, 1992, maturing through 1995[b]	1,780	676		
Other notes, with an average rate of 7.8% at January 3, 1992, maturing through 2015	209	193	Baa3	BBB
Capital lease obligations	61	62		
	3,673	3,031		
Less current portion	(75)	(52)		
	$3,598	$2,979		

Sources: MC Annual Statement; Moody's and S&P reports.

a. Includes approximately $230 million (current valuation) of 8.25% Liquid Yield Option Notes, maturing in June 2006 for the face amount of $675 million and rated Ba1 (Moody's) and not rated by S&P.

b. By year-end 1992, MC expected to have reduced its revolving loan borrowings by $500 million and its other debt by approximately $150 million.

c. On April 29, 1992, MC issued $200 million of 10% 20-year senior notes, and on May 5, 1992, $200 million of 9.5% 10-year senior notes. Both issues were rated as Baa3 (Moody's) and BBB (S&P) and sold at yields in line with other Baa3 issues at the date of issue (see Exhibit A1 in Appendix).

EXHIBIT 3

Marriott Corporation Consolidated Statements of Income
(millions of dollars except per share data)

	1989	1990	1991
Sales			
Lodging			
Rooms	$2,093	$2,374	$2,699
Food and beverages	1,082	1,146	1,194
Other	371	422	486
	3,546	3,942	4,379
Contract services	3,990	3,704	3,952
	7,536	7,646	8,331
Operating costs and expenses			
Lodging			
Departmental direct costs			
Rooms	481	554	628
Food and beverages	816	870	915
Other, including payments to hotel owners and net restructuring charges of $65 million in 1990 and $194 million in 1989	2,117	2,279	2,511
Contract services, including restructuring charges of $57 million in 1990 and $51 million in 1989	3,818	3,590	3,799
	7,232	7,293	7,853
Operating profit			
Lodging	132	239	325
Contract services, including $231 million gain on divestiture of airline catering business in 1989	403	114	153
Operating profits before corporate expenses and taxes	535	353	478
Corporate expenses, including restructuring charges of $31 million in 1990 and $11 million in 1989	(107)	(137)	(111)
Interest expense	(185)	(183)	(265)
Interest income	55	47	43
Income from continuing operations before income taxes	298	80	145
Provision for income taxes	117	33	63
Income from continuing operations	181	47	82
Discontinued operations, net of income taxes			
Income from discontinued operations	35	—	—
Provision for loss on disposal	(39)	—	—
	(4)	—	—
Net income	$ 117	$ 47	$ 82
Earnings (loss) per common share			
Continuing operations	$ 1.62	$ .46	$ .80
Discontinued operations	(.04)	—	—
	$ 1.58	$ .46	$ .80

Source: MC Annual Report.

EXHIBIT 4
Marriott Corporation Consolidated Balance Sheets (millions of dollars)

	1990	*1991*
Assets		
Current assets		
Cash and equivalents	$ 283	$ 36
Accounts receivable	654	524
Inventories, at lower of average cost or market	261	243
Other current assets	230	220
	1,428	1,023
Property and equipment	2,774	2,485
Assets held for sale	1,274	1,524
Investments in affiliates	462	455
Intangibles	494	476
Notes receivable and other	494	437
	$6,926	$6,400
Liabilities and Shareholders' Equity		
Current liabilities		
Accounts payable	$ 675	$ 579
Accrued payroll and benefits	305	313
Other payables and accruals	582	391
Notes payable and capital leases	75	53
	1,637	1,335
Long-term debt	3,598	2,979
Other long-term liabilities	388	351
Deferred income	312	232
Deferred income taxes	584	614
Convertible subordinated debt	—	210
Shareholders' equity		
Convertible preferred stock	—	200
Common stock, issued 105.0 million shares	105	105
Additional paid-in capital	69	35
Retained earnings	528	583
Treasury stock, 9.5 million and 11.4 million common shares, respectively, at cost	(295)	(244)
Total shareholders' equity	407	679
	$6,926	$6,400

Source: MC Annual Report.

EXHIBIT 5

Marriott Corporation Consolidated Statements of Cash Flows (millions of dollars)

	1989	1990	1991
Operating Activities			
Income from continuing operations	$ 181	$ 47	$ 82
Adjustments to reconcile to cash from operations			
Depreciation and amortization	186	208	272
Income taxes	41	18	27
Net restructuring charges	256	153	—
Proceeds from sale of timeshare notes receivable	—	—	83
Amortization of deferred income	(31)	(50)	(38)
Losses (gains) on sales of assets	(273)	(1)	3
Other	98	50	3
Working capital changes			
Accounts receivable	(100)	(76)	88
Inventories	(39)	(22)	63
Other current assets	(19)	(5)	13
Accounts payable and accruals	123	63	(47)
Cash from continuing operations	423	385	549
Cash from discontinued operations	86	(10)	3
Cash from operations	$ 509	$ 375	$ 552
Investing Activities			
Proceeds from sales of assets	$1,648	$ 990	$ 84
Less noncash proceeds	(258)	(15)	—
Cash received from sales of assets	1,390	975	84
Capital expenditures	(1,368)	(1,094)	(427)
Acquisitions	(242)	(118)	—
Other	(223)	(129)	(126)
Cash used in investing activities	(443)	(366)	(469)
Financing Activities			
Issuance of convertible preferred stock	—	—	$ 195
Issuances of long-term and convertible subordinated debt	873	1,317	815
Issuances of common stock	41	24	3
Repayments of long-term debt	(581)	(846)	(1,316)
Purchases of treasury stock	(280)	(294)	—
Dividends payments	(26)	(27)	(27)
Cash from (used in) financing activities	$ 27	$ 174	$ (330)
Increase (decrease) in cash and equivalents	93	183	(247)
Cash and equivalents, beginning of year	7	100	283
Cash and equivalents, end of year	$ 100	$ 283	$ 36

Source: MC Annual Report.

EXHIBIT 6
Marriott Corporation 10-Year Financial Summary (millions of dollars except per share data)

	1982	1983	1984	1985	1986	1987	1988	1989	1990[a]	1991
Reported sales growth		19%	21%	26%	29%	26%	13%	14%	1%	9%
Rate of general inflation		5	4	3	2	3	4	4	3	3
Real growth		14	17	23	27	23	9	10	(2%)	6
Increase in Marriott hotel rooms		11	11	10	16	32	14	14	12	7
Capital expenditures		$462	$627	$911	$821	$1,053	$1,359	$1,368	$1,094	$ 427
Asset Management										
Sales/total assets	.97	.95	.99	.99	1.02	1.09	1.11	1.16	1.10	1.30
Profitability										
Earnings per share	$ .41	$ .56	$ .74	$ .96	$ 1.16	$ 1.40	$ 1.59	$ 1.62	$ .46	$ .80
EBIT as % of sales	8.2%	8.2%	8.2%	8.4%	7.7%	7.3%	6.8%	6.4%	3.4%	4.9%
Net income as % of sales	4.7	4.8	4.9	4.6	4.1	3.8	3.5	2.4	0.6	1.0
Return on equity	20.0	20.0	22.1	22.1	20.6	22.2	30.4	23.8	9.7	18.3
Return on invested capital	8.5	7.6	7.5	7.4	6.3	6.4	6.7	5.7	3.9	6.5
Financial Leverage										
Long-term debt as % capital	54%	53%	48%	42%	47%	59%	61%	60%	68%	59%
Times interest earned	2.3	3.1	3.8	4.0	6.0	4.7	3.3	2.6	1.4	1.5
Senior debt rating	A2	A2	A2	A2	A2	A2	A3	A3	Baa2	Baa3
Valuation										
Share price	$11.70	$ 14.25	$ 14.70	$ 21.58	$ 29.75	$ 30.00	$ 31.63	$ 33.38	$ 10.50	$ 16.50
Earnings per share	.41	.56	.74	.96	1.16	1.40	1.59	1.62	.46	.80
Dividends per share	.06	.08	.09	.11	.14	.17	.21	.25	.28	.28
Price/earnings ratio	29	25	20	22	26	21	20	21	23	21
Market/book ratio	3.0	3.1	2.8	3.3	3.9	4.4	4.8	5.5	2.4	3.3

a. Operating results in 1990 included pretax restructuring charges and writeoffs, net of certain nonrecurring gains, of $153 million related to continuing operations. Operating results in 1989 included pretax restructuring charges and writeoffs of $256 million related to continuing operations, a $231 million pretax gain on the transfer of the airline catering division, and a $39 million after-tax charge recorded in conjunction with the planned disposal of the restaurant division.

EXHIBIT 7
Unconsolidated Affiliates

Marriott Corporation held ownership positions ranging from 1% to 50% in 267 hotels. This financial interest was reported as a $445 million "Investment in Affiliates," under either the cost or equity method of accounting (depending on the percent ownership). Marriott held management contracts and ground leases on these properties, and it provided limited guarantees on the debt of some of the properties in the form of a commitment to advance additional amounts to affiliates, if necessary, to cover certain debt requirements. Such commitments were limited to $349 million. Marriott Corporation's pretax income from affiliates was $97 million in 1991 and included management fees, net of direct costs, $81 million; ground rental income, $18 million; interest income, $19 million; and equity in net losses, ($21 million). Pretax income from affiliates was $47 million in 1986.

In 1991 the affiliates reported sales of $1,855 million, down slightly from the $1,900 million reported in 1990. Operating expense before interest totaled $2,076 million in 1991 versus $2,082 million in 1990.

Operating Results of Unconsolidated Affiliates (millions of dollars)

	1986	1990	1991	1992
Sales	$889	$1,801	$1,855	$1,900
Cash operating expenses		1,709	1,729	1,735
Depreciation	811	344	347	347
EBIT	$ 78	($252)	($221)	($182)
Interest expenses	213			
Net loss	($135)			

Balance Sheets of Unconsolidated Affiliates at December 31 (millions of dollars)

Assets	1986	1991	1992	Liabilities & Equity	1986	1991	1992
Current	$ 194	$ 158	$ 204	Current liabilities	$ 154	$ 445	$1,464
Noncurrent	2,721	4,842	4,589	Long-term debt	2,377	4,233	3,162
Total	$2,915	$5,000	$4,793	Other liabilities	242	565	694
				Equity	142	(243)	(527)
				Total	$2,915	$5,000	$4,793

Marriott Corporation Pretax Income from Unconsolidated Affiliates (millions of dollars)

	1986	1990	1991	1992
Management fees, net of cost		$76	$81	$82
Ground rents	$63	17	18	19
Interest income		21	19	16
Equity in net loss	(16)	(16)	(21)	(24)
Total	$47	$98	$97	$93

Appendix
Explanation of Bond Ratings[18]

Since the early 1900s, bonds have been assigned quality ratings that reflect their probability of going into default. The two major rating agencies are Moody's Investors Service (Moody's) and Standard & Poor's Corporation (S&P). These agencies' rating designations are shown in Exhibit A1. The AAA and AA bonds are extremely safe. A and BBB bonds are strong enough to be called investment grade bonds, and they are the lowest-rated bonds that many banks and other institutional investors are permitted by law to hold. BB and lower bonds are speculations, or junk bonds; they have a significant probability of going into default, and many financial institutions are prohibited from buying them.

Bond Rating Criteria

Although the rating assignments are judgmental, they are based on both qualitative and quantitative factors, some of which are listed below:

1. Debt ratio.
2. Times-interest-earned ratio.
3. Fixed charge coverage ratio.
4. Current ratio.
5. Mortgage provisions: Is the bond secured by a mortgage?
6. Subordination provisions: Is the bond subordinated to other debt?
7. Guarantee provisions: Some bonds are guaranteed by other firms.
8. Sinking fund: Does the bond have a sinking fund to ensure systematic repayment?
9. Maturity: Other things the same, a bond with a shorter maturity will be judged less risky than a longer-term bond.
10. Stability: Are the issuer's sales and earnings stable?
11. Regulation: Is the issuer regulated, and could an adverse regulatory climate cause the company's economic position to decline?
12. Antitrust and legal: Are any antitrust actions or lawsuits pending against the firm that could erode its position?
13. Overseas operations: What percentage of the firm's sales, assets, and profits are from overseas operations, and what is the political climate in the host countries?
14. Environmental factors: Is the firm likely to face heavy expenditures for pollution-control equipment?
15. Pension liabilities: Does the firm have unfunded pension liabilities that could pose a future problem?
16. Labor unrest: Are there potential labor problems on the horizon that could weaken the firm's position?

---

18. Based on Eugene F. Brigham and Louis C. Gapenski, *Financial Management,* 5th ed. (New York: The Dryden Press, 1988), pp. 545–547. Data on bond yield have been added.

17. Resource availability: Is the firm likely to face supply shortages that could force it to curtail operations?

18. Accounting policies: Conservative accounting policies are a plus factor in bond ratings.

Representatives of the rating agencies have consistently stated that no precise formula is used to set a firm's rating—all the factors listed, plus others, are taken into account, but not in a mathematically precise manner. Statistical studies have borne out this contention, for researchers who have tried to predict bond ratings on the basis of quantitative data have had only limited success, indicating that the agencies do indeed use a good deal of subjective judgment when establishing a firm's rating.

EXHIBIT A1
Comparison of Bond Ratings

	Moody's	*S&P*	*Yields*[a]
High quality	Aaa	AAA	7.80%
	Aa	AA	8.07
Investment grade	A	A	8.26
	Baa	BBB	8.72
Junk bonds substandard	Ba	BB	9.04
	B	B	10.81
Speculative	Caa	CCC	—
	C	D	—

Note: Moody's and S&P use "modifiers" for bonds rated below AAA. S&P uses a plus and minus system; thus, A+ designates the strongest A-rated bonds, and A− the weakest. Moody's uses a 1, 2, or 3 designation, with 1 denoting the strongest and 3 the weakest; thus, within the AA category, Aa1 is the best, Aa2 is average, and Aa3 is the weakest.

a. Yields of corporate bonds with 10-year maturities as of September 28, 1992.

EXHIBIT A2
Bond Ratings of Industrial Corporations (1987–1989 Medians)

	AAA	AA	A	BBB	BB	B	CCC
Times interest earned	12.0	9.1	5.5	3.6	2.3	1.0	.8
Long-term debt as percent of capital	12%	19%	30%	38%	51%	66%	62%

Duckworth Industries, Inc.—Incentive Compensation Programs

In early 1992, Mr. John Duckworth, president and controlling shareholder of Duckworth Industries, was considering a change in Duckworth Industries' management incentive compensation systems. If implemented, the new plan for Duckworth management would, it was hoped, align more closely the interests of management and shareholders. Several industrial firms that were pioneers in value-based management had recently adopted similar management compensation systems. Adopting the new system would keep Duckworth in the vanguard of management incentive compensation planning.

Background

Mr. Duckworth was a strong believer in the power of incentives to guide management action. When he was first promoted to a plant management job in the 1950s, Mr. Duckworth took over a plant that had an operating loss of $2.7 million on sales of $9.0 million. He implemented what was then a state-of-the-art plan for factory incentives. The plan applied to all supervisors. Achievement of specified goals earned a 15% premium over an individual's base rate of pay. As noted by Mr. Duckworth:

> The more sobering side of the plan consisted of docking supervisors 12% of their base rate when goals were not achieved. Paychecks having a 12% deduction for failure were distributed in bright red envelopes. At that time I was plant manager of the operation, and I got several red pay envelopes. Some 15–18 months after the "12% Club" was profitably and smoothly functioning, the National Labor Relations Board issued a cease and desist order predicated on the fact you cannot tamper with an individual's base pay. Naturally, I complied, but the results were already in—the division was profitable.

Mr. Duckworth founded his own business in 1971. Sales grew from $400,000 in that year to almost $125 million in 1992 (Exhibit 1). In 1986 a holding company, Duckworth Industries, was established. It included the original business, Worth Corporation, which was a highly profitable producer of proprietary fasteners and adhesives. In 1986, Hospitality Equipment Service was acquired at a purchase price of $5.5 million. In 1988, Hotel Telecom Services was acquired for about $15.0 million. The two newer acquisitions were service businesses rather than manufacturers and to date had not yet generated satisfactory levels of profitability. In 1992, Duckworth Industries employed 755 people. The structure of the organization is shown in Exhibit 2.

The Duckworth Incentive Plans

Pay for performance was firmly embedded in the corporate culture at Duckworth Industries. In the words of one senior executive, "We put incentives, within reason, behind everything we can."

For plant-level employees, Duckworth had an attendance bonus. A pay incentive of 60¢ per hour was earned for each pay period during which an employee was never more than two minutes late for work.

For plant-level employees up to the shift supervisory level, there was also a quality incentive plan (Exhibits 3 and 4). Quality measures included many variables, such as meeting promised shipment dates and reducing customer complaints of any nature. The quality incentive payment target equaled $100 per employee per month. Performance was often a team effort, and the average employee working under this incentive plan received about $600 per year from it. Employees received a separate check each month for the quality bonus to highlight the importance of quality in the company culture.

All Duckworth employees were participants in a profit-sharing plan. At the level of each business unit, a profit-sharing pool was created. The pool was equal in size to 15% of pre-tax profits after a deduction equal to 10% of the beginning-of-year net worth allocated to the business unit. At the end of each year, the profit-sharing pool was allocated to employees, pro rata, based on their individual share of total wages and salaries in the business unit. At the Worth business unit, profit sharing had grown from about 2% of pay to about 15% of pay in recent years. A plant worker earning $15,000 per year would get $2,250. Information sharing with plant personnel as to profit and margin levels was common at Duckworth, so an estimate of the size of their individual profit-sharing allocation could be made by employees as the year progressed.

The company also had individual incentive plans for all sales and supervisory personnel. These typically afforded an employee the opportunity to earn incentives ranging from 10% to 40% of base pay. The incentive plan targets for a typical customer service representative are included as Exhibit 5.

The Existing Senior Management Incentive Plans

The more senior managers at Duckworth (a group comprised of up to 40 people) all participated in an annual incentive compensation plan. A smaller subset of this group also participated in a long-term incentive program.

The incentive plans (both annual and long-term) for the senior managers had undergone considerable change in the 1983–1992 decade. Prior to 1990, the annual incentive plan would target for each manager a bonus of 20–50% of base salary if certain target levels of performance at the business unit level were reached during the year. Typical measures of performance (depending on the manager's area of responsibility) included at least three of the following:

- Cash flow.
- Sales growth of proprietary products.
- Direct labor variances.
- Inventory turns.
- Accounts receivable (days sales outstanding).
- Gross margins (less purchase price variances).
- Special individual projects.

In 1990, Duckworth abandoned the narrowly defined annual targets and opted to tie the annual bonus to a matrix built around sales growth and profitability goals. Annually, goals for each business unit were set for both sales growth and profitability (Exhibit 6). These were determined with reference to the performance levels achieved by various peer group companies (Exhibit 7). Individual managers were assigned bonus targets (generally ranging from 25% to 50% of base compensation). Depending on the level of sales growth and profitability achieved, a manager could read directly from the matrix the factor by which his or her target bonus would be multiplied to determine the actual bonus he or she would receive. The incentive compensation matrix for the Worth business unit (Exhibit 6) indicated the following: If, in fiscal 1992, a manager working at the Worth business unit had a target bonus of 40%, and the business unit provided a 20% return on assets and 10% sales growth, the manager would receive 1.00 times his or her 40% target bonus. Table A shows the percentages of target bonuses business unit managers at Duckworth received from the annual incentive plan in 1991 and 1992.

While Duckworth's annual incentive plan for senior managers covered several dozen employees by 1992, the long-term incentive plan covered fewer participants, particularly in the early part of the decade from 1983 to 1992. In 1983, Duckworth implemented a 5-year, long-term management incentive plan. The plan covered only two employees, the then vice president and general manager at Worth (now retired) and the then vice president of sales and marketing at Worth (now president of the Hotel Telecom Services operation). The plan made one payment at the end of 5 years; it was a phantom stock plan tied to the increase in book value per share multiplied by a performance factor (Exhibit 8). The performance factor was determined by several measures including (1) the spread separating annual ROE from the sum of the bank prime rate plus two percentage points, and (2) the annual growth in net book value per share.

According to one of the participants, the plan was a horror in complexity, but the fact that a manager could have 1 or 2 bad years and still get a payment was an attractive feature. Because the plan paid only once at the end of 5 years, it was somewhat like a forced savings plan. According to one manager, "The size of the payment at the end made a meaningful difference in what you could do lifestyle-wise.

TABLE A
Annual Incentive Plan Bonuses, 1991 and 1992

	1991	*1992*
Worth Corporation	170%	0%
Hotel Telecom	0	24
Hospitality Equipment	0	0
Duckworth Industries	90	0

TABLE B
Long-Term Incentive Plan Bonuses, 1989–1992

	1989	*1990*	*1991*	*1992*
Worth Corporation	112%	97%	92%	91%
Hotel Telecom	—	40	20	0
Hospitality Equipment	—	—	40	45
Duckworth Industries	85	80	75	73

A check for $150,000 is quite significant when you bring it home. You are willing to make significant personal sacrifices along the way to make it happen."

In 1986 a new long-term management incentive plan was put in place at Duckworth. This plan was broadened to include more managers (15 by 1989) and was designed to begin payments in 1989 after the expiration of the previously described 5-year plan. At the start of each year, beginning in 1986, new targets would be established so that incentive payments could be received annually. The business unit management participants in this plan would be awarded a specified percentage of base salary (generally from 25% to 40%) if a Challenge Earnings level of cumulative earnings before interest and taxes (approved by Duckworth's board of directors) was achieved by their business unit during the period. Lesser levels of earnings achievement would produce a proportionately reduced level of award (as shown in Exhibit 9 for the Worth business unit).

The incentive system established in 1986 continued for 4 years. The last update was put in place in 1989 and covered the 3-year time period ending in 1992. Table B presents the percentages of target bonuses that business unit managers received from the long-term incentive plan between 1989 and 1992.

For the top management team at Duckworth, the target and actual bonus payments (measured as a percentage of base salary) are presented as Exhibit 10.

A Proposed New EVA Incentive System

As fiscal 1992 unfolded, both management and Mr. Duckworth (the controlling shareholder) were looking for ways to more closely align the interests of management and shareholders through the incentive plan for senior management. A number of factors had contributed to dissatisfaction with the existing plans. One major factor had to do with operation of the annual incentive plan of Worth in 1992. In many ways, as Table C shows, Worth's performance in 1992 was improved over that of 1991.

The return on gross performing assets had increased, but sales had declined slightly (versus a 10% goal and a minimum 5% sales growth requirement to achieve any annual incentive plan payment). The sales decline was caused by the loss of a very large

TABLE C
Gross Performing Asset Return and Sales Growth, 1991–1992

	Worth Corporation	
	1991	*1992*
Return on gross performing assets	23.6%	23.9%
Sales growth	13.9	(2.3)

customer buying a product with commodity-type profit margins. Most of the lost sales in 1992 had been replaced by new customers purchasing proprietary products at higher margins. The change in customer mix was good for enhancing long-run shareholder value, but given the structure of the existing annual incentive plan (Exhibit 6), Worth's management failed to achieve any annual incentive bonus as a result of the change.

Near the close of fiscal 1992, Mr. John Duckworth began reading a book by G. Bennett Stewart entitled *The Quest for Value*. Stewart's book outlined a management incentive plan that promised to link management pay directly to the creation of long-run economic value for shareholders. Implementation of the plan required the services of Stern Stewart & Co., a financial consulting firm.

The economic valued-added (EVA) compensation system developed by Stern Stewart would require (1) considerable data analysis and (2) some reorienting in thinking about how to approach the business going forward for Duckworth's senior management. The EVA system was predicated on the following logic:

1. Economic value for shareholders is created when a firm earns a rate of return on invested capital that exceeds the cost of capital. The economic value-added in a particular year should equal the product of
   a. The average capital employed during the year multiplied by
   b. The spread separating the cost of capital from the return on capital earned during the year.
2. The EVA during a year can be calculated for each business unit. The management of each unit can be directly compensated for its success in adding economic value via a compensation formula that automatically adjusts the baseline for calculating next year's bonus to reflect the actual performance of the prior year.

The Key Drivers of EVA

Exhibit 11 shows a calculation of the EVA by the Worth division of Duckworth Industries from 1988 through 1992. It also shows the forecasted EVA for the period 1993–1997.

The key variables in determining the EVA by a business unit were:

1. Net operating profit after taxes (NOPAT) (Exhibit 11, Line 9).
   This excludes corporate overhead, and capitalizes R&D expenses and then amortizes them over 3 years. NOPAT excludes noneconomic, noncash charges.[1]
2. Average capital (Exhibit 11, Line 15).
   This excludes construction in progress, and assumes FIFO inventory valuation and the add-back of bad debt reserves. Noneconomic, noncash writeoffs are added back to average capital.[2]
3. Cost of capital (Exhibit 11, Line 17).
   This is determined annually for each business unit by using an assumed capital structure and riskiness factor (β value) for peer group firms comparable to each business unit. The formula for calculating capital cost was tied to the yield on 30-year Treasury obligations plus a risk premium.

---

1. Items such as the one-time writeoff of a divested business would be a noneconomic, noncash charge. Items such as depreciation or the amortization of debt discount would be economic, noncash charges.

2. This was designed to prevent managers from escaping responsibility for poor prior investment decisions by simply divesting the poorly performing assets.

The Mechanism for Calculating Incentive Compensation

Stern Stewart recommended a mechanism for linking EVA in a business unit during a given year to the incentive compensation paid to management in that year.

First, a bonus target was established. At Worth, this might equal 37% of base pay (Exhibit 12, Line 1). Bonus units (like phantom stock) would be assigned to each manager in an amount such that if the bonus unit was valued at $1.00, the desired level of bonus would be earned by the manager (Exhibit 12, Line 3).

Second, a baseline EVA level was established (Exhibit 12, Line 4). At the end of each year, the baseline EVA for the following year would change by one-half of the difference between the actual EVA achieved and the baseline EVA for the prior year (Exhibit 12, Lines 8–10). This made the system self-adjusting. If EVA performance improved each year, the new base would click up by one-half the amount of the improvement. If EVA performance deteriorated for several years, the base level would decline so that the targets would not be so far away as to be unreachable in ensuing years.

Third, a base unit value was established for each ensuing year (Exhibit 12, Lines 6 and 14). This base unit value defined, to a large degree, how much of the target bonus could be earned by just maintaining the existing level of business performance. If EVA hit exactly the baseline EVA each year, and the base unit value was set at $1.00, then exactly the target bonus would be earned each year. In the case of Worth, after the first year, the base unit value dropped to $.80. This meant that simply repeating the EVA baseline performance after 1993 would produce only 80% of the targeted bonus.

Fourth, a bonus sensitivity factor (Exhibit 12, Lines 7 and 11) was established that could either add to or subtract from the base unit value to create a total unit value. In the Worth example, the bonus sensitivity factor was set at $1,625,000. In any year that EVA varied from the baseline EVA, the amount of the gap was divided by $1,625,000, and the resulting amount (called the performance unit value, Exhibit 12, Lines 12 and 13) was added to the base unit value to determine the total unit value (Exhibit 12, Line 15). In order to earn one times the target bonus solely from the performance unit factor, management of the business unit had to beat the baseline EVA by the amount of the bonus sensitivity factor.

As indicated in Exhibit 12, if Worth hit the forecasted level of EVA in each year, Worth's management would earn the percentage shown in Table D of its target bonus in each of the next 5 years.

TABLE D
Forecasted Earned Target Bonuses, 1993–1997

	% of Target Bonus Earned, Worth Corporation
1993	100%
1994	51
1995	122
1996	170
1997	211[a]

a. Bonuses up to two times the target bonus were paid immediately. One-third of the amount over this maximum was also paid in cash. Remaining amounts were allocated to a "bonus bank" to be paid out in the future. Negative charges for deteriorating performance reduced the bonus bank. Negative charges could even create a negative balance in the bonus bank that would have to be overcome in order to resume bonus payments in future years.

TABLE E
Forecasted Earned Target Bonuses, 1993–1997

	% of Target Bonus Earned	
	Hotel Telecom	**Hospitality Equipment**
1993 . . . . 45%		79%
1994 99		85
1995 69		71
1996 66		65
1997 62		66

As indicated in Exhibits 13 through 16, if the Hotel Telecom Services and Hospitality Equipment Services business units hit their forecasted levels of EVA in each year, Hotel Telecom's and Hospitality Equipment's managements would earn the percentage shown in Table E of their targeted bonus in each of the next 5 years. (See line 15 in Exhibits 14 and 16.)

According to Bennett Stewart, the beauty of the EVA incentive compensation system was that it was "a self-motivated, self-adjusting corporate governance system that linked capital budgeting and strategic investment decisions to the compensation system."

From John Duckworth's perspective, not only were the interests of management and shareholders aligned, but in addition, the bogeys for determining bonus compensation would not have to be renegotiated each year. What had been two plans (an annual plan and a long-term plan) could be combined into one plan that paid on annual results but was designed to build long-term shareholder value. The system was like a self-winding watch. You set it once, and it might keep going, all by itself, for quite some time.

EXHIBIT 1

Consolidated Financial Statements, 1975–1992, Fiscal Years Ended May 31 (millions of dollars)

	1975	1980	1985	1990	1991	1992
Net sales	$5,811	$15,109	$40,793	$116,220	$123,545	$122,570
Cost of goods sold	4,294	11,164	30,142	85,875	89,865	86,720
Selling, gen'l & admin.	1,231	3,199	8,638	24,610	25,080	28,800
Operating income	287	746	2,013	5,735	8,595	7,050
Investment income	68	177	479	1,365	1,375	1,545
Interest expense	129	334	902	2,570	2,390	1,635
Profit sharing expense	55	142	383	1,090	1,595	1,850
Income before taxes	172	447	1,207	3,440	5,985	5,105
Taxes	50	130	351	1,000	1,850	1,565
Net income	122	317	856	2,440	4,135	3,540
Cash & marketable securities[a]	1,067	2,775	7,492	21,345	24,790	26,085
Accounts receivable	578	1,502	4,056	11,555	12,760	13,210
Inventory	572	1,487	4,014	11,435	11,380	12,995
Less: LIFO reserves	51	131	355	1,010	1,111	1,125
Net inventories	522	1,356	3,661	10,430	10,270	11,870
Other current assets	46	119	321	915	960	990
Total current assets	2,212	5,752	15,530	44,245	48,780	52,155
Construction in progress	25	65	176	500	485	3,105
Other net PP&E	799	2,076	5,605	15,970	15,450	14,330
Other assets[b]	290	753	2,032	5,790	5,735	5,685
Total assets	$3,325	$ 8,646	$23,343	$ 66,505	$ 70,450	$ 75,275
Short-term debt	$ 734	$ 1,909	$ 5,154	$ 14,685	$ 17,390	$ 15,910
Other current liabilities	1,048	2,724	7,355	20,955	19,790	23,700
Total current liabilities	1,782	4,633	12,510	35,640	37,180	39,610
Long-term borrowings	496	1,290	3,482	9,920	8,355	7,175
Other liabilities	63	164	444	1,265	1,105	1,140
Net worth	984	2,558	6,908	19,680	23,810	27,350
Total liab. & net worth	$3,325	$ 8,646	$23,343	$ 66,505	$ 70,450	$ 75,275

a. Marketable securities were carried at the lower of cost or market. Market exceeded cost by $4,090 in 1990; $7,870 in 1991; and $10,940 in 1992.

b. Other assets included goodwill of $5,130 in 1990; $4,995 in 1991; and $4,855 in 1992.

EXHIBIT 2

Organization Chart, Duckworth Industries, Inc., June 1, 1992

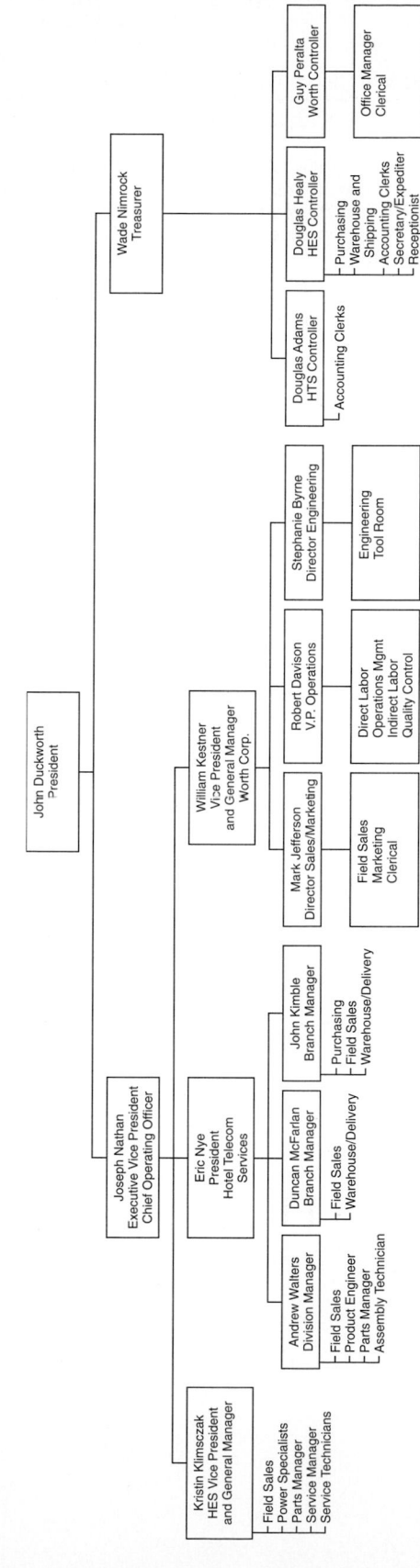

Supplementary Employment Data, Fiscal Years 1991–1993

Headcount (fiscal year)

	1993	1992	1991
Duckworth Industries	10	10	12
Worth Corporation	500	485	410
HES	135	155	170
Hotel Telecom	110	95	95
Total	755	745	687

EXHIBIT 3
Duckworth Corporation, Quality Incentive Bonus Plan, Fiscal Year 1993

The Quality Incentive bonus plan has been in its current form since FY90 (June of 1989).

As we have improved as a company, it is important that our plan be modified to reflect these changes and more accurately represent what the "real world" reflects in terms of total quality performance. After a thorough review of this year's quality performance, the following changes are being made to the Quality Incentive bonus plan effective June 1, 1992 (FY93). The monthly complaint ratio and bonus payout levels will be as follows:

Complaint Ratio	Monthly Bonus Payout
.6% or less	$100.00
More than .6%, less than 2.0%	$ 75.00
More than 2.0, less than 3.5%	$ 50.00

As you can see, the lower limits have been changed and the bottom payout of $25 eliminated, but we have increased the top-level payout by 25% to $100.00. The total potential maximum yearly payout is now $1,200, compared to $900 with the old plan. This year, through the first 11 months, we have paid $800 in incentives to each participant. As you can see from the above, superior performance will be rewarded with high-level bonus payouts.

Duckworth quality performance in FY91 improved dramatically to an average **2.7%** complaint ratio, with the **last six months** of the year averaging **2%**. The revised plan is designed to build on this success and increase our performance to "world-class" levels.

The procedures for analyzing, charging responsibility, and tallying total number of complaints by Richard Sterling all remain the same as in the past. The only additional reporting will be a new category recording invoicing errors, such as billing errors or wrong prices on orders. Complete quality is a total system—from the first customer inquiry to billing of parts and all processes in between.

With constant dedication to teamwork, continuous quality improvement, and satisfying our **customers' requirements**, we are confident that our new goals will be achieved and even surpassed. You are doing it now, and we are counting on you to make Duckworth—**Your Company**—the best quality company possible!

William Kestner
Vice President and General Manager

cc: John Duckworth
    Joseph Nathan

EXHIBIT 4
Worth Corporation, Quality Incentive Program, FY93 October Results

```
No. of shipments . . . . . . . . . . . . .   207
No. of chargeable complaints . . . . . .     4
Complaint ratio . . . . . . . . . . . . . .  1.9%
Quality bonus—October . . . . . . . . . $ 75
Quality bonus—YTD . . . . . . . . . . . $300
```

With a record number of shipments, this month had the potential of being a great quality month, but we fell short because preventable errors were not caught. Without the large shipment level, the monthly payout would not have been $75.00.

If you look at the customer complaints listed below, you will see that these problems could have been detected by our systems. The key to continued improvement is your using the systems and informing others when the systems do not work.

The XXX and YYY complaints are cases in which the system in place was not followed; the result was a complaint. The AAA and BBB complaints are cases in which people could have come forth to say that the system does not adequately detect these kinds of defects.

The task of improvement needs to be continually addressed by all. We cannot just let things go on and expect good results. Good results are achieved by good people doing the right things at the right time.

Type of Complaint	Customer	Complaint
Manufacturing process	AAA	Cracked AX47 parts; inventory not rotated
Manufacturing process	BBB	Cracked AX47 parts; inventory not rotated
Color	YYY	Color significantly off standard (yellow)
Label	XXX	Label printed with wrong code

Joy Meadow
Quality Assurance Manager

Thomas Spencer
Production Manager

EXHIBIT 5
Worth Corporation, FY93 Incentive Plan for Customer Service Representatives

	Item Results	% of Bonus	% of Salary
Order Accuracy			
4% maximum potential			
Accuracy equals percentage of	98.0% or higher	40.00%	4.00%
acceptance of orders that have	96.5	30.00	3.00
correct pricing and other	95.0	20.00	2.00
critical information. This	<95.0	0.00	0.00
accuracy is tracked by Director			
of Sales, with bonus being paid based			
on overall FY93 results.			
Order Acknowledgment/Turnaround			
3% maximum potential			
(effective 9/1/92–9-month period)			
Average number of days	2 days or less	30.00%	3.00%
(excluding holidays & weekends)	3 days	15.00	1.50
from order placement until	4 days	5.00	0.50
printing of order acknowledgment	>4 days	0.00	0.00
for all orders received (except			
those requiring new part numbers).			
Results to be tracked weekly on			
late shipments report.			
Sales Growth			
3% maximum potential			
Total net company sales growth	$7,000M	30.00%	3.00%
over FY92 net sales of	$6,000	15.00	1.50
$63.5 million	$3,000	5.00	0.50
	<$3,000	0.00	0.00

Note: Maximum award = 10% of average base salary.

EXHIBIT 6
Duckworth Industries, Inc., Fiscal 1992 Incentive Compensation

		Annual Sales Growth (%)					
		4.90	5.00	7.50	10.00	12.50	15.00
					Goal		
25.0		0	1.74	1.81	1.88	1.95	2.03
24.0		0	1.55	1.61	1.67	1.74	1.81
23.0		0	1.37	1.42	1.48	1.55	1.61
22.0		0	1.20	1.25	1.31	1.37	1.42
21.0		0	1.05	1.10	1.15	1.20	1.25
20.0	Goal	0	0.91	0.95	1.00	1.05	1.10
19.0		0	0.78	0.82	0.87	0.91	0.95
18.0		0	0.67	0.71	0.74	0.78	0.82
17.0		0	0.57	0.60	0.63	0.67	0.71
16.0		0	0.48	0.51	0.54	0.57	0.60
15.0		0	0.40	0.42	0.45	0.48	0.51
14.9		0	0	0	0	0	0

Return on gross assets (%) (row label, left side)

Return on gross performing assets will be determined by dividing operational cash flow earnings (OCFE) into average gross performing assets (AGPA).

OCFE is net profit adjusted to add depreciation and to eliminate (a) interest expense, (b) acquisition expenses, (c) net investment income, (d) expense or profit relating to LIFO, and (e) gains or losses from the disposition of depreciable assets. All adjustments will be made on an after-tax basis, using Worth Corporation's effective tax rate.

AGPA is a 13-month average of the company's gross book assets, with cumulative depreciation and the LIFO reserve added back, but investment securities and intercompany receivables eliminated.

The Board of Directors reserves the right to adjust the formula and its components, even after the fact, in any way it determines to be appropriate in order to better effectuate the plan and its purposes.

EXHIBIT 7
ROA/Growth Matrix for Worth Peer Group

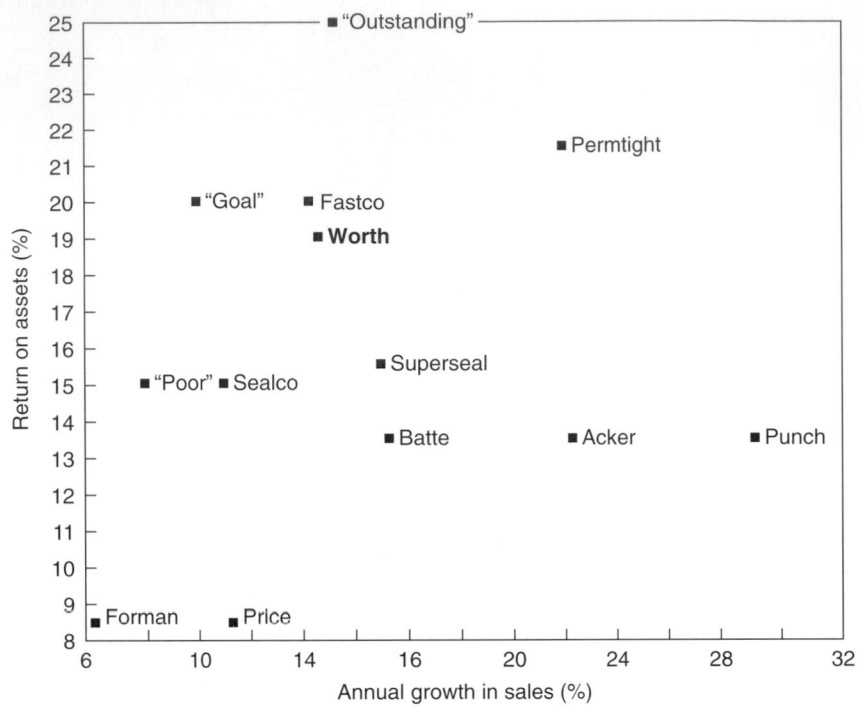

EXHIBIT 8
Worth Corporation, Inc., Executive Long-Term Incentive Plan

Summary	May 31, 1983	May 31, 1988	5–Year Change
Total shareholder's equity at year-end	$8,616,500	$16,379,000	
Per share, using standard of 500,000 shares	$ 17.23	$ 32.76	
Value-weighting "performance factor".	0.50	1.70	
Weighted share price. . . . . (= Equity per share × Performance factor)	$ 8.62	$ 55.69	$47.07
Per participant . . . . $47.07 × 3000 shares		=	$141,210
In total . . . . × 2 participants		=	$282,420

EXHIBIT 9

Worth Division of Duckworth Industries, Management Long-Term Plan: Targets Established for Successive 3-Year Plans versus Results Achieved

Plan Years	Challenge Earnings Levels (3-yr. cumulative EBIT)	% of Target Award Earned	Actual Results during Period
1986–1989	$12.0 million	100%	$13.4 million and 112%
	10.0	50	
	7.5	10	
	< 7.5	0	
1987–1990	$20.0	100	$19.3 million and 97%
	12.5	10	
	<12.5	0	
1988–1991	$28.75	100	$26.1 million and 92%
	20.0	10	
	<20.0	0	
1989–1992	$33.0	100	$30.1 million and 91%
	25.0	10	
	<25.0	0	

Award Determination

Each participant will, at the start of a performance period, be assigned a target award expressed as a percentage of the participant's average annual base salary to be paid during the performance period. The percent of the target award earned by each participant will be based upon the relationship of performance period earnings to various challenge earnings levels specified by the board for such performance period.

The percent of target award earned will awarded on a pro rata basis if the actual results fall between specified challenge earnings levels. If a participant significantly changes responsibility or positions during the performance period, the board will consider the propriety of an equitable adjustment in the target award assigned.

A participant's award is subject to organizational and environmental constraints affecting performance period earnings. Unforeseen problems (other than those referred to in the next paragraph) or opportunities, as well as peer group performance, will be taken into account during the evaluation process. As soon as practicable after the end of a performance period, the board will determine how successfully objectives were met. The board will evaluate how unforeseen difficulties, as well as unexpected opportunities, were addressed. To allow recognition for quality of results and level of effort, award amounts may be adjusted (to a maximum of plus or minus 25% of the award) by the board.

The plan also recognizes that actions of participants may be negated or overstated due to the occurrence of certain extraordinary events. Examples of extraordinary events include, but are not limited to, "acts of God," financial difficulty of a major supplier or customer, unexpected tax law changes and acquisitions, divestitures, mergers, or significant structural changes. Should such extraordinary occurrences take place, the board may adjust the incentive awards (or the various formula components thereof) in any manner reasonably intended to reflect the impact of the extraordinary occurrence.

EXHIBIT 10

Target and Actual Payments for Annual and Long-Term Incentive Compensation Plans (as a % of base salary)

		Target	1990 Actual	Target	1991 Actual	Target	1992 Actual
Manager A	Annual bonus	—	—	40[a]	68	40[a]	0
	Long-term incentive	—	—	35[a]	32	35[a]	32
Manager B	Annual bonus	—	—	25[a]	35	25[a]	0
	Long-term incentive	—	—	25[a]	23	25[a]	23
Manager C	Annual bonus	50[a]	50	50[a]	85	50[b]	0
	Long-term incentive	40[a]	39	40[a]	37	40[b]	0
Manager D	Annual bonus	25[a]	25	40[a]	35	25[a]	0
	Long-term incentive	25[a]	24	40[a]	37	40[a]	36
Manager E	Annual bonus	40[a]	40	40[a]	68	40[a]	0
	Long-term incentive	40[a]	39	35[a]	32	35[a]	32
Manager F	Annual bonus	—	—	25[b]	0	25[b]	6
	Long-term incentive	—	—	25[b]	5	25[b]	0
Manager G	Annual bonus	40[a]	40	50[b]	0	50[b]	12
	Long-term incentive	40[a]	39	40[b]	8	40[b]	0
Manager H	Annual bonus	—	—	25[b]	0	25[b]	6
	Long-term incentive	—	—	25[b]	5	25[b]	0
Manager I	Annual bonus	25[a]	25	50[d]	46	50[d]	0
	Long-term incentive	25[a]	25	25[c]	10	60[d]	44
Manager J	Annual bonus	—	—	—	—	25[c]	0
	Long-term incentive	—	—	—	—	—	—
Manager K	Annual bonus	30[c]	0	30[c]	0	30[c]	0
	Long-term incentive	30[c]	0	30[c]	12	30[c]	14
Manager L	Annual bonus	40[c]	0	40[c]	0	50[c]	0
	Long-term incentive	35[c]	0	35[c]	14	35[c]	16
Manager M	Annual bonus	50[c]	0	50[c]	0	50[c]	0
	Long-term incentive	50[c]	0	50[c]	20	50[c]	46
Manager N	Annual bonus	—	—	35[a]	60	35[a]	0
	Long-term incentive	40[a]	39	40[a]	37	40[a]	36
Manager O	Annual bonus	40[a]	40	40[a]	68	40[a]	0
	Long-term incentive	25[a]	24	25[a]	23	25[a]	23
Manager P	Annual bonus	20[a]	20	20[a]	34	20[a]	0
	Long-term incentive	20[a]	19	20[a]	18	20[a]	18

a. Worth.

b. Hotel Telecom Services.

c. Hospitality Equipment Services.

d. Duckworth Industries.

EXHIBIT 11
Worth Corporation, Summary of Historical and Projected Operating Performance (millions of dollars)

Line #		History						Forecast			
		1988	1989	1990	1991	1992	1993	1994	1995	1996	1997
	Operating results										
1	Revenue	$47,255	$54,615	$57,125	$65,035	$63,565	$69,500	$76,100	$83,330	$91,250	$99,915
2	% Growth	15.0%	15.6%	4.6%	13.9%	(2.3%)	9.3%	9.5%	9.5%	9.5%	9.5%
3	– Cost of sales	34,985	40,305	41,760	46,020	42,025	47,355	51,950	56,915	62,415	68,445
4	% Sales	74.0%	73.8%	73.1%	70.8%	66.1%	68.1%	68.3%	68.3%	68.4%	68.5%
5	– SG&A	6,620	6,700	6,905	6,905	8,585	9,695	10,865	11,715	12,680	13,585
6	% Sales	14.0%	12.3%	12.1%	10.6%	13.5%	13.9%	14.3%	14.1%	13.9%	13.6%
7	– Cash taxes	$ 2,280	$ 1,965	$ 2,615	$ 3,500	$ 3,650	$ 4,225	$ 4,855	$ 5,310	$ 5,785	$ 6,215
8	% Operating income	40.4%	25.8%	30.9%	28.9%	28.2%	33.9%	36.5%	36.1%	35.8%	34.8%
9	**NOPAT**	**$ 3,370**	**$ 5,645**	**$ 5,840**	**$ 8,615**	**$ 9,305**	**$ 8,225**	**$ 8,430**	**$ 9,390**	**$10,370**	**$11,670**
	Capital										
10	Net accounts receivable	$ 5,310	$ 4,855	$ 5,460	$ 5,525	$ 6,060	$ 6,185	$ 6,760	$ 7,395	$ 8,090	$ 8,850
11	Inventory	2,865	2,965	3,360	3,865	4,020	4,030	4,260	4,585	4,945	5,325
12	PP&E	5,540	9,415	13,775	13,505	12,180	19,465	21,555	21,825	20,915	21,200
13	Other assets	620	350	1,455	1,565	3,765	3,210	2,450	1,800	1,245	1,185
14	– NIBCL's[a]	(10,775)	(9,790)	(11,545)	(10,025)	(13,125)	(9,940)	(10,860)	(12,040)	(13,360)	(14,725)
15	**Capital**	**$ 3,555**	**$ 7,795**	**$12,505**	**$14,440**	**$12,900**	**$22,945**	**$24,165**	**$23,560**	**$21,830**	**$21,835**
	Operating analysis										
16	NOPAT/Avg cap (r)	51.4%	99.5%	57.5%	63.9%	68.1%	45.9%	35.8%	39.3%	45.7%	53.5%
17	– Cost of capital (c)	13.0%	12.6%	12.7%	12.4%	12.2%	12.2%	12.2%	12.2%	12.2%	12.2%
18	Spread (r – c)	38.4%	86.9%	44.8%	51.5%	55.9%	33.7%	23.6%	27.2%	33.5%	41.3%
19	× Average capital	$ 6,550	$ 5,675	$10,150	$13,470	$13,670	$17,925	$23,555	$23,865	$22,695	$21,830
20	**Economic value added**	**$ 2,515**	**$ 4,935**	**$ 4,550**	**$ 6,945**	**$ 7,640**	**$ 6,045**	**$ 5,565**	**$ 6,485**	**$ 7,605**	**$ 9,010**

a. Non-interest-bearing current liabilities.

EXHIBIT 12
Worth Corporation

A. Input Table

Line #		1993	1994	1995	1996	1997
	Bonus Pool Characteristics					
1	Target bonus	37%	37%	37%	37%	37%
2	Base salary (000)	$1,710	$1,795	$1,885	$1,980	$2,075
3	Number of units (000)	630	660	695	730	765
	Bonus Calculation Framework					
4	Baseline EVA (000)	$6,045				
5	Annual target adjustment factor	50%				
6	Base unit value	$ 1.00	$ 0.80	$ 0.80	$ 0.80	$ 0.80
	EVA Bonus Sensitivity Factor					
7	EVA bonus sensitivity factor (000)	$1,625				

B. Current Bonus Calculation

Line #		1993	1994	1995	1996	1997	Average
	Performance Unit Value						
8	EVA (000)	$6,045	$5,565	$6,485	$7,605	$9,010	$6,940
9	− Baseline EVA (000)	$6,045	$6,045	$5,805	$6,145	$6,875	$6,180
10	= EVA vs baseline EVA (000)	$ 0	($ 480)	$ 680	$1,460	$2,135	$ 760
11	/ EVA bonus sensitivity factor (000)	$1,625	$1,625	$1,625	$1,625	$1,625	$1,625
12	= Performance unit value	$ 0.00	($ 0.29)	$ 0.42	$ 0.90	$ 1.31	$ 0.47
	Total Unit Value						
13	Performance unit value	$ 0.00	($ 0.29)	$ 0.42	$ 0.90	$ 1.31	$ 0.47
14	+ Base unit value	$ 1.00	$ 0.80	$ 0.80	$ 0.80	$ 0.80	$ 0.84
15	= Total unit value	$ 1.00	$ 0.51	$ 1.22	$ 1.70	$ 2.11	$ 1.31
	Current Bonus						
16	Total unit value	$ 1.00	$ 0.51	$ 1.22	$ 1.70	$ 2.11	$ 1.31
17	Number of units (000)	630	660	695	730	765	695
18	Current bonus earned (000)	$ 630	$ 335	$ 850	$1,240	$1,620	$ 935

C. Past Bonus If System Had Been In Place Prior 5 Years

Line #		1988	1989	1990	1991	1992	Average
	Current Bonus						
19	Total unit value	$ 1.00	$ 2.29	$ 1.31	$ 2.53	$ 2.09	$ 1.84
20	Number of units (000)	695	720	720	740	530	680
21	Current bonus earned (000)	$ 695	$1,645	$ 945	$1,875	$1,115	$1,255

EXHIBIT 13
Hotel Telecom Services, Summary of Historical and Projected Operating Performance (millions of dollars)

Line #		History					Forecast			
		1989	1990	1991	1992	1993	1994	1995	1996	1997
	Operating Results									
1	Revenue	$29,115	$32,540	$29,980	$32,285	$46,600	$55,920	$60,115	$64,625	$69,470
2	% Growth	NMF	11.8%	(7.9%)	7.7%	44.3%	20.0%	7.5%	7.5%	7.5%
3	− Cost of sales	20,750	24,120	22,395	24,730	36,150	43,435	46,735	50,205	54,005
4	% of sales	71.3%	74.1%	74.7%	76.6%	77.6%	77.7%	77.7%	77.7%	77.7%
5	− SG&A	5,610	5,475	5,560	5,820	7,935	9,150	9,820	10,550	11,320
6	% of sales	19.3%	16.8%	18.5%	18.0%	17.0%	16.4%	16.3%	16.3%	16.3%
7	− Cash taxes	$ 455	$ 1,000	$ 700	$ 500	$ 815	$ 1,060	$ 1,135	$ 1,235	$ 1,325
8	% Operating income	16.5%	33.9%	34.5%	28.9%	32.4%	31.8%	31.8%	31.9%	31.9%
9	**NOPAT**	**$ 2,300**	**$ 1,950**	**$ 1,325**	**$ 1,230**	**$ 1,700**	**$ 2,275**	**$ 2,425**	**$ 2,640**	**$ 2,825**
	Capital									
10	Net accounts receivable	$ 3,370	$ 3,240	$ 3,935	$ 4,365	$ 6,115	$ 7,265	$ 7,805	$ 8,385	$ 9,010
11	Inventory	4,525	4,145	4,570	6,245	7,120	8,520	9,150	9,820	10,550
12	PP&E	1,365	1,250	1,355	1,525	1,520	1,405	1,395	1,255	1,085
13	Goodwill	4,395	4,395	4,395	4,400	4,400	4,400	4,400	4,400	4,400
14	Other assets	230	715	1,260	1,935	290	320	330	345	360
15	− NIBCL's[a]	(4,720)	(3,860)	(4,630)	(5,490)	(5,575)	(6,985)	(7,505)	(8,085)	(8,685)
16	**Capital**	**$ 9,170**	**$ 9,890**	**$10,891**	**$12,975**	**$13,870**	**$14,920**	**$15,570**	**$16,115**	**$16,710**
	Operating Analysis									
17	NOPAT/Avg cap (r)	22.3%	20.5%	12.8%	10.3%	12.7%	15.8%	15.9%	16.7%	17.2%
18	− Cost of capital (c)	13.1%	13.2%	12.9%	12.7%	12.7%	12.7%	12.7%	12.7%	12.7%
19	Spread (r − c)	9.2%	7.3%	(0.1%)	(2.4%)	0.0%	3.1%	3.2%	4.0%	4.5%
20	× Average capital	$10,345	$ 9,530	$10,390	$11,935	$13,420	$14,395	$15,245	$15,840	$16,410
21	**Economic value added**	**$ 950**	**$ 695**	**($ 10)**	**($ 280)**	**$ 0**	**$ 450**	**$ 495**	**$ 630**	**$ 745**

a. Non-interest-bearing current liabilities.

EXHIBIT 14
Hotel Telecom Services

A. Input Table

Line #		1993	1994	1995	1996	1997
	Bonus Pool Characteristics					
1	Target bonus	38%	38%	38%	38%	38%
2	Base salary (000)	$905	$950	$1,000	$1,050	$1,100
3	Number of units (000)	345	360	380	400	420
	Bonus Calculation Framework					
4	Baseline EVA (000)	($140)				
5	Annual target adjustment factor	50%				
6	Base unit value	$0.25	$0.25	$0.25	$0.25	$0.25
	EVA Bonus Sensitivity Factor					
7	= EVA bonus sensitivity factor (000)	$700				

B. Current Bonus Calculation

Line #		1993	1994	1995	1996	1997	Average
	Performance Unit Value						
8	EVA (000)	$ 0	$450	$495	$630	$745	$465
9	− Baseline EVA (000)	($140)	($70)	$190	$340	$485	$160
10	= EVA vs baseline EVA (000)	$140	$520	$305	$290	$255	$300
11	/ EVA bonus sensitivity factor (000)	$700	$700	$700	$700	$700	$700
12	= Performance unit value	$0.20	$0.74	$0.44	$0.41	$0.37	$0.43
	Total Unit Value						
13	Performance unit value	$0.20	$0.74	$0.44	$0.41	$0.37	$0.43
14	+ Base unit value	$0.25	$0.25	$0.25	$0.25	$0.25	$0.25
15	= Total unit value	$0.45	$0.99	$0.69	$0.66	$0.62	$0.68
	Current Bonus						
16	Total unit value	$0.45	$0.99	$0.69	$0.66	$0.62	$0.68
17	Number of units (000)	345	360	380	400	420	380
18	Current bonus earned (000)	$155	$360	$260	$265	$260	$260

C. Past Bonus If System Had Been In Place Prior 4 Years

Line #		1989	1990	1991	1992	Average
	Current Bonus					
19	Total unit value	$1.27	$0.39	($0.68)	($.60)	$0.08
20	Number of units (000)	50	150	325	340	215
21	Current bonus earned (000)	$ 60	$ 60	($225)	($205)	($ 78)

EXHIBIT 15
Hospitality Equipment Service Co., Summary of Historical and Projected Operating Performance (millions of dollars)

Line #		History							Forecast		
		1988	1989	1990	1991	1992	1993	1994	1995	1996	1997
	Operating results										
1	Revenue	$24,770	$28,670	$26,555	$28,525	$26,720	$29,220	$31,410	$33,765	$36,300	$39,020
2	% Growth	49.2%	15.8%	(7.4%)	7.4%	(6.3%)	9.4%	7.5%	7.5%	7.5%	7.5%
3	– Cost of sales	18,560	21,545	19,545	20,955	14,305	21,190	22,500	24,170	25,965	27,895
4	% Sales	74.9%	75.1%	73.6%	73.5%	72.2%	72.5%	71.6%	71.6%	71.5%	71.5%
5	– SG&A	5,765	6,100	7,240	6,495	7,135	7,065	7,480	7,950	8,455	8,985
6	% Sales	23.3%	21.3%	27.3%	22.8%	26.7%	24.2%	23.8%	23.5%	23.3%	23.0%
7	– Cash taxes	$ 275	$ 440	$ 55	$ 420	$ 320	$ 420	$ 545	$ 615	$ 690	$ 780
8	% Operating income	62.0%	43.0%	(23.7%)	38.8%	113.3%	43.6%	38.0%	37.2%	36.7%	36.4%
9	**NOPAT**	$ 170	$ 585	$ (290)	$ 660	$ (35)	$ 545	$ 885	$ 1,035	$ 1,190	$ 1,365
	Capital										
10	Net accounts receivable	$ 2,655	$ 3,775	$ 3,075	$ 3,525	$ 3,010	$ 3,660	$ 6,288	$ 4,220	$ 4,530	$ 4,865
11	Inventory	2,830	3,420	4,115	3,205	3,105	3,365	3,560	3,815	4,085	4,380
12	PP&E	545	965	815	515	360	950	1,160	1,370	1,580	1,790
13	Other assets	535	355	335	835	850	675	770	805	805	810
14	– NIBCL's[a]	(4,295)	(4,845)	(4,095)	(3,250)	(4,045)	(3,295)	(3,520)	(3,805)	(4,110)	(4,440)
15	**Capital**	$ 2,270	$ 3,675	$ 4,250	$ 4,825	$ 3,280	$ 5,355	$ 5,900	$ 6,405	$ 6,890	$ 7,400
	Operating Analysis										
16	NOPAT/Avg cap (r)	7.8%	19.7%	(7.3%)	14.5%	(0.9%)	12.6%	15.7%	16.8%	17.9%	19.1%
17	– Cost of capital (c*)	13.4%	13.4%	13.4%	13.4%	13.4%	13.5%	13.5%	13.5%	13.5%	13.5%
18	Spread (r – c*)	(5.6%)	6.3%	(20.7%)	1.1%	(14.3%)	(1.0%)	2.2%	3.3%	4.4%	5.5%
19	× Average capital	$ 2,155	$ 2,970	$ 3,960	$ 4,535	$ 4,055	$ 4,315	$ 5,625	$ 6,150	$ 6,645	$ 7,145
20	**Economic value added**	($ 120)	$ 185	($ 820)	$ 50	($ 580)	($ 40)	$ 125	$ 205	$ 290	$ 395

a. Non-interest-bearing current liabilities.

EXHIBIT 16
Hospitality Equipment Service Co.

A. Input Table

Line #		1993	1994	1995	1996	1997	
	Bonus Pool Characteristics						
1	Target bonus	42%	42%	42%	42%	42%	
2	Base salary (000)	$705	$740	$775	$815	$855	
3	Number of units (000)	300	315	330	345	365	
	Bonus Calculation Framework						
4	Baseline EVA (000)	($310)					
5	Annual target adjustment factor	50%					
6	Base unit value	$0.25	$0.25	$0.25	$0.25	$0.25	
	EVA Bonus Sensitivity Factor						
7	= EVA bonus sensitivity factor (000)	$500					

B. Current Bonus Calculation

Line #		1993	1994	1995	1996	1997	Average
	Performance Unit Value						
8	EVA (000)	($40)	$125	$205	$290	$395	$195
9	− Baseline EVA (000)	($310)	($175)	($25)	$90	$190	($45)
10	= EVA vs baseline EVA (000)	$270	$300	$230	$200	$205	$240
11	/ EVA bonus sensitivity factor (000)	$500	$500	$500	$500	$500	$500
12	= Performance unit value	$0.54	$0.60	$0.46	$0.40	$0.41	$0.48
	Total Unit Value						
13	Performance unit value	$0.54	$0.60	$0.46	$0.40	$0.41	$0.48
14	+ Base unit value	$0.25	$0.25	$0.25	$0.25	$0.25	$0.25
15	= Total unit value	$0.79	$0.85	$0.71	$0.65	$0.66	$0.73
	Current Bonus						
16	Total unit value	$0.79	$0.85	$0.71	$0.65	$0.66	$0.73
17	Number of units (000)	300	315	330	345	365	330
18	Current bonus earned (000)	$235	$265	$235	$225	$240	$240

C. Past Bonus If System Had Been In Place Prior 5 Years

Line #		1988	1989	1990	1991	1992	Average
	Current Bonus						
19	Total unit value	$0.71	$1.10	($1.34)	$1.20	($0.54)	$0.22
20	Number of units (000)	285	525	315	335	255	345
21	Current bonus earned (000)	$205	$575	($425)	$405	($140)	$125

Part IV

Review and Synthesis

Atlantic Corporation—Abridged

On April 10, 1984, Patrick Halloran and Steven Winters, chairman of Atlantic Corporation and Royal Paper Corporation, respectively, met over lunch to discuss a possible cash sale of a group of Royal assets to Atlantic. The assets Halloran sought to buy included a linerboard mill and 16 plants that converted linerboard into corrugated cardboard boxes. Some observers considered the package Royal Paper's "crown jewels." If Halloran could acquire them at a reasonable price, he could accomplish an important strategic goal of Atlantic Corporation—to increase linerboard capacity firmwide.

Halloran wondered how the events of the past few months might influence Winters. One month earlier, Royal Paper had paid a handsome and well-publicized premium to repurchase a large block of stock from a potentially hostile investor. Almost immediately after the repurchase, a second speculator bought approximately 8% of Royal Paper's stock. Halloran's telephone call to Winters, inquiring whether Royal Paper might want to sell the mill package, had come only hours after the second investor's actions were made public. Halloran's tone had been clear: "We want the Monticello mill, and you probably want your stock in more friendly hands." Although Winters had rebuffed Halloran's earlier requests to discuss selling the assets, he now seemed attentive.

Atlantic Corporation

Atlantic Corporation was one of the nation's largest forest products/paper firms, with 1983 sales of $6.5 billion and net income of $105 million (see Exhibit 1). The firm competed in three businesses: building products, paper and pulp, and chemicals. Analysts tended to classify Atlantic as a "forest products" firm due to the fact that 60% of its 1983 sales and 70% of its operating profits stemmed from the firm's building products division, which was the world's largest producer of plywood.

The forest products industry, on the whole, responded rapidly and dramatically to changes in the overall economy. Sales and profits of products like plywood were tied to construction activity, which in turn, was directly linked to interest rate fluctuations.

The Market for Linerboard

Linerboard, a stiffened paper product, was transformed into corrugated cardboard boxes, which were used to pack over 90% of all U.S. goods shipped. The demand for boxes and for linerboard was related to the amount of goods being shipped in the nation. Analysts, in search of a measure to quantify the latter, found that changes in the level of industrial production were closely tied to box shipments and linerboard sales (see Exhibit 2).

Even though the fortunes of the linerboard industry, like those of the forest products industry, were tied to the performance of the overall economy, linerboard sales and profits tended to respond less quickly and less directly to economic shifts. Industrial production and the packaging of goods in boxes did not stop in periods of high interest rates, but high interest rates could bring new home starts nearly to a halt.

Linerboard producers and Wall Street analysts expected 1984 to be a healthy year for the linerboard industry. Strong demand, limited supply, and no new capacity were expected to cause the industry to operate at nearly 100% utilization. Given the high level of fixed costs in the industry, high operating rates generally meant high profits.

Linerboard and box sales were predicted to rise nearly 7%, as real GNP and industrial production strengthened with the forecasted economic expansion. Yet, only 1–2% new capacity was expected to become available through the end of 1986. Therefore, linerboard makers would operate at historically high levels of production, with operating rates expected to reach 99%, up significantly from the 1982 level of 84% (see Exhibit 2). In response to this strong demand, analysts predicted that linerboard prices would top $420 per ton by the end of 1986.

Atlantic Corporation's Interest in Linerboard

Atlantic Corporation's intention to add linerboard capacity was well known in the paper industry. The firm's existing Toledo, Ohio, linerboard mill produced 780 tons of linerboard per day. This represented only 1.8% of domestic linerboard capacity, and thus the firm could share in only a small way in the expected healthy linerboard market. More pressing was the fact that Atlantic Corporation was the only major paper producer that was a net buyer of linerboard. Atlantic Corporation purchased approximately 150,000 tons of linerboard each year from its competitors to feed its box plants. Given the current tight market, linerboard could either become unavailable or available only at extremely high prices. In the former case, Atlantic Corporation's box plants might be forced to turn away profitable orders. In the latter case, rising raw materials prices could erode the box division's profits.

As a result, the Atlantic Corporation's staff had studied steps to remedy its linerboard shortage. It calculated that a new 2,000-ton-per-day linerboard mill would have an economic life of 30 years, would cost $750 million, and would take 2 years to build.[1] With cash costs estimated at $300 per ton (1984 dollars) and interest rates at historically high levels, the economic flows from the project could not justify this price

---

1. The operation would also require an investment of $60 million in working capital.

tag. The absence of new linerboard plants throughout the industry indicated that Atlantic Corporation was not alone in reaching this conclusion.

The Atlantic Corporation's staff then surveyed the existing U.S. linerboard mills and rated each A, B, or C, depending on factors such as their capacities and ages. Halloran called the owners of the 11 A-rated mills, testing whether they had any interest in selling their mills. None was interested, including Winters, whose Monticello mill was ranked as the fourth best in the country.

In late 1983, Halloran became aware that the Continental Group, Inc. was interested in selling a package including three of its linerboard mills, with a combined capacity of over 1.1 million tons per year (or 3,143 daily tons), or over four times Atlantic Corporation's existing capacity. Halloran submitted a bid for the mills, but Stone Container Corporation's bid was chosen. Stone Container's product line consisted almost exclusively of linerboard and box products. Roger Stone, Stone Container's chairman and CEO, summarized the deal:

> "The three mills were purchased for around $120,000 per daily ton, excluding working capital and without assigning any value to the corrugated box plants included in the deal. This represents only about 30% of the cost of building new capacity, which if started today, could probably not be brought in for less than $375,000/daily ton three years later." This would be a total replacement cost of $1.4 billion for the three mills, while the 20 converting (box) plants could have a replacement value of $200 million.[2]

The Royal Paper Package: Mill, Box Plants, and Timberland

The assets Halloran sought to buy from Winters comprised an integrated system in Royal Paper's paper operations.

The Monticello, Mississippi Mill.   Completed in 1968, the $121 million "state-of-the-art" mill produced both linerboard and kraft paper. (Kraft paper is used to manufacture grocery bags.) In December 1983, Winters announced a "master plan to modernize the Monticello Mill" that called for Royal to spend $70–80 million over 20–22 months to convert all of the mill's kraft capacity to linerboard capacity. This move would increase the mill's linerboard capacity from 661,000 tons annually to 747,000 tons per year (or 2,134 daily tons), which would be purchased from Royal Paper as part of the transaction. Part of the output would be transformed into corrugated boxes in the 16 box plants. The rest of the mill's output would be used by Atlantic Corporation's own box plants. As of April 1984, the conversion process had not yet started.

Corrugated Box Plants.   Box plants were generally located near end users due to the relatively high cost of shipping. Royal Paper's 16 corrugated box plants were almost ideally suited for a combination with Atlantic's plants. Atlantic's box plants were located in the West, South, and Midwest, while the Royal Paper plants were in the South, Midwest, and East. Together, the box plants would cover most major U.S. markets.

Exhibit 3 shows estimates prepared by Atlantic's staff for both the Monticello mill and the 16 corrugated box plants. The forecasts are based on capital expenditures totaling $140.8 million to convert all of the mill's kraft capacity to linerboard capacity, to improve efficiency in the box plants, and to maintain the facilities (see Table A). It

---

2. "Stone Container Doubles Capacity," *Pulp & Paper*, December 1983, p. 65.

TABLE A
Planned Capital Expenditures—Monticello Mill and Box Plants (millions of dollars)

1984	1985	1986	1987	1988	1989	1990	1991	1992	1993
$19.2	$30.5	$41.7	$10.2	$10.2	$8.2	$6.2	$6.2	$4.2	$4.2

was anticipated that the mill and the box plants would have a 15-year economic life (through 1998), at which time management would decide whether or not to maintain the operation by investing in new capacity to replace the mill and box plants. No salvage value was expected to be obtained at the end of their lives.

The depreciation expense shown in Exhibit 3 includes depreciation of the capital expenditures forecast for 1984–1993, as well as the depreciation of the existing mill and box plant assets that Atlantic would purchase. Atlantic's finance staff believed that the tax basis and the financial reporting basis of the Monticello mill and the 16 box plants would be "stepped up" to reflect the price paid by Atlantic Corporation, less the amount of the purchase price assigned to the net working capital that would be transferred with the mill and box plants to Atlantic. Exhibit 3 assumes a total purchase price of $319 million, of which $270 million is assigned to the mill and box plants and $49 million is assigned to the net working capital. (See Table B for a breakdown and forecast of the net working capital required to support the operations of the Monticello mill and the box plants.)

Royal Paper Corporation

From 1974 to 1981, Royal Paper's sales and net profits grew consistently 8–9% each year, but an industry downturn in 1982 and 1983 did not leave Royal Paper unscathed. Sales and profits fell, and in 1982, Royal Paper's stock price plummeted to a price lower than at any other time in the past 15 years. This downturn was precipitated by a weakening of most of Royal Paper's major forest product/paper markets, offset in part by the stable performance of its printing papers division.

In response, Royal Paper management cut its workforce by 10% and divested itself of over a dozen money-losing mills. By the end of 1983, Royal Paper stock had climbed back to prices in the mid-$30 range, and in a presentation to securities analysts, Winters stressed the company's strong product lines; its capital investment plans, including conversion of the Monticello Mill to 100% linerboard production; and its generally upbeat prospects as it looked forward to "participating in the present economic recovery."

Steven Winters's sudden interest on April 18 in discussing the sale of the Monticello Mill package to Atlantic Corporation seemed linked to his besieged firm's recent

TABLE B
Net Working Capital—Monticello Mill and Box Plants (millions of dollars)

	Actual 1983	1984	1985	1986	1987	1988	1989	1990	1991	1992	1993
Accounts receivable	$32	$38	$48	$55	$58	$61	$64	$ 67	$ 70	$ 74	$ 77
Inventories	31	37	47	53	56	59	62	65	68	71	75
Accounts payable	14	17	21	24	25	27	28	29	31	32	34
Net working capital	$49	$58	$74	$84	$89	$93	$98	$103	$107	$113	$118

dealings with significant shareholders. Early 1984 had proved to be a difficult period for Royal Paper. While the company was recovering from an industrywide slump, Winters found himself in an uncomfortable position as prominent investors accumulated large blocks of Royal Paper stock and threatened to take over the firm.

Then, on February 9, 1984, *The Wall Street Journal*'s "Heard on the Street" column reported: "Royal Paper Seen Likely Takeover Target as Buyer Pays 2-Point Premium for Huge Block of Shares." Days later, on Monday, February 13, 1984, *The Wall Street Journal* identified the buyer as Sir James Goldsmith, a well-known British businessman and reputed "corporate raider."

Goldsmith's personal and business exploits were well covered by the media. *Fortune* described him as "dominating, clever, hot-tempered, intransigent. Goldsmith is an engaging tyrant. . . . When challenged, Goldsmith turns nasty. He revels in feuds, savors the chance to ruin an adversary."[3]

One month after Goldsmith's interest was announced, on March 12, 1984, Royal Paper announced that it had purchased Goldsmith's stock back from him at a substantial premium. At the time of the March announcement, Goldsmith's group had purchased 3,062,900 shares, or 8.6% of Royal Paper's common stock, at an average price of $33.50 per share. Royal Paper paid the Goldsmith group $52 per share, giving Goldsmith a profit of approximately $51 million.

Just six days after Royal Paper announced its purchase of the Goldsmith group shares, Royal announced that Loews Corporation, an insurance, hotel, entertainment, and tobacco company, had acquired a 7.7% share of Royal Paper, or 2.77 million shares. Lawrence Tisch, Loews' chief, was considered by at least one writer to be "the smartest investor around."[4]

Meanwhile, Back at the Meeting

How much were the assets worth? What would Winters accept? Halloran wondered what Winters planned to do about Loews' investment in Royal Paper. Public statements notwithstanding, Halloran was confident that Winters was determined to protect the independence of Royal Paper and would use the proceeds from the sale of assets to repurchase and to retire the shares held by Loews Corporation.

Halloran's staff believed that a cash offer of $319 million would be necessary to gain Royal Paper's acceptance and to complete the transaction quickly. This would create financing pressures in addition to those projected for Atlantic Corporation without the purchase of the Royal assets (see Exhibit 4). With earnings depressed and raiders and takeover experts on the prowl, Halloran did not wish to expose Atlantic to the risk of a hostile takeover bid. Something needed to be done to assure the support of the shareholders while also protecting (and hopefully strengthening) Atlantic's bond rating. An increase in the dividend rate, which had been slashed from $1.20 in 1981 to $.80 in 1983, was an obvious possibility.

Halloran's staff had been investigating a variety of financing sources. While the financial markets had been quite volatile in the late 1970s and early 1980s, the situation in April 1984 was relatively calm. Yields on investment-grade bonds had increased somewhat in recent months but were still well below the levels in 1979–1981. Further declines were anticipated as inflationary fears lessened. The stock market also

3. "Jimmy Goldsmith's U.S. Bonanza," *Fortune*, October 17, 1983, p. 156.
4. "Tips from a Master," *Forbes*, August 2, 1982, p. 96.

seemed poised to move higher on the strength of a recovery in corporate earnings and further declines in interest rates (see Exhibit 5).

In this environment of possibly improving markets, Atlantic could consider (1) drawing on its bank credit line of $200 million, which bore interest at the prime rate plus 1½% (current prime rate, 9.25%); (2) issuing up to $400 million of 25-year debentures at a yield of 10¼% to be repaid in equal installments over 10 years starting in the sixth year, and noncallable except for annual repayment purposes; or (3) up to $300 million in common stock issued at an estimated price of $30 per share with net proceeds to the company of $28 per share (current stock price, $32). Halloran was cognizant that the board of directors was concerned that Atlantic's debt might slip further within the BBB category. Atlantic already had one of the lowest bond ratings among its major peer group competitors (see Exhibit 6 for a comparison of major forest product and paper companies), and management was not anxious to explore the outer limits.

EXHIBIT 1
Atlantic Corporation Financial Performance, 1979–1983 (millions of dollars except per share data)

	1979	1980	1981	1982	1983
			Year Ended December 31,		
Net sales	$5,207	$5,026	$5,414	$5,402	$6,469
Cost of goods sold	4,328	4,269	4,720	4,791	5,653
Selling, general, and administrative	279	290	327	377	399
Earnings before interest and taxes	600	467	367	234	417
Interest	93	105	137	155	140
Profit before tax	507	362	230	79	277
Extraordinary loss	0	0	0	0	118
Tax	181	119	70	27	54
Net income	$ 326	$ 243	$ 160	$ 52	$ 105
Current assets	$1,161	$1,238	$1,417	$1,449	$1,516
Net fixed assets	2,957	3,274	3,643	3,701	3,463
Total assets	$4,118	$4,512	$5,060	$5,150	$4,979
Short-term debt	$ 62	$ 192	$ 257	$ 167	$ 10
Accounts payable and accrued expenses	539	520	552	568	627
Current maturities, long-term debt	75	75	85	95	95
Long-term debt	1,109	1,227	1,487	1,618	1,523
Other liabilities and deferred taxes	382	429	475	480	482
Common equity	1,951	2,069	2,204	2,222	2,242
Total	$4,118	$4,512	$5,060	$5,150	$4,979
Percent of Sales					
Cost of goods sold	83.1%	84.9%	87.2%	88.7%	87.4%
Selling, general, and administrative	5.4	5.8	6.0	7.0	6.2
Current assets	22.3	24.6	26.2	26.8	23.4
Net fixed assets	56.8	65.1	67.3	68.5	53.4
Accounts payable and accrued expenses	10.4	10.4	10.2	10.5	9.7
Tax as percent profit before tax	36	33	30	34	34
Per-Share Data					
Earnings per share	$ 3.10	$ 2.34	$ 1.54	$ .49	$ .98
Dividends per share	1.20	1.20	1.20	1.05	.80
Market price					
High	30	35	32	27	32
Low	23	21	18	13	22
Average	27	28	25	20	27
Book value per share	19	20	21	21	21
Number of shares (millions)	105	104	104	107	107
Beta					1.35
Average market price ÷ EPS	8.7	12.0	16.2	40.8	27.6
Average market price ÷ Book value	1.4	1.4	1.2	.95	1.3
Leverage Ratios					
Debt as % of book capital	39	42	48	47	42
Debt as % of market capital	29	32	40	45	35
Times interest earned	6.5	4.4	2.7	1.5	3.0
Bond rating					BBB

EXHIBIT 2
Linerboard Production and Pricing Data

	Actual						Estimated	
	1978	*1979*	*1980*	*1981*	*1982*	*1983*	*1984*	*1985*
U.S. production (000 tons)	13,228	13,951	14,232	14,540	13,494	14,900	15,900	16,470
U.S. consumption	12,092	12,331	11,658	12,000	11,707	12,775	13,600	13,870
Exports	1,540	1,645	2,527	1,974	1,886	2,275	2,500	2,700
Inventory change	−404	−25	47	566	−99	−150	−200	−100
U.S. capacity (000 tons)	13,864	14,199	14,586	15,372	16,032	16,266	16,430	16,670
Operating rates	95.4%	98.3%	97.6%	94.6%	84.2%	91.6%	96.8%	98.8%
Pricing ($ per ton)								
Annual average	$ 205	$ 241	$ 270	$ 297	$ 272	$ 270	$ 320	$ 360
By quarter								
First	192	230	270	297	290	250		
Second	200	235	270	300	280	263		
Third	208	240	270	300	263	277		
Fourth	220	257	270	300	255	290		
Percent change in								
Consumption	6.9%	2.0%	−5.5%	2.9%	−2.4%	9.1%	6.5%	2.0%
Real GNP	5.0	2.8	−0.4	1.9	−1.8	8.8	5.2	2.3
Index of industrial production	5.8	4.4	−3.6	2.6	−8.1	6.6	11.4	2.7
Box shipments	7.4	2.8	−3.7	2.0	−4.5	7.5	6.5	2.0

Source: Morgan Stanley Investment Research, January 1984.

EXHIBIT 3
Financial Projections Prepared by Atlantic Corporation Staff for the Monticello Mill and Box Plants (assumes a purchase price of $319 million for the mill and box plants)

	1984	1985	1986	1987	1988	1989	1990	1991	1992	1993
Monticello Mill										
Annual capacity (000 tons)[a]	661	699	747	747	747	747	747	747	747	747
Utilization rate	95%	93%	93%	95%	95%	95%	95%	95%	95%	95%
Production rate (000 tons)	628	650	695	710	710	710	710	710	710	710
Price per ton[b]	$ 320	$ 360	$ 400	$ 410	$ 430	$ 452	$ 475	$ 498	$ 523	$ 549
Mill sales ($ millions)	201.0	234.0	277.9	291.1	305.3	320.9	337.3	353.6	371.3	389.8
Cash costs ($ millions)[b]	160.3	176.1	194.2	211.3	221.5	232.7	244.2	256.4	269.2	282.8
Operating profit before depreciation and taxes	$ 40.7	$ 57.9	$ 83.7	$ 79.8	$ 83.8	$ 88.2	$ 93.1	$ 97.2	$102.1	$107.0
Box Plants ($ millions)										
Operating profit before depreciation and taxes	$ 11.6	$ 14.8	$ 16.3	$ 17.1	$ 18.0	$ 18.9	$ 19.8	$ 20.8	$ 21.8	$ 22.9
Combined Mill and Plants ($ millions)										
Operating profit before depreciation and taxes[c]	$ 52.3	$ 72.7	$100.0	$ 96.0	$101.8	$107.1	$112.9	$118.0	$123.9	$129.9
Depreciation expense[c]	20.9	28.3	35.0	39.3	41.3	39.3	34.3	27.1	26.3	25.3
EBIT	31.4	44.4	65.0	57.6	60.5	67.8	78.6	90.9	97.6	104.6
Tax @ 36%	11.3	16.0	23.4	20.7	21.8	24.4	28.3	32.7	35.1	37.6
EBIAT	$ 20.1	$ 28.4	$ 41.6	$ 36.9	$ 38.7	$ 43.4	$ 50.3	$ 58.2	$ 62.5	$ 67.0

a. Assumes conversion of kraft capacity to linerboard.

b. Inflation of 5% per year is incorporated in the forecasts.

c. Assumes that $270 million of the $319 million purchase price is assigned to net working capital. Atlantic Corporation planned to use the same depreciation methods for tax and financial reporting. At year-end 1993, the book value of the Monticello Mill and the box plants would be $93.7 million. (See below for year-end book values.)

1983	1984	1985	1986	1987	1988	1989	1990	1991	1992	1993
$270.0	$268.3	$270.5	$277.2	$248.1	$217.0	$185.9	$157.8	$136.9	$114.8	$93.7

EXHIBIT 4

Financial Forecasts for Atlantic Corporation (millions of dollars)

	Actual 1983	Forecasts			
		1984	1985	1986	1987
Sales (6% p.a. growth)	$6,469	$6,857	$7,269	$7,705	$8,167
Cost of goods sold	5,653	5,993	6,251	6,626	6,942
Selling, general, and administrative	399	425	436	462	490
Earnings before interest and taxes	417	439	582	617	735
Interest					
Existing debt	140	132	124	116	108
New debt	0	—	—	—	—
Profit before tax	277	307	458	501	627
Extraordinary loss	118	0	0	0	0
Taxes at 36%	54	111	165	180	226
Net income	105	196	293	321	401
Dividends	86	a	a	a	a
Percent of Sales					
Cost of goods sold	87.4%	87.4%	86.0%	86.0%	85.0%
Selling, general, and administrative	6.2	6.2	6.0	6.0	6.0
Assets					
Current assets	$1,516	$1,577	$1,672	$1,772	$1,878
Net fixed assets	3,463	3,566	3,707	3,930	4,165
Total assets	$4,979	$5,143	$5,379	$5,702	$6,043
Liabilities and Net Worth					
Short-term loans	$ 10	$ 0	$ 0	$ 0	$ 0
Accounts payable and accruals	627	686	727	771	817
Current maturities, long-term debt	95	95	95	95	95
Total current	732	781	822	866	912
Other liabilities	482	500	530	563	600
Long-term debt	1,523	1,428	1,333	1,238	1,143
Common equity	2,242	a	a	a	a
Financing shortfall	0	a	a	a	a
Total	$4,979	$5,143	$5,379	$5,702	$6,043
Percent of Sales					
Current assets	23%	23%	23%	23%	23%
Net fixed assets	53	52	51	51	51
Accounts payable and accruals	10	10	10	10	10
Other liabilities	7	7	7	7	7

Note: Forecasts do not include the assets that Atlantic may purchase from Royal Paper.

a. Future values not yet determined.

EXHIBIT 5
Atlantic Corporation Capital Markets Data

Bond Yields, as of April 9, 1984

U.S. Government T-Bills	U.S. Government 30-Year Bonds	Corporate Bonds			
		AAA	**AA**	**A**	**BBB**
7.53%	8.49%	8.73%	8.99%	9.46%	10.05%

Bond Ratings in 1984	**AAA**	**AA**	**A**	**BBB**
Industrials				
Debt % total book capital	18%	25%	30%	40%
Times interest earned	14.1	9.7	5.4	4.1
Forest Products and Paper				
Debt % total book capital	—	32%	38%	40%
Times interest earned	—	8.0	4.4	3.6

Value Line Industrial Composite[a]	*1979*	*1980*	*1981*	*1982*	*1983*	*April 1984*
Market price	$9.05	$9.91	$10.83	$ 9.89	$13.45	$13.10
EPS	1.35	1.18	1.19	.97	1.14	1.38[b]
DPS	.44	.45	.48	.48	.49	.53[b]
Book value	7.64	7.82	8.51	8.75	9.23	9.38
Price/Earnings	6.7	8.4	9.1	10.2	11.8	9.5
Market/Book	1.2	1.3	1.3	1.1	1.5	1.4

a. Composite of 780 major industrial companies.

b. Estimated.

EXHIBIT 6
Atlantic Corporation, Statistics on Selected Forest Products, Paper, and Linerboard Producers

	Atlantic Corporation					Stone Container				
	1979	1980	1981	1982	1983	1979	1980	1981	1982	1983
Sales ($ millions)	$5,207	$5,016	$5,414	$5,402	$6,469	$328	$379	$411	$427	$660
Net income ($ millions)	326	243	160	52	105	15	21	24	14	22
EPS	3.10	2.34	1.54	0.49	0.98	1.61	2.22	2.48	1.46	1.56
DPS	1.20	1.20	1.20	1.05	0.80	.32	.38	.51	.60	.62
Book value per share					$19					$25
Stock price										
High	$ 30	$ 35	$ 32	$ 27	$ 32	$ 16	$ 14	$ 23	$ 24	$ 45
Low	24	22	18	13	22	6	9	12	13	20
Average	27	28	25	20	27	11	12	17	18	33
Capitalization at book										
% debt	39%	42%	48%	47%	43%	45%	40%	49%	51%	67%
% common	61	58	52	53	57	55	60	51	49	33
Capitalization at market										
% debt	29%	32%	40%	45%	35%	42%	39%	44%	46%	45%
% common	71	68	60	55	65	58	61	56	54	55
Bond rating					BBB					—
Beta					1.35					1.15
Linerboard capacity[a]					273					1,295
Linerboard sales ($ millions)					$74					$350

	International Paper					Royal Paper				
	1979	1980	1981	1982	1983	1979	1980	1981	1982	1983
Sales ($ millions)	$4,533	$5,043	$4,983	$4,015	$4,357	$2,498	$2,713	$2,819	$2,556	$2,775
Net income ($ millions)	525	314	525	161	131	164	177	177	45	55
EPS	10.96	5.97	1.25	2.72	2.46	4.76	5.12	5.12	1.29	1.40
DPS	2.40	2.40	2.40	2.40	2.40	1.83	2.03	2.15	1.68	1.12
Book value per share					$67					$22
Stock price										
High	$ 48	$ 48	$ 52	$ 52	$ 60	$ 35	$ 37	$ 43	$ 32	$ 37
Low	36	31	37	33	46	27	25	29	18	24
Average	42	39	44	42	53	31	31	36	25	30
Capitalization at book										
% debt	29%	25%	21%	23%	22%	31%	37%	37%	40%	34%
% common	71	75	79	77	78	69	63	63	60	66
Capitalization at market										
% debt	34%	32%	27%	31%	25%	36%	44%	41%	53%	40%
% common	6	68	73	69	75	64	56	59	47	60
Bond rating					AA/A					BBB
Beta					1.15					1.25
Linerboard capacity[a]					1,527					603
Linerboard sales ($ millions)					$412					$163

a. In thousands of tons.

Friendly Cards, Inc.

In early 1988, Wendy Beaumont, president of Friendly Cards, Inc., met with Amy McConville, a friend and financial consultant. They had been discussing the future of Friendly in relation to the research Ms. McConville had been doing on the firm. (Exhibits 1 and 2 show the company's income statements, balance sheets, and financial projections.) Mrs. Beaumont commented:

> Money is tight and, quite frankly, the cost of financing growth is now so high that I wish we could sit still for a year. But we really can't do that. You know the record and you saw our growth for last year. We're projecting a 20% increase in sales and an even larger increase in earnings for next year. I hope you can come up with some suggestions concerning the financing of our expansion, so we can talk about them on Friday morning.

Industry Background Data

In 1988 the greeting card industry consisted of over 100 companies; the "Big Three" (see Exhibit 3) dominated the scene with an overwhelming market share. Of these three, two were publicly owned (American Greetings and Gibson), and one was private (Hallmark). (See Exhibit 5 for financial data on American Greetings and Gibson.)

The rest of the industry was made up predominantly of small firms, many of which were privately owned and family controlled. Growth, however, was most prominent in the larger firms, which had larger, more diversified product lines and more efficient national distribution channels. Smaller companies were often crippled by the expense of setting up a large sales system, of producing a full line and constantly reviewing it, and of designing and preparing new cards. As a result, the total number of firms in the industry had declined by about 15% each decade since 1954. Most of this decline occurred among companies of less than 50 employees.

In order to compete successfully, all firms had to deal effectively with high fixed costs. Companies ran large inventory costs because of the necessity of keeping stock

Copyright © 1993 by the President and Fellows of Harvard College.
Harvard Business School case 293–135.

for reorders. Production was costly and long lead times prevented rerunning successful designs. In addition, many retailers could return unsold or soiled cards to the manufacturer for full refund or credit.

Because of these high fixed costs and the overall competitiveness of the industry, distribution costs were very important to overall firm profitability. The large companies used their own sales forces to sell directly to various outlets. Often companies would try to increase sales by expanding the distribution network. Sales trends within the industry were often characterized (especially in the case of smaller companies) by seasonal peaks, as most of the actual sales occurred in a short period of time even though cards were in production all year. As an example, 32% of industry dollar sales occurred at Christmas, with Valentine's Day (7% of sales), Mother's Day (5%), and Father's Day (2%) being other examples in which the selling season was short but the revenues were large. Within the industry, companies were placing an increasing emphasis on a larger variety of cards and on the rapid replacement of slow sellers to encourage more impulse buying of everyday cards. This had been successful to the extent that in 1969, 40% of card volume was represented by everyday sales, and in 1987, this figure was above 50%.

Within the industry, trends included a conscious move away from sole reliance on greeting card sales. Hallmark, for example, also marketed glassware, jewelry, candles, silverware, and giftbooks; American Greetings diversified into gift wrap and stationery goods, such as playing cards, giftbooks, and college study guides.

Friendly Cards, Inc.

In 1978, Wendy Beaumont founded Beaumont Greeting Card Company in New York City with $15,000. Shortly thereafter, she acquired the bankrupt Lithograph Publishing Company of Reading, Connecticut and moved all operations to the new plant. A year later, the renamed firm, Friendly Cards, Inc., went public through a stock offering at $3 per share.

In the years that followed, Friendly expanded rapidly through internal growth and acquisitions. Glitter Greetings of Lansing, Michigan, a firm that primarily sold cards to supermarkets, became a wholly owned subsidiary in a deal involving both cash and stock. In 1986, Friendly acquired Edwards & Company (Long Beach, New York) for cash. Edwards was a small company that sold juvenile valentines through a distribution system that included chain, drug, variety, and discount stores as well as wholesalers, rack jobbers, and supermarkets. Still another market was opened with the acquisition of a California firm, again by means of cash and stock. The California firm was renamed Friendly Artists and provided the company with distribution on the West Coast as well as an operation specializing in direct sales of packaged personalized Christmas cards to the retailer.

Friendly Cards' Operations

Unlike most small companies, Friendly manufactured a full line of greeting cards, with 1,200 designs in its 1988 line. Approximately 30% of dollar sales were accounted for by Christmas sales and 25% by valentines, with the remainder made up of everyday and spring holiday cards. Twenty-five percent of total sales were of packaged boxes of cards, which were either "title" cards (i.e., Brother's Birthday) or assortments. The sale of packaged boxes helped to cut costs because the manufacturer did not have to supervise racks and take reorders of individual cards in every outlet. Returns expense was also low because once the package was sold to a store, it was generally not returnable. In addition, the giants of the industry were not as active in packaged sales, concentrating more heavily on the sale of individual cards.

None of Friendly's designs were higher fashion studio cards. Friendly sold primarily to the over-40-year-old market. Ms. Beaumont characterized a large part of her market as cost conscious. She felt that most of the purchasers of her cards would not spend the time or the money to select *the* perfect card for each occasion but would prefer to have the less expensive, more convenient packages at home whenever a card was needed.

The designing, printing, and packaging of all cards and giftwrap were done at the 250-employee plant in Reading. The plant was operating at capacity, but much of the printing work could be done by outside printers if necessary.

Friendly Cards' Distribution Method

Distribution itself was not a large expense at Friendly. The 25-person company sales force (one-third of which worked on a full-commission basis) sold either directly to the central buyers for such stores as Kmart Corp., Wal-Mart, and Bradlees or to rack jobbers and wholesalers. This system, however, was a prime factor in the low margins earned by Friendly, for there were often two intermediaries between the manufacturer and the ultimate customer. As a reflection of this, Ms. Beaumont estimated that dollar sales of her cards at the retail level were three times the sales figures shown in her income statement.

Operations at Friendly were closely supervised. Management included three production and shipping managers, one art director, and a sales manager and an assistant to the president. Besides Ms. Beaumont, there were nine officers, six of whom were also directors.

Financial Problems

According to Ms. Beaumont, Friendly had never been without financing problems. The business was capital intensive, and Ms. Beaumont attributed much of her success to the company's good relations with its banks and suppliers. Its line of credit with nearby banks totaled $6.25 million. The company borrowed at 2½% above the prime rate, with the current prime rate being 8.5%. Because of the seasonal nature of the industry, Ms. Beaumont estimated that the company's peak needs for bank and trade credit (which amounted to over $9.0 million at the end of 1987) occurred in December and January. She also stated that the company's low-borrowing point following each selling season occurred in April, at which point bank and trade credit was reduced to about 50% of peak needs.

Although the company had a good relationship with its banks, Ms. Beaumont had been urged to seek additional equity capital. Friendly's bankers felt uneasy about the extent to which the company was depending on debt capital to finance its operations. Early in 1988, they suggested that their willingness to finance the company through an enormous sales expansion in 1986 was based on an expectation that sales growth would thereafter slow substantially. Under these expected circumstances, growth in the equity account through earnings retentions would have rapidly reduced the firm's liabilities/equity ratio to the 1985 level, a point substantially below the lofty 5.2 to 1 reached in 1986 (Exhibit 2). Given the firm's performance in 1987 and Ms. Beaumont's sales projections (Exhibits 1 and 2), however, a return to the 1985 level in Friendly's liabilities/equity ratio was at best still several years away. Friendly's bankers, therefore, insisted that the firm take some action before its peak borrowing season to make sure that the company would stay safely within two restrictions that the bankers planned to impose on future loans to Friendly. These two restrictions, which would apply at the end of 1988, were as follows:

1. The bank loans outstanding at any time could not exceed 85% of Friendly's accounts receivable.
2. Friendly's total liabilities could not exceed three times the book value of the company's net worth.

For planning purposes, Ms. Beaumont had decided to retain some margin of safety by holding Friendly's ratio of all interest-bearing debt/equity to a maximum of 2 to 1.

Decisions Confronting Friendly Cards

Ms. McConville was familiar with the background information on the greeting card industry and on Friendly Cards. Ms. Beaumont had also referred three other questions to Ms. McConville:

1. Should Friendly invest in equipment to enable the company to make rather than to buy its envelopes?
2. Should Friendly Cards acquire Creative Designs, Inc., a small midwestern manufacturer of studio cards?
3. Should Friendly go to the market to raise additional equity capital in order to relieve the pressure on its financial position?

Envelope Machine Proposal

The cost of envelopes was one of the largest components of total costs. Friendly was still purchasing its entire supply of envelopes. During 1987, it had spent $1.5 million to purchase the 100 million envelopes used by the company that year. Ms. Beaumont estimated that she could buy equipment for $500,000 that, when operated at full capacity, would enable her to manufacture all the envelopes she had used in 1987. She estimated that the envelope-making equipment would have an economic life of about 8 years.

Ms. Beaumont estimated that the people required to run the envelope-making operation would have an annual cost of $91,000. These and other expenses are shown in Exhibit 4. From these data, Ms. McConville calculated that the envelope machine project would generate a positive cash flow annually for an 8-year period, disregarding working capital and financing requirements.

The additional warehouse space included in Exhibit 4 would be needed because, if the machine was purchased, the company would be producing envelopes at a level rate substantially in excess of shipments during the spring and summer months so as to build the large inventories needed to meet year-end shipping schedules. If she started manufacturing her own envelopes, Ms. Beaumont anticipated that her average net working capital requirement would immediately increase by $200,000 and remain at that level during the life of the machine.

Possible Acquisition of Creative Designs, Inc.

Ms. Beaumont had also been investigating a possible acquisition candidate, Creative Designs, Inc. (CD), a small midwestern manufacturer of studio cards. Creative Designs was privately owned and had sales of about $5 million in 1987 (Exhibit 6). Ms.

Beaumont had spent considerable time over a four-month period examining the details of CD's operations. She had become convinced that under her management, CD could almost immediately reduce its cost of goods sold by 5%, or $154,000 at current sales levels. She also anticipated that by eliminating duplication, she could reduce CD's other expenses by 10% (or $155,000). She estimated that if Friendly acquired CD in early 1988, CD's sales would remain flat during the year of ownership change, but beyond 1988, the company would achieve sales increases of about 6% per year. What particularly interested Ms. Beaumont about the potential acquisition was the strength of CD's balance sheet (Exhibit 7). She felt CD's suppliers would be willing to go a good deal further in providing trade credit than they had in the past, and she knew that the company had unused bank credit lines. In her discussion with the three present owners of CD, all of whom were approaching retirement age, Ms. Beaumont concluded that the company could be acquired for 11 times its 1987 earnings. The principals were willing to take Friendly common stock valued at $9.50 a share, which would give them a total of 198,000 shares. A check with her public accounting firm convinced Ms. Beaumont that the exchange of securities would be a tax-free exchange. The acquisition would be treated as a "pooling of interests" for accounting purposes, so that the balance sheet for the resulting firm would simply be the sum of the two companies' statements.

Ms. Beaumont had asked Ms. McConville for a recommendation as to whether she should acquire Creative Designs on these terms. Ms. McConville knew that she would have to consider the impact of the acquisition on the earnings position of Friendly, and also the implications of the acquisition for Friendly's financial position.

Possible Sale of New Common Stock

In order to sustain the projected rapid growth for the next several years and in view of Friendly's extremely tight financial position (Exhibits 1 and 2), Ms. Beaumont was aware that she might have to raise additional equity capital. Ms. McConville knew that Ms. Beaumont would be most reluctant to accept a policy recommendation that would force her to curtail the growth in sales projected in Exhibit 1. As already indicated, Ms. Beaumont believed that if potential increases in orders from new or existing customers were turned down, it would be very difficult and perhaps impossible to retain these customers in subsequent years. Ms. Beaumont was also concerned that restrictions on the acceptance of new orders would be demoralizing to the company's sales force and perhaps would cause some of the most valuable sales representatives to shift to a competing firm.

Ms. McConville was also troubled by the fact that this was a most difficult and expensive time for any company to raise new equity capital, especially for a small company like Friendly with unseasoned securities.

Friendly Cards' stock was traded in the over-the-counter market. Volume was light, averaging about 3,000 shares a week. Due to extremely light trading volume in the stock of Friendly Cards, Inc., it was difficult to compute a β value for the stock of this company directly from stock price data. During the past two months, the stock price had held at about $9.50. During 1986 and 1987, the price of the stock had ranged from a low of $9.50 to a high of $15 per share. Ms. Beaumont owned about 55% of the stock currently outstanding. Another 20% was owned by employees and officers of the company. About 25% of the outstanding stock was owned by the public.

Ms. McConville knew that Ms. Beaumont had recently received an offer from a group of West Coat investors who had a long-term interest in the company. They had offered to buy 200,000 shares of Friendly's common stock at $8 per share. If this offer was accepted, Friendly would have to pay a finder's fee of $80,000, or 10,000 shares, to the individual who had brought this offer to Ms. Beaumont's attention.

In considering this offer, Ms. McConville approached Samuel Hexter, a friend of hers and a partner in the Boston office of the investment banking firm of Stoddard, White & Driscoll, to inquire about the feasibility of a public offering of Friendly stock. Mr. Hexter was not encouraging. He commented:

> Now is a tough time to raise equity money, especially for a small company like Friendly. The October stock market crash was a killer. The Dow Jones index of industrial stocks has fallen from 2596 in September 1987 to under 2000 right now, and there's no telling what will happen tomorrow. This is a bad time for a small company to raise money. I hate to say so, but I don't see how we could possibly take Friendly's stock to the market at more than $8 a share. Frankly, I am uncertain how many shares we could sell even at a price as low as $8.

This conversation confirmed Ms. McConville's initial impression that the only realistic prospect for raising new capital was to accept the offer of the West Coast group.

EXHIBIT 1

Consolidated Income Statements, 1985–1987, and Projected Income Statements, 1988–1990[a] (years ending December 31; in thousands of dollars except per share data)

	Actual Data			Projected Data			
	1985	1986	1987	1988	1989	1990	
Net sales	$8,055	$12,765[b]	$16,253	$19,500	$23,250	$28,000	
Cost of goods sold	5,690	8,785	10,540	12,675	15,112	18,200	(65% of proj. sales)
Gross profit on sales	$2,365	$ 3,980	$ 5,713	$ 6,825	$ 8,138	$ 9,800	(35% of proj. sales)
Expenses							
Selling, delivery, and warehousing	$1,015	$ 1,793	$ 2,373	$ 2,828	$ 3,371	$ 4,060	(14.5% of proj. sales)
General and administrative	547	945	1,125	1,365	1,628	1,960	(7.0% of proj. sales)
Total expenses	$1,562	$ 2,738	$ 3,498	$ 4,193	$ 4,999	$ 6,020	
Earnings before interest and taxes	803	1,243	2,215	2,633	3,139	3,780	
Interest	495	605	950	1,075[d]	1,188[d]	1,320[d]	
Income before federal income taxes	$ 308	$ 638	$ 1,265	$ 1,558	$ 1,951	$ 2,460	
Provision for federal income taxes	113	225	481	592	742	935	(38% of proj. PBT)
Net income	$ 195	$ 413	$ 784	$ 966	$ 1,209	$ 1,525	
Shares outstanding (000)	534	550	580	580	580	580	
Earnings per share (in dollars)	.37	.75[c]	1.35	1.67	2.08	2.63	

Source: Annual reports and management projections.

a. Net sales and net income for 1982–1984 were as follows:

	Net Sales (millions)	Net Income (thousands)
1982	$5.5	$ 53
1983	6.3	105
1984	7.0	148

b. $1.5 million of 1986 sales were from the Edwards acquisition.

c. 0.16 was from the Edwards acquisition.

d. Additional financing required beyond 1987 is assumed to carry an interest cost equal to the prime rate of 8½% plus 2½%.

EXHIBIT 2
Consolidated Balance Sheets, 1985–1987, and Projected Balance Sheets, 1988–1990 (years ending December 31; thousands of dollars)

	Actual Data			Projected Data			
	1985	1986	1987	1988	1989	1990	
Assets							
Cash	$ 200	$ 370	$ 240	$ 250	$ 250	$ 250	
Notes and accounts receivable	2,920	5,883	7,013	8,385	9,998	12,040	(43% of proj. sales)
Inventory	2,500	3,708	5,588	6,630	7,905	9,520	(34% of proj. sales)
Prepaid expenses	43	117	192	195	232	280	(1% of proj. sales)
Total current assets	$5,663	$10,078	$13,033	$15,460	$18,385	$22,090	
Net fixed assets	903	2,208	2,433	2,925	3,488	4,200	(15% of proj. sales)
Other assets	184	907	892	905	905	905	
Total assets	$6,750	$13,193	$16,358	$19,290	$22,778	$27,195	
Liabilities							
Bank loans	$2,323	$ 4,350	$ 6,070	$ 7,586[a]	$ 9,321[a]	$11,404[a]	(19% of proj. sales)
Accounts and trade notes payable	1,503	2,748	3,057	3,705	4,417	5,320	(7.5% of proj. sales)
Accrued expenses and other items	332	683	1,231	1,462	1,744	2,100	
Current portion of long-term debt	117	350	433	450	450	450	
Other	0	187	246	250	250	250	
Total current liabilities	$4,275	$ 8,318	$11,037	$13,453	$16,182	$19,524	
Long-term debt	787	2,752	2,458	2,008	1,558	1,108	
Total liabilities	$5,062	$11,070	$13,495	$15,461	$17,740	$20,632	
Common stock ($0.10 par value)	53	55	58	58	58	58	
Paid-in capital	740	763	815	815	815	815	
Retained earnings	895	1,305	1,990	2,956	4,165	5,690	
Total liabilities and net worth	$6,750	$13,193	$16,358	$19,290	$22,778	$27,195	
Ratio Data							
Bank loan/receivables	.80	.74	.87	.90	.93	.95	
Liabilities/equity	3.00	5.22	4.72	4.04	3.52	3.11	
Interest-bearing debt/equity	1.91	3.51	3.13	2.62	2.25	1.98	

a. For convenience in forecasting, additional financing required beyond 1987 is assumed to be borrowed from banks. Due to loan covenant tests, this might not be possible.

EXHIBIT 3
Greeting Card Industry Data, 1987

Company	Sales[a] (in millions)	Income after Taxes (in millions)	Earnings per share (in dollars)	Stock Price/ Earnings Ratio
Hallmark	$2,000	NA	NA	NA
American Greetings	1,174	$33.4	$1.04	13[a]
Gibson Greetings	359	24.1	1.53	8[a]
Friendly Cards	16	.8	1.35	7[a]

a. Sales include all products of these companies, but they consist primarily of greeting cards.

EXHIBIT 4
Estimated Annual Savings from Operation of Envelope Machine, Years 1 through 8
(thousands of dollars)

Savings: Outlays for envelopes purchased in 1987	$1,500
Incremental expenses from manufacturing envelopes:	
Materials	$ 902
Warehouse	94
Labor	91
Depreciation	62
Total expenses	$1,149
Increase in profits before taxes	351
Increase in income taxes @ .38	133
Increase in profit after taxes	$ 218

EXHIBIT 5
Financial Data on Large Publicly Traded Greeting Card Firms

	American Greetings			Gibson Greetings		
	1985	*1986*	*1987*	*1985*	*1986*	*1987*
Sales (millions)	$1,012	$1,102	$1,174	$ 330	$ 323	$ 359
Net income (millions)	74.2	63.4	33.4	31.5	22.6	24.1
EPS	2.32	1.97	1.04	1.99	1.43	1.53
Closing stock price	32⅝	26¼	14	19⅝	16	12⅝
Total debt (millions)	168	271	341	85	75	75
Net worth (millions)	483	524	539	119	138	154
Beta[a]			1.07			.93
Interest coverage	8.1x	5.1x	2.7x	8.3x	8.2x	9.0x

a. Based on previous 5 years.

	1988 Interest Rates
Treasury bills	6.1%
Long-term government bond	8.4%
AAA corporate bond	8.7%
Corporate bond	11.5%
(similar in quality to Friendly Cards at current time)	

EXHIBIT 6

Income Statements for Creative Designs, Inc.; Actual, 1985–1987, and Projected, 1988–1990[a] (years ending December 31; thousands of dollars)

	Actual Data			Projected Data		
	1985	*1986*	*1987*	*1988*	*1989*	*1990*
Net sales	$4,175	$4,575	$5,000	$5,000[a]	$5,300[a]	$5,618[a]
Cost of goods sold[b]	2,532	2,770	3,075			
Gross profit on sales	$1,643	$1,805	$1,925			
Expenses						
Selling, delivery, and warehousing	$1,050	$1,180	$1,200			
General and administrative	280	300	350			
Total expenses	$1,330	$1,480	$1,550			
Earnings before interest and taxes	$ 313	$ 325	$ 375			
Interest	75	95	100			
Income before federal income taxes	$ 238	$ 230	$ 275			
Provision for federal income taxes	95	85	104			
Net income	$ 143	$ 145	$ 171			
Dividends	80	80	96			
Retained earnings	$ 63	$ 65	$ 75			

a. Projection made by Ms. Beaumont.

b. The bulk of the depreciation expense for Creative Designs was included in the cost-of-goods-sold expense category.

EXHIBIT 7
Balance Sheets of Creative Designs, Inc. 1985–1987 (years ending December 31; thousands of dollars)

	1985	1986	1987
Assets			
Cash	$ 68	$ 58	$ 88
Notes and accounts receivable	1,360	1,533	1,600
Inventory	1,338	1,550	1,500
Prepaid expenses	32	54	62
Total current assets	$2,798	$3,195	$3,250
Net fixed assets [a]	1,090	1,225	1,250
Total assets	$3,888	$4,420	$4,500
Liabilities			
Bank loans	$ 0	$ 125	$ 250
Accounts payable	440	550	500
Current portion of long-term debt	38	50	50
Other	427	470	450
Total current liabilities	$ 905	$1,195	$1,250
Long-term debt	873	1,050	1,000
Total liabilities	$1,778	$2,245	$2,250
Common stock	100	100	100
Paid-in capital	300	300	300
Retained earnings	1,710	1,775	1,850
Total liabilities and net worth	$3,888	$4,420	$4,500
		Ratio Data	
Bank loan/receivables	0	.08	.16
Total liabilities/equity	.84	1.03	1.00
Interest-bearing debt/equity	.43	.56	.58

a. Reconciliation of net fixed assets:

	1985	1986	1987
Net fixed assets at beginning of year	$1,050	$1,090	$1,225
(+) Capital spending	190	297	190
(–) Depreciation expense	(150)	(162)	(165)
Net fixed assets at end of year	$1,090	$1,225	$1,250

Pinkerton (A)

Late one afternoon in November 1987, Tom Wathen, sole owner and CEO of California Plant Protection (CPP), sat in his office staring at two financing plans. Wathen was trying to decide whether or not he should increase his $85 million bid to purchase Pinkerton's—the legendary security guard firm—from its current owner, American Brands.

On the previous day, Wathen had been told by Morgan Stanley, American Brands' investment banker, that his bid of $85 million had been rejected and that nothing less than $100 million would be accepted. While Wathen was elated at still being in the deal, he had a problem. CPP's board of directors had reluctantly approved the earlier $85 million bid and was sure to balk at a $100 million bid. Wathen desperately wanted to buy Pinkerton's, but he was not sure how much it was worth or how to finance it. Wathen knew he had to act now or miss this unprecedented growth opportunity and probably his last chance to be one of the industry's biggest players.

The Security Guard Industry

The security guard industry had two segments: (1) proprietary guards and (2) contract guards. While both types of guards performed similar services, a proprietary guard was an employee on the payroll of a nonsecurity firm. Contract guards were "rented" from specialist suppliers like Pinkerton's, CPP, Wackenhut, and Baker Industries. The historical growth of the contract guard segment of the industry was due in part to companies concluding that they gained operating flexibility by contracting out their security needs as opposed to managing their own security operations. By late 1987, security guard services was a $10 billion industry growing at 6% a year. But the industry was also mature, fragmented, and price competitive. As a result, there was an

This case was prepared by Adam S. Berger (MBA 1991) under the supervision of Professor Scott P. Mason.

ongoing trend toward consolidation at the expense of smaller, local guard companies, whose employees were often imperfectly screened and poorly trained.

Pinkerton's

The security guard industry began in 1850 when Allan Pinkerton founded the Pinkerton's Detective Agency. The firm gained fame in the nineteenth century with its pursuit of such outlaws as Butch Cassidy and the Sundance Kid. In the film portrayal of that pair, Paul Newman repeatedly asks Robert Redford, "Who are those guys?" The "guys" were Pinkerton's men and women.

Pinkerton ran his firm until he died in 1884. The company was then headed by four generations of Pinkertons until the family's reign ended in 1967 with the death of Robert Pinkerton. American Brands, the $5 billion consumer goods company, with brand names such as Lucky Strike cigarettes, Jim Beam bourbon, Master Lock padlocks, and Titleist golf balls, purchased Pinkerton's for $162 million in 1982. American Brands made the acquisition in order to expand the service side of its business and because it saw the Pinkerton's brand name as a great addition to "a company of great brand names." The Pinkerton family sold the company to American Brands because they felt the industry was becoming extremely price competitive and that, as a result, the company needed a strong parent to compete and grow. In 1987, Pinkerton's was among the largest security guard firms in the United States, with sales of over $400 million; 150 offices in the United States, Canada, and the United Kingdom; and a particular strength in the eastern United States. Exhibit 1 gives selected financial data for Pinkerton's.

California Plant Protection

When Wathen bought CPP in 1963, the firm had 18 employees and revenues of $163,000. By 1987, Wathen had built CPP into a $250 million security guard company with 20,000 employees and 125 offices in 38 states and Canada. Exhibit 2 gives selected financial data for CPP. Wathen built CPP with his consummate marketing skills and the strategy of differentiating the firm with employee screening and continual training. CPP's expansion was aided by the explosive growth of California's economy and by the failure of the bigger, more established East Coast security guard firms to enter the West Coast aggressively.

While Wathen was the sole owner of CPP, he had a board of directors that he used as advisors. The board had three members: Albert Berger, James Hall, and Gerald Murphy. Berger was an entrepreneur, COO of an electrical connector firm, and a CPP director since 1975. Hall was an attorney, a former vice president of MCA, the former California secretary of health, education and welfare, and a CPP director since 1976. Murphy was president of ERLY Industries, a director of several companies, and a CPP director since 1975.

CPP's Acquisition of Pinkerton's

Wathen wanted to buy Pinkerton's for several reasons. First, he had always had the goal of creating the largest firm in the security guard industry. The acquisition of Pinkerton's would put him in a virtual tie with Baker Industries, a subsidiary of Borg Warner, and the largest provider of contract guard services. Second, Wathen had been convinced for some time that American Brands was mismanaging Pinkerton's and destroying a great brand name with its pricing strategy.

In October 1987, American Brands announced its decision to sell Pinkerton's because of its poor fit with Brands' long-range business strategy. Upon this announcement, Jerry Brown, CPP's secretary and general counsel, recalls, "Tom [Wathen] called me in, and from that moment I knew he was going to do whatever it took to buy Pinkerton's. Tom was always hung up on being the largest, and on Pinkerton's name."

Morgan Stanley, an investment bank, was to represent American Brands in the sale, and the bidding promised to be hotly contested. A task force of senior managers was quickly formed to prepare CPP's bid, which it knew, given the time pressures of the sale, would not have the benefit of adequate preparation.

The task force believed there were three ways CPP could create value by acquiring Pinkerton's. The most obvious source of value would come from the consolidation of the operations of CPP and Pinkerton's. This would eliminate common overhead expenses such as corporate headquarters, support staff, and redundant offices. Second, the task force believed that significant improvements could be made in the management of Pinkerton's net working capital.

The third source of value, and possibly a unique insight by Wathen and the CPP task force, was Pinkerton's pricing strategy. American Brands had instituted a strategy of low price and high market share at Pinkerton's in 1985. While the strategy had been successful in attracting new customers, it adversely affected profitability.

Wathen and the CPP task force planned to capitalize on the strength of the Pinkerton brand name by charging a premium price for services. The new pricing strategy would result in the loss of price-sensitive customers. Pinkerton's revenues would shrink, in a smooth fashion, to 70% of its 1987 level by the end of 1990, and would then grow at 5% per year thereafter. However, the new pricing strategy seemed likely to improve Pinkerton's gross profit margins from 8.5% in 1988 to 9.0% in 1989, 9.5% in 1990, and 10.25% thereafter. The task force further expected the new strategy to produce higher margins for CPP, increasing the operating profit from CPP's own projected business by $1.2 million in 1989, $1.5 million in 1990, $2.0 million in 1991, and $3 million in 1992. This increase in CPP's projected operating profit was expected to grow at 5% a year, in line with sales, beyond 1992. (Exhibit 3 gives a 5-year forecast of CPP's net income and cash flow assuming Pinkerton's is *not* acquired.) However, the task force realized there was a distinct possibility that the new pricing strategy might have little or no impact on CPP's projected operating profits and that Pinkerton's gross margins might improve to only 8.5% in 1988, 8.75% in 1989, 9% in 1990, and 9.5% thereafter.

The task force was confident that, as a result of eliminating common overhead, Pinkerton's operating expenses, as a percentage of sales, could be reduced to 6% in 1988, 5.9% in 1989, and 5.8% in 1990 and beyond. The task force was also confident that Pinkerton's net plant and equipment could be reduced to 4% of sales and could be kept there for the foreseeable future.

The task force was somewhat less confident in its estimate of improvements in the management of Pinkerton's net working capital. This was due to concerns over the ability of CPP's accounting department to handle a much larger and more geographically diverse operation. The task force expected that Pinkerton's net working capital, as a percentage of sales, could be reduced to 8.6% in 1988, 7.4% in 1989, and 6.2% thereafter. However, if CPP's accounting department experienced difficulties in integrating the two firms' operations, Pinkerton's net working capital would remain at 9.5% of sales.

The acquisition of Pinkerton's by CPP was not universally popular. Most of the investment banks and lenders contacted by CPP expressed negative feelings about the potential acquisition, citing inadequate cash flow and weak market conditions following the dramatic dislocation of the stock market in the previous month. However, a representative of Sutro & Company, a prominent West Coast investment bank, indicated that he was "highly confident" he could get financing for the acquisition from either Manufacturers Hanover Trust Corporation or General Electric Credit Corporation.

In addition, Wathen had some problems with CPP's board of directors. For example, Berger thought there would be obvious synergies in merging the two businesses, but he believed that CPP did not have enough management depth to run the combined firms. According to Berger, there was no COO, no CFO, no marketing manager, and nobody to handle the day-to-day details of operating a $650 million firm. The last thing CPP needed was growth, Berger argued. He felt that the field people could handle a larger firm but the corporate management could not.

Nonetheless, the task force pressed on with its analysis of Pinkerton's. In addition to current financial market conditions, the analysis took special notice of Wackenhut, the only publicly traded security guard firm. (See Exhibits 4 and 5.) Only 12 days after receiving the details of the sale from Morgan Stanley, and with the reluctant approval of his board, Wathen bid $85 million for Pinkerton's.

Wathen did not receive a response to his bid for two weeks. Through his own network, Wathen knew another firm had bid more than CPP and that Morgan Stanley was negotiating with that firm. Wathen was disappointed that he might miss his last opportunity to be one of the biggest in the business. When Morgan Stanley finally called and told Wathen that his $85 million bid was too low and that nothing less than $100 million would be accepted, Wathen was elated that he had another chance to buy Pinkerton's. But he suspected the reason Morgan Stanley had finally called him was that the other buyer had been unable to finance its higher bid.

Financing a $100 Million Bid

In a last ditch effort to improve his bid for Pinkerton's, Wathen asked his investment banker to determine the options for financing a $100 million bid. The banker responded with only two alternatives. The first alternative came from an investment firm that would provide both debt and equity financing. The debt, in the amount of $75 million, would have a 7-year maturity and an 11½% interest rate. The loan principal would not be amortized prior to maturity, at which time the entire $75 million would come due. Finally, this debt would be a senior obligation and would be backed by all the assets of the newly combined firm. The equity, in the amount of $25 million, would be provided for 45% of the equity in the newly combined firm.

The second alternative was a 100% debt financing offered by a bank. The bank would lend $100 million at the rate of 13½% a year. The loan principal would be amortized at the rate of $5 million a year for 6 years, with a final payment of $70 million at the end of the seventh year. This loan would be collateralized by all of the assets of the newly combined firm.

Under either financing alternative, Wathen was very concerned about the required debt service. The newly combined firm's nonpublic, as well as high-leverage, status could make any cash flow problems over the next 5 years highly problematic. The task force also reminded Wathen that a $100 million purchase price would result in the creation of goodwill on his balance sheet that would have to be amortized at the rate of $5 million per year for the next 10 years.[1]

Wathen sat in his office and prepared to make the biggest decision of his career. As an entrepreneur and an experienced security guard executive, Wathen was sure Pinkerton's was a good buy. However, he had routinely relied on his board and other advisers for financial advice. His board had reluctantly approved his earlier bid of $85 million and was sure to balk at a $100 million bid. How could he justify a $100 million bid for Pinkerton, particularly in light of his earlier bid of $85 million? And if he was successful in convincing the board, how was he going to finance the acquisition?

EXHIBIT 1
Selected Pinkerton's Financial Data (millions of dollars)

	1983	1984	1985	1986	1987 (E)
Income from services	$296.4	$307.7	$312.4	$367.7	$408.3
Cost of services provided	264.5	275.4	286.3	342.5	381.7
Gross profit	31.9	32.3	26.1	25.2	26.6
Operating expenses	15.5	17.1	24.9	24.5	27.0
Operating profit	$ 16.4	$ 15.2	$ 1.2	$ 0.7	$ −0.4
Cash	$ 3.8	$ 2.7	$ 2.3	$ 0.0	$ 1.1
Accounts receivable, net	48.7	51.0	55.0	62.8	67.3
Other current assets	0.0	0.0	0.6	0.6	1.0
Total current assets	52.5	53.7	57.9	$ 63.4	69.4
Net property, plant, and equipment	11.0	11.3	13.1	15.1	17.6
Total assets	$ 63.5	$ 65.0	$ 71.0	$ 78.5	$ 87.0
Accounts payable	$ 0.4	$ 1.0	$ 2.4	$ 4.7	$ 3.4
Accrued expenses and other current liabilities	29.3	29.1	25.6	22.6	27.2
Total current liabilities	$ 29.7	$ 30.1	$ 28.0	$ 27.3	$ 30.6

---

1. Amortization of goodwill had to be expensed for financial reporting purposes and could not be expensed for tax purposes. The current corporate tax rate was 34%.

EXHIBIT 2
Selected CPP Financial Data (millions of dollars)

	Year Ending 12/31/86	Year Ending 12/31/87(E)
Income from services	$243.6	$251.5
Cost of services provided	221.9	229.4
Gross profit	21.7	22.1
Operating expenses	16.1	14.5
Operating profit	5.6	7.6
Interest expense, net	0.7	0.4
Amortization of goodwill	0.3	0.3
Income before tax	4.6	6.9
Taxes	2.4	2.9
Net income	$ 2.2	$ 4.0
Cash	$ 1.0	$ 1.2
Accounts receivable, net	33.8	34.0
Other current assets	8.3	13.4
Total current assets	$ 43.1	$ 48.6
Notes receivable	$ 2.4	$ 2.4
Goodwill	1.8	1.5
Net property, plant, and equipment	1.8	2.6
Total assets	$ 49.1	$ 55.1
Notes payable	$ 1.0	$ 1.6
Current portion of long-term debt	1.0	1.1
Accounts payable	2.7	2.1
Accrued expenses and other current liabilities	26.5	30.4
Total current liabilities	$ 31.2	$ 35.2
Long-term debt, less current portion	$ 3.1	$ 2.0
Shareholders' equity	14.7	18.0
Total liabilities and equities	$ 49.0	$ 55.2

EXHIBIT 3
Five-Year Forecast of CPP Income and Cash Flow (millions of dollars)[a]

	1988	1989	1990	1991	1992
Net income	$4.1	$4.3	$4.6	$4.8	$5.0
Plus amortization of goodwill	0.3	0.3	0.3	0.3	0.3
Less change in net property, plant, and equipment	0.1	0.1	0.1	0.1	0.1
Less change in net working capital	1.2	0.7	0.7	0.7	0.8
Less amortization of long-term debt	1.1	1.0	1.0	0.0	0.0
Total cash flow	$2.0	$2.8	$3.1	$4.3	$4.4

a. Under the assumption CPP does not acquire Pinkerton's.

EXHIBIT 4
Wackenhut 1987 Financial Data (millions of dollars except share data)[a]

Sales	$382.0	Debt	$ 10.6
Earnings	5.7	Assets	130.4
Earnings per share	1.47	Stock price ($)	18.00
Book equity	39.7	Beta	0.89
Shares outstanding (millions)	3.9		

a. Wackenhut Corporation provides guard and investigative services to industry and government.

EXHIBIT 5
Selected Capital Markets Information as of November 1987

3-month Treasury bill rate	5.78%
30-year Treasury bond rate	8.58
Corporate bond yields	
AAA	9.38%
AA	9.68
A	9.99
BBB	10.58

Appendixes

Appendix A

Tax Table

This table has been prepared for use in connection with cases in this book. It is not a complete statement of applicable rates, and it should not be used as a reference for general purposes.

Federal Tax Rates on Corporate Income and Payment Dates

Income Years	Rate[a]	Income Years	Rate[a]
1946–1949	38%	1965–1967	48 %
1950	47	1968–1969[c]	52.8
1951–1953[b]	52	1970[c]	49.2
1954–1963	52	1971–1978	48
1964	50	1979–1986[d]	46
		1986–1993	34
		1993[e]–	35

a. Rate applicable to top bracket of tax, excluding the excess profits tax, when in effect.

b. Excess profits tax also in effect for part or all of year.

c. Includes special surcharge.

d. For 1984 through 1986, the top bracket rate on taxable income between $1,000,000 and $1,405,000 was 51%. See text.

e. As of 1995, the top bracket rate on taxable income between $100,000 and $335,000 was 39%; and between $15,000,000 and $18,333,333, 38%. See table on corporate income tax rates for 1995.

The 52% rate in effect from 1951 through 1963 consisted of a normal tax of 30% of taxable income and a surtax of 22% of taxable income in excess of $25,000. The 50% rate in effect in 1964 consisted of a normal tax of 22% and a surtax of 28%. The 48% rate in effect from 1965 through 1974 consisted of a normal tax of 22% and a surtax of 26% on taxable income in excess of $25,000.

In addition, in 1968 a special surcharge of 10% was imposed, making the effective rate for that year 52.8%. This rate held for 1969, but the special surcharge was phased out gradually by quarters during 1970 so that the overall effective rate for that year was 49.2%, and by 1971 the rate was again 48%.

For tax years ending after 1974 and before 1979 the normal tax rates were 20% on the first $25,000 of taxable income and 22% on taxable income over $25,000. The surtax rate was 26% on taxable income over $50,000. For tax years beginning after 1978, the taxable income of corporations was subject to graduated tax rates.

Corporate Graduated Tax Rate, 1979–1986

Amount of Taxable Income ($000s)	Applicable Tax Rate		
	1979–1981	1982	1983–1986
Zero–25	17%	16%	15%
Over 25–50	20	19	18
Over 50–75	30	30	30
Over 75–100	40	40	40
Over 100	46	46	46

For taxable years beginning after December 31, 1983, the benefit of the graduated rates on corporations with taxable income in excess of $1 million was phased out by imposing an additional 5% tax on the portion of taxable income over $1,000,000 and up to $1,405,000. Thus, the tax rate on income in this bracket was 51%. For taxable income in excess of $1,405,000, the tax rate dropped back to 46%. The effect of this provision was to impose a flat 46% rate on all corporations with taxable incomes in excess of $1,405,000.

The Tax Reform Act of 1986 reduced the top corporate tax rate from 46% to 34%, effective July 1, 1987, for corporations with taxable incomes in excess of $335,000. Graduated rates, from 15% to 39%, applied to corporations with taxable incomes of less than $335,000. The corporate income tax rates in effect in 1995 are shown below.

Corporation Income Tax Rates, 1995

Taxable Income ($000)	Tax Rate
Zero–50	15%
Over 50–75	25
Over 75–100	34
Over 100–335	39
Over 335–10,000	34
Over 10,000–15,000	35
Over 15,000–18,333	38
Over 18,333	35

Since 1950 corporate income tax payments have moved closer to current payment. Beginning in 1950, payments were gradually accelerated until, in 1954, they were brought entirely within the first half of the year following the tax liability. The Revenue Acts of 1954 and 1964 and the Tax Adjustment Act of 1966 set up even more accelerated schedules. Through 1967, all tax liabilities up to $100,000 were payable in equal amounts on March 15 and June 15 of the year following the tax liability. The Revenue Act of 1968 provided for a gradual acceleration of tax payments for corporations with tax liabilities of less than $100,000 as well as for corporations with tax liabilities of more than $100,000. Tax liabilities over $100,000, for companies on a calendar year, were payable according to the following schedule. For 1967 through

1982, if the actual tax liability for the year exceeded the amount of estimated tax payments made on this liability during the year, the balance had to be paid in equal installments on March 15 and June 15 of the following year for corporations filing their tax returns on a calendar year basis. For taxable years beginning after December 31, 1982, the entire balance had to be paid when the return was due, March 15 of the following year for corporations filing on a calendar year basis.

Corporate Tax Liabilities, 1949–1967 and After

Income Year	Percentage Paid in Income Year[a]				Percentage Paid in Following Year[b]			
	Apr. 15	June 15	Sept. 15	Dec. 15	Mar. 15	June 15	Sept. 15	Dec. 15
1949	—	—	—	—	25	25	25	25
1950	—	—	—	—	30	30	20	20
1951	—	—	—	—	35	35	15	15
1952	—	—	—	—	40	40	10	10
1953	—	—	—	—	45	45	5	5
1954	—	—	—	—	50	50	—	—
1955	—	—	5	5	45	45	—	—
1956	—	—	10	10	40	40	—	—
1957	—	—	15	15	35	35	—	—
1958	—	—	20	20	30	30	—	—
1959–1963	—	—	25	25	25	25	—	—
1964	1	1	25	25	24	24	—	—
1965	4	4	25	25	21	21	—	—
1966	12	12	25	25	13	13	—	—
1967 and after . . .	25	25	25	25	—	—	—	—

a. These are percentages of the estimated tax liability on income of the current year.

b. These are percentages of the tax liability on income of the previous year.

Appendix *B*

*Note on Investment Tax Credit**

Most recently repealed by the Tax Reform Act of 1986, a tax credit subsidy for business purchases of capital goods was first enacted by the U.S. Congress in 1962. Its purpose was twofold. First, the United States was emerging from a small economic recession in 1961, and it was hoped that the credit would encourage business spending for new plants and equipment. While the primary goal of the credit probably was to bolster a sagging economy, it also promised a substantial secondary benefit. For a number of years trade groups from numerous basic American industries had complained that European producers with lower labor costs and more modern physical facilities were slowly exporting more and more of their production to the United States. It was hoped that a tax subsidy encouraging new investment in capital goods would allow American producers to modernize their facilities and reduce their costs enough to be more competitive in the U.S. market with European producers.

Between 1962 and 1968 the investment credit underwent several revisions. It was "permanently" repealed (there had been a temporary suspension in 1966) by the Tax Reform Act of 1969. Because of a continuing business recession and rising unemployment in 1971, the investment tax credit was reenacted in the Revenue Act of 1971 under the name "job-development credit." As the law stood after reenactment, a purchaser of "Sec. 38"[1] property could deduct from federal income tax liability 7% of the cost of new "Sec. 38" property in the year it was purchased, as long as the property had an expected useful life of 7 years or more. For property with a life of 5 to 7 years, the credit was equal to two thirds of this 7%, and for property with a useful life of 3 to 5 years, the credit was equal to one third of 7%. Property with a useful life of less than 3 years did not qualify for the credit. (Under the old investment tax credit repealed in 1969, the required lives were 1 year longer; that is, the upper limit was 8 years and the lower limit was 4 years.)

The investment credit was increased from 7% to 10% for qualified business property acquired and placed in service after January 21, 1975. Since 1975 a variety of

---

*This note has been prepared for use in connection with cases in this book. It is not a definitive statement, and it should not be used as a reference for general purposes.

1. For purposes of the credit, "Sec. 38" property is defined as all depreciable property (not including buildings) used as an integral part of (1) manufacturing, (2) mining, (3) production, and (4) furnishings of services such as transportation, energy, water, and sewage disposal.

additional tax credits have been enacted to stimulate such activities as increasing expenditures on research; the clinical testing of certain drugs; the production of fuel from nonconventional sources; alcohol used as fuel; contributions to employee stock ownership plans (ESOP); the targeted jobs credit; and outlays for designated "energy property." Many of these credits have since been abolished or curtailed; in any event, they are far too specialized to be discussed in this brief summary statement.

The Tax Reform Act of 1984 created a new concept—the general business credit. It combined the available investment credit (both the regular and energy credits), targeted job credit, alcohol fuel credit, and ESOP credit into a single, general business credit (including any carrybacks and carryovers). For "Sec. 38" property depreciated on a 5-year accelerated cost recovery system (ACRS), the credit was 10%; for a 3-year recovery period, the credit was 6%.

Exhibit 1 of the Pressco, Inc. (1985) case spells out some of the technical provisions of the investment tax credit as they existed at the time of this case, just prior to the enactment of the Tax Recovery Act of 1984.

The investment tax credit (or general business credit) represents a direct credit against the total income tax liability. For a company with a 46% marginal tax rate, a tax credit of $100,000 can save as much in income taxes as a $217,391 deduction from pre-tax income. Taxpayers who have a total tax liability of $25,000 or less in a given year are allowed to credit up to 100% of the liability. For those whose tax liability exceeds $25,000, the limit on the credit is $25,000 plus the following percentage of the liability in excess of $25,000:

1979	60%
1980	70
1981	80
1982	90
1983–1985	85
1986 and after	75

Any credit that cannot be used in a given year may be carried back or forward to offset the tax liabilities of other years. In 1986 unused credits could be carried back for 3 years and forward for 15 years.

The Tax Reform Act of 1986 terminated the regular investment tax credit for virtually all otherwise qualified property placed in service after December 31, 1985. Exceptions include "transition" property (e.g., property placed in service after 1985 but acquired under a written contract that was binding prior to December 31, 1985), certain qualified progress expenditures, and qualified timber property. The latter category continues to be eligible for a 10% investment tax credit. The other two categories of qualified property are eligible for an investment credit at the following rates:

1986	10.00%
1987	8.25
1988 and after	6.50

The carrying forward of unused investment credits was also reduced, but not terminated, for years after 1986.

It cannot safely be assumed that the repeal of the investment tax credit will long endure. As noted, this credit has been repealed (even "permanently" repealed) in earlier years only to be reenacted under the pressure of the next business recession.

Appendix C

Present Value Tables

TABLE C1
Present Value of $1

Periods until Payment	1%	2%	2½%	3%	4%	5%	6%	8%	10%	12%	14%	15%	16%	18%	20%	22%	24%	25%	26%	30%	40%	50%
1	0.990	0.980	0.976	0.971	0.962	0.952	0.943	0.926	0.909	0.893	0.877	0.870	0.862	0.847	0.833	0.820	0.806	0.800	0.794	0.769	0.714	0.667
2	0.980	0.961	0.952	0.943	0.925	0.907	0.890	0.857	0.826	0.797	0.769	0.756	0.743	0.718	0.694	0.672	0.650	0.640	0.630	0.592	0.510	0.444
3	0.971	0.942	0.929	0.915	0.889	0.864	0.840	0.794	0.751	0.712	0.675	0.658	0.641	0.609	0.579	0.551	0.524	0.512	0.500	0.455	0.364	0.296
4	0.961	0.924	0.906	0.888	0.855	0.823	0.792	0.735	0.683	0.636	0.592	0.572	0.552	0.516	0.482	0.451	0.423	0.410	0.397	0.350	0.260	0.198
5	0.951	0.906	0.884	0.863	0.822	0.784	0.747	0.681	0.621	0.567	0.519	0.497	0.476	0.437	0.402	0.370	0.341	0.328	0.315	0.269	0.186	0.132
6	0.942	0.888	0.862	0.837	0.790	0.746	0.705	0.630	0.564	0.507	0.456	0.432	0.410	0.370	0.335	0.303	0.275	0.262	0.250	0.207	0.133	0.088
7	0.933	0.871	0.841	0.813	0.760	0.711	0.665	0.583	0.513	0.452	0.400	0.376	0.354	0.314	0.279	0.249	0.222	0.210	0.198	0.159	0.095	0.059
8	0.923	0.853	0.821	0.789	0.731	0.677	0.627	0.540	0.467	0.404	0.351	0.327	0.305	0.266	0.233	0.204	0.179	0.168	0.157	0.123	0.068	0.039
9	0.914	0.837	0.801	0.766	0.703	0.645	0.592	0.500	0.424	0.361	0.308	0.284	0.263	0.225	0.194	0.167	0.144	0.134	0.125	0.094	0.048	0.026
10	0.905	0.820	0.781	0.744	0.676	0.614	0.558	0.463	0.386	0.322	0.270	0.247	0.227	0.191	0.162	0.137	0.116	0.107	0.099	0.073	0.035	0.017
11	0.896	0.804	0.762	0.722	0.650	0.585	0.527	0.429	0.350	0.287	0.237	0.215	0.195	0.162	0.135	0.112	0.094	0.086	0.079	0.056	0.025	0.012
12	0.887	0.788	0.744	0.701	0.625	0.557	0.497	0.397	0.319	0.257	0.208	0.187	0.168	0.137	0.112	0.092	0.076	0.069	0.062	0.043	0.018	0.008
13	0.879	0.773	0.725	0.681	0.601	0.530	0.469	0.368	0.290	0.229	0.182	0.163	0.145	0.116	0.093	0.075	0.061	0.055	0.050	0.033	0.013	0.005
14	0.870	0.758	0.708	0.661	0.577	0.505	0.442	0.340	0.263	0.205	0.160	0.141	0.125	0.099	0.078	0.062	0.049	0.044	0.039	0.025	0.009	0.003
15	0.861	0.743	0.690	0.642	0.555	0.481	0.417	0.315	0.239	0.183	0.140	0.123	0.108	0.084	0.065	0.051	0.040	0.035	0.031	0.020	0.006	0.002
16	0.853	0.728	0.674	0.623	0.534	0.458	0.394	0.292	0.218	0.163	0.123	0.107	0.093	0.071	0.054	0.042	0.032	0.028	0.025	0.015	0.005	0.002
17	0.844	0.714	0.657	0.605	0.513	0.436	0.371	0.270	0.198	0.146	0.108	0.093	0.080	0.060	0.045	0.034	0.026	0.023	0.020	0.012	0.003	0.001
18	0.836	0.700	0.641	0.587	0.494	0.416	0.350	0.250	0.180	0.130	0.095	0.081	0.069	0.051	0.038	0.028	0.021	0.018	0.016	0.009	0.002	0.001
19	0.828	0.686	0.626	0.570	0.475	0.396	0.331	0.232	0.164	0.116	0.083	0.070	0.060	0.043	0.031	0.023	0.017	0.014	0.012	0.007	0.002	
20	0.820	0.673	0.610	0.554	0.456	0.377	0.312	0.215	0.149	0.104	0.073	0.061	0.051	0.037	0.026	0.019	0.014	0.012	0.010	0.005	0.001	
21	0.811	0.660	0.595	0.538	0.439	0.359	0.294	0.199	0.135	0.093	0.064	0.053	0.044	0.031	0.022	0.015	0.011	0.009	0.008	0.004	0.001	
22	0.803	0.647	0.581	0.522	0.422	0.342	0.278	0.184	0.123	0.083	0.056	0.046	0.038	0.026	0.018	0.013	0.009	0.007	0.006	0.003	0.001	
23	0.795	0.634	0.567	0.507	0.406	0.326	0.262	0.170	0.112	0.074	0.049	0.040	0.033	0.022	0.015	0.010	0.007	0.006	0.005	0.002		
24	0.788	0.622	0.553	0.492	0.390	0.310	0.247	0.158	0.102	0.066	0.043	0.035	0.028	0.019	0.013	0.008	0.006	0.005	0.004	0.002		
25	0.780	0.610	0.539	0.478	0.375	0.295	0.233	0.146	0.092	0.059	0.038	0.030	0.024	0.016	0.010	0.007	0.005	0.004	0.003	0.001		
26	0.772	0.598	0.526	0.464	0.361	0.281	0.220	0.135	0.084	0.053	0.033	0.026	0.021	0.014	0.009	0.006	0.004	0.003	0.002	0.001		
27	0.764	0.586	0.513	0.450	0.347	0.268	0.207	0.125	0.076	0.047	0.029	0.023	0.018	0.011	0.007	0.005	0.003	0.002	0.002	0.001		
28	0.757	0.574	0.501	0.437	0.333	0.255	0.196	0.116	0.069	0.042	0.026	0.020	0.016	0.010	0.006	0.004	0.002	0.002	0.002	0.001		
29	0.749	0.563	0.489	0.424	0.321	0.243	0.185	0.107	0.063	0.037	0.022	0.017	0.014	0.008	0.005	0.003	0.002	0.002	0.001			
30	0.742	0.552	0.477	0.412	0.308	0.231	0.174	0.099	0.057	0.033	0.020	0.015	0.012	0.007	0.004	0.003	0.002	0.001	0.001			
40	0.672	0.453	0.372	0.307	0.208	0.142	0.097	0.046	0.022	0.011	0.005	0.004	0.003	0.001	0.001							
50	0.608	0.372	0.291	0.228	0.141	0.087	0.054	0.021	0.009	0.003	0.001	0.001	0.001									

TABLE C2
Present Value of $1 Received Annually

Periods to Be Paid	1%	2%	2½%	3%	4%	5%	6%	8%	10%	12%	14%	15%	16%	18%	20%	22%	24%	25%	26%	30%	40%	50%
1	0.990	0.980	0.976	0.971	0.962	0.952	0.943	0.926	0.909	0.893	0.877	0.870	0.862	0.847	0.833	0.820	0.806	0.800	0.794	0.769	0.714	0.667
2	1.970	1.942	1.927	1.914	1.886	1.859	1.833	1.783	1.736	1.690	1.647	1.626	1.605	1.566	1.528	1.492	1.457	1.440	1.424	1.361	1.224	1.111
3	2.941	2.884	2.856	2.829	2.775	2.723	2.673	2.577	2.487	2.402	2.322	2.283	2.246	2.174	2.106	2.042	1.981	1.952	1.923	1.816	1.589	1.407
4	3.902	3.808	3.762	3.717	3.630	3.546	3.465	3.312	3.170	3.037	2.914	2.855	2.798	2.690	2.589	2.494	2.404	2.362	2.320	2.166	1.849	1.605
5	4.853	4.713	4.646	4.580	4.452	4.330	4.212	3.993	3.791	3.605	3.433	3.352	3.274	3.127	2.991	2.864	2.745	2.689	2.635	2.436	2.035	1.737
6	5.795	5.601	5.508	5.417	5.242	5.076	4.917	4.623	4.355	4.111	3.889	3.784	3.685	3.498	3.326	3.167	3.020	2.951	2.885	2.643	2.168	1.824
7	6.728	6.472	6.349	6.230	6.002	5.786	5.582	5.206	4.868	4.564	4.288	4.160	4.039	3.812	3.605	3.416	3.242	3.161	3.083	2.802	2.263	1.883
8	7.652	7.325	7.170	7.020	6.733	6.463	6.210	5.747	5.335	4.968	4.639	4.487	4.344	4.078	3.837	3.619	3.421	3.329	3.241	2.925	2.331	1.922
9	8.566	8.162	7.971	7.786	7.435	7.108	6.802	6.247	5.759	5.328	4.946	4.772	4.607	4.303	4.031	3.786	3.566	3.463	3.366	3.019	2.379	1.948
10	9.471	8.983	8.752	8.530	8.111	7.722	7.360	6.710	6.145	5.650	5.216	5.019	4.833	4.494	4.192	3.923	3.682	3.571	3.465	3.092	2.414	1.965
11	10.368	9.787	9.514	9.253	8.760	8.306	7.887	7.139	6.495	5.938	5.453	5.234	5.029	4.656	4.327	4.035	3.776	3.656	3.544	3.147	2.438	1.977
12	11.255	10.575	10.258	9.954	9.385	8.863	8.384	7.536	6.814	6.194	5.660	5.421	5.197	4.793	4.439	4.127	3.851	3.725	3.606	3.190	2.456	1.985
13	12.134	11.348	10.983	10.635	9.986	9.394	8.853	7.904	7.103	6.424	5.842	5.583	5.342	4.910	4.533	4.203	3.912	3.780	3.656	3.223	2.468	1.990
14	13.004	12.106	11.691	11.296	10.563	9.899	9.295	8.244	7.367	6.628	6.002	5.724	5.468	5.008	4.611	4.265	3.962	3.824	3.695	3.249	2.478	1.993
15	13.865	12.849	12.381	11.938	11.118	10.380	9.712	8.559	7.606	6.811	6.142	5.847	5.576	5.092	4.676	4.315	4.001	3.859	3.726	3.268	2.484	1.995
16	14.718	13.578	13.055	12.561	11.652	10.838	10.106	8.851	7.824	6.974	6.265	5.954	5.668	5.162	4.730	4.357	4.033	3.887	3.751	3.283	2.488	1.997
17	15.562	14.292	13.712	13.166	12.166	11.274	10.477	9.122	8.022	7.120	6.373	6.047	5.749	5.222	4.775	4.391	4.059	3.910	3.771	3.295	2.492	1.998
18	16.398	14.992	14.353	13.754	12.659	11.690	10.828	9.372	8.201	7.250	6.467	6.128	5.818	5.273	4.812	4.419	4.080	3.928	3.786	3.304	2.494	1.999
19	17.226	15.678	14.979	14.324	13.134	12.085	11.158	9.604	8.365	7.366	6.550	6.198	5.878	5.316	4.844	4.442	4.097	3.942	3.799	3.311	2.496	1.999
20	18.046	16.351	15.589	14.877	13.590	12.462	11.470	9.818	8.514	7.469	6.623	6.259	5.929	5.353	4.870	4.460	4.110	3.954	3.808	3.316	2.497	1.999
21	18.857	17.011	16.185	15.415	14.029	12.821	11.764	10.017	8.649	7.562	6.687	6.312	5.973	5.384	4.891	4.476	4.121	3.963	3.816	3.320	2.498	2.000
22	19.660	17.658	16.765	15.937	14.451	13.163	12.042	10.201	8.772	7.645	6.743	6.359	6.011	5.410	4.909	4.488	4.130	3.970	3.822	3.323	2.498	2.000
23	20.456	18.292	17.332	16.444	14.857	13.489	12.303	10.371	8.883	7.718	6.792	6.399	6.044	5.432	4.924	4.499	4.137	3.976	3.827	3.325	2.499	2.000
24	21.243	18.914	17.885	16.936	15.247	13.799	12.550	10.529	8.985	7.784	6.835	6.434	6.073	5.451	4.937	4.507	4.143	3.981	3.831	3.327	2.499	2.000
25	22.023	19.523	18.424	17.413	15.622	14.094	12.783	10.675	9.077	7.843	6.873	6.464	6.097	5.467	4.948	4.514	4.147	3.985	3.834	3.329	2.499	2.000
26	22.795	20.121	18.951	17.877	15.983	14.375	13.003	10.810	9.161	7.896	6.906	6.491	6.118	5.480	4.956	4.520	4.151	3.988	3.837	3.330	2.500	2.000
27	23.560	20.707	19.464	18.327	16.330	14.643	13.211	10.935	9.237	7.943	6.935	6.514	6.136	5.492	4.964	4.524	4.154	3.990	3.839	3.331	2.500	2.000
28	24.316	21.281	19.965	18.764	16.663	14.898	13.406	11.051	9.307	7.984	6.961	6.534	6.152	5.502	4.970	4.528	4.157	3.992	3.840	3.331	2.500	2.000
29	25.066	21.844	20.454	19.188	16.984	15.141	13.591	11.158	9.370	8.022	6.983	6.551	6.166	5.510	4.975	4.531	4.159	3.994	3.841	3.332	2.500	2.000
30	25.808	22.396	20.930	19.600	17.292	15.372	13.765	11.258	9.427	8.055	7.003	6.566	6.177	5.517	4.979	4.534	4.160	3.995	3.842	3.332	2.500	2.000
40	32.835	27.355	25.103	23.115	19.793	17.159	15.046	11.925	9.779	8.244	7.105	6.642	6.234	5.548	4.997	4.544	4.166	3.999	3.846	3.333	2.500	2.000
50	39.196	31.424	28.362	25.730	21.482	18.256	15.762	12.233	9.915	8.304	7.133	6.660	6.246	5.554	4.999	4.545	4.167	4.000	3.846	3.333	2.500	2.000

TABLE C3
Future Value of $1 at End of Period n

Periods until Payment	1%	2%	2½%	3%	4%	5%	6%	8%	10%	12%	14%	15%	16%	18%	20%	22%	24%	25%	26%	30%	40%	50%
1	1.010	1.020	1.025	1.030	1.040	1.050	1.060	1.080	1.100	1.120	1.140	1.150	1.160	1.180	1.200	1.220	1.240	1.250	1.260	1.300	1.400	1.500
2	1.020	1.040	1.051	1.061	1.082	1.103	1.124	1.166	1.210	1.254	1.300	1.323	1.346	1.392	1.440	1.488	1.538	1.563	1.588	1.690	1.960	2.250
3	1.030	1.061	1.077	1.093	1.125	1.158	1.191	1.260	1.331	1.405	1.482	1.521	1.561	1.643	1.728	1.816	1.907	1.953	2.000	2.197	2.744	3.375
4	1.041	1.082	1.104	1.126	1.170	1.216	1.263	1.361	1.464	1.574	1.689	1.749	1.811	1.939	2.074	2.215	2.364	2.441	2.520	2.856	3.842	5.063
5	1.051	1.104	1.131	1.159	1.217	1.276	1.338	1.469	1.611	1.762	1.925	2.011	2.100	2.288	2.488	2.703	2.932	3.052	3.176	3.713	5.378	7.594
6	1.062	1.126	1.160	1.194	1.265	1.340	1.419	1.587	1.772	1.974	2.195	2.313	2.436	2.700	2.986	3.297	3.635	3.815	4.002	4.827	7.530	11.391
7	1.072	1.149	1.189	1.230	1.316	1.407	1.504	1.714	1.949	2.211	2.502	2.660	2.826	3.186	3.583	4.023	4.508	4.768	5.042	6.275	10.541	17.086
8	1.083	1.172	1.218	1.267	1.369	1.478	1.594	1.851	2.144	2.476	2.853	3.059	3.278	3.759	4.300	4.908	5.590	5.961	6.353	8.157	14.758	25.629
9	1.094	1.195	1.249	1.305	1.423	1.551	1.690	1.999	2.358	2.773	3.252	3.518	3.803	4.436	5.160	5.987	6.931	7.451	8.005	10.604	20.661	38.443
10	1.105	1.219	1.280	1.344	1.480	1.629	1.791	2.159	2.594	3.106	3.707	4.046	4.411	5.234	6.192	7.305	8.594	9.313	10.086	13.786	28.925	57.665
11	1.116	1.243	1.312	1.384	1.540	1.710	1.898	2.332	2.853	3.479	4.226	4.652	5.117	6.176	7.430	8.912	10.657	11.642	12.708	17.922	40.496	86.498
12	1.127	1.268	1.345	1.426	1.601	1.796	2.012	2.518	3.138	3.896	4.818	5.350	5.936	7.288	8.916	10.872	13.215	14.552	16.012	23.298	56.694	129.75
13	1.138	1.294	1.379	1.469	1.665	1.886	2.133	2.720	3.452	4.364	5.492	6.153	6.886	8.599	10.699	13.364	16.386	18.190	20.175	30.288	79.371	194.62
14	1.150	1.320	1.413	1.513	1.732	1.980	2.261	2.937	3.798	4.887	6.261	7.076	7.988	10.147	12.839	16.182	20.319	22.737	25.421	39.374	111.12	291.93
15	1.161	1.346	1.448	1.558	1.801	2.079	2.397	3.172	4.177	5.474	7.138	8.137	9.266	11.974	15.407	19.742	25.196	28.422	32.030	51.186	155.57	437.89
16	1.173	1.373	1.485	1.605	1.873	2.183	2.540	3.426	4.595	6.130	8.137	9.358	10.748	14.129	18.488	24.086	31.243	35.527	40.358	66.542	217.80	656.84
17	1.184	1.400	1.522	1.653	1.948	2.292	2.693	3.700	5.055	6.866	9.277	10.761	12.468	16.672	22.186	29.384	38.741	44.409	50.851	86.504	304.91	985.26
18	1.196	1.428	1.560	1.702	2.026	2.407	2.854	3.996	5.560	7.690	10.575	12.375	14.463	19.673	26.623	35.849	48.039	55.511	64.072	112.46	426.88	1477.9
19	1.208	1.457	1.599	1.754	2.107	2.527	3.026	4.316	6.116	8.613	12.056	14.232	16.777	23.214	31.948	43.736	59.568	69.389	80.731	146.19	597.63	2216.8
20	1.220	1.486	1.639	1.806	2.191	2.653	3.207	4.661	6.728	9.646	13.743	16.367	19.461	27.393	38.338	53.358	73.864	86.736	101.72	190.05	836.68	3325.3
21	1.232	1.516	1.680	1.860	2.279	2.786	3.400	5.034	7.400	10.804	15.668	18.822	22.574	32.324	46.005	65.096	91.592	108.42	128.17	247.06	1171.4	4987.9
22	1.245	1.546	1.722	1.916	2.370	2.925	3.604	5.437	8.140	12.100	17.861	21.645	26.186	38.142	55.206	79.418	113.57	135.53	161.49	321.18	1639.9	7481.8
23	1.257	1.577	1.765	1.974	2.465	3.072	3.820	5.872	8.954	13.552	20.362	24.891	30.376	45.008	66.247	96.889	140.83	169.41	203.48	417.54	2295.9	11223.
24	1.270	1.608	1.809	2.033	2.563	3.225	4.049	6.341	9.845	15.179	23.212	28.625	35.236	53.109	79.497	118.21	174.63	211.76	256.39	542.80	3214.2	16834.
25	1.282	1.641	1.854	2.094	2.666	3.386	4.292	6.849	10.835	17.000	26.462	32.919	40.874	62.669	95.396	144.21	216.54	264.70	323.05	705.64	4499.9	25251.
26	1.295	1.673	1.900	2.157	2.773	3.556	4.549	7.396	11.918	19.040	30.167	37.857	47.414	73.949	114.48	175.94	268.51	330.87	407.04	917.33	6299.8	37877.
27	1.308	1.707	1.948	2.221	2.883	3.734	4.822	7.988	13.110	21.325	34.390	43.535	55.000	87.260	137.37	214.64	332.95	413.59	512.87	1192.5	8819.8	56815.
28	1.321	1.741	2.000	2.288	2.999	3.920	5.112	8.627	14.421	23.884	39.204	50.066	63.800	102.97	164.84	261.86	412.86	516.99	646.21	1550.3	12348.	85223.
29	1.335	1.776	2.046	2.357	3.119	4.116	5.418	9.317	15.863	26.750	44.693	57.575	74.009	121.50	197.81	319.47	511.95	646.23	814.23	2015.4	17287.	
30	1.348	1.811	2.098	2.427	3.243	4.322	5.744	10.063	17.449	29.960	50.950	66.212	85.850	143.37	237.38	389.76	634.82	807.79	1025.9	2620.0	24201.	
40	1.489	2.208	2.685	3.262	4.801	7.040	10.286	21.725	45.259	93.051	188.88	267.86	378.72	750.38	1469.8	2847.0	5455.9	7523.2	10347.	36119.		
50	1.645	2.692	3.437	4.384	7.107	11.467	18.420	46.902	117.39	289.00	700.23	1083.7	1670.7	3927.4	9100.4	17046.	46890.	70065.				

Index of Cases